North Ame...
Road Atlas

UNITED STATES   **CANADA**   **MEXICO**

Contents

Abbreviations

UNITED STATES

Alabama	AL	Illinois	IL	Montana	MT	Rhode Island	RI
Alaska	AK	Indiana	IN	Nebraska	NE	South Carolina	SC
Arizona	AZ	Iowa	IA	Nevada	NV	South Dakota	SD
Arkansas	AR	Kansas	KS	New Hampshire	NH	Tennessee	TN
California	CA	Kentucky	KY	New Jersey	NJ	Texas	TX
Colorado	CO	Louisiana	LA	New Mexico	NM	Utah	UT
Connecticut	CT	Maine	ME	New York	NY	Vermont	VT
Delaware	DE	Maryland	MD	North Carolina	NC	Virginia	VA
District of Columbia	DC	Massachusetts	MA	North Dakota	ND	Washington	WA
Florida	FL	Michigan	MI	Ohio	OH	West Virginia	WV
Georgia	GA	Minnesota	MN	Oklahoma	OK	Wisconsin	WI
Hawaii	HI	Mississippi	MS	Oregon	OR	Wyoming	WY
Idaho	ID	Missouri	MO	Pennsylvania	PA	Puerto Rico	PR

CANADA

Alberta	AB	Northwest Territories	NT	Québec	QC
British Columbia	BC	Nova Scotia	NS	Saskatchewan	SK
Manitoba	MB	Nunavut	NU	Yukon Territory	YT
New Brunswick	NB	Ontario	ON		
Newfoundland & Labrador	NF	Prince Edward Island	PE		

MICHELIN

Travel Publications

UNITED STATES
MICHELIN TRAVEL PUBLICATIONS, ONE PARKWAY SOUTH, GREENVILLE, SOUTH CAROLINA 29615
TEL 1-800-423-0485, FAX 864-458-5665, EMAIL michelin.travel-publications-us@us.michelin.com

CANADA
MICHELIN TRAVEL PUBLICATIONS, 2540, BOUL. DANIEL-JOHNSON, SUITE 510, LAVAL, QUÉBEC, H7T 2T9
TEL. 1-800-361-8236, FAX 1-800-361-6937, EMAIL michelin.travel-publications-canada@ca.michelin.com

"Developed using **MAPQUEST** data"

City and Local Maps

Alphabetical listing of select downtown and metro area maps found within the index.

United States Key Map

0 mi   125   250   375
0 km 125 250 375 400
One inch equals 204.6 miles
One centimeter equals 129.4 kilometers

AL	Alabama
AK	Alaska
AZ	Arizona
AR	Arkansas
CA	California
CO	Colorado
CT	Connecticut
DE	Delaware
FL	Florida
GA	Georgia
HI	Hawaii
ID	Idaho
IL	Illinois
IN	Indiana
IA	Iowa
KS	Kansas
KY	Kentucky
LA	Louisiana
ME	Maine
MD	Maryland
MA	Massachusetts
MI	Michigan
MN	Minnesota
MS	Mississippi
MO	Missouri
MT	Montana
NE	Nebraska
NV	Nevada
NH	New Hampshire
NJ	New Jersey
NM	New Mexico
NY	New York
NC	North Carolina
ND	North Dakota
OH	Ohio
OK	Oklahoma
OR	Oregon
PA	Pennsylvania
RI	Rhode Island
SC	South Carolina
SD	South Dakota
TN	Tennessee
TX	Texas
UT	Utah
VT	Vermont
VA	Virginia
WA	Washington
WV	West Virginia
WI	Wisconsin
WY	Wyoming

Alaska/NW Canada 154–155

0 150 300 mi
0 150 300 km

0 50 100 mi
0 50 100 km

Map Pages	Map Scale	Map Pages	Map Scale
12–65	1:1,525,000	144–151	1:590,000
66–143,152–153	1:1,100,000	154–155	1:8,500,000

United States Key Map

Alabama	AL
Alaska	AK
Arizona	AZ
Arkansas	AR
California	CA
Colorado	CO
Connecticut	CT
Delaware	DE
Florida	FL
Georgia	GA
Hawaii	HI
Idaho	ID
Illinois	IL
Indiana	IN
Iowa	IA
Kansas	KS
Kentucky	KY
Louisiana	LA
Maine	ME
Maryland	MD
Massachusetts	MA
Michigan	MI
Minnesota	MN
Mississippi	MS
Missouri	MO
Montana	MT
Nebraska	NE
Nevada	NV
New Hampshire	NH
New Jersey	NJ
New Mexico	NM
New York	NY
North Carolina	NC
North Dakota	ND
Ohio	OH
Oklahoma	OK
Oregon	OR
Pennsylvania	PA
Rhode Island	RI
South Carolina	SC
South Dakota	SD
Tennessee	TN
Texas	TX
Utah	UT
Vermont	VT
Virginia	VA
Washington	WA
West Virginia	WV
Wisconsin	WI
Wyoming	WY

CANADA

ONTARIO · QUÉBEC · NEW BRUNSWICK · MAINE

MINNESOTA · WISCONSIN · MICHIGAN · NEW YORK · N.H. · VT. · MASS. · CONN. · R.I.

IOWA · ILLINOIS · INDIANA · OHIO · PA. · N.J. · MD. · DEL.

MISSOURI · KANSAS · KENTUCKY · WEST VIRGINIA · VIRGINIA

ARKANSAS · TENNESSEE · NORTH CAROLINA

LOUISIANA · MISSISSIPPI · ALABAMA · GEORGIA · SOUTH CAROLINA

FLORIDA

GULF OF MEXICO · ATLANTIC OCEAN · BAHAMAS · CUBA

One inch equals 235.8 miles/Un pouce équivaut à 235.8 milles
One cm equals 149.3 km/Un cm équivaut à 149.3 km

0 mi   200   400
0 km   200   400   600

AB	Alberta
BC	British Columbia
MB	Manitoba
NB	New Brunswick
NF	Newfoundland and Labrador
NT	Northwest Territories
NS	Nova Scotia
NU	Nunavut
ON	Ontario
PE	Prince Edward Island
QC	Québec
SK	Saskatchewan
YT	Yukon Territory

Map Pages/Pages	Map Scale/Échelle	Map Pages/Pages	Map Scale/Échelle
156–161,164–171,176–177,182–183	1 : 2,400,000	154–155	1 : 8,500,000
162–163,172–175,178–181	1 : 1,525,000	(183)	1 : 8,000,000

Alberta	AB
Colombie-Britannique	BC
Manitoba	MB
Nouveau-Brunswick	NB
Terre-Neuve et Labrador	NF
Territoires du Nord-Ouest	NT
Nouvelle-Écosse	NS
Nunavut	NU
Ontario	ON
Île-du-Prince-Édouard	PE
Québec	QC
Saskatchewan	SK
Territoire du Yukon	YT

NOTE: Legislated standard time zone boundaries shown; observed time may differ locally.

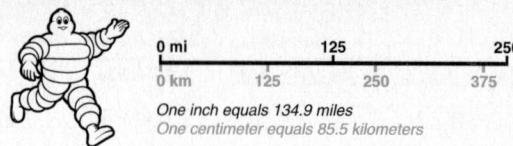

0 mi — 125 — 250
0 km — 125 — 250 — 375

One inch equals 134.9 miles
One centimeter equals 85.5 kilometers

PACIFIC

OCEAN

Islas Revillagigedo

Isla San Benedicto

Isla Roca Partida

Isla Clarión

Isla Socorro

CALIFORNIA

San Diego
Tijuana
Tecate
Calexico
Mexicali
Yuma
San Luis Río Colorado

ARIZONA

Tucson

Nogales

NEW MEXICO

Las Cruces

El Paso

Ciudad Juárez

UNITED

Midland

Isla de Todos Santos
Ensenada
El Golfo de Santa Clara
Puerto Peñasco
Sonoyta

BAJA CALIFORNIA

Isla San Martín
El Rosario
Cataviña

Vicente Guerrero
San Felipe
Pico del Diablo

Nogales
Naco
Douglas
Agua Prieta
Palomas

Nuevo Casas Grandes

El Porvenir
Villa Ahumada

Caborca
Altar
Magdalena
Santa Ana
Nacozari Viejo
Cananea

SONORA

Moctezuma

Madera
Gómez Farías

Buenaventura
Ojo de Laguna
El Sueco

Coyame
Ojinaga

Boquillas de Carmen

Ciudad Acuña
Del Río

Parque Nacional Balneario Los Novillos

El Desemboque

Isla Ángel de la Guarda

Isla Tiburón

Hermosillo

Bahía de los Ángeles
Rosarito

Bahía Kino

Presa P.E. Calles

Tonichi

Presa Álvaro Obregón

Chihuahua

Cuauhtémoc
Meoqui
Delicias

La Perla

COAHUILA

Nueva Rosita
Múzquiz

Sierra Mojada
Ocampo

San Juan de Sabinas

Cuatro Ciénegas

Frontera
Monclova

Islas San Benito
Isla Cedros
Isla Natividad
Punta Eugenia

Guerrero Negro
El Arco

Guaymas
Empalme
Cabo Haro

Yécora
Adolfo López Madero
Basaseachic

Creel

CHIHUAHUA

Hidalgo del Parral

Valle de Zaragoza
Jiménez
Saucillo
Ciudad Camargo

LLANOS LOS GIGANTES

GUAJE PLAINS

San Pedro de las Colonias

SIERRA MADRE ORIENTAL

BAJA CALIFORNIA SUR

Mulegé
Punta Concepción
Santa Rosalía

Isla Lobos

Ciudad Obregón
Navojoa
Álamos

Rosario
Samachique
Batopilas
Guachochi

Villa Ocampo

Ceballos

Mapimí

DURANGO

El Palmito
La Zarca

Gómez Palacio
Torreón
Matamoros
Viesca

Parras de la Fuente

Saltillo

Concepción del Oro

Huatabampo
Yavaros
Punta Rosa

Choix
El Fuerte

Higuera de Zaragoza
Guadalupe y Calvo

Santiago de los Caballeros

Tepehuanes

Rodeo
Nazas

Santiago Papasquiaro

Cuencamé

Loreto
Isla Carmen
Isla Santa Catalina

Villa Insurgentes
Ciudad Constitución

Isla Magdalena
Cabo San Lázaro
San Carlos

RESERVA ESPECIAL DE LA BIÓSFERA ISLAS DEL GOLFO DE CALIFORNIA

Isla San José
Isla Espíritu Santo

La Paz Bay
Pichilingue

Los Mochis
Topolobampo

SINALOA

Guasave
Guamúchil

Navolato
Culiacán

Eldorado
Cosalá

Canatlán
Francisco I. Madero
Tayoltita
Durango

Juan Aldama
San Tiburcio

ZACATECAS

Río Grande

Isla Santa Margarita

La Paz

Isla Cerralvo

La Cruz

El Salto
Mezquital
Sombrerete

Fresnillo

SAN LUIS POTOSÍ

Todos Santos

Cabo Pulmo
Parque Marino Nacional Cabo Pulmo

Mazatlán
Villa Unión
Rosario
Escuinapa

Valparaíso

Víctor Rosales
Zacatecas

Moctezuma
Salinas

Cabo Falso
Cabo San Lucas
Cabo San Lucas
San José del Cabo

Teacapan
Acaponeta

Huejuquilla
Jerez de García Salinas

Rincón de Romos

San Luis Potosí

Tuxpan

Villanueva

Ojuelos de Jalisco

NAYARIT

Tabasco
San Blas

AGU.

Aguascalientes

Lagos de Moreno
San Felipe

Isla María Madre
Isla María Magdalena
Islas Marías

Tepic

Teocaltiche
San Juan de los Lagos

León
Guanajuato

GUANAJUATO

Par. Nac. Isla Isabel

Compostela
Ixtlán

Tequila

Guadalajara

Irapuato
Celaya

Puerto Vallarta
Cabo Corrientes

Mascota
Ameca

La Piedad de Cabadas
Salamanca

Moroleón

JALISCO

Chapala
Ocotlán

Zamora de Hidalgo

Tomatlán
Autlán

Sayula

L. de Chapala

Sahuayo

Ciudad Guzmán
Los Reyes
Tecalitlán

Pátzcuaro

Morelia

Manzanillo
Tecomán

COLIMA

Colima

Cihuatlán
Nev. de Colima

Apatzingán
Nueva Italia

Uruapan
Ario de Rosales

Coalcomán

MICHOACÁN

Arteaga

Presa Infiernillo

Huetamo

Balsas

Lázaro Cárdenas
Ixtapa
Zihuatanejo
Petatlán

SIERRA

184

186

185

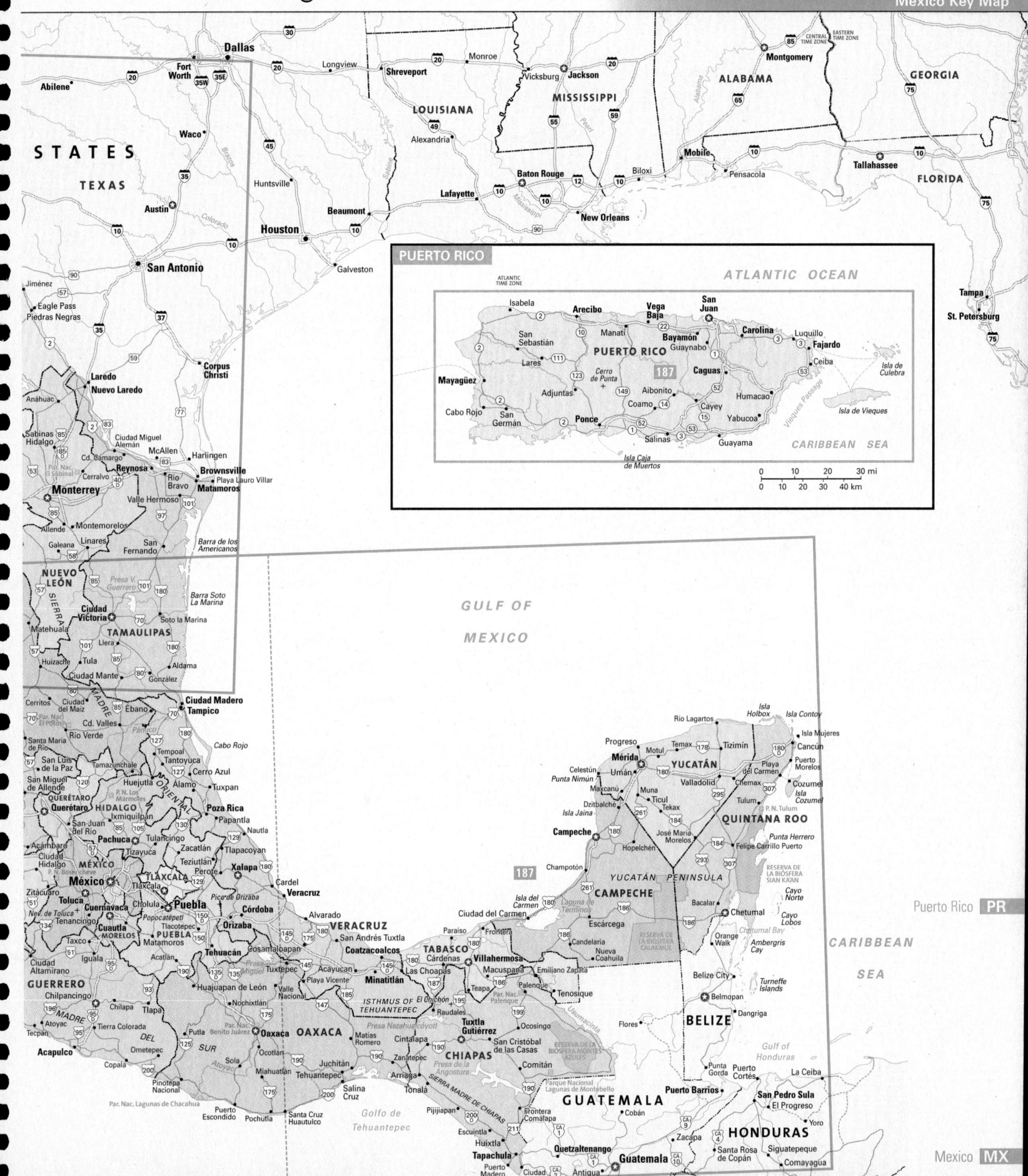

Map Pages   Map Scale
184–187 ↔ 1 : 5,000,000
187 ↔ 1 : 1,525,000

PUERTO RICO

ATLANTIC OCEAN

ATLANTIC
TIME ZONE

Isabela   Arecibo   Vega   San
Baja   Juan

San
Sebastián   Manatí   22   Carolina   Luquillo
Bayamón   Guaynabo   Caguas   3   Fajardo
Lares   PUERTO RICO   52   Ceiba
111   187   Caguas   Isla de
Culebra
Mayagüez   123   Cerro   149   Aibonito   Cayey   Humacao
de Punta   Coamo   14   53
Adjuntas   15   Yabucoa   Vieques Passage
Cabo Rojo   San   Ponce   Salinas   Isla de Vieques
Germán   2   1   53
Salinas   Guayama   CARIBBEAN SEA
Isla Caja
de Muertos

0   10   20   30 mi
0   10   20   30   40 km

GULF OF

MEXICO

Puerto Rico PR

CARIBBEAN

SEA

Mexico MX

ABQ-DEN=342

PACIFIC OCEAN

TEMPERATURE CONVERSIONS

°F	°C	°C	°F
100	37.8	35	95
90	32.2	30	86
80	26.7	25	77
70	21.1	20	68
60	15.6	15	59
50	10.0	10	50
40	4.4	5	41
32	0	0	32
30	-1.1	-5	23
20	-6.7	-10	14
10	-12.2	-15	5
0	-17.8	-20	-4
-10	-23.3	-25	-13
-20	-28.9	-30	-22
-30	-34.4	-35	-31
-40	-40.0	-40	-40
-50	-45.6	-45	-49

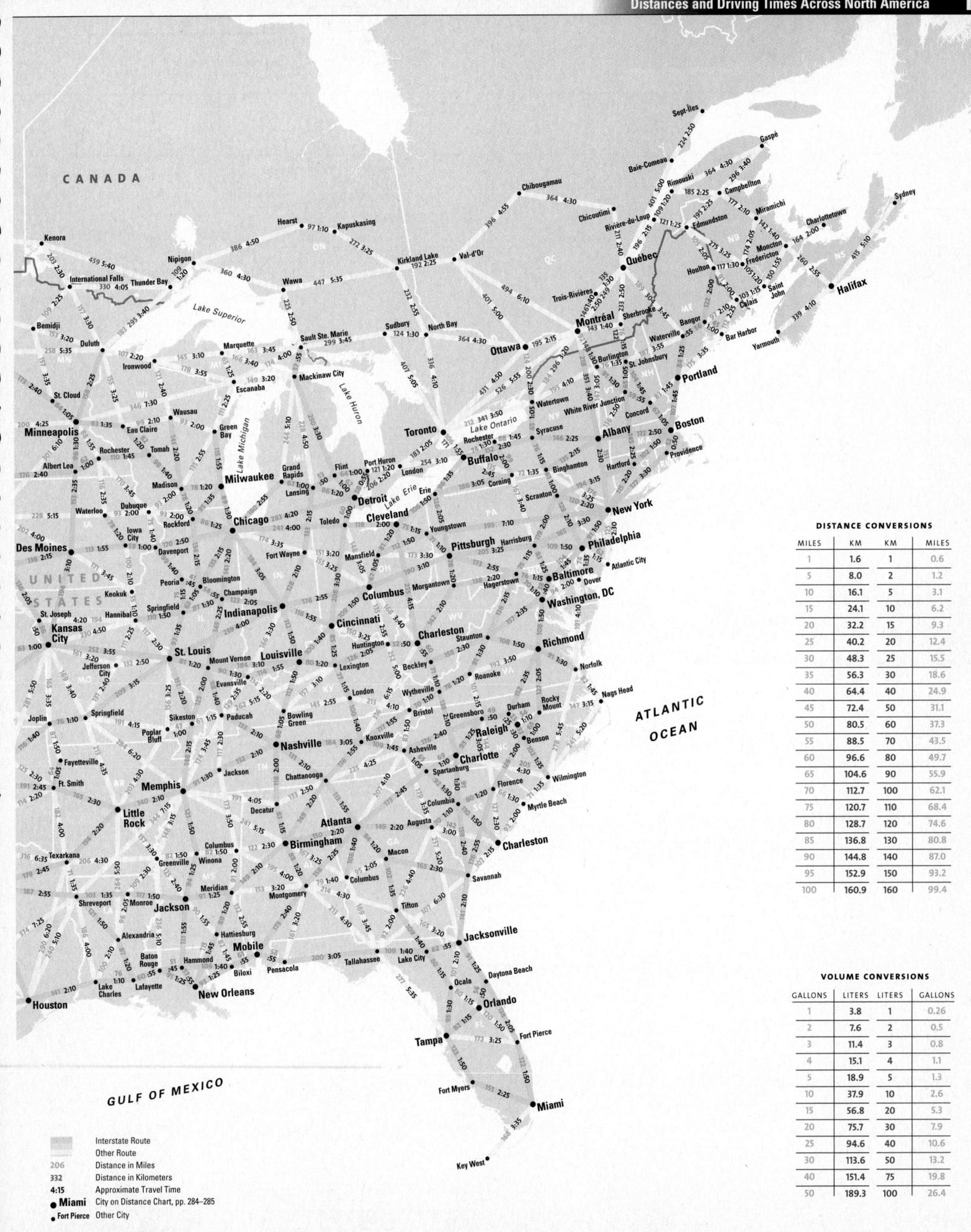

DISTANCE CONVERSIONS

MILES	KM	KM	MILES
1	1.6	1	0.6
5	8.0	2	1.2
10	16.1	5	3.1
15	24.1	10	6.2
20	32.2	15	9.3
25	40.2	20	12.4
30	48.3	25	15.5
35	56.3	30	18.6
40	64.4	40	24.9
45	72.4	50	31.1
50	80.5	60	37.3
55	88.5	70	43.5
60	96.6	80	49.7
65	104.6	90	55.9
70	112.7	100	62.1
75	120.7	110	68.4
80	128.7	120	74.6
85	136.8	130	80.8
90	144.8	140	87.0
95	152.9	150	93.2
100	160.9	160	99.4

VOLUME CONVERSIONS

GALLONS	LITERS	LITERS	GALLONS
1	3.8	1	0.26
2	7.6	2	0.5
3	11.4	3	0.8
4	15.1	4	1.1
5	18.9	5	1.3
10	37.9	10	2.6
15	56.8	20	5.3
20	75.7	30	7.9
25	94.6	40	10.6
30	113.6	50	13.2
40	151.4	75	19.8
50	189.3	100	26.4

Interstate Route
Other Route
206 Distance in Miles
332 Distance in Kilometers
4:15 Approximate Travel Time
● **Miami** City on Distance Chart, pp. 284–285
● Fort Pierce Other City

Distances and driving times may vary depending on actual
route traveled and driving conditions.

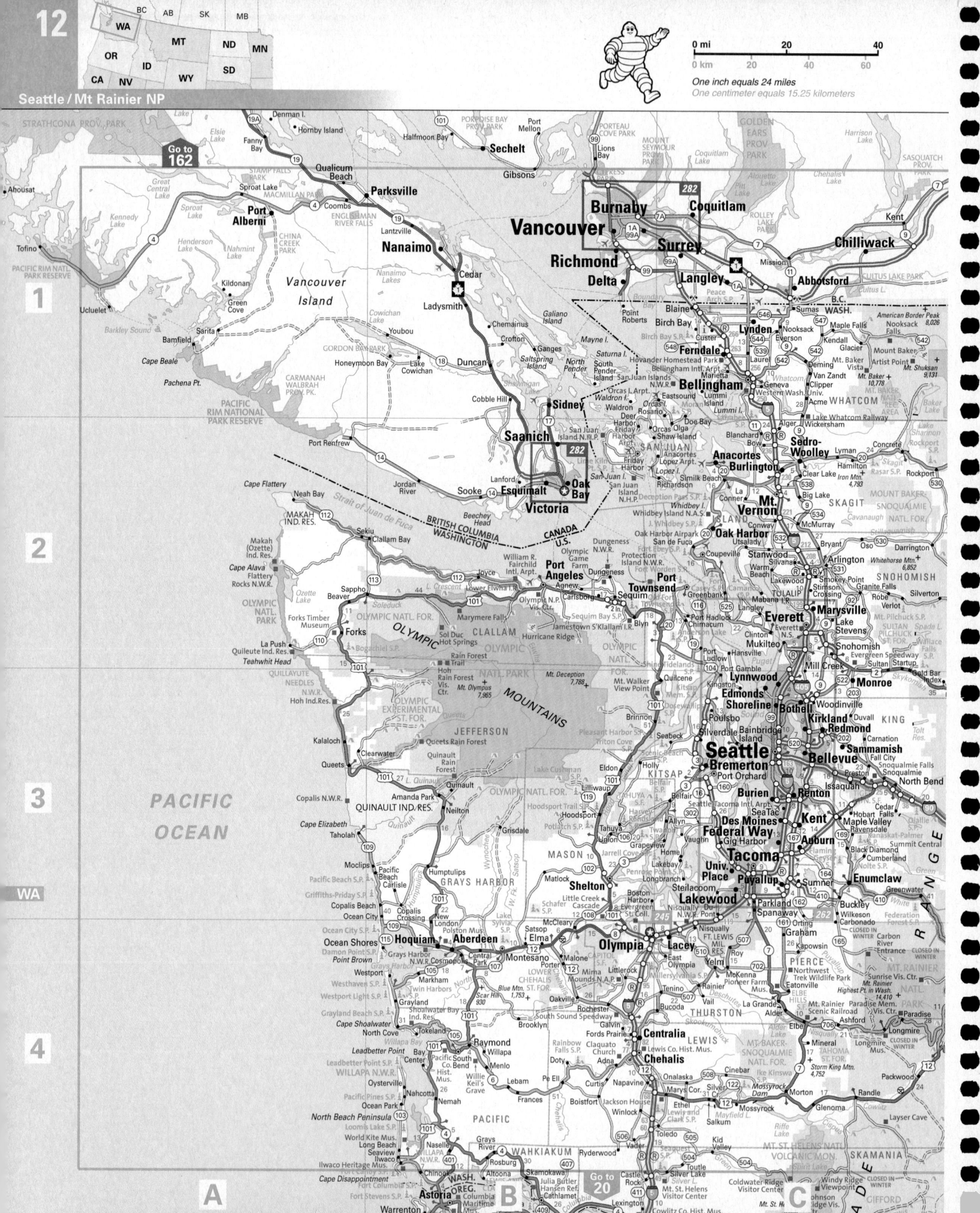

BC AB SK MB
WA
MT ND MN
OR ID WY SD
CA NV

One inch equals 24 miles
One centimeter equals 15.25 kilometers

0 mi   20   40
0 km   20   60

STRATHCONA PROV. PARK

Ahousat

Tofino

PACIFIC RIM NATL. PARK RESERVE

Ucluelet

Kennedy Lake

Kildonan

Green Cove

Sarita

Bamfield

Cape Beale

Pachena Pt.

Barkley Sound

Henderson Lake

Nahmint Lake

Port Alberni

Sproat Lake

Great Central Lake

Elsie Lake

Fanny Bay

Denman I.

Hornby Island

Qualicum Beach

Parksville

Coombs

Cedar

Nanaimo

Nanaimo Lakes

Vancouver Island

Ladysmith

Youbou

Lake Cowichan

Honeymoon Bay

GORDON BAY PARK

CARMANAH WALBRAH PROV. PK.

PACIFIC RIM NATIONAL PARK RESERVE

Cape Flattery

Neah Bay

MAKAH IND. RES.

Makah (Ozette) Ind. Res.

Cape Alava

Flattery Rocks N.W.R.

Sekiu

Clallam Bay

Ozette Lake

OLYMPIC NATL. FOR.

Sappho

Beaver

Forks

Forks Timber Museum

La Push

Quileute Ind. Res.

Teahwhit Head

QUILLAYUTE NEEDLES

Hoh Ind.Res.

PACIFIC OCEAN

Kalaloch

Clearwater

Queets

Copalis N.W.R.

Cape Elizabeth

Taholah

Moclips

Pacific Beach S.P.

Pacific Beach Carlisle

Copalis Beach

Ocean City

Ocean City S.P.

Ocean Shores

Damon Point S.P.

Point Brown

Westport

Westhaven S.P.

Westport Light S.P.

Twin Harbors S.P.

Grayland Beach S.P.

Cape Shoalwater

North Cove

Leadbetter Point

Leadbetter Point S.P.

Oysterville

Pacific Pines S.P.

Ocean Park

North Beach Peninsula

Loomis Lake S.P.

World Kite Mus.

Long Beach

Seaview

Ilwaco

Ilwaco Heritage Mus.

Cape Disappointment

Fort Columbia S.P.

Fort Stevens S.P.

Astoria

Warrenton

Go to 162

Halfmoon Bay

Sechelt

Gibsons

PORPOISE BAY PROV. PARK

Port Mellon

PORTEAU COVE PARK

Lions Bay

CYPRESS PARK

GOLDEN EARS PROV. PARK

MOUNT SEYMOUR PROM. PARK

Coquitlam Lake

Pitt Lake

ROLLEY LAKE PARK

Kent

Harrison Lake

Chehalis Lake

SASQUATCH PROV.

Vancouver

Burnaby

Coquitlam

Richmond

Surrey

Langley

Delta

Mission

Abbotsford

Chilliwack

Cultus Lake Park

Cultus L.

B.C. WASH.

Blaine

Point Roberts

Birch Bay

Birch Bay S.P.

Custer

Lynden

Everson

Nooksack

Maple Falls

Kendall

Deming

Mt. Baker Vista

Mt. Baker + 10,778

Mt. Shuksan 9,131

American Border Peak 8,026

Nooksack Falls

Artist Point

MOUNT BAKER SNOQUALMIE NATL. FOR.

Ferndale

Laurel

Marietta

Bellingham

Bellingham Intl. Arpt.

Western Wash. Univ.

Geneva

Van Zandt

Clipper

Acme

WHATCOM

Sidney

Saanich

Esquimalt

Victoria

Oak Bay

Sooke

Lanford

Jordan River

Port Renfrew

Sombrio Pt.

BRITISH COLUMBIA
WASHINGTON

Orcas I. Arpt.

Eastsound

Orcas I.

Moran S.P.

Doe Bay

Lummi Island

Waldron I.

San Juan Islands N.W.R.

South Pender Island

North Pender Island

Saltspring Island

Galiano Island

Mayne I.

Saturna I.

Shawnigan Lake

Cobble Hill

Duncan

Chemainus

Crofton

Ganges

Cowichan Lake

CHINA CREEK PARK

STAMP FALLS PROV. PARK

MACMILLAN PARK

ENGLISHMAN RIVER FALLS

Lantzville

Sproat Lake

Friday Harbor

San Juan Island N.H.P.

Lopez I.

Lopez Arpt.

Richardson

SAN JUAN

Shaw Island

Rosario

Lummi I.

Deer Harbor

Olga

Blanchard

Bow

Alger

Lake Whatcom Railway

Wickersham

Sedro-Woolley

Lyman

Clear Lake

Burlington

Concrete

Hamilton

Rockport

Rasar S.P.

Baker Lake

Lake Shannon

SKAGIT

Anacortes

Lime Kiln

Deception Pass S.P.

Whidbey I.

Whidbey Island N.A.S.

J. Whidbey S.P.

Oak Harbor Airpark

Oak Harbor

Usalady

Camano I.

Camano I. S.P.

Stanwood

Silvana

Arlington

Darrington

Oso

Whitehorse Mtn. + 6,852

MT. BAKER SNOQUALMIE NATL. FOR.

Mt. Vernon

Conway

McMurray

Big Lake

Cavanaugh

Iron Mtn. 4,793

Ronald

San de Fuca

Coupeville

Fort Casey S.P.

Keystone

Greenbank

Fort Ebey S.P.

Mabana

Tulalip I.R.

Marysville

Lake Stevens

Mt. Pilchuck S.P.

SNOHOMISH

Smokey Point

Stimson Crossing

Granite Falls

Robe

Verlot

Silverton

Spada L.

PILCHUCK SPAMA L.

WALLACE FALLS S.P.

Startup

Gold Bar

Index

Everett

Everett N.S.

Mukilteo

Clinton

Hansville

Langley

Port Susan

Port Gamble

Port Ludlow

Kingston

Edmonds

Lynnwood

Mountlake

Shoreline

Bothell

Woodinville

Duvall

KING

Carnation

Fall City

Snoqualmie

Snoqualmie Falls

North Bend

Kirkland

Redmond

Sammamish

Bellevue

Preston

Issaquah

Tolt Res.

Spencer

Snohomish

Evergreen Speedway

Monroe

Sultan

Port Angeles

Agnew

Dungeness

Port Townsend

Sequim

Carlsborg

Sequim Bay S.P.

Blyn

Jamestown S'Klallam I.R.

Chimacum

Port Hadlock

Anderson Lake

Hadlock

Fort Worden S.P.

Protection Island N.W.R.

Indian Island

William R. Fairchild Intl. Arpt.

Joyce

Lower Elwha I.R.

L. Crescent

Marymere Falls

Sol Duc Hot Springs

OLYMPIC NATL. PARK

Hurricane Ridge

OLYMPIC NATL. PARK

Mt. Deception 7,788 +

Mt. Olympus 7,965

Mt. Walker View Point

Quilcene

Dosewallips S.P.

Brinnon

Pleasant Harbor S.P.

Triton Cove

Seabeck

Silverdale

Bremerton

Port Orchard

Bainbridge Island

Poulsbo

Bangor

KITSAP

Belfair

Seattle

Seattle Tacoma Intl. Arpt.

SeaTac

Burien

Des Moines

Federal Way

Renton

Kent

Maple Valley

Hobart

Ravensdale

Black Diamond

Cedar Falls

Summit Central

Cumberland

MASON

Eldon

Holly

Tahuya

Union

Hoodsport

Lake Cushman

Lilliwaup

Potlatch S.P.

Lilliwaup

Shelton

Little Creek Cascade

Schafer S.P.

Matlock

Dayton

Vaughn

Gig Harbor

Kopachuck S.P.

Purdy

Lakebay

Penrose Pt. S.P.

Longbranch

Grapeview

Allyn

Home

Tacoma

Univ. Place

Puyallup

Sumner

Parkland

Spanaway

Lakewood

Steilacoom

FT. LEWIS MIL. RES.

DuPont

Nisqually N.W.R.

Auburn

Kent

Sumner

Enumclaw

Buckley

Wilkeson

Carbonado

Graham

Kapowsin

Orting

Carbon River Entrance CLOSED IN WINTER

MT. RAINIER NATL. PARK

Mt. Rainier Highest Pt. in Wash. 14,410 +

Sunrise Vis. Ctr.

Paradise

Mt. Rainier Paradise Mem. Vis. Ctr.

PIERCE

Roy

Rainier

McKenna

Yelm

Eatonville

Northwest Trek Wildlife Park

Pioneer Farm Mus.

Elbe

Ashford

Longmire

Storm King Mtn. 4,752

Packwood

GIFFORD

La Grande

Alder

Mt. Rainier Scenic Railroad

ELBE HILLS ST. FOR.

Mineral

TAHOMA ST. FOR.

Morton

Randle

Glenoma

Mossyrock

Mossyrock Dam

Mayfield L.

Riffe Lake

Cowlitz R.

MT. ST. HELENS NATL. VOLCANIC MON.

Layser Cave

SKAMANIA

CASCADE RANGE

Windy Ridge Viewpoint CLOSED IN WINTER

Mt. St. Helens

Coldwater Ridge Visitor Center

Mt. St. Helens Visitor Center

Johnston Ridge Vis.

Lacey

Olympia

Lakewood

Tumwater

Tenino

Bucoda

Tono

Vail

Rainier

Centralia

Chehalis

Lewis Co. Hist. Mus.

THURSTON

LEWIS

Rochester

Grand Mound

Littlerock

Mima Mounds N.A.P.

Capitol S.F.

Gate

East Olympia

Millersylvania S.P.

Scar Hill 930

Blue Mtn. 1,753

Oakville

Galvin

Adna

Napavine

Onalaska

Silver Cr.

Cinebar

Salkum

Toledo

Vader

Ryderwood

Castle Rock

Kelso

Silver L.

Seaquest S.P.

Kid Valley

Toutle

Cowlitz Co. Hist. Mus.

Lexington

Winlock

Toledo

Ethel

Jackson House

Boistfort

Curtis

Pe Ell

Doty

Rainbow Falls S.P.

Claquato Church

Fords Prairie

Willapa

Raymond

South Bend

Pacific South Co. Hist. Mus.

Willie Keil's Grave

Lebam

Menlo

Frances

WAHKIAKUM

Cathlamet

Skamokawa

Julia Butler Hansen Ref.

Altoona

Columbia R.

OREG.

Puget I.

WILLAPA N.W.R.

Naselle

Nahcotta

Nemah

Bay Center

Willapa Bay

Tokeland

GRAYS HARBOR

Aberdeen

Hoquiam

Cosmopolis

Central Park

Montesano

Satsop

Elma

McCleary

Malone

Porter

Satsop S.F.

Bordeaux

Boston Harbor

MASON

Kamilche

Arcadia

Grisdale

Neilton

Amanda Park

QUINAULT IND. RES.

Quinault

Quinault Rain Forest

L. Quinault

JEFFERSON

Queets Rain Forest

OLYMPIC EXPERIMENTAL ST. FOR.

Hoh Rain Forest Vis. Ctr.

Rain Forest Trail

Bogachiel S.P.

Humptulips

New London

Polston Mus.

Satsop

Brooklyn

W. Fk. Satsop

E. Fk. Satsop

Montesano

Wynoochee

Lake Sylvia S.P.

Cloquallum

Deschutes

Nisqually

Nisqually N.W.R. Pont.

Evergreen St. Coll.

Yelm

Harvey Field

Kitsap

Brinnon

Chinook

Fort Columbia S.P.

Warrenton

Astoria

COLUMBIA

Columbia R.

Go to 20

Go to 20

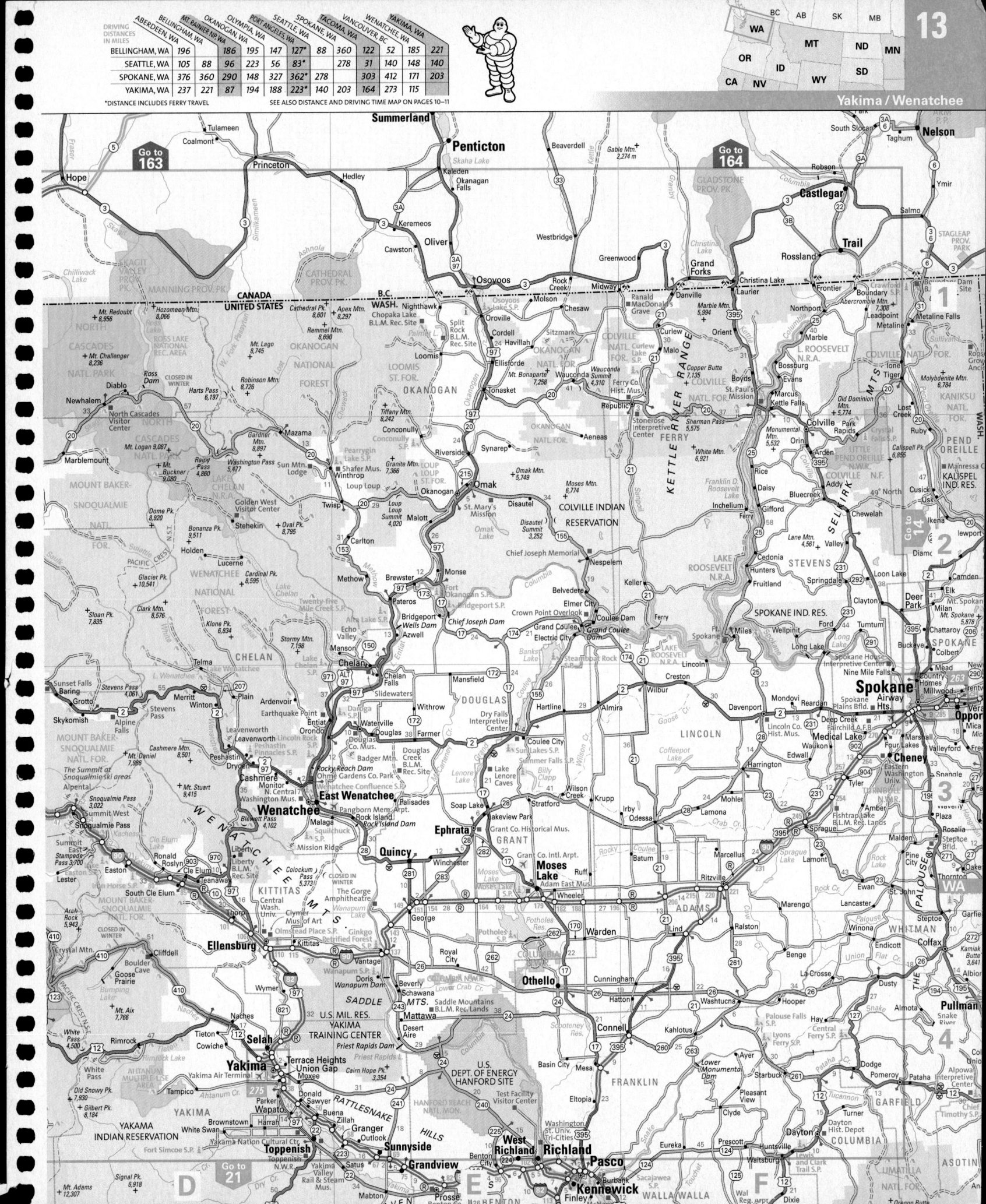

DRIVING DISTANCES IN MILES	ABERDEEN, WA	BELLINGHAM, WA	MT. RAINIER NP WA	OKANOGAN, WA	OLYMPIA, WA	PORT ANGELES, WA	SEATTLE, WA	SPOKANE, WA	TACOMA, WA	VANCOUVER, BC	WENATCHEE, WA	YAKIMA, WA
BELLINGHAM, WA	196		186	195	147	127*	88	360	122	52	185	221
SEATTLE, WA	105	88	96	223	56	83*		278	31	140	148	140
SPOKANE, WA	376	360	290	148	327	362*	278		303	412	171	203
YAKIMA, WA	237	221	87	194	188	223*	140	203	164	273	115	

*DISTANCE INCLUDES FERRY TRAVEL   SEE ALSO DISTANCE AND DRIVING TIME MAP ON PAGES 10–11

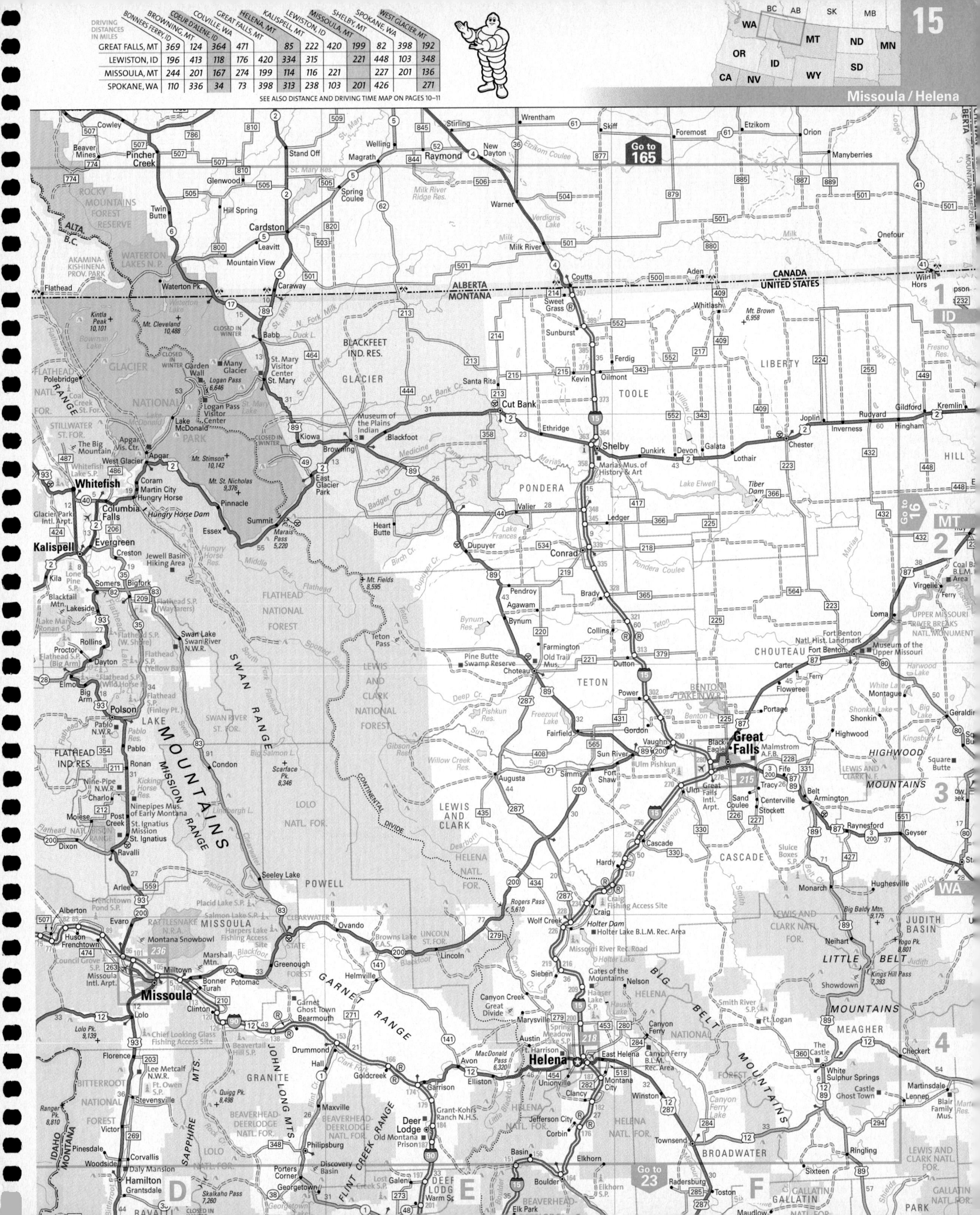

DRIVING DISTANCES IN MILES	BONNERS FERRY, ID	BROWNING, MT	COEUR D'ALENE, ID	COLVILLE, WA	GREAT FALLS, MT	HELENA, MT	KALISPELL, MT	LEWISTON, ID	MISSOULA, MT	SHELBY, MT	SPOKANE, WA	WEST GLACIER, MT
GREAT FALLS, MT	369	124	364	471		85	222	420	199	82	398	192
LEWISTON, ID	196	413	118	176	420	334	315		221	448	103	348
MISSOULA, MT	244	201	167	274	199	114	116	221		227	201	136
SPOKANE, WA	110	336	34	73	398	313	238	103	201	426		271

SEE ALSO DISTANCE AND DRIVING TIME MAP ON PAGES 10–11

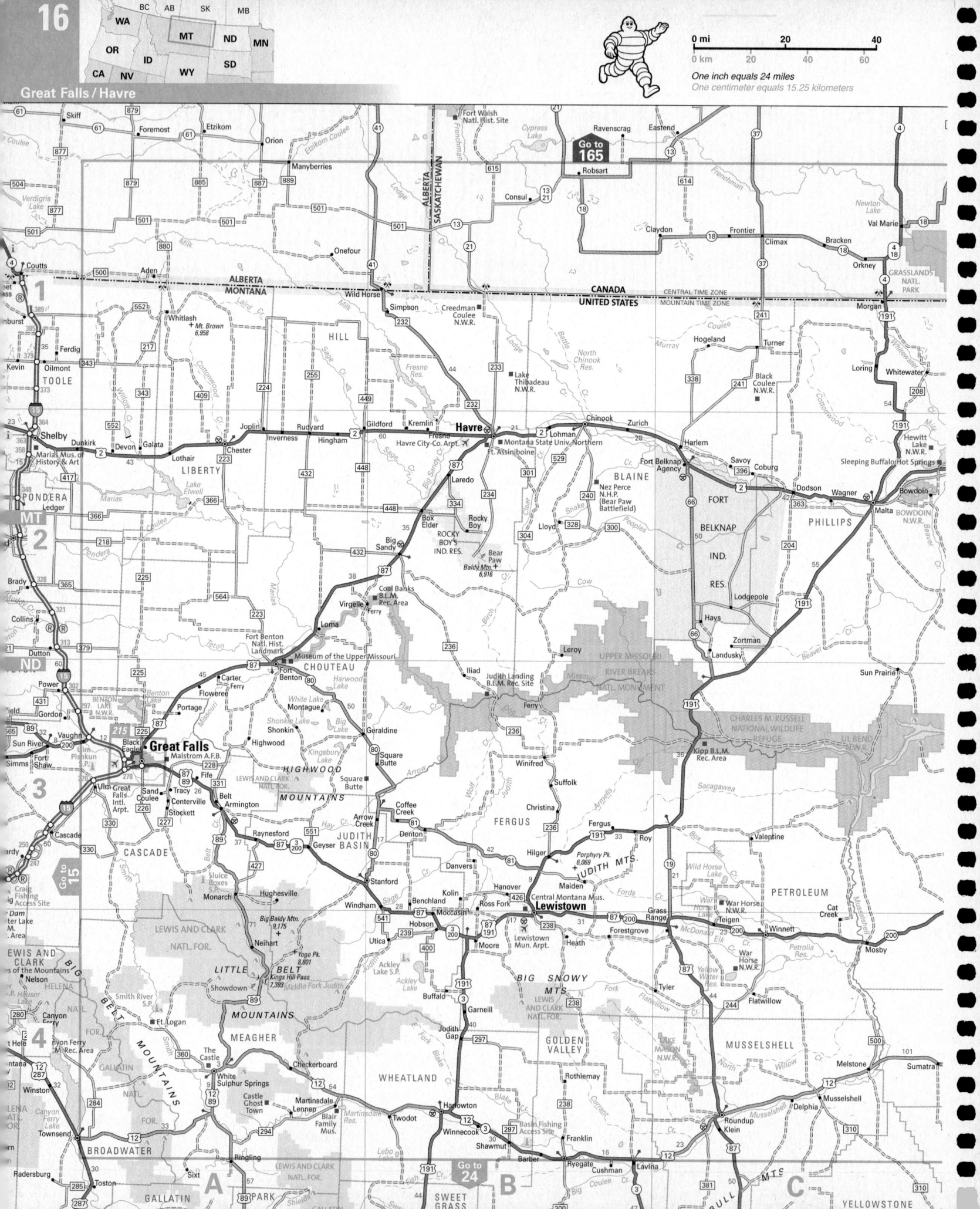

One inch equals 24 miles
One centimeter equals 15.25 kilometers

0 mi   20   40
0 km   20   40   60

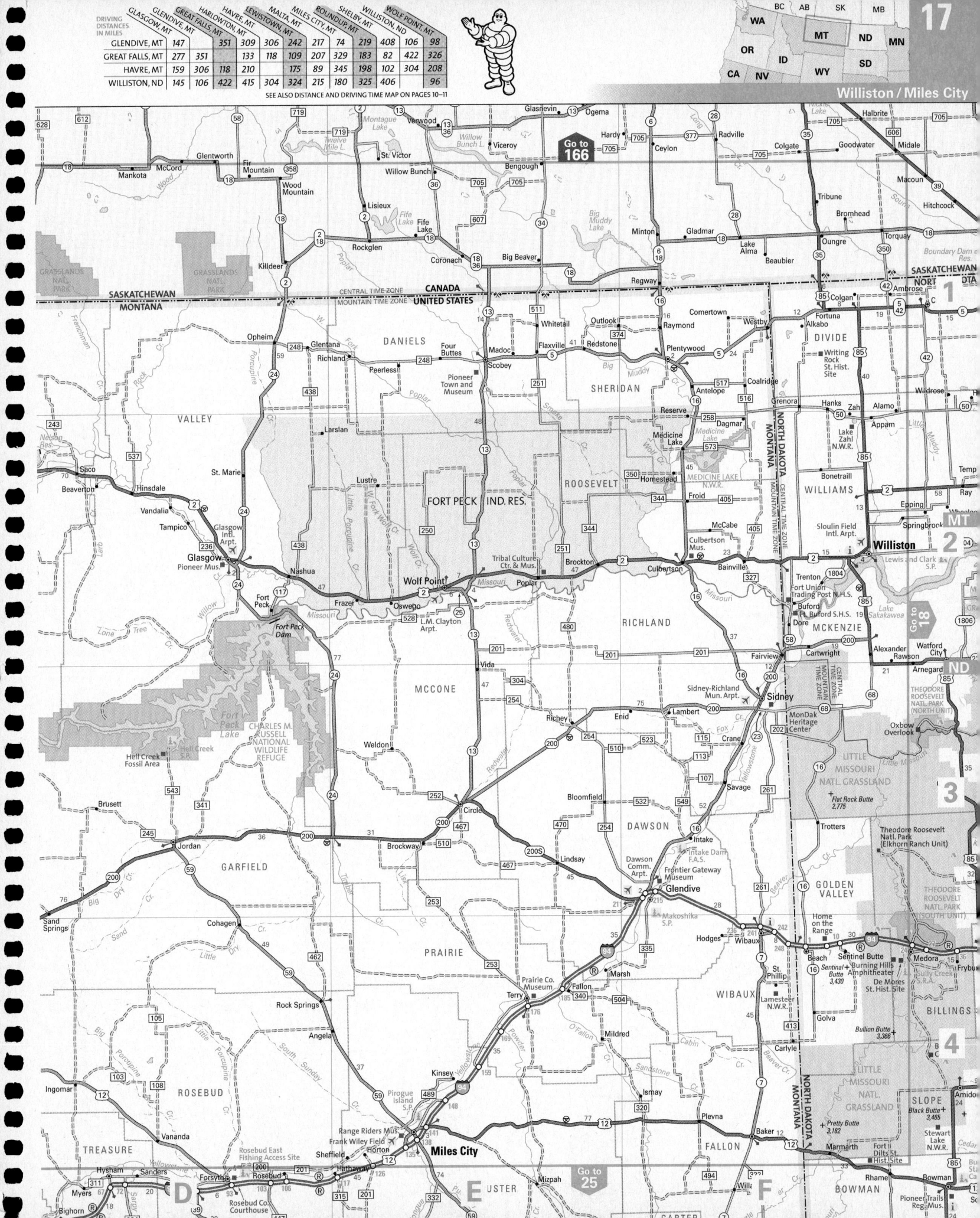

DRIVING DISTANCES IN MILES

	GLENDIVE, MT	GREAT FALLS, MT	HARLOWTON, MT	HAVRE, MT	LEWISTOWN, MT	MALTA, MT	MILES CITY, MT	ROUNDUP, MT	SHELBY, MT	WILLISTON, ND	WOLF POINT, MT
GLENDIVE, MT	147	351	309	306	242	217	74	219	408	106	98
GREAT FALLS, MT	277	351		133	118	109	207	329	183	82	422	326
HAVRE, MT	159	306	118		210	175	89	345	102	304	208
WILLISTON, ND	145	106	422	415	304	324	215	180	325	406	96

SEE ALSO DISTANCE AND DRIVING TIME MAP ON PAGES 10–11

Go to 166

Go to 18

Go to 25

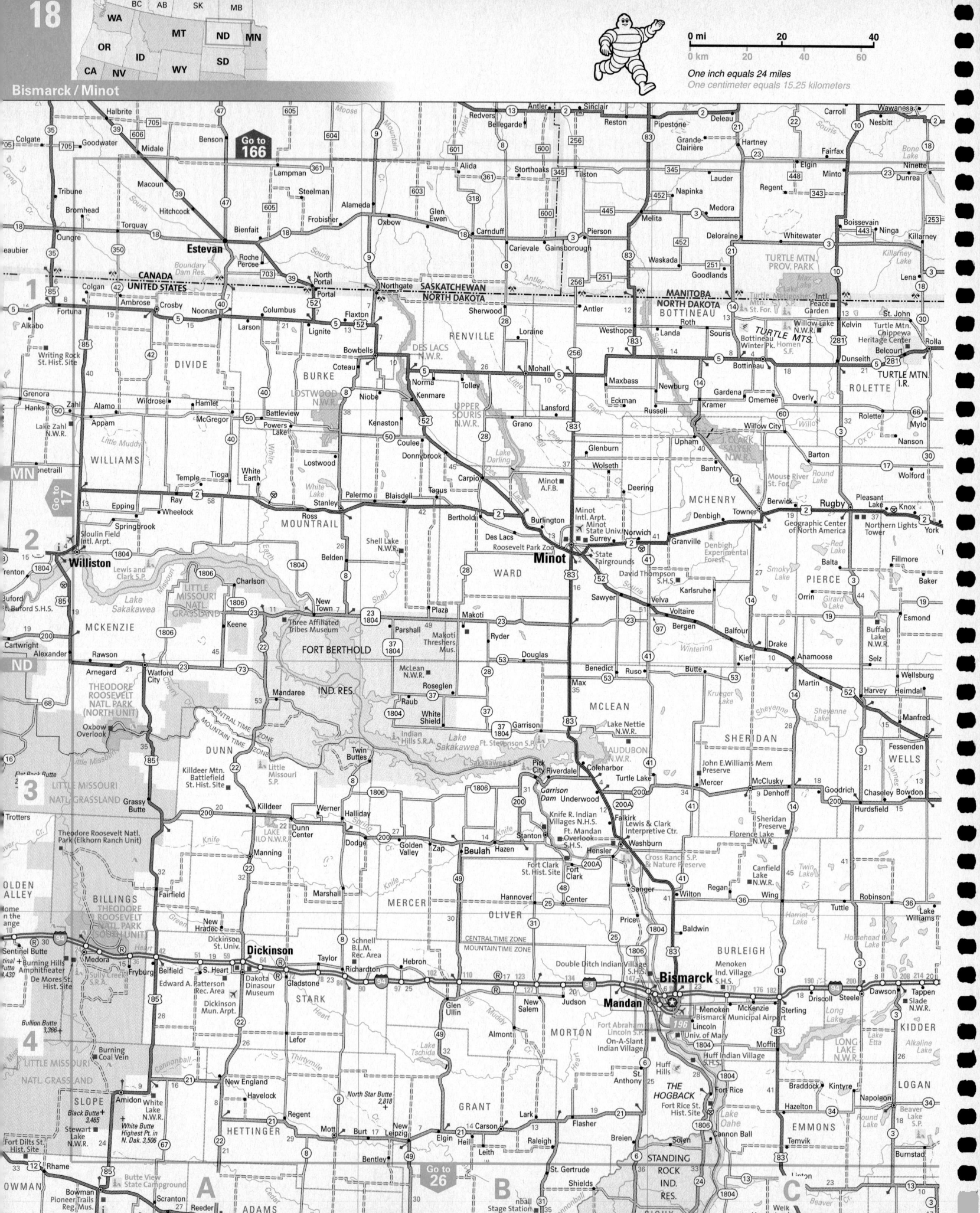

One inch equals 24 miles
One centimeter equals 15.25 kilometers

Go to 166

Go to 17

Go to 26

DRIVING DISTANCES IN MILES	BISMARCK, ND	BOTTINEAU, ND	DETROIT LAKES, MN	DICKINSON, ND	FARGO, ND	GRAND FORKS, ND	JAMESTOWN, ND	MINOT, ND	PEMBINA, ND	RUGBY, ND	THIEF RIVER FALLS, ND	WILLISTON, ND
BISMARCK, ND		189	244	97	199	274	105	116	347	153	319	229
FARGO, ND	199	271	45	291		79	97	268	152	221	113	424
GRAND FORKS, ND	274	198	125	367	79		173	212	77	148	61	340
MINOT, ND	116	76	313	178	268	212	171		238	64	276	128

SEE ALSO DISTANCE AND DRIVING TIME MAP ON PAGES 10–11

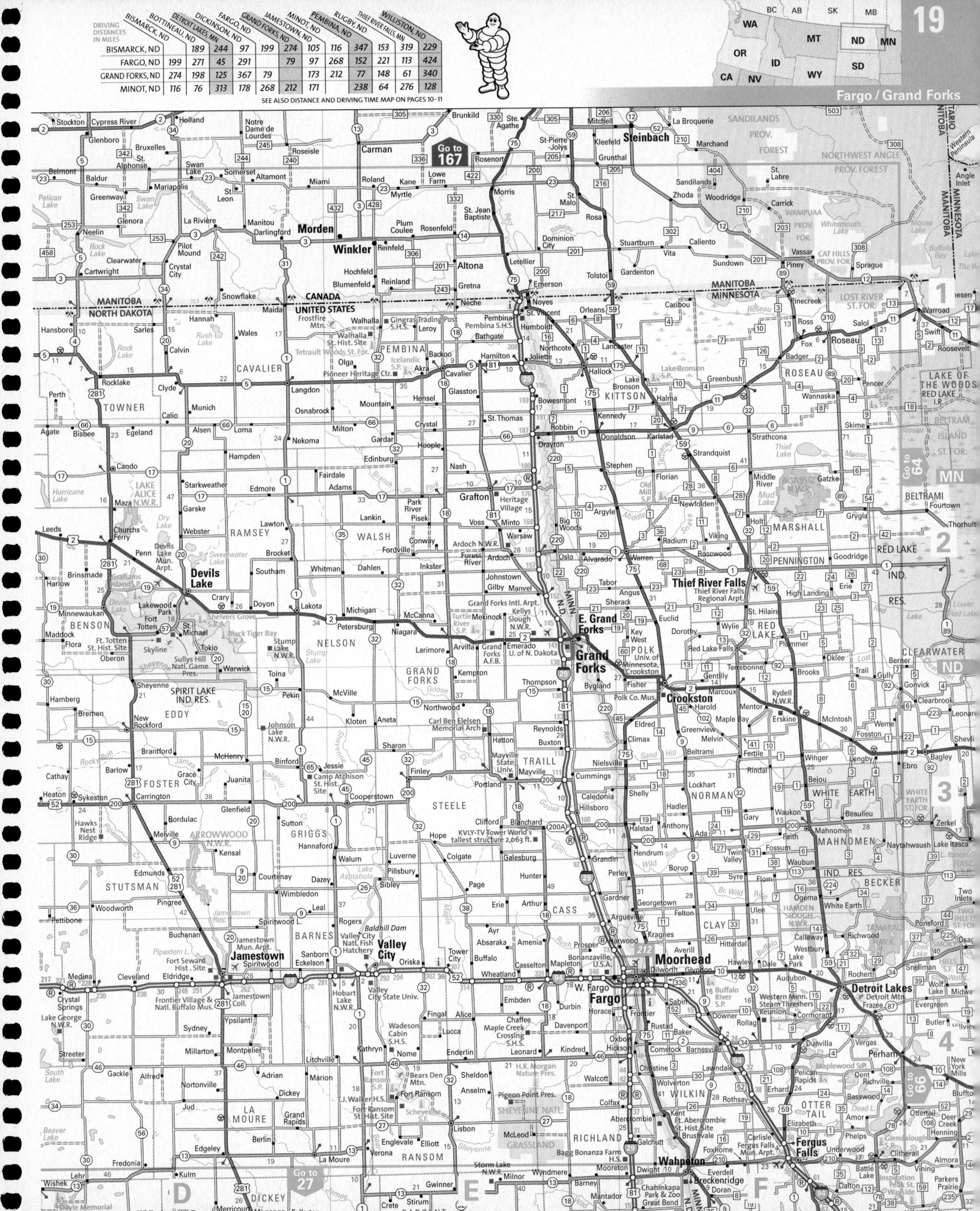

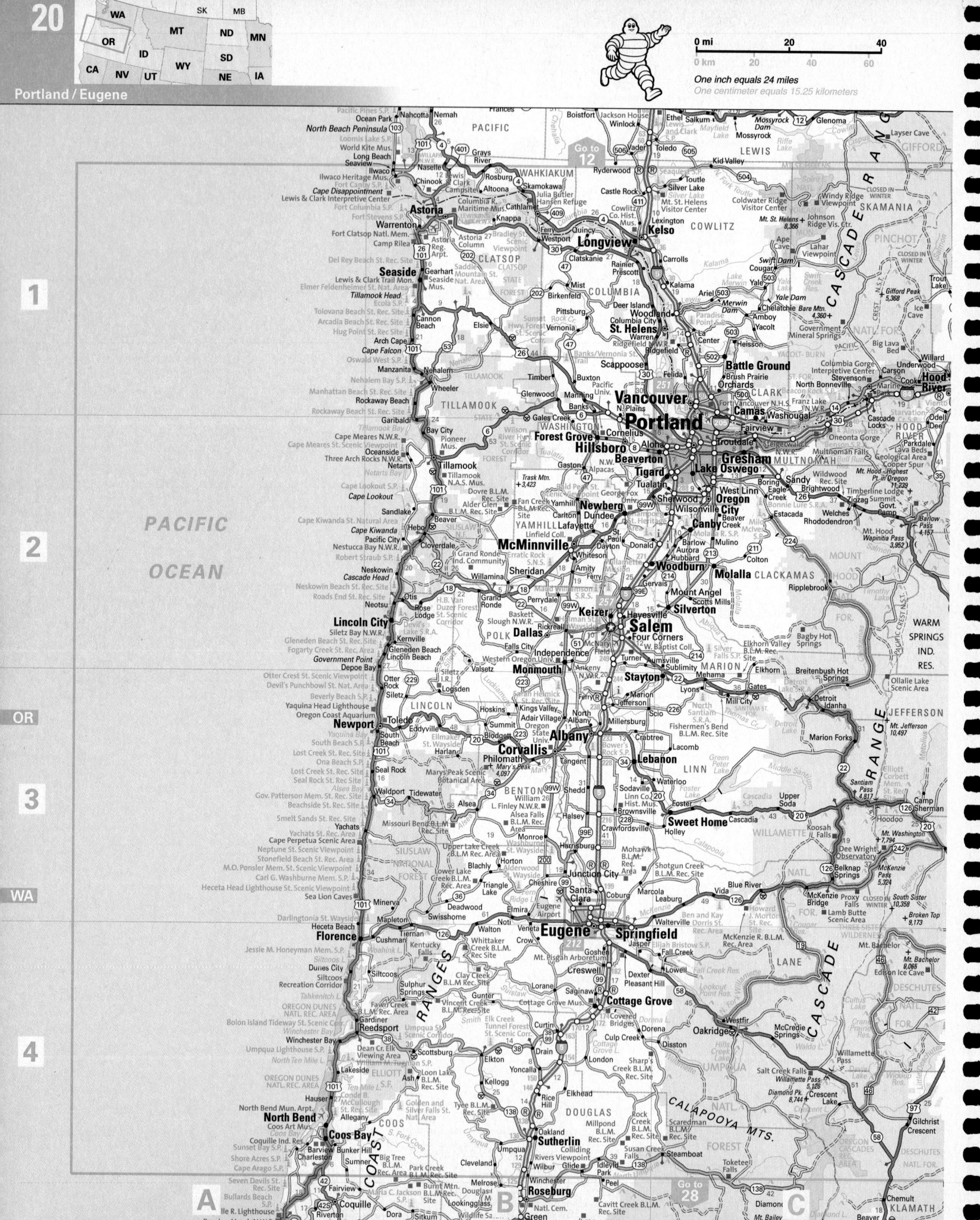

0 mi   20   40
0 km   20   40   60
One inch equals 24 miles
One centimeter equals 15.25 kilometers

WA SK MB
OR MT ND MN
ID WY SD
CA NV UT NE IA

Go to 12

Go to 28

PACIFIC OCEAN

CASCADE RANGE

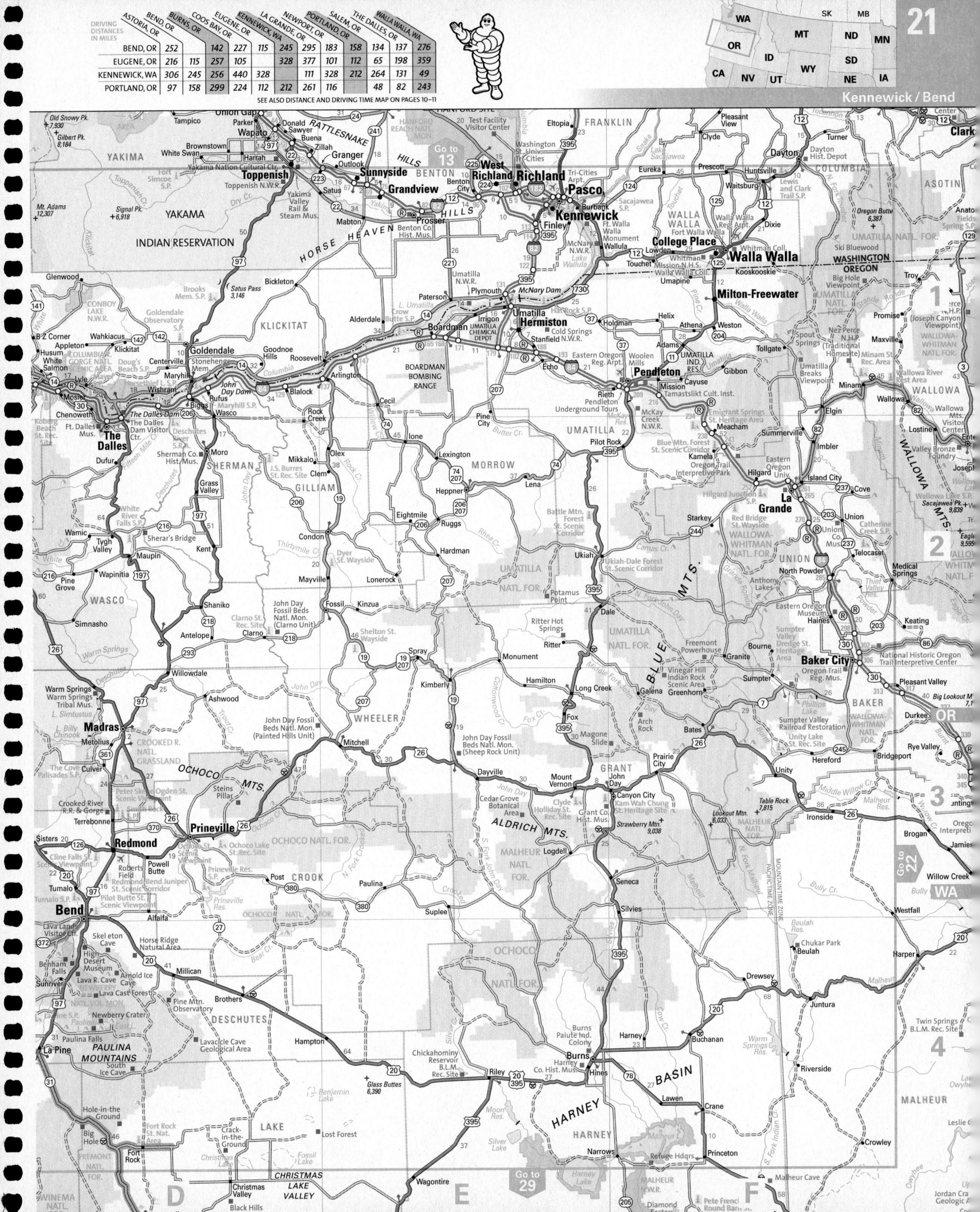

DRIVING DISTANCES IN MILES	ASTORIA, OR	BEND, OR	BURNS, OR	COOS BAY, OR	EUGENE, OR	KENNEWICK, WA	LA GRANDE, OR	NEWPORT, OR	PORTLAND, OR	SALEM, OR	THE DALLES, OR	WALLA WALLA, WA
BEND, OR	252			142	227	115	245	295	183	158	134	137	276
EUGENE, OR	216	115	257	105		328	377	101	112	65	198	359
KENNEWICK, WA	306	245	256	440	328		111	328	212	264	131	49
PORTLAND, OR	97	158	299	224	112	212	261	116		48	82	243

SEE ALSO DISTANCE AND DRIVING TIME MAP ON PAGES 10-11

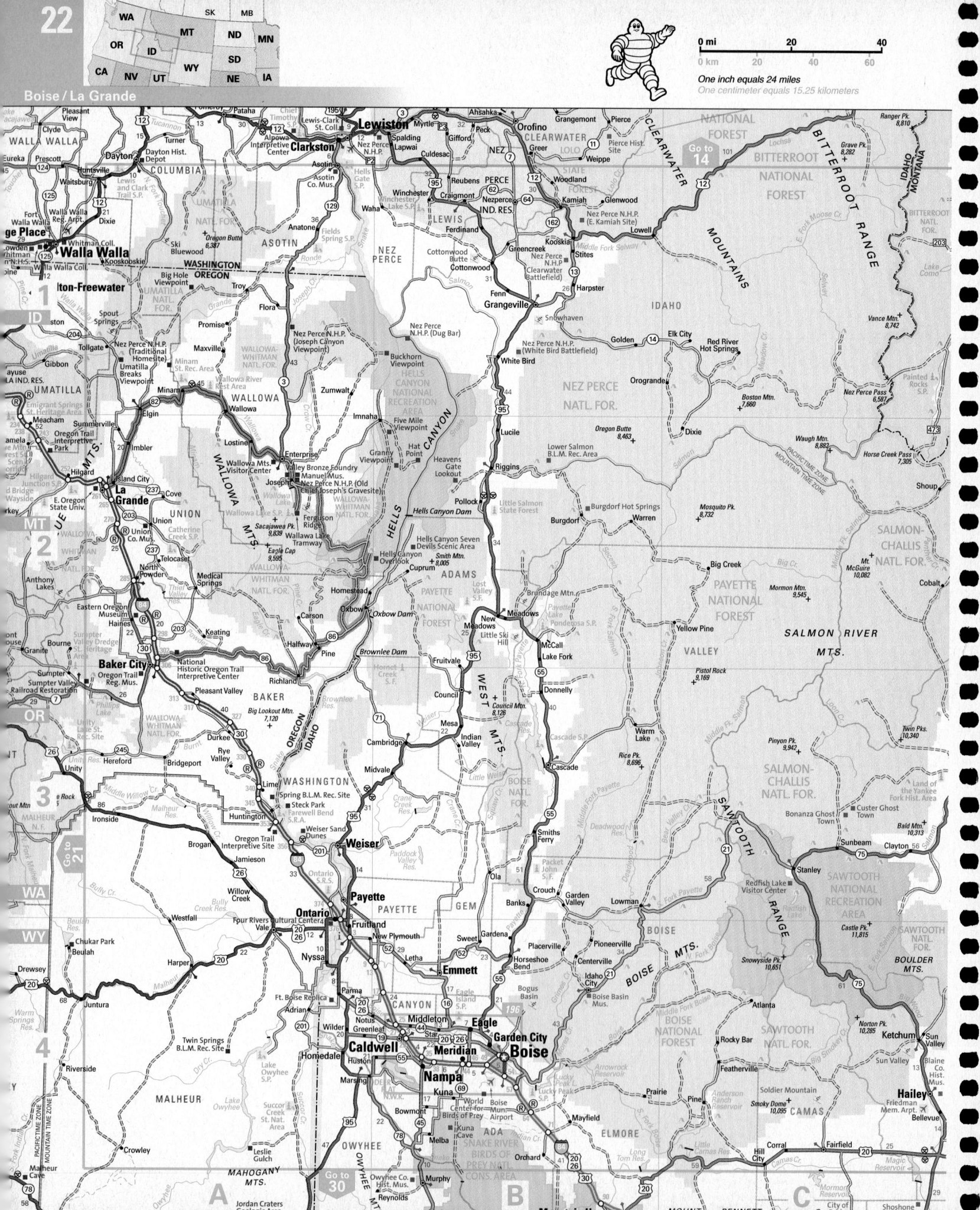

One inch equals 24 miles
One centimeter equals 15.25 kilometers

0 mi   20   40
0 km   20   40   60

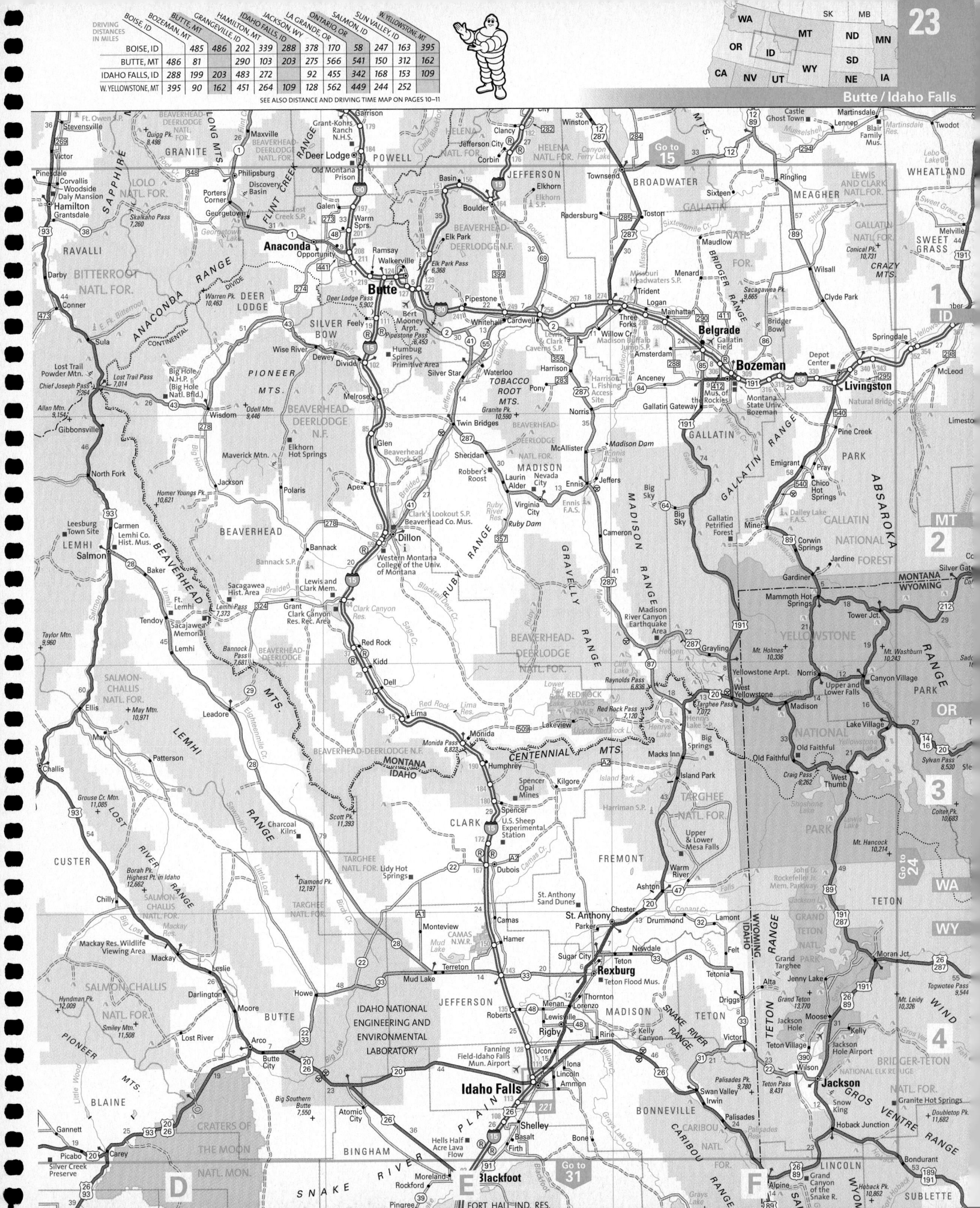

DRIVING DISTANCES IN MILES	BOISE, ID	BOZEMAN, MT	BUTTE, MT	GRANGEVILLE, ID	HAMILTON, MT	IDAHO FALLS, ID	JACKSON, WY	LA GRANDE, OR	ONTARIO, OR	SALMON, ID	SUN VALLEY, ID	W. YELLOWSTONE, MT
BOISE, ID		485	486	202	339	288	378	170	58	247	163	395
BUTTE, MT	486	81		290	103	203	275	566	541	150	312	162
IDAHO FALLS, ID	288	199	203	483	272		92	455	342	168	153	109
W. YELLOWSTONE, MT	395	90	162	451	264	109	128	562	449	244	252	

SEE ALSO DISTANCE AND DRIVING TIME MAP ON PAGES 10–11

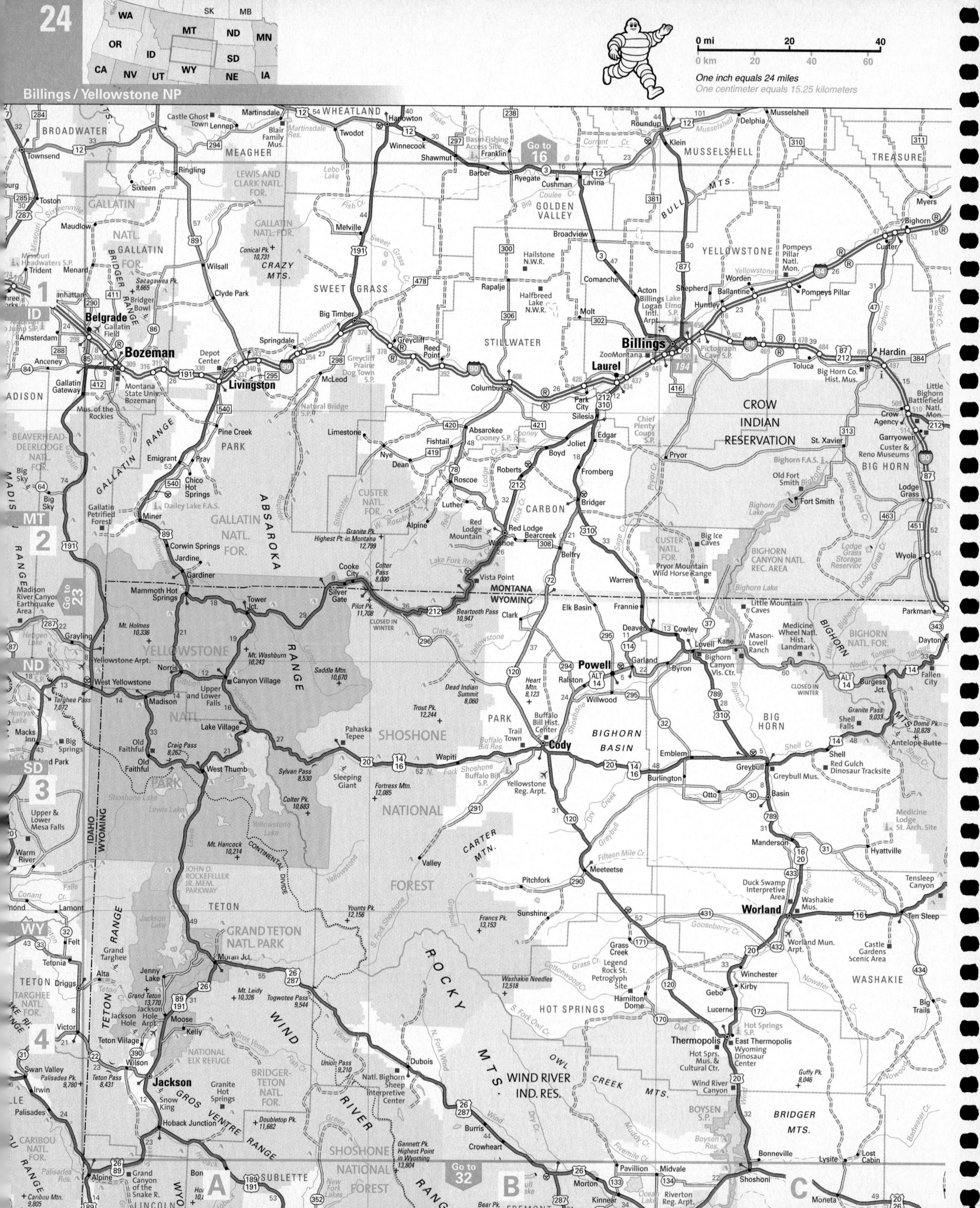

One inch equals 24 miles
One centimeter equals 15.25 kilometers

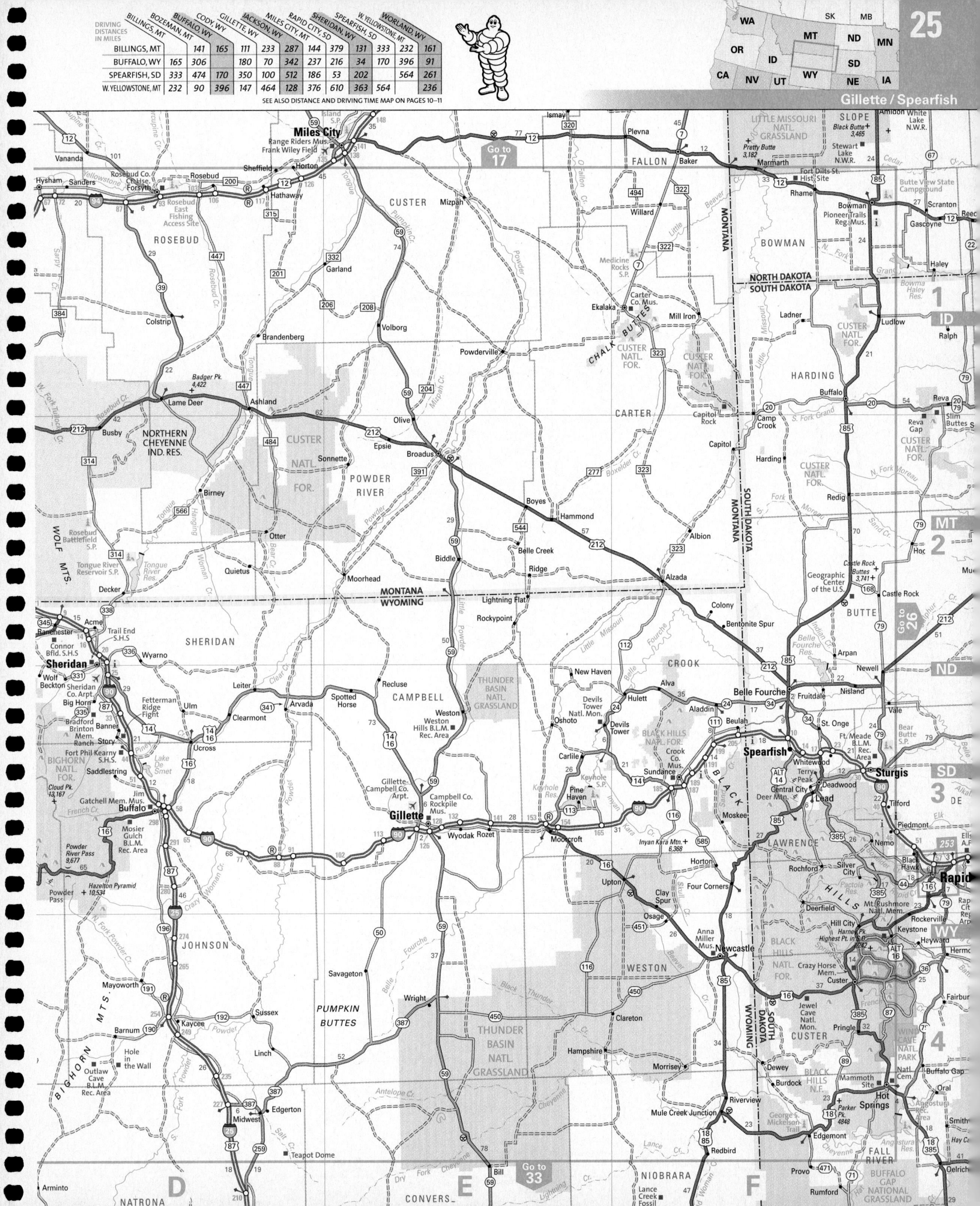

DRIVING DISTANCES IN MILES

	BILLINGS, MT	BOZEMAN, MT	BUFFALO, WY	CODY, WY	GILLETTE, WY	JACKSON, WY	MILES CITY, MT	RAPID CITY, SD	SHERIDAN, WY	SPEARFISH, SD	W. YELLOWSTONE, MT	WORLAND, WY
BILLINGS, MT		141	165	111	233	287	144	379	131	333	232	161
BUFFALO, WY	165	306		180	70	342	237	216	34	170	396	91
SPEARFISH, SD	333	474	170	350	100	512	186	53	202		564	261
W. YELLOWSTONE, MT	232	90	396	147	464	128	376	610	363	564		236

SEE ALSO DISTANCE AND DRIVING TIME MAP ON PAGES 10–11

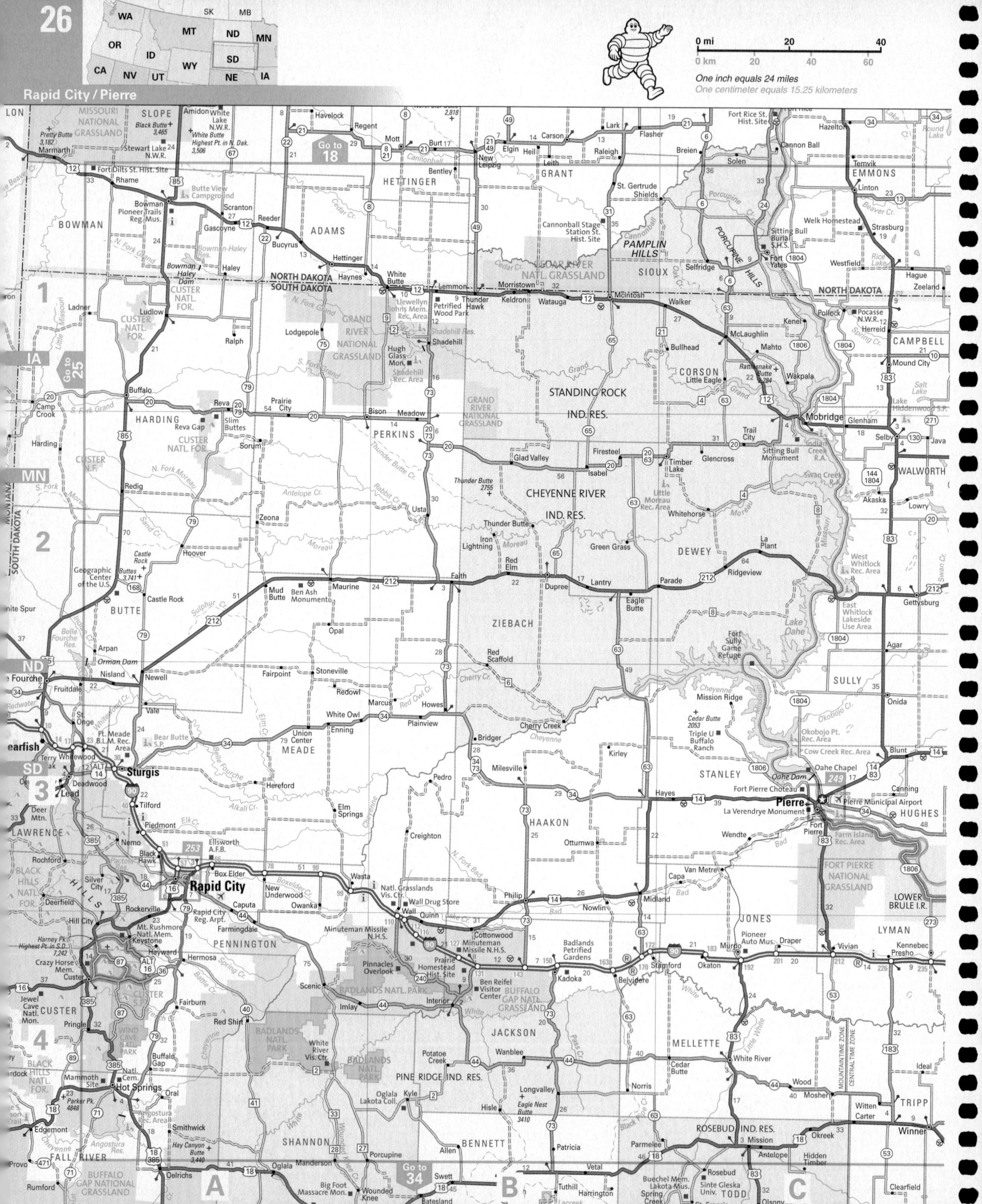

0 mi   20   40
0 km   20   60
One inch equals 24 miles
One centimeter equals 15.25 kilometers

WA SK MB
MT ND MN
OR ID WY SD IA
CA NV UT NE

Go to 18
Go to 25
Go to 34

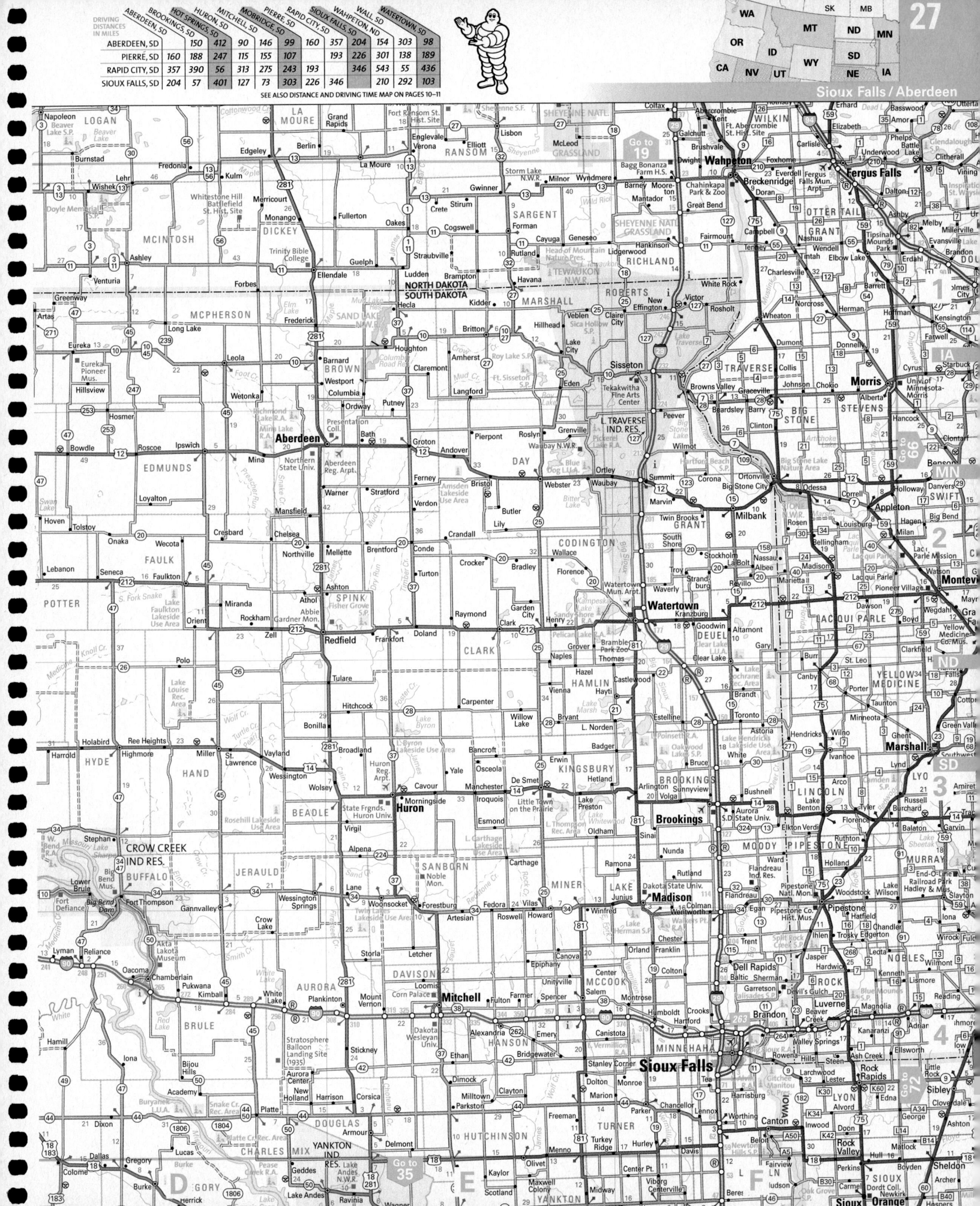

DRIVING DISTANCES IN MILES	ABERDEEN, SD	BROOKINGS, SD	HOT SPRINGS, SD	HURON, SD	MITCHELL, SD	MOBRIDGE, SD	PIERRE, SD	RAPID CITY, SD	SIOUX FALLS, SD	WAHPETON, SD	WALL, SD	WATERTOWN, SD
ABERDEEN, SD		150	412	90	146	99	160	357	204	154	303	98
PIERRE, SD	160	188	247	115	155	107		193	226	301	138	189
RAPID CITY, SD	357	390	56	313	275	243	193		346	543	55	436
SIOUX FALLS, SD	204	57	401	127	73	303	226	346		210	292	103

SEE ALSO DISTANCE AND DRIVING TIME MAP ON PAGES 10–11

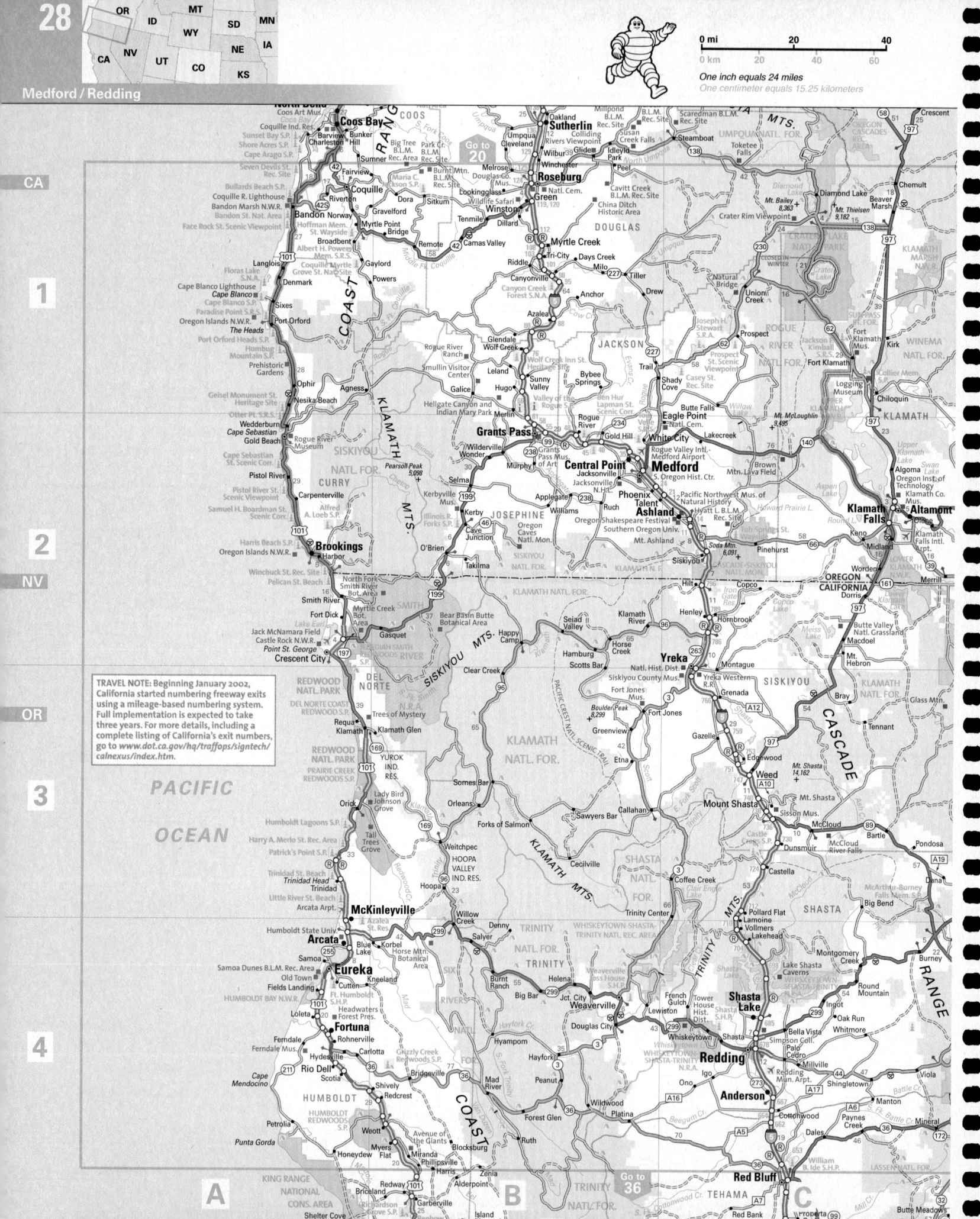

One inch equals 24 miles
One centimeter equals 15.25 kilometers

TRAVEL NOTE: Beginning January 2002, California started numbering freeway exits using a mileage-based numbering system. Full implementation is expected to take three years. For more details, including a complete listing of California's exit numbers, go to www.dot.ca.gov/hq/traffops/signtech/calnexus/index.htm.

PACIFIC OCEAN

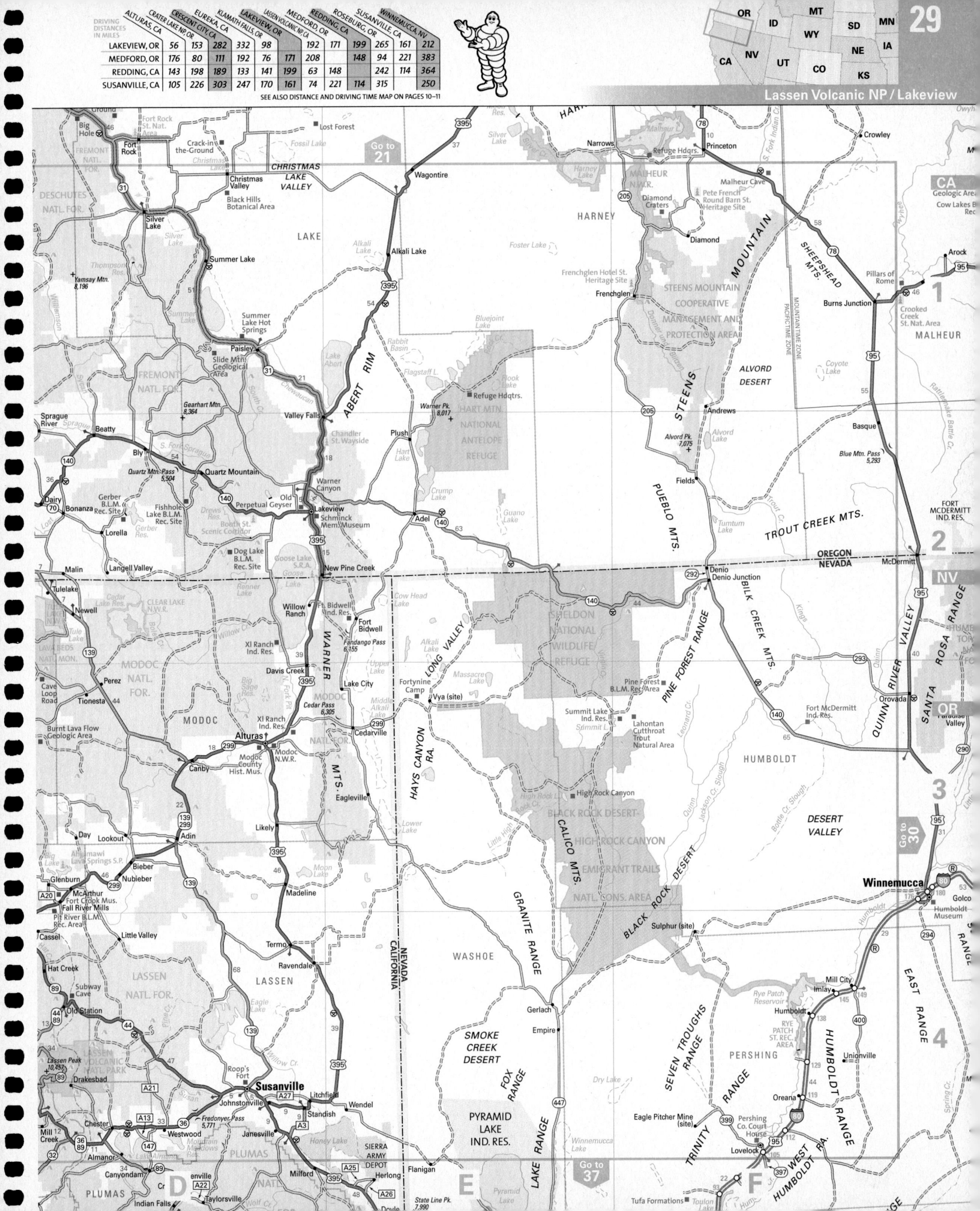

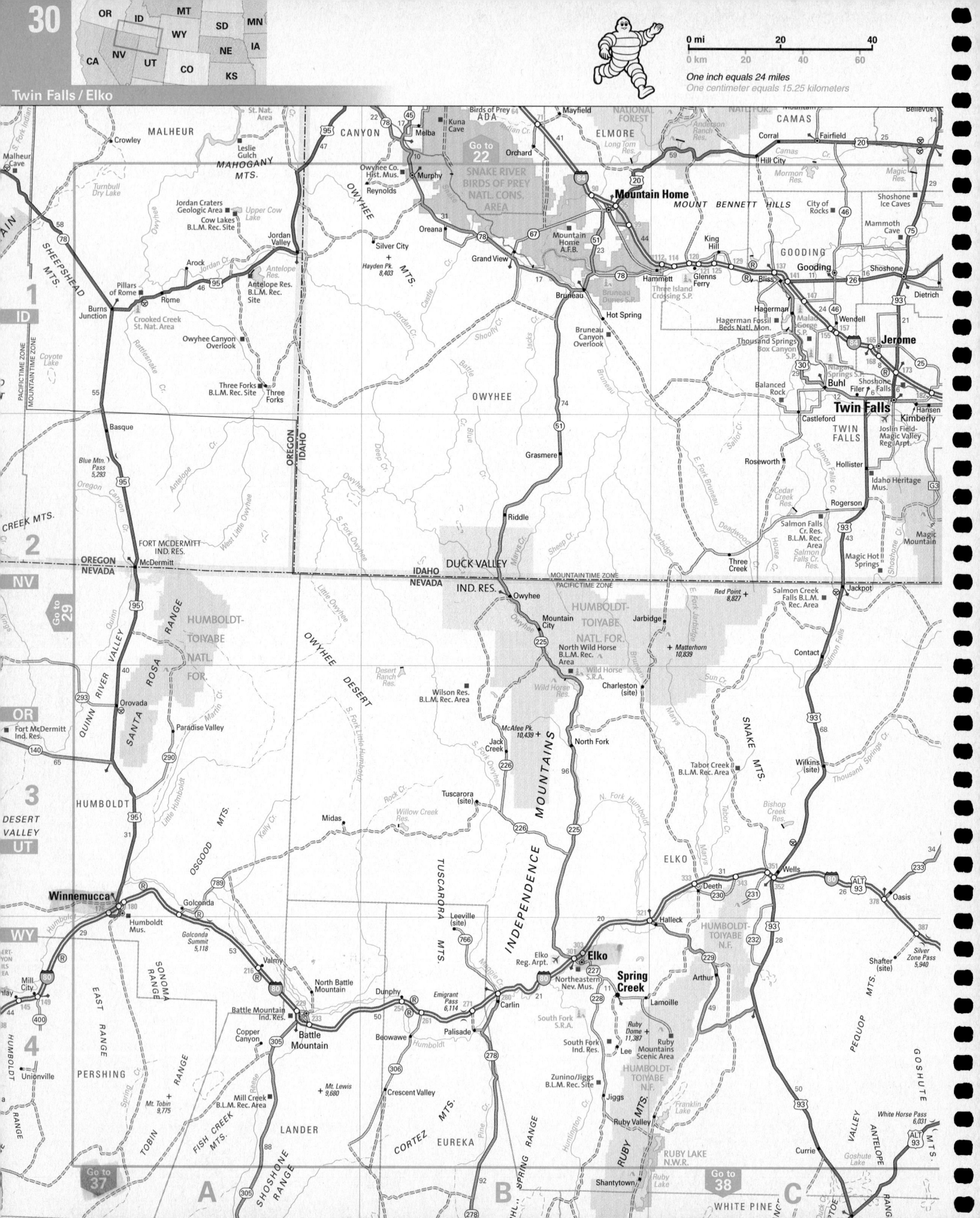

One inch equals 24 miles
One centimeter equals 15.25 kilometers

0 mi   20   40
0 km   20   40   60

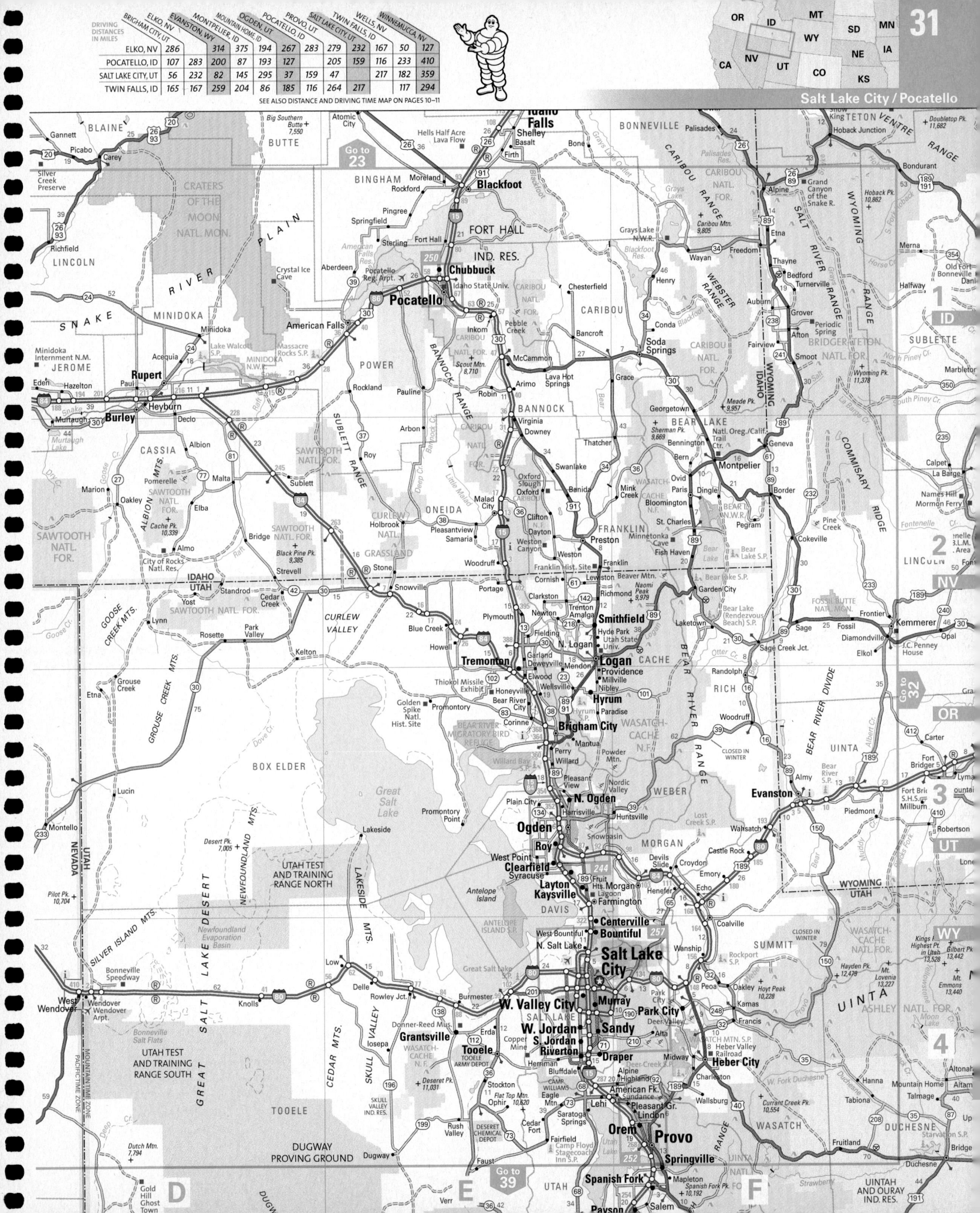

SEE ALSO DISTANCE AND DRIVING TIME MAP ON PAGES 10–11

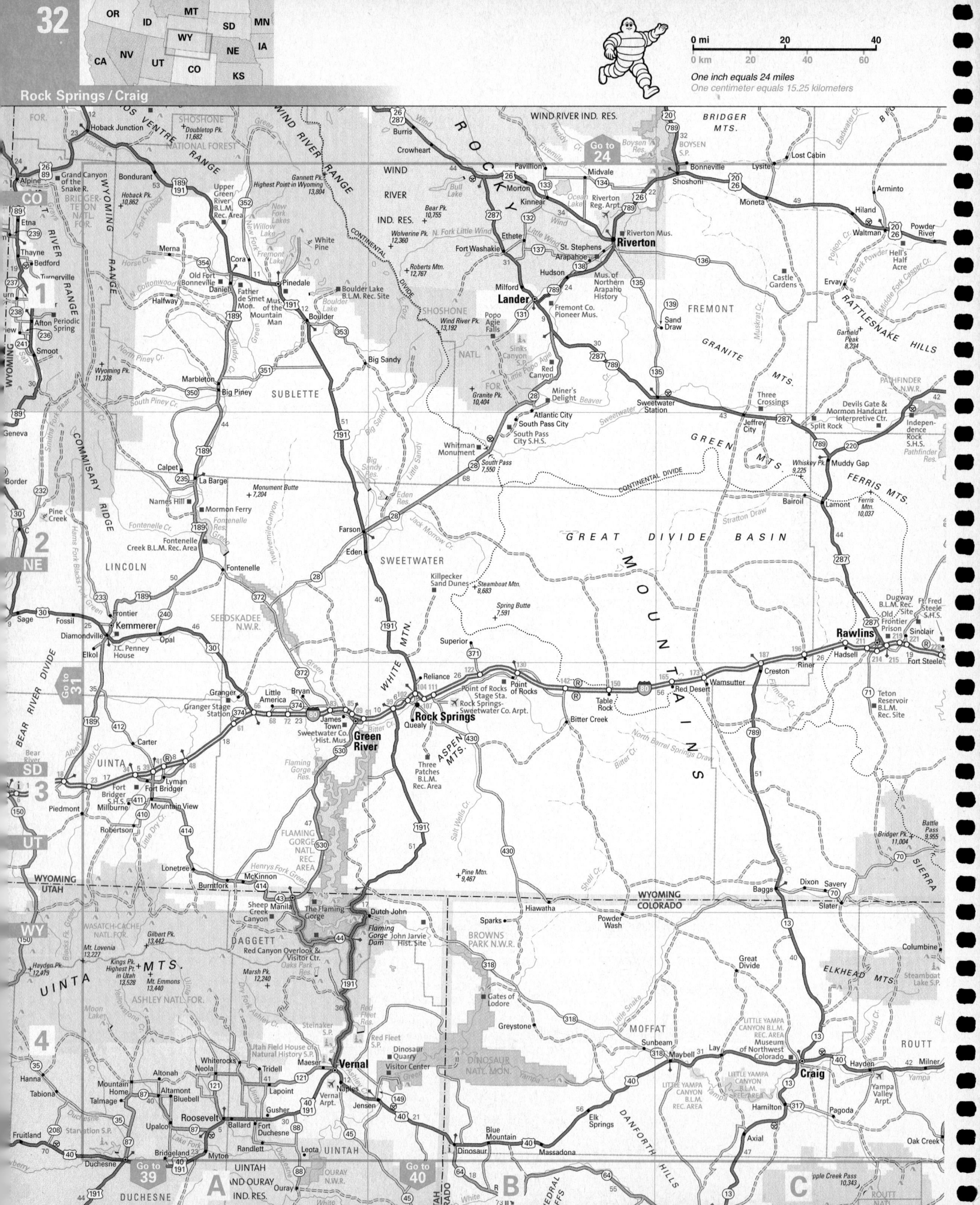

One inch equals 24 miles
One centimeter equals 15.25 kilometers

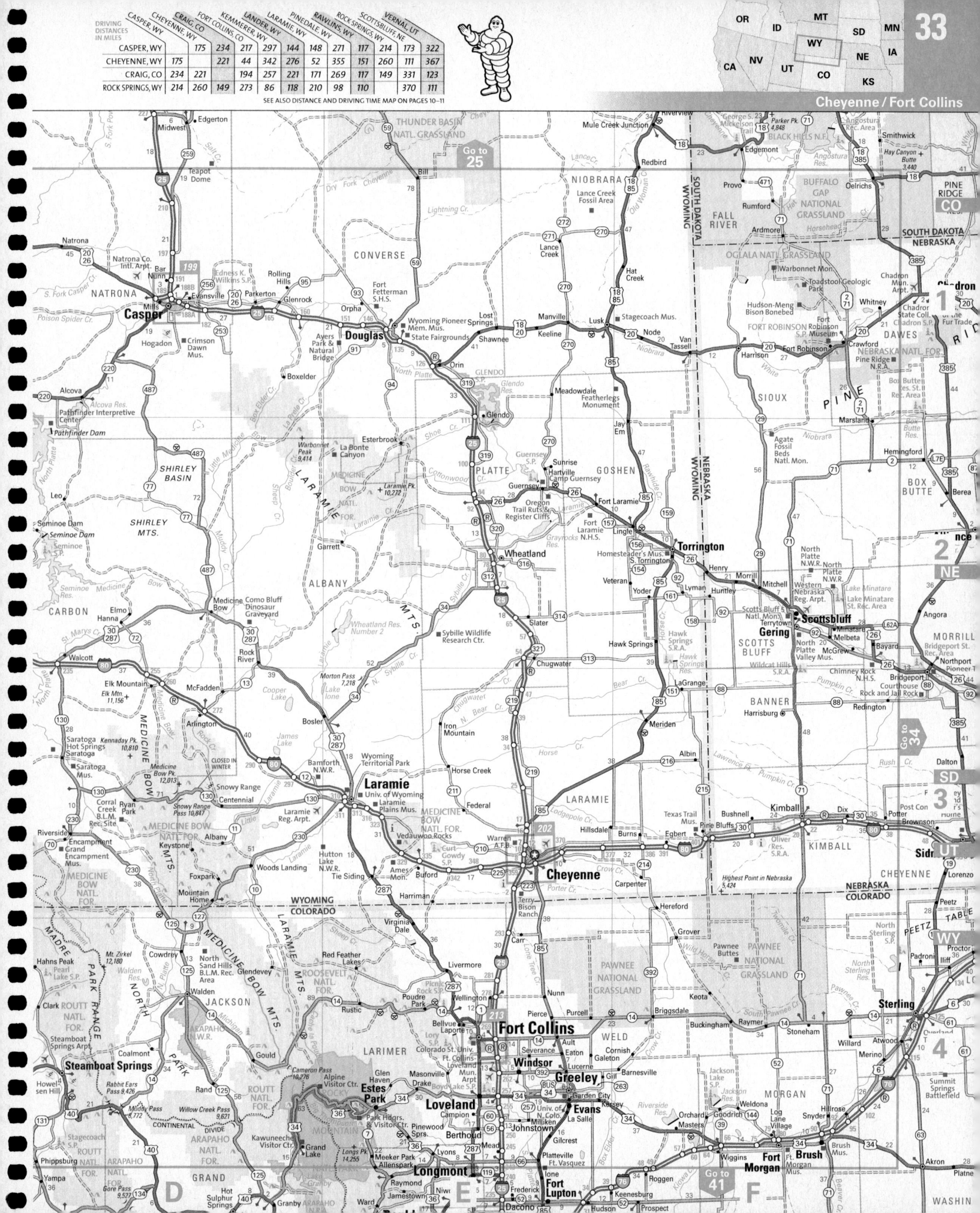

SEE ALSO DISTANCE AND DRIVING TIME MAP ON PAGES 10-11

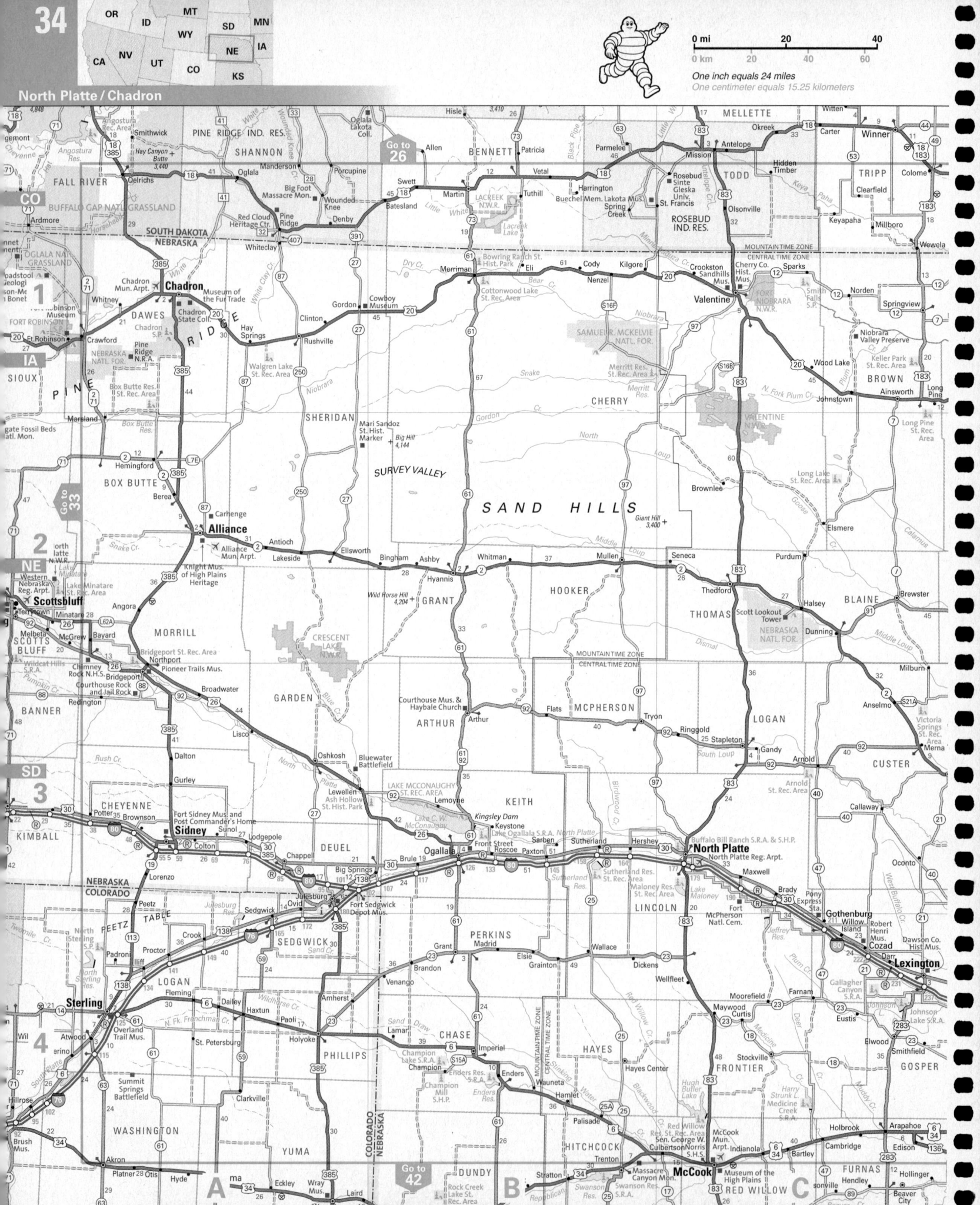

One inch equals 24 miles
One centimeter equals 15.25 kilometers

0 mi   20   40
0 km   20   40   60

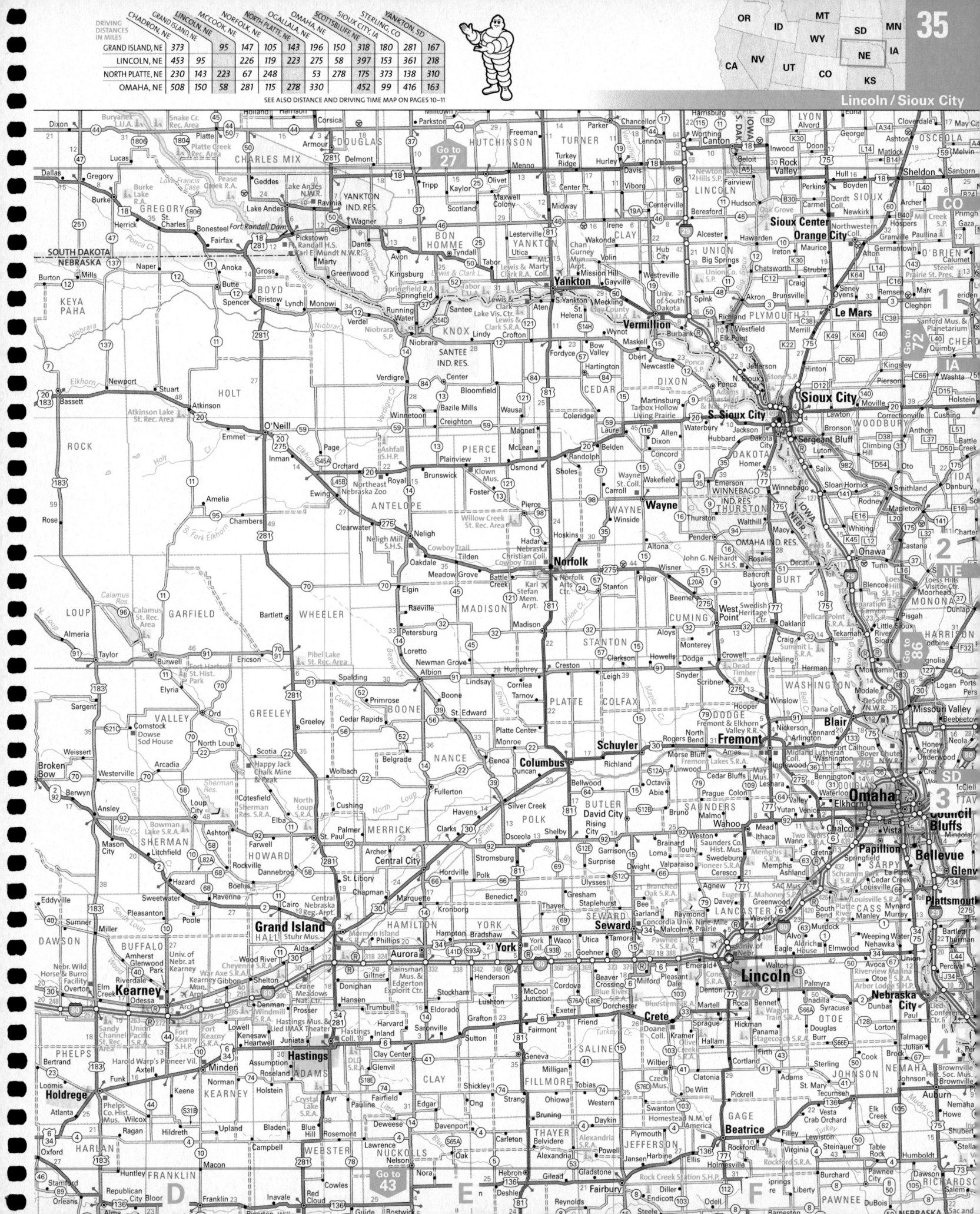

35

San Francisco / Sacramento

One inch equals 24 miles
One centimeter equals 15.25 kilometers

0 mi   20   40
0 km   20   40   60

TRAVEL NOTE: Beginning January 2002,
California started numbering freeway exits
using a mileage-based numbering system.
Full implementation is expected to take
three years. For more details, including a
complete listing of California's exit numbers,
go to www.dot.ca.gov/hq/traffops/signtech/
calnexus/index.htm.

DRIVING DISTANCES IN MILES

	AUSTIN NV	CHICO, CA	MERCED, CA	RENO, NV	SACRAMENTO CA	SAN FRANCISCO CA	SAN JOSE, CA	S. LAKE TAHOE, CA	STOCKTON, CA	TONOPAH, NV	UKIAH, CA	YOSEMITE VIL., CA
RENO, NV	171	164	243		132	217	245	59	177	237	261	199
SACRAMENTO, CA	302	88	118	132		87	115	100	48	329	153	170
SAN FRANCISCO, CA	387	182	131	217	87		43	185	82	352	116	183
YOSEMITE VIL., CA	280	257	79	199	170	183	168	180	123	199	289	

SEE ALSO DISTANCE AND DRIVING TIME MAP ON PAGES 10–11

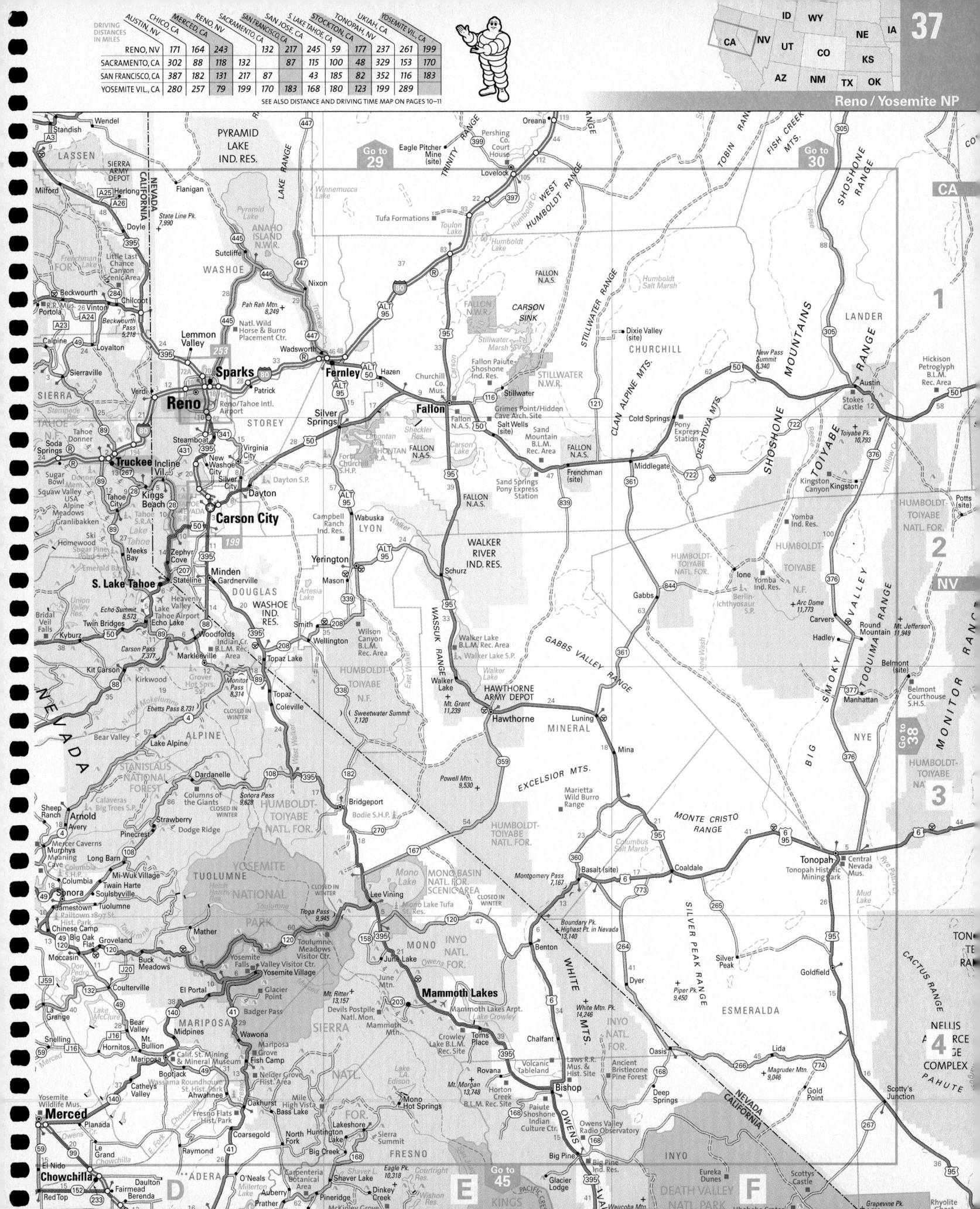

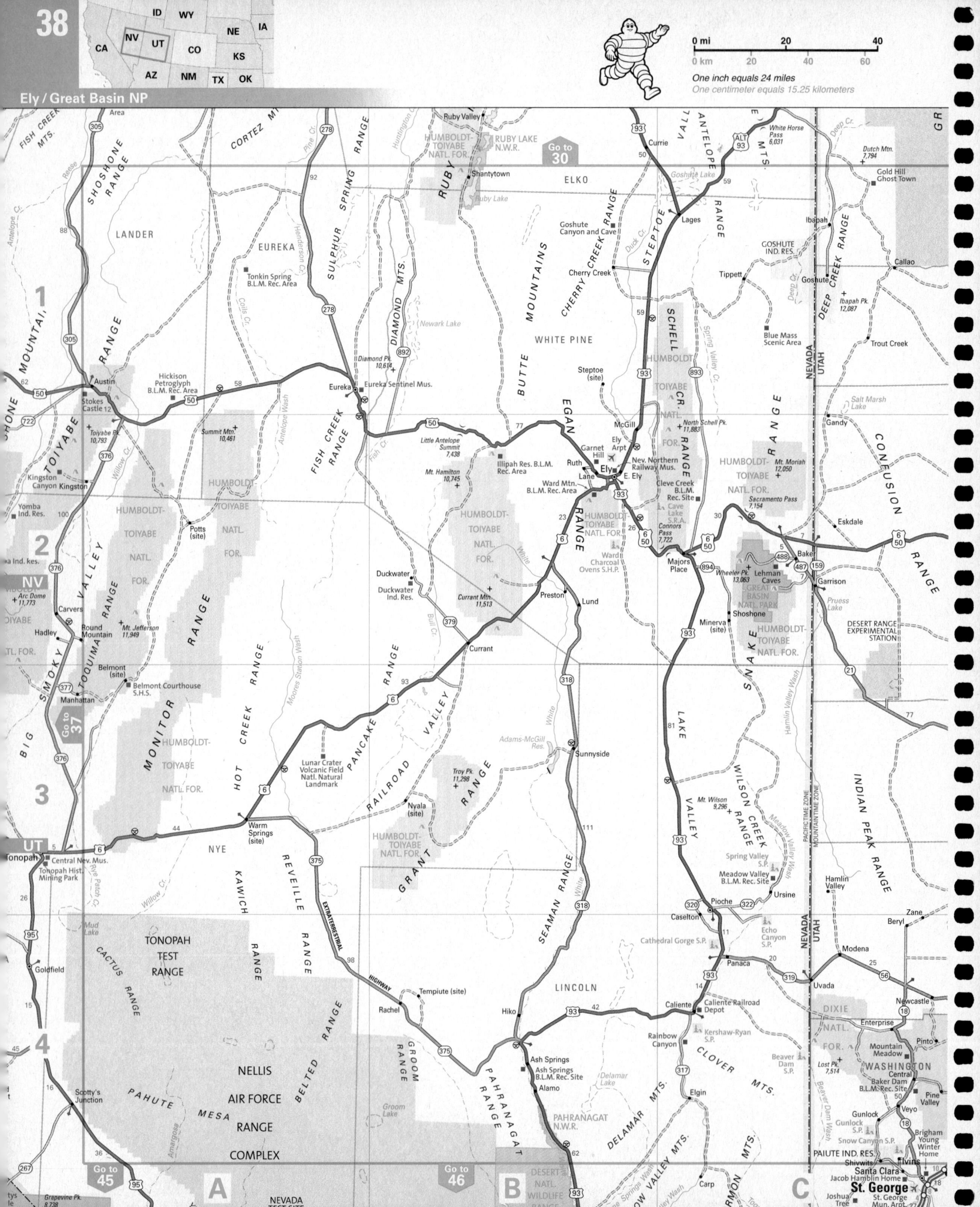

ID WY
NV UT
CA CO
AZ NM
NE IA
KS
TX OK

0 mi 20 40
0 km 20 40 60

One inch equals 24 miles
One centimeter equals 15.25 kilometers

FISH CREEK MTS.

SHOSHONE RANGE

CORTEZ MTS.

305

LANDER

EUREKA

278

Pine Cr.

RUBY VALLEY
Ruby Lake
Shantytown
Ruby Lake
HUMBOLDT-
TOIYABE
NATL. FOR.
RUBY LAKE N.W.R.

Go to 30

ELKO

93
50
Currie

ANTELOPE VALLEY

White Horse Pass 8,031

ALT 93

Dutch Mtn. 7,794

Gold Hill
Ghost Town

SULPHUR SPRING RANGE

Tonkin Spring B.L.M. Rec. Area

Newark Lake

DIAMOND MTS.

892

Diamond Pk. 10,614

Eureka
Eureka Sentinel Mus.

50
58

Hickison Petroglyph B.L.M. Rec. Area

Stokes Castle 12

Toiyabe Pk. 10,793

Summit Mtn. 10,461

Austin

50

62

722

SHOSHONE

305

TOIYABE RANGE

376

Kingston
Kingston Canyon

Yomba Ind. Res.

100

376

NV
UT

Arc Dome 11,773

Carvers

Hadley

Round Mountain

Mt. Jefferson 11,949

Belmont (site)

Belmont Courthouse S.H.S.

377

Manhattan

Go to 37

376

BIG SMOKY VALLEY

TOQUIMA RANGE

MONITOR RANGE

HUMBOLDT-TOIYABE NATL. FOR.

Potts (site)

Duckwater

Duckwater Ind. Res.

FISH CREEK RANGE

Fish Cr.

50

77

Little Antelope Summit 7,438

Mt. Hamilton 10,745

Illipah Res. B.L.M. Rec. Area

Currant Mtn. 11,513

HUMBOLDT-TOIYABE NATL. FOR.

BUTTE MOUNTAINS

WHITE PINE

CHERRY CREEK RANGE

Goshute Canyon and Cave

Cherry Creek

Steptoe (site)

McGill

Ely Arpt
Garnet Hill
Nev. Northern Railway Mus.
Ruth
Ely
E. Ely
Lane

Ward Mtn. B.L.M. Rec. Area

EGAN RANGE

93

6

23

HUMBOLDT-TOIYABE NATL. FOR.

Ward Charcoal Ovens S.H.P.

26

6
50

Connors Pass 7,722

Majors Place

894

STEPTOE VALLEY

Goshute Lake

50
59

59

Lages

893

North Schell Pk. 11,883

SCHELL CR. RANGE

Cleve Creek B.L.M. Rec. Site

Cave Lake S.R.A.

Tippett

GOSHUTE IND. RES.

Goshute

Ibapah

Ibapah Pk. 12,087

Blue Mass Scenic Area

HUMBOLDT-TOIYABE NATL. FOR.

Mt. Moriah 12,050

30

7

Sacramento Pass 7,154

6
50

488
487
159
7

Baker

Wheeler Pk. 13,063
Lehman Caves
GREAT BASIN NATL. PARK

Minerva (site)

Shoshone

HUMBOLDT-TOIYABE NATL. FOR.

Garrison

Pruess Lake

NEVADA
UTAH

DEEP CREEK RANGE

Deep Cr.

Callao

Trout Creek

Salt Marsh Lake

Gandy

Eskdale

CONFUSION RANGE

6
50

DESERT RANGE EXPERIMENTAL STATION

21

77

Duckwater

379

Preston

Lund

Currant

93

6

HUMBOLDT-TOIYABE NATL. FOR.

318

Adams-McGill Res.

Sunnyside

SNAKE RANGE

LAKE VALLEY

81

WILSON CREEK RANGE

Mt. Wilson 9,296

HAMLIN VALLEY

INDIAN PEAK RANGE

Lunar Crater Volcanic Field Natl. Natural Landmark

HOT CREEK RANGE

PANCAKE RANGE

RAILROAD VALLEY

Nyala (site)

Troy Pk. 11,298

GRANT RANGE

SEAMAN RANGE

White

111

Spring Valley S.P.

Meadow Valley B.L.M. Rec. Site

Ursine

Hamlin Valley

PACIFIC TIME ZONE
MOUNTAIN TIME ZONE

Warm Springs (site)

6

44

NYE

KAWICH RANGE

REVEILLE RANGE

EXTRATERRESTRIAL HIGHWAY

375

98

HUMBOLDT-TOIYABE NATL. FOR.

320

Pioche

322

Caselton

11

Echo Canyon S.P.

Cathedral Gorge S.P.

Panaca

20

319

Uvada

56

Modena

25

Zane

Beryl

Newcastle

18

UT
5

Tonopah

Central Nev. Mus.
Tonopah Hist. Mining Park

26

95

Mud Lake

Goldfield

15

Scotty's Junction

CACTUS RANGE

PAHUTE MESA

TONOPAH TEST RANGE

BELTED RANGE

Rachel

Tempiute (site)

GROOM RANGE

Groom Lake

NELLIS AIR FORCE RANGE COMPLEX

93

Hiko

Ash Springs
Ash Springs B.L.M. Rec. Area
Alamo

375

LINCOLN

42

Caliente
Caliente Railroad Depot

14

Rainbow Canyon

Kershaw-Ryan S.P.

317

Elgin

Delamar Lake

PAHRANAGAT RANGE

PAHRANAGAT N.W.R.

DELAMAR MTS.

CLOVER MTS.

Beaver Dam S.P.

Carp

MEADOW VALLEY MTS.

93

DIXIE NATL. FOR.

Enterprise

Pinto

Mountain Meadow

WASHINGTON

Central

Baker Dam B.L.M. Rec. Site

50

Pine Valley

Veyo

Gunlock
Gunlock S.P.
Snow Canyon S.P.

18

Beaver Dam S.P.

Lost Pk. 7,514

BRIGHAM YOUNG WINTER HOME

PAIUTE IND. RES.

Shiwits

Santa Clara
Jacob Hamblin Home

St. George

Ivins

Joshua Tree

St. George Mun. Arpt.

18

10

27

45
267

Grapevine Pk. 8,738

95

NEVADA
TEST SITE

Go to 45

A

Go to 46

B

DESERT NATL. WILDLIFE RANGE

C

36

16

62

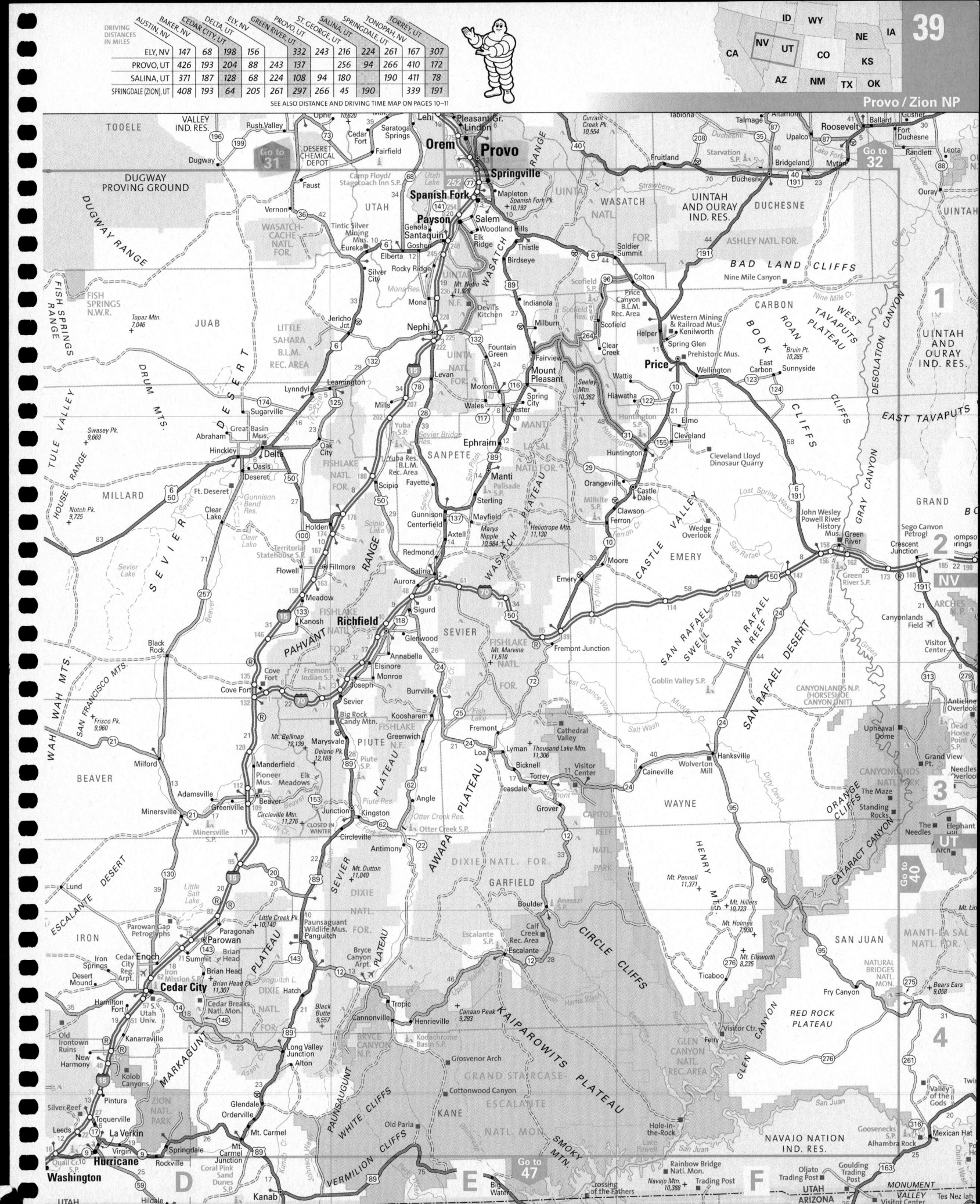

DRIVING DISTANCES IN MILES

	AUSTIN, NV	BAKER, NV	CEDAR CITY, UT	DELTA, UT	ELY, NV	GREEN RIVER, UT	PROVO, UT	ST. GEORGE, UT	SALINA, UT	SPRINGDALE, UT	TONOPAH, NV	TORREY, UT
ELY, NV	147	68	198	156		332	243	216	224	261	167	307
PROVO, UT	426	193	204	88	243	137		256	94	266	410	172
SALINA, UT	371	187	128	68	224	108	94	180		190	411	78
SPRINGDALE (ZION), UT	408	193	64	205	261	297	266	45	190		339	191

SEE ALSO DISTANCE AND DRIVING TIME MAP ON PAGES 10–11

One inch equals 24 miles
One centimeter equals 15.25 kilometers

0 mi   20   40
0 km   20   40   60

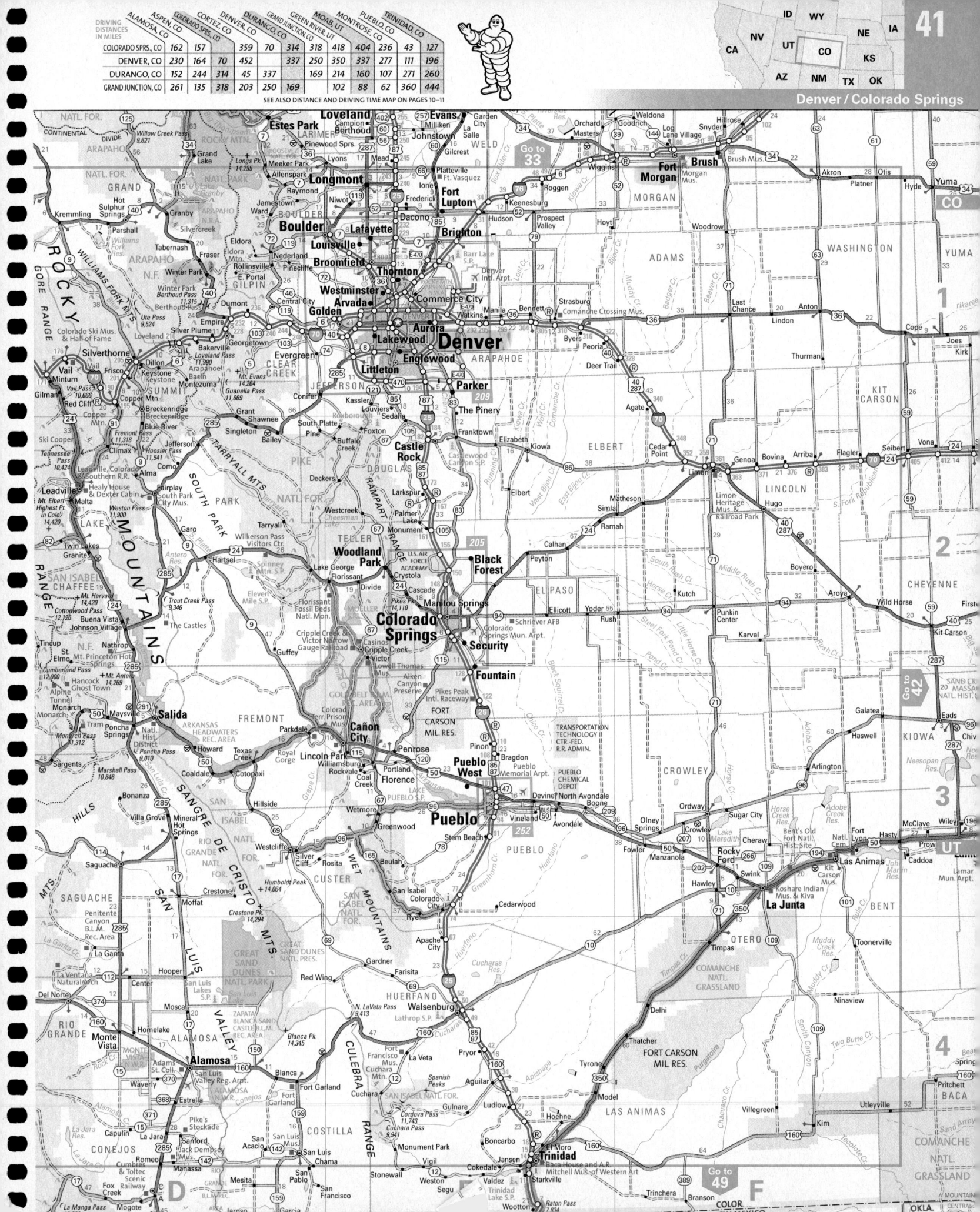

DRIVING DISTANCES IN MILES

	ALAMOSA, CO	ASPEN, CO	COLORADO SPRS., CO	CORTEZ, CO	DENVER, CO	DURANGO, CO	GRAND JUNCTION, CO	GREEN RIVER, UT	MOAB, UT	MONTROSE, CO	PUEBLO, CO	TRINIDAD, CO
COLORADO SPRS., CO	162	157		359	70	314	318	418	404	236	43	127
DENVER, CO	230	164	70	452		337	250	350	337	277	111	196
DURANGO, CO	152	244	314	45	337		169	214	160	107	271	260
GRAND JUNCTION, CO	261	135	318	203	250	169		102	88	62	360	444

SEE ALSO DISTANCE AND DRIVING TIME MAP ON PAGES 10–11

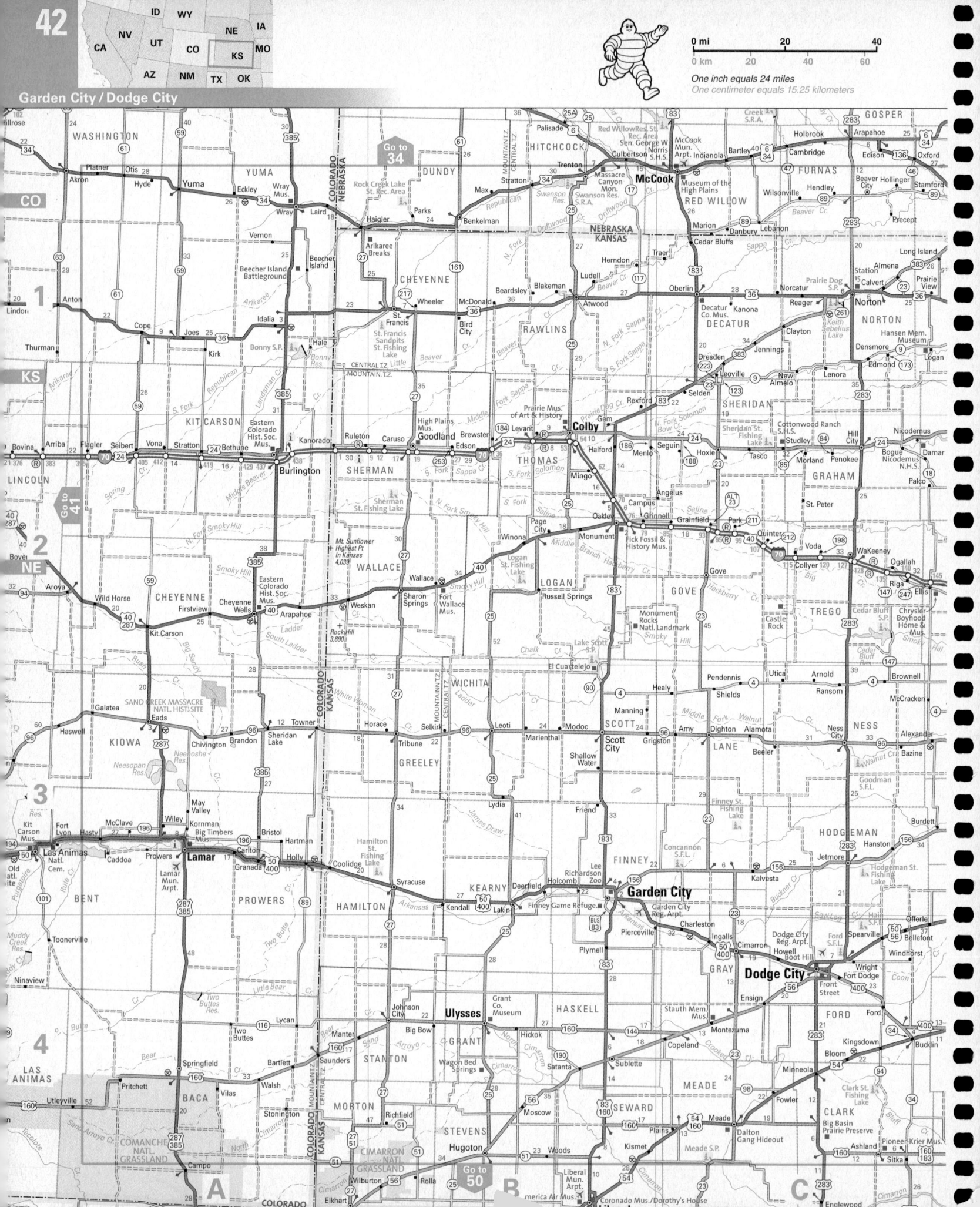

0 mi   20   40
0 km   20   40   60
One inch equals 24 miles
One centimeter equals 15.25 kilometers

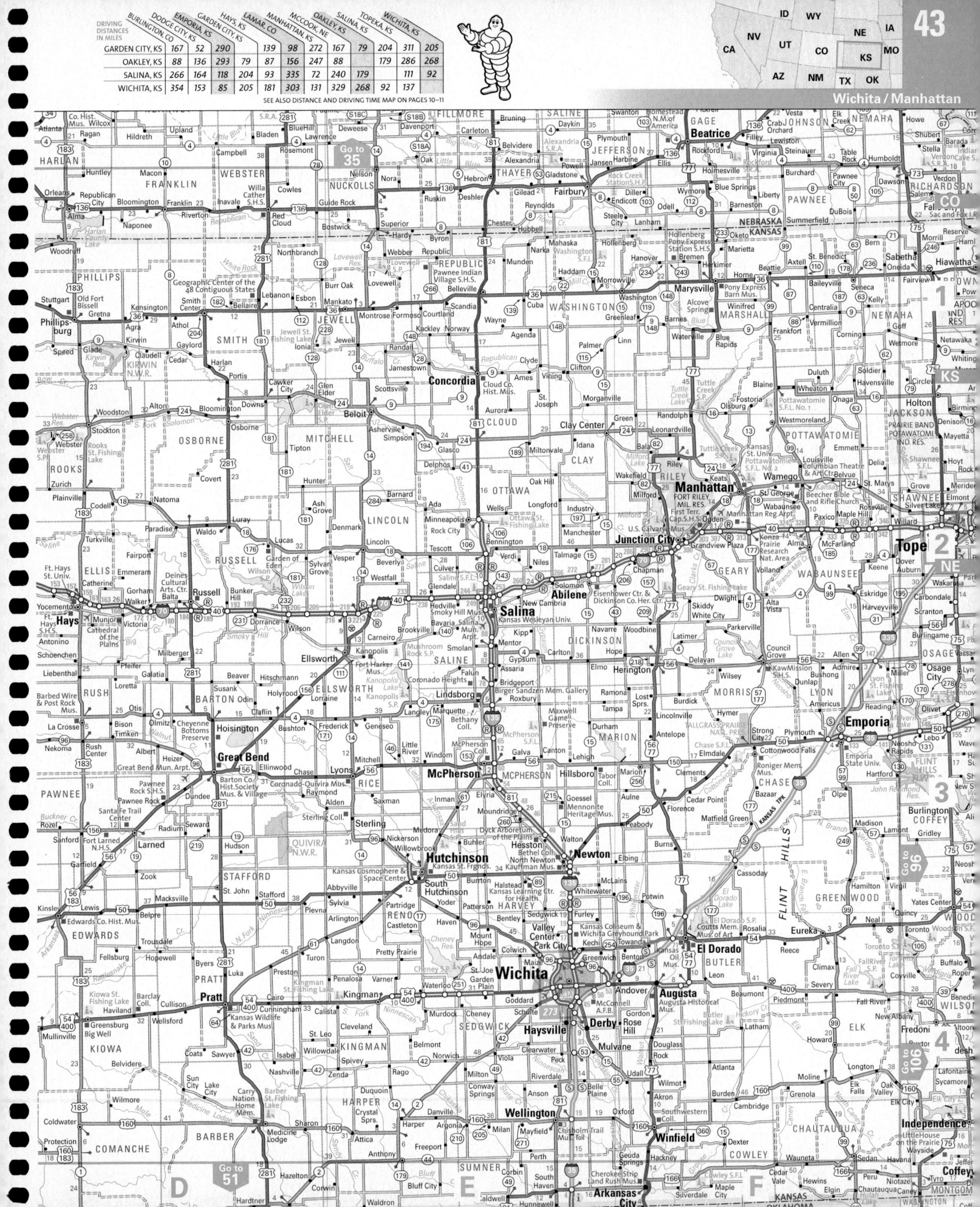

DRIVING DISTANCES IN MILES

	BURLINGTON, CO	DODGE CITY, KS	EMPORIA, KS	GARDEN CITY, KS	HAYS, KS	LAMAR, CO	MANHATTAN, KS	MCCOOK, NE	OAKLEY, KS	SALINA, KS	TOPEKA, KS	WICHITA, KS
GARDEN CITY, KS	167	52	290		139	98	272	167	79	204	311	205
OAKLEY, KS	88	136	293	79	87	156	247	88		179	286	268
SALINA, KS	266	164	118	204	93	335	72	240	179		111	92
WICHITA, KS	354	153	85	205	181	303	131	329	268	92	137	

SEE ALSO DISTANCE AND DRIVING TIME MAP ON PAGES 10–11

NV UT CO NE KS
CA AZ NM TX OK

0 mi   20   40
0 km   20   60
One inch equals 24 miles
One centimeter equals 15.25 kilometers

CA

1

NV

2

3

PACIFIC

OCEAN

4

TRAVEL NOTE: Beginning January 2002,
California started numbering freeway exits
using a mileage-based numbering system.
Full implementation is expected to take
three years. For more details, including a
complete listing of California's exit numbers,
go to www.dot.ca.gov/hq/traffops/signtech/
calnexus/index.htm.

A   B   C

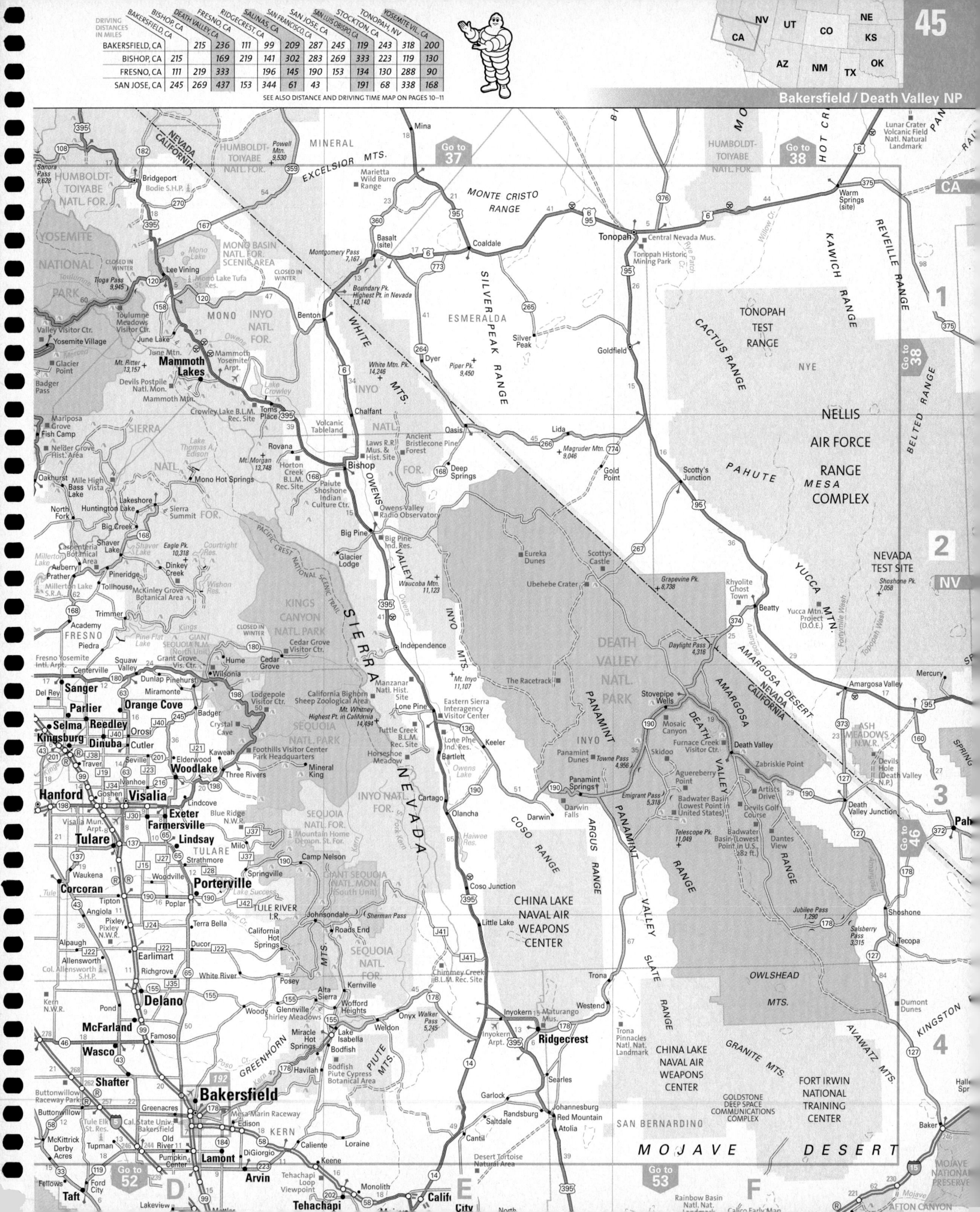

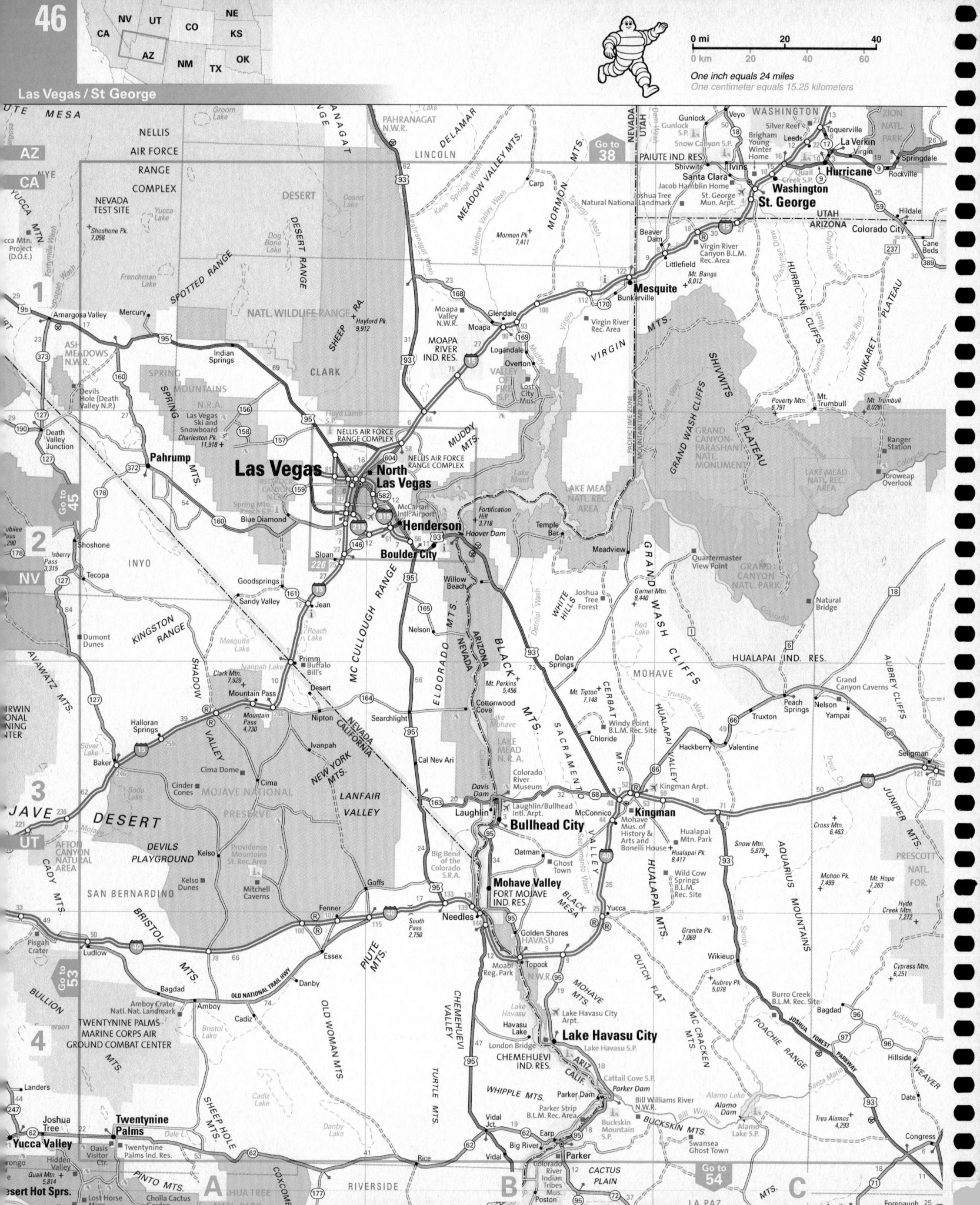

One inch equals 24 miles
One centimeter equals 15.25 kilometers

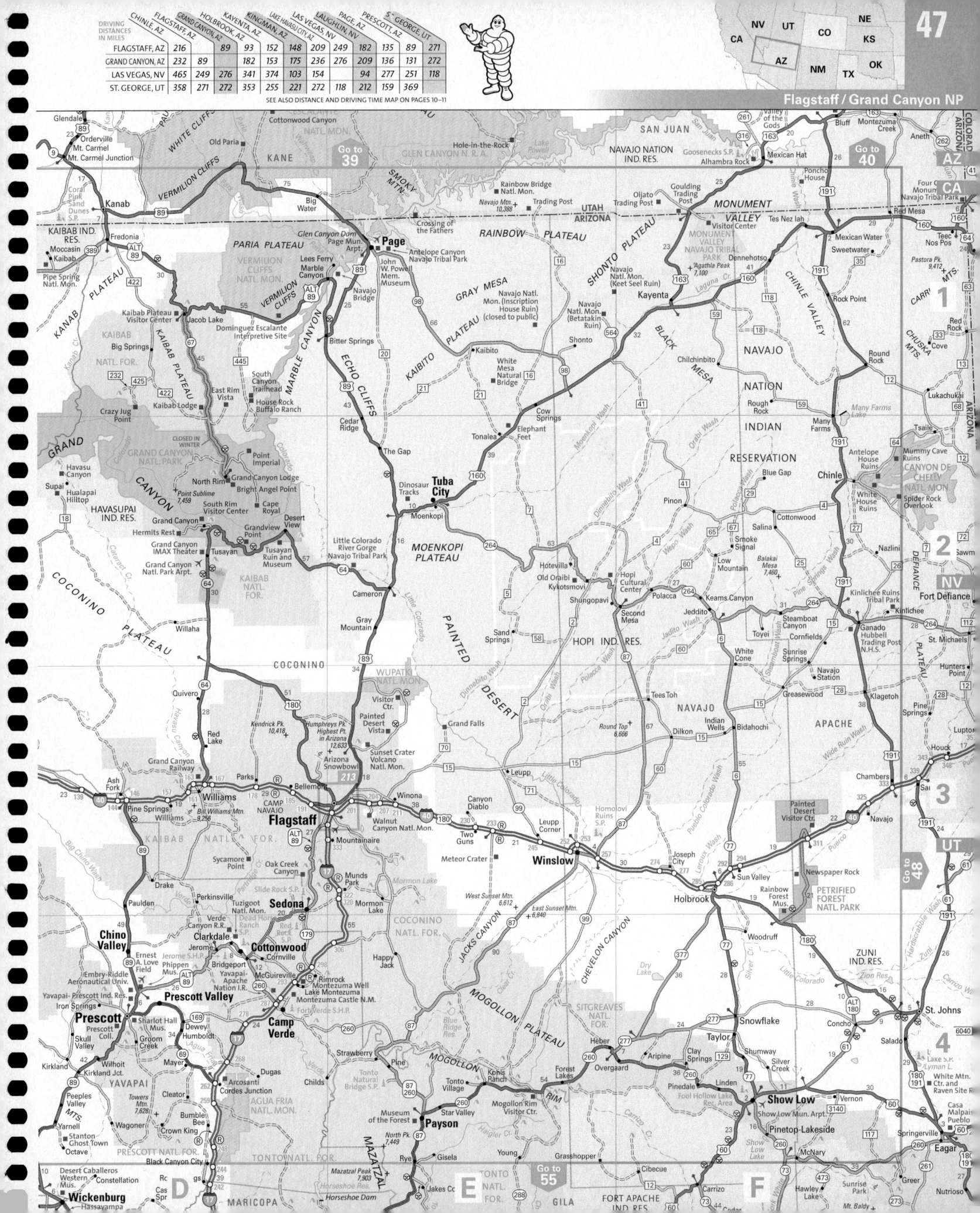

DRIVING DISTANCES IN MILES	CHINLE, AZ	FLAGSTAFF, AZ	GRAND CANYON, AZ	HOLBROOK, AZ	KAYENTA, AZ	KINGMAN, AZ	LAKE HAVASU CITY, AZ	LAS VEGAS, NV	LAUGHLIN, NV	PAGE, AZ	PRESCOTT, AZ	S. GEORGE, UT
FLAGSTAFF, AZ	216		89	93	152	148	209	249	182	135	89	271
GRAND CANYON, AZ	232	89		182	153	175	236	276	209	136	131	272
LAS VEGAS, NV	465	249	276	341	374	103	154		94	277	251	118
ST. GEORGE, UT	358	271	272	353	255	221	212	118	212	159	369	

SEE ALSO DISTANCE AND DRIVING TIME MAP ON PAGES 10–11

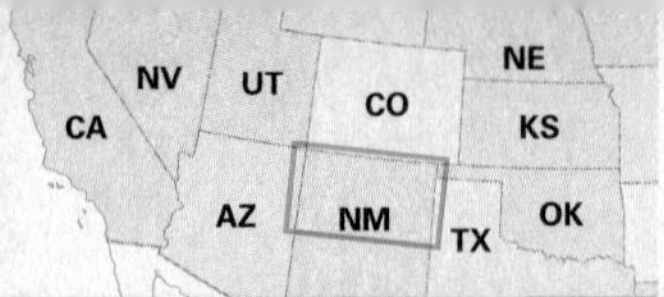

NV UT CO NE
CA KS
AZ NM TX OK

0 mi 20 40
0 km 20 40 60
One inch equals 24 miles
One centimeter equals 15.25 kilometers

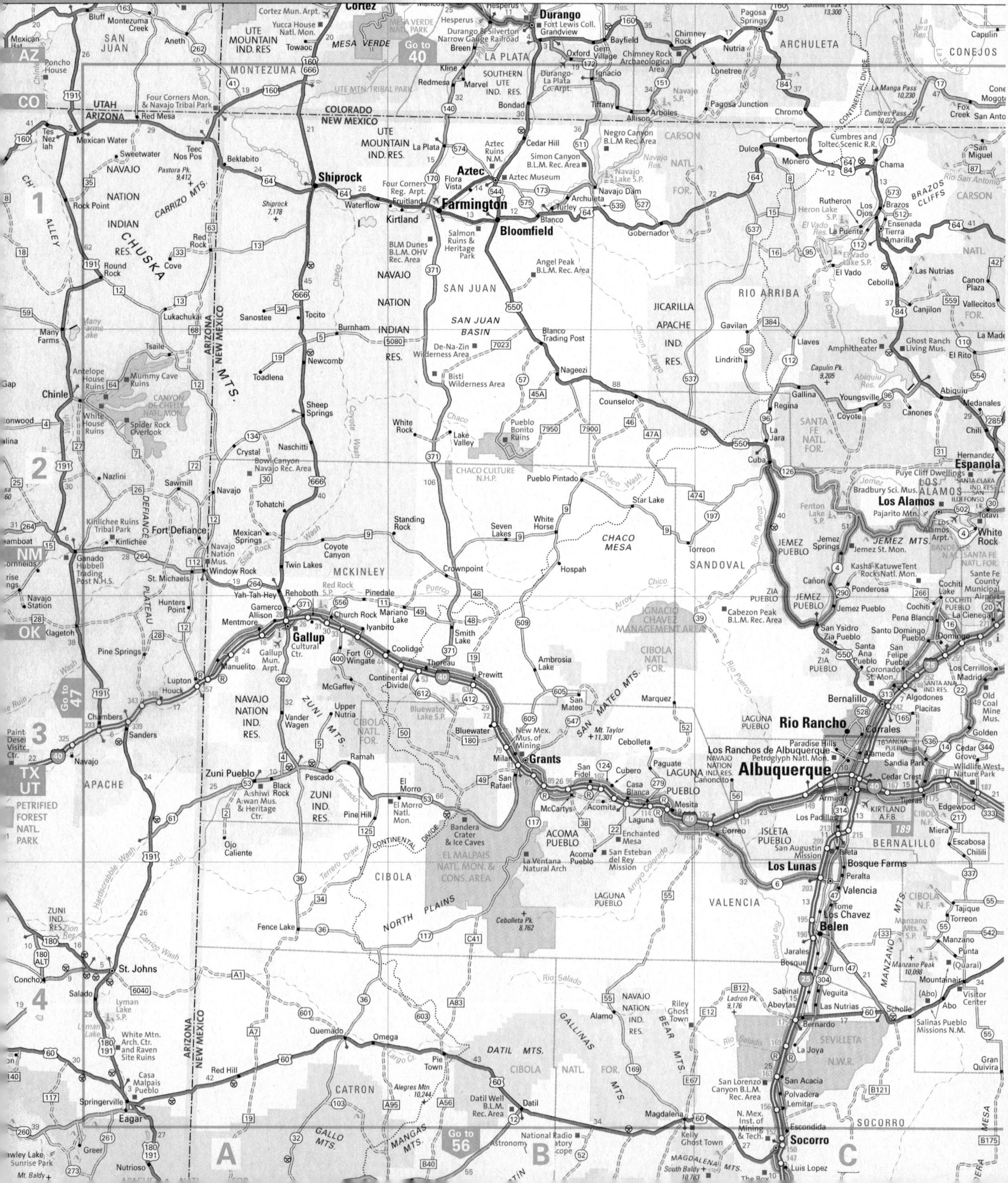

Major cities and towns: Cortez, Durango, Hesperus, Silverton, Grandview, Bayfield, Pagosa Springs, Chimney Rock, Archuleta, Capulin

Bluff, Montezuma Creek, Yucca House Natl. Mon., Mancos, Mesa Verde Natl. Park, La Plata, Oxford, Gem Village, Ignacio, Nutria, Chromo

Aneth, Towaoc, Mesa Verde, Breen, Durango–La Plata Co. Arpt., Lonetree, La Manga Pass 10,230, Cumbres Pass 10,022, Summit Peak 13,300

Mexican Hat, Poncho House, San Juan, Ute Mountain Ind. Res., Montezuma, Ute Mtn. Tribal Park, Southern Ute Ind. Res., Redmesa, Marvel, Bondad, Tiffany, Allison, Arboles, Pagosa Junction, Navajo Res., Navajo Lake S.P., Navajo Dam, Lumberton, Dulce, Monero, Chama, Cumbres and Toltec Scenic R.R., San Miguel, Fox Creek, San Anto

Mexican Water, Sweetwater, Teec Nos Pos, Beklabito, Red Mesa, Four Corners Mon. & Navajo Tribal Park, La Plata, Aztec Ruins N.M., Cedar Hill, Simon Canyon B.L.M. Rec. Area, Negro Canyon B.L.M. Rec. Area, Rutheron, Los Ojos, Brazos, Capulin

Teec Nos Pos, Rock Point, Round Rock, Red Rock, Cove, Shiprock 7,178, Four Corners Reg. Arpt., Flora Vista, Aztec, Aztec Museum, Farmington, Bloomfield, Blanco, Gobernador, Heron Lake S.P., La Puente, Tierra Amarilla, Ensenada, Canon Plaza, Las Nutrias, Cebolla, El Vado, El Vado Lake S.P.

CHUSKA MTS., Navajo Nation Indian Reservation, Many Farms, Lukachukai, Tsaile, Sanostee, Tocito, Burnham, BLM Dunes B.L.M. OHV Rec. Area, Salmon Ruins & Heritage Park, Angel Peak B.L.M. Rec. Area, San Juan Basin, Blanco Trading Post, Rio Arriba, Gavilan, Lindrith, Llaves, Echo Amphitheater, Ghost Ranch Living Mus., El Rito, La Madera, Vallecitos, Canjilon

Chinle, Antelope House Ruins, Mummy Cave Ruins, Canyon De Chelly Natl. Mon., White House Ruins, Spider Rock Overlook, Crystal, Naschitti, Sheep Springs, Newcomb, Toadlena, De-Na-Zin Wilderness Area, Bisti Wilderness Area, Nageezi, Counselor, Pueblo Bonito Ruins, Chaco Culture N.H.P., Star Lake, Cuba, La Jara, Regina, Gallina, Youngsville, Canones, Abiquiu, Medanales, Chili, Hernandez, Espanola

Cottonwood, Ganado, Nazlini, Sawmill, Navajo, Tohatchi, Standing Rock, White Rock, Lake Valley, White Horse, Seven Lakes, Torreon, Chaco Mesa, Jemez Pueblo, Jemez Springs, Los Alamos, White Rock, Pajarito Mtn., Bandelier N.M., Santa Fe Natl. For.

Fort Defiance, Kinlichee Ruins Tribal Park, Kinlichee, St. Michaels, Window Rock, Navajo Nation Mus., Twin Lakes, Coyote Canyon, Crownpoint, Hospah, Torreon, Cañon, Ponderosa, Jemez St. Mon., Zia Pueblo, Cabezon Peak B.L.M. Rec. Area, Cochiti Lake, Cochiti Pueblo, Pena Blanca, La Cienega, Santo Domingo Pueblo, San Felipe Pueblo, Algodones, Placitas, Sandia Park, Cedar Crest

Hunters Point, Yah-Tah-Hey, Gamerco, Allison, Rehoboth, Red Rock S.P., Pinedale, Church Rock, Mariano Lake, Iyanbito, Smith Lake, Ambrosia Lake, San Mateo, Mt. Taylor 11,301, Marquez, Zia Pueblo, Santa Ana Pueblo, Coronado St. Mon., Bernalillo, Rio Rancho, Corrales, Los Cerrillos, Madrid, Golden, Cedar Grove

Gallup, Gallup Cultural Ctr., Gallup Mun. Arpt., Manuelito, Lupton, Houck, Fort Wingate, Coolidge, McGaffey, Thoreau, Continental Divide, Prewitt, Bluewater, Bluewater Lake S.P., Milan, Grants, New Mex. Mus. of Mining, Cebolleta, Laguna Pueblo, San Ysidro, Zia Pueblo, Santo Domingo, Bernalillo, Rio Rancho, Corrales, Paradise Hills, Alameda, Sandia Pueblo, Los Ranchos de Albuquerque, Petroglyph Natl. Mon., Albuquerque, Kirtland A.F.B., Tijeras, Edgewood, Cibola N.F.

Chambers, Sanders, Navajo, Zuni Pueblo, A:shiwi A:wan Mus. & Heritage Ctr., Black Rock, Pescado, Ramah, El Morro, El Morro Natl. Mon., Pine Hill, McCartys, Acomita, Acoma Pueblo, San Rafael, San Fidel, Cubero, Casa Blanca, Laguna, Enchanted Mesa, Acoma Pueblo, San Esteban del Rey Mission, Mesita, Isleta Pueblo, Los Padillas, Correo, Los Lunas, Bosque Farms, Peralta, Valencia, Los Chavez, Belen, Tajique, Torreon, Manzano

Petrified Forest Natl. Park, St. Johns, Concho, Salado, Lyman Lake, White Mtn. Arch. Ctr. and Raven Site Ruins, Zuni Ind. Res., Zion Res., Ojo Caliente, Fence Lake, Cebolleta Pk. 8,762, North Plains, Cibola, Laguna Pueblo, El Malpais Natl. Mon. & Cons. Area, La Ventana Natural Arch, Bandera Crater & Ice Caves, Acoma Pueblo, Jarales, Bosque, Turn, Sabinal, Veguita, Las Nutrias, Scholle, Abo, Manzano Peak 10,098, Punta (Quarai), Mountainair, Abo, Salinas Pueblo Missions N.M., Gran Quivira

Springerville, Eagar, Casa Malpais Pueblo, Lyman Lake S.P., Greer, Red Hill, Quemado, Omega, Pie Town, Datil Mts., Datil Well B.L.M. Rec. Area, Datil, Alamo, Riley Ghost Town, Ladron Pk. 9,176, La Joya, Bernardo, Abeytas, Sevilleta N.W.R., Polvadera, Lemitar, San Acacia, Escondida, Socorro, Luis Lopez

Aragon, National Radio Astronomy Observatory, Gallo Mts., Mangas Mts., Catron, Alegres Mtn. 10,244, Datil, Magdalena, Magdalena Mts., South Baldy 10,783, Kelly Ghost Town, N. Mex. Inst. of Mining & Tech., Socorro, The Box, San Lorenzo Canyon B.L.M. Rec. Area, San Augustin Mission

Go to 40
Go to 47
Go to 56

ARIZONA / NEW MEXICO state line

Grid references: 1, 2, 3, 4 (rows) and A, B, C (columns)

UTAH / ARIZONA, COLORADO / NEW MEXICO, ARIZONA / NEW MEXICO state boundaries

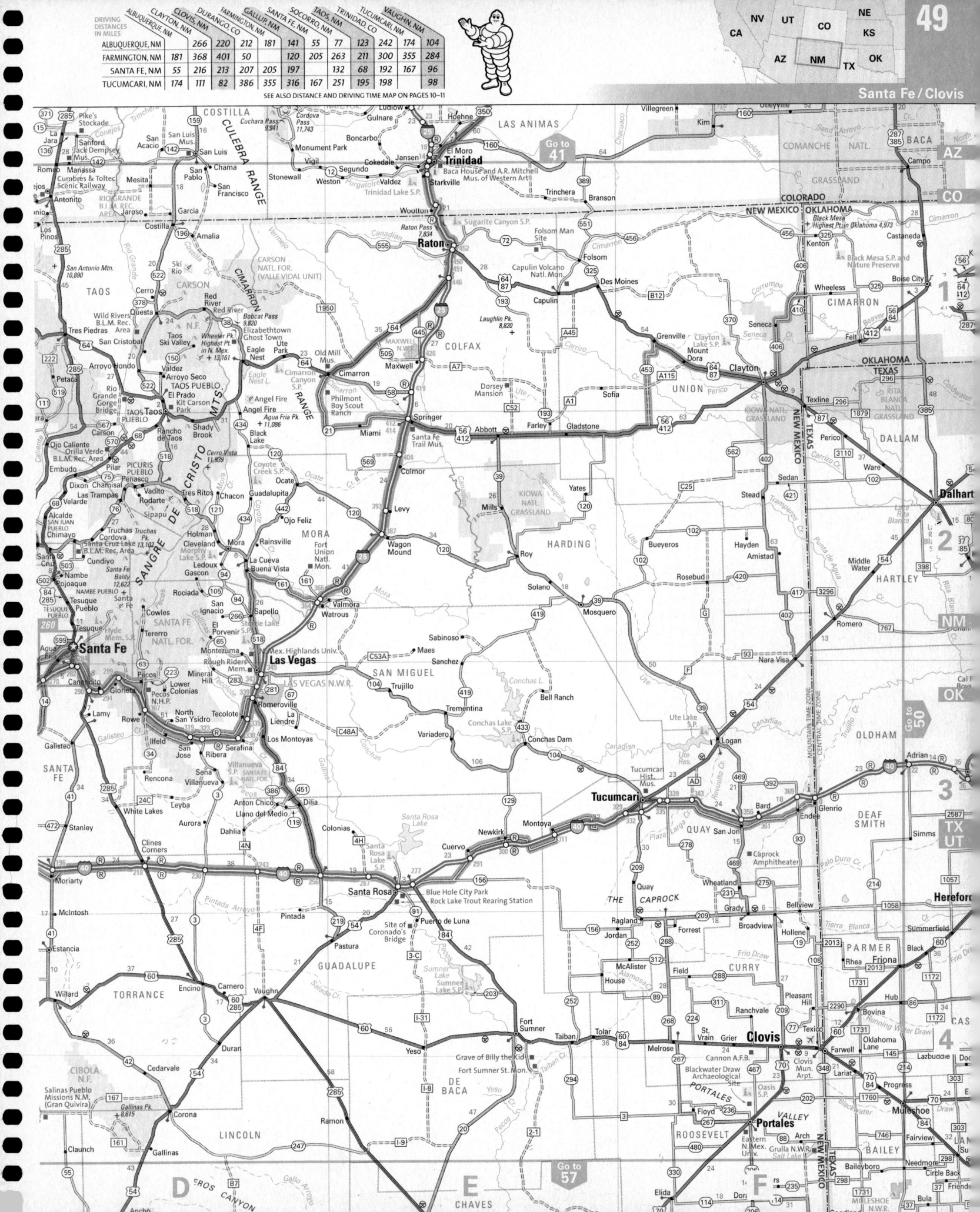

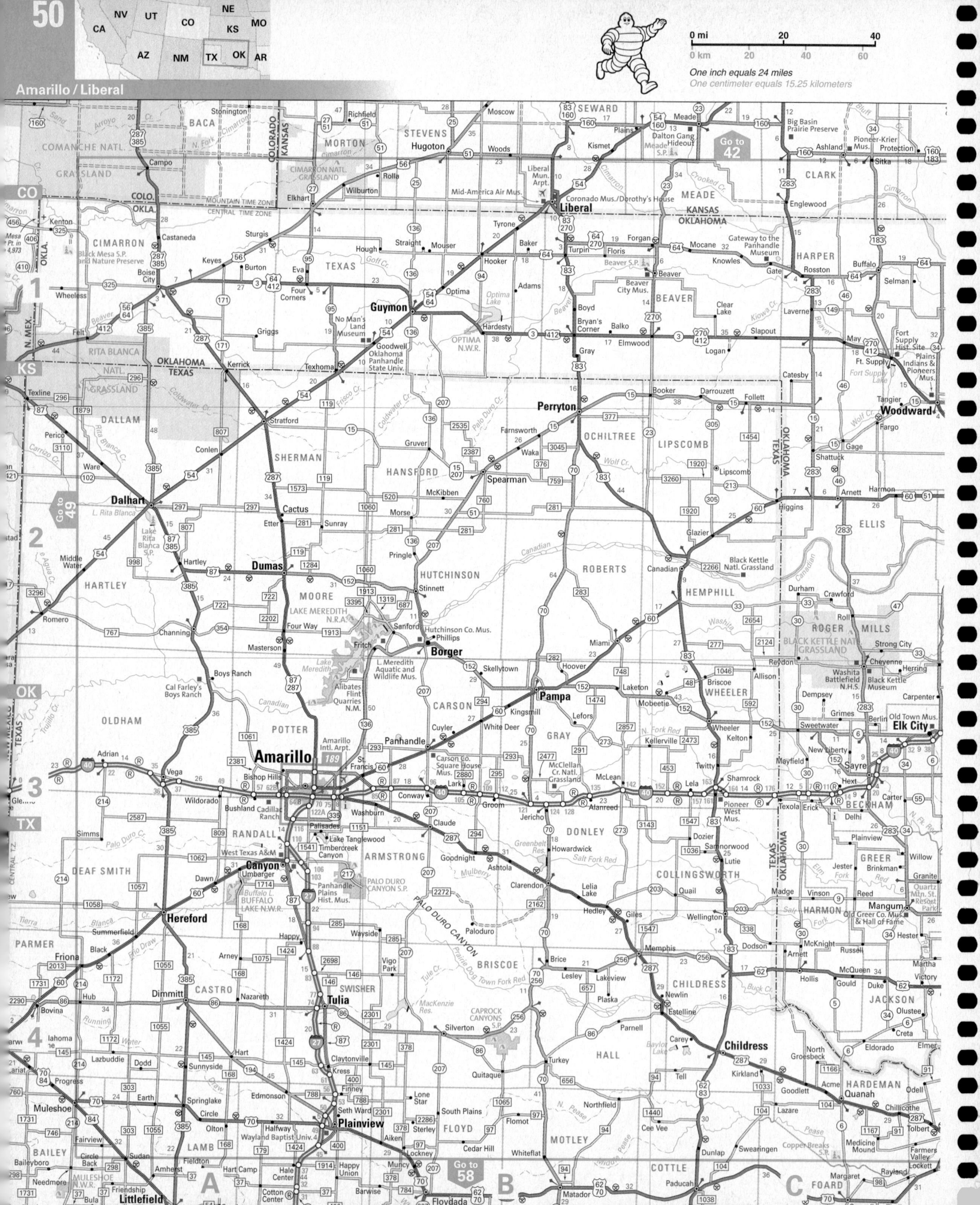

One inch equals 24 miles
One centimeter equals 15.25 kilometers

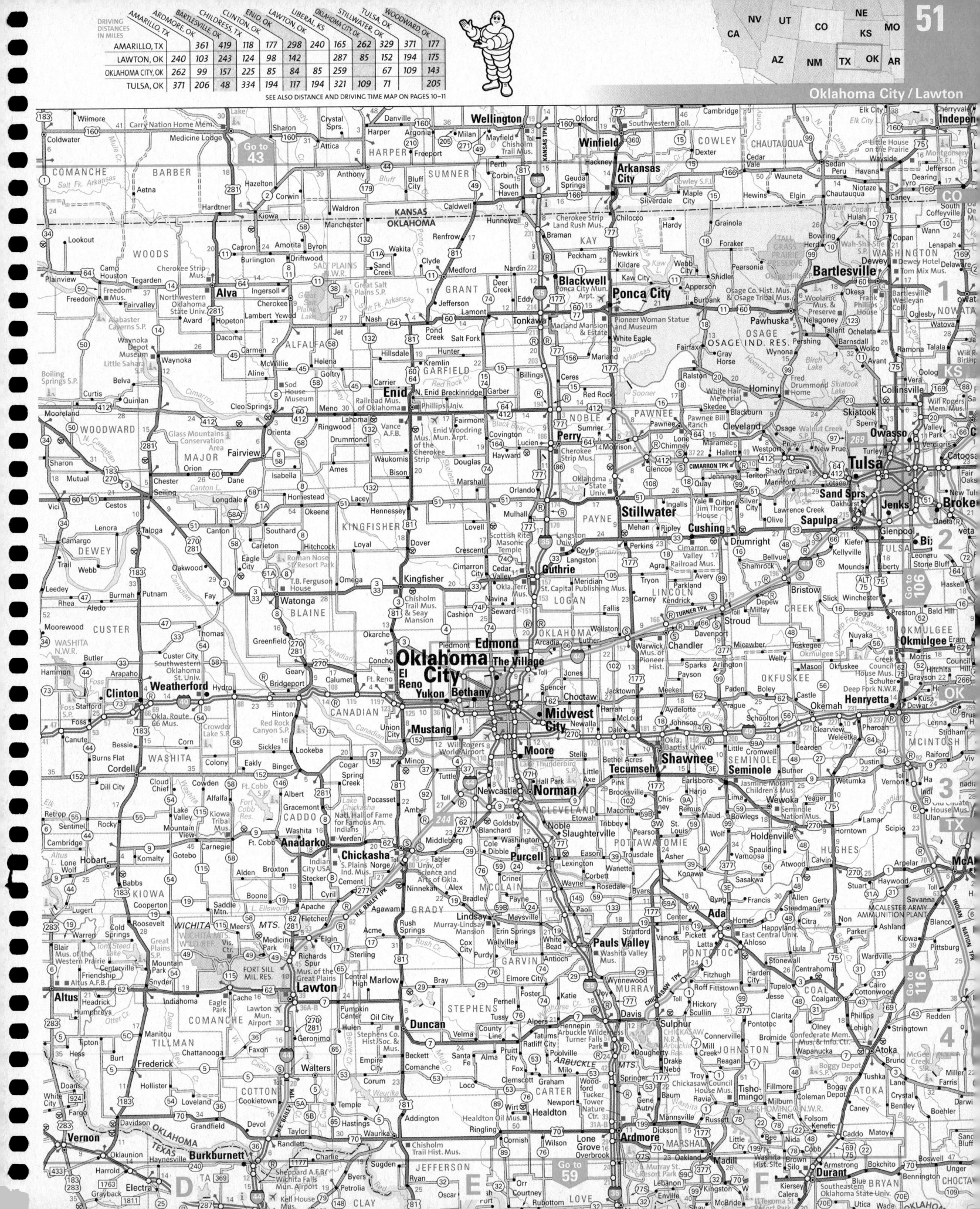

DRIVING DISTANCES IN MILES	AMARILLO, TX	ARDMORE, OK	BARTLESVILLE, OK	CHILDRESS, TX	CLINTON, OK	ENID, OK	LAWTON, OK	LIBERAL, KS	OKLAHOMA CITY, OK	STILLWATER, OK	TULSA, OK	WOODWARD, OK
AMARILLO, TX		361	419	118	177	298	240	165	262	329	371	177
LAWTON, OK	240	103	243	124	98	142		287	85	152	194	175
OKLAHOMA CITY, OK	262	99	157	225	85	84	85	259		67	109	143
TULSA, OK	371	206	48	334	187	117	194	321	109	71		205

SEE ALSO DISTANCE AND DRIVING TIME MAP ON PAGES 10–11

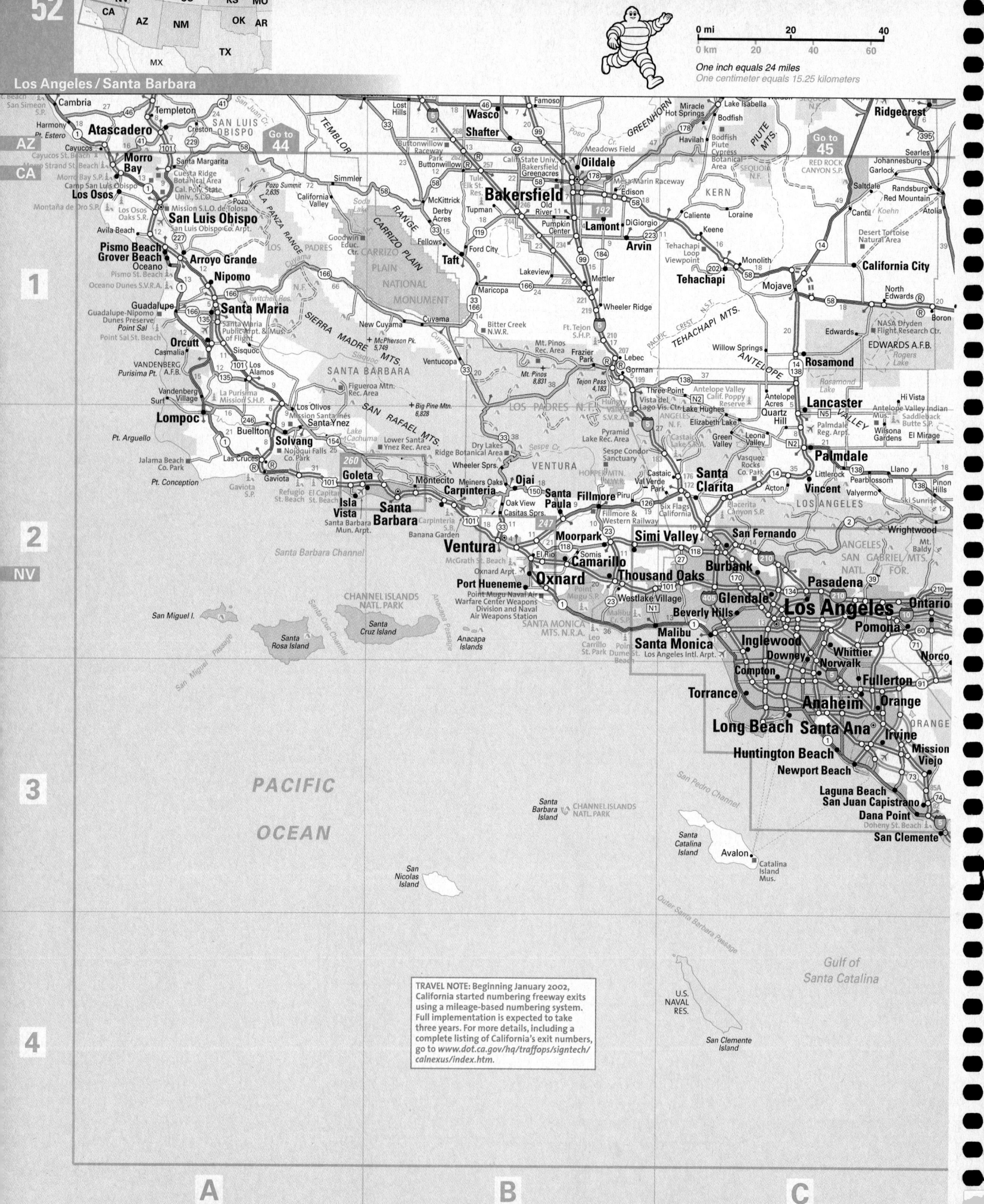

One inch equals 24 miles
One centimeter equals 15.25 kilometers

0 mi   20   40
0 km   20   40   60

PACIFIC

OCEAN

Gulf of
Santa Catalina

TRAVEL NOTE: Beginning January 2002,
California started numbering freeway exits
using a mileage-based numbering system.
Full implementation is expected to take
three years. For more details, including a
complete listing of California's exit numbers,
go to www.dot.ca.gov/hq/traffops/signtech/
calnexus/index.htm.

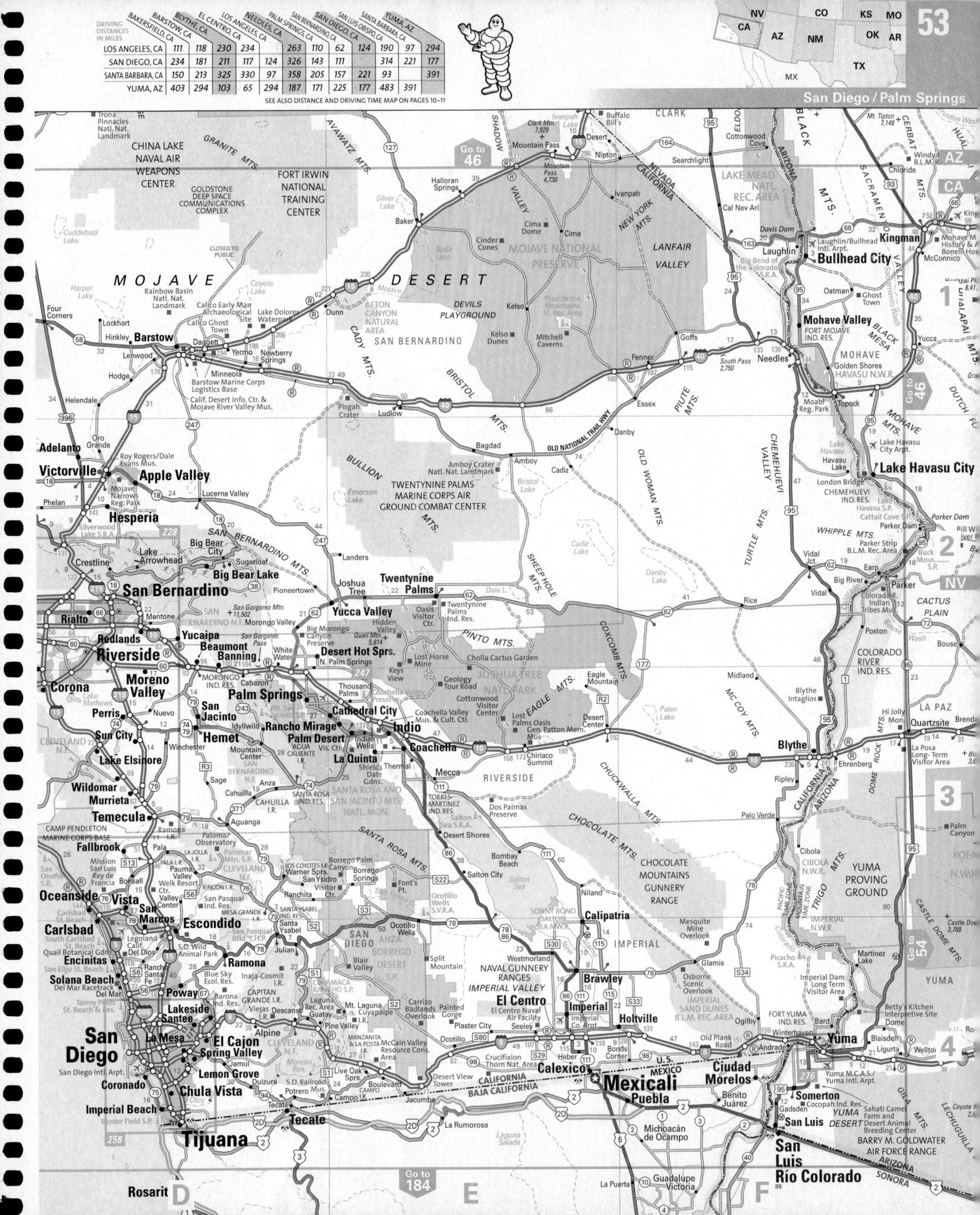

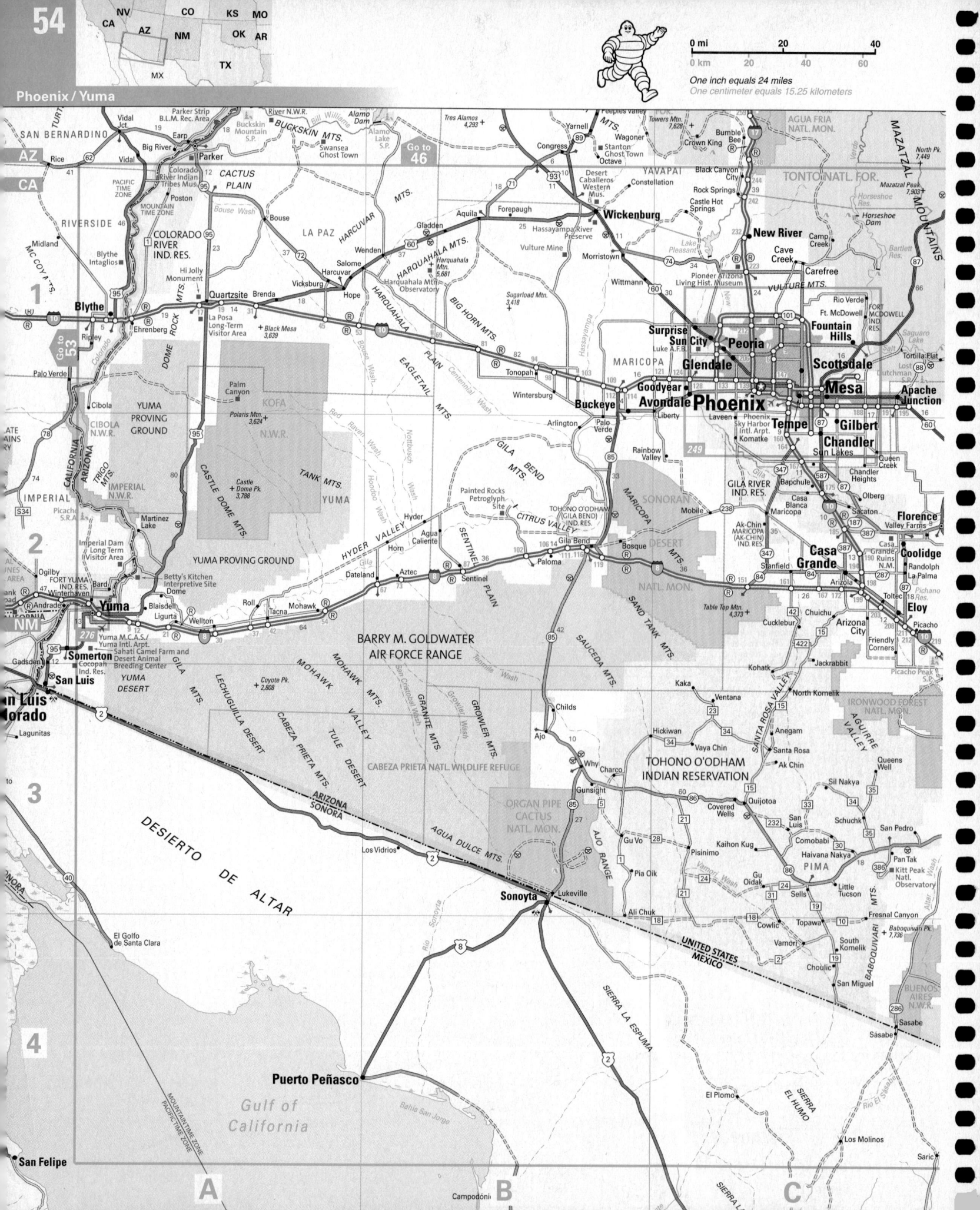

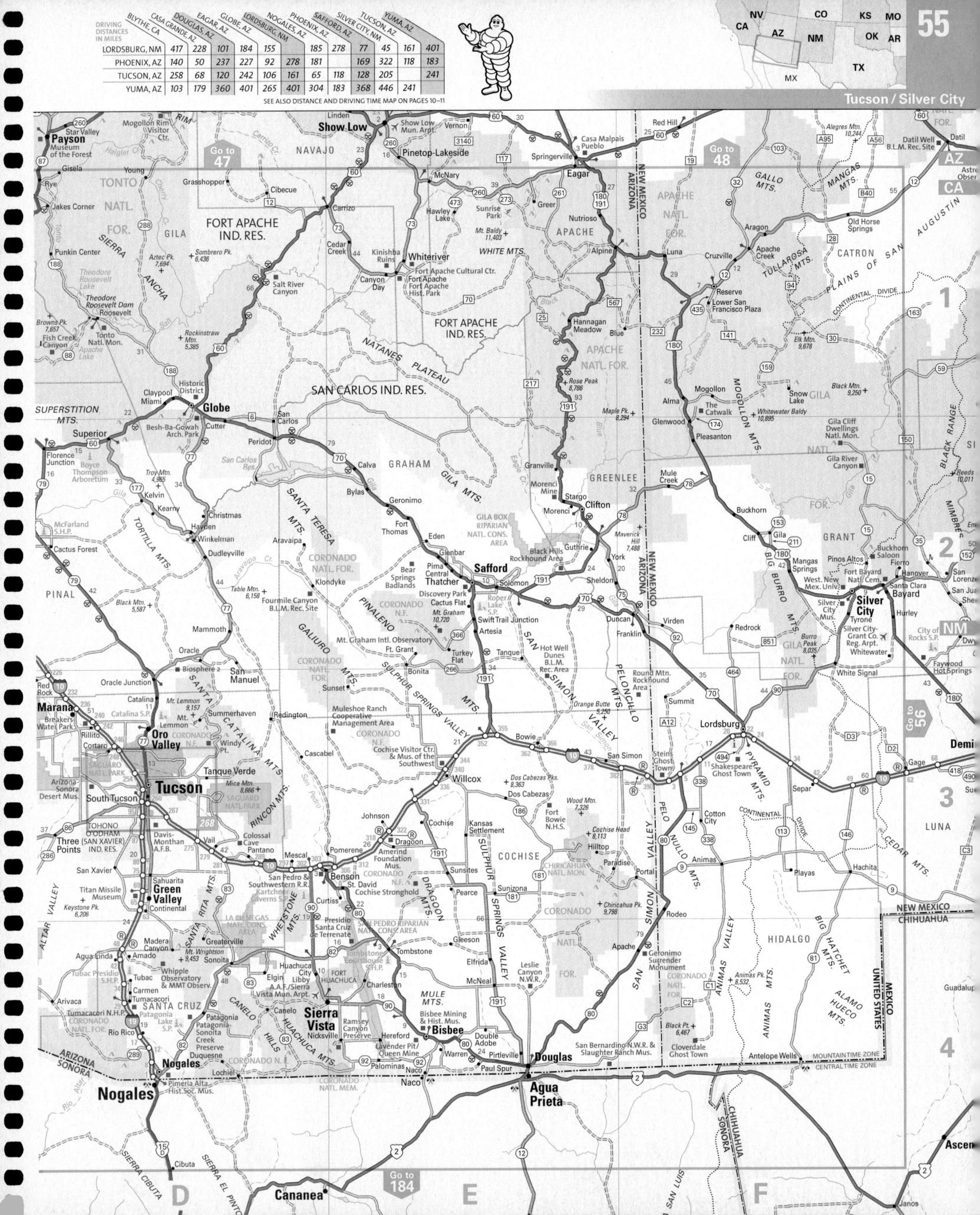

DRIVING DISTANCES IN MILES

	BLYTHE, CA	CASA GRANDE, AZ	DOUGLAS, AZ	EAGAR, AZ	GLOBE, AZ	LORDSBURG, NM	NOGALES, AZ	PHOENIX, AZ	SAFFORD, AZ	SILVER CITY, NM	TUCSON, AZ	YUMA, AZ
LORDSBURG, NM	417	228	101	184	155		185	278	77	45	161	401
PHOENIX, AZ	140	50	237	227	92	278	181		169	322	118	183
TUCSON, AZ	258	68	120	242	106	161	65	118	128	205		241
YUMA, AZ	103	179	360	401	265	401	304	183	368	446	241	

SEE ALSO DISTANCE AND DRIVING TIME MAP ON PAGES 10–11

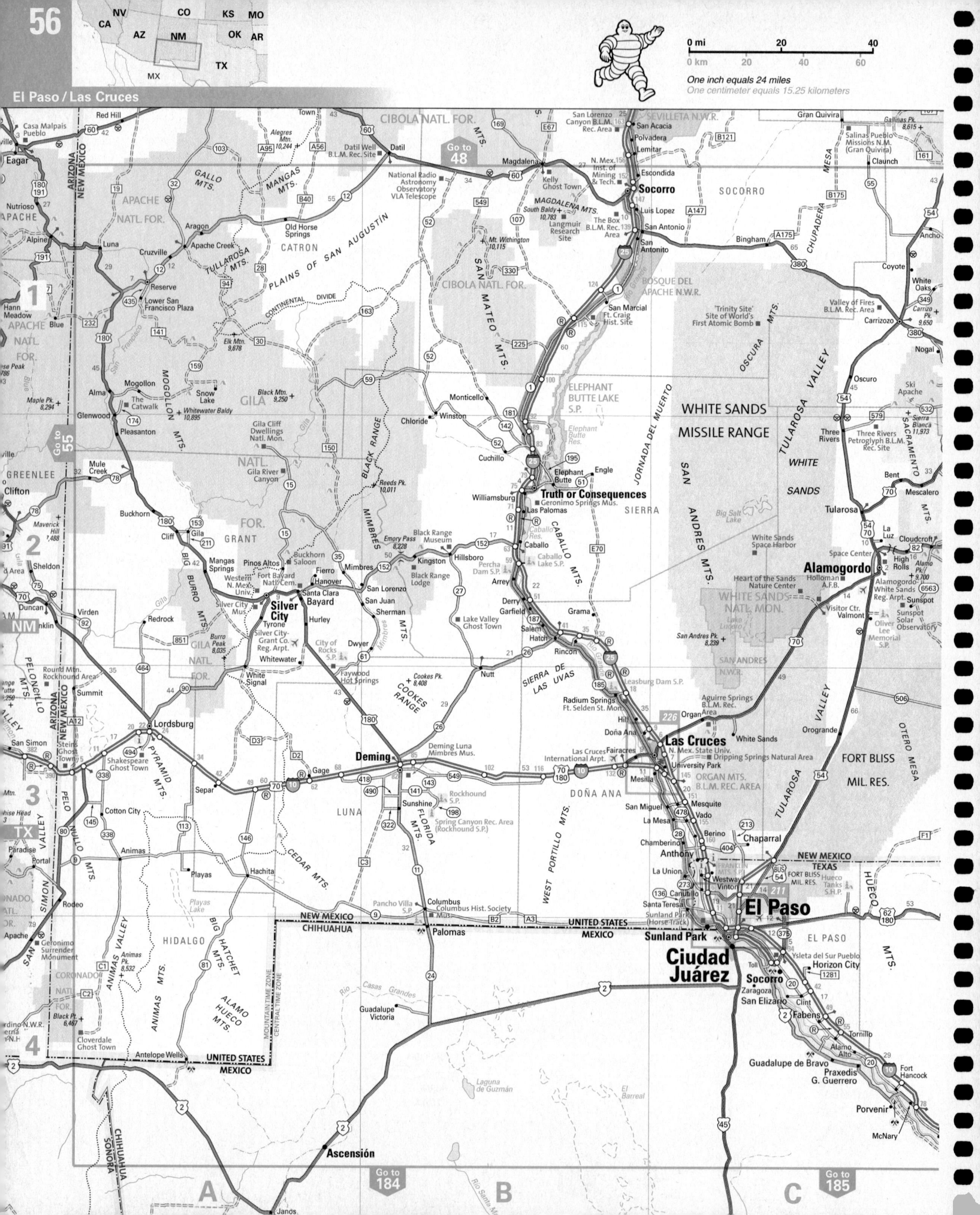

DRIVING DISTANCES IN MILES

	ALAMOGORDO NM	CARLSBAD NM	EL PASO TX	HOBBS NM	LAS CRUCES NM	LORDSBURG NM	ODESSA TX	PECOS TX	PORTALES NM	ROSWELL NM	SILVER CITY NM	SOCORRO NM
CARLSBAD, NM	144		162	70	203	321	137	87	168	76	311	241
EL PASO, TX	86	162		232	42	160	285	209	295	203	150	190
LAS CRUCES, NM	65	203	42	250		122	325	250	274	182	111	146
ROSWELL, NM	117	76	203	117	182	304	201	163	92		293	164

SEE ALSO DISTANCE AND DRIVING TIME MAP ON PAGES 10–11

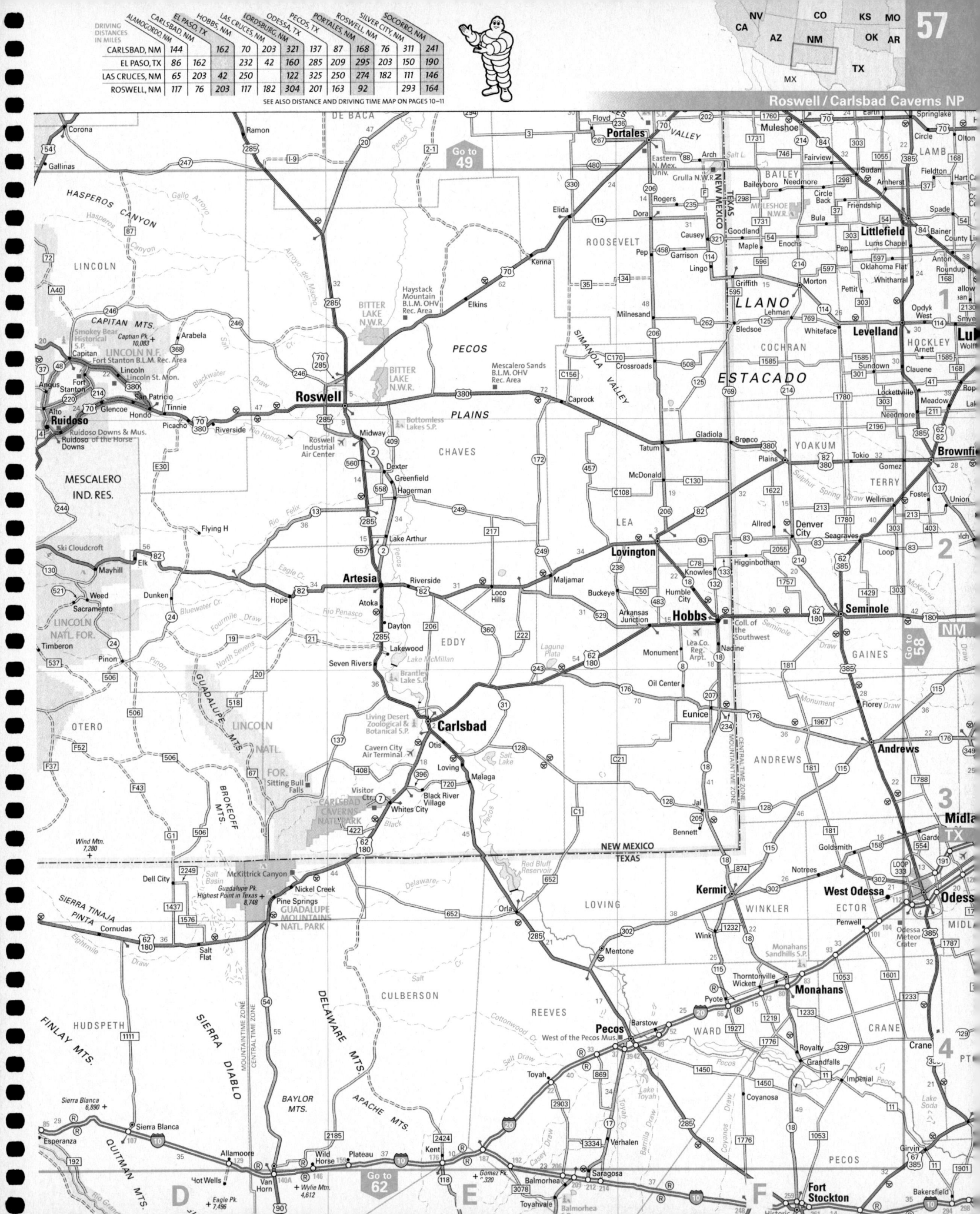

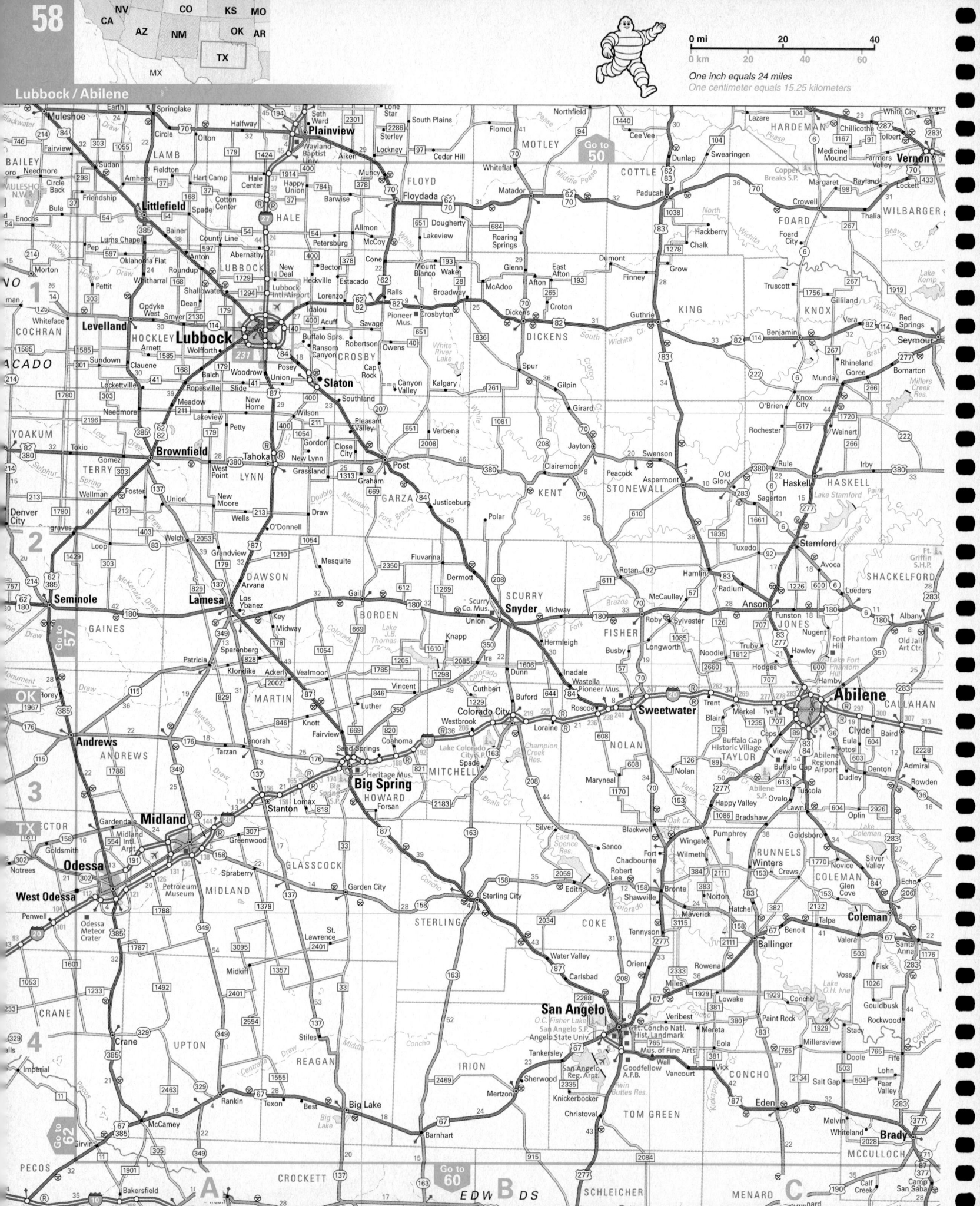

One inch equals 24 miles
One centimeter equals 15.25 kilometers

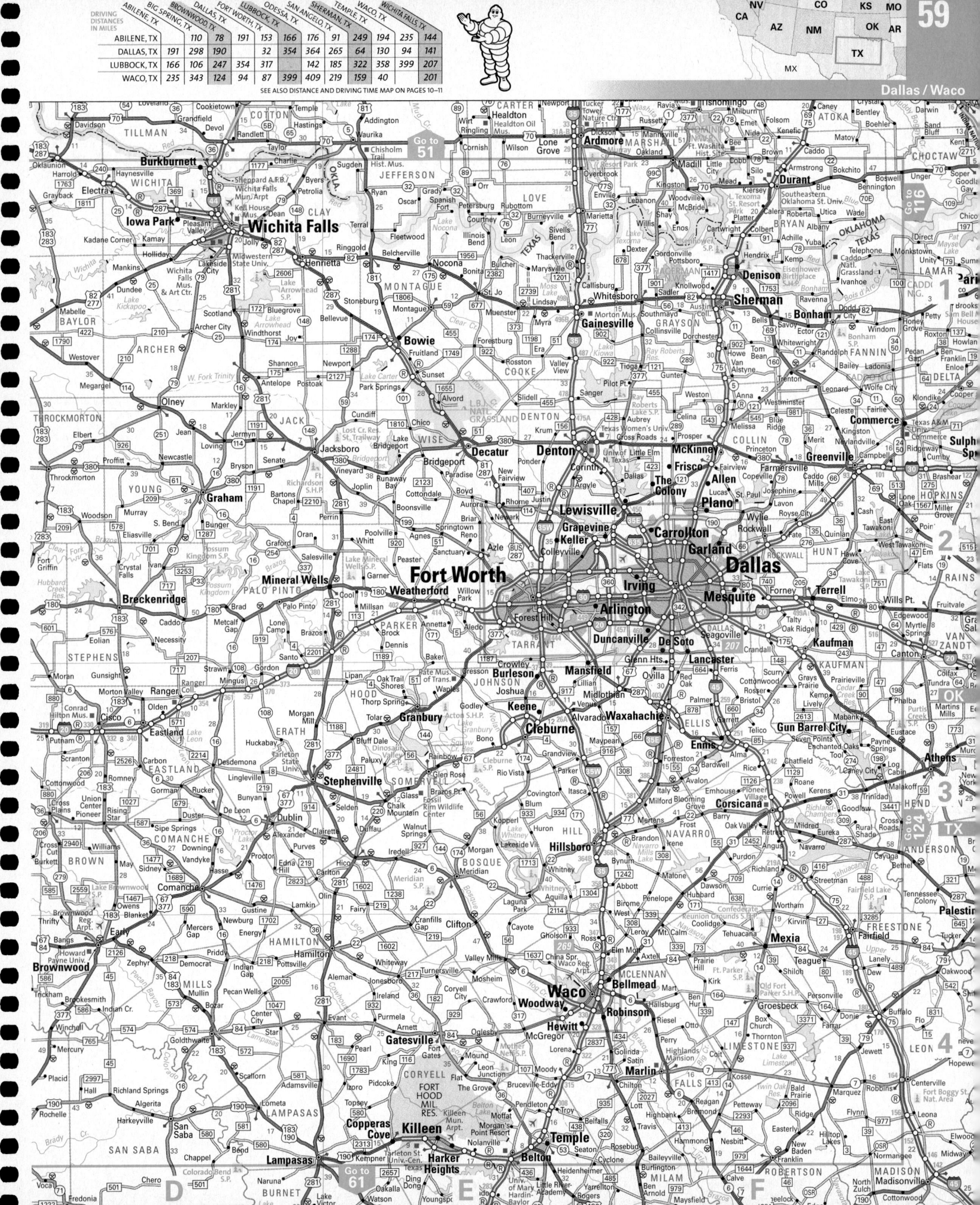

DRIVING DISTANCES IN MILES

	ABILENE, TX	BIG SPRING, TX	BROWNWOOD, TX	DALLAS, TX	FORT WORTH, TX	LUBBOCK, TX	ODESSA, TX	SAN ANGELO, TX	SHERMAN, TX	TEMPLE, TX	WACO, TX	WICHITA FALLS, TX
ABILENE, TX		110	78	191	153	166	176	91	249	194	235	144
DALLAS, TX	191	298	190		32	354	364	265	64	130	94	141
LUBBOCK, TX	166	106	247	354	317		142	185	322	358	399	207
WACO, TX	235	343	124	94	87	399	409	219	159	40		201

SEE ALSO DISTANCE AND DRIVING TIME MAP ON PAGES 10–11

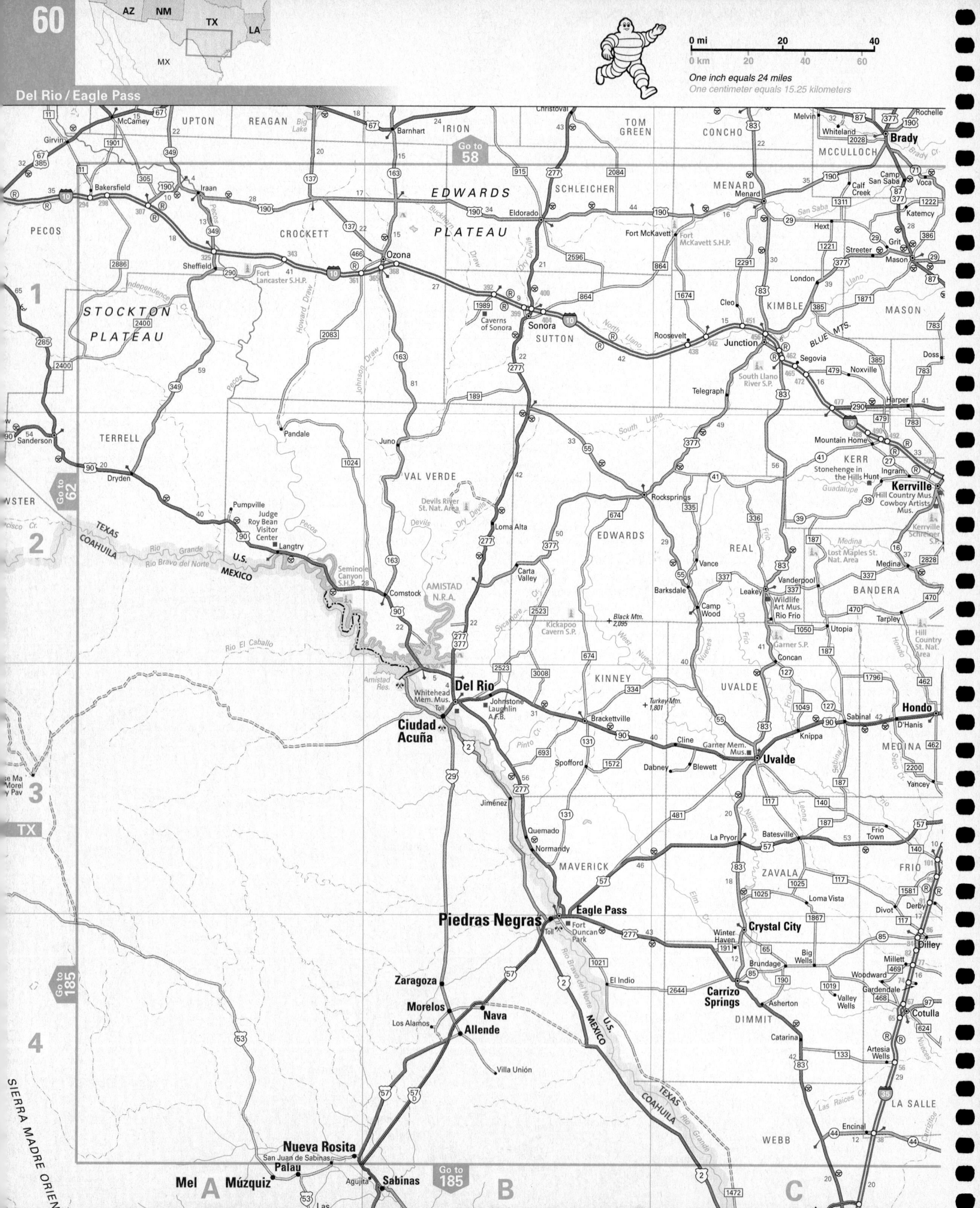

AZ NM
TX LA
MX

0 mi   20   40
0 km   20   40   60
One inch equals 24 miles
One centimeter equals 15.25 kilometers

1

McCamey
Girvin
Bakersfield
Iraan
PECOS
Sheffield
Fort Lancaster S.H.P.
STOCKTON PLATEAU
UPTON   REAGAN
Big Lake
Barnhart
IRION
Christoval
TOM GREEN
SCHLEICHER
Eldorado
CONCHO
Menard
MENARD
Whiteland
Brady
McCULLOCH
Camp San Saba
Voca
Calf Creek
Melvin
Rochelle
MASON
Mason
Grit
Katemcy
Streeter
London
Hext
Fort McKavett
Fort McKavett S.H.P.
Cleo
KIMBLE
Roosevelt
Junction
Segovia
Noxville
Harper
Doss
BLUE MTS.
EDWARDS PLATEAU
Ozona
CROCKETT
Sonora
SUTTON
Caverns of Sonora
San Saba

2

Sanderson
TERRELL
Dryden
Langtry
Pumpville
Judge Roy Bean Visitor Center
Pandale
Juno
VAL VERDE
Devils River St. Nat. Area
Loma Alta
Carta Valley
EDWARDS
Rocksprings
Vance
REAL
Barksdale
Camp Wood
Leakey
Vanderpool
Wildlife Art Mus. Rio Frio
Concan
Utopia
Tarpley
Medina
BANDERA
Lost Maples St. Nat. Area
Hill Country St. Nat. Area
Kerrville
Hill Country Mus.
Cowboy Artists Mus.
Kerrville-Schreiner S.P.
Ingram
Mountain Home
KERR
Stonehenge in the Hills Hunt
Guadalupe
TEXAS
COAHUILA
Rio Grande
Rio Bravo del Norte
MEXICO
U.S.
Seminole Canyon S.H.P.
Comstock
AMISTAD N.R.A.
Kickapoo Cavern S.P.
Black Mtn. 2,095
KINNEY
Turkey Mtn. 1,801
UVALDE
Garner S.P.
MEDINA
Hondo
D'Hanis
Sabinal
Knippa
Uvalde
Garner Mem. Mus.
Cline
Brackettville
Spofford
Dabney
Blewett
Yancey

3

Amistad Res.
Del Rio
Whitehead Mem. Mus.
Toll
Johnstone Laughlin A.F.B.
Ciudad Acuña
Jiménez
Quemado
Normandy
MAVERICK
La Pryor
Batesville
Frio Town
ZAVALA
Loma Vista
FRIO
Dilley
Crystal City
Winter Haven
Brundage
Big Wells
Derby
Divot
Millett
Woodward
Gardendale
Valley Wells
Asherton
DIMMIT
Carrizo Springs
Cotulla
Catarina
Artesia Wells
El Indio
Nueces

4

SIERRA MADRE ORIEN
Piedras Negras
Fort Duncan Park
Toll
Eagle Pass
Zaragoza
Morelos
Los Alamos
Nava
Allende
Villa Unión
COAHUILA
TEXAS
Rio Bravo del Norte
Rio Grande
MEXICO
U.S.
Las Raíces Cr.
WEBB
LA SALLE
Encinal
Nueva Rosita
San Juan de Sabinas
Palau
Múzquiz
Mel
Agujita
Sabinas
Las

Go to 58
Go to 62
Go to 185
TX
Go to 185

A   **B**   **C**

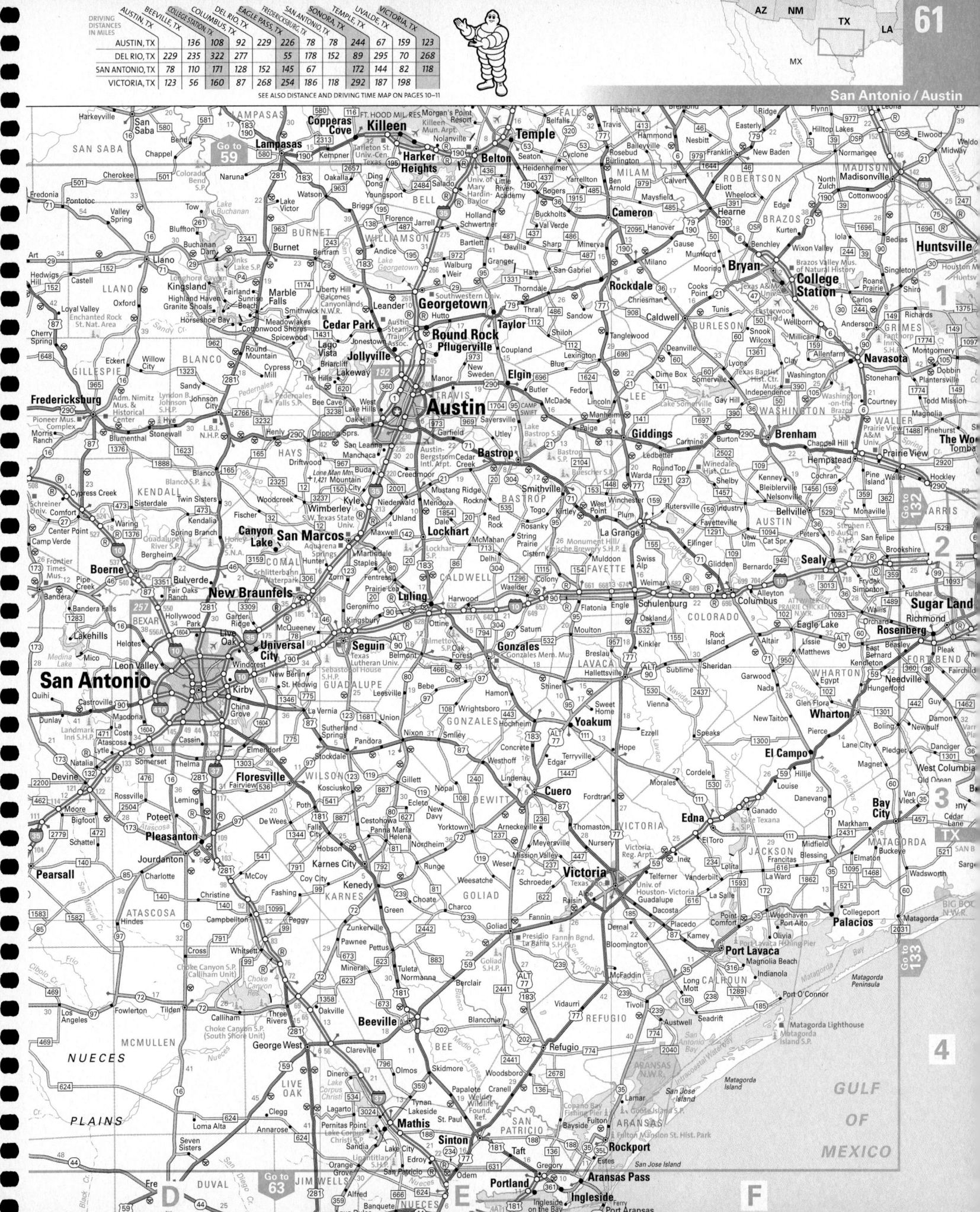

DRIVING DISTANCES IN MILES

	AUSTIN, TX	BEEVILLE, TX	COLLEGE STATION, TX	COLUMBUS, TX	DEL RIO, TX	EAGLE PASS, TX	FREDERICKSBURG, TX	SAN ANTONIO, TX	SONORA, TX	TEMPLE, TX	UVALDE, TX	VICTORIA, TX
AUSTIN, TX		136	108	92	229	226	78	78	244	67	159	123
DEL RIO, TX	229	235	322	277		55	178	152	89	295	70	268
SAN ANTONIO, TX	78	110	171	128	152	145	67		172	144	82	118
VICTORIA, TX	123	56	160	87	268	254	186	118	292	187	198	

SEE ALSO DISTANCE AND DRIVING TIME MAP ON PAGES 10–11

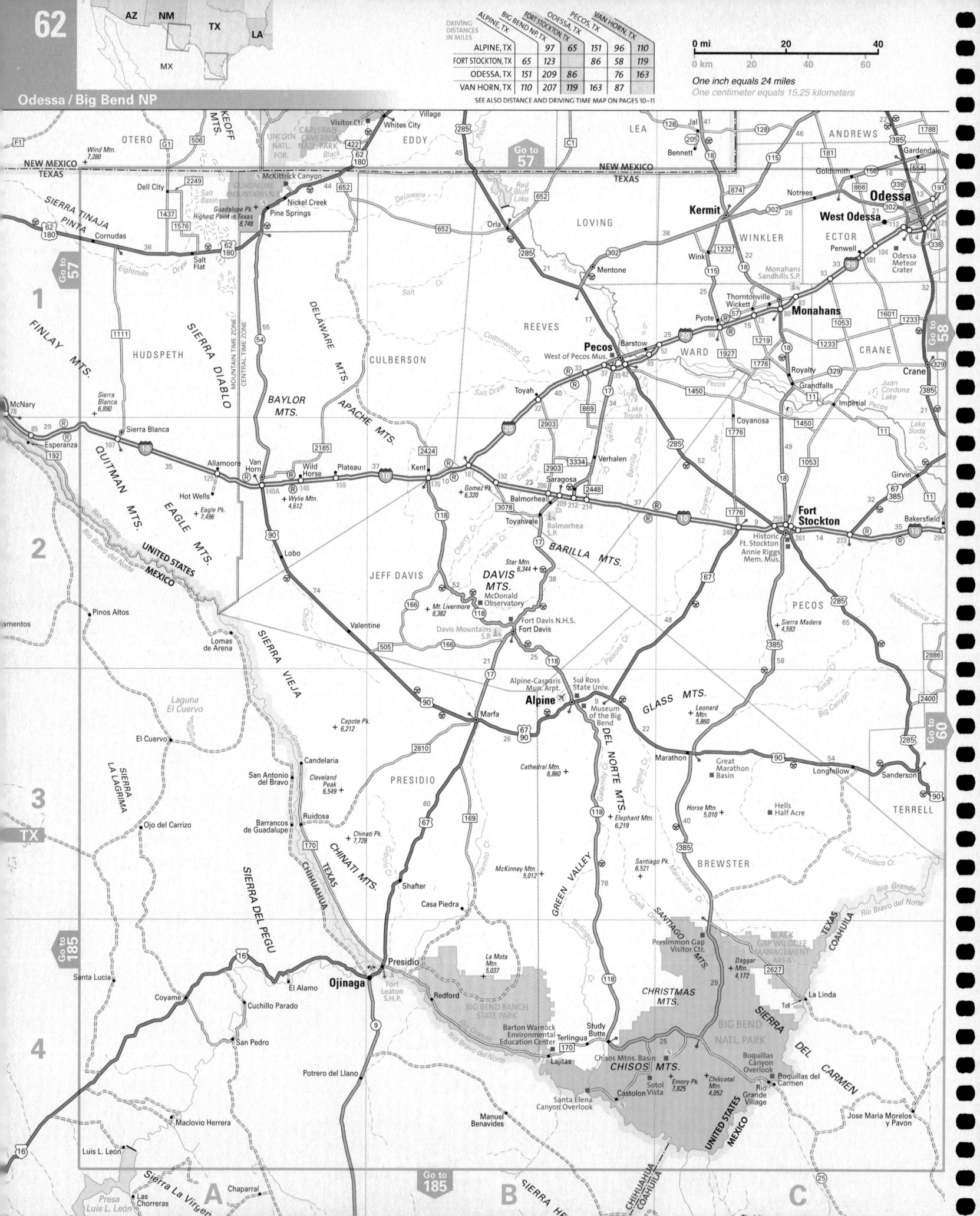

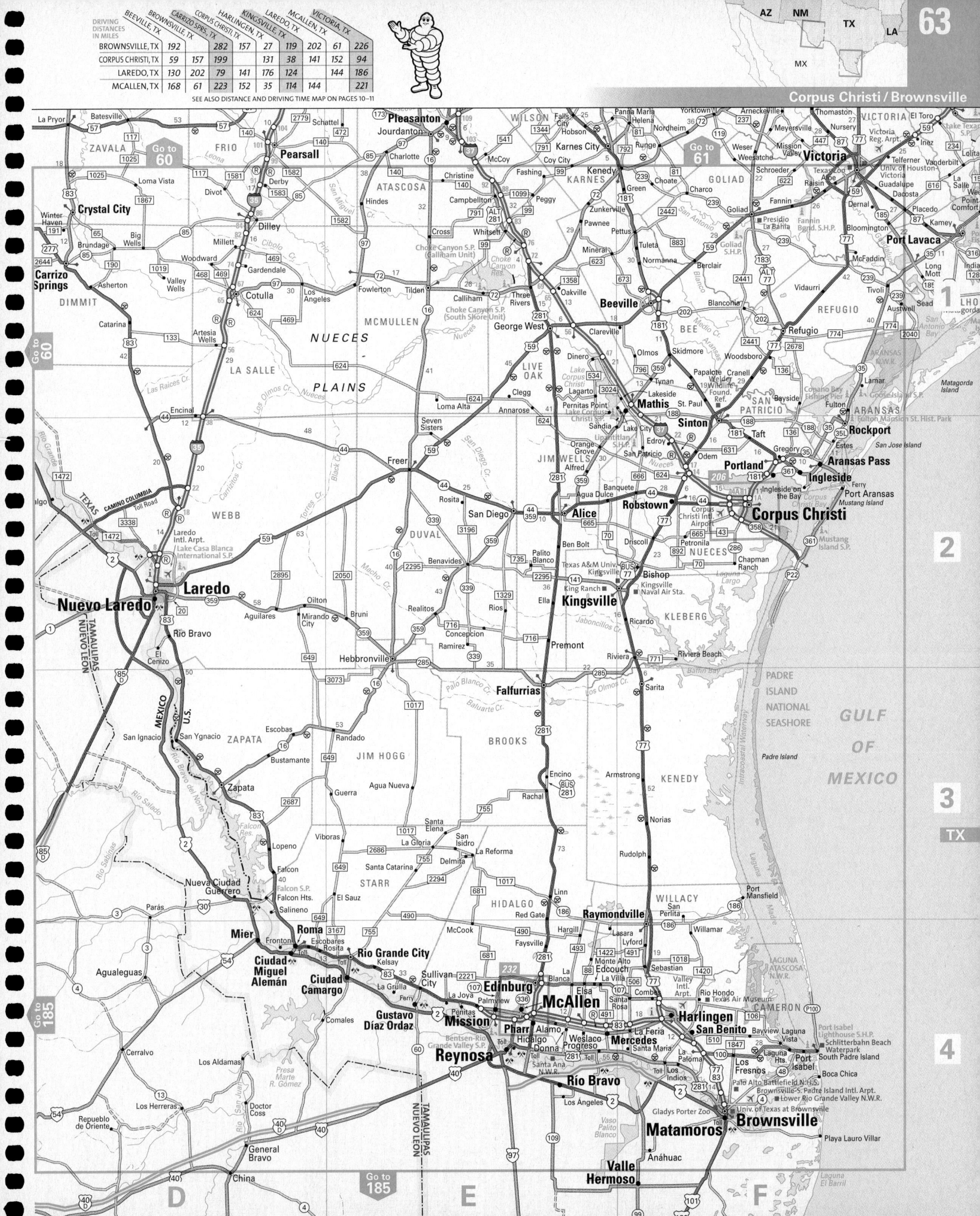

AZ NM TX LA

MX

DRIVING DISTANCES IN MILES	BEEVILLE, TX	BROWNSVILLE, TX	CARRIZO SPRS, TX	CORPUS CHRISTI, TX	HARLINGEN, TX	KINGSVILLE, TX	LAREDO, TX	MCALLEN, TX	VICTORIA, TX
BROWNSVILLE, TX	192		282	157	27	119	202	61	226
CORPUS CHRISTI, TX	59	157	199		131	38	141	152	94
LAREDO, TX	130	202	79	141	176	124		144	186
MCALLEN, TX	168	61	223	152	35	114	144		221

SEE ALSO DISTANCE AND DRIVING TIME MAP ON PAGES 10–11

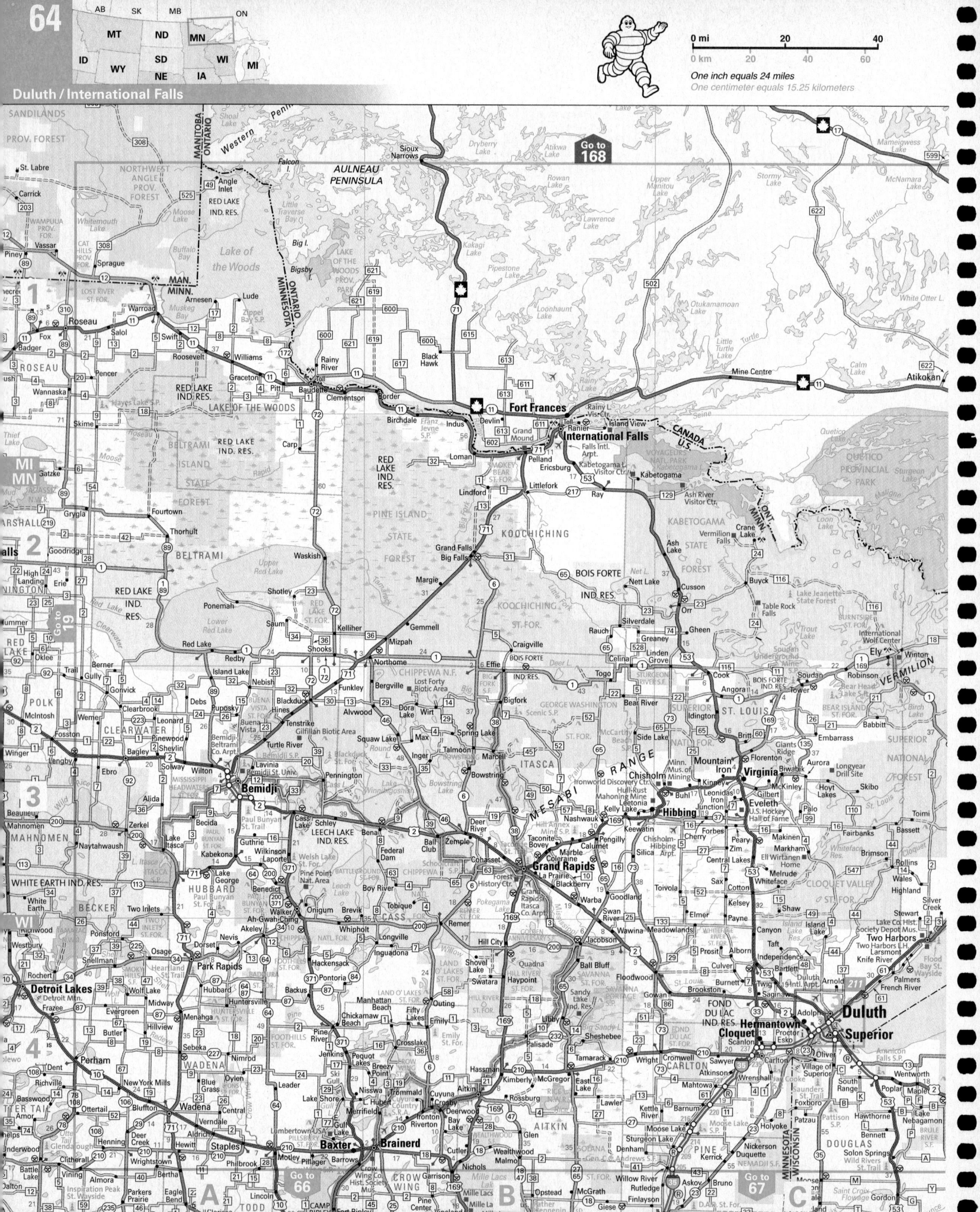

DRIVING DISTANCES IN MILES

	ASHLAND, WI	BEMIDJI, MN	BRAINERD, MN	DETROIT LAKES, MN	DULUTH, MN	GRAND PORTAGE, MN	HOUGHTON, MI	INTERNAT'L FALLS, MN	IRONWOOD, MI	ISHPEMING, MI	THUNDER BAY, ON	VIRGINIA, MN
BEMIDJI, MN	239		96	91	153	295	362	109	254	384	314	124
DULUTH, MN	92	153	116	202		143	215	157	107	238	183	61
HOUGHTON, MI	132	362	325	412	215	358		370	108	87	654	274
INTERNAT'L FALLS, MN	247	109	190	200	157	245	370		262	393	205	97

SEE ALSO DISTANCE AND DRIVING TIME MAP ON PAGES 10–11

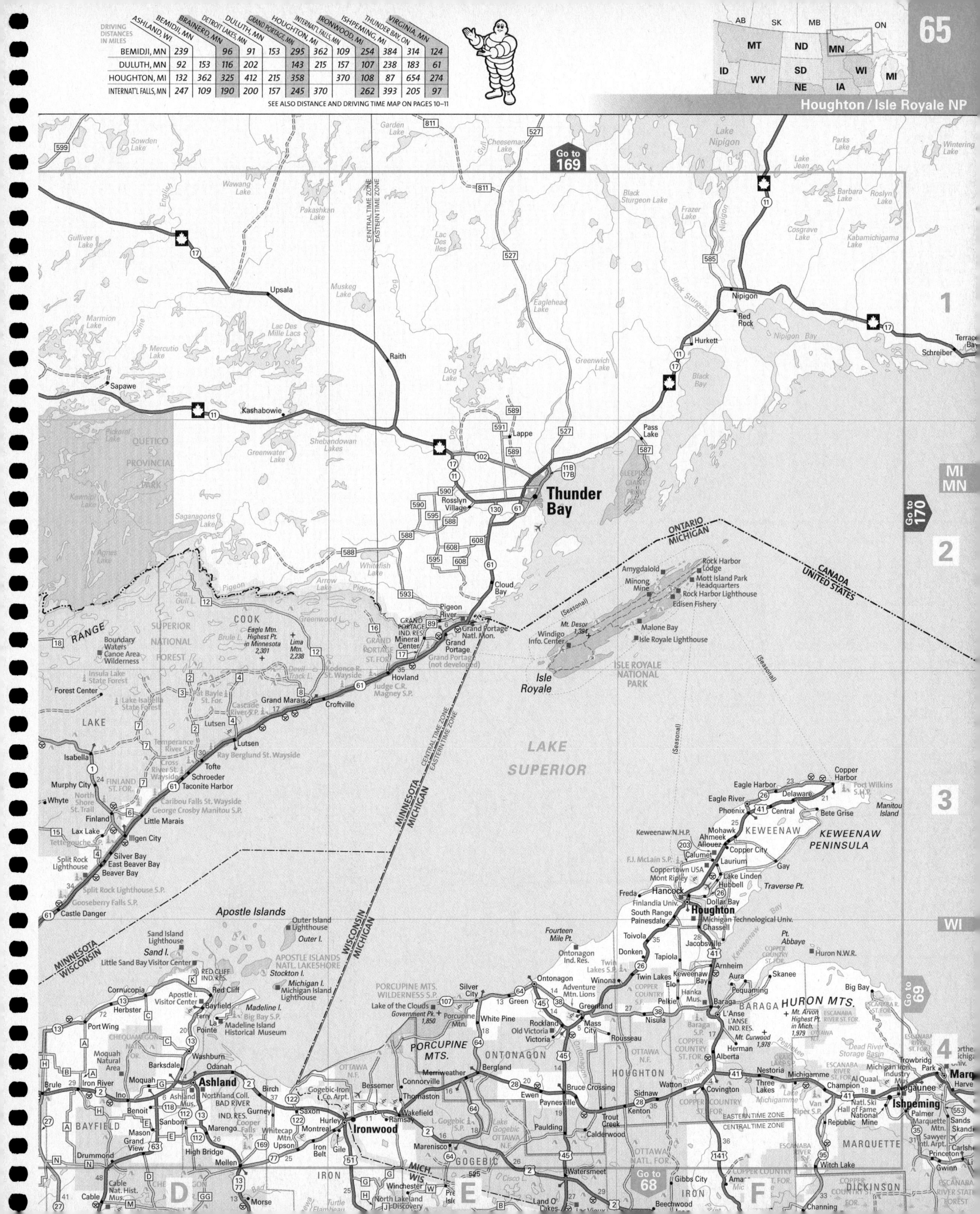

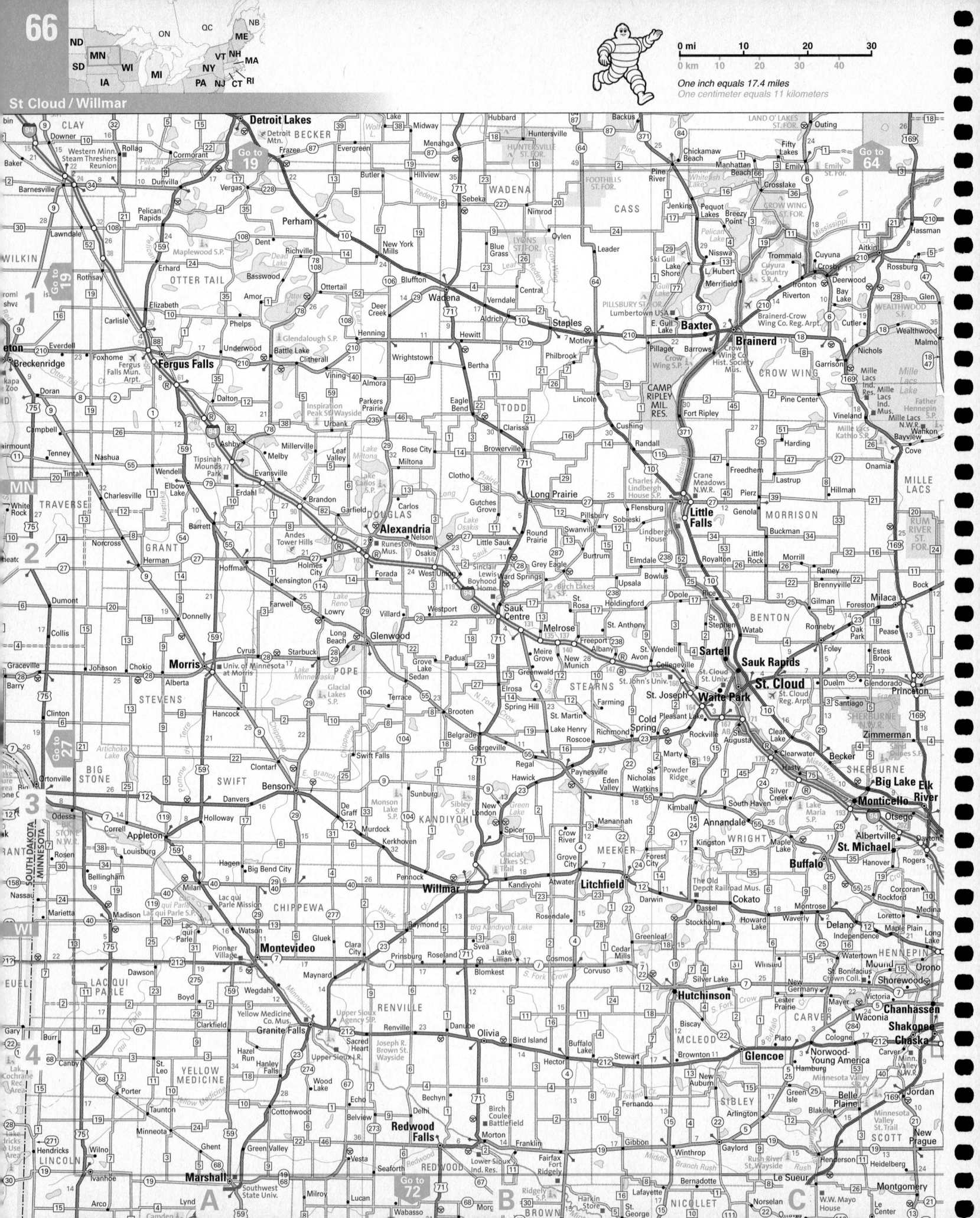

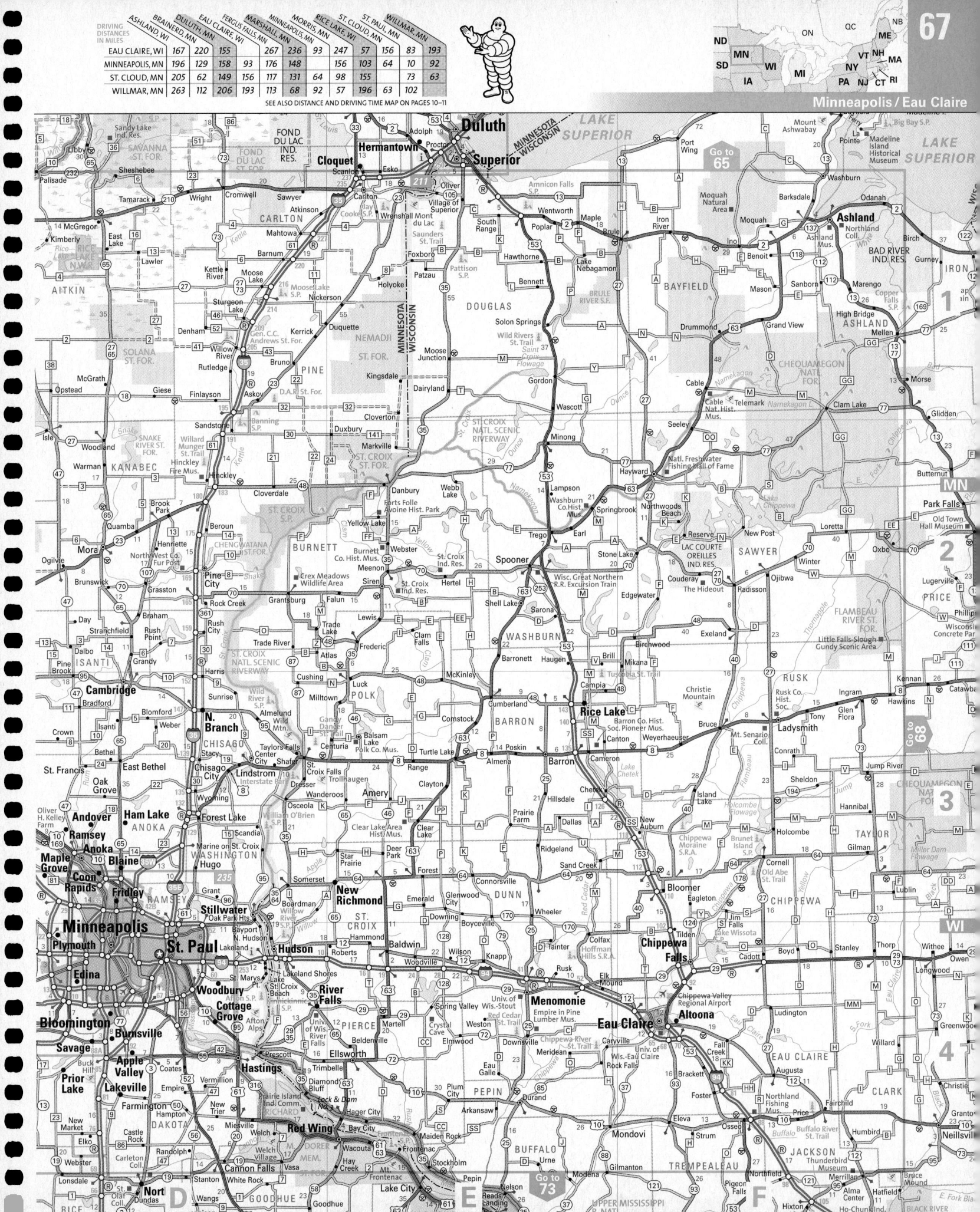

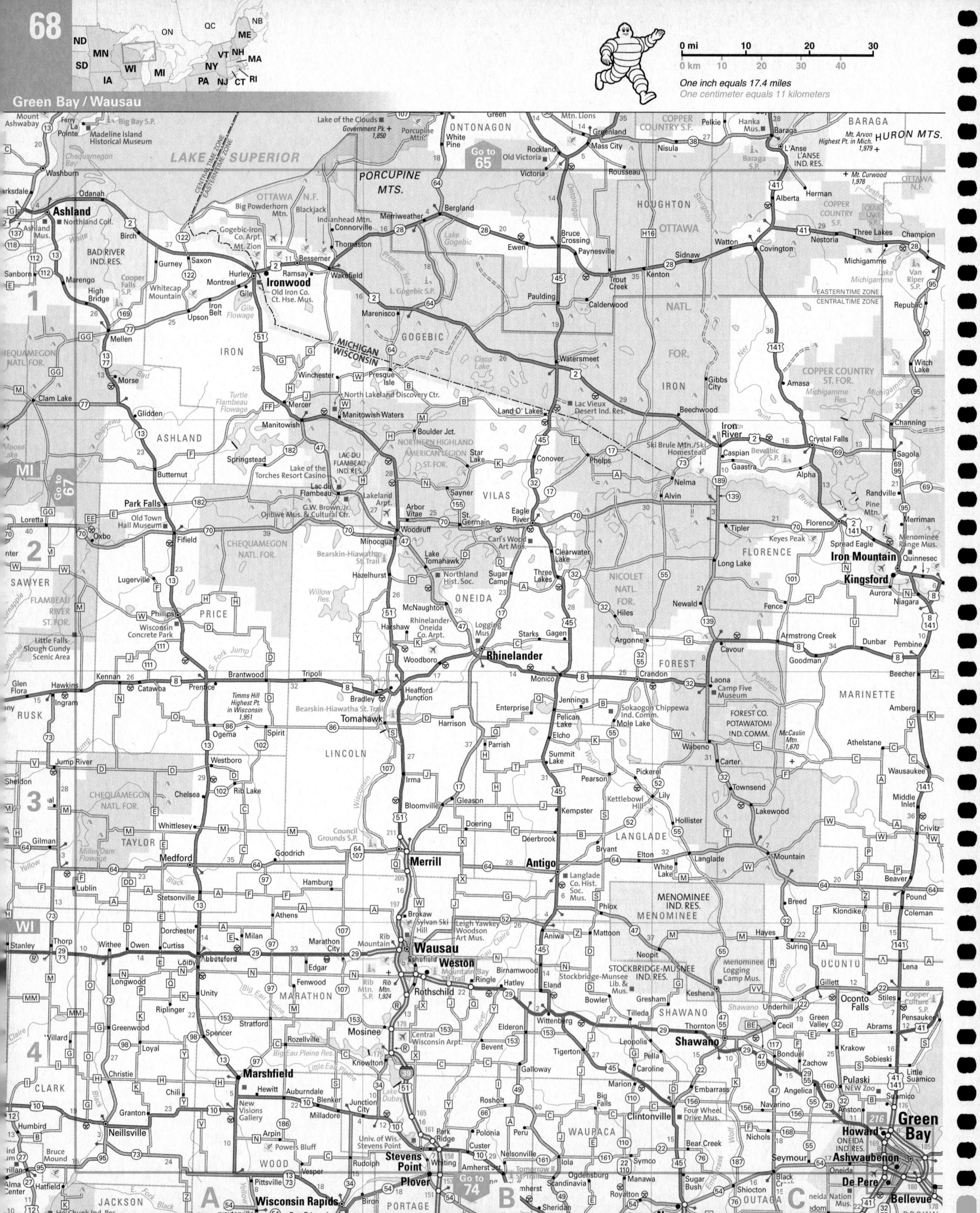

68
ND
SD MN
IA WI MI
ON QC
NB
ME
VT NH MA
NY
PA NJ CT RI
Green Bay / Wausau

0 mi 10 20 30
0 km 10 20 30 40
One inch equals 17.4 miles
One centimeter equals 11 kilometers

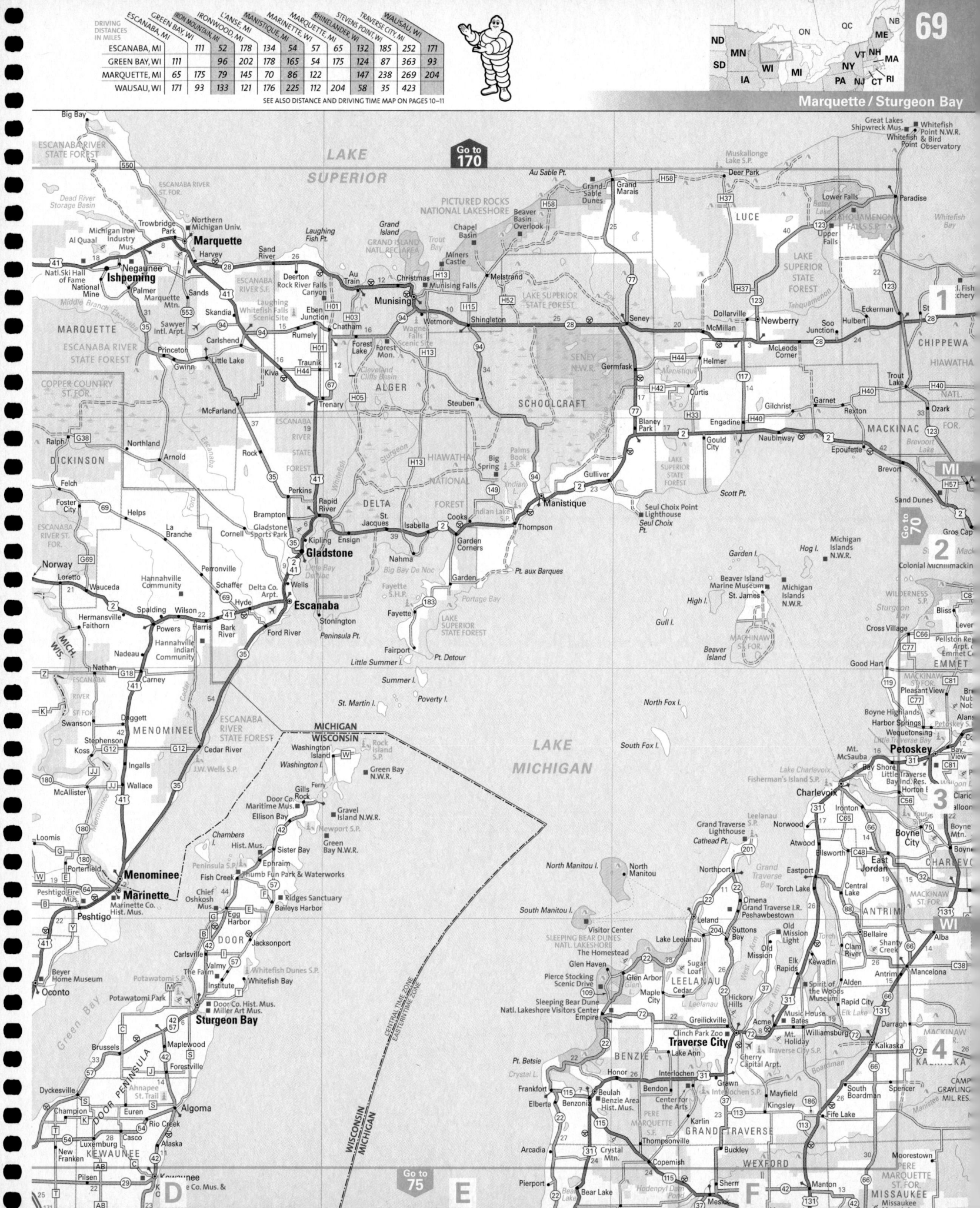

DRIVING DISTANCES IN MILES	ESCANABA, MI	GREEN BAY, WI	IRON MOUNTAIN, MI	IRONWOOD, MI	L'ANSE, MI	MANISTIQUE, MI	MARINETTE, WI	MARQUETTE, MI	RHINELANDER, WI	STEVENS POINT, WI	TRAVERSE CITY, MI	WAUSAU, WI
ESCANABA, MI		111	52	178	134	54	57	65	132	185	252	171
GREEN BAY, WI	111		96	202	178	165	54	175	124	87	363	93
MARQUETTE, MI	65	175	79	145	70	86	122		147	238	269	204
WAUSAU, WI	171	93	133	121	176	225	112	204	58	35	423	

SEE ALSO DISTANCE AND DRIVING TIME MAP ON PAGES 10–11

0 mi   10   20   30
0 km 10 20 30 40
One inch equals 17.4 miles
One centimeter equals 11 kilometers

DRIVING DISTANCES IN MILES	ALPENA, MI	CHEBOYGAN, MI	GAYLORD, MI	GRAYLING, MI	MACKINAW CITY, MI	MANISTIQUE, MI	MUNISING, MI	PETOSKEY, MI	ROGERS CITY, MI	SAULT STE. MARIE, MI	SUDBURY, ON	TRAVERSE CITY, MI
ALPENA, MI		78	76	95	94	187	215	101	38	148	334	141
MACKINAW CITY, MI	94	16	60	87		95	123	38	58	57	242	106
SAULT STE. MARIE, MI	148	71	114	142	57	120	120	93	112		186	160
TRAVERSE CITY, MI	141	115	65	52	106	198	226	67	135	160	346	

SEE ALSO DISTANCE AND DRIVING TIME MAP ON PAGES 10–11

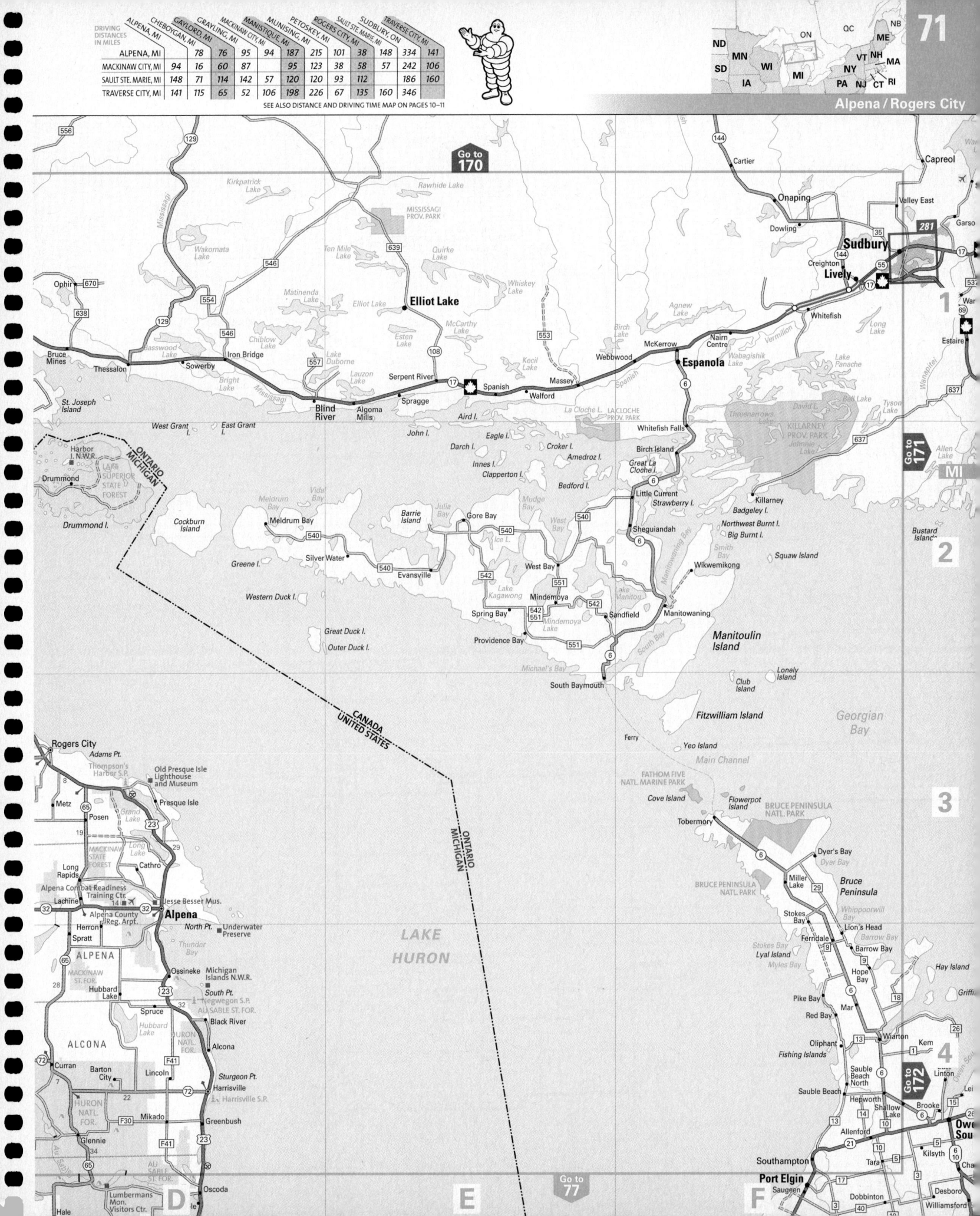

One inch equals 17.4 miles
One centimeter equals 11 kilometers

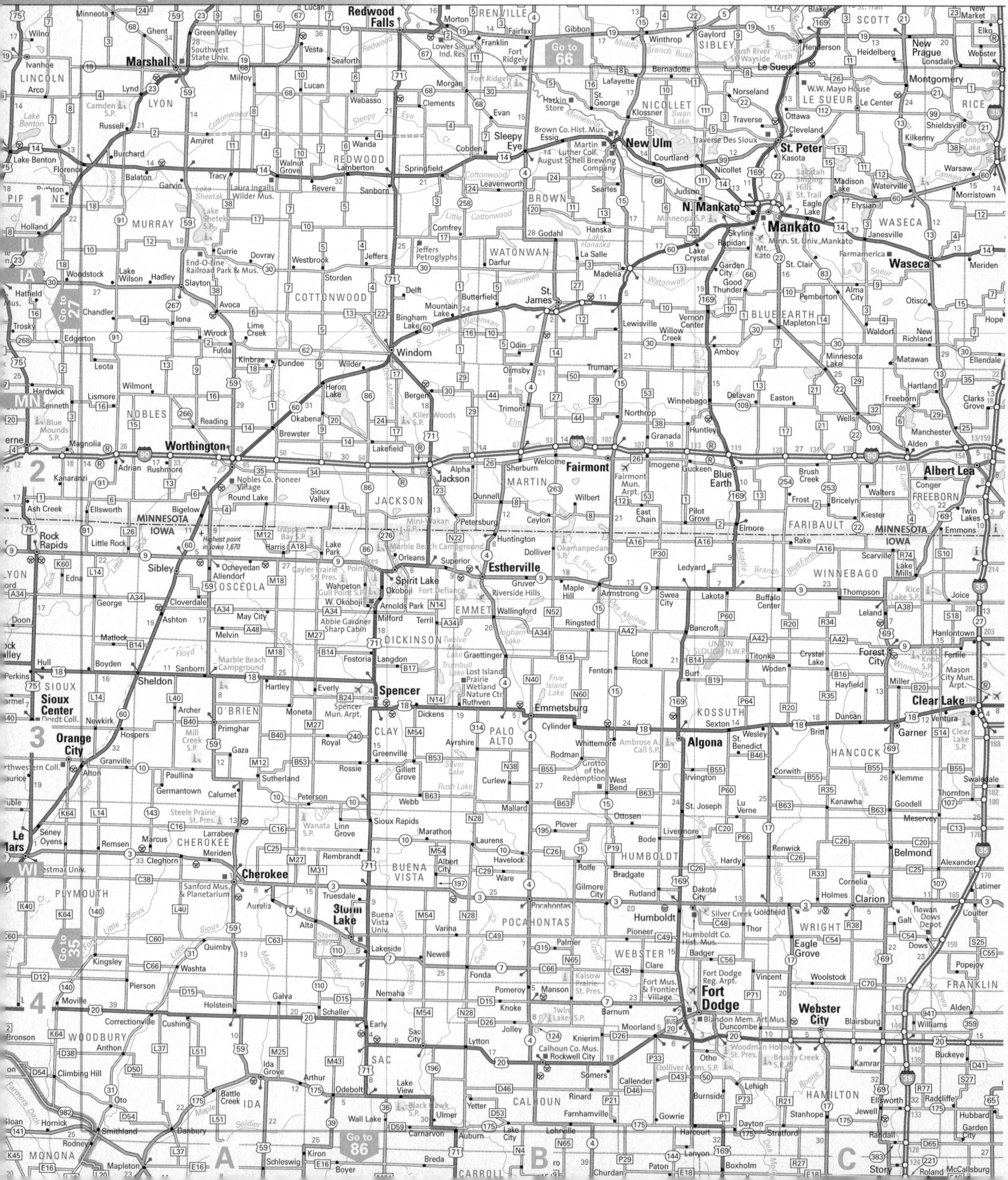

0 mi 10 20 30
0 km 10 20 30 40

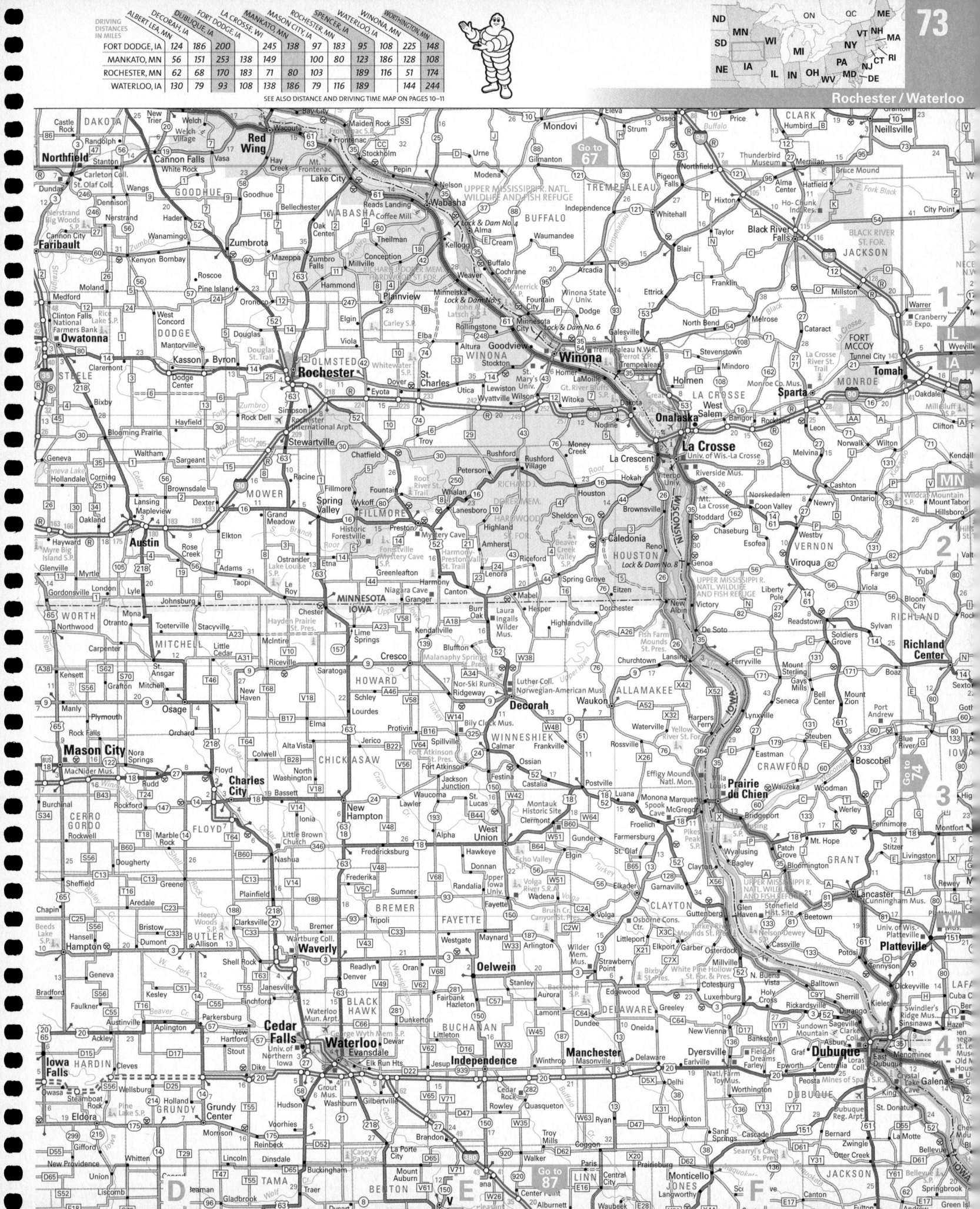

DRIVING DISTANCES IN MILES

	DECORAH, IA	DUBUQUE, IA	FORT DODGE, IA	LA CROSSE, WI	MANKATO, MN	MASON CITY, IA	ROCHESTER, MN	SPENCER, IA	WATERLOO, IA	WINONA, MN	WORTHINGTON, MN
ALBERT LEA, MN											
FORT DODGE, IA	124	186	200	245	138	97	183	95	108	225	148
MANKATO, MN	56	151	253	138	149		100	80	123	186	128	108
ROCHESTER, MN	62	68	170	183	71	80	103		189	116	51	174
WATERLOO, IA	130	79	93	108	138	186	79	116	189		144	244

SEE ALSO DISTANCE AND DRIVING TIME MAP ON PAGES 10–11

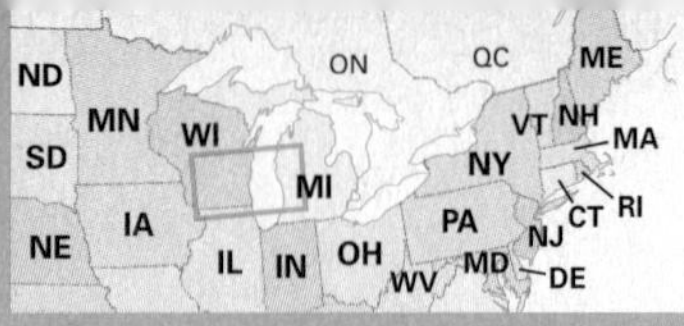

One inch equals 17.4 miles
One centimeter equals 11 kilometers

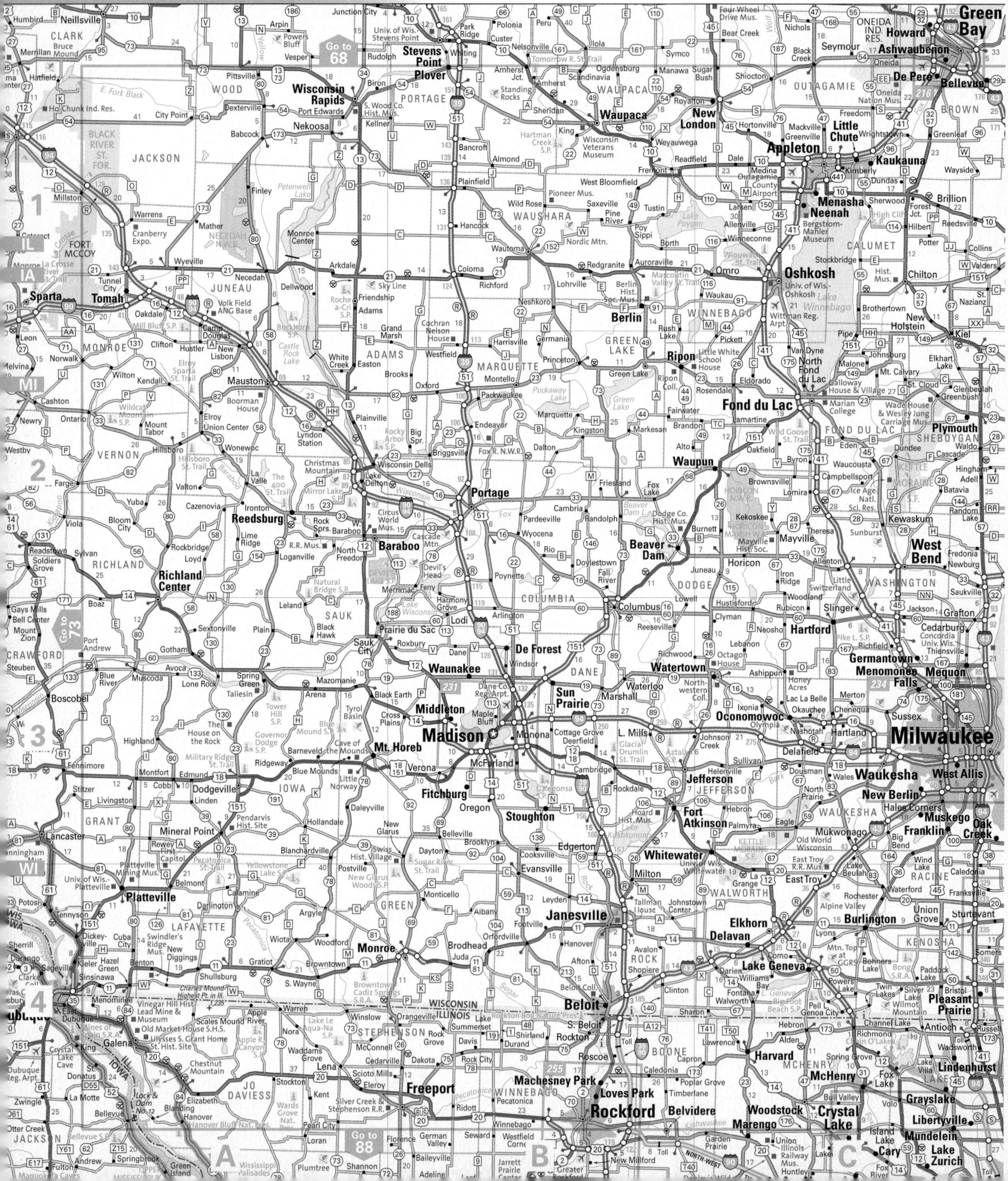

0 mi 10 20 30
0 km 10 20 30 40

Go to 68

Go to 73

Go to 88

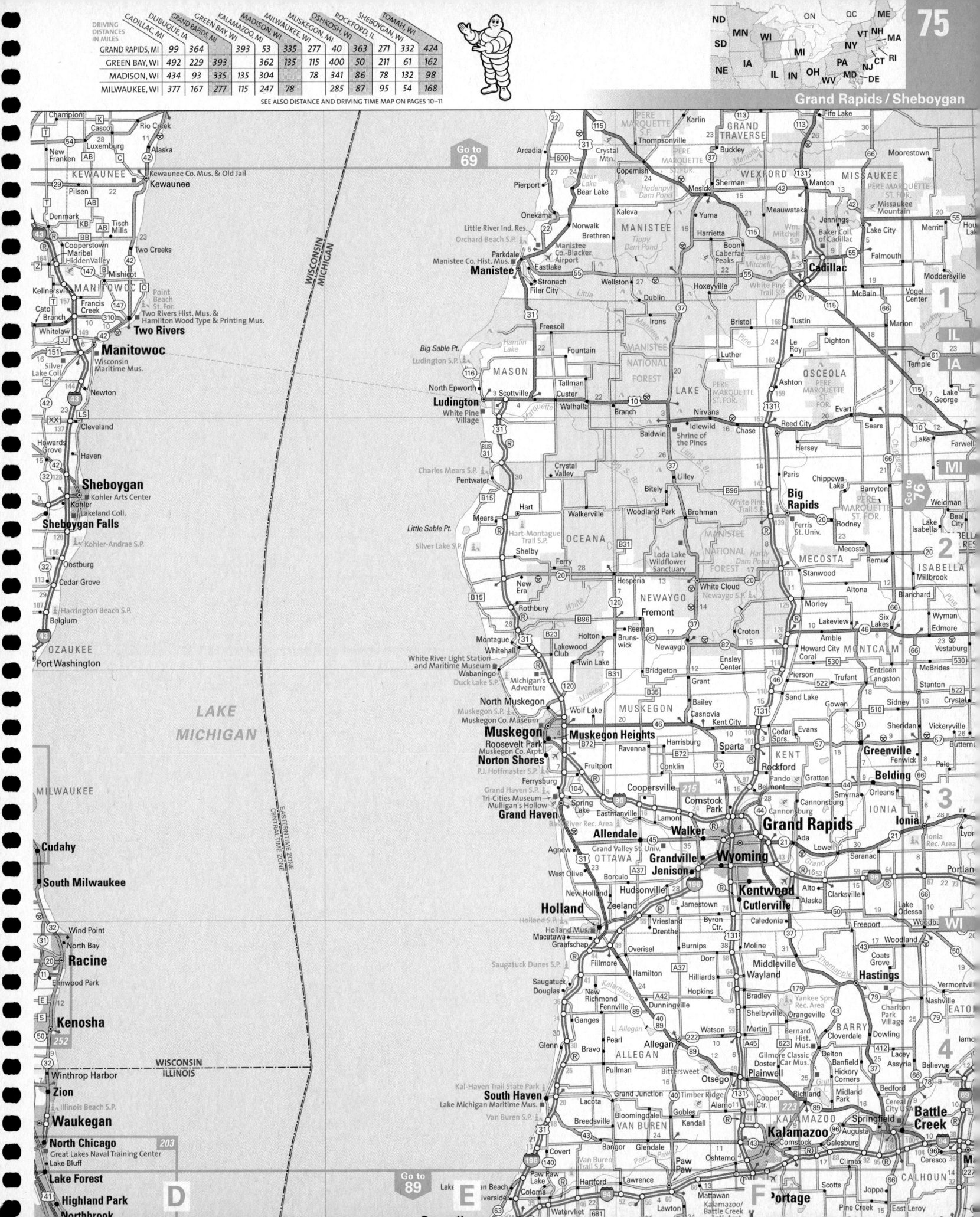

SEE ALSO DISTANCE AND DRIVING TIME MAP ON PAGES 10–11

Go to 69

Go to 76

Go to 89

LAKE MICHIGAN

EASTERN TIME ZONE / CENTRAL TIME ZONE

WISCONSIN / MICHIGAN

WISCONSIN / ILLINOIS

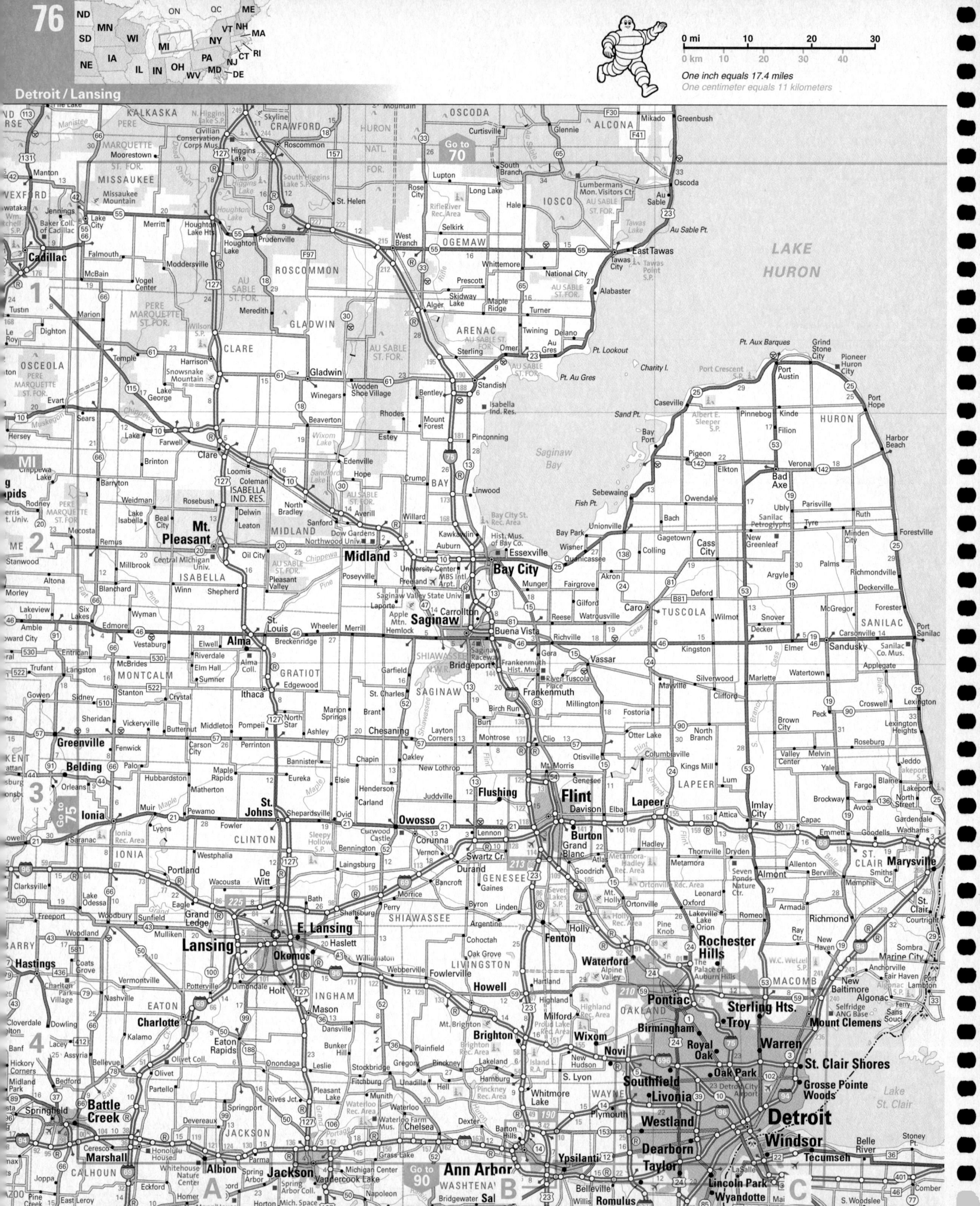

One inch equals 17.4 miles
One centimeter equals 11 kilometers

0 mi   10   20   30
0 km 10 20 30 40

LAKE HURON

Lake St. Clair

DRIVING DISTANCES IN MILES

	ANN ARBOR, MI	BAD AXE, MI	BATTLE CREEK, MI	CADILLAC, MI	DETROIT, MI	FLINT, MI	HAMILTON, ON	LANSING, MI	LONDON, ON	MT. PLEASANT, MI	PORT HURON, MI	SAGINAW, MI
DETROIT, MI	42	107	116	209		62	203	86	128	149	58	97
LANSING, MI	63	140	56	131	86	53	270		191	67	117	86
PORT HURON, MI	101	81	175	211	58	64	154	117	75	155		100
SAGINAW, MI	87	64	142	116	97	36	253	86	174	60	100	

SEE ALSO DISTANCE AND DRIVING TIME MAP ON PAGES 10–11

One inch equals 17.4 miles
One centimeter equals 11 kilometers

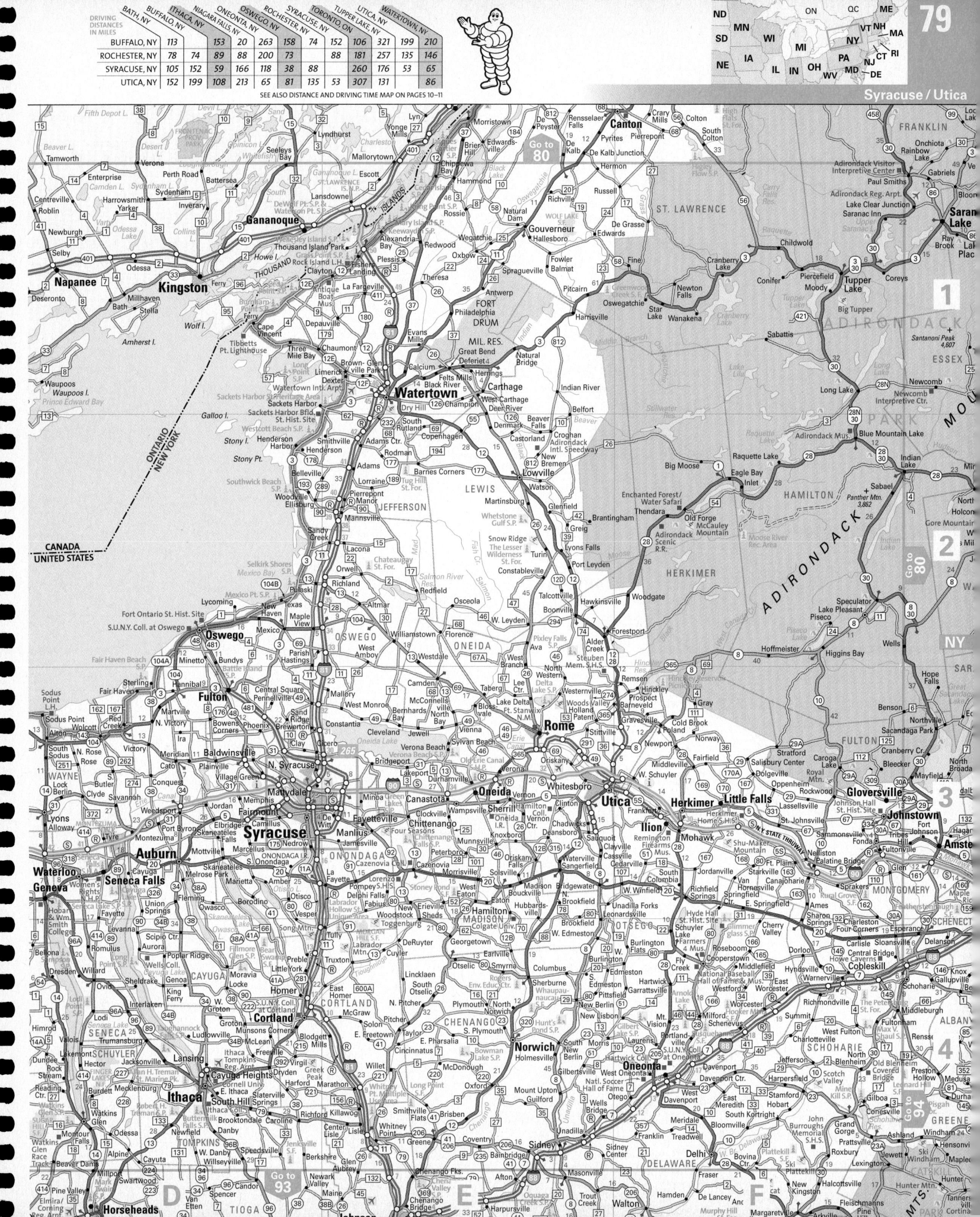

DRIVING DISTANCES IN MILES

	BATH, NY	BUFFALO, NY	ITHACA, NY	NIAGARA FALLS, NY	ONEONTA, NY	OSWEGO, NY	ROCHESTER, NY	SYRACUSE, NY	TORONTO, ON	TUPPER LAKE, NY	UTICA, NY	WATERTOWN, NY
BUFFALO, NY	113		153	20	263	158	74	152	106	321	199	210
ROCHESTER, NY	78	74	89	88	200	73		88	181	257	135	146
SYRACUSE, NY	105	152	59	166	118	38	88		260	176	53	65
UTICA, NY	152	199	108	213	65	81	135	53	307	131		86

SEE ALSO DISTANCE AND DRIVING TIME MAP ON PAGES 10–11

One inch equals 17.4 miles
One centimeter equals 11 kilometers

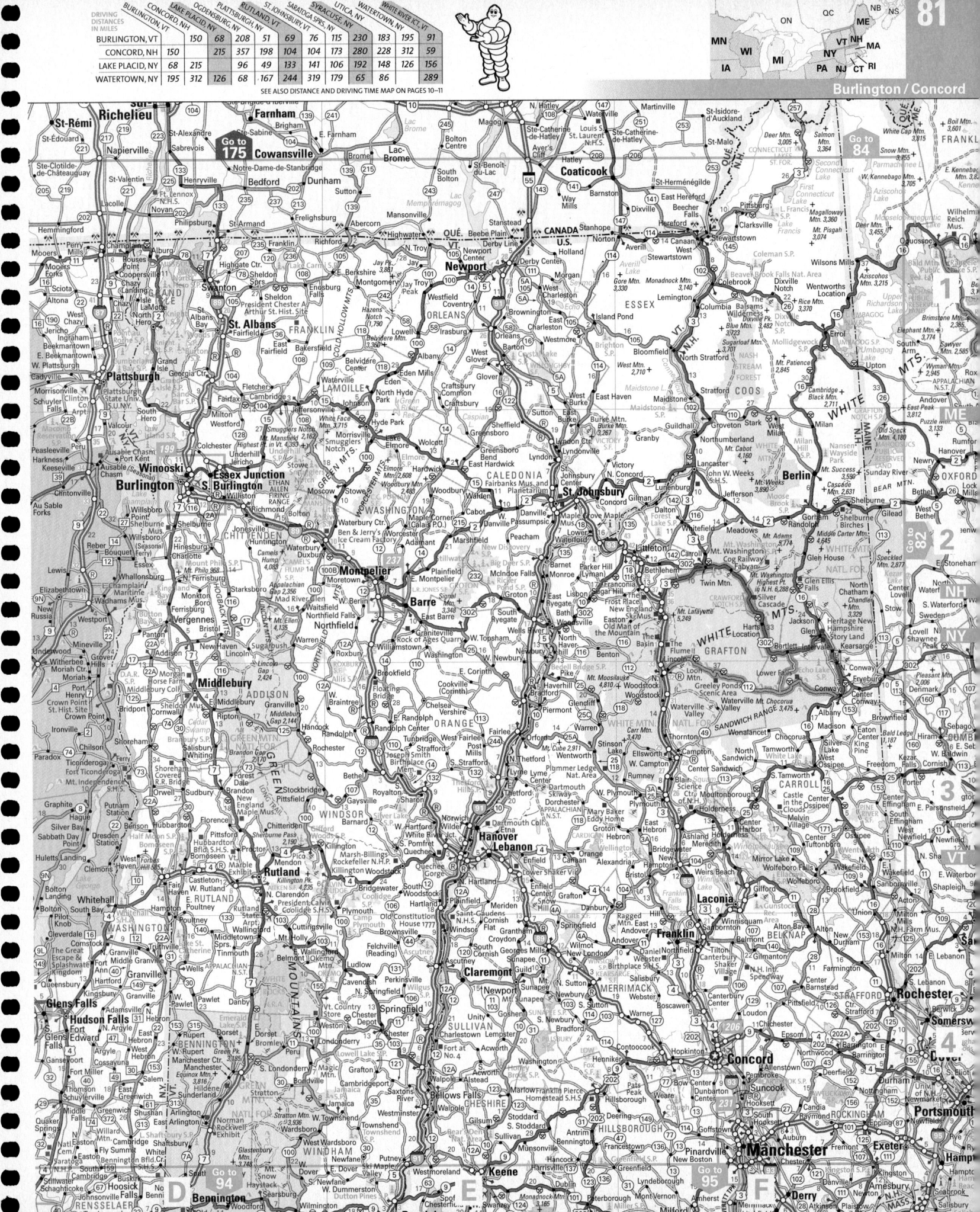

SEE ALSO DISTANCE AND DRIVING TIME MAP ON PAGES 10–11

DRIVING DISTANCES IN MILES	BURLINGTON, VT	CONCORD, NH	LAKE PLACID, NY	OGDENSBURG, NY	PLATTSBURGH, NY	RUTLAND, VT	ST. JOHNSBURY, VT	SARATOGA SPGS., NY	SYRACUSE, NY	UTICA, NY	WATERTOWN, NY	WHITE RIVER JCT., VT
BURLINGTON, VT		150	68	208	51	69	76	115	230	183	195	91
CONCORD, NH	150		215	357	198	104	104	173	280	228	312	59
LAKE PLACID, NY	68	215		96	49	133	147	106	192	148	126	156
WATERTOWN, NY	195	312	126	68	167	244	319	179	65	86		289

One inch equals 17.4 miles
One centimeter equals 11 kilometers

Go to 84

Go to 81

Go to 95

Gulf of
Maine

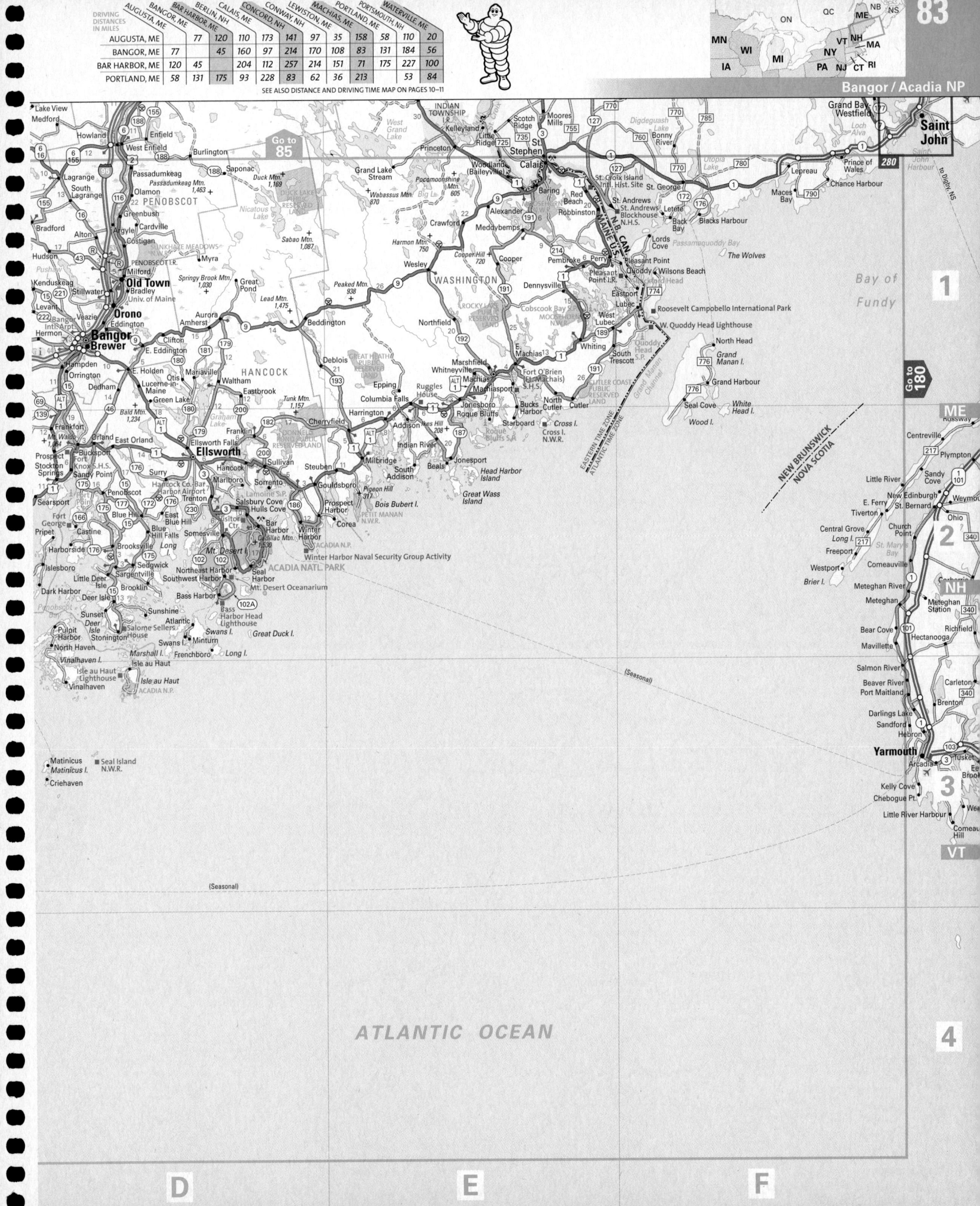

Go to 85

Go to 180

DRIVING DISTANCES IN MILES

	AUGUSTA, ME	BANGOR, ME	BAR HARBOR, ME	BERLIN, NH	CALAIS, ME	CONCORD, NH	CONWAY, NH	LEWISTON, ME	MACHIAS, ME	PORTLAND, ME	PORTSMOUTH NH	WATERVILLE NH
AUGUSTA, ME		77	120	110	173	141	97	35	158	58	110	20
BANGOR, ME	77		45	160	97	214	170	108	83	131	184	56
BAR HARBOR, ME	120	45		204	112	257	214	151	71	175	227	100
PORTLAND, ME	58	131	175	93	228	83	62	36	213		53	84

SEE ALSO DISTANCE AND DRIVING TIME MAP ON PAGES 10–11

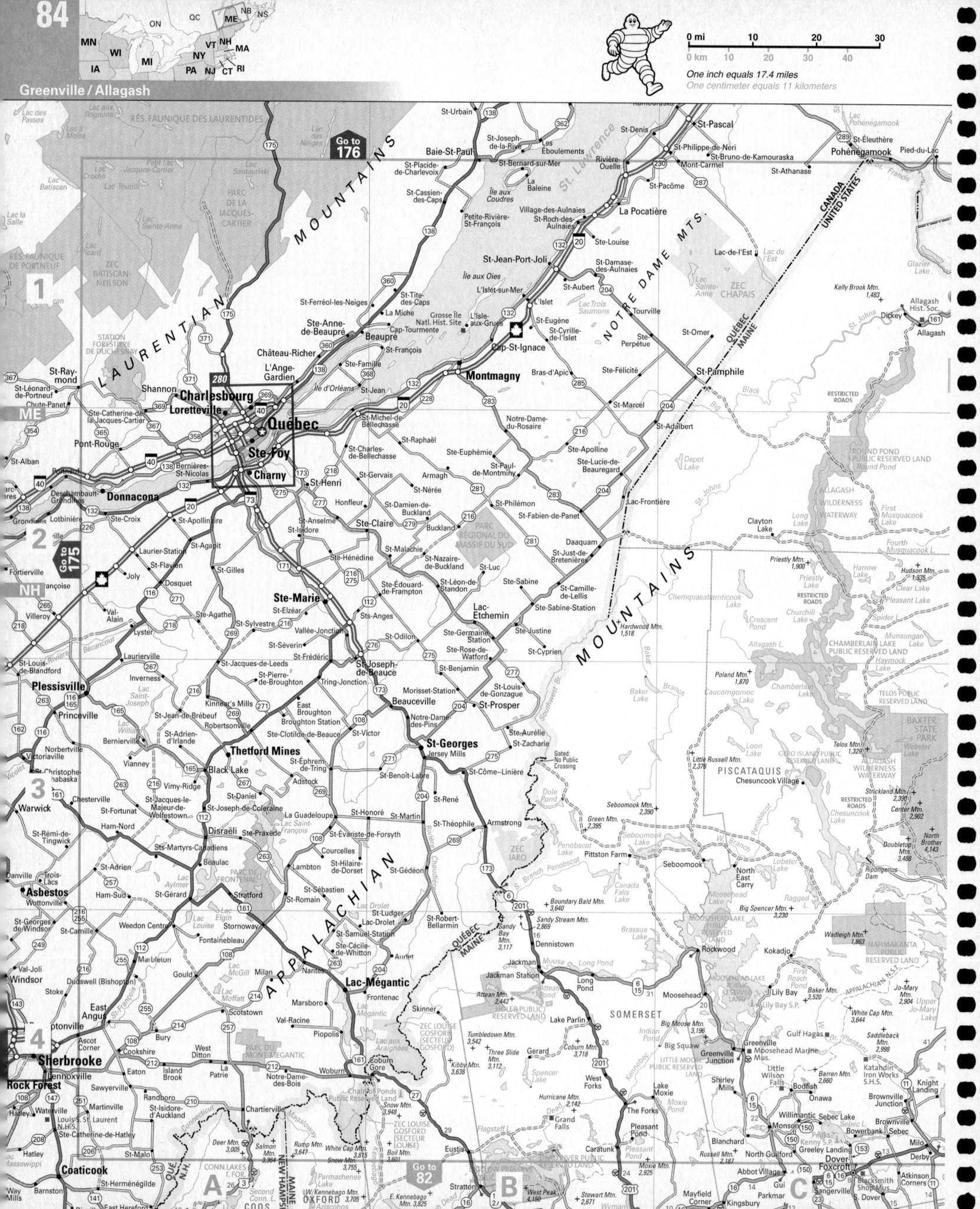

One inch equals 17.4 miles
One centimeter equals 11 kilometers

0 mi   10   20   30
0 km   10   20   30   40

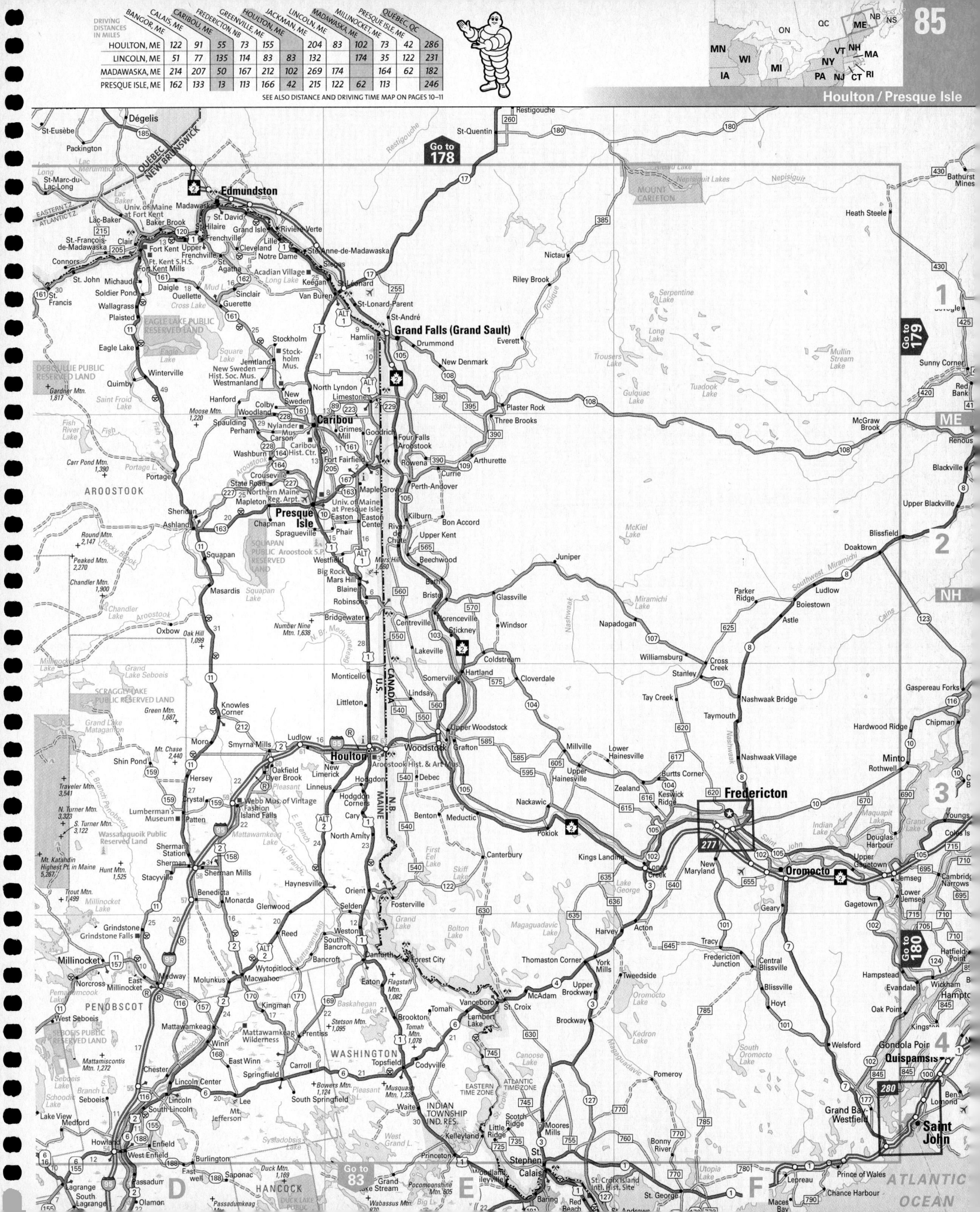

Go to 178
Go to 179
Go to 180
Go to 83

DRIVING
DISTANCES
IN MILES

	BANGOR, ME	CALAIS, ME	CARIBOU, ME	FREDERICTON, NB	GREENVILLE, ME	HOULTON, ME	JACKMAN, ME	LINCOLN, ME	MADAWASKA, ME	MILLINOCKET, ME	PRESQUE ISLE, ME	QUEBEC, QC
HOULTON, ME	122	91	55	73	155		204	83	102	73	42	286
LINCOLN, ME	51	77	135	114	83	83	132		174	35	122	231
MADAWASKA, ME	214	207	50	167	212	102	269	174		164	62	182
PRESQUE ISLE, ME	162	133	13	113	166	42	215	122	62	113		246

SEE ALSO DISTANCE AND DRIVING TIME MAP ON PAGES 10–11

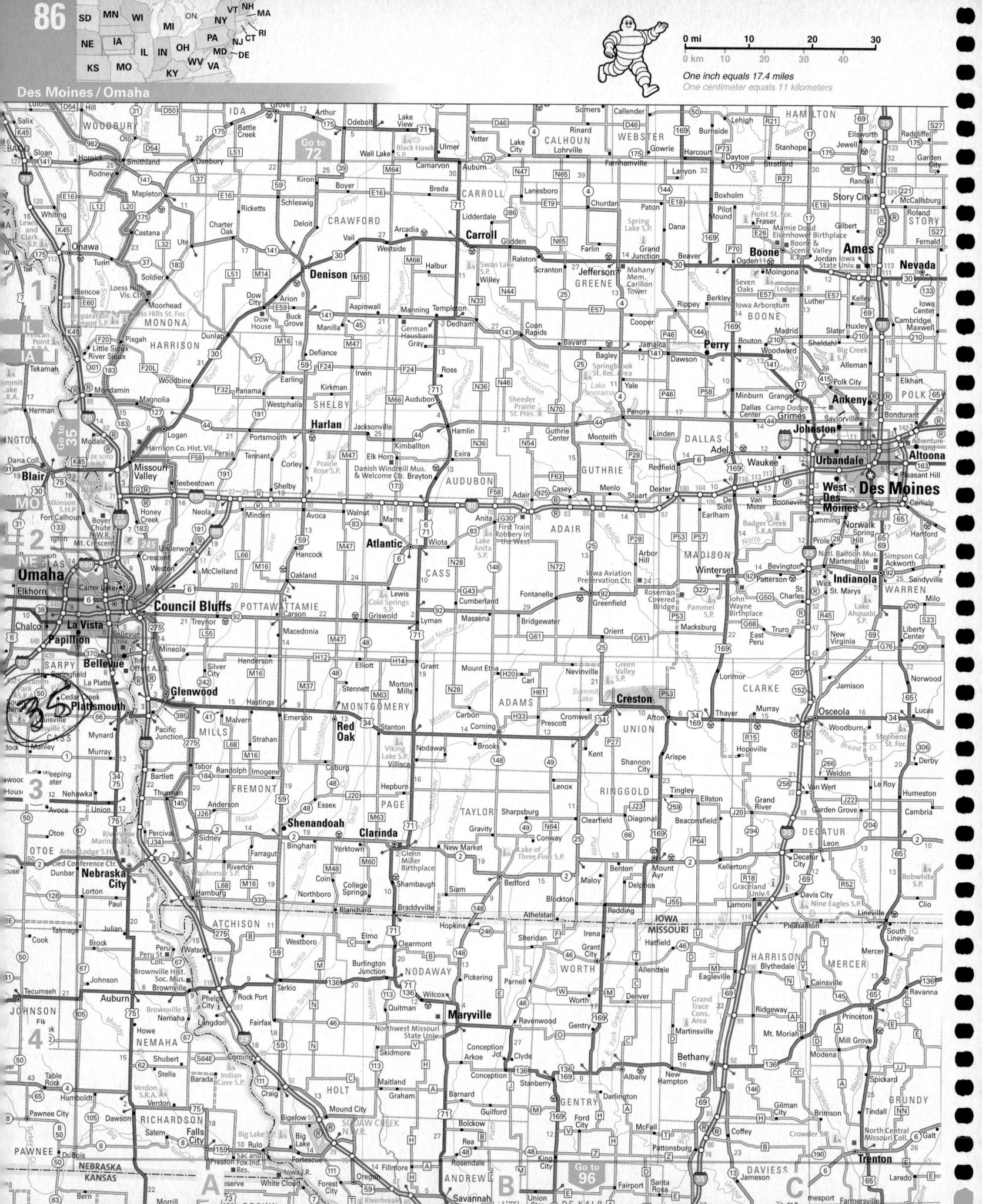

One inch equals 17.4 miles
One centimeter equals 11 kilometers

SEE ALSO DISTANCE AND DRIVING TIME MAP ON PAGES 10–11

DRIVING DISTANCES IN MILES	AMES, IA	BURLINGTON, IA	CARROLL, IA	CEDAR RAPIDS, IA	CRESTON, IA	DAVENPORT, IA	DES MOINES, IA	IOWA CITY, IA	KIRKSVILLE, MO	MARYVILLE, MO	OMAHA, NE	OTTUMWA, IA
CEDAR RAPIDS, IA	108	106	173		211	87	129	28	170	276	266	111
DES MOINES, IA	34	157	90	129	81	171		113	145	146	136	86
IOWA CITY, IA	136	82	195	28	195	59	113		143	260	250	83
OMAHA, NE	171	328	97	266	98	308	136	250	275	112		221

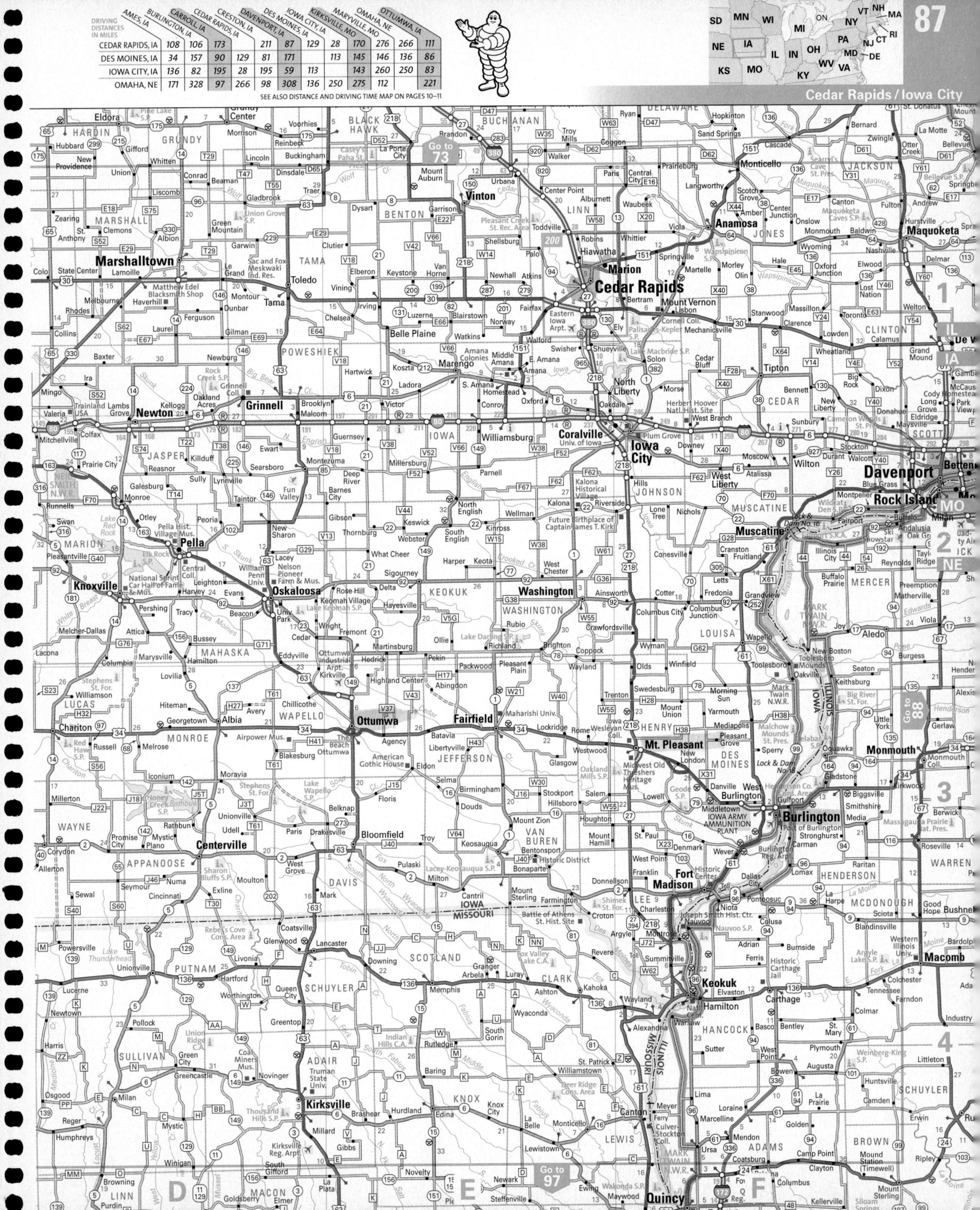

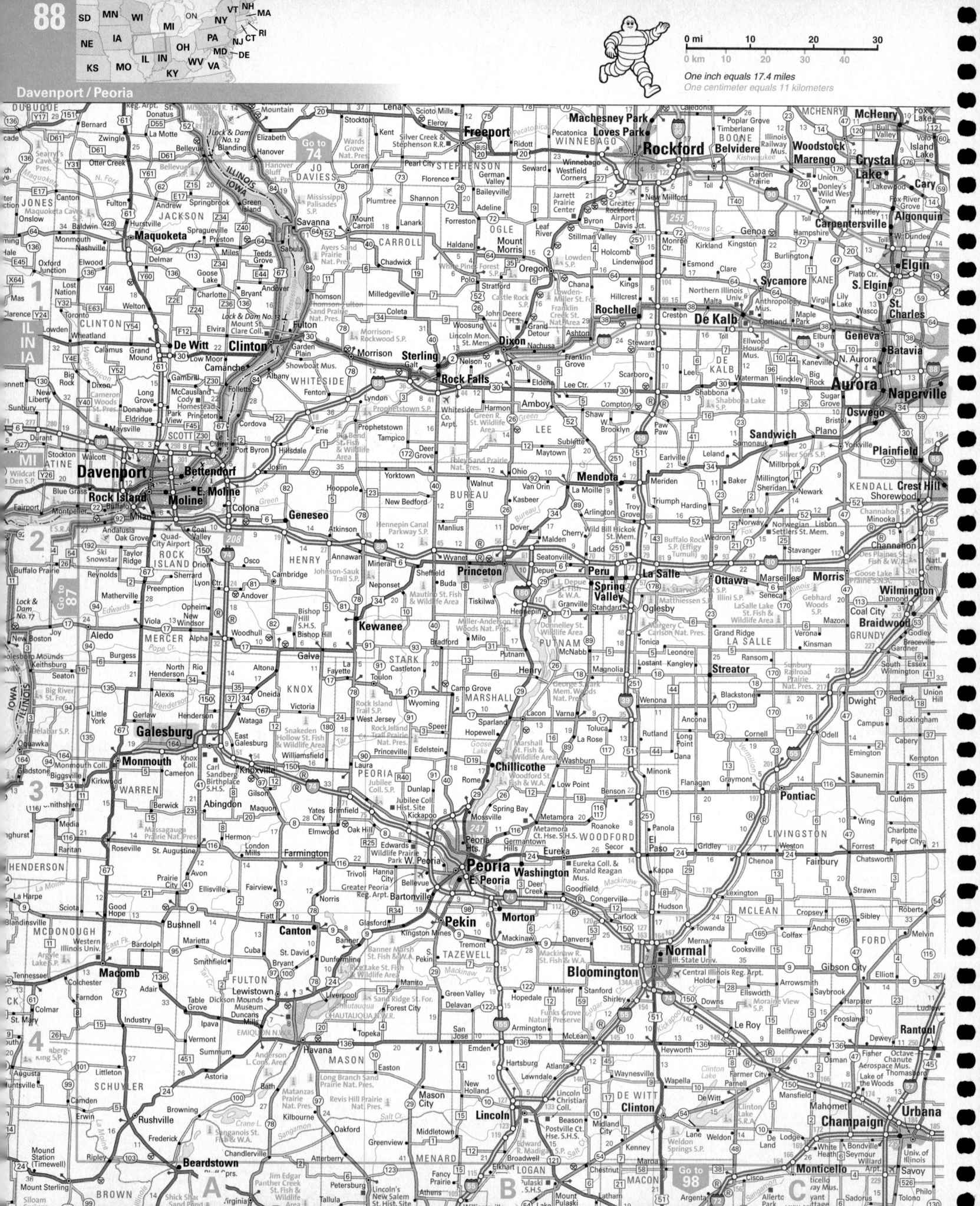

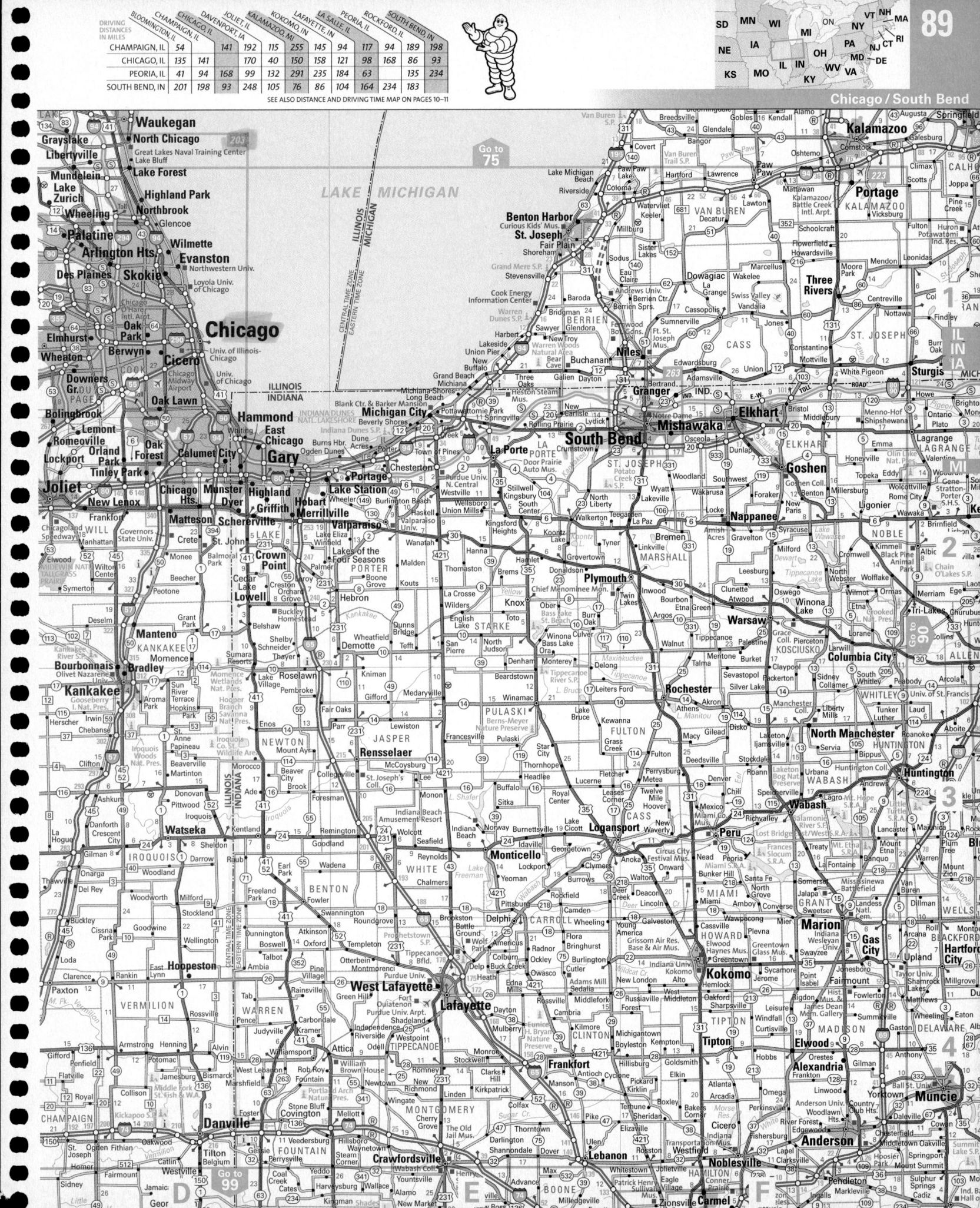

DRIVING DISTANCES IN MILES

	BLOOMINGTON, IL	CHAMPAIGN, IL	CHICAGO, IL	DAVENPORT, IA	JOLIET, IL	KALAMAZOO, MI	KOKOMO, IN	LAFAYETTE, IN	LA SALLE, IL	PEORIA, IL	ROCKFORD, IL	SOUTH BEND, IN
CHAMPAIGN, IL	54		141		192	115	255	145	94	117	94	189	198
CHICAGO, IL	135	141		170	40	150	158	121	98	168	86	93
PEORIA, IL	41	94	168		99	132	291	235	184	63		135	234
SOUTH BEND, IN	201	198	93	248	105	76	86	104	164	234	183	

SEE ALSO DISTANCE AND DRIVING TIME MAP ON PAGES 10–11

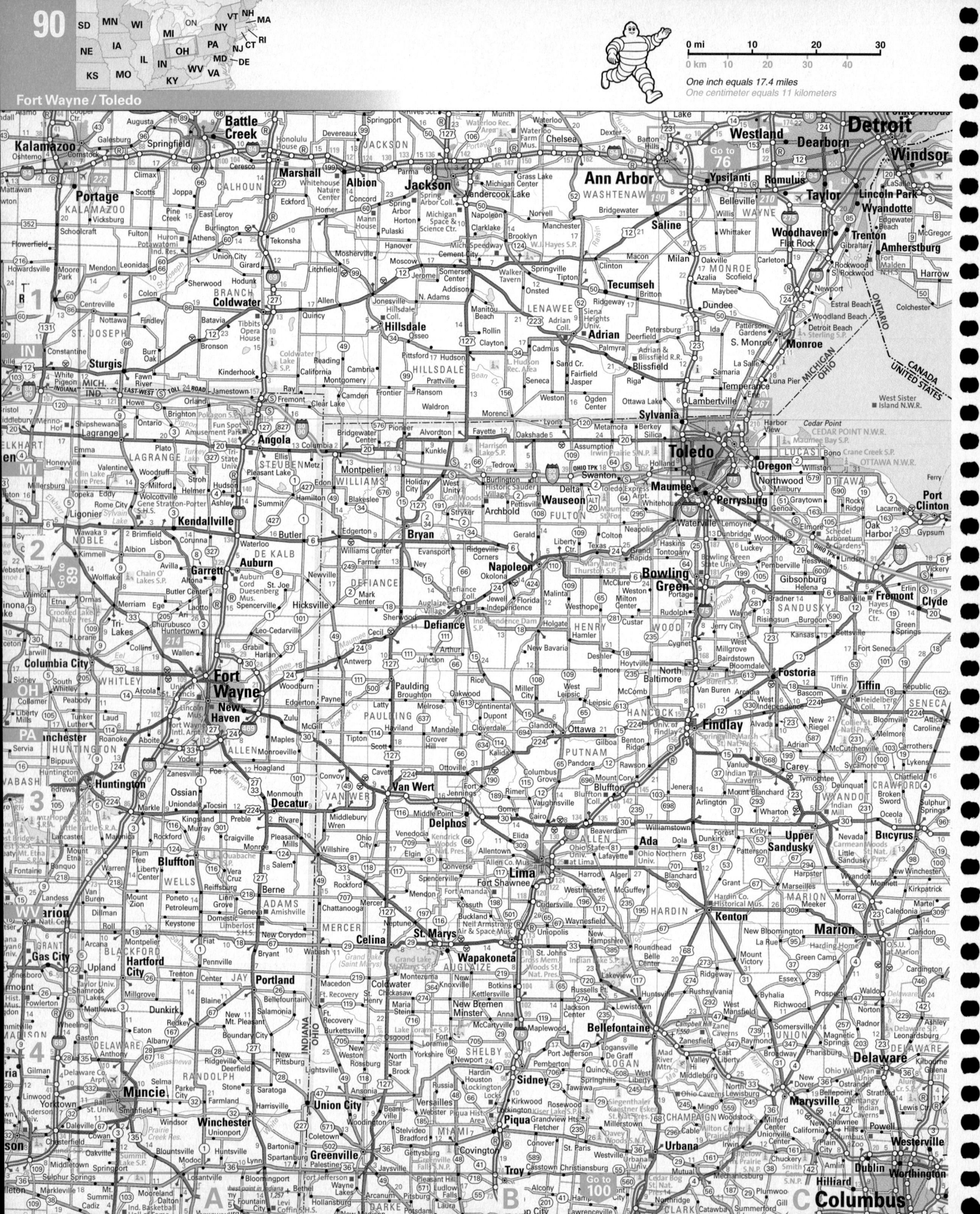

One inch equals 17.4 miles
One centimeter equals 11 kilometers

DRIVING DISTANCES IN MILES	AKRON, OH	CLEVELAND, OH	COLUMBUS, OH	DETROIT, MI	ERIE, PA	FORT WAYNE, IN	LIMA, OH	MANSFIELD, OH	MUNCIE, IN	TOLEDO, OH	WHEELING, WV	YOUNGSTOWN, OH
CLEVELAND, OH	38		144	171	106	214	163	81	287	119	16	275
FORT WAYNE, IN	237	214	186	170	322		66	151	75	109	290	274
MANSFIELD, OH	66	81	67	156	179	151	93		209	105	141	112
TOLEDO, OH	142	119	148	60	227	109	83	105	180		261	179

SEE ALSO DISTANCE AND DRIVING TIME MAP ON PAGES 10–11

One inch equals 17.4 miles
One centimeter equals 11 kilometers

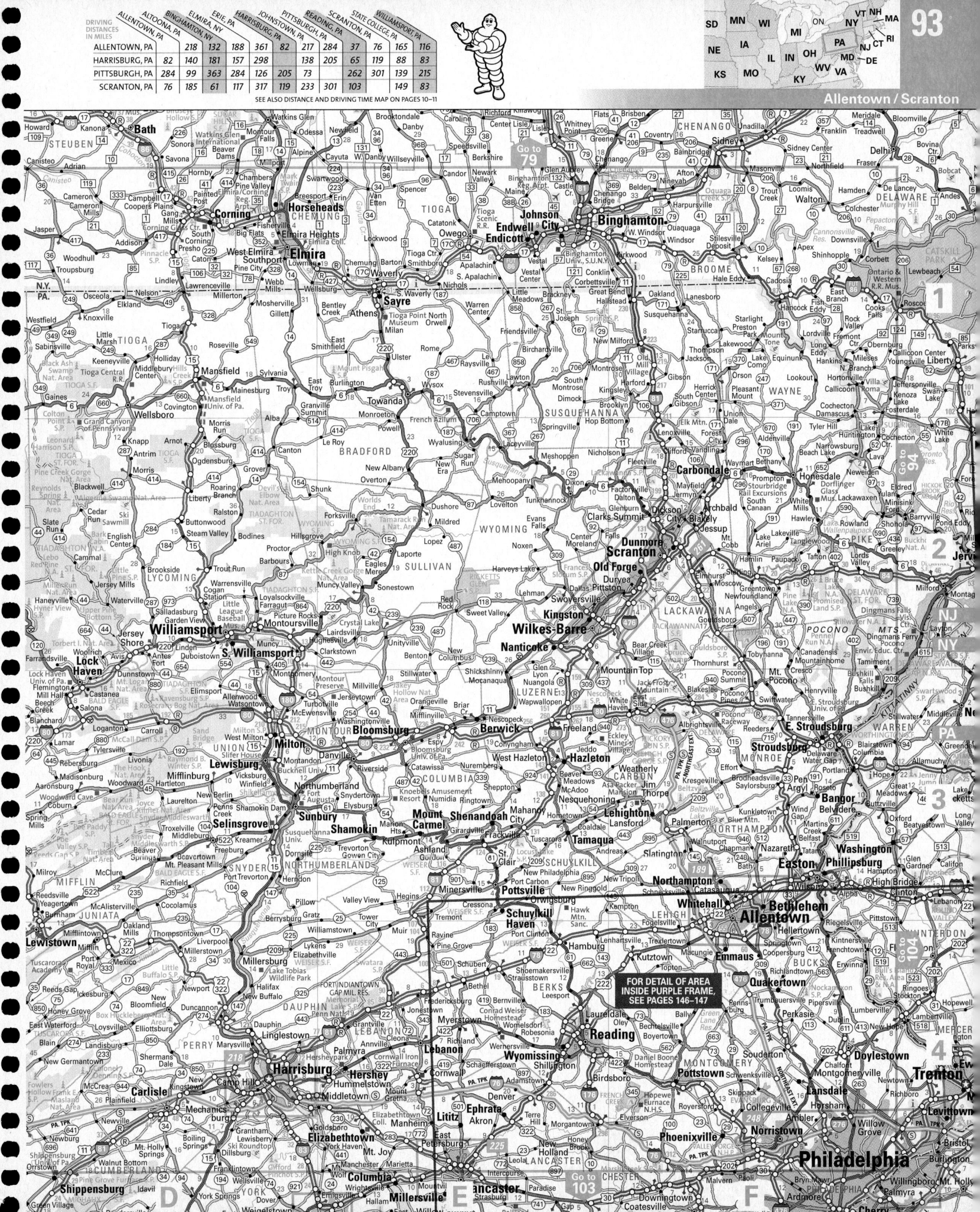

DRIVING DISTANCES IN MILES	ALLENTOWN, PA	ALTOONA, PA	BINGHAMTON, NY	ELMIRA, NY	ERIE, PA	HARRISBURG, PA	JOHNSTOWN, PA	PITTSBURGH, PA	READING, PA	SCRANTON, PA	STATE COLLEGE, PA	WILLIAMSPORT, PA	
ALLENTOWN, PA		218	132	188	361	82	217	284	37	76	165	116
HARRISBURG, PA	82	140	181	157	298		138	205	65	119	88	83
PITTSBURGH, PA	284	99	363	284	126	205	73		262	301	139	215
SCRANTON, PA	76	185	61	117	317	119	233	301	103		149	83

SEE ALSO DISTANCE AND DRIVING TIME MAP ON PAGES 10–11

FOR DETAIL OF AREA INSIDE PURPLE FRAME, SEE PAGES 146–147

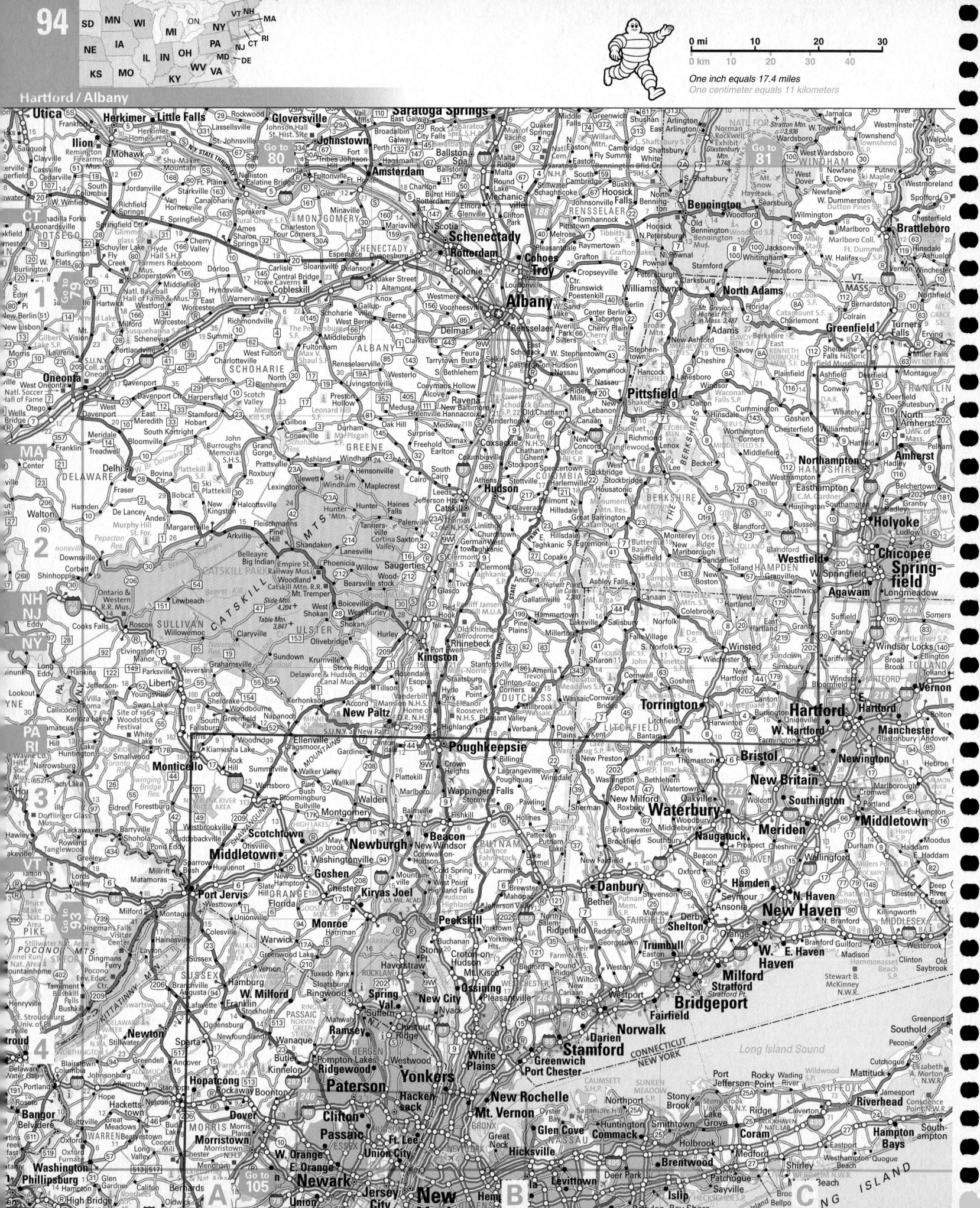

Go to 82

DRIVING DISTANCES IN MILES	ALBANY, NY	BOSTON, MA	HARTFORD, CT	MANCHESTER NH	NEWBURGH, NY	NEW HAVEN, CT	NEW YORK, NY	ONEONTA, NY	PROVIDENCE, RI	PROVINCETOWN MA	SPRINGFIELD, MA	WORCESTER, MA
ALBANY, NY		172	111	145	89	150	151	81	170	271	86	133
BOSTON, MA	172		102	54	201	139	215	251	52	117	95	46
HARTFORD, CT	111	102		131	99	39	115	190	73	200	25	62
NEW YORK, NY	151	215	115	245	56	78		193	177	292	141	176

SEE ALSO DISTANCE AND DRIVING TIME MAP ON PAGES 10–11

FOR DETAIL OF AREA INSIDE PURPLE FRAME, SEE PAGES 148–151

ATLANTIC OCEAN

ATLANTIC OCEAN

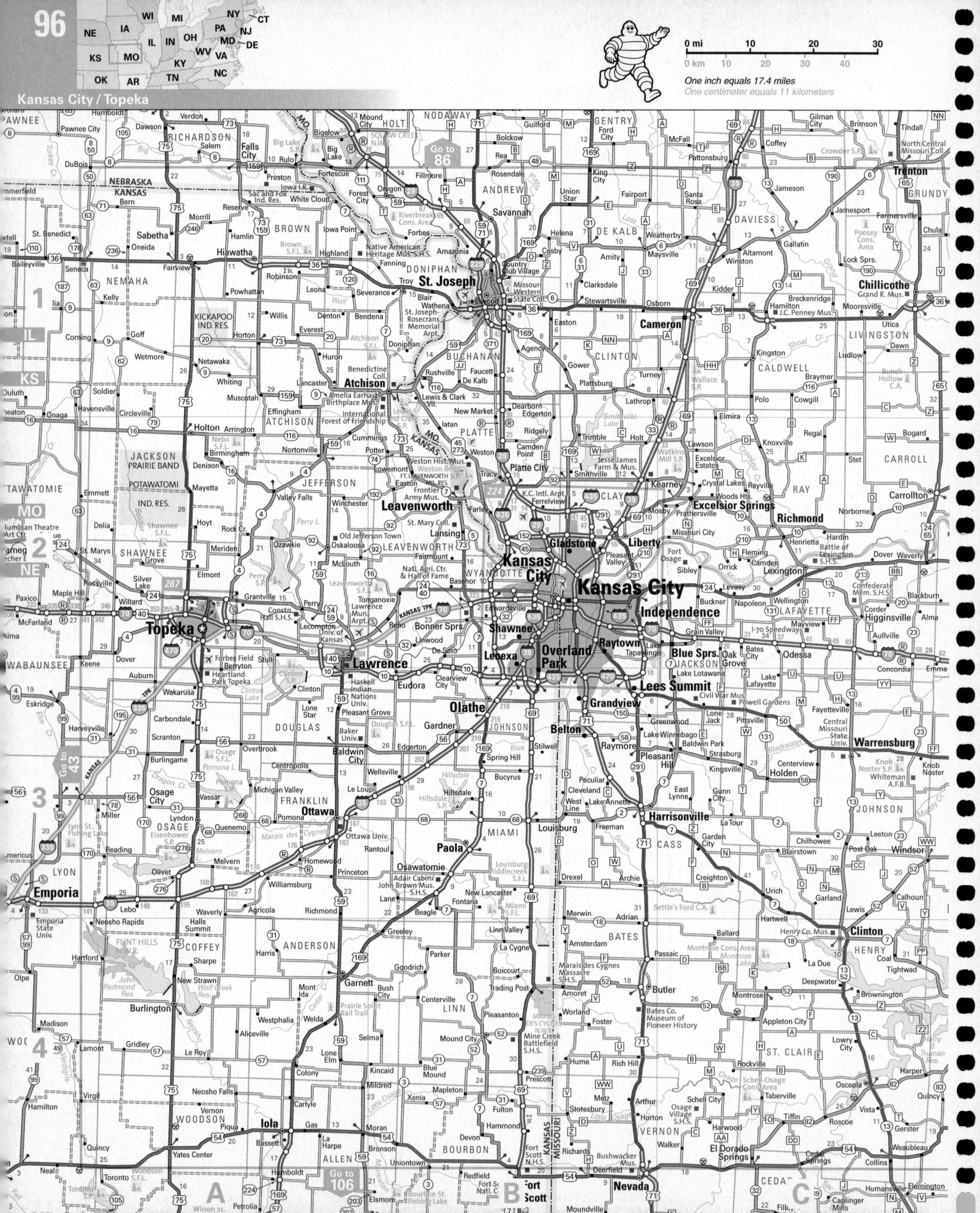

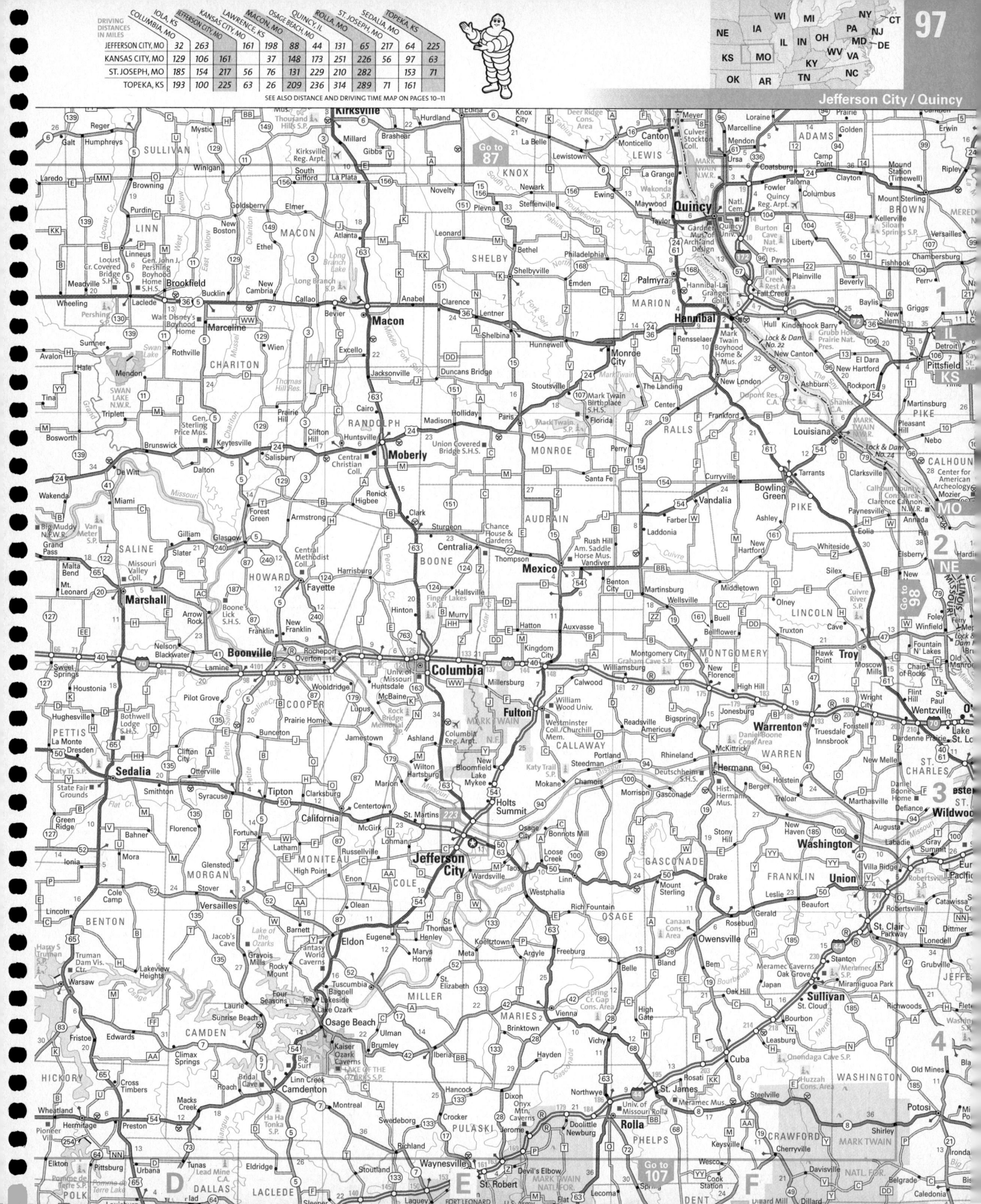

DRIVING DISTANCES IN MILES	COLUMBIA, MO	IOLA, KS	JEFFERSON CITY, MO	KANSAS CITY, KS	LAWRENCE, KS	MACON, MO	OSAGE BEACH, MO	QUINCY, IL	ROLLA, MO	ST. JOSEPH, MO	SEDALIA, KS	TOPEKA, KS
JEFFERSON CITY, MO	32	263		161	198	88	44	131	65	217	64	225
KANSAS CITY, MO	129	106	161		37	148	173	251	226	56	97	63
ST. JOSEPH, MO	185	154	217	56	76	131	229	210	282		153	71
TOPEKA, KS	193	100	225	63	26	209	236	314	289	71	161	

SEE ALSO DISTANCE AND DRIVING TIME MAP ON PAGES 10–11

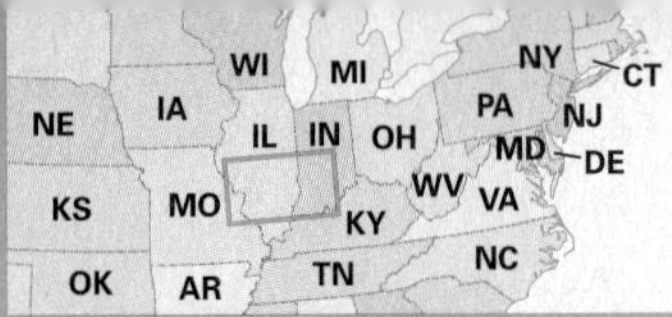

0 mi   10   20   30
0 km 10 20 30 40

One inch equals 17.4 miles
One centimeter equals 11 kilometers

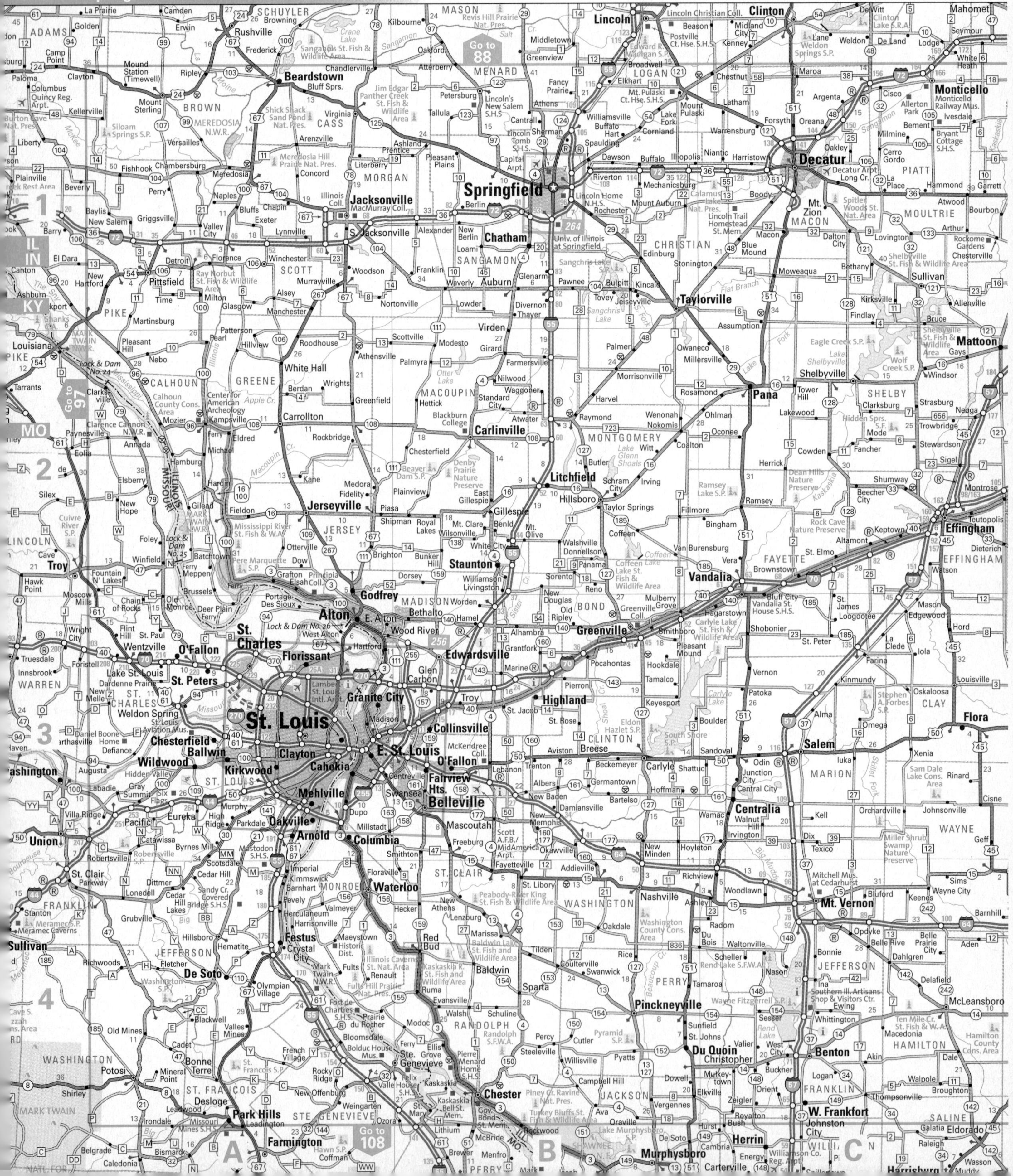

Go to 88

Go to 97

Go to 108

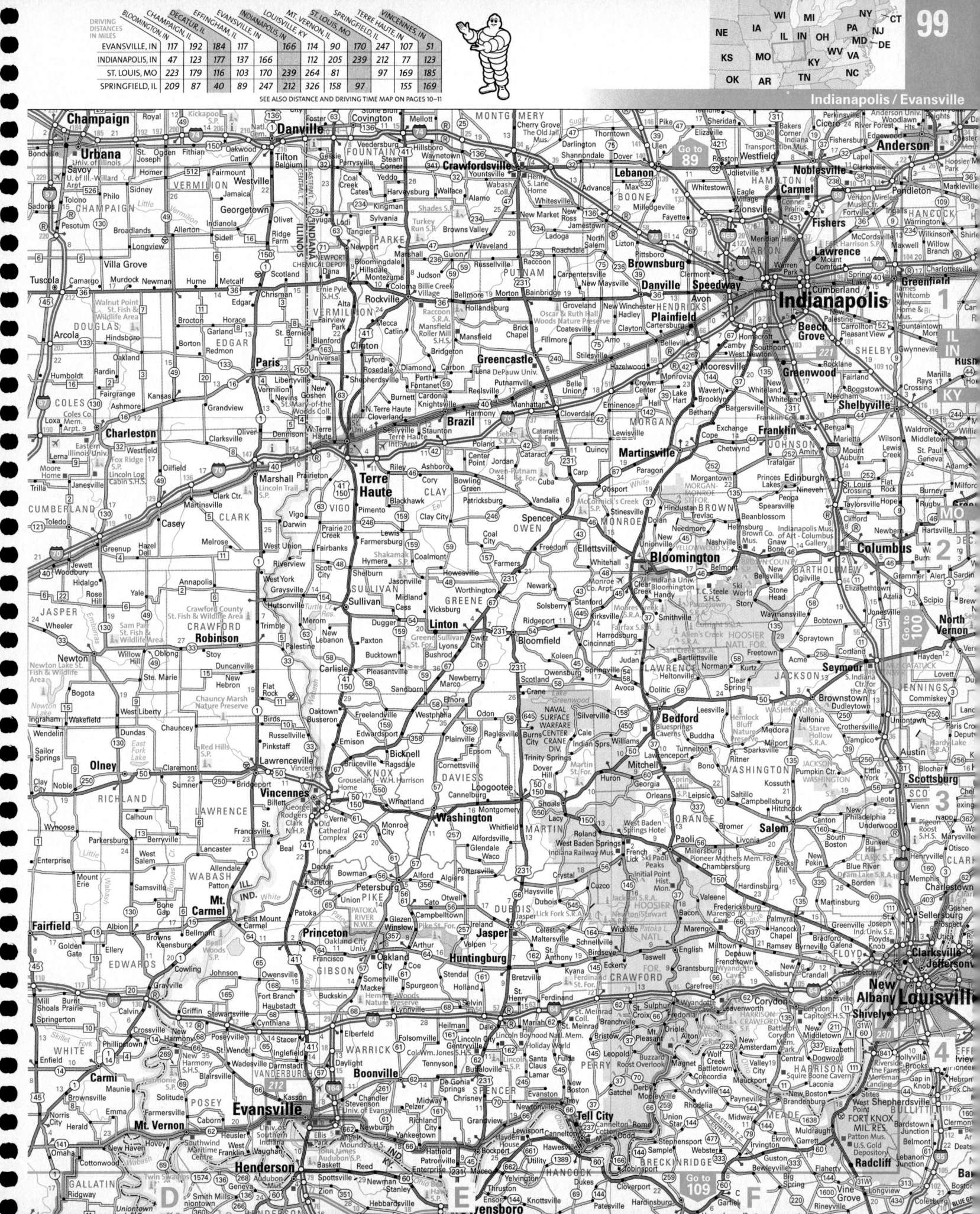

DRIVING DISTANCES IN MILES	CHAMPAIGN, IL	DECATUR, IL	EFFINGHAM, IL	EVANSVILLE, IN	INDIANAPOLIS, IN	LOUISVILLE, KY	MT. VERNON, IL	ST. LOUIS, MO	SPRINGFIELD, IL	TERRE HAUTE, IN	VINCENNES, IN
EVANSVILLE, IN	117	192	184	117		166	114	90	170	247	107	51
INDIANAPOLIS, IN	47	123	177	137	166		112	205	239	212	77	123
ST. LOUIS, MO	223	179	116	103	170	239	264	81		97	169	185
SPRINGFIELD, IL	209	87	40	89	247	212	326	158	97		155	169

SEE ALSO DISTANCE AND DRIVING TIME MAP ON PAGES 10–11

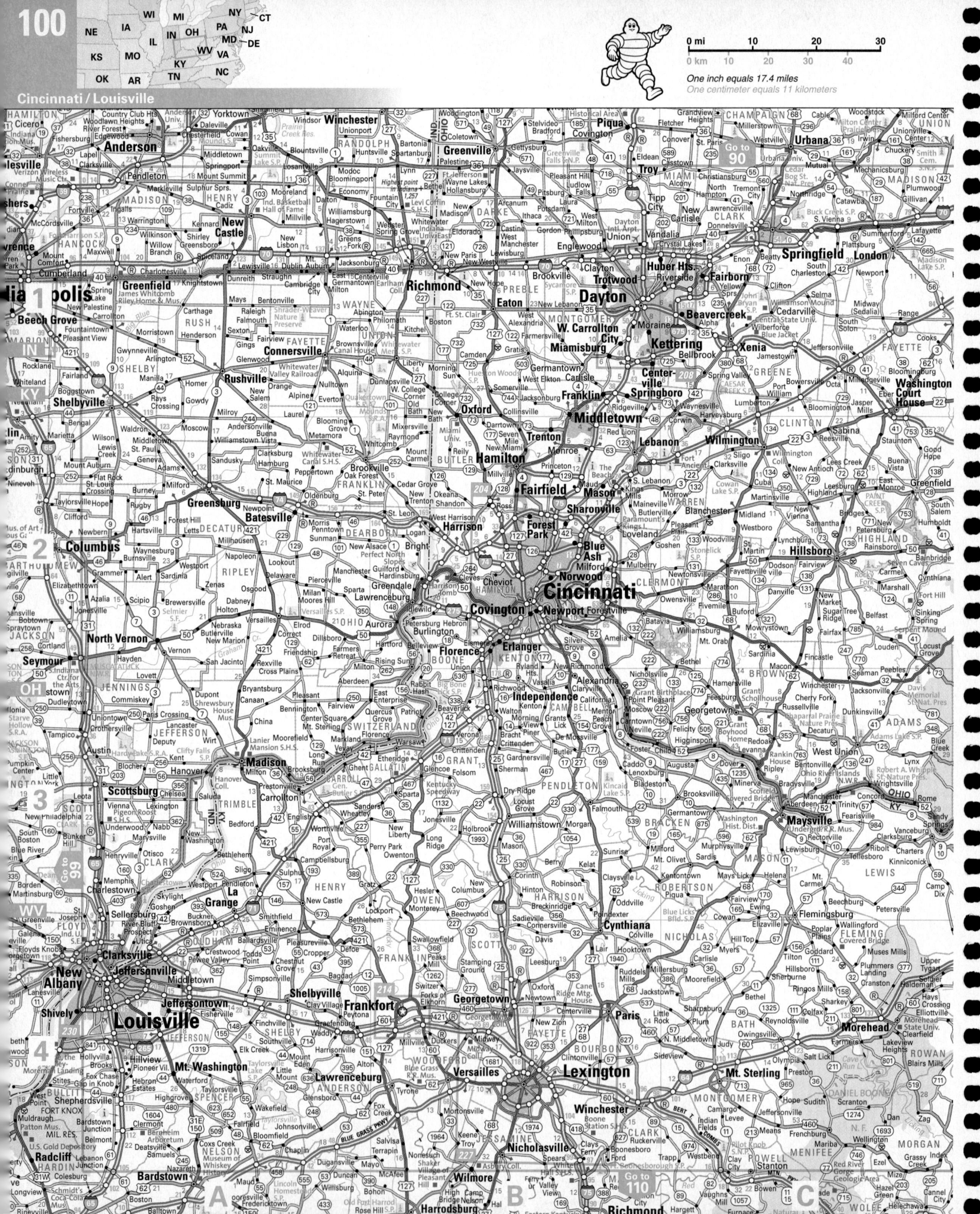

One inch equals 17.4 miles
One centimeter equals 11 kilometers

DRIVING DISTANCES IN MILES	CHARLESTON, WV	CHILLICOTHE, OH	CINCINNATI, OH	COLUMBUS, OH	DAYTON, OH	HUNTINGTON, WV	LEXINGTON, KY	LOUISVILLE, KY	MAYSVILLE, KY	PARKERSBURG, WV	WHEELING, WV	ZANESVILLE, OH
CHARLESTON, WV		121	202	168	198	52	176	251	155	73	176	155
CINCINNATI, OH	202	108		109	52	150	85	100	63	191	235	164
COLUMBUS, OH	168	47	109		70	135	193	207	114	108	130	58
LEXINGTON, KY	176	191	85	193	135	126		80	67	249	319	247

SEE ALSO DISTANCE AND DRIVING TIME MAP ON PAGES 10–11

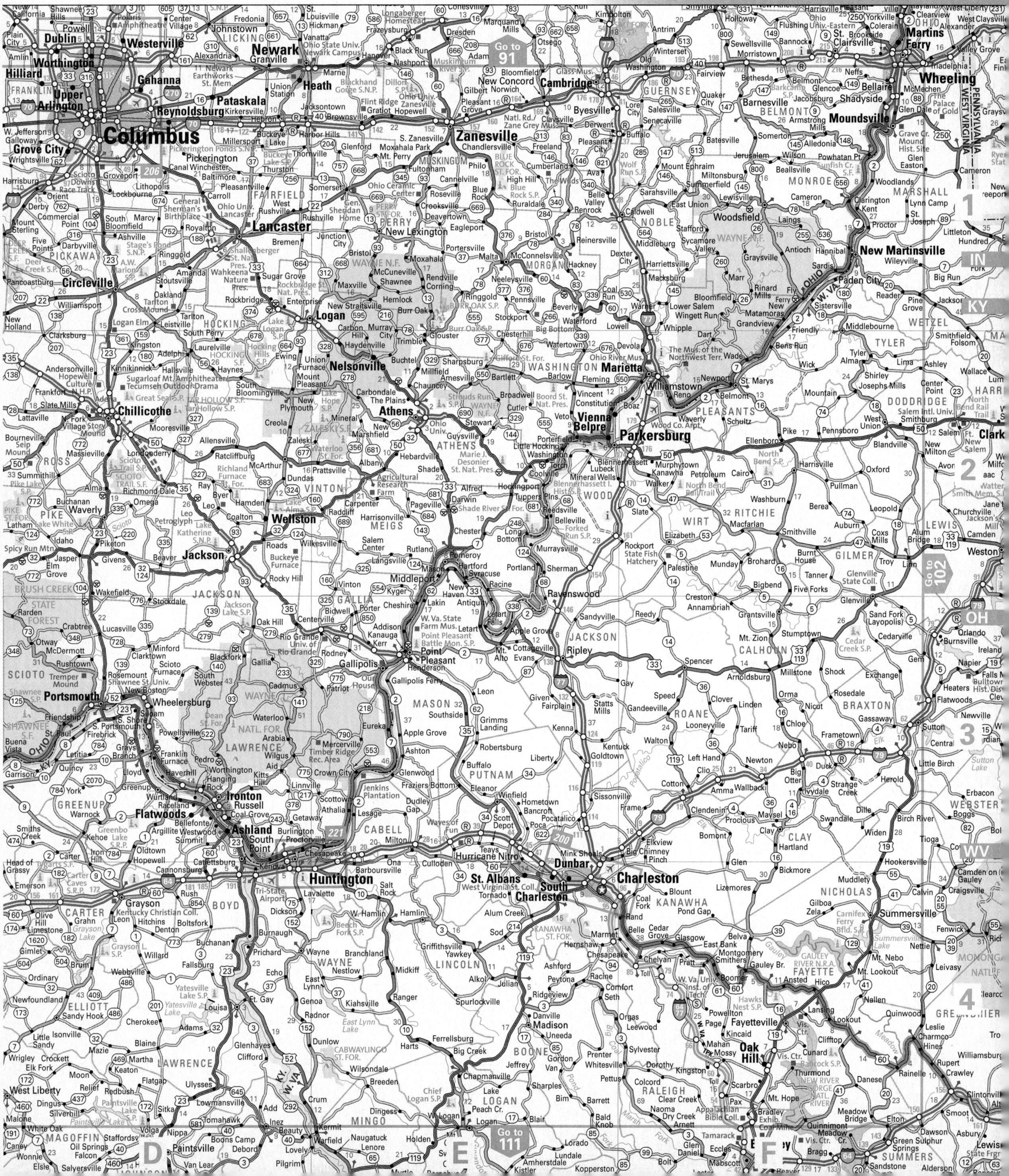

One inch equals 17.4 miles
One centimeter equals 11 kilometers

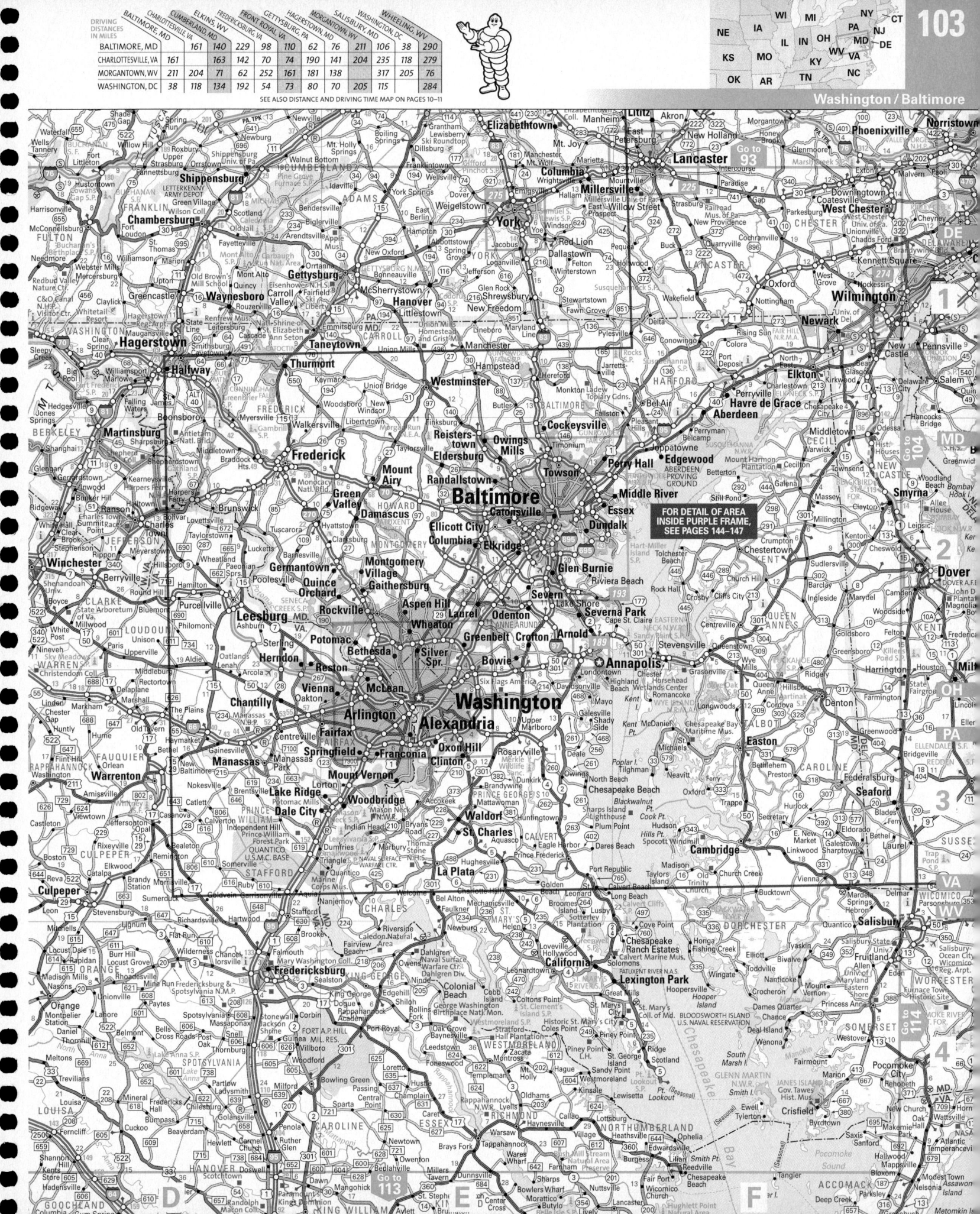

SEE ALSO DISTANCE AND DRIVING TIME MAP ON PAGES 10–11

FOR DETAIL OF AREA
INSIDE PURPLE FRAME,
SEE PAGES 144–147

Go to 93
Go to 104
Go to 114
Go to 113

DRIVING DISTANCES IN MILES	BALTIMORE, MD	CHARLOTTESVILLE, VA	CUMBERLAND, MD	ELKINS, WV	FREDERICKSBURG, VA	FRONT ROYAL, VA	GETTYSBURG, PA	HAGERSTOWN, MD	MORGANTOWN, WV	SALISBURY, MD	WASHINGTON, DC	WHEELING, WV
BALTIMORE, MD		161	140	229	98	110	62	76	211	106	38	290
CHARLOTTESVILLE, VA	161		163	142	70	74	190	141	204	235	118	279
MORGANTOWN, WV	211	204	71	62	252	161	181	138		317	205	76
WASHINGTON, DC	38	118	134	192	54	73	80	70	205	115		284

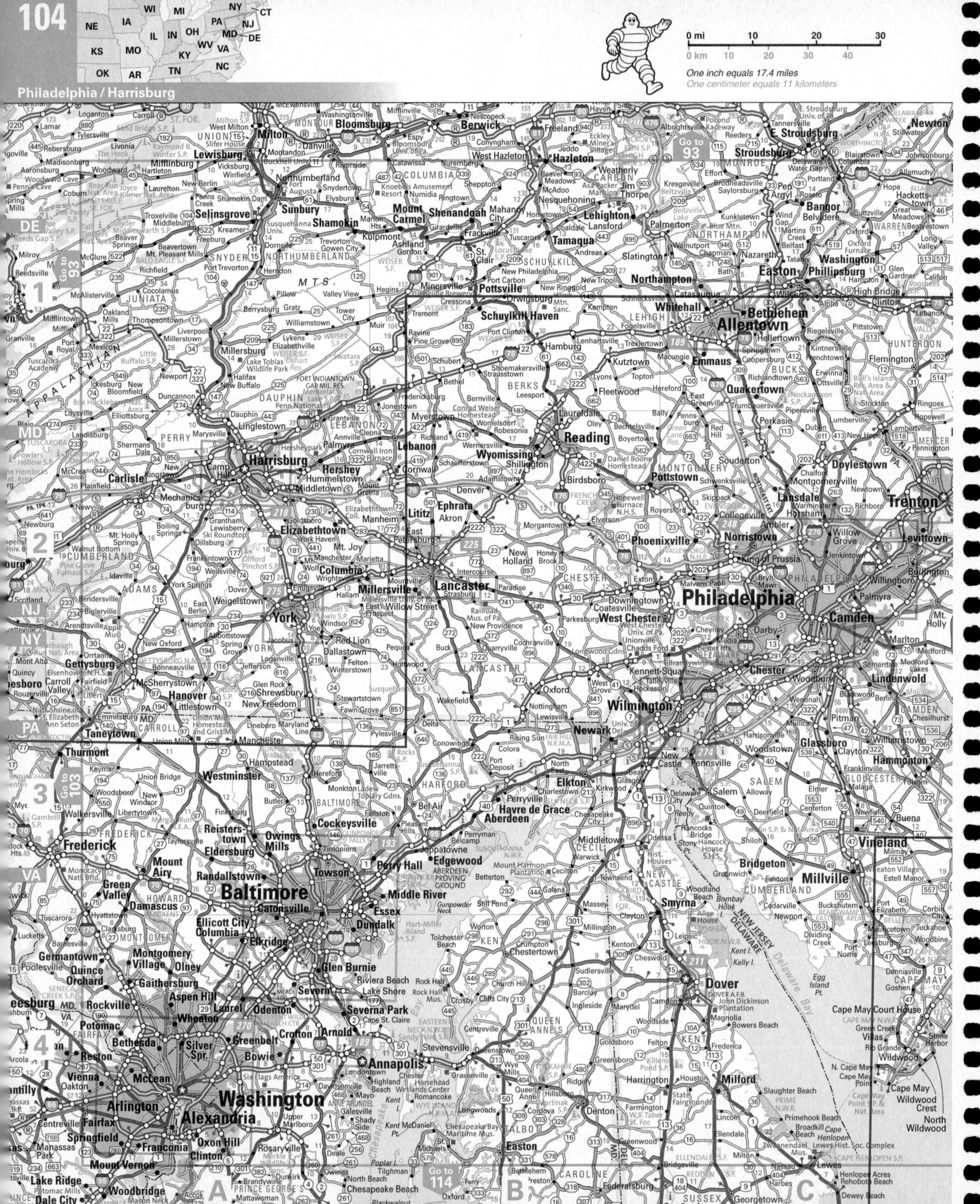

One inch equals 17.4 miles
One centimeter equals 11 kilometers

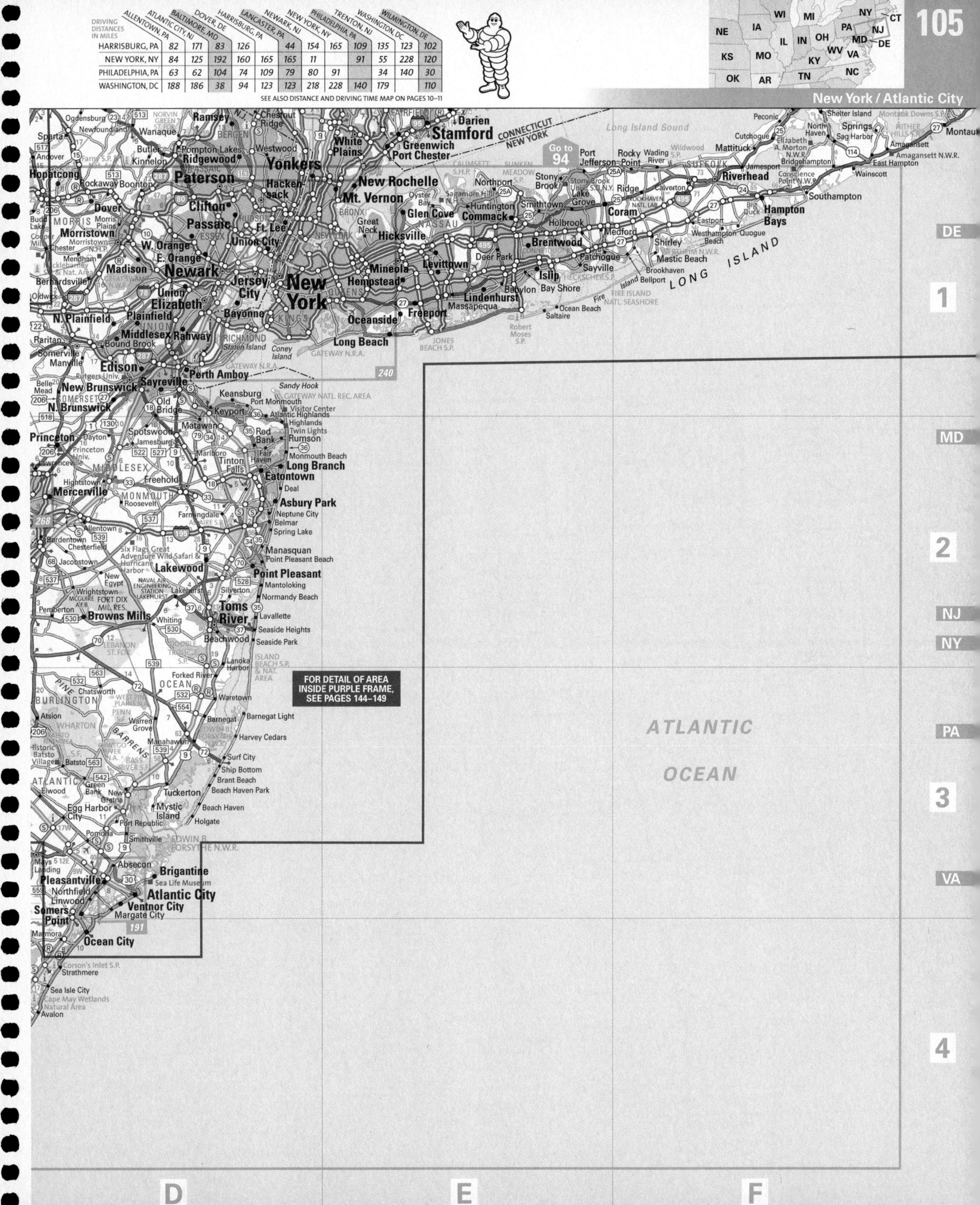

DRIVING DISTANCES IN MILES	ALLENTOWN, PA	ATLANTIC CITY, NJ	BALTIMORE, MD	DOVER, DE	HARRISBURG, PA	LANCASTER, PA	NEWARK, NJ	NEW YORK, NY	PHILADELPHIA, PA	TRENTON, NJ	WASHINGTON, DC	WILMINGTON, DE
HARRISBURG, PA	82	171	83	126		44	154	165	109	135	123	102
NEW YORK, NY	84	125	192	160	165	165	11		91	55	228	120
PHILADELPHIA, PA	63	62	104	74	109	79	80	91		34	140	30
WASHINGTON, DC	188	186	38	94	123	123	218	228	140	179		110

SEE ALSO DISTANCE AND DRIVING TIME MAP ON PAGES 10–11

FOR DETAIL OF AREA INSIDE PURPLE FRAME, SEE PAGES 144–149

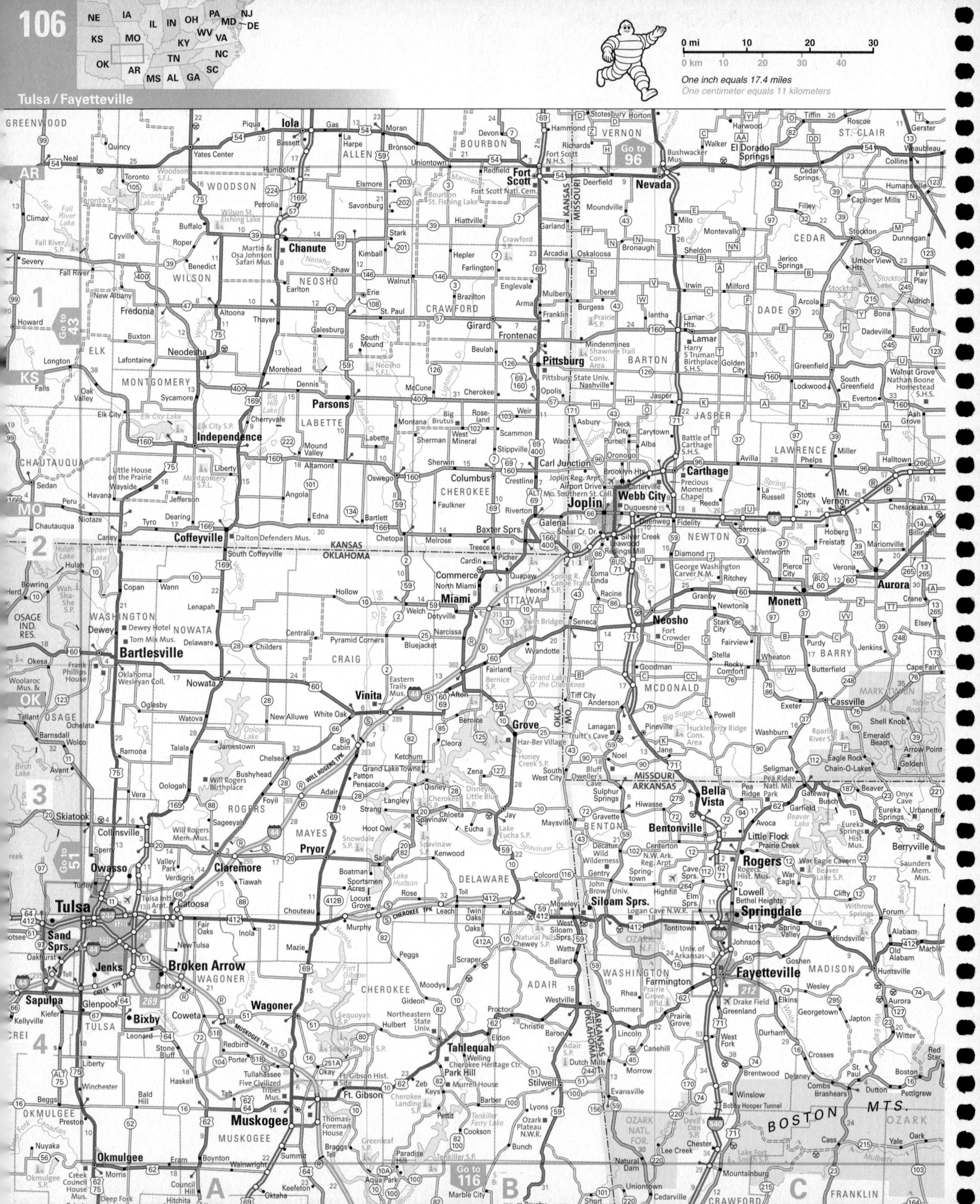

One inch equals 17.4 miles
One centimeter equals 11 kilometers

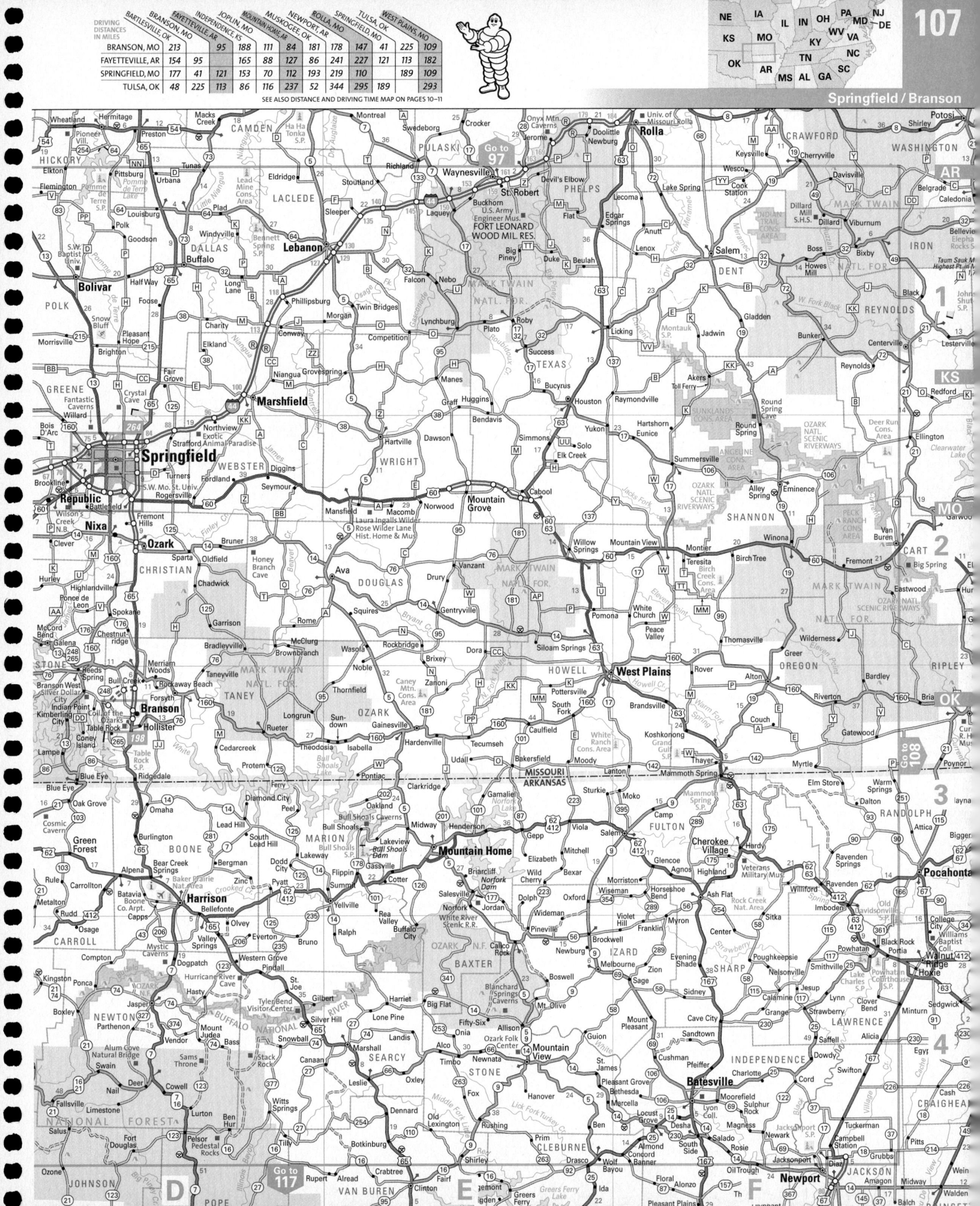

SEE ALSO DISTANCE AND DRIVING TIME MAP ON PAGES 10-11

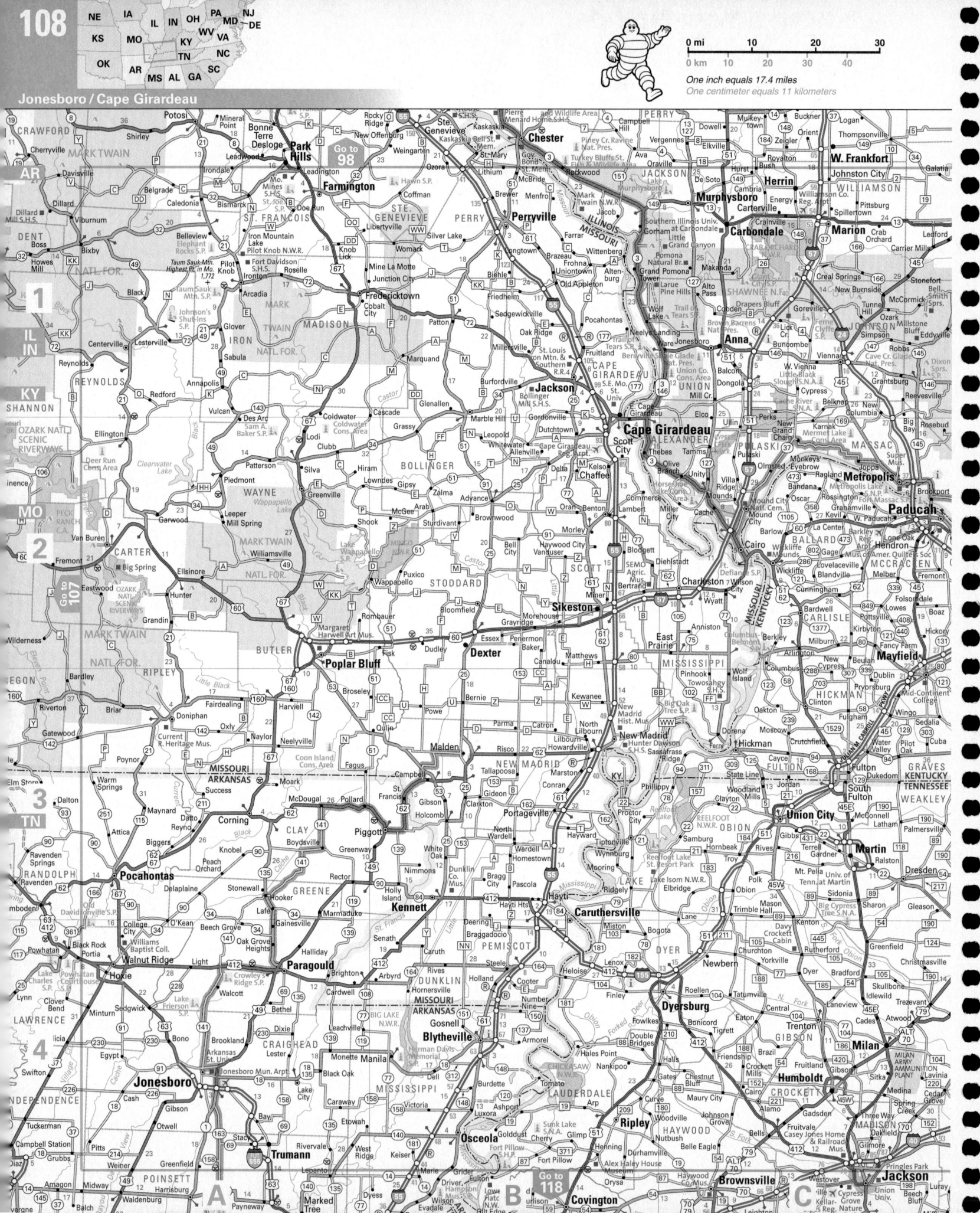

NE IA PA NJ
IL IN OH MD DE
KS MO KY VA
WV
OK TN NC
AR
MS AL GA

0 mi 10 20 30
0 km 10 20 30 40
One inch equals 17.4 miles
One centimeter equals 11 kilometers

SEE ALSO DISTANCE AND DRIVING TIME MAP ON PAGES 10–11

DRIVING DISTANCES IN MILES	BOWLING GREEN, KY	CAPE GIRARDEAU, MO	CARBONDALE, IL	CLARKSVILLE, TN	DYERSBURG, TN	HOPKINSVILLE, KY	JACKSON, TN	JONESBORO, AR	NASHVILLE, TN	OWENSBORO, KY	PADUCAH, KY	POPLAR BLUFF, MO
BOWLING GREEN, KY		199	206	63	217	63	196	349	68	76	135	239
CAPE GIRARDEAU, MO	199		46	155	112	136	161	155	197	168	67	75
JONESBORO, AR	349	155	199	268	101	249	160		285	304	178	81
NASHVILLE, TN	68	197	204	46	178	68	132	285		141	133	237

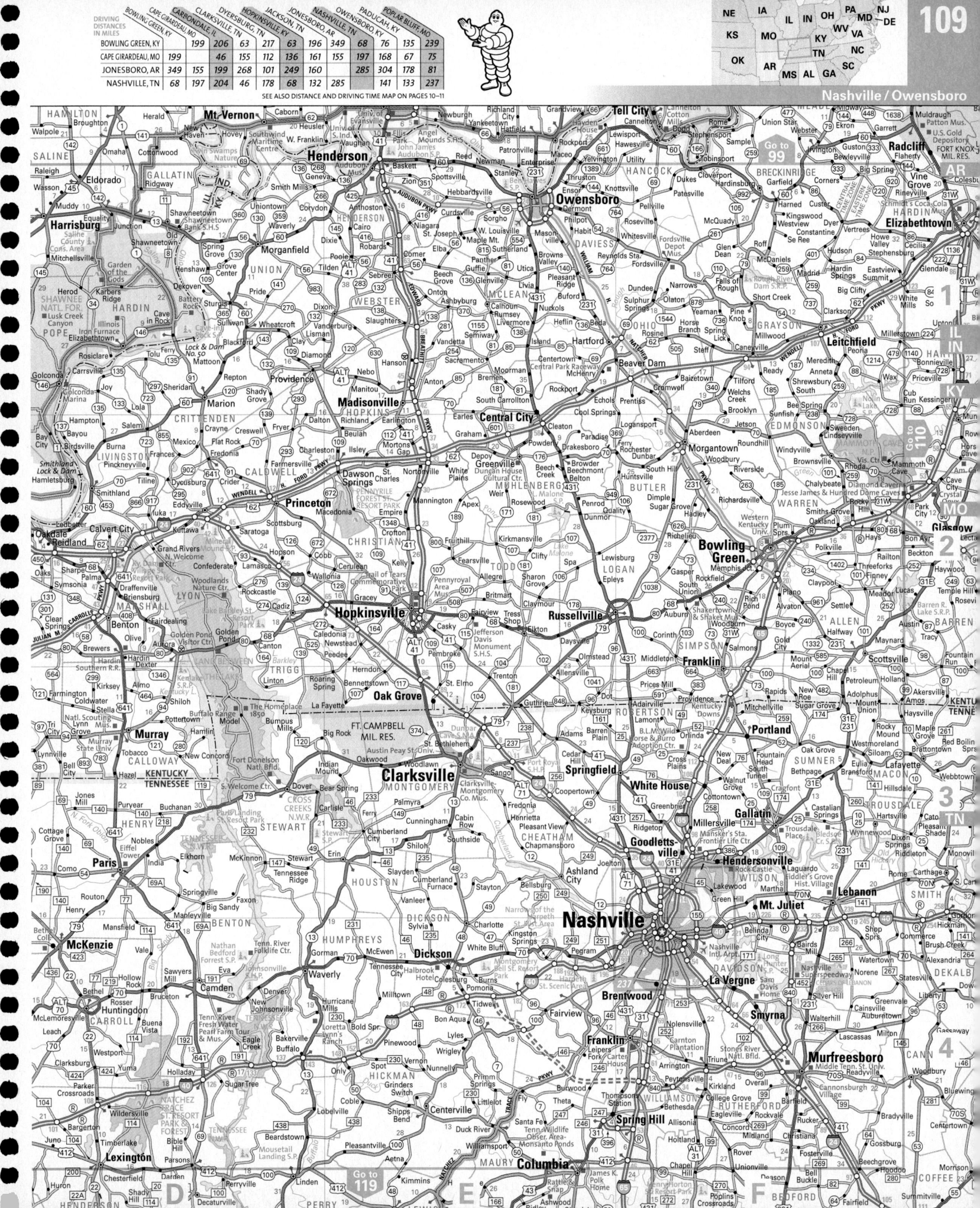

NE IA IL IN OH PA NJ MD DE
KS MO WV VA
KY
OK TN NC
AR SC
MS AL GA

0 mi 10 20 30
0 km 10 20 30 40

One inch equals 17.4 miles
One centimeter equals 11 kilometers

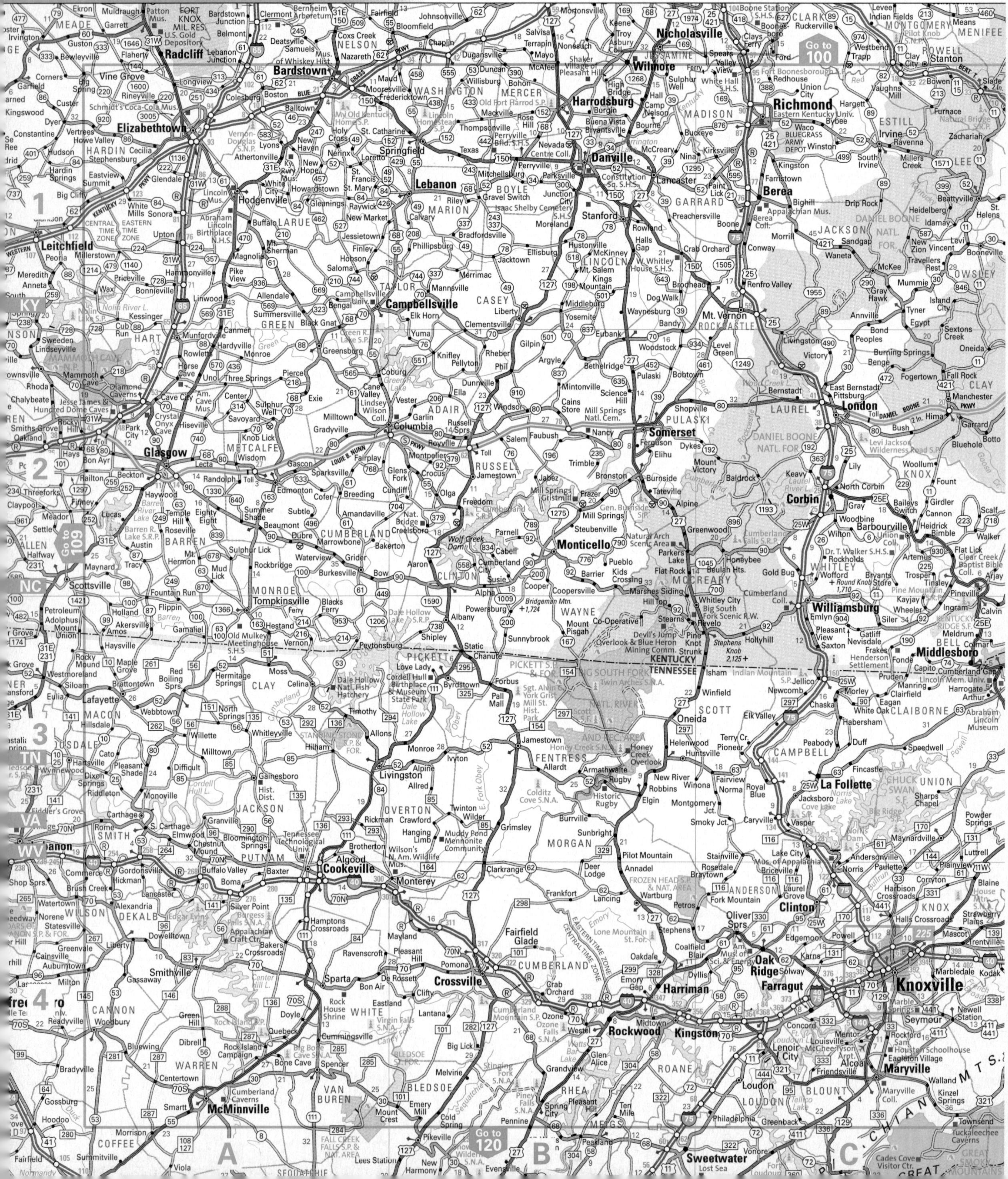

Go to 100

Go to 109

Go to 120

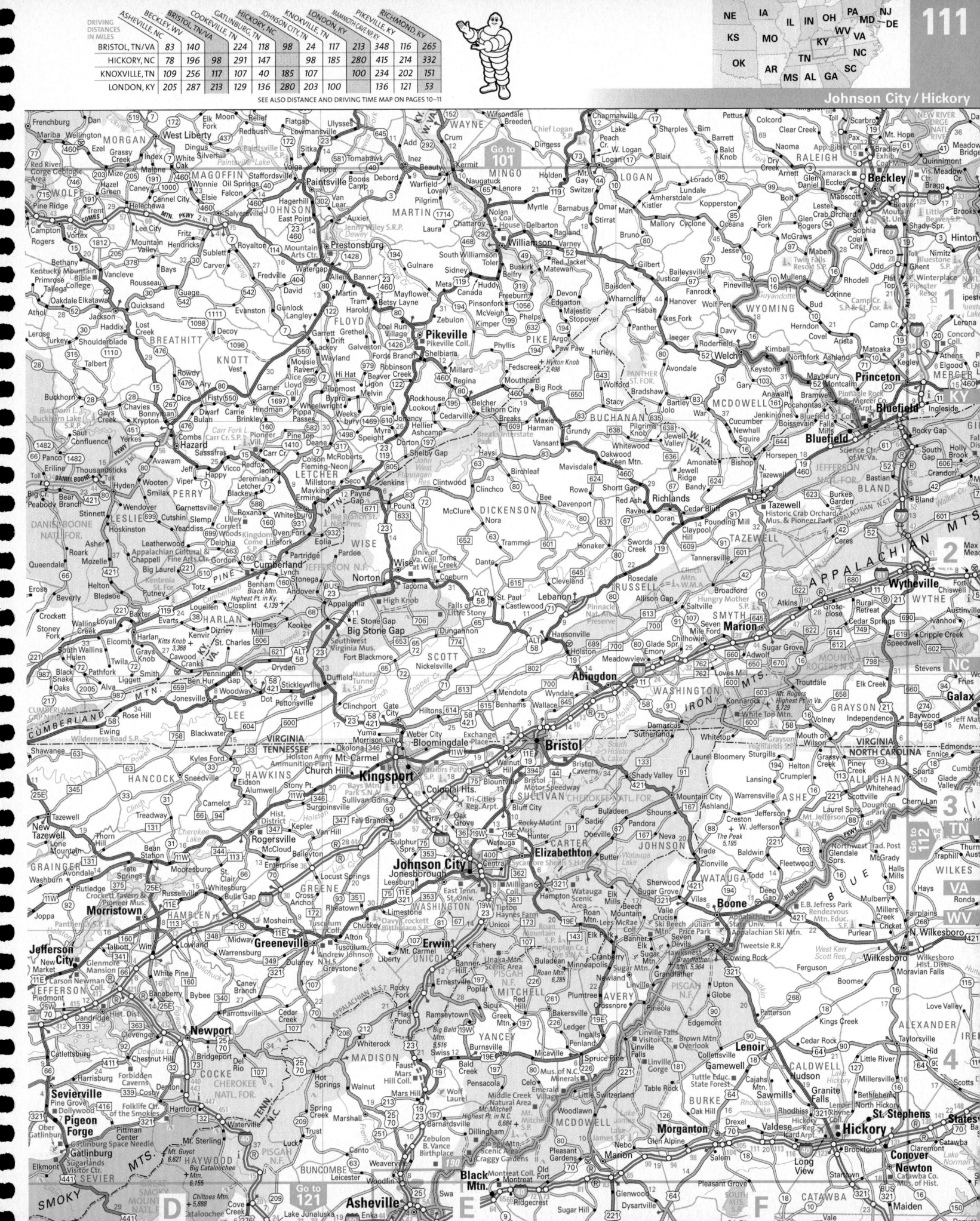

DRIVING DISTANCES IN MILES	ASHEVILLE, NC	BECKLEY, WV	BRISTOL, TN/VA	COOKEVILLE, TN	GATLINBURG, TN	HICKORY, NC	JOHNSON CITY, TN	KNOXVILLE, TN	LONDON, KY	MAMMOTH CAVE NP, KY	PIKEVILLE, KY	RICHMOND, KY
BRISTOL, TN/VA	83	140		224	118	98	24		213	348	116	265
HICKORY, NC	78	196	98	291	147		98	185	280	415	214	332
KNOXVILLE, TN	109	256	117	107	40	185	107		100	234	202	151
LONDON, KY	205	287	213	129	136	280	203	100		136	121	53

SEE ALSO DISTANCE AND DRIVING TIME MAP ON PAGES 10–11

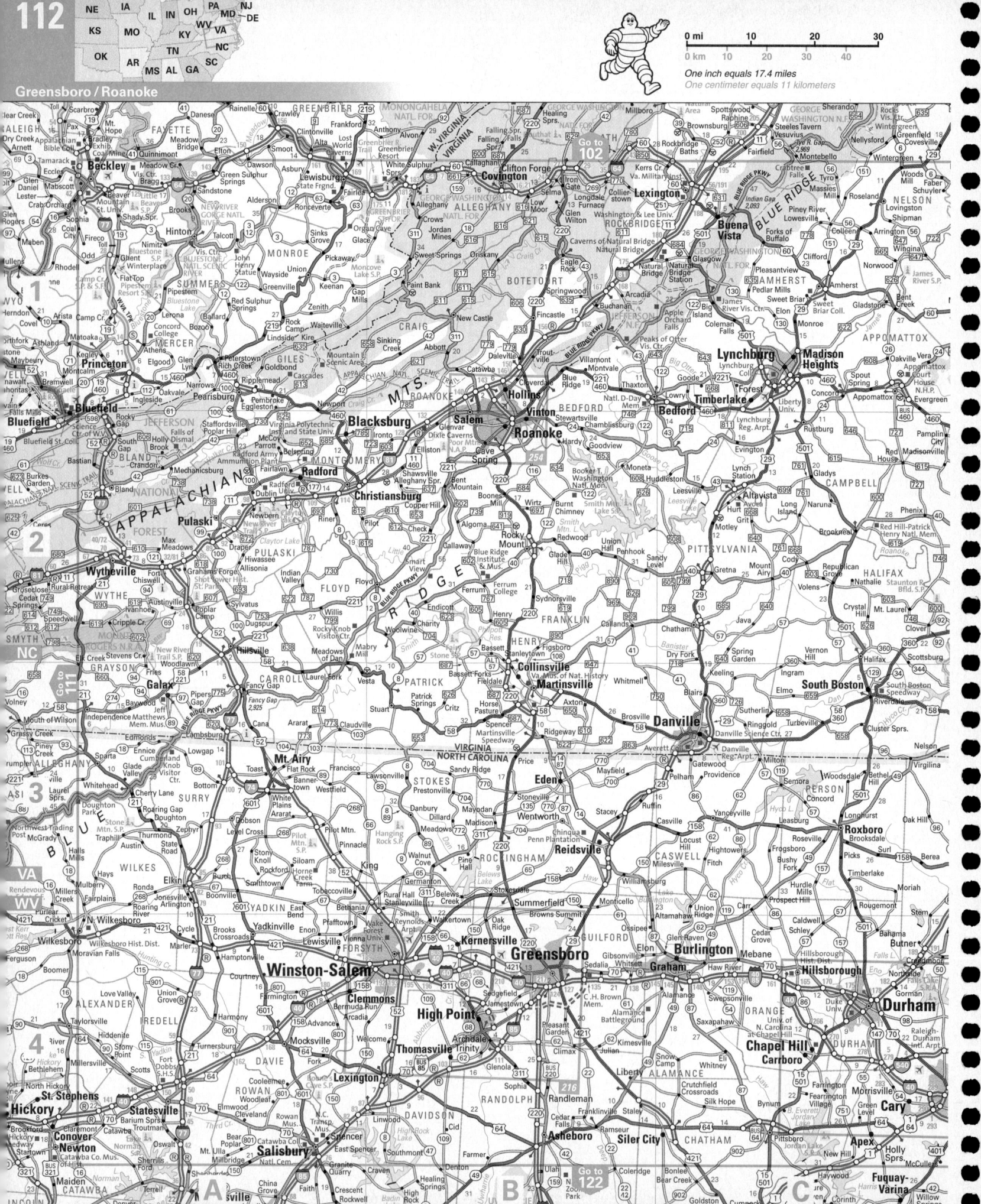

One inch equals 17.4 miles
One centimeter equals 11 kilometers

Go to 102

Go to 111

Go to 122

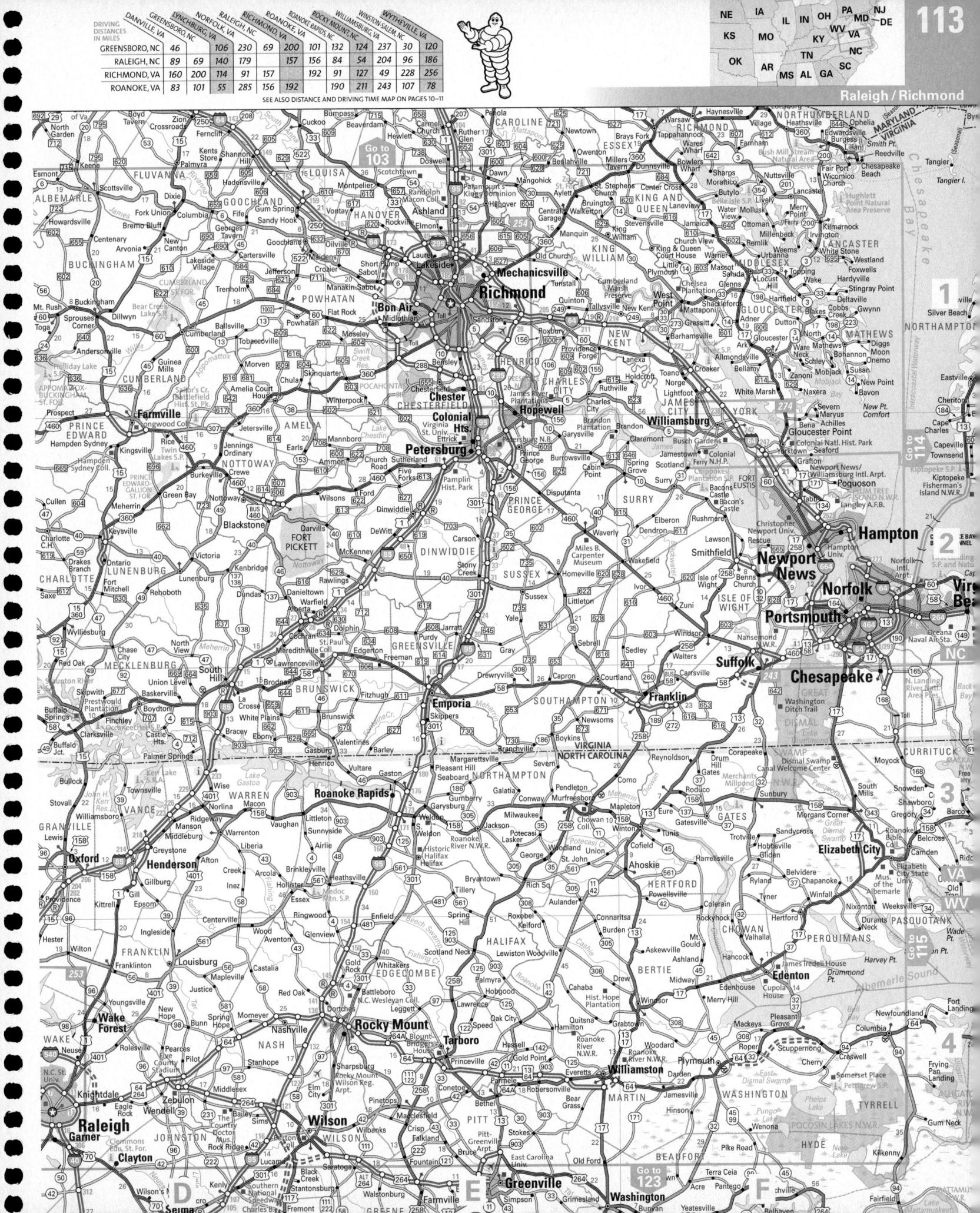

DRIVING DISTANCES IN MILES

	DANVILLE, NC	GREENSBORO, NC	LYNCHBURG, VA	NORFOLK, VA	RALEIGH, NC	RICHMOND, VA	ROANOKE, VA	ROANOKE RAPIDS, NC	ROCKY MOUNT, NC	WILLIAMSBURG, VA	WINSTON-SALEM, NC	WYTHEVILLE, VA
GREENSBORO, NC	46		106	230	69	200	101	132	124	237	30	120
RALEIGH, NC	89	69	140	179		157	156	84	54	204	96	186
RICHMOND, VA	160	200	114	91	157		192	91	127	49	228	256
ROANOKE, VA	83	101	55	285	156	192		190	211	243	107	78

SEE ALSO DISTANCE AND DRIVING TIME MAP ON PAGES 10–11

One inch equals 17.4 miles
One centimeter equals 11 kilometers

FOR DETAIL OF AREA
INSIDE PURPLE FRAME,
SEE PAGES 144-145

ATLANTIC OCEAN

DRIVING DISTANCES IN MILES

	GREENVILLE, NC	MOREHEAD CITY, NC	NAGS HEAD, NC	NEW BERN, NC	OCEAN CITY, MD	RICHMOND, VA	SALISBURY, MD	VIRGINIA BEACH, VA	WASHINGTON, DC	WILLIAMSBURG, VA
MOREHEAD CITY, NC	150	82		184	35	185	326	241	321	206	352	221
NAGS HEAD, NC	59	135	184		149	82	214	179	209	94	284	131
NORFOLK, VA	50	130	185	82	151		138	91	133	18	196	43
WASHINGTON, DC	243	270	352	284	317	196		139	108	115	212	153

SEE ALSO DISTANCE AND DRIVING TIME MAP ON PAGES 10–11

Go to 114
Go to 113
Go to 123

NE IA IN OH PA NJ
KS MO IL WV MD DE
OK AR TN KY VA NC
MS AL GA SC

DE
1
MD
2
NJ
NC
3
VA
4

D E F

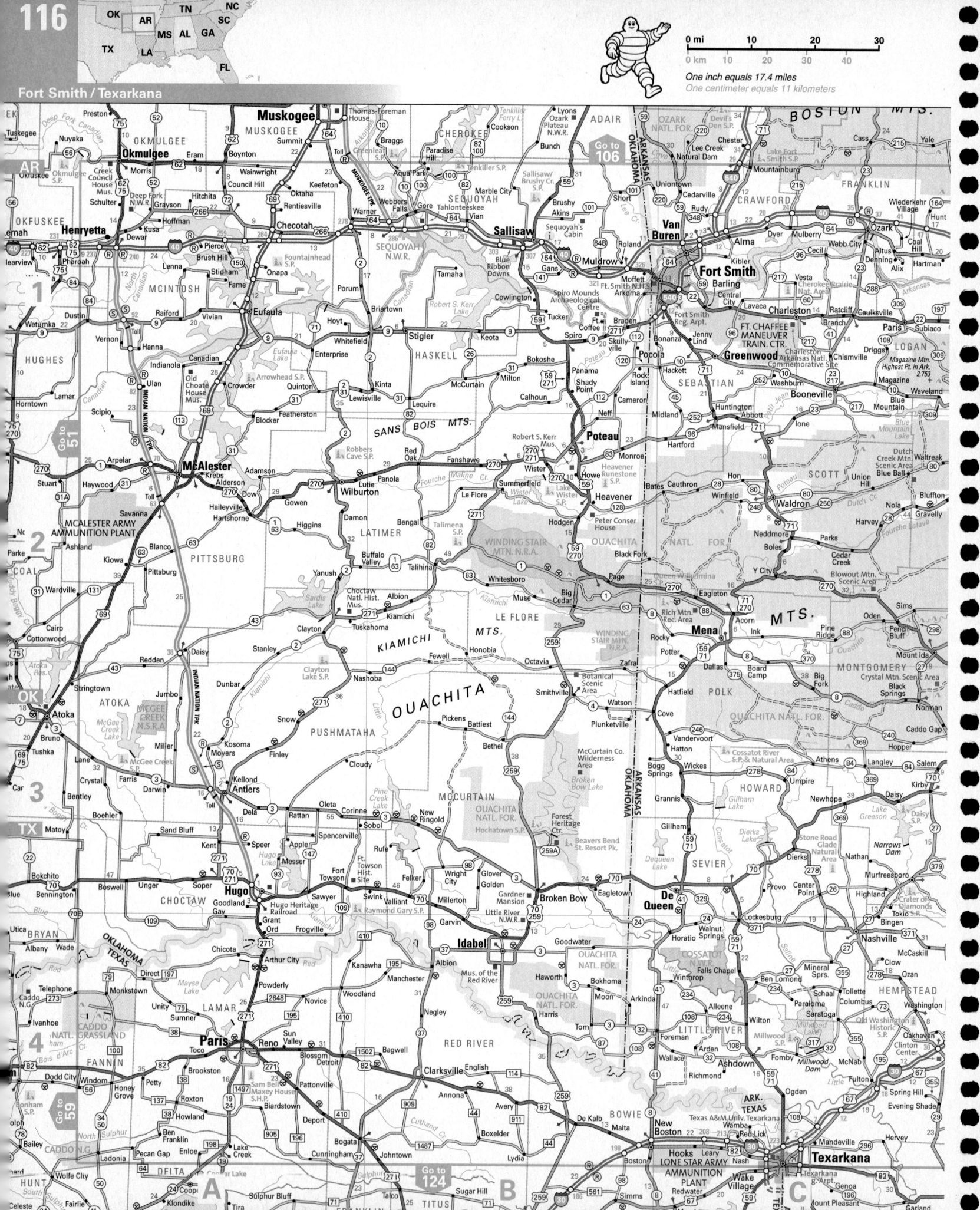

One inch equals 17.4 miles
One centimeter equals 11 kilometers

0 mi 10 20 30
0 km 10 20 30 40

Go to 106
Go to 51
Go to 59
Go to 124

DRIVING DISTANCES IN MILES	ARKADELPHIA, AR	FORT SMITH, AR	HENRYETTA, OK	HOT SPRINGS, AR	LITTLE ROCK, AR	McALESTER, OK	MENA, AR	NEWPORT, AR	PARIS, TX	PINE BLUFF, AR	RUSSELLVILLE, AR	TEXARKANA, AR/TX
FORT SMITH, AR	152		100	126	165	114	81	220	214	210	87	180
HOT SPRINGS, AR	37	126	224		65	193	75	154	207	76	67	117
LITTLE ROCK, AR	72	165	263	65		278	141	89	242	45	81	153
TEXARKANA, AR/TX	83	180	227	117	153	188	99	241	92	163	180	

SEE ALSO DISTANCE AND DRIVING TIME MAP ON PAGES 10–11

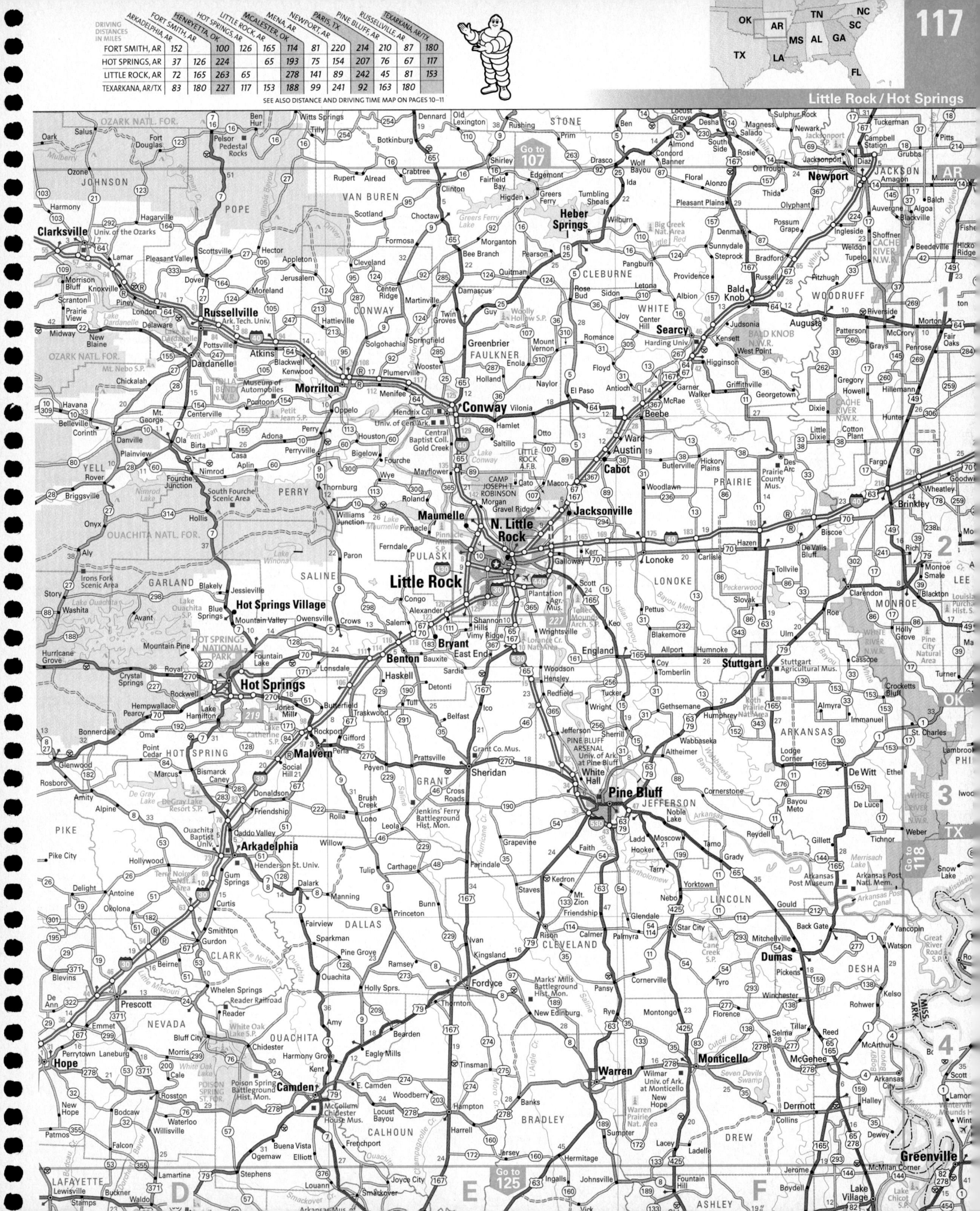

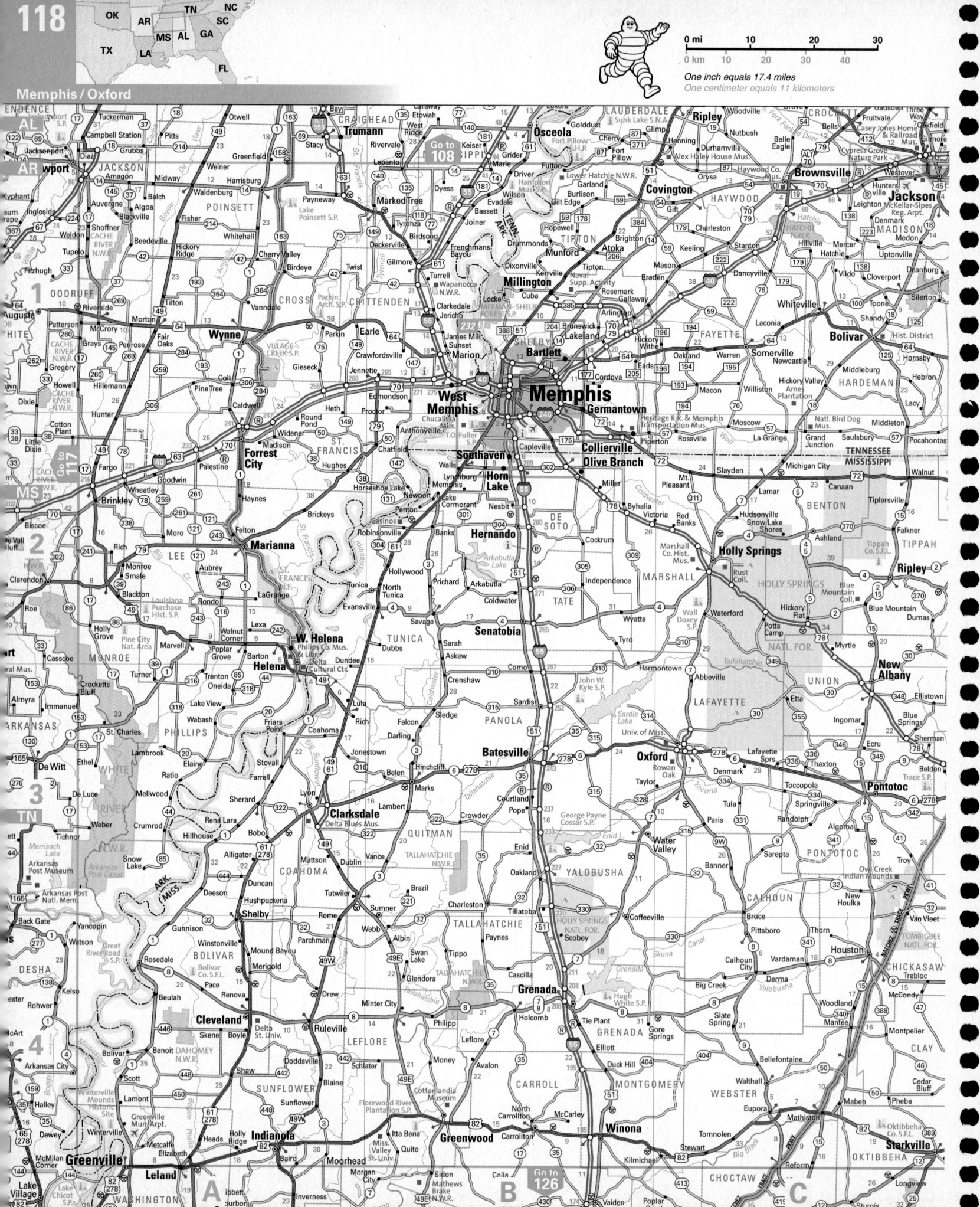

One inch equals 17.4 miles
One centimeter equals 11 kilometers

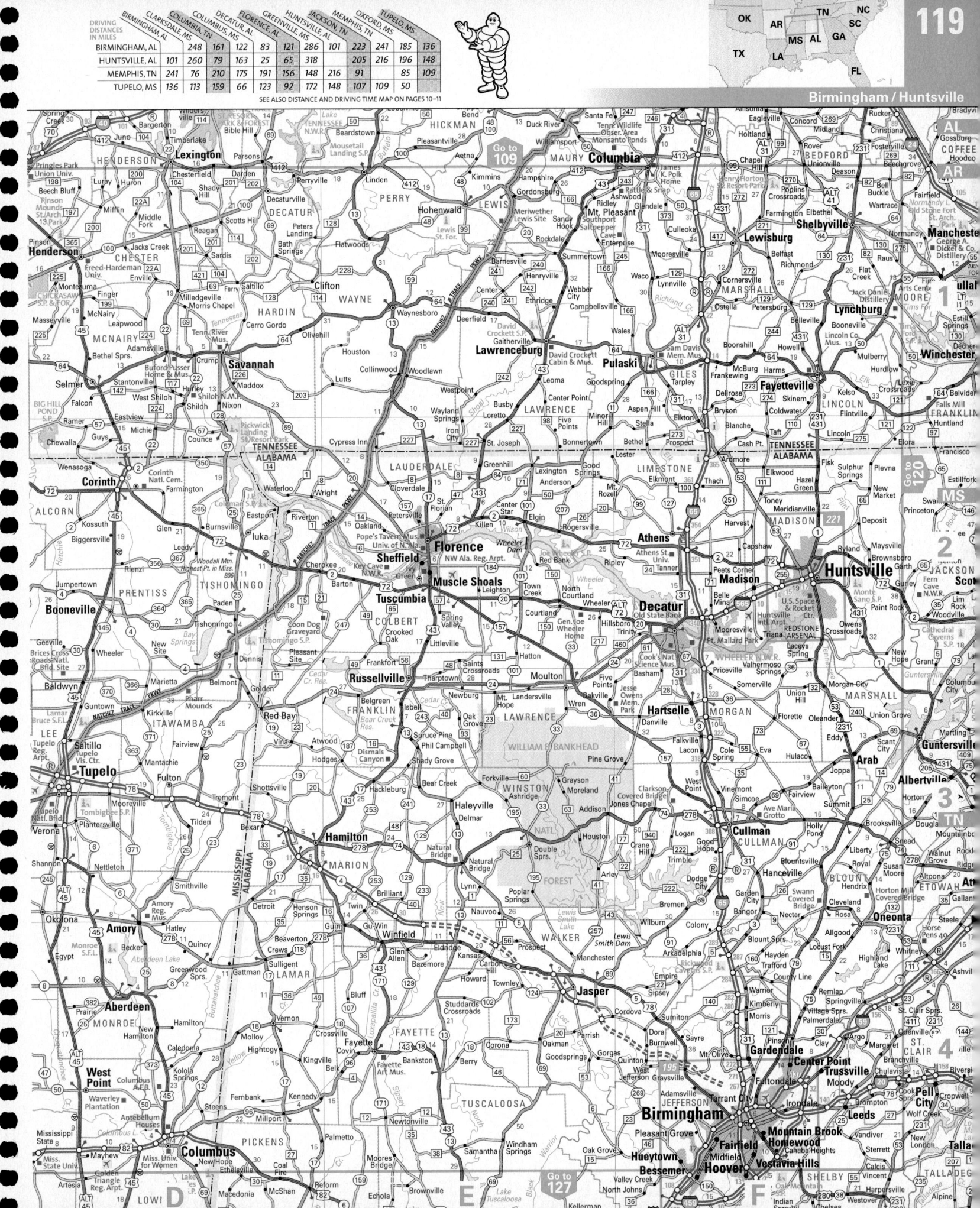

One inch equals 17.4 miles
One centimeter equals 11 kilometers

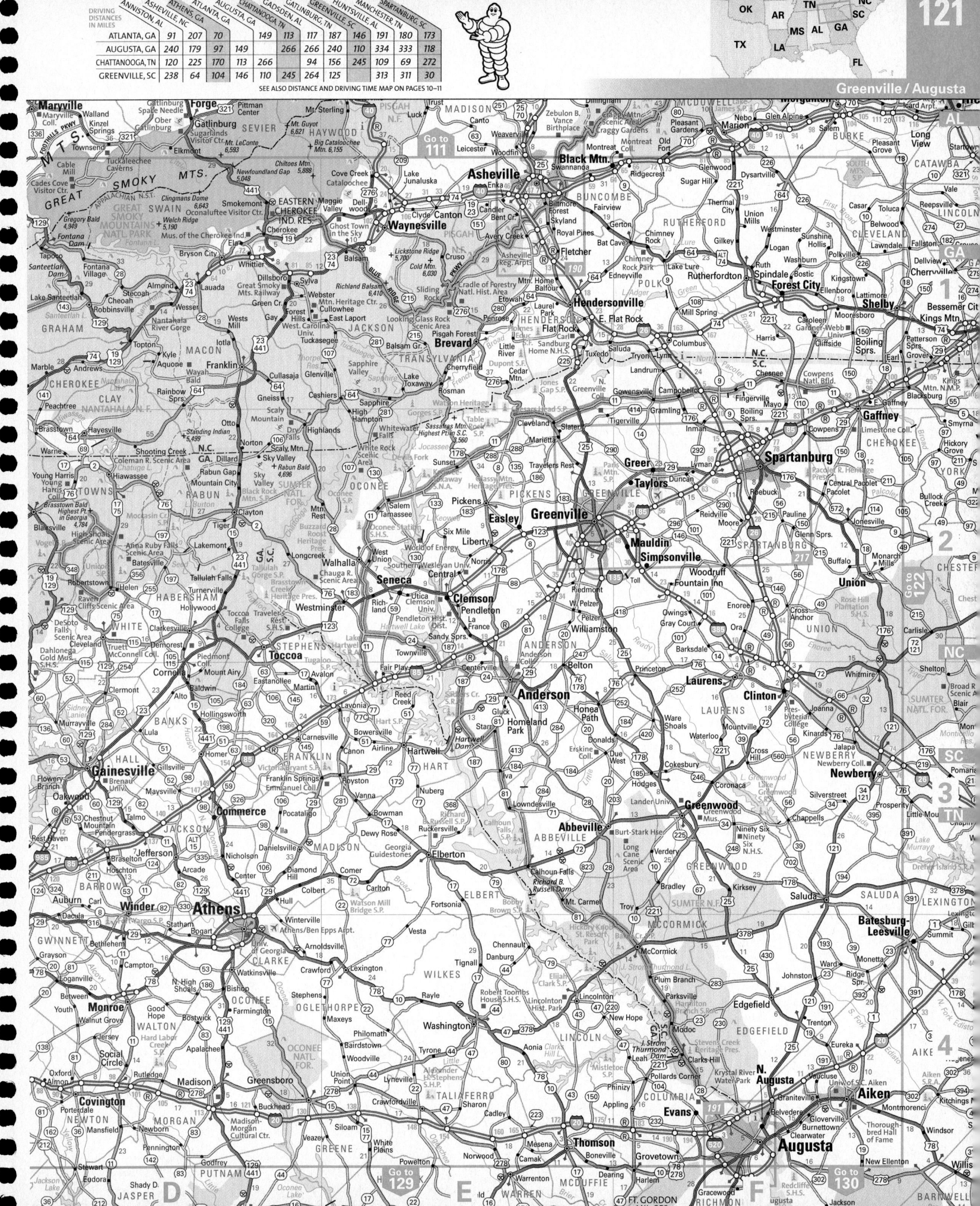

One inch equals 17.4 miles
One centimeter equals 11 kilometers

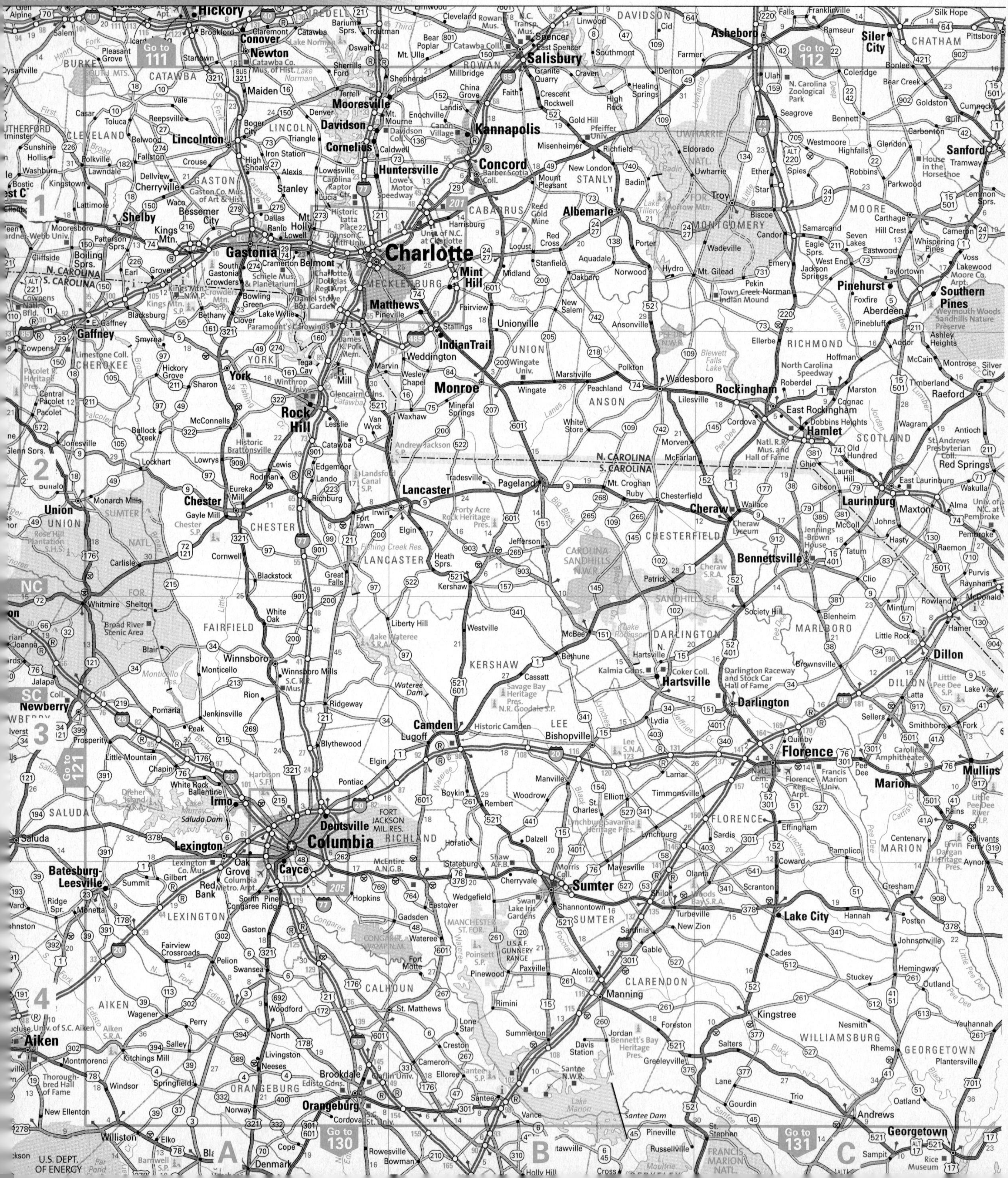

0 mi 10 20 30
0 km 10 20 30 40

DRIVING DISTANCES IN MILES	CHARLOTTE, NC	COLUMBIA, SC	FAYETTEVILLE, NC	FLORENCE, SC	GOLDSBORO, NC	HICKORY, NC	LUMBERTON, NC	MOREHEAD CITY, NC	MYRTLE BEACH, SC	ROCK HILL, SC	SUMTER, SC	WILMINGTON, NC
CHARLOTTE, NC		91	139	107	208	47	128	298	173	26	115	205
COLUMBIA, SC	91		170	80	240	139	139	289	146	70	45	199
MYRTLE BEACH, SC	173	146	116	66	170	220	83	165		181	93	71
WILMINGTON, NC	205	199	92	120	100	292	77	95	71	220	158	

SEE ALSO DISTANCE AND DRIVING TIME MAP ON PAGES 10–11

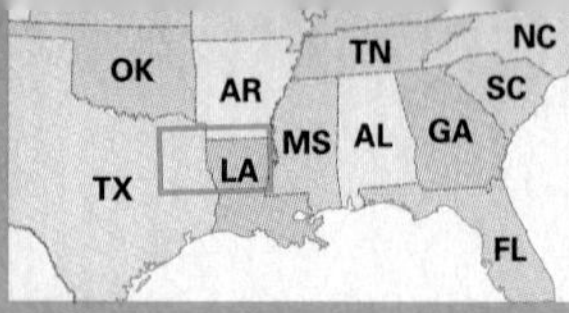

OK TN NC
AR SC
TX LA MS AL GA
FL

One inch equals 17.4 miles
One centimeter equals 11 kilometers

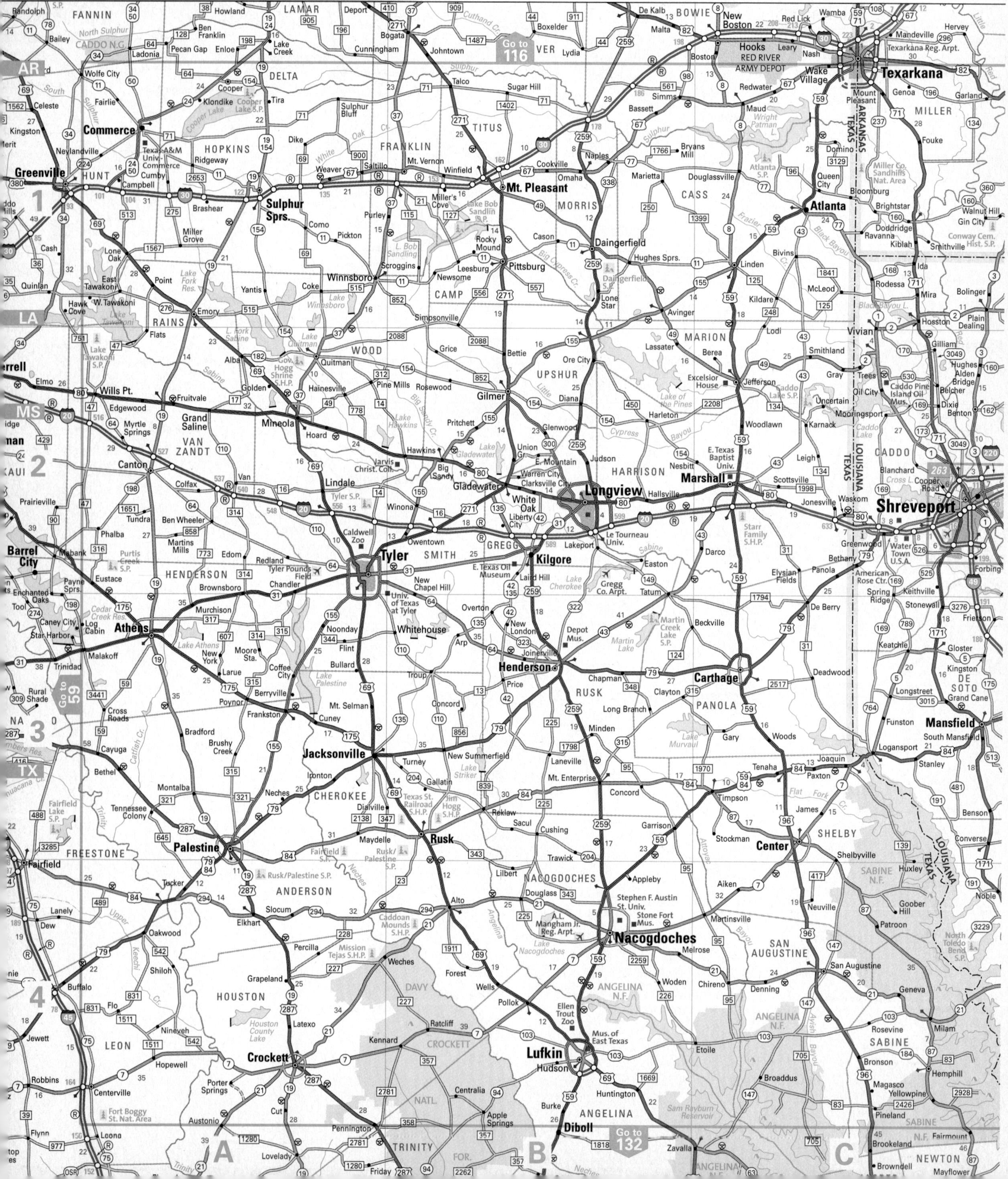

0 mi   10   20   30
0 km 10 20 30 40

Go to 116
Go to 132
Go to 59

Texarkana
Shreveport
Tyler
Longview
Marshall
Kilgore
Henderson
Carthage
Mansfield
Center
Nacogdoches
Lufkin
Diboll
Palestine
Jacksonville
Rusk
Crockett
Athens
Canton
Mineola
Gilmer
Pittsburg
Mt. Pleasant
Atlanta
Daingerfield
Sulphur Sprs.
Greenville
Commerce
New Boston
Whitehouse

COUNTIES: FANNIN, LAMAR, BOWIE, MILLER, HUNT, DELTA, HOPKINS, TITUS, MORRIS, CASS, MARION, CADDO, VAN ZANDT, WOOD, CAMP, UPSHUR, HARRISON, RAINS, SMITH, GREGG, RUSK, PANOLA, DE SOTO, HENDERSON, CHEROKEE, NACOGDOCHES, SHELBY, SAN AUGUSTINE, ANDERSON, FREESTONE, HOUSTON, LEON, TRINITY, ANGELINA, SABINE, NEWTON

ARKANSAS / TEXAS
LOUISIANA / TEXAS

RED RIVER ARMY DEPOT

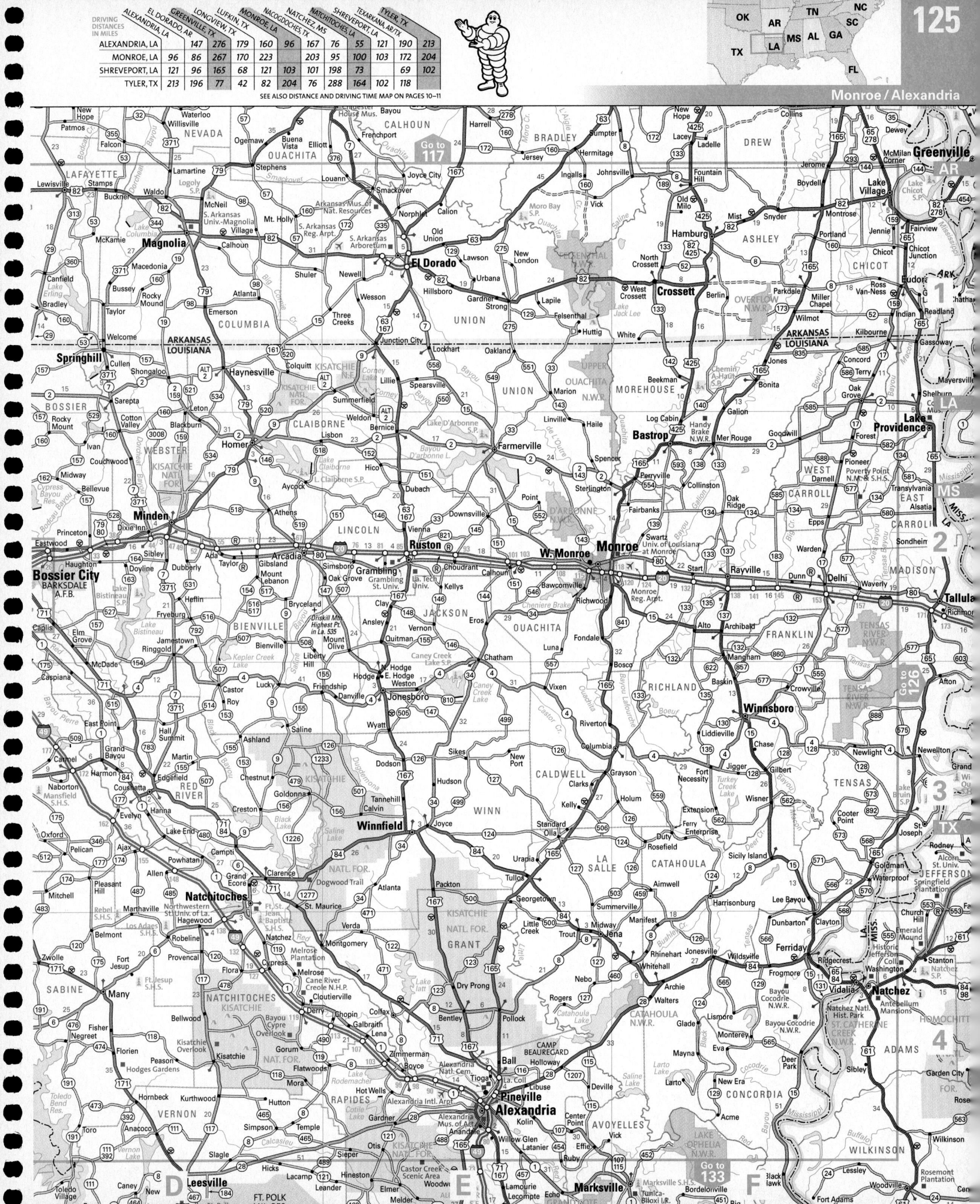

SEE ALSO DISTANCE AND DRIVING TIME MAP ON PAGES 10–11

DRIVING DISTANCES IN MILES	ALEXANDRIA, LA	EL DORADO, AR	GREENVILLE, TX	LONGVIEW, TX	LUFKIN, TX	MONROE, LA	NACOGDOCHES, TX	NATCHEZ, MS	NATCHITOCHES, LA	SHREVEPORT, LA	TEXARKANA, AR/TX	TYLER, TX
ALEXANDRIA, LA		147	276	179	160	96	167	76	55	121	190	213
MONROE, LA	96	86	267	170	223		203	95	100	103	172	204
SHREVEPORT, LA	121	96	165	68	121	103	101	198	73		69	102
TYLER, TX	213	196	77	42	82	204	76	288	164	102	118	

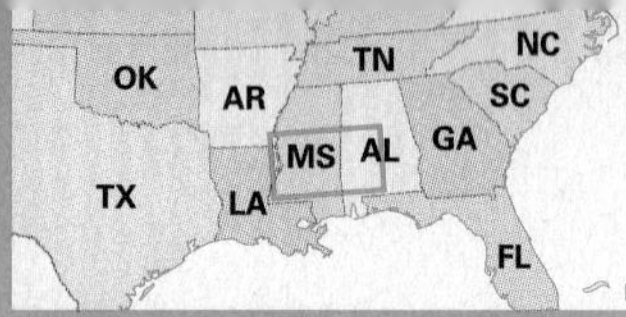

0 mi 10 20 30
0 km 10 20 30 40

One inch equals 17.4 miles
One centimeter equals 11 kilometers

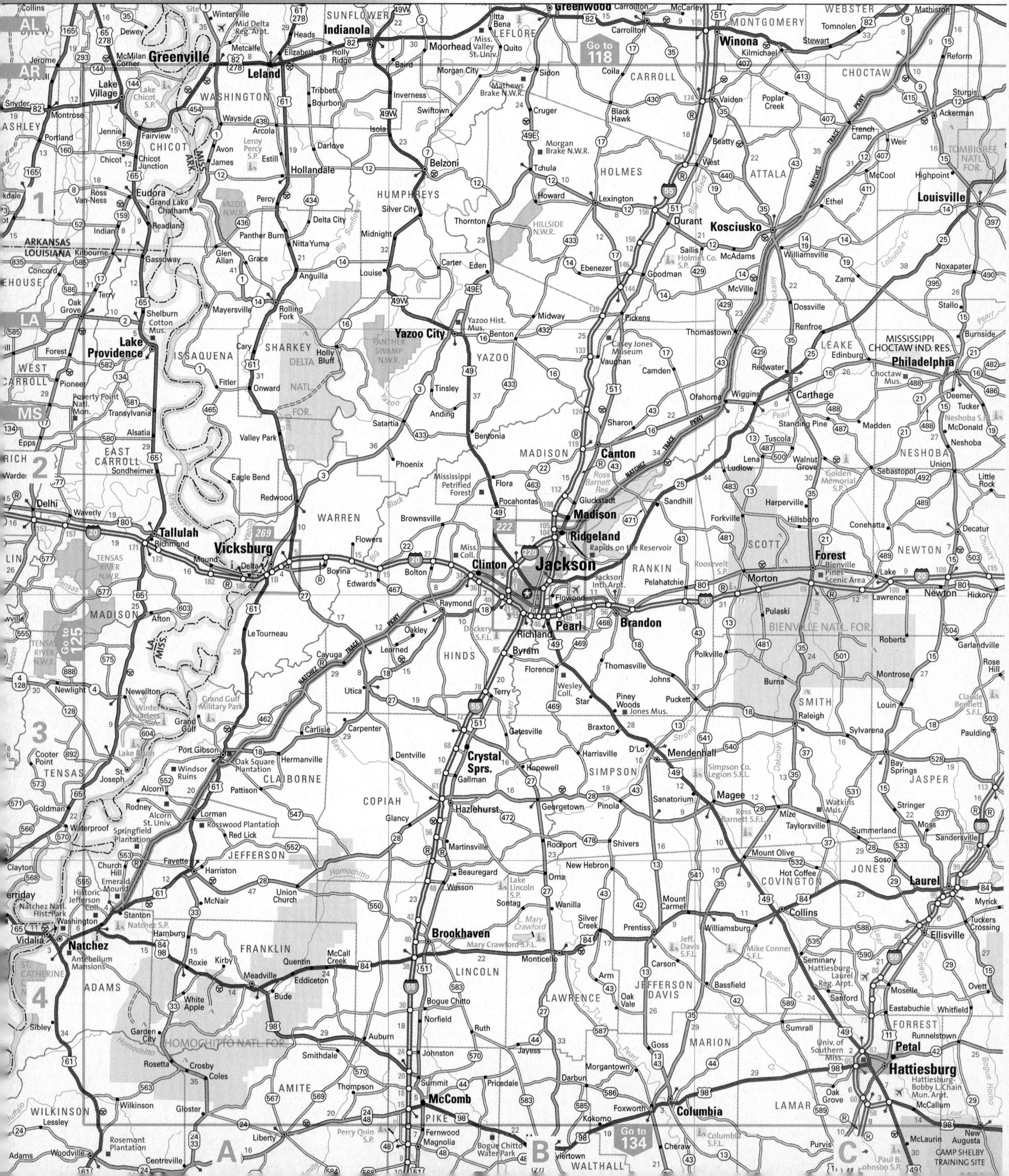

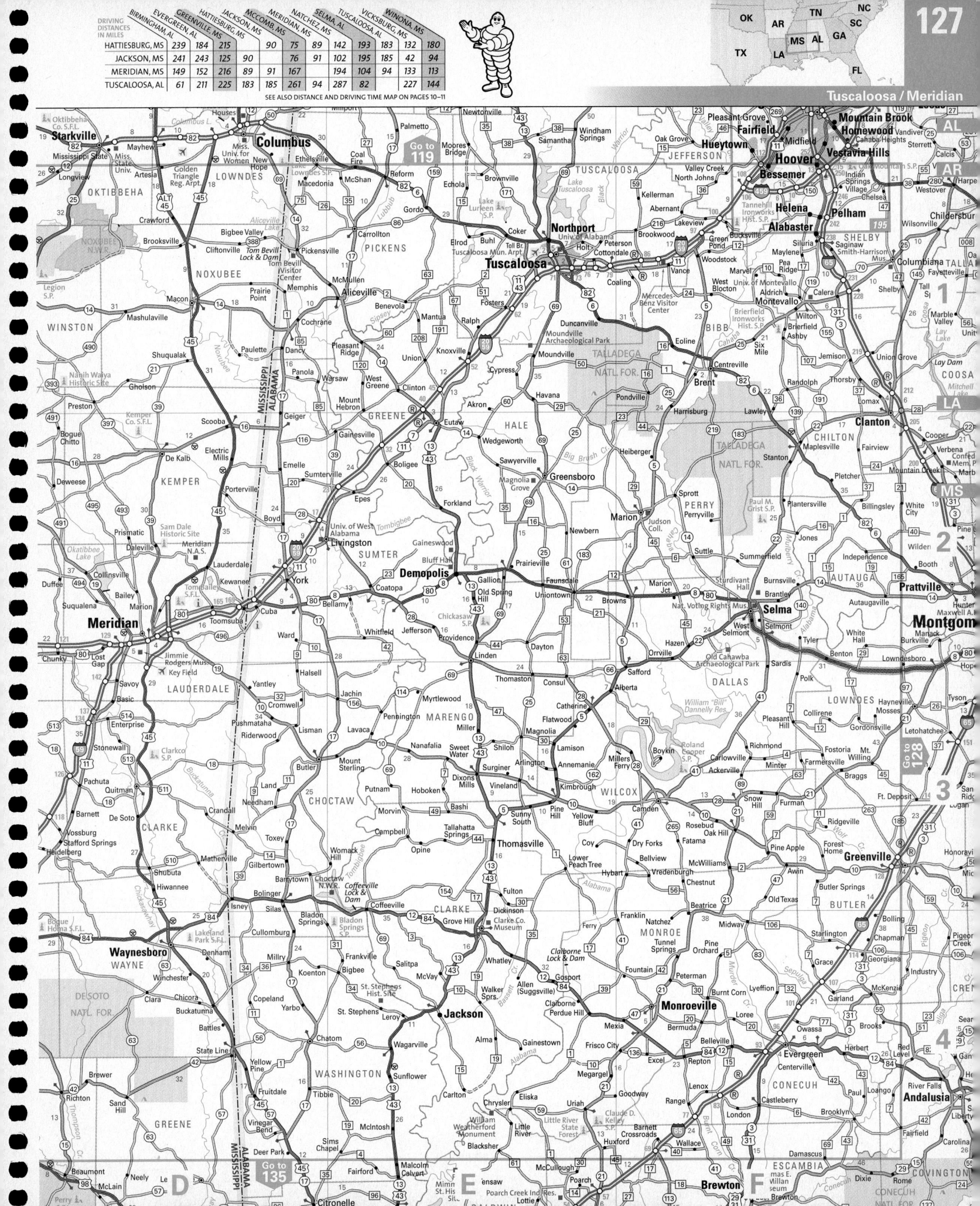

DRIVING DISTANCES IN MILES	BIRMINGHAM, AL	EVERGREEN, AL	GREENVILLE, MS	HATTIESBURG, MS	JACKSON, MS	McCOMB, MS	MERIDIAN, MS	NATCHEZ, MS	SELMA, AL	TUSCALOOSA, AL	VICKSBURG, MS	WINONA, MS
HATTIESBURG, MS	239	184	215		90	75	89	142	193	183	132	180
JACKSON, MS	241	243	125	90		76	91	102	195	185	42	94
MERIDIAN, MS	149	152	216	89	91	167		194	104	94	133	113
TUSCALOOSA, AL	61	211	225	183	185	261	94	287	82		227	144

OK TN NC
AR SC
TX MS AL GA
LA FL

0 mi 10 20 30
0 km 10 20 30 40
One inch equals 17.4 miles
One centimeter equals 11 kilometers

AL

Birmingham   Leeds
Mountain Brook   Homewood
Cahaba Heights
Vestavia Hills   Hoover   Bessemer

Helena   Pelham
Alabaster

GA

Talladega
Talladega Coll.

Sylacauga

Childersburg

Columbiana

Shelby

Clanton

CHILTON

Prattville   Millbrook

Montgomery

Maxwell A.F.B.

Wetumpka   Tallassee

ELMORE

Alexander City

Dadeville

Opelika

Auburn   Auburn Univ.

Tuskegee   Tuskegee Inst. N.H.S.   Tuskegee Univ.

Smiths
Phenix City

Columbus
Columbus Metro. Airport

FT. BENNING MIL. RES.
U.S. Army Infantry Mus.

LaGrange   LaGrange Coll.

Lanett

Valley

West Point

Newnan

Peachtree City

Thomaston

Manchester

Roanoke

Lafayette

CHAMBERS

TALLAPOOSA

LEE

MACON

RUSSELL

Union Springs

BULLOCK

Troy   Troy St. Univ.

Greenville

BUTLER

Luverne

PIKE

CRENSHAW

Brundidge

Eufaula

QUITMAN

STEWART

BARBOUR

Clayton

Abbeville

HENRY

Ozark
FT. RUCKER MIL. RES.
U.S. Army Aviation Mus.

Enterprise

DALE

Andalusia

Opp

COVINGTON

COFFEE

Dothan
Wiregrass Mus. of Art

Blakely

EARLY

Cuthbert

Dawson

TERRELL

Montgomery

Go to 127

Go to 136   A   B   Go to 137   C

Go to 120

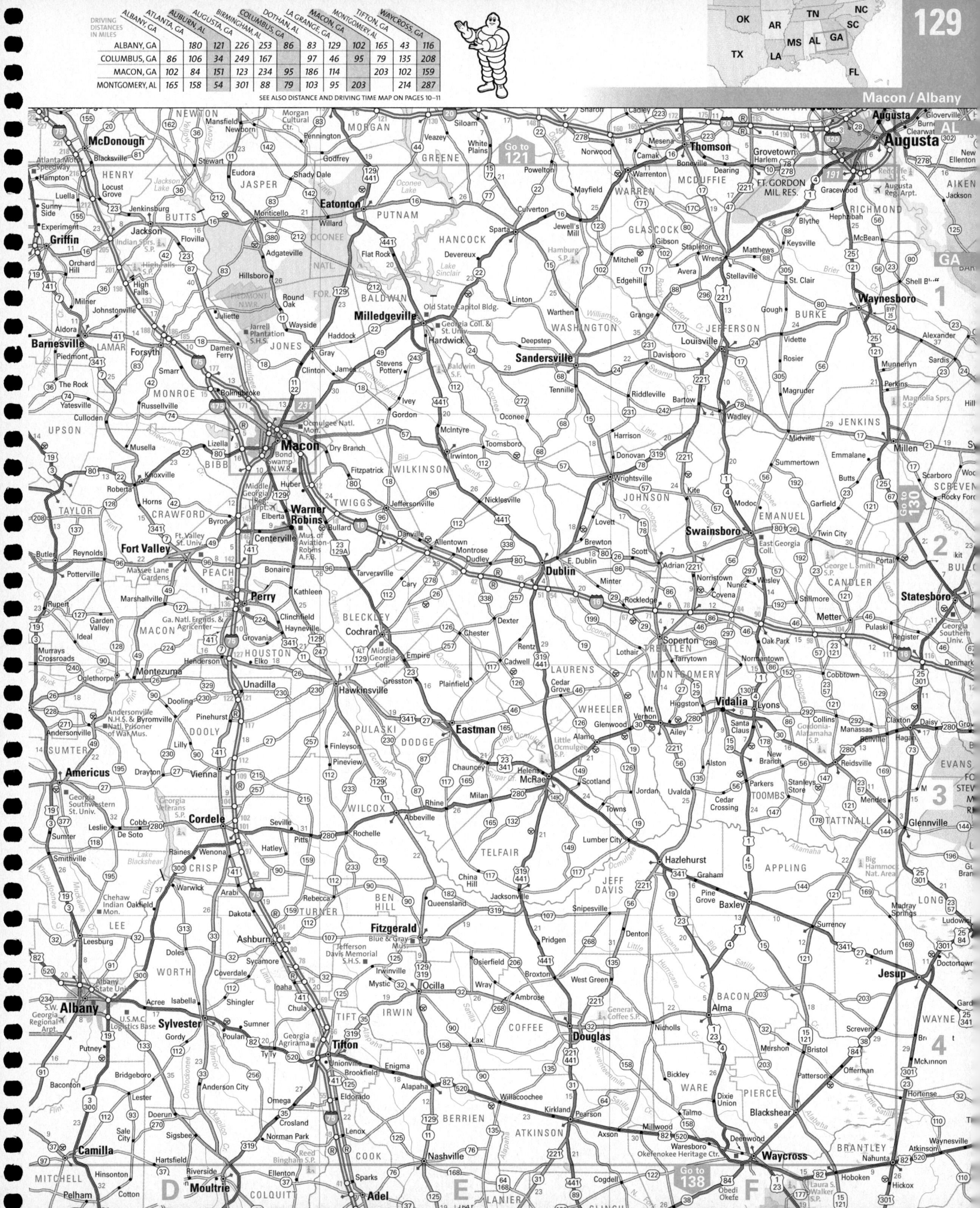

DRIVING DISTANCES IN MILES	ALBANY, GA	ATLANTA, GA	AUBURN, AL	AUGUSTA, GA	BIRMINGHAM, AL	COLUMBUS, GA	DOTHAN, AL	LA GRANGE, GA	MACON, GA	MONTGOMERY, AL	TIFTON, GA	WAYCROSS, GA
ALBANY, GA		180	121	226	253	86	83	129	102	165	43	116
COLUMBUS, GA	86	106	34	249	167		97	46	95	79	135	208
MACON, GA	102	84	151	123	234	95	186	114		203	102	159
MONTGOMERY, AL	165	158	54	301	88	79	103	95	203		214	287

SEE ALSO DISTANCE AND DRIVING TIME MAP ON PAGES 10–11

DRIVING DISTANCES IN MILES

	BEAUFORT, SC	BRUNSWICK, GA	CHARLESTON, SC	GEORGETOWN, SC	HILTON HEAD I., SC	HINESVILLE, GA	ORANGEBURG, SC	SAVANNAH, GA	STATESBORO, GA	WALTERBORO, SC	WAYCROSS, GA
AUGUSTA, GA	126	194	142	181	127	157	74	135	81	111	184
CHARLESTON, SC	142	66	175	58	95	138	73	107	150	51	203
HILTON HEAD I., SC	127	32	113	95	157	75	116	35	88	64	141
SAVANNAH, GA	135	42	78	107	163	35	41	123	53	71	106

SEE ALSO DISTANCE AND DRIVING TIME MAP ON PAGES 10–11

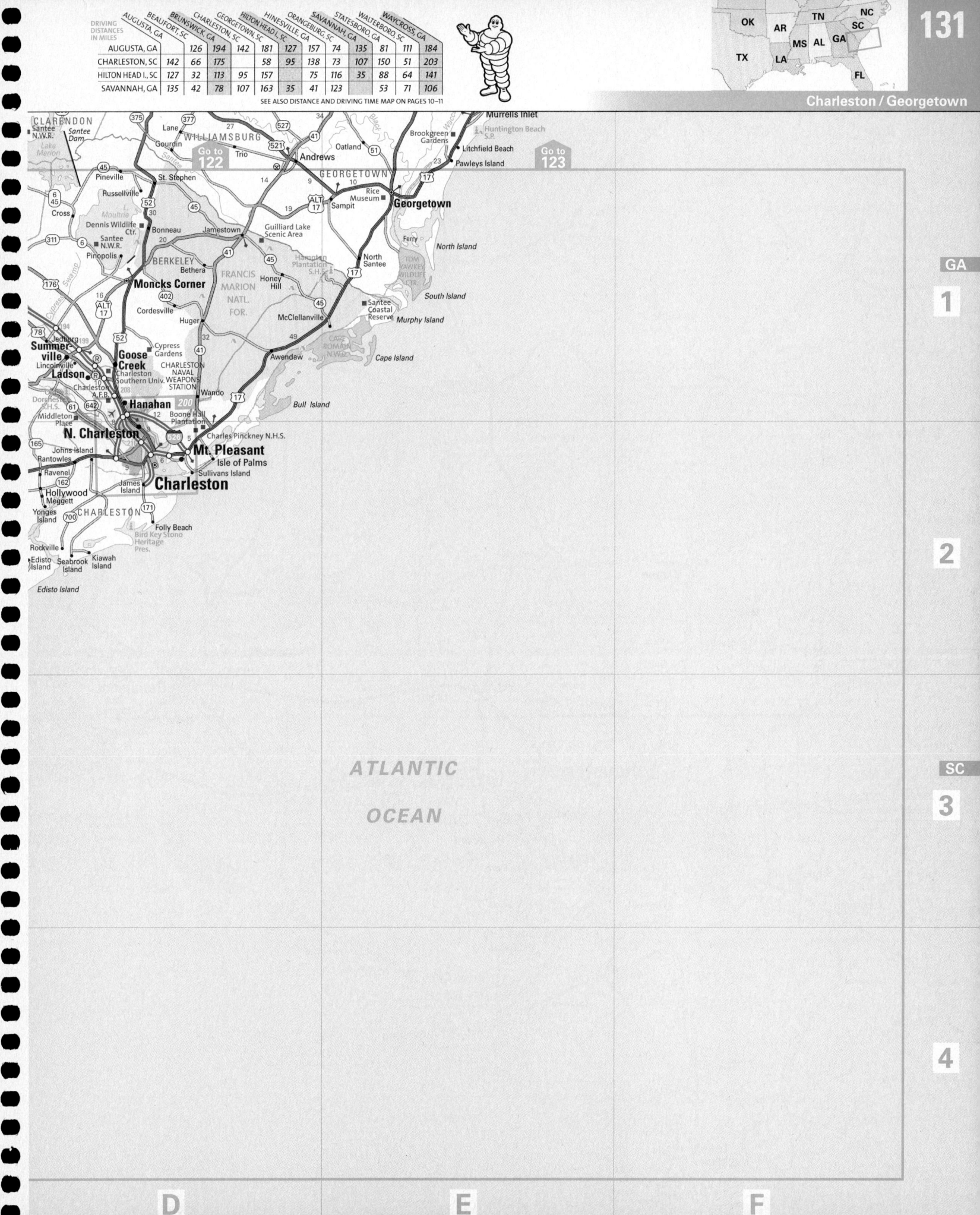

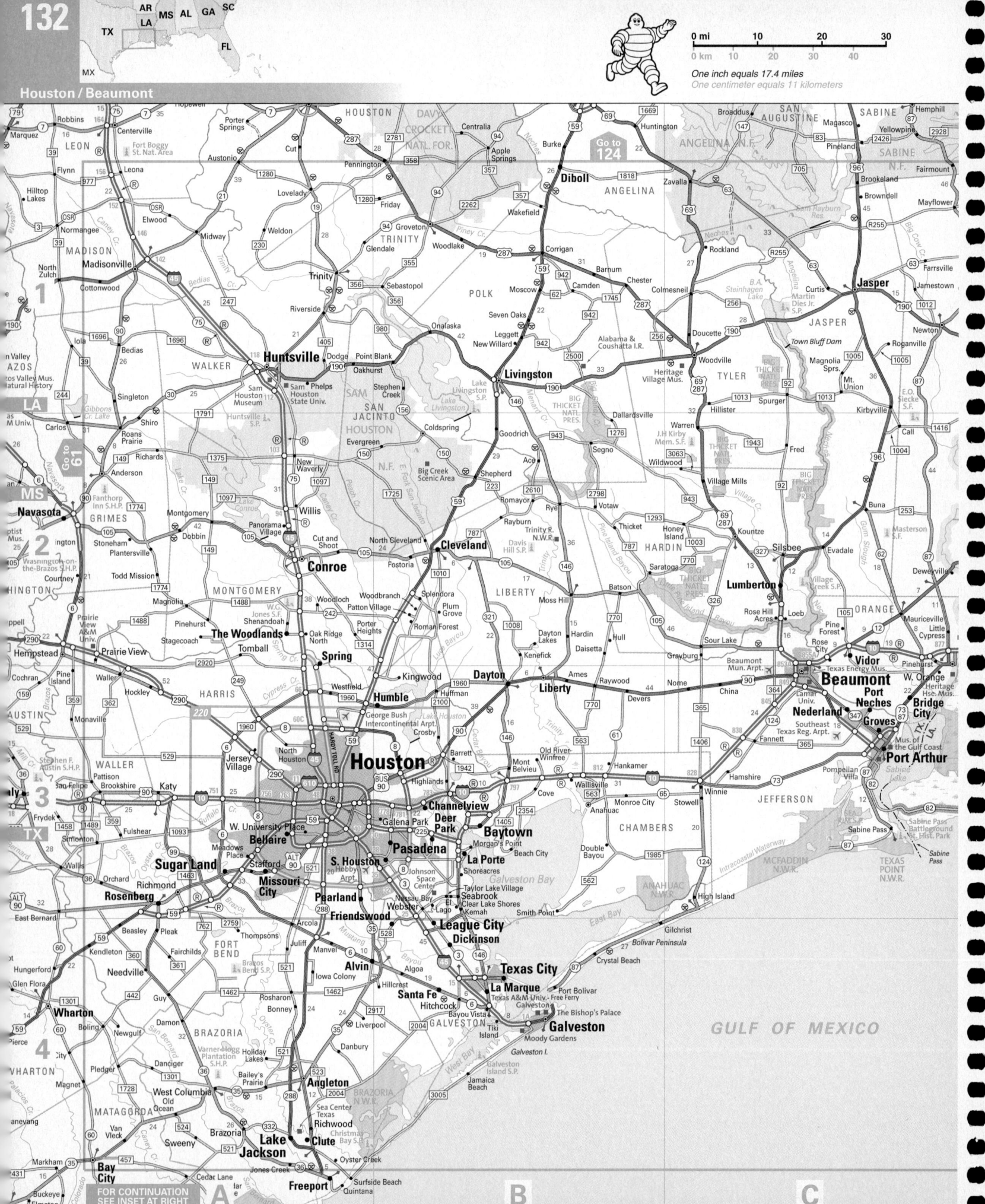

One inch equals 17.4 miles
One centimeter equals 11 kilometers

GULF OF MEXICO

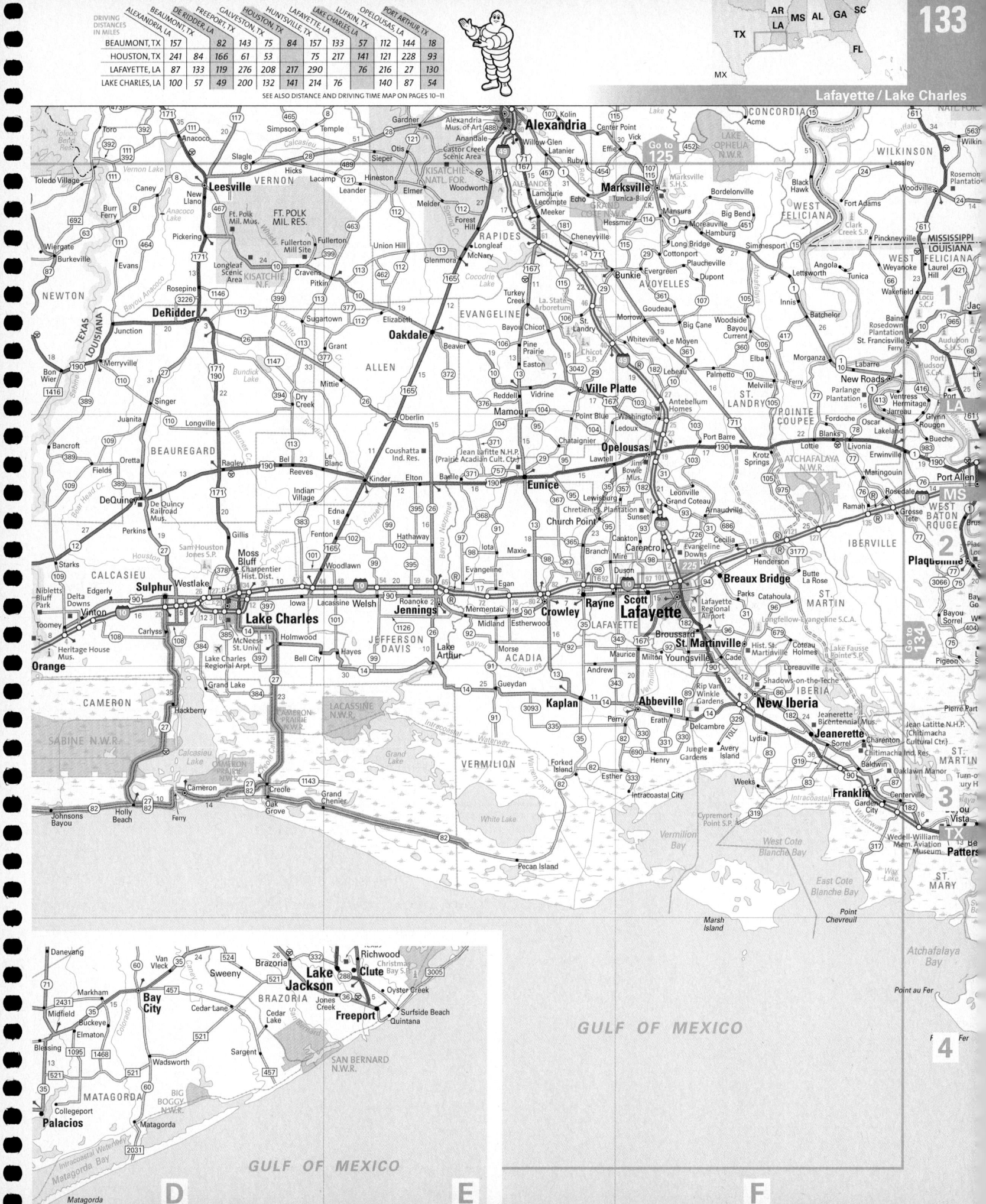

DRIVING DISTANCES IN MILES

	ALEXANDRIA, LA	BEAUMONT, TX	DE RIDDER, LA	FREEPORT, TX	GALVESTON, TX	HOUSTON, TX	HUNTSVILLE, TX	LAFAYETTE, LA	LAKE CHARLES, LA	LUFKIN, TX	OPELOUSAS, LA	PORT ARTHUR, TX
Beaumont, TX	157		82	143	75	84	157	133	57	112	144	18
Houston, TX	241	84	166	61	53		75	217	141	121	228	93
Lafayette, LA	87	133	119	276	208	217	290		76	216	27	130
Lake Charles, LA	100	57	49	200	132	141	214	76		140	87	54

SEE ALSO DISTANCE AND DRIVING TIME MAP ON PAGES 10–11

D E F

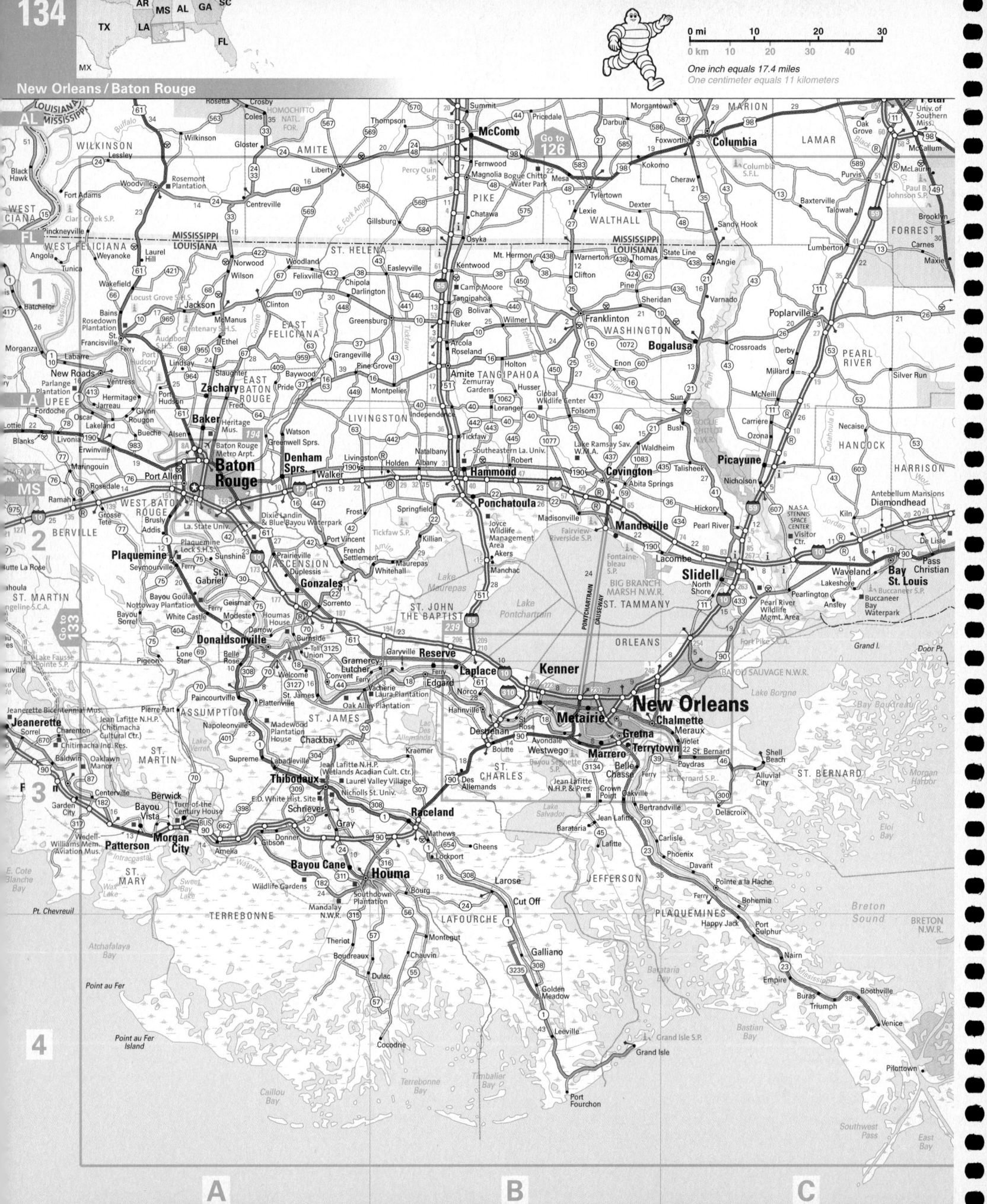

New Orleans / Baton Rouge

One inch equals 17.4 miles
One centimeter equals 11 kilometers

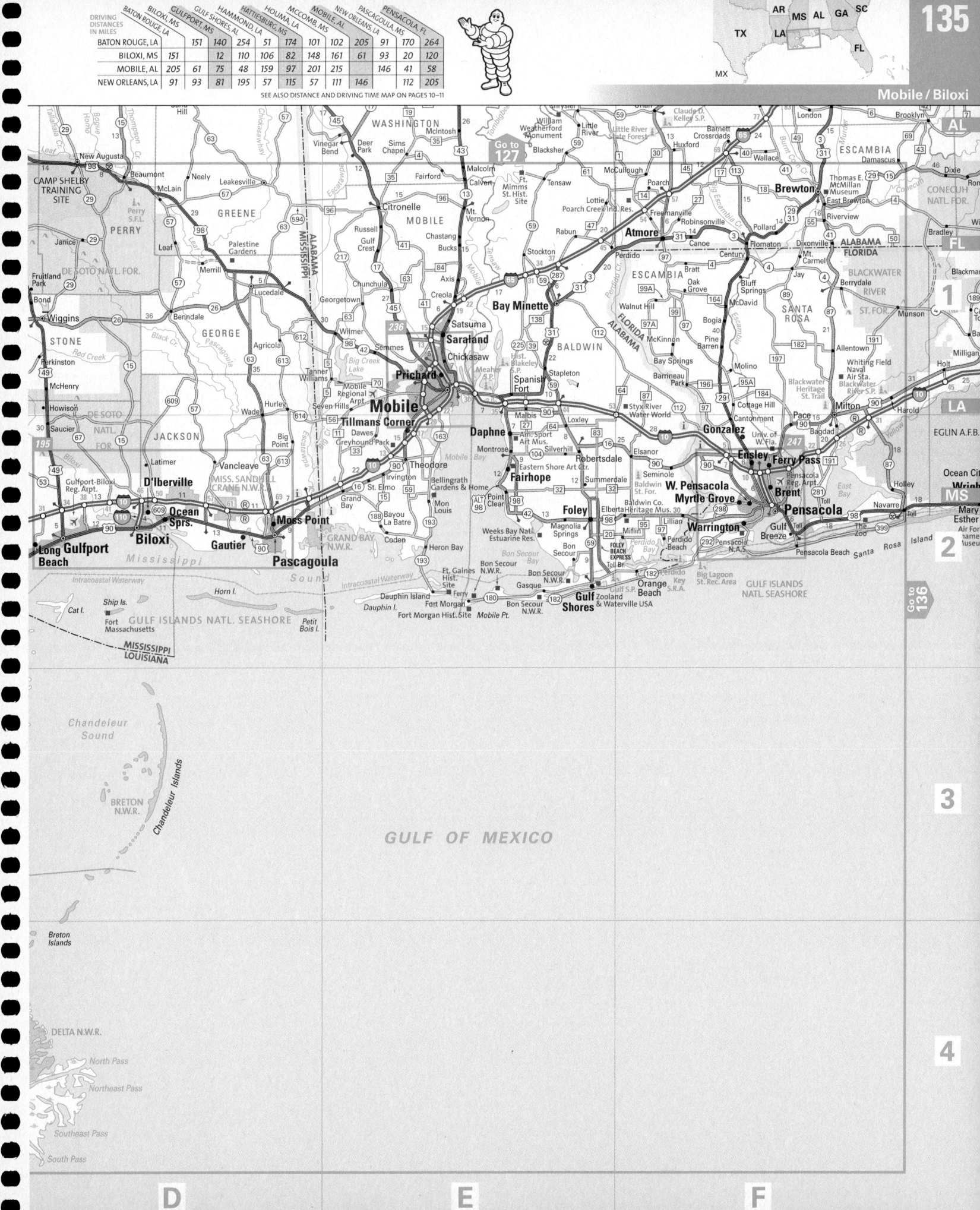

DRIVING DISTANCES IN MILES

	BATON ROUGE, LA	BILOXI, MS	GULFPORT, MS	GULF SHORES, AL	HAMMOND, LA	HATTIESBURG, MS	HOUMA, LA	McCOMB, MS	MOBILE, AL	NEW ORLEANS, LA	PASCAGOULA, MS	PENSACOLA, FL
BATON ROUGE, LA		151	140	254	51	174	101	102	205	91	170	264
BILOXI, MS	151		12	110	106	82	148	161	61	93	20	120
MOBILE, AL	205	61	75	48	159	97	201	215		146	41	58
NEW ORLEANS, LA	91	93	81	195	57	115	57	111	146		112	205

SEE ALSO DISTANCE AND DRIVING TIME MAP ON PAGES 10-11

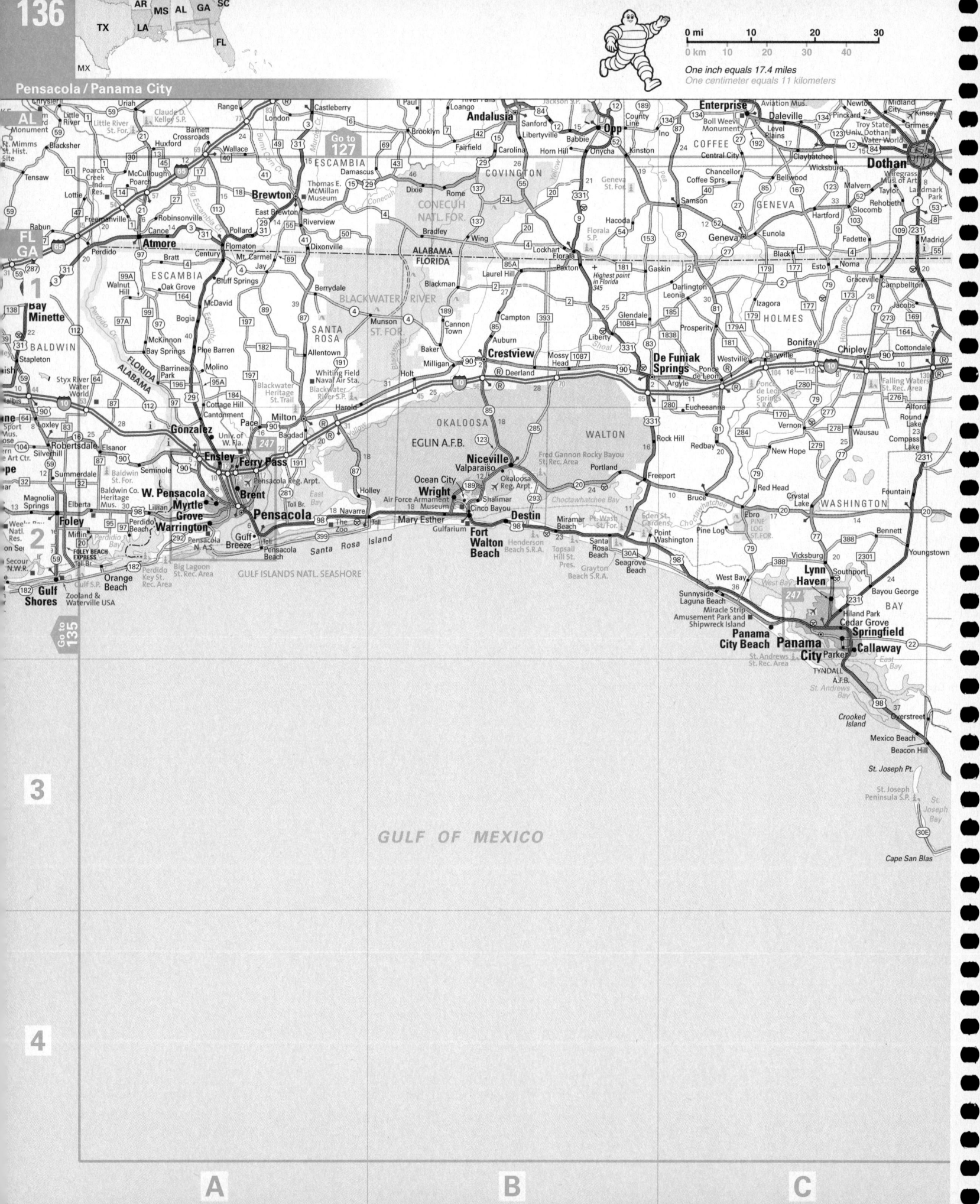

One inch equals 17.4 miles
One centimeter equals 11 kilometers

GULF OF MEXICO

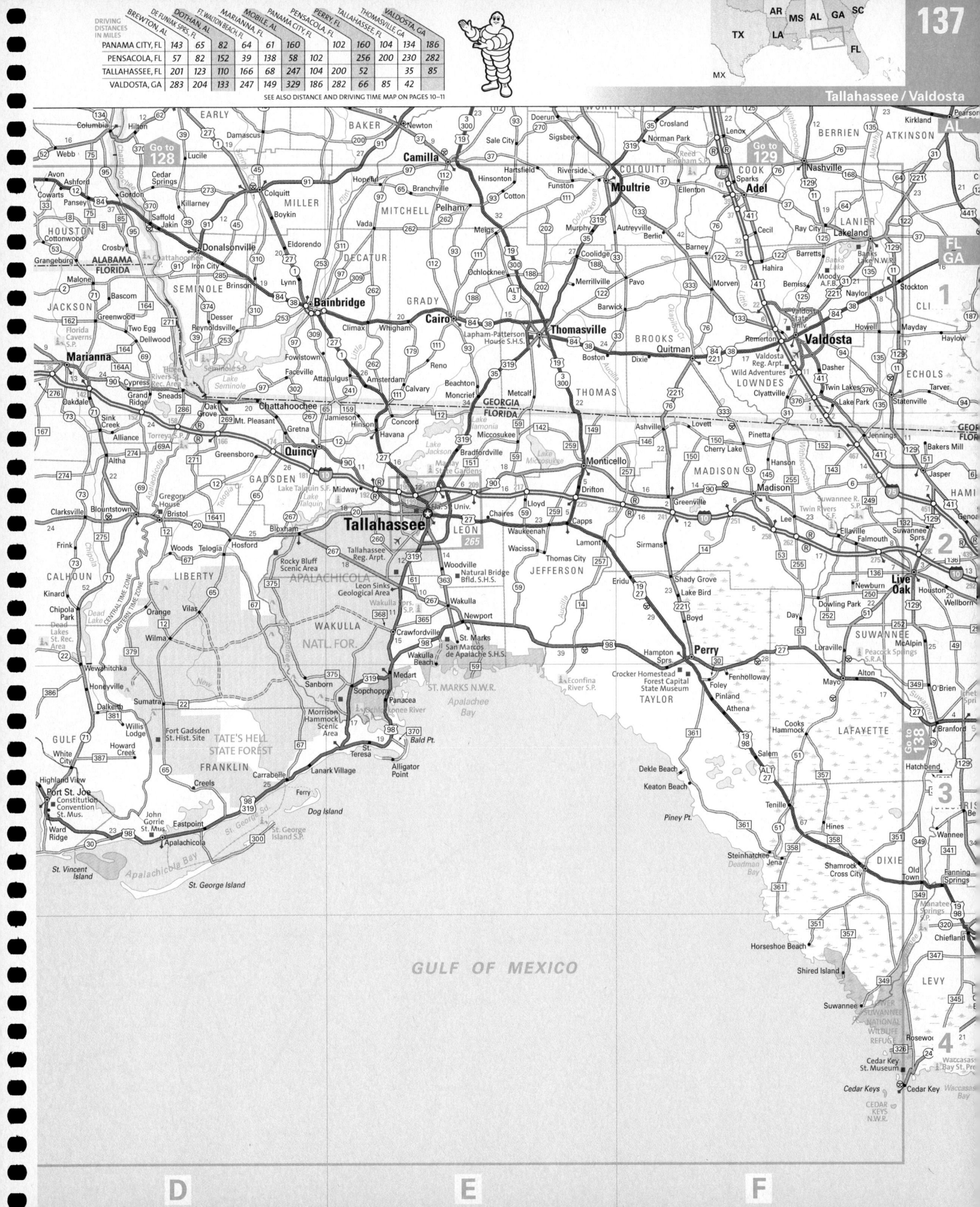

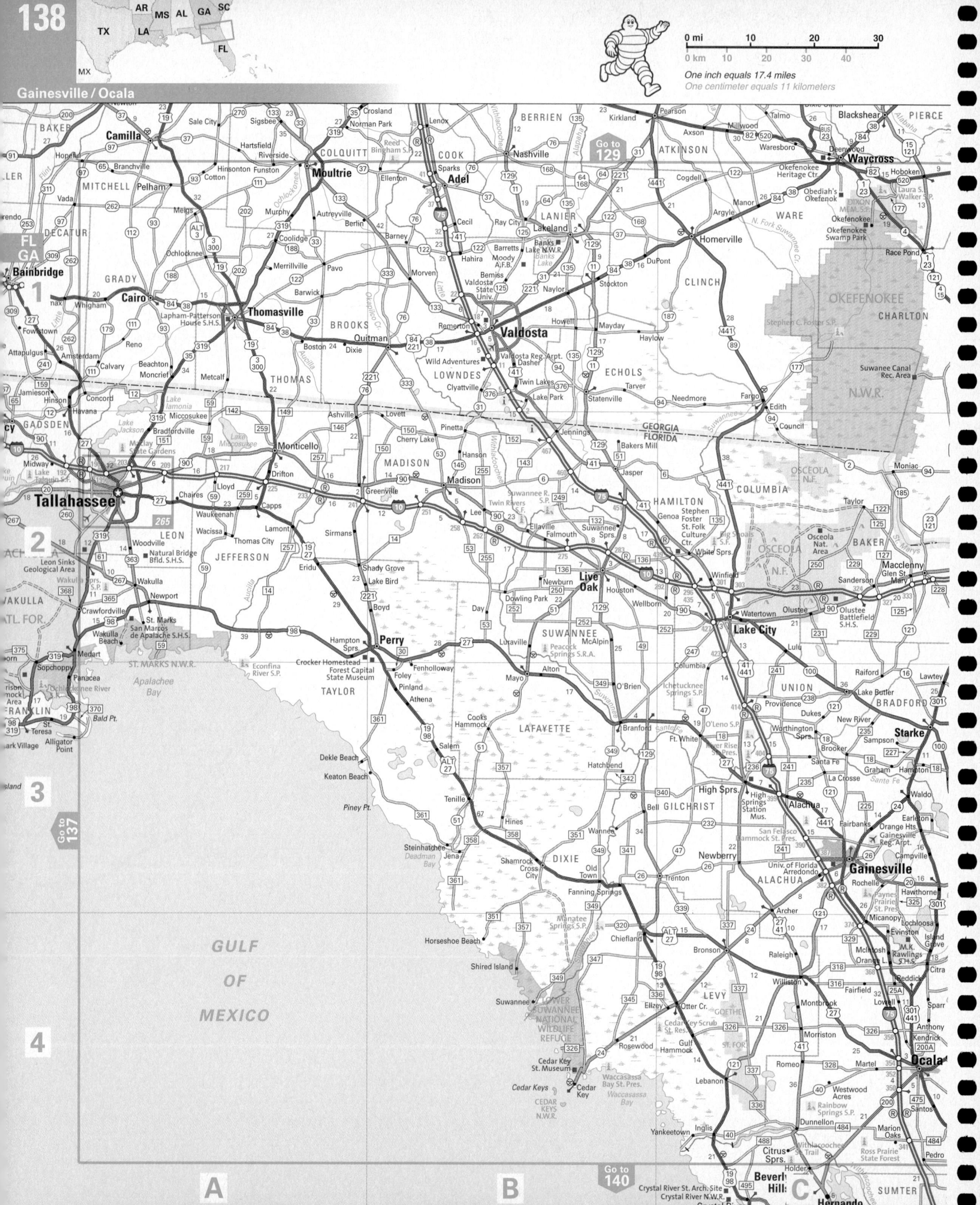

DRIVING DISTANCES IN MILES	BRUNSWICK, GA	DAYTONA BEACH, FL	GAINESVILLE, FL	JACKSONVILLE, FL	LAKE CITY, FL	OCALA, FL	PERRY, FL	ST. AUGUSTINE, FL	STARKE, FL	TALLAHASSEE, FL	VALDOSTA, GA	WAYCROSS, GA
DAYTONA BEACH, FL	160		99	91	154	77	225	53	92	258	209	173
JACKSONVILLE, FL	69	91	70		62	101	133	41	45	166	117	78
OCALA, FL	171	77	40	101		80	120	81	57	186	137	170
TALLAHASSEE, FL	235	258	152	166	109	186	52	207	145		85	146

SEE ALSO DISTANCE AND DRIVING TIME MAP ON PAGES 10–11

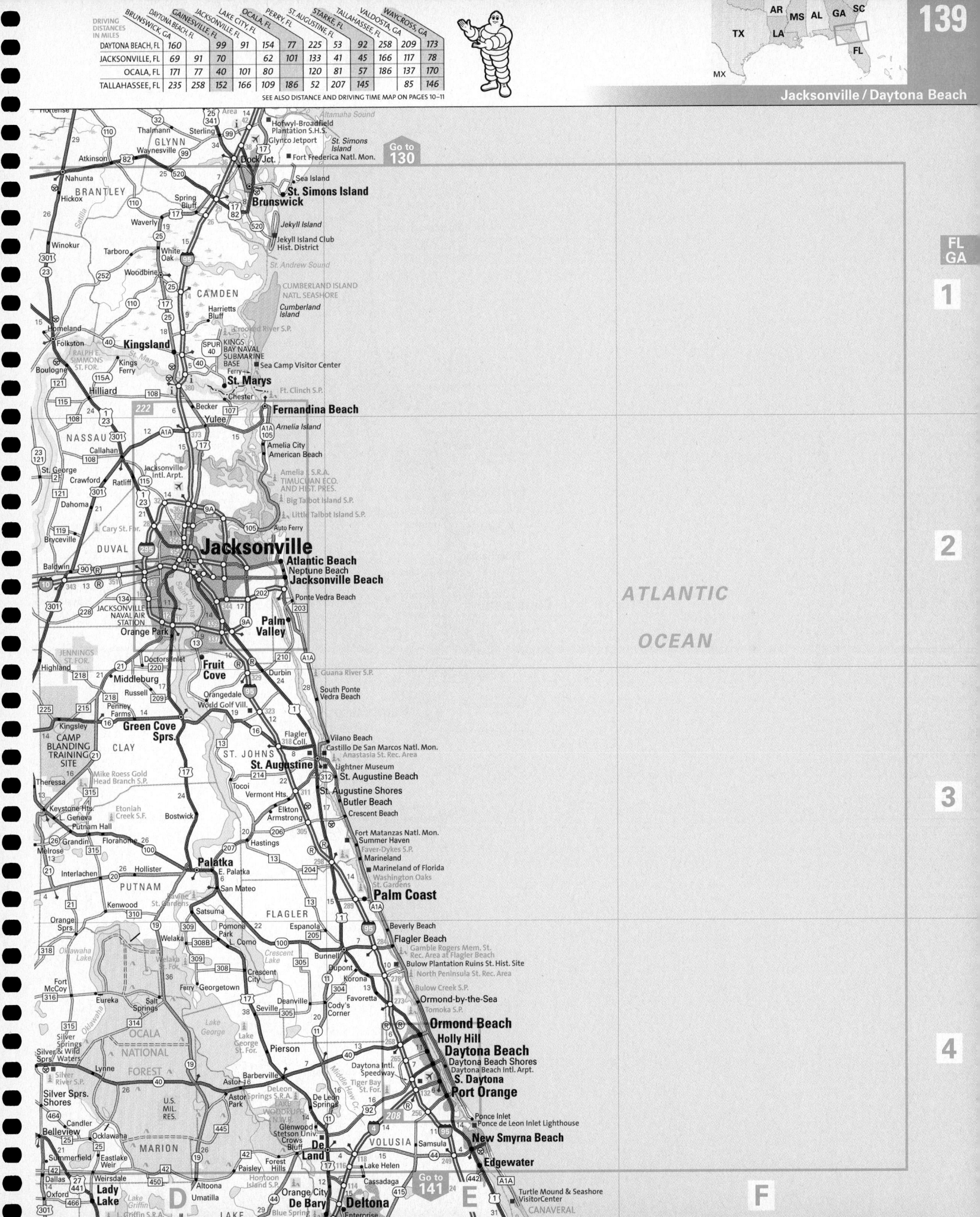

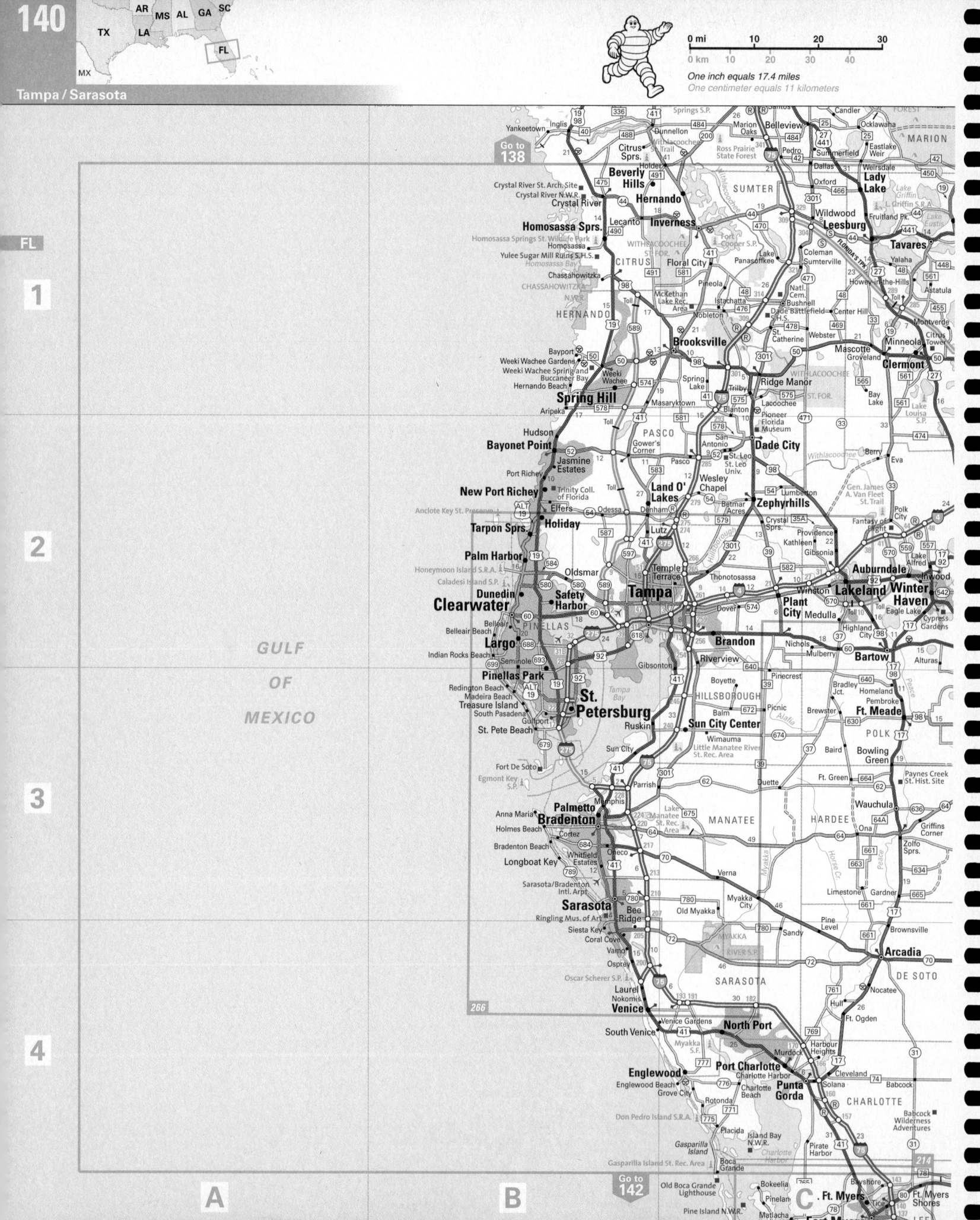

One inch equals 17.4 miles
One centimeter equals 11 kilometers

GULF

OF

MEXICO

Go to 138

Go to 142

DRIVING DISTANCES IN MILES

	FORT MYERS, FL	FORT PIERCE, FL	LAKELAND, FL	MELBOURNE, FL	OKEECHOBEE, FL	ORLANDO, FL	PUNTA GORDA, FL	ST. PETERSBURG, FL	SARASOTA, FL	TAMPA, FL	TITUSVILLE, FL	W PALM BEACH, FL
FORT PIERCE, FL	126	122	57	36	120	127	197	150	172	95	57	
ORLANDO, FL	155	120	56	72	108		131	107	130	82	40	169
SARASOTA, FL	74	150	85	190	114	130	50	35		60	170	184
TAMPA, FL	123	172	37	142	162	82	99	25	60		121	223

SEE ALSO DISTANCE AND DRIVING TIME MAP ON PAGES 10–11

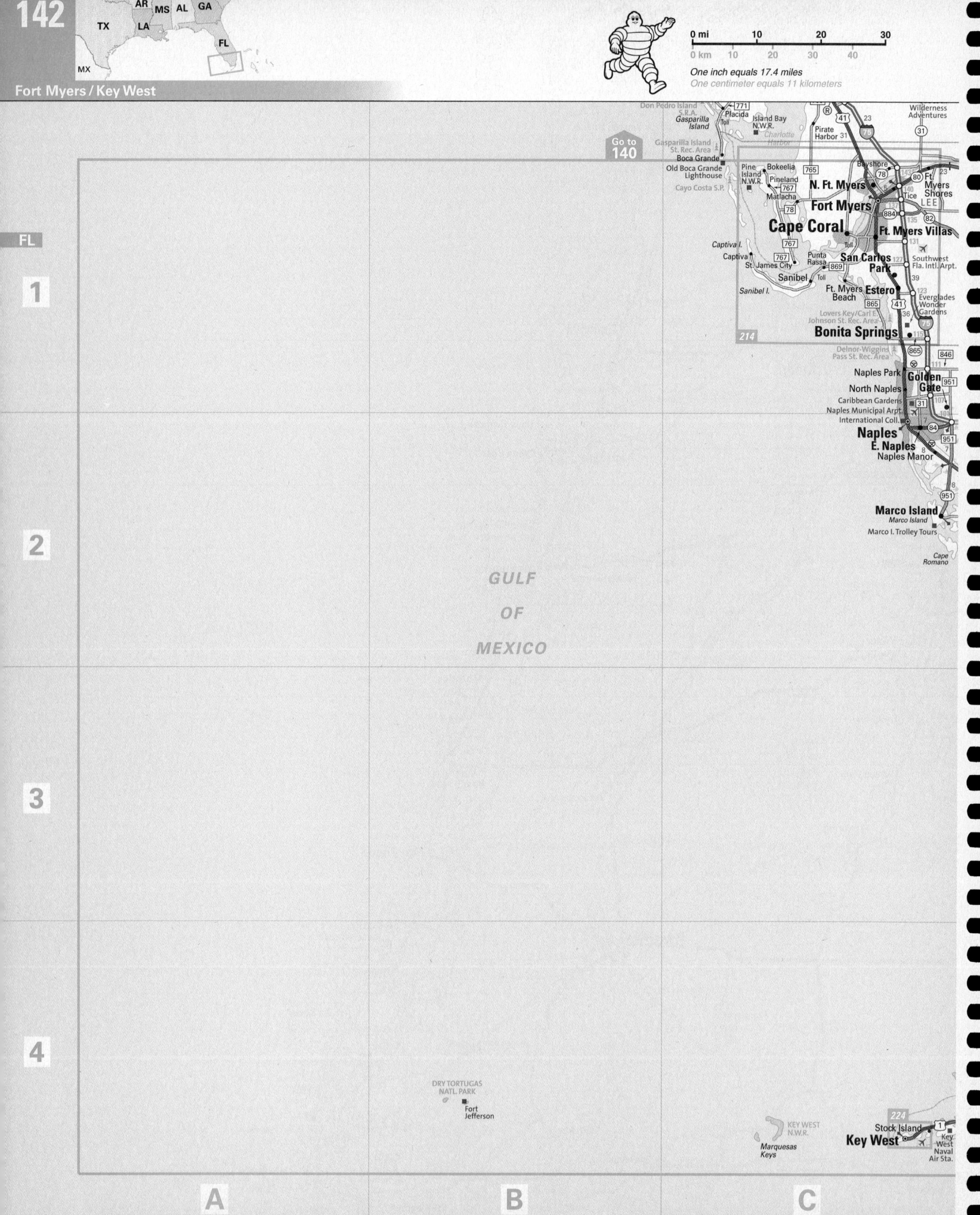

0 mi · 10 · 20 · 30
0 km 10 20 30 40

One inch equals 17.4 miles
One centimeter equals 11 kilometers

Go to 140

Don Pedro Island S.R.A.
Gasparilla Island
Placida Toll
771
Island Bay N.W.R.
Charlotte Harbor
Pirate Harbor 31
Wilderness Adventures
41
23
75
31
Gasparilla Island St. Rec. Area
Boca Grande
Old Boca Grande Lighthouse
Cayo Costa S.P.
Bayshore
Bokeelia
Pine Island N.W.R.
Pineland
765
78
Ft. Myers Shores
80
23
N. Ft. Myers
Rice
140
LEE
Matlacha
78
Fort Myers
884
157
135
82
Captiva I.
Cape Coral
767
Ft. Myers Villas
131
Captiva
767
Punta Rassa
San Carlos Park
127
Southwest Fla. Intl. Arpt.
St. James City
869
Sanibel Toll
39
Sanibel I.
Sanibel
Ft. Myers Beach
Estero
41
123
865
Everglades Wonder Gardens
75
36
Lovers Key/Carl E. Johnson St. Rec. Area
214
Bonita Springs
115
Delnor-Wiggins Pass St. Rec. Area
865
846
111
Naples Park
Golden Gate
951
North Naples
Caribbean Gardens
31
107
Naples Municipal Arpt.
103
International Coll.
84
Naples
951
E. Naples
8
Naples Manor
7
8
951
Marco Island
Marco Island
8
Marco I. Trolley Tours
Cape Romano

GULF OF MEXICO

DRY TORTUGAS NATL. PARK
Fort Jefferson

224
KEY WEST N.W.R.
Stock Island
1
Marquesas Keys
Key West
Key West Naval Air Sta.

FL

1

2

3

4

A   B   C

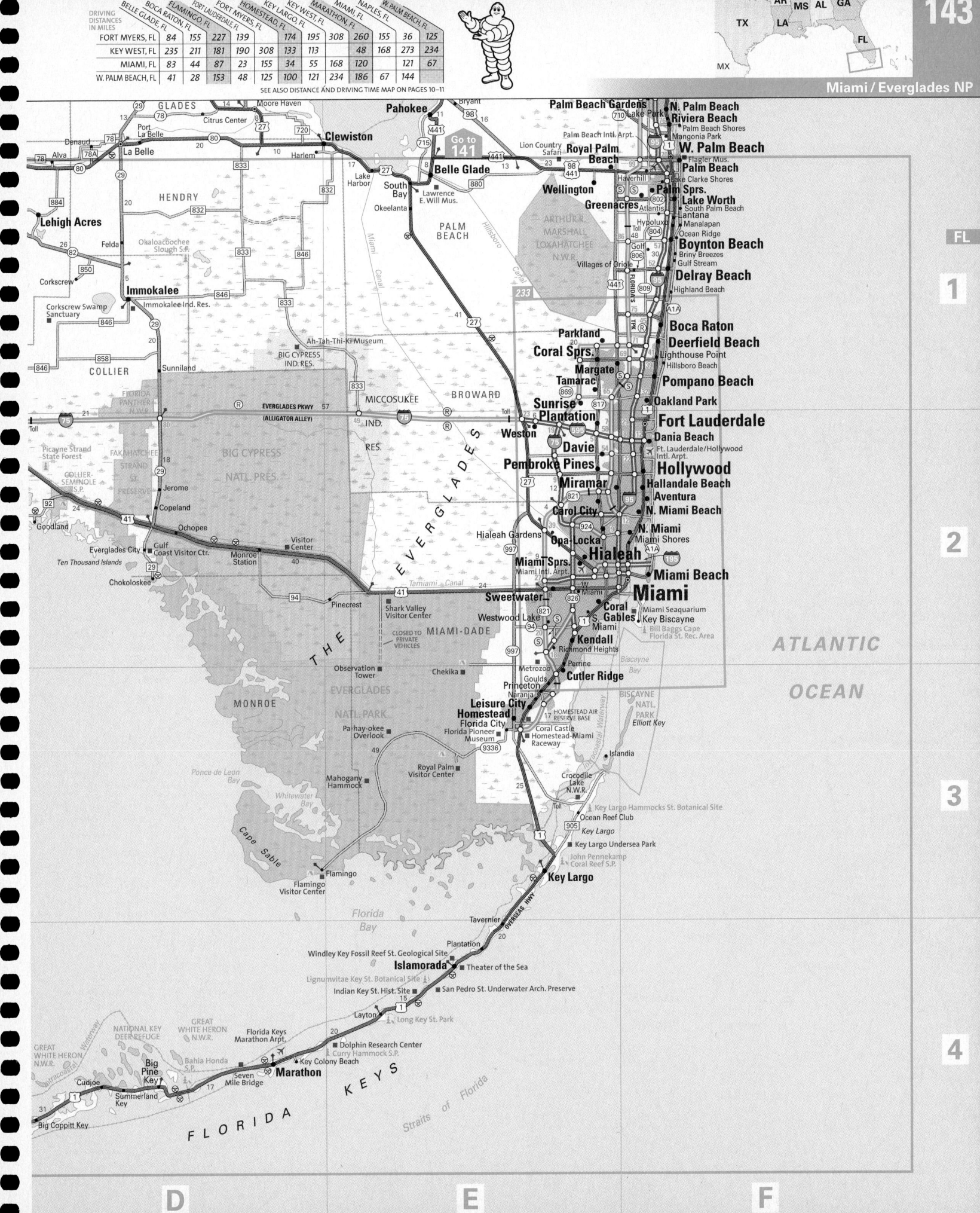

One inch equals 9.3 miles
One centimeter equals 5.9 kilometers

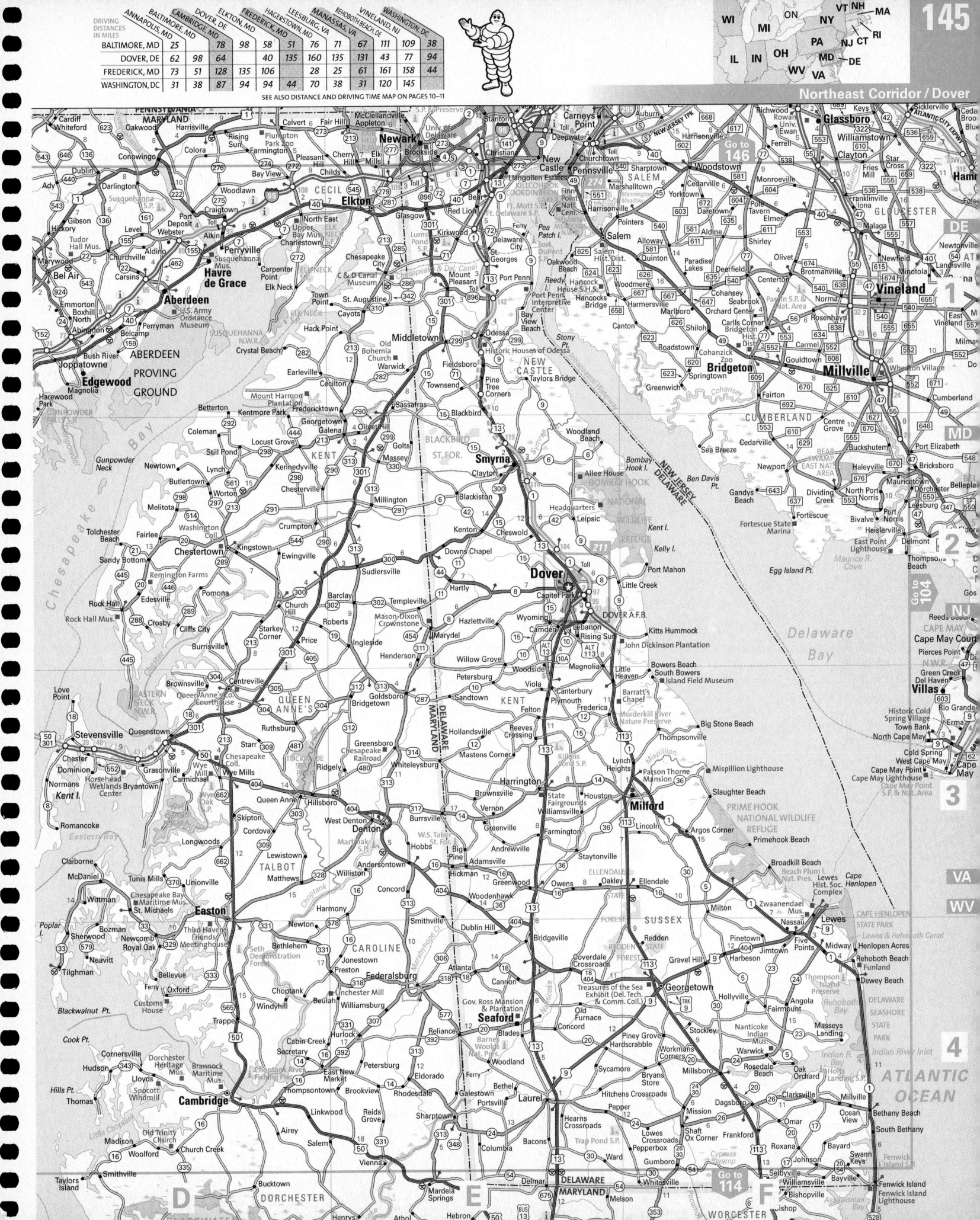

DRIVING DISTANCES IN MILES	ANNAPOLIS, MD	BALTIMORE, MD	CAMBRIDGE, MD	DOVER, DE	ELKTON, MD	FREDERICK, MD	HAGERSTOWN, MD	LEESBURG, VA	MANASSAS, VA	REHOBOTH BEACH, DE	VINELAND, NJ	WASHINGTON, DC
BALTIMORE, MD	25		78	98	58	51	76	71	67	111	109	38
DOVER, DE	62	98	64		40	135	160	135	131	43	77	94
FREDERICK, MD	73	51	128	135	106		28	25	61	161	158	44
WASHINGTON, DC	31	38	87	94	94	44	70	38	31	120	145	

SEE ALSO DISTANCE AND DRIVING TIME MAP ON PAGES 10–11

WI MI ON NY VT NH MA
IL IN OH PA NJ CT RI
WV VA MD DE

0 mi 5 10 15
0 km 5 10 15 20

One inch equals 9.3 miles
One centimeter equals 5.9 kilometers

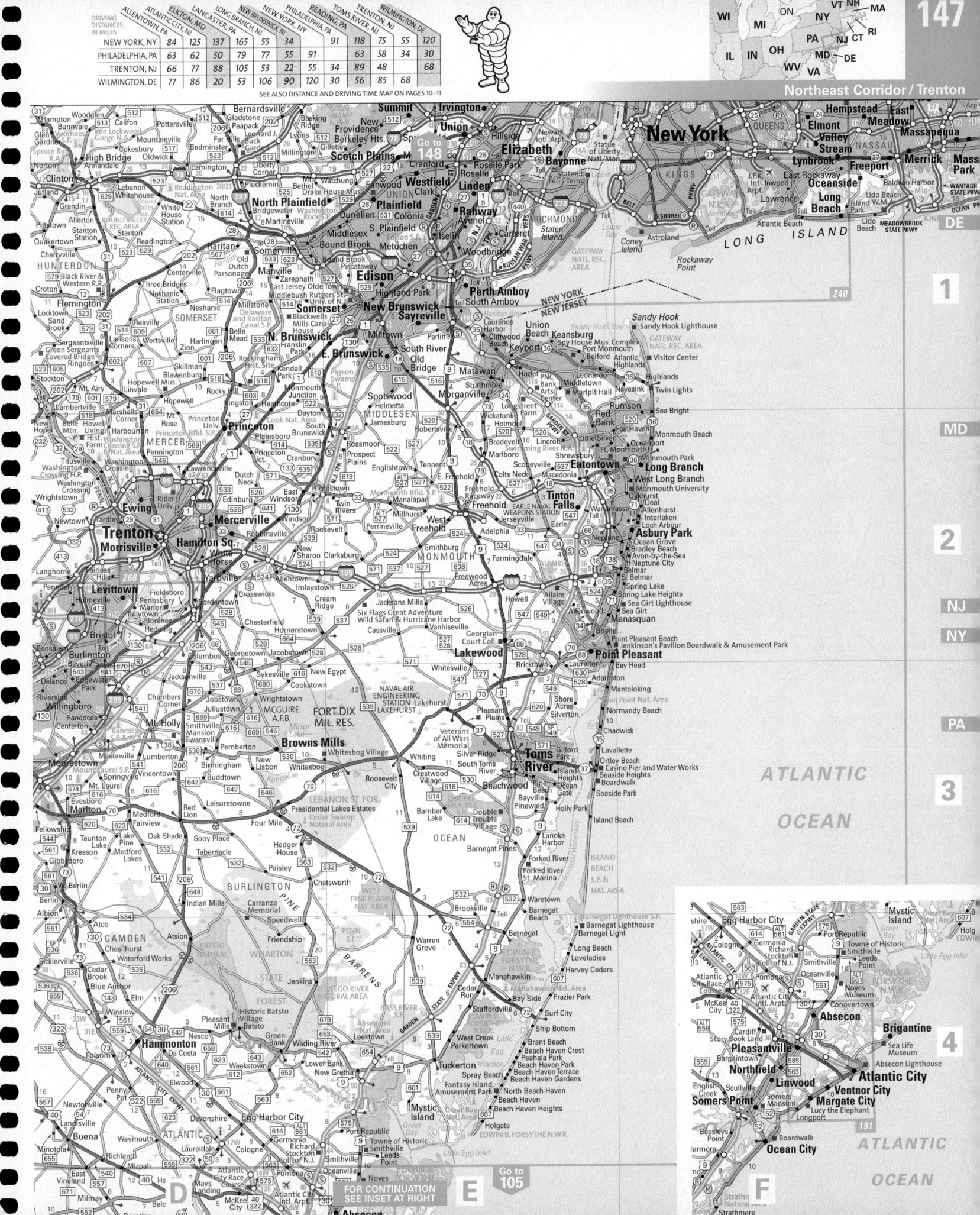

DRIVING DISTANCES IN MILES	ALLENTOWN, PA	ATLANTIC CITY, NJ	ELKTON, MD	LANCASTER, PA	LONG BRANCH, NJ	NEW BRUNSWICK, NJ	NEW YORK, NY	PHILADELPHIA, PA	READING, PA	TOMS RIVER, NJ	TRENTON, NJ	WILMINGTON, DE
NEW YORK, NY	84	125	137	165	55	34		91	118	75	55	120
PHILADELPHIA, PA	63	62	50	79	77	55	91		63	58	34	30
TRENTON, NJ	66	77	88	105	53	22	55	34	89	48		68
WILMINGTON, DE	77	86	20	53	106	90	120	30	56	85	68	

SEE ALSO DISTANCE AND DRIVING TIME MAP ON PAGES 10-11

FOR CONTINUATION
SEE INSET AT RIGHT

Go to 148

Go to 105

One inch equals 9.3 miles
One centimeter equals 5.9 kilometers

0 mi   5   10   15
0 km   5   10   15   20

SEE ALSO DISTANCE AND DRIVING TIME MAP ON PAGES 10–11

One inch equals 9.3 miles
One centimeter equals 5.9 kilometers

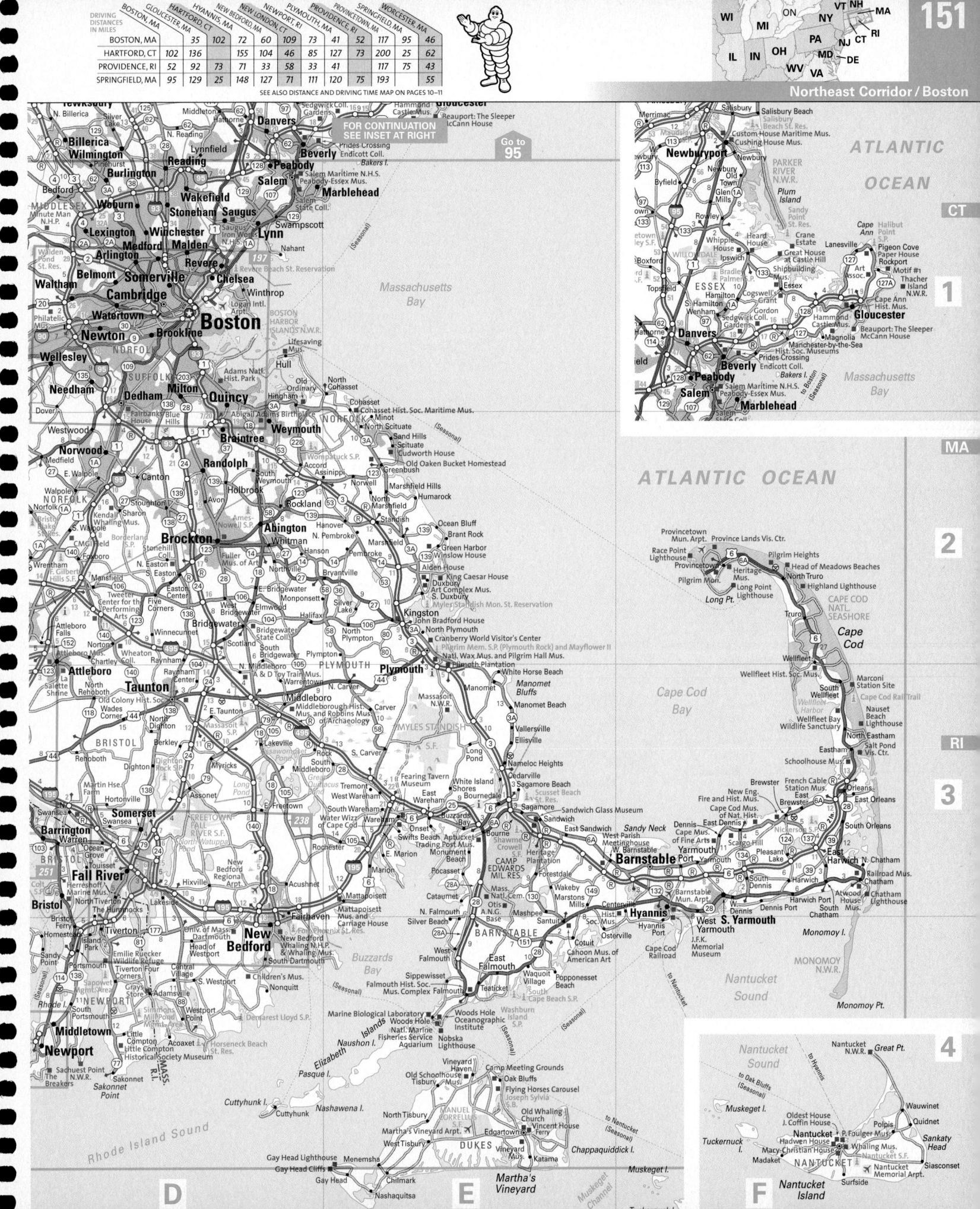

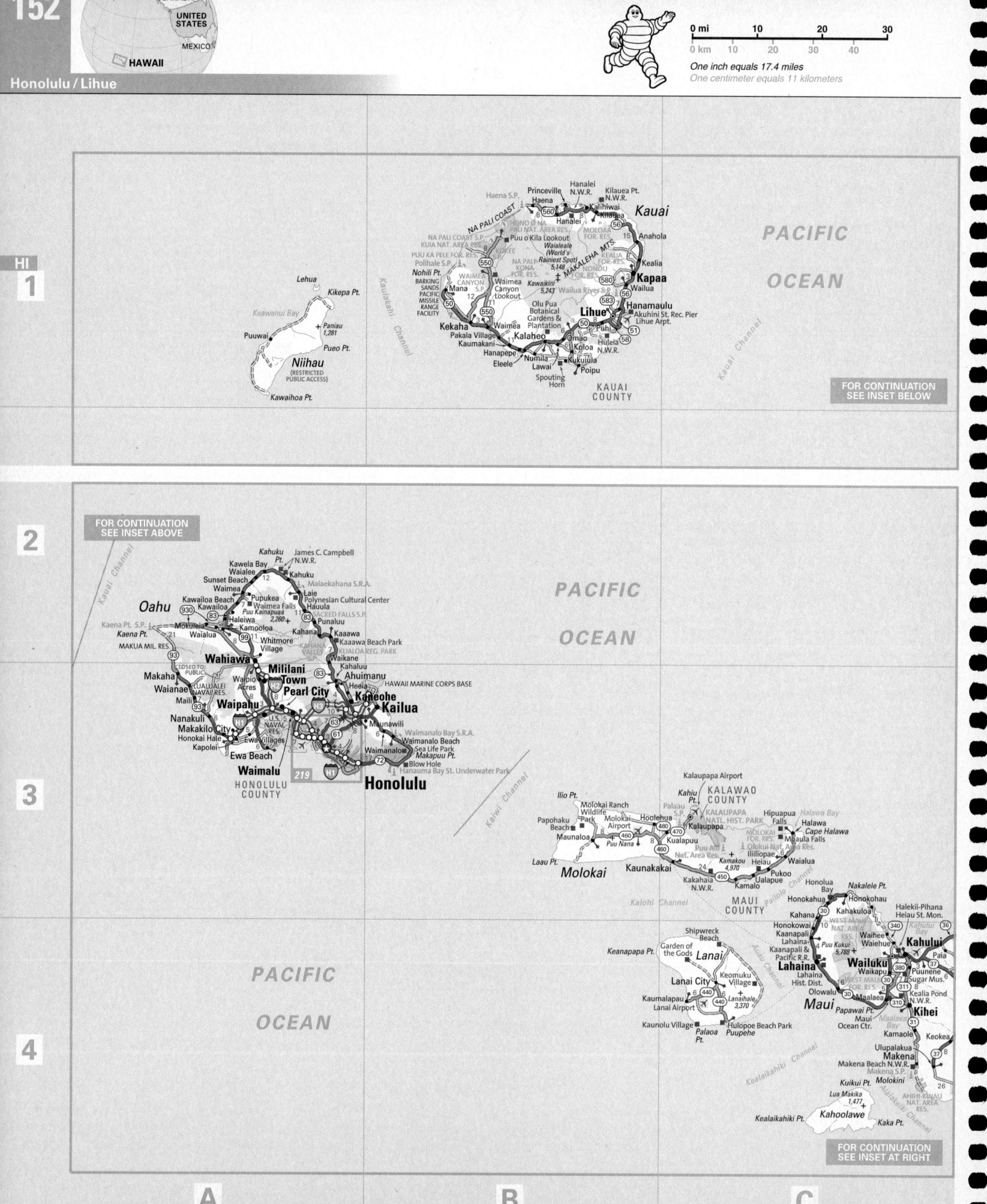

0 mi 10 20 30
0 km 10 20 30 40
One inch equals 17.4 miles
One centimeter equals 11 kilometers

HI 1

PACIFIC OCEAN

Kauai

Princeville · Hanalei · Kilauea Pt. N.W.R.
Haena S.P. · Haena · Kalihiwai · Kilauea
Kilauea N.W.R.
NA PALI COAST
HONO O NA PALI NAT. AREA RES.
Anahola
NA PALI COAST S.P.
KUIA NAT. AREA RES.
Puu o Kila Lookout
MOLOAA FOR. RES.
15
Waialeale (World's Rainiest Spot) 5,148
KOKEE
KEALIA FOR. RES.
PUU KA PELE FOR. RES.
Kealia
MAKALEHA MTS.
Polihale S.P.
550
NA PALI KONA FOR. RES.
Nohili Pt.
NONOU FOR. RES.
Kapaa
BARKING SANDS
Waimea Canyon S.P.
580
Wailua
Mana
Kawaikini 5,243
Waimea Canyon Lookout
PACIFIC MISSILE RANGE FACILITY
Waialua River S.P.
583
50
550
Olu Pua Botanical Gardens & Plantation
Lihue
Hanamaulu
Akuhini St. Rec. Pier
Lihue Arpt.
Kekaha
3
Waimea
50
Puhi
51
Pakala Village
Kalaheo
Omao
Koloa
Kaumakani
11
Hulea
58
Hanapepe · Numila · Lawai · HULEA N.W.R.
Eleele · Spouting Horn · Poipu · Kukuiula
KAUAI COUNTY

Lehua
Kikepa Pt.
Keawanui Bay
Paniau 1,281
Puuwai
Pueo Pt.
Niihau (RESTRICTED PUBLIC ACCESS)
Kawaihoa Pt.

Kaulakahi Channel

Kauai Channel

FOR CONTINUATION SEE INSET BELOW

2

FOR CONTINUATION SEE INSET ABOVE

PACIFIC OCEAN

Kauai Channel

Oahu

Kahuku Pt.
James C. Campbell N.W.R.
Kawela Bay
Waialee
Kahuku
Sunset Beach
12
Waimea
Malaekahana S.R.A.
Kawailoa Beach
Pupukea
Laie
Polynesian Cultural Center
Kawailoa
Waimea Falls
Haleiwa
Puu Kainapuaa 2,260
83
Hauula
SACRED FALLS S.P.
930
Mokuleia
Punaluu
Kaena Pt. S.P.
Kamooloa
99
Kahana
Kaaawa
Kaena Pt.
21
Waialua
11
Kaaawa Beach Park
MAKUA MIL. RES.
Whitmore Village
KUALOA REG. PARK
Wahiawa
Waikane
93
Waipio Acres
Kahaluu
CLOSED TO PUBLIC
Mililani Town
83
Ahimanu
Makaha
Pearl City
Heeia
Makua
Waianae
KUAUALEI NAVAL RES.
H2
Kaneohe
Kailua
Maili
Waipahu
HAWAII MARINE CORPS BASE
93
H3
63
Nanakuli
H1
U.S. NAVAL RES.
Maunawili
Makakilo City
Honokai Hale
Ewa Villages
61
Waimanalo Bay S.R.A.
Kapolei
Ewa Beach
Waimanalo Beach
Sea Life Park
Waimanalo
Makapuu Pt.
Waimalu
219
H1
72
Blow Hole
HONOLULU COUNTY
Hanauma Bay St. Underwater Park
Honolulu

3

Kaiwi Channel

Kalaupapa Airport

KALAWAO COUNTY

Ilio Pt.
Molokai Ranch Wildlife Park
Kahiu Pt.
Papohaku Beach
Molokai Airport
Palaau
Hoolehua
KALAUPAPA NATL. HIST. PARK
Hipuapua Falls
Halawa Bay
Maunaloa
8
460
470
Kalaupapa
Halawa
Cape Halawa
Kualapuu
480
MOLOKAI FOR. RES.
Maaula Falls
Puu Nana
460
Nat. Area Res.
Iliiliopae
Puu Ata
Waialua
Laau Pt.
Kamakou 4,970
Heiau
6
Molokai
Kaunakakai
24
Pukoo
Honolua Bay
Ualapue
Nakalele Pt.
Kakahaia N.W.R.
Kamalo
Honokohau
450
MAUI COUNTY
Honokahua
Halekii-Pihana Heiau St. Mon.
Kalohi Channel
Kahakuloa
30
Kahana
WEST MAUI NAT. AREA RES.
Waihee
340
Kahului
36
Kaanapali
Shipwreck Beach
Honokowai
10
Kahului Bay
Keanapapa Pt.
Garden of the Gods
Kaanapali & Pacific R.R.
Puu Kukui 5,788
Waihee
Paia
Lanai
Lahaina
Wailuku
380
Lahaina Hist. Dist.
WEST MAUI FOR. RES.
Waikapu
Puunene
Sugar Mus.
Lanai City
Keomuku Village
30
Olowalu
311
Lanaihale 3,370
Maalaea
310
440
Kaumalapau
Maui
Kihei
Lanai Airport
6
Papawai Pt.
Maui Ocean Ctr.
Kealia Pond N.W.R.
Kaunolu Village
440
Maalaea Bay
Palaoa Pt.
Hulopoe Beach Park
Kamaole
Puupehe
Ulupalakua
Makena
31
Kuikui Pt.
Makena Beach N.W.R.
37
Lua Makika 1,477
Molokini
Keokea
Kealaikahiki Pt.
Kahoolawe
AHIHI-KINAU NAT. AREA RES.
Kealaikahiki Channel
Alalakeiki Channel
26
Kaka Pt.

PACIFIC OCEAN

4

FOR CONTINUATION SEE INSET AT RIGHT

A · B · C

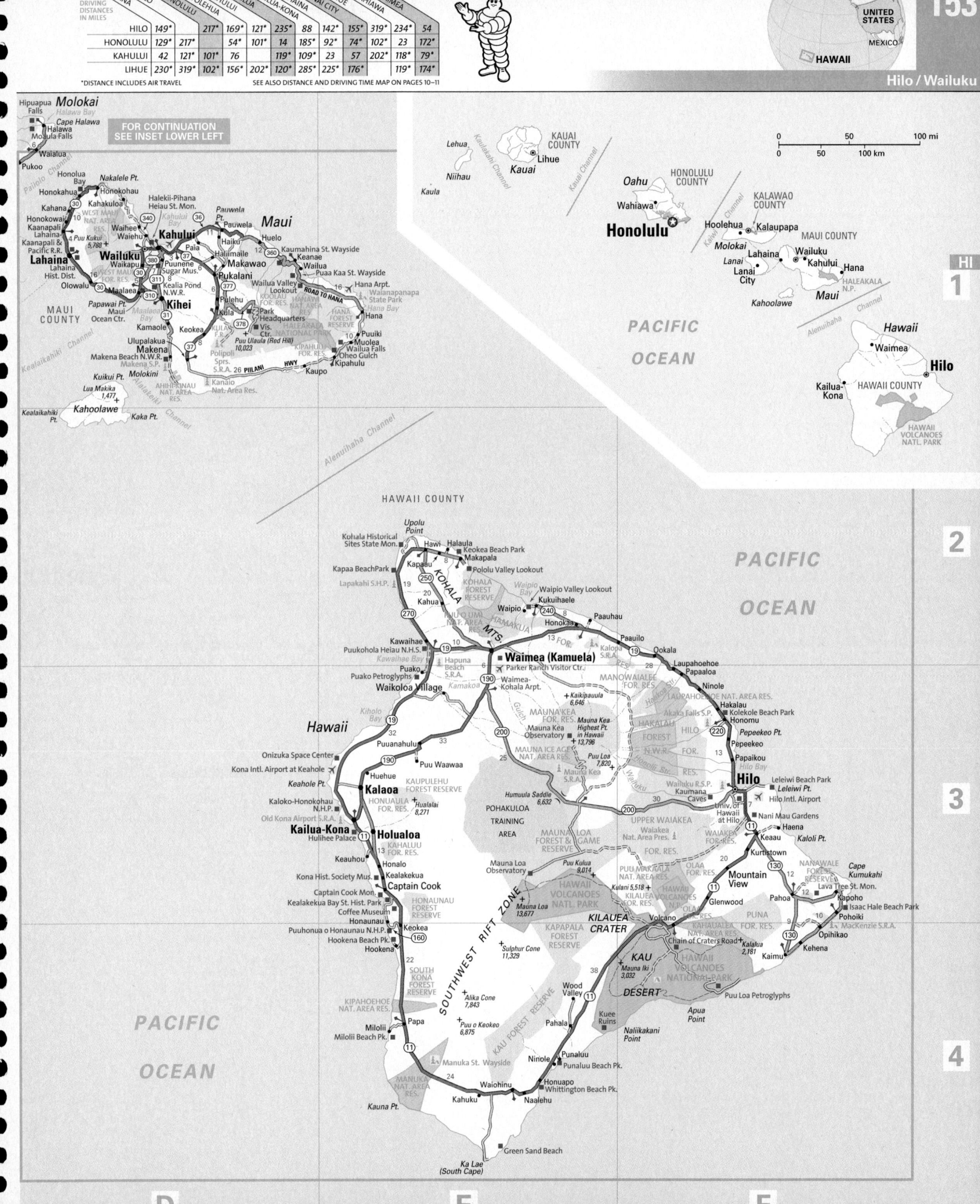

	HANA	HILO	HONOLULU	HOOLEHUA	KAHULUI	KAILUA	KAILUA-KONA	LAHAINA	LANAI CITY	LIHUE	WAHIAWA	WAIMEA
HILO	149*		217*	169*	121*	235*	88	142*	155*	319*	234*	54
HONOLULU	129*	217*		54*	101*	14	185*	92*	74*	102*	23	172*
KAHULUI	42	121*	101*		76	119*	109*	23	57	202*	118*	79*
LIHUE	230*	319*	102*	156*	202*	120*	285*	225*	176*		119*	174*

*DISTANCE INCLUDES AIR TRAVEL   SEE ALSO DISTANCE AND DRIVING TIME MAP ON PAGES 10–11

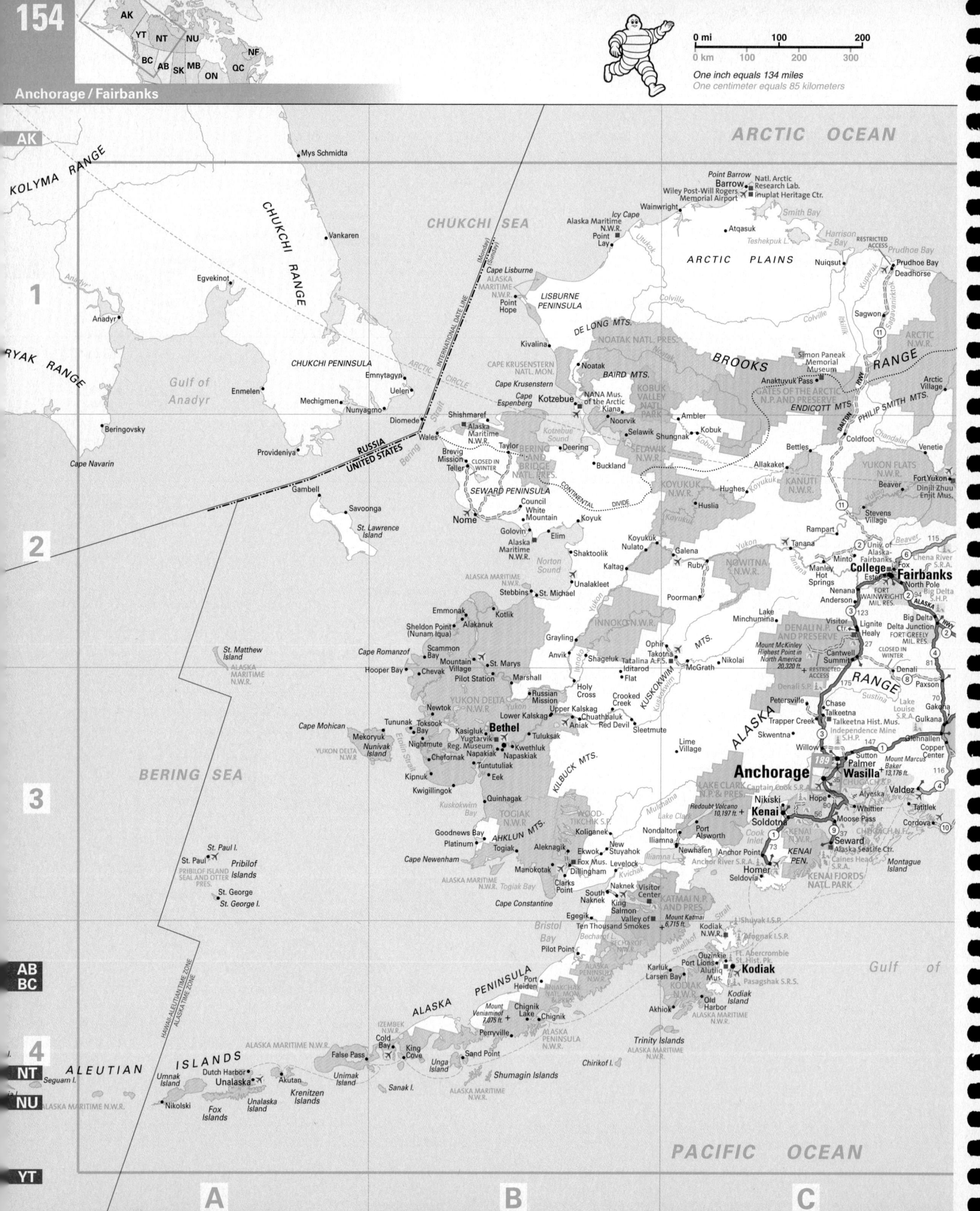

0 mi   100   200
0 km   100   200   300
One inch equals 134 miles
One centimeter equals 85 kilometers

ARCTIC OCEAN

PACIFIC OCEAN

Gulf of

KOLYMA RANGE

CHUKCHI SEA

CHUKCHI RANGE

CHUKCHI PENINSULA

RYAK RANGE

Gulf of Anadyr

BERING SEA

ALEUTIAN ISLANDS

ALASKA PENINSULA

BROOKS RANGE

ARCTIC PLAINS

ALASKA RANGE

Anchorage
Fairbanks
College
Bethel
Kenai
Kodiak
Nome
Kotzebue
Barrow

A   B   C

DRIVING DISTANCES IN MILES	ANCHORAGE AK	DAWSON CREEK, BC	DENALI NP AK	FAIRBANKS, AK	HOMER, AK	JUNEAU, AK	PRINCE GEORGE, BC	PRINCE RUPERT, BC	SKAGWAY, AK	TOK, AK	WHITEHORSE, YT	YELLOWKNIFE, NT
ANCHORAGE, AK		1516	275	378	225	841*	1679	1514	807	323	697	1844
DAWSON CREEK, BC	1516		1503	1400	1740	963*	224	625	862	1193	819	741
FAIRBANKS, AK	378	1400	103		603	726*	1564	1398	691	207	581	1729
WHITEHORSE, YT	697	819	684	581	921	211*	982	817	110	374		1147

*DISTANCE INCLUDES FERRY TRAVEL   SEE ALSO DISTANCE AND DRIVING TIME MAP ON PAGES 10–11

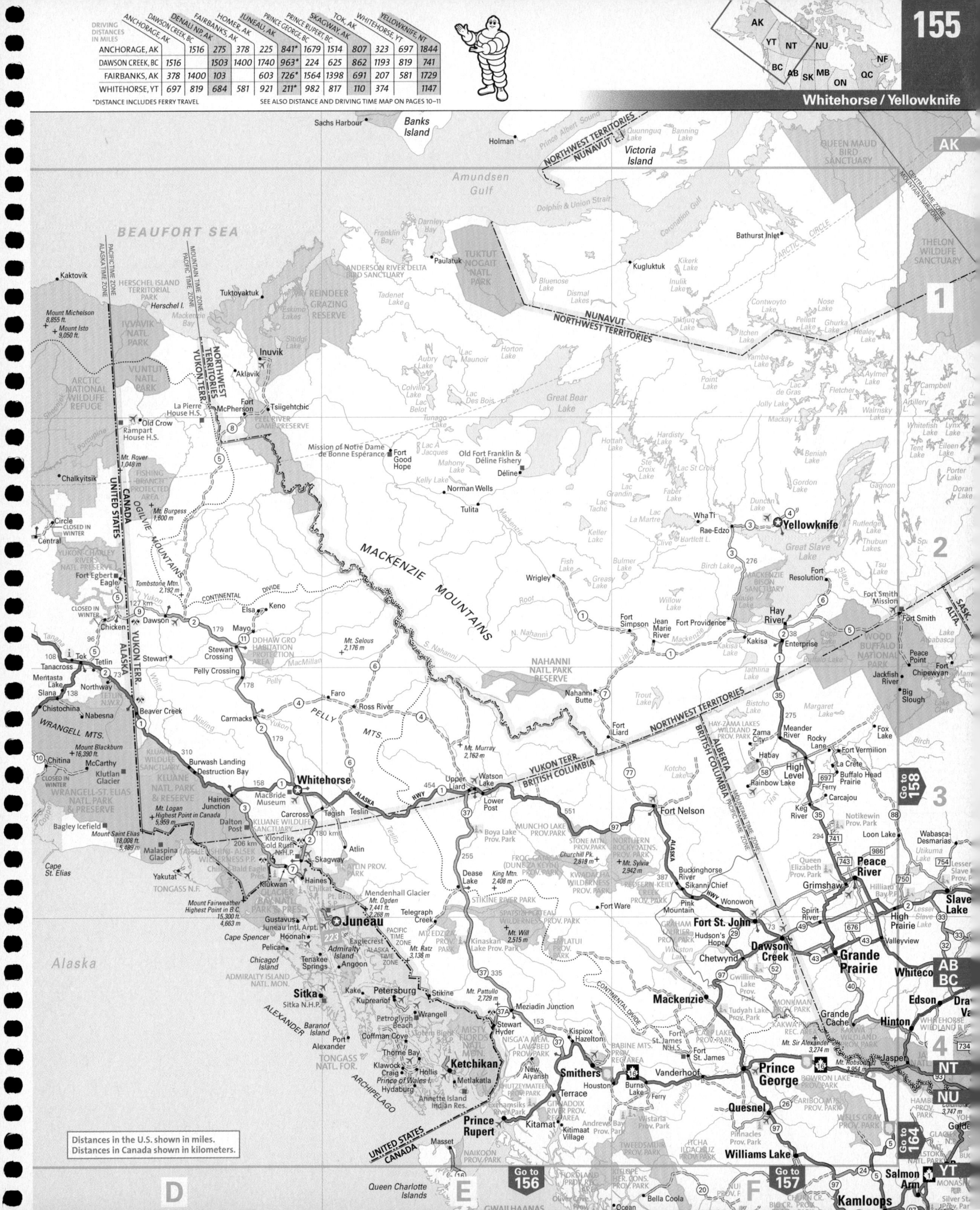

Distances in the U.S. shown in miles.
Distances in Canada shown in kilometers.

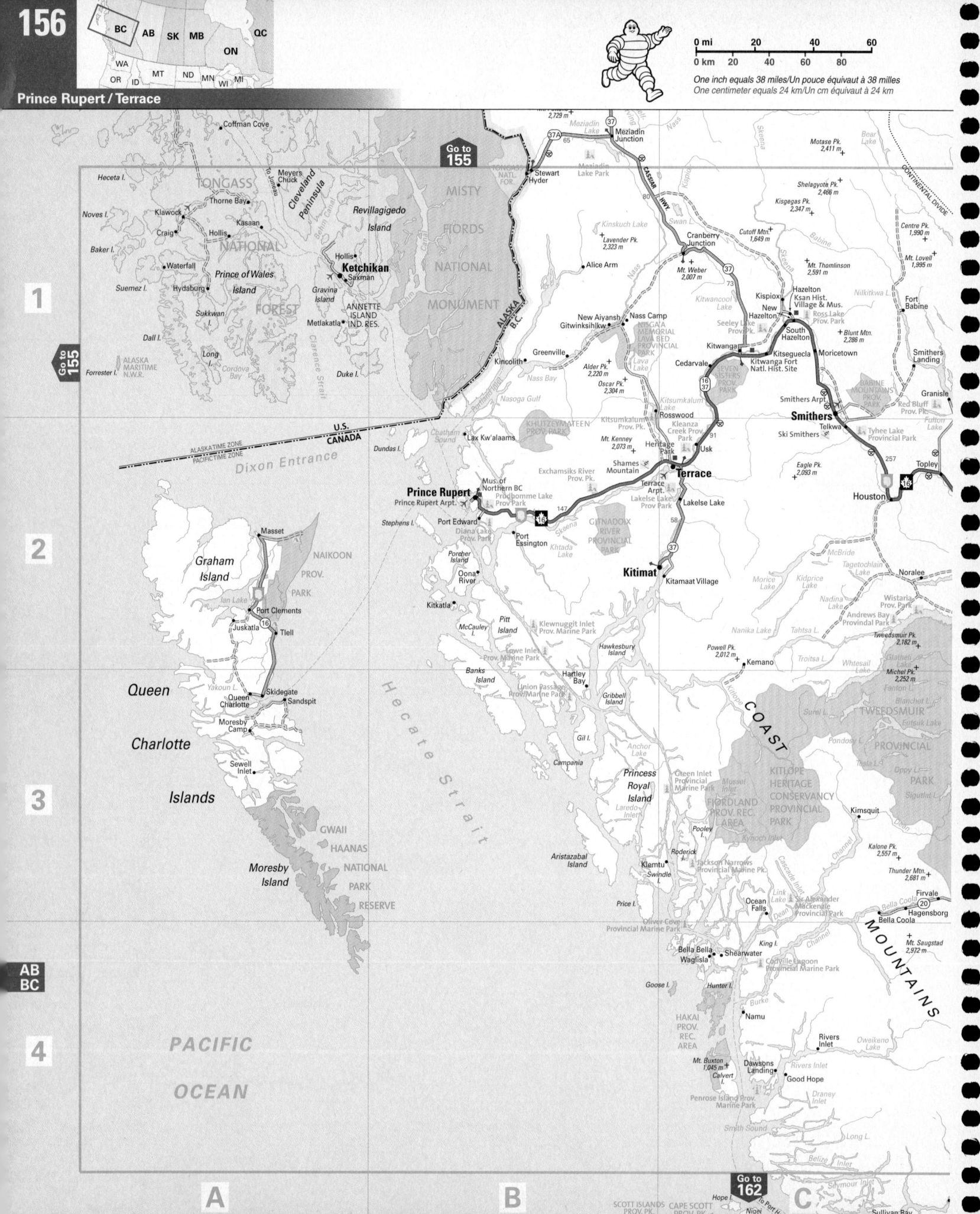

BC AB SK MB QC
WA   ON
OR ID MT ND MN WI MI

0 mi   20   40   60
0 km 20   40   60   80

One inch equals 38 miles/Un pouce équivaut à 38 milles
One centimeter equals 24 km/Un cm équivaut à 24 km

Go to 155

Go to 155

1

2

3

4

AB
BC

A   B   C

Go to 162

TONGASS

Coffman Cove
Heceta I.
Meyers Chuck
Thorne Bay
Klawock
Kasaan
Hollis
Craig
Baker I.
Waterfall
Suemez I.
Hydaburg
Sukkwan I.
Dall I.
Long I.
Forrester I.
Noyes I.

Cleveland Peninsula
Revillagigedo Island
Ketchikan
Saxman
Hollis
Gravina Island
ANNETTE ISLAND IND. RES.
Metlakatla
NATIONAL FOREST

To Jumbo

MISTY FJORDS NATIONAL MONUMENT

ALASKA MARITIME N.W.R.
Cordova Bay
Clarence Strait

ALASKA B.C.
ALASKA HWY.

U.S.
CANADA

ALASKA TIME ZONE
PACIFIC TIME ZONE

Dixon Entrance

PACIFIC

OCEAN

Queen Charlotte Islands

Graham Island
Masset
NAIKOON PROV. PARK
Ian Lake
Port Clements
Juskatla
Tlell
Yakoun L.
Queen Charlotte
Skidegate
Sandspit
Moresby Camp
Sewell Inlet
Moresby Island
GWAII HAANAS NATIONAL PARK RESERVE

Hecate Strait

Dundas I.
Stephens I.
Porcher Island
Lax Kw'alaams
Chatham Sound
Prince Rupert
Prince Rupert Arpt.
Port Edward
Diana Lake Prov. Park
Port Essington
Oona River
Kitkatla
McCauley I.
Pitt Island
Lowe Inlet Prov. Marine Park
Banks Island
Union Passage Prov. Marine Park
Hartley Bay
Gil I.
Campania I.
Princess Royal Island
Aristazabal Island
Klemtu
Swindle I.
Price I.
Pooley I.
Roderick I.
Ocean Falls
Bella Bella
Waglisla
Shearwater
Goose I.
Hunter I.
Burke
Namu
Calvert I.
Mt. Buxton 1,045 m
Dawsons Landing
Good Hope
Draney Inlet
Penrose Island Prov. Marine Park
Rivers Inlet
Oweekeno Lake
Smith Sound
Long L.
Belize Inlet
Sullivan Bay

Meziadin Lake 2,729 m
Meziadin Junction
37A 65
Meziadin Lake Park
CASSIAR HWY.
Stewart
Hyder
Kinskuch Lake
Swan R.
Motase Pk. 2,411 m
Bear Lake
CONTINENTAL DIVIDE

Lavender Pk. 2,323 m
Cranberry Junction
Cutoff Mtn. 1,649 m
Shelagyote Pk. 2,466 m
Kisgegas Pk. 2,347 m
Centre Pk. 1,990 m

Mt. Weber 2,007 m
Alice Arm
37
Mt. Thomlinson 2,591 m
Mt. Lovell 1,995 m

New Aiyansh
Nass Camp
Gitwinksihlkw
Kincolith
Greenville
NISGA'A MEMORIAL LAVA BED PROVINCIAL PARK
Lava Lake
Kitwancool Lake
Kispiox
New Hazelton
Hazelton
Ksan Hist. Village & Mus.
Seeley Lake Prov. Pk.
South Hazelton
Ross Lake Prov. Park
Blunt Mtn. 2,286 m
Fort Babine
Nilkitkwa L.
Smithers Landing

Nass Bay
Nasoga Gulf
Alder Pk. 2,220 m
Oscar Pk. 2,304 m
Cedarvale
Kitwanga
Kitwanga Fort Natl. Hist. Site
SEVEN SISTERS PROV. PARK
16 37
Kitseguecla
Moricetown
Smithers Arpt.
Smithers
Telkwa
Ski Smithers
Tyhee Lake Provincial Park
BABINE MOUNTAINS PROV. PARK
Red Bluff Prov. Pk.
Granisle
Fulton Lake

KHUTZEYMATEEN PROV. PARK
Kitsumkalum Lake
Kitsumkalum Prov. Park
Rosswood
Kleanza Creek Prov. Park
91
Eagle Pk. 2,093 m
257
Topley
Houston
16

Mt. Kenney 2,073 m
Heritage Park
Usk
Shames Mountain
Mus. of Northern BC
Prodhomme Lake Prov Park
147
Terrace
Terrace Arpt.
Lakelse Lake Prov. Park
Lakelse Lake
Exchamsiks River Prov. Pk.
GITNADOIX RIVER PROVINCIAL PARK

16
58
37
Kitimat
Kitamaat Village
McBride
Tagetochlain Lake
Noralee
Morice Lake
Kidprice Lake
Tahtsa L.
Wistaria Prov. Park
Andrews Bay Provindal Park
Tweedsmuir Pk. 2,182 m
Michel Pk. 2,252 m
Nanika Lake
Nadina Lake
Whtesail Lake
Glatheli Lake
Fanton L.
Blanchet L.

COAST

TWEEDSMUIR PROVINCIAL PARK
Surel L.
Pondosy L.
Eutsuk Lake
Sigutlat L.

Powell Pk. 2,012 m
Kemano
Troitsa L.
Kitlope Inlet
Kitimat

Kalone Pk. 2,557 m
Kimsquit
Thunder Mtn. 2,681 m
Firvale
20

KITLOPE HERITAGE CONSERVANCY PROVINCIAL PARK
FIORDLAND PROV. REC. AREA
Laredo Inlet
Green Inlet Provincial Marine Park
Mussel Inlet
Kynoch Inlet
Jackson Narrows Provincial Marine Pk.
Link Lake
Cascade Inlet
Sir Alexander Mackenzie Provincial Park
Dean Channel
Bella Coola
Hagensborg
Mt. Saugstad 2,972 m
King I.
Mt. Saugstad

HAKAI PROV. REC. AREA
Coryille Lagoon Provincial Marine Park
Oliver Cove Provincial Marine Park

MOUNTAINS

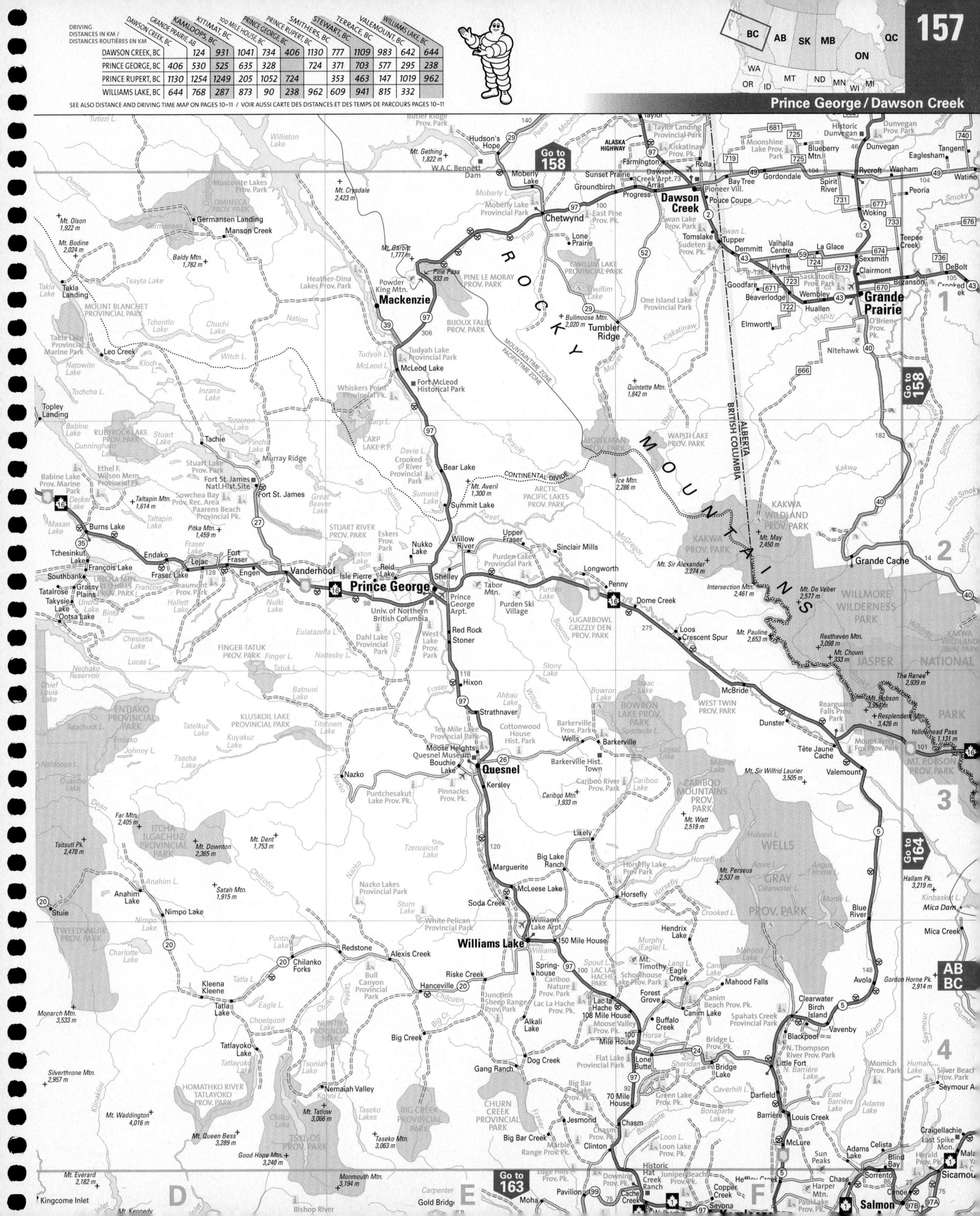

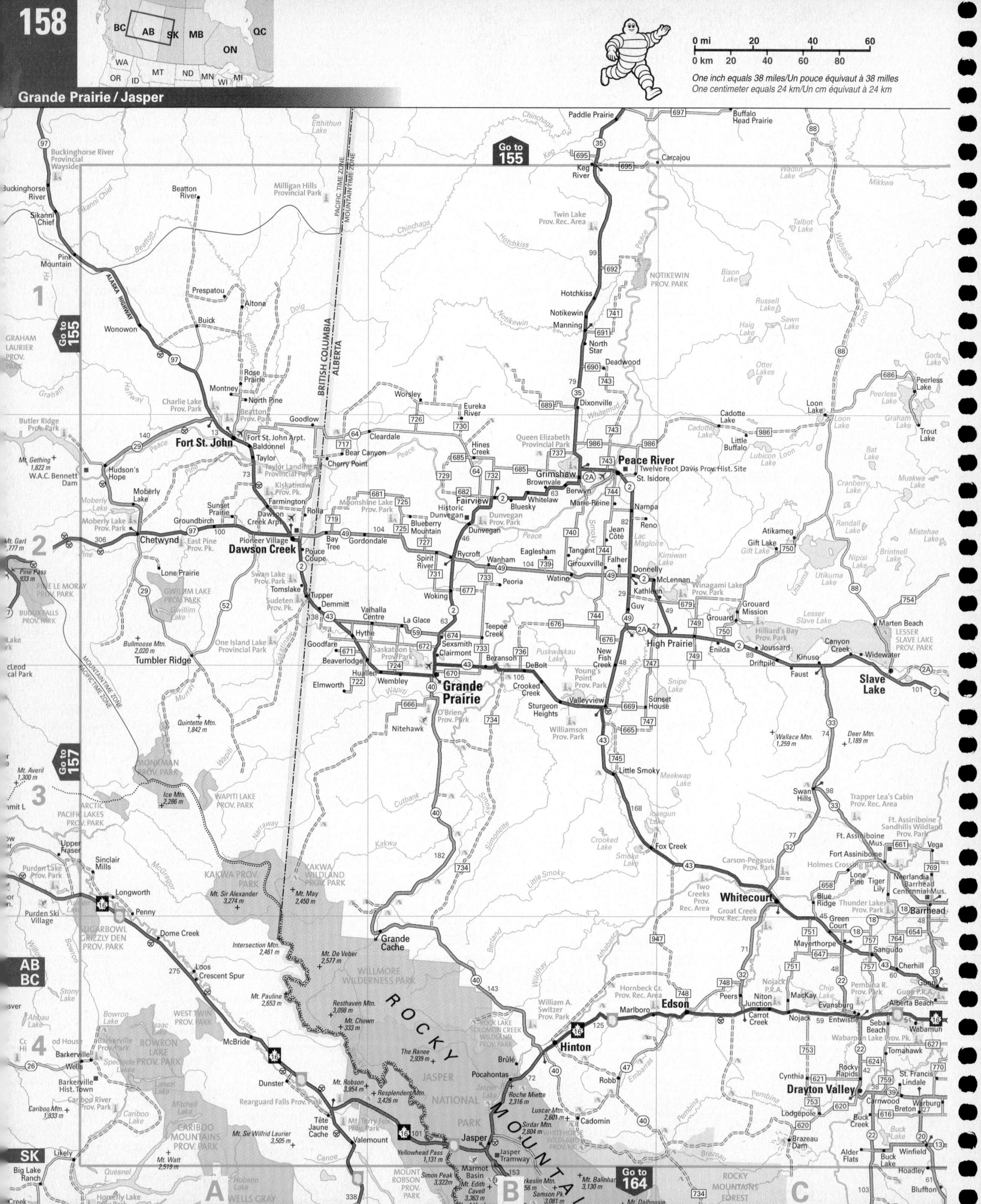

BC · AB · SK · MB · QC
ON
WA · OR · ID · MT · ND · MN · WI · MI

0 mi   20   40   60
0 km 20 40   80
One inch equals 38 miles/Un pouce équivaut à 38 milles
One centimeter equals 24 km/Un cm équivaut à 24 km

Go to 155
Go to 155
Go to 157
Go to 164

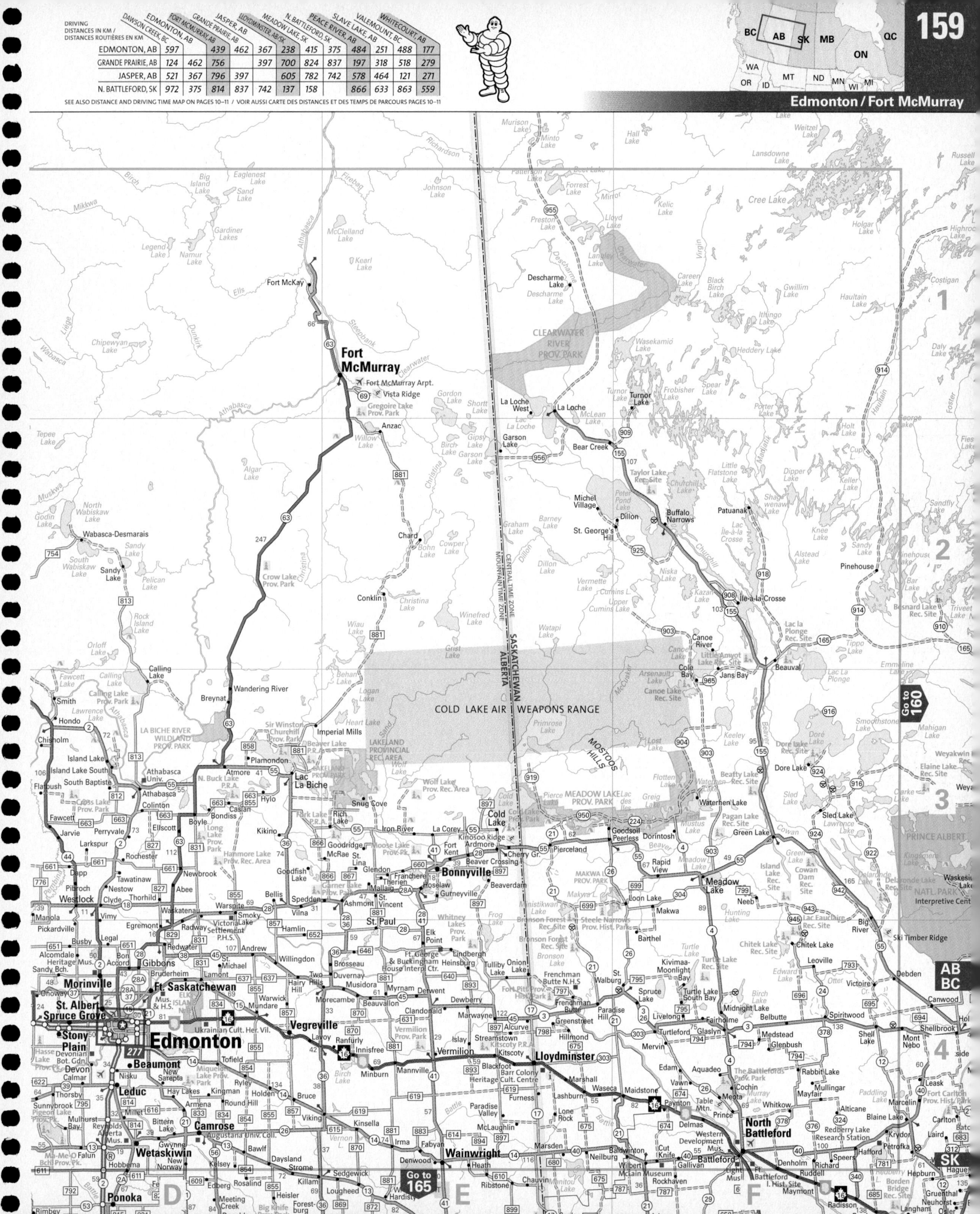

DRIVING
DISTANCES IN KM /
DISTANCES ROUTIÈRES EN KM

	DAWSON CREEK, BC	EDMONTON, AB	FORT McMURRAY, AB	GRANDE PRAIRIE, AB	JASPER, AB	LLOYDMINSTER, AB/SK	MEADOW LAKE, SK	N. BATTLEFORD, SK	PEACE RIVER, AB	SLAVE LAKE, AB	VALEMOUNT, BC	WHITECOURT, AB
EDMONTON, AB	597		439	462	367	238	415	375	484	251	488	177
GRANDE PRAIRIE, AB	124	462	756		397	700	824	837	197	318	518	279
JASPER, AB	521	367	796	397		605	782	742	578	464	121	271
N. BATTLEFORD, SK	972	375	814	837	742	137	158		866	633	863	559

SEE ALSO DISTANCE AND DRIVING TIME MAP ON PAGES 10–11 / VOIR AUSSI CARTE DES DISTANCES ET DES TEMPS DE PARCOURS PAGES 10–11

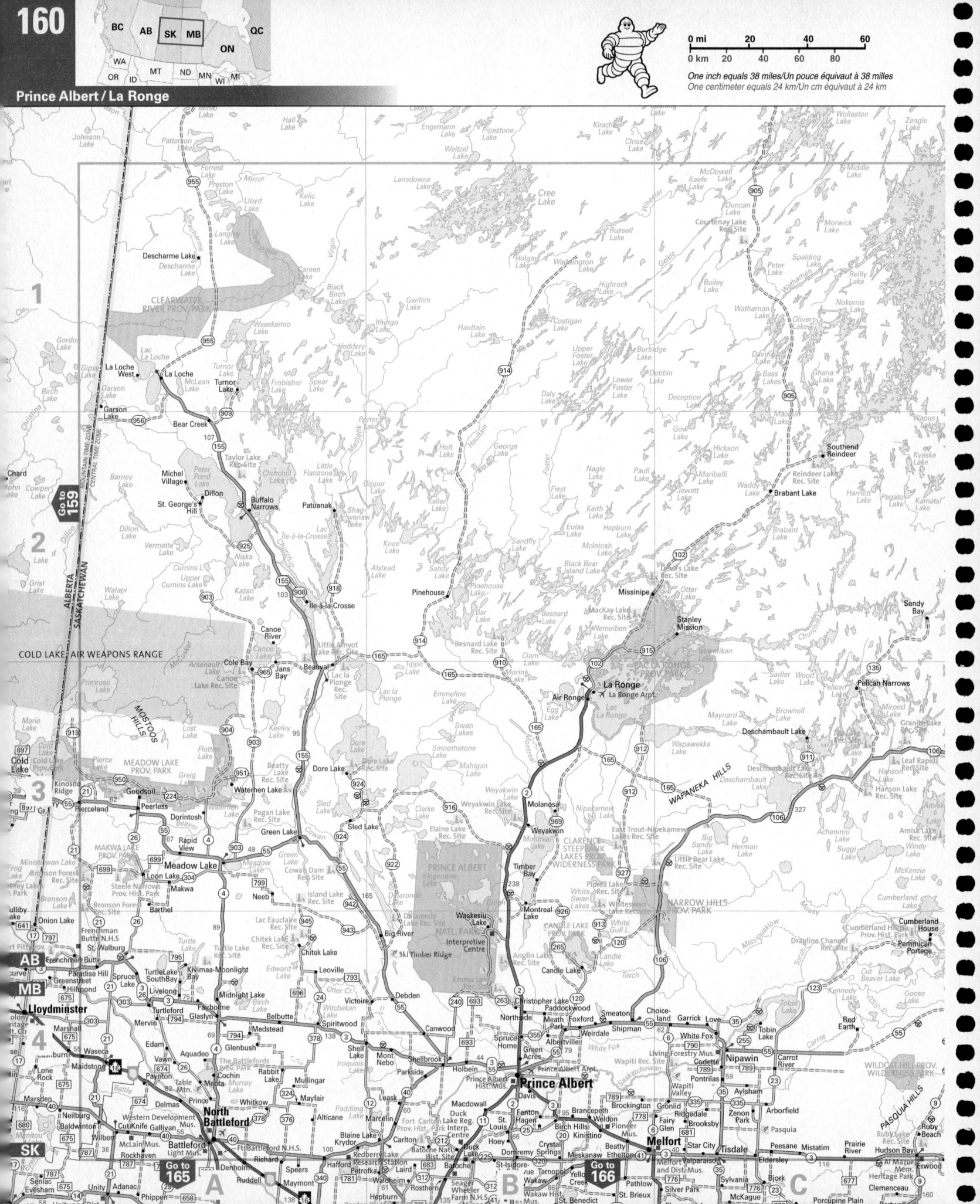

One inch equals 38 miles/Un pouce équivaut à 38 milles
One centimeter equals 24 km/Un cm équivaut à 24 km

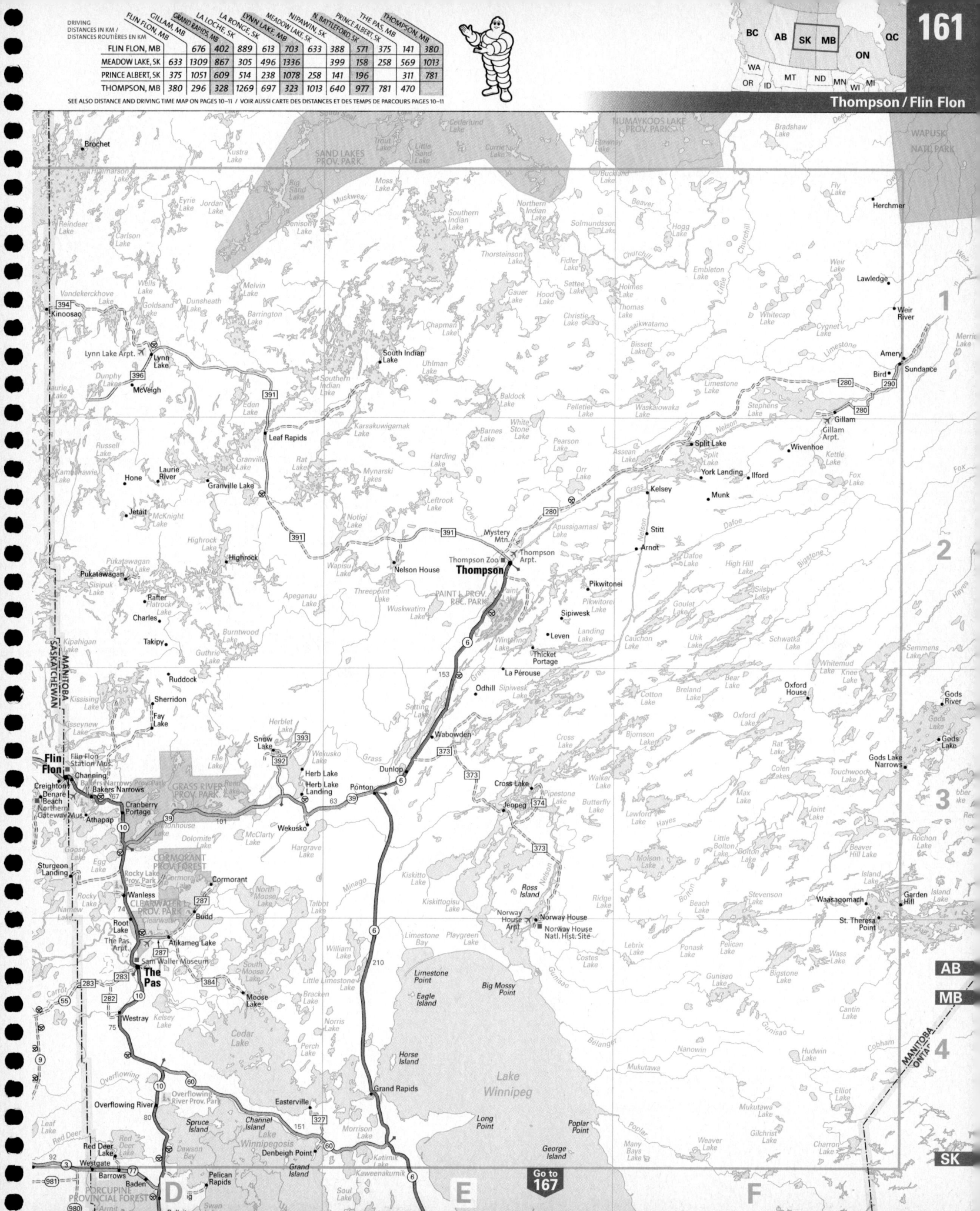

DRIVING DISTANCES IN KM / DISTANCES ROUTIÈRES EN KM

	FLIN FLON, MB	GILLAM, MB	GRAND RAPIDS, MB	LA LOCHE, SK	LA RONGE, SK	LYNN LAKE, MB	MEADOW LAKE, SK	NIPAWIN, SK	N. BATTLEFORD, SK	PRINCE ALBERT, SK	THE PAS, MB	THOMPSON, MB
FLIN FLON, MB		676	402	889	613	703	633	388	571	375	141	380
MEADOW LAKE, SK	633	1309	867	305	496	1336		399	158	258	569	1013
PRINCE ALBERT, SK	375	1051	609	514	238	1078	258	141	196		311	781
THOMPSON, MB	380	296	328	1269	697	323	1013	640	977	781	470	

SEE ALSO DISTANCE AND DRIVING TIME MAP ON PAGES 10–11 / VOIR AUSSI CARTE DES DISTANCES ET DES TEMPS DE PARCOURS PAGES 10–11

Go to 167

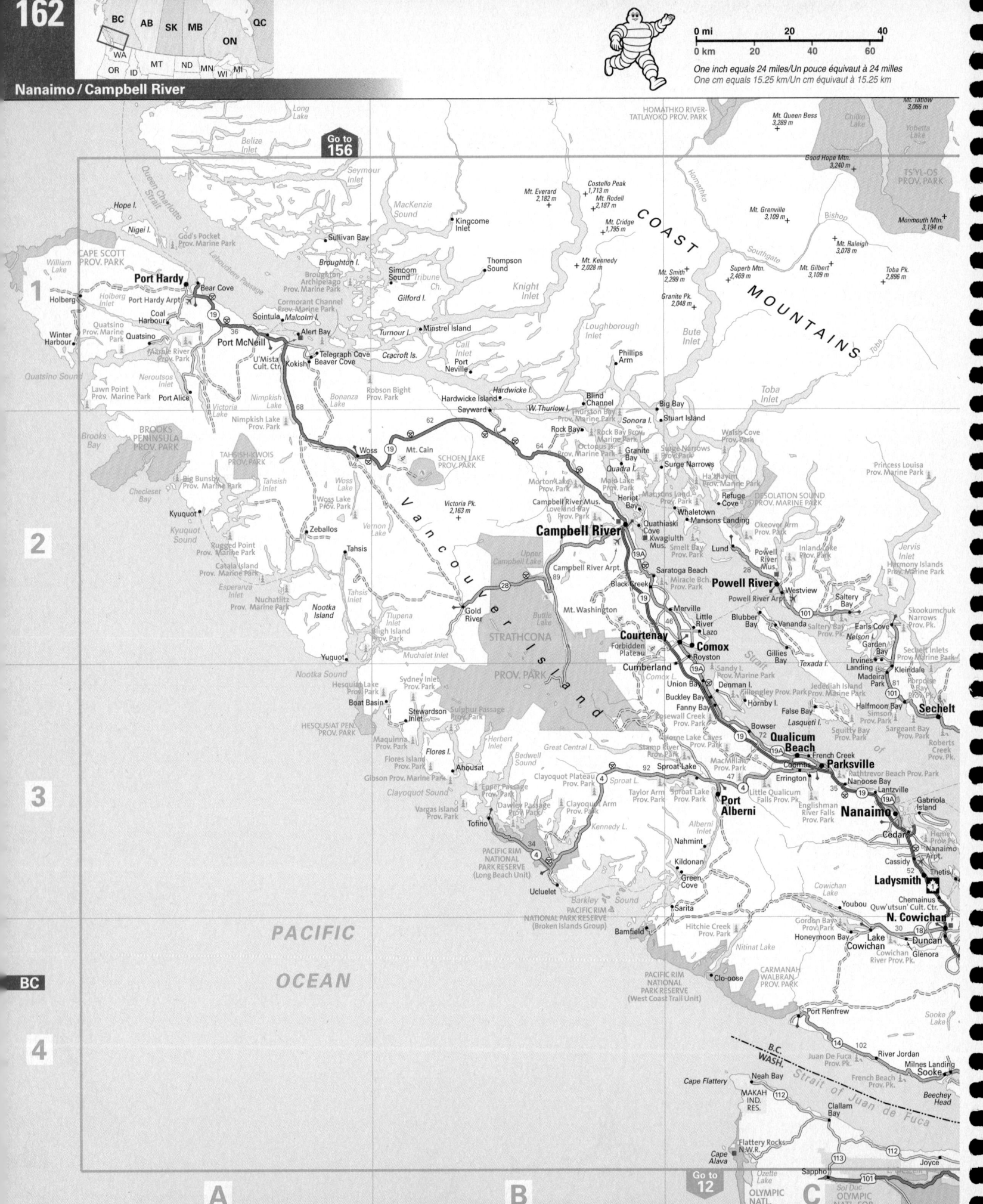

0 mi   20   40
0 km   20   40   60
One inch equals 24 miles/Un pouce équivaut à 24 milles
One cm equals 15.25 km/Un cm équivaut à 15.25 km

Go to 156

Go to 12

PACIFIC OCEAN

COAST MOUNTAINS

Vancouver Island

STRATHCONA PROV. PARK

Port Hardy
Port McNeill
Campbell River
Powell River
Courtenay
Comox
Qualicum Beach
Parksville
Nanaimo
Port Alberni
Tofino
Ucluelet
Gold River
Sechelt
Ladysmith
N. Cowichan
Duncan

BC

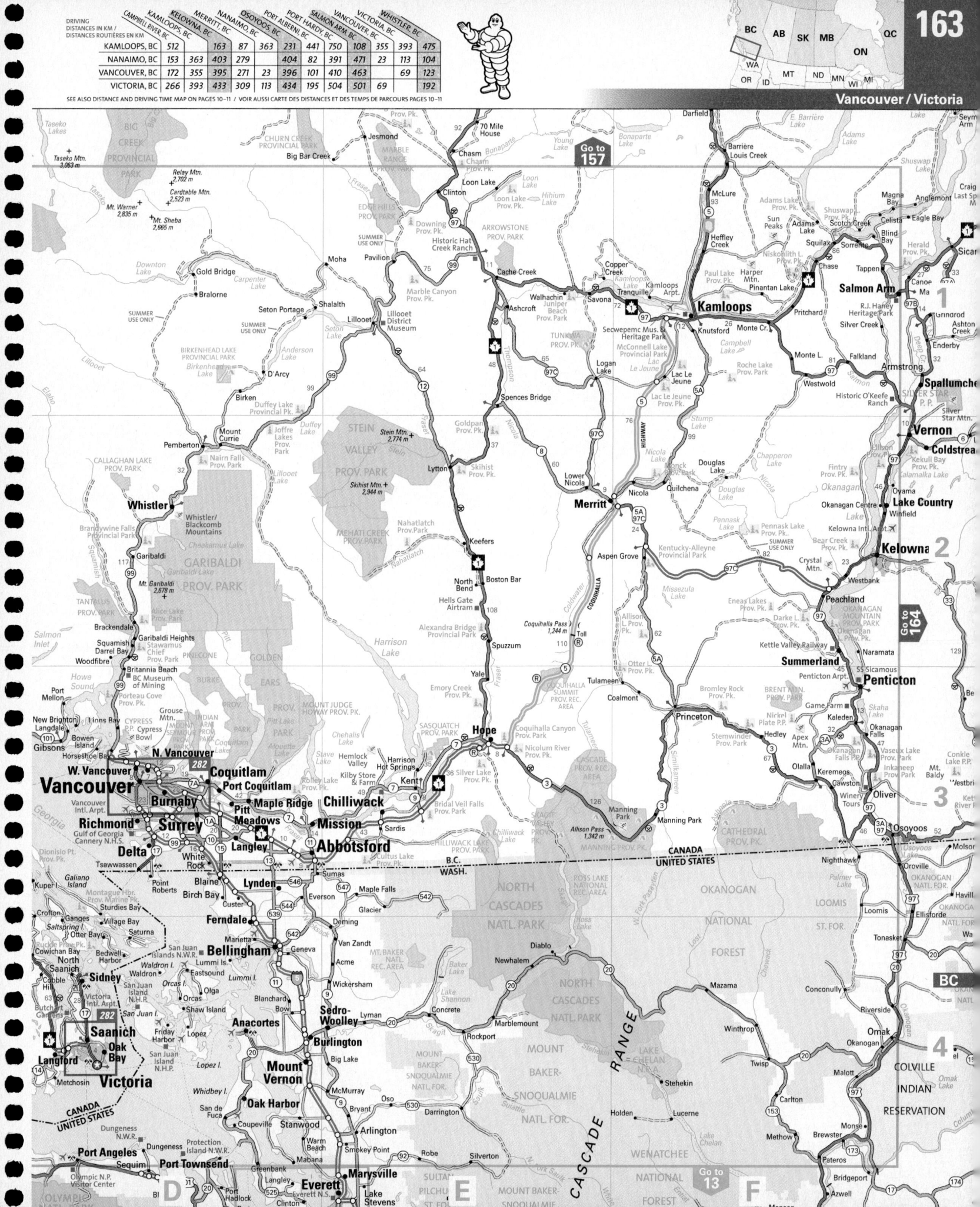

DRIVING
DISTANCES IN KM /
DISTANCES ROUTIÈRES EN KM

	CAMPBELL RIVER, BC	KAMLOOPS, BC	KELOWNA, BC	MERRITT, BC	NANAIMO, BC	OSOYOOS, BC	PORT ALBERNI, BC	PORT HARDY, BC	SALMON ARM, BC	VANCOUVER, BC	VICTORIA, BC	WHISTLER, BC
KAMLOOPS, BC	512		163	87	363	231	441	750	108	355	393	475
NANAIMO, BC	153	363	403	279		404	82	391	471	23	113	104
VANCOUVER, BC	172	355	395	271	23	396	101	410	463		69	123
VICTORIA, BC	266	393	433	309	113	434	195	504	501	69		192

SEE ALSO DISTANCE AND DRIVING TIME MAP ON PAGES 10–11 / VOIR AUSSI CARTE DES DISTANCES ET DES TEMPS DE PARCOURS PAGES 10–11

Go to 157

Go to 164

Go to 13

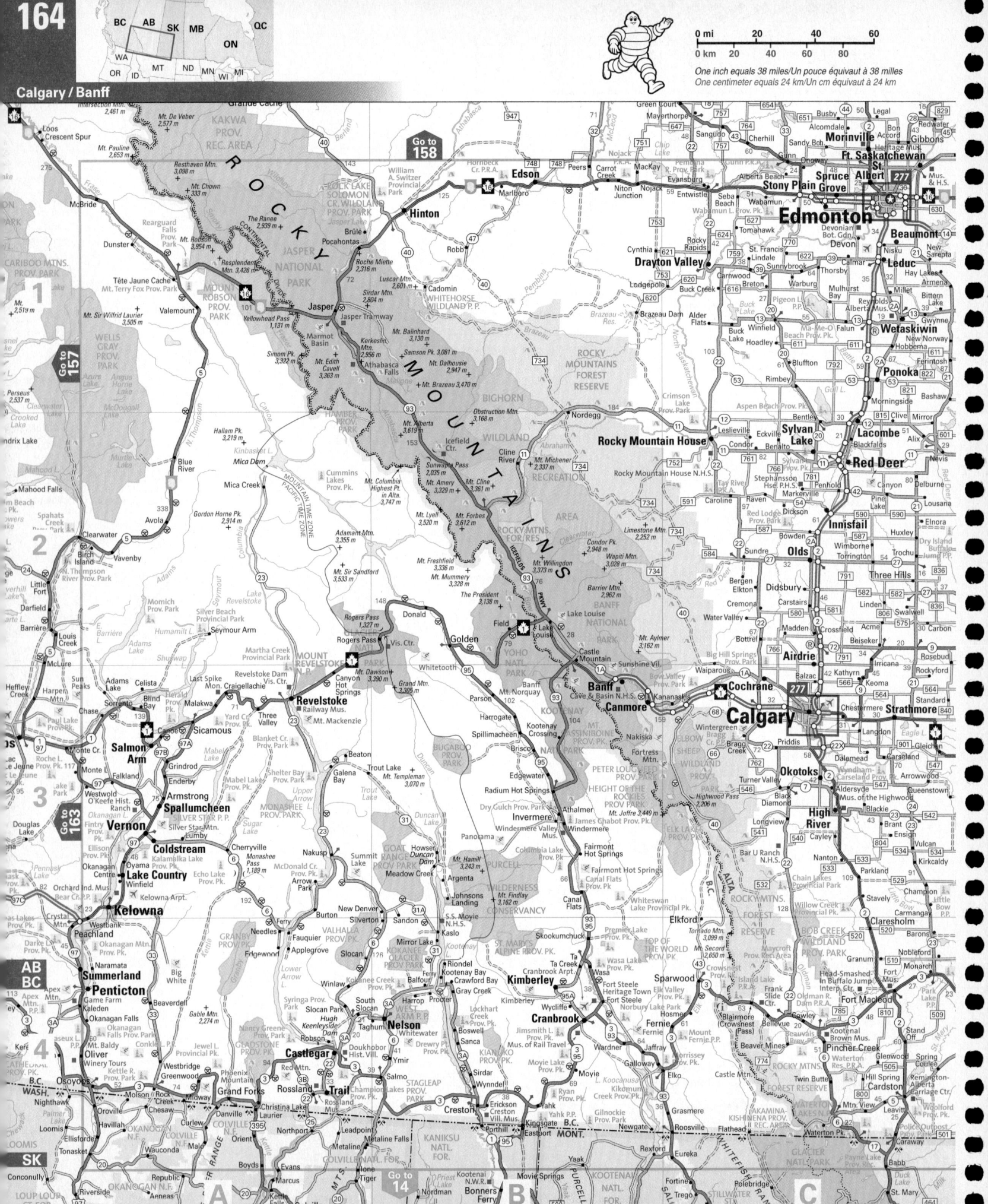

One inch equals 38 miles/Un pouce équivaut à 38 milles
One centimeter equals 24 km/Un cm équivaut à 24 km

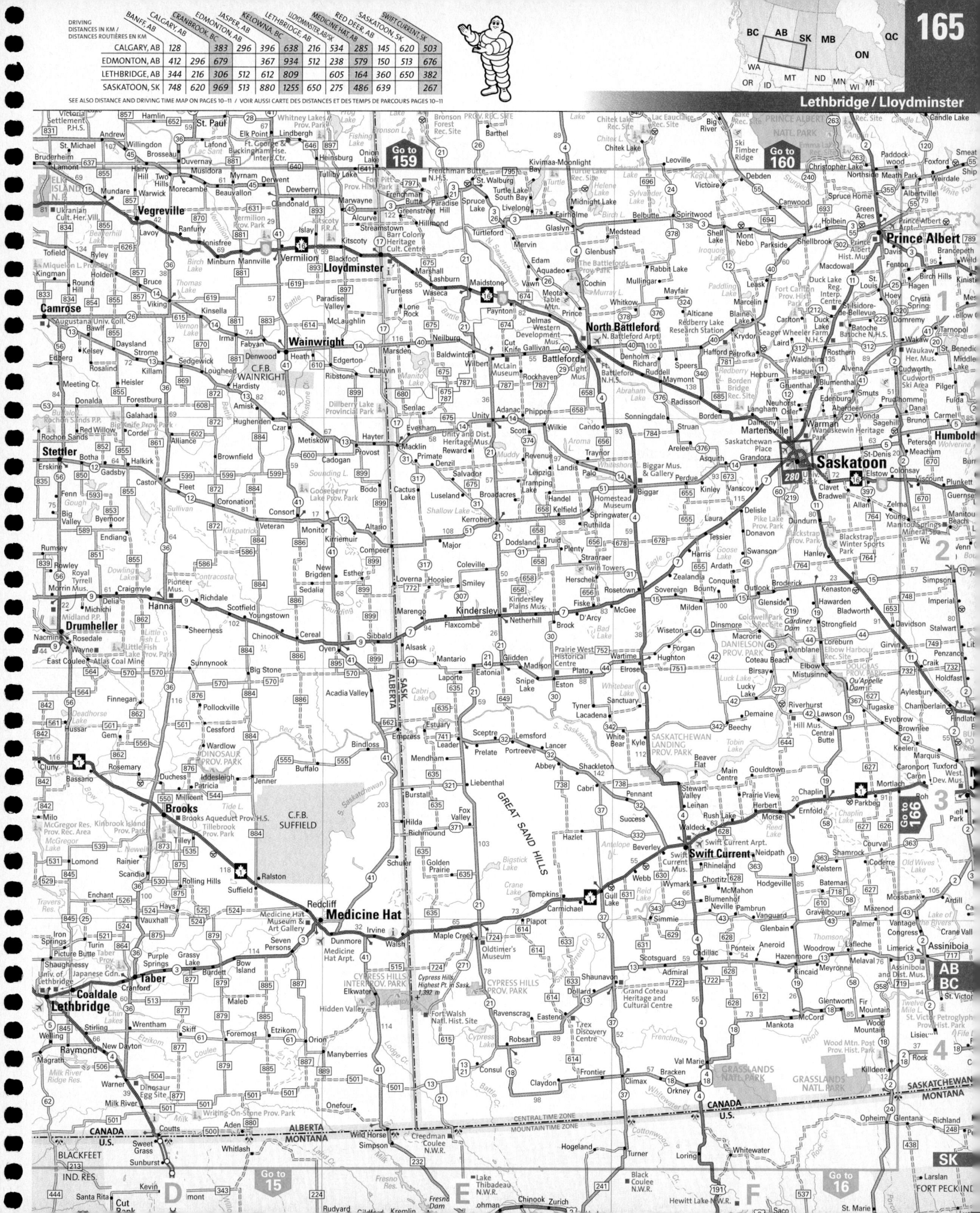

DRIVING DISTANCES IN KM / DISTANCES ROUTIÈRES EN KM

	BANFF, AB	CALGARY, AB	CRANBROOK, BC	EDMONTON, AB	JASPER, AB	KELOWNA, BC	LETHBRIDGE, AB	LLOYDMINSTER, AB/SK	MEDICINE HAT, AB	RED DEER, AB	SASKATOON, SK	SWIFT CURRENT, SK
CALGARY, AB	128		383	296	396	638	216	534	285	145	620	503
EDMONTON, AB	412	296	679		367	934	512	238	579	150	513	676
LETHBRIDGE, AB	344	216	306	512	612	809		605	164	360	650	382
SASKATOON, SK	748	620	969	513	880	1255	650	275	486	639		267

SEE ALSO DISTANCE AND DRIVING TIME MAP ON PAGES 10-11 / VOIR AUSSI CARTE DES DISTANCES ET DES TEMPS DE PARCOURS PAGES 10-11

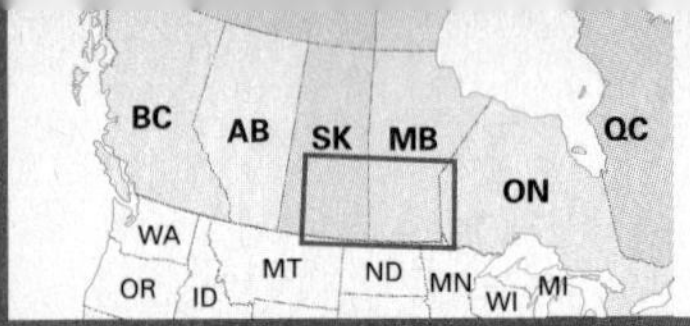

BC AB SK MB QC
WA MT ND MN WI ON
OR ID

0 mi   20   40   60
0 km 20 40 60 80

One inch equals 38 miles/Un pouce équivaut à 38 milles
One centimetre equals 24 km/Un cm équivaut à 24 km

Go to 160

Go to 165

Go to 17   Go to 18

A   B   C

1   2   3   4

MB   ON   SK

CANADA
U.S.

SASKATCHEWAN
MONTANA   N. DAK.
SASK.
N. DAK.

Major places: North Battleford, Battleford, Prince Albert, Melfort, Nipawin, Tisdale, Hudson Bay, Swan River, The Pas, Saskatoon, Humboldt, Yorkton, Melville, Esterhazy, Moosomin, Moose Jaw, Regina, Swift Current, Assiniboia, Weyburn, Estevan

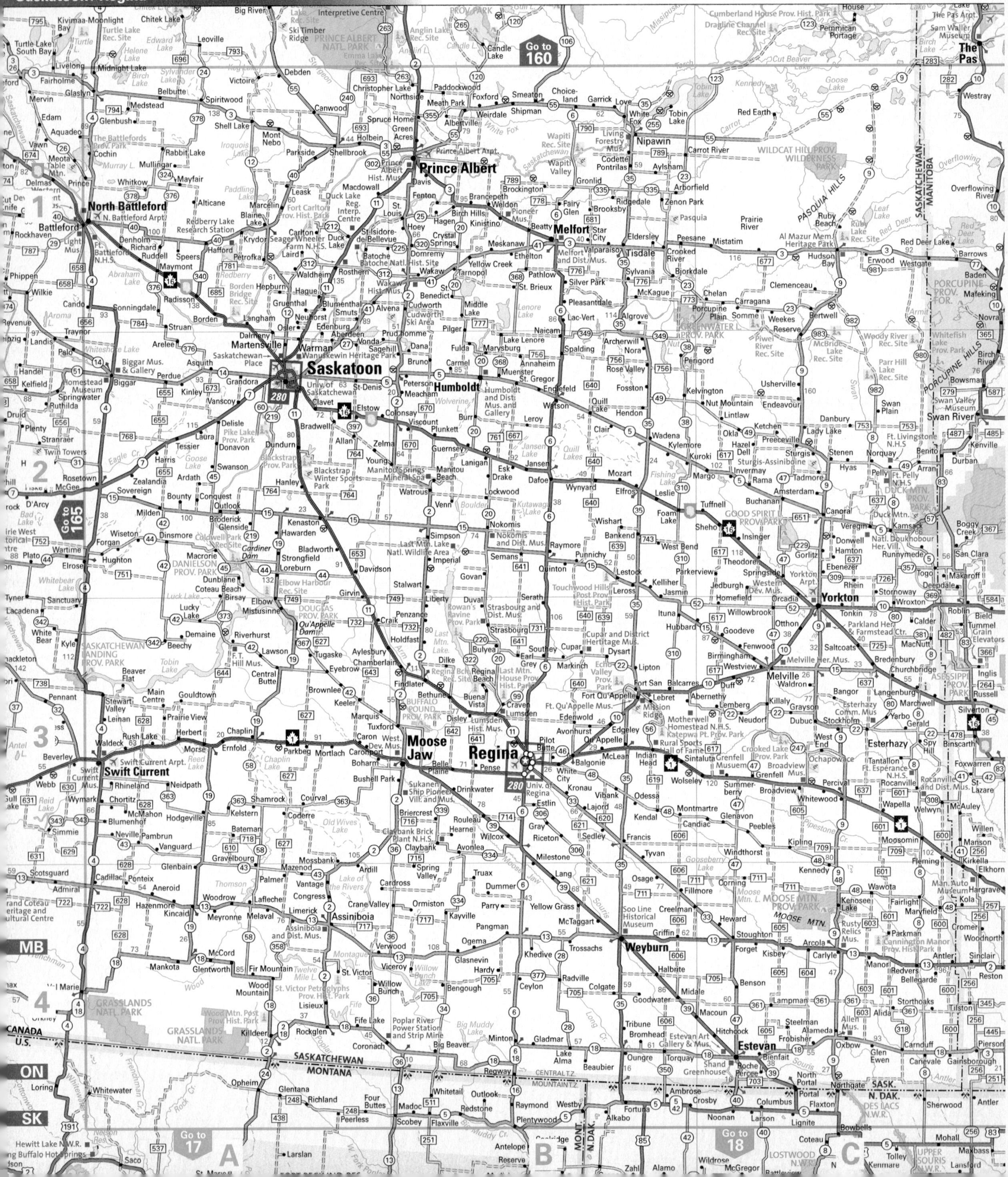

SEE ALSO DISTANCE AND DRIVING TIME MAP ON PAGES 10–11 / VOIR AUSSI CARTE DES DISTANCES ET DES TEMPS DE PARCOURS PAGES 10–11

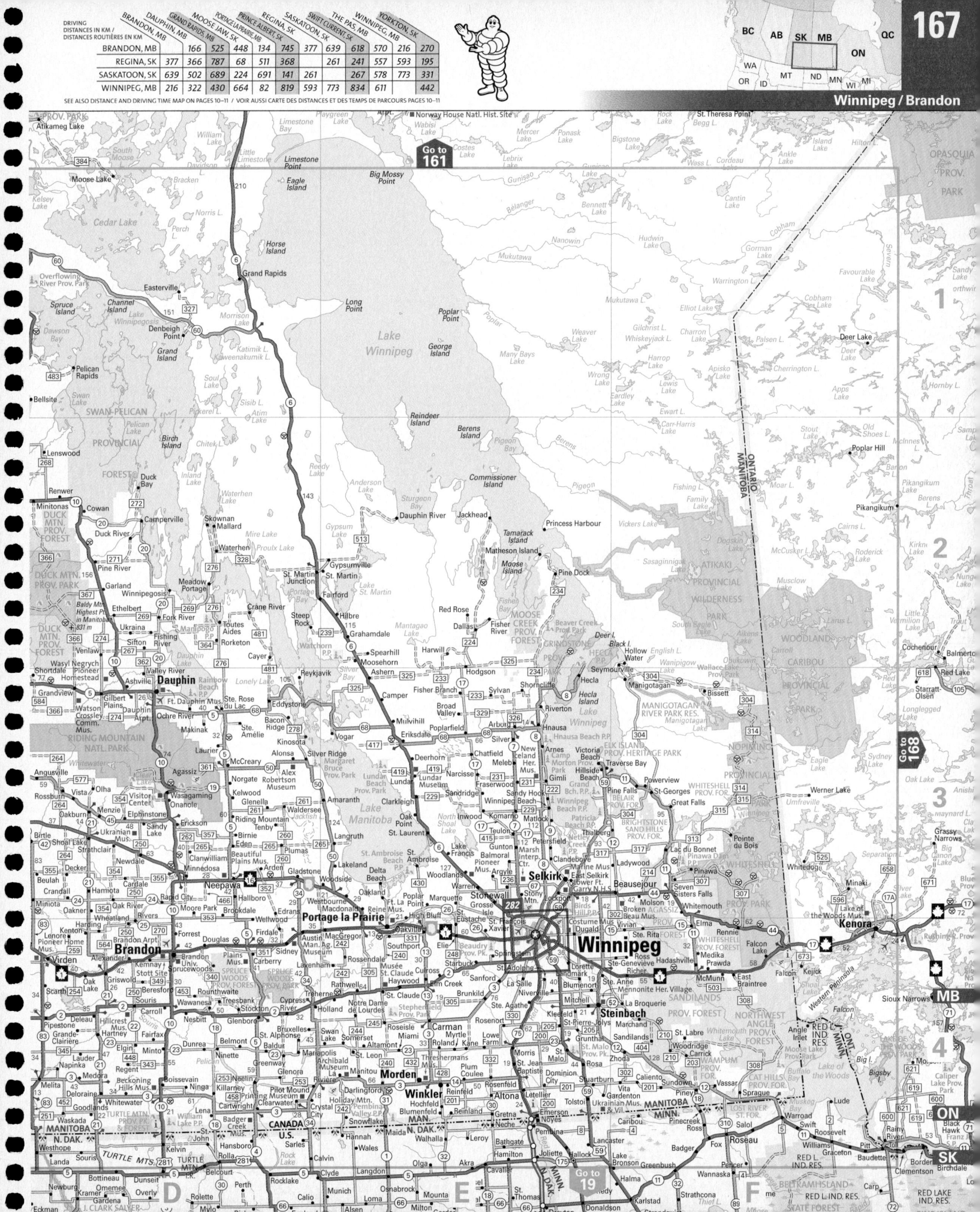

0 mi 20 40 60
0 km 20 40 60 80
One inch equals 38 miles/Un pouce équivaut à 38 milles
One centimeter equals 24 km/Un cm équivaut à 24 km

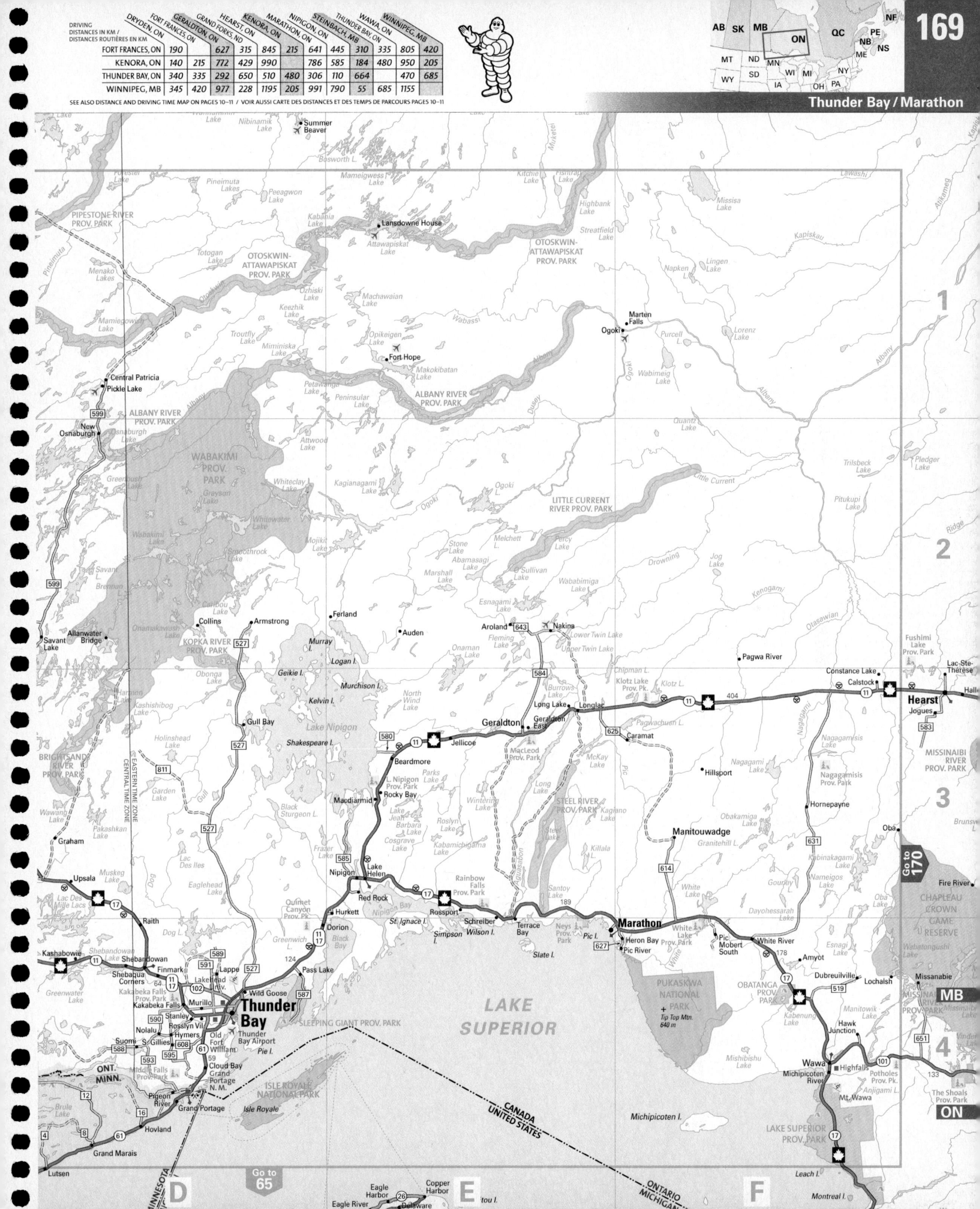

	DRYDEN, ON	FORT FRANCES, ON	GERALDTON, ON	GRAND FORKS, ND	HEARST, ON	KENORA, ON	MARATHON, ON	NIPIGON, ON	STEINBACH, MB	THUNDER BAY, ON	WAWA, ON	WINNIPEG, MB
FORT FRANCES, ON	190		627	315	845	215	641	445	310	335	805	420
KENORA, ON	140	215	772	429	990		786	585	184	480	950	205
THUNDER BAY, ON	340	335	292	650	510	480	306	110	664		470	685
WINNIPEG, MB	345	420	977	228	1195	205	991	790	55	685	1155	

SEE ALSO DISTANCE AND DRIVING TIME MAP ON PAGES 10–11 / VOIR AUSSI CARTE DES DISTANCES ET DES TEMPS DE PARCOURS PAGES 10–11

Go to 170

Go to 65

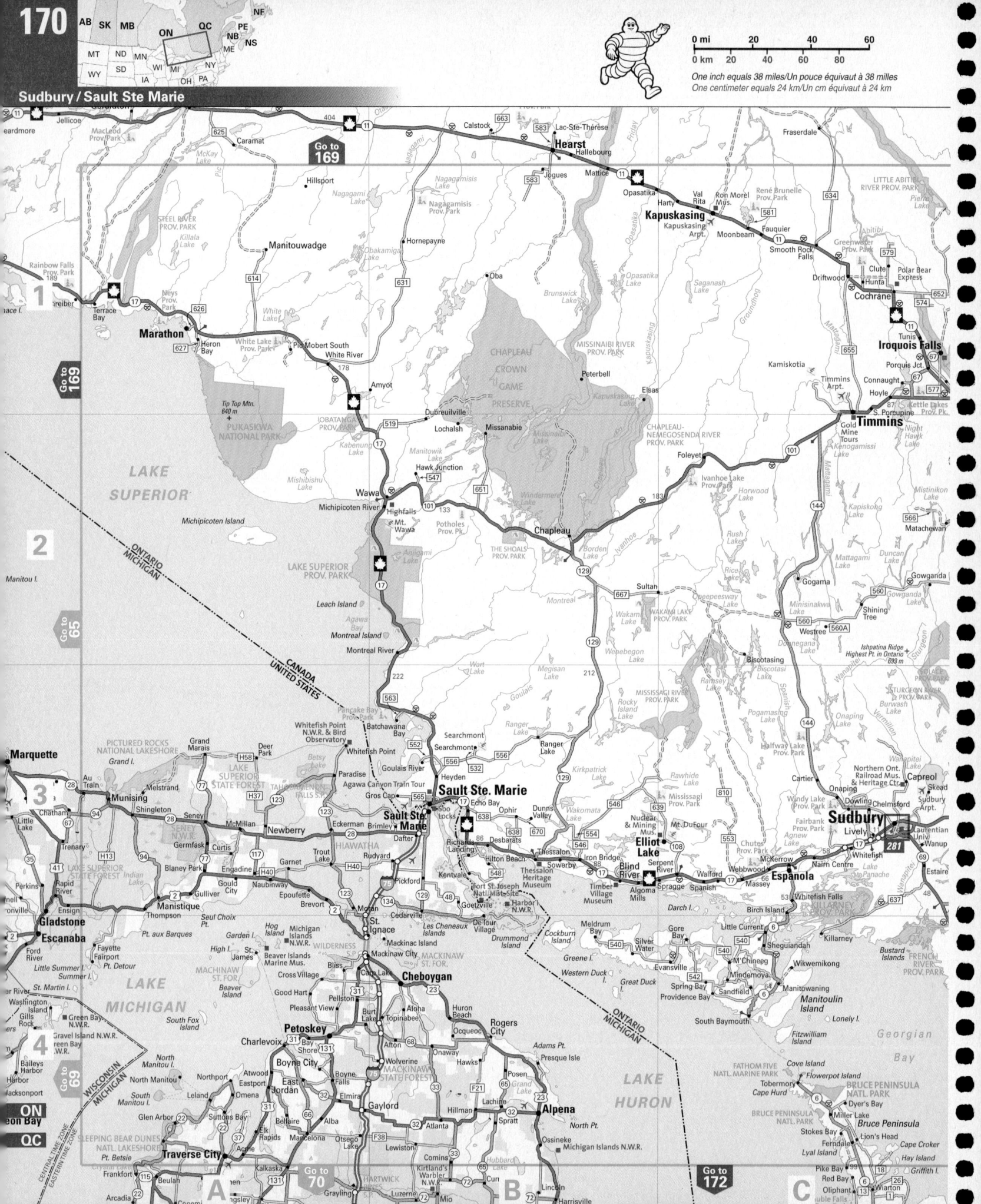

AB SK MB ON QC PE NB NS NF
MT ND MN WI MI OH PA NY ME
WY SD IA

One inch equals 38 miles/Un pouce équivaut à 38 milles
One centimeter equals 24 km/Un cm équivaut à 24 km

0 mi 20 40 60
0 km 20 40 60 80

Go to 169
Go to 169
Go to 65
Go to 69
Go to 70
Go to 172

ON
eon Bay
QC

LAKE SUPERIOR

LAKE MICHIGAN

LAKE HURON

Georgian Bay

ONTARIO MICHIGAN

CANADA UNITED STATES

Hearst
Hallebourg
Lac-Ste-Thérèse
Calstock
Fraserdale
Jogues
Mattice
Opasatika
Harty
Val Rita
Ron Morel Mus.
René Brunelle Prov. Park
Kapuskasing
Kapuskasing Arpt.
Moonbeam
Fauquier
Smooth Rock Falls
Greenwater Prov. Park
Clute
Hunta
Driftwood
Cochrane
Polar Bear Express
Tunis
Iroquois Falls
Porquis Jct.
Connaught
Hoyle
Kamiskotia
Timmins Arpt.
S. Porcupine
Kettle Lakes Prov. Pk.
Timmins
Gold Mine Tours
Matachewan
Elsas
Peterbell
CHAPLEAU CROWN GAME PRESERVE
CHAPLEAU-NEMEGOSENDA RIVER PROV. PARK
MISSINAIBI RIVER PROV. PARK
Foleyet
Ivanhoe Lake Prov. Park
Gogama
Westree
Shining Tree
Gowganda
Biscotasing
Ishpatina Ridge Highest Pt. in Ontario 693 m
Sultan
THE SHOALS PROV. PARK
Chapleau
Missanabie
Lochalsh
Dubreuilville
Amyot
Oba
White River
Mobert South
Pic
Heron Bay
Marathon
Terrace Bay
Neys Prov. Park
Schreiber
Rainbow Falls Prov. Park
Jellicoe
MacLeod Prov. Park
Caramat
Hillsport
Manitouwadge
Hornepayne
Nagagami Lake
Nagagamisis Prov. Park
Killala Lake
STEEL RIVER PROV. PARK
White Lake Prov. Park
Tip Top Mtn. 640 m
PUKASKWA NATIONAL PARK
OBATANGA PROV. PARK
Wawa
Mt. Wawa
Highfalls
Michipicoten River
Potholes Prov. Pk.
Hawk Junction
Kabenung Lake
Manitowik Lake
Mishibishu Lake
LAKE SUPERIOR PROV. PARK
Agawa Bay
Montreal Island
Montreal River
Leach Island
Anjigami Lake
Michipicoten Island
Manitou I.
Pancake Bay Prov. Park
Batchawana Bay
Searchmont
Ranger Lake
Goulais River
Heyden
Whitefish Point N.W.R. & Bird Observatory
Whitefish Point
Paradise
Agawa Canyon Train Tour
Gros Cap
Sault Ste. Marie
Echo Bay
Ophir
Dunns Valley
Desbarats
Thessalon
Sowerby
Iron Bridge
Blind River
Algoma Mills
Spragge
Spanish
Massey
Walford
Webbwood
Espanola
Nairn Centre
McKerrow
Whitefish
Lively
Sudbury
Sudbury Arpt.
Chelmsford
Dowling
Onaping
Windy Lake Prov. Park
Cartier
Capreol
Northern Ont. Railroad Mus. & Heritage Ctr.
Laurentian Univ.
Wanup
Estaire
FRENCH RIVER PROV. PARK
Nuclear & Mining Mus.
Mt. DuFour
Elliot Lake
Serpent River
Chutes Prov. Park
Agnew Lake
Rawhide Lake
Kirkpatrick Lake
Wakomata Lake
Hilton Beach
Richards Landing
Fort St. Joseph Natl. Hist. Site
St. Joseph I.
Thessalon Heritage Museum
Timber Village Museum
Darch I.
Birch Island
Whitefish Falls
Little Current
Meldrum Bay
Cockburn Island
Silver Water
Gore Bay
Killarney
Sheguiandah
M'Chineeg
Evansville
Wikwemikong
Manitowaning
Mindemoya
Spring Bay
Sandfield
Providence Bay
South Baymouth
Manitoulin Island
Bustard Islands
Lonely I.
Western Duck I.
Great Duck I.
Cove Island
Flowerpot Island
BRUCE PENINSULA NATL. PARK
Cape Hurd
FATHOM FIVE NATL. MARINE PARK
Tobermory
Miller Lake
Dyer's Bay
Bruce Peninsula
Stokes Bay
Lion's Head
Ferndale
Cape Croker
Lyal Island
Double Falls Prov. Park
Pike Bay
Red Bay
Mar
Oliphant
Wiarton
Griffith I.
Hay Island
Marquette
PICTURED ROCKS NATIONAL LAKESHORE
Grand I.
Grand Marais
Au Train
Munising
Chatham
Little Lake
Trenary
Melstrand
Shingleton
Seney
McMillan
Newberry
Germfask
Curtis
HIAWATHA
Trout Lake
Rudyard
Dafter
Brimley
Sault Ste. Marie
Soo Locks
Eckerman
LAKE SUPERIOR STATE FOREST
Deer Park
TAHQUAMENON FALLS S.P.
Betsy Lake
SENEY N.W.R.
Blaney Park
Engadine
Gould City
Naubinway
Epoufette
Brevort
Garnet
Kentvale
Goetzville
De Tour Village
Cedarville
Les Cheneaux Islands
Drummond Island
Meldrum Bay
Moran
St. Ignace
Mackinac Island
Mackinaw City
MACKINAW ST. FOR.
WILDERNESS S.P.
Cap Lake
Cross Village
Good Hart
Pellston
Bliss
Burt Lake
Topinabee
Aloha
Cheboygan
Huron Beach
Rogers City
Posen
Presque Isle
Adams Pt.
North Pt.
Onaway
Hawks
Afton
Wolverine
MACKINAW STATE FOREST
Alpena
Ossineke
Lachine
Hillman
Comins
Atlanta
Spratt
Gaylord
Elmira
Boyne Falls
East Jordan
Boyne City
Petoskey
Charlevoix
Bay Shore
Atwood
Eastport
Northport
Omena
Suttons Bay
Bellaire
Alba
Mancelona
Otsego Lake
Elk Rapids
Acme
Traverse City
SLEEPING BEAR DUNES NATL. LAKESHORE
Pt. Betsie
Frankfort
Beulah
Arcadia
Glen Arbor
Leland
North Manitou I.
South Manitou I.
Empire
Kingsley
Fife
Copemish
Kalkaska
HARTWICK PINES S.P.
Grayling
Lewiston
Mio
Luzerne
Mikado
Lincoln
Harrisville
Kirtland's Warbler N.W.R.
Michigan Islands N.W.R.
Hubbard Lake
Lake Huron
Munuscong
Pickford
Gladstone
Escanaba
Ford River
Fayette
Fairport
Pt. Detour
Little Summer I.
Summer I.
Washington Island
Gills Rock
St. Martin I.
Green Bay N.W.R.
Gravel Island N.W.R.
Green Island N.W.R.
Baileys Harbor
Jacksonport
Ensign
Rapid River
Perkins
Gulliver
Thompson
Manistique
Seul Choix Pt.
Garden I.
Pt. aux Barques
Hog Island
High I.
St. James
Beaver Islands
Beaver Islands Marine Mus.
Beaver Island
WISCONSIN MICHIGAN
CENTRAL TIME ZONE
EASTERN TIME ZONE

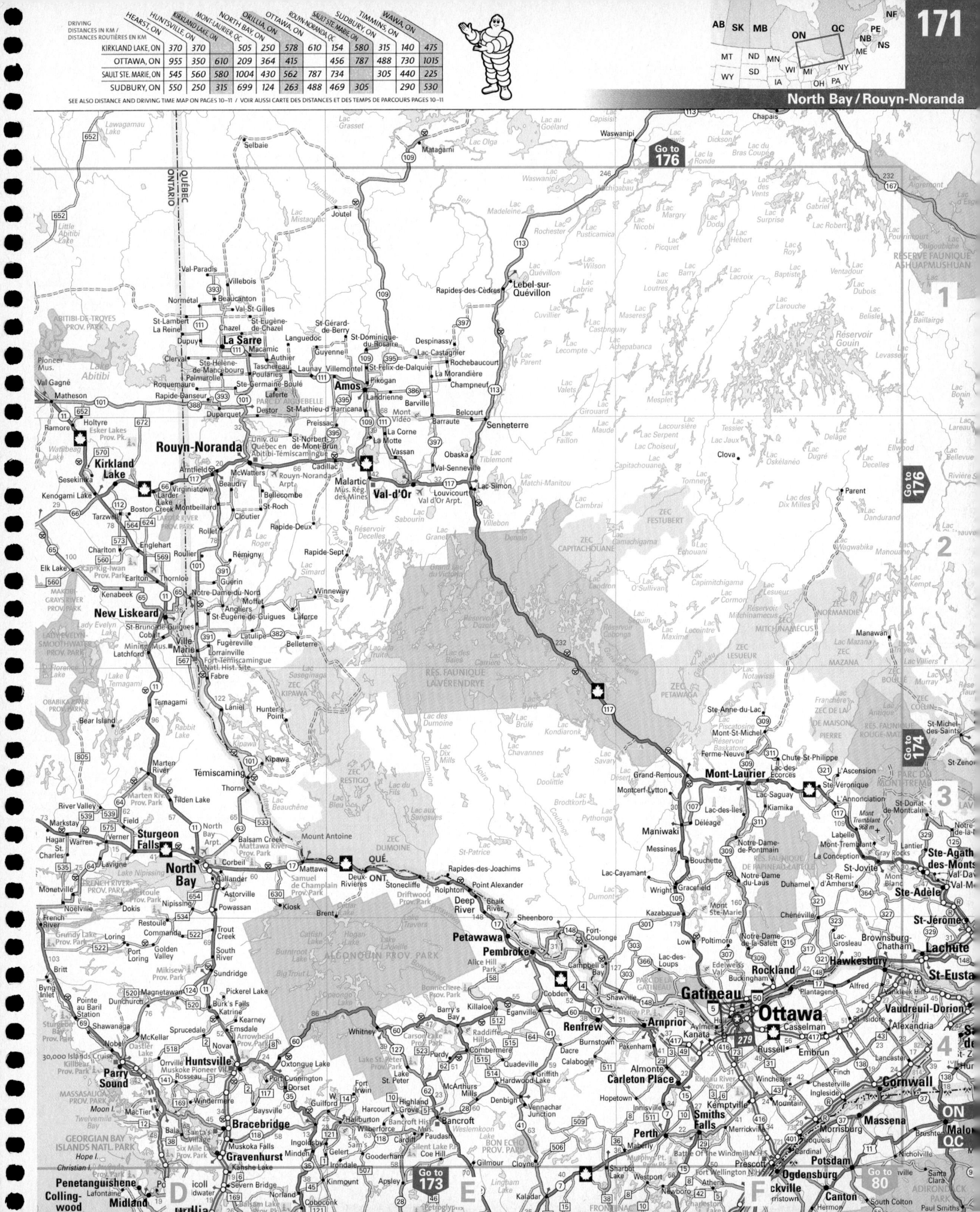

DRIVING DISTANCES IN KM /
DISTANCES ROUTIÈRES EN KM

	HEARST, ON	HUNTSVILLE, ON	KIRKLAND LAKE, ON	MONT-LAURIER, QC	NORTH BAY, ON	ORILLIA, ON	OTTAWA, ON	ROUYN-NORANDA, QC	SAULT STE. MARIE, ON	SUDBURY, ON	TIMMINS, ON	WAWA, ON
KIRKLAND LAKE, ON	370	370		505	250	578	610	154	580	315	140	475
OTTAWA, ON	955	350	610	209	364	415		456	787	488	730	1015
SAULT STE. MARIE, ON	545	560	580	1004	430	562	787	734		305	440	225
SUDBURY, ON	550	250	315	699	124	263	488	469	305		290	530

SEE ALSO DISTANCE AND DRIVING TIME MAP ON PAGES 10–11 / VOIR AUSSI CARTE DES DISTANCES ET DES TEMPS DE PARCOURS PAGES 10–11

AB SK MB ON QC PE NB NS NF
MT ND MN WI MI NY ME
WY SD IA IL IN OH PA

ON

Go to **170**

0 mi   20   40
0 km   20   40   60
One inch equals 24 miles/Un pouce équivaut à 24 miles
One cm equals 15.25 km/Un cm équivaut à 15.25 km

LAKE HURON

LAKE ERIE

LAKE ST. CLAIR

Georgian Bay

CANADA / UNITED STATES

ONTARIO / MICHIGAN

Detroit

Windsor

Sarnia

Port Huron

London

Kitchener

Guelph

Hamilton

Owen Sound

Goderich

Chatham

St. Thomas

Woodstock

Brantford

Stratford

Waterloo

Cambridge

Leamington

Kingsville

Toledo

Erie

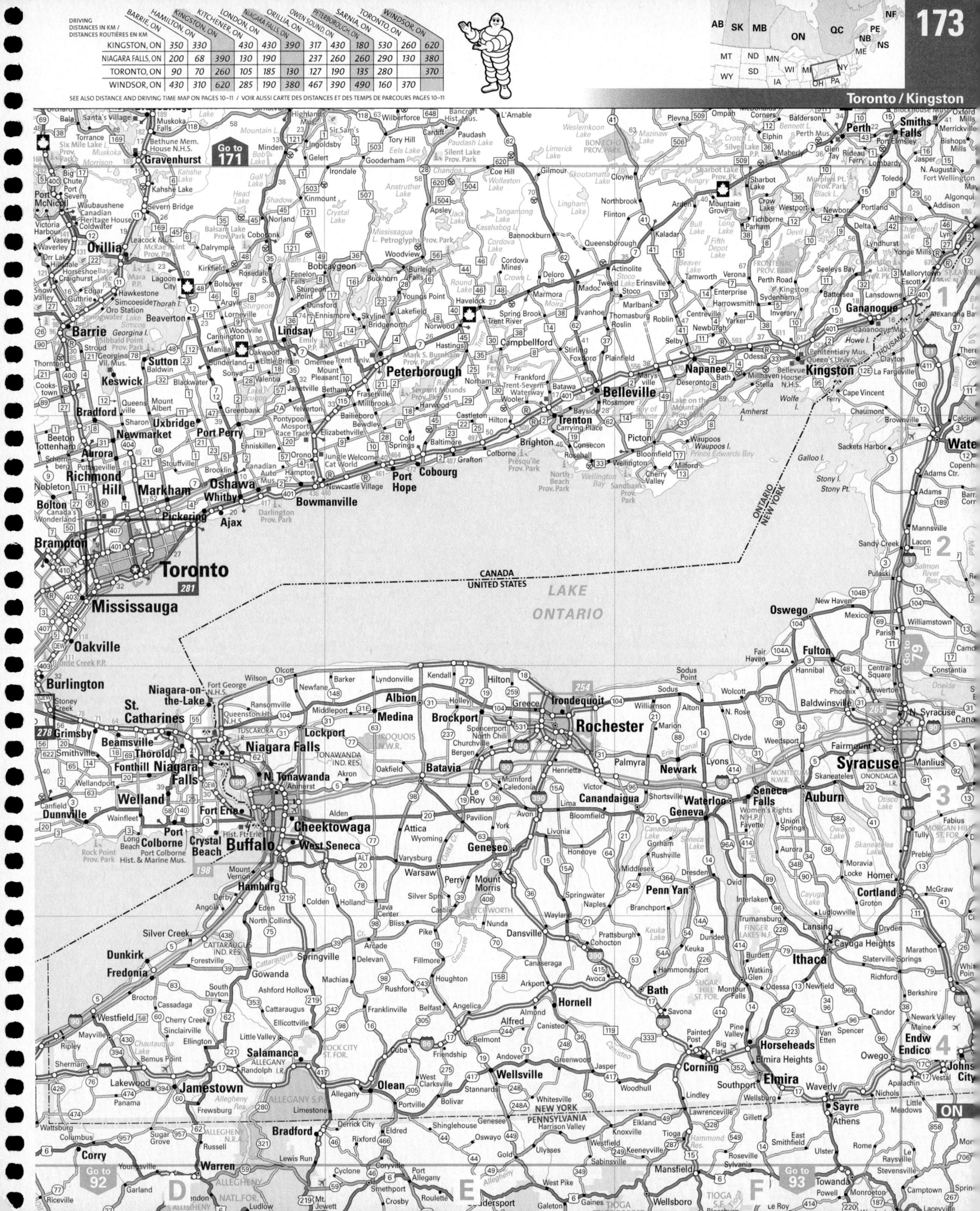

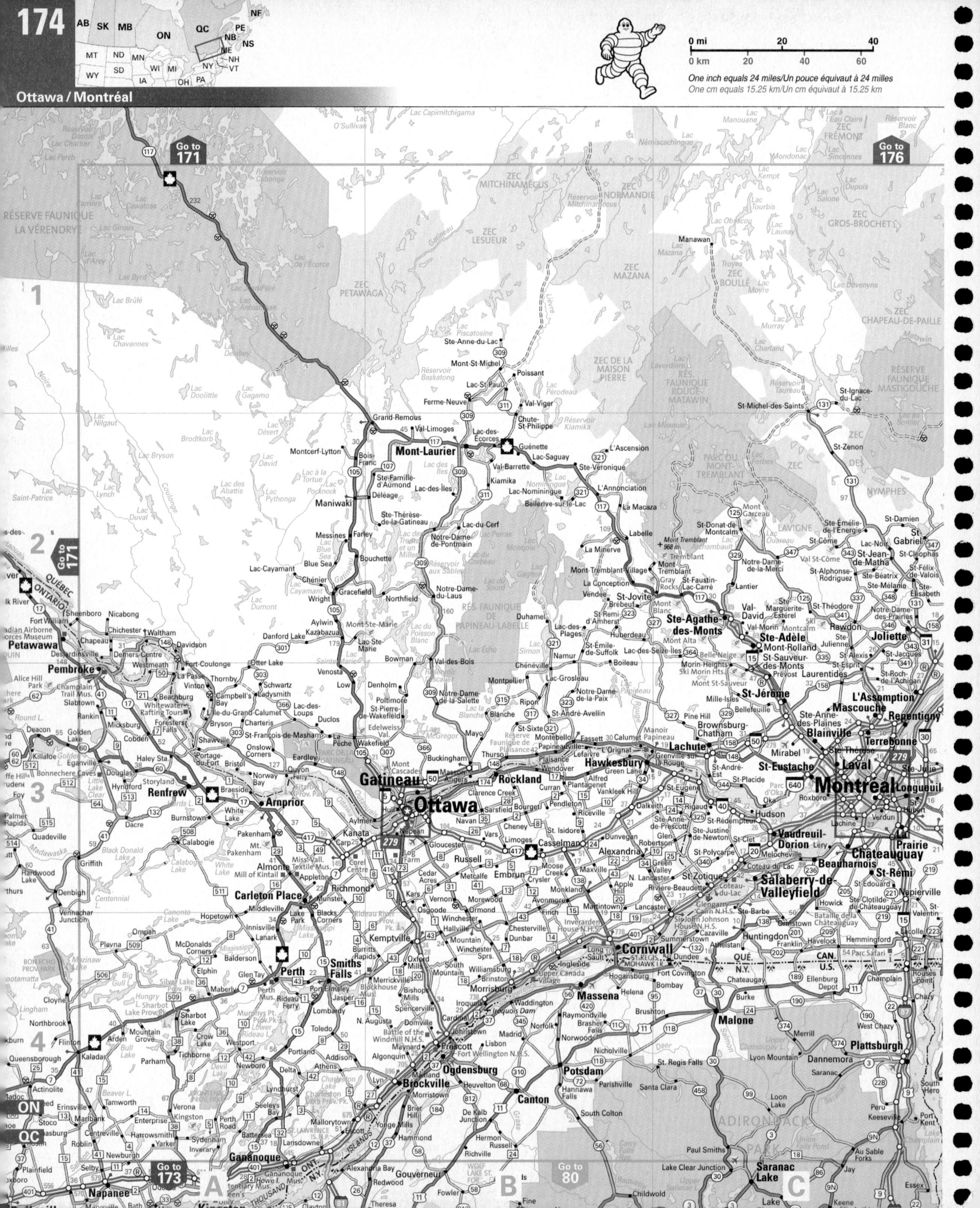

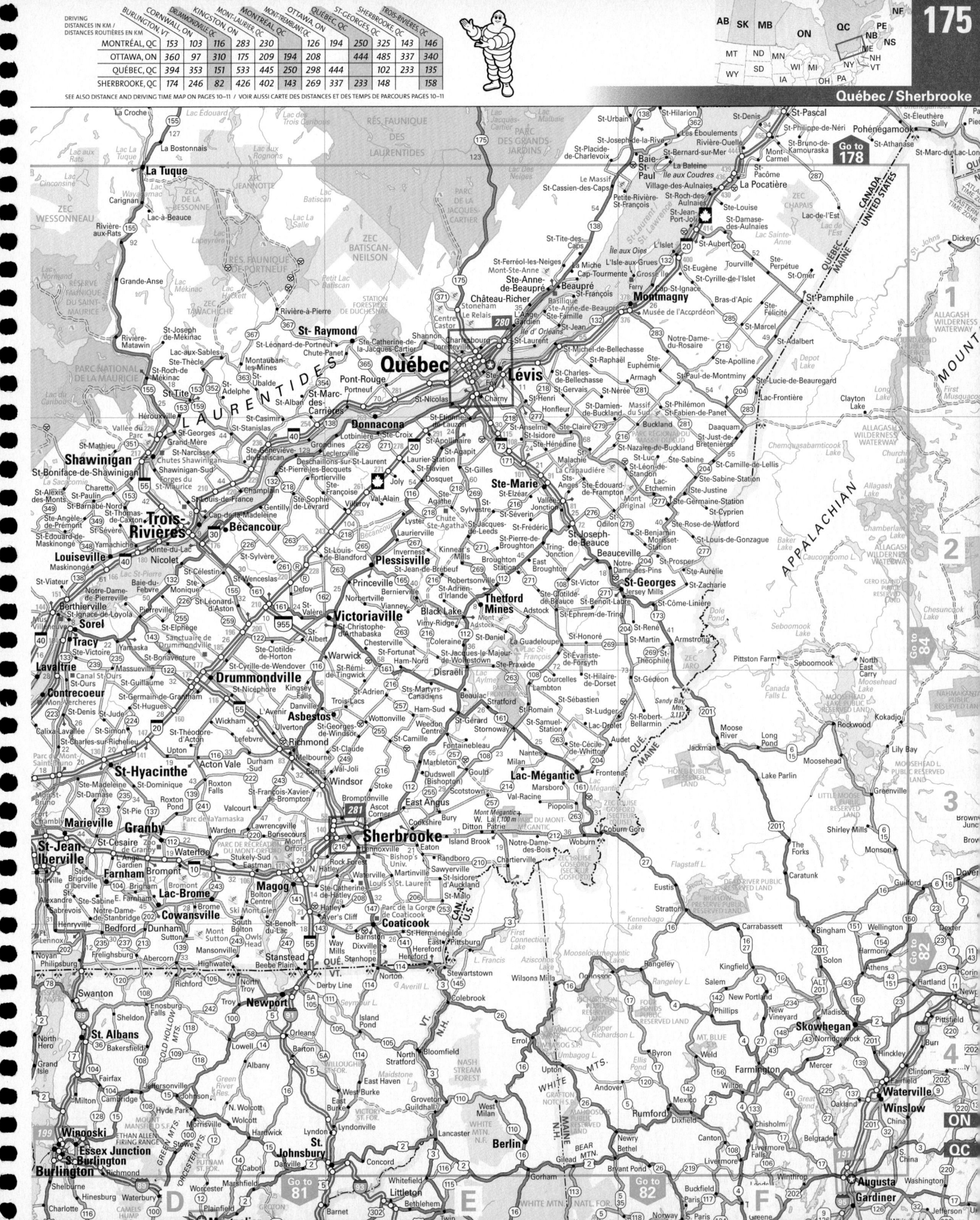

DRIVING
DISTANCES IN KM /
DISTANCES ROUTIÈRES EN KM

	BURLINGTON, VT	CORNWALL, ON	DRUMMONDVILLE, QC	KINGSTON, ON	MONT-LAURIER, QC	MONTRÉAL, QC	MONT-TREMBLANT, QC	OTTAWA, ON	QUÉBEC, QC	ST-GEORGES, QC	SHERBROOKE, QC	TROIS-RIVIÈRES, QC
MONTRÉAL, QC	153	103	116	283	230		126	194	250	325	143	146
OTTAWA, ON	360	97	310	175	209	194	208		444	485	337	340
QUÉBEC, QC	394	353	151	533	445	250	298	444		102	233	135
SHERBROOKE, QC	174	246	82	426	402	143	269	337	233	148		158

SEE ALSO DISTANCE AND DRIVING TIME MAP ON PAGES 10–11 / VOIR AUSSI CARTE DES DISTANCES ET DES TEMPS DE PARCOURS PAGES 10–11

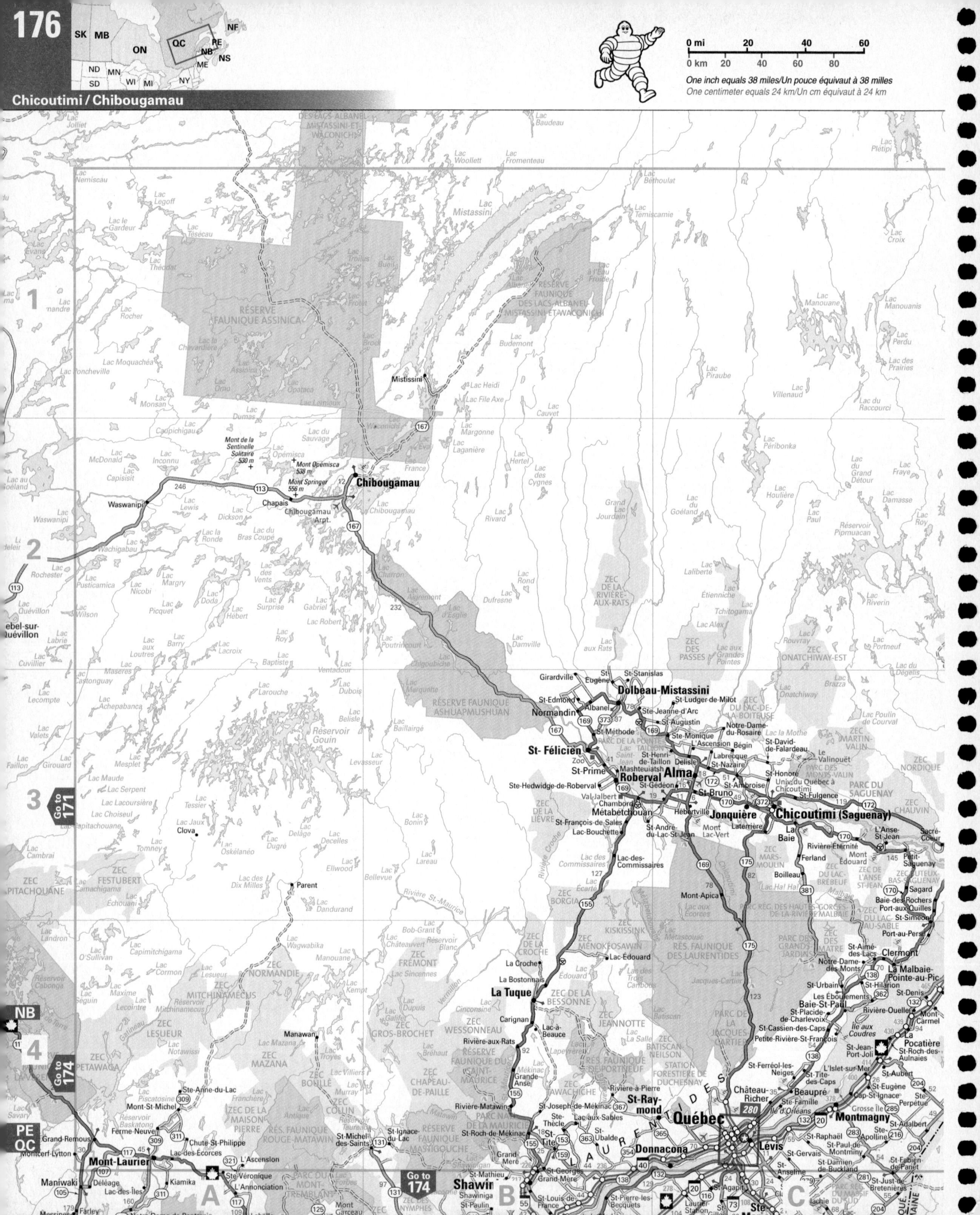

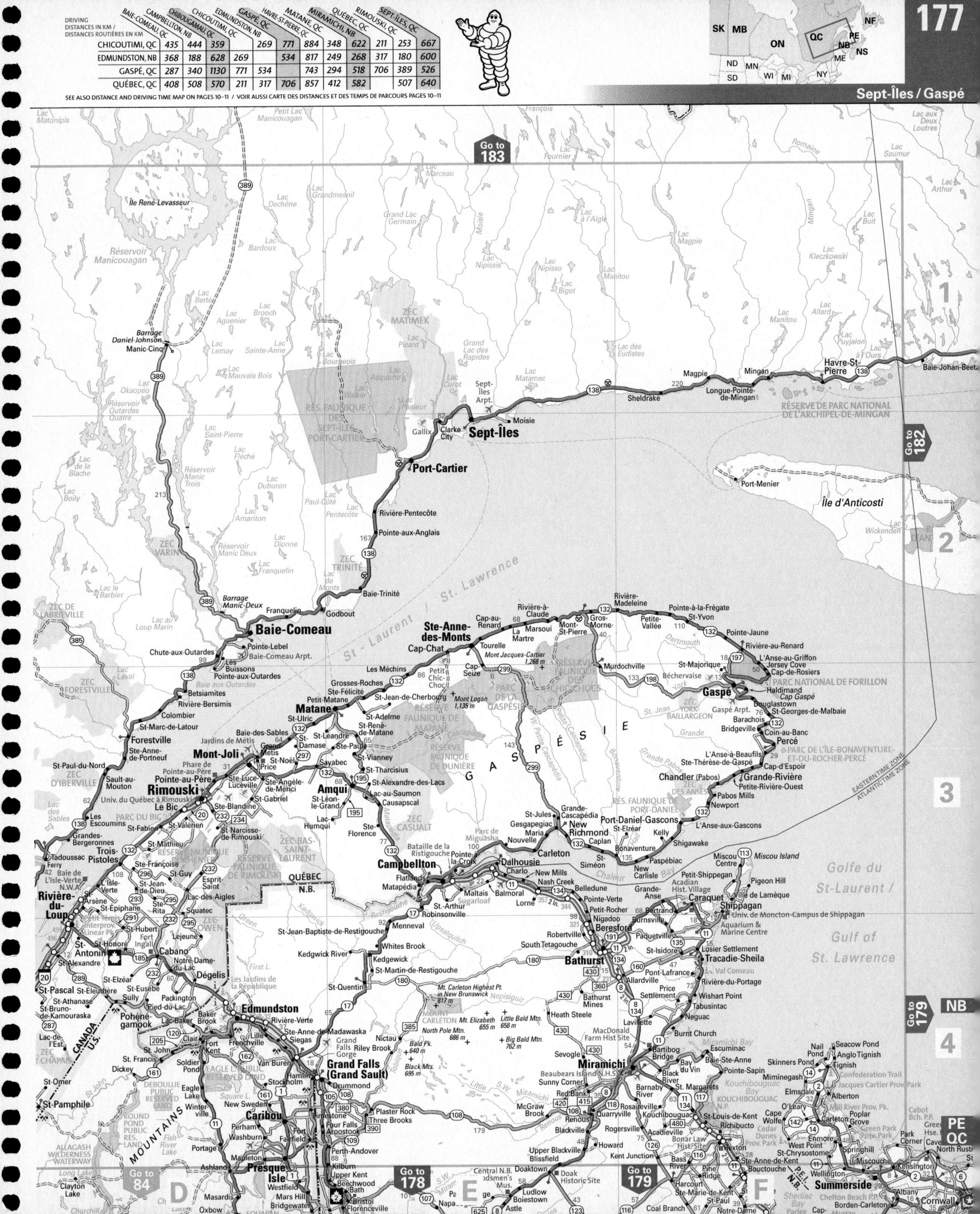

DRIVING DISTANCES IN KM / DISTANCES ROUTIÈRES EN KM

	CAMPBELLTON, NB	CHIBOUGAMAU, QC	CHICOUTIMI, QC	EDMUNDSTON, NB	GASPÉ, QC	HAVRE-ST-PIERRE, QC	MATANE, QC	MIRAMICHI, NB	QUÉBEC, QC	RIMOUSKI, QC	SEPT-ÎLES, QC	BAIE-COMEAU, QC
CHICOUTIMI, QC	435	444	359		269	771	884	348	622	211	253	667
EDMUNDSTON, NB	368	188	628	269		534	817	249	268	317	180	600
GASPÉ, QC	287	340	1130	771	534		743	294	518	706	389	526
QUÉBEC, QC	408	508	570	211	317	706	857	412	582		507	640

SEE ALSO DISTANCE AND DRIVING TIME MAP ON PAGES 10–11 / VOIR AUSSI CARTE DES DISTANCES ET DES TEMPS DE PARCOURS PAGES 10–11

Go to 183
Go to 182
Go to 179
Go to 84
Go to 178
Go to 179

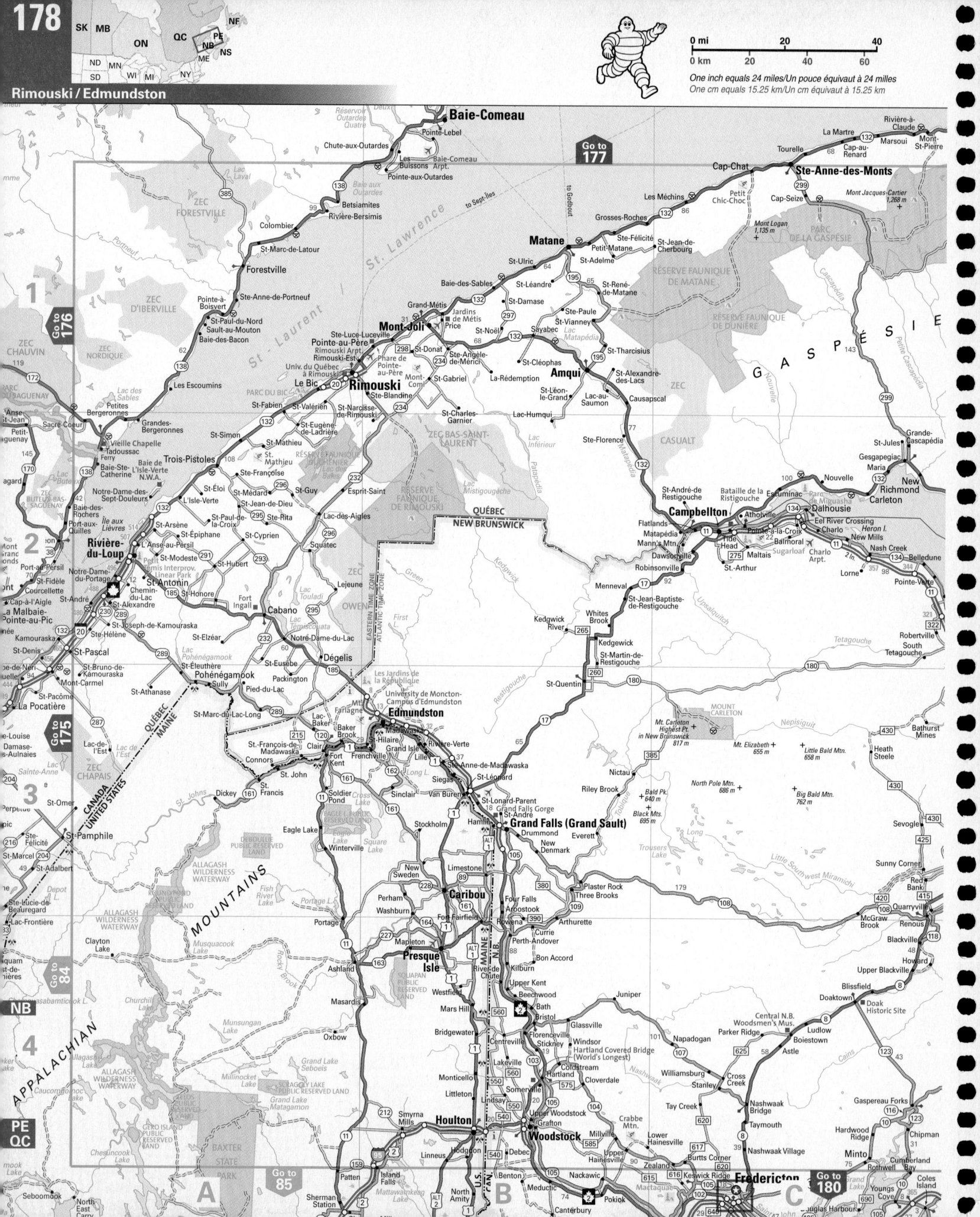

One inch equals 24 miles/Un pouce équivaut à 24 milles
One cm equals 15.25 km/Un cm équivaut à 15.25 km

DRIVING DISTANCES IN KM / DISTANCES ROUTIÈRES EN KM

	BATHURST, NB	BORDEN-CARLETON, PE	CAMPBELLTON, NB	CHARLOTTETOWN, PE	EDMUNDSTON, NB	FREDERICTON, NB	GASPÉ, QC	GRAND FALLS, NB	MATANE, QC	MIRAMICHI, NB	MONCTON, NB	RIMOUSKI, QC
CHARLOTTETOWN, PE	338	56	438		629	362	791	581	562	273	164	596
EDMUNDSTON, NB	189	428	188	638		279	534	57	249	268	447	180
MATANE, QC	262	506	168	562	249	553	294	331		346	487	95
MONCTON, NB	206	108	306	164	447	170	659	390	487	141		502

SEE ALSO DISTANCE AND DRIVING TIME MAP ON PAGES 10–11 / VOIR AUSSI CARTE DES DISTANCES ET DES TEMPS DE PARCOURS PAGES 10–11

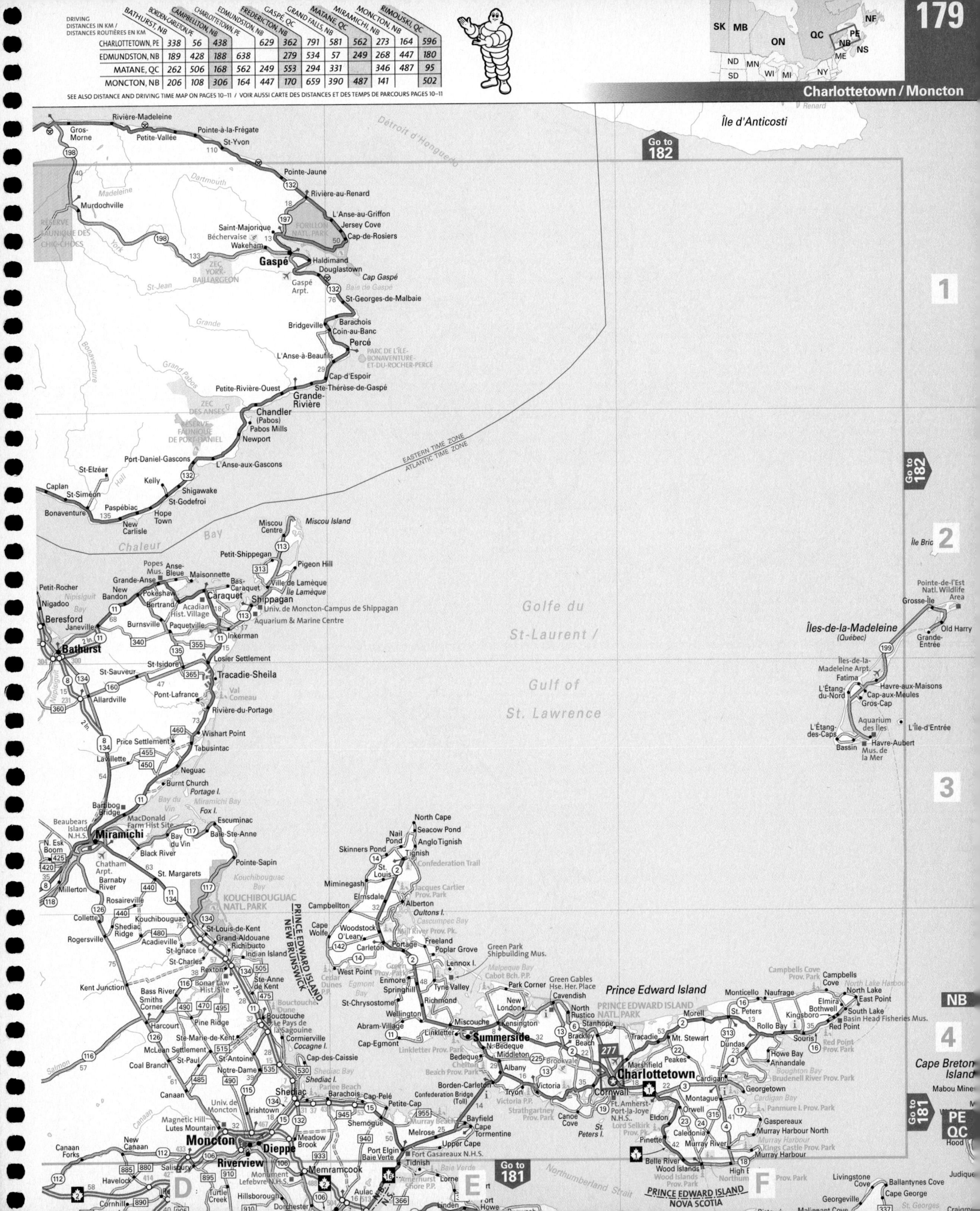

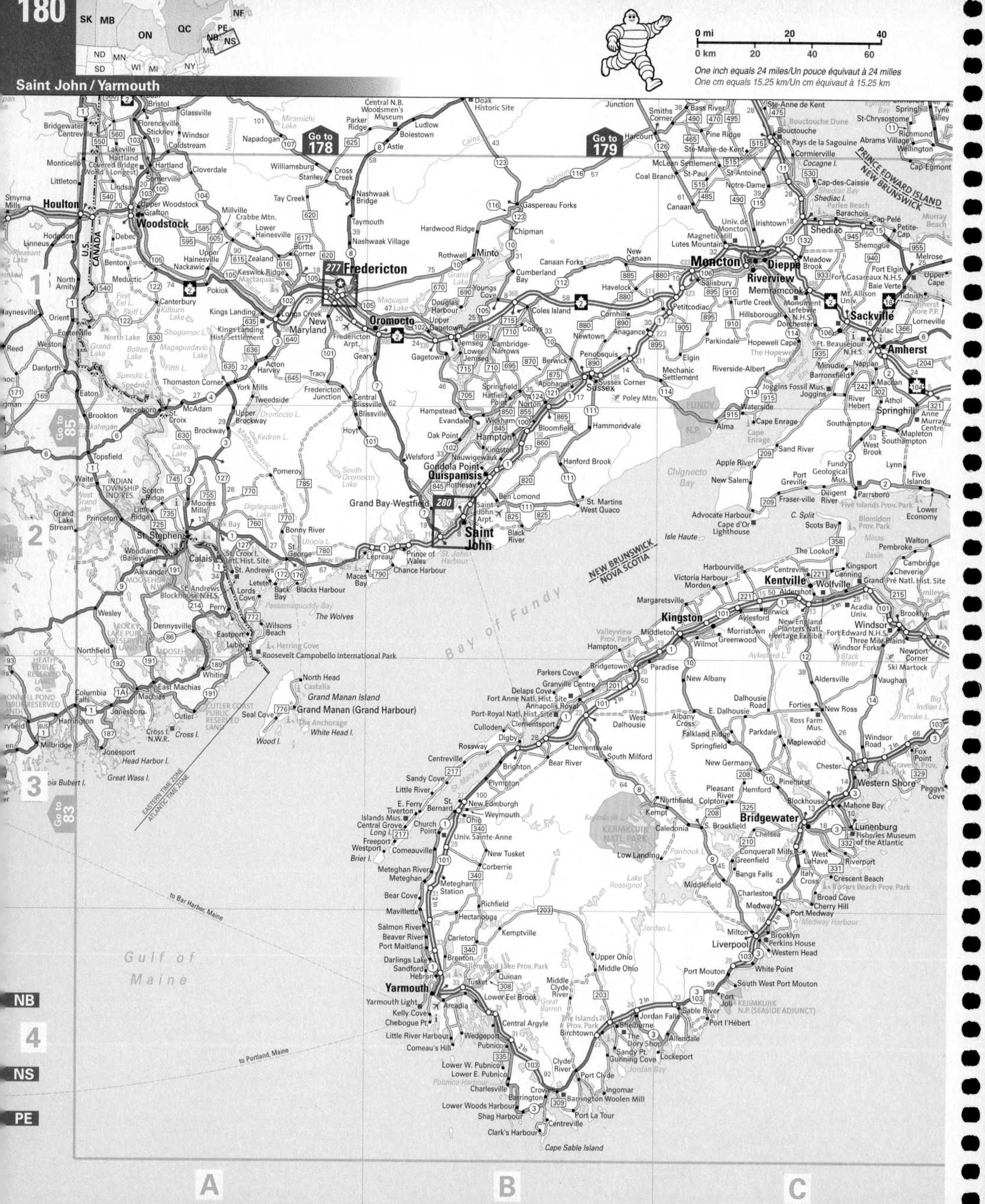

One inch equals 24 miles/Un pouce équivaut à 24 miles
One cm equals 15.25 km/Un cm équivaut à 15.25 km

Go to 178
Go to 179
Go to 85
Go to 83

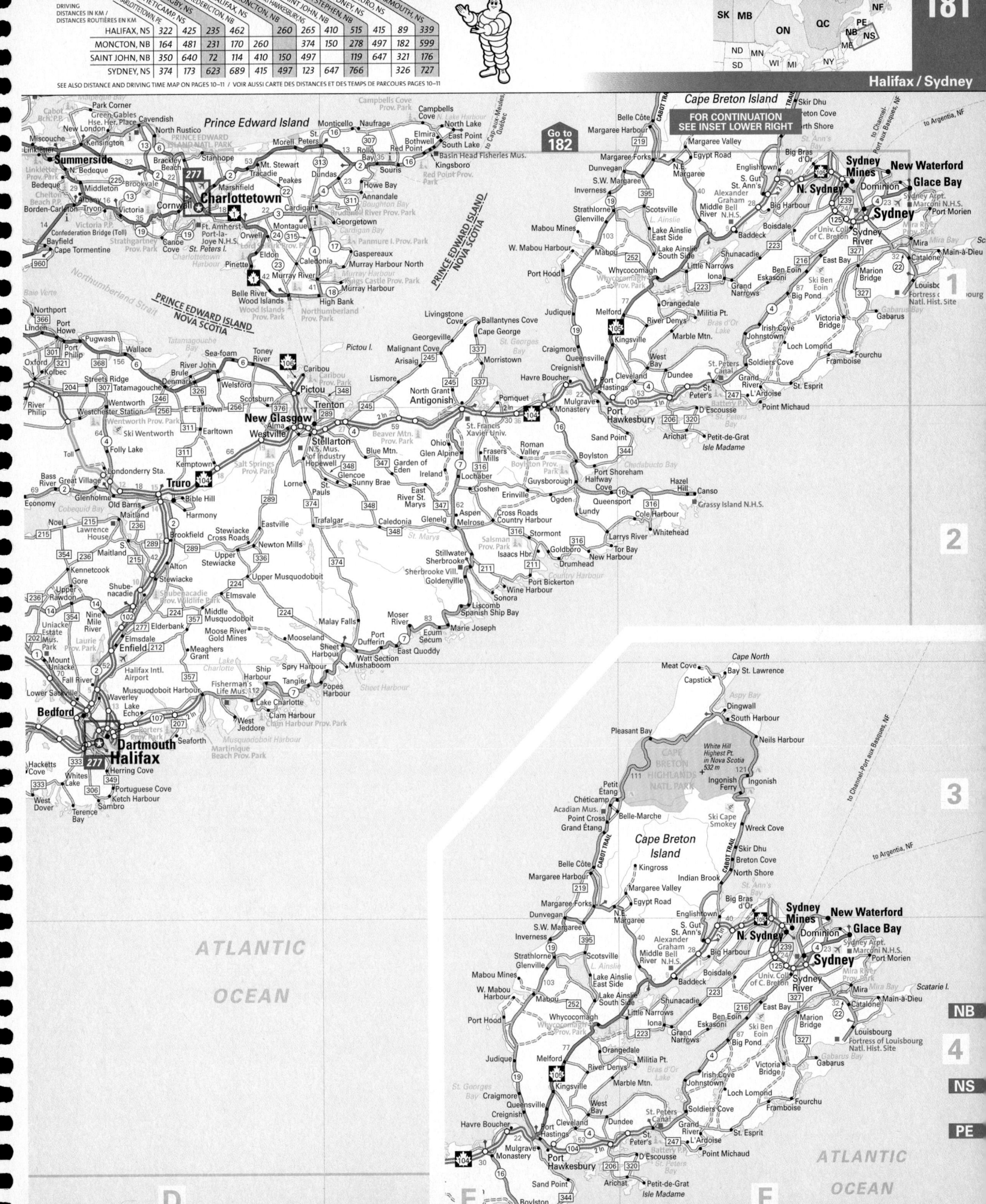

DRIVING DISTANCES IN KM / DISTANCES ROUTIÈRES EN KM

	CHARLOTTETOWN, PE	CHÉTICAMP, NS	DIGBY, NS	FREDERICTON, NB	HALIFAX, NS	MONCTON, NB	PORT HAWKESBURY, NS	SAINT JOHN, NB	ST. STEPHEN, NB	SYDNEY, NS	TRURO, NS	YARMOUTH, NS
HALIFAX, NS	322	425	235	462		260	265	410	515	415	89	339
MONCTON, NB	164	481	231	170	260		374	150	278	497	182	599
SAINT JOHN, NB	350	640	72	114	410	150	497		119	647	321	176
SYDNEY, NS	374	173	623	689	415	497	123	647	766		326	727

SEE ALSO DISTANCE AND DRIVING TIME MAP ON PAGES 10–11 / VOIR AUSSI CARTE DES DISTANCES ET DES TEMPS DE PARCOURS PAGES 10–11

Go to 182

FOR CONTINUATION SEE INSET LOWER RIGHT

Cape Breton Island

ATLANTIC OCEAN

SK MB
ON   QC
ND MN   NB
NF
NF
PE
ME   NS

0 mi   20   40   60
0 km   20   40   60   80
One inch equals 38 miles/Un pouce équivaut à 38 milles
One centimeter equals 24 km/Un cm équivaut à 24 km

FOR CONTINUATION
SEE INSET AT RIGHT

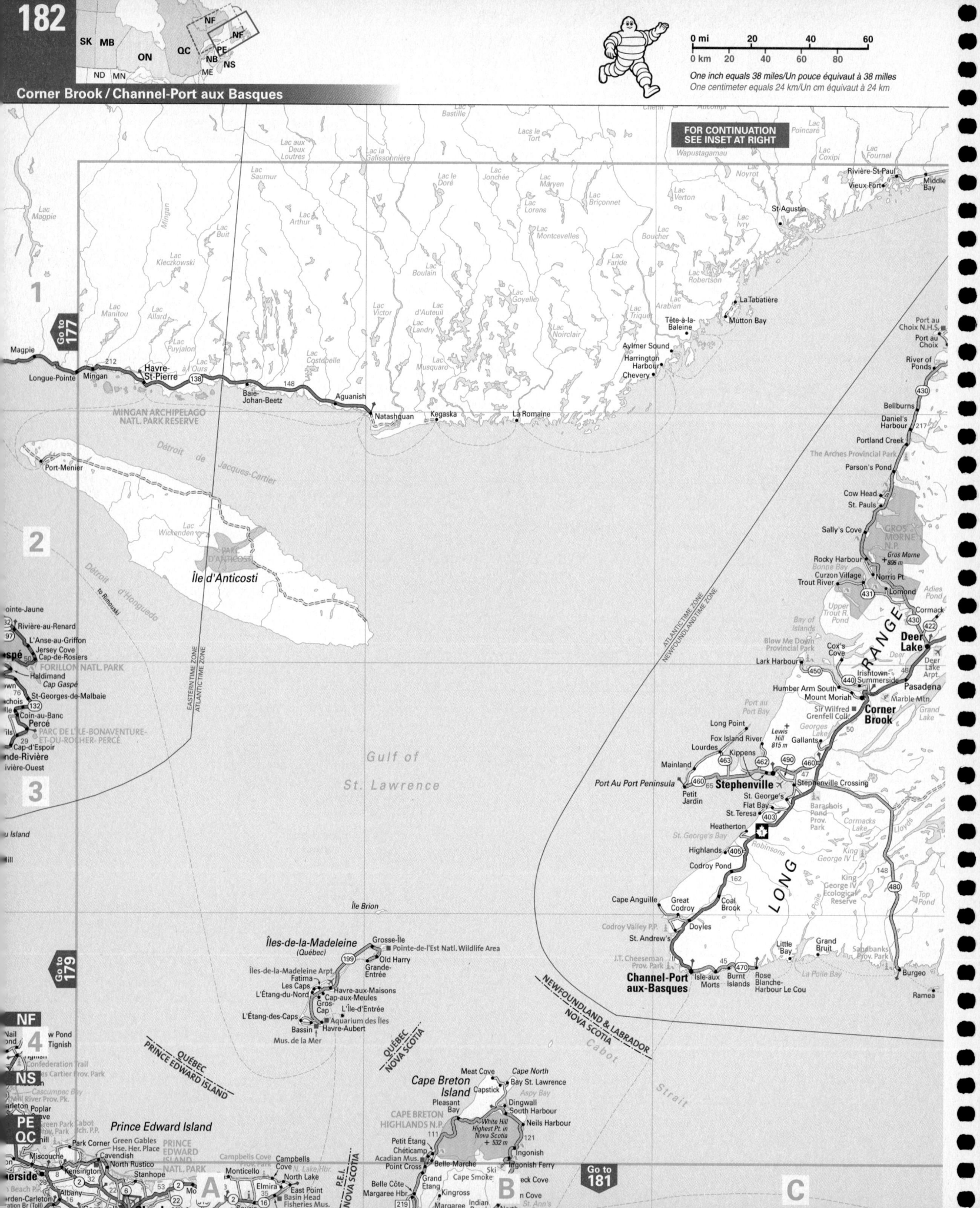

1

Lac Magpie

Magpie   Go to 177

Longue-Pointe   Mingan   Havre-St-Pierre   138   212   148   Baie-Johan-Beetz   Aguanish

MINGAN ARCHIPELAGO NATL. PARK RESERVE

Natashquan   Kegaska   La Romaine

Lac aux Deux Loutres   Lac la Galissonnière   Lacs le Tort   Wapustagamau   Lac Poincaré   Lac Coxipi

Lac Saumur   Lac le Doré   Lac Jonchée   Lac Maryen   Lac Briçonnet   Lac Verton   Lac Fournel

Lac Buit   Lac Arthur   Lac Boulain   Lac Faride   Lac Robertson   Rivière-St-Paul   Vieux-Fort   Middle Bay

Lac Manitou   Lac Allard   Lac Puyjalon   Lac l'Ours   Lac Costebelle   Lac Goyelle   Lac d'Auteuil   Lac Triquet   Lac Arabian   La Tabatière   St-Augustin

Lac Victor   Lac Landry   Lac Noirclair   Tête-à-la-Baleine   Mutton Bay

Lac Montcevelles   Lac Ivry   Aylmer Sound   Harrington Harbour   Chevery

Port au Choix N.H.S.   Port au Choix   River of Ponds

2

Port-Menier   Lac Wickenden   PARC D'ANTICOSTI   Île d'Anticosti

Détroit de Jacques-Cartier

Détroit d'Honguedo   to Rimouski

Gulf of St. Lawrence

430   Bellburns   Daniel's Harbour   217   Portland Creek   The Arches Provincial Park   Parson's Pond   Cow Head   St. Pauls   Sally's Cove   GROS MORNE N.P.   Rocky Harbour   Gros Morne 806 m   Curzon Village   Trout River   Norris Pt.   Lomond   Adies Pond   431

3

Pointe-Jaune   Rivière-au-Renard   97   L'Anse-au-Griffon   Jersey Cove   Cap-de-Rosiers   Gaspé   FORILLON NATL. PARK   Haldimand   Cap Gaspé   St-Georges-de-Malbaie   132   Coin-au-Banc   Percé   PARC DE L'ÎLE-BONAVENTURE-ET-DU-ROCHER-PERCÉ   Cap-d'Espoir   Grande-Rivière   Rivière-Ouest

Gulf of St. Lawrence

Île Brion

RANGE   Upper Trout R. Pond   Cormack   430   422   DEER LAKE   Deer Lake Arpt.   450   440   Irishtown-Summerside   Pasadena   Marble Mtn.   Bay of Islands   Blow Me Down Provincial Park   Cox's Cove   Lark Harbour   Humber Arm South   Mount Moriah   Sir Wilfred Grenfell Coll.   CORNER BROOK   Grand Lake   Long Point   Georges Lake   Lewis Hill 815 m   Fox Island River   Lourdes   Kippens   Gallants   50   Mainland   463   462   490   460   Stephenville Crossing   47   Port Au Port Peninsula   460   65   Stephenville   Petit Jardin   St. George's   Flat Bay   St. Teresa   403   Heatherton   Barachois Pond Prov. Park   Cormacks Lake   Lloyds   St. George's Bay   Highlands   405   Robinsons   King George IV L.   Codroy Pond   162   King George IV Ecological Reserve   148   480   Top Pond

4

NF

Nail Pond   w Pond   Tignish   Confederation Trail   Cartier Prov. Park

NS

Cascumpec Bay   NH River Prov. Pk   Carleton   Poplar   Green Park P.P.   tion Br (Toll)   Miscouche   Albany   32   6   Park Corner   Green Gables Hse. Her. Place   Cavendish   North Rustico   Stanhope   PRINCE EDWARD ISLAND NATL. PARK   Monticello   Campbells Cove   East Point   North Lake   Basin Head Fisheries Mus.   35   16   Souris

PE
QC

Go to 179

QUÉBEC   PRINCE EDWARD ISLAND   Prince Edward Island   PRINCE EDWARD ISLAND

Îles-de-la-Madeleine (Québec)   199   Grosse-Île   Pointe-de-l'Est Natl. Wildlife Area   Old Harry   Grande-Entrée   Îles-de-la-Madeleine Arpt.   Fatima   Les Caps   Havre-aux-Maisons   L'Étang-du-Nord   Cap-aux-Meules   Gros-Cap   L'Île-d'Entrée   L'Étang-des-Caps   Aquarium des Îles   Bassin   Havre-Aubert   Mus. de la Mer

Cape Breton Island   Meat Cove   Cape North   Bay St. Lawrence   Capstick   Pleasant Bay   Dingwall   South Harbour   CAPE BRETON HIGHLANDS N.P.   Neils Harbour   White Hill Highest Pt. in Nova Scotia 532 m   111   121   Ingonish   Ski   Ingonish Ferry

NEWFOUNDLAND & LABRADOR   NOVA SCOTIA

Codroy Valley P.P.   J.T. Cheeseman Prov. Park   St. Andrew's   Doyles   Great Codroy   Coal Brook   Cape Anguille   45   470   Channel-Port aux Basques   Isle-aux-Morts   Burnt Islands   Rose Blanche-Harbour Le Cou   Little Bay   Grand Bruit   Sandbanks Prov. Park   La Poile Bay   Burgeo   Ramea

Cabot   Strait

A   B   Go to 181   C

rside   8   2   32   Kensington   53   22   North Lake   2   Elmira

arden-Carleton   Beach P.P.

QUÉBEC   NOVA SCOTIA   Petit Étang   Chéticamp   Acadian Mus.   Point Cross   Belle Marche   Belle Côte   Grand Étang   Margaree Hbr.   219   Margaree   Indian Brook   Cape Smoke   Kingross   Wreck Cove   North   n Cove   St. Ann's

Cornwall

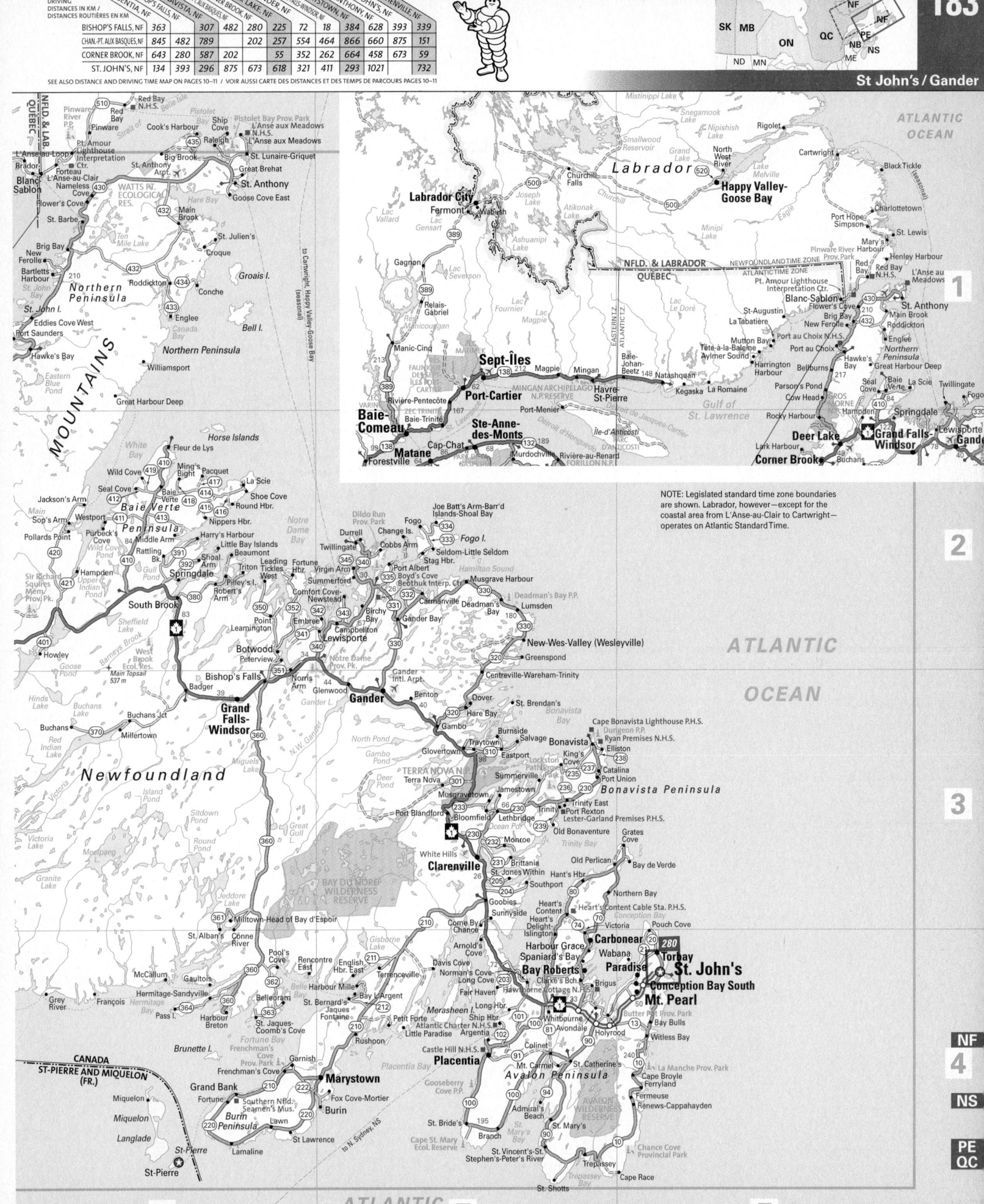

DRIVING DISTANCES IN KM / DISTANCES ROUTIÈRES EN KM

	ARGENTIA, NF	BISHOP'S FALLS, NF	BONAVISTA, NF	CHAN.-PT. AUX BASQUES, NF	CORNER BROOK, NF	DEER LAKE, NF	GANDER, NF	GRAND FALLS-WINDSOR, NF	MARYSTOWN, NF	ST. ANTHONY, NF	ST. JOHN'S, NF	STEPHENVILLE, NF
BISHOP'S FALLS, NF	363		307	482	280	225	72	18	384	628	393	339
CHAN.-PT. AUX BASQUES, NF	845	482	789		202	257	554	464	866	660	875	151
CORNER BROOK, NF	643	280	587	202		55	352	262	664	458	673	59
ST. JOHN'S, NF	134	393	296	875	673	618	321	411	293	1021		732

SEE ALSO DISTANCE AND DRIVING TIME MAP ON PAGES 10–11 / VOIR AUSSI CARTE DES DISTANCES ET DES TEMPS DE PARCOURS PAGES 10–11

NOTE: Legislated standard time zone boundaries are shown. Labrador, however—except for the coastal area from L'Anse-au-Clair to Cartwright—operates on Atlantic Standard Time.

AZ NM TX
MEXICO

0 mi 50 100 150
0 km 50 100 150 200
One inch equals 79 miles
One centimeter equals 50 kilometers

1 **2** **3** **4**

A **B** **C**

San Diego
CALIFORNIA
El Centro
Tijuana
Tecate
Calexico
Rosarito
La Rumorosa
Par. Nac. Constitución de 1857
Mexicali
Yuma
San Luis Río Colorado
El Descanso
Guadalupe
Ojos Negros
La Puerta
Riito
El Sauzal
Ensenada
Maneadero
Isla de Todos Santos
La Bufadora
Santo Tomás
San Vicente
El Golfo de Santa Clara
Colonet
Isla Montague
San Felipe
Puerto Peñasco
Pico del Diablo 3,100 m
Parque Nacional Sierra de San Pedro Mártir
Punta Estrella
Vicente Guerrero
San Quintín
Isla San Martín
El Socorro
Puertecitos
El Rosario
Punta Baja
Punta San Carlos
Puerto San Luis Gonzaga
Cataviña
Punta Canoas
BAJA CALIFORNIA
Isla Ángel de la Guarda
Cabo Tepoca
Cabo Lobos
La Libertad
RESERVA ESPECIAL DE LA BIÓSFERA ISLAS DEL GOLFO DE CALIFORNIA
Punta Prieta
Punta Maria
Bahía de los Ángeles
Punta de las Ánimas
Isla Tiburón
Rosarito
Bahía Sebastián Vizcaíno
Islas San Benito
Isla Cedros
Puerto San Francisquito
Punta Baja
Puerto Venustiano Carranza
El Arco
Misión Santa Gertrudis
Punta San Carlos
Isla Natividad
Punta Eugenia
Guerrero Negro
Scammon's Lagoon
Bahía Tortugas
Morro Hermoso
Volcán las Virgenes 1,920 m
Santa Rosalía
RESERVA DE LA BIÓSFERA EL VIZCAÍNO
Punta San Pablo
Punta San Pablo
San Ignacio
Magdalena
Punta Concepción
BAJA CALIFORNIA SUR
Mulegé
El Coyote
Punta Abreojos
SIERRA
La Purisima
Rosarito
Punta Púlpito
Comondú
Loreto
Isla Carmen
La Paz
Santo Domingo
Misión San Javier
Puerto Escondido
Ligui
Isla Santa Catalina
Adolfo López Mateos
Villa Insurgentes
Punta San Marcial
Isla Magdalena
Ciudad Constitución
San Evaristo
Isla San José
GIGANTA
Cabo San Lázaro
San Carlos
Santa Rita
La Paz Bay
Isla Espíritu Santo
Isla Santa Margarita
San Hilario
Pichilingue
Isla Cerralvo
PACIFIC OCEAN
La Paz
San Pedro
Punta Arena
Los Planes
San Antonio
San Bartolo
Buenavista
Todos Santos
El Triunfo
Santiago
El Pescadero
Miraflores
Parque Marino Nacional Cabo Pulmo
Cabo Pulmo
Reserva de la Biósfera Sierra de la Laguna
Candelaria
Santa Rosa
San José del Cabo
Cabo Falso
Cabo San Lucas

Phoenix
Casa Grande
ARIZONA
Safford
Tucson
SAGUARO N.P.
SAGUARO NATL. PARK
Lordsburg
Deming
Los Vidrios
Sonoyta
UNITED STATES
MÉXICO
Nogales
Douglas
Palomas
Quitovac
Sásabe
Nogales
Naco
Guadalupe Victoria
Ascensión
Saric
Cibuta
Agua Prieta
Janos
Fernández Leal
San Francisco
Caborca
Atil
Imuris
Cananea
Fronteras
Esqueda
Reserva Forestal Nacional Sierra de los Ajos
Buenos Aires
Casa de Janos
Pitiquito
Altar
El Ocuca Toll
Magdalena de Kino
Bacoachi
Casas Grandes
Dublán
Nuevo Casas Grandes
El Desemboque
Las Trincheras
El Claro
Santa Ana
Arizpe
Nacozari Viejo
Paquimé Ruins
Juárez
Ricardo Flores Magón
Galeana
Benjamin Hill
Cucurpé
Los Hoyos
Cúmpas
Huasabas
Buenaventura
Querobabi
Aconchi
SIERRA
Zaragoza
Las Varas
SONORA
Carbó
Baviácora
Moctezuma
Gómez Farías
Namiquipa
Santa Clara
Divisadero
Tepache
Madera
Topahue
Ures
Nácori Chico
Yepómera
San Lorenzo
Hermosillo
Guadalupe
San Pedro de la Cueva
Bacanora
Sahuaripa
Temósachic
Matachic
Bachiniva
Bahía Kino
La Colorada
Rebeico
Tacupeto
Cd. Guerrero
Kino Nuevo
Torres
Soyopa
MADRE
San Rafael
Carbó
Tecoripa
Tonichi
Yecora
Adolfo López Madero
Tastiota
Res. Especial de la Biósfera Cajón del Diablo
Ortiz
San Javier
Onavas
Yepachic
Basaseachic
Punta Baja
La Misa
Suaqui Grande
Vécora
Par. Nac. Cascada de Basaseachic
Cajurichi
San Carlos
Movas
Nuri
Maguarichic
Creel
Empalme
Guásimas
Guaymas
Cabo Haro
Vícam Toll
Bácum
Ciudad Obregón
Barranca del Cobre (Copper Canyon)
Carichic
Pótam
Fundición Toll
San Bernardo
Chinipas
Guazapares
Uruachic
Isla Lobos
Yaqui
Navojoa
Alamos
Temoris
Urique
La Bufa
Samachique
Batopilas
Guachochi
San Pedro
Etchojoa
Bacabachi
Huatabampo
Yavaros
Toll
Punta Rosa
Choix
OCCIDENTAL
Baborigame
Don
Toll
El Fuerte
San Miguel Zapotitlán
San Blas
Higuera de Zaragoza
Charay
Guadalupe y Calvo
Ahome
Mochicahui
Sinaloa de Leyva
SINALOA
Los Mochis
Tameapa
Topolobampo
Guasave
Caimanero
Bamoa
Burrioncito
Mocorito
Santiago de los Caballeros
Tamazula
Guamúchil
Toll
Badiraguato
Boca del Río
Angostura
Culiacancito
Culiacán
Navolato
Pericos
Altata
Costa Rica
El Salado
Península de Lucenilla
Toll
Eldorado
Quilá
Península de Quevedo
La Cruz
to Mazatlán

Go to 53
Go to 55

MOUNTAIN TIME ZONE
CENTRAL TIME ZONE
PACIFIC TIME ZONE

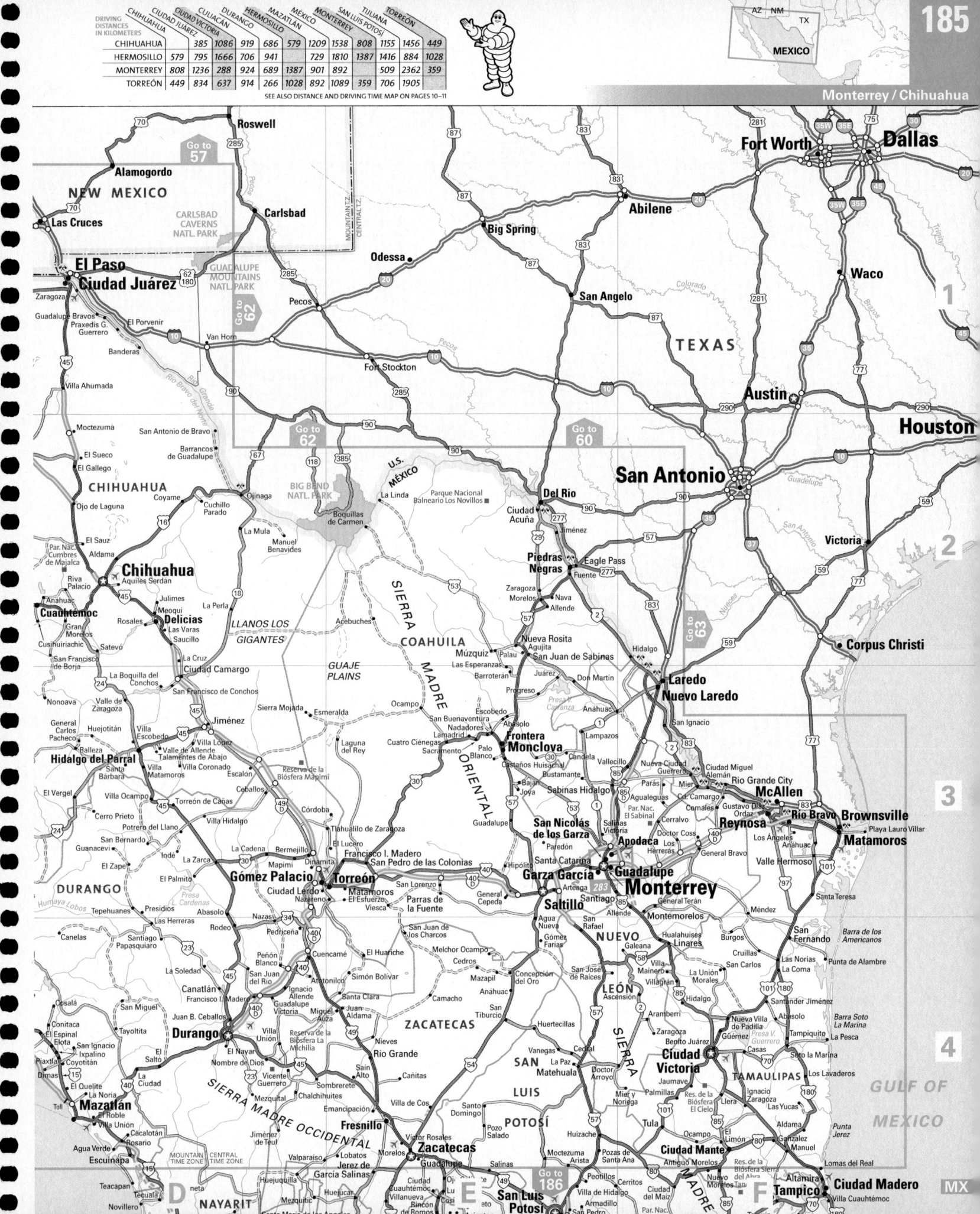

DRIVING DISTANCES IN KILOMETERS	CHIHUAHUA	CIUDAD JUÁREZ	CIUDAD VICTORIA	CULIACÁN	DURANGO	HERMOSILLO	MAZATLÁN	MÉXICO	MONTERREY	SAN LUIS POTOSÍ	TIJUANA	TORREÓN
CHIHUAHUA		385	1086	919	686	579	1209	1538	808	1155	1456	449
HERMOSILLO	579	795	1666	706	941		729	1810	1387	1416	884	1028
MONTERREY	808	1236	288	924	689	1387	901	892		509	2362	359
TORREÓN	449	834	637	914	266	1028	892	1089	359	706	1905	

SEE ALSO DISTANCE AND DRIVING TIME MAP ON PAGES 10-11

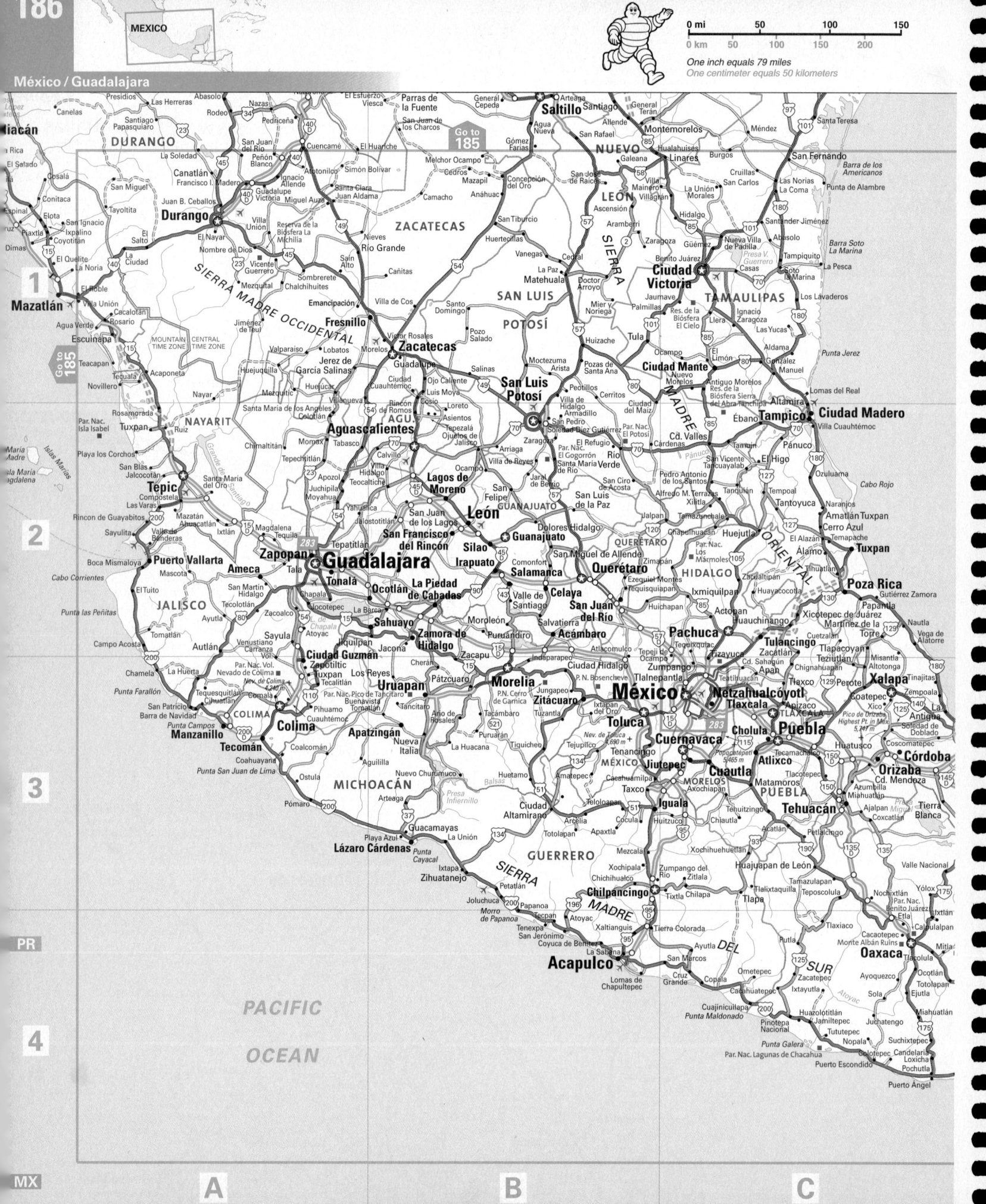

DRIVING DISTANCES IN KILOMETERS

	ACAPULCO	CANCÚN	CIUDAD VICTORIA	DURANGO	GUADALAJARA	MAZATLÁN	MÉRIDA	MÉXICO	PUEBLA	SAN LUIS POTOSÍ	TUXTLA GUTIÉRREZ	VERACRUZ
GUADALAJARA	897	2275	774	599		523	1904	578	691	336	1510	943
MÉRIDA	1777	321	1725	2182	1904	2408		1326	1282	1707	786	995
MÉXICO	422	1736	682	856	578	1081	1326		133	381	932	365
SAN LUIS POTOSÍ	834	2161	438	475	336	687	1707	381	496		1313	747

SEE ALSO DISTANCE AND DRIVING TIME MAP ON PAGES 10–11

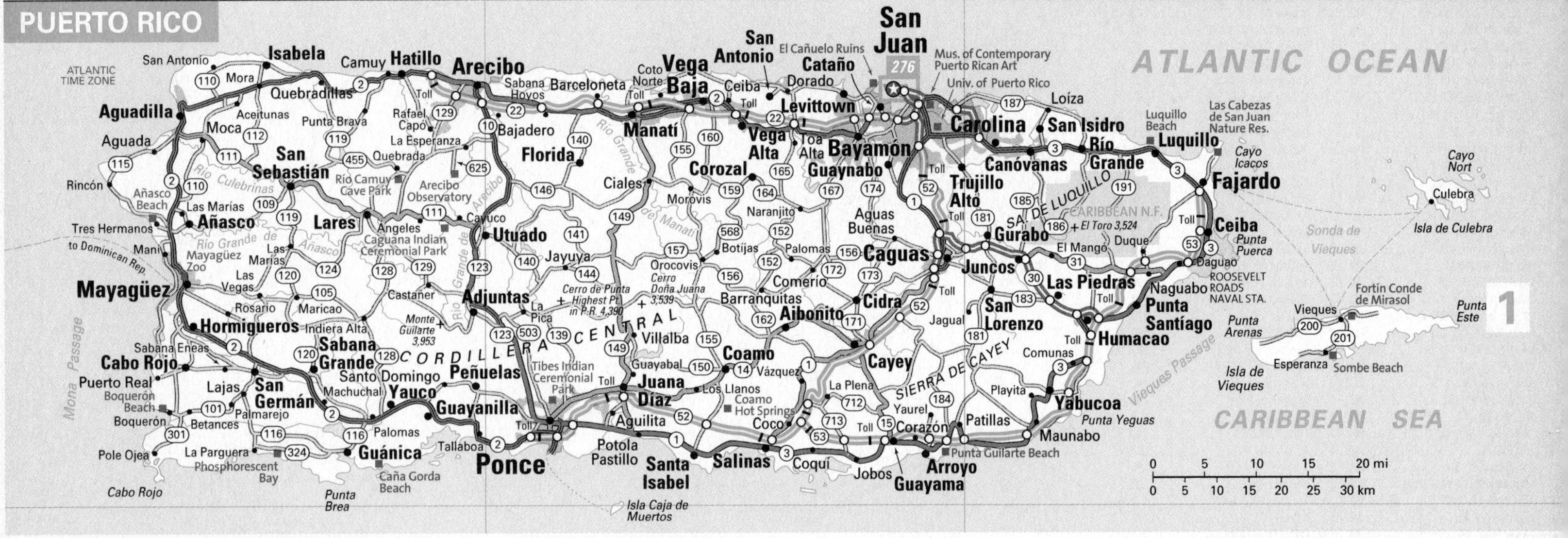

PUERTO RICO

ATLANTIC OCEAN

CARIBBEAN SEA

GULF OF MEXICO

YUCATÁN PENINSULA

Golfo de Tehuantepec

ATLANTIC TIME ZONE

0   5   10   15   20 mi
0 5 10 15 20 25 30 km

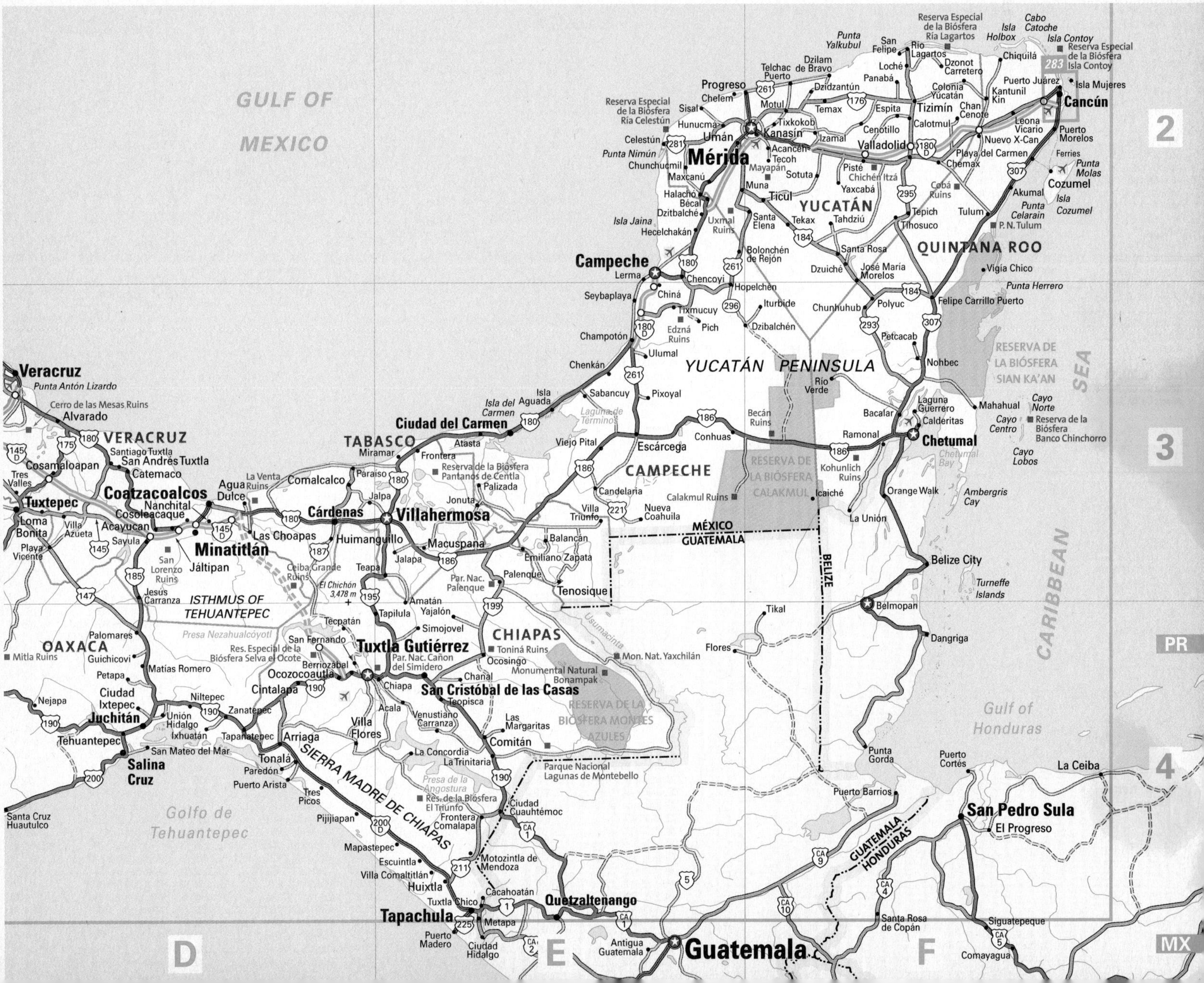

D   E   F   MX

188 Abbeville—Allenwood

Figures after entries indicate population, page number, and grid reference.

UNITED STATES

A

Abbeville AL, 2987	128	B4
Abbeville GA, 2298	129	E3
Abbeville LA, 11887	133	F3
Abbeville MS, 423	118	C4
Abbeville SC, 5840	121	D4
Abbeville Co. SC, 26167	121	E3
Abbotsford WI, 1956	68	A4
Abbottstown PA, 905	103	E1
Abercrombie ND, 296	19	F4
Aberdeen ID, 1840	31	E1
Aberdeen MD, 13842	145	D1
Aberdeen MS, 6415	119	D4
Aberdeen NC, 3400	122	C1
Aberdeen OH, 1603	100	C3
Aberdeen SD, 24658	27	E2
Aberdeen WA, 16461	12	B4
Abernathy TX, 2839	58	A1
Abilene KS, 6543	43	E2
Abilene TX, 115930	58	C3
Abingdon IL, 3612	88	A3
Abingdon MD, 950	145	D1
Abingdon VA, 7780	111	E3
Abington MA, 14605	151	D2
Abita Sprs. LA, 1957	134	B2
Absarokee MT, 1234	24	B2
Absecon NJ, 7638	147	F4
Acadia Par. LA, 58861	133	E2
Accokeek MD, 7349	144	B3
Accokeek Acres MD, 1500	144	B4
Accomac VA, 547	114	C3
Accomack Co. VA, 38305	114	C3
Accord MA, 2300	151	D2
Accord NY, 622	94	A3
Achille OK, 506	59	F1
Achilles VA, 650	115	F2
Ackerman MS, 1696	126	C1
Ackley IA, 1809	73	D4
Acme MI, 650	69	F4
Acomita NM, 288	48	B3
Acton CA, 2390	52	C2
Acton MA, 2700	150	C1
Acushnet MA, 3171	151	D3
Acworth GA, 13422	120	C3
Ada MN, 1657	19	F3
Ada OH, 5582	90	B3
Ada OK, 15691	51	F4
Ada Co. ID, 300904	22	B4
Adair IA, 839	86	B2
Adair OK, 704	106	A3
Adair Co. IA, 8243	86	B2
Adair Co. KY, 17244	110	B2
Adair Co. MO, 24977	87	D4
Adair Co. OK, 21038	106	B4
Adairsville GA, 2542	120	B3
Adair Vil. OR, 536	20	B3
Adairville KY, 920	109	F3
Adams MA, 5784	94	C1
Adams MN, 800	73	D2
Adams NE, 489	35	F4
Adams NY, 1624	79	E2
Adams OR, 297	21	F1
Adams TN, 566	109	E3
Adams WI, 1914	74	A1
Adams Ctr. NY, 1500	79	E2
Adams Co. CO, 348618	41	F1
Adams Co. ID, 3476	22	B2

Adams Co. IL, 68277	87	F4
Adams Co. IN, 33625	90	A3
Adams Co. IA, 4482	86	B3
Adams Co. MS, 34340	126	A4
Adams Co. NE, 31151	35	D4
Adams Co. ND, 2593	26	A3
Adams Co. OH, 27330	100	C3
Adams Co. PA, 91292	103	E1
Adams Co. WA, 16428	13	D4
Adams Co. WI, 18643	74	A1
Adamston NJ, 4900	147	E3
Adamstown MD, 650	144	A2
Adamstown PA, 1203	146	B1
Adamsville AL, 4965	119	F4
Adamsville RI, 550	151	D4
Adamsville TN, 1983	119	D1
Addis LA, 2238	134	A2
Addison AL, 723	119	E3
Addison IL, 35914	203	C4
Addison ME, 300	83	E2
Addison MI, 627	90	B1
Addison NY, 1797	93	D1
Addison TX, 14166	207	D1
Addison Co. VT, 35974	81	D3
Adel GA, 5307	137	F1
Adel IA, 3435	86	C2
Adelanto CA, 18130	53	D2
Adelphi MD, 14998	270	E1
Adelphia NJ, 700	147	E2
Adena OH, 815	91	F4
Adrian GA, 579	129	F2
Adrian MI, 21574	90	B1
Adrian MN, 1234	72	A2
Adrian MO, 1780	96	B4
Advance IN, 562	99	E1
Advance MO, 1244	108	B2
Adwolf VA, 1457	111	F3
Affton MO, 20535	256	B3
Afton IA, 917	86	C3
Afton NY, 836	93	F1
Afton OK, 1118	106	B3
Afton WY, 1818	31	F1
Agawam MA, 28144	150	A2
Agency IA, 622	87	E3
Agency MO, 599	96	B1
Agoura Hills CA, 20537	228	A2
Agua Dulce TX, 737	63	E2
Agua Fria NM, 2051	49	D2
Aguilar CO, 593	41	E4
Ahoskie NC, 4523	113	F1
Ahsahka ID, 600	14	B4
Ahuimanu HI, 8506	152	A3
Aiken SC, 25337	121	F4
Aiken Co. SC, 142552	122	A4
Ainsworth IA, 524	87	F2
Ainsworth NE, 1862	34	C1
Airmont NY, 7799	148	B3
Airport Drive MO, 622	106	B2
Airway Hts. WA, 4500	13	F1
Aitkin MN, 1984	64	B4
Aitkin Co. MN, 15301	64	B4
Ajo AZ, 3705	54	B3
Ak-Chin AZ, 669	54	C2
Akiachak AK, 585	154	B3
Akins OK, 449	116	B1

Akron NY, 3085	78	B3
Akron OH, 217074	91	E3
Akron PA, 4046	146	A2
Akron IN, 1076	89	F3
Akron IA, 1489	35	F1
Akron MI, 461	76	B2
Akron AL, 521	127	E1
Akron CO, 1711	41	F1

Alachua FL, 6098	138	C3
Alachua Co. FL, 217955	138	C3
Alakanuk AK, 652	154	B2
Akutan AK, 713	154	A4
Alabaster AL, 22619	127	F1
Alameda CA, 72259	259	C2
Alameda NM, 4200	48	C3
Alameda Co. CA, 1443741	36	B4
Alamo CA, 15626	259	D2
Alamo GA, 1943	129	E3
Alamo NM, 1183	48	B4
Alamo TN, 2392	108	C4
Alamo TX, 14760	63	E4
Alamogordo NM, 35582	56	C2
Alamo Hts. TX, 7319	257	E2
Alamosa CO, 7960	41	D4
Alamosa Co. CO, 14966	41	D4
Alanson MI, 785	70	C3
Alapaha GA, 682	129	E4
Alba MO, 588	106	B2
Albany CA, 16444	259	C2
Albany GA, 76939	129	D4
Albany IL, 895	88	A1
Albany IN, 2368	90	A4
Albany KY, 2220	110	B3
Albany LA, 865	134	B2
Albany MN, 1796	66	B2
Albany MO, 1937	86	B4
Albany NY, 95658	94	B1
Albany OH, 808	101	E2
Albany OR, 40852	20	B3
Albany TX, 1921	58	C2
Albany WI, 1191	74	B4
Albany Co. NY, 294565	94	B1
Albany Co. WY, 32014	33	E2
Albemarle NC, 15680	122	B1
Albemarle Co. VA, 79236	102	C4
Albers IL, 878	98	B3
Albert City IA, 709	72	B4
Albert Lea MN, 18356	72	C2
Alberton MT, 374	15	D4
Albertville AL, 17247	120	A3
Albertville MN, 3621	66	C3
Albia IA, 3706	87	D3
Albin VA, 700	102	C3
Albion ID, 262	31	D2
Albion IL, 1933	99	D4
Albion IN, 2284	90	A2
Albion IA, 592	87	D1

Albion MI, 9144	76	A4
Albion NE, 1797	35	E3
Albion NY, 7438	78	B3
Albion PA, 1607	91	F1
Albion WI, 616	14	A4
Albuquerque NM, 448607	48	C3
Alburg VT, 488	81	D1
Alburnett IA, 559	87	E1
Alburtis PA, 2117	146	B1
Alcalde NM, 377	49	D2
Alcester SD, 880	35	F1
Alcoa TN, 7734	110	C4
Alcona Co. MI, 11719	71	D4
Alcorn MS, 1200	126	A3
Alcorn Co. MS, 34558	119	D2
Alda NE, 652	35	D4
Aldan PA, 4313	248	B4
Alden IA, 804	72	C4
Alden MN, 652	72	C2
Alden NY, 2666	78	B3
Alderson WV, 1091	112	A1
Alderwood Manor WA, 15329	262	B2
Aldine TX, 13979	220	C1
Aledo IL, 3613	87	F2
Aledo TX, 1726	59	E2
Alex OK, 635	51	E4
Alexander AR, 614	117	E2
Alexander City AL, 15008	128	A1
Alexander Co. IL, 9590	108	C2
Alexander Co. NC, 33603	112	A4
Alexandria AL, 3692	120	A4

Alexandria IN, 6260	89	F4
Alexandria LA, 46342	125	E3
Alexandria MN, 8820	66	B2
Alexandria SD, 563	27	E4
Alexandria TN, 814	110	A4
Alexandria VA, 128283	144	B3
Alexandria Bay NY, 1088	79	E1
Alexis IL, 863	88	A3
Alford FL, 466	136	C1
Alfred ME, 700	82	B4
Alfred NY, 3954	92	C1
Alger OH, 888	90	B3
Alger Co. MI, 9862	69	E1
Algoa TX, 900	132	B4
Algodones NM, 688	48	C3
Algoma MS, 508	118	C3
Algoma WI, 3357	69	D4
Algona IA, 5741	72	B3
Algona WA, 2460	262	B5
Algonac MI, 4613	76	C4
Algonquin IL, 23276	88	C1
Algood TN, 2942	110	A3
Alhambra CA, 85804	228	D2
Alhambra IL, 630	98	B3
Alice TX, 19010	63	E2
Aliceville AL, 2567	127	E1
Ali Chuk AZ, 450	54	B3
Aliquippa PA, 11734	91	F3
Aliso Viejo CA, 40166	229	G6
Allamakee Co. IA, 14675	73	F1

Allamuchy NJ, 3125	94	A4
Allardt TN, 642	110	B3
Allegan MI, 4838	75	F4
Allegan Co. MI, 105665	75	F4
Allegany NY, 1883	92	C1
Allegany Co. MD, 74930	102	C1
Allegany Co. NY, 49927	78	C4
Alleghany Co. NC, 10677	111	F3
Alleghany Co. VA, 12926	102	A4
Allegheny Co. PA, 1281666	92	A4
Allen NE, 411	35	F2
Allen OK, 951	51	F3
Allen SD, 419	26	B4
Allen TX, 43554	59	F2
Allen Co. IN, 331849	90	A3
Allen Co. KS, 14385	96	A4
Allen Co. KY, 17800	109	F3
Allen Co. OH, 108473	90	B3
Allendale MI, 11555	75	F3
Allendale NJ, 6699	148	B3
Allendale SC, 4052	130	B1
Allendale Co. SC, 11211	130	B1
Allenhurst GA, 788	130	B3
Allenhurst NJ, 718	147	F2
Allen Par. LA, 25440	133	E1
Allen Park MI, 29376	210	B4
Allenspark CO, 496	41	D1
Allenton WI, 1400	150	C4
Allentown NJ, 1882	147	E2
Allentown PA, 106632	146	B1
Allenwood NJ, 935	147	E2

Albany / Schenectady / Troy NY

Albany	D3	E. Greenbush	E3	Maywood	D2	Scotia	C1
Alplaus	C1	Elsmere	D3	McCormack Corners	C2	Sherwood Park	E3
Best	E3	Ft. Hunter	C2	McKownville	D3	Slingerlands	D3
Bethlehem Ctr.	D3	Glenmont	D3	Meadowdale	C3	Snyders Corners	E3
Boght Corners	E1	Glenridge	C1	Menands	E3	Speigletown	E1
Calico Colony	D1	Grant Hollow	E1	Mohawk View	D2	Sycaway	E2
Clifton Gardens	D1	Green Island	E2	New Salem	C3	Troy	E2
Clifton Park	D1	Grooms Corners	D1	New Scotland	C3	Unionville	D3
Clifton Park Ctr.	D1	Guilderland	C2	Newtonville	E2	Verdoy	D1
Clinton Park	D1	Guilderland Ctr.	C2	Niskayuna	D2	Vischer Ferry	D1
Cohoes	E2	Halfmoon	E1	Normanville	D3	Voorheesville	C3
Colonie	E2	Hartmans Corners	C2	N. Bethlehem	D3	Waterford	E1
Crescent	E1	Hawthorne Hill	D1	Rensselaer	E3	Watervliet	E2
Defreestville	E3	Latham	E2	Rexford	D1	W. Hill	C1
Delmar	D3	Loudonville	E2	Roessleville	D2	Westmere	D2
Dunnsville	C2	Luther	E3	Rotterdam	C1	Wynantskill	E2
Dunsbach Ferry	E1	Maple Wood	E2	Schenectady	C1		

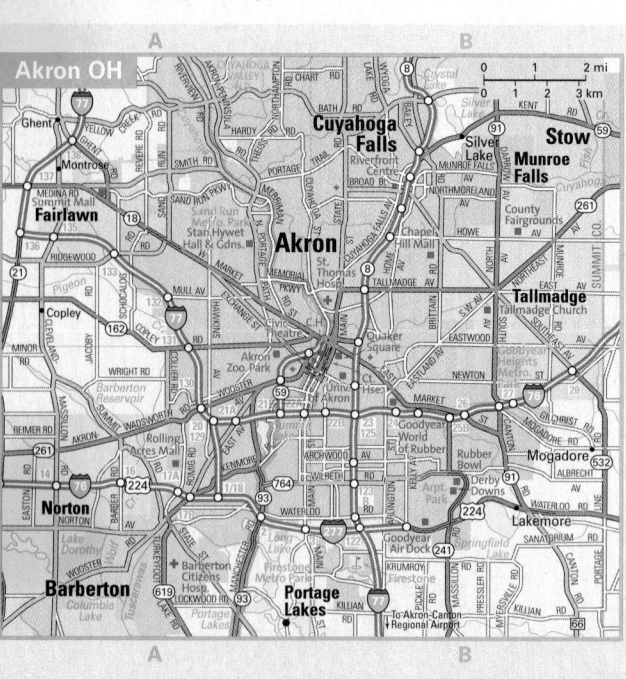

Akron OH

Akron	A1
Barberton	A2
Copley	A1
Cuyahoga Falls	B1
Fairlawn	A1
Ghent	A1
Lakemore	B2
Mogadore	B2
Montrose	A1
Munroe Falls	B1
Norton	A2
Portage Lakes	A2
Silver Lake	B1
Stow	B1
Tallmadge	B1

Allerton IA, *559* **87** D3
Allgood AL, *629* **119** F4
Alliance NE, *8959* **34** A2
Alliance NC, *781* **115** D3
Alliance OH, *23253* **91** E3
Allison IA, *1006* **73** D4
Allison Gap VA, *900* **111** F2

Alpharetta GA, *34854* **120** C3
Alpine CA, *13143* **53** D4
Alpine NJ, *2183* **148** B3
Alpine TX, *5786* **62** B3
Alpine UT, *7146* **31** F4
Alpine WY, *550* **31** F1
Alpine Co. CA, *1208* **37** D3

Alton KY, *750* **100** B4
Alton MO, *668* **107** F3
Alton NH, *650* **81** F4
Altona IL, *570* **88** A3
Alton NY, *1056* **79** D1
Alton MO, *2561* **88** B1
Alton Bay NH, *400* **81** F4

Amawalk NY, *1500* **148** B2
Amber OK, *490* **51** E3
Amberley OH, *3425* **204** B2
Amboy CA, *6426* **146** C2
Amboy IL, *2561* **88** B1
Amboy MN, *575* **72** C2
Amboy WA, *2085* **20** C1

Amherstdale WV, *1785* **111** F1
Amidon ND, *26* **18** A4
Amissville VA, *550* **103** D3
Amite LA, *4110* **134** B1
Amite Co. MS, *13599* **126** A4

Anahola HI, *1932* **152** B1
Anahuac TX, *2210* **132** B3
Anamoose ND, *282* **18** C2
Anamosa IA, *5494* **87** F1
Anchorage AK, *260283* **154** C3
Anchorage KY, *2264* **230** F1
Anchor Pt. AK, *1845* **154** C3

Anderson Co. SC, *165740* **121** E2
Anderson Co. TN, *71330* **110** C4
Anderson Co. TX, *55109* **124** A4
Andersonville OH, *800* **101** D2
Andover CT, *800* **150** A3
Andover IL, *594* **88** A2
Andover KS, *6698* **43** F4
Andover MA, *7900* **95** E1
Andover MN, *26588* **67** D3
Andover NJ, *658* **94** A4
Andover NY, *1073* **92** C1
Andover OH, *1269* **91** F2
Andrew Co. MO, *16492* **96** B1
Andrews IN, *1290* **89** F3
Andrews NC, *1602* **121** D1
Andrews SC, *3068* **122** C4
Andrews TX, *9652* **57** F3
Andrews Co. TX, *13004* **57** F3
Androscoggin Co. ME, *103793* **82** B2
Aneta ND, *284* **19** E3
Aneth UT, *598* **40** A4
Angel Fire NM, *1048* **49** D2
Angelica NY, *903* **78** B4
Angelina Co. TX, *80130* **124** B4
Angels Camp CA, *3004* **36** C3
Angier NC, *3419* **123** D1
Angleton TX, *18130* **132** A4
Angola IN, *7344* **90** A2
Angola NY, *2266* **78** A4
Angola on the Lake NY, *1771* **78** A4
Angoon AK, *572* **155** E4
Anguilla MS, *907* **126** A1
Angwin CA, *3148* **36** B3
Aniak AK, *572* **154** B3
Anita IA, *1049* **86** B2
Ankeny IA, *27117* **86** C1
Anmoore WV, *685* **102** A2
Anna IL, *5136* **108** C1
Anna OH, *1319* **90** B4
Anna TX, *1225* **59** F4
Annabella UT, *603* **39** E2
Anna Maria FL, *1814* **140** B3
Annandale MN, *2684* **66** C3
Annandale NJ, *1276* **147** D1
Annandale VA, *54994* **144** B3
Annapolis MD, *35838* **144** C3
Ann Arbor MI, *114024* **76** B4
Annawan IL, *868* **88** A2
Anne Arundel Co. MD, *489656* **144** C3
Annetta TX, *1108* **59** E2
Anniston AL, *24276* **120** A4
Annsville NY, *850* **148** B2
Annville KY, *589* **110** C1
Annville PA, *4518* **93** E4

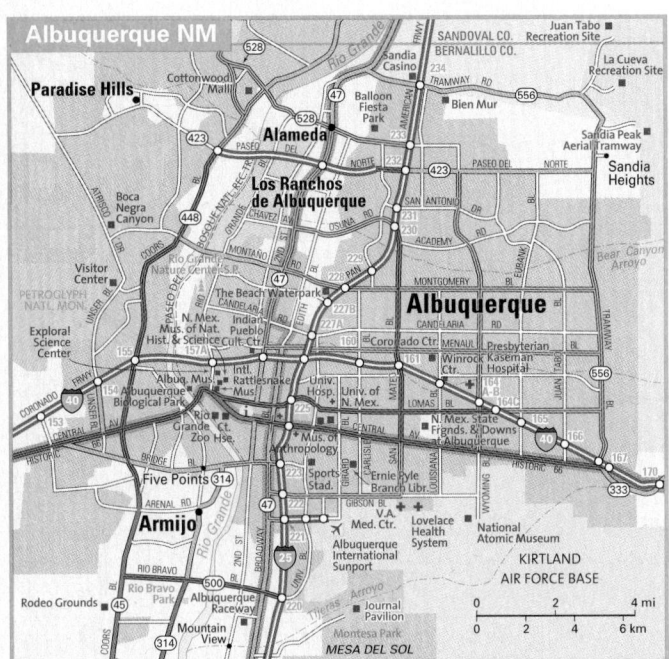

Albuquerque NM

Paradise Hills
Alameda
Los Ranchos de Albuquerque
Sandia Heights
Albuquerque
Armijo

Amarillo TX

Cliffside
Bishop Hills
Amarillo

Alloway NJ, *1128* **145** F1
Allyn WA, *2004* **12** C3
Alma AR, *4160* **116** C1
Alma GA, *3236* **129** F4
Alma KS, *797* **43** F2
Alma MI, *9275* **76** A2
Alma NE, *1214* **43** D1
Alma WI, *942* **73** E1
Almena KS, *469* **42** C1
Almena WI, *720* **67** E3
Almon GA, *1000* **121** D4
Almont MI, *2803* **76** C3
Aloe TX, *850* **61** E3
Aloha OR, *41741* **20** B2
Alorton IL, *2749* **256** C3
Alpaugh CA, *761* **45** D4
Alpena MI, *11304* **71** D3
Alpena SD, *265* **27** E3
Alpena Co. MI, *31314* **71** D4
Alpha IL, *726* **88** A2
Alpha NJ, *2482* **146** C1

Alsen LA, *950* **134** A2
Alsip IL, *19725* **203** D6
Alta IA, *1865* **72** A4
Alta UT, *370* **31** F4
Alta WV, *400* **23** F4
Altadena CA, *42610* **228** D1
Altamahaw NC, *996* **112** B4
Altamont IL, *2283* **98** C2
Altamont KS, *1092* **106** A2
Altamont NY, *1737* **94** B1
Altamont OR, *19603* **28** C2
Altamont TN, *1136* **120** A1
Altamonte Sprs. FL, *41200* **141** D2
Alta Vista KS, *442* **43** F2
Altavista VA, *3425* **112** C2
Altha FL, *506* **137** D2
Altheimer AR, *1192* **117** F3
Alto GA, *876* **121** D3
Alto TX, *1190* **124** B4
Alton IL, *30496* **98** A3
Alton IA, *1095* **35** F1

Altoona IA, *10345* **86** C2
Altoona KS, *485* **106** A1
Altoona PA, *49523* **92** C4
Altoona WI, *6698* **67** F4
Altona IL, *570* **29** D3
Altus OK, *21447* **51** D4
Altus AR, *817* **116** C1
American Fork UT, *21941* **31** F4
Americus GA, *17013* **129** D3
Americus KS, *938* **43** F3
Amery WI, *2845* **67** E3
Ames IA, *50731* **86** C1
Ames TX, *1079* **132** B3
Amesbury MA, *12327* **95** E1
Ama LA, *1285* **239** B2
Amado AZ, *275* **55** D4
Amagansett NY, *1067* **149** F3
Amalga UT, *427* **31** E2
Amana IA, *700* **87** E1
Amanda OH, *707* **101** D1
Amarillo TX, *173627* **50** A3

Ambridge PA, *7769* **92** A3
Amelia LA, *2423* **134** A3
Amelia OH, *2752* **100** B2
Amelia City FL, *1300* **139** D2
Amelia Co. VA, *11400* **113** D2
Amelia C.H. VA, *400* **113** D1
Amenia NY, *1115* **94** B3
American Beach FL, *800* **139** D2
American Canyon CA, *9774* **36** B3
American Falls ID, *4111* **31** E1
Americus GA (dup) ....
Amityville NY, *9441* **148** C4
Ammon ID, *6187* **23** E4
Amory MS, *6956* **119** D4
Amsterdam MT, *727* **23** F1
Amsterdam NY, *18355* **94** A1
Amsterdam OH, *568* **91** F4
Anacoco LA, *866* **125** D4
Anaconda MT, *9417* **23** D1
Anacortes WA, *14557* **12** C1
Anadarko OK, *6645* **51** D3
Anaheim CA, *328014* **52** C3

Amityville NY (dup)
Ammon ID
Amory MS
Andale KS, *766* **43** E4
Andalusia AL, *8794* **128** A4
Andalusia IL, *1050* **87** F2
Anderson CA, *9022* **28** C4
Anderson IN, *59734* **89** F4
Anderson MO, *1856* **106** B3
Anderson SC, *25514* **121** E3
Anderson TX, *257* **61** F1
Anderson Co. KS, *8110* **96** A4
Anderson Co. KY, *19111* **100** A4

Anchorville MI, *3200* **76** C4

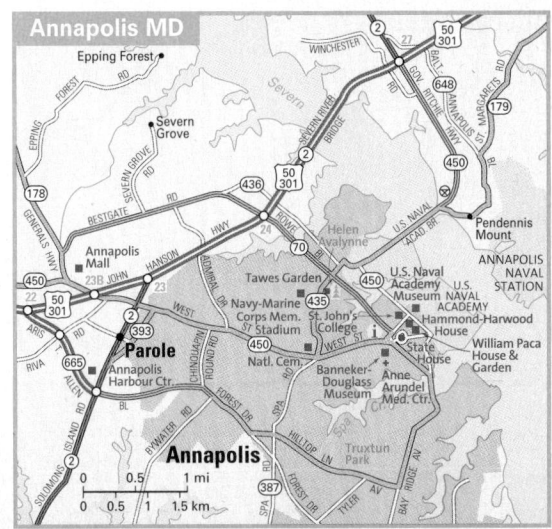

Anchorage AK

ELMENDORF AIR FORCE BASE
FORT RICHARDSON MILITARY RESERVATION
Anchorage

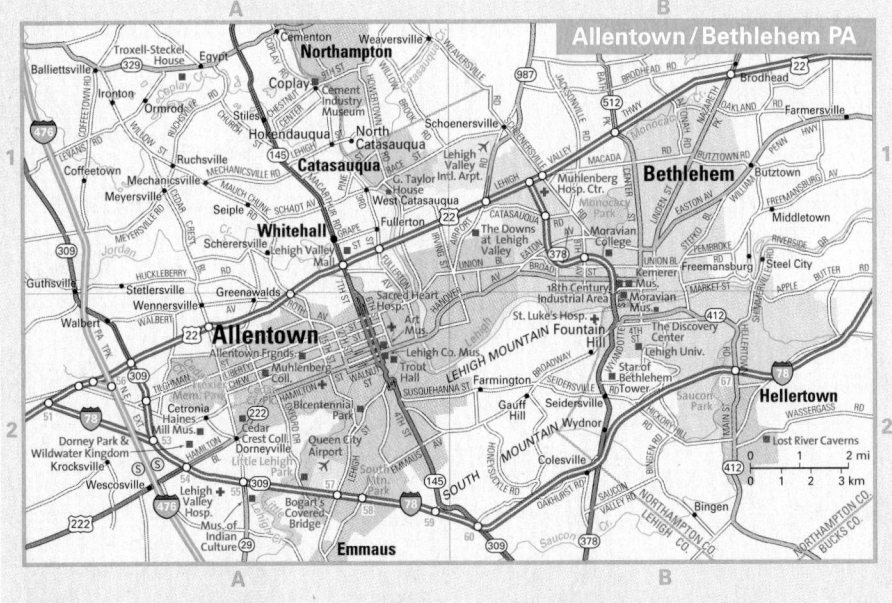

Allentown / Bethlehem PA

Northampton
Catasauqua
Whitehall
Allentown
Emmaus
Bethlehem
Hellertown

Annapolis MD

Epping Forest
Annapolis Mall
Parole
Annapolis

Allentown A2
Ballietsville B1
Bethlehem B1
Bingen B2
Brodhead B1
Butztown B1
Catasauqua A1
Cementon A1
Cetronia A1
Coffeetown A1
Colesville B2
Coplay A1
Dorneyville A2
Egypt A1
Emmaus A2
Farmersville B1
Farmington A1
Fountain Hill A2
Freemansburg B1
Fullerton A1
Gauff Hill B2
Greenawalds A2
Guthsville A1
Hellertown B2
Hokendauqua A1
Ironton A1
Krocksville A1
Mechanicsville A1
Meyersville A1
Middletown B1
Northampton A1
N. Catasauqua A1
Ormrod A1
Ruchsville A1
Schoenersville B1
Seidersville B2
Seiple A1
Steel City B1
Stetlersville A1
Stiles A1
Walbert A2
Weaversville A1
Wennersville A2
W. Catasauqua A1
Whitehall A1
Wydnor B2

190 Anoka—Arbyrd

Figures after entries indicate population, page number, and grid reference.

Ann Arbor MI

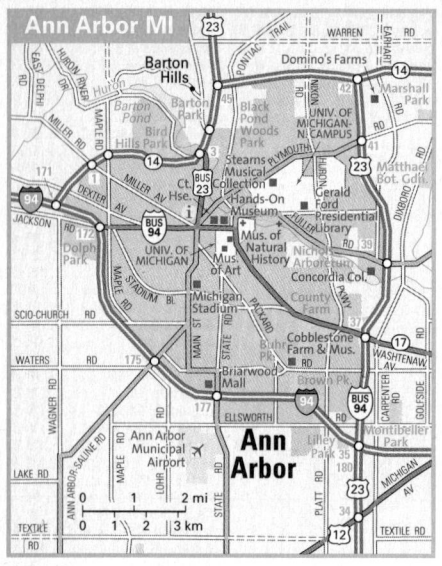

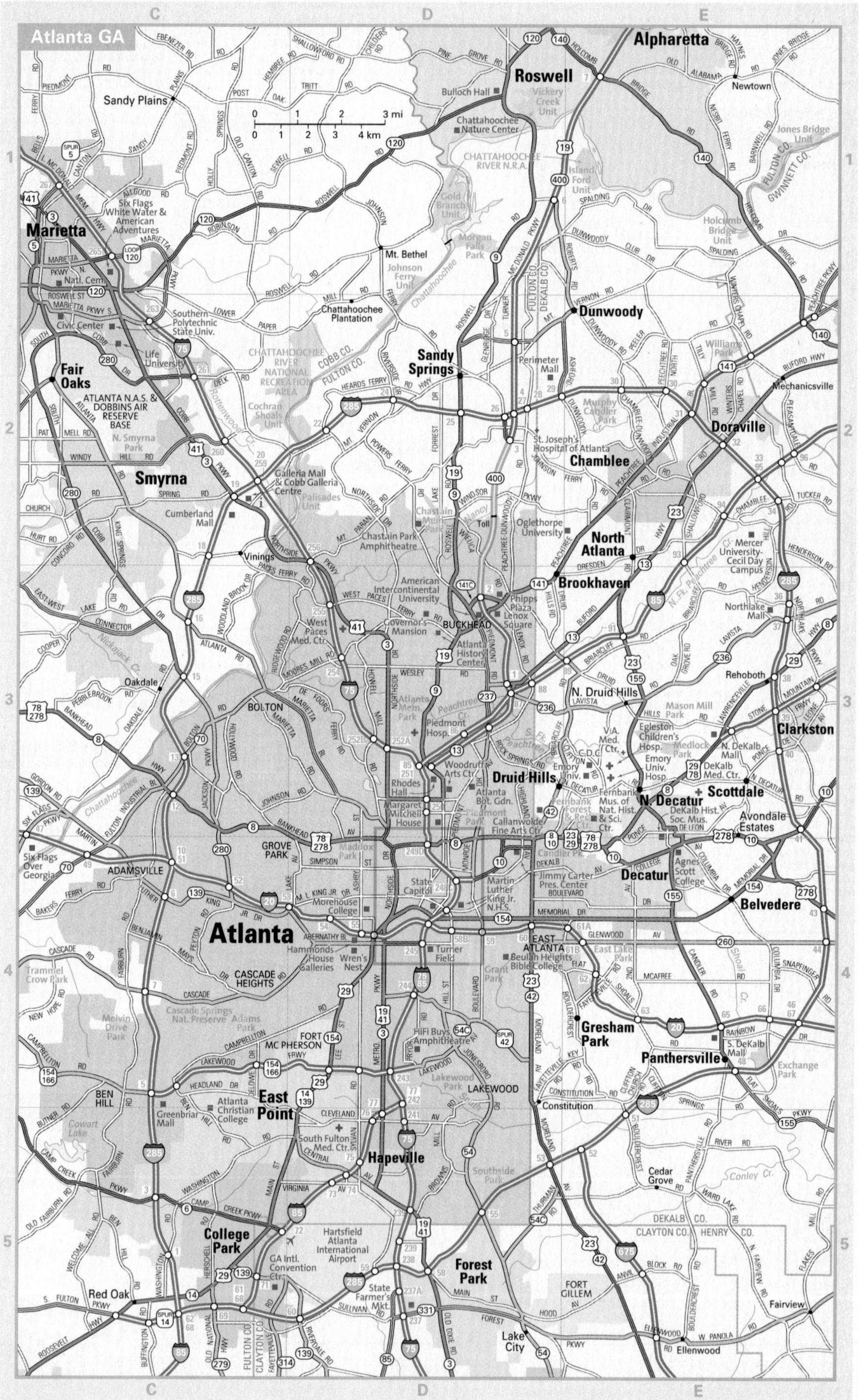

Atlanta GA

Asheville NC

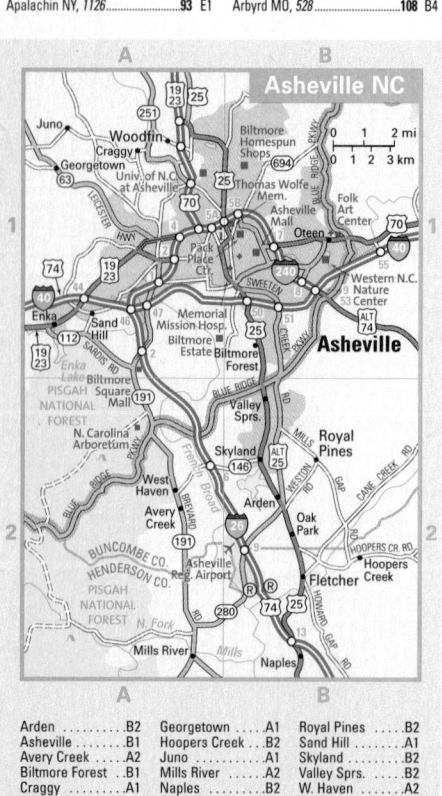

Entries in **bold** indicate counties or parishes. Entries in color indicate cities with detailed inset maps.

Arcade—Augusta **191**

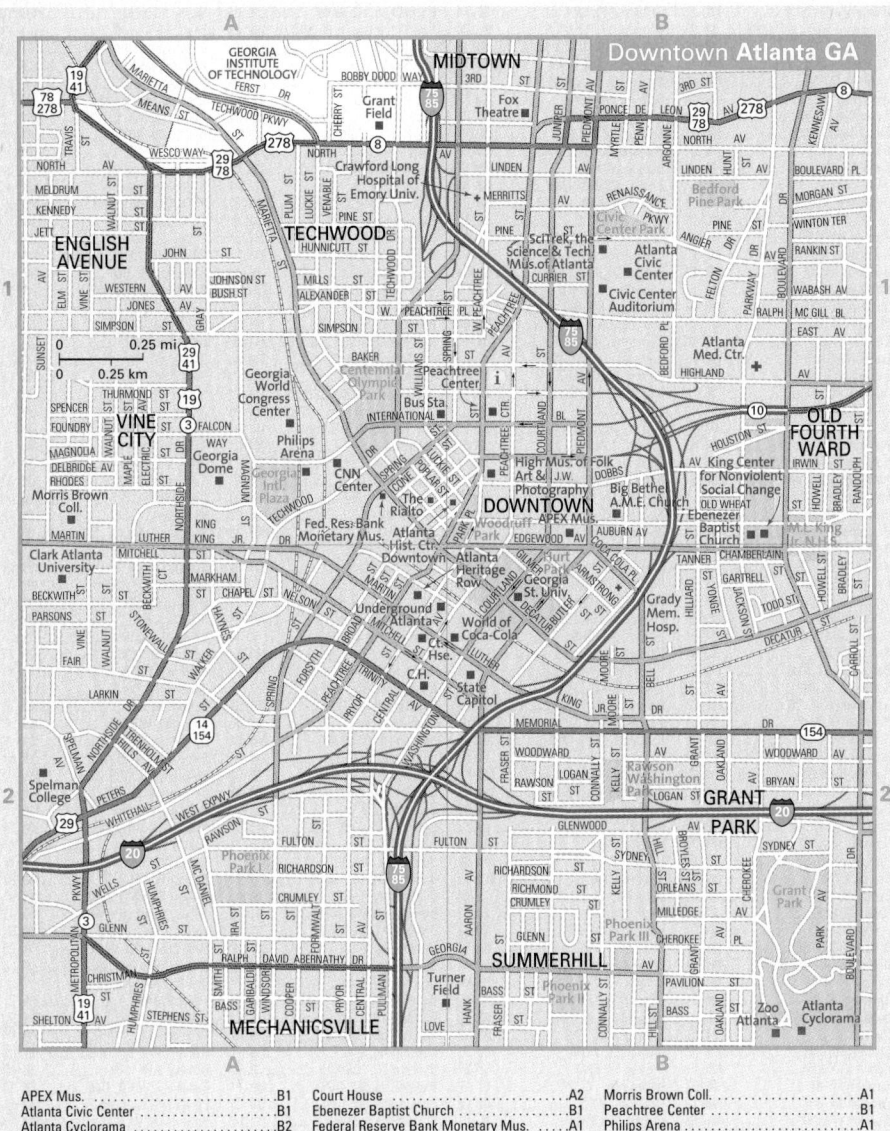

Downtown Atlanta GA

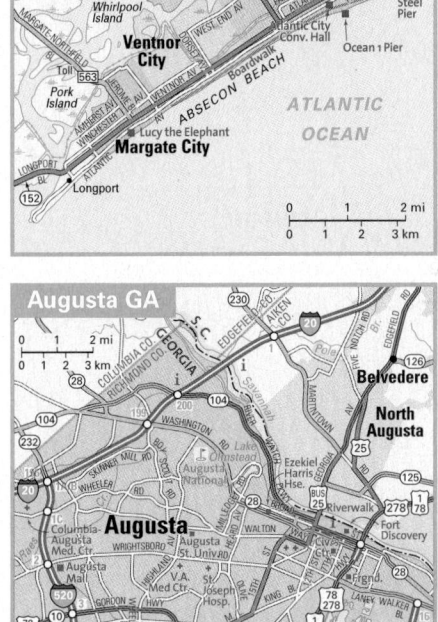

Atlantic City NJ

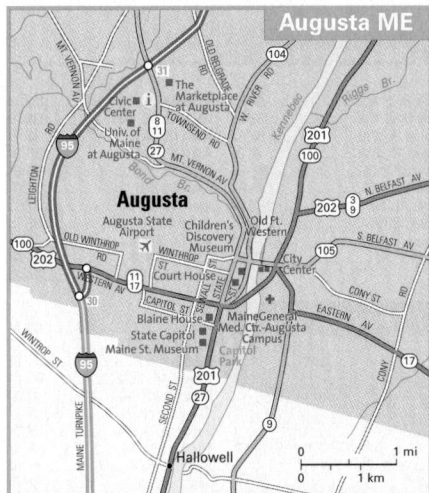

Augusta GA

Augusta ME

APEX Mus. B1
Atlanta Civic Center B1
Atlanta Cyclorama B2
Atlanta Heritage Row A2
Atlanta Historic Center Downtown B1
Big Bethel African
 Methodist Episcopal Church B1
Bus Station A1
City Hall A2
Civic Center Auditorium B1
Clark Atlanta Univ. A2
CNN Center A1
Court House A2
Ebenezer Baptist Church B1
Federal Reserve Bank Monetary Mus. ...A1
Fox Theatre B1
Georgia Dome A1
Georgia Institute of Technology A1
Georgia State Univ. B2
Georgia World Congress Center A1
Grant Field A1
High Mus. of Folk Art & Photography ...B1
King Center for Nonviolent Social Change ...B1
Martin Luther King, Jr. Natl. Hist. Site ...B1
Morris Brown Coll. A1
Peachtree Center B1
Philips Arena A1
SciTrek, the Science & Technology
 Mus. of Atlanta B1
Spelman Coll. A2
State Capitol B2
The Rialto A1
Turner Field A2
Underground Atlanta A2
World of Coca-Cola B2
Zoo Atlanta B2

192 Augusta County—Belmont
Figures after entries indicate population, page number, and grid reference.

Augusta Co. VA, 65615 102 B4
Aulander NC, 888 113 E3
Ault CO, 1432 33 E4
Aumsville OR, 3003 20 B2
Aurelia IA, 1062 72 A4
Aurora CO, 276393 41 E1
Aurora IL, 142990 88 C1
Aurora IN, 3965 100 B2
Aurora MN, 1850 64 C3
Aurora MO, 7014 106 C2
Aurora NE, 4225 35 E4
Aurora NY, 720 79 D4
Aurora NC, 583 115 D3
Aurora OH, 13556 91 E2
Aurora OR, 655 20 C2
Aurora SD, 500 27 F3
Aurora TX, 853 59 E2
Aurora UT, 947 39 E2
Aurora Co. SD, 3058 27 D4

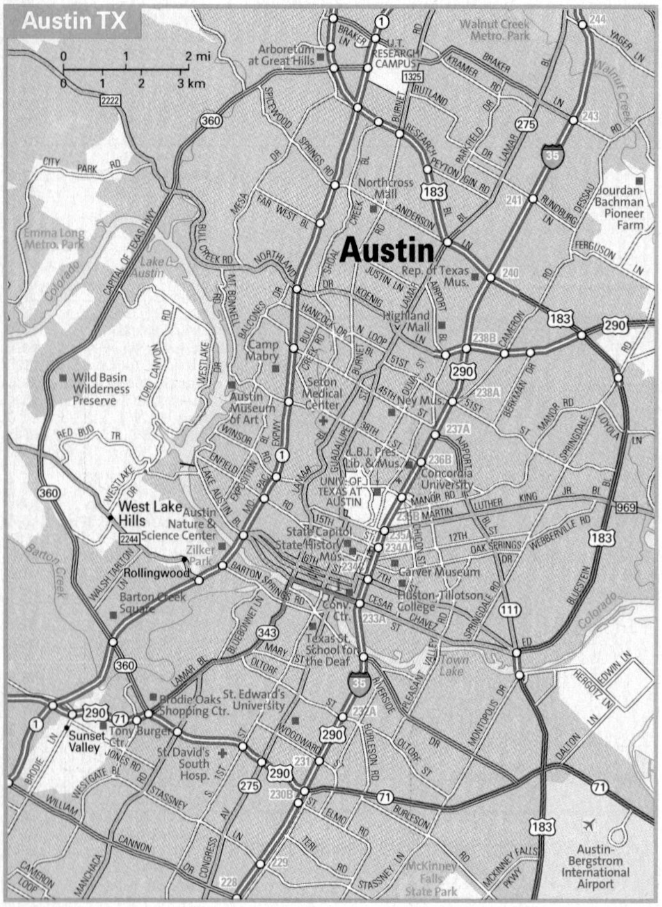
Austin TX
Austin
Arboretum at Great Hills
U.T. Research Campus
Walnut Creek Metro. Park
Northcross Mall
Jourdan-Bachman Pioneer Farm
Emma Long Metro. Park
Lake Austin
Rep. of Texas Mus.
Highland Mall
Camp Mabry
Seton Medical Center
Austin Museum of Art
Wild Basin Wilderness Preserve
L.B.J. Pres. Lib. & Mus.
Univ. of Texas at Austin
Concordia University
West Lake Hills
Austin Nature & Science Center
Zilker Park
State Capitol
Carver Museum
Rollingwood
Huston-Tillotson College
Barton Creek Square
Texas St. School for the Deaf
Town Lake
St. Edward's University
Brodie Oaks Shopping Ctr.
Sunset Valley
St. David's South Hosp.
Austin Bergstrom International Airport
McKinney Falls State Park
Colorado
Barton Creek

Au Sable MI, 1533 76 C1
Au Sable Forks NY, 670 81 D2
Austin AR, 605 117 E2
Austin IN, 4724 99 F3
Austin MN, 23314 73 D2
Austin NV, 600 37 F1
Austin PA, 623 92 C2
Austin TX, 656562 61 E1
Austin Co. TX, 23590 61 F2
Austintown OH, 31627 91 F3
Autauga Co. AL, 43671 127 F2
Autaugaville AL, 820 127 F2
Auxvasse MO, 901 97 E2
Ava IL, 662 98 B4
Ava MO, 3021 107 E2
Avalon CA, 3127 52 C3
Avalon NJ, 2143 105 D4
Avalon PA, 5294 250 A1
Avawam KY, 450 111 D2
Avella PA, 750 91 F4
Avenal CA, 14674 44 C3
Avenel NJ, 17552 147 E1
Aventura FL, 25267 143 F2
Averill Park NY, 1517 94 B1
Avery CA, 672 37 D3
Avery Co. NC, 17167 111 F4
Avery Creek NC, 1405 121 E1
Avilla IN, 2049 90 A2
Avis PA, 1492 93 D2
Aviston IL, 1231 98 B3
Avoca AR, 423 106 C3
Avoca IA, 1610 86 A2
Avoca NY, 1008 78 C4
Avoca PA, 2851 261 C2
Avoca WI, 608 74 A3
Avon AL, 466 137 D1
Avon CO, 5561 40 C1
Avon CT, 1500 94 C3
Avon IL, 915 88 A3

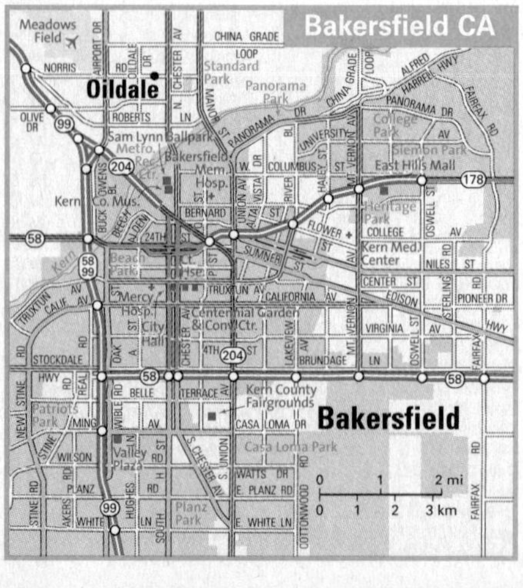
Bakersfield CA
Bakersfield
Oildale
Meadows Field
Standard Park
Panorama Park
College Park
Sam Lynn Ballpark
Bakersfield Mem. Hosp.
Stiern Park
East Hills Mall
Kern Co. Mus.
Heritage Park
Kern Med. Center
Beach Park
Mercy Hosp.
Centennial Garden & Conv. Ctr.
City Hall
Kern County Fairgrounds
Casa Loma Park
Planz Park
Patriots Park
Valley Plaza

Avon IN, 6248 99 F1
Avon MN, 1242 66 C2
Avon NY, 2977 78 C3
Avon NC, 550 115 F3
Avon OH, 11446 91 D2
Avon PA, 2856 146 A2
Avon SD, 561 35 E1
Avon-by-the-Sea NJ, 2244 147 F2
Avondale AZ, 35883 54 C1
Avondale CO, 754 41 E3
Avondale LA, 5441 134 B3
Avondale MO, 529 224 C2
Avondale PA, 1108 146 B3
Avondale RI, 425 149 F2
Avondale Estates GA, 2609 190 E3
Avonia PA, 1331 91 F1
Avon Lake OH, 18145 91 D2
Avonmore PA, 820 92 A4
Avon Park FL, 8542 141 D3
Avoyelles Par. LA, 41481 125 F4
Awendaw SC, 1195 131 D1
Axtell KS, 445 43 F1
Axtell NE, 696 35 D4
Ayden NC, 4622 115 D3
Ayer MA, 2960 95 D1
Aynor SC, 587 122 C3
Azalea Park FL, 11073 246 D2
Azle TX, 9600 59 E2
Aztec NM, 6378 48 B1
Azusa CA, 44712 228 E2

B

Babbie AL, 627 128 A4
Babbitt MN, 1670 64 C3
Babson Park FL, 1182 141 D3
Babylon NY, 12615 148 C4
Baca Co. CO, 4517 42 A4
Bacon Co. GA, 10103 129 F4
Baconton GA, 804 129 D4
Bad Axe MI, 3462 76 C2
Baden PA, 4377 92 A3
Badger IA, 610 72 C4
Badin NC, 1154 122 B1
Bagdad AZ, 1578 46 C4
Bagdad FL, 1490 135 F2
Baggs WY, 348 32 C3
Bagley MN, 1235 64 A3
Bahama NC, 550 112 C4
Bailey NC, 670 113 D4
Bailey Co. TX, 6594 49 F4
Bailey Island ME, 400 82 B3
Baileys Crossroads VA, 23166 270 B4
Bailey's Prairie TX, 694 132 A4
Baileyton AL, 684 119 F3
Baileyton TN, 504 111 D3
Bainbridge GA, 11722 137 D1
Bainbridge IN, 743 99 E1
Bainbridge NY, 1365 79 E4
Bainbridge OH, 1012 101 D2
Bainbridge Island WA, 20308 12 C3
Baird TX, 1623 58 C3
Baiting Hollow NY, 1449 149 E3
Baker LA, 13793 134 A2
Baker MT, 1695 17 F4
Baker City OR, 9860 21 F2
Baker Co. FL, 22259 138 C2
Baker Co. GA, 4074 128 C4
Baker Co. OR, 16741 21 F3
Bakersfield CA, 247057 45 D4
Bakersville NC, 357 111 E4
Bala-Cynwyd PA, 10300 146 C3
Balaton MN, 637 72 A1
Balch Sprs. TX, 19375 207 E3
Balcones Hts. TX, 3016 257 E2
Bald Knob AR, 3210 117 F1
Baldwin FL, 1634 139 D2
Baldwin GA, 2425 121 D3
Baldwin IL, 3627 98 B4
Baldwin LA, 2497 133 F3
Baldwin MD, 850 144 C1
Baldwin MI, 1107 75 F2
Baldwin PA, 19999 250 C3
Baldwin WI, 2667 67 E4
Baldwin City KS, 3400 96 A3
Baldwin Co. AL, 140415 135 E1
Baldwin Co. GA, 44700 129 E1
Baldwin Harbor NY, 8147 147 F1
Baldwin Park CA, 75837 228 E2
Baldwinsville NY, 7053 79 D3
Baldwinville MA, 1852 95 D1
Baldwyn MS, 3321 119 D3
Balfour NC, 1200 121 E1
Bal Harbour FL, 3305 233 B3
Ball LA, 3681 125 E4
Ballantine MT, 346 24 C1
Ballard UT, 566 32 A4
Ballard Co. KY, 8286 108 C2
Ballentine SC, 850 122 A3
Ball Ground GA, 730 120 C3
Ballinger TX, 4243 58 C4
Ballouville CT, 950 150 B3
Ballston Spa NY, 5556 80 C4
Ballville OH, 3255 90 C2
Ballwin MO, 31283 98 A3
Bally PA, 1062 146 B1
Balmorhea TX, 527 62 B2
Balmville NY, 3339 148 B1
Balsam Lake WI, 950 67 E3
Baltic CT, 1500 149 F1
Baltic OH, 743 91 E4
Baltic SD, 811 27 F4
Baltimore MD, 651154 144 C2
Baltimore OH, 2881 101 D1
Baltimore Co. MD, 754292 144 C1
Baltimore Highlands MD, 15724 193 C4
Bamberg SC, 3733 130 C1
Bamberg Co. SC, 16658 130 B1
Bancroft ID, 382 31 E1
Bancroft IA, 808 72 B3
Bancroft KY, 536 230 F1
Bancroft MI, 616 76 B3
Bancroft NE, 520 35 F2
Bancroft WV, 367 101 E3
Bandera TX, 957 61 D2
Bandera Co. TX, 17645 60 C2
Bandon OR, 2833 28 A1
Bangor ME, 31473 83 D1
Bangor MI, 1933 75 E4
Bangor PA, 5319 93 F3
Bangor WI, 1400 73 F2
Bangs TX, 1620 59 D4
Banks OR, 1286 20 B1
Banks Co. GA, 14422 121 D3
Banner Co. NE, 819 33 F3
Banner Elk NC, 811 111 F4
Banner Hill TN, 1053 111 E4
Bannertown NC, 950 112 A3
Banning CA, 23562 53 D2
Bannockburn IL, 1429 203 C2
Bannock Co. ID, 75565 31 E1
Banquete TX, 850 63 F2
Bantam CT, 802 94 C3
Baraboo WI, 10711 74 A2
Baraga MI, 1285 65 F4
Baraga Co. MI, 8746 65 F4
Barataria LA, 1333 134 B3
Barber Co. KS, 5307 43 D4
Barberton OH, 27899 91 E3
Barbour Co. AL, 29038 128 B3
Barbour Co. WV, 15557 102 A2
Barbourmeade KY, 1260 230 F1
Barboursville WV, 3183 101 E4
Barbourville KY, 3589 110 C2
Bardstown KY, 10374 110 A1
Bardwell KY, 799 108 C2
Bardwell TX, 583 59 F3
Bareville PA, 6625 146 A2
Bargersville IN, 2120 99 F1
Bar Harbor ME, 2680 83 D2
Barker NY, 577 78 B3
Barling AR, 4176 116 C1
Barlow KY, 715 108 C2
Bar Mills ME, 800 82 B3
Barnegat NJ, 1690 147 E4
Barnegat Light NJ, 764 147 E4
Barnegat Pines NJ, 1300 147 E3
Barnes Co. ND, 11775 19 D4
Barnesville GA, 5972 129 D1
Barnesville MN, 2173 19 F4
Barnesville OH, 4225 101 F1
Barneveld WI, 1088 74 A3
Barnhart MO, 6108 98 A4
Barnsboro NJ, 2500 146 C4
Barnsdall OK, 1325 51 F1
Barnstable MA, 47821 151 F3
Barnstable Co. MA, 222230 151 E4
Barnum MN, 525 64 C4
Bar Nunn WY, 936 33 D1
Baroda MI, 858 89 E1
Barrackville WV, 1288 102 A1
Barre MA, 1150 150 B1
Barre VT, 9291 81 E2
Barren Co. KY, 38033 110 A2
Barre Plains MA, 1200 150 B1
Barrett TX, 2872 132 B3
Barrington IL, 10168 203 B2
Barrington NH, 600 81 F4
Barrington NJ, 7084 248 D4
Barrington RI, 16819 151 D3
Barrington Hills IL, 3915 203 A2
Barron WI, 3248 67 E3
Barron Co. WI, 44963 67 E3
Barrow AK, 4581 154 C1
Barrow Co. GA, 46144 121 D3
Barry IL, 1368 97 F1
Barry Co. MI, 56755 75 F4
Barry Co. MO, 34010 106 C2
Barstow CA, 21119 53 D1
Barstow MD, 750 144 C4
Bartelso IL, 593 98 B3
Bartholomew Co. IN, 71435 99 F2
Bartlesville OK, 34748 51 F1
Bartlett IL, 36706 203 A3
Bartlett NE, 128 35 D2
Bartlett NH, 500 81 F2
Bartlett TN, 40543 118 B1
Bartlett TX, 1675 61 E1
Barton MD, 478 102 C1
Barton VT, 742 81 E1
Barton Co. KS, 28205 43 D3
Barton Co. MO, 12541 106 B1
Bartonsville MD, 12529 144 A1
Bartonville IL, 6310 88 B3
Bartow FL, 15340 140 C2
Bartow Co. GA, 76019 120 B3
Barview OR, 1872 20 A4
Basalt CO, 2681 40 C2
Basalt ID, 419 23 E4
Basehor KS, 2238 96 B2
Basile LA, 1660 133 E2
Basin MT, 255 15 E4
Basin WY, 1238 24 C3
Basin City WA, 968 13 E4
Baskett KY, 550 99 E4
Basking Ridge NJ, 3600 148 A4
Bassett NE, 743 35 D1
Bassett VA, 1338 112 B2
Bass Harbor ME, 600 83 D2
Bass Lake IN, 1249 89 E2
Bastrop LA, 12988 125 F2
Bastrop TX, 5340 61 E2
Bastrop Co. TX, 57733 61 E2
Basye VA, 986 102 C3
Batavia IL, 23866 88 C1
Batavia IA, 500 87 E3
Batavia NY, 16256 78 B3
Batavia OH, 1617 100 B2
Batesburg-Leesville SC, 5517 122 A4
Bates Co. MO, 16653 96 B4
Batesville AR, 9445 107 F4
Batesville IN, 6033 100 A2
Batesville MS, 7113 118 B3
Batesville TX, 1298 60 C3
Bath ME, 9266 82 C3
Bath MI, 1200 76 A3
Bath NY, 5641 78 C4
Bath PA, 2678 93 F3
Bath Co. KY, 11085 100 C4
Bath Co. VA, 5048 102 B4
Baton Rouge LA, 227818 134 A2
Battle Creek IA, 743 72 A4
Battle Creek MI, 53364 75 F4
Battle Creek NE, 1158 35 E2
Battlefield MO, 2385 107 D2
Battle Ground IN, 1323 89 E4
Battle Ground WA, 9296 20 C1
Battle Lake MN, 686 19 F4
Battlement Mesa CO, 3497 40 B2
Battle Mtn. NV, 2871 30 A4
Baudette MN, 1104 64 A1
Baumstown PA, 1000 146 B2
Bauxite AR, 432 117 E2
Bawcomville LA, 7616 125 E2
Baxley GA, 4150 129 F3
Baxter IA, 1052 87 D1
Baxter MN, 5555 64 B4
Baxter TN, 1279 110 A4
Baxter Co. AR, 38386 107 E4
Baxter Estates NY, 1006 241 G2
Baxter Sprs. KS, 4602 106 B2
Bay AR, 1800 108 A4
Bayard IA, 536 86 B1
Bayard NE, 1247 33 F2
Bayard NM, 2534 55 F2
Bayboro NC, 741 115 D3
Bay City MI, 36817 76 B2
Bay City OR, 1149 20 B2
Bay City TX, 18667 61 F3
Bay Co. FL, 148217 136 C2
Bay Co. MI, 110157 76 B2
Bayfield CO, 1549 40 C4
Bayfield WI, 611 65 D4
Bayfield Co. WI, 15013 65 D4
Bay Harbor Islands FL, 5146 233 C4
Bay Head NJ, 1238 147 E3
Bay Hill FL, 5177 246 B3
Baylor Co. TX, 4093 59 D1
Bay Minette AL, 7820 135 E1
Bayonet Pt. FL, 23577 140 B2
Bayonne NJ, 61842 148 B4
Bayou Cane LA, 17046 134 A3
Bayou George FL, 800 136 C2
Bayou Goula LA, 750 134 A2
Bayou La Batre AL, 2313 135 E2
Bayou Vista LA, 4351 134 A3
Bayou Vista TX, 1644 132 B4
Bay Park NY, 2300 241 G5
Bay Pines FL, 3065 266 A3
Bay Pt. CA, 21534 259 D1
Bayport MN, 3162 67 D4
Bayport NY, 8662 149 D4
Bay Ridge MD, 2300 144 C3
Bay St. Louis MS, 8209 134 C2
Bayshore FL, 750 142 C1
Bay Shore NY, 23852 149 D4
Bayshore Gardens FL, 17350 266 B5
Bay Side NJ, 1800 147 E4
Bayside WI, 4518 234 D1
Bay Sprs. MS, 2097 126 C3
Baytown TX, 66430 132 B3
Bay View OH, 692 91 D2
Bay Vil. OH, 16087 204 D2
Bayville NJ, 4700 147 E3
Bayville NY, 7135 148 C3
Beach ND, 1116 17 F4
Beach City OH, 1137 91 E3
Beach City TX, 1645 132 B3
Beach Haven NJ, 1278 147 E4
Beach Haven Gardens NJ, 1200 147 E4
Beach Haven Terrace NJ, 1100 147 E4
Beachwood NJ, 10375 147 E3
Beachwood OH, 12186 204 G2
Beacon IA, 518 87 D2
Beacon NY, 13808 148 B1
Beacon Falls CT, 1500 149 D1
Beadle Co. SD, 17023 27 D3
Bealeton VA, 2100 103 D3
Beals ME, 750 83 E2
Bean Sta. TN, 1400 111 D3
Bear DE, 17593 145 E1
Bear Creek AL, 1053 119 E3
Bearden AR, 1125 117 E4
Beardstown IL, 5766 98 A1
Bear Lake Co. ID, 6411 31 F2
Bear River City UT, 750 31 E3
Beasley TX, 590 132 A4
Beatrice AL, 412 127 F4
Beatrice NE, 12496 35 F4
Beatty NV, 1154 45 F2
Beattyville KY, 1193 110 C1
Beatyestown NJ, 3223 94 A4
Beaufort NC, 3771 115 E4
Beaufort SC, 12950 130 C2
Beaufort Co. NC, 44958 113 F4
Beaufort Co. SC, 120937 130 C3
Beaumont CA, 11384 53 D2
Beaumont MS, 977 135 D1
Beaumont TX, 113866 132 C3
Beaumont Place TX, 4500 220 D2
Beauregard Par. LA, 32986 133 D2
Beaver OK, 1570 50 C1
Beaver PA, 4775 91 F3
Beaver UT, 2454 39 D3
Beaver WV, 1378 111 F1
Beaver City NE, 641 42 C1
Beaver Co. OK, 5857 50 C1
Beaver Co. PA, 181412 91 F3
Beaver Co. UT, 6005 39 D3
Beavercreek OH, 37984 100 C1
Beaver Crossing NE, 457 35 E4
Beaverdale PA, 1230 92 B4
Beaver Dam KY, 3033 109 E1
Beaver Dam WI, 15169 74 B2
Beaver Falls PA, 9920 91 F3
Beaverhead Co. MT, 9202 23 D2
Beaver Meadows PA, 968 93 E3
Beaver Sprs. PA, 634 93 D3
Beaverton MI, 1106 76 A2
Beaverton OR, 76129 20 C2
Beavertown PA, 870 93 D3
Bechtelsville PA, 931 146 B1
Beckemeyer IL, 1043 98 B3
Becker MN, 2673 66 C3
Becker Co. MN, 30000 19 F3
Beckett NJ, 4726 146 C4
Beckham Co. OK, 19799 50 C3
Beckley WV, 17254 111 F1
Beckville TX, 752 124 C3
Bedford IN, 13768 99 F3
Bedford IA, 1620 86 B3
Bedford KY, 677 100 A3
Bedford MA, 12595 151 D1
Bedford NH, 1800 95 D1
Bedford NY, 1724 148 C2
Bedford OH, 14214 204 G3
Bedford PA, 3141 102 C1
Bedford TX, 47152 207 B2
Bedford VA, 6299 112 B1
Bedford Co. PA, 49984 92 C4
Bedford Co. TN, 37586 120 A1
Bedford Co. VA, 60371 112 B1
Bedford Hts. OH, 11375 204 G3
Bedford Hills NY, 5500 148 C2
Bedford Park IL, 574 203 D5
Beebe AR, 4930 117 F2
Bee Cave TX, 656 61 E1
Beech Bottom WV, 606 91 F4
Beech Creek PA, 717 93 D3
Beecher IL, 2033 89 D2
Beech Grove IN, 14880 99 F1
Beechwood Vil. KY, 1173 230 E1
Bee Co. TX, 32359 61 E4
Beemer NE, 773 35 F2
Bee Ridge FL, 8744 140 B4
Beersheba Sprs. TN, 553 120 A1
Beesleys Pt. NJ, 1400 147 F4
Beeville TX, 13129 61 E4
Beggs OK, 1364 51 F2
Belcamp MD, 1900 145 D1
Belchertown MA, 2626 150 A1
Belcourt ND, 2440 18 C1
Belding MI, 5877 75 F3
Belen NM, 6901 48 C4
Belfair WA, 700 12 C3
Belfast ME, 6381 82 C2
Belfast NY, 800 78 B4
Belfast PA, 1301 93 F3
Belfield ND, 866 18 A4
Belford NJ, 1340 147 E1
Belfry MT, 219 24 B2
Belgium WI, 1678 75 D2
Belgrade MN, 692 66 B3
Belgrade MT, 5728 23 F1
Belgrade Lakes ME, 350 82 B2
Belhaven NC, 1968 115 E3
Belinda City TN, 2100 109 F4
Belington WV, 1788 102 A2
Belknap Co. NH, 56325 81 F4
Bell CA, 36664 228 D3
Bellair FL, 16539 222 C4
Bellaire OH, 4892 101 F1
Bellaire TX, 15642 132 A3
Bellamy AL, 600 127 E2
Bella Villa MO, 687 256 B3
Bella Vista AR, 16582 106 C3
Bella Vista CA, 550 28 C4
Bellbrook OH, 7009 100 C1
Bell Buckle TN, 391 119 F1
Bell Co. KY, 30060 110 C3
Bell Co. TX, 237974 61 E1
Belle MO, 1344 97 F4
Belle WV, 1259 101 F4
Belleair FL, 4067 140 B2
Belleair Beach FL, 1751 140 B2
Belleair Bluffs FL, 2243 266 A2
Belle Ctr. OH, 807 90 C4
Belle Chasse LA, 9848 134 B3
Bellefontaine OH, 13069 90 B4
Bellefontaine Neighbors MO, 11271 256 C1
Bellefonte AR, 400 107 D3
Bellefonte DE, 1249 146 B4
Bellefonte KY, 837 101 D3
Bellefonte PA, 6395 92 C3
Belle Fourche SD, 4565 25 F3
Belle Glade FL, 14906 143 E1
Belle Haven VA, 480 114 B3
Belle Isle FL, 5531 141 D1
Bellemeade KY, 871 230 F2
Belle Plaine IA, 2878 87 E1
Belle Plaine KS, 1708 43 E4
Belle Plaine MN, 3789 66 C4
Belle Rose LA, 1944 134 A3
Bellerose NY, 1193 241 G3
Bellerose Terrace NY, 2157 241 G3
Belle Terre NY, 832 149 D3
Belle Vernon PA, 1211 92 A4
Belleview FL, 3478 139 D4
Belleville IL, 41410 98 B3
Belleville KS, 2239 43 E1
Belleville MI, 3997 90 C1
Belleville NJ, 35928 148 B4
Belleville PA, 1386 92 C4
Belleville WI, 1908 74 B3
Bellevue ID, 1876 22 C4
Bellevue IL, 1887 88 B3
Bellevue IA, 2350 74 A4
Bellevue KY, 6480 204 B3
Bellevue MI, 1365 76 A4
Bellevue NE, 44382 86 A2
Bellevue OH, 8193 204 B3
Bellevue PA, 8770 92 A4
Bellevue WA, 109569 12 C3
Bellevue WI, 11828 74 C1
Bellflower CA, 72878 228 D3
Bell Gardens CA, 44054 228 D3
Bellingham MA, 4497 150 C2
Bellingham WA, 67171 12 C1
Bellmawr NJ, 11262 146 C3
Bellmead TX, 9214 59 E4
Bellows Falls VT, 3165 81 E4
Bellport NY, 2363 149 D4
Bells TN, 2171 108 C4
Bells TX, 1190 59 F1
Bellview FL, 21201 247 A1
Bellville OH, 1773 91 D3
Bellville TX, 3794 61 F2
Bellwood IL, 20535 203 C4
Bellwood NE, 446 35 E3
Bellwood PA, 2016 92 C4
Bellwood VA, 5974 254 B3
Belmar NJ, 6045 147 F2
Belmond IA, 2560 72 C3
Belmont CA, 25123 259 B4
Belmont MA, 24194 151 D1

Entries in **bold** indicate counties or parishes. Entries in color indicate cities with detailed inset maps.

193

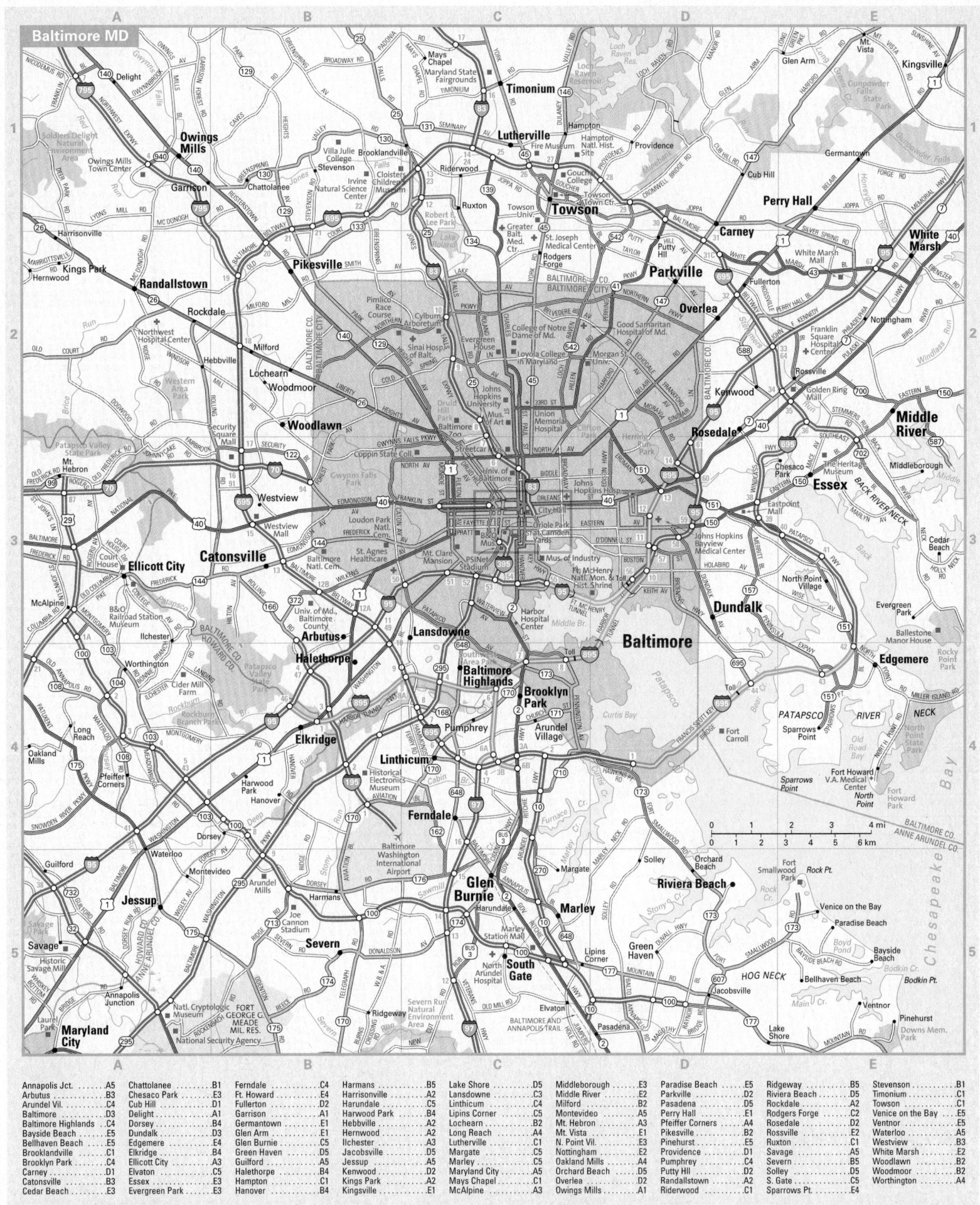

Baltimore MD

194 Belmont—Blair County

Figures after entries indicate population, page number, and grid reference.

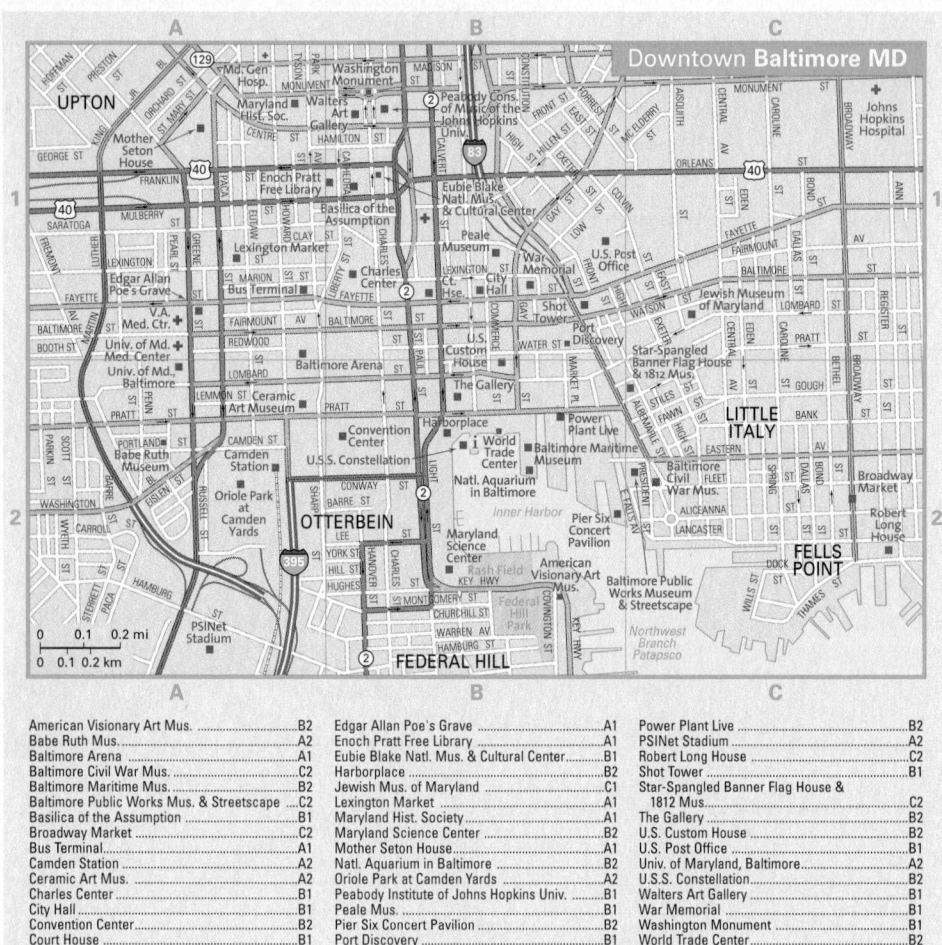

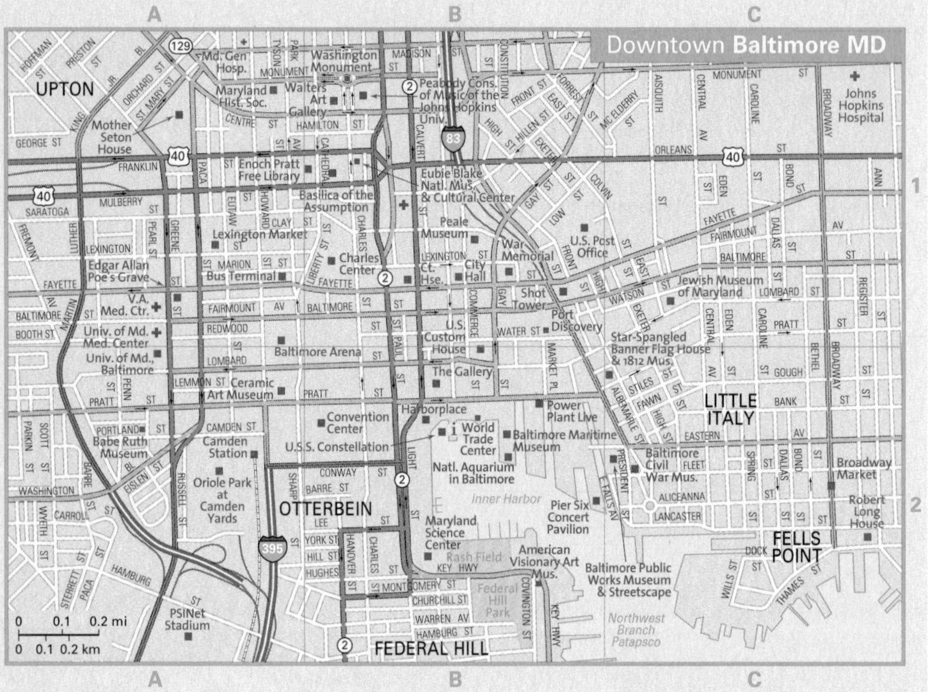
Downtown Baltimore MD
A
B
C
1
2
UPTON
LITTLE ITALY
FELLS POINT
OTTERBEIN
FEDERAL HILL
Mt. Vernon
Johns Hopkins Hospital
Washington Monument
Peabody Cons. of Music of the Johns Hopkins Univ.
Maryland Hist. Soc.
Walters Art Gallery
Mother Seton House
Enoch Pratt Free Library
Eubie Blake Natl. Mus. & Cultural Center
Basilica of the Assumption
Lexington Market
Peale Museum
War Memorial
U.S. Post Office
Charles Center
City Hall
Ct. Hse.
Edgar Allan Poe's Grave
Bus Terminal
V.A. Med. Ctr.
Univ. of Md. Med. Center
Univ. of Md., Baltimore
Baltimore Arena
Ceramic Art Museum
Jewish Museum of Maryland
Shot Tower
Port Discovery
U.S. Custom House
The Gallery
Star-Spangled Banner Flag House & 1812 Mus.
Power Plant Live
Harborplace
World Trade Center
Baltimore Maritime Museum
Convention Center
U.S.S. Constellation
Babe Ruth Museum
Camden Station
Oriole Park at Camden Yards
Natl. Aquarium in Baltimore
Inner Harbor
Pier Six Concert Pavilion
Maryland Science Center
American Visionary Art Mus.
Baltimore Public Works Museum & Streetscape
Baltimore Civil War Mus.
Broadway Market
Robert Long House
Federal Hill Park
PSINet Stadium
Rash Field
Northwest Branch Patapsco
0 0.1 0.2 mi
0 0.1 0.2 km

American Visionary Art Mus. B2
Babe Ruth Mus. A2
Baltimore Arena A1
Baltimore Civil War Mus. C2
Baltimore Maritime Mus. B2
Baltimore Public Works Mus. & Streetscape C2
Basilica of the Assumption B1
Broadway Market C2
Bus Terminal A1
Camden Station A2
Ceramic Art Mus. A2
Charles Center B1
City Hall B1
Convention Center B2
Court House B1
Edgar Allan Poe's Grave A1
Enoch Pratt Free Library A1
Eubie Blake Natl. Mus. & Cultural Center B1
Harborplace B2
Jewish Mus. of Maryland C1
Lexington Market A1
Maryland Hist. Society A1
Maryland Science Center B2
Mother Seton House A1
Natl. Aquarium in Baltimore B2
Oriole Park at Camden Yards A2
Peabody Institute of Johns Hopkins Univ. B1
Peale Mus. B1
Pier Six Concert Pavilion B2
Port Discovery B1
Power Plant Live B2
PSINet Stadium A2
Robert Long House C2
Shot Tower B1
Star-Spangled Banner Flag House & 1812 Mus. C2
The Gallery B2
U.S. Custom House B2
U.S. Post Office B1
Univ. of Maryland, Baltimore A2
U.S.S. Constellation B2
Walters Art Gallery B1
War Memorial B1
Washington Monument B1
World Trade Center B2

Belmont MS, *1961* **119** D3
Belmont NH, *950* **81** F4
Belmont NY, *952* **92** C1
Belmont NC, *8705* **122** A1
Belmont WV, *1036* **101** F2
Belmont WI, *871* **74** A4
Belmont Corner ME, *375* **82** C2
Belmont Co. OH, *70226* **101** F1
Bel-Nor MO, *1598* **256** B2
Beloit KS, *4019* **43** E1
Beloit OH, *1024* **91** F3
Beloit WI, *35775* **74** B4
Belpre OH, *6660* **101** E2
Bel-Ridge MO, *3082* **256** B2
Belt MT, *633* **15** F3
Belton KY, *500* **109** E2
Belton MO, *21730* **96** B3
Belton SC, *4461* **121** E3
Belton TX, *14623* **59** E4
Beltrami Co. MN, *39650* **64** A2
Beltsville MD, *15690* **144** B3
Belvedere CA, *2125* **259** B2
Belvedere GA, *11100* **190** E4
Belvedere SC, *5631* **121** F4
Belvidere IL, *20820* **74** B4
Belvidere NJ, *2771* **93** F3
Belwood NC, *962* **121** F1
Belzoni MS, *2663* **126** B1
Bement IL, *1784* **98** C1
Bemidji MN, *11917* **64** A3
Bemiss GA, *1500* **137** F1
Benavides TX, *1686* **63** E2
Ben Avon PA, *1917* **250** A1
Benbrook TX, *20208* **207** A3
Bend OR, *52029* **21** D3
Bendersville PA, *576* **103** E1
Benewah Co. ID, *9171* **14** B3
Benham KY, *599* **111** D2
Ben Hill Co. GA, *17484* **129** E3
Benicia CA, *26865* **36** B3
Benjamin TX, *264* **58** C1
Benkelman NE, *1006* **42** B1
Benld IL, *1541* **98** B2
Ben Lomond CA, *2364* **44** A2
Bennet NE, *570* **35** F4
Bennett CO, *2021* **41** E1
Bennett Co. SD, *3574* **26** B4
Bennettsville SC, *9425* **122** C2
Bennington KS, *623* **43** E2
Bennington NE, *937* **35** F3
Bennington NH, *425* **81** E4
Bennington VT, *9168* **94** C1
Bennington Co. VT, *36994* **81** D4
Benoit MS, *611* **118** A4
Bensenville IL, *20703* **203** C4
Bensley VA, *5435* **113** E1
Benson AZ, *4711* **55** D3
Benson MD, *950* **144** C1
Benson MN, *3376* **66** A3
Benson NC, *2923* **123** D1
Benson Co. ND, *6964* **19** D2
Bent Co. CO, *5998* **41** F3
Bent Creek NC, *1389* **121** E1
Bentleyville OH, *947* **204** G3
Bentleyville PA, *2502* **92** A4
Benton AR, *21906* **117** E2
Benton IL, *6880* **98** C4
Benton KS, *827* **43** F4
Benton KY, *4197* **109** D2
Benton LA, *2035* **124** C2
Benton ME, *500* **82** C2
Benton MO, *732* **108** B2
Benton PA, *955* **93** E2
Benton TN, *1138* **120** C1
Benton WI, *976* **74** A4
Benton City WA, *2624* **21** E1
Benton Co. AR, *153406* **106** B3
Benton Co. IN, *9421* **89** D3
Benton Co. IA, *25308* **87** E1
Benton Co. MN, *34226* **66** C2
Benton Co. MS, *8026* **118** C2
Benton Co. MO, *17180* **97** D4
Benton Co. OR, *78153* **20** B3
Benton Co. TN, *16537* **109** D4
Benton Co. WA, *142475* **21** E1
Benton Harbor MI, *11182* **89** E1
Bentonia MS, *500* **126** B2
Bentonville AR, *19730* **106** C3
Benzie Co. MI, *15998* **69** F4
Benzonia MI, *519* **69** E4
Berea KY, *9851* **110** C1
Berea OH, *18970* **91** E2
Berea SC, *14158* **217** A2
Beresford SD, *2006* **35** F1
Bergen NY, *1240* **78** B3
Bergen Co. NJ, *884118* **148** B3
Bergenfield NJ, *26247* **148** B3
Bergholz OH, *769* **91** F4
Bergman AR, *407* **107** D3
Berino NM, *900* **56** C3
Berkeley CA, *102743* **36** B4
Berkeley IL, *5245* **203** C4
Berkeley MO, *10063* **256** B1
Berkeley RI, *2800* **150** C3
Berkeley Co. SC, *142651* **131** D1
Berkeley Co. WV, *75905* **103** D2
Berkeley Hts. NJ, *13407* **148** A4
Berkeley Sprs. WV, *663* **102** C1
Berkley MA, *850* **151** D3
Berkley MI, *15531* **210** B2
Berks Co. PA, *373638* **146** B1
Berkshire CT, *950* **149** D2
Berkshire Co. MA, *134953* **94** C2
Berlin CT, *1000* **149** E1
Berlin GA, *595* **137** F1
Berlin MD, *3491* **114** C2
Berlin MA, *650* **150** C1
Berlin NH, *10331* **81** F2
Berlin NJ, *6149* **147** D3
Berlin OH, *1300* **91** E4
Berlin PA, *2192* **102** C1
Berlin WI, *5305* **74** B1
Berlin Hts. OH, *685* **91** D2
Bermuda Run NC, *1431* **112** A4
Bernalillo NM, *6611* **48** C3
Bernalillo Co. NM, *556678* **48** C3
Bernardston MA, *1000* **94** C1
Bernardsville NJ, *7345* **148** A4
Berne IN, *4150* **90** A3
Bernice LA, *1809* **125** E2
Bernice OK, *504* **106** B3
Bernie MO, *1777* **108** B3
Bernstadt KY, *475* **110** C2
Bernville PA, *865* **146** A1
Berrien Co. GA, *16235* **129** E4
Berrien Co. MI, *162453* **89** E1
Berrien Sprs. MI, *1862* **89** E1
Berry AL, *1238* **119** E4
Berryville AR, *4433* **106** C3
Berryville TX, *891* **124** A3
Berryville VA, *2963* **103** D2
Berthold ND, *466* **18** B2
Berthoud CO, *4839* **33** E4
Bertie Co. NC, *19773* **113** F4
Bertram IA, *681* **87** F1
Bertram TX, *1122* **61** D1
Bertrand MI, *1700* **89** F1
Bertrand MO, *740* **108** B2
Bertrand NE, *786* **35** D4
Berwick LA, *4418* **134** A3
Berwick ME, *1993* **82** A4
Berwick PA, *10774* **93** E3
Berwyn IL, *54016* **89** D1
Berwyn PA, *5067* **146** B3
Berwyn Hts. MD, *2942* **270** E2
Bessemer AL, *29672* **127** F1
Bessemer MI, *2148* **65** E4
Bessemer PA, *1172* **91** F3
Bessemer City NC, *5119* **122** A1
Bethalto IL, *9454* **98** B3
Bethany CT, *900* **149** D1
Bethany IL, *1287* **98** C1
Bethany MO, *3087* **86** C4
Bethany OK, *20307* **51** E3
Bethany WV, *985* **91** F4
Bethany Beach DE, *903* **145** F4
Bethel AK, *5471* **154** B3
Bethel CT, *9137* **148** C2
Bethel DE, *184* **145** E4
Bethel ME, *475* **82** B2
Bethel NC, *1681* **113** E4
Bethel OH, *2637* **100** C2
Bethel VT, *800* **81** E3
Bethel VA, *500* **103** D3
Bethel Acres OK, *2735* **51** F3
Bethel Hts. AR, *714* **106** C3
Bethel Park PA, *33556* **92** A4
Bethel Sprs. TN, *763* **119** D1
Bethesda MD, *55277* **144** B3
Bethesda OH, *1413* **101** F1
Bethlehem CT, *2022* **149** D1
Bethlehem GA, *716* **121** D4
Bethlehem MD, *600* **145** D4
Bethlehem NH, *700* **81** F2
Bethlehem NC, *3713* **111** F4
Bethlehem PA, *71329* **146** C1
Bethlehem Ctr. NY, *2500* **188** D3
Bethpage NY, *16543* **148** C4
Betmar Acres FL, *4000* **140** C2
Bettendorf IA, *31275* **88** A2
Bettsville OH, *784* **90** C2
Beulah CO, *1164* **41** E3
Beulah MI, *363* **69** E4
Beulah MS, *473* **118** A4
Beulah ND, *3152* **18** B3
Beulaville NC, *1067* **123** E2
Beverly MA, *39862* **151** F1
Beverly NJ, *2661* **147** D3
Beverly OH, *1282* **101** E1
Beverly WV, *651* **102** B3
Beverly Beach FL, *547* **139** E4
Beverly Beach MD, *1600* **144** C3
Beverly Hills CA, *33784* **52** C2
Beverly Hills FL, *8317* **140** B1
Beverly Hills MI, *10437* **210** B2
Beverly Hills MO, *603* **256** B2
Beverly Shores IN, *708* **89** E2
Bevier MO, *723* **97** E1
Bevil Oaks TX, *1346* **132** C2
Bevis OH, *5700* **204** A1
Bexar Co. TX, *1392931* **61** D2
Bexley OH, *13203* **206** C2
Bibb Co. AL, *20826* **127** F1
Bibb Co. GA, *153887* **129** D2
Bicknell IN, *3378* **99** E3
Bicknell UT, *353* **39** E3
Biddeford ME, *20942* **82** B4
Bienville Par. LA, *15752* **125** D2
Big Bear City CA, *5779* **53** D2
Big Bear Lake CA, *5438* **53** D2
Big Beaver PA, *2186* **91** F3
Big Bend WI, *1278* **74** C3
Big Chimney WV, *600* **101** F3
Big Coppitt Key FL, *2595* **143** D4
Big Delta AK, *749* **154** C2
Big Flats NY, *2482* **93** D1
Bigfork MT, *1421* **15** D2
Biggs CA, *1793* **36** B2
Big Horn Co. MT, *12671* **24** C2
Big Horn Co. WY, *11461* **24** C3
Big Lake MN, *6063* **66** C3
Big Lake TX, *2885* **58** A4
Big Lake WA, *1153* **12** C2
Biglerville PA, *1101* **103** E1
Big Oak Flat CA, *3388* **37** D4
Big Pine CA, *1350* **37** E4
Big Pine Key FL, *5032* **143** D4
Big Piney WY, *408* **32** A1
Big Rapids MI, *10849* **75** F2
Big River CA, *1266* **46** B4
Big Run PA, *686* **92** B3
Big Sandy MT, *703* **16** B2
Big Sandy TN, *518* **109** D3
Big Sandy TX, *1288* **124** B2
Big Sky MT, *1221* **23** F2
Big Spr. TX, *25233* **58** A3
Big Sprs. NE, *418* **34** B3
Big Stone City SD, *605* **27** F2
Big Stone Co. MN, *5820* **27** F2
Big Stone Gap VA, *4856* **111** E2
Big Timber MT, *1650* **24** A1
Big Water UT, *417* **47** D1
Big Wells TX, *704* **60** C4
Billerica MA, *38981* **95** E1
Billings MO, *1091* **106** C2
Billings MT, *89847* **24** C1
Billings NY, *800* **148** B1
Billings OK, *436* **51** E1
Billings Co. ND, *888* **18** A3
Billington Hts. NY, *1691* **78** B4
Biloxi MS, *50644* **135** D2
Biltmore Forest NC, *1440* **121** E1
Bingen PA, *1300* **189** B2
Binger OK, *708* **51** D3
Bingham ME, *856* **82** B1
Bingham Co. ID, *41735* **23** E4
Bingham Farms MI, *1030* **210** B2
Binghamton NY, *47380* **93** E1
Biola CA, *1037* **44** C2
Birch Bay WA, *4961* **12** C1
Birch Run MI, *1653* **76** B3
Birch Tree MO, *634* **107** F2
Birchwood Vil. MN, *968* **235** E1
Bird City KS, *482* **42** B1
Bird Island MN, *1195* **66** B4
Birdsboro PA, *5064* **146** B2
Birmingham AL, *242820* **119** F4
Birmingham MI, *19291* **76** C4
Birnamwood WI, *795* **68** B4
Biron WI, *915* **74** A1
Bisbee AZ, *6090* **55** E4
Biscayne Park FL, *3269* **233** B4
Biscoe AR, *476* **117** F2
Biscoe NC, *1700* **122** C1
Bishop CA, *3575* **37** E4
Bishop TX, *3305* **63** F2
Bishopville SC, *3670* **122** B3
Bismarck MO, *1470* **108** A1
Bismarck ND, *55532* **18** C4
Bison SD, *373* **26** A2
Bithlo FL, *4626* **141** D1
Bitter Sprs. AZ, *547* **47** D1
Biwabik MN, *954* **64** C3
Bixby OK, *13336* **106** A4
Blackbird DE, *700* **145** E1
Black Canyon City AZ, *2697* **47** D4
Black Creek NC, *714* **123** E1
Black Creek WI, *1192* **68** C4
Black Diamond WA, *3970* **12** C3
Blackduck MN, *696* **64** A3
Black Eagle MT, *914* **15** F3
Black Earth WI, *1320* **74** A3
Blackfoot ID, *10419* **31** E1
Blackford Co. IN, *14048* **90** A4
Black Forest CO, *13247* **41** E2
Black Hawk SD, *2432* **26** A3
Black Hawk Co. IA, *128012* **73** E4
Black Jack MO, *6792* **256** B1
Black Lick PA, *1438* **92** B4
Blacklick Estates OH, *9518* **206** C3
Black Mtn. NC, *7511* **121** E1
Black River NY, *1285* **79** E1
Black River Falls WI, *3618* **73** F1
Black Rock AR, *717* **107** F4
Black Rock NM, *1252* **48** A3
Blacksburg SC, *1880* **122** A1
Blacksburg VA, *39573* **112** A2
Blackshear GA, *3283* **129** F4
Blackstone MA, *2900* **150** C2
Blackstone VA, *3675* **113** D2
Blackville SC, *2973* **130** B1
Blackwell OK, *7668* **51** E1
Blackwells GA, *2200* **120** C3
Blackwood NJ, *4692* **146** C3
Bladenboro NC, *1718* **123** D3
Bladen Co. NC, *32278* **123** D2
Bladensburg MD, *7661* **270** E3
Blades DE, *956* **145** E4
Blaine ME, *1428* **85** E2
Blaine MN, *44942* **67** D3
Blaine TN, *1585* **110** C4
Blaine WA, *3770* **12** C1
Blaine Co. ID, *18991* **23** D4
Blaine Co. MT, *7009* **16** B2
Blaine Co. NE, *583* **34** C2
Blaine Co. OK, *11976* **51** D2
Blair NE, *7512* **35** F3
Blair OK, *894* **51** D4
Blair WI, *1273* **73** F1
Blair Co. PA, *129144* **92** C4

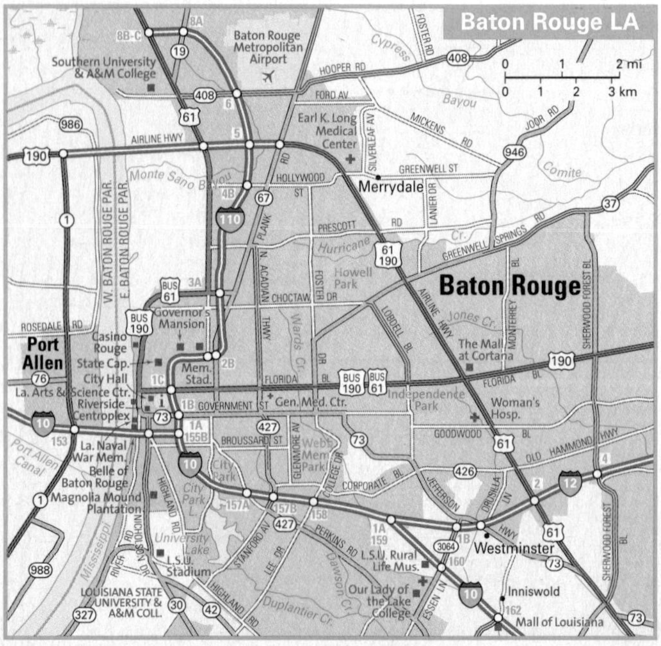
Baton Rouge LA
Baton Rouge
Baton Rouge Metropolitan Airport
Southern University & A&M College
Earl K. Long Medical Center
Merrydale
Governor's Mansion
Port Allen
Casino Rouge
State Cap.
City Hall
La. Arts & Science Ctr.
Riverside Centroplex
Mem. Stad.
Gen. Med. Ctr.
Independence Park
Woman's Hosp.
The Mall at Cortana
La. Naval War Mem.
Belle of Baton Rouge
Magnolia Mound Plantation
City Park
University Lake
L.S.U. Stadium
L.S.U. Rural Life Mus.
Our Lady of the Lake College
LOUISIANA STATE UNIVERSITY & A&M COLL.
Westminster
Inniswold
Mall of Louisiana
Howell Park
0 1 2 mi
0 1 2 3 km

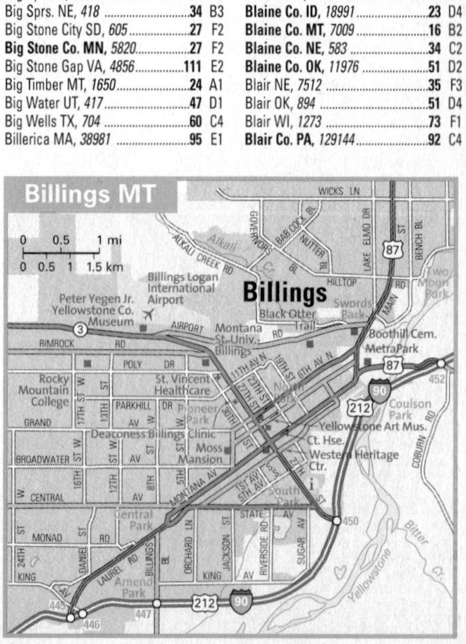
Billings MT
Billings
Billings Logan International Airport
Peter Yegen Jr. Yellowstone Co. Museum
Montana St.-Univ.-Billings
Rocky Mountain College
St. Vincent Healthcare
Deaconess Billings Clinic
Moss Mansion
Yellowstone Art Mus.
Ct. Hse.
Western Heritage Ctr.
Boothill Cem.
MetraPark
Coulson Park
Black Otter Trail
Two Moon Park
Swords Park
South Park
Central Park
Amend Park
0 0.5 1 mi
0 0.5 1 1.5 km

Entries in **bold** indicate counties or parishes. Entries in color indicate cities with detailed inset maps.

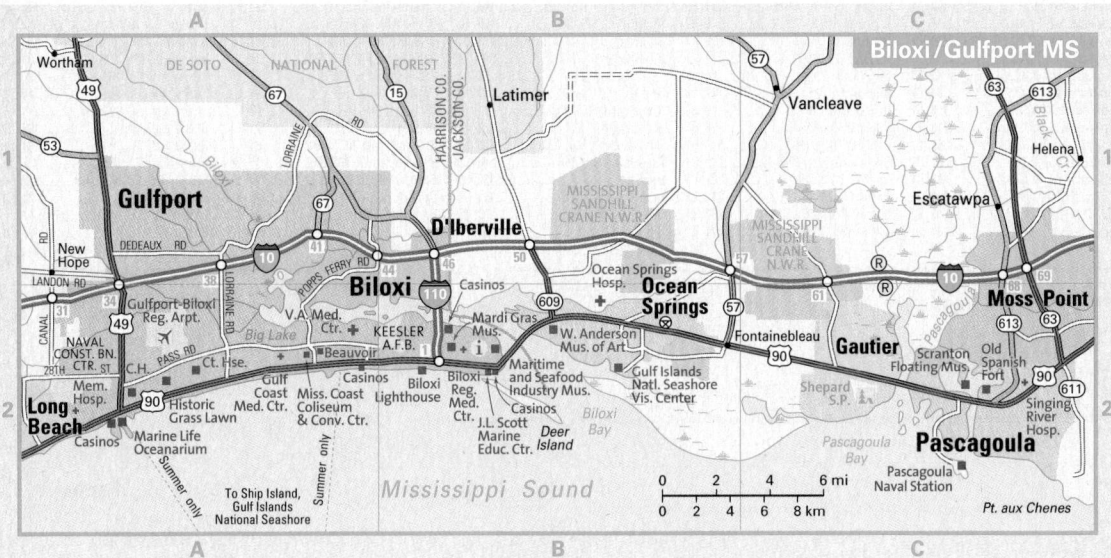

Bowdoinham ME, 600 82 B3
Bowdon GA, 1959 120 B4
Bowers Beach DE, 305 145 F3
Bowie AZ, 550 55 E3
Bowie MD, 50269 144 C3
Bowie TX, 5219 59 E1
Bowie Co. TX, 89306 116 B4
Bowleys Quarters MD, 6314 144 C2
Bowling Green FL, 2892 140 C3
Bowling Green KY, 49296 109 F2
Bowling Green MO, 3260 97 F2
Bowling Green OH, 29636 90 C2
Bowling Green VA, 936 103 D4
Bowman GA, 898 121 E3
Bowman ND, 1600 25 F1
Bowman SC, 1198 130 C1
Bowman Co. ND, 3242 25 F1
Bow Mar CO, 847 209 B4
Boxborough MA, 1400 150 C1
Box Butte Co. NE, 12158 34 A2
Box Elder MT, 794 16 B2
Box Elder SD, 2841 26 A3
Box Elder Co. UT, 42745 31 D3
Boxford MA, 2340 151 F1
Boxhill North MD, 2900 145 D1
Boyce LA, 1190 125 E4
Boyce VA, 426 103 D2
Boyceville WI, 1043 67 E3
Boyd TX, 1099 59 E2
Boyd WI, 680 67 F4
Boyd Co. KY, 49752 101 D4
Boyd Co. NE, 2438 35 D1
Boyden IA, 672 35 F1
Boydton VA, 454 113 D3
Boyertown PA, 3940 146 B2
Boyette FL, 5895 140 C3
Boykins VA, 620 113 E3
Boyle MS, 720 118 A4
Boyle Co. KY, 27697 110 B1
Boyne City MI, 3503 70 B3
Boynton Beach FL, 60389 143 F1
Boys Town NE, 818 245 A2
Bozeman MT, 27509 23 F1
Braceville IL, 792 88 C2
Bracken Co. KY, 8279 100 C3
Brackettville TX, 1876 60 B3
Bradbury CA, 855 228 E2
Braddock PA, 2912 250 C2
Braddock Hts. MD, 4627 144 A1
Braddock Hills PA, 1998 250 C2
Bradenton FL, 49504 140 B3
Bradenton Beach FL, 1482 140 B3
Bradford AR, 800 117 F1
Bradford IL, 787 88 B2
Bradford NH, 600 81 E4
Bradford OH, 1859 90 B4
Bradford PA, 9175 92 B1
Bradford RI, 1497 150 C4
Bradford TN, 1113 108 C4
Bradford VT, 815 81 E3
Bradford Co. FL, 26088 138 C3
Bradford Co. PA, 62761 93 E2
Bradfordville FL, 1100 137 E2
Bradford Woods PA, 1149 92 A3
Bradley AR, 563 125 D1

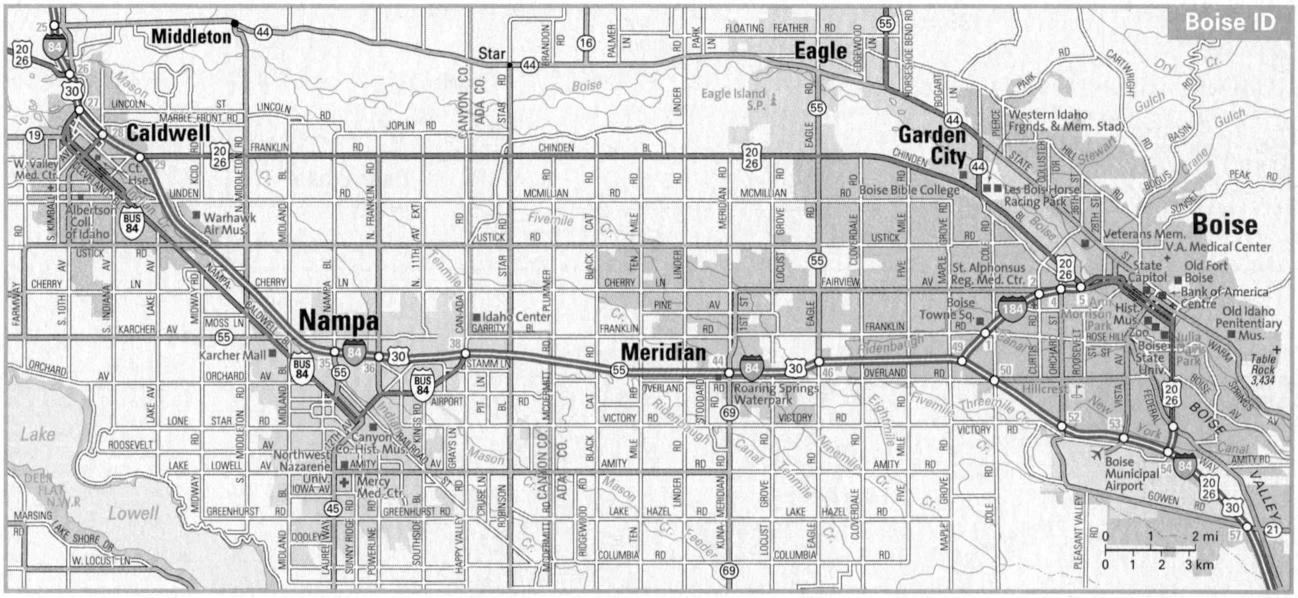
Boise ID
Middleton
Star
Eagle
Caldwell
Garden City
Boise
Nampa
Meridian
Western Idaho Frgnds. & Mem. Stad.
Boise Bible College
Les Bois Horse Racing Park
Veterans Mem.
V.A. Medical Center
State Capitol
Old Fort Boise
Bank of America Centre
Old Idaho Penitentiary
Boise State Univ.
Boise Municipal Airport
Table Rock 3,434
Roaring Springs Waterpark
Karcher Mall
Idaho Center
Warhawk Air Mus.
Northwest Nazarene Univ.
Mercy Med. Ctr.
Canyon Co. Hist. Mus.
Albertson Coll. of Idaho
St. Alphonsus Reg. Med. Ctr.
Boise Towne Sq.
Eagle Island S.P.
Lake Lowell
Deer Flat N.W.R.
0 1 2 mi
0 1 2 3 km

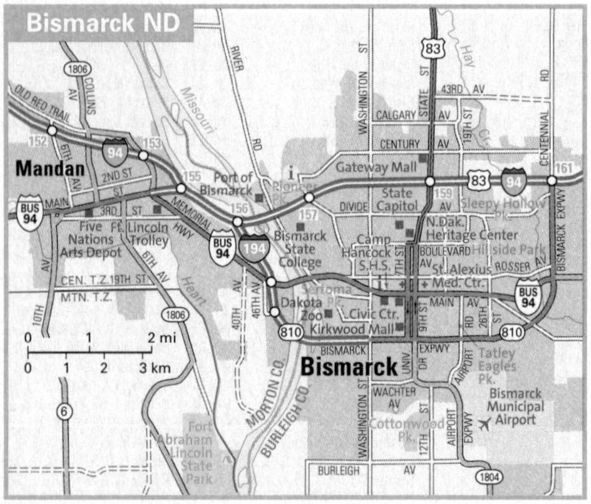
Bismarck ND
Mandan
Bismarck
Gateway Mall
State Capitol
Port of Bismarck
Five Nations Arts Depot
Lincoln Trolley
Bismarck State College
Camp Hancock S.H.S.
N.Dak. Heritage Center
St. Alexius Med. Ctr.
Dakota Zoo
Civic Ctr.
Kirkwood Mall
Sleepy Hollow Pk.
Hillside Park
Tatley Eagles Pk.
Bismarck Municipal Airport
Cottonwood Pk.
Fort Abraham Lincoln State Park
CEN. T.Z.
MTN. T.Z.
0 1 2 mi
0 1 2 3 km

Bradley IL, 12784 89 D3
Bradley ME, 650 83 D1
Bradley WV, 2371 101 F4
Bradley Beach NJ, 4793 147 F2
Bradley Co. AR, 12600 117 E4
Bradley Co. TN, 87965 120 C1
Bradley Jct. FL, 850 140 C3
Bradner OH, 1171 90 C2
Brady TX, 5523 58 C4
Braham MN, 1276 67 D2
Braidwood IL, 5203 88 C2
Brainerd MN, 13178 64 B4
Braintree MA, 33698 151 D2
Bramwell WV, 426 111 F1
Branch Co. MI, 45787 90 A1
Branchville AL, 825 119 F4
Branchville NJ, 845 94 A4
Branchville SC, 1083 130 C1
Brandenburg KY, 2049 99 F4
Brandon FL, 77895 140 C2
Brandon MS, 16436 126 B3
Brandon SD, 5693 27 F4
Brandon VT, 1684 81 D3
Brandon WI, 912 74 C2
Brandywine MD, 1410 144 B4
Brandywine Manor PA, 1200 146 B3
Branford CT, 5735 149 D2
Branford FL, 695 138 B3
Branson MO, 6050 107 D3
Brant Beach NJ, 800 147 E4
Brantley AL, 920 128 A4
Brantley Co. GA, 14629 129 F4
Brant Rock MA, 5100 151 E2
Braselton GA, 1206 121 D3
Brasher Falls NY, 1140 80 B1
Bratenahl OH, 1337 204 F1
Brattleboro VT, 8289 94 C1
Brawley CA, 22052 53 E4
Braxton Co. WV, 14702 101 F3
Bray OK, 1035 51 E4
Braymer MO, 910 96 C1
Brazil IN, 8188 99 E1
Brazoria TX, 2787 132 A4
Brazoria Co. TX, 241767 132 A4
Brazos Co. TX, 152415 61 F1
Brea CA, 35410 229 F3
Breathitt Co. KY, 16100 111 D1
Breaux Bridge LA, 7281 133 F2
Breckenridge CO, 2408 41 D1
Breckenridge MI, 1339 76 A2
Breckenridge MN, 3559 27 F1
Breckenridge TX, 5868 59 D2
Breckenridge Hills MO, 4817 256 B2
Breckinridge Co. KY, 18648 99 F4
Brecksville OH, 13382 204 F3
Breese IL, 4048 98 B3
Breezy Pt. MD, 800 144 C4
Breezy Pt. MN, 979 64 B4
Breinigsville PA, 1700 146 B1
Bremen GA, 4579 120 B4
Bremen IN, 4486 89 F2
Bremen KY, 365 109 E1
Bremen OH, 1265 101 D1
Bremer Co. IA, 23325 73 E3
Bremerton WA, 37259 12 C3
Bremond TX, 876 59 F4
Brenham TX, 13507 61 F2
Brent AL, 4024 127 F1
Brent FL, 22257 135 F2
Brentsville VA, 650 144 A4
Brentwood CA, 23302 36 B3
Brentwood MD, 2844 270 E2
Brentwood MO, 7693 256 B2
Brentwood NY, 53917 149 D4
Brentwood PA, 10466 250 B3
Brentwood TN, 23445 109 F4
Bressler PA, 2809 218 C2
Brevard NC, 6789 121 E1
Brevard Co. FL, 476230 141 E2
Brewer ME, 8987 83 D1
Brewerton NY, 3453 79 D3
Brewster MA, 2212 151 F3
Brewster MN, 502 72 A2
Brewster NE, 29 34 C2
Brewster NY, 2162 148 C2
Brewster OH, 2324 91 E3
Brewster WA, 2189 13 E2
Brewster Co. TX, 8866 62 C3
Brewster Hill NY, 2226 148 C1
Brewton AL, 5498 135 F1
Briar TX, 5350 59 E2
Briarcliff TX, 895 61 D1
Briarcliffe Acres SC, 470 123 D4
Briarcliff Manor NY, 7696 148 B2
Briar Creek PA, 651 93 E3
Briarwood KY, 554 230 F1
Briceville TN, 650 110 C4
Brickerville PA, 1287 146 A2
Bridge City LA, 8323 239 B2
Bridge City TX, 8651 132 C3
Bridgehampton NY, 1381 149 F3
Bridgeport AL, 2728 120 A2
Bridgeport CA, 200 37 E3
Bridgeport CT, 139529 149 D2
Bridgeport IL, 2168 99 D3
Bridgeport MD, 2700 144 A1
Bridgeport MI, 7849 76 B3
Bridgeport NE, 1594 34 A3
Bridgeport NY, 1665 79 E3
Bridgeport PA, 4371 248 A1
Bridgeport TX, 4309 59 E2
Bridgeport WA, 2059 13 E2
Bridgeport WV, 7306 102 A2
Bridger MT, 745 24 B2
Bridgeton MO, 15550 256 B1
Bridgeton NJ, 22771 145 F1
Bridgetown OH, 12569 204 A2
Bridgeview IL, 15335 203 D5
Bridgeville DE, 1436 145 E4
Bridgeville PA, 5341 250 A3
Bridgewater MA, 6664 151 D2
Bridgewater NJ, 3200 147 D1
Bridgewater NY, 579 79 E3
Bridgewater SD, 607 27 E4
Bridgewater VA, 5203 102 C4
Bridgman MI, 2428 89 E1
Bridgton ME, 2359 82 B3
Brielle NJ, 4893 147 E2
Brier WA, 6383 262 B2
Brigantine NJ, 12594 147 F4
Brigham City UT, 17411 31 E3
Bright IN, 5405 100 B2
Brighton AL, 3640 195 D2
Brighton CO, 20905 41 E1
Brighton IL, 2196 98 A2
Brighton IA, 687 87 E2
Brighton MI, 6701 76 B4
Brighton NY, 35584 78 C3
Brighton TN, 1719 118 B1
Brightwaters NY, 3248 149 D4
Brightwood VA, 500 102 C3
Brilliant AL, 762 119 E3
Brilliant OH, 1600 91 F4
Brillion WI, 2937 74 C1
Brimfield IL, 933 88 B3
Brinckerhoff NY, 2734 148 B1
Brinkley AR, 3940 117 F2
Brinnon WA, 803 12 C3
Brisbane CA, 3597 259 B3
Briscoe Co. TX, 1790 50 B4
Bristol CT, 60062 149 D1
Bristol FL, 845 137 D2
Bristol IN, 1382 89 F1
Bristol NH, 1670 81 F3
Bristol PA, 9923 147 D2
Bristol RI, 22469 151 D3
Bristol SD, 377 27 E2
Bristol TN, 24821 111 E3
Bristol VT, 1800 81 D2
Bristol VA, 17367 111 E3
Bristol WI, 1100 74 C4
Bristol Co. MA, 534678 151 D3
Bristol Co. RI, 50648 151 D3
Bristow OK, 4325 51 F2
Britt IA, 2052 72 C3
Brittany Farms PA, 3268 146 C2
Britton MI, 699 90 B1
Britton SD, 1328 27 E1
Broadalbin NY, 1411 80 C4
Broad Brook CT, 3469 150 A3
Broadmoor CA, 4026 259 B3
Broadus MT, 451 25 E2
Broadview IL, 8264 203 C4
Broadview Hts. OH, 15967 204 F3
Broadwater Co. MT, 4385 15 F4
Broadway NC, 1015 123 D1
Broadway VA, 2192 102 C3
Brock Hall MD, 1200 144 C3
Brockport NY, 8103 78 C3
Brockton MA, 94304 151 D2
Brockton MT, 245 17 E2
Brockway PA, 2182 92 B2
Brocton NY, 1547 78 A4
Brodhead KY, 1193 110 C1
Brodhead WI, 3180 74 B4
Brodheadsville PA, 1637 93 F3
Brogden NC, 2907 123 E1
Broken Arrow OK, 74859 106 A4
Broken Bow NE, 3491 35 D3
Broken Bow OK, 4230 116 B3
Bromley KY, 838 204 A3
Bronson FL, 964 138 C4
Bronson MI, 2421 90 A1
Bronte TX, 1076 58 C3
Bronwood GA, 513 128 C3
Bronx Co. NY, 1332650 148 B4
Brook IN, 1062 89 D3
Brookdale SC, 4724 122 A4
Brooke VA, 650 103 D4
Brooke Co. WV, 25447 91 F4
Brookfield CT, 2700 148 C1
Brookfield IL, 19085 203 C5
Brookfield MA, 1200 150 B2
Brookfield MO, 4769 97 D1
Brookfield OH, 1288 276 C1
Brookfield WI, 38649 234 B2
Brookfield Ctr. CT, 1800 148 C1
Brookhaven MS, 9861 126 B4
Brookhaven NY, 3570 149 D4
Brookhaven PA, 7985 248 A4
Brookings OR, 5447 28 A2
Brookings SD, 18504 27 F3
Brookings Co. SD, 28220 27 F3
Brookland AR, 1332 108 A4
Brooklandville MD, 2200 193 C1
Brooklawn NJ, 2354 248 C4
Brooklet GA, 1113 130 B2
Brookline MA, 57107 151 D1
Brookline NH, 650 95 D1
Brooklyn CT, 1100 150 B3
Brooklyn IL, 676 256 C2
Brooklyn IN, 1545 99 F1
Brooklyn IA, 1367 87 E1
Brooklyn MI, 1176 90 B1
Brooklyn OH, 11586 204 E2
Brooklyn WI, 916 74 B3
Brooklyn Ctr. MN, 29172 235 B1
Brooklyn Hts. OH, 1558 204 F2
Brooklyn Park MD, 10938 193 C4
Brooklyn Park MN, 67388 235 B1
Brookneal VA, 1259 112 C2
Brook Park OH, 21218 204 E3
Brookport IL, 1054 108 C2
Brooks GA, 553 128 C1
Brooks KY, 2678 100 A4
Brooks ME, 550 82 C2
Brooks Co. GA, 16450 137 F1
Brooks Co. TX, 7976 63 E3
Brookshire TX, 3450 61 F2
Brookside AL, 1393 195 D1
Brookside DE, 14806 146 B4
Brookside OH, 644 91 F4
Brookside Vil. TX, 1960 220 C4
Brookston IN, 1717 89 E3
Brooksville FL, 7264 140 C1
Brooksville KY, 589 100 C3
Brooksville MS, 1182 127 D1
Brookville IN, 2652 100 A2
Brookville NY, 2126 148 C4
Brookville OH, 5289 100 B1
Brookville PA, 4230 92 B3
Brookwood AL, 1483 127 F1
Broomall PA, 11046 146 C3
Broome Co. NY, 200536 93 F1
Broomfield CO, 38272 41 E1
Broomfield Co. CO, 38272 41 E1
Brooten MN, 649 66 B3
Broussard LA, 5874 133 F2
Broward Co. FL, 1623018 143 E1
Browerville MN, 735 66 B2
Brown City MI, 1334 76 C3
Brown Co. IL, 6950 87 F4
Brown Co. IN, 14957 99 F2
Brown Co. KS, 10724 96 A1
Brown Co. MN, 26911 72 B1
Brown Co. NE, 3525 34 C1
Brown Co. OH, 42285 100 C3
Brown Co. SD, 35460 27 E1
Brown Co. TX, 37674 59 D3
Brown Co. WI, 226778 74 C1
Brown Deer WI, 12170 234 C1
Brownfield TX, 9488 58 A2
Browning MT, 1065 15 E2
Brownsboro TX, 796 124 A3
Brownsburg IN, 14520 99 F1
Brownsdale MN, 718 73 D2
Browns Mills NJ, 11257 147 D3
Brownstown IL, 705 98 C2
Brownstown IN, 2978 99 F3
Browns Valley MN, 690 27 F1
Brownsville CA, 1069 36 C1
Brownsville KY, 921 109 F2
Brownsville MN, 466 73 F2
Brownsville OR, 1449 20 B3
Brownsville PA, 2804 102 B1
Brownsville TN, 10748 118 C1
Brownsville TX, 139722 63 F4
Brownsville WI, 570 74 C2
Brownton MN, 807 66 C4
Brownville NY, 1022 79 E1
Brownville Jct. ME, 750 84 C4
Brownwood TX, 18813 59 D4
Broxton GA, 1428 129 E4
Broyhill Park VA, 17000 270 B4
Bruce MS, 2097 118 C3
Bruce SD, 272 27 F3
Bruce WI, 787 67 F3
Bruceton TN, 1554 109 D4
Bruceville-Eddy TX, 1490 59 E4
Brule Co. SD, 5364 27 D4
Brundidge AL, 2341 128 B4
Brunson SC, 589 130 B1
Brunswick GA, 15600 139 D1
Brunswick ME, 14816 82 B3
Brunswick MD, 4894 144 A2
Brunswick MO, 925 97 D2
Brunswick OH, 33388 91 E2
Brunswick Co. NC, 73143 123 E3
Brunswick Co. VA, 18419 113 D3
Brush CO, 5117 33 F4
Brush Prairie WA, 2384 20 C1
Brushy OK, 787 116 B1
Brusly LA, 2020 134 A2
Bryan OH, 8333 90 B2
Bryan TX, 65660 61 F1
Bryan Co. GA, 23417 130 B3
Bryan Co. OK, 36534 59 F1
Bryans Road MD, 4912 144 B4
Bryant AR, 9764 117 E2
Bryant SD, 396 27 E3
Bryantville MA, 2600 151 E2
Bryn Athyn PA, 1351 248 D1
Bryn Mawr PA, 4382 146 C3
Bryson TX, 528 59 D2
Bryson City NC, 1411 121 D1
Buchanan GA, 941 120 B4
Buchanan MI, 4681 89 E1
Buchanan NY, 2189 148 B2
Buchanan VA, 1233 112 B1
Buchanan Co. IA, 21093 73 E4
Buchanan Co. MO, 85998 96 B1
Buchanan Co. VA, 26978 111 F2
Buchanan Dam TX, 1688 61 D1
Buchtel OH, 574 101 E2
Buckeye AZ, 6537 54 B1
Buckeye Lake OH, 3049 101 D1
Buckfield ME, 325 82 B2
Buckhannon WV, 5725 102 A2
Buckhead Ridge FL, 1390 141 E4
Buckingham PA, 1400 146 C2
Buckingham VA, 175 113 D1
Buckingham Co. VA, 15623 113 D1
Buckland AK, 406 154 B2
Buckley IL, 593 89 D4
Buckley MI, 550 69 F4
Buckley WA, 4145 12 C3
Bucklin KS, 725 42 C4
Bucklin MO, 524 97 D1
Buckner KY, 4000 100 A4
Buckner MO, 2725 96 C2
Bucks Co. PA, 597635 146 C1
Bucksport ME, 2970 83 D2
Bucksport SC, 1117 123 D4
Bucoda WA, 628 12 C4
Bucyrus OH, 13224 90 C3
Buda IL, 592 88 B2
Buda TX, 2404 61 E2
Budd Lake NJ, 8100 94 A4
Bude MS, 1037 126 A4
Buellton CA, 3828 52 A2
Buena NJ, 3873 147 D4
Buena WA, 950 13 D4
Buena Park CA, 78282 228 E3
Buena Ventura Lakes FL, 14100 246 C5
Buena Vista CO, 2195 41 D2
Buena Vista GA, 1664 128 C2
Buena Vista MI, 7845 76 B2
Buena Vista VA, 6349 112 C1
Buena Vista Co. IA, 20411 72 B4
Buffalo IN, 672 89 E3
Buffalo IA, 1321 87 F2
Buffalo KY, 475 110 A1
Buffalo MN, 10097 66 C3
Buffalo MO, 2781 107 D1
Buffalo NY, 292648 78 B3
Buffalo ND, 209 19 E4
Buffalo OK, 1200 50 C1
Buffalo SC, 1426 121 F2
Buffalo SD, 380 25 F1
Buffalo TX, 1804 59 F4
Buffalo WV, 1171 101 E3
Buffalo WI, 1040 73 E1
Buffalo WY, 3900 25 D3
Buffalo Ctr. IA, 963 72 C2
Buffalo Co. NE, 42259 35 D4
Buffalo Co. SD, 2032 27 D3
Buffalo Co. WI, 13804 67 E4
Buffalo Grove IL, 42909 203 C2
Buffalo Lake MN, 768 66 B4
Buford GA, 10668 120 C3
Buhl ID, 3985 30 C1
Buhl MN, 1000 64 C3
Buhler KS, 1358 43 E3
Buies Creek NC, 2215 123 D1
Bullard TX, 1150 124 A3
Bullhead SD, 308 26 C1
Bullhead City AZ, 33769 46 B3
Bullitt Co. KY, 61236 99 F4
Bulloch Co. GA, 55983 130 B2
Bullock Co. AL, 11714 128 B3
Bulls Gap TN, 714 111 D3
Bull Shoals AR, 2000 107 E3
Bull Valley IL, 726 74 C4
Bulverde TX, 3761 61 D2
Buna TX, 2269 132 C2
Buncombe Co. NC, 206330 111 E4
Bunker Hill IL, 1801 98 B2
Bunker Hill IN, 987 89 F3
Bunker Hill OR, 1462 20 A4
Bunker Hill WV, 700 103 D2
Bunker Hill Vil. TX, 3654 220 B2
Bunkerville NV, 1014 46 B1
Bunkie LA, 4662 133 E1
Bunnell FL, 2122 139 E4
Buras LA, 3358 134 C4
Burbank CA, 100316 52 C2
Burbank IL, 27902 203 D5
Burbank WA, 3303 21 E1
Burden KS, 564 43 F4

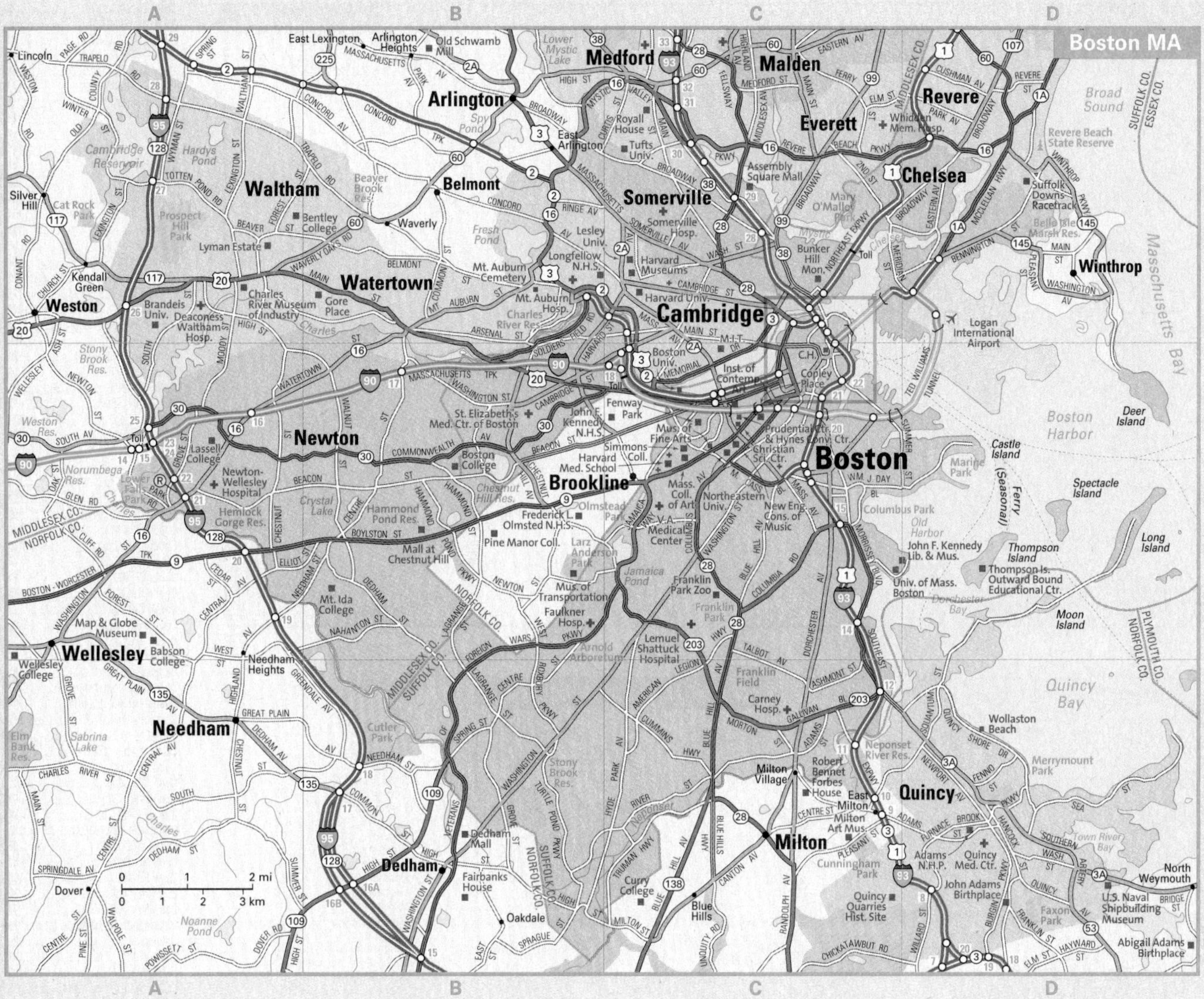

Entries in **bold** indicate counties or parishes. Entries in color indicate cities with detailed inset maps.

Bureau County—Butte County **197**

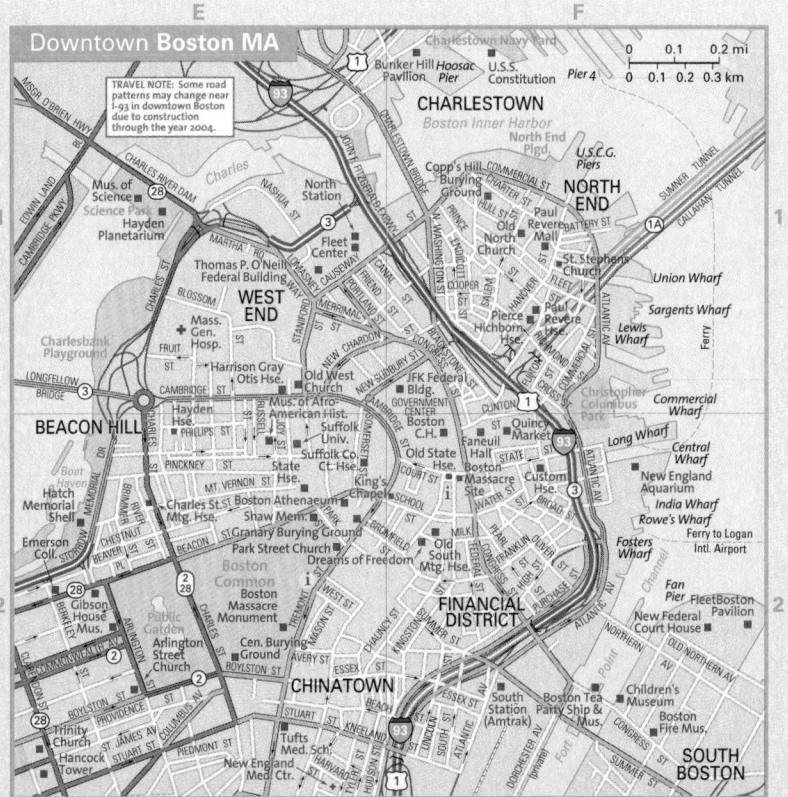

Boston MA

Downtown Boston MA

TRAVEL NOTE: Some road patterns may change near I-93 in downtown Boston due to construction through the year 2004.

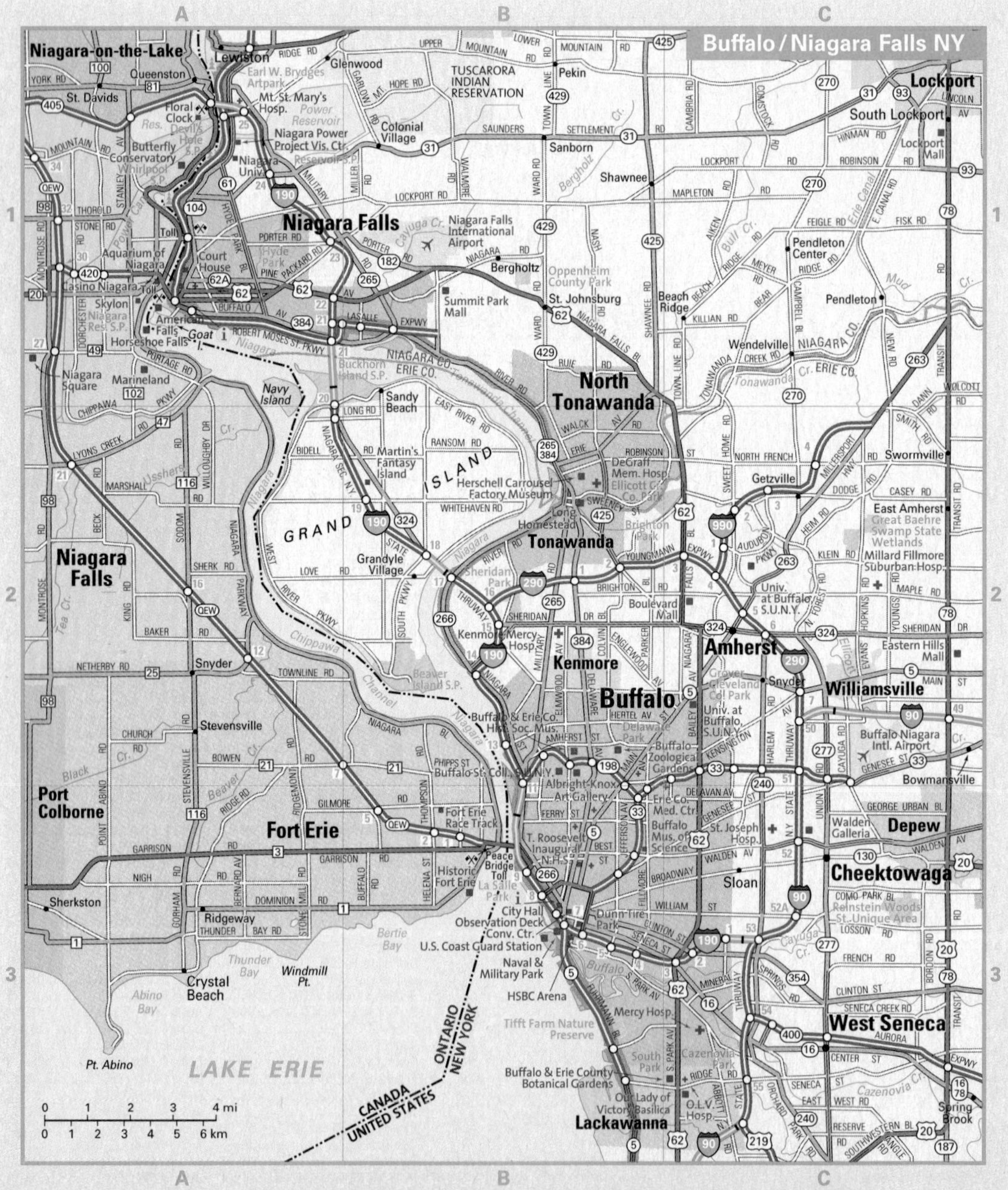

198 Butte County—Calion

Figures after entries indicate population, page number, and grid reference.

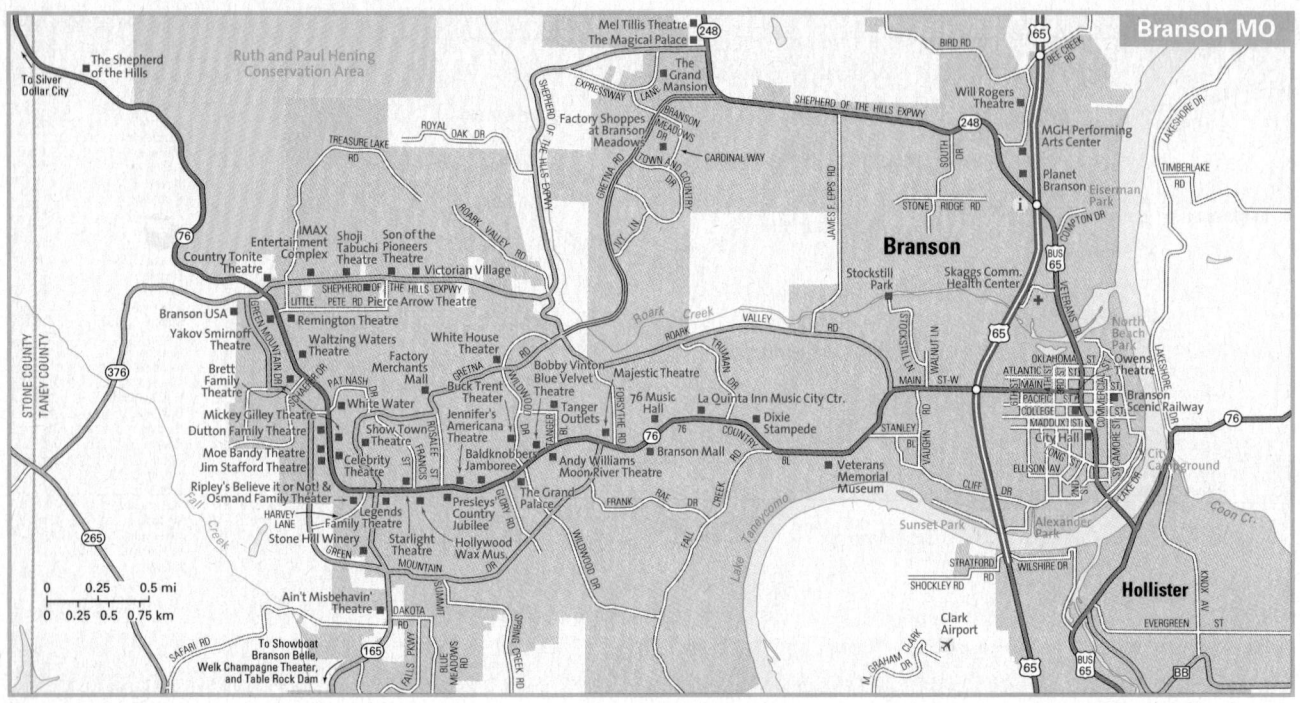

Branson MO

Buffalo / Niagara Falls NY

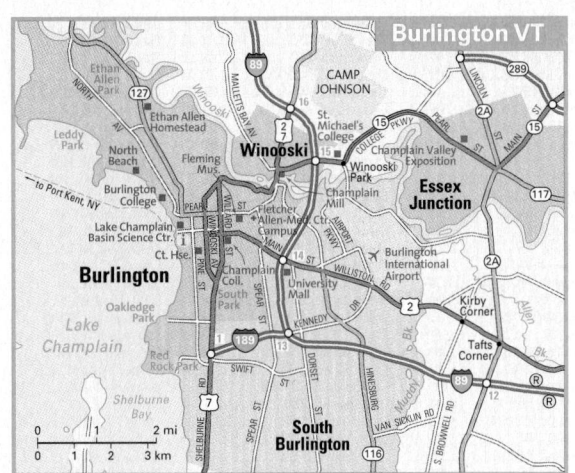

Burlington VT

Carson City NV

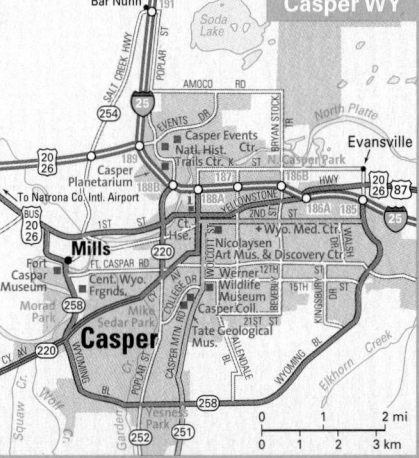

Casper WY

Canton OH inset map

Cairo	B1
Canton	B1
Crystal Sprs.	A1
Fairhope	B1
Green	A1
Hills and Dales	A1
Louisville	B1
Massillon	B1
McDonaldsville	A1
Meyers Lake	B2
Middlebranch	B1
N. Canton	B1
Perry Hts.	A2
Reedurban	A2
Richville	A2
Waco	B2

Calipatria CA, 7289 ... 53 E4
Calistoga CA, 5190 ... 36 B3
Callahan FL, 962 ... 139 D2
Callahan Co. TX, 12905 ... 58 C3
Callaway FL, 14233 ... 136 C2
Callaway NE, 637 ... 34 C3
Callaway Co. MO, 40766 ... 97 E3
Calloway Co. KY, 34177 ... 109 D3
Calmar IA, 1058 ... 73 E4
Cal Nev Ari NV, 278 ... 46 B3
Calpella CA, 950 ... 36 A2
Calumet MI, 879 ... 65 F3
Calumet OK, 535 ... 51 E3
Calumet City IL, 39071 ... 89 D2
Calumet Co. WI, 40631 ... 74 C1
Calumet Park IL, 8516 ... 203 E6
Calvert TX, 1426 ... 61 F1
Calvert Beach MD, 2487 ... 103 E4
Calvert City KY, 2701 ... 109 D2
Calvert Co. MD, 74563 ... 144 C4
Calvert Manor MD, 650 ... 144 B4
Calverton MD, 12610 ... 144 B3
Calverton NY, 5704 ... 149 E3
Calverton Park MO, 1322 ... 256 D1
Camanche IA, 4215 ... 88 A1
Camargo KY, 923 ... 100 C4
Camarillo CA, 57077 ... 52 B2
Camas WA, 12534 ... 20 C1
Camas Co. ID, 991 ... 22 C4
Cambria CA, 6232 ... 44 B4
Cambria IL, 1330 ... 108 C1
Cambria WI, 762 ... 74 B2
Cambria Co. PA, 152598 ... 92 B4
Cambridge ID, 360 ... 22 B3
Cambridge IL, 2180 ... 88 A2
Cambridge IA, 819 ... 86 C1
Cambridge MD, 10911 ... 145 D4
Cambridge MA, 101355 ... 151 D1
Cambridge MN, 5520 ... 67 D3
Cambridge NE, 1041 ... 34 C4
Cambridge NY, 1925 ... 81 D4
Cambridge OH, 11520 ... 101 E1
Cambridge VT, 235 ... 81 D1
Cambridge WI, 1101 ... 74 B3
Cambridge City IN, 2121 ... 100 A1
Cambridge Sprs. PA, 2363 ... 92 A1
Camden AL, 2257 ... 127 F3
Camden AR, 13154 ... 117 D4
Camden DE, 2100 ... 145 E2
Camden IN, 582 ... 89 E3
Camden ME, 3934 ... 82 C2
Camden MI, 550 ... 90 A1
Camden NJ, 79904 ... 146 C3
Camden NY, 2330 ... 79 E3
Camden NC, 350 ... 115 E1
Camden OH, 2302 ... 100 B1
Camden SC, 6682 ... 122 B3
Camden TN, 3828 ... 109 D4
Camden Co. GA, 43664 ... 139 D1
Camden Co. MO, 37051 ... 97 D4
Camden Co. NJ, 508932 ... 147 E4
Camden Co. NC, 6885 ... 115 E1
Camden Pt. MO, 484 ... 96 B2
Camdenton MO, 2779 ... 97 D4
Cameron AZ, 978 ... 47 E2
Cameron LA, 1965 ... 133 D3
Cameron MO, 8312 ... 96 C1
Cameron SC, 449 ... 122 B4
Cameron TX, 5634 ... 61 E1
Cameron WV, 1212 ... 102 A1
Cameron WI, 1546 ... 67 E3
Cameron Co. PA, 5974 ... 92 C2
Cameron Co. TX, 335227 ... 63 F4
Cameron Par. LA, 9991 ... 133 D3
Camilla GA, 5669 ... 129 D4
Camillus NY, 1249 ... 79 D3
Camino CA, 1100 ... 36 C2
Campbell CA, 38138 ... 36 B4
Campbell FL, 2677 ... 141 D2
Campbell MO, 1883 ... 108 B3
Campbell OH, 9460 ... 91 F3
Campbell TX, 734 ... 59 F2
Campbell Co. KY, 88616 ... 100 B3
Campbell Co. SD, 1782 ... 26 C1
Campbell Co. TN, 39854 ... 110 C3

Campbell Co. VA, 51078 ... 112 C2
Campbell Co. WY, 33698 ... 25 E3
Campbell Hall NY, 750 ... 148 A1
Campbellsburg IN, 578 ... 99 F3
Campbellsburg KY, 705 ... 100 A3
Campbellsport WI, 1913 ... 74 C2
Campbellsville KY, 10498 ... 110 A1
Campbellton FL, 212 ... 136 C1
Camp Douglas WI, 592 ... 74 A1
Camp Hill AL, 1273 ... 128 B2
Camp Hill PA, 7636 ... 93 D4
Campion CO, 1832 ... 33 E4
Campobello SC, 449 ... 121 F1
Camp Pt. IL, 1244 ... 87 F4
Camp Sprs. MD, 17968 ... 144 B3
Campton KY, 424 ... 111 D1
Campton NH, 450 ... 81 F3
Camp Verde AZ, 9451 ... 47 D4
Camp Wood TX, 822 ... 60 C2
Cana VA, 1228 ... 112 A3
Canaan CT, 1288 ... 94 B2
Canaan ME, 300 ... 82 C1
Canaan NH, 800 ... 81 E3
Canaan VT, 550 ... 81 F1
Canadian TX, 2233 ... 50 C2
Canadian Co. OK, 87697 ... 51 E3
Canajoharie NY, 2257 ... 79 E3
Canal Fulton OH, 5061 ... 91 E3
Canal Pt. FL, 525 ... 141 E4
Canal Winchester OH, 4478 ... 101 D1
Cantua Creek CA, 655 ... 44 C3
Canute OK, 524 ... 51 D3
Canandaigua NY, 11264 ... 78 C3
Canaseraga NY, 425 ... 79 D4
Canastota NY, 4425 ... 79 E3
Canby MN, 1903 ... 27 F3
Canby OR, 12790 ... 20 C2
Candler Co. GA, 9577 ... 129 F2
Cando ND, 1342 ... 19 D2
Candor NY, 855 ... 93 E1

Candor NC, 825 ... 122 C1
Caney KS, 2092 ... 51 F1
Caneyville KY, 627 ... 109 F1
Canfield OH, 7374 ... 91 F3
Canistee NY, 2336 ... 78 C4
Canistota SD, 700 ... 27 E4
Cannelton IN, 1209 ... 99 E4
Cannon Ball ND, 864 ... 18 C4
Cannon Co. TN, 12826 ... 110 A4
Cannondale CT, 1400 ... 148 C2
Cannon Falls MN, 3795 ... 67 D4
Cannonsburg KY, 1300 ... 101 D4
Canon GA, 755 ... 121 E3
Canon City CO, 15431 ... 41 E3
Canonsburg PA, 8607 ... 92 A4
Canterbury DE, 1200 ... 145 E2
Canton CT, 1565 ... 94 C3
Canton GA, 7709 ... 120 C3
Canton IL, 15288 ... 88 A4
Canton KS, 829 ... 43 E3
Canton MA, 20775 ... 151 D2
Canton MS, 12911 ... 126 B2
Canton MO, 2557 ... 87 F4
Canton NY, 5882 ... 80 B2
Canton NC, 4029 ... 121 E1
Canton OK, 618 ... 51 D2
Canton PA, 1807 ... 93 D2
Canton SD, 3110 ... 27 F4
Canton TX, 3292 ... 124 A2
Canton OH, 80806 ... 91 E3
Cantonment FL, 2300 ... 135 F2
Carls Corner NJ, 1100 ... 145 F1
Carlsbad CA, 78247 ... 53 D4
Carlsbad NM, 25625 ... 57 D4
Canton Day AZ, 1092 ... 55 E1
Canyon Lake CA, 9952 ... 229 J5

Canyon Lake TX, 16870 ... 61 D2
Canyonville OR, 1293 ... 28 B1
Capac MI, 1775 ... 76 C3
Cape Canaveral FL, 8829 ... 141 E2
Cape Carteret NC, 1214 ... 115 D4
Cape Charles VA, 1134 ... 114 B3
Cape Coral FL, 102286 ... 142 C1
Cape Cottage ME, 2300 ... 251 B2
Cape Elizabeth ME, 1100 ... 82 B3
Cape Girardeau MO, 35349 ... 108 B1
Cape Girardeau Co. MO, 68693 ... 108 B1
Cape May NJ, 4034 ... 104 C4
Cape May Co. NJ, 102326 ... 104 C4
Cape May C.H. NJ, 4704 ... 104 C4
Cape Neddick ME, 2997 ... 82 B4
Cape Porpoise ME, 650 ... 82 B3
Cape St. Claire MD, 8022 ... 144 C3
Cape Vincent NY, 760 ... 79 D1
Capitan NM, 1443 ... 57 D1
Capitola CA, 10033 ... 44 B2
Capitol Hts. MD, 4138 ... 270 C3
Capitol Park DE, 700 ... 145 E2
Capron IL, 961 ... 74 C4
Captain Cook HI, 3206 ... 153 F6
Caraway AR, 1349 ... 108 A4
Carbonado WA, 621 ... 12 C4
Carbon Cliff IL, 1689 ... 208 C2

Carlyle IL, 3406 ... 98 B3
Carlyss LA, 4049 ... 133 D3
Carmel IN, 37733 ... 99 F1
Carmel ME, 400 ... 82 C1
Carmel NY, 5650 ... 148 C1
Carmel-by-the-Sea CA, 4081 ... 44 B3
Carmel Valley CA, 4700 ... 44 B3
Carmen AZ, 569 ... 55 D4
Carmi IL, 5422 ... 99 D4
Carmichael CA, 49742 ... 255 C2
Carnation WA, 1893 ... 12 C3
Carnegie OK, 1637 ... 51 D3
Carnegie PA, 8389 ... 250 A2
Carnesville GA, 541 ... 121 D3
Carney MD, 28264 ... 193 D1
Carney OK, 649 ... 51 F2
Carneys Pt. NJ, 6914 ... 146 B4
Caro MI, 4145 ... 76 C2
Carol City FL, 59443 ... 143 E2
Caroleen NC, 1200 ... 121 F1
Carolina RI, 850 ... 150 C4
Carolina Beach NC, 4701 ... 123 E3
Carolina Shores NC, 1482 ... 123 D4
Caroline Co. MD, 29772 ... 145 E4
Caroline Co. VA, 22121 ... 103 E4
Carol Stream IL, 40438 ... 203 B3
Carpendale WV, 954 ... 102 C1

Carson City NV, 52457 ... 37 D2
Carson Co. TX, 6516 ... 50 B3
Carsonville MI, 502 ... 76 C2
Carter Co. KY, 26889 ... 101 D4
Carter Co. MO, 5941 ... 108 A2
Carter Co. MT, 1360 ... 25 F3
Carter Co. OK, 45621 ... 51 E4
Carter Co. TN, 56742 ... 111 E3
Carter Lake IA, 3248 ... 86 A2
Cartersville GA, 15925 ... 120 B3
Carterville IL, 4616 ... 108 C1
Carterville MO, 1826 ... 106 B2
Carthage AR, 442 ... 117 E3
Carthage IL, 2725 ... 87 F4
Carthage IN, 928 ... 100 A1
Carthage MS, 4637 ... 126 C2
Carthage MO, 12668 ... 106 C2
Carthage NY, 3721 ... 79 E1
Carthage NC, 1871 ... 122 C1
Carthage TN, 2251 ... 110 A3
Carthage TX, 6664 ... 124 C3
Caruthers CA, 2103 ... 44 C3
Caruthersville MO, 6760 ... 108 B4
Carver MA, 900 ... 151 E2
Carver MN, 1266 ... 66 C4
Carver Co. MN, 70205 ... 66 C4
Cary IL, 15531 ... 88 C1
Cary MS, 427 ... 126 A2
Cary NC, 94536 ... 112 C4
Caryville TN, 2243 ... 110 C3
Casa Blanca AZ, 300 ... 54 C2
Casa Blanca NM, 669 ... 48 B3
Casa Grande AZ, 25224 ... 54 C2
Cascade CO, 1709 ... 41 E2
Cascade ID, 997 ... 22 B3
Cascade IA, 1958 ... 73 E1
Cascade MD, 1141 ... 103 D1
Cascade MT, 819 ... 15 D1
Cascade Co. MT, 80357 ... 15 D1
Cascade Locks OR, 1115 ... 20 C1
Casco ME, 400 ... 82 B3
Casco WI, 572 ... 69 D4
Caseville MI, 888 ... 76 C1
Casey IL, 2942 ... 99 D2
Casey Co. KY, 15447 ... 110 B1
Caseyville IL, 4310 ... 256 D2
Cashion OK, 635 ... 51 E3
Cashmere WA, 2965 ... 13 D3
Cashton WI, 1005 ... 73 F2
Casitas Sprs. CA, 1000 ... 52 B2
Casper WY, 49644 ... 33 D1
Caspian MI, 997 ... 68 C2
Cassadaga NY, 650 ... 141 D1
Cassadaga NY, 676 ... 78 A4
Cass City MI, 2643 ... 76 C2
Cass Co. IL, 13695 ... 98 A1
Cass Co. IN, 40930 ... 89 F3

Cass Co. IA, 14684 ... 86 B2
Cass Co. MI, 51104 ... 89 F1
Cass Co. MN, 27150 ... 64 B4
Cass Co. MO, 82092 ... 96 C3
Cass Co. NE, 24334 ... 35 F3
Cass Co. ND, 123138 ... 19 E3
Cass Co. TX, 30438 ... 124 C1
Casselberry FL, 22629 ... 141 D1
Casselton ND, 1855 ... 19 E4
Cassia Co. ID, 21416 ... 31 D2
Cass Lake MN, 860 ... 64 A3
Cassopolis MI, 1740 ... 89 F1
Cassville MO, 2890 ... 106 C3
Cassville NJ, 900 ... 147 E2
Cassville WV, 1586 ... 102 A1
Cassville WI, 1085 ... 73 F4
Castaic CA, 1100 ... 52 C2
Castalia OH, 935 ... 91 D2
Castanea PA, 1189 ... 93 D3
Castle NY, 1051 ... 78 B4
Castine ME, 900 ... 83 D2
Castleberry AL, 590 ... 127 F4
Castle Dale UT, 1657 ... 39 F2
Castleford ID, 277 ... 30 C1
Castle Hayne NC, 1116 ... 123 E3
Castle Hills TX, 4202 ... 257 C2
Castle Rock CO, 20224 ... 41 E2
Castle Rock WA, 2130 ... 20 B1
Castle Shannon PA, 8556 ... 250 B3
Castleton VT, 1566 ... 81 D3
Castleton-on-Hudson NY, 1619 ... 94 B1
Castle Valley UT, 349 ... 40 A3
Castlewood SD, 666 ... 27 F3
Castlewood VA, 2036 ... 111 E2
Castro Co. TX, 8285 ... 50 A4
Castro Valley CA, 57292 ... 259 D3
Castroville CA, 6724 ... 44 B2
Castroville TX, 2664 ... 61 D3
Caswell Co. NC, 23501 ... 112 C3
Catahoula Par. LA, 10920 ... 125 E2
Catalina AZ, 7025 ... 55 D3
Catasauqua PA, 6588 ... 146 B1
Catawba NC, 698 ... 112 A4
Catawba SC, 700 ... 122 A2
Catawba Co. NC, 141685 ... 122 A1
Catawba Island OH, 850 ... 91 D2
Catawissa PA, 1589 ... 93 E3
Catharpin VA, 600 ... 144 A3
Cathcart WA, 3015 ... 262 B2
Cathedral City CA, 42647 ... 53 E3
Cathlamet WA, 565 ... 20 B1
Catlettsburg KY, 1960 ... 101 D3
Catlin IL, 2087 ... 89 D4
Cato NY, 601 ... 79 D3
Catonsville MD, 39820 ... 144 C2
Catoosa OK, 5449 ... 106 A3
Catoosa Co. GA, 53282 ... 120 B3
Catron Co. NM, 3543 ... 48 A4
Catskill NY, 4392 ... 94 B2
Cattaraugus NY, 1075 ... 78 A4

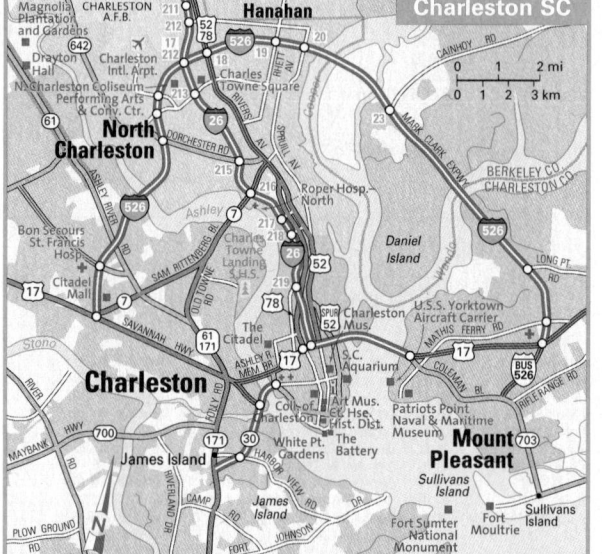

Charleston SC

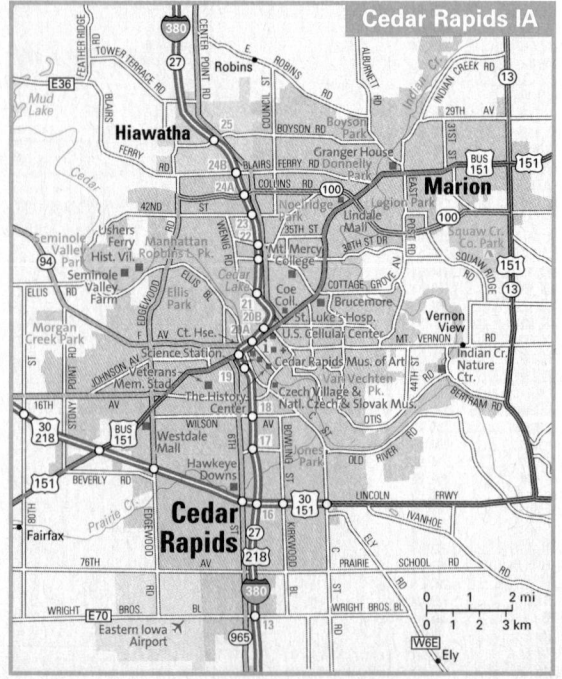

Cedar Rapids IA

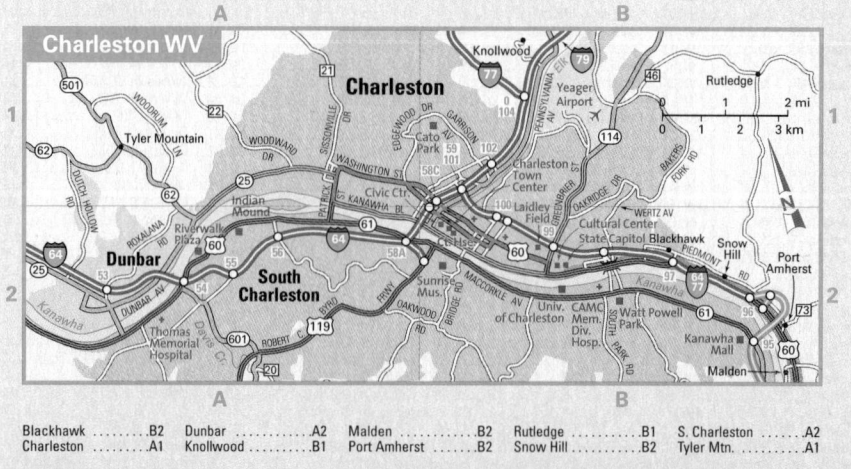

Charleston WV

Blackhawk B2
Charleston A1
Dunbar A2
Knollwood B1
Malden B2
Port Amherst B2
Rutledge B1
Snow Hill B2
S. Charleston A2
Tyler Mtn. A1

Entries in **bold** indicate counties or parishes. Entries in color indicate cities with detailed inset maps.

Charlotte NC

Charlottesville VA

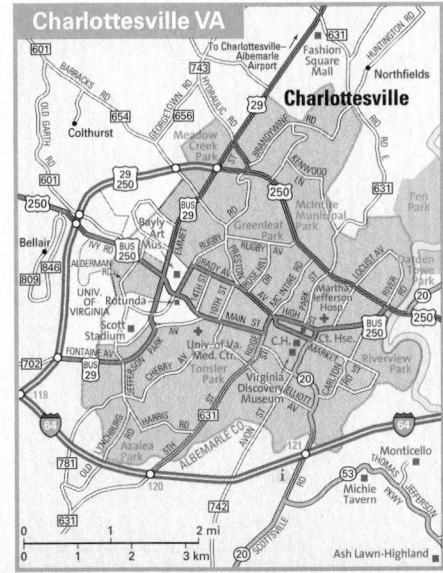

Chattanooga TN

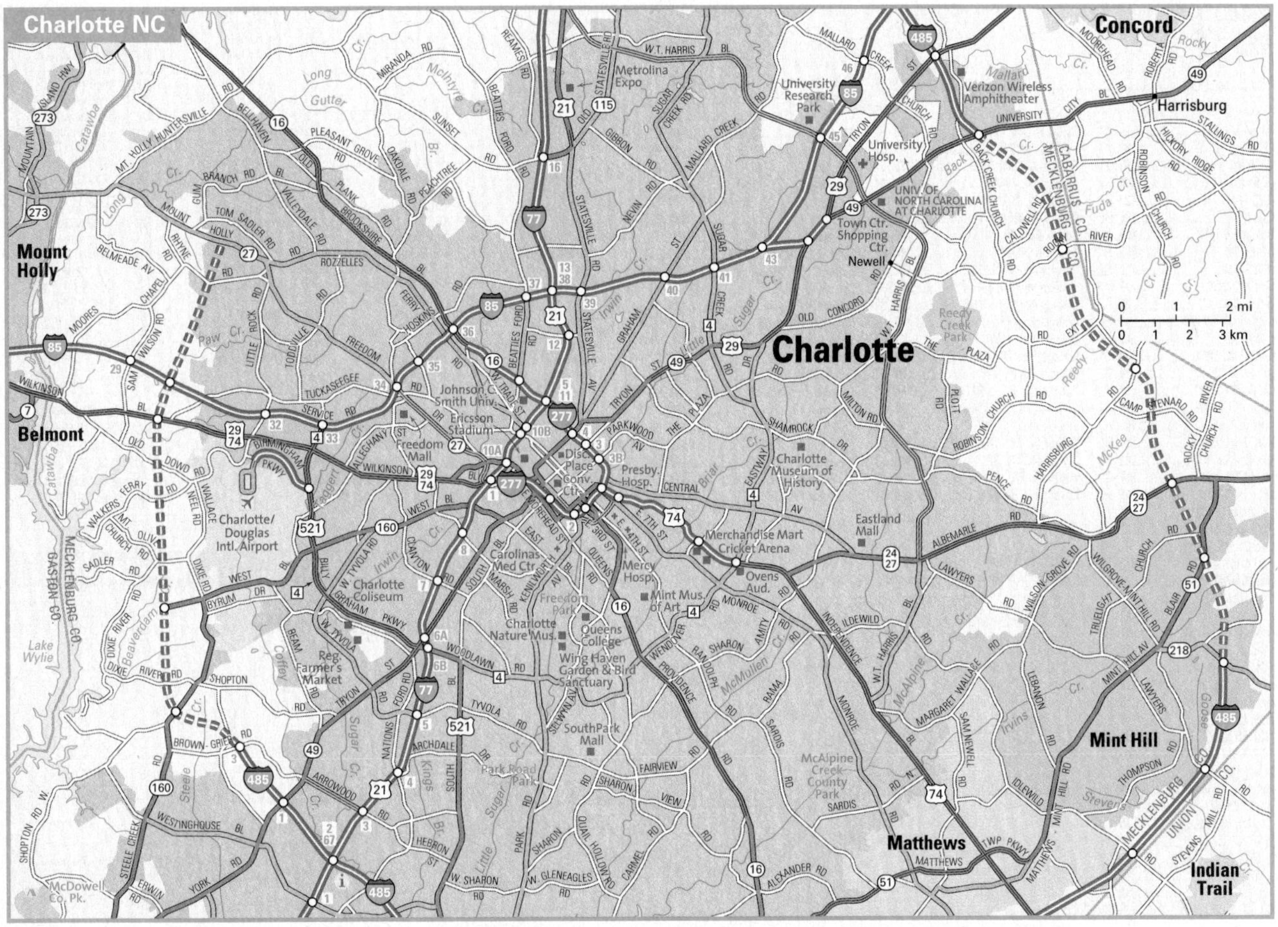

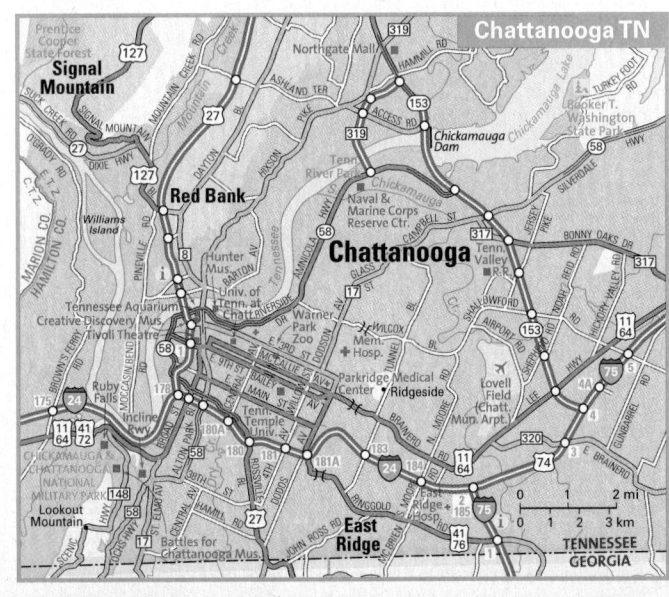

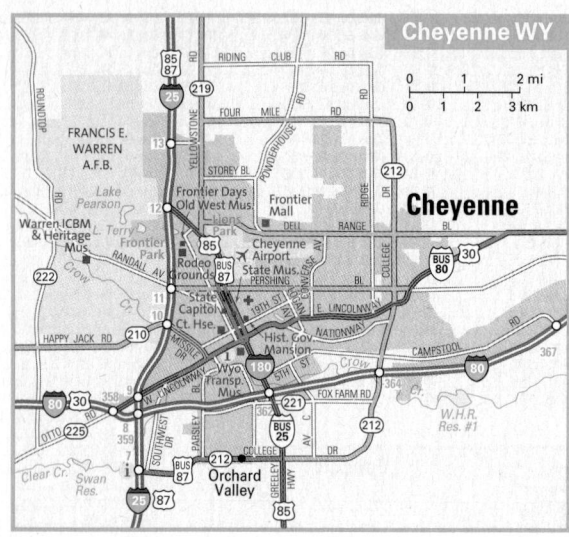

Cheyenne WY

Cheyenne

Orchard Valley

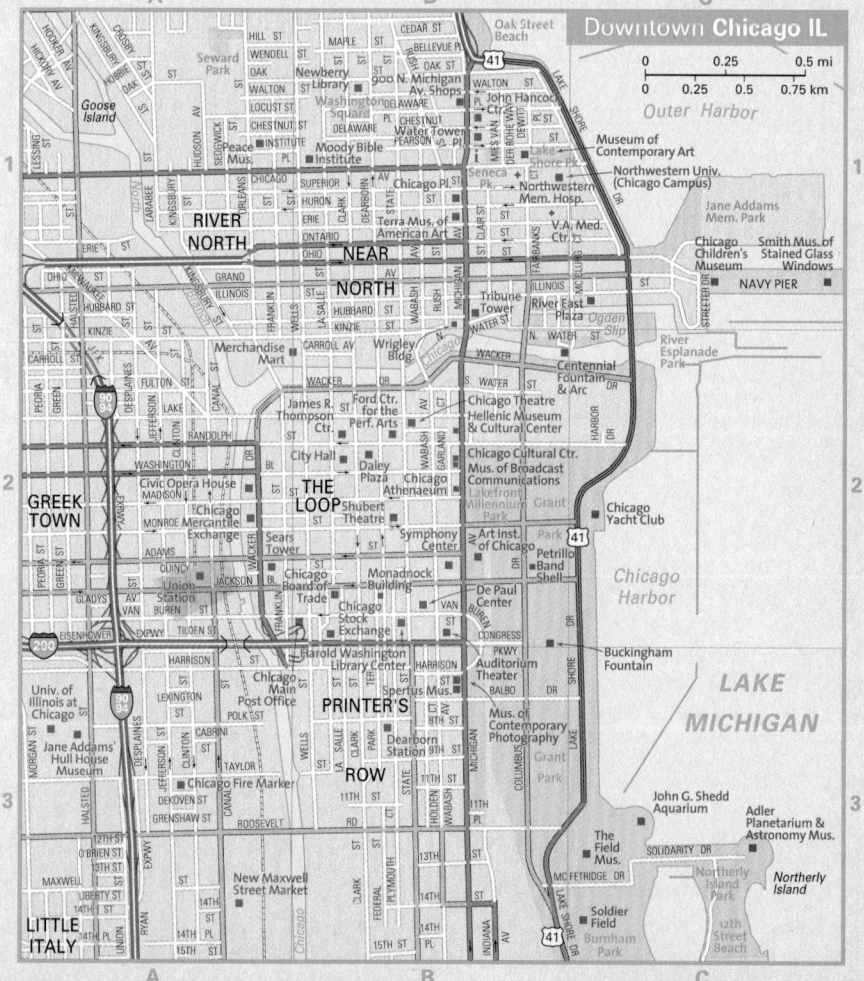

Downtown **Chicago** IL

Entries in **bold** indicate counties or parishes. Entries in color indicate cities with detailed inset maps.

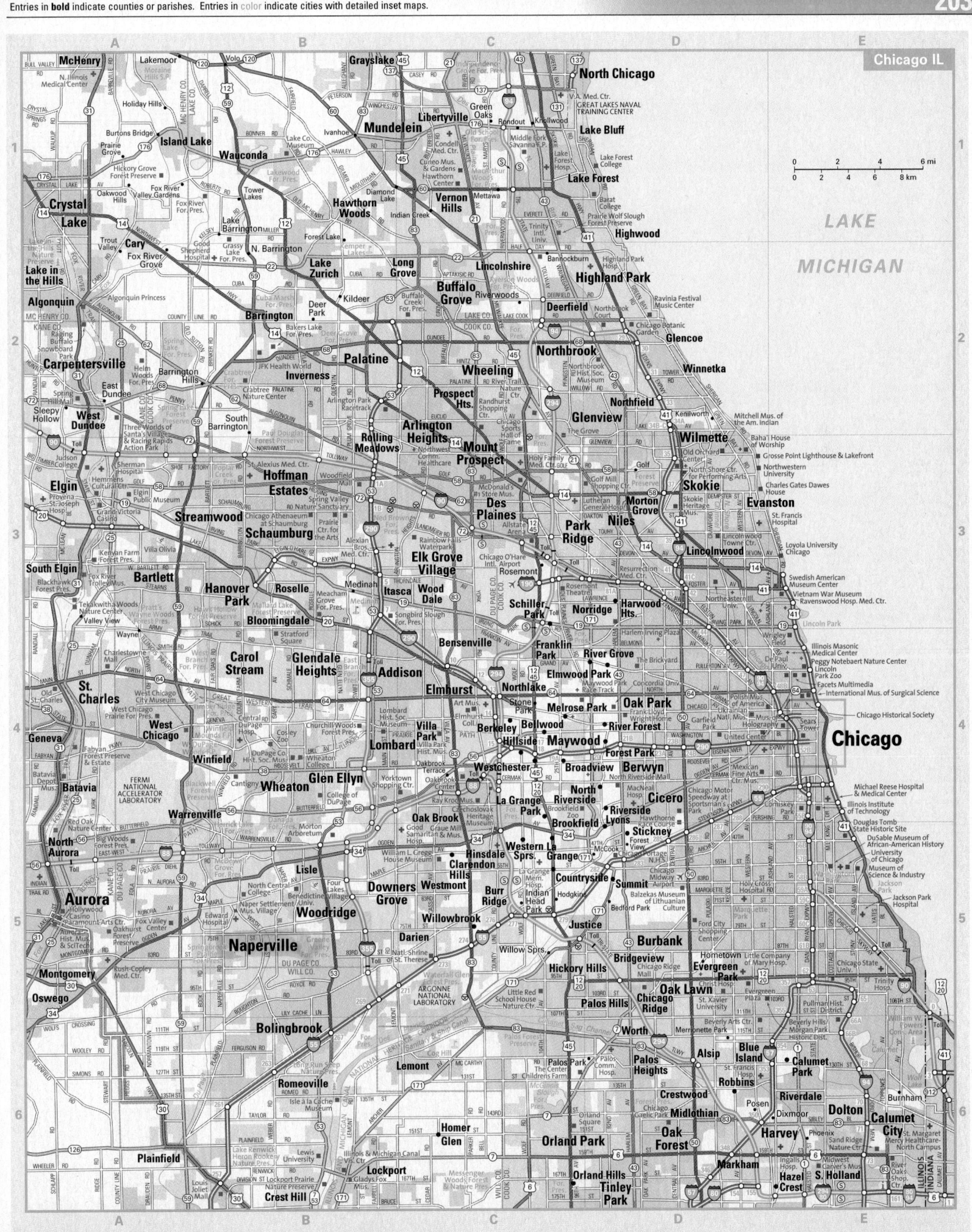

Chicago IL

Figures after entries indicate population, page number, and grid reference.

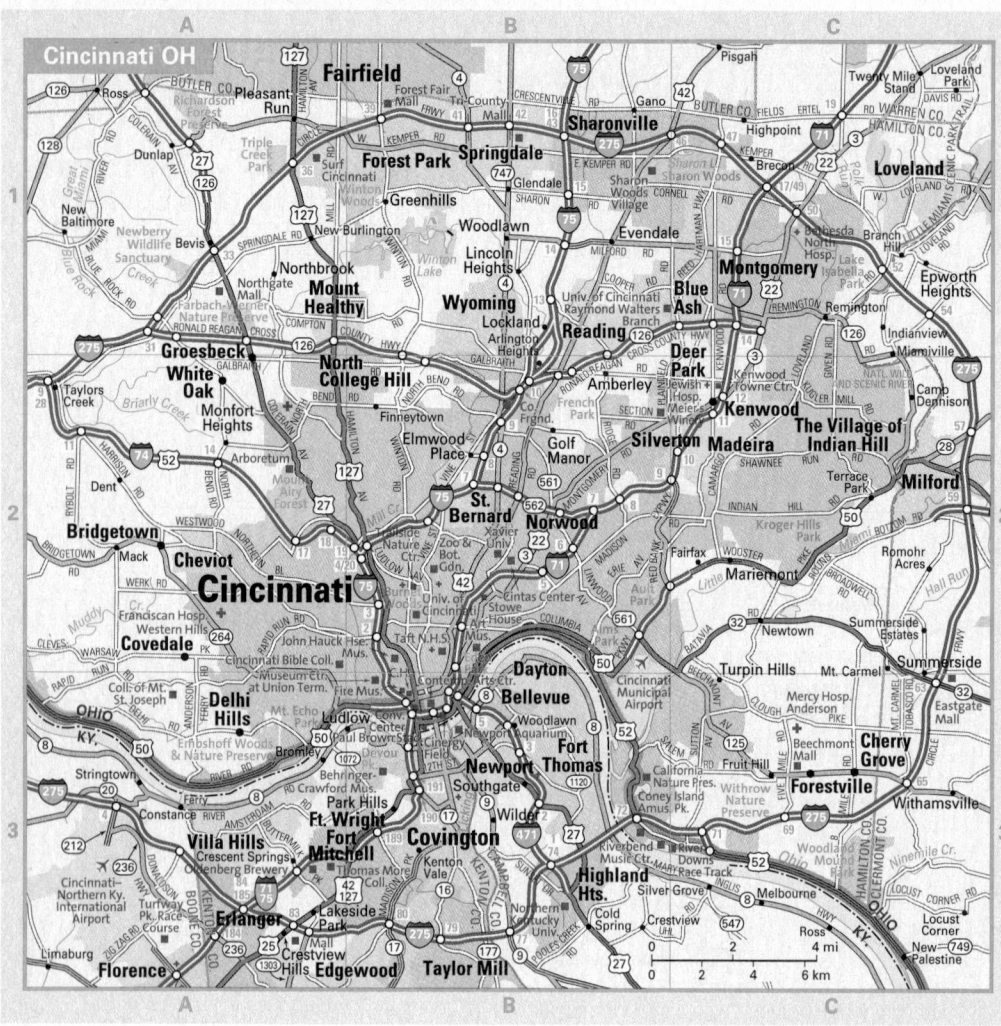

Cincinnati OH

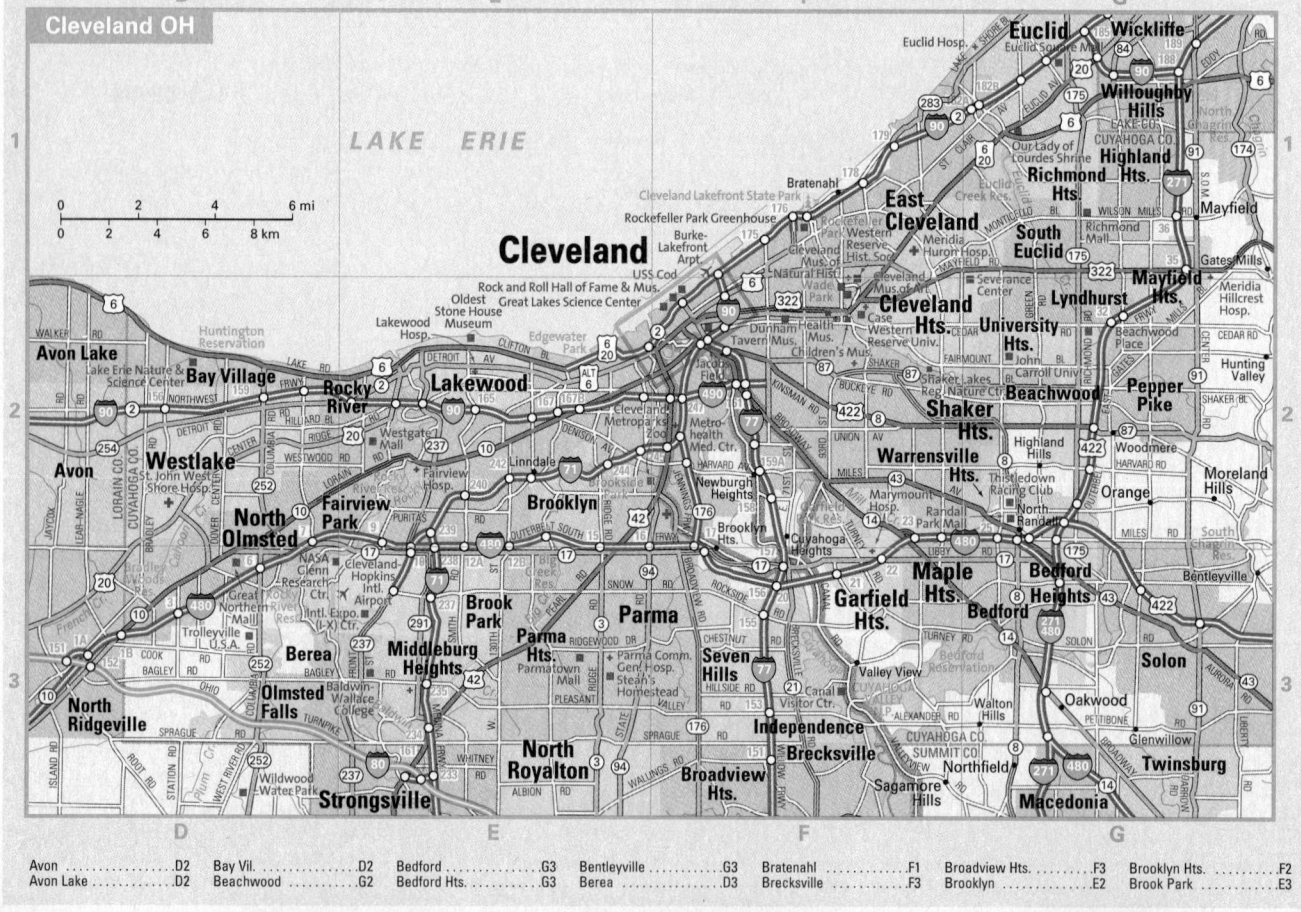

Cleveland OH

Entries in **bold** indicate counties or parishes. Entries in color indicate cities with detailed inset maps.

Comstock Park—Crescent **205**

Colorado Springs CO

Black Forest ...D1
Cascade ...C1
Chipita Park ...C1
Colorado Sprs. ...D1
Crystola ...C1
Fountain ...D2
Green Mtn. Falls ...C1
Manitou Sprs. ...C2
Security ...D2
Stratmoor Hills ...D2
Widefield ...D2

Columbia SC

Arcadia Lakes ...F1
Arthurtown ...F2
Cayce ...E2
Columbia ...F2
Denny Terrace ...E1
Dentsville ...F1
Dixiana ...E2
Forest Acres ...F1
Olympia ...E2
Pineridge ...E2
St. Andrews ...E1
Springdale ...E2
W. Columbia ...E2

Downtown Cleveland OH

Amtrak Station ...A1
Burke-Lakefront Arpt. ...A1
City Hall ...A1
Cleveland Arcade ...A1
Cleveland Browns Stadium ...A1
Cleveland Police Mus. ...A1
Cleveland State Univ. ...B2
Convention Center ...A1
Court House ...A1
Federal Court House ...A2
Galleria at Erieview ...B1
Great Lakes Science Center ...A1
Gund Arena ...A2
Jacobs Field ...A2
Playhouse Square ...B2
Rock and Roll Hall of Fame & Mus. ...A1
Terminal Tower/Tower City ...A2
U.S.S. Cod ...B1
West Side Market ...A1
William G. Mather Mus. ...B1

Columbus GA

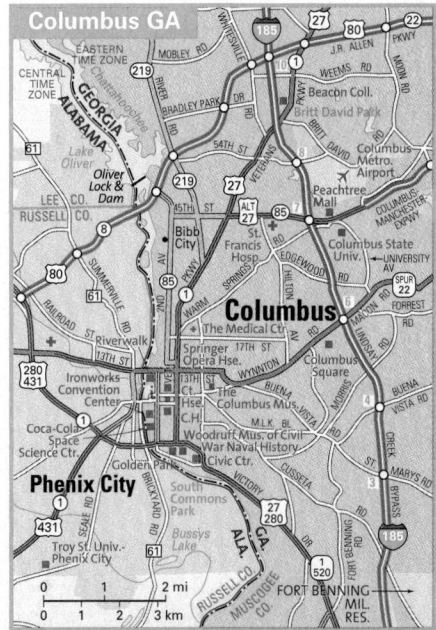

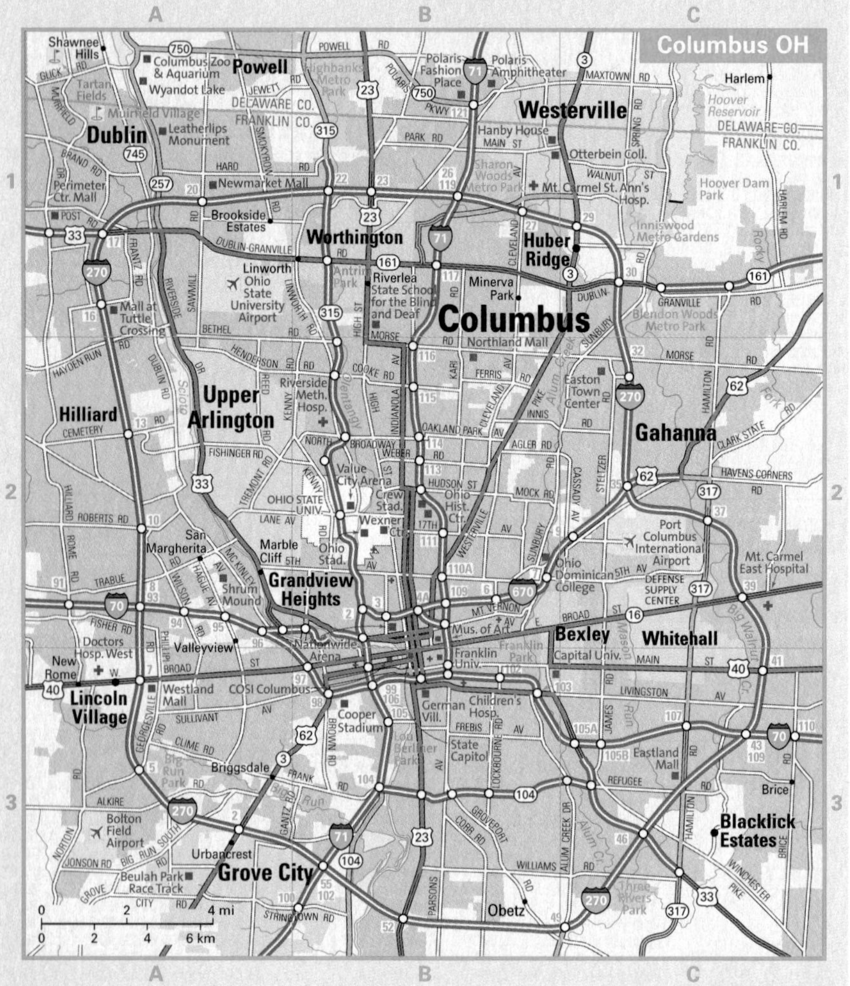
Columbus OH
Powell
Dublin
Westerville
Worthington
Huber Ridge
Columbus
Upper Arlington
Hilliard
Gahanna
Grandview Heights
Bexley
Whitehall
Lincoln Village
Grove City
Blacklick Estates
Obetz

Bexley C2
Blacklick Estates C3
Brice C3
Briggsdale A3
Brookside Estates A1
Columbus B1
Dublin A1
Gahanna C2
Grandview Hts. B2
Grove City A3
Harlem C1
Hilliard A2
Huber Ridge C1
Lincoln Vil. A3
Linworth B1
Marble Cliff A2
Minerva Park B1
New Rome A3
Obetz B3
Powell A1
Riverlea B1
San Margherita A2
Shawnee Hills A1
Upper Arlington A2
Urbancrest A3
Valleyview A2
Westerville C1
Whitehall C2
Worthington B1

Crescent OK, *1281* **51** E2
Crescent Beach FL, *985* **139** E3
Crescent City CA, *4006* **28** A2
Crescent City FL, *1776* **139** D4
Crescent City IL, *631* **89** D3
Crescent Sprs. KY, *3931* **204** A3
Cresco IA, *3905* **73** E2
Cresson PA, *1631* **92** B4
Cressona PA, *1635* **146** A1
Crested Butte CO, *1529* **40** C2
Crest Hill IL, *13329* **89** D2
Crestline CA, *10218* **53** D2
Crestline OH, *5088* **91** D3
Creston IA, *7597* **86** B3
Creston OH, *2161* **91** E3
Crestview FL, *14766* **136** B1
Crestview KY, *471* **204** B3
Crestview Hills KY, *2889* **204** A3
Crestwood IL, *11251* **203** D6
Crestwood KY, *1999* **100** A4
Crestwood MO, *11863* **256** B3
Crestwood Vil. NJ, *8392* **147** E3

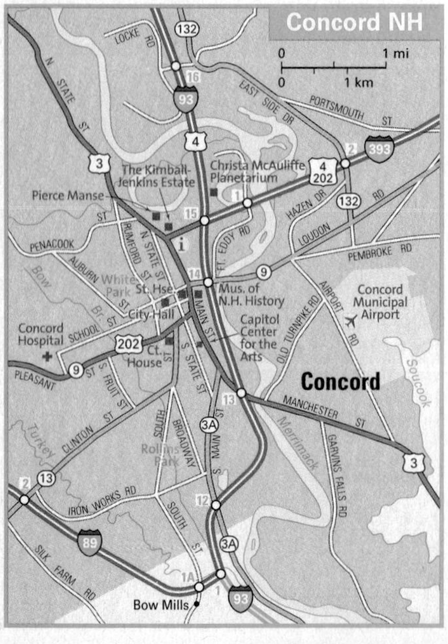
Concord NH
Concord

Creswell OR, *3579* **20** B4
Crete IL, *7346* **89** D2
Crete NE, *6028* **35** F4
Creve Coeur MO, *16500* **256** A2
Crewe VA, *2378* **113** D2
Cricket NC, *2053* **111** F4
Cridersville OH, *1817* **90** B3
Crimora VA, *1796* **102** C4
Cripple Creek CO, *1115* **41** E2
Crisfield MD, *2723* **103** F4
Crisp Co. GA, *21996* **129** D3
Crittenden KY, *2401* **100** B3
Crittenden Co. AR, *50866* **118** B1
Crittenden Co. KY, *9384* **109** D2
Crivitz WI, *998* **68** C3
Crocker MO, *1033* **97** E4
Crockett CA, *3194* **259** C1
Crockett TX, *7141* **124** A4
Crockett Co. TN, *14532* **108** C4
Crockett Co. TX, *4099* **60** A1
Crofton KY, *838* **109** E2
Crofton MD, *20091* **144** C3
Crofton NE, *754* **35** E1
Croghan NY, *665* **79** E2
Crompond NY, *2050* **148** B2
Cromwell CT, *750* **149** E1
Crook Co. OR, *19182* **21** D3
Crook Co. WY, *5887* **25** F3
Crooked Lake Park FL, *1682* **141** D3
Crooks SD, *859* **27** F4
Crookston MN, *8192* **19** F3
Crooksville OH, *2483* **101** E1
Crosby MN, *2299* **64** B4
Crosby ND, *1089* **18** A1
Crosby TX, *1714* **132** B3
Crosby Co. TX, *7072* **58** A1
Crosbyton TX, *1874* **58** B1
Cross City FL, *1775* **137** F3
Cross Co. AR, *19526* **118** A1
Crossett AR, *6097* **125** F1
Cross Hill SC, *601* **121** F3
Cross Keys NJ, *3600* **146** C4
Crosslake MN, *1893* **64** B4
Cross Plains TN, *1381* **109** F3
Cross Plains TX, *1068* **59** D3
Cross Plains WI, *3084* **74** B3
Cross Roads TX, *603* **59** F2
Crossville AL, *1431* **120** A3
Crossville IL, *782* **99** D4
Crossville TN, *8981* **110** B4
Crosswicks NJ, *900* **147** D2
Croswell MI, *2467* **76** C3
Crothersville IN, *1570* **99** F3
Croton Falls NY, *1200* **148** C2
Croton-on-Hudson NY, *7606* **148** B2
Crow Agency MT, *1552* **24** C1
Crowder MS, *766* **118** B3
Crowder OK, *436* **116** A1
Crowell TX, *1141* **58** C1
Crowley LA, *14225* **133** E2
Crowley TX, *7467* **59** E2
Crowley Co. CO, *5518* **41** F3
Crown Hts. NY, *2992* **148** B1
Crown Pt. IN, *19806* **89** D2
Crown Pt. LA, *650* **134** B3
Crownpoint NM, *2630* **48** B2
Crown Pt. NY, *650* **81** D3
Crownsville MD, *1670* **144** C3
Crow Wing Co. MN, *55099* **66** C1
Croydon PA, *9993* **248** E2
Crozet VA, *2820* **102** C4
Cruger MS, *449* **126** B1
Crump TN, *1521* **119** D1
Crystal MN, *22698* **235** B2
Crystal NM, *347* **48** A2
Crystal Beach FL, *4000* **266** A1
Crystal City MO, *4247* **98** A4
Crystal City TX, *7190* **60** C4
Crystal Falls MI, *1791* **68** C2
Crystal Lake CT, *1459* **150** A3
Crystal Lake IL, *38000* **88** C1
Crystal Lakes OH, *1411* **100** C1
Crystal River FL, *3485* **140** B1
Crystal Sprs. FL, *1175* **140** C2
Crystal Sprs. MS, *5873* **126** B3
Cuba IL, *1418* **88** A4
Cuba MO, *3230* **97** F4
Cuba NM, *590* **48** C2
Cuba NY, *1633* **92** C1
Cuba City WI, *2156* **74** A4
Cudahy CA, *24208* **228** D3
Cudahy WI, *18429* **75** D3
Cuddebackville NY, *750* **148** A1
Cudjoe FL, *1695* **143** D4
Cuero TX, *6571* **61** E3
Culberson Co. TX, *2975* **57** E4
Culbertson MT, *716* **17** F2
Culbertson NE, *594* **34** C4
Culdesac ID, *378* **14** B4
Cullen LA, *1296* **125** D1
Cullman AL, *13995* **119** F3
Cullman Co. AL, *77483* **119** F3
Culloden WV, *2940* **101** E3
Cullowhee NC, *3579* **121** D1
Culpeper VA, *9664* **103** D3
Culpeper Co. VA, *34262* **103** D3
Culver IN, *1539* **89** E2
Culver OR, *802* **21** D3
Culver City CA, *38816* **228** C3
Cumberland IN, *5500* **99** F1
Cumberland KY, *2611* **111** D2
Cumberland MD, *21518* **102** C1
Cumberland NC, *4400* **123** D2
Cumberland VA, *125* **113** D1
Cumberland WI, *2280* **67** E3
Cumberland Ctr. ME, *2596* **82** B3
Cumberland Co. IL, *11253* **99** D2
Cumberland Co. KY, *7147* **110** A2
Cumberland Co. ME, *265612* **82** B3
Cumberland Co. NJ, *146438* **145** F2
Cumberland Co. NC, *302963* **123** D2
Cumberland Co. PA, *213674* **103** D1
Cumberland Co. TN, *46802* **110** B4
Cumberland Co. VA, *9017* **113** D1
Cumberland Foreside ME, *500* **82** B3
Cumberland Hill RI, *7738* **150** C2
Cumby TX, *616* **124** A1
Cuming Co. NE, *10203* **35** F2
Cumming GA, *4220* **120** C3
Cunningham KS, *514* **43** D4
Cupertino CA, *50546* **36** B4
Curlew FL, *5900* **266** A1
Currituck NC, *125* **115** E1
Currituck Co. NC, *18190* **115** E1
Curry Co. NM, *45044* **49** F4
Curry Co. OR, *21137* **28** A2
Curtis NE, *832* **34** C4
Curwensville PA, *2650* **92** B3
Cushing OK, *8371* **51** F2
Cushing TX, *637* **124** B3
Cushman AR, *461* **107** F4
Cusseta GA, *1196* **128** C3
Custer SD, *1860* **25** F4
Custer Co. CO, *3503* **41** E3
Custer Co. ID, *4342* **23** D3
Custer Co. MT, *11696* **25** E1
Custer Co. NE, *11793* **34** C3
Custer Co. OK, *26142* **51** D2
Custer Co. SD, *7275* **25** F4
Cut and Shoot TX, *1158* **132** A2
Cut Bank MT, *3105* **15** E1
Cutchogue NY, *2849* **149** E3
Cuthbert GA, *3731* **128** C3
Cutler CA, *4491* **45** D3
Cutler Ridge FL, *24781* **143** E3
Cutlerville MI, *15114* **75** F3
Cut Off LA, *5635* **134** B3
Cutten CA, *2933* **28** A4
Cuyahoga Co. OH, *1393978* **91** E2
Cuyahoga Falls OH, *49374* **91** E3
Cuyahoga Hts. OH, *599* **204** F2
Cygnet OH, *564* **90** C2
Cynthiana IN, *693* **99** D4
Cynthiana KY, *6258* **100** B4
Cypress CA, *46229* **228** E4
Cypress Quarters FL, *1150* **141** E4
Cyril OK, *1168* **51** E3

D

Dacono CO, *3015* **41** E1
Dacula GA, *3848* **121** D3
Dade City FL, *6188* **140** C2
Dade Co. GA, *15154* **120** B2
Dade Co. MO, *7923* **106** C1
Dadeville AL, *3212* **128** B2
Daggett CA, *600* **53** D1
Daggett Co. UT, *921* **32** A4
Dagsboro DE, *519* **145** F4
Dahlgren VA, *997* **103** E4
Dahlonega GA, *3638* **120** C3
Daingerfield TX, *2517* **124** B1
Daisetta TX, *1034* **132** B2
Dakota City IA, *911* **72** C4
Dakota City NE, *1821* **35** F2
Dakota Co. MN, *355904* **67** D4
Dakota Co. NE, *20253* **35** F2
Dale IN, *1568* **99** E4
Dale City VA, *55971* **144** A4
Dale Co. AL, *49129* **128** B4
Daleville AL, *4653* **128** B4
Daleville IN, *1658* **89** F4
Daleville VA, *1454* **112** B1
Dalhart TX, *7237* **50** A2
Dallam Co. TX, *6222* **50** A2
Dallas GA, *5056* **120** B4
Dallas NC, *3402* **122** A1
Dallas OR, *12459* **20** B2
Dallas PA, *2557* **93** E2
Dallas TX, *1188580* **59** F2
Dallas Ctr. IA, *1595* **86** C2
Dallas City IL, *1055* **87** F3
Dallas Co. AL, *46365* **127** F3
Dallas Co. AR, *9210* **117** E4
Dallas Co. IA, *40750* **86** C2
Dallas Co. MO, *15661* **107** D1
Dallas Co. TX, *2218899* **59** F2
Dallastown PA, *4087* **103** E1
Dalton GA, *27912* **120** B2
Dalton MA, *4100* **94** C1
Dalton OH, *1605* **91** E3
Dalton PA, *1294* **93** F2
Dalton City IL, *581* **98** C1
Dalton Gardens ID, *2278* **14** B3
Dalworthington Gardens TX, *2186* **207** B3
Daly City CA, *103621* **36** B4
Dalzell SC, *2260* **122** B3
Damariscotta ME, *1751* **82** C3
Damascus MD, *11430* **144** B2
Damascus VA, *981* **111** F3
Damon TX, *535* **132** A4
Dana IN, *662* **99** E1
Dana Pt. CA, *35110* **52** C3
Danboro PA, *1500* **146** C2
Danbury CT, *74848* **148** C2
Danbury NC, *108* **112** B3
Danbury TX, *1611* **132** A4
Dandridge TN, *2078* **111** D4
Dane WI, *799* **74** B3
Dane Co. WI, *426526* **74** B3
Danforth IL, *587* **89** D3
Dania Beach FL, *20061* **143** F2
Daniel MD, *650* **144** B1
Daniels Co. MT, *2017* **17** E1
Danielson CT, *4265* **150** B3
Danielsville GA, *457* **121** D3
Dannemora NY, *4129* **80** C1
Dansville NY, *4832* **78** C4
Dante VA, *650* **111** E2
Danube MN, *529* **66** B4
Danvers IL, *1183* **88** B4
Danvers MA, *25212* **151** F1
Danville AR, *2392* **117** D2
Danville CA, *41715* **36** B4
Danville IL, *33904* **89** D4
Danville IN, *6418* **99** F1
Danville IA, *914* **87** F3
Danville KY, *15477* **110** B1
Danville NH, *1300* **95** E1
Danville OH, *1104* **91** D4
Danville PA, *4897* **93** E3
Danville VT, *475* **81** E2
Danville VA, *48411* **112** C3
Danville WV, *550* **101** E4
Daphne AL, *16581* **135** E2
Darby MT, *710* **23** D1
Darby PA, *10299* **146** C3
Dardanelle AR, *4228* **117** D1
Dardenne Prairie MO, *4384* **98** A3
Dare Co. NC, *29967* **115** F2
Dares Beach MD, *1400* **144** C4
Darien CT, *19607* **148** C3
Darien GA, *1719* **130** B4
Darien IL, *22860* **203** C5
Darien WI, *1572* **74** C4
Darke Co. OH, *53309* **100** B1
Darlington IN, *854* **89** E4
Darlington SC, *6720* **122** C3
Darlington WI, *2418* **74** A4
Darlington Co. SC, *67394* **122** B3
Darmstadt IN, *1313* **99** D4
Darnestown MD, *6378* **144** B2
Darrington WA, *1136* **12** C2
Dasher GA, *834* **137** F1
Dassel MN, *1233* **66** C3
Dauphin PA, *773* **93** D4
Dauphin Co. PA, *251798* **93** D4
Dauphin Island AL, *1371* **135** E2
Davenport FL, *1924* **141** D2
Davenport IA, *98359* **88** A2
Davenport ND, *261* **19** E4
Davenport OK, *881* **51** F2
Davenport WA, *1730* **13** F3
David City NE, *2597* **35** F3
Davidson NC, *7139* **122** A1
Davidson Co. NC, *147246* **112** B4
Davidson Co. TN, *569891* **109** F4
Davidsville PA, *1119* **92** B4
Davie FL, *75720* **143** E2
Davie Co. NC, *34835* **112** A4
Daviess Co. IN, *29820* **99** E3
Daviess Co. KY, *91545* **109** E1
Daviess Co. MO, *8016* **96** C1
Davis CA, *60308* **36** B3
Davis IL, *662* **74** B4
Davis OK, *2610* **51** F4
Davis WV, *624* **102** B2
Davisboro GA, *1544* **129** F1
Davis Co. IA, *8541* **87** E3
Davis Co. UT, *238994* **31** E3
Davison MI, *5536* **76** B3
Davison Co. SD, *18741* **27** E4
Davy WV, *373* **111** F1
Dawes Co. NE, *9060* **34** A1
Dawson GA, *5058* **128** C3
Dawson MN, *1539* **27** F2
Dawson TX, *852* **59** F3
Dawson Co. GA, *15999* **120** C3
Dawson Co. MT, *9059* **17** F3
Dawson Co. NE, *24365* **35** D4
Dawson Co. TX, *14985* **58** A2
Dawson Sprs. KY, *2980* **109** E2
Dawsonville GA, *619* **120** C3
Day Co. SD, *6267* **27** E2
Dayton ID, *444* **31** E2
Dayton IN, *1120* **89** E4
Dayton IA, *884* **72** C4
Dayton KY, *5966* **204** B2
Dayton MN, *4699* **66** C3
Dayton NV, *5907* **37** D2
Dayton NJ, *6235* **147** D1
Dayton OH, *166179* **100** B1
Dayton OR, *2119* **20** B2
Dayton TN, *6180* **120** B1
Dayton TX, *5709* **132** B3
Dayton VA, *1344* **102** C3
Dayton WA, *2655* **13** F4
Dayton WY, *678* **24** C2
Daytona Beach FL, *64112* **139** E4
Daytona Beach Shores FL, *4299* **139** E4
Dayville CT, *1600* **150** B3
Deadwood SD, *1380* **25** F3
Deaf Smith Co. TX, *18561* **49** F3
Deal NJ, *1070* **147** F2
Deale MD, *4796* **144** C3
Deal Island MD, *578* **103** F4
Dearborn MI, *97775* **76** C4
Dearborn MO, *529* **96** B1
Dearborn Co. IN, *46109* **100** B2
Dearborn Hts. MI, *58264* **210** B3
Dearing KS, *415* **106** A2
DeArmanville AL, *700* **120** A4
Deary ID, *552* **14** B4
Deaver WY, *177* **24** B2
De Baca Co. NM, *2240* **49** E4
De Bary FL, *15559* **141** D1
De Beque CO, *451* **40** B2
Decatur AL, *53929* **119** F2
Decatur AR, *1314* **106** B3
Decatur GA, *18147* **120** C4

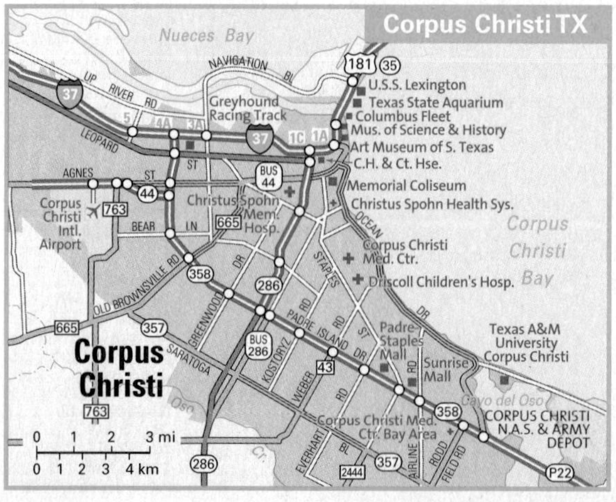
Corpus Christi TX
Nueces Bay
Corpus Christi Bay
Corpus Christi

Entries in **bold** indicate counties or parishes. Entries in color indicate cities with detailed inset maps.

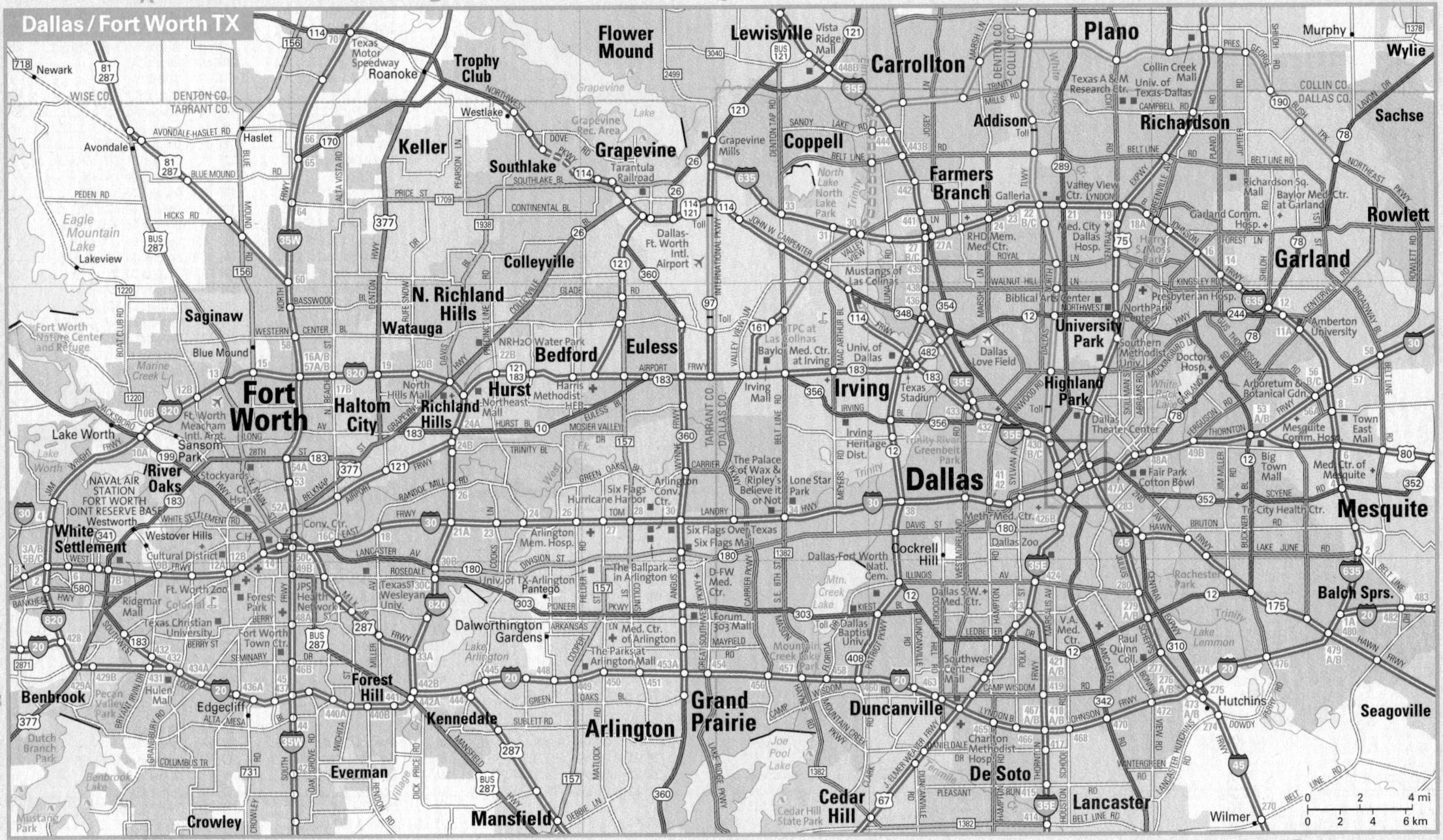

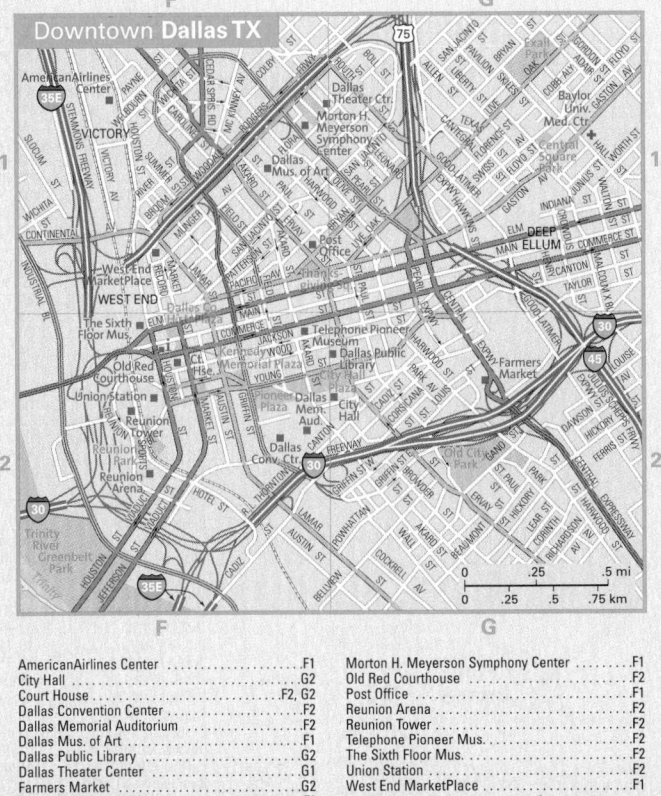

Dallas / Fort Worth TX

Downtown Dallas TX

208 Des Plaines—Duck Hill

Figures after entries indicate population, page number, and grid reference.

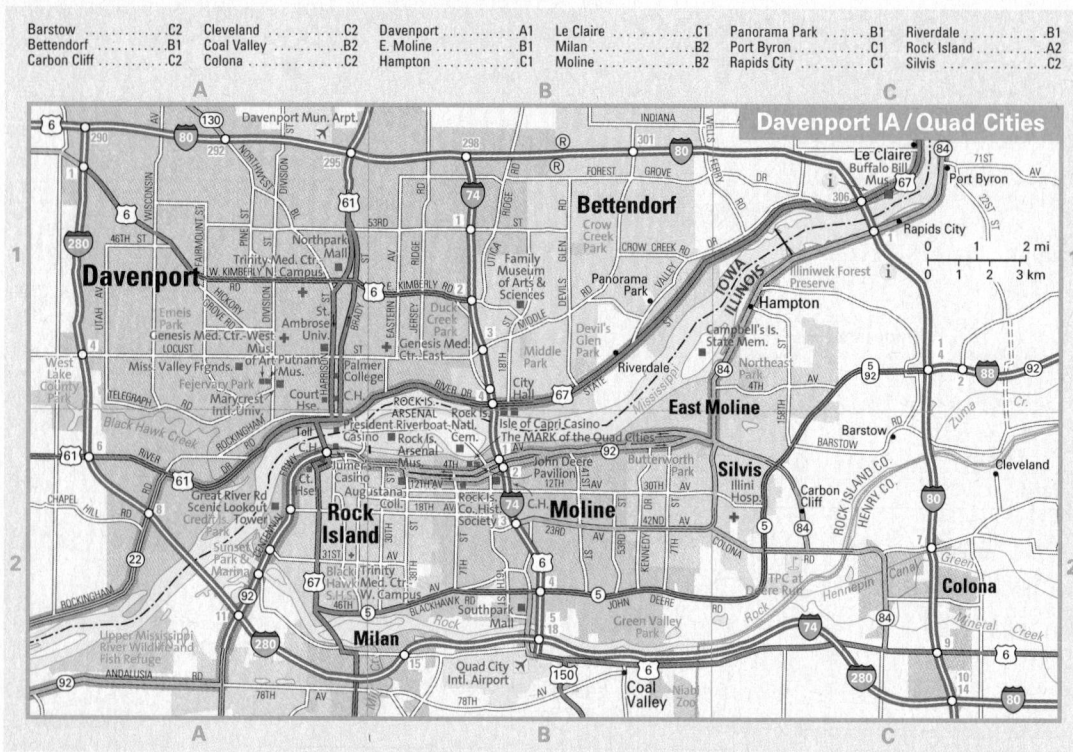

Davenport IA / Quad Cities

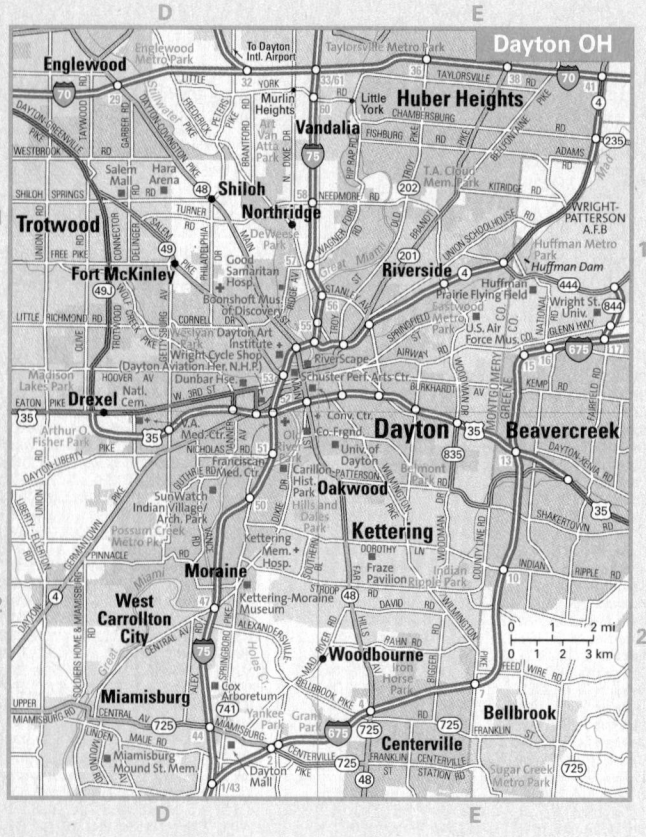

Dayton OH

Daytona Beach FL

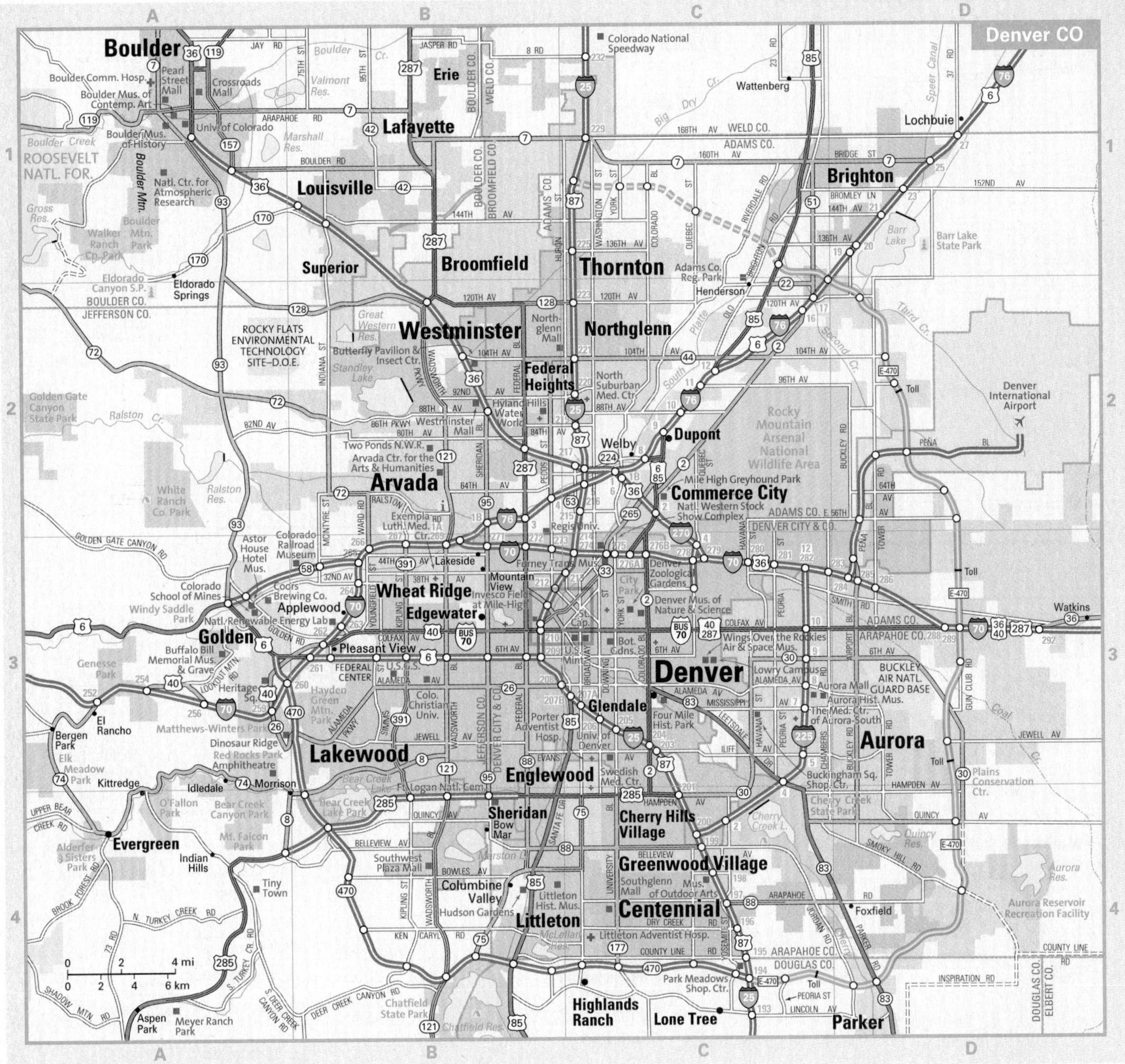

Entries in **bold** indicate counties or parishes. Entries in color indicate cities with detailed inset maps.

Ducktown—Durand **209**

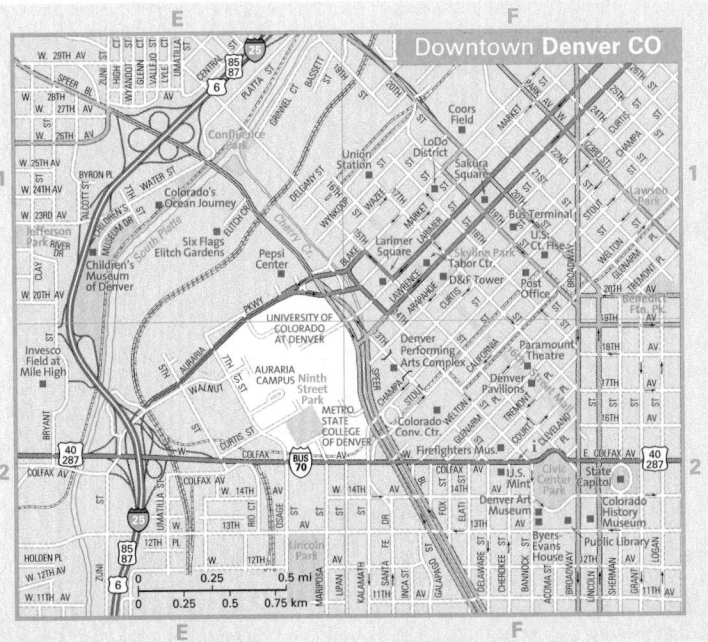

Denver CO

Downtown Denver CO

Auraria Campus	E2
Bus Terminal	F1
Byers-Evans House	F2
Children's Mus. of Denver	E1
Colorado Convention Center	F2
Colorado History Mus.	F2
Colorado's Ocean Journey	E1
Coors Field	F1
Currigan Hall	F2
D&F Tower	F1
Denver Art Mus.	F2
Denver Pavilions	F2
Denver Performing Arts Complex	F2
Firefighters Mus.	F2
Invesco Field at Mile High	E2
Larimer Square	F1
LoDo District	F1
Metropolitan State Coll. of Denver	E2
Pepsi Center	E1
Post Office	F1
Public Library	F2
Sakura Square	F1
Six Flags Elitch Gardens	E1
State Capitol	F2
Tabor Center	F1
Union Station	F1
U.S. Court House	F2
U.S. Mint	F2
Univ. of Colorado at Denver	E2

Figures after entries indicate population, page number, and grid reference.

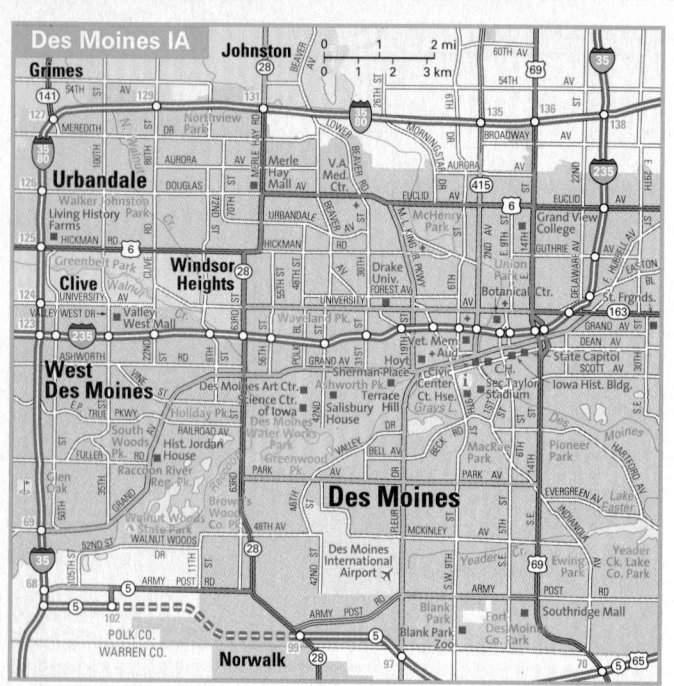

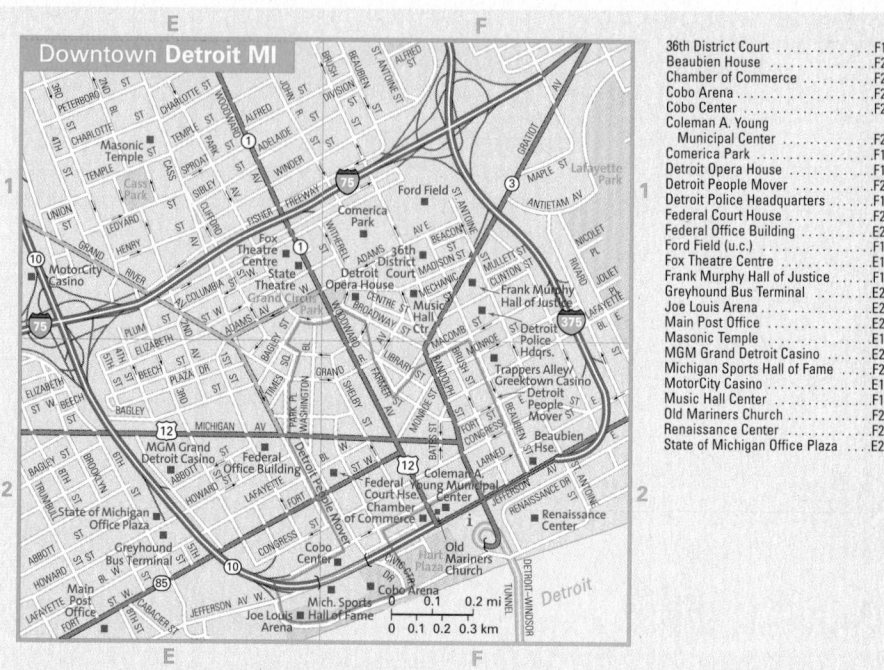

Des Moines IA

Downtown Detroit MI

Detroit MI

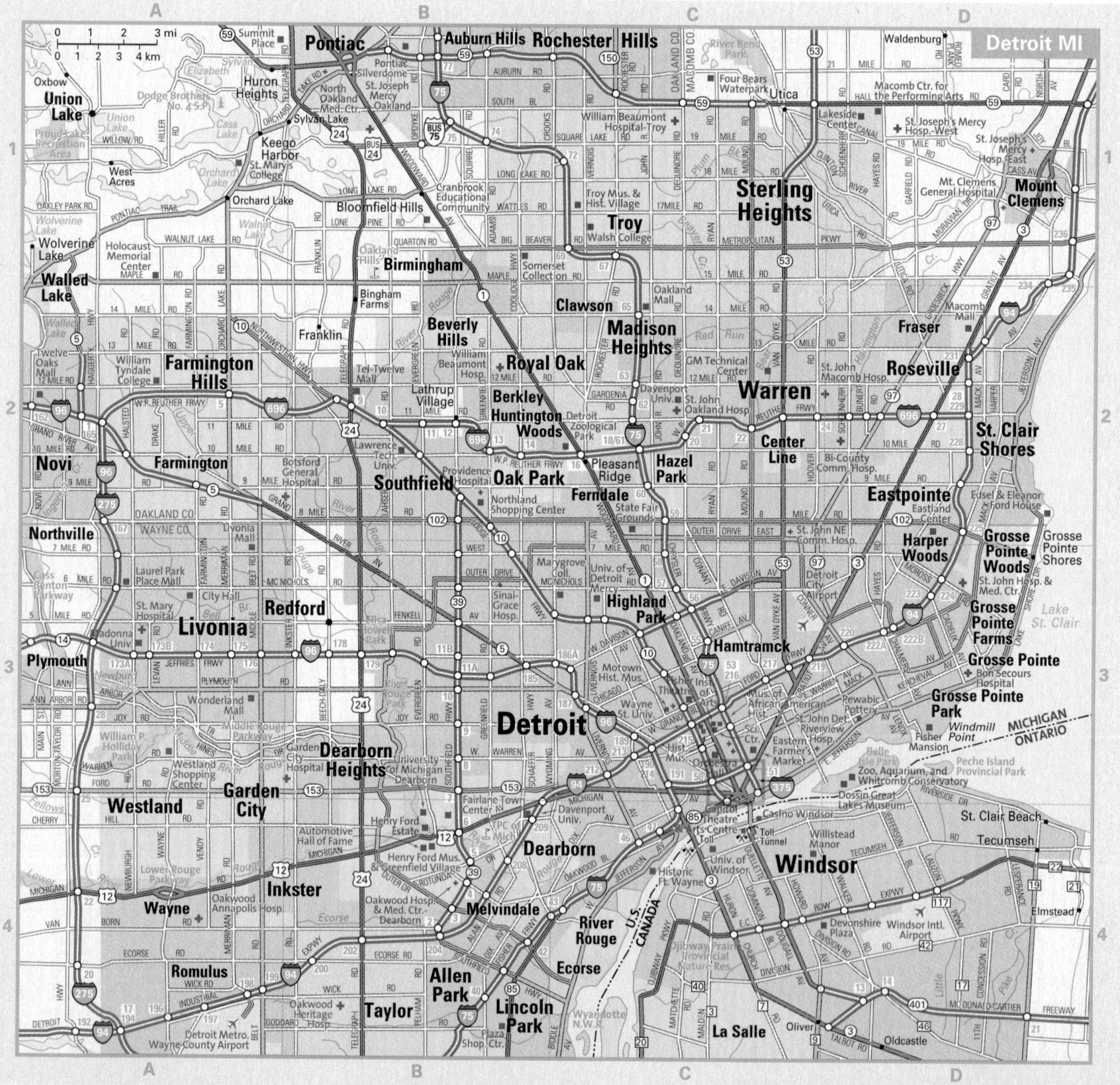

Entries in **bold** indicate counties or parishes. Entries in color indicate cities with detailed inset maps.

Durand—Elizabeth Lake **211**

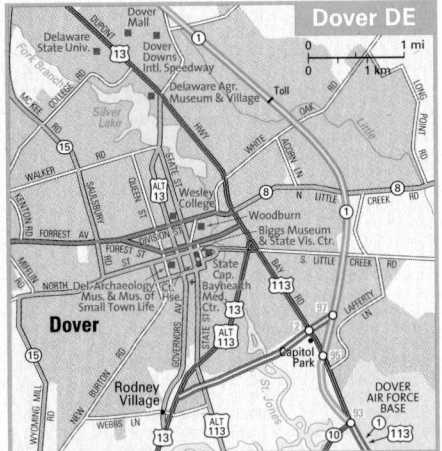

Dover DE

Dover

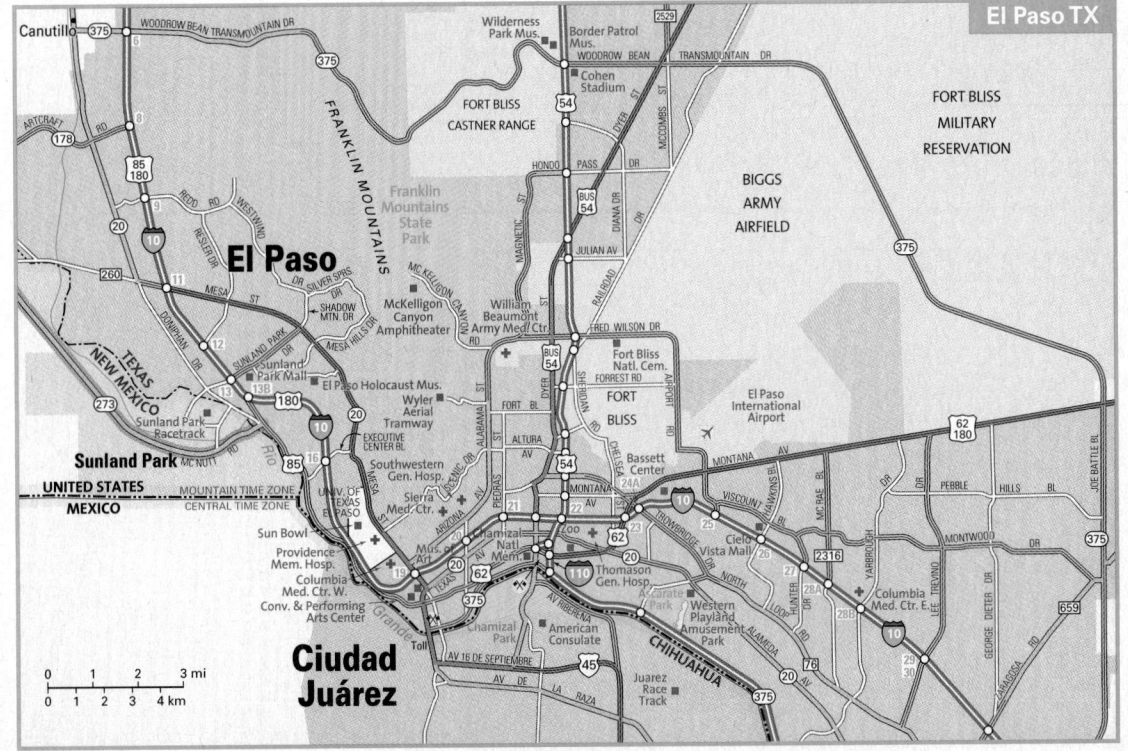

Duluth MN

Hermantown

Duluth

Superior

Proctor

LAKE SUPERIOR

El Paso TX

Canutillo

El Paso

Sunland Park

UNITED STATES
MEXICO

FRANKLIN MOUNTAINS

FORT BLISS
CASTNER RANGE

FORT BLISS
MILITARY
RESERVATION

BIGGS ARMY AIRFIELD

Ciudad Juárez

Elizabethton TN, 13372 ......111 E3
Elizabethtown IL, 348 ......109 D1
Elizabethtown KY, 22542 ......110 A1
Elizabethtown NY, 750 ......81 D2
Elizabethtown NC, 3698 ......123 D2
Elizabethtown PA, 11887 ......93 E4
Elizabethville PA, 1344 ......93 D4
El Jebel CO, 4488 ......40 C2
Elkader IA, 1465 ......73 F3
Elk City OK, 10510 ......50 C3
Elk Co. KS, 3261 ......43 F4
Elk Co. PA, 35112 ......92 B2
Elk Grove CA, 59984 ......36 C3
Elk Grove Vil. IL, 34727 ......203 C3
Elkhart IN, 51874 ......89 F2
Elkhart KS, 2233 ......50 A1
Elkhart TX, 1215 ......124 C4
Elkhart Co. IN, 182791 ......89 F2
Elkhart Lake WI, 1021 ......74 C2
Elkhorn CA, 1591 ......236 C3
Elk Horn IA, 649 ......86 B2
Elkhorn NE, 6062 ......35 F3
Elkhorn WI, 7305 ......74 C4
Elkhorn City KY, 1060 ......111 E1

Elkin NC, 4109 ......112 A3
Elkins AR, 1251 ......106 C4
Elkins WV, 7032 ......102 A3
Elkland PA, 1786 ......93 D1
Elkmont AL, 470 ......119 F2
Elk Pt. SD, 1714 ......35 F1
Elk Rapids MI, 1700 ......69 F4
Elk Ridge UT, 1838 ......39 E1
Elk River MN, 16447 ......66 C3
Elk Run Hts. IA, 1052 ......73 E4
Elkton KY, 1984 ......109 E2
Elkton MD, 11893 ......145 E1
Elkton MI, 863 ......76 C2
Elkton SD, 677 ......27 F3
Elkton TN, 510 ......119 F2
Elkton VA, 2042 ......102 C3
Elkview WV, 1182 ......101 F3
Elkville IL, 1001 ......98 B4
El Lago TX, 3075 ......132 B3
Ellaville GA, 1609 ......129 D3

Ellenboro NC, 479 ......121 F1
Ellenboro WV, 373 ......101 F2
Ellendale DE, 327 ......145 F3
Ellendale MN, 590 ......72 C2
Ellendale ND, 1559 ......27 D1
Ellensburg WA, 15414 ......13 D4
Ellenton FL, 3142 ......266 B4
Ellenville NY, 4130 ......94 A3
Ellerbe NC, 1021 ......122 C2
Ellerslie MD, 600 ......102 C1
Ellettsville IN, 5078 ......99 F2
Ellicott NY, 2200 ......78 B4
Ellicott City MD, 56397 ......144 C2
Ellijay GA, 1584 ......120 C2
Elliston MT, 225 ......15 E4
Elliston VA, 1241 ......112 B2
Ellisville MS, 3465 ......126 C4
Ellisville MO, 9104 ......256 A2
Elloree SC, 742 ......122 B4
Ellsworth IA, 531 ......72 C4
Ellsworth KS, 2965 ......43 E2
Ellsworth ME, 6456 ......83 D2
Ellsworth MI, 483 ......69 F3
Ellsworth MN, 540 ......27 F4
Ellsworth PA, 1083 ......92 A4
Ellsworth WI, 2909 ......67 E4
Ellsworth Co. KS, 6525 ......43 E3
Ellwood City PA, 8688 ......91 F3
Elma IA, 598 ......73 D3
Elma NY, 2491 ......78 B3
Elma WA, 3049 ......12 B4
Elm City NC, 1165 ......113 D4
Elm Creek NE, 894 ......35 D4
Elmendorf TX, 664 ......61 D3
Elmer NJ, 1384 ......145 F1
Elm Grove WI, 6249 ......234 B2
Elmhurst IL, 42762 ......89 D1
Elmira NY, 30940 ......93 D1
El Mirage AZ, 7609 ......249 A1
Elmira Hts. NY, 4170 ......93 D1
Elm Mott TX, 1200 ......59 E4
Elmo UT, 368 ......39 F2
Elmont NY, 32657 ......148 C4
Elmont VA, 500 ......113 E1
El Monte CA, 115965 ......228 C4
Elmore MN, 735 ......72 C2
Elmore OH, 1426 ......90 C2

Elmore City OK, 756 ......51 E4
Elmore Co. AL, 65874 ......128 E4
Elmore Co. ID, 29130 ......22 B4
Elm Sprs. AR, 1044 ......106 C3
Elmsford NY, 1945 ......88 A3
Elmwood NE, 668 ......35 F4
Elmwood WI, 841 ......67 E4
Elmwood Park IL, 25405 ......203 B4
Elmwood Park NJ, 18925 ......240 C1
Elmwood Place OH, 2681 ......204 B2
Elnora IN, 721 ......99 E3
Elnora NY, 2700 ......94 B1
Elon NC, 6738 ......112 C4
Eloy AZ, 10375 ......54 C2
El Paso IL, 2695 ......88 B3
El Paso TX, 563662 ......56 C4
El Paso Co. CO, 516929 ......41 E2
El Paso Co. TX, 679622 ......56 C4
El Portal FL, 2505 ......233 B4
El Prado NM, 400 ......49 D1
El Reno OK, 16212 ......51 E3
El Rio CA, 6193 ......52 B2
El Rito NM, 425 ......48 C2
Elroy WI, 1578 ......74 A2
Elsa TX, 5549 ......63 E4
Elsah IL, 635 ......98 A2
Elsberry MO, 2047 ......98 A2
El Segundo CA, 16033 ......228 C3
Erda UT, 2473 ......31 E4
Elsie MI, 1055 ......76 A3
Elsinore UT, 733 ......39 E3
Elsmere DE, 5800 ......146 B4
Elsmere KY, 8139 ......100 B2
Elsmere NY, 3200 ......188 D3
El Sobrante CA, 12260 ......259 C1
Elton LA, 1261 ......133 E2
Elvaton MD, 3500 ......193 C5
Elverson PA, 959 ......146 B2
Elwood IL, 1620 ......89 D2
Elwood IN, 9737 ......89 F4
Elwood KS, 1145 ......96 B1
Elwood NE, 761 ......34 C4
Elwood NJ, 1392 ......147 D4
Elwood UT, 678 ......31 E3
Ely IA, 1149 ......87 E1
Ely MN, 3724 ......64 C2
Ely NV, 4041 ......38 B2
Elyria OH, 55953 ......91 D2
Elysburg PA, 2067 ......93 E3
Elysian MN, 486 ......72 C1
Emanuel Co. GA, 21837 ......129 F2
Emerado ND, 510 ......19 E2
Emerald Isle NC, 3488 ......115 D4
Emerson GA, 1092 ......120 C3
Emerson NE, 817 ......35 F2
Emerson NJ, 7197 ......148 B3
Emery SD, 439 ......27 E4
Emery UT, 308 ......39 E2
Emery Co. UT, 10860 ......39 F2
Emery Mills ME, 350 ......82 A4
Emigsville PA, 2467 ......103 E1
Emily MN, 847 ......64 B4
Eminence KY, 2231 ......100 A4
Eminence MO, 548 ......107 F2
Emlenton PA, 784 ......92 A2
Emmaus PA, 11313 ......146 B1
Emmet AR, 506 ......117 D4
Emmet Co. IA, 11027 ......72 B3
Emmet Co. MI, 31437 ......70 B3
Emmetsburg IA, 3958 ......72 B3
Emmett ID, 5490 ......22 B4
Emmitsburg MD, 2290 ......103 D1
Emmonak AK, 767 ......154 B2
Emmons Co. ND, 4331 ......18 C4
Emmorton MD, 4000 ......145 D1
Emory TX, 1021 ......124 A1
Emory VA, 2266 ......111 F2
Empire CO, 355 ......41 D1
Empire LA, 2211 ......134 C4
Empire NV, 499 ......29 E4
Empire City OK, 734 ......51 E4
Emporia KS, 26760 ......43 F3
Emporia VA, 5665 ......113 E3
Emporium PA, 2526 ......92 C2
Emsworth PA, 2598 ......250 A1
Encampment WY, 443 ......33 D3
Encinal TX, 629 ......60 C4
Encinitas CA, 58014 ......53 D4
Enderlin ND, 947 ......19 E4
Endicott NY, 13038 ......93 E1
Endicott WA, 621 ......13 F4
Endwell NY, 11706 ......93 E1
Energy IL, 1175 ......108 C1
Enfield CT, 8125 ......150 A2
Enfield IL, 625 ......99 D4
Enfield NH, 1698 ......81 E3
Enfield NC, 2347 ......113 E4
Enfield Ctr. NH, 600 ......81 E3
England AR, 2972 ......117 E2
Englewood CO, 31727 ......41 E1
Englewood FL, 16196 ......140 C4
Englewood NJ, 26203 ......148 B3
Englewood OH, 12235 ......100 B1
Englewood TN, 1590 ......120 C1
Englewood Beach FL, 1000 ......140 C4
Englewood Cliffs NJ, 5322 ......240 D1
English IN, 673 ......99 F4
Englishtown NJ, 1764 ......147 E2
Enhaut PA, 2809 ......218 C2
Enid OK, 47045 ......51 E1
Enigma GA, 869 ......129 E4
Enka NC, 1500 ......121 E1

Ennis MT, 840 ......23 E2
Ennis TX, 16045 ......59 F3
Enoch UT, 3467 ......39 D4
Enochville NC, 2851 ......122 B1
Enola PA, 5627 ......218 A1
Enon OH, 2638 ......100 C1
Enoree SC, 700 ......121 F2
Enosburg Falls VT, 1473 ......81 D1
Ensley FL, 18752 ......135 F2
Ensor KY, 500 ......109 E1
Enterprise AL, 21178 ......128 B4
Enterprise KS, 836 ......43 F2
Enterprise MS, 474 ......127 D3
Enterprise OR, 1895 ......22 A2
Enterprise UT, 1285 ......38 C4
Enterprise WV, 939 ......102 A2
Entiat WA, 957 ......13 D3
Enumclaw WA, 11116 ......12 C3
Ephraim UT, 4505 ......39 E2
Ephrata PA, 13213 ......146 A2
Ephrata WA, 6808 ......13 E3
Epping NH, 1673 ......81 F4
Epps LA, 1153 ......125 F2
Epworth IA, 1428 ......73 F4
Epworth Hts. OH, 3300 ......204 D1
Equality IL, 721 ......109 D1
Erath LA, 2187 ......133 F3
Erath Co. TX, 33001 ......59 D3
Erda UT, 2473 ......31 E4
Erial NJ, 6200 ......146 C4
Erick OK, 1023 ......50 C3
Erie CO, 6291 ......209 B1
Erie IL, 1589 ......88 A2
Erie KS, 1211 ......106 A1
Erie Co. NY, 950265 ......78 B4
Erie Co. OH, 79551 ......91 D2
Erie Co. PA, 280843 ......92 A1
Erin TN, 1490 ......109 E3
Erlanger KY, 16676 ......100 B2
Erwin NC, 4537 ......123 D1
Erwin TN, 5610 ......111 E4
Erwinville LA, 700 ......134 A2
Escalante UT, 818 ......39 E4
Escalon CA, 5963 ......36 C4

Escambia Co. AL, 38440 ......136 A1
Escambia Co. FL, 294410 ......135 F1
Escanaba MI, 13140 ......69 D2
Escatawpa MS, 3566 ......195 C1
Escobares TX, 1954 ......63 D4
Escondido CA, 133559 ......53 D4
Esko MN, 1300 ......64 C3
Eskridge KS, 589 ......43 F2
Esmeralda Co. NV, 971 ......37 F4
Espanola NM, 9688 ......49 D2
Espanoy NJ, 2700 ......148 A3
Esparto CA, 1858 ......36 B2
Espy PA, 1428 ......93 E3
Essex CT, 2573 ......149 E2
Essex IA, 884 ......86 A3
Essex MD, 39078 ......144 C2
Essex MA, 1426 ......151 F1
Essex MO, 524 ......108 B2
Essex Co. MA, 723419 ......151 F1
Essex Co. NJ, 793633 ......148 A3
Essex Co. NY, 38851 ......80 C3
Essex Co. VT, 6459 ......81 F1
Essex Co. VA, 9989 ......103 E4
Essex Fells NJ, 2162 ......240 A2
Essex Jct. VT, 8591 ......81 D2
Essexville MI, 3766 ......76 B2
Essexville MI, 3766 ......76 B2
Estacada OR, 2371 ......20 C2
Estancia NM, 1584 ......49 D4
Estelle LA, 15880 ......239 C3
Estelline SD, 655 ......27 F3
Estell Manor NJ, 1585 ......104 C1
Ester AK, 1680 ......154 C2
Estero FL, 9503 ......142 C1
Estes Park CO, 5413 ......33 E4
Estherville IA, 6656 ......72 B2
Estherwood LA, 807 ......133 E2
Estill SC, 2425 ......130 B2
Estill Co. KY, 15307 ......110 C1
Estill Sprs. TN, 2152 ......120 B1
Ethan SD, 330 ......27 E4
Ethel MS, 452 ......126 C1
Ethete WY, 1455 ......32 B1
Ethridge TN, 536 ......119 F1
Etna CA, 781 ......28 B3

Etna PA, 3924 ......250 C1
Etna Green IN, 663 ......89 F2
Etowah NC, 2766 ......121 E1
Etowah TN, 3663 ......120 C1
Etowah Co. AL, 103459 ......120 A3
Ettrick VA, 5627 ......113 E2
Ettrick WI, 521 ......73 F1
Eubank KY, 358 ......110 B2
Euclid OH, 52717 ......91 E2
Eudora AR, 2819 ......126 A1
Eudora KS, 4307 ......96 B3
Eufaula AL, 13908 ......128 B3
Eufaula OK, 2639 ......116 A1
Eugene OR, 137893 ......20 B4
Euharlee GA, 3208 ......120 B3
Euless TX, 46005 ......207 C2
Eunice LA, 11499 ......133 E2
Eunice NM, 2562 ......57 F3
Eupora MS, 2326 ......118 C4
Eureka CA, 26128 ......28 A4
Eureka IL, 4871 ......88 B3
Eureka KS, 2914 ......43 F4
Eureka MO, 7676 ......98 A3
Eureka MT, 1017 ......14 C1
Eureka NV, 550 ......38 A1
Eureka SD, 1101 ......27 D1
Eureka Co. NV, 1651 ......30 B4
Eureka Mill SC, 1737 ......122 A2
Eureka Sprs. AR, 2278 ......106 C3
Eustace TX, 798 ......59 F3
Eustis FL, 15106 ......140 C1
Eustis NE, 464 ......34 C4
Eutaw AL, 1878 ......127 E2
Eva AL, 491 ......119 F3
Evadale TX, 1430 ......132 C2
Evangeline Par. LA, 35434 ......133 E1
Evans CO, 9514 ......33 E4
Evans GA, 17727 ......121 F4
Evans WV, 750 ......101 E3
Evans City PA, 2009 ......92 A3
Evans Co. GA, 10495 ......130 B3
Evansdale IA, 4526 ......73 E4
Evans Mills NY, 605 ......79 E1
Evanston IL, 74239 ......89 D1
Evanston WY, 11507 ......31 F3
Evansville IL, 724 ......98 A4
Evansville IN, 121582 ......99 D4
Evansville MN, 566 ......66 A3
Evansville WI, 4039 ......74 B4
Evansville WY, 2255 ......33 D1
Evaro MT, 329 ......15 D4
Evart MI, 1738 ......75 F1
Eveleth MN, 3865 ......64 C3
Evendale OH, 3090 ......204 B1
Evening Shade AR, 465 ......107 F4
Everett MA, 38037 ......197 C1
Everett PA, 1905 ......102 C1
Everett WA, 91488 ......12 C2
Everglades City FL, 479 ......143 D2
Evergreen AL, 3630 ......127 F4
Evergreen CO, 9216 ......41 D1
Evergreen MT, 6215 ......15 D2
Evergreen Park IL, 20821 ......203 B6
Everly IA, 647 ......72 A3
Everman TX, 5836 ......207 B3
Everson PA, 842 ......92 A4
Everson WA, 2035 ......12 C1
Evesboro NJ, 2400 ......147 D3
Ewa Beach HI, 14650 ......152 A3

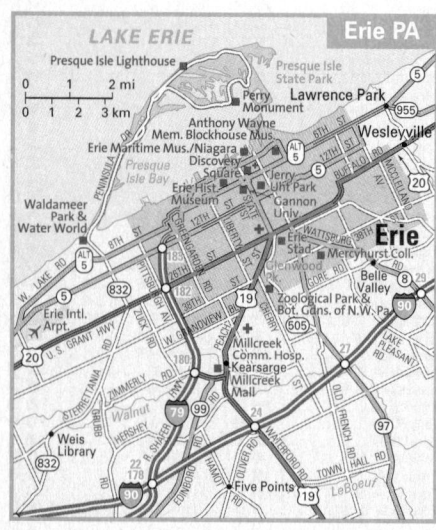
Erie PA

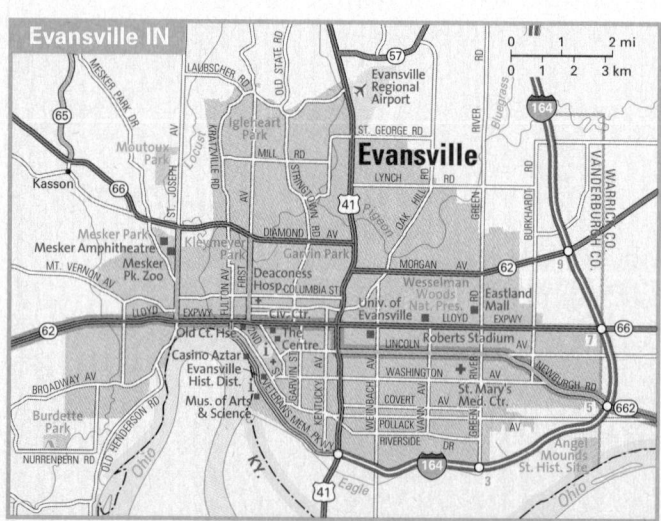
Eugene OR

Evansville IN

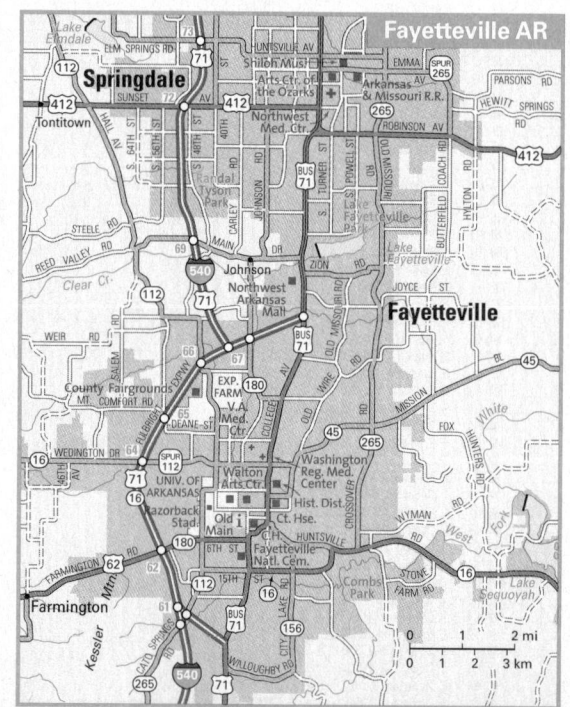
Fargo ND

Fayetteville AR

Entries in **bold** indicate counties or parishes. Entries in color indicate cities with detailed inset maps.
Ewa Villages—Fogelsville 213

Ewa Villages HI, 4741 ....152 A3
Ewing NE, 433 ....35 E2
Ewing NJ, 35707 ....147 D2
Ewing VA, 436 ....111 D3
Excel AL, 582 ....127 F4
Excelsior Sprs. MO, 10847 ....96 C2
Exeter CA, 9168 ....45 D3
Exeter MO, 707 ....106 C3
Exeter NE, 712 ....35 E4
Exeter NH, 9759 ....82 A4
Exeter PA, 5955 ....261 C1
Exeter RI, 1000 ....150 C4
Exira IA, 810 ....86 B2
Exmore VA, 1136 ....114 B3
Experiment GA, 3233 ....129 D1
Exton PA, 4267 ....146 B3
Eyota MN, 1644 ....73 E1

F
Fabens TX, 8043 ....56 C4
Factoryville PA, 1144 ....93 F2
Fairacres NM, 1100 ....56 B3
Fairbank IA, 1041 ....73 E4
Fairbanks AK, 30224 ....154 C2
Fairbanks FL, 750 ....138 C3
Fairbanks ME, 700 ....82 B1
Fair Bluff NC, 1181 ....123 D3
Fairborn OH, 32052 ....100 C1
Fairburn GA, 5464 ....120 C4
Fairbury IL, 3968 ....88 C3
Fairbury NE, 4262 ....43 E1
Fairchance PA, 2174 ....102 B1
Fairchild WI, 564 ....67 F4
Fairchilds TX, 678 ....132 A4
Fairfax CA, 7319 ....36 B3
Fairfax DE, 2300 ....274 E1
Fairfax IA, 889 ....87 E1
Fairfax MN, 1295 ....66 B4
Fairfax MO, 645 ....86 A4
Fairfax OH, 1938 ....204 C2
Fairfax OK, 1555 ....51 F1
Fairfax SC, 3206 ....130 B1
Fairfax VT, 600 ....81 D1
Fairfax VA, 21498 ....144 A3
Fairfax Co. VA, 969749 ....144 A3
Fairfield AL, 12381 ....119 F4
Fairfield CA, 96178 ....36 B3
Fairfield CT, 57340 ....149 D2
Fairfield ID, 395 ....22 C4
Fairfield IL, 5421 ....99 D4
Fairfield IA, 9509 ....87 E3
Fairfield ME, 2569 ....82 C2
Fairfield MT, 659 ....15 E3
Fairfield NE, 467 ....35 E4
Fairfield NJ, 7063 ....240 A1
Fairfield OH, 42097 ....100 B2
Fairfield TX, 3094 ....59 F4
Fairfield WA, 494 ....14 B3
Fairfield Bay AR, 2460 ....117 E1
Fairfield Co. CT, 882567 ....149 D2
Fairfield Co. OH, 122759 ....101 D1
Fairfield Co. SC, 23454 ....122 A3
Fairfield Glade TN, 4885 ....110 B4
Fairgrove MI, 627 ....76 B2
Fair Grove MO, 1107 ....107 D1
Fairhaven MA, 16159 ....151 D3
Fair Haven MI, 1500 ....76 C4
Fair Haven NJ, 5937 ....147 E2
Fair Haven NY, 884 ....79 D3
Fair Haven VT, 2435 ....81 D3
Fairhope AL, 12480 ....135 E2
Fairland IN, 1276 ....99 F1
Fairland MD, 21738 ....144 B2
Fairland OK, 1025 ....106 B3
Fair Lawn NJ, 31637 ....148 B3
Fairlawn OH, 7307 ....188 A1
Fairlawn VA, 2211 ....112 A2
Fairlea WV, 1706 ....112 A1
Fairless Hills PA, 8365 ....147 D2
Fairmead CA, 750 ....44 C2
Fairmont MN, 10889 ....72 B2
Fairmont NE, 691 ....35 E4
Fairmont NC, 2604 ....123 D3
Fairmont WV, 19097 ....102 A2
Fairmont City IL, 2436 ....256 C2
Fairmount GA, 745 ....120 C3
Fairmount IL, 640 ....99 D1
Fairmount IN, 2992 ....89 F4
Fairmount MD, 537 ....103 F4
Fairmount NY, 10795 ....79 D3
Fairmount ND, 406 ....27 F1
Fairmount TN, 2600 ....120 B1
Fairmount Hts. MD, 1508 ....270 E3
Fair Oaks CA, 28008 ....255 C1
Fair Oaks GA, 8443 ....120 C4
Fair Oaks Ranch TX, 4695 ....61 D2
Fair Plain MI, 7828 ....89 E1
Fairplains NC, 2051 ....111 F3
Fairplay CO, 679 ....41 D2
Fairport NY, 5740 ....78 C3
Fairport Harbor OH, 3180 ....91 E1
Fairton NJ, 1264 ....145 F1
Fairview AL, 522 ....119 F3
Fairview GA, 6601 ....120 B2
Fairview MI, 600 ....70 C4
Fairview MT, 709 ....17 F2
Fairview NJ, 13255 ....148 B3
Fairview NC, 2495 ....121 E1
Fairview OK, 2733 ....51 D2
Fairview OR, 7561 ....20 C2
Fairview PA, 1900 ....91 F1
Fairview TN, 5800 ....109 E4
Fairview TX, 2644 ....59 F2
Fairview UT, 1160 ....39 E1
Fairview WV, 435 ....102 A1
Fairview WY, 277 ....31 F1
Fairview Hts. IL, 15034 ....98 B3
Fairview Park IN, 1496 ....99 E1
Fairview Park OH, 17572 ....204 D2
Fairview Shores FL, 13898 ....246 C1
Fairway KS, 3952 ....224 B3
Faison NC, 744 ....123 E1
Faith NC, 695 ....122 B1
Faith SD, 489 ....26 B2
Falconer NY, 2540 ....92 B1
Falcon Hts. MN, 5572 ....235 C2
Falfurrias TX, 5297 ....63 E3
Falkville AL, 1202 ....119 F3
Fall Branch TN, 1313 ....111 E3
Fallbrook CA, 29100 ....53 D3
Fall City WA, 1638 ....12 C3
Fall Creek WI, 1236 ....67 F4
Falling Waters WV, 650 ....103 D1
Fallon NV, 7536 ....37 E1
Fallon Co. MT, 2837 ....17 F4
Fall River MA, 91938 ....151 D3
Fall River WI, 1097 ....74 B2
Fall River Co. SD, 7453 ....33 F1
Fall River Mills CA, 648 ....29 D3
Falls Church VA, 10377 ....144 B3
Falls City NE, 4671 ....86 A4
Falls City OR, 966 ....20 B2
Falls City TX, 591 ....61 E3
Falls Co. TX, 18576 ....59 F4
Falls Creek PA, 983 ....92 B3
Fallston MD, 8427 ....144 C1
Fallston NC, 603 ....122 A1
Falmouth KY, 2058 ....100 B3
Falmouth MA, 4115 ....151 E4
Falmouth VA, 3624 ....103 D4
Falmouth Foreside ME, 1964 ....82 B3
Fancy Farm KY, 500 ....108 C2
Fannett TX, 1000 ....132 C3
Fannin Co. GA, 19798 ....120 C2
Fannin Co. TX, 31242 ....59 F1
Fanning Sprs. FL, 737 ....138 B3
Fanwood NJ, 7174 ....147 E1
Fargo ND, 90599 ....19 F4
Far Hills NJ, 859 ....148 A4
Faribault MN, 20818 ....73 D1
Faribault Co. MN, 16181 ....72 C2
Farley IA, 1334 ....73 F4
Farmer City IL, 2055 ....88 C4
Farmers Branch TX, 27508 ....207 D1
Farmersburg IN, 1180 ....99 E2
Farmers Mills NY, 800 ....148 C1
Farmersville CA, 8737 ....45 D3
Farmersville IL, 768 ....98 B2
Farmersville OH, 980 ....100 B1
Farmersville PA, 2400 ....189 B1
Farmersville TX, 3118 ....59 F2
Farmerville LA, 3808 ....125 E2
Farmingdale ME, 1935 ....82 C2
Farmingdale NJ, 1587 ....147 E2
Farmingdale NY, 8399 ....148 C4
Farmington AR, 3605 ....106 C4
Farmington CT, 1600 ....94 C3
Farmington IL, 2601 ....88 A3
Farmington IA, 756 ....87 E3
Farmington ME, 4098 ....82 B1
Farmington MI, 10423 ....210 A2
Farmington MN, 12365 ....67 D4
Farmington MS, 1810 ....119 D2
Farmington MO, 13924 ....108 A1
Farmington NH, 3468 ....81 F4
Farmington NM, 37844 ....48 B1
Farmington UT, 12081 ....31 E3
Farmington WV, 387 ....102 A1
Farmington Hills MI, 82111 ....210 A2
Farmingville NY, 16458 ....149 D3
Farmland IN, 1456 ....90 A4
Farmville NC, 4302 ....115 C2
Farmville VA, 6845 ....113 D2
Farragut IA, 509 ....86 A3
Farragut TN, 17720 ....110 C4
Farrell PA, 6050 ....91 F2
Farr West UT, 3094 ....244 A1
Farson WY, 242 ....32 A2
Farwell MI, 855 ....76 A2
Farwell TX, 1364 ....49 F4
Faulk Co. SD, 2640 ....27 D2
Faulkner Co. AR, 86014 ....117 E1
Faulkton SD, 785 ....27 D2
Fauquier Co. VA, 55139 ....144 A4
Favoretta FL, 650 ....139 E4
Fayette AL, 4922 ....119 E4
Fayette IA, 1300 ....73 E3
Fayette MS, 2242 ....126 A4
Fayette MO, 2793 ....97 D2
Fayette OH, 1340 ....90 B2
Fayette Co. AL, 18495 ....119 E4
Fayette Co. GA, 91263 ....120 C4
Fayette Co. IL, 21802 ....98 C2
Fayette Co. IN, 25588 ....100 A1
Fayette Co. IA, 22008 ....73 E4
Fayette Co. KY, 260512 ....100 B4
Fayette Co. OH, 28433 ....100 C1
Fayette Co. PA, 148644 ....102 B1
Fayette Co. TN, 28806 ....118 C1
Fayette Co. TX, 21804 ....61 E2
Fayette Co. WV, 47579 ....101 F4
Fayetteville AR, 58047 ....106 C4
Fayetteville GA, 11148 ....120 C4
Fayetteville NY, 4190 ....79 E3
Fayetteville NC, 121015 ....123 D2
Fayetteville PA, 2774 ....103 D1
Fayetteville TN, 6994 ....119 F1
Fayetteville WV, 2754 ....101 F4
Fearrington Vil. NC, 903 ....112 C4
Feasterville PA, 6525 ....248 D1
Federal Hts. CO, 12065 ....209 B2
Federalsburg MD, 2620 ....145 E4
Federal Way WA, 83259 ....12 C3
Felicity OH, 922 ....100 C3
Felida WA, 5683 ....20 C1
Fellowship NJ, 4900 ....147 D3
Fellsmere FL, 3813 ....141 E3
Felton CA, 1051 ....236 D1
Felton DE, 784 ....145 E3
Fennimore WI, 2387 ....73 F3
Fennville MI, 1459 ....75 E4
Fenton MI, 10582 ....76 B4
Fenton MO, 4360 ....256 A3
Fentress Co. TN, 16625 ....110 B3
Fenwick Island DE, 342 ....114 C1
Ferdinand IN, 2277 ....99 E4
Fergus Co. MT, 11893 ....16 B3
Fergus Falls MN, 13471 ....19 F4
Ferguson KY, 881 ....110 B2
Ferguson MO, 22406 ....256 B1
Fernandina Beach FL, 10549 ....139 D1
Fernan Lake Vil. ID, 186 ....14 B3
Ferndale CA, 1382 ....28 A4
Ferndale MD, 16056 ....193 C4
Ferndale MI, 22105 ....210 C2
Ferndale PA, 900 ....146 C1
Ferndale WA, 8758 ....12 C1
Fernley NV, 8543 ....37 E1
Fern Park FL, 8318 ....246 C1
Ferrell NJ, 1100 ....146 C4
Ferrellsburg WV, 500 ....101 E4
Ferrelview MO, 593 ....96 B2
Ferriday LA, 3723 ....125 F4
Ferris TX, 2175 ....59 F3
Ferron UT, 1623 ....39 E2
Ferrum VA, 1313 ....112 B2
Ferry Co. WA, 7260 ....13 F2
Ferry Pass FL, 27176 ....135 F2
Ferrysburg MI, 3040 ....75 E3
Fertile MN, 893 ....19 F3
Fessenden ND, 625 ....18 C3
Festus MO, 9660 ....98 A4
Fieldale VA, 929 ....112 B3
Fielding UT, 448 ....31 E2
Fieldsboro NJ, 522 ....147 D2
Fife WA, 4784 ....262 B5
Fife Lake MI, 466 ....69 F4
Filer ID, 1620 ....30 C1
Fillmore CA, 13643 ....52 B2
Fillmore IN, 545 ....99 E1
Fillmore UT, 2253 ....39 D2
Fillmore Co. MN, 21122 ....73 E2
Fillmore Co. NE, 6634 ....35 E4
Fincastle KY, 825 ....230 F1
Fincastle VA, 359 ....112 B1
Findlay IL, 723 ....98 C1
Findlay OH, 38967 ....90 C3
Finley ND, 515 ....19 E3
Finley WA, 5770 ....21 E1
Finney Co. KS, 40523 ....42 B3
Finneytown OH, 13492 ....204 B2
Fircrest WA, 5868 ....262 A5
Firebaugh CA, 5743 ....44 C2
Firth ID, 408 ....23 E4
Firth NE, 564 ....35 F4
Fitchcliffe NY, 4970 ....148 B1
Fisher IL, 1647 ....88 C4
Fisher Co. TX, 4344 ....58 B2
Fishers IN, 37835 ....99 F1
Fishersville VA, 4998 ....102 C4
Fishkill NY, 1735 ....148 B1
Fishkill Plains NY, 900 ....148 B1
Fiskdale MA, 2156 ....150 B2
Fitchburg MA, 39102 ....95 D1
Fitchburg WI, 20501 ....74 B3
Fitchville CT, 750 ....149 F1
Fitzgerald GA, 8758 ....129 E4
Fitzwilliam NH, 500 ....95 D1
Five Corners MA, 2100 ....151 D2
Flagler CO, 612 ....41 F2
Flagler Beach FL, 4954 ....139 E4
Flagler Co. FL, 49832 ....139 D3
Flagstaff AZ, 52894 ....47 E3
Flagtown NJ, 3000 ....147 D1
Flanagan IL, 1083 ....88 C3
Flanders NY, 3646 ....149 E3
Flanders (E. Lyme) CT, 1800 ....149 F2
Flandreau SD, 2376 ....27 F3
Flasher ND, 285 ....18 B4
Flathead Co. MT, 74471 ....14 C2
Flat Lick KY, 700 ....110 C2
Flatonia TX, 1377 ....61 E2
Flat Rock MI, 8488 ....90 C1
Flat Rock NC, 1690 ....112 A3
Flat Rock NC, 2565 ....121 E1
Flatwoods KY, 7605 ....101 D3
Flatwoods WV, 348 ....102 A3
Fleetwood PA, 4018 ....146 B1
Fleming CO, 426 ....34 A4
Fleming Co. KY, 13792 ....100 C4
Fleming-Neon KY, 840 ....111 E2
Flemingsburg KY, 3010 ....100 C3
Flemington NJ, 4200 ....147 D1
Flemington PA, 1319 ....93 D3
Fletcher NC, 4185 ....121 E1
Fletcher OK, 1022 ....51 D4
Flint MI, 124943 ....76 B3
Flint TX, 1200 ....124 A3
Flippin AR, 1357 ....107 E3
Flohrville MD, 950 ....144 B1
Flomaton AL, 1588 ....135 F1
Floodwood MN, 503 ....64 C4
Flora IL, 5086 ....98 C3
Flora IN, 2227 ....89 E4
Flora MS, 1546 ....126 B2
Florala AL, 1964 ....136 B1
Floral City FL, 4989 ....140 C1
Floral Park NY, 15967 ....241 G3
Flora Vista NM, 1383 ....48 B1
Flordell Hills MO, 931 ....256 C1
Florence AL, 36264 ....119 E2
Florence AZ, 17054 ....54 C2
Florence CA, 60197 ....228 D3
Florence CO, 3653 ....41 E3
Florence KS, 671 ....43 F3
Florence KY, 23551 ....100 B2
Florence MS, 3994 ....126 B3
Florence MT, 901 ....15 D4
Florence NJ, 8200 ....147 D2
Florence OR, 7263 ....20 B4
Florence SC, 30248 ....122 C3
Florence SD, 299 ....27 E2
Florence TX, 1054 ....61 E1
Florence WI, 750 ....68 C2
Florence Co. SC, 125761 ....122 C3
Florence Co. WI, 5088 ....68 C2
Florence Jct. AZ, 275 ....55 D2
Floresville TX, 5868 ....61 D3
Florham Park NJ, 8857 ....148 A4
Florida NY, 2571 ....148 A2
Florida City FL, 7843 ....143 E3
Florien LA, 692 ....125 D4
Florin CA, 27653 ....36 C3
Florissant MO, 50497 ....98 A3
Floritown PA, 4669 ....248 B1
Flovilla GA, 652 ....129 D1
Flower Hill NY, 4508 ....241 G2
Flower Mound TX, 50702 ....207 C1
Flowery Branch GA, 1806 ....121 D3
Flowood MS, 4750 ....126 B3
Floyd VA, 432 ....112 B2
Floydada TX, 3676 ....58 B1
Floyd Co. GA, 90565 ....120 B3
Floyd Co. IN, 70823 ....99 F4
Floyd Co. IA, 16900 ....73 D3
Floyd Co. KY, 42441 ....111 E1
Floyd Co. TX, 7771 ....50 B4
Floyd Co. VA, 13874 ....112 A2
Flushing MI, 8348 ....76 B3
Flushing OH, 900 ....91 F4
Fluvanna Co. VA, 20047 ....113 D1
Flying Hills PA, 1191 ....146 A2
Foard Co. TX, 1622 ....58 C1
Fogelsville PA, 950 ....146 B1

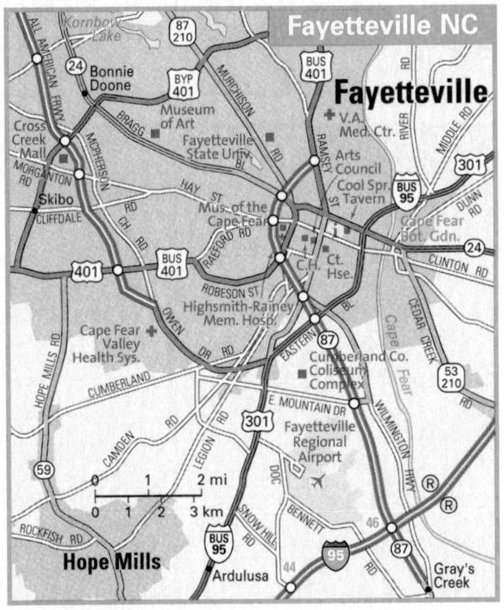
Fayetteville NC
Fayetteville
Bonnie Doone
Cross Creek Mall
Skibo
Museum of Art
Fayetteville State Univ.
V.A. Med. Ctr.
Arts Council
Cool Spr. Tavern
Mus. of the Cape Fear
Cape Fear Bot. Gdn.
Ct. Hse.
Highsmith-Rainey Mem. Hosp.
Cape Fear Valley Health Sys.
Cumberland Co. Coliseum Complex
Fayetteville Regional Airport
Hope Mills
Ardulusa
Gray's Creek

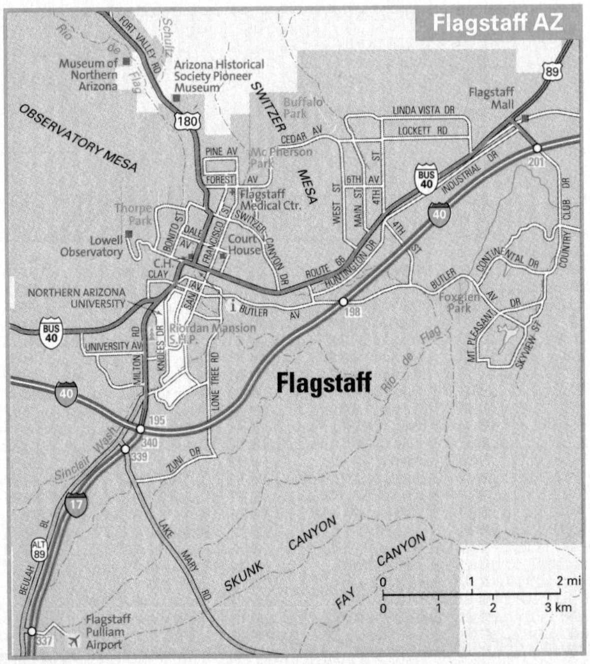
Flagstaff AZ
Museum of Northern Arizona
Arizona Historical Society Pioneer Museum
OBSERVATORY MESA
Buffalo Park
Flagstaff Mall
Flagstaff Medical Ctr.
Lowell Observatory
Court House
NORTHERN ARIZONA UNIVERSITY
Riordan Mansion S.H.P.
Foxglenn Park
Flagstaff
SKUNK CANYON
FAY CANYON
Flagstaff Pulliam Airport

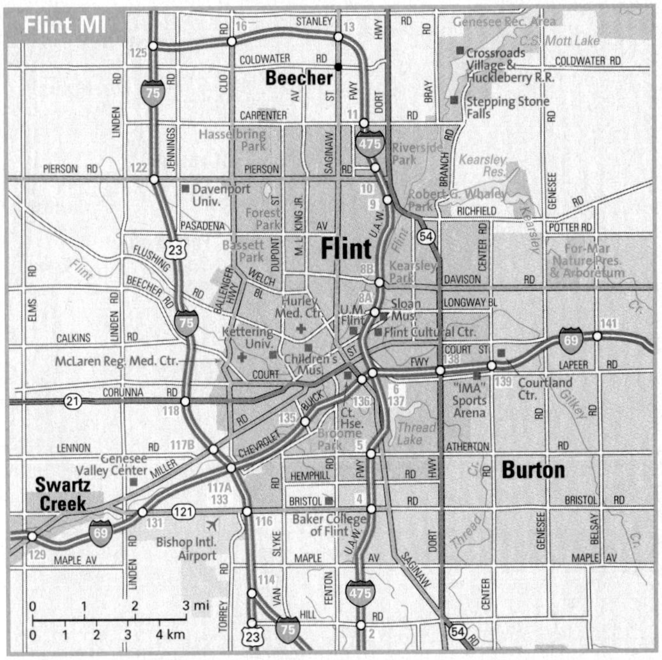
Flint MI
Genesee Rec. Area
C.S. Mott Lake
Crossroads Village & Huckleberry R.R.
Beecher
Stepping Stone Falls
Hasselbring Park
Riverside Park
Kearsley Res.
Davenport Univ.
Forest Park
Flint
Bassett Park
Kearsley Park
For-Mar Nature Pres. & Arboretum
Hurley Med. Ctr.
U.M. Flint
Sloan Mus.
Flint Cultural Ctr.
Kettering Univ.
McLaren Reg. Med. Ctr.
Children's Mus.
Courtland Ctr.
"IMA" Sports Arena
Broome Park
Thread Lake
Burton
Swartz Creek
Genesee Valley Center
Baker College of Flint
Bishop Intl. Airport

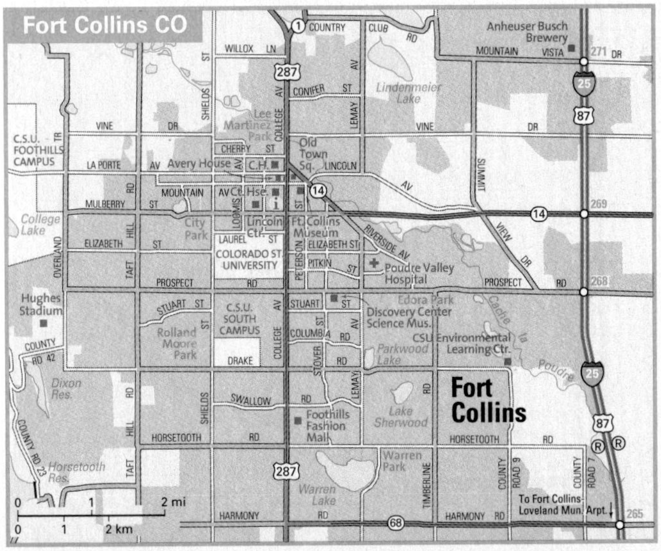
Fort Collins CO
Anheuser Busch Brewery
Lindenmeier Lake
Lee Martinez Park
Old Town Sq.
C.S.U. - FOOTHILLS CAMPUS
Avery House
College Lake
City Park
Ft. Collins Museum
COLORADO ST. UNIVERSITY
Poudre Valley Hospital
Hughes Stadium
C.S.U. SOUTH CAMPUS
Rolland Moore Park
Discovery Center Science Mus.
Edora Park
CSU Environmental Learning Ctr.
Dixon Res.
Foothills Fashion Mall
Fort Collins
Horsetooth Res.
Warren Lake
Warren Park
To Fort Collins Loveland Mun. Arpt.

Figures after entries indicate population, page number, and grid reference.

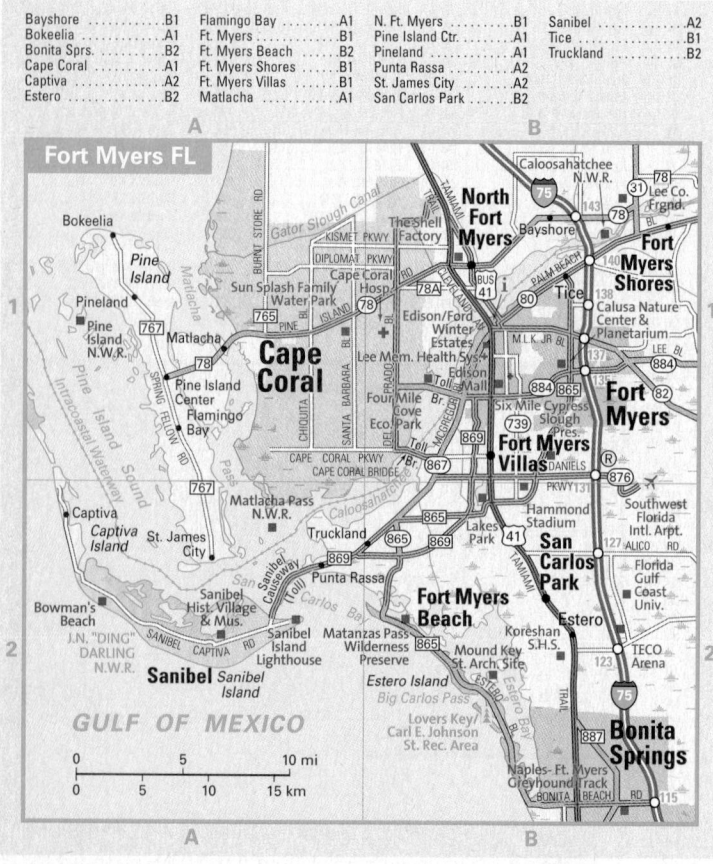

Fort Myers FL

Frankfort KY

Fresno CA

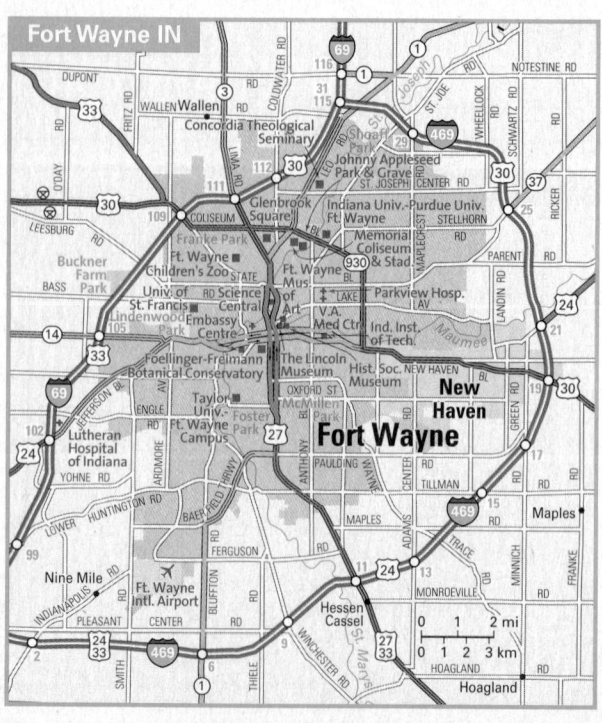

Fort Wayne IN

Entries in **bold** indicate counties or parishes. Entries in color indicate cities with detailed inset maps.
Franklin County—Glen Elder 215

Franklin Co. IA, 10704 72 C4
Franklin Co. KS, 24784 96 A3
Franklin Co. KY, 47687 100 B4
Franklin Co. ME, 29467 82 B1
Franklin Co. MA, 71535 150 A1
Franklin Co. MS, 8448 126 A4
Franklin Co. MO, 93807 97 F3
Franklin Co. NE, 3574 43 D1
Franklin Co. NY, 51134 80 C2
Franklin Co. NC, 47260 113 D4
Franklin Co. OH, 1068978 101 D1
Franklin Co. PA, 129313 103 D1
Franklin Co. TN, 39270 120 A1
Franklin Co. TX, 9458 124 B1
Franklin Co. VT, 45417 81 D1
Franklin Co. VA, 47286 112 B2
Franklin Co. WA, 49347 13 F4
Franklin Furnace OH, 1537 101 D3
Franklin Grove IL, 1052 88 B1
Franklin Par. LA, 21263 125 F2
Franklin Park IL, 19434 203 C4
Franklin Park PA, 11364 92 A3
Franklin Sprs. GA, 762 121 E3
Franklin Square NY, 29342 241 G4
Franklinton LA, 3657 134 B1
Franklinton NC, 1745 113 D4
Franklinville NJ, 1500 145 F1
Franklinville NY, 1855 78 B4
Franklinville NC, 1258 112 B4
Frankston TX, 1209 124 A3
Franksville WI, 1789 74 C4
Frankton IN, 1905 89 F4
Frannie WY, 209 24 B2
Fraser CO, 910 41 D1
Fraser MI, 15297 210 D2
Frazee MN, 1377 19 F4
Frazer MT, 452 17 E2
Frazeysburg OH, 1201 91 D4
Frazier Park CA, 2348 52 B1
Frederic WI, 1262 67 E2
Frederica DE, 648 145 E3
Frederick CO, 2467 41 E1
Frederick MD, 52767 144 A1
Frederick OK, 4637 51 D4
Frederick SD, 255 27 D1
Frederick Co. MD, 195277 144 A1
Frederick Co. VA, 59209 102 C2
Fredericksburg IA, 984 73 E3
Fredericksburg PA, 1140 92 A2
Fredericksburg PA, 987 93 E4
Fredericksburg TX, 8911 61 D2
Fredericksburg VA, 19279 103 D4
Fredericktown MO, 3928 108 A1
Fredericktown OH, 2428 91 D4
Fredonia AZ, 1036 47 D1
Fredonia KS, 2600 106 A1
Fredonia KY, 420 109 D2
Fredonia NY, 10706 78 A4
Fredonia PA, 652 91 F2
Fredonia WI, 1934 74 C2
Freeborn Co. MN, 32584 72 C2
Freeburg IL, 3872 98 B3
Freeburg PA, 584 93 D3
Freedom CA, 6000 44 B2
Freedom WI, 1500 74 C1
Freehold NJ, 10976 147 E2
Freeland MI, 5147 76 B2
Freeland PA, 3643 93 E3
Freeland WA, 1313 262 A1
Freeman MO, 521 96 B3
Freeman SD, 1317 27 E4
Freemansburg PA, 1897 146 C1
Freeport FL, 1190 136 B2
Freeport IL, 26443 74 B4
Freeport ME, 1813 82 B3
Freeport NY, 43783 147 F1
Freeport PA, 1962 92 A3
Freeport TX, 12708 133 E4
Freer TX, 3241 63 E2
Freestone Co. TX, 17867 59 F4
Freetown IN, 600 99 F2
Freetown NY, 2400 149 F3
Freeville NY, 505 79 D4
Freewood Acres NJ, 3100 147 E2
Fremont CA, 203413 36 B4
Fremont IN, 1696 90 A1
Fremont IA, 704 87 E2
Fremont MI, 4224 75 F2
Fremont NE, 25174 35 F3
Fremont NH, 500 81 F4
Fremont NC, 1463 123 E1
Fremont OH, 17375 90 C2
Fremont WI, 666 74 B1
Fremont Co. CO, 46145 41 D3
Fremont Co. ID, 11819 23 F3
Fremont Co. IA, 8010 86 A3
Fremont Co. WY, 35804 32 C1
Fremont Hills MO, 597 107 D2
Frenchburg KY, 551 100 C4
French Camp CA, 4109 36 C4
French Lick IN, 1941 99 F3
French Settlement LA, 945 134 A2
Frenchtown MT, 883 15 D4
Frenchtown NJ, 1488 146 C1
Frenchville ME, 350 85 D1
Fresno CA, 427652 44 C3
Fresno TX, 6603 220 B4
Fresno Co. CA, 799407 37 E4
Frewsburg NY, 1965 92 B1
Friant CA, 519 44 C2
Friars Pt. MS, 1480 118 A3
Friday Harbor WA, 1989 12 B2
Fridley MN, 27449 67 D3
Friedens PA, 1673 102 C1
Friedensburg PA, 828 146 A1
Friend NE, 1174 35 E4
Friendly MD, 10938 144 B4
Friendship ME, 475 82 C3
Friendship NY, 1176 92 C1
Friendship TN, 608 108 C4
Friendship WI, 698 74 A1
Friendsville MD, 539 102 B1
Friendsville TN, 890 110 C4
Friendswood TX, 29037 132 B4
Fries VA, 614 112 A3
Frio Co. TX, 16252 60 C3
Friona TX, 3854 49 F4
Frisco CO, 2443 41 D1
Frisco TX, 33714 59 F2
Frisco City AL, 1460 127 F4
Fritch TX, 2235 50 B2
Froid MT, 195 17 F2
Fromberg MT, 486 24 B2
Frontenac FL, 1900 232 A1
Frontenac KS, 2996 106 B1
Frontenac MO, 3483 256 B2
Frontier ND, 273 19 F4
Frontier Co. NE, 3099 34 C4
Fronton TX, 599 63 D4
Front Royal VA, 13589 102 C3
Frost TX, 648 59 F3
Frostburg MD, 7873 102 C1
Frostproof FL, 2975 141 D3
Fruita CO, 6478 40 B2
Fruit Cove FL, 16077 139 D2
Fruit Hts. UT, 4701 31 E3
Fruit Hill OH, 3945 204 C3
Fruitland ID, 3805 22 A4
Fruitland IA, 703 87 F2
Fruitland MD, 3774 103 F4
Fruitland NM, 650 48 B1
Fruitland Park FL, 3186 140 C1
Fruitport MI, 1124 75 E3
Fruitville FL, 12741 266 C5
Fryeburg ME, 1549 81 F3
Fulda MN, 1283 72 A2
Fullerton CA, 126003 52 C3
Fullerton MD, 10100 193 D2
Fullerton NE, 1378 35 E3
Fulshear TX, 716 132 A3
Fulton IL, 3881 88 A1
Fulton KY, 2775 108 C3
Fulton MD, 850 144 B2
Fulton MS, 3882 119 D3
Fulton MO, 12128 97 E3
Fulton NY, 11855 79 D3
Fulton TX, 1553 61 E4
Fulton Co. AR, 11642 107 F3
Fulton Co. GA, 816006 120 C4
Fulton Co. IL, 38250 88 A4
Fulton Co. IN, 20511 89 F3
Fulton Co. KY, 7752 108 C3
Fulton Co. NY, 55073 79 F3
Fulton Co. OH, 42084 90 B2
Fulton Co. PA, 14261 103 D1
Fultondale AL, 6595 119 F4
Fultonville NY, 710 79 F3
Fuquay-Varina NC, 7898 123 D1
Furnas Co. NE, 5324 42 C1
Fyffe AL, 971 120 A3

G
Gabbs NV, 318 37 F2
Gackle ND, 335 19 D4
Gadsden AL, 38978 120 A3
Gadsden AZ, 953 53 F4
Gadsden TN, 553 108 C4
Gadsden Co. FL, 45087 137 D2
Gaffney SC, 12968 121 F2
Gage Co. NE, 22993 35 F4
Gahanna OH, 32636 101 D1
Gail TX, 70 58 B2
Gainesboro TN, 879 110 A3
Gaines Co. TX, 14467 57 F2
Gainesville FL, 95447 138 C3
Gainesville GA, 25578 121 D3
Gainesville MO, 632 107 E3
Gainesville TX, 15538 59 E1
Gainesville VA, 4382 144 A3
Gaithersburg MD, 52613 144 B2
Galatia IL, 1013 108 C1
Galax VA, 6837 112 A3
Galena AK, 675 154 C2
Galena IL, 3460 74 A4
Galena IN, 1831 99 F4
Galena KS, 3287 106 B2
Galena MO, 451 107 D2
Galena Park TX, 10592 220 C3
Galesburg IL, 33706 88 A3
Galesburg MI, 1988 75 F4
Gales Ferry CT, 2400 149 F1
Galesville WI, 1427 73 F1
Galeton PA, 1325 92 C1
Galeville NY, 4476 265 A1
Galien MI, 593 89 E1
Galilee RI, 700 150 C4
Galion OH, 11341 91 D3
Galisteo NM, 265 49 D3
Gallatin MO, 1789 96 C1
Gallatin TN, 23230 109 F3
Gallatin Co. IL, 6445 109 D1
Gallatin Co. KY, 7870 100 B3
Gallatin Co. MT, 67831 23 F2
Gallatin Gateway MT, 350 23 F1
Gallaway TN, 666 118 B1
Gallia Co. OH, 31069 101 E3
Galliano LA, 7356 134 B4
Gallipolis OH, 4180 101 E3
Gallitzin PA, 1756 92 B4
Gallup NM, 20209 48 A3
Galt CA, 19472 36 C3
Galva IL, 2758 88 A2
Galva KS, 701 43 E3
Galveston IN, 1532 89 F3
Galveston KY, 450 111 E1
Galveston TX, 57247 132 B4
Galveston Co. TX, 250158 132 B4
Gamaliel KY, 439 110 A3
Gambell AK, 649 154 A2
Gamber MD, 1000 144 B1
Gambier OH, 1871 91 D4
Gamewell NC, 3644 111 F4
Ganado AZ, 1505 47 F2
Ganado TX, 1915 61 F3
Gang Mills NY, 3304 93 D1
Gannvalley SD, 20 27 D3
Gansevoort NY, 800 81 D4
Gantt SC, 13962 217 A2
Gap PA, 1611 146 A3
Garber OK, 845 51 E1
Gardena CA, 57746 228 C4
Garden City AL, 564 119 F3
Garden City CO, 357 33 E4
Garden City GA, 11289 130 B3
Garden City ID, 10624 22 B4
Garden City KS, 28451 42 B3
Garden City MI, 30047 210 A3
Garden City MO, 1500 96 C3
Garden City NY, 21672 241 G3
Garden City SC, 9357 123 D4
Garden City TX, 200 58 A3
Garden City UT, 357 31 F2
Garden City South NY, 3974 241 G4
Garden Co. NE, 2292 34 A3
Gardendale AL, 11626 119 F4
Gardendale MI, 800 76 C3
Gardendale TX, 1197 58 A3
Garden Grove CA, 165196 228 E4
Garden Home OR, 6931 251 C2
Garden Plain KS, 797 43 E4
Garden Ridge TX, 1882 61 D2
Garden View PA, 2679 93 D2
Gardenville PA, 1000 146 C1
Gardiner ME, 6198 82 C2
Gardiner MT, 851 23 F2
Gardiner NY, 856 148 B1
Gardner IL, 1406 88 C2
Gardner KS, 9396 96 B3
Gardner MA, 20770 95 D1
Gardnertown NY, 4533 148 B1
Gardnerville NV, 3357 37 D2
Garfield AR, 490 106 C3
Garfield NJ, 29786 148 B3
Garfield TX, 1660 61 E2
Garfield WA, 641 14 B4
Garfield Co. CO, 43791 40 B1
Garfield Co. MT, 1279 17 D3
Garfield Co. NE, 1902 35 D2
Garfield Co. OK, 57813 51 E1
Garfield Co. UT, 4735 39 E3
Garfield Co. WA, 2397 14 A4
Garfield Hts. OH, 30734 91 E2
Garibaldi OR, 899 20 B2
Garland NC, 808 123 D2
Garland TX, 215768 59 F2
Garland UT, 1943 31 E2
Garland Co. AR, 88068 117 D2
Garnavillo IA, 754 73 F3
Garner IA, 2922 72 C3
Garner KY, 600 111 D1
Garner NC, 17757 113 D4
Garnett KS, 3368 96 A4
Garrard Co. KY, 14792 110 C1
Garretson SD, 1165 27 F4
Garrett IN, 5803 90 A2
Garrett Co. MD, 29846 102 B2
Garrett Park MD, 917 270 C1
Garrettsville OH, 2262 91 F2
Garrison KY, 950 101 D3
Garrison MD, 7969 193 A1
Garrison ND, 1318 18 B3
Garrison TX, 844 124 B3
Garrisonville VA, 2700 144 A4
Garvin Co. OK, 27210 51 E4
Garwin IA, 565 87 D1
Gary IN, 102746 89 D2
Gary SD, 231 27 F2
Gary WV, 917 111 F1
Garysburg NC, 1254 113 E3
Garyville LA, 2775 134 B3
Garza Co. TX, 4872 58 B2
Gas KS, 556 96 A4
Gas City IN, 5940 89 F4
Gasconade Co. MO, 15342 97 F3
Gasport NY, 1248 78 B3
Gassaway WV, 901 101 F4
Gassville AR, 1706 107 E3
Gaston IN, 1010 89 F4
Gaston NC, 973 113 E3
Gaston OR, 600 20 B2
Gaston SC, 1304 122 A4
Gaston Co. NC, 190365 122 A1
Gastonia NC, 66277 122 A1
Gate City VA, 2159 111 E3
Gates NY, 15138 78 C3
Gates OR, 471 20 C3
Gates TN, 901 108 B4
Gates Co. NC, 10516 113 F3
Gates Mills OH, 2493 204 G1
Gatesville NC, 281 113 F3
Gatesville TX, 15591 59 E4
Gatlinburg TN, 3382 111 D4
Gauley Bridge WV, 738 101 F4
Gautier MS, 11681 135 D2
Gayle Mill SC, 1094 122 A2
Gaylord MI, 3681 70 C3
Gaylord MN, 2279 66 C4
Gaylordsville CT, 750 148 C1
Gays Mills WI, 625 73 F3
Gayville SD, 418 35 E1
Gearhart OR, 995 20 B1
Geary OK, 1258 51 D3
Geary Co. KS, 27947 43 F2
Geauga Co. OH, 90895 91 E2
Geddes SD, 208 35 D1
Geistown PA, 2555 92 B4
Gem Co. ID, 15181 22 B3
Genesee ID, 946 14 B4
Genesee MI, 1800 76 B3
Genesee Co. MI, 436141 76 B3
Genesee Co. NY, 60370 78 B3
Geneseo IL, 6480 88 A2
Geneseo NY, 7579 78 C4
Geneva AL, 4388 136 C1
Geneva FL, 2601 141 D1
Geneva IL, 19515 88 C1
Geneva IN, 1368 90 A3
Geneva NE, 2226 35 E4
Geneva NY, 13617 79 D3
Geneva OH, 6595 91 F1
Geneva WA, 2257 12 C1
Geneva Co. AL, 25764 136 C1
Geneva-on-the-Lake OH, 1545 91 F1
Genoa IL, 4169 88 C1
Genoa NE, 981 35 E3
Genoa OH, 2230 90 C2
Genoa City WI, 1949 74 C4
Genola UT, 965 39 E1
Gentry AR, 2165 106 B3
Gentry Co. MO, 6861 86 B4
George IA, 1051 72 A2
George WA, 528 13 E4
George Co. MS, 19144 135 D1
Georgetown CA, 962 36 C2
Georgetown CO, 1088 41 D1
Georgetown CT, 1650 148 C2
Georgetown DE, 4643 145 F4
Georgetown GA, 973 128 C3
Georgetown ID, 538 31 F1
Georgetown IL, 3628 99 D1
Georgetown IN, 2227 99 F4
Georgetown KY, 18080 100 B4
Georgetown MA, 3000 151 F1
Georgetown OH, 3691 100 C3
Georgetown PA, 850 146 A3
Georgetown PA, 2200 261 A2
Georgetown SC, 8950 131 E1
Georgetown TX, 28339 61 E1
Georgetown Co. SC, 55797 122 C4
George West TX, 2524 61 D4
Georgia Ctr. VT, 375 81 D1
Georgiana AL, 1737 127 F4
Gerald MO, 1171 97 F3
Geraldine AL, 786 120 A3
Geraldine MT, 284 16 A3
Gerber CA, 1389 36 B1
Gering NE, 7751 33 F2
Gerlach NV, 499 29 E4
Germania NJ, 750 147 D4
Germantown IL, 1118 98 B3
Germantown MD, 55419 144 B2
Germantown NY, 862 94 B2
Germantown OH, 4884 100 B1
Germantown TN, 37348 118 B1
Germantown WI, 18260 74 C3
Germantown Hills IL, 2111 88 B3
Geronimo OK, 959 51 D3
Geronimo TX, 619 61 E2
Gerrardstown WV, 550 103 D2
Gervais OR, 2009 20 C2
Gettysburg OH, 558 90 B4
Gettysburg PA, 7490 103 E1
Gettysburg SD, 1352 26 C2
Geyserville CA, 700 36 A2
Ghent KY, 371 100 A3
Ghent NY, 586 94 B2
Ghent OH, 5261 188 A1
Gholson TX, 922 59 E4
Giants Neck CT, 1000 149 F2
Gibbon MN, 808 66 B4
Gibbon NE, 1759 35 D4
Gibbsboro NJ, 2435 147 D3
Gibbstown NJ, 3758 146 C3
Gibraltar MI, 4264 90 C1
Gibsland LA, 1119 125 D2
Gibson GA, 694 129 F1
Gibson MD, 650 145 D1
Gibson NC, 584 122 C2
Gibsonburg OH, 2506 90 C2
Gibson City IL, 3373 88 C4
Gibson Co. IN, 32500 99 E4
Gibson Co. TN, 48152 108 C4
Gibsonia FL, 4507 140 C2
Gibsonton FL, 8752 140 C3
Gibsonville NC, 4372 112 B4
Giddings TX, 5105 61 F2
Gideon MO, 1113 108 B3
Gifford FL, 7599 141 E3
Gifford IL, 815 89 D4
Gig Harbor WA, 6465 12 C3
Gila Bend AZ, 1980 54 B2
Gila Co. AZ, 51335 55 D1
Gilbert AZ, 109697 54 C2
Gilbert IA, 987 86 C1
Gilbert LA, 561 125 F3
Gilbert MN, 1847 64 C3
Gilbert SC, 500 122 A4
Gilbert WV, 417 111 F1
Gilbertsville PA, 4242 146 B2
Gilbertville IA, 767 73 E4
Gilbertville MA, 1000 150 B1
Gilby ND, 243 19 E2
Gilchrist Co. FL, 14437 138 C3
Gilcrest CO, 1162 33 E4
Giles Co. TN, 29447 119 F1
Giles Co. VA, 16657 112 A1
Gilford NH, 600 81 F3
Gilford Park NJ, 8700 147 E3
Gillespie IL, 3412 98 B2
Gillespie Co. TX, 20814 61 D1
Gillett AR, 819 117 F3
Gillett WI, 1256 68 C4
Gillette WY, 19646 25 E3
Gilliam Co. OR, 1915 21 D2
Gilman IL, 1793 89 D3
Gilman IA, 600 87 D1
Gilman VT, 375 81 F2
Gilmer TX, 4799 124 B2
Gilmer Co. GA, 23456 120 C2
Gilmer Co. WV, 7160 101 F2
Gilmore City IA, 556 72 B4
Gilpin Co. CO, 4757 41 D1
Gilroy CA, 41464 44 B2
Gilt Edge TN, 489 118 B1
Girard IL, 2245 98 B2
Girard KS, 2773 106 B1
Girard OH, 10902 91 F2
Girard PA, 3164 91 F1
Girardville PA, 1742 93 E3
Gisela AZ, 532 47 E4
Glacier Co. MT, 13247 15 E1
Gladbrook IA, 1015 87 D1
Gladden AZ, 400 54 B1
Glades Co. FL, 10576 141 D4
Glade Spr. VA, 1374 111 F2
Gladewater TX, 6078 124 B2
Gladstone MI, 5032 69 D2
Gladstone MO, 26365 96 B2
Gladstone NJ, 2433 148 A4
Gladstone ND, 248 18 A4
Gladstone OR, 11438 251 D3
Gladwin MI, 3001 76 A1
Gladwin Co. MI, 26023 76 A1
Glandorf OH, 919 90 B3
Glasco KS, 536 43 E2
Glasco NY, 1692 94 B2
Glascock Co. GA, 2556 129 F1
Glasford IL, 1076 88 B4
Glasgow DE, 12840 145 E1
Glasgow KY, 13019 110 A2
Glasgow MO, 1263 97 D2
Glasgow MT, 3253 17 D2
Glasgow VA, 1046 112 C1
Glasgow WV, 783 101 F4
Glasgow Vil. MO, 5234 256 C1
Glassboro NJ, 19068 146 C4
Glasscock Co. TX, 1406 58 A3
Glassmanor MD, 35355 270 D5
Glassport PA, 4993 250 C3
Glastonbury CT, 7157 150 A3
Gleason TN, 1463 108 C3
Glenaire MO, 553 224 C2
Glen Allen AL, 442 119 E4
Glen Allen VA, 12562 254 B1
Glen Alpine NC, 1090 111 F4
Glenarden MD, 6318 144 B3
Glen Avon CA, 14853 229 H3
Glenburn ND, 374 18 B2
Glenburn PA, 1212 93 F2
Glen Burnie MD, 38922 144 C2
Glen Carbon IL, 10425 98 B3
Glencoe AL, 5152 120 A4
Glencoe IL, 8762 89 D1
Glencoe MN, 5453 66 C4
Glencoe OK, 583 51 F2
Glen Cove ME, 375 82 C2
Glen Cove NY, 26622 148 C3
Glendale AZ, 218812 54 C1
Glendale CA, 194973 52 C2
Glendale CO, 4547 209 C3
Glendale MO, 5767 256 B2
Glendale OH, 2188 204 B1
Glendale OR, 855 28 B1
Glendale RI, 800 150 C2
Glendale UT, 355 39 D4
Glen Dale WV, 1552 101 F1
Glendale WI, 13367 234 C1
Glendale Hts. IL, 31765 203 B4
Glendive MT, 4729 17 F3
Glendo WY, 229 33 E1
Glendora CA, 49415 229 F2
Glendora NJ, 4907 146 C3
Glen Elder KS, 439 43 D1

Ada B2	E. Grand Rapids B2	Jenison A2	Tallmadge A1
Cascade B2	Grand Rapids B1	Kentwood B2	Walker A2
Comstock Park A1	Grandville A2	Marne A1	Wyoming A2

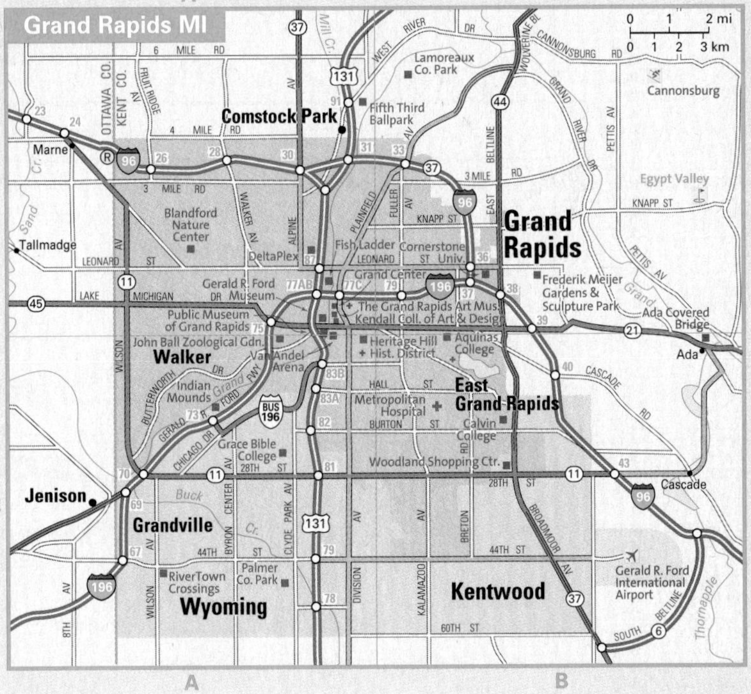
Grand Rapids MI
Comstock Park
Marne
Tallmadge
Walker
Grand Rapids
East Grand Rapids
Jenison
Grandville
Wyoming
Kentwood
Ada
Cascade
Cannonsburg
Egypt Valley
Fifth Third Ballpark
Blandford Nature Center
DeltaPlex
Fish Ladder
Cornerstone Univ.
Gerald R. Ford Museum
Public Museum of Grand Rapids
John Ball Zoological Gdn.
Van Andel Arena
Frederik Meijer Gardens & Sculpture Park
Ada Covered Bridge
Heritage Hill Hist. District
Aquinas College
Indian Mounds
Metropolitan Hospital
Calvin College
Grace Bible College
Woodland Shopping Ctr.
RiverTown Crossings
Palmer Co. Park
Gerald R. Ford International Airport
0 1 2 mi
0 1 2 3 km

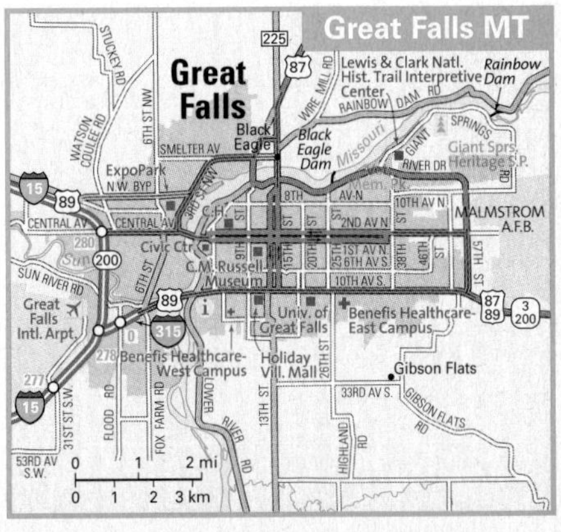
Great Falls MT
Great Falls
Black Eagle
Black Eagle Dam
Rainbow Dam
Lewis & Clark Natl. Hist. Trail Interpretive Center
Giant Sprs. Heritage S.P.
MALMSTROM A.F.B.
ExpoPark
Civic Ctr.
C.M. Russell Museum
Great Falls Intl. Arpt.
Univ. of Great Falls
Benefis Healthcare-East Campus
Benefis Healthcare-West Campus
Holiday Vil. Mall
Gibson Flats
0 1 2 mi
0 1 2 3 km

Glen Ellen CA, 992 ... 36 B3
Glen Ellyn IL, 26999 ... 203 B4
Glen Gardner NJ, 1902 ... 104 C1
Glenham NY, 4300 ... 148 B1
Glen Lyon PA, 1881 ... 93 E2
Glen Mills MA, 750 ... 151 F1
Glenmoor OH, 2192 ... 91 F3
Glenmora LA, 1558 ... 133 E1
Glennallen AK, 554 ... 154 C3
Glenn Co. CA, 26453 ... 36 B1
Glenn Dale MD, 12609 ... 144 C3
Glenn Hts. TX, 7224 ... 59 F3
Glenns Ferry ID, 1611 ... 30 C1
Glennville GA, 3641 ... 130 A3
Glenolden PA, 7476 ... 146 C3
Glenpool OK, 8123 ... 51 F2
Glen Raven NC, 2750 ... 112 C4
Glen Ridge NJ, 7271 ... 240 B2
Glen Rock NJ, 11546 ... 148 B3
Glen Rock PA, 1809 ... 103 E1
Glenrock WY, 2231 ... 33 D1
Glen Rose TX, 2122 ... 59 E3
Glen St. Mary FL, 473 ... 138 C2
Glens Falls NY, 14354 ... 81 D4
Glenside PA, 7914 ... 146 C2
Glen Ullin ND, 865 ... 18 B4
Glenview IL, 41847 ... 203 D2
Glenview KY, 558 ... 230 E1
Glenview Hills KY, 337 ... 230 E1
Glenville MN, 720 ... 73 D2
Glenville WV, 1544 ... 101 F3
Glenwood AR, 1751 ... 117 D3
Glenwood GA, 884 ... 129 F3
Glenwood IA, 5358 ... 86 A3
Glenwood MD, 650 ... 144 B2
Glenwood MN, 2594 ... 66 B2
Glenwood UT, 437 ... 39 E2
Glenwood City WI, 1183 ... 67 E3
Glenwood Sprs. CO, 7736 ... 40 C1
Glidden IA, 1253 ... 86 B1
Glide OR, 1690 ... 20 B4
Globe AZ, 7486 ... 55 D1
Glorieta NM, 859 ... 49 D3
Gloster MS, 1073 ... 126 A4
Gloucester MA, 30273 ... 151 F1
Gloucester VA, 2269 ... 113 F1
Gloucester City NJ, 11484 ... 146 C3
Gloucester Co. NJ, 254673 ... 146 C4
Gloucester Co. VA, 34780 ... 113 F1
Gloucester Pt. VA, 9429 ... 113 F2
Glouster OH, 1972 ... 101 E2
Gloversville NY, 15413 ... 79 F3
Gloverville SC, 2805 ... 121 F4
Glyndon MD, 1200 ... 144 C1
Glyndon MN, 1049 ... 19 F4
Glynn Co. GA, 67568 ... 130 B4
Gnadenhutten OH, 1280 ... 91 E4
Gobles MI, 815 ... 75 F4
Goddard KS, 2037 ... 43 E4
Godeffroy NY, 650 ... 148 A1
Godfrey IL, 16286 ... 98 A2
Godley IL, 594 ... 88 C2
Godley TX, 879 ... 59 E3
Goessel KS, 565 ... 43 E3
Goffstown NH, 2400 ... 81 F4
Gogebic Co. MI, 17370 ... 65 E4
Golconda IL, 726 ... 109 D1
Golconda NV, 175 ... 30 A3
Gold Bar WA, 2014 ... 12 C2
Gold Beach OR, 1897 ... 28 A2
Golden CO, 17159 ... 41 E1
Golden IL, 629 ... 87 F4
Golden Beach FL, 919 ... 233 C3
Golden Beach MD, 2665 ... 144 C4
Golden Bridge NY, 1578 ... 148 C2
Golden City MO, 884 ... 106 C1
Goldendale WA, 3760 ... 21 D1
Golden Gate FL, 20951 ... 142 C1
Golden Meadow LA, 2193 ... 134 B4
Goldenrod FL, 12871 ... 246 D1
Golden Valley MN, 20281 ... 235 B2
Golden Valley Co. MT, 1042 ... 16 B4
Golden Valley Co. ND, 1924 ... 17 F3
Goldfield IA, 680 ... 72 C4
Goldfield NV, 175 ... 37 F4
Gold Hill OR, 1073 ... 28 B2
Goldonna LA, 457 ... 125 D3
Goldsboro NC, 39043 ... 123 E1
Goldsboro PA, 939 ... 93 D4
Goldsby OK, 1204 ... 51 E3
Goldthwaite TX, 1802 ... 59 D4
Goleta CA, 55204 ... 52 B2
Golf Manor OH, 3999 ... 204 B2
Goliad TX, 1975 ... 61 E4
Goliad Co. TX, 6928 ... 61 E3
Gonzales CA, 7525 ... 44 B3
Gonzales LA, 8156 ... 134 A2
Gonzales TX, 7202 ... 61 E2
Gonzales Co. TX, 18628 ... 61 E3
Gonzalez FL, 11365 ... 135 F2
Goochland VA, 1100 ... 113 D1
Goochland Co. VA, 16863 ... 113 D1
Goodfield IL, 686 ... 88 B3
Good Hope AL, 1966 ... 119 F3
Goodhue MN, 779 ... 73 D1
Goodhue Co. MN, 44127 ... 73 D1
Gooding ID, 3384 ... 30 C1
Gooding Co. ID, 14155 ... 30 C1
Goodland IN, 1096 ... 89 D3
Goodland KS, 4948 ... 42 B2
Goodlettsville TN, 13780 ... 109 F3
Goodman MS, 1252 ... 126 B1
Goodman MO, 1183 ... 106 B3
Goodrich MI, 1353 ... 76 B3
Goodsprings NV, 232 ... 46 A2
Good Thunder MN, 592 ... 72 C1
Goodview MN, 3373 ... 73 E1
Goodwater AL, 1633 ... 128 A1
Goodwell OK, 1192 ... 50 B1
Goodyear AZ, 18911 ... 54 C1
Goose Creek SC, 29208 ... 131 D1
Gordo AL, 1677 ... 127 E1
Gordon AL, 408 ... 137 D1
Gordon GA, 2152 ... 129 E1
Gordon NE, 1756 ... 34 A1
Gordon PA, 781 ... 93 E3
Gordon Co. GA, 44104 ... 120 B3
Gordonsville TN, 1066 ... 110 A4
Gordonsville VA, 1498 ... 102 C4
Gordonville PA, 800 ... 146 A3
Gore OK, 850 ... 116 B1
Goreville IL, 938 ... 108 C1
Gorham ME, 4164 ... 82 B3
Gorham NH, 1773 ... 81 F2
Gorham NY, 650 ... 78 C4
Gorman NC, 1002 ... 112 C4
Gorman TX, 1236 ... 59 D3
Goshen AR, 752 ... 106 C4
Goshen CA, 2394 ... 45 D3
Goshen IN, 29383 ... 89 F2
Goshen KY, 907 ... 100 A3
Goshen MD, 1300 ... 144 B2
Goshen NY, 5676 ... 148 A2
Goshen OR, 650 ... 20 B4
Goshen UT, 874 ... 39 E1
Goshen VA, 406 ... 102 B4
Goshen Co. WY, 12538 ... 33 F2
Gosnell AR, 3968 ... 108 B4
Gosper Co. NE, 2143 ... 34 C4
Gosport IN, 715 ... 99 E2
Gotha FL, 731 ... 246 A2
Gothenburg NE, 3619 ... 34 C4
Gould AR, 1305 ... 117 F3
Goulding FL, 4484 ... 247 B1
Goulds FL, 7453 ... 143 E3
Gouldtown NJ, 2300 ... 145 F1
Gouverneur NY, 4263 ... 79 E1
Gove KS, 105 ... 42 C2
Gove Co. KS, 3068 ... 42 C2
Gowanda NY, 2842 ... 78 A4
Gower MO, 1399 ... 96 B1
Gowrie IA, 1038 ... 72 B4
Grabill IN, 1113 ... 90 A2
Grace ID, 990 ... 31 F1
Graceville FL, 2402 ... 136 C1
Graceville MN, 605 ... 27 F1
Grady AR, 523 ... 117 F3
Grady Co. GA, 23659 ... 137 E1
Grady Co. OK, 45516 ... 51 E4
Graettinger IA, 900 ... 72 B3
Graford TX, 578 ... 59 D2
Grafton IL, 609 ... 98 A2
Grafton MA, 2400 ... 150 C2
Grafton ND, 4516 ... 19 E2
Grafton OH, 2302 ... 91 D2
Grafton WV, 5489 ... 102 A2
Grafton WI, 10312 ... 74 C3
Grafton Co. NH, 81743 ... 81 F2
Graham KY, 475 ... 109 E2
Graham NC, 12833 ... 112 C4
Graham TX, 8716 ... 59 D2
Graham WA, 8739 ... 12 C4
Graham Co. AZ, 33489 ... 55 E2
Graham Co. KS, 2946 ... 42 C2
Graham Co. NC, 7993 ... 121 D1
Grainger Co. TN, 20659 ... 111 D3
Grain Valley MO, 5160 ... 96 C2
Grambling LA, 4693 ... 125 E2
Gramercy LA, 3066 ... 134 B3
Granada CO, 640 ... 42 A3
Granbury TX, 5718 ... 59 E3
Granby CO, 1525 ... 41 D1
Granby CT, 2453 ... 94 C2
Granby MA, 1344 ... 150 A1
Granby MO, 2121 ... 106 C2
Grand Bay AL, 3918 ... 135 E2
Grand Blanc MI, 8242 ... 76 B3
Grand Canyon AZ, 1460 ... 47 D2
Grand Coteau LA, 1040 ... 133 F2
Grand Coulee WA, 897 ... 13 E2
Grand Co. CO, 12442 ... 41 D1
Grand Co. UT, 8485 ... 40 A2
Grandfield OK, 1110 ... 51 D4
Grand Forks ND, 49321 ... 19 E2
Grand Forks Co. ND, 66109 ... 19 E3
Grand Haven MI, 11168 ... 75 E3
Grandin NJ, 1800 ... 147 D1
Grand Island NE, 42940 ... 35 E4
Grand Isle LA, 1541 ... 134 B4
Grand Isle VT, 350 ... 81 D1
Grand Isle Co. VT, 6901 ... 81 D1
Grand Jct. CO, 41986 ... 40 B2
Grand Jct. IA, 964 ... 86 C1
Grand Lake CO, 447 ... 33 D4
Grand Ledge MI, 7813 ... 76 A4
Grand Marais MN, 1353 ... 65 D3
Grand Meadow MN, 945 ... 73 D2
Grand Mound IA, 676 ... 88 A1
Grand Prairie TX, 127427 ... 207 C3
Grand Rapids MI, 197800 ... 75 F3
Grand Rapids MN, 7764 ... 64 B3
Grand Rapids OH, 1002 ... 90 B2
Grand Ridge FL, 792 ... 137 D1
Grand Rivers KY, 343 ... 109 D2
Grand Saline TX, 3028 ... 124 A2
Grand Terrace CA, 11626 ... 229 J3
Grand Tower IL, 624 ... 108 B1
Grand Traverse Co. MI, 77654 ... 69 F4
Grandview CO, 600 ... 40 B4
Grand View ID, 470 ... 30 B1
Grandview IN, 696 ... 99 E4
Grandview IA, 600 ... 87 F2
Grandview MO, 24881 ... 96 B3
Grandview TX, 1358 ... 59 E3
Grandview WA, 8377 ... 21 E1
Grandview Hts. OH, 6695 ... 206 B2
Grandview Plaza KS, 1184 ... 43 F2
Grandville MI, 16263 ... 75 F3
Grandy NC, 1000 ... 115 F1
Granger IN, 28284 ... 89 F1
Granger IA, 583 ... 86 C1
Granger TX, 1299 ... 61 E1
Granger WA, 2530 ... 13 E4
Grangeville ID, 3228 ... 22 B1
Granite OK, 1844 ... 50 C3
Granite UT, 2018 ... 257 B3
Granite City IL, 31301 ... 98 A3
Granite Co. MT, 2830 ... 15 D4
Granite Falls MN, 3070 ... 66 A4
Granite Falls NC, 4612 ... 111 F4
Granite Falls WA, 2347 ... 12 C2
Granite Quarry NC, 2175 ... 122 B1
Granite Shoals TX, 2040 ... 61 D1
Granite Sprs. NY, 2300 ... 148 B2
Graniteville SC, 2700 ... 121 F4
Graniteville VT, 2136 ... 81 E2
Grannis AR, 575 ... 116 C3
Grant AL, 665 ... 120 A2
Grant MI, 881 ... 75 F3
Grant MN, 4026 ... 67 D3
Grant NE, 1225 ... 34 B4
Grant City MO, 926 ... 86 B4
Grant Co. AR, 16464 ... 117 E3
Grant Co. IN, 73403 ... 89 F3
Grant Co. KS, 7909 ... 42 B4
Grant Co. KY, 22384 ... 100 B3
Grant Co. MN, 6289 ... 27 F1
Grant Co. NE, 747 ... 34 B2
Grant Co. NM, 31002 ... 55 F2
Grant Co. ND, 2841 ... 18 B4
Grant Co. OK, 5144 ... 51 E1
Grant Co. OR, 7935 ... 21 F3
Grant Co. SD, 7847 ... 27 F2
Grant Co. WA, 74698 ... 13 E3
Grant Co. WV, 11299 ... 102 B2
Grant Co. WI, 49597 ... 73 F3
Grant Hollow NY, 700 ... 188 E1
Grant Par. LA, 18698 ... 125 E4
Grant Park IL, 1358 ... 89 D2
Grants NM, 8806 ... 48 B3
Grantsburg WI, 1369 ... 67 D2
Grantsdale MT, 750 ... 23 D1
Grants Pass OR, 23003 ... 28 B2
Grantsville MD, 619 ... 102 B1
Grantsville UT, 6015 ... 31 E4
Grantsville WV, 565 ... 101 F3
Grant Town WV, 657 ... 102 A1
Grantville GA, 1309 ... 128 C1
Grantville PA, 1000 ... 93 E4
Granville IL, 1414 ... 88 B2
Granville NY, 2644 ... 81 D4
Granville ND, 286 ... 18 C2
Granville OH, 3167 ... 91 D4
Granville Co. NC, 48498 ... 113 D3
Grapeland TX, 1451 ... 124 A4
Grapeview WA, 2004 ... 12 C3
Grapevine TX, 42059 ... 59 E2
Grasonville MD, 2193 ... 145 D3
Grass Lake MI, 1082 ... 76 B4
Grass Valley CA, 10922 ... 36 C2
Graterford PA, 1400 ... 146 B2
Gratiot Co. MI, 42285 ... 76 A3
Gratis OH, 934 ... 100 B1
Graton CA, 1815 ... 36 A3
Gratz PA, 676 ... 93 E4
Gravel Ridge AR, 3232 ... 117 E2
Graves Co. KY, 37028 ... 108 C3
Gravette AR, 1810 ... 106 B3
Grawn MI, 1600 ... 69 F4
Gray GA, 1811 ... 129 D1
Gray KY, 650 ... 110 C2
Gray LA, 4958 ... 134 A3
Gray ME, 800 ... 82 B3
Gray TN, 1273 ... 111 E3
Gray Co. KS, 5904 ... 42 C4
Gray Co. TX, 22744 ... 50 B3
Gray Court SC, 1021 ... 121 F2
Grayland WA, 1002 ... 12 B4
Grayling MI, 1952 ... 70 C4
Graymoor-Devondale KY, 2925 ... 230 E1
Grays Harbor Co. WA, 67194 ... 12 B3
Grayslake IL, 18506 ... 74 C4
Grayson GA, 765 ... 121 D4

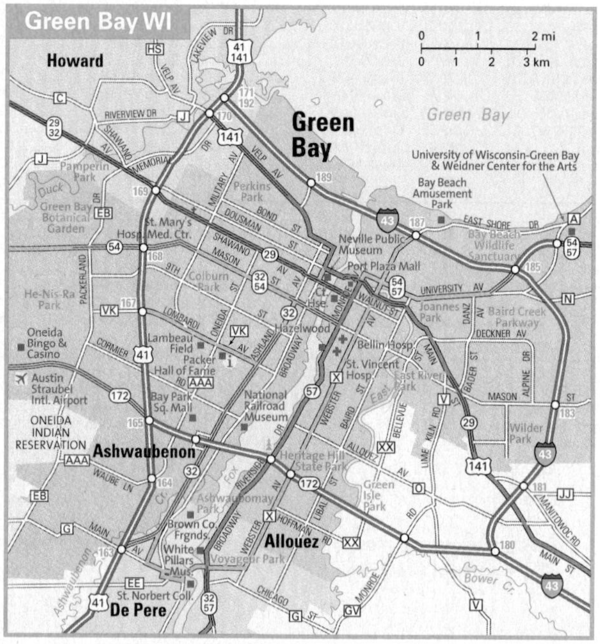
Green Bay WI
0 1 2 mi
0 1 2 3 km
Howard
Green Bay
Green Bay
University of Wisconsin-Green Bay & Weidner Center for the Arts
Bay Beach Amusement Park
Bay Beach Wildlife Sanctuary
Neville Public Museum
Port Plaza Mall
St. Mary's Hosp. Med. Ctr.
Green Bay Botanical Garden
Pamperin Park
Perkins Park
Colburn Park
He-Nis-Ra Park
Joannes Park
Baird Creek Parkway
Oneida Bingo & Casino
Lambeau Field
Packer Hall of Fame
Hazelwood
Bellin Hosp.
St. Vincent Hosp.
East River Park
Austin Straubel Intl. Airport
Bay Park Sq. Mall
National Railroad Museum
ONEIDA INDIAN RESERVATION
Ashwaubenon
Heritage Hill State Park
Wilder Park
Ashwaubomay Park
Green Isle Park
Brown Co. Frgnds.
White Pillars Mus.
Allouez
Voyageur Park
St. Norbert Coll.
De Pere
Bower Cr.

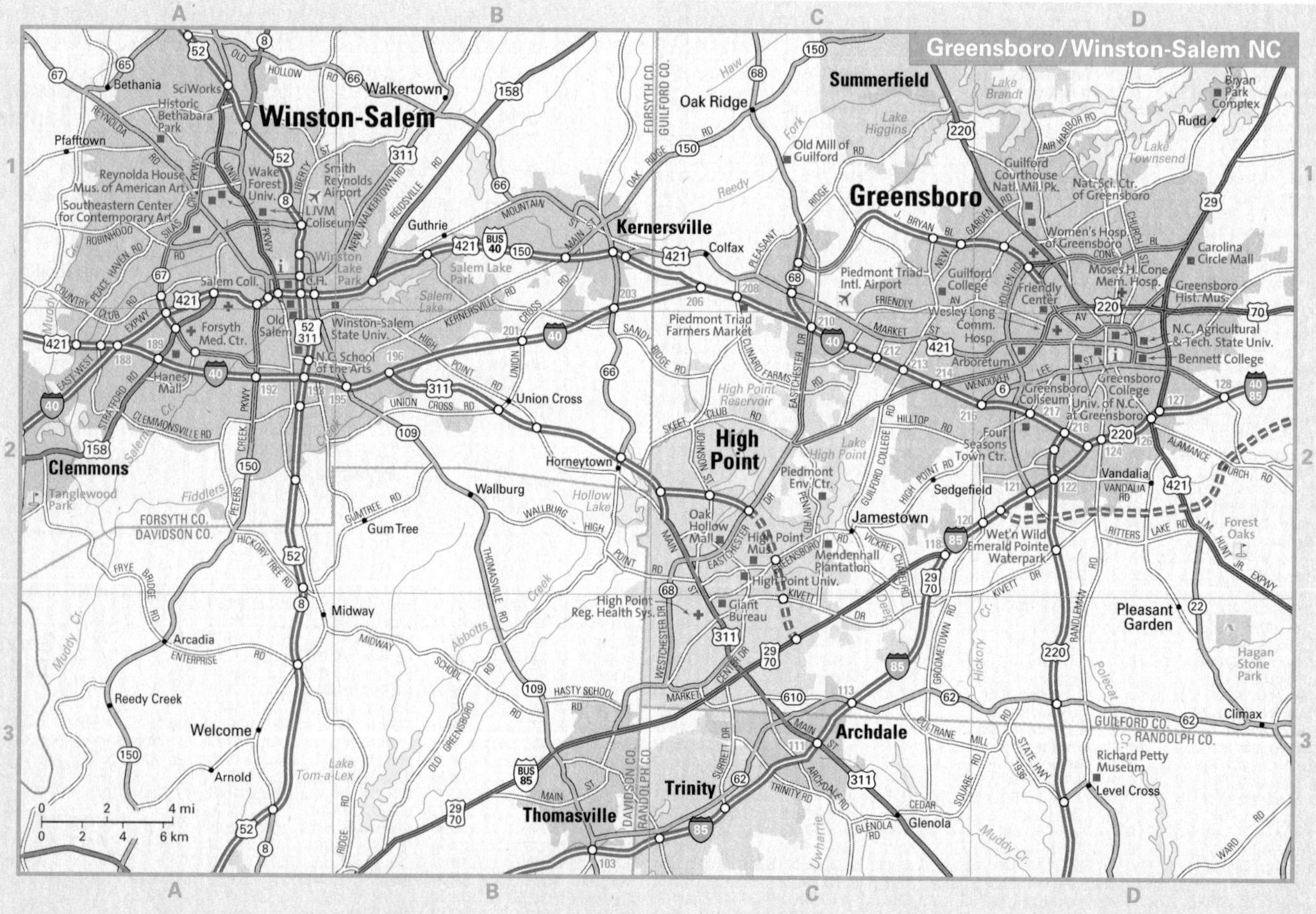
Greensboro / Winston-Salem NC
A B C D
1 2 3
Bethania
SciWorks
Historic Bethabara Park
Walkertown
Winston-Salem
Pfafftown
Reynolda House Mus. of American Art
Wake Forest Univ.
Smith Reynolds Airport
Southeastern Center for Contemporary Art
LJVM Coliseum
Guthrie
Kernersville
Colfax
Salem Lake Park
Winston Lake Park
Salem Coll.
Old Salem
Winston-Salem State Univ.
Forsyth Med. Ctr.
N.C. School of the Arts
Hanes Mall
Union Cross
Clemmons
Tanglewood Park
FORSYTH CO.
DAVIDSON CO.
Horneytown
Wallburg
Gum Tree
Midway
Arcadia
Reedy Creek
Welcome
Arnold
Thomasville
Trinity
Archdale
Glenola
Oak Ridge
Summerfield
Lake Brandt
Lake Higgins
Lake Townsend
Old Mill of Guilford
Guilford Courthouse Natl. Mil. Pk.
Nat. Sci. Ctr. of Greensboro
Greensboro
Piedmont Triad Intl. Airport
Guilford College
Friendly Center
Wesley Long Comm. Hosp.
Women's Hosp. of Greensboro
Moses H. Cone Mem. Hosp.
Greensboro Hist. Mus.
Carolina Circle Mall
N.C. Agricultural & Tech. State Univ.
Bennett College
Arboretum
Greensboro Coliseum
Greensboro College
Univ. of N.C. at Greensboro
Four Seasons Town Ctr.
Piedmont Triad Farmers Market
High Point Reservoir
High Point
Piedmont Env. Ctr.
Oak Hollow Mall
High Point Mus.
High Point Univ.
Mendenhall Plantation
Jamestown
Sedgefield
Wet'n Wild Emerald Pointe Waterpark
Vandalia
Forest Oaks
High Point Reg. Health Sys.
Gilbert Bureau
Pleasant Garden
Hagan Stone Park
Climax
GUILFORD CO.
RANDOLPH CO.
Richard Petty Museum
Level Cross
Rudd
Bryan Park Complex
0 2 4 mi
0 2 4 6 km

Arcadia ... A3	Climax ... D3	Guthrie ... B1	Level Cross ... D3	Reedy Creek ... A3	Trinity ... C3	Welcome ... A3
Archdale ... C3	Colfax ... C1	High Pt. ... C2	Midway ... A3	Rudd ... D1	Union Cross ... B2	Winston-Salem ... A1
Arnold ... A3	Glenola ... C3	Horneytown ... B2	Oak Ridge ... C1	Sedgefield ... C2	Vandalia ... D2	
Bethania ... A1	Greensboro ... C1	Jamestown ... C2	Pfafftown ... A1	Summerfield ... C1	Walkertown ... B1	
Clemmons ... A2	Gum Tree ... B2	Kernersville ... B1	Pleasant Garden ... D3	Thomasville ... B3	Wallburg ... B2	

Grayson KY, 3877 101 D4
Grayson LA, 531 125 E3
Grayson Co. KY, 24053 109 F1
Grayson Co. TX, 110595 59 F1
Grayson Co. VA, 17917 111 F3
Gray Summit MO, 2640 98 A3
Graysville AL, 2344 119 F4
Graysville TN, 1411 120 B1
Grayville IL, 1725 99 D4
Greasewood AZ, 581 47 F3
Great Barrington MA, 2459 94 B2
Great Bend KS, 15345 43 D3
Great Bend NY, 801 79 E1
Great Bend PA, 700 93 F1
Great Falls MT, 56690 15 F3
Great Falls SC, 2194 122 A2
Great Falls VA, 8549 144 B3
Great Meadows NJ, 1264 94 A4
Great Mills MD, 2600 103 E4
Great Neck NY, 9538 148 B4
Great Neck Estates NY, 2756 241 G3
Great Neck Gardens NY, 1089 241 G2
Great Neck Plaza NY, 6433 241 G2
Great River NY, 1546 149 D4
Greece NY, 14614 78 C3
Greeley CO, 76930 33 E4
Greeley NE, 531 35 D3
Greeley Co. KS, 1534 42 B3
Greeley Co. NE, 2714 35 D3
Greeleyville SC, 452 122 B4
Green OH, 22817 91 E3
Green OR, 6174 28 B1
Greenacres CA, 7400 45 D4
Greenacres FL, 27569 143 F1
Greenback TN, 954 110 C4
Green Bay WI, 102313 68 C4
Greenbelt MD, 21456 144 B3
Greenbrier AR, 3042 117 E1
Greenbrier TN, 4940 109 F3
Greenbrier Co. WV, 34453 102 A4
Greenbush MA, 550 151 E2
Greenbush MN, 784 19 F1
Greencastle IN, 9880 99 E1
Greencastle PA, 3722 103 D1
Green City MO, 688 87 D4
Green Co. KY, 11518 110 A1
Green Co. WI, 33647 74 B4
Green Cove Sprs. FL, 5378 139 D3
Green Creek NJ, 1300 104 C4
Greendale IN, 4296 100 B2
Greendale MO, 722 256 B2
Greendale WI, 14405 234 C3
Greene IA, 1099 73 D3
Greene ME, 950 82 B2
Greene NY, 1701 79 E4
Greene Co. AL, 9974 127 E2
Greene Co. AR, 37331 108 A3
Greene Co. GA, 14406 121 E4
Greene Co. IL, 14761 98 A2
Greene Co. IN, 33157 99 E2
Greene Co. IA, 10366 86 B1
Greene Co. MS, 13299 127 D4
Greene Co. MO, 240391 107 D1
Greene Co. NY, 48195 94 A2
Greene Co. NC, 18974 115 C3
Greene Co. OH, 147886 100 C1
Greene Co. PA, 40672 102 A1
Greene Co. TN, 62909 111 D3
Greene Co. VA, 15244 102 C4
Greenevers NC, 560 123 E2
Greeneville TN, 15198 111 D4
Greenfield CA, 12583 44 B3
Greenfield IL, 1179 98 A2
Greenfield IN, 14600 99 F1
Greenfield IA, 2129 86 B2
Greenfield MA, 13716 94 C1
Greenfield MO, 1358 106 C1
Greenfield NH, 375 95 D1
Greenfield OH, 4906 100 C2
Greenfield TN, 2208 108 C4
Greenfield WI, 35476 234 C3
Green Forest AR, 2717 107 D3
Green Harbor MA, 2397 151 E2
Green Haven MD, 17415 144 C2
Green Haven NY, 3000 148 C1
Green Hill TN, 7068 109 F3
Greenhills OH, 4103 204 B1
Green Island NY, 2278 188 E2
Green Lake WI, 1100 74 B2
Green Lake Co. WI, 19105 74 B2
Greenland AR, 907 106 C4
Greenland NH, 1100 82 A4
Green Lane PA, 584 146 B2
Greenleaf ID, 862 22 A4
Greenlee Co. AZ, 8547 55 E2
Greenmount MD, 600 144 B1
Green Mtn. Falls CO, 773 205 C1
Green Oaks IL, 3572 203 C1
Green Park MO, 2666 256 B3
Green Pond NJ, 1400 148 A3
Greenport NY, 2048 149 E3
Green River UT, 973 39 F2
Green River WY, 11808 32 A3
Greensboro AL, 2731 127 E2
Greensboro FL, 619 137 D2
Greensboro GA, 3238 121 D4
Greensboro MD, 1632 145 E3
Greensboro NC, 223891 112 B4
Greensboro Bend VT, 350 81 E2
Greensburg IN, 10260 100 A2
Greensburg KS, 1574 43 D4
Greensburg KY, 2396 110 A2
Greensburg LA, 631 134 B1
Greensburg PA, 15889 92 A4
Green Sprs. OH, 1247 90 C2
Greensville Co. VA, 11560 113 E2
Greentown IN, 2546 89 F4
Greentown OH, 3154 91 E3
Green Tree PA, 4719 250 B2
Greenup IL, 1532 99 D2
Greenup KY, 1198 101 D3
Greenup Co. KY, 36891 101 D3
Green Valley AZ, 17283 55 D3
Green Valley CA, 600 52 C2
Green Valley IL, 728 88 B4
Green Valley MD, 12262 144 B2
Greenview IL, 862 88 B4
Green Vil. PA, 1100 103 D1
Greenville AL, 7228 128 A3
Greenville CA, 1160 36 C1
Greenville DE, 2332 146 B3
Greenville FL, 837 137 F2
Greenville GA, 946 128 C1
Greenville IL, 6955 98 B3
Greenville IN, 591 99 F4
Greenville KY, 4398 109 E2
Greenville ME, 1319 84 C4
Greenville MI, 7935 75 F3
Greenville MS, 41633 126 A1
Greenville MO, 451 108 A2
Greenville NH, 1131 95 D1
Greenville NY, 493 94 B2
Greenville NC, 60476 115 D2
Greenville OH, 13294 90 A4
Greenville PA, 6380 91 F2
Greenville RI, 8626 150 C3
Greenville SC, 56002 121 E2
Greenville TX, 23960 59 F2
Greenville VA, 886 102 B4
Greenville WI, 950 74 C1
Greenville Co. SC, 379616 121 E2
Greenville Jct. ME, 850 84 C4
Greenwich CT, 61101 148 C3
Greenwich NY, 1902 81 D4
Greenwich OH, 1525 91 D3
Greenwood AR, 7112 116 C1
Greenwood DE, 837 145 E3
Greenwood FL, 735 137 D1
Greenwood IN, 36037 99 F1
Greenwood LA, 2458 124 C2
Greenwood MS, 18425 118 B4
Greenwood MO, 3952 96 B3
Greenwood NE, 544 35 F3
Greenwood SC, 22071 121 F3
Greenwood WI, 1079 68 A4
Greenwood Co. KS, 7673 43 F3
Greenwood Co. SC, 66271 121 F3
Greenwood Lake NY, 3411 148 A2
Greenwood Vil. CO, 11035 209 C4
Greer SC, 16843 121 F2
Greer Co. OK, 6061 50 C3
Greers Ferry AR, 930 117 E1
Gregg Co. TX, 111379 124 B2
Gregory SD, 1342 35 D1
Gregory TX, 2318 63 F2
Gregory Co. SD, 4792 35 D1
Greilickville MI, 1415 69 F4
Grenada MS, 14879 118 B4
Grenada Co. MS, 23263 118 B4
Gresham OR, 90205 20 C2
Gresham WI, 575 68 C4
Gresham Park GA, 9215 190 E4
Gretna FL, 1709 137 D2
Gretna LA, 17423 134 B3
Gretna NE, 2355 35 F3
Gretna VA, 1257 112 C2
Greybull WY, 1815 24 C3
Gridley CA, 5382 36 B2
Gridley IL, 1411 88 C3
Gridley KS, 372 96 A4
Griffin GA, 23451 129 D1
Griffith IN, 17334 89 D2
Grifton NC, 2073 115 D3
Griggs Co. ND, 2754 19 D3
Griggsville IL, 1258 98 A1
Grimes AL, 459 128 B4
Grimes IA, 5098 86 C2
Grimes Co. TX, 23552 132 A2
Grinnell IA, 9105 87 D1
Griswold IA, 1039 86 B2
Groesbeck OH, 7202 204 A2
Groesbeck TX, 4291 59 F4
Groom TX, 587 50 B3
Grosse Pointe MI, 5670 210 D3
Grosse Pointe Farms MI, 9764 210 D3
Grosse Pointe Park MI, 12443 210 D3
Grosse Pointe Shores MI, 2823 210 D3
Grosse Pointe Woods MI, 17080 76 C4
Grosse Tete LA, 670 133 F2
Grosvenor Dale CT, 700 150 B2
Groton CT, 10010 149 F2
Groton MA, 1113 95 D1
Groton NY, 2470 79 D4
Groton SD, 1356 27 E2
Groton VT, 450 81 E2
Groton Long Pt. CT, 667 149 F2
Grottoes VA, 2114 102 C4
Grove OK, 5131 106 B3
Grove City FL, 2092 140 C4
Grove City MN, 608 66 B3
Grove City OH, 27075 101 D1
Grove City PA, 8024 92 A2
Grove Hill AL, 1438 127 E4
Groveland CA, 3388 37 D4
Groveland FL, 2360 140 C1
Groveland MA, 2800 95 E1
Groveport OH, 3865 101 D1
Grover NC, 698 122 A1
Grover Beach CA, 13067 52 A1
Groves TX, 15733 132 C3
Groveton NH, 1197 81 F2
Groveton TX, 1107 132 B1
Groveton VA, 21296 144 B4
Grovetown GA, 6089 121 F4
Grubbs AR, 438 107 F4
Gruetli-Laager TN, 1867 120 A1
Grundy VA, 1105 111 E2
Grundy Ctr. IA, 2596 73 D4
Grundy Co. IL, 37535 88 C2
Grundy Co. IA, 12369 73 D4
Grundy Co. MO, 10432 86 C4
Grundy Co. TN, 14332 120 A1
Gruver TX, 1162 50 B2
Guadalupe AZ, 5228 249 C3
Guadalupe CA, 5659 52 A1
Guadalupe Co. NM, 4680 49 E4
Guadalupe Co. TX, 89023 61 E3
Guerneville CA, 2441 36 A3
Guernsey WY, 1147 33 E2
Guernsey Co. OH, 40792 91 E4
Gueydan LA, 1598 133 E3
Guilderland NY, 1700 188 C2
Guildhall VT, 40 81 F2
Guilford CT, 2603 149 E2
Guilford ME, 945 82 C1
Guilford MD, 2700 193 A5
Guilford Co. NC, 421048 112 B4
Guin AL, 2389 119 E4
Gulf Breeze FL, 5665 135 F2
Gulf Co. FL, 13332 137 D3
Gulfcrest AL, 600 135 E1
Gulf Gate Estates FL, 10911 140 B4
Gulfport FL, 12527 140 B3
Gulfport MS, 71127 135 D2
Gulf Shores AL, 5044 135 E2
Gulf Stream FL, 716 143 F1
Gun Barrel City TX, 5145 59 F3
Gunnison CO, 5409 40 C3
Gunnison MS, 633 118 A4
Gunnison UT, 2394 39 E2
Gunnison Co. CO, 13956 40 C2
Gunter TX, 1230 59 F1
Guntersville AL, 7395 120 A3
Guntown MS, 1183 119 D3
Gurdon AR, 2276 117 D4
Gurley AL, 876 119 F2
Gurn Spr. NY, 600 80 C4
Gustavus AK, 429 155 D4
Gustine CA, 4698 36 C4
Guthrie KY, 1469 109 E3
Guthrie OK, 9925 51 E2
Guthrie TX, 10 58 C1
Guthrie Ctr. IA, 1668 86 B2
Guthrie Co. IA, 11353 86 B2
Guthriesville PA, 1800 146 B3
Guttenberg IA, 1987 73 F4
Guttenberg NJ, 10807 240 D2
Guymon OK, 10472 50 B1
Guys TN, 483 119 D2
Guyton GA, 917 130 B2
Gwinn MI, 1965 69 D1
Gwinner ND, 717 27 E1
Gwinnett Co. GA, 588448 121 D4
Gwynn VA, 600 113 F1
Gypsum CO, 3654 40 C1
Gypsum KS, 414 43 E2

H

Haakon Co. SD, 2196 26 B3
Habersham Co. GA, 35902 121 D2
Hacienda Hts. CA, 53122 228 E3
Hackberry LA, 1699 133 D3
Hackensack NJ, 42677 148 B3
Hackett AR, 694 116 C1
Hackettstown NJ, 10403 94 A4
Hackleburg AL, 1527 119 E3
Haddam CT, 650 149 E1
Haddonfield NJ, 11659 146 C3
Haddon Hts. NJ, 7547 248 D4
Hadley MA, 1200 150 A1
Hadley NY, 2240 80 C4
Hagaman NY, 1357 80 C4
Hagan GA, 898 129 F3
Hagerhill KY, 900 111 D1
Hagerman ID, 656 30 C1
Hagerman NM, 1168 57 E2
Hagerstown IN, 1768 100 A1
Hagerstown MD, 36687 144 A1
Hahira GA, 1626 137 F1
Hahnville LA, 2792 134 B3
Haiku HI, 6578 153 D1
Hailey ID, 6200 22 C4
Haileyville OK, 891 116 A2
Haines AK, 1811 155 D3
Haines OR, 416 21 F2
Haines City FL, 13174 141 D2
Halaula HI, 495 153 E2
Halawa HI, 13891 152 C3
Hale Ctr. TX, 2263 58 A1
Hale Co. AL, 17185 127 E2
Hale Co. TX, 36602 58 A1
Haledon NJ, 8252 148 B3
Haleiwa HI, 2225 152 A2
Hales Corners WI, 7765 74 C3
Haleyville AL, 4182 119 E3
Halfmoon NY, 2300 188 E1
Half Moon NC, 6645 115 D4
Half Moon Bay CA, 11842 36 B4
Halfway MD, 10065 144 A1
Halfway OR, 337 22 A2
Halifax MA, 1000 151 D2
Halifax NC, 344 113 E3
Halifax PA, 875 93 D4
Halifax VA, 1389 112 C2
Halifax Co. NC, 57370 113 E4
Halifax Co. VA, 37355 112 C2
Haliimaile HI, 895 153 D1
Hallam PA, 1532 103 E1
Hallandale Beach FL, 34282 143 F2
Hall Co. GA, 139277 121 D3
Hall Co. NE, 53534 35 D4
Hall Co. TX, 3782 50 B4
Hallettsville TX, 2345 61 F3
Halliday ND, 227 18 A3
Hallock MN, 1196 19 E1
Hallowell ME, 2467 82 C2
Hall Park OK, 1088 51 E3
Halls TN, 2311 108 C4
Hallsburg TX, 518 59 F4
Halls Crossroads TN, 2100 110 C4
Halls Gap KY, 450 110 B1
Hallstead PA, 1216 93 F1
Hallsville MO, 978 97 E2
Hallsville TX, 2772 124 B2
Halsey OR, 724 20 B3
Halstad MN, 622 19 F3
Halstead KS, 1873 43 E3
Haltom City TX, 39018 207 B2
Hamblen Co. TN, 58128 111 D3
Hamburg AR, 3039 125 F1
Hamburg IA, 1240 86 A3
Hamburg MN, 538 66 C4
Hamburg NY, 3105 148 A2
Hamburg NY, 10116 78 B4
Hamburg PA, 4114 146 A1
Hamden CT, 56913 149 D2
Hamden OH, 871 101 D2
Hamel IL, 570 98 B3
Hamilton AL, 6786 119 D3
Hamilton GA, 307 128 C2
Hamilton IL, 3029 87 F4
Hamilton IN, 1233 90 A2
Hamilton MI, 1300 75 F4
Hamilton MO, 1813 96 C1
Hamilton MT, 3705 23 D1
Hamilton NY, 3509 79 E3
Hamilton NC, 516 113 E4
Hamilton OH, 60690 100 B2
Hamilton RI, 2500 150 C4
Hamilton TX, 2977 59 E4
Hamilton VA, 562 144 A2
Hamilton City CA, 1903 36 B1
Hamilton Co. FL, 13327 138 C2
Hamilton Co. IL, 8621 98 C4
Hamilton Co. IN, 182740 99 F1
Hamilton Co. IA, 16438 72 C4
Hamilton Co. KS, 2670 42 A3
Hamilton Co. NE, 9403 35 E4
Hamilton Co. NY, 5379 79 F2
Hamilton Co. OH, 845303 100 B2
Hamilton Co. TN, 307896 120 B1
Hamilton Co. TX, 8229 59 D4
Hamilton Square NJ, 26419 147 D2
Ham Lake MN, 12710 67 D3
Hamler OH, 650 90 B2
Hamlet IN, 820 89 E2
Hamlet NC, 6018 122 C2
Hamlin TX, 2248 58 C2
Hamlin WV, 1119 101 E4
Hamlin Co. SD, 5540 27 E3
Hammon OK, 469 50 C3
Hammond IN, 83048 89 D2
Hammond LA, 17639 134 B2
Hammond WI, 1153 67 E4
Hammondsport NY, 731 78 C4
Hammondville AL, 486 120 A2
Hammonton NJ, 12604 147 D4
Hamorton PA, 1400 146 B3
Hampden ME, 4126 83 D1
Hampden Co. MA, 456228 150 A2
Hampden Sydney VA, 1264 113 D2
Hampshire IL, 2900 88 C1
Hampshire Co. MA, 152251 94 C2
Hampshire Co. WV, 20203 102 C2
Hampstead MD, 5060 144 B1
Hampstead NH, 1100 95 E1
Hampton AR, 1579 117 E4
Hampton FL, 431 138 C3
Hampton GA, 3857 129 D1
Hampton IL, 1626 208 C1
Hampton IA, 4218 73 D4
Hampton MD, 5004 193 C1
Hampton NE, 439 35 E4
Hampton NH, 9126 95 E1
Hampton NJ, 1546 104 C1
Hampton PA, 633 103 E1
Hampton SC, 2837 130 B2
Hampton TN, 1300 111 E3
Hampton VA, 146437 113 F2
Hampton Bays NY, 12236 149 E3
Hampton Beach NH, 1800 95 E1
Hampton Co. SC, 21386 130 B2
Hampton Park NY, 950 149 E3
Hamtramck MI, 22976 210 C3
Hana HI, 709 153 E1
Hanahan SC, 12937 131 D1
Hanamaulu HI, 3272 152 B1
Hanapepe HI, 2153 152 B1
Hanceville AL, 2951 119 F3
Hancock MD, 1725 102 C1
Hancock MI, 4323 65 F3
Hancock MN, 717 66 A3
Hancock NH, 375 81 E4
Hancock NY, 1189 93 F1
Hancock Co. GA, 10076 129 E1
Hancock Co. IL, 20121 87 F4
Hancock Co. IN, 55391 100 A1
Hancock Co. IA, 12100 72 C3
Hancock Co. KY, 8392 109 F1
Hancock Co. ME, 51791 83 D1
Hancock Co. MS, 42967 134 C2
Hancock Co. OH, 71295 90 B3
Hancock Co. TN, 6786 111 D3
Hancock Co. WV, 32667 91 F4
Hand Co. SD, 3741 27 D3
Hanford CA, 41686 45 D3
Hankinson ND, 1058 27 F1
Hanley Hills MO, 2124 256 B2
Hanna WY, 873 33 D2
Hanna City IL, 1013 88 B3
Hannibal MO, 17757 97 F1
Hannibal NY, 542 79 D3
Hanover CT, 700 149 F1
Hanover IL, 836 74 A4
Hanover IN, 2834 100 A3
Hanover KS, 653 43 F1
Hanover MA, 2200 151 E2
Hanover MN, 1355 66 C3
Hanover NH, 8162 81 E3
Hanover NJ, 11500 148 A3
Hanover OH, 885 91 D4
Hanover PA, 14535 103 E1
Hanover VA, 225 113 E1
Hanover Co. VA, 86320 103 D4
Hanover Park IL, 38278 203 B3
Hansen ID, 970 30 C1
Hansford Co. TX, 5369 50 B2
Hanson KY, 625 109 E1
Hanson MA, 2044 151 D2
Hanson Co. SD, 3139 27 E4
Hapeville GA, 6180 190 D5
Happy TX, 647 50 A4
Happy Camp CA, 800 28 B2
Happy Valley OR, 4519 251 D2
Harahan LA, 9885 239 B2
Haralson Co. GA, 25690 120 B4
Harbert MI, 1619 89 E1
Harbeson DE, 375 145 F4
Harbor OR, 2622 28 A2
Harbor Beach MI, 1837 76 C2
Harbor Bluffs FL, 2807 266 A2
Harbor Hills NY, 563 241 G2
Harbor Hills OH, 1303 101 D1
Harbor Sprs. MI, 1567 70 B3
Harbour Hts. FL, 2873 140 C4
Hardee Co. FL, 26938 140 C3
Hardeeville SC, 1793 130 B3
Hardeman Co. TN, 28105 118 C1
Hardeman Co. TX, 4724 50 C4
Hardin IL, 959 98 A2
Hardin KY, 564 109 D2
Hardin MO, 614 96 C2
Hardin MT, 3384 24 C1
Hardin TX, 755 132 B2
Hardin Co. IL, 4800 109 D1
Hardin Co. IA, 18812 73 D4
Hardin Co. KY, 94174 110 A1
Hardin Co. OH, 31945 90 C3
Hardin Co. TN, 25578 119 D1
Hardin Co. TX, 48073 132 C2
Harding Co. NM, 810 49 E2
Harding Co. SD, 1353 25 F1
Hardinsburg KY, 2345 109 F1
Hardwick GA, 5135 129 E1
Hardwick VT, 1100 81 E2
Hardy AR, 578 107 F3
Hardy Co. WV, 12669 102 C2
Harewood Park MD, 3400 145 D1
Harford Co. MD, 218590 144 C1
Hargill TX, 900 63 E4
Harker Hts. TX, 17308 59 E4
Harkers Island NC, 1525 115 E4
Harlan IA, 5282 86 A2
Harlan KY, 2081 111 D2
Harlan Co. KY, 33202 111 D2
Harlan Co. NE, 3786 35 D4
Harlem FL, 2730 141 D4
Harlem GA, 1814 129 F1
Harlem MT, 848 16 C2
Harleysville PA, 8795 146 C2
Harleyville SC, 594 130 C1
Harlingen TX, 57564 63 F4
Harlowton MT, 1062 16 B4
Harmon Co. OK, 3283 50 C4
Harmony IN, 589 99 E1
Harmony MN, 1080 73 E2
Harmony NC, 526 112 A4
Harmony PA, 937 92 A3
Harmony RI, 850 150 C3
Harnett Co. NC, 91025 123 D1
Harney Co. OR, 7609 21 E4
Harold KY, 1400 111 E1
Harper KS, 1567 43 E4
Harper TX, 1006 60 C1
Harper Co. KS, 6536 43 E4
Harper Co. OK, 3562 50 C1
Harpersville AL, 1620 128 A1
Harper Woods MI, 14254 210 D2
Harrah OK, 4719 51 E3
Harrah WA, 542 13 D4
Harriman NY, 2252 148 B2
Harriman TN, 6744 110 B4
Harrington DE, 3174 145 E3

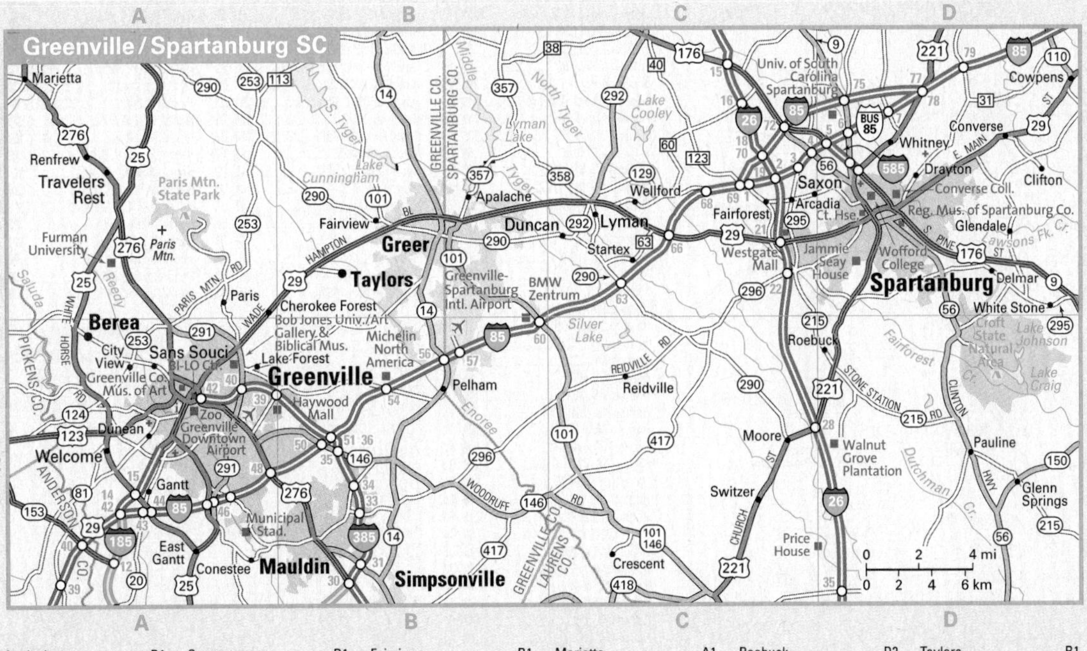

Greenville / Spartanburg SC
A
B
C
D
1
2
Marietta
Renfrew
Travelers Rest
Paris Mtn. State Park
Furman University
Paris Mtn.
Cunningham
Apalache
Fairview
Greer
Taylors
Duncan
Lyman
Startex
Wellford
Lake Cooley
Lyman Lake
Fairforest
Westgate Mall
Jammie Seay House
Univ. of South Carolina Spartanburg
Cowpens
Whitney
Converse
Drayton
Clifton
Saxon
Arcadia
Converse Coll.
Reg. Mus. of Spartanburg Co.
Glendale
Wofford College
Spartanburg
Delmar
White Stone
Croft State Natural Area
Lake Johnson
Lake Craig
Paris
Cherokee Forest
Bob Jones Univ./Art Gallery & Biblical Mus.
Berea
Sans Souci
City View
Greenville Co. Mus. of Art
Lake Forest
Greenville
Michelin North America
Greenville-Spartanburg Intl. Airport
BMW Zentrum
Silver Lake
Pelham
Reidville
Roebuck
Haywood Mall
Greenville Downtown Airport
Zoo
Dunean
Welcome
Gantt
Municipal Stad.
East Gantt
Conestee
Mauldin
Simpsonville
Crescent
Moore
Switzer
Walnut Grove Plantation
Pauline
Glenn Springs
Price House
GREENVILLE CO.
SPARTANBURG CO.
GREENVILLE CO.
LAURENS CO.
PICKENS CO.
0 2 4 mi
0 2 4 6 km

Apalache B1
Arcadia C1
Berea A2
Cherokee Forest A1
City View A2
Clifton D1
Conestee A2
Converse D1
Cowpens D1
Crescent C2
Delmar D1
Drayton D1
Duncan C1
Dunean A2
E. Gantt A2
Fairforest C1
Fairview B1
Gantt A2
Glendale D1
Glenn Sprs. D2
Greenville A2
Greer B1
Lake Forest A2
Lyman C1
Marietta A1
Mauldin B2
Moore C2
Paris A2
Pauline D2
Pelham B2
Reidville C2
Renfrew A1
Roebuck D2
Sans Souci A2
Saxon C1
Simpsonville B2
Slater A1
Spartanburg D1
Startex C1
Switzer C2
Taylors B1
Travelers Rest A1
Welcome A2
Wellford C1
White Stone D1
Whitney D1

Figures after entries indicate population, page number, and grid reference.

Harrington ME, 425 .... 83 E2
Harrington WA, 426 .... 13 F3
Harris MN, 1121 .... 67 D3
Harrisburg AR, 2192 .... 118 A1
Harrisburg IL, 9860 .... 109 D1
Harrisburg NE, 75 .... 33 F3
Harrisburg NC, 4493 .... 122 B1
Harrisburg OR, 2795 .... 20 B3
Harrisburg PA, 48950 .... 93 D4
Harrisburg SD, 958 .... 27 F4
Harris Co. GA, 23695 .... 128 C2
Harris Co. TX, 3400578 .... 132 A3
Harrison AR, 12152 .... 107 D3
Harrison GA, 509 .... 129 F2
Harrison ID, 267 .... 14 B3
Harrison ME, 375 .... 82 B2
Harrison MI, 2108 .... 76 A1
Harrison NE, 279 .... 33 F1
Harrison NJ, 14424 .... 148 B4
Harrison NY, 24154 .... 148 C3

Bressler C2	Fair Acres B2	Marsh Run C2	Penbrook B1	Summerdale A1
Camp Hill A2	Good Hope A1	Mechanicsburg A2	Progress B1	W. Enola A1
Colonial Park C1	Green Lane Farms B2	New Cumberland B2	Reesers Summit B2	W. Fairview A1
Eberlys Mill B2	Harrisburg B1	Oakleigh C2	Rossmoyne A2	White Hill A2
Edgemont B1	Highland Park B2	Oberlin C2	Rossmoyne Manor A2	Wormleysburg B2
Enhaut C2	Highspire C2	Paxtang B1	Rutherford Hts. C1	
Enola A1	Lawnton C1	Paxtang Manor C1	Shiremanstown A2	
Estherton B1	Lemoyne B2	Paxtonia C1	Steelton B2	

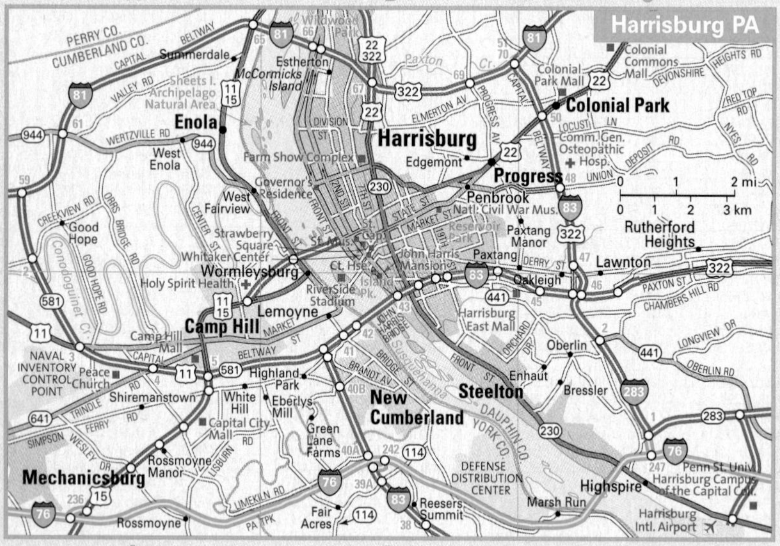

Harrisburg PA
Harrisburg
Enola
Colonial Park
Progress
Camp Hill
Lemoyne
Wormleysburg
New Cumberland
Steelton
Mechanicsburg
Highspire
Penbrook
Edgemont
Rutherford Heights
Lawnton
Oakleigh
Paxtang
Summerdale
Estherton
West Enola
West Fairview
Good Hope
Shiremanstown
Rossmoyne
Oberlin
Enhaut
Bressler
Marsh Run
Reesers Summit
Fair Acres
Harrisburg Intl. Airport

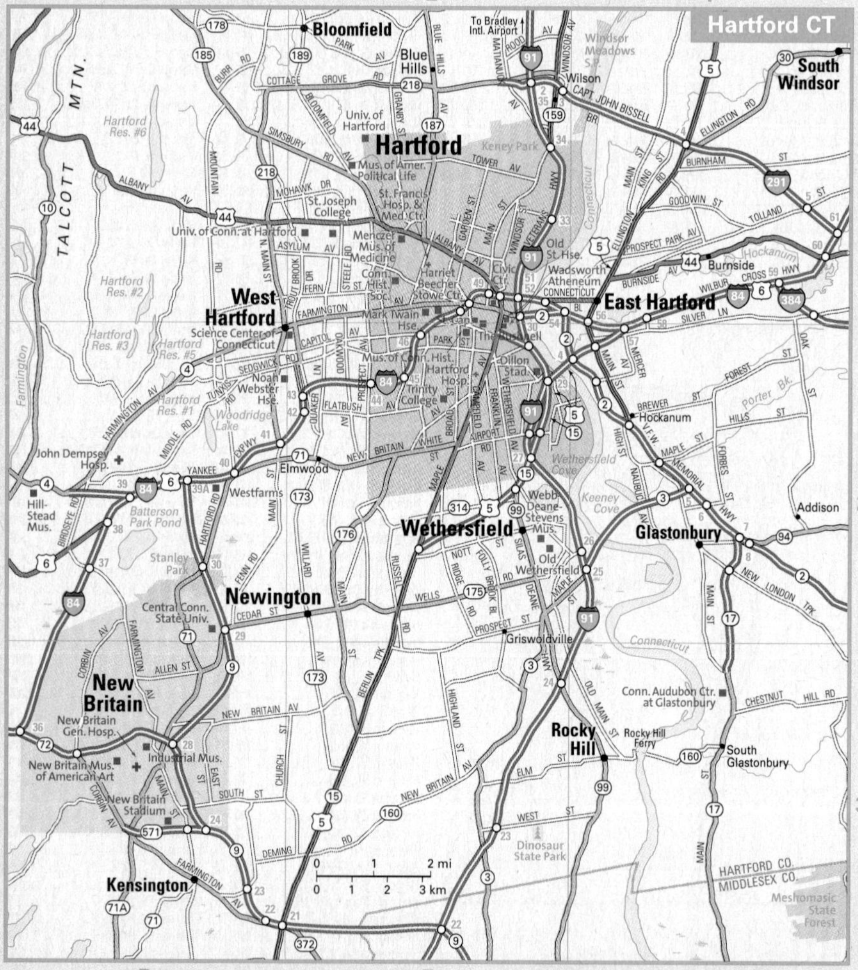

Hartford CT
Hartford
West Hartford
East Hartford
Bloomfield
Blue Hills
South Windsor
Wilson
Burnside
Elmwood
Newington
Wethersfield
Glastonbury
New Britain
Rocky Hill
Kensington
Addison
Hockanum
Griswoldville
South Glastonbury

Addison F2	E. Hartford F1	Hartford E1	Newington E2	W. Hartford D2
Bloomfield E1	Elmwood E2	Hockanum F2	Rocky Hill F3	Wethersfield E2
Blue Hills E1	Glastonbury F2	Kensington D3	S. Glastonbury F3	Wilson E1
Burnside F1	Griswoldville E2	New Britain D3	S. Windsor F1	

Harrison OH, 7487 .... 100 B2
Harrison TN, 7630 .... 120 B1
Harrisonburg LA, 746 .... 125 F3
Harrisonburg VA, 40468 .... 102 C3
Harrison Co. IN, 34325 .... 99 F4
Harrison Co. IA, 15666 .... 86 A1
Harrison Co. KY, 17983 .... 100 B3
Harrison Co. MS, 189601 .... 134 C2
Harrison Co. MO, 8850 .... 86 C4
Harrison Co. OH, 15856 .... 91 E4
Harrison Co. TX, 62110 .... 124 B2
Harrison Co. WV, 68652 .... 102 A2
Harrisonville MO, 8946 .... 96 B3
Harristown IL, 1338 .... 98 C1
Harrisville MD, 600 .... 146 A4
Harrisville MI, 514 .... 71 D4
Harrisville NH, 400 .... 95 D1
Harrisville NY, 653 .... 79 E1
Harrisville PA, 883 .... 92 A3
Harrisville RI, 1561 .... 150 C2
Harrisville UT, 3645 .... 31 E3
Harrisville WV, 1842 .... 101 F2
Harrodsburg KY, 8014 .... 110 B1
Harrogate TN, 2865 .... 110 C3
Harrold SD, 209 .... 27 D3
Hart MI, 1950 .... 75 E2
Hart TX, 1198 .... 50 A4
Hart Co. GA, 22997 .... 121 E3
Hart Co. KY, 17445 .... 110 A2
Hartford AL, 2369 .... 136 C1
Hartford AR, 772 .... 116 C2
Hartford CT, 121578 .... 150 A3
Hartford IL, 1545 .... 98 A3
Hartford IA, 759 .... 86 C2
Hartford KS, 500 .... 43 F3
Hartford KY, 2571 .... 109 E1
Hartford MI, 2476 .... 89 F1
Hartford SD, 1844 .... 27 F4
Hartford WV, 519 .... 101 E2
Hartford WI, 10905 .... 74 C3
Hartford City IN, 6928 .... 90 A4
Hartford Co. CT, 857183 .... 150 A3
Hartington NE, 1640 .... 35 E1
Hartland ME, 872 .... 82 C1
Hartland VT, 500 .... 81 E3
Hartland WI, 7905 .... 74 C3
Hartley IA, 1733 .... 72 A3
Hartley Co. TX, 5537 .... 50 A2
Hartly DE, 78 .... 145 E2
Hartman AR, 596 .... 116 C1
Harts WV, 2361 .... 101 E4
Hartselle AL, 12019 .... 119 F3
Hartshorne OK, 2102 .... 116 A2
Hartsville SC, 7556 .... 122 B3
Hartsville TN, 2395 .... 109 F3
Hartville MO, 607 .... 107 E2
Hartville OH, 2174 .... 91 E3
Hartwell GA, 4188 .... 121 E3
Harvard IL, 7996 .... 74 C4
Harvard MA, 800 .... 150 C1
Harvard NE, 998 .... 35 E4
Harvest AL, 3054 .... 119 F2
Harvey IL, 30000 .... 203 E6
Harvey LA, 22226 .... 239 C2
Harvey MI, 1321 .... 69 D1
Harvey ND, 1989 .... 18 C3
Harvey Co. KS, 32869 .... 43 E3
Harveysburg OH, 563 .... 100 C2
Harveys Lake PA, 2888 .... 93 E2
Harwich MA, 1832 .... 151 F3
Harwich Port MA, 1809 .... 151 F3
Harwinton CT, 3242 .... 94 C3
Harwood ND, 607 .... 19 F4
Harwood Hts. IL, 8297 .... 203 D3
Hasbrouck Hts. NJ, 11662 .... 240 C1
Haskell AR, 2645 .... 117 E3
Haskell OK, 1765 .... 106 A4
Haskell TX, 3106 .... 58 C2
Haskell Co. KS, 4307 .... 42 B4
Haskell Co. OK, 11792 .... 116 B1
Haskell Co. TX, 6093 .... 58 C2
Haskins OH, 638 .... 90 C2
Haslet TX, 1134 .... 207 A1
Haslett MI, 11283 .... 76 A4
Hastings FL, 521 .... 139 D3
Hastings MI, 7095 .... 75 F4
Hastings MN, 18204 .... 67 D4
Hastings NE, 24064 .... 35 E4
Hastings PA, 1398 .... 92 B3
Hatboro PA, 7393 .... 146 C2
Hatch NM, 1673 .... 56 B2
Hatfield AR, 402 .... 116 C3
Hatfield IN, 1000 .... 99 E4
Hatfield MA, 1298 .... 150 A1
Hatfield PA, 2605 .... 146 C2
Hatley MS, 476 .... 119 D4
Hatteras NC, 650 .... 115 F3
Hattiesburg MS, 44779 .... 126 C4
Hatton ND, 707 .... 19 E3
Haubstadt IN, 1529 .... 99 D4
Haughton LA, 2792 .... 125 D2
Hauppauge NY, 20100 .... 149 D3
Hauser ID, 668 .... 14 B3
Hauula HI, 3651 .... 152 A2
Havana FL, 1713 .... 137 E2
Havana IL, 3577 .... 88 A4
Havelock NC, 22442 .... 115 D4
Haven KS, 1175 .... 43 E4
Haverhill FL, 1454 .... 143 F1
Haverhill MA, 58969 .... 95 E1
Haverhill NH, 500 .... 81 E3
Haverstraw NY, 10117 .... 148 B2
Havertown PA, 22300 .... 248 B3
Haviland KS, 612 .... 43 D4
Havre MT, 9621 .... 16 B2
Havre de Grace MD, 11331 .... 145 D1
Hawaiian Gardens CA, 14779 .... 228 E4
Hawaii Co. HI, 148677 .... 153 E2
Hawarden IA, 2478 .... 35 F1
Hawesville KY, 971 .... 99 E4
Hawi HI, 938 .... 153 E2
Hawkins TX, 1331 .... 124 B2
Hawkins Co. TN, 53563 .... 111 D3
Hawkinsville GA, 3280 .... 129 E3
Hawley MN, 1882 .... 19 F4
Hawley PA, 1303 .... 93 F2
Hawley TX, 646 .... 58 C2
Hawleyville CT, 800 .... 148 C1
Haw River NC, 1908 .... 112 C4
Hawthorn PA, 587 .... 92 B3
Hawthorne CA, 84112 .... 228 C3
Hawthorne FL, 1415 .... 138 C3
Hawthorne NV, 3311 .... 37 E3
Hawthorne NJ, 18218 .... 148 B3
Hawthorne NY, 5083 .... 148 B3
Hawthorn Woods IL, 6002 .... 203 B1
Haxtun CO, 982 .... 34 A4
Hayden AL, 470 .... 119 F4
Hayden AZ, 892 .... 55 D2
Hayden CO, 1634 .... 32 C4
Hayden ID, 9159 .... 14 B3
Hayden Lake ID, 494 .... 14 B3
Haydenville MA, 700 .... 150 A1
Hayes LA, 750 .... 133 E2
Hayes Ctr. NE, 240 .... 34 B4
Hayes Co. NE, 1068 .... 34 B4
Hayesville NC, 297 .... 121 D2
Hayesville OR, 18222 .... 20 B2
Hayfield MN, 1325 .... 73 D2
Hayfork CA, 2315 .... 28 B4
Haymarket VA, 879 .... 144 A3
Haynesville LA, 2679 .... 125 D1
Haynesville VA, 550 .... 103 E4
Hayneville AL, 1177 .... 128 A3
Hays KS, 20013 .... 43 D2
Hays MT, 702 .... 16 C2
Hays NC, 1731 .... 112 A3
Hays Co. TX, 97589 .... 61 D2
Hay Sprs. NE, 652 .... 34 A1
Haysville KS, 8502 .... 43 E4
Hayti MO, 3207 .... 108 B3
Hayti SD, 367 .... 27 F3
Hayti Hts. MO, 771 .... 108 B3
Hayward CA, 140030 .... 36 B4
Hayward WI, 2129 .... 67 F2
Haywood Co. NC, 54033 .... 111 D4
Haywood Co. TN, 19797 .... 108 C4
Hazard KY, 4806 .... 111 D2
Hazardville CT, 4900 .... 150 A2
Hazel KY, 440 .... 109 D3
Hazel Crest IL, 14816 .... 203 E6
Hazel Green AL, 3805 .... 119 F2
Hazel Green WI, 1183 .... 74 A4
Hazel Park MI, 18963 .... 210 C2
Hazelton ID, 687 .... 31 D1
Hazelton ND, 237 .... 18 C4
Hazelwood MO, 26206 .... 256 B1
Hazen AR, 1637 .... 117 F2
Hazen ND, 2457 .... 18 B3
Hazlehurst GA, 3787 .... 129 F3
Hazlehurst MS, 4400 .... 126 B3
Hazleton IA, 950 .... 73 E4
Hazleton PA, 23329 .... 93 E3
Hazlettville DE, 450 .... 145 E2
Headland AL, 3523 .... 128 B4
Head of the Harbor NY, 1447 .... 149 D3
Healdsburg CA, 10722 .... 36 B3
Healdton OK, 2786 .... 51 E4
Healy AK, 1000 .... 154 C2
Heard Co. GA, 11012 .... 128 B1
Hearne TX, 4690 .... 61 F1
Heart Butte MT, 698 .... 15 E2
Heath OH, 8527 .... 101 D1
Heathcote NJ, 4755 .... 147 D1
Heath Sprs. SC, 864 .... 122 B2
Heathsville VA, 30 .... 103 E4
Heavener OK, 3201 .... 116 B2
Hebbronville TX, 4498 .... 63 E2
Hebbville MD, 10900 .... 193 A2
Heber AZ, 2722 .... 47 E4
Heber CA, 2988 .... 53 E4
Heber City UT, 7291 .... 31 F4
Heber Sprs. AR, 6432 .... 117 E1
Hebron CT, 1200 .... 149 E1
Hebron IL, 1038 .... 74 C4
Hebron IN, 3596 .... 89 E2
Hebron KY, 1300 .... 100 B2
Hebron MD, 807 .... 103 F3
Hebron NE, 1565 .... 43 E1
Hebron ND, 803 .... 18 B4
Hebron OH, 2034 .... 101 D1
Hebron Estates KY, 1104 .... 100 A4
Hecla SD, 314 .... 27 E1
Hector AR, 506 .... 117 D1
Hector MN, 1166 .... 66 B4
Hedrick IA, 837 .... 87 E2
Hedwig Vil. TX, 2334 .... 220 B2
Heeia HI, 4944 .... 152 A3
Heflin AL, 3002 .... 120 A4
Heidelberg MS, 840 .... 127 D3
Heidelberg PA, 1225 .... 250 A3
Heilwood PA, 786 .... 92 B3
Helena AL, 10296 .... 127 F1
Helena AR, 6323 .... 118 A2
Helena GA, 2307 .... 129 E3
Helena MS, 778 .... 195 C1
Helena MT, 25780 .... 15 E4
Helena OK, 443 .... 51 D1
Helenwood TN, 846 .... 110 B3
Hellertown PA, 5606 .... 146 C1
Helmetta NJ, 1825 .... 147 E1
Helotes TX, 4285 .... 61 D2
Helper UT, 2025 .... 39 F1
Hemet CA, 58812 .... 53 D3
Hemingford NE, 993 .... 34 A2
Hemingway SC, 573 .... 122 C4
Hemlock MI, 1585 .... 76 B2
Hemphill TX, 1106 .... 124 C4
Hemphill Co. TX, 3351 .... 50 C2
Hempstead NY, 56554 .... 148 C4
Hempstead TX, 4691 .... 61 F2
Hempstead Co. AR, 23587 .... 116 C4
Henagar AL, 2400 .... 120 A2
Henderson KY, 27373 .... 109 E1
Henderson LA, 1531 .... 133 F2
Henderson MN, 910 .... 66 C4
Henderson NE, 986 .... 35 E4
Henderson NV, 175381 .... 46 B2
Henderson NC, 16095 .... 113 D3
Henderson TN, 5670 .... 119 D1
Henderson TX, 11273 .... 124 B3
Henderson Co. IL, 8213 .... 87 F3
Henderson Co. KY, 44829 .... 109 E1
Henderson Co. NC, 89173 .... 121 E1
Henderson Co. TN, 25522 .... 109 D4
Henderson Co. TX, 73277 .... 124 A2
Hendersonville NC, 10420 .... 121 E1
Hendersonville TN, 40620 .... 109 F3
Hendricks MN, 725 .... 27 F3
Hendricks Co. IN, 104093 .... 99 F1
Hendron KY, 4239 .... 108 C2
Hendry Co. FL, 36210 .... 143 D1
Henefer UT, 684 .... 31 F3
Henlopen Acres DE, 139 .... 145 F4
Hennepin IL, 707 .... 88 B2
Hennepin Co. MN, 1116200 .... 66 C4
Hennessey OK, 2058 .... 51 E2
Henniker NH, 1627 .... 81 F4
Henning MN, 719 .... 64 A4
Henning TN, 970 .... 108 B4
Henrico Co. VA, 262300 .... 113 E1
Henrietta NY, 6600 .... 78 C3
Henrietta TX, 3264 .... 59 D1
Henry IL, 2540 .... 88 B3
Henry SD, 268 .... 27 E2
Henry TN, 520 .... 109 D3
Henry Co. AL, 16310 .... 128 B4
Henry Co. GA, 119341 .... 129 D1
Henry Co. IL, 51020 .... 88 A2
Henry Co. IN, 48508 .... 100 A1
Henry Co. IA, 20336 .... 87 F3
Henry Co. KY, 15060 .... 100 A3
Henry Co. MO, 21997 .... 96 C4
Henry Co. OH, 29210 .... 90 B2
Henry Co. TN, 31115 .... 109 D3

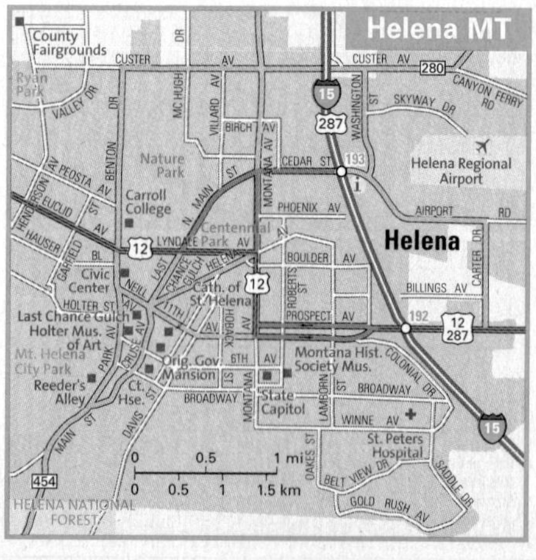

Helena MT
Helena
Helena Regional Airport
Carroll College
Nature Park
County Fairgrounds
Ryan Park
Civic Center
Last Chance Gulch
Holter Mus. of Art
Mt. Helena City Park
Reeder's Alley
Cath. of St. Helena
State Capitol
Montana Hist. Society Mus.
St. Peters Hospital
HELENA NATIONAL FOREST

Entries in **bold** indicate counties or parishes. Entries in color indicate cities with detailed inset maps.
Henry County—Hopkins County 219

Henry Co. VA, 57930 ... 112 B2
Henryetta OK, 6096 ... 51 F3
Henryville IN, 1545 ... 100 A3
Hephzibah GA, 3880 ... 129 F1
Heppner OR, 1395 ... 21 E2
Herculaneum MO, 2805 ... 98 A4
Hercules CA, 19488 ... 259 C1
Hereford PA, 1400 ... 146 B1
Hereford TX, 14597 ... 50 A4
Herington KS, 2563 ... 43 F3
Herkimer NY, 7498 ... 79 F3
Herkimer Co. NY, 64427 ... 79 F2
Hermann MO, 2674 ... 97 F3
Hermantown MN, 7448 ... 64 C4
Herminie PA, 856 ... 92 A4
Hermiston OR, 13154 ... 21 E1
Hialeah FL, 226419 ... 143 E2
Hialeah Gardens FL, 19297 ... 143 E2
Hiawassee GA, 808 ... 121 D2
Hiawatha IA, 6480 ... 87 E1
Hiawatha KS, 3417 ... 96 A1
Hibbing MN, 17071 ... 64 B3
Hickman KY, 2560 ... 108 C3
Hickman NE, 1084 ... 35 F4
Hickman Co. KY, 5262 ... 108 C3
Hickman Co. TN, 22295 ... 109 E4
Hickory MS, 499 ... 126 C2
Hickory NC, 37222 ... 111 F4
Hickory Co. MO, 8940 ... 97 D4
Hickory Flat MS, 565 ... 118 C2
Hickory Hills IL, 13926 ... 203 D5
Hickory Withe TN, 2574 ... 118 C1
Highland Park TX, 8842 ... 207 D2
Highlands NJ, 5097 ... 147 F1
Highlands NC, 909 ... 121 D2
Highlands TX, 7089 ... 132 B3
Highlands Co. FL, 87366 ... 141 D4
Highland Sprs. VA, 15137 ... 254 C2
Highlands Ranch CO, 70931 ... 209 C4
Highlandville MO, 872 ... 107 D2
Highmore SD, 851 ... 27 D3
High Pt. FL, 5800 ... 266 B2
High Pt. NC, 85839 ... 112 B4
High Ridge MO, 4236 ... 98 A3
High Rolls NM, 425 ... 56 C2
High Shoals NC, 729 ... 122 A1
Highspire PA, 2720 ... 218 C2
High Sprs. FL, 3863 ... 138 C3
Hillsborough NH, 1842 ... 81 E4
Hillsborough NC, 5446 ... 112 C4
Hillsborough Co. FL, 998948 ... 140 C3
Hillsborough Co. NH, 380841 ... 81 F4
Hillsdale IL, 588 ... 88 A2
Hillsdale MI, 8233 ... 90 B1
Hillsdale MO, 1477 ... 256 B2
Hillsdale NJ, 10087 ... 148 B3
Hillsdale Co. MI, 46527 ... 90 B1
Hillside IL, 8155 ... 203 C4
Hillside NJ, 21747 ... 148 A4
Hillside Lake NY, 2022 ... 148 B1
Hillsville VA, 2607 ... 112 A2
Hilltop MN, 766 ... 235 C1
Hillview KY, 7037 ... 100 A4
Hilmar CA, 4807 ... 36 C4
Hodgeman Co. KS, 2085 ... 42 C3
Hodgenville KY, 2874 ... 110 A1
Hodgkins IL, 2134 ... 203 C5
Hoffman MN, 672 ... 66 A2
Hoffman NC, 624 ... 122 C2
Hoffman Estates IL, 49495 ... 203 B3
Hogansville GA, 2774 ... 128 C1
Hohenwald TN, 3754 ... 119 E1
Hoisington KS, 2975 ... 43 D3
Hokah MN, 614 ... 73 F2
Hoke Co. NC, 33646 ... 123 D2
Hokendauqua PA, 3411 ... 189 A1
Hokes Bluff AL, 4149 ... 120 A3
Holbrook AZ, 4917 ... 47 F3
Holbrook MA, 10785 ... 151 D2
Holbrook NY, 27512 ... 149 D4
Holcomb KS, 2026 ... 42 B3
Holcomb MO, 696 ... 108 B3
Holden MA, 4200 ... 150 B1
Holden MO, 2510 ... 96 C3
Holden UT, 400 ... 39 E2
Holden WV, 1105 ... 111 E1
Holden Beach NC, 787 ... 123 E4
Holdenville OK, 4732 ... 51 F3
Holdingford MN, 736 ... 66 B2
Holdrege NE, 5636 ... 35 D4
Holgate OH, 1194 ... 90 B2
Holiday FL, 21904 ... 140 B2
Holiday Hills IL, 831 ... 203 A1
Holiday Lakes TX, 1095 ... 132 A4
Holladay UT, 14561 ... 257 B2
Holland AR, 577 ... 117 E1
Holland IN, 695 ... 99 E4
Holland MA, 1444 ... 150 B2
Holland MI, 35048 ... 75 E4
Holland NY, 1261 ... 78 B4
Holland OH, 1306 ... 90 C2
Holland TX, 1102 ... 61 E1
Hollandale MS, 3437 ... 126 A1
Holley FL, 650 ... 135 F2
Holley NY, 1802 ... 78 B3
Holliday TX, 1632 ... 59 D1
Hollidaysburg PA, 5368 ... 92 C4
Hollins VA, 14309 ... 112 B1
Hollis NH, 550 ... 95 D1
Hollis OK, 2264 ... 50 C4
Hollis Ctr. ME, 450 ... 82 B3
Hollister CA, 34413 ... 44 B2
Hollister ID, 237 ... 30 C2
Hollister MO, 3867 ... 107 D3
Hollister NC, 600 ... 113 D3
Holliston MA, 3400 ... 150 C2
Hollow Creek KY, 815 ... 230 E3
Hollow Rock TN, 963 ... 109 D4
Holly CO, 1048 ... 42 A3
Holly MI, 6135 ... 76 B4
Holly Grove AR, 722 ... 117 F2
Holly Hill FL, 12119 ... 139 E4
Holly Hill SC, 1281 ... 130 C1
Holly Park NJ, 2200 ... 147 E3
Holly Pond AL, 645 ... 119 F3
Holly Ridge NC, 831 ... 115 C4
Holly Sprs. GA, 3195 ... 120 C3
Holly Sprs. MS, 7957 ... 118 C2
Holly Sprs. NC, 9192 ... 112 C4
Hollyvilla KY, 481 ... 100 A4
Hollywood AL, 950 ... 120 A2
Hollywood FL, 139357 ... 143 F2
Hollywood MD, 650 ... 103 E4
Hollywood SC, 3946 ... 131 D2
Hollywood Park TX, 2983 ... 61 D2
Holmdel NJ, 1200 ... 147 E2
Holmen WI, 6200 ... 73 F1
Holmes Beach FL, 4966 ... 140 B3
Holmes Co. FL, 18564 ... 136 C1
Holmes Co. MS, 21609 ... 126 B1
Holmes Co. OH, 38943 ... 91 D4
Holstein IA, 1470 ... 72 A4
Holt AL, 4103 ... 127 E1
Holt MI, 11315 ... 76 A4
Holt Co. MO, 5351 ... 86 A4
Holt Co. NE, 11551 ... 35 D1
Holton KS, 3353 ... 96 A2
Holts Summit MO, 2935 ... 97 E3
Holtville CA, 5612 ... 53 E4
Holualoa HI, 6107 ... 153 E3
Holyoke CO, 2261 ... 34 A4
Holyoke MA, 39838 ... 150 A2
Holyrood KS, 464 ... 43 D3
Homecroft IN, 751 ... 99 F1
Homedale ID, 2528 ... 22 A4
Home Gardens CA, 9461 ... 229 H4
Homeland CA, 3710 ... 229 K4
Homeland GA, 765 ... 139 D1
Homeland Park SC, 6337 ... 121 E3
Homer AK, 3946 ... 154 C3
Homer GA, 950 ... 121 D3
Homer IL, 1200 ... 99 D1
Homer LA, 3788 ... 125 D2
Homer MI, 1851 ... 90 A1
Homer NE, 590 ... 35 F2
Homer NY, 3368 ... 79 D4
Homer City PA, 1844 ... 92 B4
Homer Glen IL, 22269 ... 203 C6
Homerville GA, 2803 ... 138 C1
Homestead FL, 31909 ... 143 E3
Homestead PA, 3569 ... 250 C2
Homestead Valley CA, 10691 ... 259 A2
Hometown IL, 4467 ... 203 D5
Hometown PA, 1399 ... 93 E3
Hometown WV, 750 ... 101 E3
Homewood AL, 25043 ... 119 F4
Hominy OK, 2584 ... 51 F1
Homosassa FL, 2294 ... 140 B1
Homosassa Sprs. FL, 12458 ... 140 B1
Honaker VA, 945 ... 111 E2
Honalo HI, 1987 ... 153 E3
Honaunau HI, 2414 ... 153 E3
Hondo TX, 7897 ... 60 C3
Honea Path SC, 3504 ... 121 E3
Honeoye NY, 800 ... 78 C4
Honeoye Falls NY, 2595 ... 78 C3
Honesdale PA, 4874 ... 93 F2
Honey Brook PA, 1287 ... 146 B2
Honey Grove TX, 1746 ... 59 F1
Honeyville UT, 1214 ... 31 E3
Honokaa HI, 2233 ... 153 E2
Honokowai HI, 6788 ... 153 D1
Honolulu HI, 371657 ... 152 A3
Honolulu Co. HI, 876156 ... 152 A3
Honomu HI, 541 ... 153 F3
Hood Co. TX, 41100 ... 59 E3
Hood River OR, 5831 ... 21 D1
Hood River Co. OR, 20411 ... 20 C2
Hooker OK, 1788 ... 50 B1
Hooker Co. NE, 783 ... 34 B2
Hooks TX, 2973 ... 116 C4
Hooksett NH, 3609 ... 81 F4
Hoonah AK, 860 ... 155 D4
Hooper NE, 827 ... 35 F3
Hooper UT, 3926 ... 244 A2
Hooper Bay AK, 1014 ... 154 B3
Hoopeston IL, 5965 ... 89 D4
Hoople ND, 292 ... 19 E2
Hoosick Falls NY, 3436 ... 94 B1
Hoover AL, 62742 ... 127 F1
Hooverson Hts. WV, 2909 ... 91 F4
Hooversville PA, 779 ... 92 B4
Hopatcong NJ, 15888 ... 148 A3
Hope AR, 10616 ... 117 D4
Hope IN, 2140 ... 99 F2
Hope ND, 303 ... 19 E3
Hope RI, 1900 ... 150 C3
Hopedale IL, 929 ... 88 B4
Hopedale MA, 4158 ... 150 C2
Hopedale OH, 984 ... 91 F4
Hope Mills NC, 11237 ... 123 D2
Hope Valley RI, 1649 ... 150 C4
Hopewell NJ, 2035 ... 147 D1
Hopewell TN, 1815 ... 120 B1
Hopewell VA, 22354 ... 113 E1
Hopewell Jct. NY, 2610 ... 148 B1
Hopkins MI, 592 ... 75 F4
Hopkins MN, 17145 ... 235 A3
Hopkins MO, 579 ... 86 B4
Hopkins Co. KY, 46519 ... 109 E2

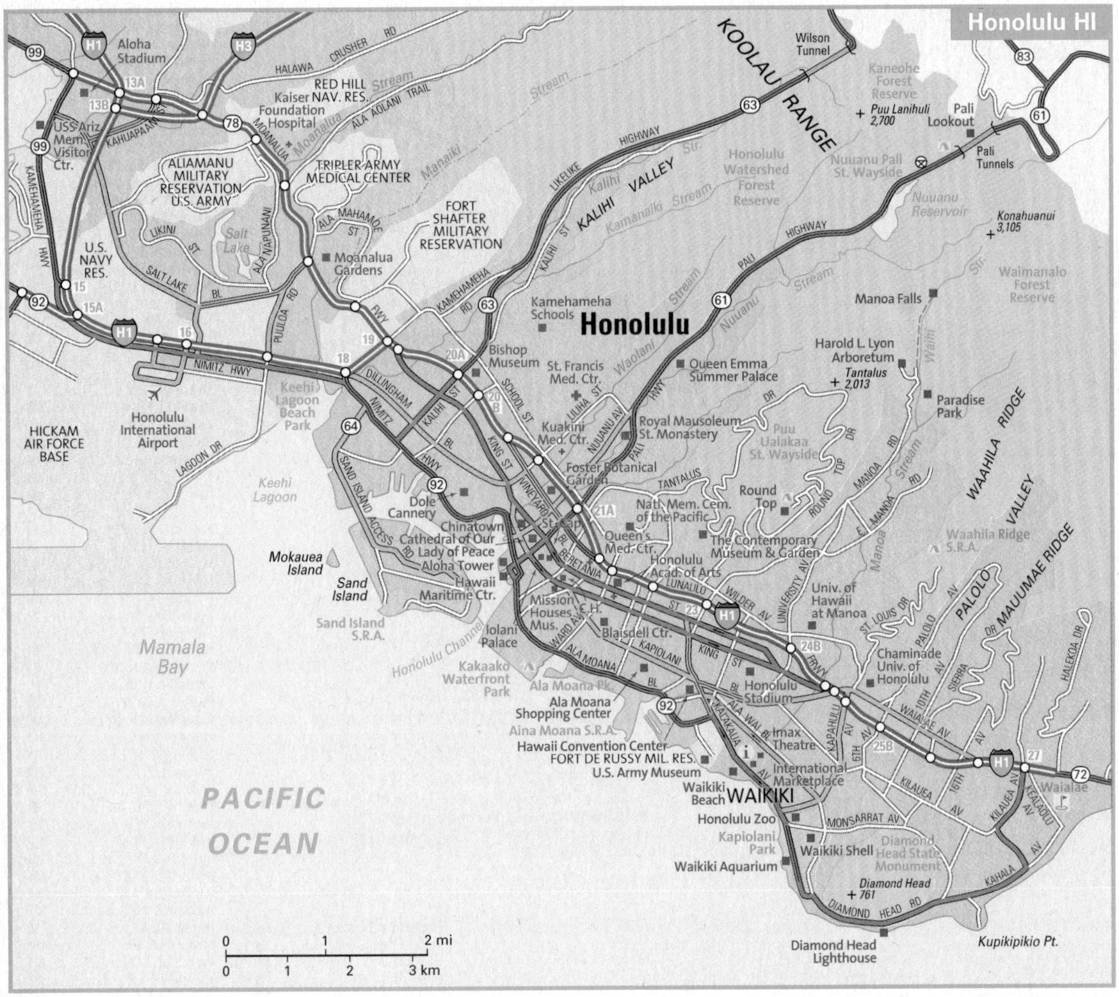
Honolulu HI
KOOLAU RANGE
Aloha Stadium
RED HILL
Kaiser NAV. RES.
Foundation Hospital
USS Ariz. Mem. Visitor Ctr.
ALIAMANU MILITARY RESERVATION U.S. ARMY
TRIPLER ARMY MEDICAL CENTER
FORT SHAFTER MILITARY RESERVATION
Salt Lake
U.S. NAVY RES.
Moanalua Gardens
KALIHI VALLEY
Honolulu Watershed Forest Reserve
Nuuanu Pali St. Wayside
Wilson Tunnel
Kaneohe Forest Reserve
Puu Lanihuli 2,700
Pali Lookout
Pali Tunnels
Nuuanu Reservoir
Konahuanui 3,105
Waimanalo Forest Reserve
Manoa Falls
Kamehameha Schools
Honolulu
Bishop Museum
St. Francis Med. Ctr.
Queen Emma Summer Palace
Harold L. Lyon Arboretum
Tantalus 2,013
Paradise Park
WAAHILA RIDGE
HICKAM AIR FORCE BASE
Honolulu International Airport
Keehi Lagoon Beach Park
Keehi Lagoon
Kuakini Med. Ctr.
Royal Mausoleum St. Monastery
Puu Ualakaa St. Wayside
Foster Botanical Garden
Round Top
VALLEY
Dole Cannery
Chinatown
Natl. Mem. Cem. of the Pacific
Queen's Med. Ctr.
The Contemporary Museum & Garden
Waahila Ridge S.R.A.
Mokauea Island
Cathedral of Our Lady of Peace
Aloha Tower
Hawaii Maritime Ctr.
Honolulu Acad. of Arts
Sand Island
Sand Island S.R.A.
Mission Houses Mus.
Iolani Palace
Blaisdell Ctr.
Univ. of Hawaii at Manoa
PALOLO
MAUUMAE RIDGE
Mamala Bay
Kakaako Waterfront Park
Ala Moana Pk.
Ala Moana Shopping Center
Aina Moana S.R.A.
Hawaii Convention Center
FORT DE RUSSY MIL. RES.
U.S. Army Museum
Chaminade Univ. of Honolulu
Honolulu Stadium
Imax Theatre
International Marketplace
Waialae
PACIFIC OCEAN
Waikiki Beach
WAIKIKI
Honolulu Zoo
Kapiolani Park
Waikiki Shell
Diamond Head State Monument
Waikiki Aquarium
Diamond Head 761
Diamond Head Lighthouse
Kupikipikio Pt.
0 1 2 mi
0 1 2 3 km

Hermitage AR, 769 ... 117 E4
Hermitage MO, 406 ... 97 D4
Hermitage PA, 16157 ... 91 F2
Hermon ME, 750 ... 83 D1
Hermosa CO, 700 ... 40 B4
Hermosa SD, 315 ... 26 A4
Hermosa Beach CA, 18566 ... 228 C4
Hernandez NM, 600 ... 48 C2
Hernando FL, 8253 ... 140 C1
Hernando MS, 6812 ... 118 B2
Hernando Beach FL, 2185 ... 140 B1
Hernando Co. FL, 130802 ... 140 B1
Herndon VA, 21655 ... 144 A3
Heron Lake MN, 768 ... 72 A2
Herreid SD, 482 ... 26 C1
Herricks NY, 4076 ... 241 G3
Herriman UT, 1523 ... 31 E4
Herrin IL, 11298 ... 108 C1
Herscher IL, 1523 ... 89 D3
Hershey NE, 572 ... 34 B3
Hershey PA, 12771 ... 93 E4
Hertford NC, 2070 ... 113 F3
Hertford Co. NC, 22601 ... 113 F3
Hesperia CA, 62582 ... 53 D2
Hesperia MI, 954 ... 75 E2
Hessmer LA, 642 ... 133 F1
Hesston KS, 3509 ... 43 E3
Hettinger ND, 1307 ... 26 A1
Hettinger Co. ND, 2715 ... 18 A4
Heuvelton NY, 804 ... 80 B2
Hewitt TX, 11085 ... 59 E4
Hewitt WI, 670 ... 68 A4
Hewlett NY, 7060 ... 241 G4
Hewlett Harbor NY, 1271 ... 241 G5
Hewlett Neck NY, 504 ... 241 G5
Heyburn ID, 2899 ... 31 D1
Heyworth IL, 2431 ... 88 C4
Hicksville NY, 41260 ... 148 C4
Hicksville OH, 3649 ... 90 A2
Hico TX, 1341 ... 59 E3
Hidalgo TX, 7322 ... 63 E4
Hidalgo Co. NM, 5932 ... 55 F4
Hidalgo Co. TX, 569463 ... 63 E3
Hidden Hills CA, 1875 ... 228 A2
Hiddenite NC, 650 ... 112 A4
Higbee MO, 623 ... 97 E2
Higganum CT, 1671 ... 149 E1
Higginsville MO, 4682 ... 96 C2
High Bridge NJ, 3776 ... 104 C1
Highgate Ctr. VT, 600 ... 81 D1
Highgrove CA, 3445 ... 229 J3
Highland AR, 986 ... 107 F3
Highland CA, 44605 ... 229 K2
Highland IL, 8438 ... 98 B3
Highland IN, 23546 ... 89 D2
Highland KS, 976 ... 96 A1
Highland MD, 800 ... 144 B2
Highland NY, 5060 ... 94 B3
Highland UT, 8172 ... 31 F4
Highland WI, 855 ... 74 A3
Highland Beach FL, 3775 ... 143 F1
Highland City FL, 2051 ... 140 C2
Highland Co. OH, 40875 ... 100 C2
Highland Co. VA, 2536 ... 102 B4
Highland Falls NY, 3678 ... 148 B2
Highland Hts. KY, 6554 ... 204 B3
Highland Hts. OH, 8082 ... 204 G1
Highland Hills OH, 1618 ... 204 G2
Highland Lakes NJ, 5051 ... 148 A2
Highland Mills NY, 3468 ... 148 B2
Highland Park IL, 31365 ... 89 D1
Highland Park MI, 16746 ... 210 C3
Highland Park NJ, 13999 ... 147 E1
Highland Park PA, 4900 ... 218 B2
Hightstown NJ, 5216 ... 147 D2
Hightsville NC, 759 ... 275 A1
Highwood IL, 4143 ... 203 D1
Higley AZ, 425 ... 249 D3
Hiland Park FL, 999 ... 136 C2
Hilbert WI, 1089 ... 74 C1
Hilda SC, 436 ... 130 B1
Hildale UT, 1895 ... 46 C1
Hillandale MD, 3054 ... 270 E1
Hillburn NY, 881 ... 148 B2
Hill City KS, 1604 ... 42 C2
Hill City MN, 479 ... 64 B4
Hill City SD, 780 ... 25 F4
Hill Country Vil. TX, 1028 ... 257 E1
Hill Co. MT, 16673 ... 16 A1
Hill Co. TX, 32321 ... 59 E3
Hillcrest IL, 1158 ... 88 B1
Hillcrest NY, 7106 ... 148 B2
Hillcrest TX, 722 ... 132 B4
Hillcrest Hts. MD, 16359 ... 144 B3
Hilliard FL, 2702 ... 139 D1
Hilliard OH, 24230 ... 101 D1
Hillman MI, 685 ... 70 C3
Hills IA, 679 ... 87 F2
Hills MN, 565 ... 27 F4
Hillsboro AL, 608 ... 119 E2
Hillsboro IL, 4359 ... 98 B2
Hillsboro IN, 489 ... 89 E4
Hillsboro KS, 2854 ... 43 E3
Hillsboro MO, 1675 ... 98 A4
Hillsboro ND, 1563 ... 19 E3
Hillsboro OH, 6368 ... 100 C2
Hillsboro OR, 70186 ... 20 B2
Hillsboro TX, 8232 ... 59 E3
Hillsboro WI, 1302 ... 74 A2
Hillsboro Beach FL, 2163 ... 143 F1
Hillsborough CA, 10825 ... 259 B4
Hilo HI, 40759 ... 153 F3
Hilshire Vil. TX, 720 ... 220 B2
Hilton NY, 5856 ... 78 C3
Hilton Head Island SC, 33862 ... 130 C3
Hinckley IL, 1994 ... 88 C1
Hinckley MN, 1291 ... 67 D2
Hinckley UT, 698 ... 39 D2
Hindman KY, 787 ... 111 D1
Hinds Co. MS, 250800 ... 126 B3
Hines OR, 1623 ... 21 E4
Hinesburg VT, 900 ... 81 D2
Hinesville GA, 30392 ... 130 B3
Hingham MA, 5352 ... 151 D1
Hinsdale IL, 17349 ... 203 C5
Hinsdale MA, 750 ... 94 C1
Hinsdale NH, 1713 ... 94 C1
Hinsdale Co. CO, 790 ... 40 C4
Hinson FL, 750 ... 137 E2
Hinton IA, 808 ... 35 F1
Hinton OK, 2175 ... 51 D3
Hinton WV, 2880 ... 112 A1
Hiram GA, 1361 ... 120 C4
Hiram OH, 1242 ... 91 E2
Hitchcock TX, 6386 ... 132 B4
Hitchcock Co. NE, 3111 ... 34 B4
Hitchins KY, 475 ... 101 D4
Hobart IN, 25363 ... 89 D2
Hobart OK, 3997 ... 51 D3
Hobart WA, 6251 ... 12 C3
Hobbs NM, 28657 ... 57 F2
Hobe Sound FL, 11376 ... 141 F4
Hoboken NJ, 38577 ... 148 B4
Hobson MT, 244 ... 16 B4
Hockessin DE, 12902 ... 146 B3
Hocking Co. OH, 28241 ... 101 D1
Hockley Co. TX, 22716 ... 58 A1
Hodge LA, 492 ... 125 E3

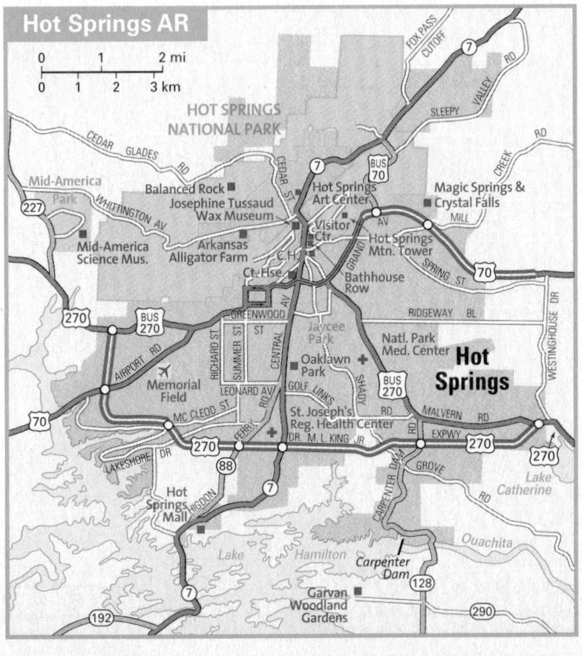
Hot Springs AR
0 1 2 mi
0 1 2 3 km
HOT SPRINGS NATIONAL PARK
Mid-America Park
Balanced Rock
Josephine Tussaud Wax Museum
Hot Springs Art Center
Magic Springs & Crystal Falls
Mid-America Science Mus.
Arkansas Alligator Farm
Visitor Ctr.
Hot Springs Mtn. Tower
Bathhouse Row
Jaycee Park
Oaklawn Park
Natl. Park Med. Center
Hot Springs
Memorial Field
St. Joseph's Reg. Health Center
Hot Springs Mall
Lake Hamilton
Carpenter Dam
Lake Catherine
Ouachita
Garvan Woodland Gardens

220 Hopkins County—Humboldt County

Figures after entries indicate population, page number, and grid reference.

Houston TX area index

Aldine	C1	Channelview	D2	Four Corners	A3	Houmont Park	D2	League City	D4	N. Houston	B1	Southside Place	B3
Barrett	D1	Clodine	A3	Fresno	B4	Houston	C2	Lynchburg	D2	Pasadena	D3	Spring Valley	B2
Beaumont Place	D2	Cloverleaf	D2	Friendswood	D4	Humble	C1	Magnolia Gardens	D1	Pearland	C4	Stafford	B4
Bellaire	B3	Crabb	A4	Galena Park	C3	Hunters Creek Vil.	B2	Meadows Place	A3	Piney Pt. Vil.	B2	Sugar Land	A3
Booth	A4	Crosby	D1	Hedwig Vil.	B2	Jacinto City	C2	Mission Bend	A3	Satsuma	A1	Webster	D4
Brookside Vil.	C4	Cypress	A1	Highlands	D2	Jersey Vil.	A1	Missouri City	B4	Sheldon	D2	W. University Place	B3
Bunker Hill Vil.	B2	Deer Park	D3	Hilshire Vil.	B2	La Porte	D3	Nassau Bay	D4	S. Houston	C3	

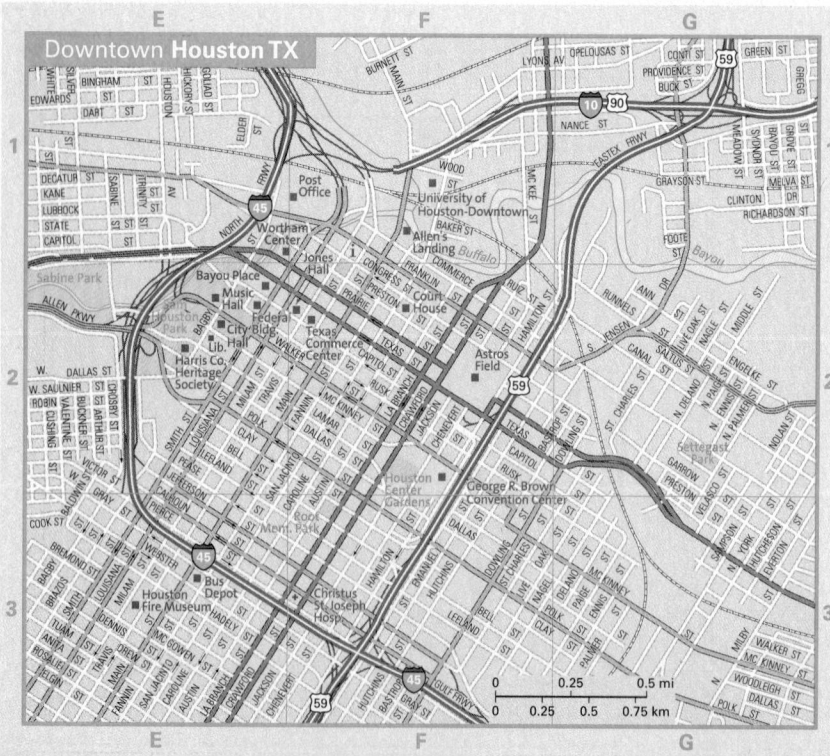

Houston TX

Downtown **Houston TX**

Allen's Landing	F1
Astros Field	F2
Bayou Place	E2
Bus Depot	E3
City Hall	F2
Court House	F2
Federal Building	F2
George R. Brown Convention Center	F2
Harris County Heritage Society	E2
Houston Fire Mus.	E3
Jones Hall	F2
Library	E2
Music Hall	E2
Post Office	F1
Texas Commerce Center	F2
Univ. of Houston-Downtown	F1
Wortham Center	E1

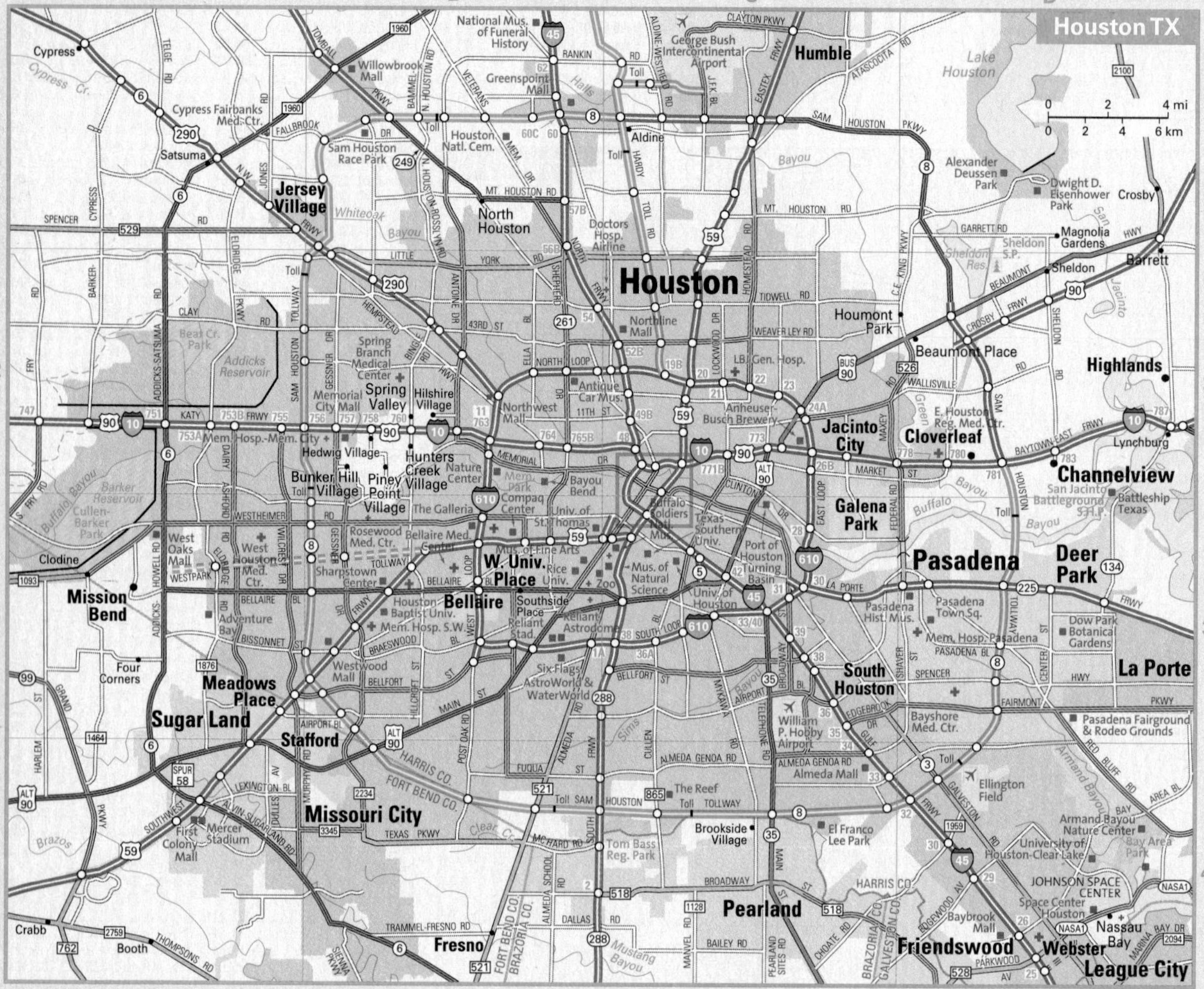

Entries in **bold** indicate counties or parishes. Entries in color indicate cities with detailed inset maps.

Huntington WV

Huntsville AL

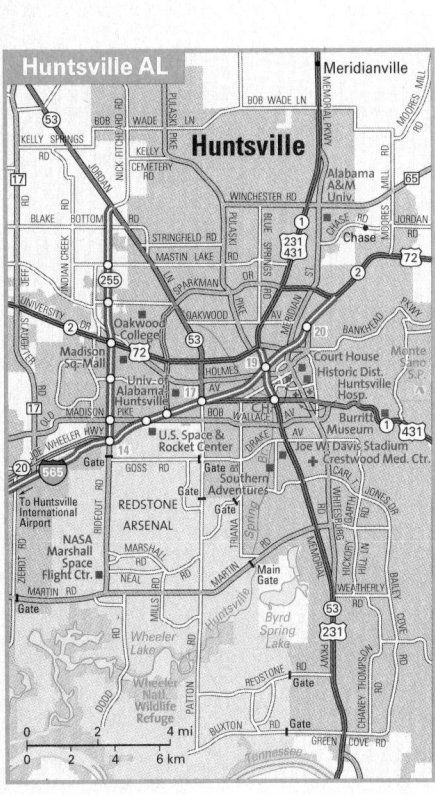

Idaho Falls ID

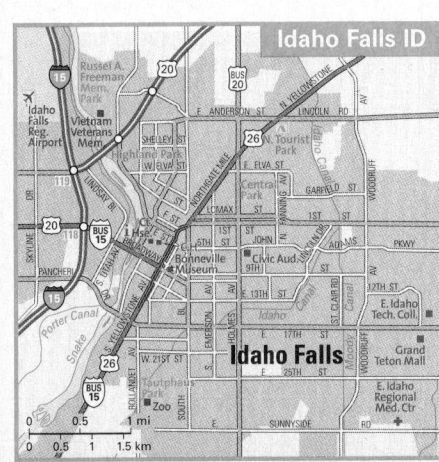

Indianapolis IN

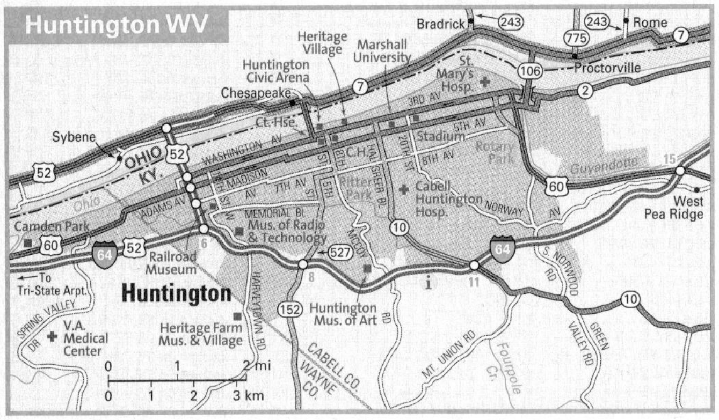

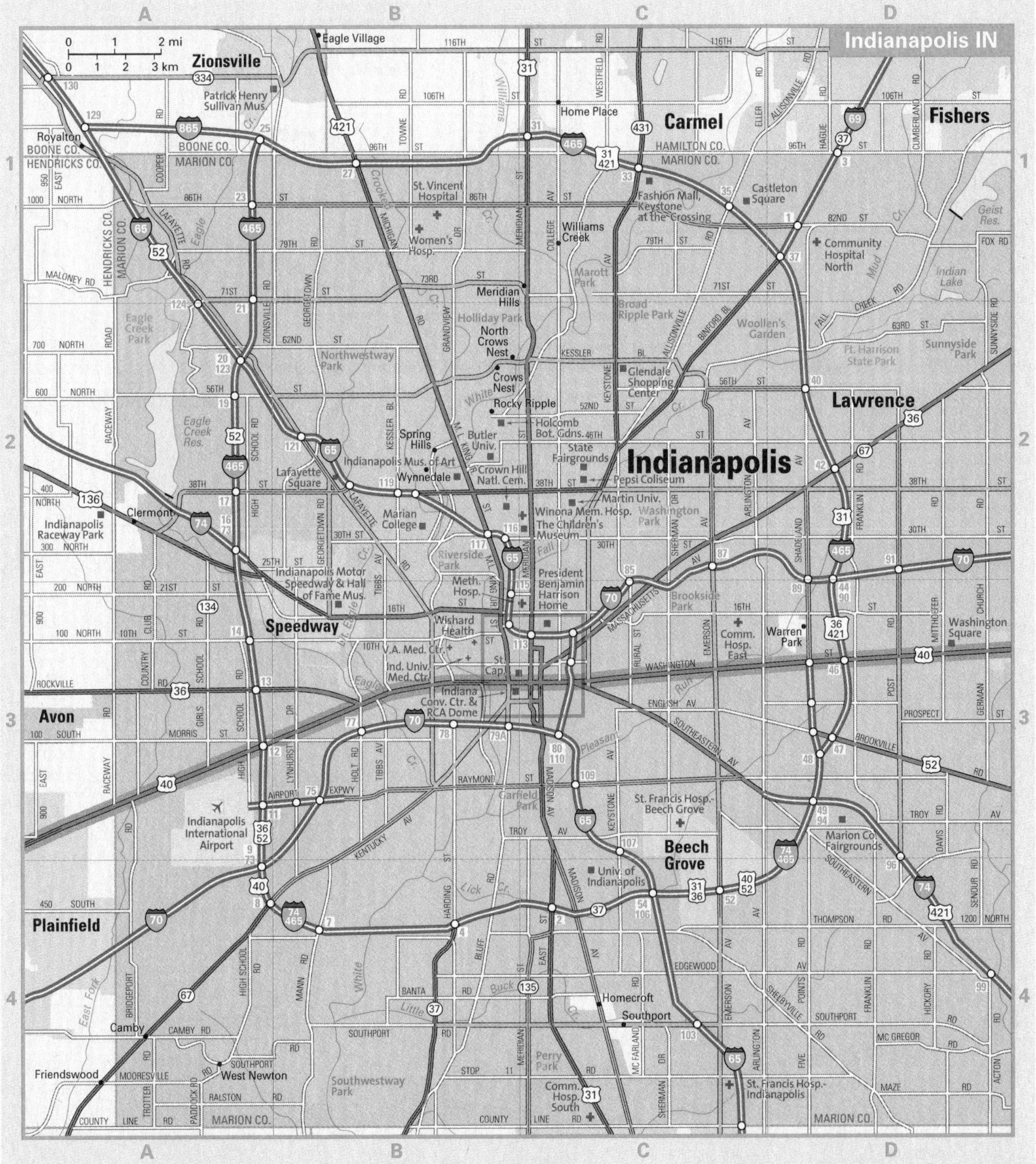

222 Indian Springs—Jacksonville

Figures after entries indicate population, page number, and grid reference.

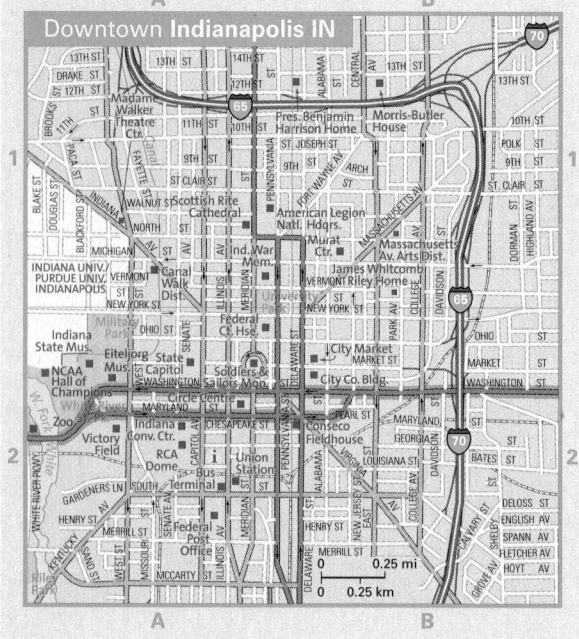

Downtown Indianapolis IN

American Legion National Headquarters ...A1	James Whitcomb Riley Home ...B1
Bus Terminal ...A2	Madame Walker Theatre Center ...A1
Canal Walk District ...A1	Massachusetts Avenue Arts District ...B1
Circle Centre ...A2	Morris-Butler House ...B1
City County Building ...B2	Murat Center ...B1
City Market ...B2	NCAA Hall of Champions ...A2
Conseco Fieldhouse ...A2	President Benjamin Harrison Home ...A1
Eiteljorg Mus. ...A2	RCA Dome ...A2
Federal Court House ...A2	Scottish Rite Cathedral ...A1
Federal Post Office ...A2	Soldiers & Sailors Monument ...A2
Indiana Convention Center ...A2	State Capitol ...A2
Indiana State Mus. ...A2	Union Station ...A2
Indiana Univ./Purdue Univ. Indianapolis ...A1	Victory Field ...A2
Indiana War Memorial ...A1	Zoo ...A2

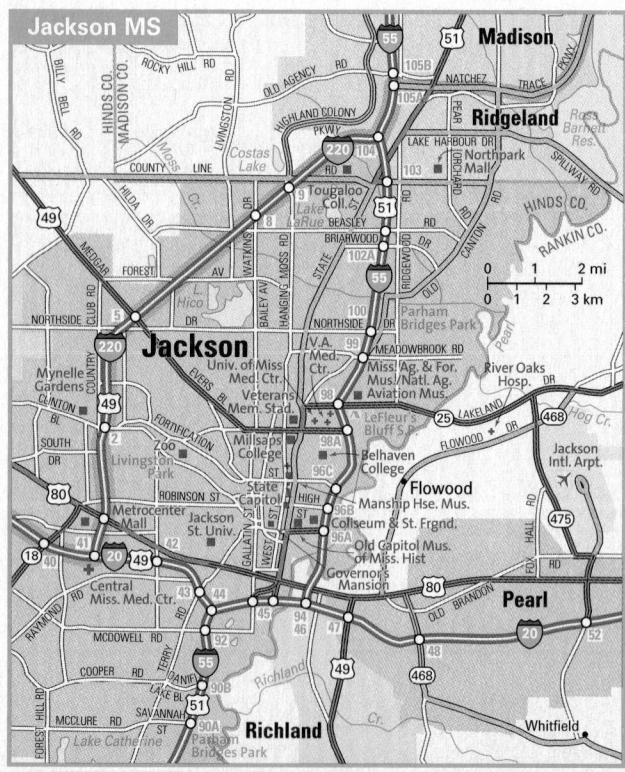

Jackson MS

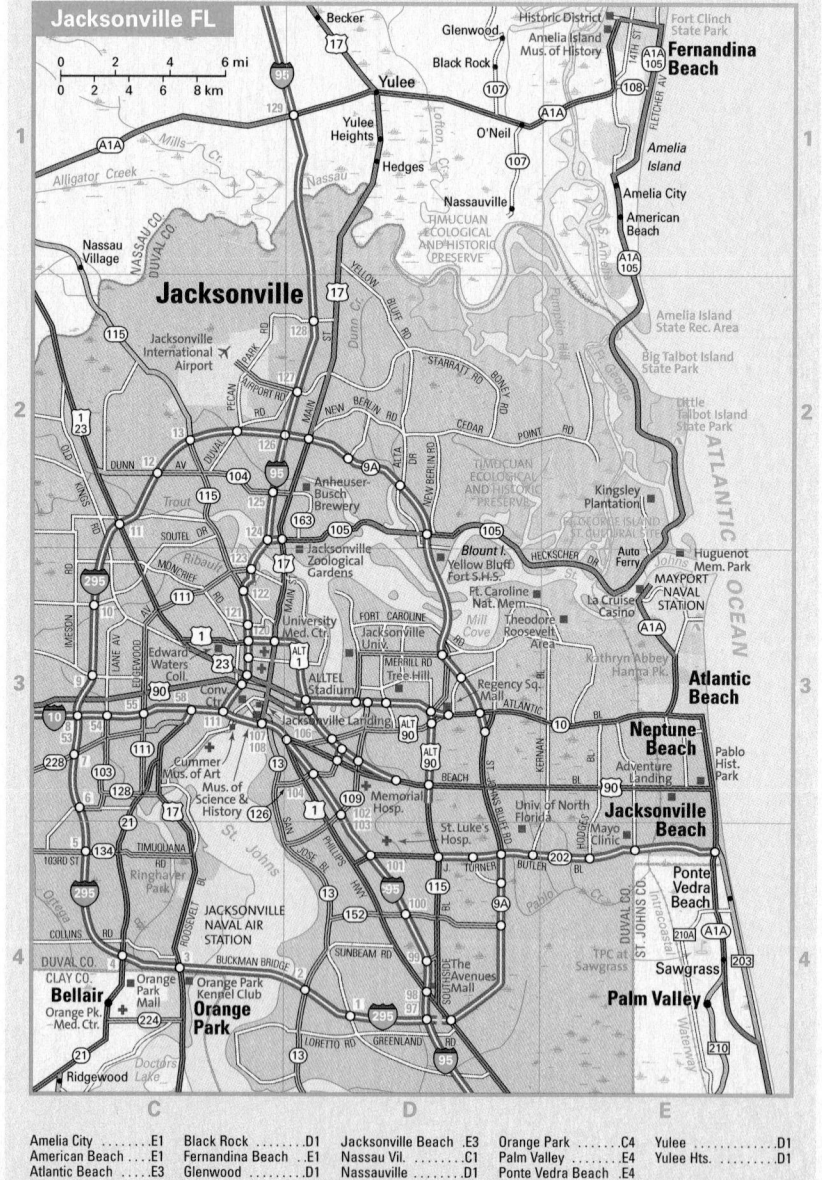

Jacksonville FL

Jacksonville—Keystone Heights 223

Entries in **bold** indicate counties or parishes. Entries in color indicate cities with detailed inset maps.

Jacksonville IL, 18940 98 A1
Jacksonville MD, 900 144 C1
Jacksonville NC, 66715 115 D4
Jacksonville OR, 2235 28 B2
Jacksonville PA, 675 92 B4
Jacksonville TX, 13868 124 A3
Jacksonville VT, 237 94 C1
Jacksonville Beach FL, 20990 139 D2
Jacobstown NJ, 950 147 D2
Jacobus PA, 1203 103 E1
Jaffrey NH, 2802 95 D1
Jal NM, 1996 57 F3
Jamaica Beach TX, 1075 132 B4
Jamesburg NJ, 6025 147 E2
James City NC, 5420 115 D3
James City Co. VA, 48102 113 F1
Jamesport MO, 505 96 C1
Jamesport NY, 1526 149 E3
Jamestown CA, 3017 37 D3
Jamestown IN, 886 99 E1
Jamestown KS, 399 43 E1
Jamestown KY, 1624 110 B2
Jamestown MI, 750 75 F3
Jamestown NY, 31730 92 B1
Jamestown NC, 3088 112 B4
Jamestown ND, 15527 19 D4
Jamestown OH, 1917 100 C1
Jamestown PA, 636 91 F2
Jamestown RI, 5622 150 C4
Jamestown TN, 1839 110 B3
James Town WY, 552 32 A3
Jamesville NC, 502 113 F4
Jamul CA, 5920 53 D4
Jane Lew WV, 406 102 A2
Janesville CA, 550 29 D4
Janesville IA, 829 73 D4
Janesville MN, 2109 72 C1
Janesville WI, 59498 74 B4
Jarales NM, 1434 48 C4
Jarratt VA, 589 113 E2
Jarrettsville MD, 2756 144 C1
Jasmine Estates FL, 18213 140 B2
Jasonville IN, 2490 99 E2
Jasper AL, 14052 119 E4
Jasper AR, 498 107 D4
Jasper FL, 1780 138 B2
Jasper GA, 2167 120 C3
Jasper IN, 12100 99 E4
Jasper MN, 597 27 F4
Jasper MO, 1011 106 C1
Jasper OR, 700 20 B4
Jasper TN, 3214 120 A2
Jasper TX, 8247 132 C1
Jasper Co. GA, 11426 129 D1
Jasper Co. IL, 10117 99 D2
Jasper Co. IN, 30043 89 E3
Jasper Co. IA, 37213 87 D2
Jasper Co. MS, 18149 126 C3
Jasper Co. MO, 104686 106 C2
Jasper Co. SC, 20678 130 C3
Jasper Co. TX, 35604 132 C1
Jay FL, 579 135 F1
Jay ME, 325 82 B2
Jay OK, 2482 106 B3
Jay Co. IN, 21806 90 A4
Jayton TX, 513 58 B2
Jeanerette LA, 5997 133 F3
Jean Lafitte LA, 2137 134 B3
Jeannette PA, 10654 92 A4
Jeddito AZ, 390 47 F2
Jeff Davis Co. GA, 12684 129 F3
Jeff Davis Co. TX, 2207 62 B2
Jefferson GA, 3825 121 D3
Jefferson IA, 4626 86 B1
Jefferson LA, 11843 239 B1
Jefferson MA, 1600 150 B1
Jefferson NC, 1422 111 F3
Jefferson OH, 3572 91 F1
Jefferson OR, 2487 20 B3
Jefferson PA, 631 103 E1
Jefferson SC, 704 122 B2
Jefferson SD, 586 35 F1
Jefferson TX, 2024 124 C2
Jefferson WI, 7338 74 B3
Jefferson City MO, 39636 97 E3
Jefferson City MT, 295 15 E4
Jefferson City TN, 7760 111 D4
Jefferson Co. AL, 662047 119 F4
Jefferson Co. AR, 84278 117 F3
Jefferson Co. CO, 525507 41 E1
Jefferson Co. FL, 12902 137 E2
Jefferson Co. GA, 17266 129 F1
Jefferson Co. ID, 19155 23 E4
Jefferson Co. IL, 40045 98 C4
Jefferson Co. IN, 31705 100 A3
Jefferson Co. IA, 16181 87 E3
Jefferson Co. KS, 18426 96 A2
Jefferson Co. KY, 693604 100 A4
Jefferson Co. MS, 9740 126 A3
Jefferson Co. MO, 198099 98 A4
Jefferson Co. MT, 10049 23 E1
Jefferson Co. NE, 8333 35 F4
Jefferson Co. NY, 111738 79 E2
Jefferson Co. OH, 73894 91 F4
Jefferson Co. OK, 6818 59 E1
Jefferson Co. OR, 19009 20 C3
Jefferson Co. PA, 45932 92 B2
Jefferson Co. TN, 44294 111 D4

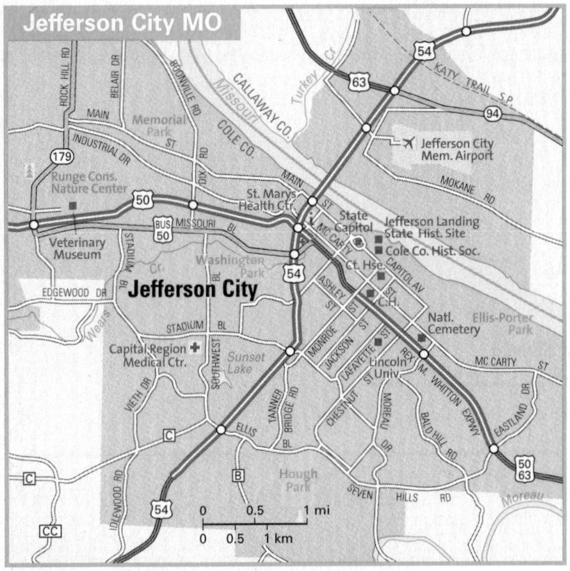

Jefferson City MO
Jefferson City
Missouri
Jefferson City Mem. Airport
Runge Cons. Nature Center
Veterinary Museum
St. Marys Health Ctr.
State Capitol
Jefferson Landing State Hist. Site
Cole Co. Hist. Soc.
Ct. Hse.
Capital Region Medical Ctr.
Natl. Cemetery
Ellis-Porter Park
Lincoln Univ.
Memorial Park
Washington Park
Sunset Lake
Hough Park
Moreau
KATY TRAIL S.P.
CALLAWAY CO.
COLE CO.
0 0.5 1 mi
0 0.5 1 km

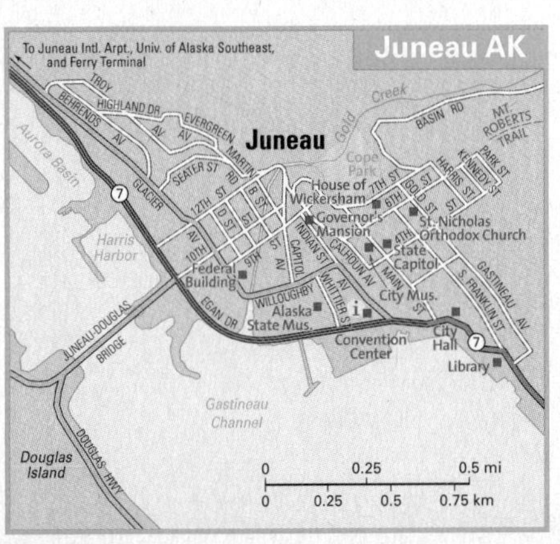

Juneau AK
To Juneau Intl. Arpt., Univ. of Alaska Southeast, and Ferry Terminal
Juneau
Aurora Basin
Harris Harbor
House of Wickersham
Governor's Mansion
St. Nicholas Orthodox Church
State Capitol
Federal Building
Alaska State Mus.
City Mus.
Convention Center
City Hall
Library
Gastineau Channel
Douglas Island
0 0.25 0.5 mi
0 0.25 0.5 0.75 km

Jefferson Co. TX, 252051 132 C3
Jefferson Co. WA, 25953 12 B3
Jefferson Co. WV, 42190 103 D2
Jefferson Co. WI, 74021 74 C3
Jefferson Davis Co. MS, 13962 126 B4
Jefferson Davis Par. LA, 31435 133 E2
Jefferson Hts. NY, 1104 94 B2
Jefferson Hills PA, 9666 92 A4
Jefferson Par. LA, 455466 134 B3
Jeffersontown KY, 26633 100 A4
Jefferson Valley NY, 14891 148 B2
Jeffersonville GA, 1209 129 E2
Jeffersonville IN, 27362 100 A4
Jeffersonville KY, 1804 100 C4
Jeffersonville OH, 1288 100 C1
Jeffersonville PA, 10200 248 A1
Jeffersonville VT, 568 81 D1
Jellico TN, 2448 110 C3
Jemez Pueblo NM, 1953 48 C3
Jemez Sprs. NM, 375 48 C2
Jemison AL, 2248 127 F1
Jena LA, 2971 125 E4
Jenison MI, 17211 75 F3
Jenkins KY, 2401 111 E2
Jenkins Co. GA, 8575 129 F2
Jenkintown PA, 4478 146 C2
Jenks OK, 9557 51 F2
Jennerstown PA, 714 92 B4
Jennings FL, 833 137 F2
Jennings LA, 10986 133 E2
Jennings MO, 15469 256 B1
Jennings Co. IN, 27554 100 A3
Jenny Lind AR, 650 116 C1
Jensen Beach FL, 11100 141 E4
Jerauld Co. SD, 2295 27 D3
Jericho NY, 13045 148 C4
Jericho VT, 1457 81 D2
Jermyn PA, 2287 93 F2
Jerome AZ, 329 47 D4
Jerome ID, 7780 30 C1
Jerome PA, 1068 92 B4
Jerome Co. ID, 18342 31 D1
Jersey City NJ, 240055 148 B4
Jersey Co. IL, 21668 98 A2
Jersey Shore PA, 4482 93 D2
Jersey Vil. TX, 6880 132 A3
Jerseyville IL, 7984 98 A2
Jerseyville NJ, 1000 147 E2
Jerusalem RI, 800 150 C4
Jessamine Co. KY, 39041 100 B4
Jessup MD, 7865 144 C2
Jessup PA, 4718 93 F2
Jesup GA, 9279 130 A4
Jesup IA, 2212 73 E4
Jetmore KS, 903 42 C3
Jewell IA, 1239 72 C4
Jewell KS, 483 43 E1
Jewell Co. KS, 3791 43 E1
Jewett OH, 784 91 F4
Jewett TX, 861 59 F4
Jewett City (Griswold) CT, 3053 149 F1
Jim Hogg Co. TX, 5281 63 E3
Jim Thorpe PA, 4804 93 F3
Jim Wells Co. TX, 39326 63 E2
Joanna SC, 1609 121 F3
Joaquin TX, 925 124 C3
Jo Daviess Co. IL, 22289 74 A4
John Day OR, 1821 21 F3
Johns Island SC, 650 131 D2
Johnson AR, 2319 106 C4
Johnson VT, 1420 81 E2
Johnsonburg PA, 3003 92 B2
Johnson City KS, 1528 42 B4
Johnson City NY, 15535 93 E1
Johnson City OR, 634 251 D3
Johnson City TN, 55469 111 E3
Johnson City TX, 1191 61 D1
Johnson Co. AR, 22781 117 D1
Johnson Co. GA, 8560 129 F2
Johnson Co. IL, 12878 108 C1
Johnson Co. IN, 115209 99 F2
Johnson Co. IA, 111006 87 F2
Johnson Co. KS, 451086 96 B3
Johnson Co. KY, 23445 111 D1
Johnson Co. MO, 48258 96 C3
Johnson Co. NE, 4488 35 F4
Johnson Co. TN, 17499 111 F3
Johnson Co. TX, 126811 59 E3
Johnson Co. WY, 7075 25 D4
Johnson Creek WI, 1581 74 C3
Johnsonville SC, 1418 122 C4
Johnston IA, 8649 86 C2
Johnston SC, 2336 121 F4
Johnston City IL, 3557 108 C1
Johnston Co. NC, 121965 113 D4
Johnston Co. OK, 10513 51 F4
Johnstown CO, 3827 33 E4
Johnstown NY, 8511 79 F3
Johnstown OH, 3440 91 D4
Johnstown PA, 23906 92 B4
Joiner AR, 540 118 B1
Joliet IL, 106221 89 D2
Joliet MT, 575 24 B2
Jollyville TX, 15813 61 E1
Jones OK, 2517 51 E3
Jonesboro AR, 55515 108 A4
Jonesboro GA, 3829 120 C4
Jonesboro IL, 1853 108 C1
Jonesboro IN, 1887 89 F4
Jonesboro LA, 3914 125 E3
Jonesborough TN, 4168 111 E3
Jonesburg MO, 695 97 F3
Jones Co. GA, 23639 129 D1
Jones Co. IA, 20221 87 F1
Jones Co. MS, 64958 126 C4
Jones Co. NC, 10381 115 D3
Jones Co. SD, 1193 26 C4
Jones Co. TX, 20785 58 C2
Jones Creek TX, 2130 132 A4
Jonesport ME, 650 83 E2
Jonestown MS, 1701 118 A3
Jonestown PA, 1028 93 E4
Jonestown TX, 1681 61 E1
Jonesville LA, 2469 125 F4
Jonesville MI, 2337 90 B1
Jonesville NC, 1464 112 A3
Jonesville SC, 982 121 F2
Jonesville VT, 375 81 D2
Jonesville VA, 995 111 D3
Joplin MO, 45504 106 B2
Joplin MT, 210 15 F2
Joppatowne MD, 11391 145 D1
Jordan MN, 3833 66 C4
Jordan MT, 364 17 D3
Jordan NY, 1314 79 D3
Joseph OR, 1054 22 A2
Joseph City AZ, 1000 47 F3
Josephine TX, 594 59 F2
Josephine Co. OR, 75726 28 B2
Joshua TX, 4528 59 E3
Joshua Tree CA, 4207 53 E2
Jourdanton TX, 3732 61 D3
Juab Co. UT, 8238 39 D1
Judith Basin Co. MT, 2329 16 A3
Judsonia AR, 1982 117 F1
Julesburg CO, 1467 34 A3
Juliaetta ID, 609 14 B4
Julian CA, 1621 53 D4
Julian NC, 600 112 B4
Jumpertown MS, 404 119 D2
Junction TX, 2618 60 C1
Junction UT, 177 39 E3
Junction City AR, 721 125 E1
Junction City KS, 18886 43 F2
Junction City KY, 2184 110 B1
Junction City LA, 652 125 E1
Junction City OH, 818 101 E1
Junction City OR, 4721 20 B3
Juneau AK, 30711 155 E4
Juneau WI, 2485 74 C2
Juneau Co. WI, 24316 74 A1
Juniata NE, 693 35 D4
Juniata Co. PA, 22821 93 D3
Junior WV, 450 102 A2
Juno Beach FL, 3262 141 F4
Jupiter FL, 39328 141 F4
Jupiter Island FL, 620 141 F4
Justice IL, 12193 203 D5
Justin TX, 1891 59 E2
Justus PA, 950 261 E1

K

Kaaawa HI, 1324 152 A2
Kaanapali HI, 1375 153 D1
Kadoka SD, 706 26 B4
Kahaluu HI, 2935 152 A3
Kahoka MO, 2241 87 E4
Kahuku HI, 2097 152 A2
Kahului HI, 20146 153 D1
Kaibab AZ, 275 47 D1
Kaibito AZ, 1607 47 E1
Kailua HI, 38635 152 B3
Kailua-Kona HI, 9870 153 E3
Kake AK, 710 155 E4
Kalaheo HI, 3913 152 B1
Kalama WA, 1783 20 C1
Kalamazoo MI, 77145 75 F4
Kalamazoo Co. MI, 238603 75 F4
Kalaoa HI, 6794 153 E3
Kalaupapa HI, 152 C3
Kalawao Co. HI, 147 152 C3
Kaleva MI, 509 75 F1
Kalida OH, 1031 90 B3
Kalihiwai HI, 717 152 B1
Kalispell MT, 14223 15 D2
Kalkaska MI, 2226 69 F4
Kalkaska Co. MI, 16571 70 B4
Kalona IA, 2293 87 E2
Kamas UT, 1274 31 F4
Kamiah ID, 1160 22 B1
Kanab UT, 3564 47 D1
Kanabec Co. MN, 14996 67 D2
Kanarraville UT, 311 39 D4
Kanawha IA, 739 72 C3
Kanawha WV, 500 101 F2
Kanawha Co. WV, 200073 101 F4
Kandiyohi MN, 555 66 B3
Kandiyohi Co. MN, 41203 66 B3
Kane PA, 4126 92 B2
Kane Co. IL, 404119 88 C1
Kane Co. UT, 6046 39 E4
Kaneohe HI, 34970 152 A3
Kankakee IL, 27491 89 D3
Kankakee Co. IL, 103833 89 D2
Kannapolis NC, 36910 122 B1
Kanopolis KS, 543 43 E2
Kanosh UT, 485 39 D2
Kansas IL, 842 99 D1
Kansas OK, 685 106 B3
Kansas City KS, 146866 96 B2
Kansas City MO, 441545 96 B2
Kapaa HI, 9472 152 B1
Kapaau HI, 1159 153 E2
Kaplan LA, 5177 133 E3
Karlstad MN, 794 19 F2
Karnak IL, 619 108 C2
Karnes City TX, 3457 61 E3
Karnes Co. TX, 15446 61 E3
Karns TN, 1500 110 C4
Kasigluk AK, 543 154 B3
Kasota MN, 680 72 C1
Kasson IN, 1500 99 D4
Kasson MN, 4398 73 D1
Kathleen FL, 3280 140 C2
Kathleen GA, 650 129 D2
Katonah NY, 3600 148 C2
Katy TX, 11775 132 A3
Keavy KY, 450 110 C2
Kechi KS, 1038 43 E4
Keedysville MD, 482 144 A1
Keegan ME, 650 85 E1
Keego Harbor MI, 2769 210 A1
Keene NH, 22563 95 D1
Keene TX, 5003 59 E3
Keeneland KY, 383 230 F1
Keener NC, 508 123 E2
Keenesburg CO, 855 41 E1
Keeseville NY, 1850 81 D2
Keewatin MN, 1164 64 B3
Keiser AR, 808 108 B4
Keith Co. NE, 8875 34 B3
Keithsburg IL, 714 87 F3
Keizer OR, 32203 20 B2
Kekaha HI, 3175 152 B1
Keller TX, 27345 59 E2
Kellogg ID, 2395 14 B3
Kellogg IA, 606 87 D1
Kellyville OK, 906 51 F2
Kelseyville CA, 2928 36 B2
Kelso MO, 527 108 B2
Kelso WA, 11895 20 B1
Kemah TX, 2330 132 B3
Kemblesville PA, 1000 146 B4
Kemmerer WY, 2651 31 F2
Kemp TX, 1133 59 F3
Kemper Co. MS, 10453 127 D2
Kempner TX, 1004 59 E4
Kenai AK, 6942 154 C3
Kenansville NC, 1149 123 E2
Kenbridge VA, 1253 113 D2
Kendall FL, 75226 143 E2
Kendall NY, 750 78 B3
Kendall Co. IL, 54544 88 C2
Kendall Co. TX, 23743 61 D2
Kendall Park NJ, 9006 147 D1
Kendallville IN, 9616 90 A2
Kendrick FL, 600 138 C4
Kendrick ID, 369 14 B4
Kenedy TX, 3487 61 E3
Kenedy Co. TX, 414 63 F3
Kenefick TX, 667 132 B2
Kenesaw NE, 873 35 D4
Kenilworth IL, 2494 203 D2
Kenilworth NJ, 7675 240 A4
Kensington KS, 529 43 D1
Kensington MD, 1873 270 C1
Kensington NY, 1209 241 G2
Kensington Park FL, 3720 266 C5
Kent CT, 650 94 B3
Kent OH, 27906 91 E3
Kent WA, 79524 12 C3
Kent City MI, 1061 75 F3
Kent Co. DE, 126697 145 E3
Kent Co. MD, 19197 145 D2
Kent Co. MI, 574335 75 F3
Kent Co. RI, 167090 150 C3
Kent Co. TX, 859 58 B2
Kentfield CA, 6351 259 A1
Kentland IN, 1822 89 D3
Kenton DE, 237 145 E2
Kenton OH, 8336 90 C3
Kenton TN, 1306 108 C3
Kenton Co. KY, 151464 100 B2
Kents Hill ME, 375 82 B2
Kentwood LA, 2205 134 B1
Kentwood MI, 45255 75 F3
Kenvil NJ, 12569 148 A3
Kenwood MD, 9800 193 D2
Kenwood OH, 7423 204 C2
Kenwood Beach MD, 600 144 C4
Kenyon MN, 1661 73 D1
Keokuk IA, 11427 87 F4
Keokuk Co. IA, 11400 87 E2
Keosauqua IA, 1066 87 E3
Keota IA, 1025 87 E2
Keota OK, 517 116 B1
Kerens TX, 1681 59 F3
Kerhonkson NY, 1732 94 A3
Kerkhoven MN, 759 66 B3
Kerman CA, 8551 44 C3
Kermit TX, 5714 57 F3
Kern Co. CA, 661645 45 D4
Kernersville NC, 17126 112 B4
Kernville CA, 1736 45 E4
Kerr Co. TX, 43653 60 C2
Kerrville TX, 20425 60 C2
Kersey CO, 1389 33 E4
Kershaw SC, 1645 122 B2
Kershaw Co. SC, 52647 122 B3
Keshena WI, 1394 68 C4
Ketchikan AK, 7922 155 E4

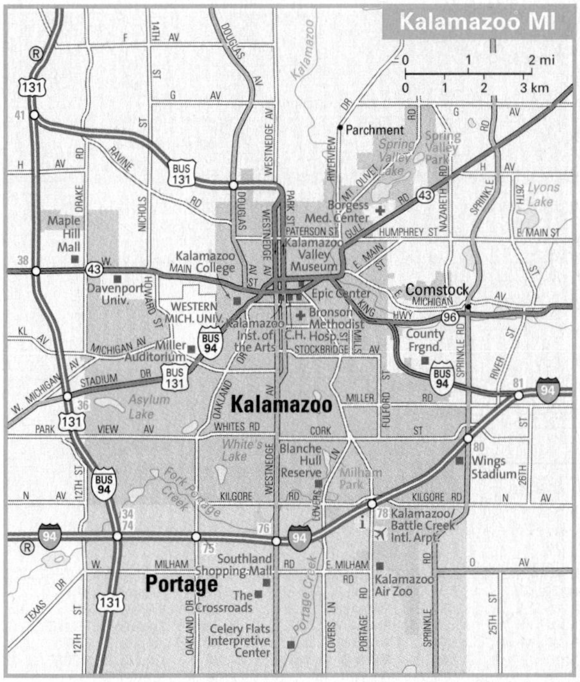

Kalamazoo MI
Kalamazoo
Portage
Comstock
Parchment
Spring Valley Park
Lyons Lake
Maple Hill Mall
Borgess Med. Center
Kalamazoo Valley Museum
Kalamazoo College
Davenport Univ.
WESTERN MICH. UNIV.
Epic Center
Bronson Methodist Hosp.
Kalamazoo Inst. of the Arts
C.H. Hosp.
Miller Auditorium
County Frgnd.
Asylum Lake
White's Lake
Blanche Hull Reserve
Milham Park
Wings Stadium
Kalamazoo/Battle Creek Intl. Arpt.
Kalamazoo Air Zoo
Southland Shopping Mall
The Crossroads
Celery Flats Interpretive Center
Fort Custer Creek
Portage Creek
0 1 2 mi
0 1 2 3 km

Kauai Co. HI, 58463 152 B1
Kaufman TX, 6490 59 F2
Kaufman Co. TX, 71313 59 F3
Kaukauna WI, 12983 74 C1
Kaumakani HI, 607 152 B1
Kaunakakai HI, 2726 152 C3
Kawkawlin MI, 1600 76 B2
Kaycee WY, 249 25 D4
Kay Co. OK, 48080 51 E1
Kayenta AZ, 4922 47 F1
Kaysville UT, 20351 31 E3
Keaau HI, 2010 153 F3
Kealakekua HI, 1645 153 E3
Keams Canyon AZ, 260 47 F2
Keansburg NJ, 10732 147 E1
Kearney MO, 8452 96 B2
Kearney NE, 27431 35 D4
Kearney Co. NE, 6882 35 D4
Kearneysville WV, 650 103 D2
Kearns UT, 33659 257 A2
Kearny AZ, 2249 55 D2
Kearny NJ, 40513 148 B4
Kearny Co. KS, 4531 42 B3
Keauhou HI, 2414 153 E3
Kenilworth PA, 1576 146 B2
Kenly NC, 1569 123 E1
Kenmare ND, 1081 18 B1
Kenmore NY, 16426 78 A3
Kenmore WA, 18678 262 B2
Kennebec SD, 286 26 C4
Kennebec Co. ME, 117114 82 B2
Kennebunk ME, 4804 82 B4
Kennebunkport ME, 1376 82 B4
Kennedale TX, 5850 207 B3
Kennedy AL, 541 119 D4
Kenner LA, 70517 134 B3
Kennesaw GA, 21675 120 C3
Kenneth City FL, 4400 266 A3
Kennett MO, 11260 108 B3
Kennett Square PA, 5273 146 B3
Kennewick WA, 54693 21 E1
Keno OR, 650 28 C2
Kenosha WI, 90352 75 D4
Kenosha Co. WI, 149577 74 C4
Kenova WV, 3485 101 D4
Kensett AR, 1791 117 F1
Kensington CA, 4936 259 C2
Kensington CT, 8541 149 E1
Ketchum ID, 3003 22 C4
Kettering OH, 57502 100 B1
Kettle Falls WA, 1527 13 F1
Kettleman City CA, 1499 44 C3
Kevil KY, 574 108 C2
Kewanee IL, 12944 88 A2
Kewanna IN, 614 89 E3
Kewaskum WI, 3274 74 C2
Kewaunee WI, 2806 75 D1
Kewaunee Co. WI, 20187 69 D4
Keweenaw Co. MI, 2301 65 F3
Keya Paha Co. NE, 983 35 D1
Key Biscayne FL, 10507 143 F2
Key Colony Beach FL, 788 143 D4
Keyes CA, 4575 36 C4
Key Largo FL, 11886 143 E3
Keyport NJ, 7568 147 E1
Keys OK, 458 106 B4
Keyser WV, 5303 102 C2
Keystone CO, 825 41 D1
Keystone IA, 687 87 E1
Keystone SD, 311 25 F4
Keystone WV, 453 111 F1
Keystone Hts. FL, 1349 139 D3

Figures after entries indicate population, page number, and grid reference.

Avondale C2
Birmingham C2
Claycomo C2
Countryside B4
Edwardsville A3
Fairway B3
Farley A1
Ferrelview B1
Gladstone C2
Glenaire C2
Houston Lake B2
Independence D3
Kansas City, KS B2
Kansas City, MO C2
Lake Quivira A3
Lake Waukomis B2
Lees Summit D4
Lenexa A4
Liberty D2
Merriam B4
Mission B3
Mission Hills B4
N. Kansas City B2
Northmoor B2
Oaks C2
Oakview C2
Oakwood C2
Oakwood Park C2
Olathe A4
Overland Park B4
Parkville B2
Platte Woods B2
Pleasant Valley C2
Prairie Vil. B4
Randolph C2
Raytown C4
River Bend D2
Riverside B2
Roeland Park B3
Shawnee A3
Smithville C1
Sugar Creek D3
Unity Vil. D4
Waldron A2
Weatherby Lake B2
Westwood B3

Keysville VA, *817* **113** D2
Keytesville MO, *533* **97** D2
Key West FL, *25478* **142** C4
Kezar Falls ME, *750* **82** A3
Kiamesha Lake NY, *700* **148** A1
Kiawah Island SC, *1163* **131** D2
Kibler AR, *969* **116** C1
Kidder Co. ND, *2753* **18** C4
Kiefer OK, *1026* **51** F2
Kiel WI, *3450* **74** C2
Kiester MN, *540* **72** C2
Kihei HI, *16749* **153** D1
Kilauea HI, *2092* **152** B1
Kilbourne LA, *436* **125** F1
Kildeer IL, *3460* **203** B2
Kilgore TX, *11301* **124** B2
Killbuck OH, *839* **91** E4
Killdeer ND, *713* **18** A3
Kill Devil Hills NC, *5897* **115** F2
Killeen TX, *86911* **59** E4
Killen AL, *1119* **119** E2
Killian LA, *1053* **134** B2
Killona LA, *797* **239** A1
Kilmarnock VA, *1244* **113** F1
Kilmichael MS, *830* **118** C4
Kiln MS, *2040* **134** C2
Kimball MN, *635* **66** C3
Kimball NE, *2559* **33** F3
Kimball SD, *745* **27** D4
Kimball TN, *1312* **120** A2
Kimball WV, *411* **111** F1
Kimball Co. NE, *4089* **33** F3
Kimberling City MO, *2253* **107** D3
Kimberly AL, *1801* **119** F4
Kimberly ID, *2614* **30** C1
Kimberly WI, *6146* **74** C1
Kimberton PA, *2500* **146** B2
Kimble Co. TX, *4468* **60** C1
Kincaid IL, *1441* **98** B1
Kinde MI, *534* **76** C1
Kinder LA, *2148* **133** E2
Kinderhook NY, *1275* **94** B2
Kindred ND, *614* **19** E4
King NC, *5952* **112** A3
King WI, *2215* **74** B1
King and Queen Co. VA, *6630* **113** F1
King and Queen C.H. VA, *50* **113** F1
King City CA, *11094* **44** B3
King City MO, *1012* **86** B4
King City OR, *1949* **251** C3
King Co. TX, *356* **58** C1
King Co. WA, *1737034* **12** C3
King Cove AK, *792* **154** B4
Kingfield ME, *600* **82** B1
Kingfisher OK, *4380* **51** E2
Kingfisher Co. OK, *13926* **51** E2
King George VA, *375* **103** E4
King George Co. VA, *16803* **103** E4
Kingman AZ, *20069* **46** B3
Kingman IN, *538* **99** E1
Kingman KS, *3387* **43** E4
Kingman Co. KS, *8673* **43** E4
King of Prussia PA, *18511* **146** C2
King Salmon AK, *442* **154** B3
Kings Beach CA, *4037* **37** D2
Kingsburg CA, *9199* **45** D3
Kingsbury TX, *652* **61** E2
Kingsbury Co. SD, *5815* **27** E3
Kings Co. CA, *129461* **44** C3
Kings Co. NY, *2465326* **147** F1
Kingsford MI, *5549* **68** C2
Kingsford Hts. IN, *1453* **89** E2
Kingsland AR, *449* **117** E4
Kingsland GA, *10506* **139** D1
Kingsland TX, *4584* **61** D1
Kingsley IA, *1245* **35** F1
Kingsley MI, *1469* **69** F4
Kings Mtn. NC, *9693* **122** A1
Kings Park NY, *16146* **149** D3
Kings Pt. NY, *5076* **148** B4
Kingsport TN, *44905* **111** E3
Kingston GA, *659* **120** B3
Kingston ID, *650* **14** B3
Kingston IL, *980* **88** C1
Kingston KY, *600* **110** C1
Kingston MA, *5380* **151** E2
Kingston MI, *450* **76** C2
Kingston MO, *287* **96** C1
Kingston NH, *1700* **95** E1
Kingston NJ, *1292* **147** D1
Kingston NY, *23456* **94** B2
Kingston OH, *1032* **101** D2
Kingston OK, *1390* **59** F1
Kingston PA, *13855* **93** E2
Kingston RI, *5446* **150** C4
Kingston TN, *5264* **110** B4

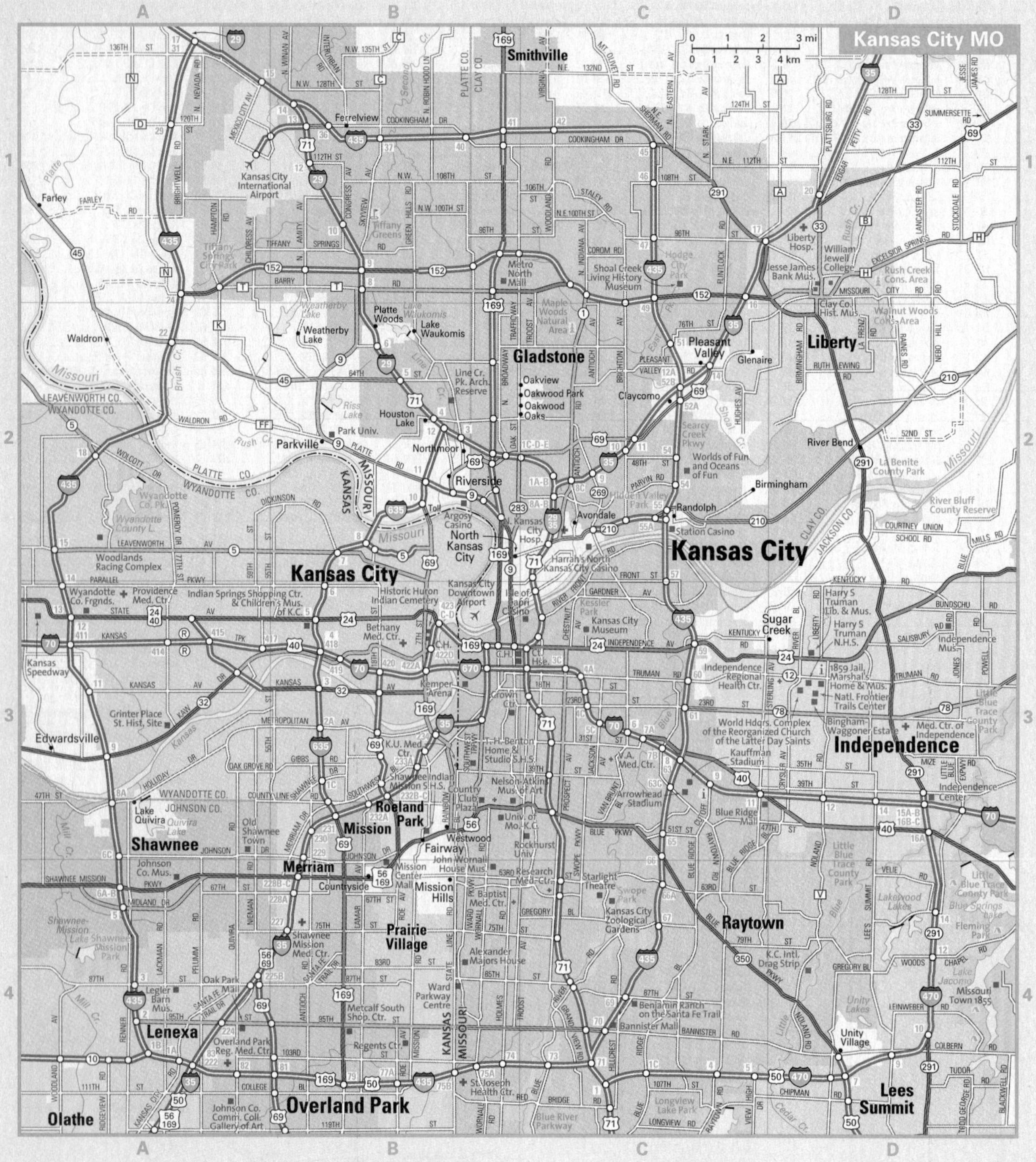

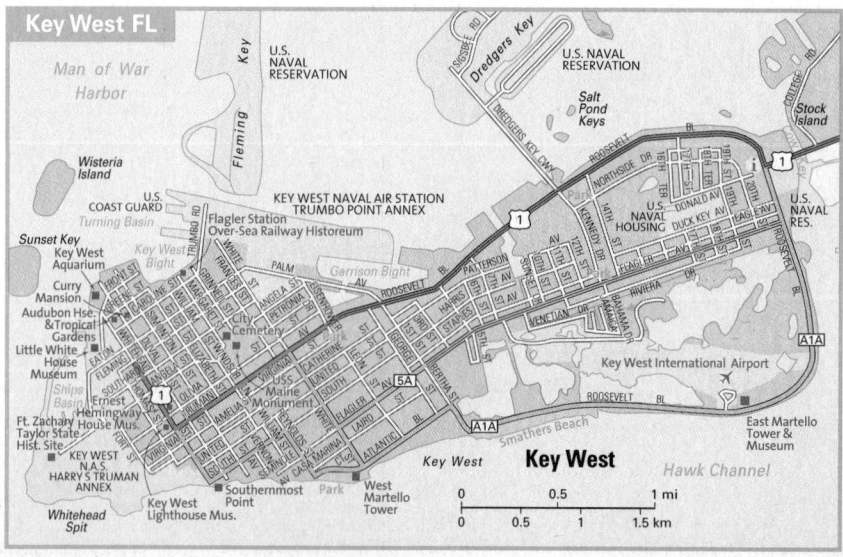

Entries in **bold** indicate counties or parishes. Entries in color indicate cities with detailed inset maps.

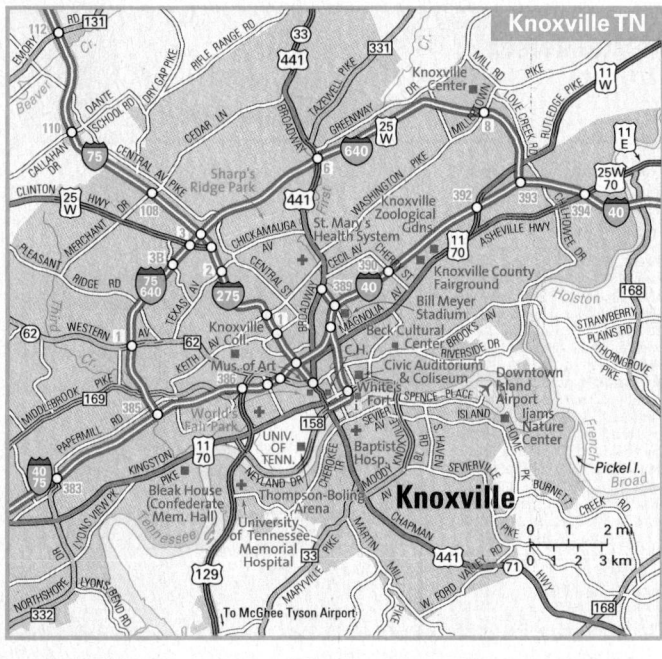

Knoxville TN

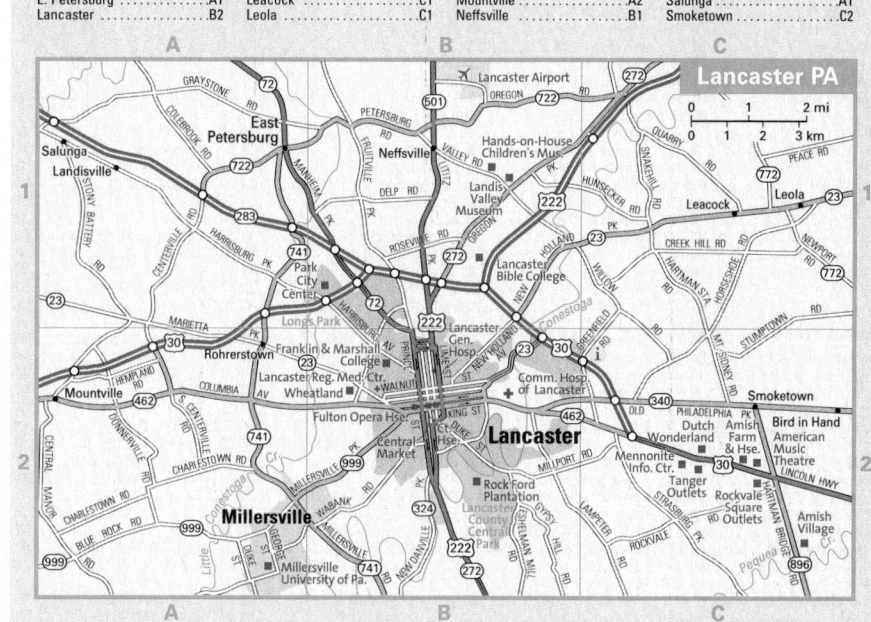

Lancaster PA

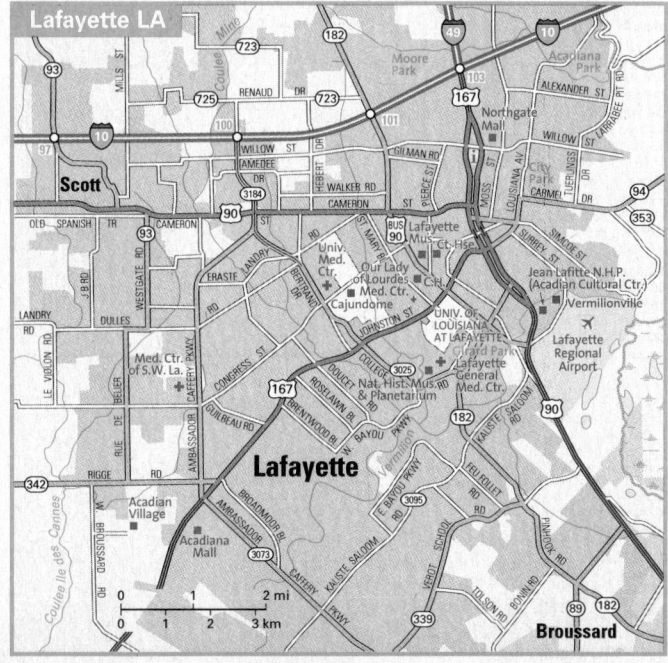

Lafayette LA

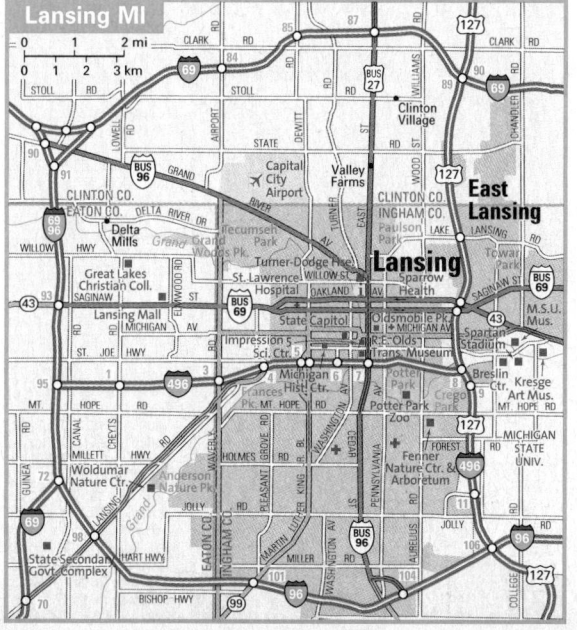

Lansing MI

226 Lake Geneva—Lawnside

Figures after entries indicate population, page number, and grid reference.

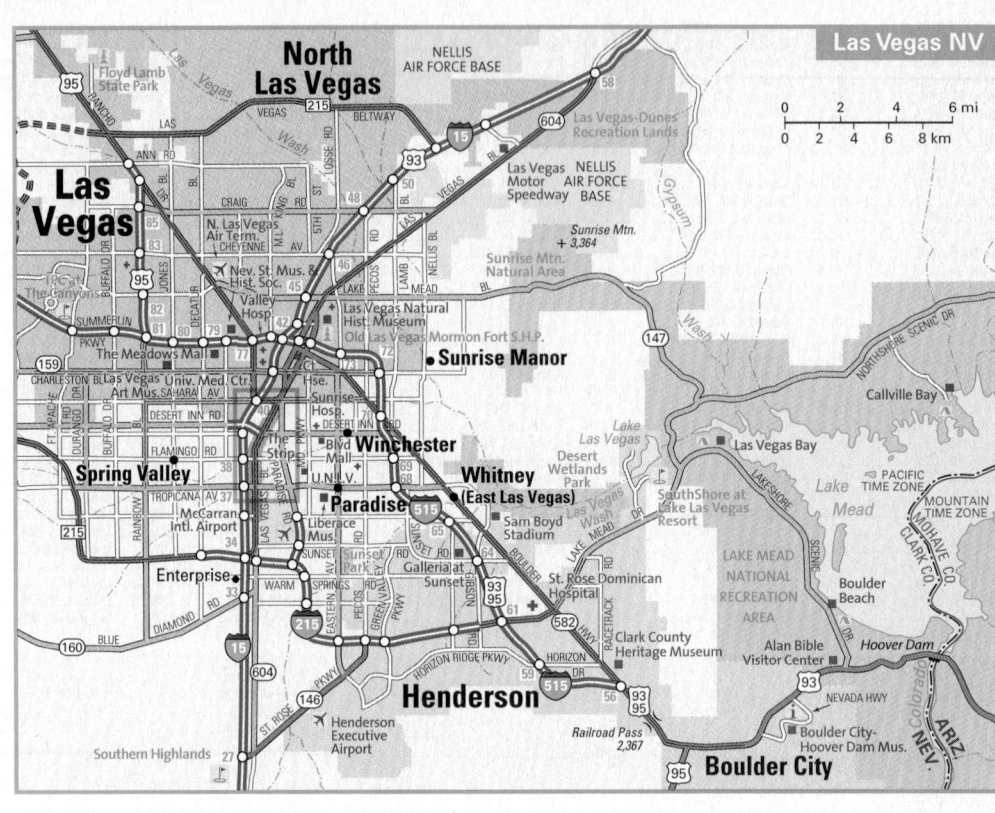

Las Vegas NV

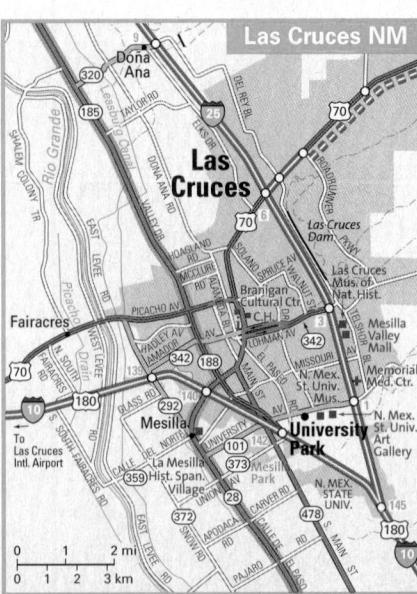

Las Cruces NM

Las Vegas Strip NV

Entries in **bold** indicate counties or parishes. Entries in color indicate cities with detailed inset maps.

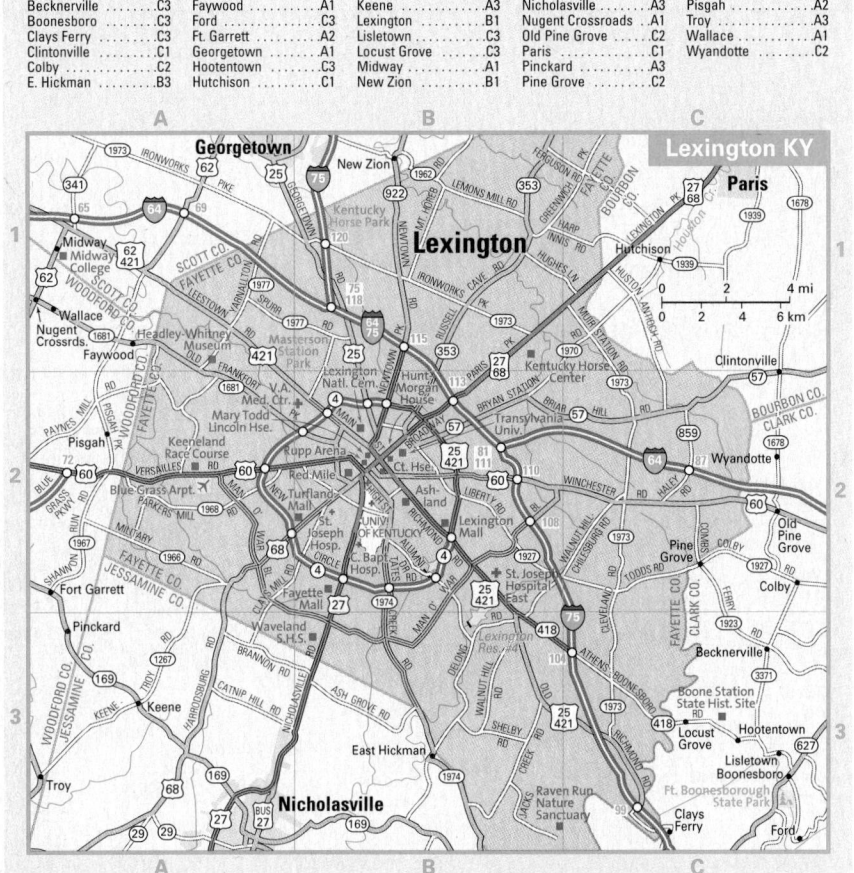

Figures after entries indicate population, page number, and grid reference.

TRAVEL NOTE: Beginning January 2002, California started numbering freeway exits using a mileage-based numbering system. Full implementation is expected to take three years. For more details, including a complete listing of California's exit numbers, go to www.dot.ca.gov/hq/traffops/signtech/calnexus/index.htm.

Entries in **bold** indicate counties or parishes. Entries in color indicate cities with detailed inset maps.

229

Los Angeles CA

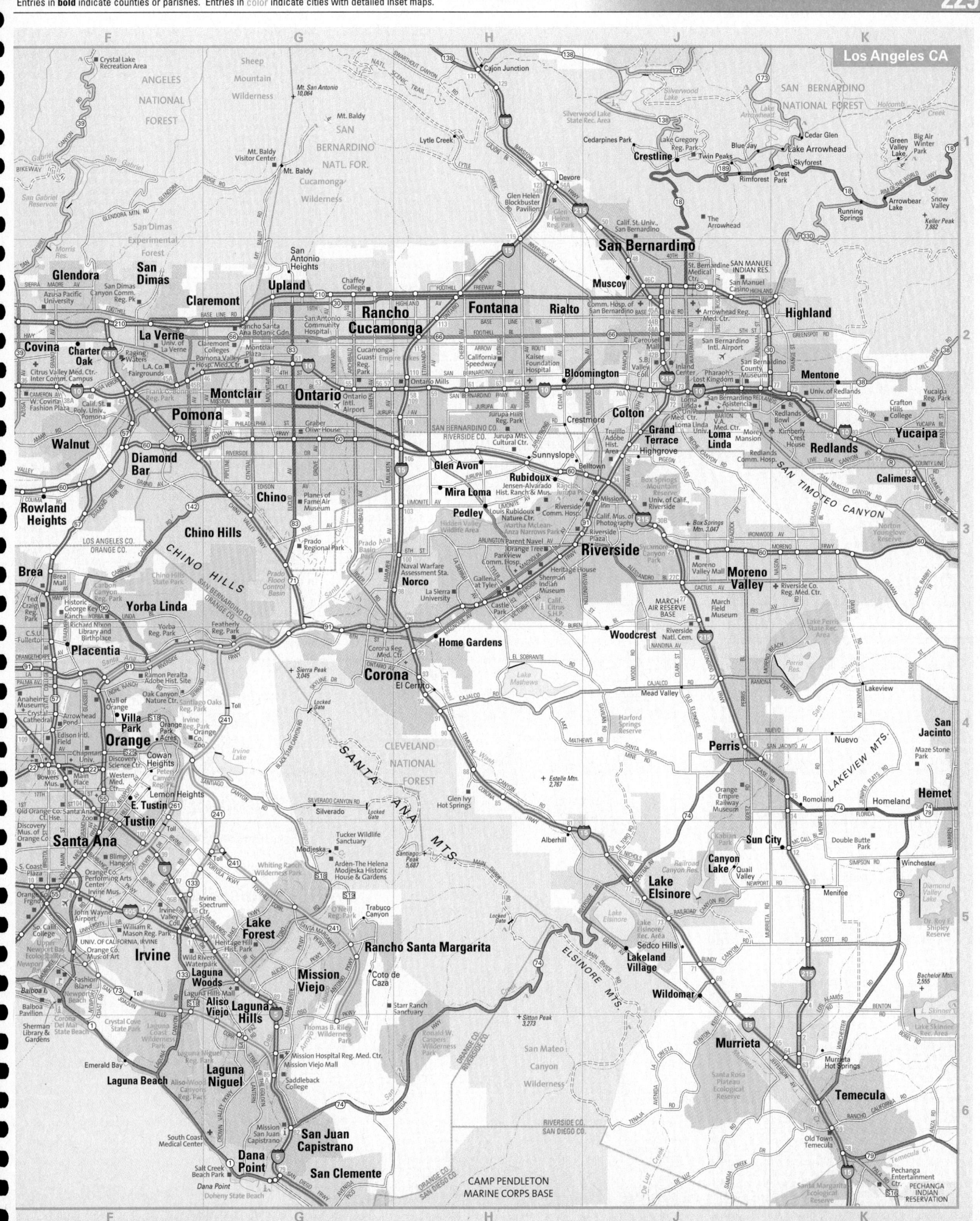

Downtown Los Angeles CA

Louisville KY

Entries in **bold** indicate counties or parishes. Entries in color indicate cities with detailed inset maps.

Logan—Macon **231**

Logan IA, 1545	86	A2
Logan KS, 603	42	C1
Logan NM, 1094	49	F3
Logan OH, 6704	101	D1
Logan UT, 42670	31	E2
Logan WV, 1630	101	E4
Logan Co. AR, 22486	116	C1
Logan Co. CO, 20504	34	A4
Logan Co. IL, 31183	98	B1
Logan Co. KS, 3046	42	B2
Logan Co. KY, 26573	109	F2
Logan Co. NE, 774	34	C3
Logan Co. ND, 2308	18	C4
Logan Co. OH, 46005	90	B4
Logan Co. OK, 33924	51	E2
Logan Co. WV, 37710	101	E4

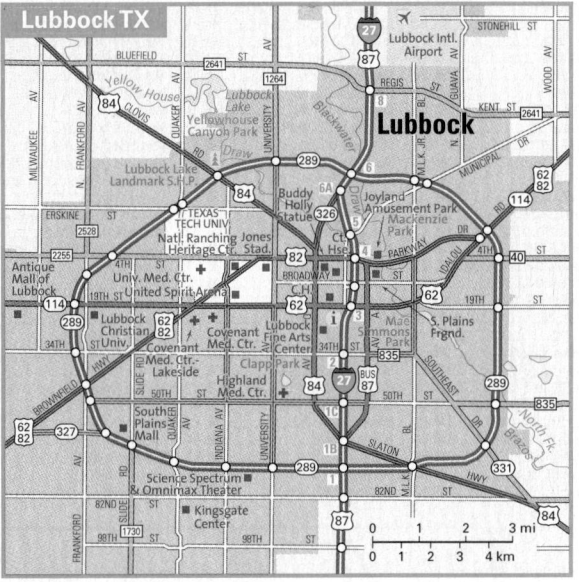

Lubbock TX

Logandale NV, 800	46	B1
Logansport IN, 19684	89	E3
Logansport LA, 1630	124	C3
Loganville GA, 5435	121	D4
Loganville PA, 908	103	E1
Log Cabin TX, 733	59	F3
Log Lane Vil. CO, 1006	33	F4
Loleta CA, 600	28	A4
Lolita TX, 548	61	F3
Lolo MT, 3388	15	D4
Loma Linda CA, 18681	229	J3
Loma Linda MO, 507	106	B2
Loma Rica CA, 2075	36	C2
Lombard IL, 42322	203	B4
Lometa TX, 782	59	D4
Lomira WI, 2233	74	C2
Lomita CA, 20046	228	C4
Lompoc CA, 41103	52	A2
Lonaconing MD, 1205	102	C1
London AR, 925	117	D1
London KY, 5692	110	C2
London OH, 8771	100	C1
Londonderry NH, 11417	95	E1
Londonderry VT, 300	81	D4
Londontown MD, 7595	144	C3
Lone Grove OK, 4631	51	E4
Lone Jack MO, 528	96	C3

Lone Oak KY, 454	108	C2
Lone Oak TX, 521	59	F2
Lone Pine CA, 1655	45	E3
Lone Rock WI, 929	74	A3
Lone Star LA, 1400	239	A2
Lone Star TX, 1631	124	B1
Lone Tree CO, 4873	209	C4
Lone Tree IA, 1151	87	F2
Lone Wolf OK, 500	51	D3
Long Beach CA, 461522	52	C3
Long Beach IN, 1559	89	E1
Long Beach MD, 2487	103	E3
Long Beach MS, 17320	135	D2
Long Beach NY, 35462	147	F1
Long Beach WA, 1283	12	A4
Long Branch NJ, 31340	147	F2
Long Co. GA, 10304	130	B3
Long Creek IL, 1364	98	C1
Long Green MD, 1000	144	C1
Long Grove IL, 6735	203	C2
Long Grove IA, 597	88	A1
Long Lake MN, 1842	66	C4
Longmeadow MA, 15633	150	A2
Longmont CO, 71093	41	E1
Long Pond MA, 1500	151	E3
Longport NJ, 1054	147	F4
Long Prairie MN, 3040	66	B2
Longton KS, 394	43	F4
Long Valley NJ, 1818	94	A4
Long View NC, 4871	111	F4
Longview TX, 73344	124	B2
Longview WA, 34660	20	B1
Longwood FL, 13745	141	D1
Lonoke AR, 4287	117	F2
Lonoke Co. AR, 52828	117	F2
Lonsdale MN, 1491	67	D4
Loogootee IN, 2741	99	E3
Lookout CA, 6260	36	C2
Loomis CA, 6260	36	C2
Loomis NE, 397	35	D4
Lorain OH, 68652	91	D2

Loraine TX, 656	58	B3
Lorane PA, 2994	146	B2
Lorain Co. OH, 284664	91	D2
Lordsburg NM, 3379	55	F3
Lordstown OH, 3633	91	F2
Loreauville LA, 938	133	F3
Lorena TX, 1433	59	E4
Lorenzo TX, 1372	58	A1
Loretto KY, 623	110	A1
Loretto MN, 570	66	C3
Loretto PA, 1190	92	B4
Loretto TN, 1665	119	E2
Loris SC, 2079	123	D3
Lorton VA, 17786	144	B3
Los Alamitos CA, 11536	228	C4
Los Alamos CA, 1372	52	A1
Los Alamos NM, 11909	48	C2
Los Alamos Co. NM, 18343	48	C2
Los Altos CA, 27693	36	A4
Los Altos Hills CA, 7902	259	C5
Los Banos CA, 25869	44	B2
Los Chavez NM, 5033	48	C4
Los Fresnos TX, 4512	63	F4
Los Gatos CA, 28592	36	B4
Los Indios TX, 1149	63	F4
Los Lunas NM, 10034	48	C4
Los Molinos CA, 1952	36	B1
Los Olivos CA, 950	52	A2
Los Osos CA, 14351	44	B4
Los Padillas NM, 1800	48	C3
Los Ranchos de Albuquerque NM, 5092	48	C3
Lost Creek WV, 467	102	A2
Lost Hills CA, 1938	44	C4
Lost Nation IA, 497	87	F1
Lott TX, 724	59	F4
Loudon TN, 4476	110	C4
Loudon Co. TN, 39086	110	C4
Loudonville NY, 10800	94	B1
Loudonville OH, 2906	91	D3
Loudoun Co. VA, 169599	144	A2

Loughman FL, 1385	141	D2
Louisa KY, 2018	101	D4
Louisa VA, 1401	103	D4
Louisa Co. IA, 12183	87	F2
Louisa Co. VA, 25627	103	D4
Louisburg KS, 2576	96	B3
Louisburg NC, 3111	113	D4
Louise TX, 977	61	F3
Louisiana MO, 3863	97	F2
Louisville AL, 612	128	B3
Louisville CO, 18937	41	E1
Louisville GA, 2712	129	F1
Louisville IL, 1242	98	C3
Louisville KY, 256231	100	A4
Louisville MS, 7006	126	C1
Louisville NE, 1046	35	F3
Louisville OH, 8904	91	E3
Louisville TN, 2001	110	C4
Loup City NE, 996	35	D3
Loup Co. NE, 712	35	D2
Love Co. OK, 8831	59	E4
Lovelady TX, 608	132	A1
Loveland CO, 50608	33	E4
Loveland OH, 11677	100	B2
Loveland Park OH, 1799	204	C1
Lovell WY, 2281	24	C1
Lovelock NV, 2003	29	F4
Loves Park IL, 20044	74	B4
Lovettsville VA, 853	144	A2
Loveville MD, 650	103	E4
Lovilia IA, 583	87	D3
Loving NM, 1326	57	E3
Loving Co. TX, 67	57	E3
Lovingston VA, 475	112	C1
Lovington IL, 1222	98	C1
Lovington NM, 9471	57	F2
Lowden IA, 794	87	F1
Lowell AR, 5013	106	A3
Lowell IN, 7505	89	D2
Lowell MA, 105167	95	E1
Lowell MI, 4013	75	F3
Lowell NC, 2662	122	A1
Lowell OH, 628	101	F1
Lowell OR, 857	20	C4
Lowellville OH, 1281	91	F3
Lower Brule SD, 599	27	D3
Lower Lake CA, 1755	36	B3
Lowesville NC, 1440	122	A1
Low Moor VA, 367	112	B1
Lowndes Co. AL, 13473	127	E1
Lowndes Co. GA, 92115	137	D3
Lowndes Co. MS, 61586	127	D1
Lowry City MO, 728	96	C4
Lowville NY, 3476	79	E2
Loxley AL, 1348	135	E2
Loyal WI, 1308	68	A4
Loyalhanna PA, 3415	92	B4
Loyall KY, 766	111	D2
Loyalton CA, 862	37	D1
Lubbock TX, 199564	58	A1
Lubbock Co. TX, 242628	58	A1
Lubec ME, 650	83	F1
Lubeck WV, 1303	101	E2
Lucama NC, 847	113	D4
Lucas OH, 620	91	D3
Lucas KS, 436	43	D2
Lucas TX, 2890	59	F2
Lucas Co. IA, 9422	87	D3
Lucas Co. OH, 455054	90	C2
Lucasville OH, 1588	101	D3
Luce Co. MI, 7024	69	F1
Lucedale MS, 2458	135	D1
Lucerne CA, 2870	36	B2
Lucerne WY, 525	24	C1
Lucernemines PA, 951	92	B4
Luck WI, 1210	67	E3
Luckey OH, 998	90	C2
Ludington MI, 8357	75	E1
Ludingtonville NY, 1000	148	C1
Ludlow KY, 4409	204	A3
Ludlow MA, 7400	150	A2
Ludlow VT, 958	81	E4
Ludowici GA, 1440	130	B4
Lufkin TX, 32709	124	A4
Lugoff SC, 6278	122	B3
Lukachukai AZ, 1565	48	A1
Lula GA, 1438	121	D3
Luling LA, 11512	239	A2
Luling TX, 5080	61	E2
Lumber City GA, 1247	129	F3
Lumberport WV, 937	102	A2
Lumberton MS, 2228	134	C1
Lumberton NJ, 2500	147	D3
Lumberton NC, 20795	123	D2
Lumberton TX, 8731	132	C2
Lumpkin GA, 1369	128	C3
Lumpkin Co. GA, 21016	120	C3
Luna Co. NM, 25016	56	A3
Luna Pier MI, 1483	90	C1
Lunenburg MA, 1695	95	D1
Lunenburg VT, 500	81	F2
Lunenburg VA, 40	113	D2
Lunenburg Co. VA, 13146	113	D2
Lupton AZ, 375	48	A3
Luray VA, 4871	102	C4
Lusby MD, 1666	103	F3
Lusk WY, 1447	33	E1
Lutcher LA, 3735	134	B3
Luther OK, 612	51	E2
Luthersville GA, 783	128	C1
Luttrell TN, 915	110	C4
Lutz FL, 17081	140	B2
Luverne AL, 2635	128	A4

Luverne MN, 4617	27	F4
Luxemburg WI, 1935	69	D4
Luxora AR, 1317	108	B4
Luzerne PA, 2952	261	B1
Luzerne Co. PA, 319250	93	E3
Lycoming Co. PA, 120044	93	D2
Lydia LA, 1079	133	F3
Lydick IN, 1300	89	E2
Lyerly GA, 488	120	B3
Lyford TX, 1973	63	F4
Lykens PA, 1937	93	E4
Lyle MN, 566	73	D2
Lyle WA, 530	21	D1
Lyman NE, 421	33	F2
Lyman SC, 2659	121	F2
Lyman WA, 409	12	C2
Lyman WY, 1938	32	A3
Lyman Co. SD, 3895	26	C4
Lynbrook NY, 19911	147	F1
Lynch KY, 900	111	D2
Lynch Hts. DE, 550	145	F3
Lynch Sta. VA, 500	112	C1
Lyndell PA, 1000	146	B3
Lynden WA, 9020	12	C1
Lyndhurst NJ, 19383	240	C1
Lyndhurst OH, 15279	204	G2
Lyndhurst VA, 1527	102	C4
Lyndon KS, 1038	96	A3
Lyndon Sta. WI, 475	74	B1
Lyndon NY, 4600	265	B2
Lyndon VT, 375	81	E2
Lyndon Ctr. VT, 1200	81	E2
Lyndonville NY, 862	78	B3
Lyndonville VT, 1227	81	E2
Lyndora PA, 6685	92	A3
Lynn AL, 597	119	E3
Lynn IN, 1143	90	A4
Lynn MA, 89050	151	E1
Lynn Haven FL, 12451	136	C2
Lynn Co. TX, 6550	58	A2
Lynnview KY, 965	230	D3
Lynnville IN, 781	99	E4
Lynnwood WA, 33847	12	C3
Lynwood CA, 69845	228	D3
Lyon MS, 418	118	A3
Lyon Co. IA, 11763	27	F4
Lyon Co. KS, 35935	43	F3
Lyon Co. KY, 8080	109	D2
Lyon Co. MN, 25425	72	A1
Lyon Co. NV, 34501	37	E2
Lyons CO, 1585	33	E4
Lyons GA, 4169	129	F3
Lyons IL, 10255	203	D5
Lyons IN, 748	99	E3
Lyons KS, 3732	43	E3
Lyons MI, 726	76	A3
Lyons NE, 963	35	F2
Lyons NY, 3695	79	D3
Lyons OH, 559	90	B2

Lyons OR, 1008	20	C3
Lyons Falls NY, 591	79	E2
Lyons Plain CT, 2100	148	C2
Lytle TX, 2383	61	D3

M

Mabank TX, 2151	59	F3
Mabel MN, 766	73	E2
Maben MS, 803	118	C4
Mableton GA, 29733	120	C4
Mabscott WV, 1403	111	F1
Mabton WA, 1891	21	E1
Mcclenny FL, 4459	138	C2
Macedon NY, 1496	78	C3
Macedonia OH, 9224	91	E2
Machesney Park IL, 20759	74	B4
Machias ME, 1376	83	E1
Machias NY, 1422	78	B4
Mack OH, 8900	204	A2
Mackay ID, 566	23	D4
Mackinac Co. MI, 11943	70	B1
Mackinac Island MI, 523	70	C1
Mackinaw IL, 1452	88	B4
Mackinaw City MI, 859	70	C1
Macksville KS, 514	43	D3
Macomb IL, 18558	88	A4
Macomb Co. MI, 788149	76	C4
Macon AR, 1100	117	E2
Macon GA, 97255	129	D2
Macon IL, 1213	98	C1
Macon MS, 2461	127	D1
Macon MO, 5538	97	E1

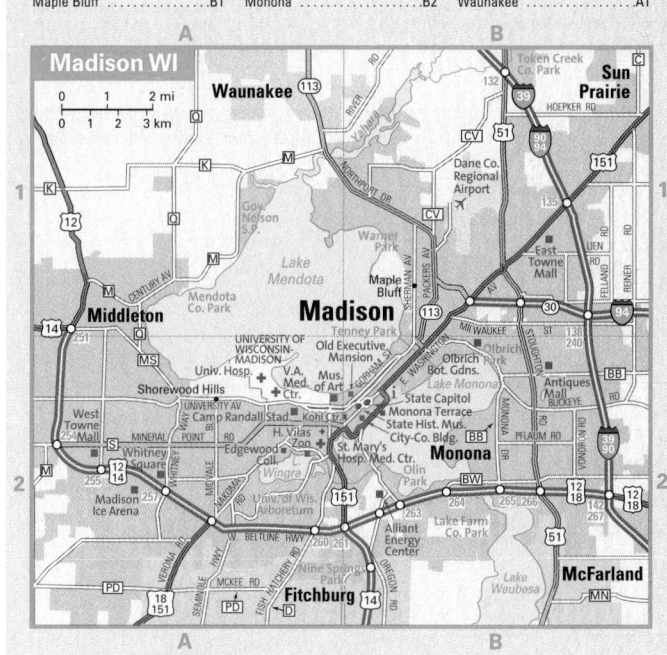

Madison WI

Fitchburg	A2	McFarland	B2	Shorewood Hills	A2
Madison	A1	Middleton	A1	Sun Prairie	B1
Maple Bluff	B1	Monona	B2	Waunakee	A1

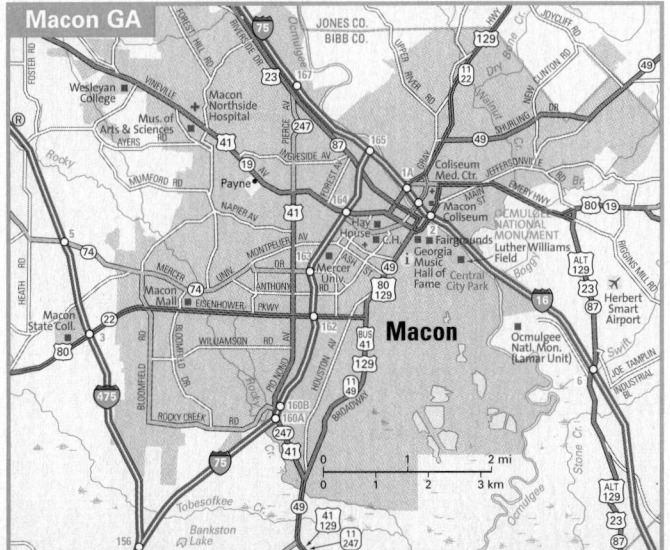

Macon GA

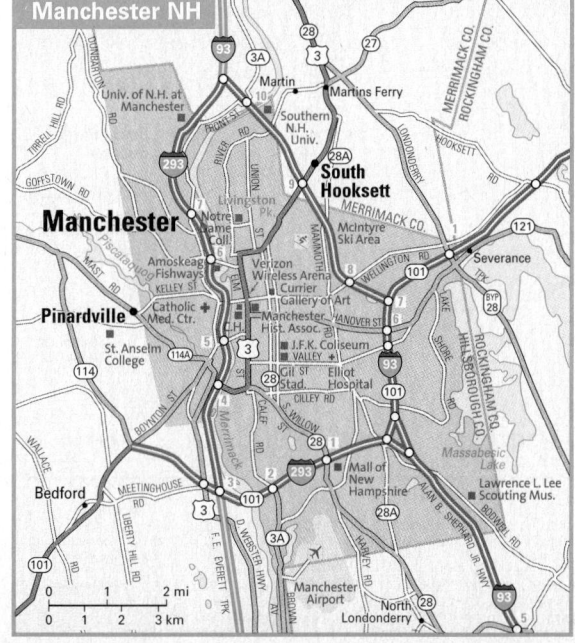

Manchester NH

Macon Co. AL, 24105 ....128 B3	Macy NE, 956 ....35 F2	Madill OK, 3410 ....51 F4	Madison Co. VA, 12520 ......102 C3	Makawao HI, 6327 ....153 D1	Manchaug MA, 850 ....150 C2	Manitowoc Co. WI, 82887 ....75 D1
Macon Co. GA, 14074 ....129 D2	Madawaska ME, 3326 ....35 F2	Madison AL, 29329 ....119 F2	Madison Hts. MI, 31101 ......210 C2	Makena HI, 5671 ....153 D1	Manchester GA, 3988 ....128 C2	Mankato KS, 976 ....43 E1
Macon Co. IL, 114706 ....98 C1	Maddock ND, 498 ....19 D2	Madison AR, 987 ....118 A2	Madison Hts. VA, 11584 .....112 C1	Malabar FL, 2622 ....141 E4	Manchester IA, 5257 ....73 F4	Mankato MN, 32427 ....72 C1
Macon Co. MO, 15762 ....97 D1	Madeira OH, 8923 ....204 C2	Madison CT, 2222 ....149 E2	Madison Lake MN, 837 ....72 C1	Malad City ID, 2158 ....31 E2	Manchester KY, 1738 ....110 C2	Manlius NY, 4819 ....79 E3
Macon Co. NC, 29811 ....121 D1	Madeira Beach FL, 4511 .....140 B3	Madison FL, 3061 ....137 F2	Madison GA, 3636 ....121 D4	Malaga CA, 1400 ....44 C2	Manchester MD, 3329 ....103 E1	Manly IA, 1342 ....73 D3
Macon Co. TN, 20386 ....110 A3	Madelia MN, 2340 ....72 B1	Madison IL, 4545 ....98 A3	Madisonville KY, 19307 ......109 E1	Malaga NJ, 1700 ....145 F1	Manchester ME, 600 ....82 B2	Mannford OK, 2095 ....51 F2
Macoupin Co. IL, 49019 .....98 B2	Madera CA, 43207 ....44 C2	Madison IN, 12004 ....100 A3	Madisonville TN, 3939 ....120 C1	Malakoff TX, 2257 ....59 F3	Manchester MI, 2160 ....90 B1	Manning IA, 1490 ....86 B1
Macungie PA, 3039 ....146 B1	Madera Co. CA, 123109 .....44 C2	Madison KS, 857 ....43 F3	Madisonville TX, 4159 ....61 F1	Malcolm NE, 413 ....35 F4	Manchester MN, 19161 ......256 A3	Manning ND, 30 ....18 A3
		Madison ME, 2733 ....82 B1	Madison MN, 1768 ....27 F2	Madras OR, 5078 ....21 D3	Malden MA, 56340 ....151 D1	Manchester MO, 19161 ......256 A3	Manning SC, 4025 ....122 B4
		Madison MN, 1768 ....27 F2	Madison NC, 2262 ....112 B3	Madrid IA, 2264 ....86 C1	Malden MO, 4782 ....108 B3	Manchester NH, 107006 .....81 F4	Mannington WV, 2124 ....102 A1
		Madison MS, 14692 ....126 B2	Madison NE, 2367 ....35 E2	Madrid NY, 650 ....79 D1	Malden WV, 750 ....200 B3	Manchester NY, 1475 ....78 C3	Mannsville NY, 587 ....51 F4
		Madison MO, 586 ....97 E2	Madison NJ, 16530 ....148 A4	Maeser UT, 2855 ....32 A4	Malheur Co. OR, 31615 ......22 A4	Manchester OH, 2043 ....100 C3	Manns Choice PA 154 B3
		Madison NE, 2367 ....35 E2	Madison NC, 2262 ....112 B3	Magalia CA, 10569 ....36 C1	Malibu CA, 12575 ....52 B2	Manchester PA, 2350 ....93 E4	Manor PA, 2796 ....92 A4
		Madison NJ, 16530 ....148 A4	Madison OH, 2921 ....91 F1	Magazine AR, 915 ....116 C1	Malin OR, 638 ....29 D2	Manchester TN, 8294 ....120 A1	Manor TX, 1204 ....61 E1
		Madison NC, 2262 ....112 B3	Madison SD, 6540 ....27 F3	Magdalena NM, 913 ....48 B4	Mallory WV, 1143 ....111 F1	Manchester VT, 602 ....81 D4	Manorhaven NY, 6138 ....241 G2
		Madison OH, 2921 ....91 F1	Madison VA, 210 ....102 C4	Magee MS, 4200 ....126 C3	Malone FL, 2007 ....137 D1	Manchester WA, 4958 ....262 A3	Manorville NY, 11131 ....149 D3
		Madison SD, 6540 ....27 F3	Mancos WV, 2677 ....101 E4	Maggie Valley NC, 607 ......121 E1	Malone NY, 6075 ....80 C1	Manchester-by-the-Sea	Mansfield AR, 1097 ....116 C2
		Madison VA, 210 ....102 C4	Madison WI, 208054 ....74 B3	Magna UT, 22770 ....257 A2	Malone WA, 473 ....12 B4	MA, 3600 ....151 F1	Mansfield IL, 949 ....88 C4
		Mancos WV, 2677 ....101 E4	Madison Co. AL, 276700 ....119 F2	Magnolia AL, 10858 ....125 D1	Malta ID, 177 ....31 E2	Manchester Ctr. VT, 2065 ....81 D4	Mansfield LA, 5582 ....124 C3
		Madison Co. AR, 14243 .....106 C4	Magnolia AR, 11215 ....136 C1	Malta IL, 969 ....88 C1	Mancos CO, 1119 ....40 B4	Mansfield MA, 7320 ....151 D2
		Madison Co. FL, 18733 .....137 F2	Magnolia DE, 226 ....145 E2	Malta MT, 2120 ....16 C2	Mandan ND, 16718 ....18 C4	Mansfield MO, 1349 ....107 E2
		Madison Co. GA, 25730 .....121 E3	Magnolia MS, 2071 ....134 B1	Malta NY, 2100 ....94 B1	Mandaree ND, 558 ....18 A3	Mansfield OH, 49346 ....91 D3
		Madison Co. ID, 27467 ......23 F4	Magnolia NC, 932 ....123 D2	Malta OH, 696 ....101 E1	Manderson SD, 626 ....26 A4	Mansfield PA, 3411 ....93 D3
		Madison Co. IL, 258941 .....98 B3	Magnolia OH, 931 ....91 E3	Maltby WA, 8267 ....262 B3	Mandeville AR, 700 ....116 C4	Mansfield TX, 28031 ....59 E3
		Madison Co. IN, 133358 .....89 F4	Magnolia TX, 1111 ....132 A2	Malvern AL, 1215 ....136 C1	Mandeville LA, 10489 ....134 B2	Mansfield Ctr. CT, 973 .....150 B3
		Madison Co. IA, 14019 ......86 C2	Mahanoy City PA, 4647 ......93 E3	Malvern AR, 9021 ....117 D3	Mangham LA, 595 ....125 F2	Mansfield Four Corners CT, 700..150 B3
		Madison Co. KY, 70872 .....110 C1	Mahaska Co. IA, 22335 ......87 D2	Malvern IA, 1256 ....86 A3	Mango FL, 8842 ....266 C2	Manson IA, 1893 ....72 B4
		Madison Co. MS, 74674 .....126 B2	Mahnomen MN, 1202 ....19 F3	Malvern OH, 1218 ....91 E3	Mangonia Park FL, 1283 ....141 F4	Manson WA, 900 ....13 E2
		Madison Co. MO, 11800 ....108 A1	Mahnomen Co. MN, 5190 ...19 F3	Malvern PA, 3059 ....146 B3	Mangum OK, 2924 ....50 C3	Mansura LA, 1573 ....133 F1
		Madison Co. MT, 6851 ....23 E2	Mahomet IL, 4877 ....88 C4	Malverne NY, 8934 ....241 G4	Manhasset NY, 8362 ....148 C4	Mantachie MS, 1107 ....119 D3
		Madison Co. NE, 35226 ......35 E2	Mahopac NY, 8478 ....148 C1	Mamaroneck NY, 18752 ....148 C3	Manhasset Hills NY, 3661 ..241 G3	Manteca CA, 49258 ....36 C4
		Madison Co. NY, 69441 ......79 E4	Mahtomedi MN, 7563 ....235 E1	Mammoth AZ, 1762 ....55 D2	Manhattan IL, 3330 ....89 D2	Manteno IL, 6414 ....89 D2
		Madison Co. NC, 19635 ....111 E4	Mahwah NJ, 5200 ....148 B3	Mammoth Hot Sprs. WY, 25..23 F2	Manhattan KS, 44831 ....43 F2	Manteo NC, 1052 ....115 F2
		Madison Co. OH, 40213 ....100 C1	Maiden NC, 3282 ....122 A1	Mammoth Lakes CA, 7093 ...37 E4	Manhattan MT, 1396 ....23 F1	Manti UT, 3040 ....39 E2
		Madison Co. TN, 91837 .....108 C4	Maili HI, 5943 ....152 A3	Mammoth Spr. AR, 1147 ....107 F3	Manhattan Beach CA, 33852 ..228 C3	Manton MI, 1221 ....75 F1
		Madison Co. TX, 12940 ......61 F1	Maine NY, 1000 ....93 E1	Mamou LA, 3566 ....133 E2	Manila AR, 3055 ....108 B4	Mantorville MN, 1054 ....73 D1
			Mainville OH, 885 ....100 B2	Man WV, 700 ....111 F1	Manila UT, 308 ....32 A3	Mantua OH, 1043 ....91 E2
			Maitland FL, 12019 ....141 D1	Manahawkin NJ, 2004 ....147 E4	Manilla IA, 839 ....86 A1	Mantua UT, 791 ....31 E3
			Maize KS, 1868 ....43 E4	Manasquan NJ, 6310 ....147 E2	Manistee MI, 6586 ....75 E1	Mantua VA, 7485 ....270 A4
			Majestic KY, 600 ....111 E1	Manassa CO, 1042 ....41 D4	Manistee Co. MI, 24527 .....70 A4	Manvel ND, 370 ....19 E2
			Major Co. OK, 7545 ....51 D2	Manassas VA, 35135 ....144 A4	Manistique MI, 3583 ....69 E2	Manvel TX, 3046 ....132 A4
			Makaha HI, 7753 ....152 A3	Manassas Park VA, 10290 ..144 A3	Manito IL, 1733 ....88 B4	Manville NJ, 10343 ....147 D1
			Makakilo City HI, 13156 .....152 A3	Manawa WI, 1330 ....74 B1	Manitou Beach MI, 2080 .....90 B1	Manville RI, 3800 ....150 C2
				Mancelona MI, 1408 ....70 B4	Manitou Sprs. CO, 4980 .....41 E2	Many LA, 2889 ....125 D2
				Manchaca TX, 1200 ....61 E2	Manitowoc WI, 34053 ....75 D1	Many Farms AZ, 1548 ....47 D2

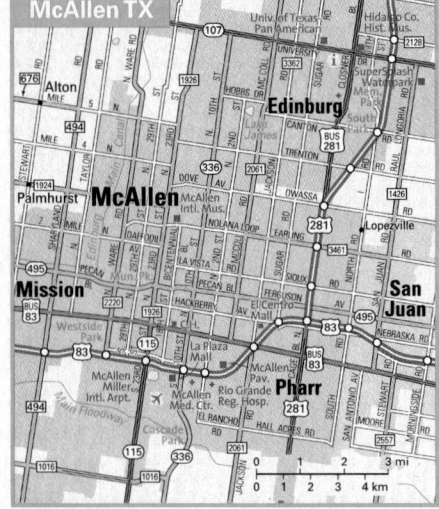

McAllen TX

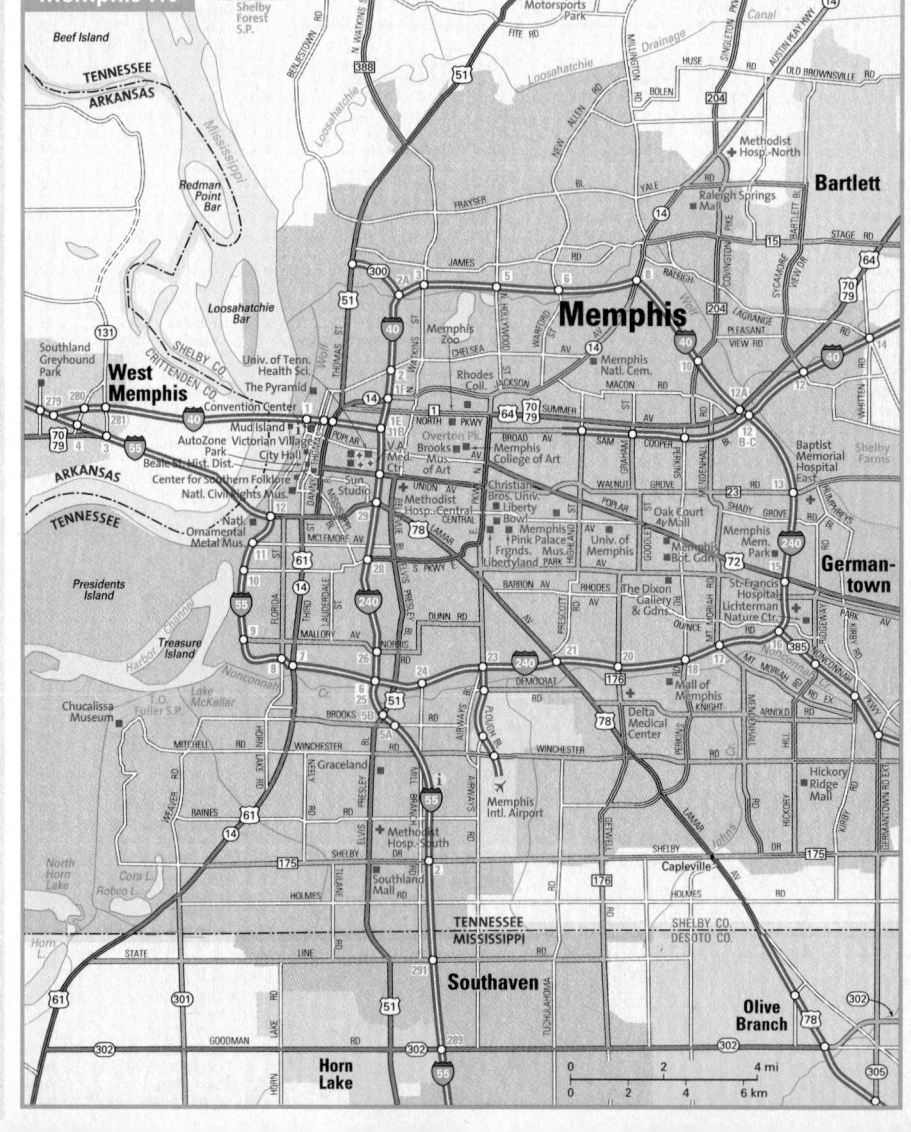

Melbourne / Titusville FL

Memphis TN

Entries in **bold** indicate counties or parishes. Entries in color indicate cities with detailed inset maps.

Miami / Fort Lauderdale FL

(Map with cities including Boca Raton, Coconut Creek, Parkland, Coral Springs, Deerfield Beach, Lighthouse Point, Pompano Beach, Margate, North Lauderdale, Tamarac, Lauderhill, Lauderdale Lakes, Oakland Park, Sunrise, Plantation, Fort Lauderdale, Weston, Davie, Cooper City, Dania Beach, Southwest Ranches, Pembroke Pines, Hollywood, Miramar, Pembroke Park, Hallandale Beach, Aventura, Carol City, North Miami Beach, Miami Lakes, Opa-Locka, North Miami, Hialeah, Hialeah Gardens, Miami Shores, Miami, Miami Springs, Miami Beach, Sweetwater, West Miami, Westwood Lake, South Miami, Coral Gables, Key Biscayne, Kendall, Pinecrest, Richmond Hts., Perrine, S. Miami Hts., Goulds, Cutler Ridge; Atlantic Ocean, Biscayne National Park)

Downtown Miami FL

Marysvale UT, 381 ... 39 E3
Marysville CA, 12268 ... 36 C2
Marysville KS, 3271 ... 43 F1
Marysville MI, 9684 ... 76 C3
Marysville OH, 22016 ... 100 B2
Marysville PA, 2306 ... 93 D4
Marysville WA, 25315 ... 12 C2
Maryville IL, 4651 ... 256 D1
Maryville MO, 10581 ... 86 B4
Maryville TN, 23120 ... 110 C4
Marywood MD, 6000 ... 145 D1
Masaryktown FL, 920 ... 140 B1
Mascot TN, 2119 ... 110 C4
Mascotte FL, 2687 ... 140 C1
Mascoutah IL, 5659 ... 98 B3
Mashpee MA, 901 ... 151 E3

Mason MI, 6714 ... 76 A4
Mason NV, 500 ... 37 E2
Mason NH, 550 ... 95 D1
Mason OH, 22016 ... 100 B2
Mason TX, 1089 ... 118 C1
Mason TX, 2134 ... 60 C1
Mason City IA, 29172 ... 73 D3
Mason City IL, 2558 ... 88 B4
Mason Co. IL, 16038 ... 88 A4
Mason Co. KY, 16800 ... 100 C3
Mason Co. MI, 28274 ... 75 E1
Mason Co. TX, 3738 ... 60 C1
Mason Co. WA, 49405 ... 12 B3
Mason Co. WV, 25957 ... 101 E3

Masontown PA, 3611 ... 102 B1
Masontown WV, 647 ... 102 B1
Masonville KY, 1075 ... 109 E1
Masonville NJ, 7300 ... 147 D3
Massac Co. IL, 15161 ... 108 C2
Massapequa NY, 22652 ... 148 C4
Massapequa Park NY, 17499 ... 148 C4
Massena NY, 11209 ... 80 B1
Massillon OH, 31325 ... 91 E3
Mastic NY, 15436 ... 149 D4
Mastic Beach NY, 11543 ... 149 D4
Masury OH, 2618 ... 91 F2
Matador TX, 740 ... 58 B1

Matewan WV, 498 ... 111 E1
Matherville IL, 772 ... 88 A2
Mathews LA, 2003 ... 134 B3
Mathews VA, 850 ... 113 F1
Mathews Co. VA, 9207 ... 113 F1
Mathis TX, 5034 ... 61 E4
Mathiston MS, 720 ... 118 C4
Matlacha FL, 735 ... 142 C1
Mattapoisett MA, 2966 ... 151 E3
Mattawa WA, 2609 ... 13 C4
Mattawamkeag ME, 400 ... 85 D4
Mattawan MI, 2536 ... 75 F4
Mattawoman MD, 3100 ... 144 B4

Matthews NC, 22127 ... 122 B1
Mattituck NY, 4198 ... 149 E3
Mattoon IL, 18291 ... 98 C2
Mattydale NY, 6367 ... 79 D3
Matunuck RI, 750 ... 150 C4
Maud OH, 4800 ... 100 B2
Maud OK, 1136 ... 51 F3
Maud TX, 1028 ... 124 C1
Maugansville MD, 2295 ... 103 D1
Mauldin SC, 15224 ... 121 F2
Maumee OH, 15237 ... 90 C2
Maumelle AR, 10557 ... 117 E2
Maunawili HI, 4869 ... 152 B3
Maupin OR, 411 ... 21 D2
Maurertown VA, 550 ... 102 C3

Maurice LA, 642 ... 133 F2
Mauriceville TX, 2743 ... 132 C2
Maury City TN, 704 ... 108 C4
Maury Co. TN, 69498 ... 109 E4
Mauston WI, 3740 ... 74 A2
Mavisdale VA, 550 ... 111 E2
Max ND, 278 ... 18 B3
Max Meadows VA, 512 ... 112 A4
Maxton NC, 2551 ... 122 C2
Maxwell CA, 900 ... 36 B2
Maxwell IA, 807 ... 86 C1
Maxwell NM, 274 ... 49 E1
Maybee MI, 505 ... 90 C1
Maybeury WV, 550 ... 111 F1
Maybrook NY, 3084 ... 148 B1
Mayer AZ, 1408 ... 47 D3
Mayersville MS, 795 ... 126 A1
Mayesville SC, 1001 ... 122 B3
Mayfield KY, 10349 ... 108 C3
Mayfield NY, 800 ... 80 C4
Mayfield OH, 3435 ... 204 G1
Mayfield PA, 1756 ... 93 F2
Mayfield UT, 420 ... 39 E3
Mayfield Hts. OH, 19386 ... 91 E2
Mayflower AR, 1631 ... 117 E2
Maynard IA, 500 ... 73 E4
Maynard MA, 10433 ... 150 C1
Maynardville TN, 1782 ... 110 C3
Mayo FL, 988 ... 137 F3
Mayo MD, 3153 ... 144 C3
Mayo SC, 1842 ... 121 F1
Mayodan NC, 2417 ... 112 B3
Maypearl TX, 746 ... 59 F3
Mays Chapel MD, 11427 ... 193 C1
Mays Landing NJ, 2321 ... 105 D3
Maysville GA, 1247 ... 121 D3
Maysville KY, 8993 ... 100 C3
Maysville MO, 1212 ... 96 B1
Maysville NC, 1002 ... 115 D4
Maysville OK, 1313 ... 51 E4
Maytown AL, 435 ... 195 D1
Mayville MI, 1055 ... 76 C3
Mayville NY, 1756 ... 78 A4
Mayville ND, 1953 ... 19 E3
Mayville WI, 4902 ... 74 C2
Maywood CA, 28083 ... 228 D3
Maywood IL, 26987 ... 203 C4
Maywood NJ, 9523 ... 240 C1
Maywood WV, 4200 ... 188 D2
Maywood Park OR, 777 ... 251 D2
Mazeppa MN, 778 ... 73 D1
Mazomanie WI, 1485 ... 74 A3
Mazon IL, 904 ... 88 C2
McAdoo PA, 2274 ... 93 E3
McAfee NJ, 2600 ... 148 A1
McAlester OK, 17783 ... 116 A4
McAlisterville PA, 765 ... 93 D3
McAllen TX, 106414 ... 63 E4
McArthur OH, 1888 ... 101 D2
McBain MI, 584 ... 75 F1
McBee SC, 714 ... 122 B3
McCall ID, 2084 ... 22 B2
McCamey TX, 1805 ... 58 A4
McCammon ID, 805 ... 31 E1
McCandless PA, 29022 ... 92 A4
McCaysville GA, 1071 ... 120 C2
McClain Co. OK, 27740 ... 51 E3
McCleary WA, 1454 ... 12 B3
McClellandville DE, 2400 ... 146 B4
McClellanville SC, 459 ... 131 E1
McCloud CA, 1343 ... 28 C3
McClure OH, 761 ... 90 B2
McClure PA, 975 ... 93 D3
McClusky ND, 415 ... 18 C3
McColl SC, 2498 ... 122 C2
McComb MS, 13337 ... 126 B4
McComb OH, 1744 ... 90 B3
McCone Co. MT, 1977 ... 17 E3
McConnellsburg PA, 1073 ... 103 D1
McConnelsville OH, 1676 ... 101 E1
McCook NE, 7994 ... 42 C1
McCook Co. SD, 5832 ... 27 E4
McCordsville IN, 1134 ... 99 F1
McCormack Corners NY, 2300 ... 188 C2
McCormick SC, 1489 ... 121 F4
McCormick Co. SC, 9958 ... 121 F4
McCracken Co. KY, 65514 ... 108 C2
McCreary Co. KY, 17080 ... 110 C2
McCrory AR, 1850 ... 117 F1
McCulloch Co. TX, 8205 ... 58 C4
McCune KS, 426 ... 106 B1
McCurtain OK, 466 ... 116 B1
McCurtain Co. OK, 34402 ... 116 B3
McDermitt NV, 269 ... 30 A2
McDonald OH, 3481 ... 276 B2
McDonald PA, 2281 ... 92 A4
McDonald Co. MO, 21681 ... 106 C3
McDonough GA, 8493 ... 120 C4
McDonough Co. IL, 32913 ... 87 F3
McDowell Co. NC, 42151 ... 111 E4
McDowell Co. WV, 27329 ... 111 F1
McDuffie Co. GA, 21231 ... 129 F1
McEwen TN, 1702 ... 109 E4
McFarland CA, 9618 ... 45 D4
McFarland WI, 6416 ... 74 B3
McGaheysville VA, 500 ... 102 C4
McGehee AR, 4570 ... 117 F4
McGill NV, 1054 ... 38 B2
McGrath AK, 401 ... 154 C2
McGraw NY, 1000 ... 79 E4

McGregor IA, 871 ... 73 F3
McGregor TX, 4727 ... 59 E4
McHenry IL, 21501 ... 74 C4
McHenry KY, 417 ... 109 E1
McHenry Co. IL, 260077 ... 74 C4
McHenry Co. ND, 5987 ... 18 C3
McIntosh FL, 453 ... 138 C4
McIntosh MN, 638 ... 19 F3
McIntosh SD, 217 ... 26 B1
McIntosh Co. GA, 10847 ... 130 B4
McIntosh Co. ND, 3390 ... 27 D1
McIntosh Co. OK, 19456 ... 116 A1
McIntyre GA, 718 ... 129 E2
McKean Co. PA, 45936 ... 92 B1
McKee KY, 878 ... 110 C1
McKee City NJ, 2800 ... 147 F4
McKeesport PA, 24040 ... 92 A4
McKees Rocks PA, 6622 ... 250 B1
McKenna WA, 800 ... 12 C4
McKenney VA, 441 ... 113 E2
McKenzie AL, 644 ... 127 F4
McKenzie TN, 5295 ... 109 D4
McKenzie Co. ND, 5737 ... 17 F2
McKinley Co. NM, 74798 ... 48 A2
McKinleyville CA, 13599 ... 28 A4
McKinney TX, 54369 ... 59 F2
McKownville NY, 2600 ... 188 D3
McLain MS, 603 ... 135 D1
McLaughlin SD, 775 ... 26 C1
McLean IL, 808 ... 88 B4
McLean TX, 830 ... 50 B3
McLean VA, 38929 ... 144 B3
McLean Co. IL, 150433 ... 88 C4
McLean Co. KY, 9938 ... 109 E1
McLean Co. ND, 9311 ... 18 B3
McLeansboro IL, 2945 ... 98 C4
McLennan Co. TX, 213517 ... 59 F4
McLeod Co. MN, 34898 ... 66 C4
McLoud OK, 3548 ... 51 E3
McLouth KS, 868 ... 96 C4
McMechen WV, 1937 ... 101 F1
McMinn Co. TN, 49015 ... 120 C1
McMinnville OR, 26499 ... 20 B2
McMinnville TN, 12749 ... 110 A4
McMullen Co. TX, 851 ... 61 D4
McMurray PA, 4726 ... 92 A4
McNairy Co. TN, 24653 ... 119 D1
McNary AZ, 349 ... 47 F4
McNeil AR, 662 ... 125 D1
McPherson KS, 13770 ... 43 E3
McPherson Co. KS, 29554 ... 43 E3
McPherson Co. NE, 533 ... 34 B3
McPherson Co. SD, 2904 ... 27 D1
McQueeney TX, 2527 ... 61 D2
McRae AR, 661 ... 117 F1
McRae GA, 2682 ... 129 E3
McRoberts KY, 921 ... 111 E2
McSherrystown PA, 2691 ... 103 E1
McVeigh KY, 550 ... 111 E1
McVille ND, 470 ... 19 E3
Mead CO, 2017 ... 33 D4
Mead NE, 564 ... 35 F3
Mead WA, 2100 ... 14 A3
Meade KS, 1672 ... 42 C4
Meade Co. KS, 4631 ... 42 C4
Meade Co. KY, 26349 ... 99 F4
Meade Co. SD, 24253 ... 26 A3
Meadow TX, 658 ... 58 A1
Meadowlakes TX, 1293 ... 61 D2
Meadows Place TX, 4912 ... 132 A3
Meadow Vale KY, 765 ... 230 F1
Meadow Valley CA, 575 ... 36 C1
Meadowview VA, 2266 ... 111 F2
Meadville MS, 519 ... 126 A4
Meadville PA, 13685 ... 92 A2
Meagher Co. MT, 1932 ... 15 F4
Mebane NC, 7284 ... 112 C4
Mecca CA, 5402 ... 53 E3
Mechanic Falls ME, 2450 ... 82 B2
Mechanicsburg OH, 1744 ... 90 C4
Mechanicsburg PA, 9042 ... 93 D4
Mechanicsville IA, 1173 ... 87 F1
Mechanicsville MD, 750 ... 103 E3
Mechanicsville VA, 30464 ... 113 E1
Mechanicville NY, 5019 ... 94 B1
Mecklenburg Co. NC, 695454 ... 122 B1
Mecklenburg Co. VA, 32380 ... 113 D2
Mecosta Co. MI, 40553 ... 75 F2
Medanales NM, 450 ... 48 C2
Medaryville IN, 565 ... 89 D3
Medfield MA, 6670 ... 151 D2
Medford MN, 984 ... 73 D1
Medford NJ, 3500 ... 147 D3
Medford NY, 21985 ... 149 D4
Medford OK, 1172 ... 51 E1
Medford OR, 63154 ... 28 B2
Medford WI, 4350 ... 68 A3
Medford Lakes NJ, 4173 ... 147 D3
Media PA, 5533 ... 146 C3
Mediapolis IA, 1644 ... 87 F3
Medical Lake WA, 3758 ... 13 F3
Medicine Bow WY, 274 ... 33 D2
Medicine Lake MT, 377 ... 17 F2
Medicine Lodge KS, 2193 ... 43 D4
Medina MN, 6415 ... 78 B3
Medina ND, 335 ... 19 D4
Medina OH, 25139 ... 91 E3
Medina TN, 969 ... 108 C4
Medina WA, 3011 ... 262 B3
Medina Co. OH, 151095 ... 91 E3
Medina Co. TX, 39304 ... 60 C3

Milwaukee WI — Community Index

Bayside	D1
Brookfield	B2
Brown Deer	C1
Butler	B1
Cudahy	D3
Elm Grove	B2
Fox Pt.	D1
Glendale	C1
Greendale	C3
Greenfield	C3
Hales Corners	B3
Lannon	A1
Menomonee Falls	B1
Milwaukee	C2
New Berlin	B3
Pewaukee (city)	A2
Pewaukee (village)	A2
River Hills	D1
St. Francis	D3
Shorewood	D2
Sussex	A1
Waukesha	A2
Wauwatosa	C2
W. Allis	C3
W. Milwaukee	C3
Whitefish Bay	D1

Downtown Milwaukee WI — Points of Interest

Amtrak Station	F2
Arena	F1
Auditorium	F1
Betty Brinn Children's Mus.	G2
Bradley Center	F2
Broadway Theater Center	F2
City Hall	F1
Court House	E1
Discovery World Mus.	E1
Federal Plaza	F2
Grain Exchange Room	F2
Grand Avenue Mall	F2
Hist. Third Ward	F2
IMAX	E1
Intercity Bus Depot	E1
Maier Festival Park	G2
Marcus Center for Performing Arts	F1
Marquette Univ.	E2
Midwest Express Center	F2
Milwaukee Art Mus. & War Memorial Center	G1
Milwaukee County Hist. Center	F1
Milwaukee Institute of Art & Design	F2
Milwaukee Public Mus.	E1
Milwaukee School of Engineering	F1
Municipal Pier	G2
Pabst Brewery	E1
Pabst Theater	F1
Post Office	F2, G1
Potawatomi Bingo & Casino	E2
St. Joan of Arc Chapel	E2
State Office Building	F1
Wisconsin Conservatory of Music	G1

Entries in **bold** indicate counties or parishes. Entries in color indicate cities with detailed inset maps.

Minneapolis / St Paul MN

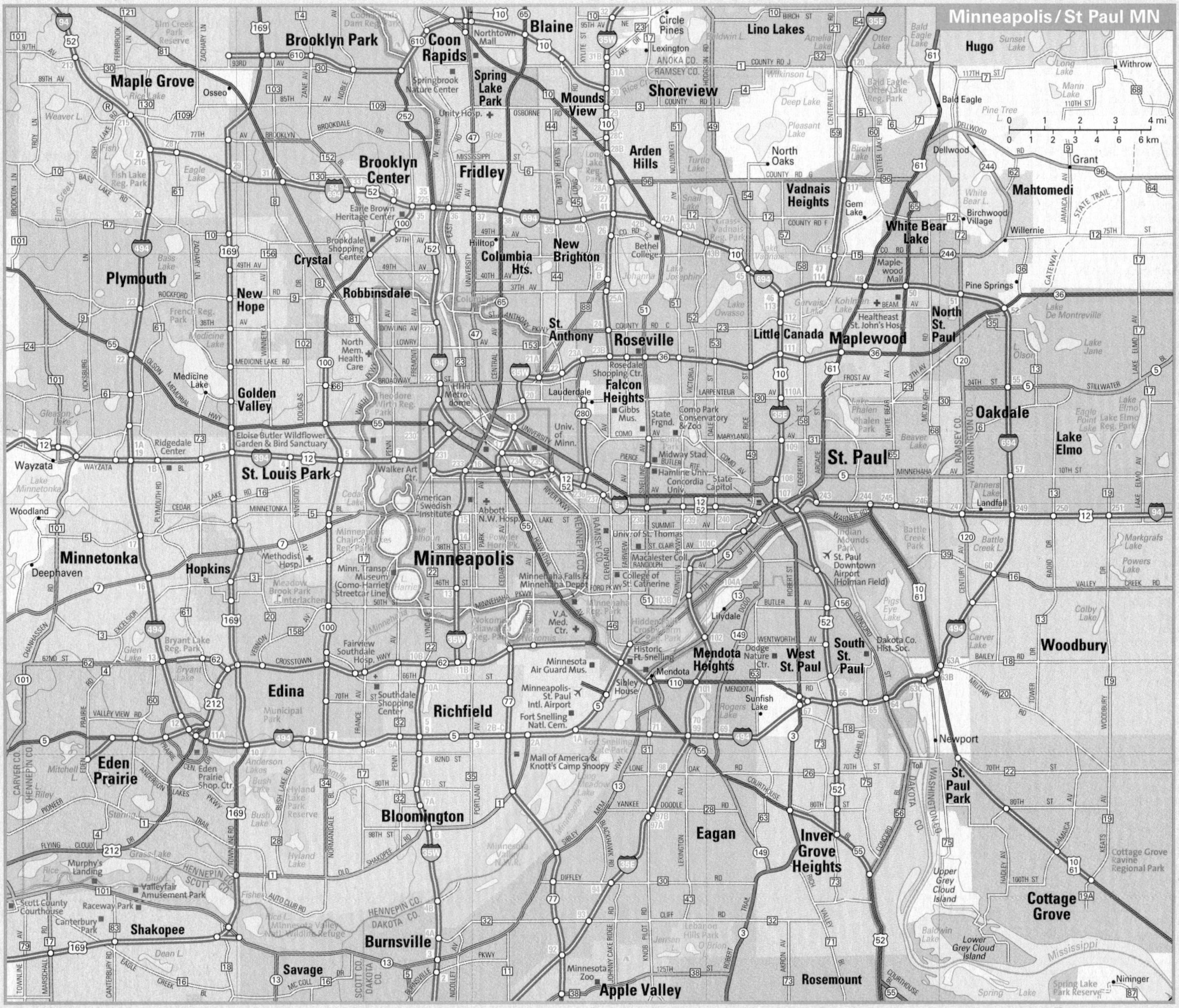

236   **Mexico—Milesburg**

Figures after entries indicate population, page number, and grid reference.

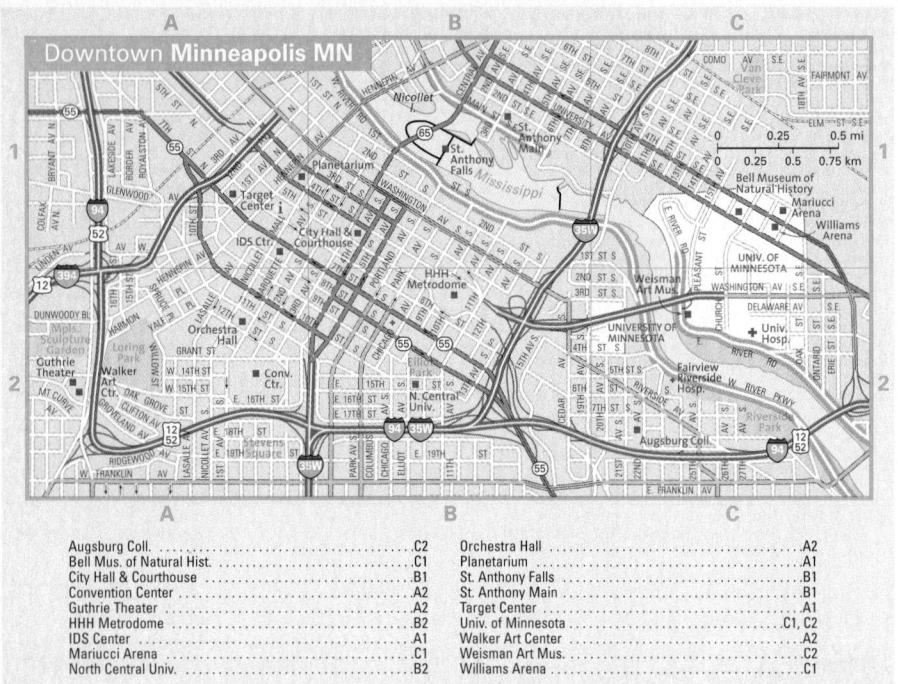

Downtown Minneapolis MN

Augsburg Coll.	C2
Bell Mus. of Natural Hist.	C1
City Hall & Courthouse	B1
Convention Center	A2
Guthrie Theater	A2
HHH Metrodome	B2
IDS Center	A1
Mariucci Arena	C1
North Central Univ.	B2
Orchestra Hall	A2
Planetarium	A1
St. Anthony Falls	B1
St. Anthony Main	B1
Target Center	A1
Univ. of Minnesota	C1, C2
Walker Art Center	A2
Weisman Art Mus.	C2
Williams Arena	C1

Index of cities (top right):

Monterey Bay index:

Aptos	D1	Del Rey Oaks	E3	Monterey	D3	Salinas	E3
Aromas	E2	Elkhorn	E2	Moss Landing	E2	Sand City	E3
Ben Lomond	D1	Felton	D1	Mt. Hermon	D1	Santa Cruz	D1
Bolsa Knolls	E2	Freedom	E1	Opal Cliffs	D1	Scotts Valley	D1
Capitola	D1	Gabilan Acres	E2	Pacific Grove	D3	Seaside	E3
Carmel-by-the-Sea	D3	Gilroy	E1	Pajaro	E1	Soquel	D1
Carmel Highlands	D3	La Selva Beach	D1	Paradise Park	D1	Spreckels	E3
Carmel Valley	E3	Las Lomas	D1	Pebble Beach	D3	Twin Lakes	D1
Castroville	E2	Live Oak	D1	Prunedale	D2	Watsonville	D1
Corralitos	E1	Marina	E2	Rio del Mar	D1	Zayante	D1

Monterey Bay CA

City index (lower left)

City	Pop.	Page	Grid
Mexico IN,	*984*	89	F3
Mexico ME,	*1946*	82	B2
Mexico MO,	*11320*	97	E2
Mexico NY,	*1572*	79	D2
Mexico Beach FL,	*1017*	136	C3
Meyersdale PA,	*2473*	102	C1
Meyers Lake OH,	*565*	199	B2
Miami AZ,	*1936*	55	D1
Miami FL,	*362470*	143	F2
Miami OK,	*13704*	106	B2
Miami TX,	*588*	50	B2
Miami Beach FL,	*87933*	143	F2
Miami Co. IN,	*36082*	89	F3
Miami Co. KS,	*28351*	96	B3
Miami Co. OH,	*98868*	90	B4
Miami-Dade Co. FL,	*2253362*	143	F2
Miami Lakes FL,	*22676*	233	A3
Miamisburg OH,	*19489*	100	B1
Miami Shores FL,	*10380*	143	F2
Miami Sprs. FL,	*13712*	143	E2
Micanopy FL,	*653*	138	C4
Micaville NC,	*750*	111	E4
Micco FL,	*9498*	141	E2
Michie TN,	*647*	119	D2
Michigan ND,	*345*	19	E2
Michigan Ctr. MI,	*4641*	90	C1
Michigan City IN,	*32900*	89	E1
Middleboro MA,	*6913*	151	D3
Middlebourne WV,	*870*	101	F3
Middleburg FL,	*10338*	139	D3
Middleburg PA,	*1382*	93	D3
Middleburg VA,	*632*	144	A3
Middleburgh NY,	*1398*	79	F4
Middleburg Hts. OH,	*15542*	204	E3
Middlebury CT,	*950*	149	C1
Middlebury IN,	*2956*	89	F2
Middlebury VT,	*6252*	81	D3
Middle Falls NY,	*750*	81	D4
Middlefield CT,	*1900*	149	E1
Middlefield OH,	*2233*	91	F2
Middle Haddam CT,	*900*	149	E1
Middle Island NY,	*9702*	149	D3
Middle Pt. OH,	*593*	90	B3
Middleport NY,	*1917*	78	B3
Middleport OH,	*2525*	101	E2
Middle River MD,	*23958*	144	C2
Middlesboro KY,	*10384*	110	C3
Middlesex NJ,	*13717*	147	D1
Middlesex NC,	*838*	113	D4
Middlesex Co. CT,	*155071*	149	E1
Middlesex Co. MA,	*1465396*	151	D1
Middlesex Co. NJ,	*750162*	147	E2
Middlesex Co. VA,	*9932*	113	F1
Middleton ID,	*2978*	22	B4
Middleton MA,	*1200*	151	F1
Middleton TN,	*602*	118	C2
Middleton WI,	*15535*	74	B3
Middletown CA,	*1020*	36	B2
Middletown CT,	*43167*	149	E1
Middletown DE,	*6161*	145	E1
Middletown IN,	*2488*	89	F4
Middletown IA,	*535*	87	F3
Middletown KY,	*5744*	100	A4
Middletown MD,	*2668*	144	A1
Middletown NY,	*25388*	148	A1
Middletown OH,	*51605*	100	B1
Middletown PA,	*9242*	93	E4
Middletown RI,	*17334*	151	D4
Middletown VA,	*1015*	102	C2
Middletown Sprs. VT,	*300*	81	D4
Middle Valley TN,	*11854*	120	B1

City	Pop.	Page	Grid
Middleville MI,	*2721*	75	F4
Middleville NY,	*550*	79	F3
Midfield AL,	*5626*	119	D4
Midland MD,	*473*	102	C1
Midland MI,	*41685*	76	B2
Midland PA,	*3137*	91	F3
Midland TX,	*94996*	58	A3
Midland WA,	*7414*	262	A5
Midland City AL,	*1703*	128	B4
Midland Co. MI,	*82874*	76	A2
Midland Co. TX,	*116009*	58	A3
Midlothian IL,	*14315*	203	D6
Midlothian TX,	*7480*	59	F3
Midlothian VA,	*3300*	113	E1
Midtown TN,	*1306*	110	B4
Midvale UT,	*27029*	257	F3
Midway AL,	*457*	128	B3
Midway DE,	*1500*	145	F4
Midway FL,	*1446*	137	C2
Midway GA,	*1100*	130	B3
Midway KY,	*1620*	100	B4
Midway LA,	*1505*	125	C4
Midway NM,	*700*	57	E2
Midway PA,	*982*	91	F4
Midway TN,	*2491*	111	D4
Midway UT,	*2121*	31	F4
Midwest WY,	*408*	25	D4

Missoula MT

Mobile AL

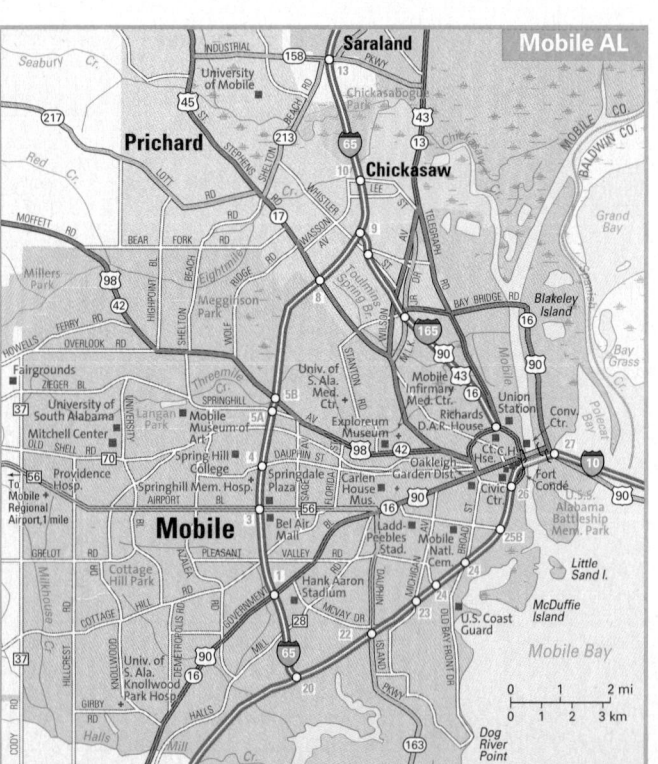

Montgomery AL

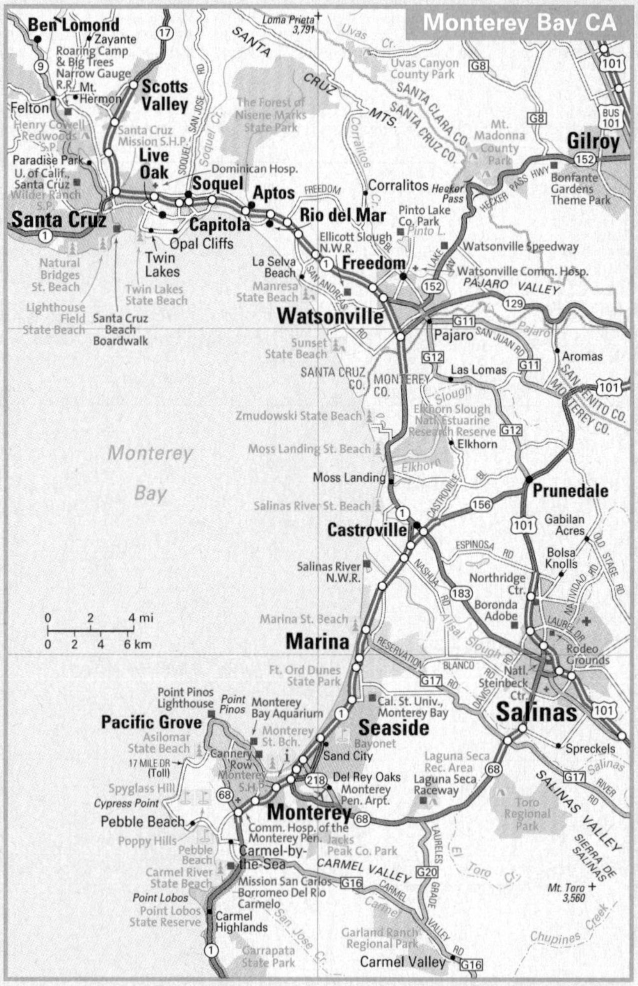

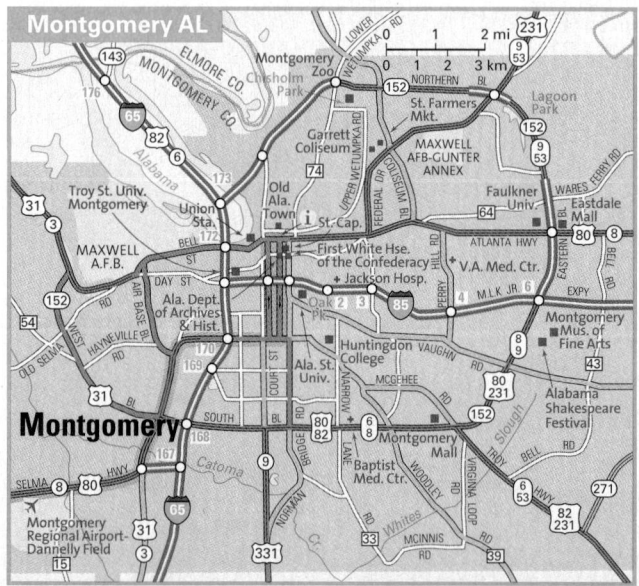

Miles City MT, 8487 ....17 E4	Mililani Town HI, 28608 ....152 A3	**Miller Co. MO,** 23564 ....97 E4	Milton NH, 950 ....81 F4	Minoa NY, 3348 ....79 E2	Modesto CA, 188856 ....36 C4	Monroe MI, 22076 ....90 C1
Milford CT, 52305 ....149 D2	**Millard Co. UT,** 12405 ....39 D2	Miller Place NY, 10580 ....149 D3	Milton NY, 1251 ....148 B1	Minocqua WI, 750 ....68 B2	**Modoc Co. CA,** 9449 ....29 D3	Monroe NY, 7780 ....148 B2
Milford DE, 6732 ....145 F3	Millbourne PA, 943 ....248 B3	Millersburg IN, 868 ....89 F2	Milton PA, 6650 ....93 D3	Minong WI, 531 ....67 E2	Moenkopi AZ, 901 ....47 E2	Monroe NC, 26228 ....122 B2
Milford IL, 1369 ....89 D3	Millbrae CA, 20718 ....259 B3	Millersburg KY, 842 ....100 B4	Milton VT, 1537 ....81 D1	Minonk IL, 2168 ....88 B3	**Moffat Co. CO,** 13184 ....32 B4	Monroe OH, 7133 ....100 B2
Milford IN, 1550 ....89 F2	Millbrook AL, 10386 ....128 A2	Millersburg OH, 3326 ....91 E4	Milton WV, 5795 ....262 B5	Minooka IL, 3971 ....88 C2	Mogadore OH, 3893 ....188 B2	Monroe OR, 607 ....20 B2
Milford IA, 2474 ....72 A3	Millbrook NJ, 1429 ....94 B3	Millersburg OR, 651 ....20 B3	Milton WV, 2206 ....101 E3	Minor Hill TN, 437 ....119 E2	Mohall ND, 812 ....18 B1	Monroe UT, 1845 ....39 E3
Milford KS, 502 ....43 F2	Millburn NJ, 19765 ....240 A1	Millersburg PA, 2562 ....93 D4	Milton WI, 5132 ....74 B4	Minot ME, 400 ....82 B2	**Mohave Co. AZ,** 155032 ....46 B3	Monroe WA, 13795 ....12 C3
Milford ME, 2197 ....83 D1	Millbury MA, 4700 ....150 C2	Millersport OH, 963 ....101 D1	Milton-Freewater OR, 6470 ....21 F1	Minot MA, 1100 ....151 E2	Mohave Valley AZ, 13694 ....46 B3	Monroe WI, 10843 ....74 B4
Milford MD, 26527 ....193 B2	Millbury OH, 1161 ....90 C2	Millerstown PA, 679 ....93 D4	Minatare NE, 810 ....33 F2	Minot ND, 36567 ....18 B2	Mohawk NY, 2660 ....79 D3	Monroe City IN, 548 ....99 E3
Milford MA, 24230 ....150 C2	Mill City NV, 300 ....29 F4	Millersville PA, 7774 ....146 A3	Minco OK, 1672 ....51 E3	Minster OH, 2794 ....90 B4	Mohawk NY, 2660 ....79 D3	Monroe City MO, 2588 ....97 E1
Milford MI, 6272 ....76 B4	Mill City OR, 1537 ....20 C3	Millersville TN, 5308 ....109 F3	Minden IA, 564 ....86 A2	Mint Hill NC, 14922 ....122 B1	**Monroe Co. AL,** 24324 ....127 F4
Milford NE, 2070 ....35 F4	Mill Creek WA, 11525 ....12 C3	Millerton NY, 925 ....94 B2	Minden LA, 13027 ....125 D2	Minto ND, 657 ....19 E2	Mohegan Lake NY, 5700 ....148 B2	**Monroe Co. AR,** 10254 ....118 A2
Milford NH, 8293 ....95 D1	Mill Creek WV, 662 ....102 A3	Millport AL, 1160 ....119 D4	Minden NE, 2964 ....35 D4	Minturn CO, 1068 ....41 D1	Mohnton PA, 2963 ....146 A2	**Monroe Co. FL,** 79589 ....143 D3
Milford NJ, 1195 ....146 C1	Mill Creek CA, 610 ....28 C4	Millry AL, 615 ....127 D4	Minden NV, 2836 ....37 D2	Mio MI, 2016 ....76 B2	Mohrsville PA, 800 ....146 A1	**Monroe Co. GA,** 21757 ....129 D1
Milford NY, 511 ....79 F4	Mill Neck NY, 825 ....148 C3	Mills WY, 2591 ....33 D1	Mineola NY, 19234 ....148 C4	Mira Loma CA, 17617 ....229 H3	Mojave CA, 3836 ....52 C1	**Monroe Co. IL,** 27619 ....98 A4
Milford OH, 6284 ....100 B1	Mill City OH, 841 ....91 E4	Mineral City OH, 841 ....91 E4	Mineola TX, 4550 ....124 A2	Miramar FL, 72739 ....143 E2	Mokelumne Hill CA, 774 ....36 C3	**Monroe Co. IN,** 120563 ....99 F2
Milford PA, 1104 ....94 A3	Miller SD, 1530 ....27 D3	Mineral CO, 2888 ....33 E4	Mineral VA, 424 ....103 D4	Miramar Beach FL, 2435 ....136 B2	Mokuleia HI, 1839 ....152 A3	**Monroe Co. IA,** 8016 ....87 D3
Milford TX, 685 ....59 F3	Miller MO, 754 ....106 D2	**Mills Co. IA,** 14547 ....86 A3	Mineral Pt. WI, 2617 ....74 A3	Misenheimer NC, 750 ....122 B1	Molalla OR, 5647 ....20 C2	**Monroe Co. KY,** 11756 ....110 A2
Milford UT, 1451 ....39 D3	**Miller Co. AR,** 40443 ....124 C1	**Mills Co. TX,** 5151 ....59 D4	Mineral Ridge OH, 3900 ....276 B2	Mishawaka IN, 46557 ....89 F2	Molena GA, 475 ....128 C1	**Monroe Co. MI,** 145945 ....90 C1
Milford Ctr. OH, 626 ....90 C4	**Miller Co. GA,** 6383 ....128 C4	Millstadt IL, 2794 ....98 A3	**Mineral Co. CO,** 831 ....40 C3	Mishicot WI, 1422 ....75 D1	Moline KS, 457 ....43 F4	**Monroe Co. MS,** 38014 ....119 D4
Milford Square PA, 1100 ....146 C1		Millstone KY, 650 ....111 E2	**Mineral Co. MT,** 3884 ....14 C3	**Missaukee Co. MI,** 14478 ....75 F1	Moline IL, 43768 ....88 A3	**Monroe Co. MO,** 9311 ....97 E2
		Milltown IN, 932 ....99 F4	**Mineral Co. NV,** 5071 ....37 E3	Mission KS, 9727 ....224 B3	Molino FL, 1312 ....135 F1	**Monroe Co. NY,** 735343 ....78 C3
		Milltown NJ, 7000 ....147 E1	**Mineral Co. WV,** 27078 ....102 C2	Mission OR, 1019 ....21 F1	Momence IL, 3171 ....89 D2	**Monroe Co. OH,** 15180 ....101 F1
		Milltown WI, 888 ....67 E3	Mineral Pt. WI, 2617 ....74 A3	Mission SD, 904 ....26 C4	Mona UT, 850 ....39 E1	**Monroe Co. PA,** 138687 ....93 F3
		Millvale PA, 4028 ....250 B1	Mineral Sprs. AR, 1264 ....116 C4	Mission TX, 45408 ....63 E4	Monaca PA, 6286 ....91 F3	**Monroe Co. TN,** 38961 ....120 C1
		Mill Valley CA, 13600 ....36 B4	Mineral Sprs. NC, 1370 ....122 B2	Mission Bend TX, 30831 ....220 A3	Monahans TX, 6821 ....57 F4	**Monroe Co. WV,** 14583 ....112 A1
		Millville CA, 610 ....28 C4	Mineral Wells TX, 16946 ....59 E2	Mission Hills KS, 3593 ....224 B4	Monarch Mills SC, 1930 ....121 F2	**Monroe Co. WI,** 40899 ....73 F1
		Millville DE, 259 ....145 F4	Mineral Wells WV, 1860 ....101 E4	Mission Viejo CA, 93102 ....52 C3	Moncks Corner SC, 5952 ....131 D1	Monroeville AL, 6862 ....127 F4
		Millville NJ, 26847 ....145 F1	**Miner Co. SD,** 2884 ....27 E3	**Mississippi Co. AR,** 51979 ....108 B4	Mondovi WI, 2634 ....67 E3	Monroeville IN, 1236 ....90 A3
		Millville OH, 817 ....100 B2	Minersville PA, 4552 ....93 E3	**Mississippi Co. MO,** 13427 ....108 C2	Monessen PA, 8669 ....92 A4	Monroeville OH, 1433 ....91 D2
		Millville PA, 991 ....93 E3	Minersville UT, 817 ....39 D3	Mississippi State MS, 3500 ....119 D4	Monett MO, 7396 ....106 C2	Monroeville PA, 29349 ....92 A4
		Millville UT, 1507 ....31 E3	Minerva OH, 3934 ....91 F3	**Missoula Co. MT,** 95802 ....15 D4	Monette AR, 1179 ....108 A4	Monrovia CA, 36929 ....228 E2
		Millwood NY, 2300 ....148 B2	Minerva Park OH, 1288 ....206 B1	Missouri City TX, 52913 ....132 A3	Monfort Hts. OH, 3880 ....204 A2	Monrovia IN, 628 ....99 F1
		Millwood WA, 1649 ....14 A3	Mineville NY, 1747 ....81 D3	Missouri Valley IA, 2992 ....86 A1	Monmouth IL, 9841 ....88 A3	Monsey NY, 14504 ....148 A4
		Milner GA, 522 ....129 D1	**Mingo Co. WV,** 28253 ....101 E4	Mitchell IN, 4567 ....99 F3	Monmouth OR, 7741 ....20 B2	Monson MA, 2103 ....150 A2
		Milnor ND, 711 ....27 E1	Mingo Jct. OH, 3631 ....91 F4	Mitchell NE, 1831 ....33 F2	Monmouth Beach NJ, 3595 ....147 F2	Montague CA, 1456 ....28 C3
		Milo IA, 839 ....86 C2	Minidoka Co. ID, 20174 ....31 D1	Mitchell SD, 14558 ....27 E3	**Monmouth Co. NJ,** 615301 ....147 E2	Montague MA, 800 ....94 C1
		Milo ME, 1898 ....84 C4	Minier IL, 1244 ....88 B4	**Mitchell Co. GA,** 23932 ....137 E1	Monmouth Jct. NJ, 2721 ....147 D1	Montague MI, 2407 ....75 E2
		Milpitas CA, 62698 ....36 B4	Minneapolis KS, 2046 ....43 E2	**Mitchell Co. IA,** 10874 ....73 D2	**Mono Co. CA,** 12853 ....37 E4	Montague TX, 225 ....59 E1
		Milroy IN, 800 ....100 A2	Minneapolis MN, 382618 ....67 D4	**Mitchell Co. KS,** 6932 ....43 E2	Monon IN, 1733 ....89 E3	**Montague Co. TX,** 19117 ....59 E1
		Milroy PA, 1386 ....93 D3	**Minnehaha Co. SD,** 148281 ....27 F4	**Mitchell Co. NC,** 15687 ....111 E4	Monona IA, 1550 ....73 F3	Mont Alto PA, 1357 ....103 D1
		Milton DE, 1657 ....145 F3	Minneola FL, 5435 ....140 C1	**Mitchell Co. TX,** 9698 ....58 B3	Monona WI, 8018 ....74 B3	Montana City MT, 2094 ....15 E4
		Milton FL, 7045 ....135 F1	Minneola KS, 717 ....42 C4	Mitchellville AR, 497 ....117 F4	**Monona Co. IA,** 10020 ....86 A1	Montara CA, 2950 ....259 A4
		Milton IN, 611 ....100 A1	Minneota MN, 1449 ....27 F3	Mitchellville IA, 1715 ....87 D2	Monongah WV, 928 ....102 A2	Montauk NY, 3851 ....149 F3
		Milton IA, 550 ....87 E3	Minnesota Lake MN, 681 ....72 C2	Mi-Wuk Vil. CA, 1485 ....37 D3	Monongahela PA, 4761 ....92 A4	Mont Belvieu TX, 2324 ....132 B3
		Milton KY, 525 ....100 A3	Minnetonka MN, 51301 ....235 A3	Moapa NV, 928 ....46 C3	**Monongalia Co. WV,** 81866 ....102 A1	Montcalm WV, 885 ....111 F1
		Milton MA, 26062 ....151 D1	Minnewaukan ND, 318 ....19 D2	Moberly MO, 11945 ....97 E2	Mononsett MA, 1700 ....151 E2	**Montcalm Co. MI,** 61266 ....75 F2
				Mobile AL, 198915 ....135 E1	Monroe CT, 3000 ....149 D2	Montclair CA, 33049 ....229 G2
				Mobile Co. AL, 399843 ....135 E1	Monroe GA, 11407 ....121 D4	Montclair NJ, 38977 ....148 A3
				Mobridge SD, 3574 ....26 C2	Monroe IA, 1808 ....87 D2	Mont Clare PA, 1900 ....146 B2
				Moclips WA, 615 ....12 B3	Monroe LA, 53107 ....125 E2	Monteagle TN, 1238 ....120 A1
				Modena NY, 1100 ....148 B1		Monte Alto TX, 1611 ....63 E4
				Modena PA, 610 ....146 B3		Montebello CA, 62150 ....228 D3
						Montecito CA, 10000 ....52 B2
						Montegut LA, 1803 ....134 B4

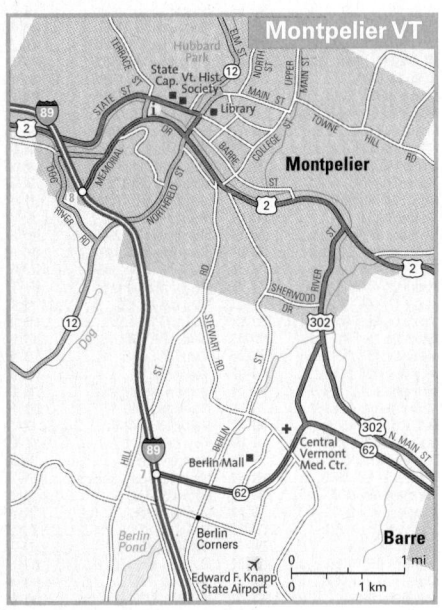

Montpelier VT

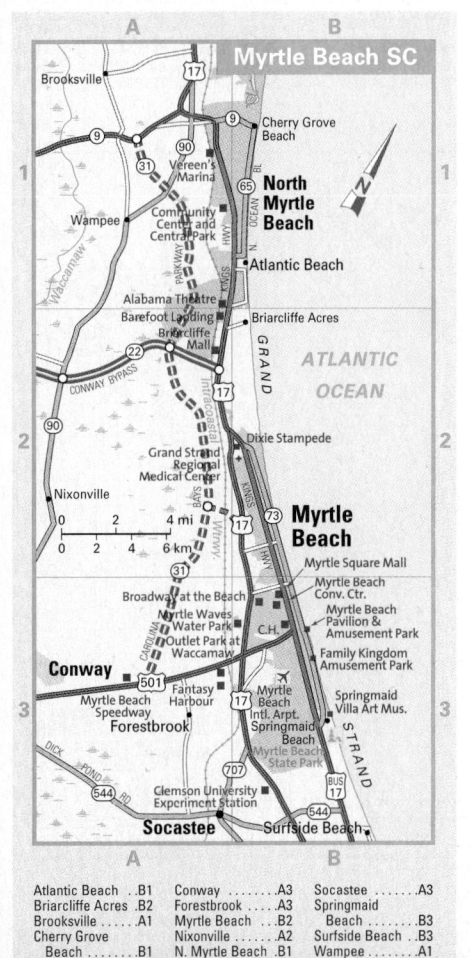

Myrtle Beach SC

Atlantic Beach ..B1	Conway A3	Socastee A3
Briarcliffe Acres .B2	Forestbrook A3	Springmaid
Brooksville A1	Myrtle Beach ..B2	Beach B3
Cherry Grove	Nixonville A3	Surfside Beach ..B3
Beach B1	N. Myrtle Beach .B1	Wampee A1

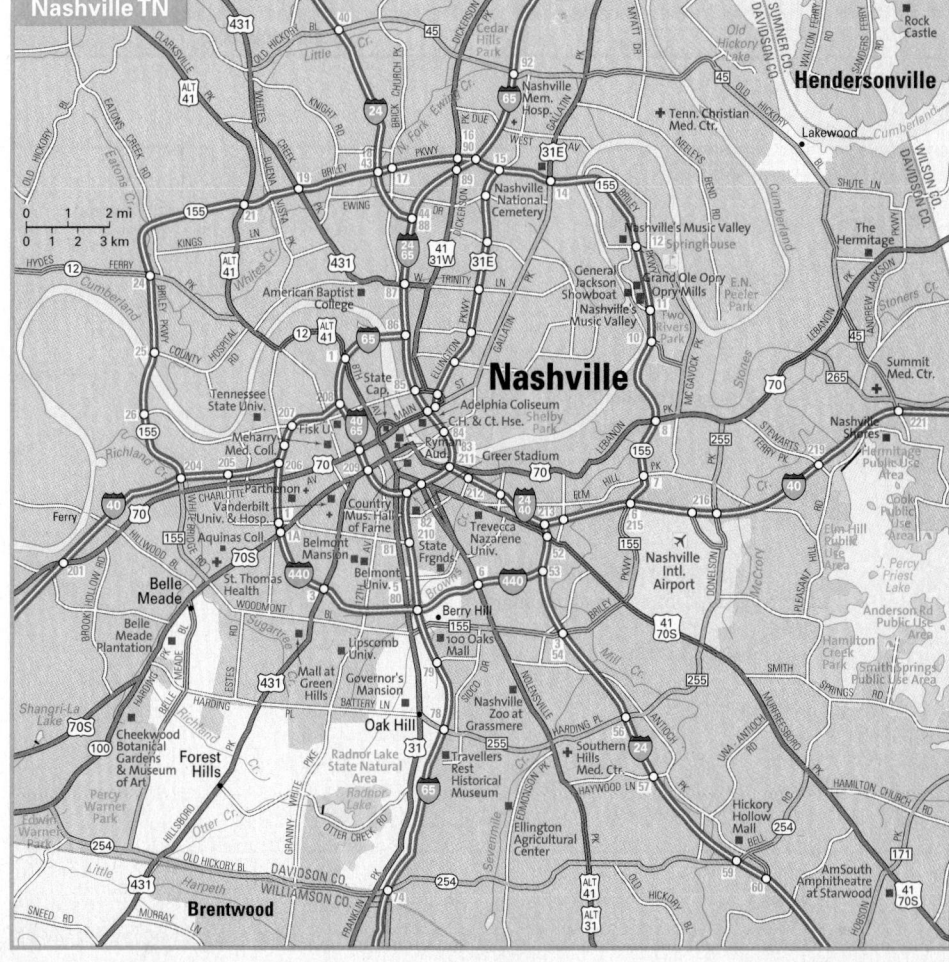

Nashville TN

238 Montello—Morris County

Figures after entries indicate population, page number, and grid reference.

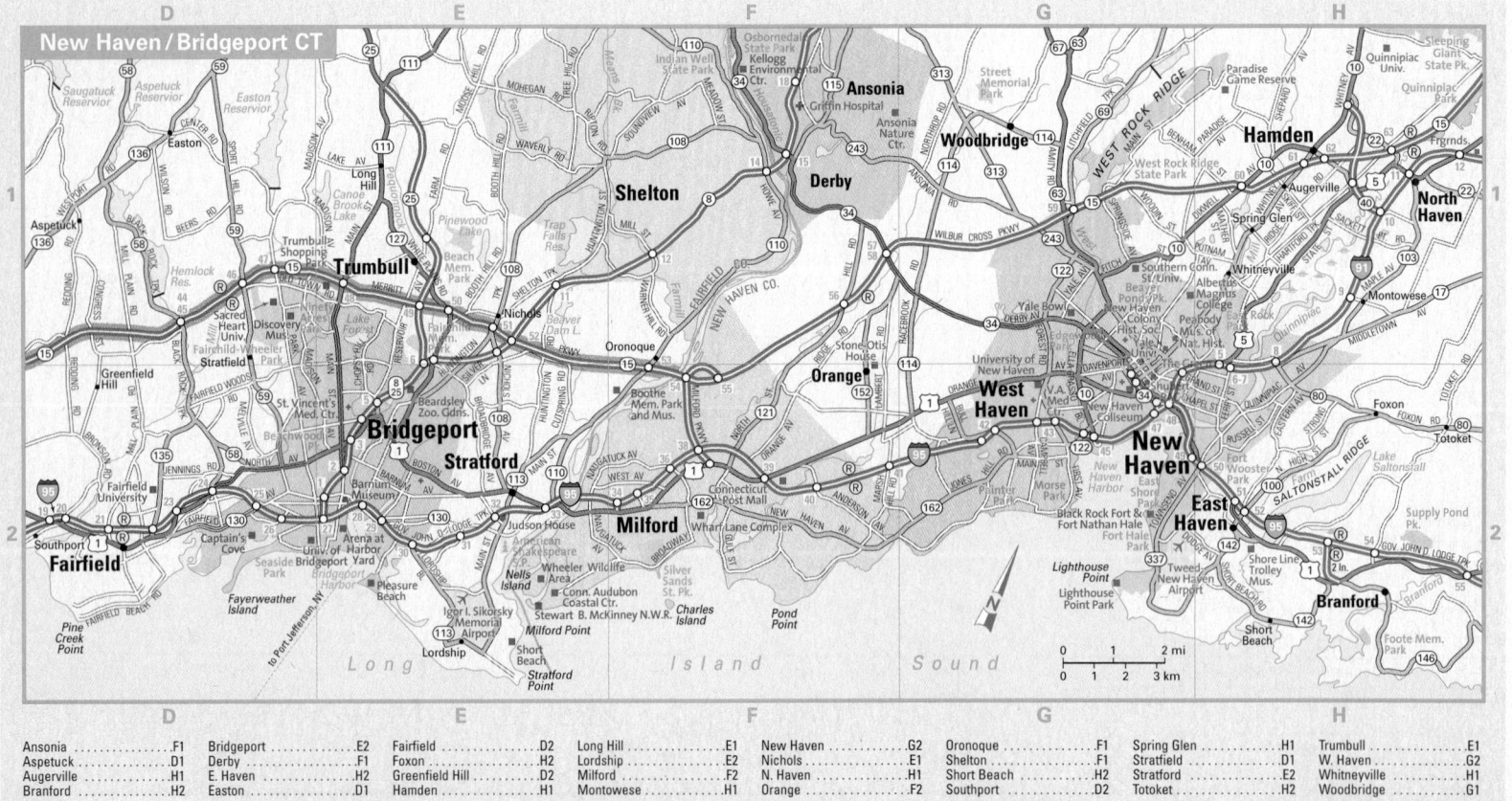

New Bedford / Fall River MA

Acushnet C1
Bliss Corner C1
Braleys C1
Coury Hts. C1
Eagleville A2
Fairhaven C2
Fall River B1
Faunce Corner C1
Head of Westport B2
Hixville B1
Idlewood C2
Island Park A2
Lakeside B2
Long Plain C1
New Bedford C2
N. Dartmouth C2
N. Fairhaven C2
N. Tiverton A2
Ocean Grove A1
Sherwood Forest C1
Somerset A1
S. Dartmouth C2
S. Swansea A1
Summit Grove B2
Swansea A1
The Hummocks A2
Tiverton A2
Westport Factory B2

New Haven / Bridgeport CT

Ansonia F1
Aspetuck D1
Branford H2
Bridgeport E2
Derby F1
E. Haven H2
Easton D1
Fairfield D2
Foxon H2
Greenfield Hill D1
Hamden H1
Idlewood E1
Lordship E2
Milford E2
Montowese H1
New Haven G2
Nichols E1
N. Haven H1
Orange F2
Oronoque F1
Shelton F1
Short Beach H2
Southport D2
Spring Glen H1
Stratfield D1
Stratford E2
Totoket H2
Trumbull E1
W. Haven G2
Whitneyville H1
Woodbridge G1

Entries in **bold** indicate counties or parishes. Entries in color indicate cities with detailed inset maps.

Ama	B2	Caernarvon	D2	Frenier	A1	Kenner	B1	Meraux	D2
Arabi	C1	Chalmette	C2	Gretna	C2	Killona	A1	Metairie	C1
Avondale	B2	Dalcour	C2	Hahnville	A2	Laplace	A1	Mimosa Park	A2
Belle Chasse	C2	Des Allemands	A2	Harahan	B2	Lone Star	A2	Montz	A1
Boutte	A2	Destrehan	A2	Harvey	C2	Lucy	A1	New Orleans	D1
Braithwaite	D2	English Turn	C2	Jefferson	B1	Luling	A2	New Sarpy	A1
Bridge City	B2	Estelle	C2	Kenilworth	D2	Marrero	C2	Norco	A1

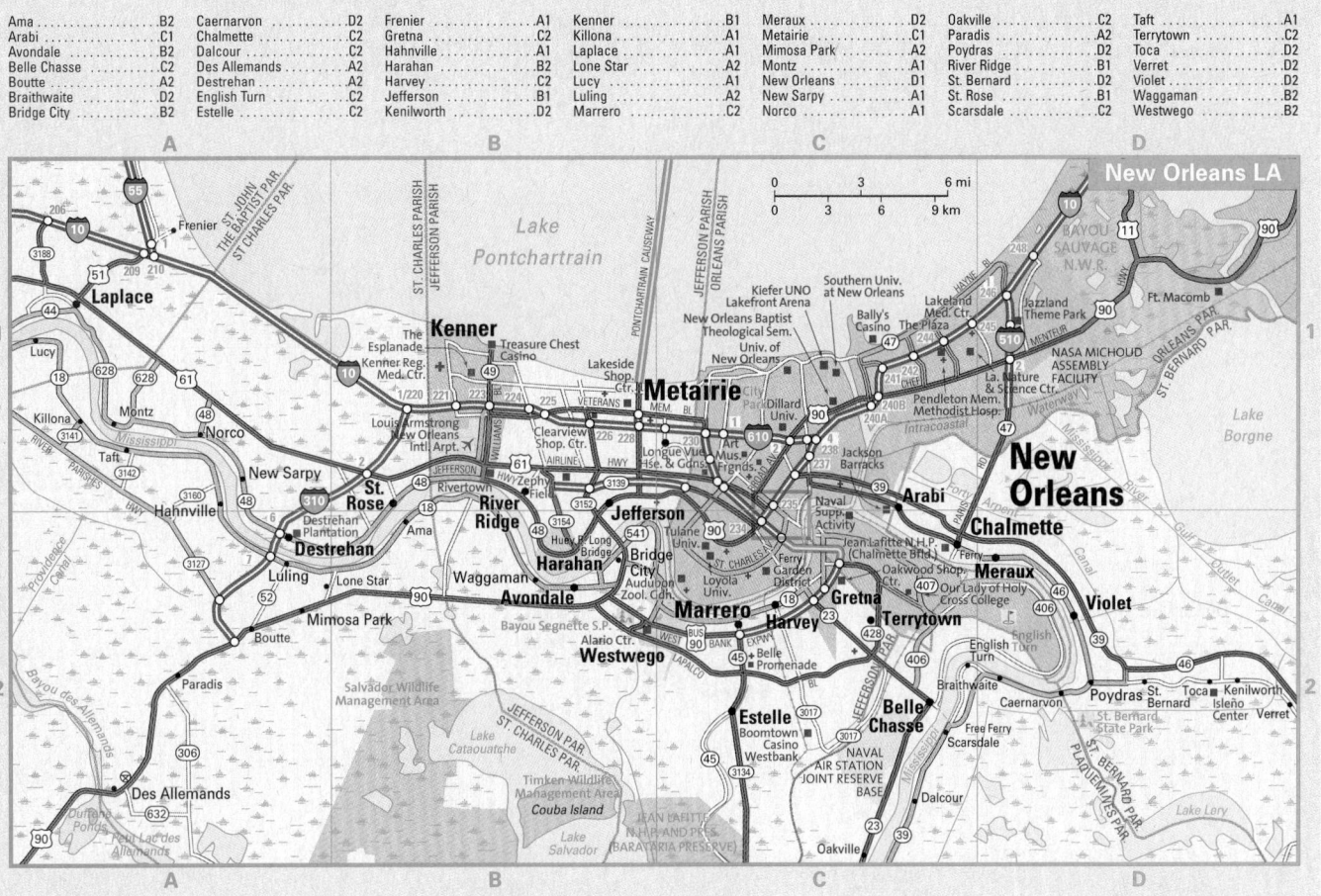

New Orleans LA

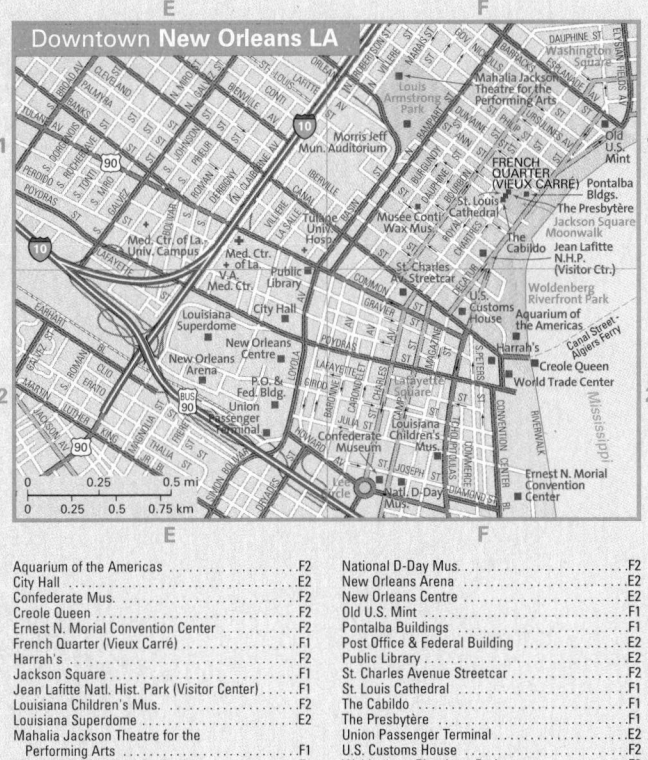

Downtown New Orleans LA

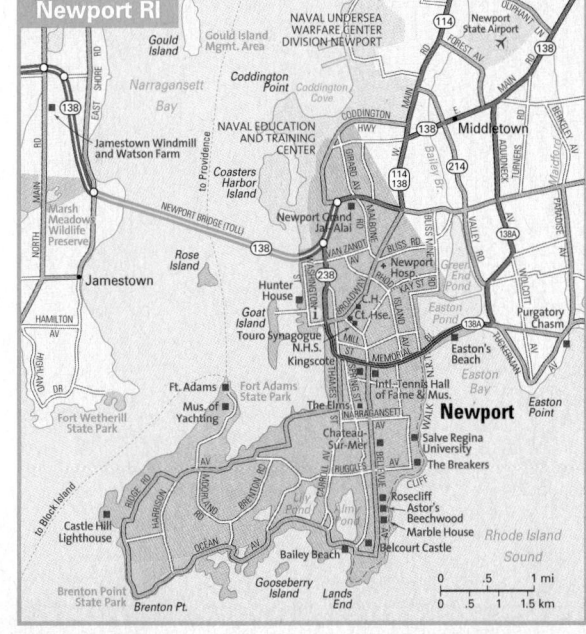

Newport RI

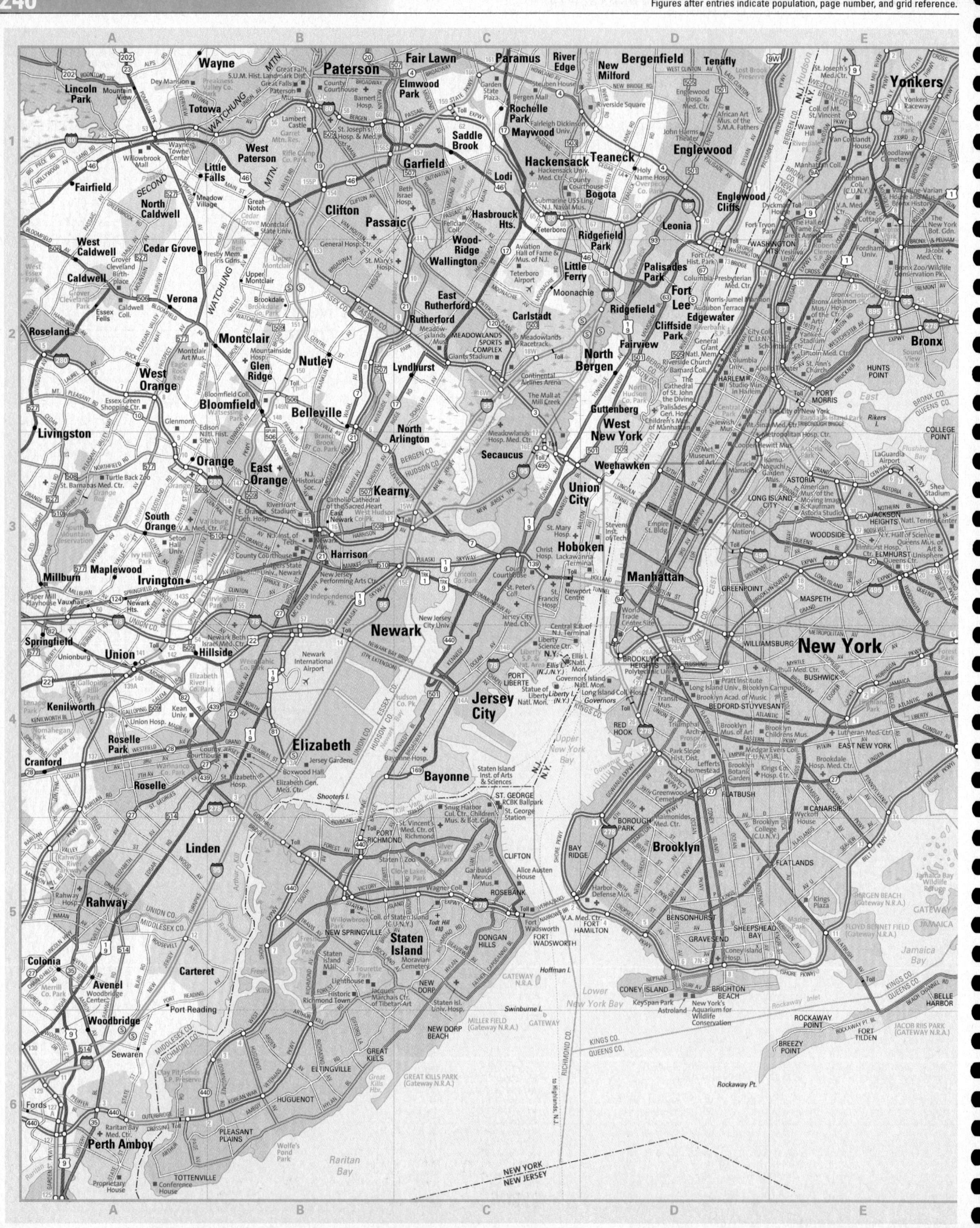

Entries in **bold** indicate counties or parishes. Entries in color indicate cities with detailed inset maps.

Mukilteo – New Castle 241

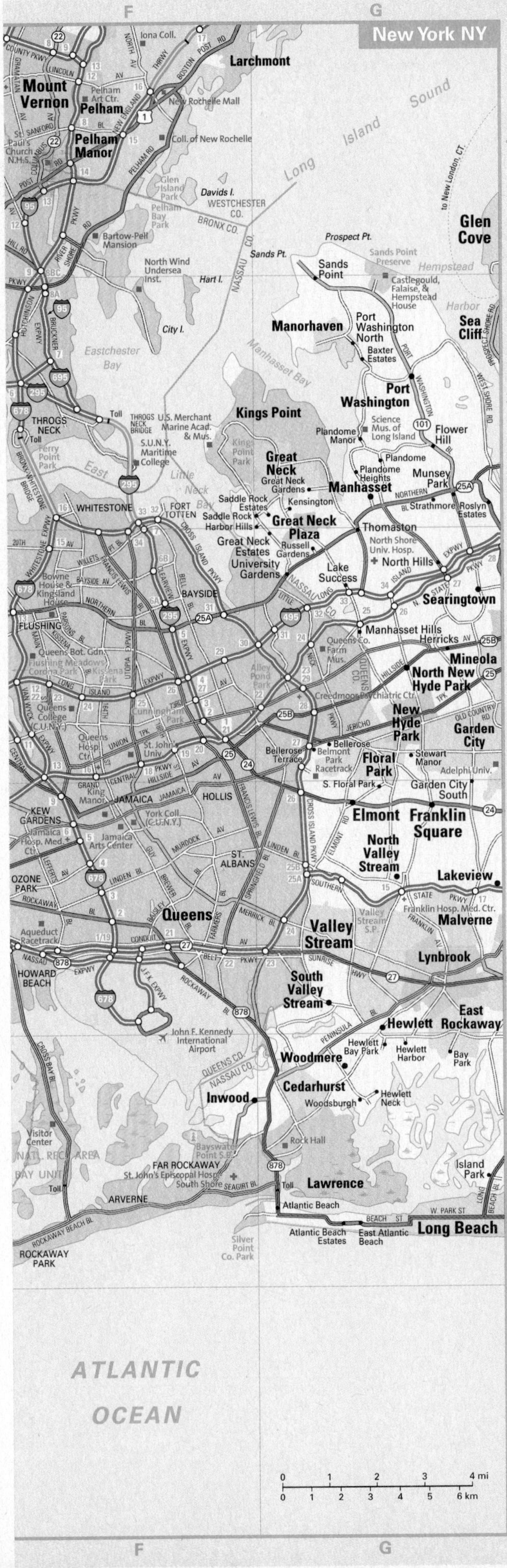

New York NY
F
G
Larchmont
Mount Vernon
Pelham
Pelham Manor
Iona Coll.
Pelham Art Ctr.
New Rochelle Mall
Coll. of New Rochelle
Long Island Sound
St. Paul's Church N.H.S.
Glen Island Park
Pelham Bay Park
Davids I.
WESTCHESTER CO.
BRONX CO.
Bartow-Pell Mansion
to New London, CT
Glen Cove
Prospect Pt.
Sands Pt.
Sands Point
Sands Point Preserve
Castlegould, Falaise, & Hempstead House
Hempstead Harbor
North Wind Undersea Inst.
Hart I.
NASSAU CO.
City I.
Eastchester Bay
Manorhaven
Port Washington North
Baxter Estates
Sea Cliff
Manhasset Bay
Port Washington
Kings Point
THROGS NECK
Toll
THROGS NECK BRIDGE
U.S. Merchant Marine Acad. & Mus.
S.U.N.Y. Maritime College
Ferry Point Park
Science Mus. of Long Island
Plandome Manor
Plandome
Plandome Heights
Flower Hill
Great Neck
Great Neck Gardens
Kensington
Manhasset
Munsey Park
Strathmore
Roslyn Estates
East River
Little Neck Bay
WHITESTONE
FORT TOTTEN
Saddle Rock Estates
Saddle Rock
Harbor Hills
Great Neck Plaza
Great Neck Estates
Russell Gardens
University Gardens
Thomaston
North Shore Univ. Hosp.
North Hills
Lake Success
Searingtown
Bowne House & Kingsland House
BAYSIDE
FLUSHING
Manhasset Hills
Herricks
Queens Co. Farm Mus.
QUEENS CO.
Mineola
North New Hyde Park
Queens Bot. Gdn.
Flushing Meadows Corona Park
Kissena Park
Alley Pond Park
Creedmoor Psychiatric Ctr.
New Hyde Park
Garden City
Queens College (C.U.N.Y.)
Cunningham Park
Queens Hosp. Ctr.
St. John's Univ.
Bellerose
Bellerose Terrace
Belmont Park Racetrack
Floral Park
Stewart Manor
Adelphi Univ.
KEW GARDENS
JAMAICA
HOLLIS
S. Floral Park
Garden City South
Elmont
Franklin Square
Jamaica Hosp. Med. Ctr.
Jamaica Arts Center
York Coll. (C.U.N.Y.)
ST. ALBANS
North Valley Stream
OZONE PARK
Lakeview
Franklin Hosp. Med. Ctr.
Malverne
Queens
Valley Stream
Valley Stream S.P.
Aqueduct Racetrack
HOWARD BEACH
Lynbrook
South Valley Stream
East Rockaway
Hewlett
John F. Kennedy International Airport
Hewlett Bay Park
Hewlett Harbor
Bay Park
Woodmere
QUEENS CO.
NASSAU CO.
Inwood
Cedarhurst
Woodsburgh
Hewlett Neck
Visitor Center
Rock Hall
NATL. REC. AREA
BAY UNIT
Bayswater Point S.P.
FAR ROCKAWAY
St. John's Episcopal Hosp. South Shore
Island Park
Lawrence
ARVERNE
Atlantic Beach
Atlantic Beach Estates
East Atlantic Beach
Long Beach
ROCKAWAY PARK
Silver Point Co. Park
ATLANTIC OCEAN
0 1 2 3 4 mi
0 1 2 3 4 5 6 km

Atlantic Beach G5
Atlantic Beach Estates ..G5
Avenel A5
Baxter Estates G2
Bayonne C4
Bay Park G5
Bellerose G3
Bellerose Terrace G3
Belleville B2
Bergenfield D1
Bloomfield B2
Bogota D1
Brookdale B2
Caldwell A2
Carlstadt C2
Carteret A5
Cedar Grove A2
Cedarhurst G5
Cliffside Park D2
Clifton B1
Colonia A5
Cranford A4
E. Atlantic Beach G5
E. Newark B3
E. Orange B3
E. Rockaway G4
E. Rutherford C2
Edgewater D2
Elizabeth B4
Elmont G4
Elmwood Park C1
Englewood D1
Englewood Cliffs D1
Essex Fells A2
Fairfield A1
Fair Lawn C1
Fairview D2
Floral Park G3
Flower Hill G2
Fords A6
Ft. Lee D2
Franklin Square G4
Garden City G3
Garden City South G4
Garfield C1
Glen Cove G1
Glen Ridge B2
Great Neck G2
Great Neck Estates G3
Great Neck Gardens G2
Great Neck Plaza G2
Great Notch B1
Guttenberg D2
Hackensack C1
Harbor Hills G2
Harrison B3
Hasbrouck Hts. C1
Herricks G3
Hewlett G4
Hewlett Bay Park G5
Hewlett Harbor G5
Hewlett Neck G5
Hillside A4
Hoboken C3
Inwood F5
Irvington A3
Island Park G5
Jersey City C4
Kearny B3
Kenilworth A4
Kensington G2
Kings Pt. G2
Lake Success G3
Lakeview G4
Larchmont F1
Lawrence G5
Leonia D1
Lincoln Park A1
Linden A5
Little Falls A1
Little Ferry C2
Livingston A2
Lodi C1
Long Beach G5
Lynbrook G4
Lyndhurst C2
Malverne G4
Manhasset G2
Manhasset Hills G3
Manorhaven G2
Maplewood A3
Maywood C1
Meadow Vil. A1
Millburn A3
Mineola G3
Montclair B2
Moonachie C2
Mtn. View A1
Mt. Vernon F1
Munsey Park G2
Newark B4
Newark Hts. A3
New Hyde Park G3
New Milford D1
New York E4
N. Arlington C2
N. Bergen D2
N. Caldwell A1
N. Hills G3
N. New Hyde Park G3
N. Valley Stream G4
Nutley B2
Orange A3
Palisades Park D2
Paramus C1
Passaic B1
Paterson B1
Pelham F1
Pelham Manor F1
Perth Amboy A6
Plandome G2
Plandome Hts. G2
Plandome Manor G2
Port Reading A5
Port Washington G2
Port Washington North ..G2
Rahway A5
Ridgefield D2
Ridgefield Park D1
River Edge C1
Rochelle Park C1
Roseland A2
Roselle A4
Roselle Park A4
Roslyn Estates G2
Russell Gardens G3
Rutherford C2
Saddle Brook C1
Saddle Rock G2
Saddle Rock Estates ...G2
Sands Pt. G2
Sea Cliff G2
Searingtown G3
Secaucus C3
Sewaren A6
S. Floral Park G4
S. Orange A3
S. Valley Stream G4
Springfield A4
Stewart Manor G3
Strathmore G2
Teaneck D1
Tenafly D1
Teterboro C1
Thomaston G3
Totowa A1
Union A4
Unionburg A4
Union City C3
University Gardens G3
Upper Montclair B2
Valley Stream G4
Vauxhall A3
Verona A2
Wallington C2
Wayne A1
Weehawken D3
W. Caldwell A2
W. New York D2
W. Orange A2
W. Paterson B1
Woodbridge A6
Woodmere G5
Wood-Ridge C2
Woodsburgh G5
Yonkers E1

Mukilteo WA, 18019 ....12 C2
Mukwonago WI, 6162 ....74 C3
Mulberry AR, 1627 ....116 C1
Mulberry FL, 3230 ....140 C2
Mulberry IN, 1387 ....89 E4
Mulberry KS, 577 ....106 B1
Mulberry NC, 2269 ....111 F3
Mulberry OH, 3139 ....100 B2
Mulberry Grove IL, 671 ....98 B3
Muldraugh KY, 1298 ....99 F4
Muldrow OK, 3104 ....116 B1
Muleshoe TX, 4530 ....49 F4
Mulga AL, 973 ....195 D1
Mullan ID, 840 ....14 C3
Mullen NE, 491 ....34 B2
Mullens WV, 1769 ....111 F1
Mullica Hill NJ, 1658 ....146 C4
Mulliken MI, 557 ....76 A4
Mullins SC, 5029 ....122 C3
Multnomah Co. OR, 660486 ....20 C2
Mulvane KS, 5155 ....43 E4
Muncie IN, 67430 ....90 A4
Muncy PA, 2663 ....93 D2
Munday TX, 1527 ....58 C1
Mundelein IL, 30935 ....74 C4
Munds Park AZ, 1250 ....47 E3
Munford AL, 2446 ....120 A4
Munford TN, 4708 ....118 B1
Munfordville KY, 1563 ....110 A2
Munhall PA, 12264 ....250 C3
Munich ND, 268 ....19 D1
Munising MI, 2539 ....69 E1
Munroe Falls OH, 5314 ....188 B1
Munsey Park NY, 2632 ....241 G2
Munsons Corners NY, 2426 ....79 D4
Munster IN, 21511 ....89 D2
Murchison TX, 592 ....124 A3
Murdo SD, 612 ....26 C4
Murfreesboro AR, 1764 ....116 C3
Murfreesboro NC, 2045 ....113 E3
Murfreesboro TN, 68816 ....109 F4
Murphy ID, 40 ....30 B1
Murphy MO, 9048 ....98 A3
Murphy NC, 1568 ....120 C2
Murphy TX, 3099 ....207 E1
Murphys CA, 2061 ....37 D3
Murphysboro IL, 13295 ....108 C1
Murray IA, 766 ....86 C3
Murray KY, 14950 ....109 D3
Murray NE, 481 ....86 A3
Murray UT, 34024 ....31 E4
Murray Co. GA, 36506 ....120 C2
Murray Co. MN, 9165 ....72 A1
Murray Co. OK, 12623 ....51 F4
Murray Hill KY, 616 ....230 F1
Murrayville IL, 644 ....98 A1
Murrells Inlet SC, 5519 ....123 D4
Murrieta CA, 44282 ....53 D3
Murrieta Hot Sprs. CA, 2948 ....229 K6
Murrysville PA, 18872 ....92 A4
Muscatine IA, 22697 ....87 F2
Muscatine Co. IA, 41722 ....87 F2
Muscle Shoals AL, 11924 ....119 E2
Muscoda WI, 1453 ....74 A3
Muscogee Co. GA, 186291 ....128 C2
Muscoy CA, 8919 ....229 J2
Muskego WI, 21397 ....74 C3
Muskegon MI, 40105 ....75 E3
Muskegon Co. MI, 170200 ....75 F3
Muskegon Hts. MI, 12049 ....75 E3
Muskingum Co. OH, 84585 ....91 E4
Muskogee OK, 38310 ....106 A4
Muskogee Co. OK, 69451 ....106 A4
Musselshell Co. MT, 4497 ....16 C4
Mustang OK, 13156 ....51 E3
Mustang Ridge TX, 785 ....61 E2
Muttontown NY, 3412 ....148 C3
Myers Corner NY, 5546 ....148 B1
Myerstown PA, 3171 ....146 A1
Myersville MD, 1382 ....144 A1
Myricks MA, 600 ....151 D3
Myrtle MS, 407 ....118 C2
Myrtle Beach SC, 22759 ....123 D4
Myrtle Creek OR, 3419 ....28 B1
Myrtle Grove FL, 17211 ....135 F2
Myrtle Grove NC, 7125 ....123 E3
Myrtle Pt. OR, 2451 ....28 A1
Mystic CT, 4001 ....149 F2
Mystic IA, 588 ....87 D3
Mystic Island NJ, 8694 ....147 E4
Myton UT, 539 ....32 A4

N

Naalehu HI, 919 ....153 E4
Naches WA, 643 ....13 D4
Naco AZ, 833 ....55 E4
Nacogdoches TX, 29914 ....124 B4
Nacogdoches Co. TX, 59203 ....124 B4
Nageezi NM, 296 ....48 B2
Nags Head NC, 2700 ....115 F2
Nahant MA, 3632 ....151 D1
Nahunta GA, 930 ....129 F4
Nain VA, 700 ....102 C2
Naknek AK, 678 ....154 B3
Nambe NM, 1200 ....49 D2
Nameloc Hts. MA, 1500 ....151 E3
Nampa ID, 51867 ....22 B4
Nanakuli HI, 10814 ....152 A3
Nance Co. NE, 4038 ....35 E3
Nanticoke PA, 10955 ....93 E2
Nantucket MA, 3830 ....151 F4
Nantucket Co. MA, 9520 ....151 F4
Nanty Glo PA, 3054 ....92 B4
Nanuet NY, 16707 ....148 B3
Napa CA, 72585 ....36 B3
Napa Co. CA, 124279 ....36 B2
Napanoch NY, 1168 ....94 A3
Napaskiak AK, 390 ....154 B3
Napavine WA, 1361 ....12 B4
Naperville IL, 128358 ....88 C1
Naples FL, 20976 ....142 C2
Naples NY, 1072 ....78 C4
Naples TX, 1410 ....124 B1
Naples UT, 1300 ....32 A4
Naples Manor FL, 5186 ....142 C2
Naples Park FL, 6741 ....142 C1
Napoleon MI, 1254 ....90 B1
Napoleon ND, 857 ....18 C4
Napoleon OH, 9318 ....90 B2
Napoleonville LA, 686 ....134 A3
Nappanee IN, 6710 ....89 F2
Naranja FL, 4034 ....143 E3
Narberth PA, 4233 ....248 B3
Narragansett Pier RI, 3671 ....150 C4
Narrows VA, 2111 ....112 A1
Naschitti NM, 360 ....48 A2
Nash TX, 2169 ....116 C4
Nash Co. NC, 87420 ....113 D4
Nashotah WI, 1266 ....74 C3
Nashua IA, 1618 ....73 D3
Nashua MT, 325 ....17 D2
Nashua NH, 86605 ....95 D1
Nashville AR, 4878 ....116 C4
Nashville GA, 4697 ....129 E4
Nashville IL, 3147 ....98 B4
Nashville IN, 825 ....99 F2
Nashville MI, 1684 ....76 A4
Nashville NC, 4309 ....113 D4
Nashville TN, 569891 ....109 F4
Nashwauk MN, 935 ....64 B3
Nassau DE, 1600 ....145 F4
Nassau NY, 1161 ....94 B1
Nassau Bay TX, 4170 ....132 B3
Nassau Co. FL, 57663 ....139 D2
Nassau Co. NY, 1334544 ....148 C4
Nassau Vil. FL, 1900 ....222 C1
Nassawadox VA, 572 ....114 B3
Natalbany LA, 1739 ....134 B2
Natalia TX, 1663 ....61 D3
Natchez LA, 583 ....125 D4
Natchez MS, 18464 ....125 F4
Natchitoches LA, 17865 ....125 D3
Natchitoches Par. LA, 39080 ....125 D4
Natick MA, 32170 ....150 C1
National City CA, 54260 ....258 B2
National Park NJ, 3205 ....146 C3
Natrona Co. WY, 66533 ....33 D1
Natrona Hts. PA, 10934 ....92 A3
Naturita CO, 635 ....40 B3
Naugatuck CT, 30989 ....149 D1
Nauvoo IL, 1063 ....87 F4
Navajo NM, 2097 ....48 A2
Navajo Co. AZ, 97470 ....47 F3
Navarre OH, 1440 ....91 E3
Navarro Co. TX, 45124 ....59 F3
Navasota TX, 6789 ....61 F1
Navesink NJ, 1962 ....147 F1
Naylor MO, 610 ....108 A3
Naytahwaush MN, 583 ....19 F3
Nazareth KY, 1000 ....100 A4
Nazareth PA, 6023 ....93 F3
Nazlini AZ, 397 ....47 F2
Neah Bay WA, 794 ....12 A2
Neapolis OH, 1000 ....90 B2
Nebraska City NE, 7228 ....86 A3
Necedah WI, 888 ....74 A1
Neche ND, 437 ....19 E1
Nederland CO, 1394 ....41 D1
Nederland TX, 17422 ....132 C3
Nedrow NY, 2265 ....79 D3
Needham MA, 28911 ....151 D1
Needles CA, 4830 ....46 B4
Needville TX, 2609 ....132 A4
Neelyville MO, 487 ....108 A3
Neenah WI, 24507 ....74 C1
Neffs OH, 1138 ....101 F1
Negaunee MI, 4576 ....65 F4
Neillsville WI, 2731 ....68 A4
Nekoosa WI, 2590 ....74 A1
Neligh NE, 1651 ....35 E2
Nelliston NY, 622 ....79 F3
Nelson GA, 626 ....120 C3
Nelson NE, 587 ....35 E4
Nelson Co. KY, 37477 ....100 A4
Nelson Co. ND, 3715 ....19 E2
Nelson Co. VA, 14445 ....112 C1
Nelsonville NY, 565 ....148 B1
Nelsonville OH, 5230 ....101 E2
Nemacolin PA, 1034 ....102 A1
Nemaha Co. KS, 10717 ....96 A1
Nemaha Co. NE, 7576 ....86 A4
Nenana AK, 402 ....154 C2
Neodesha KS, 2848 ....106 A1
Neoga IL, 1854 ....98 C2
Neola IA, 845 ....86 A2
Neola UT, 533 ....32 A4
Neopit WI, 839 ....68 C4
Neosho MO, 10505 ....106 B2
Neosho WI, 593 ....74 C3
Neosho Co. KS, 16997 ....106 A1
Neotsu OR, 650 ....20 B2
Nephi UT, 4733 ....39 E1
Neptune NJ, 9000 ....147 F2
Neptune Beach FL, 7270 ....139 D2
Neptune City NJ, 5218 ....147 F2
Nesbit MS, 700 ....118 B2
Nesconset NY, 11992 ....149 D3
Nescopeck PA, 1528 ....93 E3
Neshoba Co. MS, 28684 ....126 C2
Nesquehoning PA, 3288 ....93 F3
Ness City KS, 1534 ....42 C3
Ness Co. KS, 3454 ....42 C3
Netarts OR, 744 ....20 B2
Netcong NJ, 2580 ....94 A4
Nettleton MS, 1932 ....119 D3
Nevada IA, 6658 ....86 C1
Nevada MO, 8607 ....106 C1
Nevada OH, 814 ....90 C3
Nevada City CA, 3001 ....36 C2
Nevada Co. AR, 9955 ....117 D4
Nevada Co. CA, 92033 ....36 C2
New Albany IN, 37603 ....99 F4
New Albany MS, 7607 ....118 C3
New Albin IA, 527 ....73 F2
New Alexandria PA, 595 ....92 A4
Newark AR, 1219 ....107 F4
Newark CA, 42471 ....259 D4
Newark DE, 28547 ....146 B4
Newark IL, 887 ....88 C2
Newark NJ, 273546 ....148 B4
Newark NY, 9682 ....78 C3
Newark OH, 46279 ....91 D4
Newark TX, 887 ....59 E2
Newark Valley NY, 1071 ....93 E1
New Athens IL, 1981 ....98 B4
New Auburn MN, 488 ....66 C4
New Auburn WI, 562 ....67 F3
New Augusta MS, 715 ....126 C4
Newaygo MI, 1670 ....75 F2
Newaygo Co. MI, 47874 ....75 F2
New Baden IL, 3001 ....98 B3
New Baltimore MI, 7405 ....76 C4
New Baltimore NY, 800 ....94 B1
New Baltimore VA, 800 ....144 A3
New Beaver PA, 1677 ....91 F3
New Bedford MA, 93768 ....151 D4
Newberg OR, 18064 ....20 B2
New Berlin IL, 1030 ....98 B1
New Berlin NY, 1129 ....79 E4
New Berlin PA, 838 ....93 D3
New Berlin WI, 38220 ....74 C3
New Bern NC, 23128 ....115 D3
Newbern TN, 2988 ....108 C4
Newberry FL, 3316 ....138 C3
Newberry MI, 2686 ....69 F1
Newberry SC, 10580 ....121 F3
Newberry Co. SC, 36108 ....121 F3
New Bethlehem PA, 1057 ....92 B3
New Bloomfield MO, 599 ....97 E3
New Bloomfield PA, 1077 ....93 D4
Newborn GA, 520 ....121 D4
New Boston IL, 632 ....87 F2
New Boston NH, 550 ....81 F4
New Boston OH, 2340 ....101 D3
New Boston TX, 4808 ....116 B4
New Braunfels TX, 36494 ....61 D2
New Bremen OH, 2909 ....90 B4
New Brighton MN, 22206 ....235 C1
New Brighton PA, 6641 ....91 F3
New Britain CT, 71538 ....149 E1
New Britain PA, 3125 ....146 C2
New Brockton AL, 1250 ....128 A4
New Brunswick NJ, 48573 ....147 E1
New Buffalo MI, 2200 ....89 E1
Newburg WV, 360 ....102 B2
Newburg WI, 1119 ....74 C2
Newburgh IN, 3088 ....99 E4
Newburgh NY, 28259 ....148 B1
Newburgh Hts. OH, 2389 ....204 F2
Newbury VT, 396 ....81 E2
Newburyport MA, 17189 ....151 F1
New Canaan CT, 6600 ....148 C2
New Carlisle IN, 1505 ....89 E1
New Carlisle OH, 5735 ....100 C1
New Carrollton MD, 12589 ....144 B3
New Castle CO, 1984 ....40 C1
New Castle DE, 4862 ....146 B4
New Castle IN, 17780 ....100 A1

242 New Castle—New Lisbon

Figures after entries indicate population, page number, and grid reference.

Manhattan New York NY

Entries in **bold** indicate counties or parishes. Entries in color indicate cities with detailed inset maps.

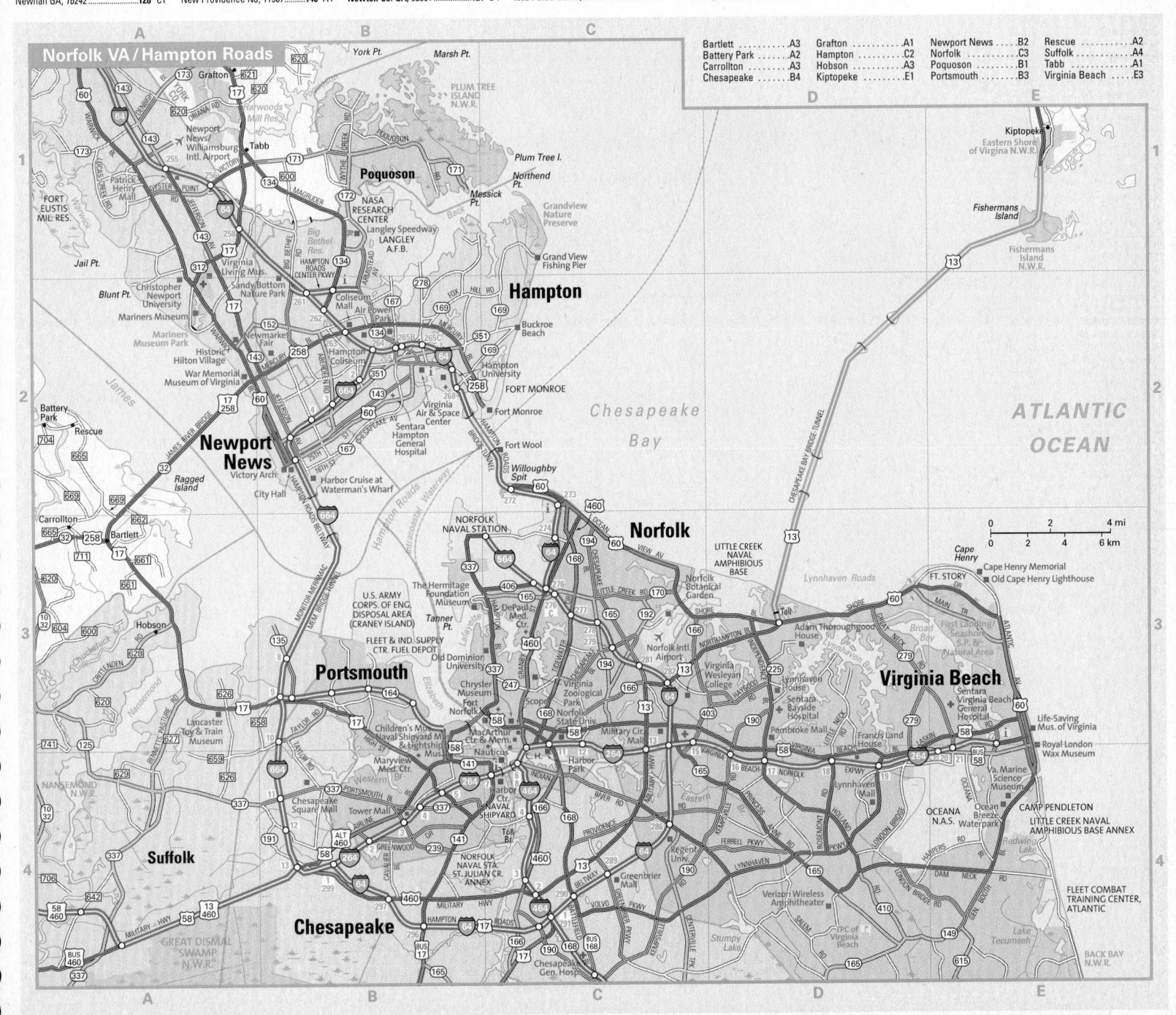

Figures after entries indicate population, page number, and grid reference.

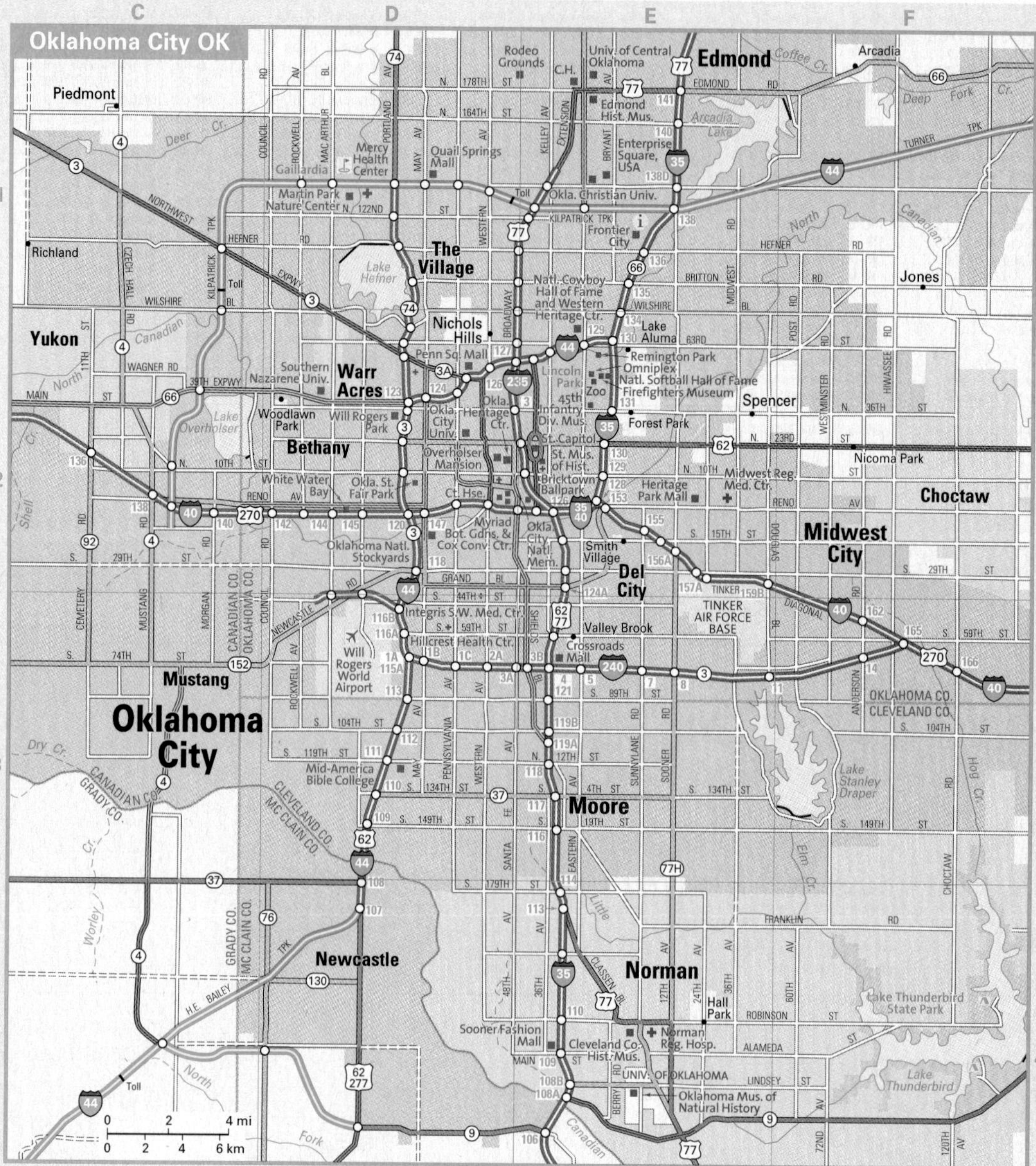

Oklahoma City OK

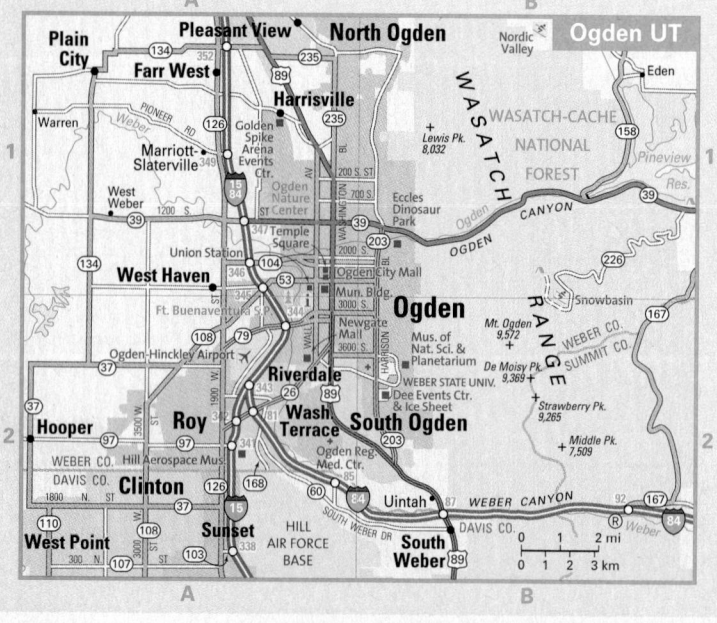

Ogden UT

Entries in **bold** indicate counties or parishes. Entries in color indicate cities with detailed inset maps.
Northwood—Ossining 245

Northwood NH, 500 81 F4
Northwood ND, 959 19 E3
Northwood OH, 5471 90 C2
Northwoods MO, 4643 256 B2
N. Woodstock NH, 750 81 F3
Northwye MO, 550 97 E4
N. York PA, 1689 275 E1
Norton KS, 3012 42 C1
Norton MA, 2618 151 D2
Norton OH, 11523 91 E3
Norton VA, 3904 111 E2
Norton Co. KS, 5953 42 C1
Norton Shores MI, 22527 75 E3
Nortonville KS, 620 96 A2
Nortonville KY, 1264 109 E2
Norwalk CA, 103298 52 C3
Norwalk CT, 82951 148 C2
Norwalk IA, 6884 86 C2
Norwalk OH, 16238 91 D2
Norwalk WI, 653 73 F2
Norway IA, 601 87 E1
Norway ME, 2623 82 B2
Norway MI, 2959 69 D2
Norwell MA, 1300 151 E2
Norwich CT, 36117 149 F1
Norwich KS, 551 43 E4
Norwich NY, 7355 79 E4
Norwich VT, 1200 81 E3
Norwood CO, 438 40 B3
Norwood KY, 395 230 F1
Norwood MA, 28587 151 D2
Norwood MO, 552 107 E2
Norwood NY, 1685 80 B1
Norwood NC, 2216 122 B1
Norwood OH, 21675 100 B2
Norwood PA, 5985 248 B4
Norwood-Young America MN, 3108 66 C4
Notasulga AL, 916 128 B2
Nottingham NH, 550 81 F4
Nottoway VA, 100 113 D2
Nottoway Co. VA, 15725 113 D2
Notus ID, 458 22 B4
Novato CA, 47630 36 B3
Novi MI, 47386 76 B4
Novinger MO, 534 87 D4
Nowata OK, 3971 106 A3
Nowata Co. OK, 10569 106 A2
Noxapater MS, 419 126 C1
Noxon MT, 230 14 C2
Noxubee Co. MS, 12548 127 D1
Noyack NY, 2696 149 E3
Nuangola PA, 671 93 E3
Nuckolls Co. NE, 5057 35 E4
Nucla CO, 734 40 B3
Nueces Co. TX, 313645 63 F2
Nuevo CA, 6135 53 D3
Nuiqsut AK, 433 154 C1
Nunda NY, 1330 78 B4
Nunn CO, 471 33 E4
Nutley NJ, 27362 148 B3
Nutter Fort WV, 1686 102 A2
Nyack NY, 6737 148 B3
Nye Co. NV, 32485 37 F3
Nyssa OR, 3163 22 A4

O

Oacoma SD, 390 27 D4
Oak Bluffs MA, 1700 151 E4
Oakboro NC, 1198 122 B1
Oak Brook IL, 8702 203 C4
Oakbrook Terrace IL, 2300 203 C4
Oak City UT, 650 39 D2
Oak Creek CO, 849 32 C4
Oak Creek WI, 28456 74 C3
Oakdale CA, 15503 36 C4
Oakdale CT, 1100 149 F1
Oakdale KY, 4937 109 D2
Oakdale LA, 8137 133 E1
Oakdale MA, 1100 150 C1
Oakdale MN, 26653 235 E2
Oakdale NY, 8075 149 D4
Oakdale PA, 1551 92 A4
Oakes ND, 1979 27 E1
Oakesdale WA, 420 14 A3
Oakfield ME, 475 85 D3
Oakfield NY, 1805 78 B3
Oakfield WI, 1012 74 C2
Oak Forest IL, 28051 89 D2
Oak Grove AL, 457 128 A1
Oak Grove IL, 1318 88 A2
Oak Grove KY, 7064 109 E3
Oak Grove LA, 2174 125 F1
Oak Grove MI, 700 70 C4
Oak Grove MN, 6903 67 D3
Oak Grove MS, 1400 126 C4
Oak Grove MO, 5535 96 C2
Oak Grove OR, 12808 251 D3
Oak Grove SC, 8183 122 A3
Oak Grove TN, 4072 111 E3
Oak Grove Hts. AR, 727 108 A4
Oak Harbor OH, 2841 90 C2
Oak Harbor WA, 19795 12 C2
Oak Hill FL, 1378 141 E1
Oak Hill OH, 1685 101 D3
Oak Hill WV, 7589 101 F4
Oak Hills IL, 2400 256 D2
Oakhurst CA, 2868 37 D4
Oakhurst NJ, 4152 147 F2
Oakhurst OK, 2731 51 F2
Oak Island NC, 6571 123 E4
Oakland CA, 399484 36 B4
Oakland FL, 936 141 D1
Oakland IL, 996 99 D1
Oakland IA, 1487 86 A2
Oakland ME, 2758 82 C2
Oakland MD, 1930 102 B2
Oakland MD, 2100 144 B1
Oakland MS, 586 118 B3
Oakland MO, 1540 256 B3
Oakland NE, 1367 35 F2
Oakland NJ, 12466 148 A3
Oakland OK, 674 51 F4
Oakland OR, 954 20 B4
Oakland PA, 622 93 F1
Oakland TN, 1279 118 C1
Oakland City IN, 2588 99 E4
Oakland Co. MI, 1194156 76 B4
Oakland Park FL, 30966 143 F1
Oak Lawn IL, 55245 89 D1
Oakley ID, 668 31 D2
Oakley KS, 2173 42 B2
Oakley UT, 948 31 F4
Oaklyn NJ, 4188 248 D4
Oakman AL, 944 119 E4
Oakmont PA, 6911 92 A4
Oak Orchard DE, 750 145 F4
Oak Park CA, 2320 228 A2
Oak Park IL, 52524 89 D1
Oak Park MI, 29793 76 C4
Oak Park Hts. MN, 3957 67 D3
Oak Ridge NJ, 750 148 A3
Oak Ridge NC, 3988 112 B4
Oakridge OR, 3148 20 C4
Oak Ridge TN, 27387 110 C4
Oak Ridge North TX, 2991 132 A2
Oak Shade NJ, 1500 147 D3
Oakton VA, 29348 144 A3
Oaktown IN, 633 99 E3
Oak Trail Shores TX, 2475 59 E3
Oak View CA, 4199 52 B2
Oakville CT, 8618 149 D1
Oakville MO, 35309 98 A3
Oakville WA, 675 12 B4
Oakwood GA, 2689 121 D3
Oakwood IL, 1502 89 D4
Oakwood OH, 607 90 B3
Oakwood OH, 3667 204 G3
Oakwood OH, 9215 208 E2
Oakwood Beach NJ, 700 145 E1
Oakwood Hills IL, 2194 203 A1
Oasis NV, 200 30 C3
Oberlin KS, 1994 42 C1
Oberlin LA, 1853 133 E2
Oberlin OH, 8195 91 D2
Oberlin PA, 2809 218 C2
Obetz OH, 3977 206 B3
Obion TN, 1134 108 C3
Obion Co. TN, 32450 108 C3
Oblong IL, 1580 99 D2
O'Brien Co. IA, 15102 72 A3
Ocala FL, 45943 138 C4
Occidental CA, 1272 36 A3
Occoquan VA, 759 144 B4
Oceana WV, 1550 111 F1
Oceana Co. MI, 26873 75 E2
Ocean Bluff MA, 5100 151 E2
Ocean Breeze Park FL, 463 141 E4
Ocean City FL, 5594 136 B2
Ocean City MD, 7173 114 C1
Ocean City NJ, 15378 147 F4
Ocean Co. NJ, 510916 147 E3
Ocean Gate NJ, 2076 147 E3
Ocean Grove MA, 3012 151 D3
Ocean Grove NJ, 4256 147 F2
Oceano CA, 7260 52 A1
Ocean Park WA, 1459 12 B4
Ocean Pines MD, 10496 114 C1
Oceanport NJ, 5807 147 F2
Ocean Reef Club FL, 1000 143 E3
Ocean Ridge FL, 1636 143 F1
Ocean Shores WA, 3836 12 B4
Oceanside CA, 161029 53 D3
Oceanside NY, 32733 147 F1
Oceanside OR, 326 20 B2
Ocean Sprs. MS, 17225 135 D2
Ocean View DE, 1006 145 F4
Ochelata OK, 494 51 F1
Ocheyedan IA, 536 72 A2
Ochiltree Co. TX, 9006 50 B2
Ochlocknee GA, 605 137 E1
Ocilla GA, 3270 129 E4
Ocoee FL, 24391 141 D1
Oconee Co. GA, 26225 121 D4
Oconee Co. SC, 66215 121 E2
Oconomowoc WI, 12382 74 C3
Oconto WI, 4708 69 D4
Oconto Co. WI, 35634 68 C4
Oconto Falls WI, 2843 68 C4
Ocracoke NC, 769 115 E3
Odebolt IA, 1153 72 A4
Odell IL, 1014 88 C3
Odell OR, 1849 20 C1
Odem TX, 2499 61 E4
Odenton MD, 20534 144 C2
Odenville AL, 1131 119 F4
Odessa DE, 286 145 E1
Odessa FL, 3173 140 B2
Odessa MO, 4818 96 C2
Odessa NY, 617 79 D4
Odessa TX, 90943 58 A3
Odessa WA, 957 13 F3
Odin IL, 1122 98 C3
Odon IN, 1376 99 E3
O'Donnell TX, 1011 58 A2
Oelwein IA, 6692 73 E4
O'Fallon IL, 21910 98 B3
O'Fallon MO, 46169 98 A3
Ogallala NE, 4930 34 B3
Ogden IL, 743 89 D4
Ogden IA, 2023 86 C1
Ogden KS, 1762 43 F2
Ogden NC, 5481 123 E3
Ogden UT, 77226 31 E3
Ogden Dunes IN, 1313 89 E2
Ogdensburg NJ, 2638 148 A3
Ogdensburg NY, 12364 80 B1
Ogemaw Co. MI, 21645 76 B1
Oglala SD, 1229 34 A1
Ogle Co. IL, 51032 88 B1
Oglesby IL, 3647 88 B2
Oglethorpe GA, 1200 129 D3
Oglethorpe Co. GA, 12635 121 E4
Ogunquit ME, 800 82 B4
Ohatchee AL, 1215 120 A4
Ohio City OH, 784 90 B3
Ohio Co. IN, 5623 100 A2
Ohio Co. KY, 22916 109 F1
Ohio Co. WV, 47427 91 F4
Ohioville PA, 3759 91 F3
Oil City LA, 1219 124 C2
Oil City PA, 11504 92 A2
Oildale CA, 27885 45 D4
Oilton OK, 1099 51 F2
Ojai CA, 7862 52 B2
Okaloosa Co. FL, 170498 136 B2
Okanogan WA, 2484 13 E2
Okanogan Co. WA, 39564 13 E1
Okarche OK, 1110 51 E2
Okauchee WI, 2100 74 C3
Okawville IL, 1355 98 B3
Okay OK, 597 106 A4
Okeechobee FL, 5376 141 E4
Okeechobee Co. FL, 35910 141 E3
Okeene OK, 1240 51 D2
Okemah OK, 3038 51 F3
Okemos MI, 22805 76 A4
Okfuskee Co. OK, 11814 51 F3
Oklahoma City OK, 506132 51 E3
Oklahoma Co. OK, 660448 51 E2
Okmulgee OK, 13022 51 F2
Okmulgee Co. OK, 39685 51 F2
Okoboji IA, 820 72 A2
Okolona MS, 3056 119 D3
Oktibbeha Co. MS, 42902 118 C4
Ola AR, 1204 117 D2
Olanta SC, 613 122 C4
Olathe CO, 1573 40 B3
Olathe KS, 92962 96 B3
Olcott NY, 1156 78 B3
Old Bennington VT, 232 94 C1
Old Bridge NJ, 22833 147 E1
Oldenburg IN, 647 100 A2
Old Field NY, 947 149 D3
Old Forge NY, 800 79 F2
Old Forge PA, 8798 93 F2
Old Fort NC, 963 111 E4
Oldham SD, 206 27 E3
Oldham Co. KY, 46178 100 A4
Oldham Co. TX, 2185 49 F3
Old Lyme CT, 850 149 E2
Old Mystic CT, 3205 149 F2
Old Orchard Beach ME, 8856 82 B4
Old River-Winfree TX, 1364 132 B3
Old Saybrook CT, 1962 149 E2
Oldsmar FL, 11910 140 B2
Oldtown ID, 190 14 B2
Old Town ME, 8130 83 D1
Old Zionsville PA, 950 146 B1
Olean NY, 15347 92 C1
Oley PA, 1100 146 B1
Olin IA, 716 87 F1
Olive Branch MS, 21054 118 B2
Olive Hill KY, 1813 101 D4
Olivehurst CA, 11061 36 C2
Oliver PA, 2925 102 B1
Oliver Co. ND, 2065 18 B4
Oliver Sprs. TN, 3303 110 C4
Olivet MI, 1758 76 A4
Olivet NJ, 1420 145 F1
Olivet SD, 70 35 E1
Olivette MO, 7438 256 B2
Olivia MN, 2570 66 B4
Olla LA, 1417 125 E3
Olmos Park TX, 2343 257 E2
Olmsted Co. MN, 124277 73 E1
Olmsted Falls OH, 7962 204 D3
Olney IL, 8631 99 D3
Olney MD, 31438 144 B2
Olney TX, 3396 59 D1
Olney Sprs. CO, 389 41 F3
Olpe KS, 504 43 F3
Olton TX, 2288 50 A4
Olustee OK, 680 50 C4
Olympia WA, 42514 12 B4
Olympian Vil. MO, 669 98 A4
Olyphant PA, 4978 261 E2
Omaha NE, 390007 86 A2
Omaha TX, 999 124 B1
Omak WA, 4721 13 E2
Omao HI, 1221 152 B1
Omega GA, 1340 129 D4
Omro WI, 3177 74 C1
Onaga KS, 704 43 F1
Onalaska TX, 1174 132 B1
Onalaska WI, 14839 73 F2
Onamia MN, 847 66 C2
Onancock VA, 1525 114 C3
Onarga IL, 1438 89 D3
Onawa IA, 3091 35 F2
Onaway ID, 230 14 B4
Onaway MI, 993 70 C3
Oneco FL, 7500 140 B3
Oneida IL, 752 88 A3
Oneida NY, 10987 79 E3
Oneida TN, 3615 110 B3
Oneida WI, 1070 68 C4
Oneida Co. ID, 4125 31 E2
Oneida Co. NY, 235469 79 E2
Oneida Co. WI, 36776 68 B2
O'Neill NE, 3733 35 D2
Onekama MI, 647 75 E1
Oneonta AL, 5576 119 F4
Oneonta NY, 13292 79 F4
Onida SD, 740 26 C3
Onley VA, 496 114 C3
Onondaga Co. NY, 458336 79 E3
Onset MA, 1292 151 E3
Onslow Co. NC, 150355 115 D4
Onsted MI, 813 90 B1
Ontario CA, 158007 52 C2
Ontario OH, 5303 91 D3
Ontario OR, 10985 22 A4
Ontario Co. NY, 100224 78 C4
Ontonagon MI, 1769 65 E4
Ontonagon Co. MI, 7818 65 E4
Onyx CA, 476 45 E4
Oolitic IN, 1152 99 F3
Oologah OK, 883 106 A3
Ooltewah TN, 5681 120 B2
Oostburg WI, 2660 75 D2
Opal Cliffs CA, 6458 236 D1
Opa-Locka FL, 14951 143 E2
Opelika AL, 23498 128 B2
Opelousas LA, 22860 133 F2
Opp AL, 6607 128 A4
Oppelo AR, 725 117 E1
Opportunity WA, 25065 14 B3
Oquawka IL, 1539 87 F3
Oracle AZ, 3563 55 D2
Oracle Jct. AZ, 550 55 D3
Oradell NJ, 8047 148 B3
Oran MO, 1264 108 B2
Orange CA, 128821 52 C3
Orange CT, 13233 149 D2
Orange MA, 3945 95 D1
Orange NJ, 32868 240 A3
Orange OH, 3236 204 G2
Orange TX, 18643 132 C2
Orange VA, 4123 103 D4
Orange Beach AL, 3784 135 F2
Orangeburg NY, 3388 148 B3
Orangeburg SC, 12765 122 A4
Orangeburg Co. SC, 91582 122 A4
Orange City FL, 6604 141 D1
Orange City IA, 5582 35 F1
Orange Co. CA, 2846289 52 C3
Orange Co. FL, 896344 141 D1
Orange Co. IN, 19306 99 F3
Orange Co. NY, 341367 148 A2
Orange Co. NC, 118227 112 C4
Orange Co. TX, 84966 132 C2
Orange Co. VT, 28226 81 E3
Orange Co. VA, 25881 103 D4
Orange Cove CA, 7722 45 D3
Orange Grove TX, 1288 61 E4
Orange Lake FL, 650 138 C4
Orange Lake NY, 6085 148 B1
Orange Park FL, 9081 139 D2
Orangeville IL, 751 74 B4
Orangeville UT, 1398 39 F2
Orchard Beach MD, 4400 193 D5
Orchard City CO, 2880 40 B2
Orchard Lake MI, 2215 210 A1
Orchard Mesa CO, 6456 40 B2
Orchard Park NY, 3294 78 B4
Orchards WA, 17852 20 C1
Orcutt CA, 28830 52 A1
Ord NE, 2269 35 D3
Orderville UT, 596 39 D4
Ordway CO, 1248 41 F3
Oreana IL, 892 98 C1
Ore City TX, 1106 124 B2
Orefield PA, 1600 146 B1
Oregon IL, 4060 88 B1
Oregon MO, 935 96 B1
Oregon OH, 19355 90 C2
Oregon WI, 7514 74 B3
Oregon City OR, 25754 20 C2
Oregon Co. MO, 10344 107 F3
Oreland PA, 5509 248 C1
Orem UT, 84324 31 F4
Orfordville WI, 1272 74 B4
Orient NY, 709 149 F2
Oriental NC, 875 115 E3
Orient Park FL, 5703 266 C2
Orinda CA, 17599 259 C2
Orion IL, 1713 88 A2
Oriskany NY, 1459 79 E3
Oriskany Falls NY, 698 79 E3
Orland CA, 6281 36 B1
Orland ME, 500 83 D2
Orland Hills IL, 6779 203 C6
Orlando FL, 185951 141 D1
Orland Park IL, 51077 89 D2
Orleans IN, 2273 99 F3
Orleans IA, 583 72 B2
Orleans MA, 1716 151 F3
Orleans NE, 425 43 D1
Orleans VT, 826 81 E1
Orleans Co. NY, 44171 78 B3
Orleans Co. VT, 26277 81 E1
Orleans Par. LA, 484674 134 B2
Orlinda TN, 594 109 F3
Orlovista FL, 6047 246 B2
Ormond Beach FL, 36301 139 E4
Ormond-by-the-Sea FL, 8430 139 E4
Orofino ID, 3247 14 B4
Orono ME, 8253 83 D1
Orono MN, 7538 66 C4
Oronoco MN, 883 73 D1
Oronogo MO, 976 106 B2
Orosi CA, 7318 45 D3
Oro Valley AZ, 29700 55 D3
Oroville CA, 13004 36 C1
Oroville WA, 1653 13 E1
Orrick MO, 889 96 C2
Orrington ME, 325 83 D1
Orrs Island ME, 550 82 B3
Orrville OH, 8551 91 E3
Orting WA, 3760 12 C3
Ortonville MI, 1535 76 B3
Ortonville MN, 2158 27 F2
Orwell OH, 1519 91 F2
Orwigsburg PA, 3106 146 A1
Osage IA, 3451 73 D3
Osage WY, 215 25 F4
Osage Beach MO, 3662 97 D4
Osage City KS, 3034 96 A3
Osage Co. KS, 16712 96 A3
Osage Co. MO, 13062 97 F4
Osage Co. OK, 44437 51 F1
Osakis MN, 1567 66 B2
Osawatomie KS, 4645 96 B3
Osborne KS, 1607 43 D2
Osborne Co. KS, 4452 43 D2
Osburn ID, 1545 14 B3
Oscawana Corners NY, 1500 148 B2
Osceola AR, 8875 108 B4
Osceola IN, 1859 89 F2
Osceola IA, 4659 86 C3
Osceola MO, 835 96 C4
Osceola NE, 921 35 E3
Osceola WI, 2421 67 D3
Osceola Co. FL, 172493 141 D2
Osceola Co. IA, 7003 72 A2
Osceola Co. MI, 23197 75 F1
Osceola Mills PA, 1249 92 C3
Oscoda MI, 992 76 C1
Oscoda Co. MI, 9418 70 C4
Osgood IN, 1669 100 A2
Oshkosh NE, 887 34 A3
Oshkosh WI, 62916 74 C1
Oskaloosa IA, 10938 87 D2
Oskaloosa KS, 1165 96 A2
Oslo FL, 1900 141 E3
Osmond NE, 796 35 E2
Osprey FL, 4143 140 B4
Osseo MN, 2434 235 A1
Osseo WI, 1669 67 F4
Ossian IN, 2943 90 A3
Ossian IA, 853 73 E3
Ossineke MI, 1059 71 D4
Ossining NY, 24010 148 B2

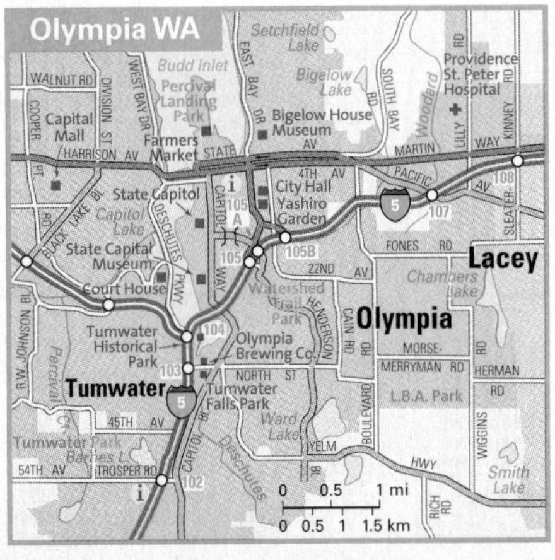
Olympia WA
Olympia
Lacey
Tumwater
State Capitol
Capitol Lake
Bigelow House Museum
Providence St. Peter Hospital
City Hall
Tumwater Falls Park
0 0.5 1 mi
0 0.5 1 1.5 km

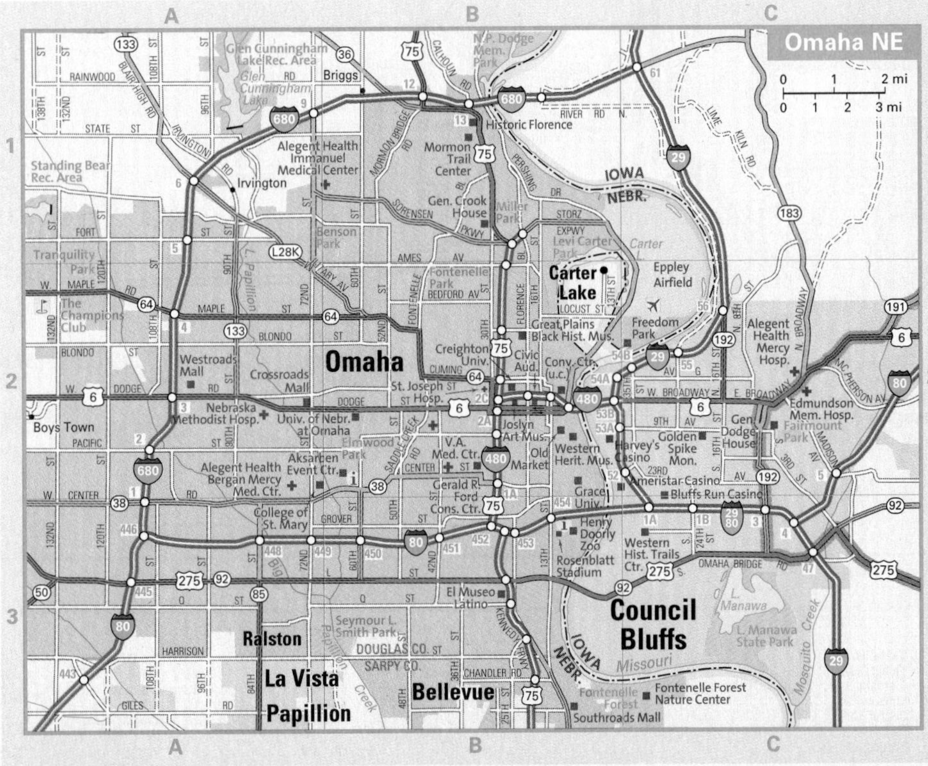
Omaha NE
Omaha
Council Bluffs
Carter Lake
Boys Town
Irvington
Ralston
La Vista
Papillion
Bellevue
Briggs
IOWA
NEBR.
Eppley Airfield
0 1 2 mi
0 1 2 3 mi

Bellevue B3
Boys Town A2
Briggs B1
Carter Lake B2
Council Bluffs C3
Irvington A1
La Vista A3
Omaha B2
Papillion A3
Ralston A3

246 Ossipee—Palm Valley

Figures after entries indicate population, page number, and grid reference.

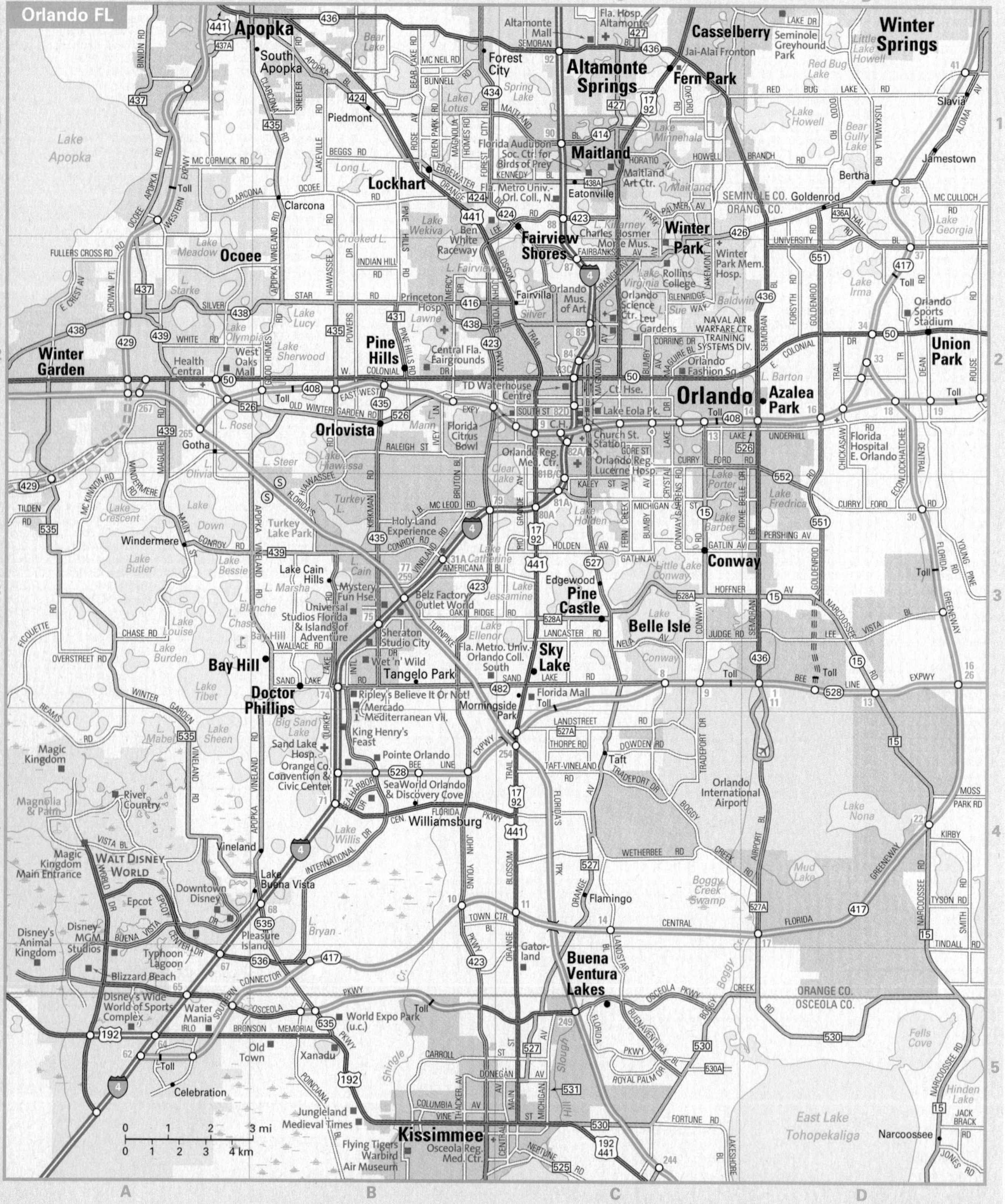

Orlando FL

Entries in **bold** indicate counties or parishes. Entries in color indicate cities with detailed inset maps.

Palmview—Patterson Springs **247**

Oxnard / Ventura CA

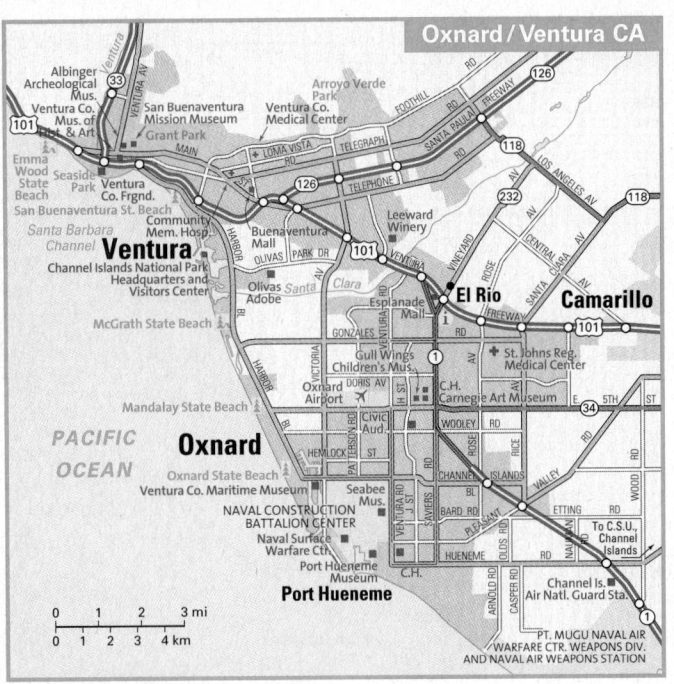

Palm Springs CA

Panama City FL

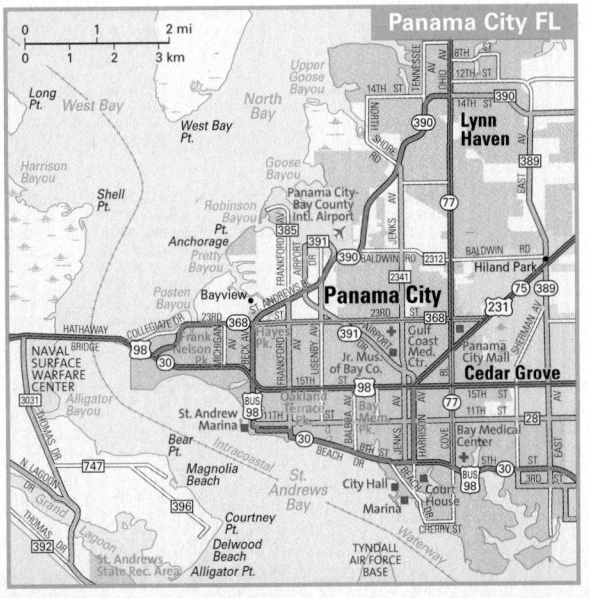

Pensacola FL

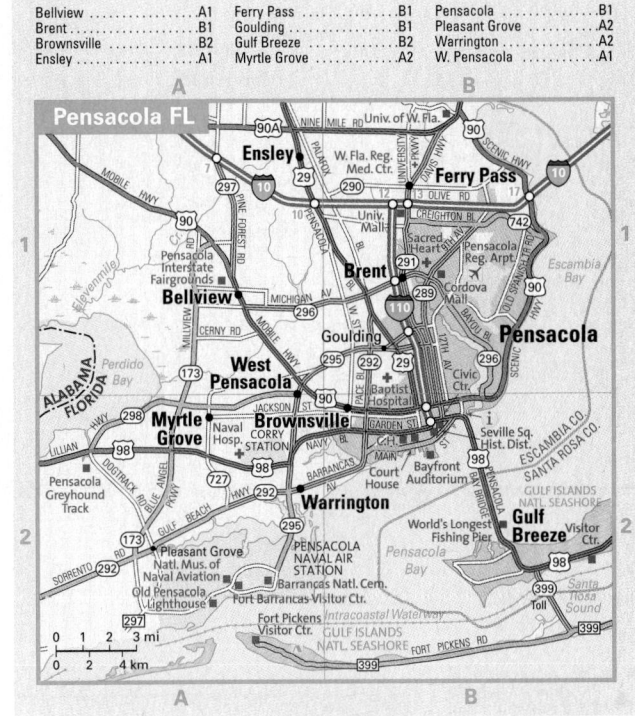

Peoria IL

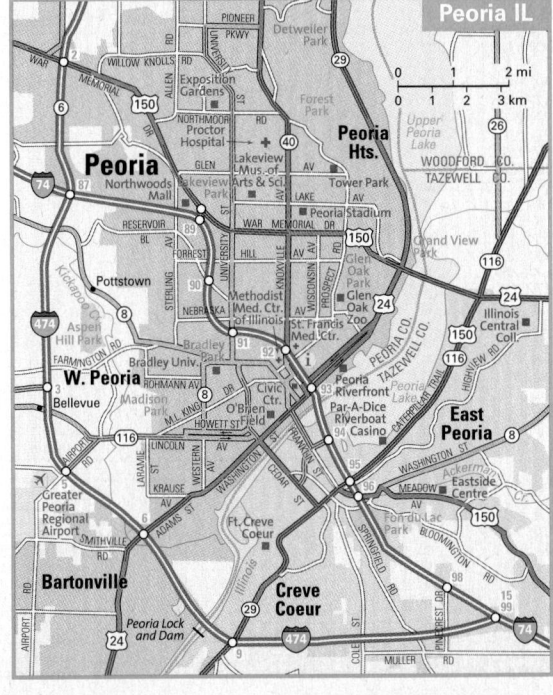

Figures after entries indicate population, page number, and grid reference.

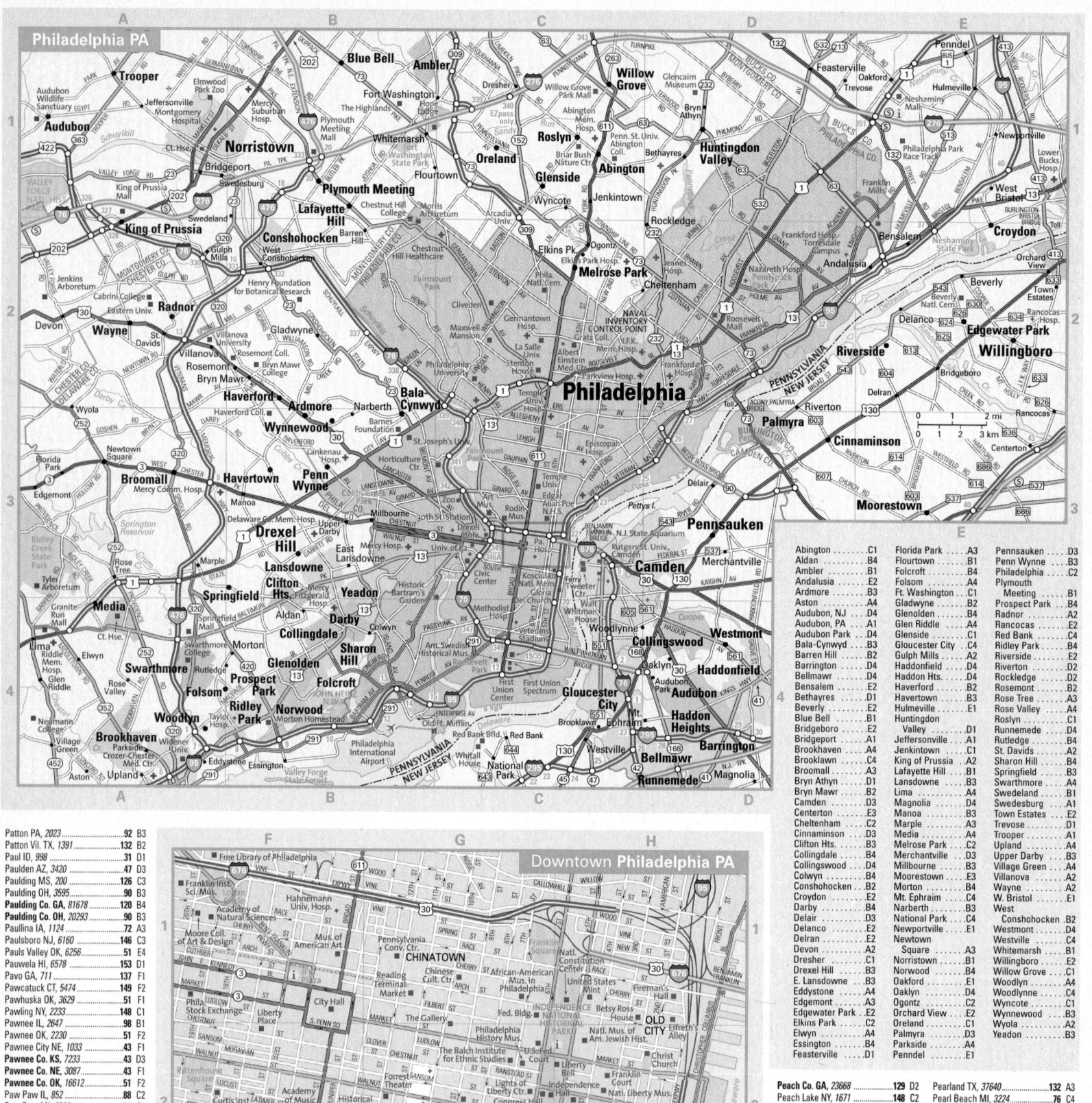

Philadelphia PA

Downtown Philadelphia PA

Entries in **bold** indicate counties or parishes. Entries in color indicate cities with detailed inset maps.

Pecatonica—Pickett County   **249**

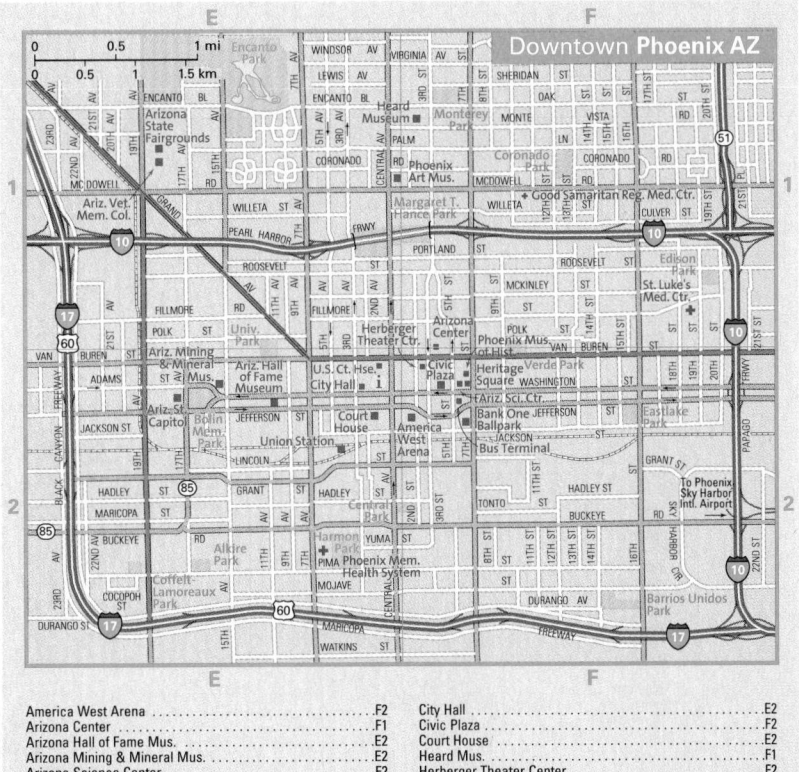

Phoenix AZ

Downtown Phoenix AZ

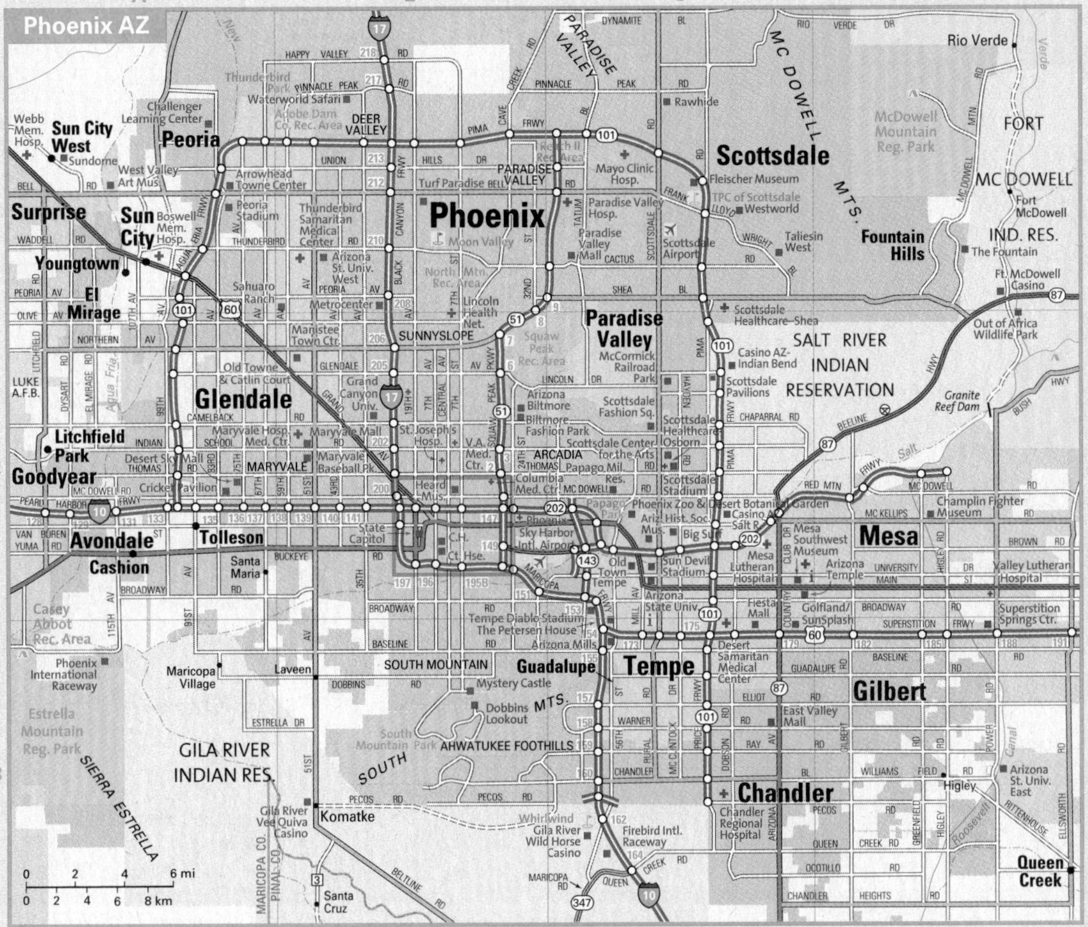

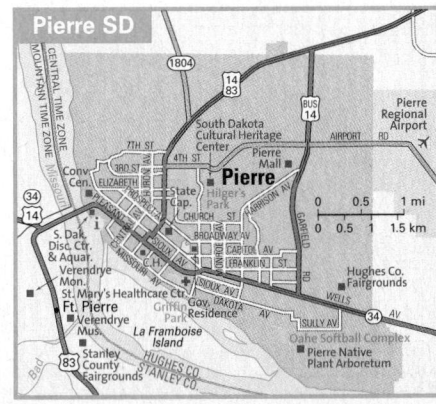

Pierre SD

Pittsburgh PA

Downtown Pittsburgh PA

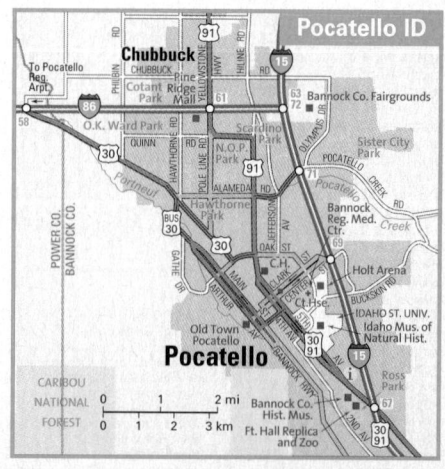

Pocatello ID

Entries in **bold** indicate counties or parishes. Entries in color indicate cities with detailed inset maps.

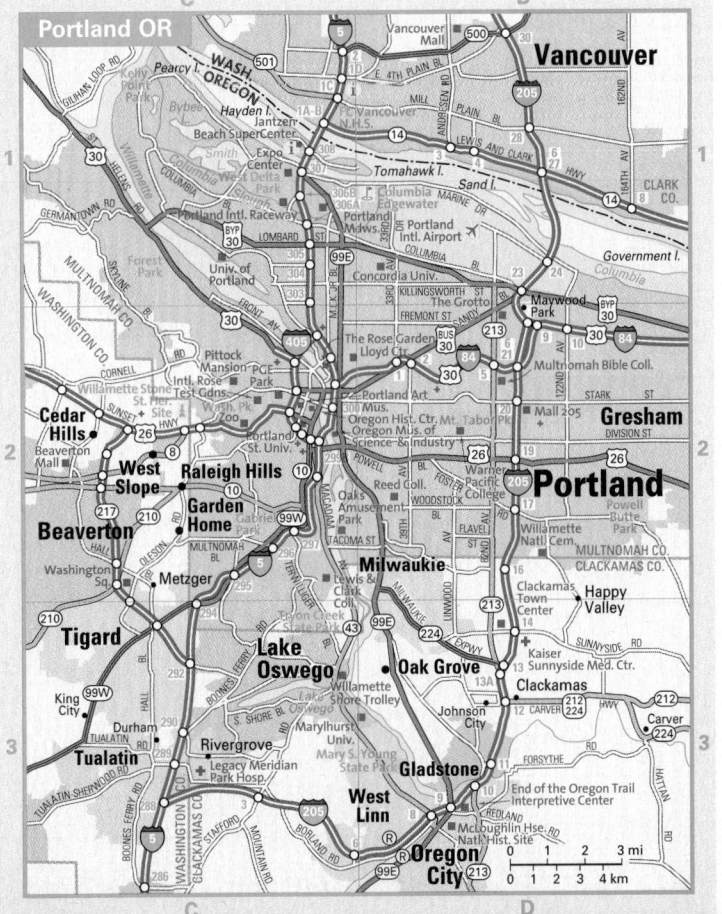

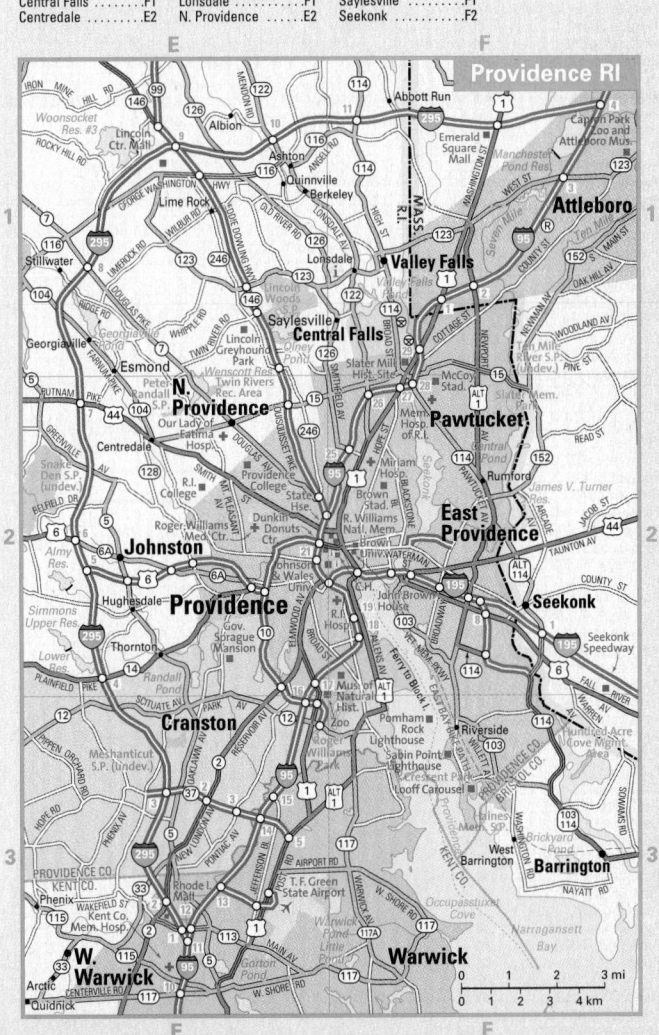

252   Point Pleasant—Quincy

Figures after entries indicate population, page number, and grid reference.

Provo UT

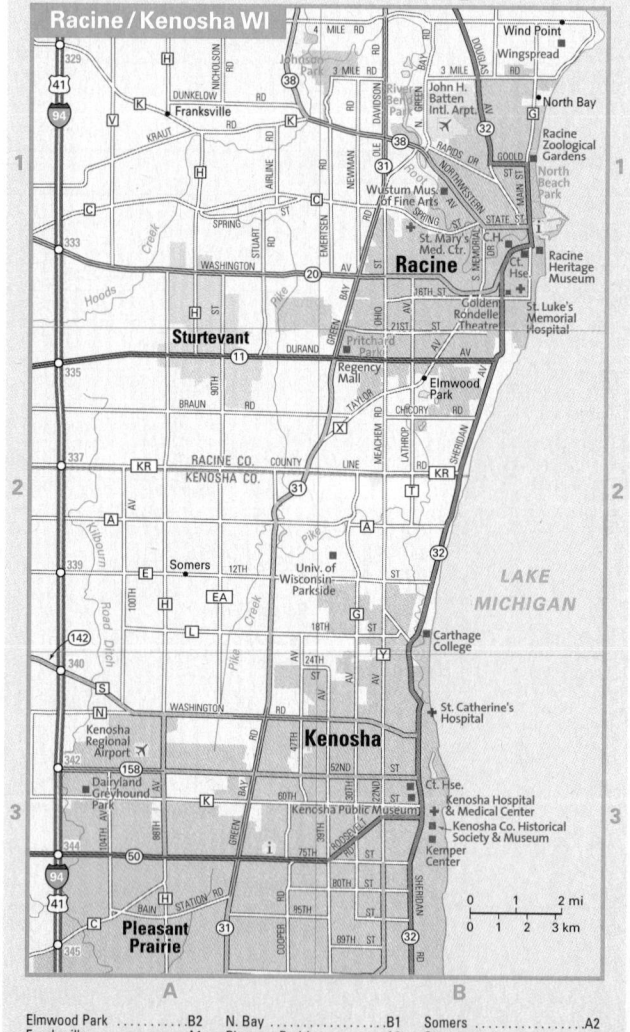

Pueblo CO

Racine / Kenosha WI

Entries in **bold** indicate counties or parishes. Entries in color indicate cities with detailed inset maps.

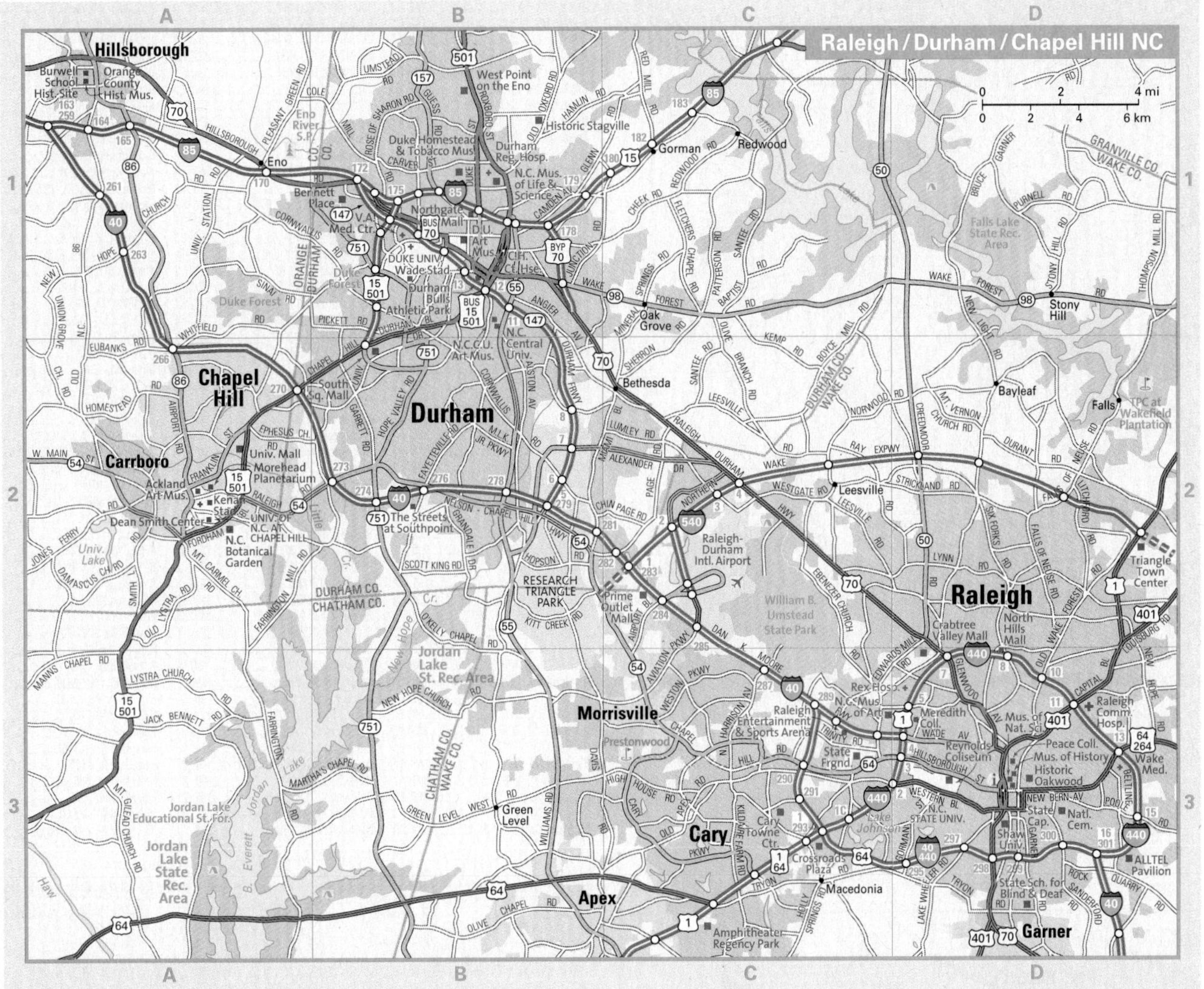

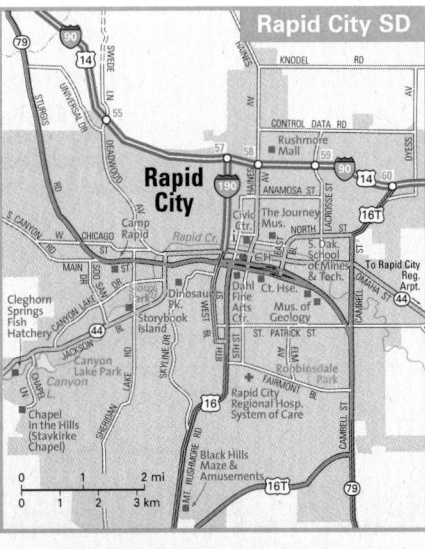

Raleigh / Durham / Chapel Hill NC

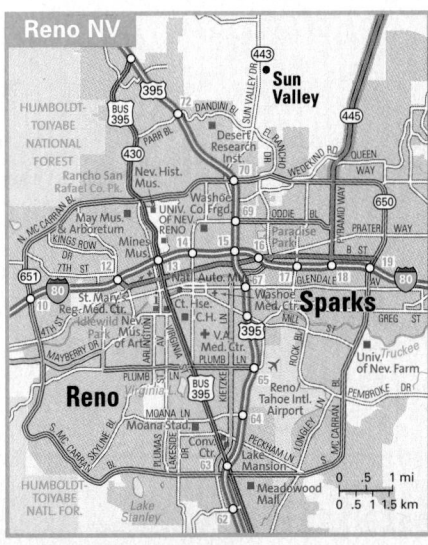

Rapid City SD

Reno NV

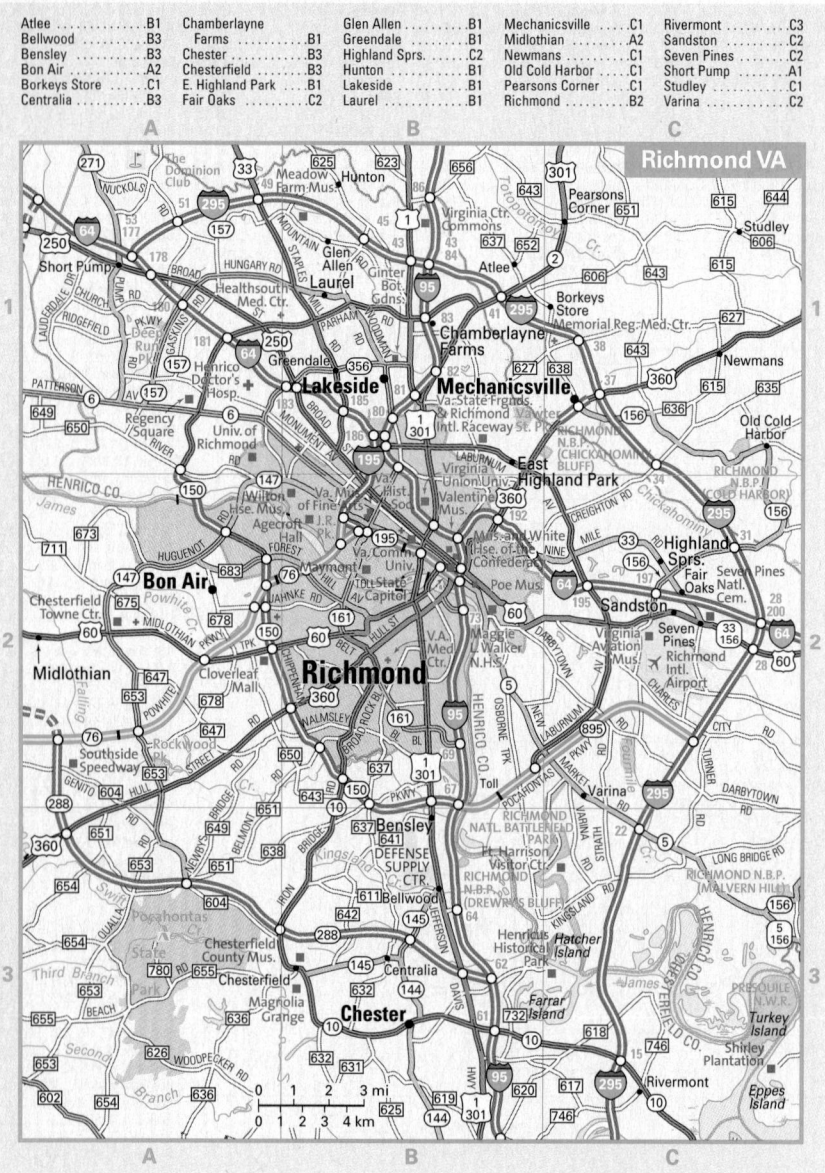

Richmond VA

Atlee	B1
Bellwood	B3
Bensley	B3
Bon Air	A2
Borkeys Store	C1
Centralia	C1

Chamberlayne Farms	B1
Chester	B3
Chesterfield	B3
E. Highland Park	B1
Fair Oaks	C2

Glen Allen	B1
Greendale	B1
Highland Sprs.	C2
Hunton	B1
Lakeside	B1
Laurel	B1

Mechanicsville	C1
Midlothian	A2
Newmans	C1
Old Cold Harbor	C1
Pearsons Corner	C1
Richmond	B2

Rivermont	C3
Sandston	C2
Seven Pines	C2
Short Pump	A1
Studley	C1
Varina	C2

Renovo PA, 1318	92	C2
Rensselaer IN, 5294	89	E3
Rensselaer NY, 7761	94	B1
Rensselaer Co. NY, 152538	94	B1
Renton WA, 50052	12	C3
Renville MN, 1323	66	B4
Renville Co. MN, 17154	66	B4
Renville Co. ND, 2610	18	B1
Republic MI, 614	65	F4
Republic MO, 8438	107	D2
Republic OH, 614	90	C3
Republic PA, 1396	102	B1
Republic WA, 954	13	F1
Republic Co. KS, 5835	43	E1
Resaca GA, 815	120	B2
Reserve LA, 9111	134	B3
Reserve NM, 387	55	F1
Reston VA, 56407	144	A3
Revere MA, 47283	151	D1
Rexburg ID, 17257	23	E4
Reyno AR, 484	108	A3
Reynolds GA, 1036	129	D2
Reynolds IN, 547	89	E3
Reynolds ND, 350	19	D2
Reynoldsburg OH, 32069	101	D1
Reynolds Co. MO, 6689	107	F1
Reynoldsville PA, 2710	92	B3
Rhea Co. TN, 28400	110	B4
Rhinebeck NY, 3077	94	B1
Rhinelander WI, 7735	68	B3
Rhome TX, 551	59	E2
Rialto CA, 91873	53	D2
Rib Lake WI, 878	68	A3
Rice MN, 711	66	C2
Rice TX, 798	59	F3
Ricebora GA, 736	130	B4
Rice City RI, 425	150	C3
Rice Co. KS, 10761	43	E3
Rice Co. MN, 56665	72	C1
Rice Lake WI, 8320	67	E3
Riceville IA, 840	73	D3
Riceville TN, 650	120	C1
Richardson TX, 91802	207	E1
Richardson Co. NE, 9531	86	A4
Richardton ND, 619	18	A4
Richboro PA, 6678	146	C2
Rich Co. UT, 1961	31	F3
Rich Creek VA, 665	112	A1
Richey MT, 189	17	E3
Richfield ID, 412	31	D1
Richfield MN, 34439	235	B3
Richfield NC, 515	122	B1
Richfield OH, 3286	91	E2
Richfield UT, 6847	39	E2
Richfield Sprs. NY, 1255	79	F3
Richford VT, 1400	81	E1
Richgrove CA, 2723	45	D4
Rich Hill MO, 1461	96	B4
Richland GA, 1794	128	C3
Richland IA, 587	87	E2
Richland MI, 593	75	F4
Richland MS, 6027	126	B3
Richland MO, 1805	97	E4
Richland NJ, 750	147	D4
Richland PA, 1508	146	A2
Richland WA, 38708	13	E4
Richland Ctr. WI, 5114	74	A3
Richland Co. IL, 16149	99	D3

Richland Co. MT, 9667	17	F2
Richland Co. ND, 17998	19	E4
Richland Co. OH, 128852	91	D3
Richland Co. SC, 320677	122	B3
Richland Co. WI, 17924	74	A2
Richland Hills TX, 8132	207	B2
Richland Par. LA, 20981	125	F3
Richlands NC, 928	115	D4
Richlands VA, 4144	111	F2
Richlandtown PA, 1283	146	C1
Richmond CA, 99216	36	B3
Richmond IL, 1091	74	C4
Richmond IN, 39124	100	B1
Richmond KS, 510	96	A3
Richmond KY, 27152	110	C1
Richmond LA, 499	126	A2
Richmond ME, 782	82	C3
Richmond MI, 4897	76	C4
Richmond MN, 1213	66	B3
Richmond MO, 6116	96	C2
Richmond TX, 11081	132	A3
Richmond UT, 2051	31	E1
Richmond VT, 950	81	D2
Richmond VA, 199770	113	E1
Richmond Co. GA, 199775	130	A1
Richmond Co. NY, 443728	147	E1
Richmond Co. NC, 46564	122	C2
Richmond Co. VA, 8809	103	E4
Richmond Hts. FL, 8479	143	E2
Richmond Hts. MO, 9602	256	B2
Richmond Hts. OH, 10944	204	G1
Richmond Hill GA, 6959	130	B3
Richmondville NY, 786	79	F4
Rich Square NC, 931	113	E3
Richton MS, 1038	127	D4
Richwood KY, 2115	125	E2
Richwood OH, 2156	90	C4
Richwood TX, 3012	132	A4
Richwood WV, 2477	102	A4
Riddle OR, 1014	28	B1
Ridge NY, 13380	149	D3
Ridgebury CT, 1200	148	C2
Ridgebury NY, 850	148	A2
Ridgecrest CA, 24927	45	E4
Ridgecrest LA, 801	125	F4
Ridge Farm IL, 912	99	D1
Ridgefield CT, 7212	148	C2
Ridgefield NJ, 10830	240	D2
Ridgefield WA, 3147	20	C1
Ridgefield Park NJ, 12873	240	D1
Ridgeland MS, 20173	126	B2
Ridgeland SC, 2518	130	C2
Ridgely MD, 1352	145	E3
Ridgely TN, 1667	108	B3
Ridge Manor FL, 4108	140	C1
Ridge Spr. SC, 823	121	F4
Ridgetop TN, 1083	109	F3
Ridgeville IN, 843	90	A4
Ridgeville SC, 1690	130	C1
Ridgeway MO, 530	86	C4
Ridgeway VA, 775	112	B3
Ridgeway WV, 790	103	D2
Ridgeway WI, 689	74	A3
Ridgewood NJ, 24936	148	B3
Ridgway CO, 713	40	B3
Ridgway IL, 928	109	D1
Ridgway PA, 4591	92	B2
Ridley Park PA, 7196	248	B4

Riegelsville PA, 863	146	C1
Riesel TX, 973	59	F4
Rifle CO, 6784	40	B2
Rigby ID, 2998	23	E4
Riggins ID, 410	22	B2
Riley KS, 886	43	F2
Riley Co. KS, 62843	43	F2
Rimersburg PA, 1051	92	A3
Rincon GA, 4376	130	B3
Rindge NH, 750	95	D1
Rineyville KY, 550	110	A1
Ringgold GA, 2422	120	B2
Ringgold LA, 1660	125	D2
Ringgold Co. IA, 5469	86	B3
Ringle WI, 1100	68	B3
Ringoes NJ, 1100	147	D1
Ringtown PA, 826	93	E3
Ringwood NJ, 12396	148	A2
Rio FL, 1028	141	E4
Rio WI, 938	74	B2
Rio Arriba Co. NM, 41190	48	C1
Rio Blanco Co. CO, 5986	40	B1
Rio Bravo TX, 5553	63	D2
Rio Dell CA, 3174	28	A4
Rio del Mar CA, 9198	236	D1
Rio Grande NJ, 2444	104	C4
Rio Grande OH, 915	101	E3
Rio Grande City TX, 11923	63	E4
Rio Grande Co. CO, 12413	41	D4
Rio Hondo TX, 1942	63	F4
Rio Linda CA, 10466	255	B1
Rio Rancho NM, 51765	48	C3
Rio Rico AZ, 3164	55	D4
Rio Verde AZ, 1419	54	C3
Rio Vista CA, 4571	36	B3
Rio Vista TX, 656	59	E3
Ripley CA, 650	53	F3
Ripley MS, 5478	118	C2
Ripley NY, 1030	78	A4
Ripley OH, 1745	100	C3
Ripley OK, 444	51	F2
Ripley TN, 7844	108	B4
Ripley WV, 3263	101	E3
Ripley Co. IN, 26523	100	A2
Ripley Co. MO, 13509	108	A3
Ripon CA, 10146	36	C3
Ripon WI, 6828	74	B2
Ririe ID, 545	23	E4
Rising Star TX, 835	59	D3
Rising Sun DE, 2458	145	E2
Rising Sun IN, 2470	100	B2
Rising Sun MD, 1702	146	A4
Risingsun OH, 620	90	C2
Rison AR, 1271	117	E4
Ritchie Co. WV, 10343	101	F3
Rittman OH, 6314	91	E3
Ritzville WA, 1736	13	F3
Riverbank CA, 15826	36	C4
River Bend NC, 2923	115	D3
River Bluff KY, 402	100	A4
Riverdale CA, 2416	44	C3
Riverdale GA, 12478	120	C4
Riverdale IL, 15055	203	E6
Riverdale LA, 656	208	B1
Riverdale ND, 273	18	B3
Riverdale UT, 7656	244	D1
Riverdale Park MD, 6690	270	E2

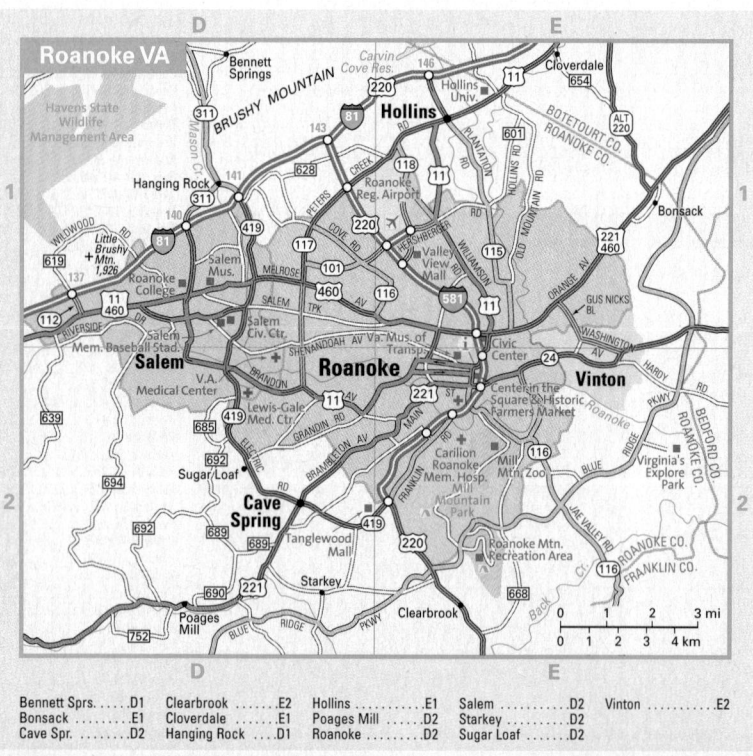

Roanoke VA

Bennett Sprs.	D1
Bonsack	E1
Cave Spr.	D2

Clearbrook	E2
Cloverdale	E1
Hanging Rock	D1

Hollins	E1
Poages Mill	D2
Roanoke	D2

Salem	D2
Starkey	D2
Sugar Loaf	D2

Vinton	E2

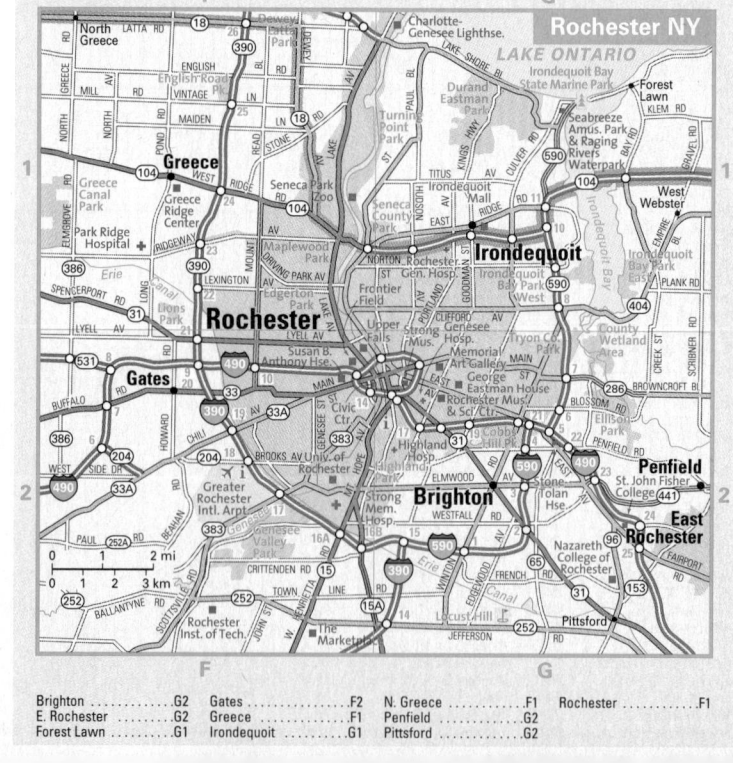

Rochester NY

Brighton	G2
E. Rochester	G2
Forest Lawn	G1

Gates	F2
Greece	F1
Irondequoit	G1

N. Greece	F1
Penfield	G2
Pittsford	G2

Rochester	F1

Entries in **bold** indicate counties or parishes. Entries in color indicate cities with detailed inset maps.

River Edge—Rusk 255

River Edge NJ, 10946 ...240 C1
River Falls AL, 616 ...128 A4
River Falls WI, 12560 ...67 D4
River Forest IL, 11635 ...203 D4
River Grove IL, 10668 ...203 D4
Riverhead NY, 10513 ...149 E3
River Hills WI, 1631 ...234 D1
River Oaks TX, 6985 ...207 A4
River Ridge LA, 14588 ...239 B1
River Rouge MI, 9917 ...210 C4
Riverside AL, 1564 ...120 A4
Riverside CA, 255166 ...53 D2
Riverside IL, 8895 ...203 D4
Riverside IL, 928 ...87 F2
Riverside MO, 2979 ...224 B2

Roby TX, 673 ...58 B2
Rochdale MA, 1400 ...150 B2
Rochelle GA, 1415 ...129 E3
Rochelle IL, 9424 ...88 B1
Rochelle Park NJ, 5528 ...240 C1
Rochester IL, 2893 ...98 B1
Rochester IN, 6414 ...89 F3
Rochester MN, 85806 ...73 D1
Rochester NH, 28461 ...81 F4
Rochester NY, 219773 ...78 C3
Rochester PA, 4014 ...91 F3
Rochester VT, 300 ...81 D3
Rochester WA, 1829 ...12 B4
Rochester WI, 1149 ...74 C4
Rochester Hills MI, 68825 ...76 C4

Rock River WY, 235 ...33 D2
Rocksprings TX, 1285 ...60 B2
Rock Sprs. WY, 18708 ...32 B3
Rockton IL, 5296 ...74 B4
Rockvale CO, 426 ...41 E3
Rock Valley IA, 2702 ...35 F1
Rockville CT, 7708 ...150 A3
Rockville IN, 2765 ...99 E1
Rockville MD, 47388 ...144 B2
Rockville MN, 749 ...66 C3
Rockville RI, 425 ...150 C4
Rockville UT, 231 ...39 E1
Rockwall Co. TX, 43080 ...59 F2
Rockwell AR, 3024 ...117 D3
Rockwell AL, 989 ...73 D3
Rockwell NC, 1971 ...122 B1

Rockwell City IA, 2264 ...72 B4
Rockwood MI, 3442 ...90 C1
Rockwood PA, 954 ...102 B1
Rockwood TN, 5774 ...110 B4
Rocky Ford CO, 4286 ...41 F3
Rocky Hill CT, 17966 ...149 E1
Rocky Hill NJ, 662 ...147 D1
Rocky Mount NC, 55893 ...113 E4
Rocky Mount VA, 4066 ...112 B2
Rocky Pt. NY, 10185 ...149 D3
Rocky Ridge UT, 403 ...39 E1
Rocky Ripple IN, 712 ...221 B2
Rocky River OH, 20735 ...204 E2
Rodarte NM, 350 ...49 D2
Rodeo CA, 8717 ...259 C4
Roebuck SC, 1725 ...121 F2
Roeland Park KS, 6817 ...224 B3
Roessleville NY, 10800 ...188 D2
Roff OK, 734 ...51 F4
Roger Mills Co. OK, 3436 ...50 C2
Rogers AR, 38829 ...106 C3
Rogers MN, 3588 ...66 C3
Rogers TX, 1117 ...61 E1
Rogers City MI, 3322 ...71 D3
Rogers Co. OK, 70641 ...106 A3
Rogersville AL, 1199 ...119 E2
Rogersville MO, 1508 ...107 D2
Rogersville TN, 4240 ...111 D3
Rogue River OR, 1847 ...28 B2
Rohnert Park CA, 42236 ...36 B3
Roland IA, 1324 ...86 C1
Roland OK, 2842 ...116 B1
Rolesville NC, 907 ...113 D4
Rolette ND, 538 ...18 C1
Rolette Co. ND, 13674 ...18 C1
Rolfe IA, 675 ...72 B3
Rolla KS, 482 ...50 B1
Rolla MO, 16367 ...97 F4
Rolla ND, 1417 ...18 C1
Rolling Fields KY, 648 ...230 E1
Rolling Fork MS, 2486 ...126 A1
Rolling Hills CA, 1871 ...228 C4
Rolling Hills KY, 907 ...230 F1
Rolling Hills WY, 449 ...33 D1
Rolling Hills Estates CA, 7676 ...228 C4
Rolling Meadows IL, 24604 ...203 B3
Rolling Prairie IN, 800 ...89 E2
Rollingstone MN, 697 ...73 E1
Rollinsford NH, 1500 ...82 A4
Roma TX, 9617 ...63 D4
Romancoke MD, 800 ...145 D3
Roman Forest TX, 1279 ...132 B2
Rome GA, 34980 ...120 B3
Rome IL, 1776 ...88 B3
Rome NY, 34950 ...79 D3
Rome City IN, 1615 ...90 A2

Romeo MI, 3721 ...76 C4
Romeoville IL, 21153 ...89 D2
Romney WV, 1940 ...102 C2
Romoland CA, 2764 ...229 K4
Romulus MI, 22979 ...90 C1
Ronan MT, 1812 ...15 D3
Ronceverte WV, 1557 ...112 A1
Ronkonkoma NY, 20029 ...149 D3
Ronan NC, 490 ...94 B3
Roodhouse IL, 2214 ...98 A2
Rooks Co. KS, 5685 ...43 D2
Roosevelt NJ, 933 ...147 E2
Roosevelt UT, 4299 ...32 A4
Roosevelt Co. MT, 10620 ...17 E2
Roosevelt Co. NM, 18018 ...49 F4
Roper NC, 613 ...113 F4
Ropesville TX, 517 ...58 A1
Rosalia WA, 648 ...14 A3
Rosamond CA, 14349 ...52 C1
Rosaryville MD, 12322 ...144 C4
Roscoe IL, 6244 ...74 B4
Roscoe NY, 597 ...94 A2
Roscoe SD, 324 ...27 D2
Roscoe TX, 1378 ...58 B3
Roscommon MI, 1133 ...76 A1
Roscommon Co. MI, 25469 ...76 A1
Roseau MN, 2756 ...19 F1
Roseau Co. MN, 16338 ...19 F1
Roseboro NC, 1267 ...123 D2
Rose Bud AR, 429 ...117 E1
Rosebud SD, 1557 ...34 C1
Rosebud TX, 1493 ...59 F4
Rosebud Co. MT, 9383 ...17 D4
Roseburg OR, 20017 ...28 B3
Rose City MI, 721 ...76 B1
Rose City TX, 519 ...132 C2
Rosedale IN, 750 ...99 E1
Rosedale LA, 753 ...133 F2
Rosedale MD, 19199 ...144 C2
Rosedale MS, 2414 ...118 A4
Rosedale Beach DE, 750 ...145 F4
Rose Haven MD, 1400 ...144 C4
Rose Hill KS, 3432 ...43 F4
Rose Hill NC, 1330 ...123 E2
Rose Hill VA, 714 ...111 D3
Rose Hill VA, 15058 ...270 C5
Roseland FL, 1775 ...141 E3
Roseland LA, 1162 ...134 B1
Roseland NJ, 5298 ...240 A2
Roselawn IN, 3933 ...89 D3
Roselle IL, 23115 ...203 B3
Roselle NJ, 21274 ...147 E1
Roselle Park NJ, 13281 ...147 E1
Rose Lodge OR, 1708 ...20 B2
Rosemead CA, 53505 ...228 E2
Rosemont CA, 22904 ...255 C3
Rosemont IL, 4224 ...203 C3

Rosemount MN, 14619 ...235 D4
Rosemount OH, 2043 ...101 D3
Rosenberg TX, 24043 ...132 A3
Rosenhayn NJ, 1099 ...145 F1
Rosepine LA, 1390 ...133 D1
Roseto PA, 1653 ...93 F3
Rose Valley PA, 944 ...248 A4
Roseville CA, 79921 ...36 C2
Roseville IL, 1083 ...88 A3
Roseville MI, 48129 ...210 D2
Roseville MN, 33690 ...235 C2
Roseville OH, 1336 ...101 E1
Roseville Park DE, 6200 ...146 B4
Rosholt SD, 419 ...27 F1
Rosiclare IL, 1213 ...109 D1
Roslyn NY, 16900 ...248 C1
Roslyn SD, 225 ...27 E2
Roslyn WA, 1017 ...13 D3
Roslyn Estates NY, 1210 ...241 G2
Rosman NC, 490 ...121 E1
Ross CA, 2329 ...259 A4
Ross OH, 1971 ...100 B2
Ross Co. OH, 73345 ...101 D2
Rossford OH, 6406 ...267 B2
Rossiter PA, 799 ...92 B3
Rossmoor CA, 10298 ...228 E4
Rossmoor NJ, 3129 ...147 E2
Rossville GA, 3511 ...120 B2
Rossville IN, 1217 ...89 E4
Rossville KS, 1014 ...43 F2
Rossville MD, 11515 ...193 E2
Rossville TN, 380 ...118 C2
Roswell GA, 79334 ...120 C3
Roswell NM, 45293 ...57 E1
Rotan TX, 1611 ...58 B2
Rothsay MN, 497 ...19 F4
Rothschild WI, 4970 ...68 B4
Rothsville PA, 3017 ...146 A2
Rotonda FL, 6574 ...140 C4
Rotterdam NY, 20536 ...94 B1
Rotterdam Jct. NY, 918 ...94 B1
Rougemont NC, 600 ...112 C4
Rough Rock AZ, 469 ...47 F1
Round Hill VA, 500 ...103 D2
Round Lake NY, 604 ...94 B1
Round Mtn. NV, 550 ...37 F2
Round Pond ME, 325 ...82 C3
Round Rock AZ, 601 ...47 F1
Round Rock TX, 61136 ...61 E1
Roundup MT, 1931 ...16 C4
Rouses Pt. NY, 2277 ...81 D1
Routt Co. CO, 19690 ...32 C4
Rouzerville PA, 862 ...103 D1
Rowan Co. KY, 22094 ...100 C4

Rowan Co. NC, 130340 ...112 A4
Rowland NC, 1146 ...122 C3
Rowland Hts. CA, 48553 ...229 F3
Rowlesburg WV, 613 ...102 B2
Rowlett TX, 44503 ...207 E4
Roxana DE, 375 ...145 F4
Roxboro NC, 8696 ...112 C4
Roxie MS, 569 ...126 A4
Roxton TX, 694 ...116 A4
Royal Ctr. IN, 832 ...89 E3
Royal City WA, 1823 ...13 E4
Royal Oak MD, 750 ...145 D4
Royal Oak MI, 60062 ...76 C4
Royal Palm Beach FL, 21523 ...143 F2
Royal Pines NC, 5334 ...121 E1
Royalton IL, 1130 ...98 C4
Royalton MN, 816 ...66 C2
Royersford PA, 4246 ...146 B2
Royse City TX, 2957 ...59 F2
Royston GA, 2493 ...121 E3
Rubidoux CA, 29180 ...229 H3
Rubonia FL, 1700 ...266 B4
Ruch OR, 700 ...28 B3
Rudyard MT, 275 ...15 F2
Rugby ND, 2939 ...18 C2
Ruidoso NM, 7698 ...57 D2
Ruidoso Downs NM, 1824 ...57 D2
Rule TX, 698 ...58 C2
Ruleville MS, 3234 ...118 B4
Rumford ME, 4795 ...82 B2
Rumson NJ, 7137 ...147 F2
Runaway Bay TX, 1104 ...59 E2
Runge TX, 1080 ...61 E3
Runnels Co. TX, 11495 ...58 C1
Runnemede NJ, 8533 ...146 C3
Running Sprs. CA, 5125 ...229 K1
Rupert ID, 5645 ...31 D1
Rupert WV, 940 ...102 A4
Rural Hall NC, 2464 ...112 B3
Rural Retreat VA, 1350 ...111 F2
Rural Valley PA, 922 ...92 B3
Rush City MN, 2102 ...67 D2
Rush Co. IN, 18261 ...100 A1
Rush Co. KS, 3551 ...43 D3
Rushford MN, 1730 ...73 E2
Rushford Vil. MN, 714 ...73 E2
Rushmere VA, 1083 ...113 F2
Rush Sprs. OK, 1231 ...59 E1
Rush Valley UT, 453 ...31 E4
Rushville IL, 3212 ...88 A4
Rushville IN, 5995 ...100 A1
Rushville NE, 999 ...34 A1
Rushville NY, 621 ...78 C4
Rusk TX, 5085 ...124 D1

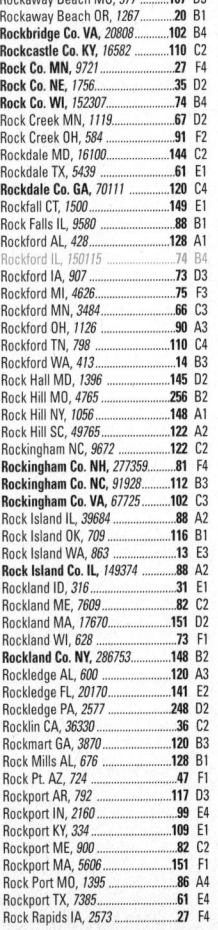

Rockford IL

Riverside NJ, 8000 ...147 D3
Riverside NY, 2875 ...149 E3
Riverside OH, 23545 ...100 C1
Riverside PA, 1861 ...93 E3
Riverside Co. CA, 1545387 ...53 E3
Riverton IL, 3048 ...98 B1
Riverton KS, 850 ...106 B2
Riverton NJ, 2759 ...146 C3
Riverton UT, 25011 ...31 E4
Riverton WY, 9310 ...32 B1
Riverview FL, 12035 ...140 C2
Riverview MO, 3146 ...256 C1
Riverwood KY, 469 ...230 E1
Riverwoods IL, 3843 ...203 C2
Rives Jct. MI, 650 ...76 A4
Rivesville WV, 913 ...102 A1
Riviera Beach FL, 29884 ...141 F4
Riviera Beach MD, 12695 ...144 C3
Roachdale IN, 975 ...99 E1
Roaming Shores OH, 1239 ...91 F2
Roane Co. TN, 51910 ...110 B4
Roane Co. WV, 15446 ...101 F3
Roan Mtn. TN, 1160 ...111 E3
Roanoke AL, 6563 ...128 B1
Roanoke IL, 1994 ...88 B3
Roanoke IN, 1495 ...90 A3
Roanoke TX, 2810 ...207 B1
Roanoke VA, 94911 ...112 B2
Roanoke Co. VA, 85778 ...112 B1
Roanoke Rapids NC, 16957 ...113 E3
Roaring Spr. PA, 2418 ...92 C4
Robards KY, 564 ...109 E1
Robbins IL, 6635 ...203 D6
Robbins NC, 1195 ...122 C1
Robbinsdale MN, 14123 ...235 B2
Robbinsville NJ, 1900 ...147 D2
Robbinsville NC, 747 ...121 D1
Robersonville NC, 1731 ...113 E4
Roberta GA, 808 ...129 D2
Robert Lee TX, 1171 ...58 B3
Roberts ID, 647 ...23 E4
Roberts WI, 969 ...67 E4
Roberts Co. SD, 10016 ...27 F1
Roberts Co. TX, 887 ...50 B2
Robertsdale AL, 3782 ...135 E2
Robertson Co. KY, 2266 ...100 C3
Robertson Co. TN, 54433 ...109 F3
Robertson Co. TX, 16000 ...61 F1
Robertsville NJ, 9800 ...147 E2
Robeson Co. NC, 123339 ...123 D2
Robesonia PA, 2036 ...146 A2
Robins IA, 1806 ...87 E1
Robinson IL, 6822 ...99 D2
Robinson TX, 7845 ...59 E4
Robstown TX, 12727 ...63 E4

Rockaway NJ, 6473 ...148 A3
Rockaway Beach MO, 577 ...107 D3
Rockaway Beach OR, 1267 ...20 B1
Rockbridge Co. VA, 20808 ...102 B4
Rockcastle Co. KY, 16582 ...110 C2
Rock Co. MN, 9721 ...27 F4
Rock Co. NE, 1756 ...35 D3
Rock Co. WI, 152307 ...74 B4
Rock Creek MN, 1119 ...67 D2
Rock Creek OH, 584 ...91 F2
Rockdale MD, 16100 ...144 C2
Rockdale TX, 5439 ...61 E1
Rockdale Co. GA, 70111 ...120 C4
Rockfall CT, 150 ...149 E1
Rock Falls IL, 9580 ...88 B1
Rockford AL, 428 ...128 A1
Rockford IL, 150115 ...74 B4
Rockford IA, 907 ...73 D3
Rockford MI, 4626 ...75 F3
Rockford MN, 3484 ...66 C3
Rockford OH, 1126 ...90 A3
Rockford WA, 413 ...14 B3
Rock Hall MD, 1396 ...145 D2
Rock Hill MO, 4765 ...256 B2
Rock Hill NY, 1056 ...148 A1
Rock Hill SC, 49765 ...122 A2
Rockingham NC, 9672 ...122 C2
Rockingham Co. NH, 277359 ...81 F4
Rockingham Co. NC, 91928 ...112 B3
Rockingham Co. VA, 67725 ...102 C3
Rock Island IL, 39684 ...88 A2
Rock Island OK, 709 ...116 B1
Rock Island WA, 863 ...13 E3
Rock Island Co. IL, 149374 ...88 A2
Rockland ID, 316 ...31 E1
Rockland ME, 7609 ...82 C3
Rockland MA, 17670 ...151 D2
Rockland WI, 628 ...73 F1
Rockledge FL, 20170 ...141 E2
Rockledge AL, 600 ...120 A3
Rockledge PA, 2577 ...248 D2
Rocklin CA, 36330 ...36 C2
Rockmark GA, 3870 ...120 B3
Rock Mills AL, 676 ...128 B1
Rock Pt. AZ, 724 ...47 F1
Rockport IN, 2160 ...99 E4
Rockport KY, 334 ...109 E1
Rockport ME, 900 ...82 C2
Rockport MA, 5606 ...151 E1
Rock Port MO, 1395 ...86 A4
Rock Rapids IA, 2573 ...27 F4

Sacramento CA

St Louis MO

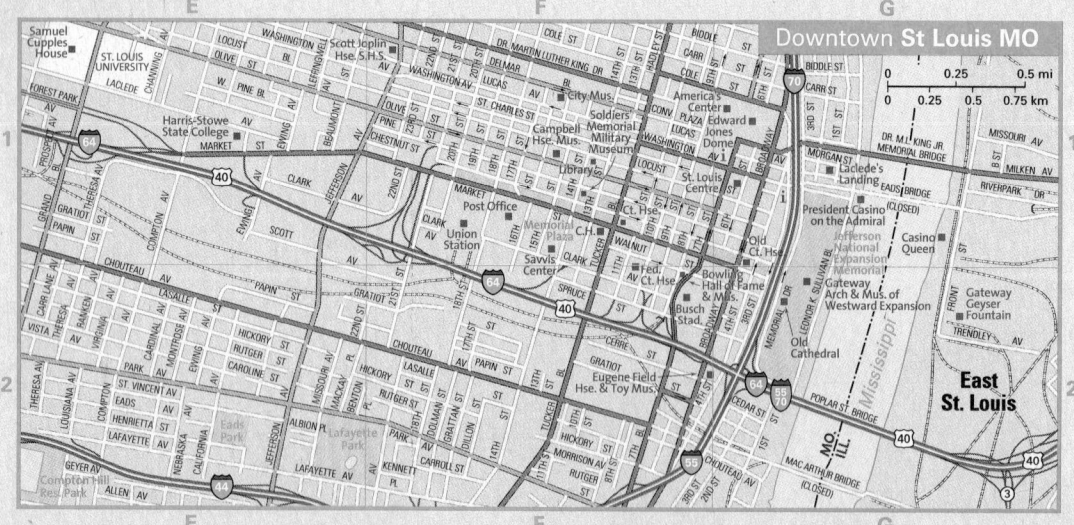

Downtown St Louis MO

Entries in **bold** indicate counties or parishes. Entries in color indicate cities with detailed inset maps.

Salem OR

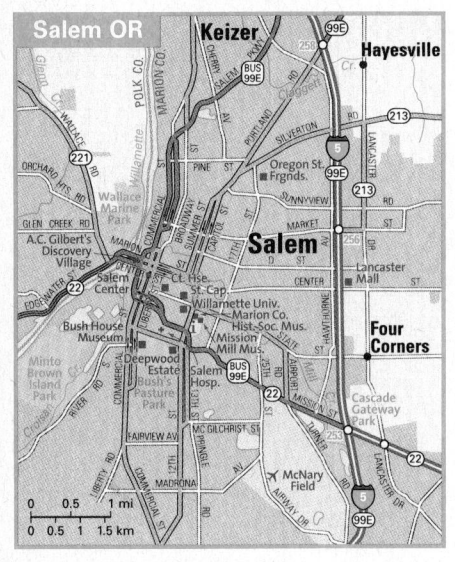

San Antonio TX

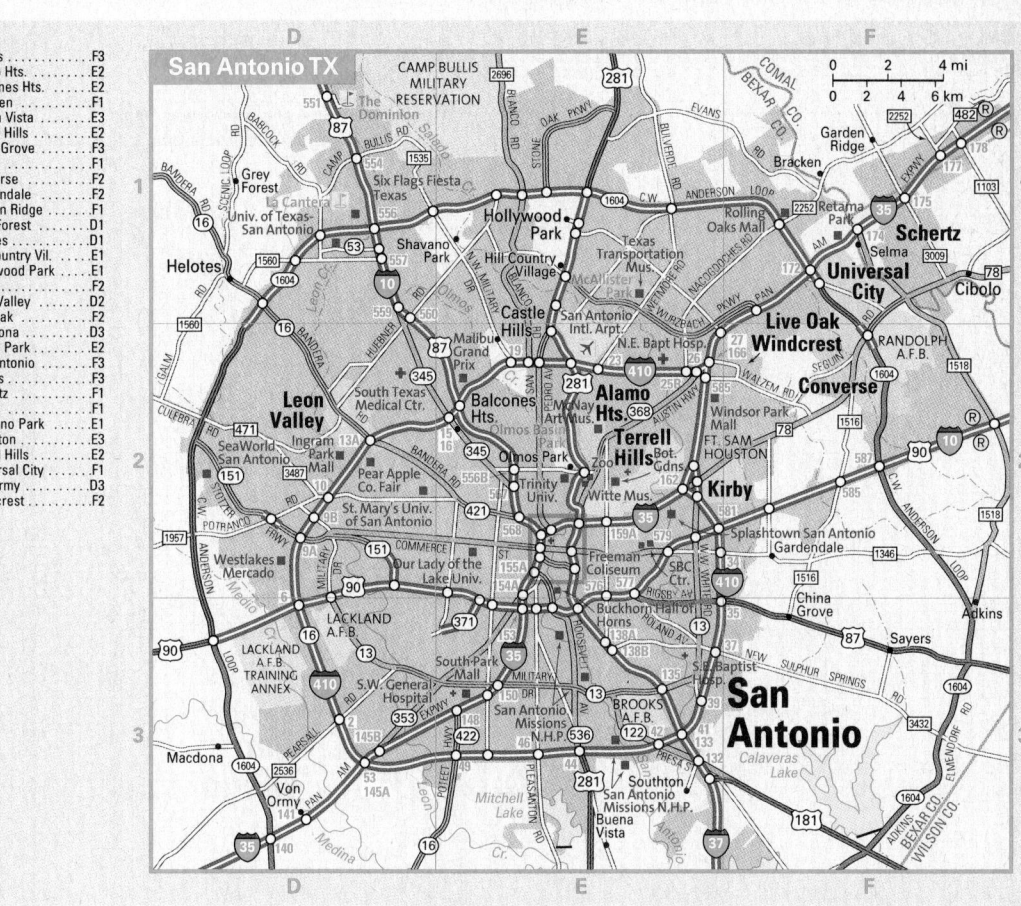

Salt Lake City UT

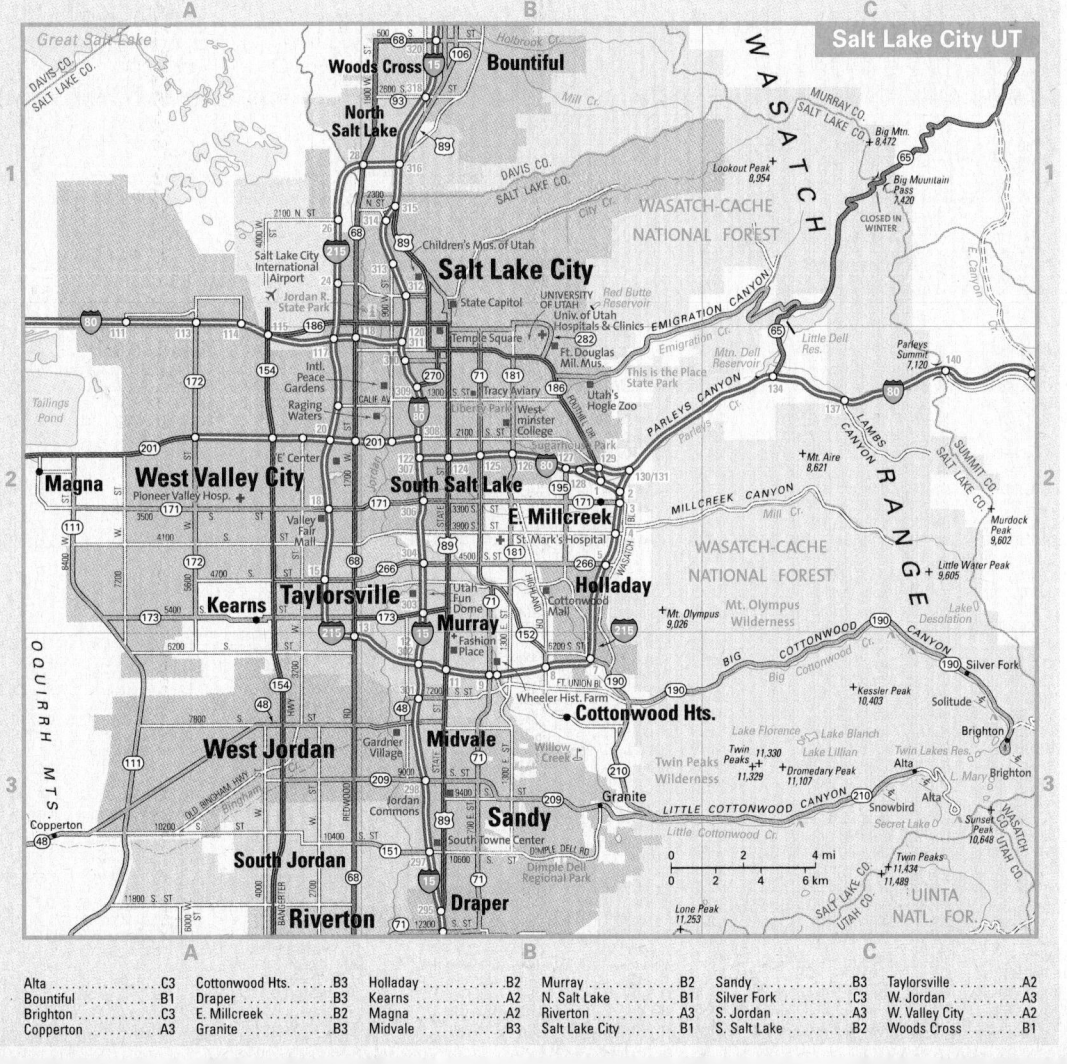

Downtown San Antonio TX

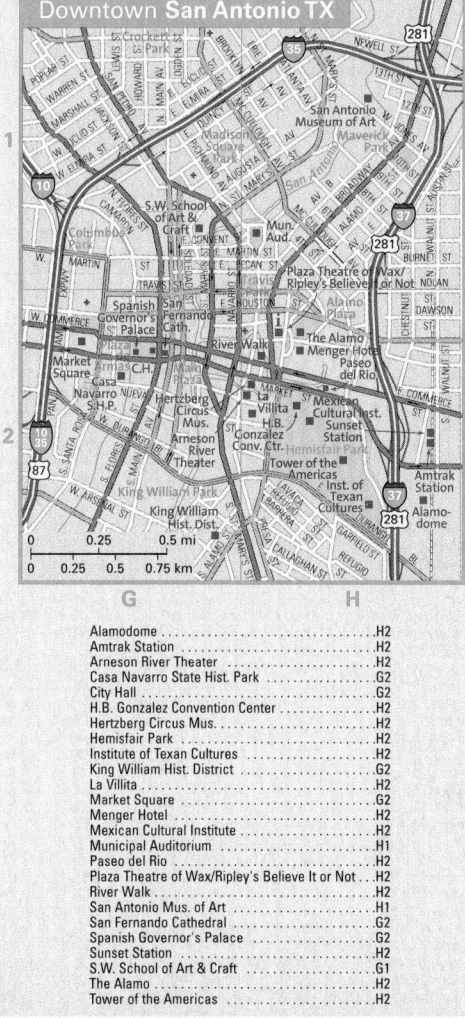

258 St Clair—Salyersville

Figures after entries indicate population, page number, and grid reference.

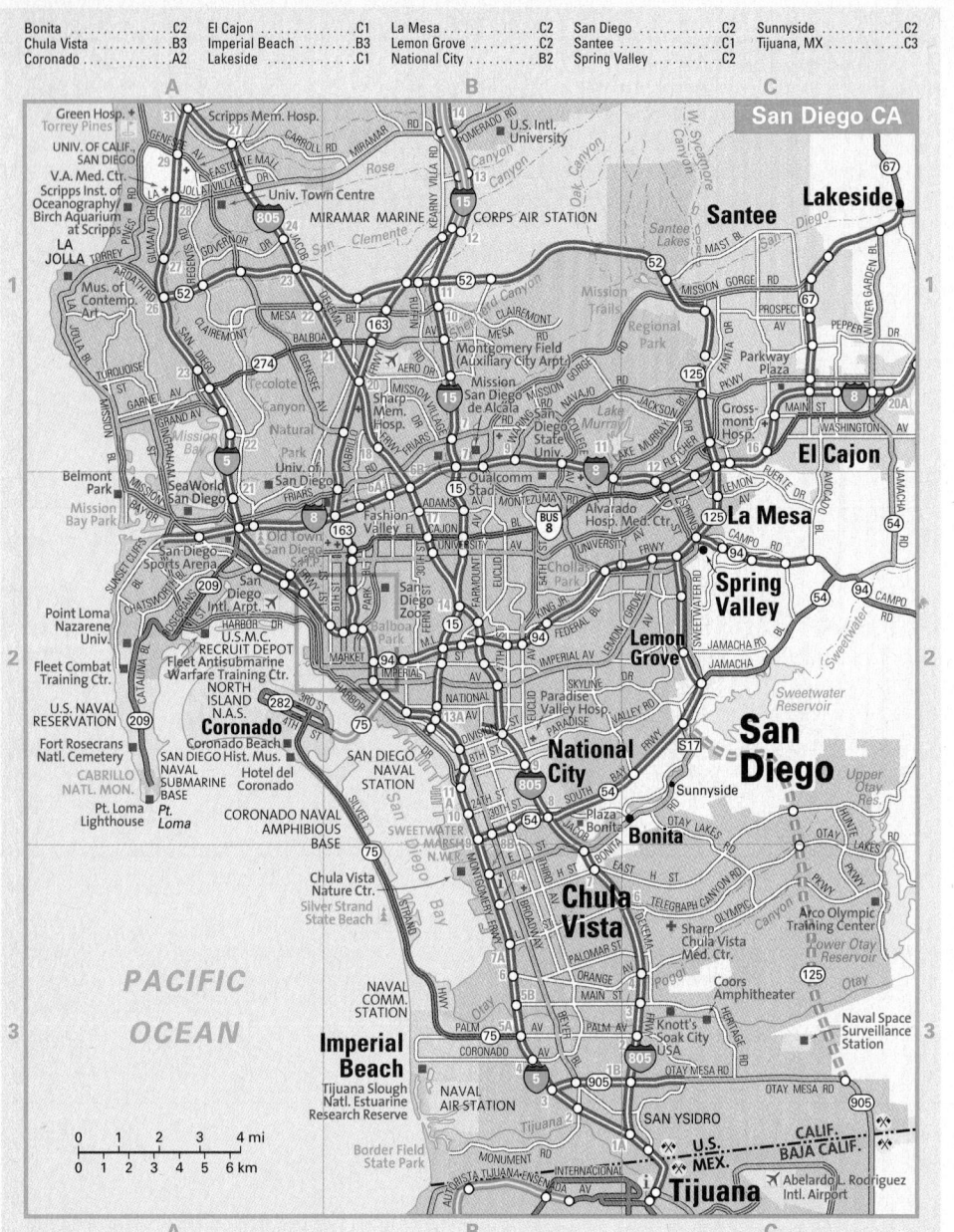

San Diego CA

Downtown San Diego CA

Bonita C2
Chula Vista B3
Coronado A2
El Cajon C1
Imperial Beach B3
Lakeside C1
La Mesa C2
Lemon Grove C2
National City B2
San Diego C2
Santee C1
Spring Valley C2
Sunnyside C2
Tijuana, MX C3

Automotive Mus. E1
Balboa Park E1
Balboa Stadium E2
Ballpark (u.c.) E2
Casa del Prado E1
Children's Mus. D2
City Hall D2
Civic Center D2
Copley Symphony Hall E2
County Court House D2
Cruise Ship Terminal D2
Edison Centre for the Performing Arts E1
Firehouse Mus. D2
Fleet & Industrial Supply Center D2
Gaslamp Quarter & W. H. Davis House ...E2
Horton Plaza D2
House of Hospitality E1
Maritime Mus. D2
Mus. of Contemporary Art, Downtown D2
Reuben H. Fleet Space Theater & Science Center E1
San Diego Aerospace Mus. E1
San Diego Convention Center D2
San Diego Intl. Arpt. (Lindbergh Field) ...D1
San Diego Museum of Art E1
San Diego Museum of Man E1
San Diego National Hist. Mus. E1
San Diego Zoo E1
Santa Fe Station D2
Seaport Village D2
Spanish Village Art Center E1
Sports Mus. E1
Spreckels Organ Pavilion E1
Starlight Bowl E1
Timken Mus. of Art E1
U.S. Court House D2

Entries in **bold** indicate counties or parishes. Entries in color indicate cities with detailed inset maps.

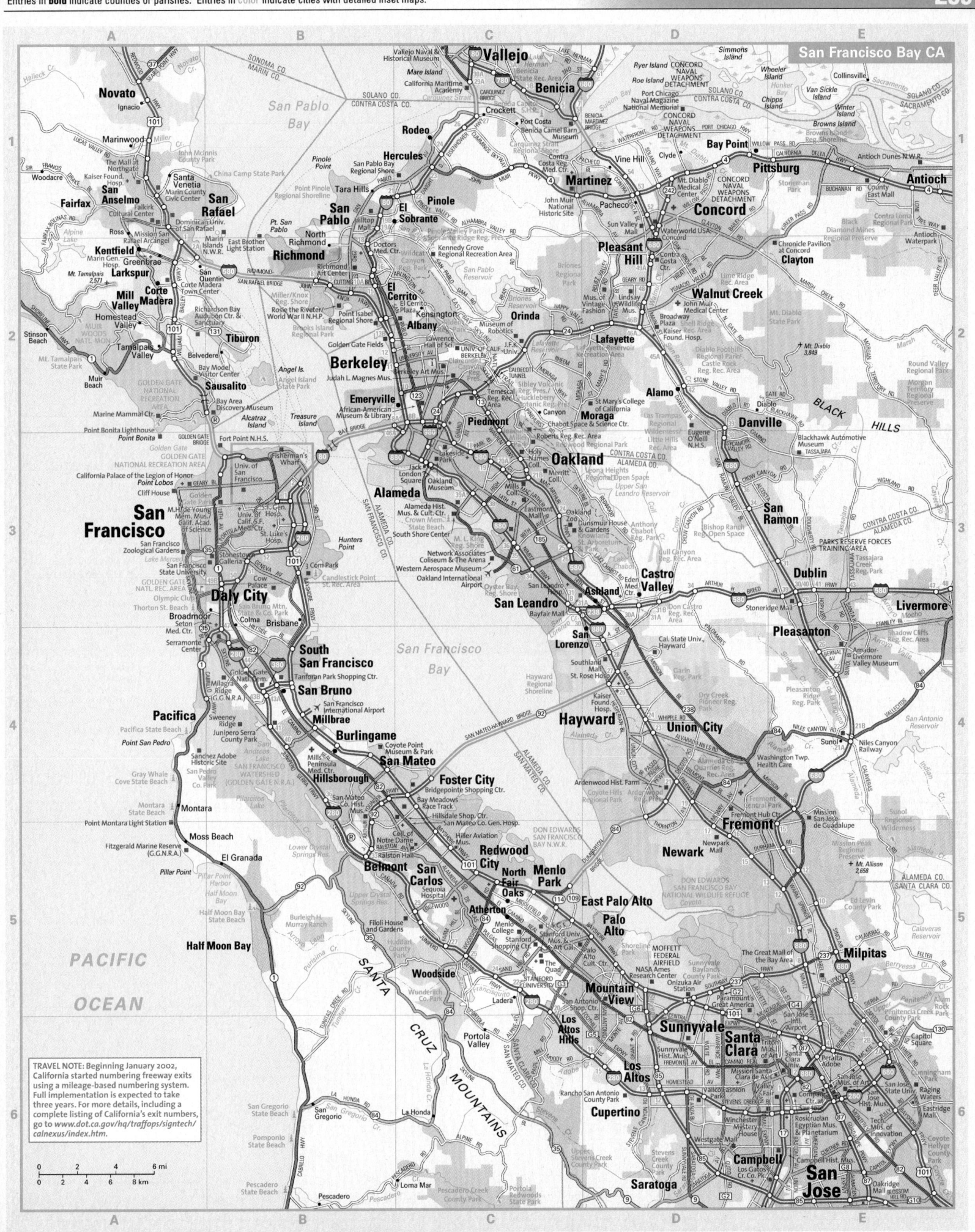

San Francisco Bay CA

TRAVEL NOTE: Beginning January 2002, California started numbering freeway exits using a mileage-based numbering system. Full implementation is expected to take three years. For more details, including a complete listing of California's exit numbers, go to www.dot.ca.gov/hq/traffops/signtech/calnexus/index.htm.

0   2   4   6 mi
0   2   4   6   8 km

Downtown San Francisco CA

Downtown San Francisco CA map index

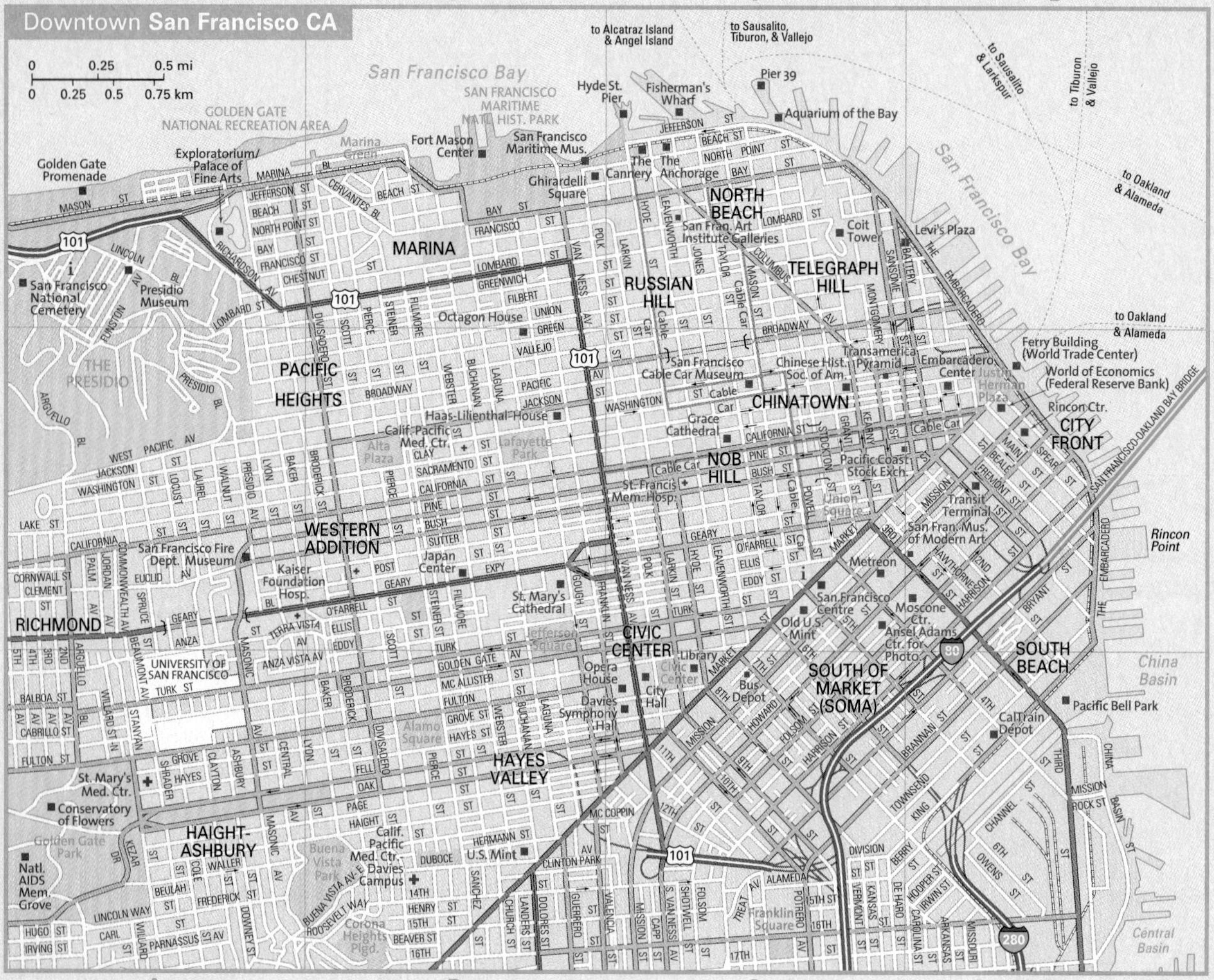

Ansel Adams Center for Photography	C2
Aquarium of the Bay	C1
Bus Depot	C3
CalTrain Depot	D3
Chinese Hist. Society of America	C2
City Hall	C3
Coit Tower	C1
Conservatory of Flowers	A3
Davies Symphony Hall	C3
Embarcadero Center	D2
Exploratorium/Palace of Fine Arts	A1
Ferry Building (World Trade Center)	D2
Fisherman's Wharf	C1
Fort Mason Center	B1
Ghirardelli Square	B1
Golden Gate Natl. Rec. Area	A1
Golden Gate Park	A3
Golden Gate Promenade	A1
Grace Cathedral	C2
Haas-Lilienthal House	B2
Hyde Street Pier	C1
Japan Center	B2
Levi's Plaza	D1
Library	C3
Metreon	C2
Moscone Center	D2
National AIDS Memorial Grove	A3
Octagon House	B2
Old U.S. Mint	C2
Opera House	C3
Pacific Bell Park	D3
Pacific Coast Stock Exchange	C2
Pier 39	C1
Presidio Mus.	A1
Rincon Center	D2
St. Mary's Cathedral	B2
San Francisco Art Institute Galleries	C1
San Francisco Cable Car Mus.	C2
San Francisco Centre	C2
San Francisco Fire Dept. Mus.	A2
San Francisco Maritime Mus.	B1
San Francisco Maritime Natl. Hist. Park	B1
San Francisco Mus. of Modern Art	D2
San Francisco Natl. Cemetery	A1
The Anchorage	C1
The Cannery	C1
The Presidio	A2
Transamerica Pyramid	C2
Transit Terminal	D2
U.S. Mint	B3
Univ. of San Francisco	A3
World of Economics (Federal Reserve Bank)	D2

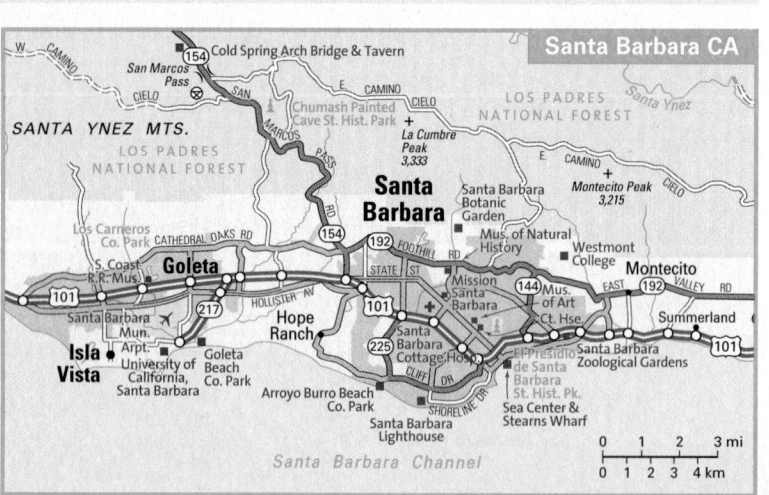

Santa Barbara CA

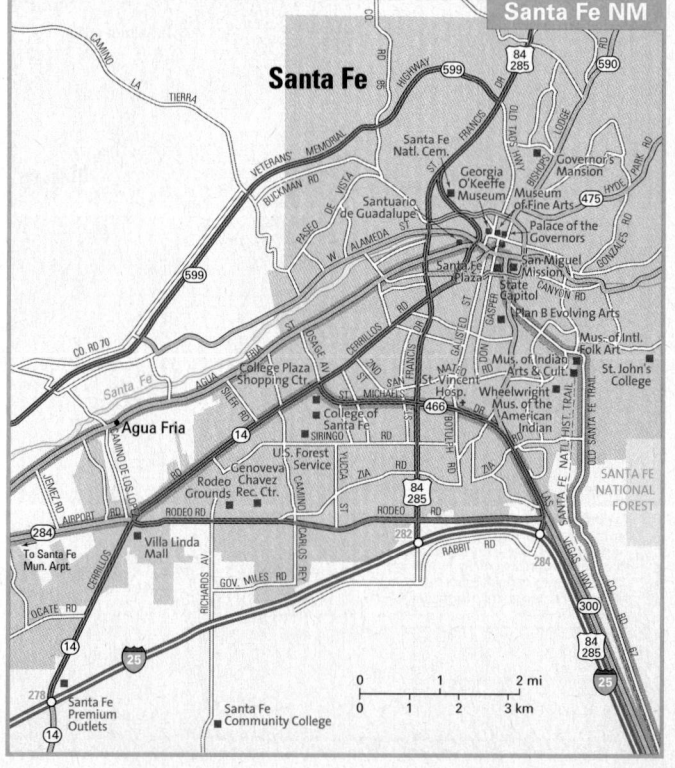

Santa Fe NM

Entries in **bold** indicate counties or parishes. Entries in color indicate cities with detailed inset maps.

Savannah GA

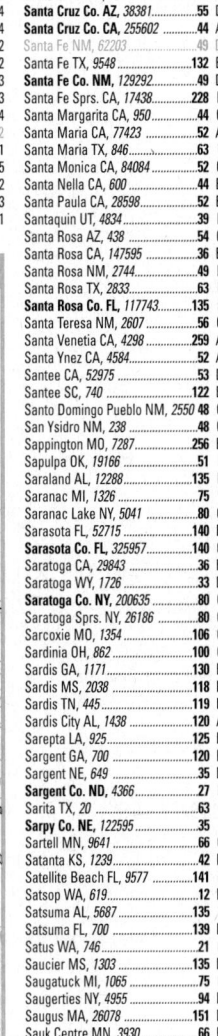
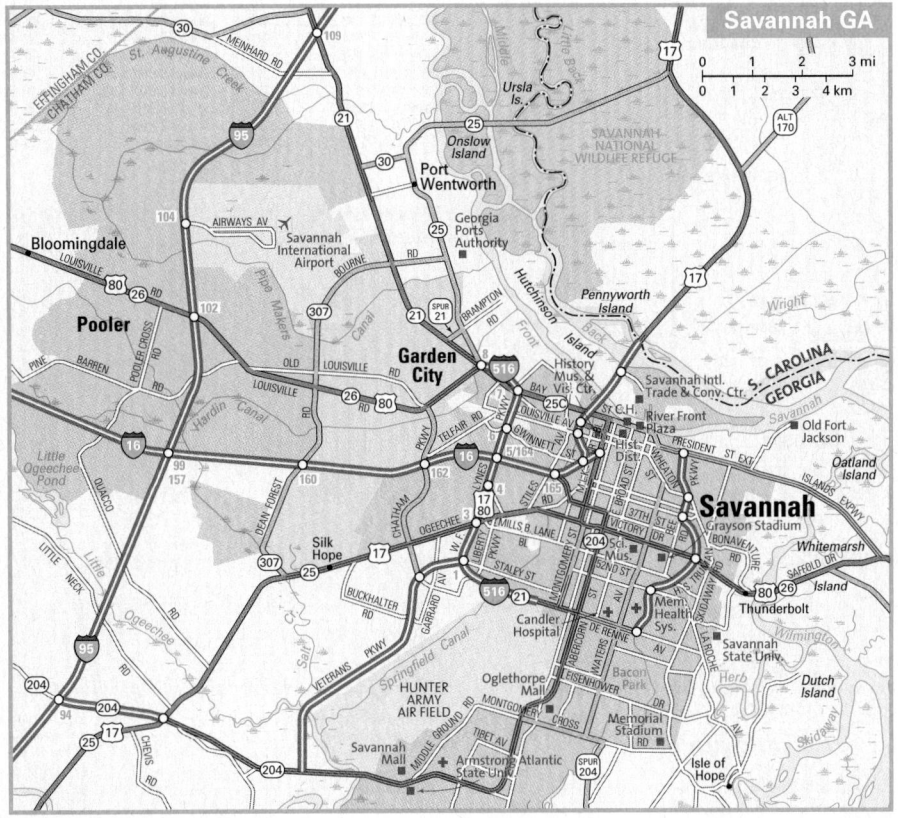

Scranton / Wilkes-Barre PA

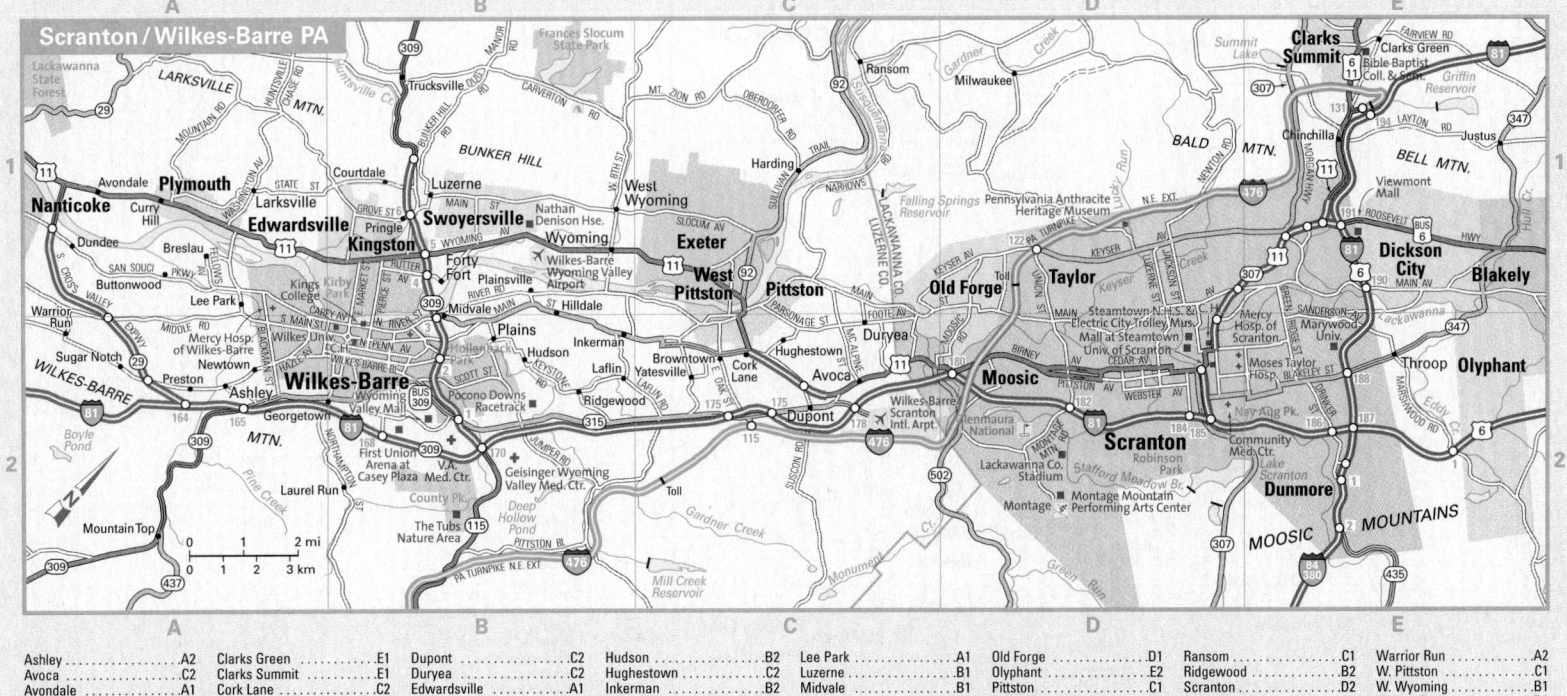

Figures after entries indicate population, page number, and grid reference.

Seattle / Tacoma WA

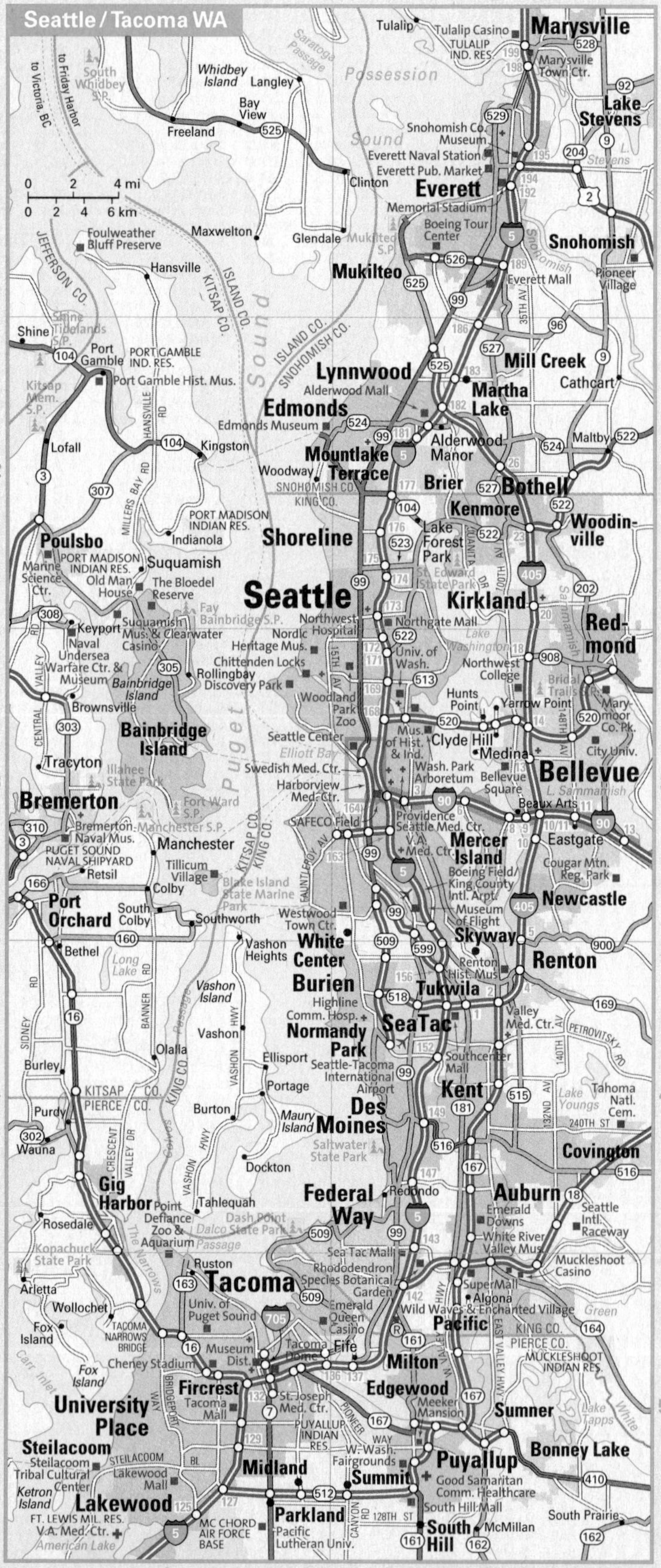

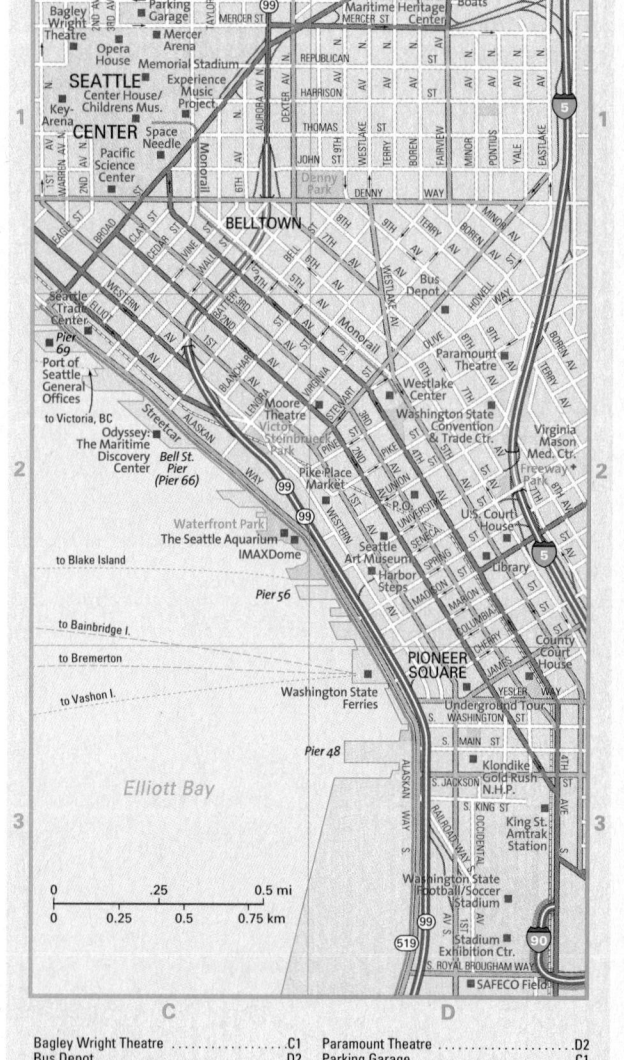

Downtown Seattle WA

Entries in **bold** indicate counties or parishes. Entries in color indicate cities with detailed inset maps.

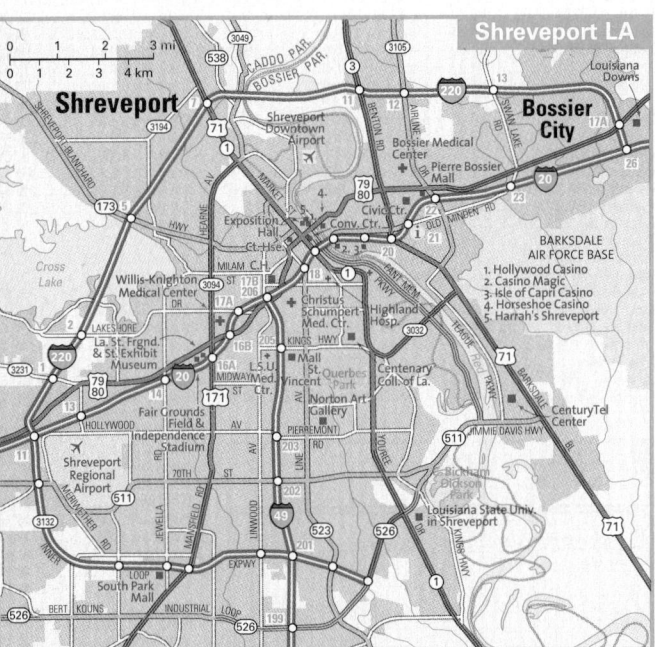

Shreveport LA

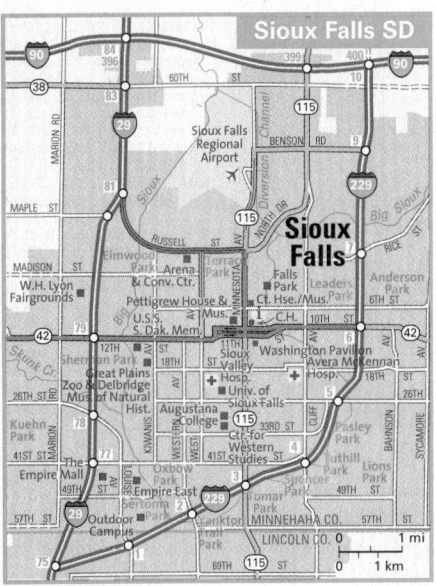

Sioux Falls SD

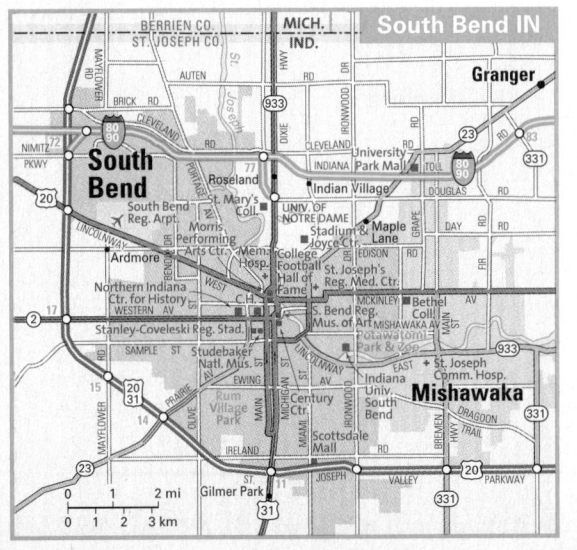

South Bend IN

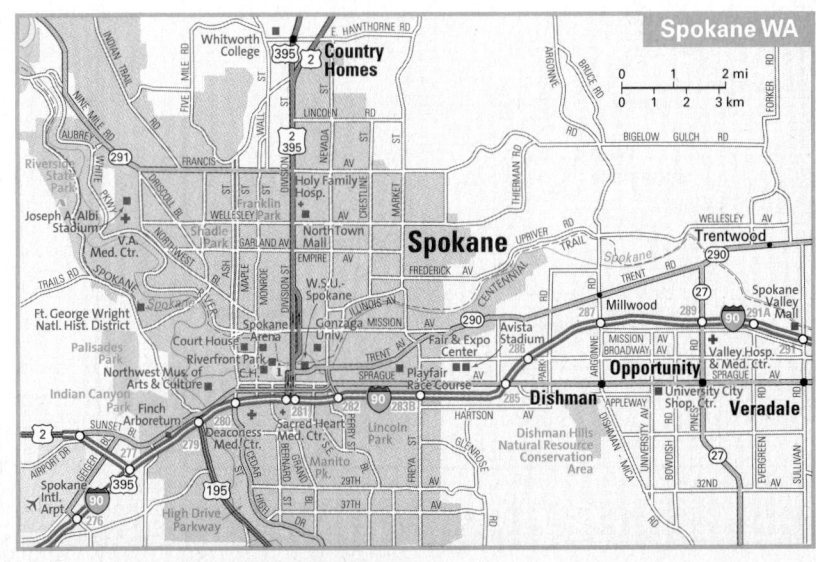

Spokane WA

Springfield IL

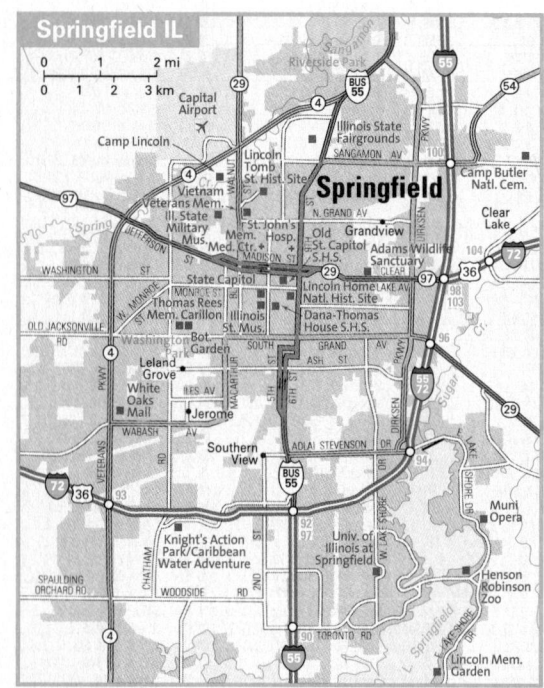

Springfield MO

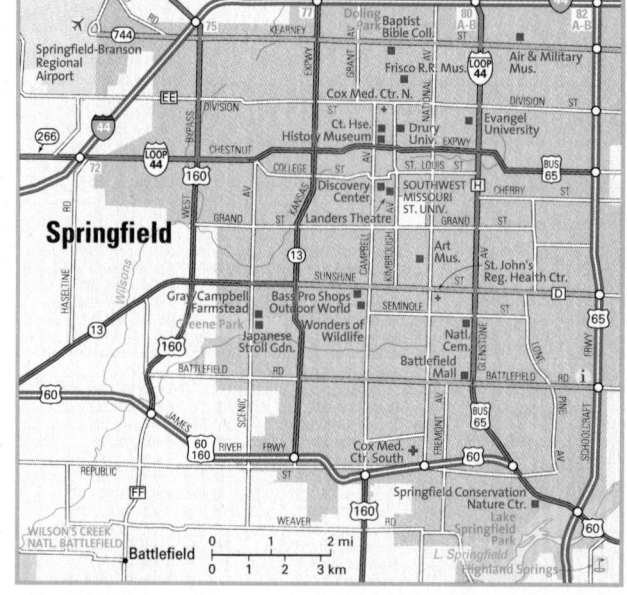

Springfield MA

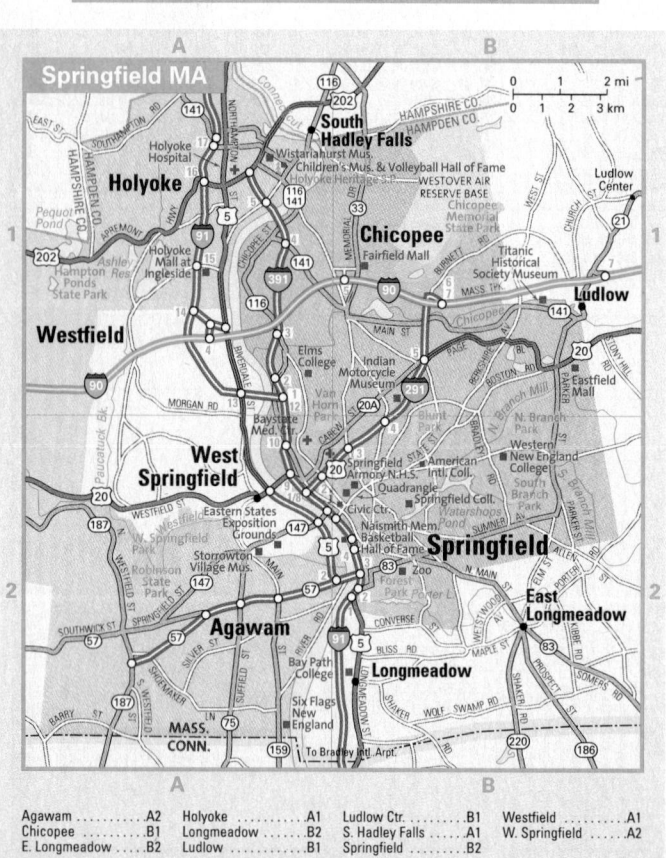

Stamford CT

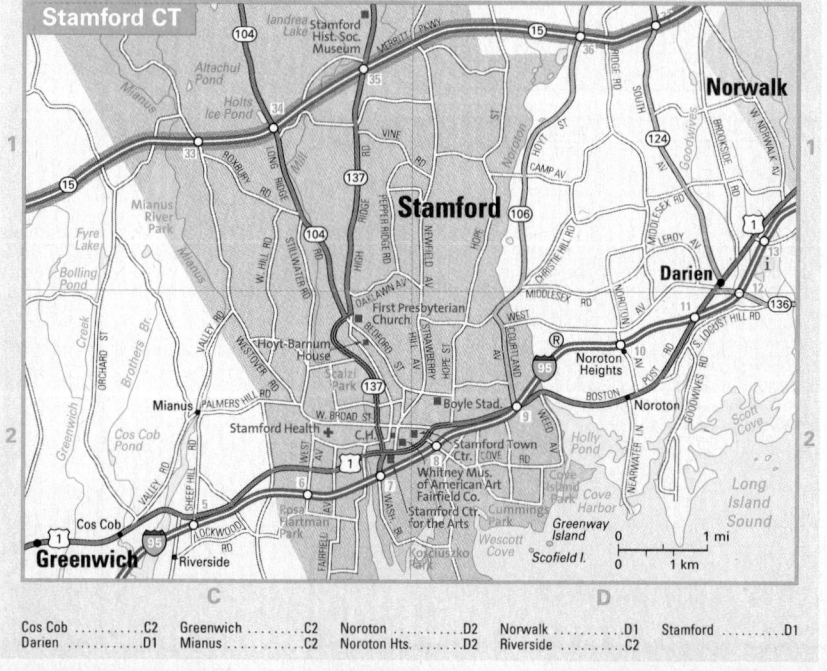

South Lebanon—Stillmore 265

Entries in **bold** indicate counties or parishes. Entries in color indicate cities with detailed inset maps.

S. Lebanon OH, 2538 100 B2
S. Lockport NY, 8552 78 B3
S. Lyon MI, 10036 76 B4
Southmayd TX, 992 59 F1
S. Miami FL, 10741 143 E2
S. Miami Hts. FL, 33522 233 A5
S. Middleboro MA, 750 151 E3
S. Mills NC, 700 113 F3
S. Milwaukee WI, 21256 75 D3
S. Monroe MI, 6370 90 C1
Southmont NC, 850 112 B4
S. Naknek AK, 137 154 B3
S. Ogden UT, 14377 244 A2
Southold NY, 5465 149 E3
S. Orange NJ, 16964 240 A3
S. Orleans MA, 1100 151 F3
S. Padre Island TX, 2422 63 F4
S. Palm Beach FL, 699 143 F1
S. Paris ME, 2237 82 B2
S. Pasadena CA, 24292 228 D2
S. Pasadena FL, 5778 140 B3
S. Patrick Shores FL, 8913 141 E2
S. Pekin IL, 1162 88 B4
S. Pittsburg TN, 3295 120 A2
S. Plainfield NJ, 21810 147 E1
S. Point OH, 3742 101 D3
Southport FL, 1500 136 C2
Southport IN, 1852 99 F1
Southport NY, 7396 93 D1
Southport NC, 2351 123 E4
S. Portland ME, 23324 82 B3
S. Pottstown PA, 2135 146 B2
S. Range MI, 727 65 F3
S. River NJ, 15322 147 E1
S. Rockwood MI, 1284 90 C1
S. Roxana IL, 1888 256 D1
S. Royalton VT, 800 81 E3
S. Russell OH, 4022 91 E2
S. St. Paul MN, 20167 235 D3
S. Salt Lake UT, 22038 257 B2
S. Sanford ME, 4173 82 B2
S. San Francisco CA, 60552 259 B3
S. San Gabriel CA, 7595 228 E2
S. Shaftsbury VT, 772 94 C1
S. Shore KY, 1226 101 D3
S. Shore SD, 270 27 F2
Southside AL, 7036 120 A4
Southside Place TX, 1546 220 B3
S. Sioux City NE, 11925 35 F2
S. Thomaston ME, 350 82 C3
S. Toms River NJ, 3634 147 E3
S. Torrington WY, 550 33 F2
S. Tucson AZ, 5490 55 D3
S. Valley Stream NY, 5638 241 G4
S. Venice FL, 13539 140 B4
S. Wallins KY, 996 111 D2
S. Walpole MA, 1900 151 D2
S. Waverly PA, 987 93 E1
S. Weber UT, 4260 244 B2
S. Webster OH, 764 101 D3
S. Weldon NC, 1414 113 E3
South West City MO, 855 106 B3
Southwest Harbor ME, 950 83 D2
S. Westport MA, 600 151 D4
S. Weymouth MA, 11100 151 D2
S. Whitley IN, 1782 89 F3
S. Whittier CA, 55193 228 E3
Southwick MA, 2000 150 A2
S. Williamson KY, 600 111 E1
S. Williamsport PA, 6412 93 D2
S. Willington CT, 1700 150 A3
S. Wilmington IL, 621 88 C2
S. Windham CT, 1278 149 F1
S. Windham ME, 1792 82 B3
S. Windsor CT, 700 150 A3
Southwood Acres CT, 8067 150 A2
S. Woodstock CT, 1211 150 B3
S. Yarmouth MA, 11603 151 F3
S. Zanesville OH, 1936 101 E1
Spalding NE, 537 35 E3
Spalding Co. GA, 58417 128 C1
Spanaway WA, 21588 12 C3
Spanish Fork UT, 20246 39 E1
Spanish Fort AL, 5423 135 E1
Spanish Lake MO, 21337 256 C1
Sparkman AR, 586 117 D4
Sparks GA, 1755 137 F1
Sparks MD, 1800 144 C1
Sparks NV, 66346 37 D1
Sparrow Bush NY, 1100 94 A3
Sparta GA, 1522 129 E1
Sparta IL, 4486 98 B4
Sparta MI, 4159 75 F3
Sparta MO, 1144 107 D2
Sparta NJ, 9755 148 A3
Sparta NC, 1817 112 A3
Sparta TN, 4599 110 A4
Sparta WI, 8648 73 F1
Spartanburg SC, 39673 121 F2
Spartanburg Co. SC, 253791 121 F2
Spavinaw OK, 563 106 B3
Spearfish SD, 8606 25 F3
Spearman TX, 3021 50 B2
Spearville KS, 813 42 C4
Speedway IN, 12881 99 F1
Speigner AL, 1700 128 A2
Spencer IN, 2508 99 E2
Spencer IA, 11317 72 A3
Spencer MA, 6032 150 B1
Spencer NE, 541 35 D1
Spencer NY, 731 93 E1
Spencer NC, 3355 112 A4
Spencer OH, 747 91 D3
Spencer OK, 3746 51 E3
Spencer TN, 1713 110 A4
Spencer WV, 2352 101 F3
Spencer WI, 1932 68 A4
Spencer Co. IN, 20391 99 E4
Spencer Co. KY, 11766 100 A4
Spencerport NY, 3559 78 C3
Spencerville OH, 2235 90 B3
Speonk NY, 2675 149 E3
Sperry OK, 981 51 F2
Spiceland IN, 807 100 A1
Spicer MN, 1126 66 B3
Spindale NC, 4022 121 F1
Spink Co. SD, 7454 27 E2
Spinnerstown PA, 1100 146 C1
Spirit Lake ID, 1376 14 B2
Spirit Lake IA, 4261 72 B2
Spiro OK, 2227 116 B1
Splendora TX, 1275 132 B2
Spofford NH, 500 94 C1
Spokane WA, 195629 14 A3
Spokane Co. WA, 417939 14 B2
Spooner WI, 2653 67 E2
Spotswood NJ, 7880 147 E1
Spotsylvania VA, 3833 103 D4
Spotsylvania Co. VA, 90395 103 D4
Spottsville KY, 600 99 E4
Spout Sprs. NC, 550 123 D1
Sprague WA, 490 13 F3
Spreckels CA, 485 236 E3
Spring TX, 36385 132 A2
Spring Arbor MI, 2188 90 B1
Springboro OH, 12380 100 B1
Spring City PA, 3305 146 B2
Spring City TN, 2025 110 B4
Spring City UT, 956 39 E1
Spring Creek NV, 10548 30 B4
Springdale AR, 45798 106 C4
Springdale OH, 10563 204 B1
Springdale PA, 3828 250 D1
Springdale SC, 2877 205 E2
Springdale UT, 457 39 D4
Springer NM, 1285 49 E2
Springer OK, 577 51 E4
Springerville AZ, 1972 48 A4
Springfield CO, 1562 42 A4
Springfield FL, 8810 136 C2
Springfield GA, 1821 130 B2
Springfield IL, 111454 98 B1
Springfield KY, 2634 110 B1
Springfield LA, 395 134 B2
Springfield MA, 152082 150 A2
Springfield MI, 5189 75 F4
Springfield MN, 2215 72 B1
Springfield MO, 151580 107 D2
Springfield NE, 1450 35 F3
Springfield NJ, 14429 148 A4
Springfield OH, 65358 100 C1
Springfield OR, 52864 20 B4
Springfield PA, 23677 146 C3
Springfield SC, 504 122 A4
Springfield SD, 792 35 E1
Springfield TN, 14329 109 F3
Springfield VT, 3938 81 E4
Springfield VA, 30417 144 B3
Spring Garden Estates MD, 2400 144 A1
Spring Glen UT, 1000 39 F1
Spring Green WI, 1444 74 A3
Spring Grove IL, 3880 74 C4
Spring Grove MN, 1304 73 E2
Spring Grove PA, 2050 103 E1
Spring Hill FL, 69078 140 B1
Spring Hill KS, 2727 96 B3
Springhill LA, 5439 125 D1
Spring Hill TN, 7715 109 E4
Spring Hope NC, 1261 113 D4
Spring Lake MI, 2514 75 E3
Spring Lake NJ, 3567 147 F2
Spring Lake NC, 8098 123 D1
Spring Lake Hts. NJ, 5227 147 E2
Spring Lake Park MN, 6772 235 C1
Springlee KY, 426 230 E2
Spring Mill KY, 380 230 E3
Springport MI, 704 76 A4
Springs NY, 4950 149 F3
Springtown TX, 2062 59 E2
Springvale ME, 3488 82 A4
Spring Valley CA, 26663 53 D4
Spring Valley IL, 5398 88 B2
Spring Valley KY, 668 230 F1
Spring Valley MN, 2518 73 D2
Spring Valley NY, 25464 148 B2
Spring Valley TX, 3611 220 B2
Spring Valley WI, 1189 67 E4
Springview NE, 244 34 C1
Springville AL, 2521 119 F4
Springville CA, 1109 45 D3
Springville IA, 1091 87 F1
Springville NJ, 2400 147 D3
Springville NY, 4252 78 B4
Springville UT, 20424 39 E1
Springwater NY, 700 78 C4
Spruce Pine NC, 2030 111 E4
Spry PA, 4903 275 F2
Spur TX, 1088 58 B1
Squaw Valley CA, 2691 45 D3
Staatsburg NY, 911 94 B3
Stacy MN, 1278 67 D3
Stafford CT, 900 150 B2
Stafford KS, 1161 43 D3
Stafford TX, 15681 132 A3
Stafford VA, 3000 103 D3
Stafford Co. KS, 4789 43 D3
Stafford Co. VA, 92446 144 A4
Stafford Sprs. CT, 4100 150 A2
Stallings NC, 3189 122 B1
Stamford CT, 117083 148 C3
Stamford NY, 1265 79 F4
Stamford TX, 3636 58 C2
Stamping Ground KY, 566 100 B4
Stamps AR, 2131 125 D1
Stanardsville VA, 476 102 C4
Stanberry MO, 1243 86 B4
Standing Pine MS, 509 126 C2
Standish ME, 600 82 B3
Standish MI, 1581 76 B1
Stanfield AZ, 651 54 C2
Stanfield NC, 1113 122 B1
Stanfield OR, 1979 21 E1
Stanford IL, 670 88 B4
Stanford KY, 3430 110 B1
Stanford MT, 454 16 B3
Stanhope NJ, 3584 94 A4
Stanislaus Co. CA, 446997 36 C4
Stanley NC, 3053 122 A1
Stanley ND, 1279 18 A2
Stanley VA, 1326 102 C3
Stanley WI, 1898 67 F4
Stanley Co. SD, 2772 26 C3
Stanleytown VA, 1515 112 B2
Stanly Co. NC, 58100 122 B1
Stannards NY, 868 92 C1
Stanton CA, 37403 228 E4
Stanton DE, 5000 146 B4
Stanton IA, 714 86 B3
Stanton KY, 3029 110 C1
Stanton MI, 1504 76 A3
Stanton NE, 1627 35 E2
Stanton ND, 345 18 B3
Stanton TN, 615 118 C1
Stanton TX, 2556 58 A3
Stanton Co. KS, 2406 42 B4
Stanton Co. NE, 6455 35 E2
Stantonsburg NC, 726 123 E1
Stanwood IA, 680 87 F1
Stanwood WA, 3923 12 C2
Staples MN, 3104 64 A4
Stapleton NE, 301 34 C3
Star ID, 1795 22 B4
Star NC, 807 122 C1
Starbuck MN, 1314 66 A2
Star City AR, 2471 117 F4
Star City WV, 1366 102 A1
Star Cross NJ, 1400 145 F1
Stark Co. IL, 6332 88 B3
Stark Co. ND, 22636 18 A4
Stark Co. OH, 378098 91 E3
Starke FL, 5593 138 C3
Starke Co. IN, 23556 89 E2
Starkey VA, 600 254 D2
Starks LA, 650 133 D2
Starkville MS, 21869 118 C4
Star Lake NY, 860 79 F1
Star Prairie WI, 574 67 E3
Starr Co. TX, 53597 63 E3
Startex SC, 988 217 C1
Startup WA, 817 12 C2
Star Valley AZ, 550 47 E4
Stateburg SC, 1264 122 B4
State Ctr. IA, 1349 87 D1
State College PA, 38420 92 C3
State Line MS, 555 127 D4
Stateline NV, 1215 37 D2
State Line PA, 1300 103 D1
Statenville GA, 50 137 F1
State Road NC, 900 112 A3
Statesboro GA, 22698 130 B2
Statesville NC, 23320 112 A4
Statham GA, 2040 121 D4
Staunton IL, 5030 98 B2
Staunton IN, 550 99 E2
Staunton VA, 23853 102 B4
Stayton OR, 6816 20 C3
Steamboat NV, 1100 37 D2
Steamboat Canyon AZ, 1100 47 F2
Steamboat Sprs. CO, 9815 33 D4
Stearns KY, 1586 110 B3
Stearns Co. MN, 133166 66 B3
Stebbins AK, 547 154 B2
Stedman NC, 664 123 D2
Steele AL, 1093 120 A4
Steele MO, 2263 108 B4
Steele ND, 761 18 C4
Steele Co. MN, 33680 73 D1
Steele Co. ND, 2258 19 E3
Steeleville IL, 2077 98 B4
Steelton PA, 5858 218 B2
Steelville MO, 1429 97 F4
Steilacoom WA, 6049 12 C3
Steinhatchee FL, 700 137 F3
Stephen MN, 708 19 E2
Stephens AR, 1152 125 D1
Stephens City VA, 1146 102 C2
Stephens Co. GA, 25435 121 D2
Stephens Co. OK, 43182 51 E4
Stephens Co. TX, 9674 59 D2
Stephenson MI, 875 69 D3
Stephenson VA, 1100 103 D2
Stephenson Co. IL, 48979 74 B4
Stephenville TX, 14921 59 D3
Sterling CO, 11360 34 A4
Sterling CT, 650 150 B3
Sterling IL, 15451 88 B1
Sterling KS, 2642 43 E3
Sterling MA, 1300 150 C1
Sterling MI, 533 76 B1
Sterling NE, 507 35 F4
Sterling OK, 762 51 E4
Sterling VA, 20500 144 A3
Sterling City TX, 1081 58 B3
Sterling Co. TX, 1393 58 B4
Sterling Forest NY, 700 148 A2
Sterling Hts. MI, 124471 76 C4
Sterlington LA, 1276 125 E2
Stetsonville WI, 563 68 A3
Steuben Co. IN, 33214 90 A2
Steuben Co. NY, 98726 78 C4
Steubenville KY, 550 110 B2
Steubenville OH, 19015 91 F4
Stevens Co. KS, 5463 42 B4
Stevens Co. MN, 10053 27 F2
Stevens Co. WA, 40066 13 F2
Stevens Creek VA, 550 112 A2
Stevenson AL, 1770 120 A2
Stevenson CT, 800 149 D2
Stevenson WA, 1200 20 C1
Stevens Pt. WI, 24551 68 B4
Stevensville MD, 5880 145 D3
Stevensville MI, 1191 89 E1
Stevensville MT, 1553 15 D4
Stewardson IL, 747 98 C2
Stewart MN, 564 66 B4
Stewart Co. GA, 5252 128 C3
Stewart Co. TN, 12370 109 D3
Stewart Manor NY, 1935 241 G3
Stewartstown PA, 1752 103 E1
Stewartsville MO, 759 96 B1
Stewartville MN, 5411 73 D2
Stickney IL, 6148 203 D5
Stickney SD, 334 27 E4
Stigler OK, 2731 116 B1
Stillman Valley IL, 1048 88 B1
Stillmore GA, 730 129 F2

Bayberry A1
Collamer B1
DeWitt B2
E. Syracuse B2
Fairmount A2
Franklin Park B1
Galeville A1
Jamesville B2
Lakeland A1
Liverpool A1
Lyndon B2
Mattydale B1
Nedrow A2
N. Syracuse B1
Onondaga Hill A2
Solvay A2
Split Rock A2
Syracuse A2
Taunton A2
Westvale A2

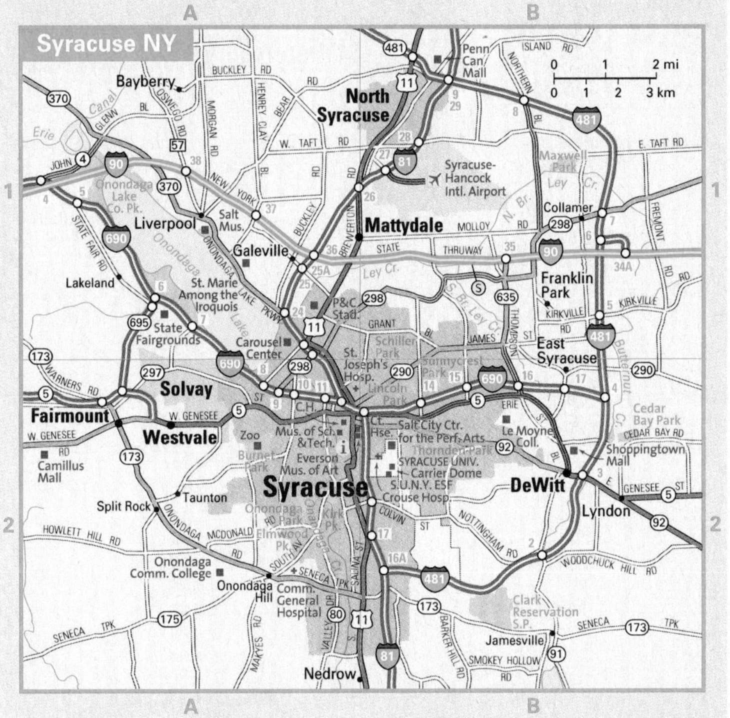

Syracuse NY
North Syracuse
Bayberry
Syracuse-Hancock Intl. Airport
Collamer
Liverpool
Mattydale
Galeville
Lakeland
Franklin Park
East Syracuse
Solvay
Fairmount
Westvale
Syracuse
DeWitt
Lyndon
Split Rock
Taunton
Jamesville
Nedrow
Onondaga Comm. College
Onondaga Hill
Shoppingtown Mall
Carousel Center
SYRACUSE UNIV.

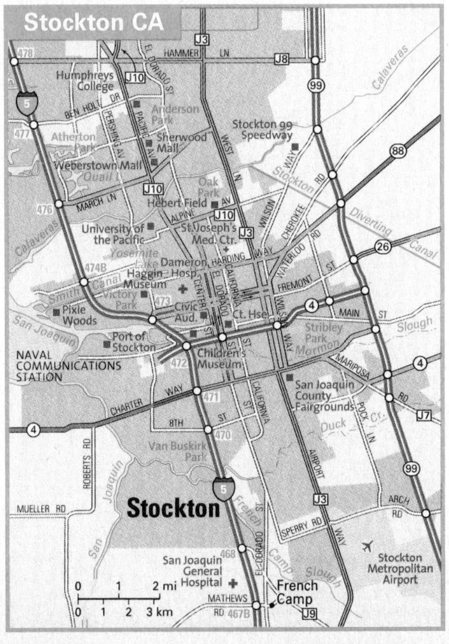

Stockton CA
Stockton
Humphreys College
Stockton 99 Speedway
Weberstown Mall
University of the Pacific
Haggin Museum
Port of Stockton
NAVAL COMMUNICATIONS STATION
San Joaquin County Fairgrounds
San Joaquin General Hospital
Stockton Metropolitan Airport
French Camp

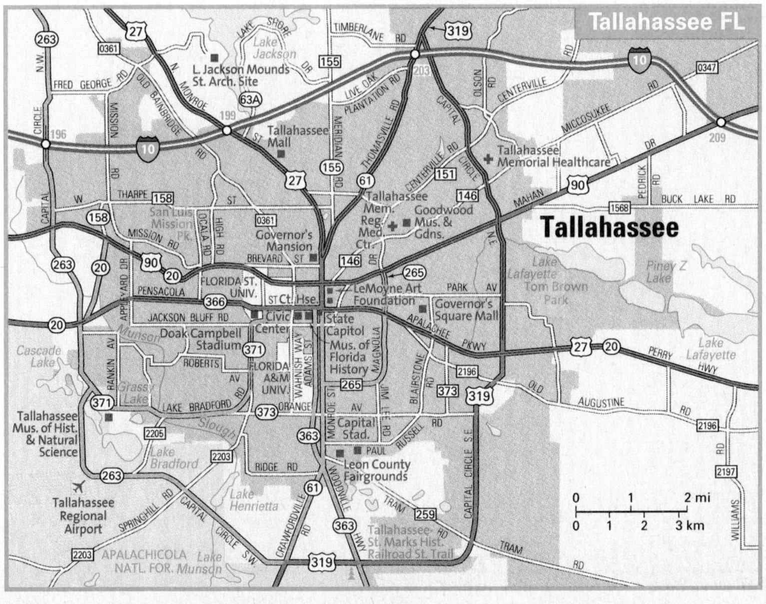

Tallahassee FL
Tallahassee
Tallahassee Mall
Tallahassee Memorial Healthcare
Governor's Mansion
FLORIDA ST. UNIV.
Doak Campbell Stadium
FLORIDA A&M UNIV.
Capitol
Tallahassee Mus. of Hist. & Natural Science
Tallahassee Regional Airport
Leon County Fairgrounds
APALACHICOLA NATL. FOR.
Lake Jackson
Lake Lafayette

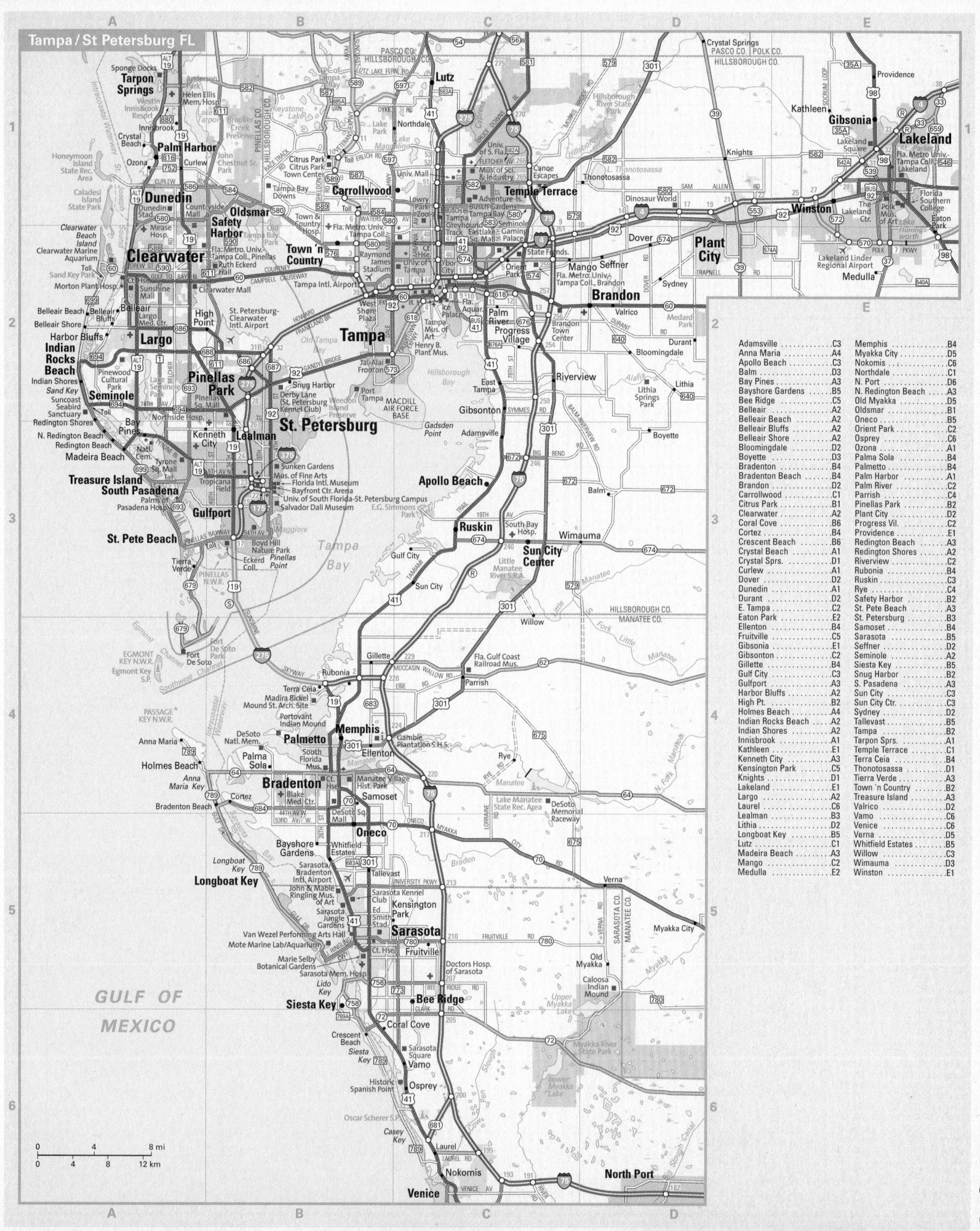

Tampa / St Petersburg FL

Stillwater—Terrebonne 267

Entries in **bold** indicate counties or parishes. Entries in color indicate cities with detailed inset maps.

Stillwater ME, 1600 83 D1
Stillwater MN, 15143 67 D3
Stillwater NY, 1644 94 B1
Stillwater OK, 39065 51 F2
Stillwater Co. MT, 8195 24 B1
Stilwell KS, 1200 96 B3
Stilwell OK, 3276 106 B4
Stimson Crossing WA, 773 12 C2
Stinnett TX, 1936 50 B2
Stinson Beach CA, 751 259 A2
Stites ID, 226 22 B1
Stockbridge GA, 9853 120 C4
Stockbridge MA, 900 94 B2
Stockbridge MI, 1260 76 B4
Stockbridge WI, 649 74 C1
Stockdale TX, 1398 61 E3
Stock Island FL, 4410 142 C4
Stockton CA, 243771 36 C3
Stockton IL, 1926 74 A4
Stockton KS, 1558 43 D2
Stockton MN, 682 73 E1
Stockton MO, 1960 106 C1
Stockton NJ, 560 146 C1
Stockton UT, 443 31 E4
Stockton Sprs. ME, 550 83 D2
Stockville NE, 36 34 C4
Stoddard WI, 815 73 F3
Stoddard Co. MO, 29705 108 B2
Stokes Co. NC, 44711 112 B3
Stokesdale NC, 3267 112 B3
Stoneboro PA, 1104 92 A2
Stone Co. AR, 11499 107 E4
Stone Co. MS, 13622 135 D1
Stone Co. MO, 28658 107 D3
Stonega VA, 475 111 D2
Stoneham MA, 22219 151 D1
Stone Harbor NJ, 1128 104 C4
Stone Mtn. GA, 7145 120 C4
Stone Park IL, 5127 203 C4
Stone Ridge NY, 1173 94 B3
Stoneville NC, 1002 112 B3
Stonewall LA, 1668 124 C3
Stonewall MS, 1149 127 D3
Stonewall OK, 465 51 F4
Stonewall Co. TX, 1693 58 B2
Stonewood WV, 1815 102 A2
Stoney Creek Mills PA, 5900 146 B2
Stonington CT, 1032 149 F2
Stonington IL, 960 98 C1
Stonington ME, 850 83 D2
Stony Brook NY, 13727 149 D3
Stony Creek CT, 900 149 E2
Stony Pt. NY, 11744 148 B2
Stony Pt. NC, 1380 112 A4
Storey Co. NV, 3399 37 D2
Storm Lake IA, 10076 72 A4
Stormstown PA, 1602 92 C3
Storrs CT, 10996 150 B3
Story WY, 887 25 D3
Story City IA, 3228 86 C1
Story Co. IA, 79981 86 C1
Stottville NY, 1355 94 B2
Stoughton MA, 11200 151 D2
Stoughton WI, 12354 74 B3
Stoutsville OH, 581 101 D1
Stover MO, 969 97 D3
Stow OH, 32139 91 E2
Stowe PA, 3585 146 B2
Stowe VT, 500 81 E2
Stowell TX, 1572 132 C3
Strafford MO, 1845 107 D2
Strafford Co. NH, 112233 81 F4
Straitsville CT, 1000 149 D1
Strasburg CO, 1402 41 E1
Strasburg IL, 603 98 C2
Strasburg ND, 549 26 C1
Strasburg OH, 2310 91 E4
Strasburg PA, 2800 146 A3
Strasburg VA, 4017 102 C2
Stratford CA, 1264 44 C3
Stratford CT, 49976 149 D2
Stratford IA, 746 72 C4
Stratford NJ, 7271 146 C3
Stratford OK, 1474 51 F4
Stratford TX, 1991 50 A2
Stratford WI, 1523 68 A4
Stratham NH, 1000 82 A4
Strathmoor Vil. KY, 625 230 E2
Strathmore CA, 2584 45 D3
Strathmore NJ, 6740 147 E1
Stratmoor Hills CO, 6650 205 D2
Stratton CO, 669 42 A2
Stratton ME, 425 82 B1
Stratton NE, 396 42 B1
Strawberry AZ, 1028 47 E4
Strawberry Pt. IA, 1386 73 E4
Strawn TX, 739 59 D3
Streamwood IL, 36407 203 B3
Streator IL, 14190 88 C3
Streetsboro OH, 12311 91 E3
Stroh IN, 700 90 A2
Stromsburg NE, 1232 35 E3
Strong AR, 651 125 E1
Strong ME, 550 82 B1
Strong City KS, 584 43 F3
Stronghurst IL, 896 87 F3
Strongsville OH, 43858 91 E2
Stroud OK, 2758 51 F2
Stroudsburg PA, 5756 93 F3
Strum WI, 1001 67 F4
Struthers OH, 11756 91 F3
Stryker OH, 1406 90 B2
Stuart FL, 14633 141 E4
Stuart IA, 1712 86 B2
Stuart NE, 625 35 D1
Stuart VA, 961 112 B3
Stuarts Draft VA, 8367 102 C4
Sturbridge MA, 2047 150 B2
Sturgeon MO, 944 97 E2
Sturgeon Bay WI, 9437 69 D4
Sturgis KY, 2030 109 D1
Sturgis MI, 11285 90 A1
Sturgis SD, 6442 25 F3
Sturtevant WI, 5287 74 C4
Stutsman Co. ND, 21908 19 D3
Stuttgart AR, 9745 117 F3
Suamico WI, 950 68 C4
Subiaco AR, 439 116 C1
Sublette KS, 1592 42 B4
Sublette Co. WY, 5920 32 A1
Sublimity OR, 2148 20 C2
Succasunna NJ, 12569 148 A3
Sudan TX, 1039 57 F1
Sudbury MA, 2300 150 C1
Suffern NY, 11006 148 B2
Suffield CT, 1244 150 A2
Suffolk VA, 63677 113 F3
Suffolk Co. MA, 689807 151 D1
Suffolk Co. NY, 1419369 149 D3
Sugar City ID, 1242 23 E4
Sugar Creek MO, 3839 224 D3
Sugarcreek OH, 2174 91 E4
Sugarcreek PA, 5331 92 A2
Sugar Grove IL, 3909 88 C1
Sugar Grove PA, 613 92 B1
Sugar Grove VA, 741 111 F2
Sugar Hill GA, 11399 120 C3
Sugar Land TX, 63328 132 A3
Sugarland Run VA, 9400 144 A3
Sugar Loaf NY, 700 148 A2
Sugar Notch PA, 1023 261 A2
Suisun City CA, 26118 36 B3
Suitland MD, 33515 144 B3
Sulligent AL, 2151 119 D4
Sullivan IL, 4326 98 C1
Sullivan IN, 4617 99 E2
Sullivan MO, 6351 97 F4
Sullivan WI, 688 74 C3
Sullivan City TX, 3998 63 E4
Sullivan Co. IN, 21751 99 E2
Sullivan Co. MO, 7219 87 D4
Sullivan Co. NH, 40458 81 E4
Sullivan Co. NY, 73966 94 A2
Sullivan Co. PA, 6556 93 E2
Sullivan Co. TN, 153048 111 E3
Sullivans Island SC, 1911 131 D2
Sully IA, 904 87 D2
Sully Co. SD, 1556 26 C3
Sulphur LA, 20512 133 D2
Sulphur OK, 4794 51 F4
Sulphur Rock AR, 421 107 F4
Sulphur Sprs. AR, 671 106 B3
Sulphur Sprs. TX, 14551 124 A1
Sultan WA, 3344 12 C3
Sumas WA, 960 12 C1
Sumiton AL, 2665 119 F4
Summerdale AL, 655 135 E2
Summerfield NC, 7018 112 B3
Summerland Key FL, 600 143 D4
Summers Co. WV, 12999 112 A1
Summerside OH, 5523 204 C2
Summersville MO, 544 107 F2
Summersville WV, 3294 101 F4
Summerton SC, 1061 122 B4
Summertown TN, 800 119 E1
Summerville GA, 4556 120 B3
Summerville SC, 27752 131 D1
Summit AR, 586 107 E3
Summit IL, 10637 203 D5
Summit KY, 3400 101 D3
Summit MS, 1428 126 B4
Summit NJ, 21131 148 A4
Summit SD, 281 27 F2
Summit WA, 8041 262 B5
Summit Co. CO, 23548 41 D1
Summit Co. OH, 542899 91 E3
Summit Co. UT, 29736 31 F4
Summitville IN, 1090 89 F4
Sumner IL, 1022 99 D3
Sumner IA, 2106 73 E3
Sumner MS, 407 118 B3
Sumner WA, 8504 12 C3
Sumner Co. KS, 25946 51 E1
Sumner Co. TN, 130449 109 F3
Sumrall MS, 1005 126 C4
Sumter SC, 39643 122 B4
Sumter Co. AL, 14798 127 E2
Sumter Co. FL, 53345 140 C1
Sumter Co. GA, 33200 129 D3
Sumter Co. SC, 104646 122 B4
Sun LA, 471 134 C1
Sunapee NH, 750 81 E4
Sunbright TN, 577 110 B3
Sunburst MT, 415 15 E1
Sunbury OH, 2630 91 D4
Sunbury PA, 10610 93 D3
Sun City AZ, 38309 54 C1
Sun City CA, 17773 53 D3
Sun City Ctr. FL, 16321 140 C3
Sun City West AZ, 26344 249 A1
Suncook NH, 5362 81 F4
Sundance WY, 1161 25 F3
Sunderland MD, 1400 144 C4
Sunderland MA, 850 150 A1
Sundown TX, 1505 57 F1
Sunfield MI, 591 76 A4
Sunfish Lake MN, 504 235 D3
Sunflower MS, 696 118 A4
Sunflower Co. MS, 34369 118 A4
Sun Lakes AZ, 11936 54 C2
Sunland Park NM, 13309 56 C4
Sunman IN, 805 100 A2
Sunnybrook MD, 2300 144 C1
Sunny Isles Beach FL, 15315 233 C3
Sunnyside UT, 404 39 F1
Sunnyside WA, 13905 13 E4
Sunnyslope CA, 4437 229 H3
Sunnyvale CA, 131760 36 B4
Sunol CA, 1332 259 E3
Sun Prairie WI, 20369 74 B3
Sunray TX, 1950 50 A2
Sunrise FL, 85779 143 E1
Sunrise Beach TX, 704 61 D1
Sunset LA, 2352 133 F2
Sunset UT, 5204 244 A2
Sunset Beach NC, 1824 123 D4
Sunset Hills MO, 8267 256 B3
Sun Valley ID, 1427 22 C4
Superior AZ, 3254 55 D2
Superior CO, 9011 209 B1
Superior MT, 893 14 C3
Superior NE, 2055 43 E1
Superior WI, 27368 64 C4
Superior WY, 244 32 B2
Supreme LA, 1119 134 A3
Suquamish WA, 3510 262 A2
Surf City NJ, 1442 147 E4
Surf City NC, 1393 123 E3
Surfside FL, 4909 233 C4
Surfside Beach SC, 4425 123 D4
Surfside Beach TX, 763 133 E4
Surgoinsville TN, 1484 111 D3
Suring WI, 605 68 C4
Surprise AZ, 30848 54 C1
Surrey ND, 917 18 B2
Surry VA, 262 113 F2
Surry Co. NC, 71219 112 A3
Surry Co. VA, 6829 113 F2
Susan VA, 475 113 F1
Susan Moore AL, 721 119 F3
Susanville CA, 13541 29 D4
Susquehanna PA, 1690 93 F1
Susquehanna Co. PA, 42238 93 E2
Sussex NJ, 2145 148 A2
Sussex VA, 125 113 E2
Sussex WI, 8828 74 C3
Sussex Co. DE, 156638 145 F4
Sussex Co. NJ, 144166 148 A2
Sussex Co. VA, 12504 113 E2
Sutcliffe NV, 281 37 D1
Sutherland IA, 707 72 A3
Sutherland NE, 1129 34 B3
Sutherlin OR, 6669 20 B4
Sutter CA, 2885 36 B2
Sutter Co. CA, 78930 36 B2
Sutter Creek CA, 2303 36 C3
Sutton AK, 1080 154 C3
Sutton MA, 650 150 C2
Sutton NE, 1447 35 E4
Sutton WV, 1011 101 F3
Sutton Co. TX, 4077 60 B1
Suttons Bay MI, 589 69 F4
Suwanee GA, 8725 120 C3
Suwannee Co. FL, 34844 138 B2
Swain Co. NC, 12968 121 D1
Swainsboro GA, 6943 129 F2
Swampscott MA, 14412 151 D1
Swannanoa NC, 4132 121 E1
Swann Keys DE, 700 145 F4
Swanquarter NC, 275 115 E3
Swansboro NC, 1426 115 D4
Swansea IL, 10579 98 B3
Swansea SC, 533 122 A4
Swanton OH, 3307 90 B2
Swanton VT, 2548 81 D1
Swan Valley ID, 213 23 F4
Swarthmore PA, 6170 146 C3
Swartz LA, 4247 125 F2
Swartz Creek MI, 5102 76 B3
Swayzee IN, 1011 89 F4
Swea City IA, 642 72 B2
Swedesboro NJ, 2055 146 C4
Sweeny TX, 3624 132 A4
Sweet Briar VA, 750 112 C1
Sweet Grass Co. MT, 3609 24 A1
Sweet Home OR, 8016 20 C3
Sweetser IN, 1229 89 F3
Sweet Sprs. MO, 1628 97 D3
Sweetwater FL, 14226 143 E2
Sweetwater TN, 5586 120 C1
Sweetwater TX, 11415 58 B3
Sweetwater Co. WY, 37613 32 B2
Swepsonville NC, 922 112 C4
Swift Co. MN, 11956 66 A3
Swifton AR, 871 107 F4
Swifts Beach MA, 2700 151 E3
Swift Trail Jct. AZ, 2195 55 E2
Swiftwater PA, 800 93 F3
Swink CO, 696 41 F3
Swisher IA, 813 87 E1
Swisher Co. TX, 8378 50 A4
Swissvale PA, 9653 250 C2
Switzer WV, 1138 111 E1
Switzerland Co. IN, 9065 100 B3
Swoyersville PA, 5157 93 E2
Sycamore GA, 496 129 D4
Sycamore IL, 12020 88 C1
Sycamore OH, 914 90 C3
Sycaway NY, 3000 188 E2
Sykesville MD, 4197 144 B1
Sykesville PA, 1246 92 B3
Sylacauga AL, 12616 128 A1
Sylva NC, 2435 121 D1
Sylvan Beach NY, 1071 79 E3
Sylvania AL, 1186 120 A2
Sylvania GA, 2675 130 B2
Sylvania OH, 18670 90 C2
Sylvan Lake MI, 1735 210 B1
Sylvan Lake NY, 1200 148 C1
Sylvan Shores FL, 2424 141 D3
Sylvan Sprs. AL, 1465 195 D2
Sylvester GA, 5990 129 D4
Symsonia KY, 450 109 D2
Syosset NY, 18544 148 C3
Syracuse IN, 3038 89 F2
Syracuse KS, 1824 42 B3
Syracuse NE, 1762 35 F4
Syracuse NY, 147306 79 D3
Syracuse OH, 879 101 E2
Syracuse UT, 9398 31 E3

T

Tabor IA, 993 86 A3
Tabor SD, 417 35 E1
Tabor City NC, 2509 123 D3
Tacna AZ, 555 54 A2
Tacoma WA, 193556 12 C3
Taft CA, 6400 52 B1
Taft FL, 1938 246 C4
Taft TX, 3396 61 E4
Tahlequah OK, 14458 106 B4
Tahoe City CA, 1761 37 D2
Tahoka TX, 2910 58 A2
Taholah WA, 824 12 A3
Takoma Park MD, 17299 270 D2
Talbot Co. GA, 6498 128 C2
Talbot Co. MD, 33812 145 D3
Talbott TN, 1400 111 D4
Talbotton GA, 1019 128 C2
Talco TX, 570 124 B1
Talcottville CT, 4500 150 A3
Talent OR, 5589 28 B2
Taliaferro Co. GA, 2077 121 E4
Talihina OK, 1211 116 B2
Talkeetna AK, 772 154 C3
Talladega AL, 15143 120 A4
Talladega Co. AL, 80321 128 A1
Tallahassee FL, 150624 137 E2
Tallahatchie Co. MS, 14903 118 B4
Tallapoosa GA, 2789 120 B4
Tallapoosa Co. AL, 41475 128 B1
Tallassee AL, 4934 128 B1
Tallevast FL, 1100 266 B5
Talleyville DE, 6300 146 B3
Tallmadge OH, 16390 91 E3
Tallula IL, 638 98 B1
Tallulah LA, 9189 126 A2
Talmage CA, 1141 36 A2
Talmo GA, 477 121 D3
Taloga OK, 372 51 D2
Talty TX, 1028 59 F2
Tama IA, 2731 87 D1
Tama Co. IA, 18103 87 D1
Tamalpais Valley CA, 10691 259 A2
Tamaqua PA, 7174 93 E3
Tamarac FL, 55588 143 E1
Tamaroa IL, 740 98 B4
Tamms IL, 724 108 C2
Tampa FL, 303447 140 B2
Tampico IL, 772 88 B2
Taney Co. MO, 39703 107 D3
Taneytown MD, 5128 103 E1
Tangelo Park FL, 2430 246 B3
Tangent OR, 933 20 B3
Tangier VA, 604 114 B2
Tangipahoa LA, 747 134 B1
Tangipahoa Par. LA, 100588 134 B1
Tanner AL, 900 119 F2
Tannersville PA, 1000 93 F3
Tanque Verde AZ, 16195 55 D3
Tantallon MD, 7900 144 B4
Taos MO, 870 97 E3
Taos NM, 4700 49 D1
Taos Co. NM, 29979 49 D1
Tappahannock VA, 2068 103 E4
Tappan NY, 6757 148 B3
Tappen ND, 210 18 C4
Tara Hills CA, 5332 259 B1
Tarboro NC, 11138 113 E4
Tarentum PA, 4993 92 A3
Tariffville CT, 1371 150 A3
Tarkiln RI, 950 150 C2
Tarkio MO, 1935 86 A4
Tarpon Sprs. FL, 21003 140 B2
Tarrant City AL, 7022 119 F4
Tarrant Co. TX, 1446219 59 E2
Tarrytown NY, 11090 148 B3
Tasso TN, 1300 120 B1
Tatamy PA, 930 93 F3
Tate Co. MS, 25370 118 B2
Tattnall Co. GA, 22305 129 F3
Tatum NM, 683 57 F2
Tatum TX, 1175 124 B2
Taunton MA, 55976 151 D3
Tavares FL, 9700 140 C1
Tavernier FL, 2173 143 E4
Tawas City MI, 2005 76 B1
Taylor AL, 1898 136 C1
Taylor AZ, 3176 47 F4
Taylor AR, 566 125 D1
Taylor MI, 65868 90 C1
Taylor NE, 207 35 D2
Taylor PA, 6475 261 D1
Taylor TX, 13575 61 E1
Taylor Co. FL, 19256 137 F3
Taylor Co. GA, 8815 129 D2
Taylor Co. IA, 6958 86 B3
Taylor Co. KY, 22927 110 B1
Taylor Co. TX, 126555 58 C3
Taylor Co. WV, 16089 102 A2
Taylor Co. WI, 19680 67 F3
Taylor Creek FL, 4289 141 E4
Taylor Lake Vil. TX, 3694 132 B3
Taylor Mill KY, 6913 204 B3
Taylors SC, 20125 121 F2
Taylors Falls MN, 951 67 D3
Taylor Sprs. IL, 583 98 B2
Taylorsville IN, 919 99 F2
Taylorsville KY, 1009 100 A4
Taylorsville MD, 900 144 B1
Taylorsville MS, 1341 126 C3
Taylorsville NC, 1799 111 F4
Taylorsville UT, 57439 257 A2
Taylortown NJ, 1200 148 A3
Taylortown NC, 845 122 C1
Taylorville IL, 11427 98 B1
Tazewell TN, 2165 111 D3
Tazewell VA, 4206 111 F2
Tazewell Co. IL, 128485 88 B4
Tazewell Co. VA, 44598 111 F2
Tchula MS, 2332 126 B1
Tea SD, 1742 27 F4
Teague TX, 4557 59 F4
Teaneck NJ, 39260 148 B3
Teaticket MA, 1907 151 E4
Teays WV, 2400 101 E3
Tecumseh MI, 8574 90 B1
Tecumseh NE, 1716 35 F4
Tecumseh OK, 6098 51 F3
Teec Nos Pos AZ, 799 48 A1
Tega Cay SC, 4044 122 A2
Tehachapi CA, 10957 52 C1
Tehama CA, 432 36 B1
Tehama Co. CA, 56039 36 B1
Tekamah NE, 1892 35 F2
Tekoa WA, 826 14 B3
Tekonsha MI, 712 90 A1
Telfair Co. GA, 11794 129 E3
Telford PA, 4680 146 C2
Tell City IN, 7845 99 E4
Teller Co. CO, 20555 41 E2
Tellico Plains TN, 859 120 C1
Telluride CO, 2221 40 B3
Temecula CA, 57716 53 D3
Tempe AZ, 158625 54 C1
Temperance MI, 7757 90 C1
Temple GA, 2383 120 B4
Temple OK, 1146 51 E4
Temple PA, 1400 146 B1
Temple TX, 54514 59 E4
Temple City CA, 33377 228 E2
Temple Hills MD, 7792 270 E5
Temple Terrace FL, 20918 140 C2
Templeton CA, 4687 44 C4
Templeton MA, 800 95 D1
Tenafly NJ, 13806 148 B3
Tenaha TX, 1046 124 C3
Tenants Harbor ME, 500 82 C3
Tenino WA, 1447 12 C4
Tennent NJ, 1100 147 E2
Tennessee Ridge TN, 1334 109 D3
Tennille GA, 1505 129 E1
Tensas Par. LA, 6618 125 F3
Ten Sleep WY, 304 24 C3
Tequesta FL, 5273 141 F4
Terra Alta WV, 1456 102 B2
Terra Bella CA, 3466 45 D4
Terrace Hts. WA, 6447 13 D4
Terrace Park OH, 2273 204 C2
Terrebonne OR, 1469 21 D3

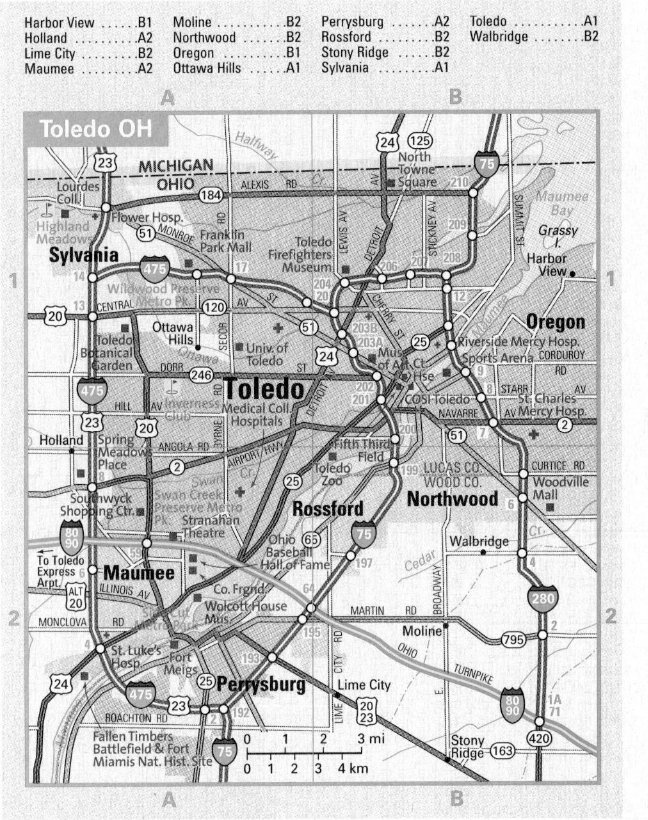

Harbor View B1
Holland A2
Lime City B2
Maumee A2
Moline B2
Northwood B2
Oregon B1
Ottawa Hills A1
Perrysburg A2
Rossford B2
Stony Ridge B2
Sylvania A1
Toledo A1
Walbridge B2
Toledo OH
MICHIGAN
OHIO
Sylvania
Toledo
Oregon
Holland
Rossford
Northwood
Maumee
Perrysburg
Walbridge
Moline
Lime City
Harbor View
Ottawa Hills
North Towne Square
Franklin Park Mall
Toledo Firefighters Museum
Univ. of Toledo
Toledo Botanical Garden
Medical Coll. Hospitals
Toledo Zoo
Fifth Third Field
COSI Toledo
Woodville Mall
Southwyck Shopping Ctr.
Ohio Baseball Hall of Fame
Wolcott House Mus.
St. Luke's Hosp.
Fort Meigs
To Toledo Express Arpt.
Fallen Timbers Battlefield & Fort Miamis Nat. Hist. Site
Stony Ridge
0 1 2 3 mi
0 1 2 3 4 km

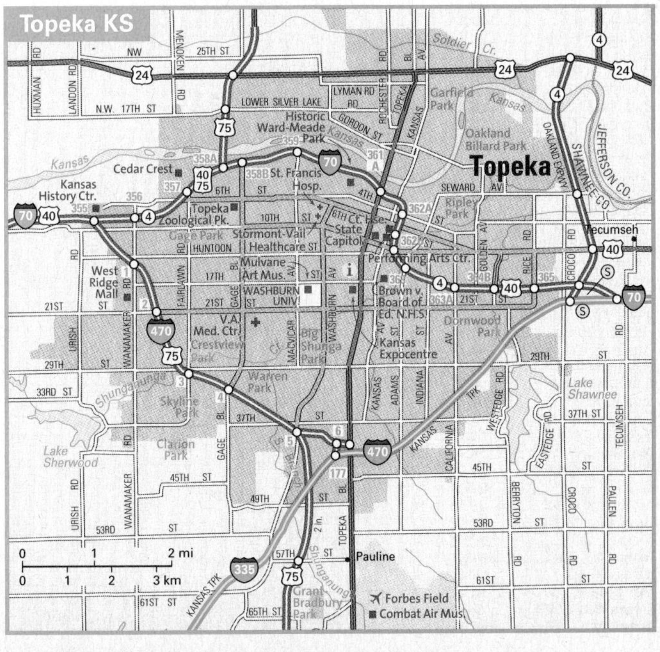

Topeka KS
Topeka
Historic Ward-Meade Park
Garfield Park
Oakland Billard Park
Cedar Crest
Kansas History Ctr.
St. Francis Hosp.
Topeka Zoological Pk.
Gage Park
Stormont-Vail Healthcare
State Capitol
Performing Arts Ctr.
West Ridge Mall
Mulvane Art Mus.
Washburn Univ.
Brown v. Board of Ed. N.H.S.
V.A. Med. Ctr.
Kansas Expocentre
Lake Shawnee
Lake Sherwood
Tecumseh
Pauline
Forbes Field
Combat Air Mus.
0 1 2 mi
0 1 2 3 km

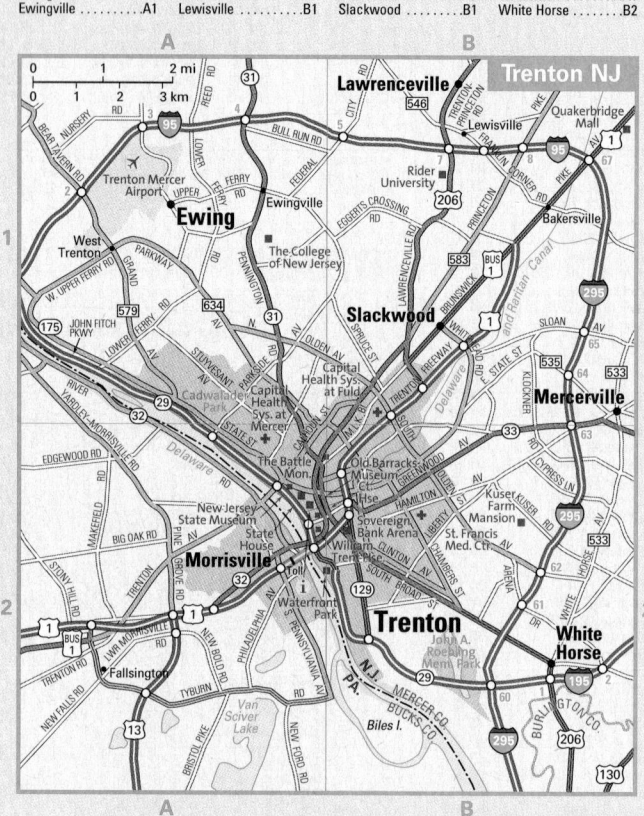

Trenton NJ

Bakersville B1
Ewing A1
Ewingville A1
Fallsington A2
Lawrenceville B1
Lewisville B1
Mercerville B1
Morrisville A2
Slackwood A2
Trenton B2
W. Trenton A1
White Horse B2

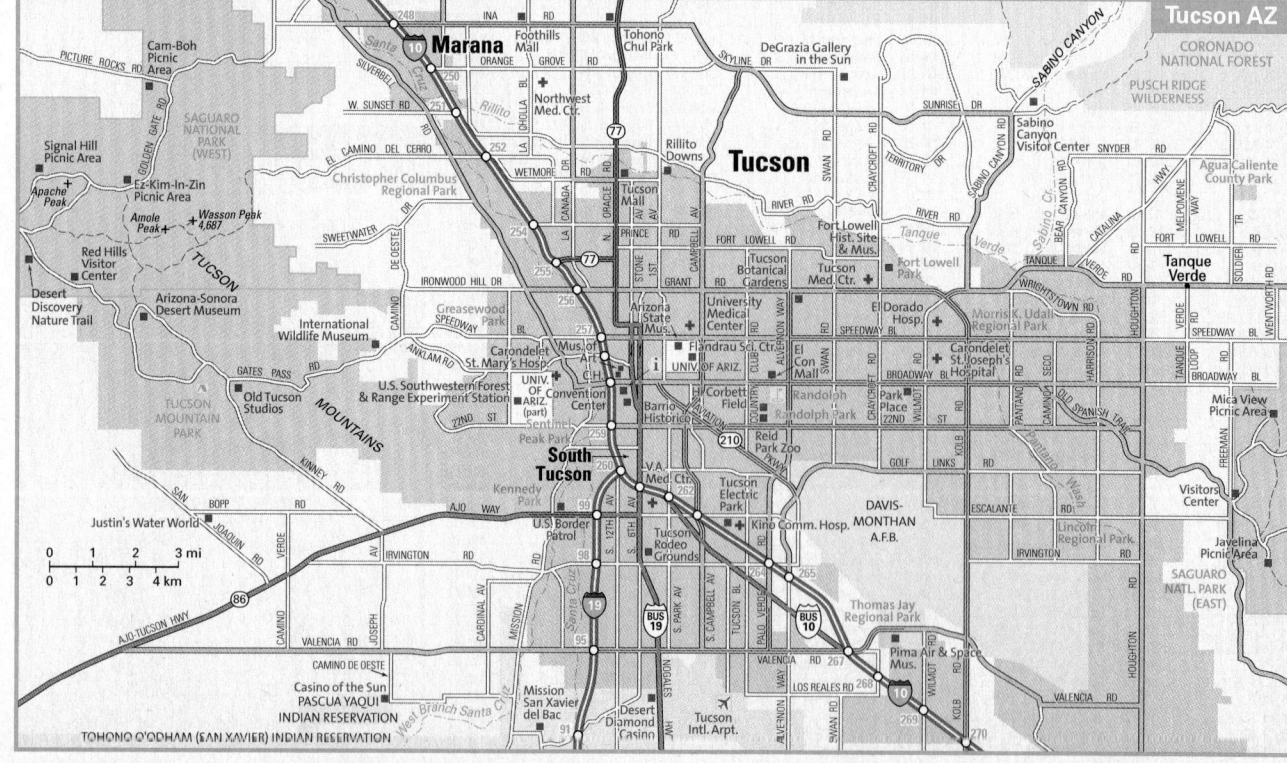

Tucson AZ

Entries in **bold** indicate counties or parishes. Entries in color indicate cities with detailed inset maps.

TROY — Vermilion County 269

Troy ID, 798 ....14 B4
Troy IL, 8524 ....98 B3
Troy KS, 1054 ....96 B1
Troy MI, 80959 ....76 C4
Troy MO, 6737 ....97 F2
Troy MT, 957 ....14 C2
Troy NH, 1300 ....95 D1
Troy NY, 49170 ....94 B1
Troy NC, 3430 ....122 C1
Troy OH, 21999 ....100 B1
Troy PA, 1508 ....93 D1
Troy TN, 1273 ....108 C3
Troy TX, 1378 ....59 E4
Troy VT, 375 ....81 E1
Truckee CA, 13864 ....37 D2
Truman MN, 1259 ....72 B2
Trumann AR, 6889 ....108 A4
Trumansburg NY, 1581 ....79 D4
Trumbauersville PA, 1059 ....146 C1
Trumbull CT, 34243 ....149 D2
Trumbull Co. OH, 225116 ....91 F2
Trussville AL, 12924 ....119 F4
Truth or Consequences NM, 7289 ....56 C2
Tryon NE, 100 ....34 B3

Tuolumne CA, 1865 ....37 D3
Tuolumne Co. CA, 54501 ....37 D3
Tupelo MS, 34211 ....119 D3
Tupper Lake NY, 3935 ....79 F1
Turbeville SC, 602 ....122 B4
Turbotville PA, 691 ....93 D3
Turley NM, 425 ....48 B1
Turley OK, 3231 ....51 F2
Turlock CA, 55810 ....36 C4
Turner ME, 550 ....82 B2
Turner OR, 1199 ....20 B2
Turner Co. GA, 9504 ....129 D4
Turner Co. SD, 8849 ....27 F4
Turners Falls MA, 4441 ....94 C1
Turnersville NJ, 3867 ....146 C4
Turon KS, 436 ....43 D4
Turpin Hills OH, 4960 ....204 C3
Turrell AR, 957 ....118 B1
Turtle Creek PA, 6076 ....250 D2
Turtle Lake ND, 580 ....18 C3
Turtle Lake WI, 1065 ....67 E3
Tusayan AZ, 562 ....47 D2
Tuscaloosa AL, 77906 ....127 E1
Tuscaloosa Co. AL, 164875 ....119 E4
Tuscarawas OH, 934 ....91 E4

Tyler MN, 1218 ....27 F3
Tyler TX, 83650 ....124 A2
Tyler Co. TX, 20871 ....132 C1
Tyler Co. WV, 9592 ....101 F2
Tylersport PA, 950 ....146 C1
Tylertown MS, 1910 ....134 B1
Tyndall SD, 1239 ....35 E1
Tyrone GA, 3916 ....120 C4
Tyrone NM, 500 ....55 F2
Tyrone OK, 880 ....50 B1
Tyrone PA, 5528 ....92 C3
Tyronza AR, 918 ....118 B1
Tyrrell Co. NC, 4149 ....113 F4
Ty Ty GA, 716 ....129 D4

U
Ubly MI, 873 ....76 C2
Ucon ID, 943 ....23 E4
Udall KS, 794 ....43 F4
Uhrichsville OH, 5662 ....91 E4
Ukiah CA, 15497 ....36 A2

Union Bridge MD, 989 ....144 B1
Union City GA, 11621 ....120 C4
Union City IN, 3622 ....90 A4
Union City IN, 1804 ....90 A1
Union City NJ, 67088 ....148 B4
Union City OH, 1767 ....90 A4
Union City OK, 1375 ....51 E3
Union City TN, 10876 ....108 C3
Union Co. AR, 45629 ....125 E1
Union Co. FL, 13442 ....138 C3
Union Co. GA, 17289 ....120 C2
Union Co. IL, 18293 ....108 C4
Union Co. IN, 7349 ....100 B1
Union Co. IA, 12309 ....86 B3
Union Co. KY, 15637 ....109 D1
Union Co. MS, 25362 ....118 C3
Union Co. NJ, 522541 ....147 E1
Union Co. NM, 4174 ....49 F1
Union Co. NC, 123677 ....122 B2
Union Co. OH, 40909 ....90 C4
Union Co. OR, 24530 ....21 F2
Union Co. PA, 41624 ....93 D3
Union Co. SC, 29881 ....121 F1

Upland CA, 68393 ....229 G2
Upland IN, 3803 ....89 F4
Upland PA, 2977 ....248 A4
Upper Arlington OH, 33686 ....101 F5
Upper Darby PA, 1900 ....248 B3
Upper Lake CA, 989 ....36 A2
Upper Marlboro MD, 648 ....144 C3
Upper Saddle River NJ, 7741 ....148 B3
Upper Sandusky OH, 6533 ....90 C3
Upshur Co. TX, 35291 ....124 B2
Upshur Co. WV, 23404 ....102 A3
Upson Co. GA, 27597 ....129 D2
Upton KY, 654 ....110 A1
Upton MA, 2326 ....150 C2
Upton WY, 872 ....25 F3
Upton Co. TX, 3404 ....58 A4
Urania LA, 700 ....125 E3
Urbana IA, 1019 ....87 E1
Urbana IL, 36395 ....88 C4
Urbana OH, 11613 ....90 B4
Urbancrest OH, 868 ....206 A3
Urbandale IA, 29072 ....86 C2
Urbanna VA, 543 ....113 F1
Urich MO, 499 ....96 C3
Ursa IL, 591 ....87 F4
Usquepaug RI, 350 ....150 C4
Utah Co. UT, 368536 ....39 E1
Utica IL, 591 ....100 A4
Utica MI, 4577 ....210 C1
Utica MS, 966 ....126 A3
Utica NE, 844 ....35 E4
Utica NY, 60651 ....79 E3
Utica OH, 2130 ....91 D4
Utica SC, 1322 ....121 E1
Uvalda GA, 530 ....129 F3
Uvalde TX, 15149 ....60 C3
Uvalde Co. TX, 25926 ....60 C3
Uxbridge MA, 3300 ....150 C2

V
Vacaville CA, 88625 ....36 B3
Vader WA, 590 ....12 B4
Vadito NM, 242 ....49 D2
Vadnais Hts. MN, 13069 ....235 D1
Vado NM, 3003 ....56 C3
Vaiden MS, 840 ....126 C1
Vail AZ, 2484 ....55 D3

Vail CO, 4531 ....41 D1
Vails Gate NY, 3319 ....148 B1
Val Verde Co. TX, 44856 ....60 B2
Val Verde Park CA, 1472 ....52 C2
Vamo FL, 5285 ....140 B4
Van TX, 2362 ....124 A2
Van Alstyne TX, 2502 ....59 F1
Van Buren AR, 18986 ....116 C1
Van Buren IN, 935 ....89 F3
Van Buren ME, 2345 ....85 E1
Van Buren MO, 845 ....107 F2
Van Buren Co. AR, 16192 ....117 E1
Van Buren Co. IA, 7809 ....87 E3
Van Buren Co. MI, 76263 ....75 F4
Van Buren Co. TN, 5508 ....110 A4
Vance AL, 600 ....127 F1
Vanceboro NC, 898 ....115 D3
Vanceburg KY, 1731 ....100 C3
Vance Co. NC, 42954 ....113 D3
Vancleave MS, 4910 ....135 D2
Vancouver WA, 143560 ....20 C1
Vandalia IL, 6975 ....98 C3
Vandalia MO, 2529 ....97 F2
Vandalia OH, 14603 ....100 B1
Vandenberg Vil. CA, 5802 ....52 A1
Vander NC, 1204 ....123 D2
Vanderbilt MI, 587 ....70 C3
Vanderburgh Co. IN, 171922 ....99 D4
Vandercook Lake MI, 4809 ....90 B1
Vandergrift PA, 5455 ....92 A4
Vandling PA, 738 ....93 F2
Vanhiseville NJ, 700 ....147 E2
Van Horn TX, 2435 ....57 D4
Van Horne IA, 716 ....87 E1
Van Lear KY, 1100 ....111 E1
Van Meter IA, 866 ....86 C2
Vansant VA, 989 ....111 E2
Van Vleck TX, 1411 ....132 A4
Van Wert OH, 10690 ....90 B3
Van Wert Co. OH, 29659 ....90 B3
Van Zandt Co. TX, 48140 ....124 A2
Vardaman MS, 1065 ....118 C4
Varnamtown NC, 481 ....123 E4
Varnell GA, 1491 ....120 B2
Varnville SC, 2074 ....130 B2
Vashon WA, 10123 ....262 A4
Vashon Hts. WA, 1100 ....262 A3
Vass NC, 750 ....122 C1
Vassalboro ME, 350 ....82 C2
Vassar MI, 2823 ....76 B3
Vaughn MT, 701 ....15 F3
Vaughn NM, 539 ....49 D4
Veazie ME, 1500 ....83 D1
Veblen SD, 281 ....27 E1
Veedersburg IN, 2299 ....89 D4
Vega TX, 936 ....50 A3
Velma OK, 664 ....51 E4
Velva ND, 1049 ....18 B2
Venango Co. PA, 57565 ....92 A2
Veneta OR, 2755 ....20 B3
Venice FL, 17764 ....140 B4
Venice IL, 2528 ....256 C2
Venice LA, 2220 ....134 C4
Venice Gardens FL, 7466 ....140 C4
Ventnor City NJ, 12910 ....147 F4
Ventura CA, 100916 ....52 B2
Ventura IA, 670 ....72 C3
Ventura Co. CA, 753197 ....52 B2
Venus TX, 910 ....59 E3
Veradale WA, 9387 ....14 B3
Verden OK, 659 ....51 E3
Verdi NV, 2949 ....37 D1
Verdigre NE, 519 ....35 E1
Vergennes VT, 2741 ....81 D2
Vermilion OH, 10927 ....91 D2
Vermilion Co. IL, 83919 ....89 D4

Tulsa OK

Bixby C3
Bowden A3
Broken Arrow C3
Catoosa C1
Jenks B3
Oakhurst A3
Sand Sprs. A2
Sapulpa A3
Tiger C1
Tulsa B2

Vicksburg MS

Tryon NC, 1760 ....121 F1
Tryon OK, 448 ....51 F2
Tsaile AZ, 1078 ....48 A2
Tualatin OR, 22791 ....20 C2
Tubac AZ, 949 ....55 D4
Tuba City AZ, 8225 ....47 E2
Tuckahoe NY, 1741 ....149 E3
Tucker MS, 534 ....126 C2
Tucker Co. WV, 7321 ....102 B2
Tuckerman AR, 1757 ....107 F4
Tuckerton NJ, 3517 ....147 E4
Tucson AZ, 486699 ....55 D4
Tucumcari NM, 5989 ....49 F3
Tukwila WA, 17181 ....262 B4
Tulalip WA, 1571 ....262 B1
Tulare CA, 43994 ....45 D3
Tulare SD, 221 ....27 E3
Tulare Co. CA, 368021 ....45 D3
Tularosa NM, 2864 ....56 C2
Tulelake CA, 1020 ....29 D2
Tulia TX, 5117 ....50 A4
Tullahoma TN, 17994 ....120 A1
Tullos LA, 419 ....125 E3
Tully NY, 924 ....79 E4
Tullytown PA, 2031 ....147 D2
Tulsa OK, 393049 ....51 F2
Tulsa Co. OK, 563299 ....106 A4
Tuluksak AK, 428 ....154 B3
Tumacacori AZ, 569 ....55 D4
Tunica MS, 1132 ....118 B2
Tunica Co. MS, 9227 ....118 B2
Tunkhannock PA, 1911 ....93 E2
Tunnel Hill GA, 1209 ....120 B2

Tuscarawas Co. OH, 90914 ....91 E4
Tuscarora PA, 939 ....93 E3
Tuscola IL, 4448 ....99 D1
Tuscola TX, 714 ....58 C3
Tuscola Co. MI, 58266 ....76 C2
Tusculum TN, 2004 ....111 E4
Tuscumbia AL, 7856 ....119 E2
Tuscumbia MO, 218 ....97 E4
Tuskegee AL, 11846 ....128 B2
Tustin CA, 67504 ....229 F5
Tuttle OK, 4294 ....51 E3
Tutwiler MS, 1364 ....118 A3
Tuxedo Park NY, 731 ....148 B2
Twain Harte CA, 2586 ....37 D3
Twentynine Palms CA, 14764 ....46 A4
Twiggs Co. GA, 10590 ....129 E2
Twin Bridges MT, 400 ....23 E1
Twin City GA, 1752 ....129 F2
Twin Falls ID, 34469 ....30 C1
Twin Falls Co. ID, 64284 ....30 C1
Twin Lake MI, 1613 ....75 F3
Twin Lakes CA, 5533 ....236 D1
Twin Lakes GA, 750 ....137 F1
Twin Lakes MN, 1069 ....48 A2
Twin Lakes WI, 5124 ....74 C4
Twin Rivers NJ, 7422 ....147 E2
Twin Valley MN, 865 ....19 F3
Twisp WA, 938 ....13 E2
Two Harbors MN, 3613 ....64 C4
Two Rivers WI, 12639 ....75 D1
Tybee Island GA, 3392 ....130 C3
Tye TX, 1158 ....58 C3

Ulah NC, 800 ....122 C1
Uledi PA, 1100 ....102 B1
Ulen MN, 532 ....19 F3
Ullin IL, 779 ....108 C2
Ulm MT, 750 ....15 F3
Ulster Co. NY, 177749 ....148 A1
Ulysses KS, 5960 ....42 B4
Ulysses PA, 684 ....92 C1
Umatilla FL, 2214 ....141 D1
Umatilla OR, 4978 ....21 E1
Umatilla Co. OR, 70548 ....21 E1
Unadilla GA, 2772 ....129 D3
Unadilla NY, 1127 ....79 E4
Unalakleet AK, 747 ....154 B2
Unalaska AK, 4283 ....154 A4
Uncasville CT, 1500 ....149 F1
Underhill VT, 1200 ....81 D2
Underwood IA, 688 ....86 A2
Underwood ND, 812 ....18 B3
Unicoi TN, 3519 ....111 E4
Unicoi Co. TN, 17667 ....111 E4
Union IL, 576 ....88 C1
Union KY, 2893 ....100 B3
Union ME, 475 ....82 C3
Union MS, 2021 ....126 C2
Union MO, 7757 ....97 F3
Union NH, 1300 ....81 F4
Union NJ, 54405 ....148 A4
Union OH, 5574 ....100 B1
Union OR, 1926 ....21 F2
Union SC, 8793 ....121 F2
Union WV, 548 ....112 A1

Union Co. SD, 12584 ....35 F1
Union Co. TN, 17808 ....110 C3
Union Gap WA, 5621 ....13 D4
Union Grove WI, 4322 ....74 C4
Union Hall VA, 957 ....112 B2
Union Lake MI, 5000 ....210 A1
Union Par. LA, 22803 ....125 E1
Union Pt. GA, 1669 ....121 E4
Union Park FL, 10191 ....246 D2
Union Sprs. AL, 3670 ....128 B3
Union Sprs. NY, 1074 ....79 D3
Uniontown AL, 1636 ....127 E2
Uniontown KY, 1064 ....109 D1
Uniontown OH, 2802 ....91 E3
Uniontown PA, 12422 ....102 B1
Unionville CT, 5100 ....149 E1
Unionville GA, 2074 ....129 E4
Unionville MI, 605 ....76 B2
Unionville MO, 2041 ....97 D1
Unionville NV, 250 ....29 F4
Unionville NY, 536 ....148 A2
Unionville NC, 4797 ....122 B2
Unionville PA, 1200 ....146 B3
Unity ME, 486 ....82 C2
Universal City TX, 14849 ....61 D2
University City MO, 37428 ....256 B2
University Hts. NY, 4138 ....241 G3
University Hts. OH, 14146 ....204 G2
University Park FL, 536 ....87 D2
University Park MD, 2318 ....270 E2
University Park NM, 2732 ....56 C3
University Park TX, 23324 ....207 D3
University Place WA, 29933 ....12 C3

Waco TX

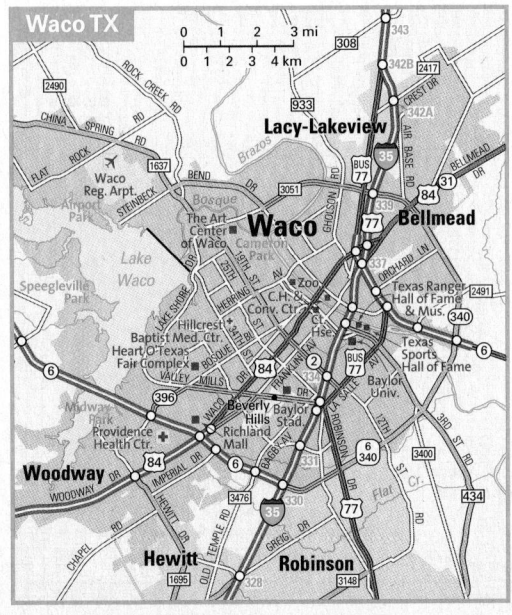

Figures after entries indicate population, page number, and grid reference.

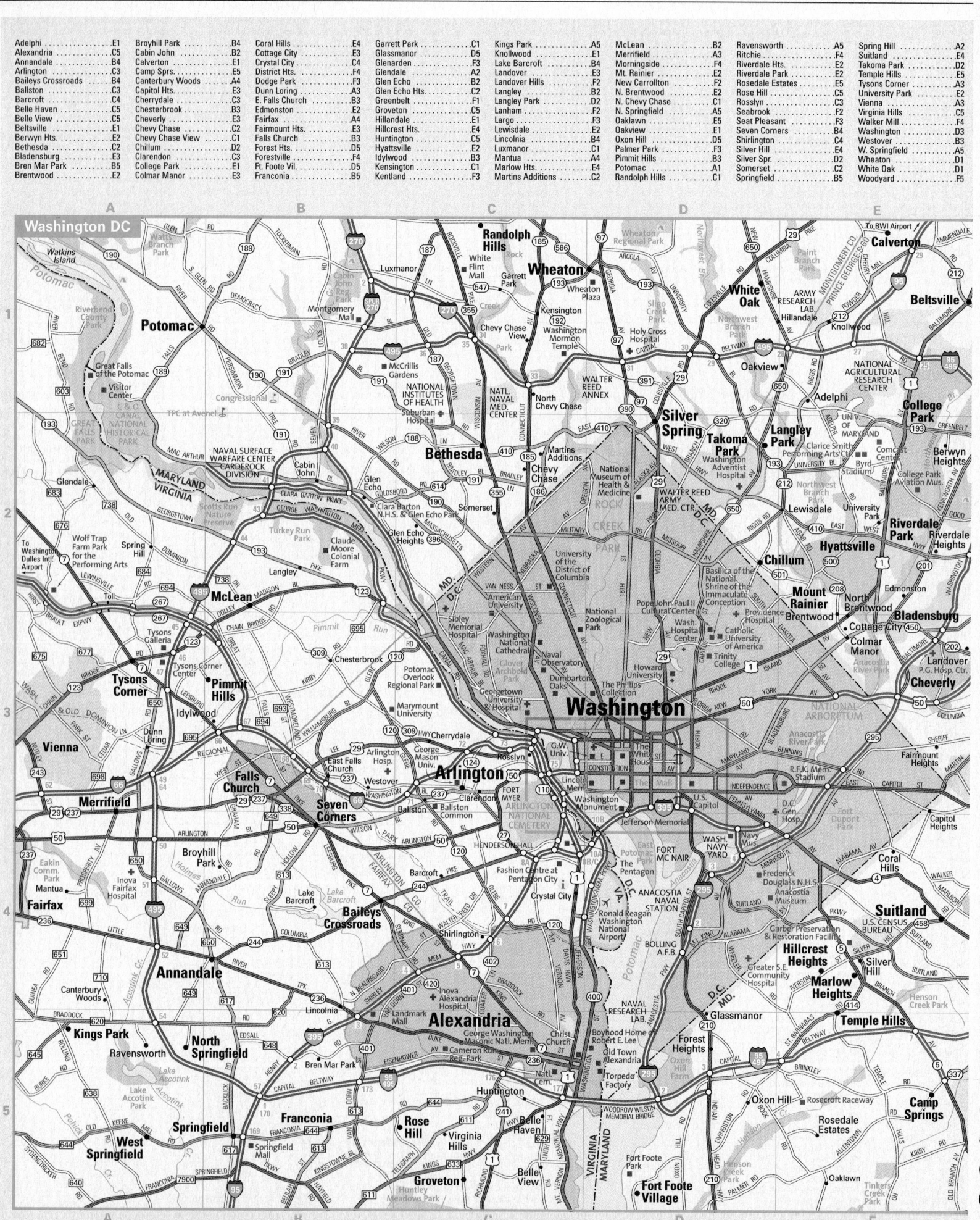

Washington DC

Vermilion Parish—Waynesboro 271

Entries in **bold** indicate counties or parishes. Entries in color indicate cities with detailed inset maps.

Vermilion Par. LA, 53807 133 E3
Vermillion SD, 9765 35 F1
Vermillion Co. IN, 16788 99 E1
Vermont IL, 792 88 A4
Vermontville MI, 789 76 A4
Vernal UT, 7714 32 A4
Verndale MN, 575 64 A4
Vernon AL, 2143 119 D4
Vernon CT, 28063 150 A3
Vernon FL, 743 136 C2
Vernon IN, 330 100 A2
Vernon MI, 847 76 B3
Vernon NY, 1155 79 E3
Vernon TX, 11660 51 D4
Vernon VT, 400 94 C1
Vernon Co. MO, 20454 96 C4
Vernon Co. WI, 28056 73 F2
Vernon Hills IL, 20120 203 C1
Vernonia OR, 2228 20 B1
Vernon Par. LA, 52531 125 D4
Vernon Valley NJ, 1737 148 A2
Vero Beach FL, 17705 141 E3
Verona MS, 3334 119 D3
Verona MO, 714 106 C2
Verona NJ, 13533 148 A3
Verona NC, 700 115 D4
Verona PA, 3124 250 D1
Verona VA, 3638 102 C4
Verona WI, 7052 74 B3
Verplanck NY, 777 148 B2
Versailles CT, 750 149 F1
Versailles IN, 1784 100 A2
Versailles KY, 7511 100 B4
Versailles MO, 2565 97 D3
Versailles OH, 2589 90 B4
Vesper WI, 541 68 A4
Vestal NY, 3900 93 E1
Vestal Ctr. NY, 850 93 E1
Vestavia Hills AL, 24476 119 F4
Vevay IN, 1735 100 A3
Vian OK, 1362 116 B1
Viborg SD, 832 35 F1
Viburnum MO, 825 107 F1
Vici OK, 668 51 D2
Vicksburg MI, 2320 89 F1
Vicksburg MS, 26407 126 A2
Victor CO, 445 41 E2
Victor ID, 840 23 F4
Victor IA, 952 87 E1
Victor MT, 859 15 D4
Victor NY, 2433 78 C3
Victoria KS, 1208 43 D2
Victoria MN, 4025 66 C4
Victoria TX, 60603 61 F3
Victoria VA, 1821 113 D2
Victoria Co. TX, 84088 61 F3
Victorville CA, 64029 53 D2
Victory Gardens NJ, 1546 148 A3
Vidalia GA, 10491 129 F3
Vidalia LA, 4543 125 F4
Vidor TX, 11440 132 C2
Vienna GA, 2973 129 D3
Vienna IL, 1234 108 C1
Vienna LA, 424 125 E2
Vienna MO, 628 97 E4
Vienna VA, 14453 144 B3
Vienna WV, 10861 101 E2
View Park CA, 10958 228 C3
Vigo Co. IN, 105848 99 E2
Vilano Beach FL, 2533 139 E3
Vilas Co. WI, 21033 68 B2
Village Green NY, 3945 79 D3
Village Green PA, 8279 248 A4
Villages of Oriole FL, 4758 143 F1
Villa Grove IL, 2553 99 D1
Villa Hills KY, 7948 204 A3
Villa Park CA, 5999 229 F4
Villa Park IL, 22075 203 C4
Villa Rica GA, 4134 120 B4
Villa Ridge MO, 2417 98 A3
Villas NJ, 9064 104 C4
Ville Platte LA, 8145 133 E1
Villisca IA, 1344 86 B3
Vilonia AR, 2106 117 E1
Vimy Ridge AR, 600 117 E2
Vinalhaven ME, 750 83 D3
Vincennes IN, 18701 99 D3
Vincent AL, 1853 128 A1
Vincent CA, 15097 52 C2
Vincentown NJ, 750 147 D3
Vinco PA, 1429 92 B4
Vine Grove KY, 4169 110 A1
Vine Hill CA, 3260 259 D1
Vineland MN, 607 66 C1
Vineland NJ, 56271 145 F1
Vinemont AL, 425 119 F3
Vineyard Haven MA, 2048 151 E4
Vinings GA, 9677 190 C2
Vinita OK, 6472 106 B3
Vinita Park MO, 1924 256 B2
Vinton CA, 387 37 D1
Vinton IA, 5102 87 E1
Vinton LA, 3338 133 D2
Vinton TX, 1892 56 C3
Vinton VA, 7782 112 B2
Vinton Co. OH, 12806 101 E2
Viola DE, 156 145 E3
Viola IL, 956 88 A2
Viola WI, 667 73 F2
Violet LA, 8555 134 C3
Virden IL, 3488 98 B2
Virgin UT, 394 39 D4
Virginia IL, 1728 98 A1
Virginia MN, 9157 64 C3
Virginia Beach VA, 425257 114 B4
Virginia City MT, 130 23 E2
Virginia City NV, 800 37 D2
Virginia Gardens FL, 2348 233 A4
Viroqua WI, 4335 73 F2
Visalia CA, 91565 45 D3
Vista CA, 89857 53 D3
Vivian LA, 4031 124 C1
Volcano HI, 2231 153 F4
Volga SD, 1435 27 F3
Volin SD, 207 35 E1
Voluntown CT, 850 149 F1
Volusia Co. FL, 443343 139 E4
Vonore TN, 1162 120 C1
Voorheesville NY, 2705 94 B1

W

Wabash IN, 11743 89 F3
Wabasha MN, 2599 73 E1
Wabasha Co. MN, 21610 73 E1
Wabash Co. IL, 12937 99 D3
Wabash Co. IN, 34960 89 F3
Wabasso FL, 918 141 E3
Wabasso MN, 643 72 A1
Wabaunsee Co. KS, 6885 43 F2
Waco TX, 113726 59 E4
Waconia MN, 6814 66 C4
Waddington NY, 923 80 B1
Wade MS, 491 135 D2
Wade NC, 480 123 D1
Wadena MN, 4294 64 A4
Wadena Co. MN, 13713 64 A4
Wadesboro NC, 5552 122 B2
Wading River NY, 6668 149 D3
Wadley AL, 640 128 B1
Wadley GA, 2088 129 F1
Wadsworth NV, 881 37 D1
Wadsworth OH, 18437 91 E3
Waelder TX, 947 61 E2
Wagener SC, 863 122 A4
Waggaman LA, 9435 239 B2
Wagner SD, 1675 35 E1
Wagoner OK, 7669 106 A4
Wagoner Co. OK, 57491 106 A4
Wagon Mound NM, 369 49 E2
Wagontown PA, 1100 146 B3
Wagram NC, 801 122 C2
Wahiawa HI, 16151 152 A2
Wahkiakum Co. WA, 3824 12 B4
Wahoo NE, 3942 35 F3
Wahpeton ND, 8586 27 F1
Waialua HI, 3761 152 A2
Waianae HI, 10506 152 A3
Waiehu HI, 7310 153 D1
Waihee HI, 7310 153 D1
Waikane HI, 726 152 A2
Waikapu HI, 1115 153 D1
Waikoloa Vil. HI, 4806 153 E3
Wailua HI, 2083 152 B1
Wailuku HI, 12296 153 D1
Waimalu HI, 29371 152 A3
Waimanalo HI, 3664 152 B3
Waimanalo Beach HI, 4271 152 B3
Waimea HI, 1787 152 B1
Waimea (Kamuela) HI, 7028 153 E2
Wainscott NY, 628 149 F3
Wainwright AK, 546 154 C1
Waipahu HI, 33108 152 A3
Waipio Acres HI, 5236 152 A3
Waite Park MN, 6568 66 C3
Waitsburg WA, 1212 13 F4
Waitsfield VT, 350 81 D2
Wakarusa IN, 1618 89 F2
Wakeby MA, 1600 151 E3
Wake Co. NC, 627846 113 D4
WaKeeney KS, 1924 42 C2
Wakefield KS, 838 43 F2
Wakefield MA, 24804 151 D1
Wakefield MI, 2085 65 E4
Wakefield NE, 1411 35 F2
Wakefield RI, 8468 150 C4
Wakefield VA, 1038 113 F2
Wake Forest NC, 12588 113 D4
Wakeman OH, 951 91 D2
Wake Vil. TX, 5129 124 C1
Wakonda SD, 374 35 F1
Wakulla Co. FL, 22863 137 E2
Walbridge OH, 2546 267 B2
Walcott IA, 1528 87 F2
Walden CO, 734 33 D4
Walden NY, 6164 148 B1
Walden TN, 1960 120 B1
Waldo AR, 1594 125 D1
Waldo FL, 821 138 C3
Waldoboro ME, 1291 82 C2
Waldo Co. ME, 36280 82 C2
Waldorf MD, 22312 144 B4
Waldport OR, 2050 20 B3
Waldron AR, 3508 116 C2
Waldron IN, 1100 100 A2
Waldron MI, 590 90 B1
Wales MA, 850 150 B2
Wales WI, 2523 74 C3
Waleska GA, 616 120 C3
Walford IA, 1224 87 E1
Walhalla ND, 1057 19 E1
Walhalla SC, 3801 121 E2
Walker IA, 750 73 E4
Walker LA, 4801 134 A2
Walker MI, 21842 75 F3
Walker MN, 1069 64 A3
Walker Co. AL, 70713 119 E4
Walker Co. GA, 61053 120 B2
Walker Co. TX, 61758 132 A1
Walker Mill MD, 11104 271 F4
Walkersville MD, 5192 144 A1
Walkerton IN, 2274 89 E2
Walkertown NC, 4009 112 B4
Walker Valley NY, 758 148 A1
Walkerville MT, 714 23 E1
Wall PA, 727 250 D3
Wall SD, 818 26 B3
Wallace ID, 960 14 B3
Wallace NC, 3344 123 E2
Wallace VA, 550 111 E3
Wallace Co. KS, 1749 42 B2
Walla Walla WA, 29686 21 F1
Walla Walla Co. WA, 55180 21 F1
Walled Lake MI, 6713 210 A2
Waller TX, 2092 61 F2
Waller Co. TX, 32663 132 A3
Wallingford CT, 17509 149 D1
Wallingford VT, 948 81 D4
Wallington NJ, 11583 148 B3
Wallis TX, 1172 61 F2
Wallkill NY, 2143 148 B1
Wall Lake IA, 841 72 B4
Wallowa OR, 869 22 A1
Wallowa Co. OR, 7226 22 A1
Walnut CA, 30004 229 F3
Walnut IL, 1461 88 B2
Walnut IA, 778 86 A2
Walnut MS, 754 118 C2
Walnut Cove NC, 1465 112 B3
Walnut Creek CA, 64296 36 B4
Walnut Creek NC, 859 123 E1
Walnut Grove AL, 710 120 A3
Walnut Grove CA, 669 36 C3
Walnut Grove GA, 1241 121 D4
Walnut Grove MN, 599 72 A1
Walnut Grove MS, 488 126 C2
Walnut Grove MO, 630 106 C1
Walnut Grove TN, 677 109 F3
Walnut Hill TN, 2756 111 E3
Walnut Park CA, 16180 228 D3
Walnutport PA, 2043 93 F3
Walnut Ridge AR, 4925 108 A4
Walnut Sprs. TX, 755 59 E3
Walpole MA, 5867 151 D2
Walpole NH, 700 81 E4
Walsenburg CO, 4182 41 E4
Walsh CO, 723 42 A4
Walsh Co. ND, 11119 19 E2
Walterboro SC, 5153 130 C1
Walterhill TN, 1523 109 F4
Walters OK, 2657 51 D4
Walthall MS, 170 118 C4
Walthall Co. MS, 15156 134 B1
Waltham MA, 59226 151 D1
Walthill NE, 909 35 F2
Walthourville GA, 4030 130 B3
Walton IN, 1069 89 F3
Walton KY, 2450 100 B3
Walton NY, 3070 93 F1
Walton Co. FL, 40601 136 B2
Walton Co. GA, 60687 121 D4
Walton Hills OH, 2400 204 G3
Walworth WI, 2304 74 C4
Walworth Co. SD, 5974 26 C2
Walworth Co. WI, 93759 74 C4
Wamac IL, 1378 98 C3
Wamego KS, 4246 43 F2
Wampsville NY, 561 79 E3
Wamsutter WY, 261 32 C3
Wanakah NY, 3200 78 A4
Wanamassa NJ, 4551 147 E2
Wanamingo MN, 1007 73 D1
Wanaque NJ, 10266 148 A3
Wanatah IN, 1013 89 E2
Wanblee SD, 641 26 B4
Wanchese NC, 1527 115 F2
Wapakoneta OH, 9474 90 B4
Wapanucka OK, 445 51 F4
Wapato WA, 4582 13 D4
Wapella IL, 651 88 C4
Wapello IA, 2124 87 F2
Wapello Co. IA, 36051 87 D3
Waples TX, 800 59 E3
Wappingers Falls NY, 4929 148 B1
War WV, 788 111 F1
Ward AR, 2580 117 F2
Ward Co. ND, 58795 18 B2
Ward Co. TX, 10909 57 F4
Warden WA, 2544 13 E4
Wardner ID, 215 14 B3
Wardsville MO, 976 97 E3
Ware MA, 6174 150 B1
Ware Co. GA, 35483 129 F4
Wareham MA, 2874 151 E3
Ware Shoals SC, 2363 121 F3
Waretown NJ, 1582 147 E3
Warm Beach WA, 2040 12 C2
Warm Sprs. GA, 485 128 C1
Warm Sprs. OR, 2431 21 D3
Warm Sprs. VA, 200 102 B4
Warner NH, 650 81 F4
Warner OK, 1430 116 A1
Warner SD, 419 27 D2
Warner Robins GA, 48804 129 D2
Warr Acres OK, 9735 244 D2
Warren AR, 6442 117 E4
Warren IL, 1496 74 A4
Warren IN, 1272 90 A3
Warren ME, 900 82 C2
Warren MA, 1452 150 B2
Warren MI, 138247 76 C4
Warren MN, 1678 19 F2
Warren OH, 46832 91 F2
Warren PA, 10259 92 B1
Warren RI, 11360 151 D3
Warren Co. GA, 6336 129 F1
Warren Co. IL, 18735 88 A3
Warren Co. IN, 8419 89 D4
Warren Co. IA, 40671 86 C2
Warren Co. KY, 92522 109 F2
Warren Co. MS, 49644 126 A2
Warren Co. MO, 24525 97 F3
Warren Co. NJ, 102437 93 F3
Warren Co. NY, 63303 80 C3
Warren Co. NC, 19972 113 D3
Warren Co. OH, 158383 100 C2
Warren Co. PA, 43863 92 B1
Warren Co. TN, 38276 110 A4
Warren Co. VA, 31584 103 D2
Warren Glen NJ, 650 146 C1
Warren Park IN, 1656 99 F1
Warrensburg IL, 1289 98 C1
Warrensburg MO, 16340 96 C3
Warrensburg NY, 3208 80 C4
Warrensville PA, 1100 93 D2
Warrensville Hts. OH, 15109 204 G2
Warrenton GA, 2013 129 F1
Warrenton MO, 5281 97 F3
Warrenton NC, 811 113 D3
Warrenton OR, 4096 20 B1
Warrenton VA, 6670 103 D3
Warrenville IL, 13363 203 A4
Warrick Co. IN, 52383 99 E4
Warrington FL, 15207 135 F2
Warrington PA, 5400 146 C2
Warrior AL, 3169 119 F4
Warrior Run PA, 624 261 A2
Warroad MN, 1722 64 A1
Warsaw IL, 1793 87 F4
Warsaw IN, 12415 89 F2
Warsaw KY, 1811 100 B3
Warsaw MN, 550 72 C1
Warsaw MO, 2070 97 D4
Warsaw NY, 3814 78 B4
Warsaw NC, 3051 123 E2
Warsaw OH, 781 91 D4
Warsaw VA, 1375 103 E4
Warson Woods MO, 1983 256 B2
Wartburg TN, 890 110 B4
Wartrace TN, 548 120 A1
Warwick NY, 6412 148 A2
Warwick RI, 85808 150 C3
Wasatch Co. UT, 15215 31 F4
Wasco CA, 21263 45 D4
Wasco OR, 381 21 D1
Wasco Co. OR, 23791 21 D2
Waseca MN, 8493 72 C1
Waseca Co. MN, 19526 72 C1
Washakie Co. WY, 8289 24 C4
Washburn IL, 1147 88 B3
Washburn IA, 1000 73 E4
Washburn ME, 800 85 D2
Washburn ND, 1389 18 B3
Washburn WI, 2280 65 D4
Washburn Co. WI, 16036 67 E2
Washington CT, 600 148 C1
Washington DC, 572059 144 B3
Washington GA, 4295 121 E4
Washington IL, 10841 88 B3
Washington IN, 11380 99 E3
Washington IA, 7047 87 E2
Washington KS, 1223 43 F1
Washington LA, 1082 133 F2
Washington MO, 13243 97 F3
Washington NJ, 6712 93 F3
Washington NC, 9583 115 D3
Washington OK, 520 51 E3
Washington PA, 15268 91 F4
Washington UT, 8186 46 C1
Washington VT, 350 81 E2
Washington VA, 183 103 D3
Washington WV, 1170 101 E2
Washington Co. AL, 18097 127 E4
Washington Co. AR, 157715 106 B4
Washington Co. CO, 4926 34 A4
Washington Co. FL, 20973 136 C2
Washington Co. GA, 21176 129 E1
Washington Co. ID, 9977 22 A3
Washington Co. IL, 15148 98 B4
Washington Co. IN, 27223 99 F3
Washington Co. IA, 20670 87 E2
Washington Co. KS, 6483 43 E1
Washington Co. KY, 10916 110 B1
Washington Co. ME, 33941 83 E1
Washington Co. MD, 131923 103 D1
Washington Co. MN, 201130 67 D3
Washington Co. MS, 62977 126 A1
Washington Co. MO, 23344 97 F4
Washington Co. NE, 18780 35 F3
Washington Co. NY, 61042 81 D4
Washington Co. NC, 13723 113 F4
Washington Co. OH, 63251 101 E2
Washington Co. OK, 48996 106 A2
Washington Co. OR, 445342 20 B2
Washington Co. PA, 202897 92 A4
Washington Co. RI, 123546 150 C4
Washington Co. TN, 107198 111 E3
Washington Co. TX, 30373 61 F2
Washington Co. UT, 90354 38 C4
Washington Co. VT, 58039 81 E2
Washington Co. VA, 51103 111 F3
Washington Co. WI, 117493 74 C2
Washington C.H. OH, 13524 100 C1
Washington Crossing NJ, 950 147 D2
Washington Crossing PA, 1300 147 D2
Washington Hts. NY, 1318 148 A1
Washington Par. LA, 43926 134 B1
Washington Park IL, 5345 256 D2
Washington Terrace UT, 8551 244 A2
Washingtonville NY, 5851 148 B1
Washingtonville OH, 789 91 F3
Washita Co. OK, 11508 51 D3
Washoe Co. NV, 339486 29 E4
Washougal WA, 8595 20 C2
Washtenaw Co. MI, 322895 90 B1
Wasilla AK, 5469 154 C3
Waskom TX, 2068 124 C2
Wataga IL, 857 88 A3
Watauga TN, 403 111 E3
Watauga TX, 21908 207 B2
Watauga Co. NC, 42695 111 F3
Watchung NJ, 5613 147 E1
Waterboro ME, 800 82 B3
Waterbury CT, 107271 149 D1
Waterbury VT, 1706 81 D2
Waterbury Ctr. VT, 850 81 E2
Waterford CA, 6924 36 C4
Waterford CT, 2935 149 F2
Waterford MI, 73150 76 B4
Waterford NY, 2204 188 E1
Waterford PA, 1449 92 A1
Waterford WI, 4048 74 C4
Waterford Works NJ, 1000 147 D4
Waterloo IL, 7614 98 A4
Waterloo IN, 2200 90 A2
Waterloo IA, 68747 73 E4
Waterloo MD, 900 144 C2
Waterloo NE, 459 35 F3
Waterloo NY, 5111 79 D3
Waterloo WI, 3259 74 B3
Waterman IL, 1224 88 C1
Water Mill NY, 1724 149 E3
Waterproof LA, 834 125 F3
Watertown CT, 5300 149 D1
Watertown FL, 2837 138 C2
Watertown MA, 32986 151 D1
Watertown MN, 3029 66 C4
Watertown NY, 26705 79 E1
Watertown SD, 20237 27 F2
Watertown TN, 1358 109 F4
Watertown WI, 21598 74 C3
Water Valley MS, 3677 118 B3
Waterville KS, 681 43 F1
Waterville ME, 15605 82 C2
Waterville MN, 1833 72 C1
Waterville NY, 1721 79 E3
Waterville OH, 4828 90 C2
Waterville WA, 1163 13 E3
Watervliet MI, 1843 89 F1
Watervliet NY, 10207 188 E2
Watford City ND, 1435 18 A3
Wathena KS, 1348 96 B1
Watkins MN, 880 66 C3
Watkins Glen NY, 2149 79 D4
Watkinsville GA, 2097 121 D4
Watonga OK, 4658 51 D2
Watonwan Co. MN, 11876 72 B1
Watseka IL, 5670 89 D3
Watson IL, 729 98 C2
Watson LA, 1400 134 A2
Watsontown PA, 2255 93 D3
Watsonville CA, 44265 44 B2
Watterson Park KY, 953 230 E2
Waubay SD, 662 27 E2
Wauchula FL, 4368 140 C3
Wauconda IL, 9448 203 B1
Waukee IA, 5126 86 C2
Waukegan IL, 87901 75 D4
Waukesha WI, 64825 74 C3
Waukesha Co. WI, 360767 74 C3
Waukomis OK, 1261 51 E2
Waukon IA, 4131 73 E3
Waunakee WI, 8995 74 B3
Wauneta NE, 625 34 B4
Waupaca WI, 5676 74 B1
Waupaca Co. WI, 51731 68 B4
Waupun WI, 10718 74 C2
Wauregan CT, 1085 150 B3
Waurika OK, 1988 51 E4
Wausa NE, 636 35 E1
Wausau WI, 38426 68 B4
Wausaukee WI, 572 68 C3
Wauseon OH, 7091 90 B2
Waushara Co. WI, 23154 74 B1
Wautoma WI, 1998 74 B1
Wauwatosa WI, 47271 234 C2
Wauzeka WI, 768 73 F3
Waveland MS, 6674 134 C2
Waverly FL, 1927 141 D2
Waverly IL, 1346 98 B1
Waverly IA, 8968 73 D4
Waverly KS, 589 96 A3
Waverly MN, 732 66 C3
Waverly MO, 806 96 C2
Waverly NE, 2448 35 F4
Waverly NY, 4607 93 E1
Waverly OH, 4433 101 D2
Waverly TN, 4028 109 D4
Waverly VA, 2309 113 E2
Waverly Hall GA, 709 128 C2
Waxahachie TX, 21426 59 F3
Waxhaw NC, 2625 122 B2
Waycross GA, 15333 129 F4
Wayland IA, 945 87 E2
Wayland MA, 1300 150 C1
Wayland MI, 3939 75 F4
Wayland NY, 1893 78 C4
Waymart PA, 1429 93 F2
Wayne IL, 2137 203 A4
Wayne MI, 19051 210 A4
Wayne NE, 5583 35 F2
Wayne NJ, 54069 148 A3
Wayne OH, 842 90 C2
Wayne OK, 714 51 E3
Wayne PA, 1000 146 C3
Wayne WV, 1105 101 D4
Wayne City IL, 1089 98 C4
Wayne Co. GA, 26565 130 A4
Wayne Co. IL, 17151 98 C3
Wayne Co. IN, 71097 100 A1
Wayne Co. IA, 6730 87 D3
Wayne Co. KY, 19923 110 B3
Wayne Co. MI, 2061162 76 B4
Wayne Co. MS, 21216 127 D4
Wayne Co. MO, 13259 108 A2
Wayne Co. NE, 9851 35 F2
Wayne Co. NY, 93765 79 D3
Wayne Co. NC, 113329 123 E1
Wayne Co. OH, 111564 91 E3
Wayne Co. PA, 47722 93 F3
Wayne Co. TN, 16842 119 E1
Wayne Co. UT, 2509 39 F3
Wayne Co. WV, 42903 101 E4
Wayne Lakes OH, 684 100 B1
Waynesboro GA, 5813 129 F1
Waynesboro MS, 5197 127 D4

F
Howard University Beltsville Campus
Capitol College
NATIONAL AGRICULTURAL RESEARCH CENTER
Greenbelt
NASA Goddard Space Flight Center
Doctors Community Hospital
New Carrollton
Seabrook
Lanham
Landover Hills
Dodge Park
Glenarden
Kentland
Palmer Park
Landover Mall
FedEx Field
Seat Pleasant
Largo
Walker Mill
Walker Mill Reg. Park
Ritchie
District Heights
Forestville
Morningside
ANDREWS AIR FORCE BASE
Woodyard
0 1 2 mi
0 1 2 3 km
1
2
3
4
5

Figures after entries indicate population, page number, and grid reference.

Entries in **bold** indicate counties or parishes. Entries in color indicate cities with detailed inset maps.

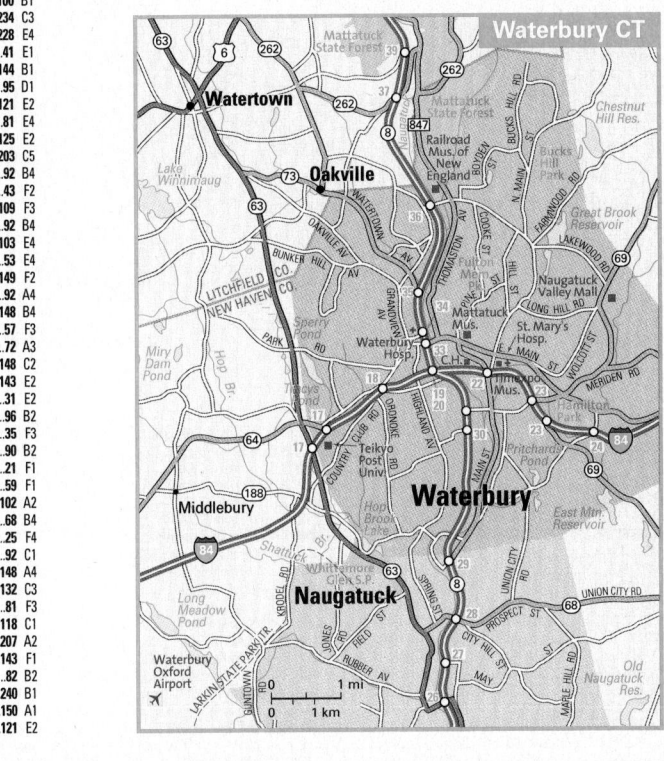

Waterbury CT

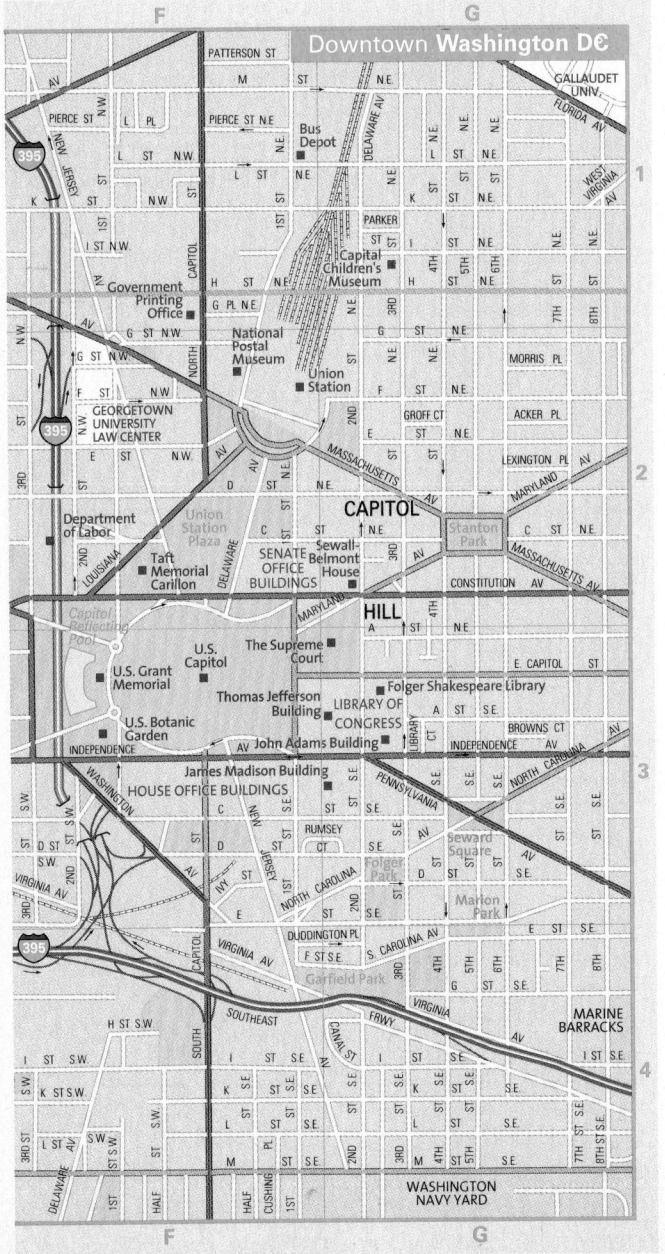

Downtown Washington DC

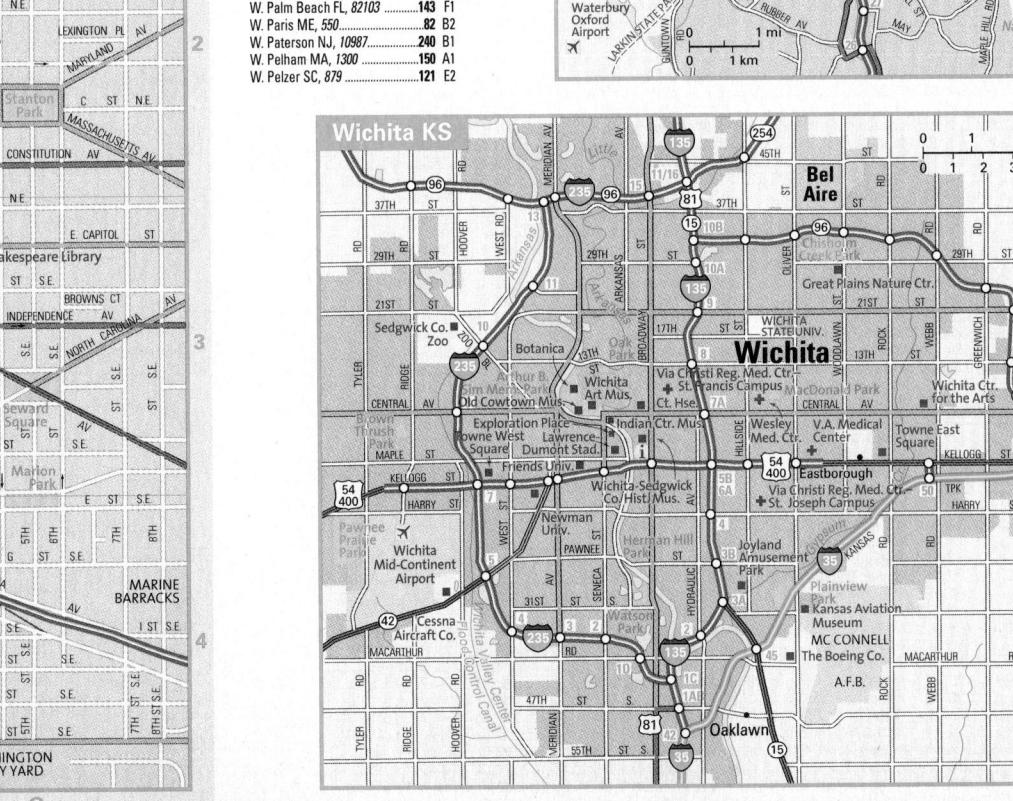

Wichita KS

274 Wewahitchka — Winnebago County

Figures after entries indicate population, page number, and grid reference.

Wewahitchka FL, *1722* ... 137 D2
Wewoka OK, *3562* ... 51 F3
Wexford Co. MI, *30484* ... 69 F4
Weyauwega WI, *1806* ... 74 B1
Weyers Cave VA, *1225* ... 102 C4
Weymouth MA, *53988* ... 151 D2
Wharton NJ, *6298* ... 148 A3
Wharton OH, *409* ... 90 C3
Wharton TX, *9237* ... 61 F3
Wharton Co. TX, *41188* ... 61 F3
What Cheer IA, *678* ... 87 E2
Whatcom Co. WA, *166814* ... 12 C1
Whately MA, *425* ... 150 A1
Wheatfield IN, *772* ... 89 E2
White Hall VA, *300* ... 103 D2
Whitehall PA, *14444* ... 250 B3
Whitehall WV, *595* ... 102 A2
Whitehall WI, *1651* ... 73 F1
White Haven PA, *1182* ... 93 F3
White Horse NJ, *9373* ... 147 D2
White Horse PA, *475* ... 146 A3
White Horse Beach MA, *2300* ... 151 E3
Whitehouse OH, *2733* ... 90 B2
White House TN, *7220* ... 109 F3
Whitehouse TX, *5346* ... 124 B3
White House Sta. NJ, *1951* ... 147 D1
White Island Shores MA, *2133* ... 151 E3
White Lake NY, *475* ... 94 A3
Whitney TX, *1833* ... 59 E3
Whitney Pt. NY, *965* ... 79 E4
Whitsett NC, *686* ... 112 B4
Whittemore IA, *530* ... 72 B3
Whittemore MI, *476* ... 76 B1
Whittier CA, *83680* ... 52 C2
Whitwell TN, *1660* ... 120 B1
Why AZ, *225* ... 54 B3
Wibaux MT, *567* ... 17 F4
Wibaux Co. MT, *1068* ... 17 F4
Wichita KS, *344284* ... 43 E4
Wichita Co. KS, *2531* ... 42 B3
Wichita Co. TX, *131664* ... 59 D1
Wichita Falls TX, *104197* ... 59 D1
Williamsburg CO, *714* ... 41 E3
Williamsburg FL, *6736* ... 246 B4
Williamsburg IA, *2622* ... 87 E2
Williamsburg KS, *351* ... 96 A3
Williamsburg KY, *5143* ... 110 C3
Williamsburg MA, *550* ... 150 A1
Williamsburg NM, *527* ... 56 B2
Williamsburg OH, *2358* ... 100 C2
Williamsburg PA, *1345* ... 92 C4
Williamsburg VA, *11998* ... 113 F2
Williamsburg Co. SC, *37217* ... 122 C4
Williams Co. ND, *19761* ... 17 F2
Williams Co. OH, *39188* ... 90 A2
Williams Creek IN, *413* ... 221 C1
Wilmar AR, *571* ... 117 F4
Wilmer AL, *500* ... 135 E1
Wilmer TX, *3393* ... 207 E3
Wilmerding PA, *2145* ... 250 D3
Wilmette IL, *27651* ... 89 D1
Wilmington DE, *72664* ... 146 B4
Wilmington IL, *5134* ... 88 C2
Wilmington NC, *75838* ... 123 E3
Wilmington OH, *11921* ... 100 C2
Wilmington VT, *800* ... 94 C1
Wilmington Island GA, *14213* ... 130 C3
Wilmington Manor DE, *8262* ... 274 D3
Wilmore KY, *5905* ... 100 B4
Wilmot AR, *786* ... 125 F1
Wilmot SD, *543* ... 27 F2
Wilsall MT, *237* ... 23 F1
Wilson AR, *939* ... 118 B1
Wilson KS, *799* ... 43 D2
Wilson LA, *668* ... 134 A1
Wilson NY, *1213* ... 78 B3
Wilson NC, *44405* ... 113 D4
Wilson OK, *1584* ... 51 E4
Wilson PA, *7682* ... 93 F3
Wilson TX, *532* ... 58 A2
Wilson WY, *1294* ... 23 F4
Wilson Co. KS, *10332* ... 106 A1
Wilson Co. NC, *73814* ... 113 E4
Wilson Co. TN, *88809* ... 109 F3
Wilson Co. TX, *32408* ... 61 E3
Wilson's Mills NC, *1291* ... 123 D1
Wilsonville AL, *1551* ... 128 A1
Wilsonville IL, *604* ... 98 B2
Wilsonville OR, *13991* ... 20 C2
Wilton AL, *580* ... 127 F1
Wilton AR, *439* ... 116 C4
Wilton CA, *4551* ... 36 C3
Wilton CT, *2000* ... 148 C2
Wilton IA, *2829* ... 87 F2
Wilton ME, *2290* ... 82 B2
Wilton NH, *1236* ... 95 D1
Wilton NY, *600* ... 80 C4
Wilton ND, *807* ... 18 C3
Wilton WI, *519* ... 73 F2
Wilton Manors FL, *12697* ... 233 C2
Wimauma FL, *4246* ... 140 C3
Wimberley TX, *3797* ... 61 D2
Wimbledon ND, *237* ... 19 D3
Winamac IN, *2418* ... 89 E3
Winchendon MA, *4246* ... 95 D1
Winchester CA, *2155* ... 53 D3
Winchester ID, *308* ... 22 B1
Winchester IL, *1650* ... 98 A1
Winchester IN, *5037* ... 90 A4
Winchester KS, *579* ... 96 A2
Winchester KY, *16724* ... 100 B4
Winchester MA, *20810* ... 151 D1
Winchester MO, *1651* ... 256 A2
Winchester NH, *1832* ... 94 C1
Winchester OH, *1025* ... 100 C3
Winchester OK, *424* ... 51 F2
Winchester OH, *1025* ... 100 C3
Winchester TN, *7329* ... 120 A1
Winchester VA, *23585* ... 103 D2
Winchester Bay OR, *488* ... 20 A4
Windber PA, *4395* ... 92 B4
Windcrest TX, *5105* ... 61 D2
Winder GA, *10201* ... 121 D3
Windermere FL, *1897* ... 141 D1
Windfall IN, *712* ... 89 F4
Wind Gap PA, *2812* ... 93 F3
Windham CT, *1000* ... 149 F1
Windham NH, *1600* ... 95 E1
Windham OH, *2806* ... 91 F2
Windham Co. CT, *109091* ... 150 B3
Windham Co. VT, *44216* ... 81 E4
Wind Lake WI, *5202* ... 74 C3
Windom MN, *4490* ... 72 B2
Window Rock AZ, *3059* ... 48 A2
Wind Pt. WI, *1853* ... 75 D4
Windsor CA, *22744* ... 36 B3
Windsor CO, *9896* ... 33 E4
Windsor CT, *3600* ... 150 A3
Windsor IL, *1125* ... 98 C2
Windsor MO, *3087* ... 96 C3
Windsor NY, *901* ... 93 F1
Windsor NC, *2283* ... 113 F4
Windsor PA, *1331* ... 103 E1
Windsor VT, *2200* ... 81 E4
Windsor VA, *916* ... 113 F2
Windsor WI, *2533* ... 74 B3
Windsor Co. VT, *57418* ... 81 E3
Windsor Hts. WV, *431* ... 91 F4
Windsor Hills CA, *10958* ... 228 C3
Windsor Locks CT, *12043* ... 150 A2
Windthorst TX, *440* ... 59 D1
Windy Hills KY, *2480* ... 230 E1
Winfall NC, *554* ... 113 F3
Winfield AL, *4540* ... 119 E4
Winfield IL, *8718* ... 203 B4
Winfield IN, *2298* ... 89 D2
Winfield IA, *1131* ... 87 F3
Winfield KS, *12206* ... 43 F4
Winfield MO, *723* ... 98 A2
Winfield TN, *911* ... 110 C3
Winfield TX, *499* ... 124 B1
Winfield WV, *1858* ... 101 E3
Wingate NC, *2406* ... 122 B2
Wingdale NY, *1500* ... 148 C1
Wingo KY, *581* ... 108 C3
Winifred MT, *156* ... 16 B3
Wink TX, *919* ... 57 F4
Winkelman AZ, *443* ... 55 D2
Winkler Co. TX, *7173* ... 57 F3
Winlock WA, *1166* ... 12 B4
Winnebago IL, *2958* ... 74 B4
Winnebago MN, *1487* ... 72 C2
Winnebago NE, *768* ... 35 F2
Winnebago Co. IL, *278418* ... 74 B4

Five Forks ... A1
Gloucester Pt. ... C2
Hayes ... C1
Lackey ... C2
Newport News ... C2
Scotland ... A2
Wicomico ... C1
Williamsburg ... A1
Yorktown ... C2

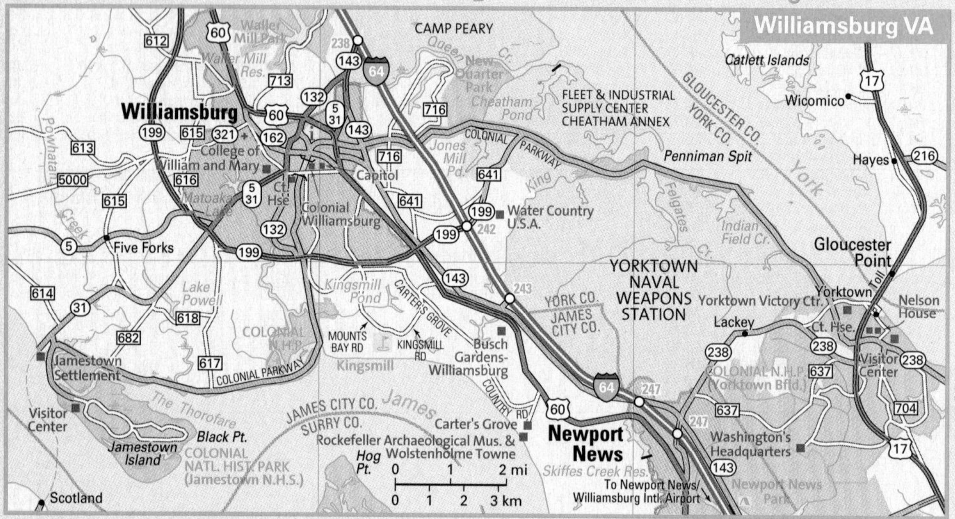

Wheatland CA, *2275* ... 36 C2
Wheatland IN, *504* ... 99 E3
Wheatland IA, *772* ... 87 F1
Wheatland WY, *3548* ... 33 E2
Wheatland Co. MT, *2259* ... 16 B4
Wheatley AR, *372* ... 118 A2
Wheaton IL, *55416* ... 89 D1
Wheaton MD, *57694* ... 144 B3
Wheaton MN, *1619* ... 27 F1
Wheaton MO, *721* ... 106 C2
Wheat Ridge CO, *32913* ... 209 B3
Wheeler MS, *300* ... 119 D2
Wheeler OR, *391* ... 20 B1
Wheeler TX, *1378* ... 50 C3
Wheeler Co. GA, *6179* ... 129 E3
Wheeler Co. NE, *886* ... 35 D2
Wheeler Co. OR, *1547* ... 21 E3
Wheeler Co. TX, *5284* ... 50 C3
Wheelersburg OH, *6471* ... 101 D3
Wheeling IL, *34496* ... 89 D1
Wheeling WV, *31419* ... 91 F4
Wheelwright KY, *1042* ... 111 E1
Wheelwright MA, *425* ... 150 B1
Whigham GA, *631* ... 137 E1
Whippany NJ, *3800* ... 148 A3
Whispering Pines NC, *2090* ... 122 C1
Whitaker PA, *1338* ... 250 C2
Whitakers NC, *799* ... 113 E4
White GA, *693* ... 120 C3
White SD, *530* ... 27 F3
White Bear Lake MN, *24325* ... 235 D1
White Bird ID, *106* ... 22 B1
White Bluff TN, *2142* ... 109 E4
White Castle LA, *1946* ... 134 A2
White Ctr. WA, *20975* ... 262 B4
White City FL, *4221* ... 141 E3
White City KS, *518* ... 43 F2
White City OR, *5466* ... 28 B2
White Cloud MI, *1420* ... 75 F2
White Co. AR, *67165* ... 117 F1
White Co. GA, *19944* ... 121 D2
White Co. IL, *15371* ... 99 D4
White Co. IN, *25267* ... 89 E3
White Co. TN, *23102* ... 110 A4
White Deer TX, *1060* ... 50 B3
White Earth MN, *424* ... 19 F3
Whiteface TX, *465* ... 57 F1
Whitefield NH, *1089* ... 81 F2
Whitefish MT, *5032* ... 15 D2
Whitefish Bay WI, *14163* ... 234 D1
Whiteford MD, *700* ... 146 A4
White Hall AL, *1014* ... 127 F2
White Hall AR, *4732* ... 117 E3
White Hall IL, *2629* ... 98 A2
Whitehall MI, *2884* ... 75 E2
Whitehall MT, *1044* ... 23 E1
Whitehall NY, *2667* ... 81 D3
Whitehall OH, *19201* ... 206 C2
Whitehall PA, *14268* ... 146 B1
Whitehall VA, *250* ... 102 C4
White Lake NC, *529* ... 123 D2
White Lake SD, *405* ... 27 D4
Whiteland IN, *3958* ... 99 F1
Whitelaw WI, *730* ... 75 D1
White Marsh MD, *8485* ... 193 E2
White Marsh VA, *600* ... 113 F1
White Oak MD, *20973* ... 270 D1
White Oak OH, *13277* ... 204 A2
White Oak PA, *8437* ... 92 A4
White Oak TX, *5624* ... 124 B2
White Pigeon MI, *1627* ... 89 F1
White Pine MI, *700* ... 65 E4
White Pine TN, *1997* ... 111 D4
White Pine Co. NV, *9181* ... 38 B1
White Plains KY, *800* ... 109 E2
White Plains MD, *3600* ... 144 B4
White Plains NY, *53077* ... 148 B3
White Plains NC, *1049* ... 112 A3
Whiteriver AZ, *5220* ... 55 E1
White River SD, *598* ... 26 C4
White River Jct. VT, *2569* ... 81 E3
White Rock NM, *6045* ... 48 C2
Whiterocks UT, *341* ... 32 A4
White Salmon WA, *2193* ... 21 D1
Whitesboro NY, *3943* ... 79 E3
Whitesboro TX, *3760* ... 59 F1
Whitesburg GA, *596* ... 120 B4
Whitesburg KY, *1600* ... 111 D2
White Settlement TX, *14831* ... 207 A2
White Shield ND, *348* ... 18 B3
Whiteside Co. IL, *60653* ... 88 A1
White Sprs. FL, *819* ... 138 C2
White Stone VA, *358* ... 113 F1
White Sulphur Sprs. MT, *984* ... 15 F4
White Sulphur Sprs. WV, *2315* ... 112 B1
Whitesville KY, *632* ... 109 F1
Whitesville NY, *400* ... 92 C1
Whitesville WV, *520* ... 101 F4
White Swan WA, *3033* ... 13 D4
Whiteville NC, *5148* ... 123 D3
Whiteville TN, *3148* ... 118 C1
Whitewater KS, *653* ... 43 E3
Whitewater WI, *13437* ... 74 C3
Whitewood SD, *844* ... 25 F3
Whitewright TX, *1740* ... 59 F1
Whitfield Co. GA, *83525* ... 120 B2
Whitfield Estates FL, *4200* ... 140 B3
Whiting IN, *5137* ... 89 D2
Whiting IA, *707* ... 35 F2
Whiting NJ, *1800* ... 147 E3
Whiting WI, *1760* ... 68 B4
Whitinsville MA, *6340* ... 150 C2
Whitley City KY, *1111* ... 110 C3
Whitley Co. IN, *30707* ... 89 F3
Whitley Co. KY, *35865* ... 110 C2
Whitman MA, *13882* ... 151 D2
Whitman Co. WA, *40740* ... 14 A4
Whitmire SC, *1512* ... 121 F3
Whitmore Lake MI, *6574* ... 76 B4
Whitmore Vil. HI, *4057* ... 152 A2
Wickenburg AZ, *5082* ... 54 B1
Wickes AR, *675* ... 116 C3
Wickett TX, *455* ... 57 F4
Wickford RI, *1900* ... 150 C4
Wickliffe KY, *794* ... 108 C2
Wickliffe OH, *13484* ... 91 E2
Wicomico Church VA, *250* ... 113 F1
Wicomico Co. MD, *84644* ... 114 C1
Widefield CO, *29845* ... 205 D2
Wiggins CO, *838* ... 33 F4
Wiggins MS, *3849* ... 135 D1
Wilbarger Co. TX, *14676* ... 58 C1
Wilber NE, *1761* ... 35 F4
Wilberforce OH, *1579* ... 100 C1
Wilbraham MA, *3544* ... 150 A2
Wilbur WA, *914* ... 13 F3
Wilbur Park MO, *475* ... 256 B3
Wilburton OK, *2972* ... 116 A2
Wilcox NE, *360* ... 35 D4
Wilcox PA, *500* ... 92 B2
Wilcox Co. AL, *13183* ... 127 F3
Wilcox Co. GA, *8577* ... 129 E3
Wilder ID, *1462* ... 22 A4
Wilder KY, *2624* ... 204 B3
Wilder VT, *1636* ... 81 E3
Wilderness VA, *300* ... 103 D4
Wildomar CA, *14064* ... 53 D3
Wild Rose WI, *765* ... 74 B1
Wildwood FL, *3924* ... 140 C1
Wildwood MO, *32884* ... 98 A3
Wildwood NJ, *5436* ... 104 C4
Wildwood TX, *550* ... 132 C2
Wildwood Crest NJ, *3980* ... 104 C4
Wiley CO, *483* ... 42 A3
Wilhoit AZ, *664* ... 47 D4
Wilkes-Barre PA, *43123* ... 93 E2
Wilkesboro NC, *3159* ... 111 F4
Wilkes Co. GA, *10687* ... 121 E4
Wilkes Co. NC, *65632* ... 111 E3
Wilkeson WA, *395* ... 12 C3
Wilkin Co. MN, *7138* ... 19 F4
Wilkinsburg PA, *19196* ... 250 C2
Wilkinson Co. GA, *10220* ... 129 E2
Wilkinson Co. MS, *10312* ... 125 F4
Willacoochee GA, *1434* ... 129 E4
Willacy Co. TX, *20082* ... 63 F3
Willamina OR, *1844* ... 20 B2
Willard MO, *3193* ... 107 D2
Willard NM, *240* ... 49 D4
Willard OH, *6806* ... 91 D3
Willard UT, *1630* ... 31 E3
Willards MD, *938* ... 114 C1
Will Co. IL, *502266* ... 89 D2
Willcox AZ, *3733* ... 55 E3
Willernie MN, *549* ... 235 E1
Williams AZ, *2842* ... 47 D3
Williams CA, *3670* ... 36 B2
Williams IA, *427* ... 72 C4
Williams OR, *200* ... 28 B2
Williams Bay WI, *2415* ... 74 C4
Williamsfield IL, *620* ... 88 A3
Williamson NY, *2100* ... 78 C3
Williamson WV, *3414* ... 111 E1
Williamson Co. IL, *61296* ... 108 C1
Williamson Co. TN, *126638* ... 109 F4
Williamson Co. TX, *249967* ... 61 E1
Williamsport IN, *1935* ... 89 D4
Williamsport MD, *1868* ... 103 D1
Williamsport OH, *1002* ... 101 D1
Williamsport PA, *30706* ... 93 D2
Williamston MI, *3441* ... 76 A4
Williamston NC, *5843* ... 113 E4
Williamston SC, *3791* ... 121 E2
Williamstown KY, *3227* ... 100 B3
Williamstown MA, *4754* ... 94 C1
Williamstown NJ, *11812* ... 146 C4
Williamstown NY, *475* ... 79 E2
Williamstown PA, *1433* ... 93 E4
Williamstown VT, *850* ... 81 E2
Williamstown WV, *2996* ... 101 F1
Williamsville DE, *350* ... 114 C1
Williamsville IL, *1439* ... 98 B1
Williamsville MS, *400* ... 126 C1
Williamsville NY, *5573* ... 198 C2
Willimantic CT, *15823* ... 150 B3
Willingboro NJ, *36300* ... 147 D3
Willis TX, *3985* ... 132 A2
Willisburg KY, *304* ... 110 B1
Williston FL, *2297* ... 138 C4
Williston MD, *425* ... 145 E3
Williston ND, *12512* ... 17 F2
Williston OH, *800* ... 90 C2
Williston SC, *3307* ... 130 B1
Williston TN, *341* ... 118 C1
Williston VT, *500* ... 81 D2
Willisville IL, *694* ... 98 B4
Willis Wharf VA, *475* ... 114 B3
Willits CA, *5073* ... 36 A2
Willmar MN, *18351* ... 66 B3
Willoughby OH, *22621* ... 91 E2
Willoughby Hills OH, *8595* ... 204 G1
Willow AK, *1658* ... 154 C3
Willowbrook CA, *34138* ... 228 D3
Willowbrook IL, *8967* ... 203 C5
Willow City ND, *221* ... 18 C2
Willow Creek CA, *1743* ... 28 B4
Willow Creek MT, *209* ... 23 E1
Willow Grove PA, *16234* ... 146 C2
Willowick OH, *14361* ... 91 E2
Willow Lake SD, *294* ... 27 E3
Willow Park TX, *2849* ... 59 E2
Willows CA, *6220* ... 36 B1
Willows MD, *900* ... 144 C4
Willow Sprs. IL, *5027* ... 203 C5
Willow Sprs. MO, *2147* ... 107 E2
Willow Street PA, *7258* ... 146 A3
Willsboro NY, *600* ... 81 D2
Willshire OH, *463* ... 90 A3
Wills Pt. TX, *3496* ... 59 F2
Willwood WY, *100* ... 24 B3

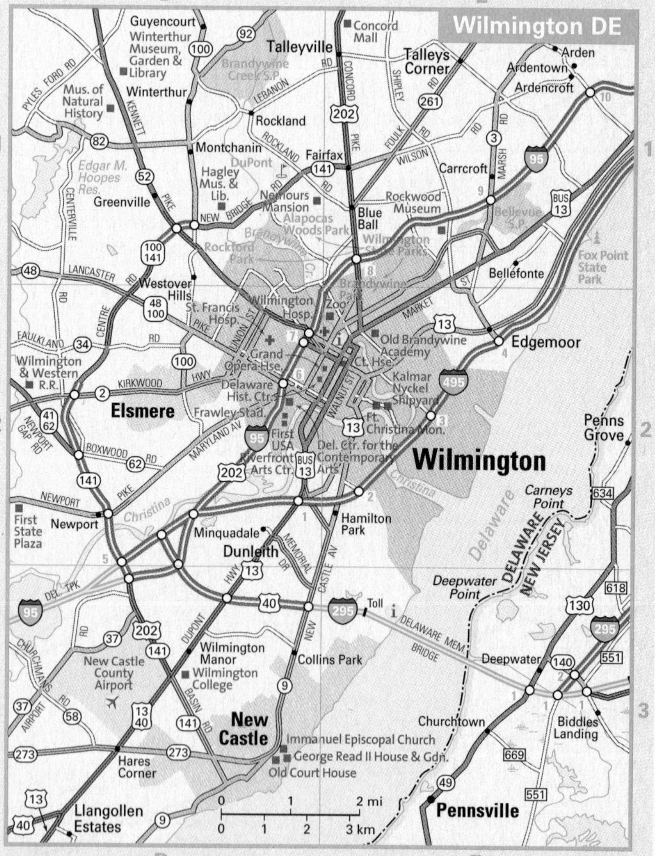

Arden ... E1
Ardencroft ... E1
Ardentown ... E1
Bellefonte ... E1
Biddles Landing ... E3
Blue Ball ... E1
Carrcroft ... E1
Churchtown ... E3
Collins Park ... D3
Deepwater ... E3
Dunleith ... D2
Edgemoor ... E2
Elsmere ... D2
Fairfax ... E1
Greenville ... D1
Guyencourt ... D1
Hamilton Park ... E2
Hares Corner ... D3
Llangollen Estates ... D3
Minquadale ... D2
Montchanin ... D1
New Castle ... D3
Newport ... D2
Penns Grove ... E2
Pennsville ... E3
Rockland ... D1
Talleys Corner ... E1
Talleyville ... E1
Westover Hills ... D1
Wilmington ... E2
Wilmington Manor ... D3
Winterthur ... D1

Entries in **bold** indicate counties or parishes. Entries in color indicate cities with detailed inset maps.

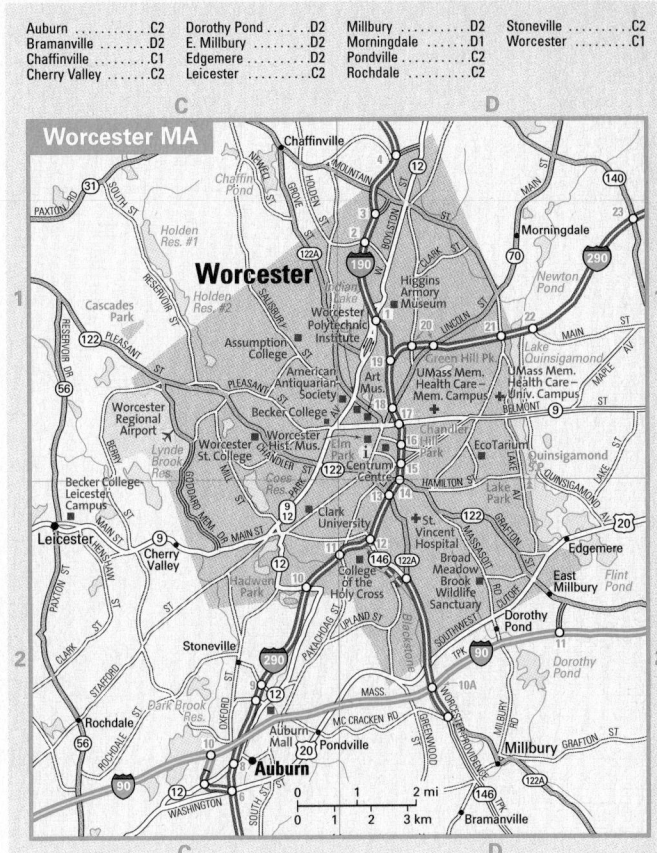

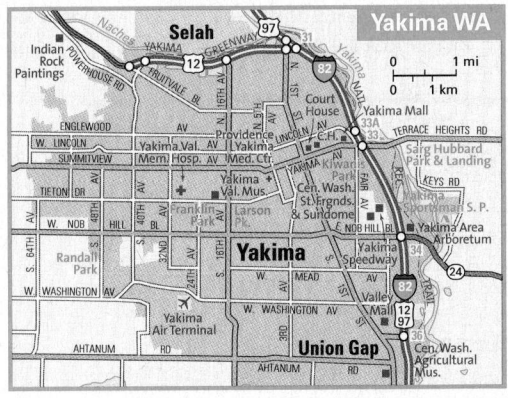

Yakima WA

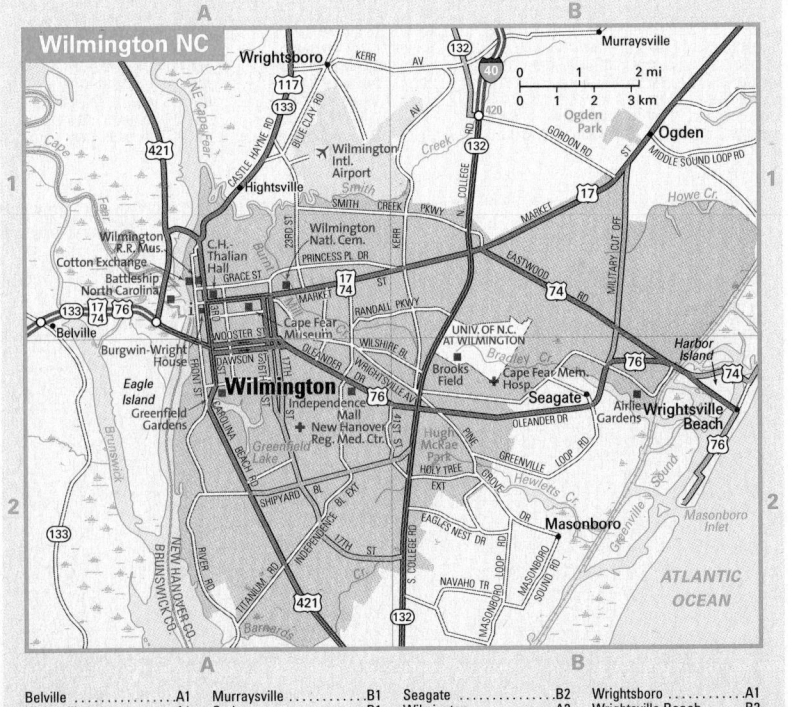

Wilmington NC

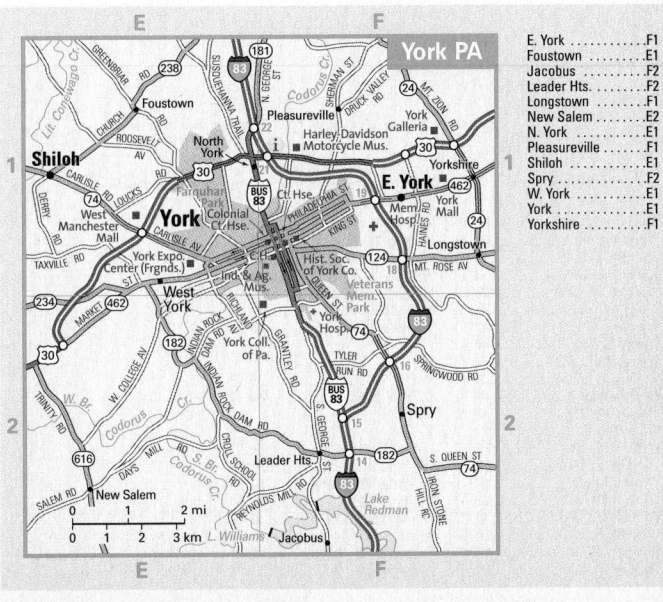

York PA

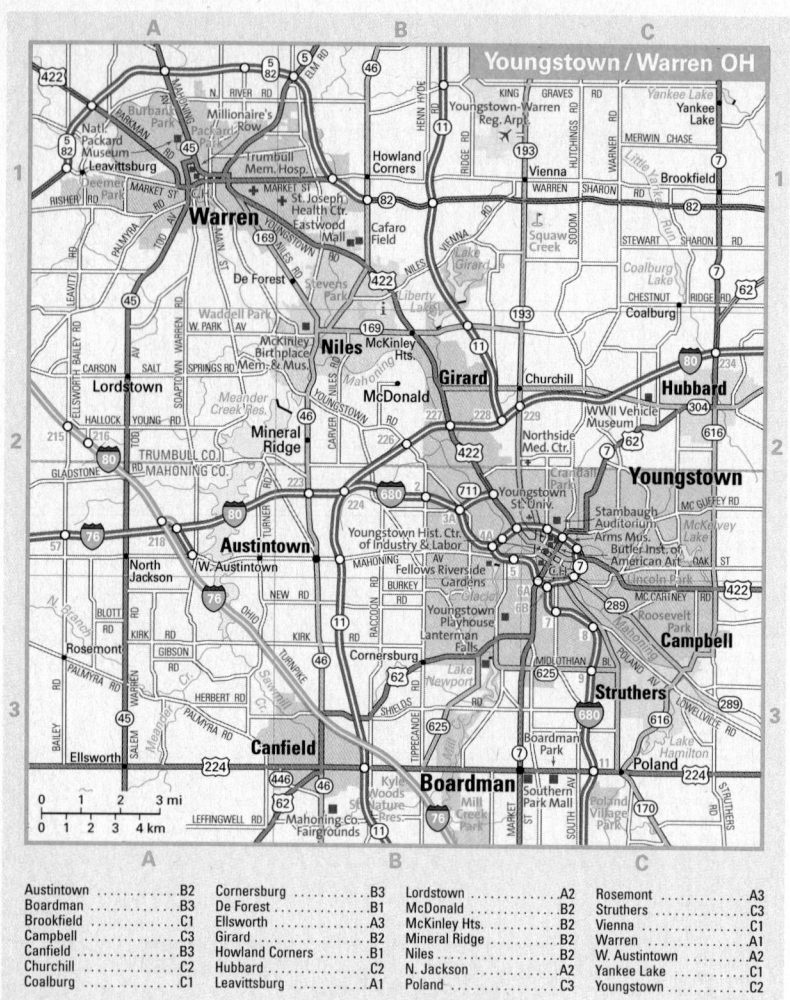

Youngstown / Warren OH

Austintown	B2	Cornersburg	B3	Lordstown	A2	Rosemont	A3
Boardman	B3	De Forest	B1	McDonald	A2	Struthers	C3
Brookfield	C1	Ellsworth	A3	McKinley Hts.	B2	Vienna	C1
Campbell	C3	Girard	B2	Mineral Ridge	B2	Warren	A1
Canfield	B3	Howland Corners	B1	Niles	B2	W. Austintown	A2
Churchill	C2	Hubbard	C2	N. Jackson	A2	Yankee Lake	C1
Coalburg	C1	Leavittsburg	A1	Poland	C3	Youngstown	C2

Yuma AZ

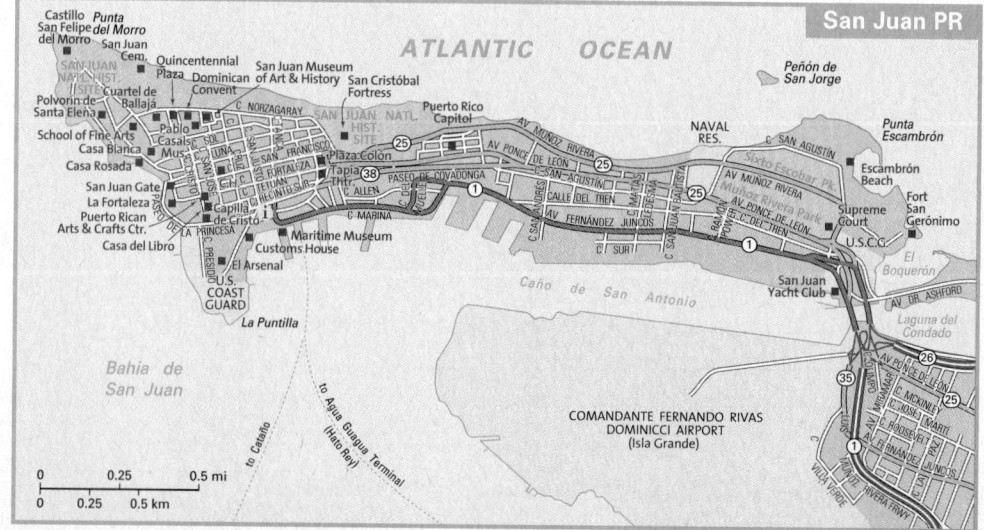

San Juan PR

Entries in color indicate cities with detailed inset maps.

CANADA

Abbotsford BC, 105403 ....163 D3
Abrams Vil. PE, 328 ....179 E4
Acme AB, 600 ....164 C2
Acton ON, 7632 ....172 C2
Acton Vale QC, 4685 ....175 D3
Adstock QC, 1613 ....175 E2
Ailsa Craig ON, 1044 ....172 B3

Airdrie AB, 15946 ....164 C3
Air Ronge SK, 957 ....160 B3
Ajax ON, 64430 ....173 D2
Aklavik NT, 727 ....155 D1
Albanel QC, 1111 ....176 B3
Alberta Beach AB, 640 ....158 C4
Alberton PE, 1084 ....179 E3
Alert Bay BC, 612 ....162 A1
Alexandria ON, 3531 ....174 B3
Alfred ON, 1228 ....174 B3
Alix AB, 765 ....164 C2
Allan SK, 702 ....165 F2
Allardville NB, 675 ....179 D3
Alliston ON, 8225 ....172 C3
Alma QC, 26127 ....176 C3
Almonte ON, 4611 ....174 A3
Alton ON, 955 ....172 C2
Altona MB, 3286 ....167 E4
Alvinston ON, 1037 ....172 B3
Amherst NS, 9669 ....180 C1
Amherstburg ON, 10245 ....172 A4
Amos QC, 13632 ....171 E1
Amqui QC, 6800 ....178 B1
Angus ON, 9723 ....172 C1
Anmore BC, 961 ....282 D1
Annapolis Royal NS, 583 ....180 B3
Anse-Bleue NB, 522 ....179 D2
Antigonish NS, 4860 ....181 E1
Arborg MB, 1012 ....167 E3
Arcadia NS, 770 ....180 B4
Arcola SK, 517 ....166 C4
Arichat NS, 886 ....181 F2
Armstrong BC, 3906 ....164 A3
Arnold's Cove NF, 1115 ....183 E4
Arnprior ON, 7113 ....174 A3
Arthur ON, 2139 ....172 C2
Asbestos QC, 6271 ....175 E3
Ascot Corner QC, 2280 ....175 E3
Ashcroft BC, 1858 ....163 E1
Ashern MB, 692 ....167 E3
Asquith SK, 533 ....165 F2
Assiniboia SK, 2653 ....166 A4
Athabasca AB, 2313 ....159 D3
Athens ON, 997 ....174 A4
Atholville NB, 1376 ....178 C2
Atikokan ON, 3961 ....168 C4
Atwood ON, 877 ....172 C2
Aurora ON, 34857 ....173 D2
Austin MB, 439 ....167 D4
Avondale NF, 765 ....183 E4
Ayer's Cliff QC, 986 ....175 D3
Aylesford NS, 1121 ....180 C2
Aylmer ON, 7018 ....172 C3
Aylmer QC, 34901 ....174 B3
Ayr ON, 3151 ....172 C3

Back Bay NB, 559 ....180 A2
Baddeck NS, 1064 ....181 F1
Badger NF, 997 ....183 D3
Baie-Comeau QC, 25554 ....177 D2
Baie-du-Febvre QC, 1196 ....175 D2
Baie-Ste-Anne NB, 1941 ....179 D3
Baie-St-Paul QC, 3569 ....176 C4
Baie Verte NF, 1708 ....183 D2
Baker Brook NB, 629 ....178 A3
Balcarres SK, 661 ....166 B3
Balgonie SK, 1132 ....166 B3
Balmoral NB, 1975 ....178 C2
Bancroft ON, 2554 ....171 E4
Banff AB, 6098 ....164 B3
Barachois NB, 783 ....179 D4
Barnston QC, 1500 ....175 D3
Barraute QC, 1159 ....171 E1
Barrhead AB, 4239 ....158 C4
Barrie ON, 79191 ....173 D1

Barrière BC, 1653 ....157 F4
Barry's Bay ON, 1086 ....171 E4
Bas-Caraquet NB, 1775 ....179 D2
Bashaw AB, 774 ....164 C1
Bassano AB, 1272 ....165 D3
Bath NB, 629 ....178 B4
Bath ON, 1389 ....173 F1
Bathurst NB, 13815 ....179 D2
Battleford SK, 3936 ....159 F4

Bay Bulls NF, 1063 ....183 F4
Bay de Verde NF, 594 ....183 F3
Bayfield ON, 833 ....172 B2
Bay Roberts NF, 5472 ....183 E4
Bay St. George NF, ...
Beachburg ON, 902 ....174 A3
Beamsville ON, 7699 ....173 D3
Bear River NS, 881 ....180 B3
Beauceville QC, 3751 ....175 E2
Beaucourt QC, 1139 ....171 D2
Beauharnois QC, 6435 ....174 C3
Beaumont AB, 5810 ....159 D4
Beaupré QC, 2799 ....175 E1
Beausejour MB, 2712 ....167 F3
Beauval SK, 785 ....159 F2
Beaverlodge AB, 1997 ....157 F1
Beaverton ON, 3009 ....173 D1
Bécancour QC, 11489 ....175 D2
Bedford NS, 13638 ....181 D3
Bedford QC, 2748 ....175 D4
Beeton ON, 2886 ....173 D2
Beiseker AB, 708 ....164 C2
Belcarra QC, 665 ....282 D1
Bella Bella BC, 1211 ....156 C4
Bella Coola BC, ...
Bellefeuille QC, 12803 ....174 C3
Belleoram NF, 564 ....183 D4
Belle River ON, 4531 ....172 A4
Belleville ON, 37083 ....173 E1
Bellevue AB, 1046 ....164 C4
Benito MB, 460 ....166 C2
Bentley AB, 987 ....164 C2
Beresford NB, 4720 ....179 D2
Bernierville QC, 1871 ....175 E2
Berthierville QC, 3952 ....175 D2
Bertrand QC, 1379 ....179 D2

Berwick NS, 2195 ....180 C2
Berwyn AB, 606 ....158 B2
Bewdley ON, 825 ....173 E2
Bienfait SK, 826 ....166 C4
Biggar SK, 2351 ....165 F2
Big River SK, 826 ....159 F3
Binscarth MB, 463 ....166 C3
Birch Hills SK, 945 ....160 B4
Birch River MB, 419 ....166 C2

Birchy Bay NF, 735 ....183 E2
Birtle MB, 720 ....167 D3
Bishop's Falls NF, 4048 ....183 D3
Black Creek BC, 1950 ....162 B2
Black Diamond AB, 1811 ....164 C3
Black Lake QC, 4408 ....175 E2
Blacks Hbr. NB, 1148 ....180 A2
Blackville NB, 957 ....178 C4
Blaine Lake SK, 516 ....160 B4
Blainville QC, 29603 ....174 C3
Blairmore AB, 2118 ....164 C4
Blanc-Sablon QC, 1248 ....183 D1
Blenheim ON, 4873 ....172 B4
Blind River ON, 3152 ....170 B3
Blockhouse NS, 700 ....180 C3
Bloomfield NF, 650 ....183 E3
Bloomfield ON, 687 ....173 F2
Blyth ON, 991 ....172 B2
Bobcaygeon ON, 2753 ....173 E1
Boissevain MB, 1544 ....167 D4
Bolton ON, 10569 ....173 D2
Bon Accord AB, 1493 ....159 D4
Bonaventure QC, 1509 ....179 D2
Bonavista NF, 4526 ....183 E3
Bonnyville AB, 5100 ....159 E3
Borden-Carleton PE, 829 ....179 E4
Bothwell ON, 990 ....172 B3
Botwood NF, 3613 ....183 D2
Bouctouche NB, 2459 ....179 D4
Bourget ON, 970 ....174 B3
Bowden AB, 1014 ....164 C2
Bowen Island BC, 1791 ....163 D3
Bow Island AB, 1688 ....165 D4
Bowmanville ON, 27594 ....173 D2
Boyle AB, 802 ....159 D3

Bracebridge ON, 13223 ....171 D4
Bradford ON, 14869 ....173 D2
Braeside ON, 715 ....174 A3
Bragg Creek AB, 591 ....164 C3
Brampton ON, 268251 ....173 D2
Brandon MB, 39175 ....167 D4
Brantford ON, 84764 ....172 C3
Bridgenorth ON, 1671 ....173 E1
Bridgetown NS, 994 ....180 B3
Bridgewater NS, 7351 ....180 C3
Brigham QC, 2290 ....175 D3
Brighton ON, 4584 ....173 E2
Brigus NF, 902 ....183 E4
Bristol NB, 707 ....178 B4
Bristol QC, 1129 ....174 A3
Broadview SK, 751 ....166 C3
Brockville ON, 21752 ....174 B4
Bromont QC, 4290 ....175 D3
Bromptonville QC, 3426 ....175 E3
Brooke ON, 991 ....172 C1
Brookfield NS, 917 ....181 D2
Brooklin ON, 2063 ....173 D2
Brooklyn NS, 610 ....180 C2
Brooklyn NS, 1253 ....180 C4
Brooks AB, 10093 ....165 D3
Brownsburg-Chatham QC, 2583 ....174 C3
Bruce Mines ON, 653 ....170 B3
Bruderheim AB, 1198 ....159 D4
Bruno SK, 648 ....166 B2
Brussels ON, 1131 ....172 B2
Buchans NF, 1056 ....183 D3
Buckingham QC, 11678 ....174 B3
Buffalo Narrows SK, 1053 ....159 F2
Burgeo NF, 2098 ....182 C4
Burin NF, 2682 ....183 E4
Burk's Falls ON, 986 ....171 D4
Burlington ON, 136976 ....173 D3
Burnaby BC, 179209 ....163 D3
Burns Lake BC, 1793 ....157 D2
Burnt Islands NF, 919 ....182 C4
Burstner Corner NB, 910 ....178 C4
Bury QC, 1151 ....175 E3

Cabano QC, 3086 ....178 A2
Cabri SK, 529 ....165 E3
Cache Creek BC, 1115 ....163 E1
Cadillac QC, 930 ....171 E2
Caledonia ON, 7038 ....172 C3
Caledon Vil. ON, 1365 ....172 C2
Calgary AB, 768082 ....164 C3
Calmar AB, 1797 ....159 D4
Cambridge ON, 101429 ....172 C3
Cambridge-Narrows NB, 634 ....180 B1
Campbellford ON, 3647 ....173 E1
Campbell River BC, 28851 ....162 B2
Campbellton AB, 8404 ....178 C2
Campbellton NF, 642 ....183 E2
Camperville MB, 579 ....167 D2
Camrose AB, 13728 ....159 D4
Canal Flats BC, 685 ....164 B3
Canmore AB, 8354 ....164 B3
Canning NS, 908 ....180 C2
Cannington ON, 2018 ....173 D1
Canora SK, 2208 ....166 C2
Canso NS, 1127 ....181 F2
Cap-aux-Meules QC, 1661 ....179 F3
Cap-Chat QC, 2847 ....178 C1
Cap-de-la-Madeleine
  QC, 33438 ....175 D2
Cape Broyle NF, 633 ....183 F4
Caplan QC, 2145 ....179 D2
Cap-Pele NB, 2242 ....179 E4
Capreol ON, 3410 ....170 C3
Cap-St-Ignace QC, 3078 ....175 F1
Caraquet NB, 4653 ....179 D2
Carberry MB, 1493 ....167 D4
Carbonear NF, 5168 ....183 E4
Cardigan PE, 371 ....179 F4
Cardinal ON, 1777 ....174 B4
Cardston AB, 3417 ....164 C4
Carleton QC, 2886 ....178 C2
Carleton Place ON, 8450 ....174 A3
Carlyle SK, 1252 ....166 C4
Carmacks YT, 466 ....155 D3
Carman MB, 2704 ....167 E4
Carmanville NF, 913 ....183 E2
Carnduff SK, 1069 ....166 C4
Caronport SK, 1147 ....166 A3
Carrot River SK, 1032 ....160 C4
Carseland AB, 578 ....164 C3
Carstairs AB, 1887 ....164 C2
Cartwright NF, 628 ....F1 183
Casselman ON, 2877 ....174 B3
Castlegar BC, 7027 ....164 A4
Castor AB, 970 ....165 D2
Catalina NF, 1155 ....183 E3
Causapscal QC, 2080 ....178 B1
Cavendish PE, 179 ....179 E4
Cawston BC, 843 ....163 F3
Cayuga ON, 1015 ....172 C3
Cedar BC, 3178 ....162 C3
Central Butte SK, 521 ....165 F3
Centreville NS, 559 ....178 B4
Centreville NS, 1086 ....180 C2
Centreville-Wareham-Trinity
  NF, 1328 ....183 E3
Chalk River ON, 974 ....171 E3
Chambord QC, 1608 ....176 B3
Champlain QC, 1608 ....175 D2
Chandler (Pabos) QC, 3358 ....179 D1
Channel-Port aux Basques
  NF, 5243 ....182 C4
Chapais QC, 2090 ....176 A2
Chapleau ON, 2934 ....170 B2

Charette QC, 962 ....175 D2
Charlesbourg QC, 70942 ....175 E1
Charlo NB, 1610 ....178 C2
Charlottetown PE, 32531 ....179 E4
Charny QC, 10661 ....175 E1
Chase BC, 2460 ....163 F1
Châteauguay QC, 41423 ....174 C3
Château-Richer QC, 3579 ....175 E1
Chatham ON, 43409 ....172 B4
Chelsea QC, 962 ....
Chesley ON, 1904 ....172 B1
Chestermere AB, 1911 ....164 C3
Chesterville ON, 1497 ....174 B4
Chéticamp NS, 979 ....181 E3
Chetwynd BC, 2980 ....157 F1
Chibougamau QC, 8664 ....176 A2
Chicoutimi (Saguenay)
  QC, 63061 ....176 C3
Chilliwack BC, 60186 ....163 E3
Chipman NB, 1518 ....178 C4
Churchbridge SK, 815 ....166 C3
Churchill Falls NF, 797 ....E1 183
Church Pt. NS, 487 ....180 B3
Chute-aux-Outardes QC, 2155 ....177 D2
Clair NB, 905 ....178 A3
Clarenville NF, 5335 ....183 E3
Claresholm AB, 3427 ....164 C4
Clark's Beach NF, 1244 ....183 E4

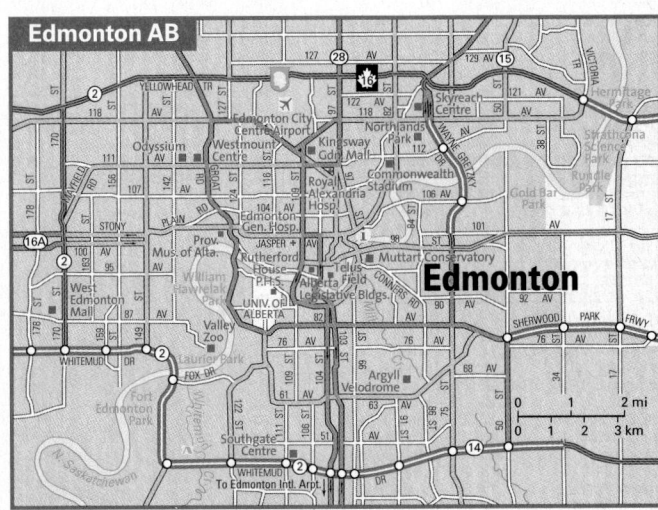

Calgary AB

Calgary

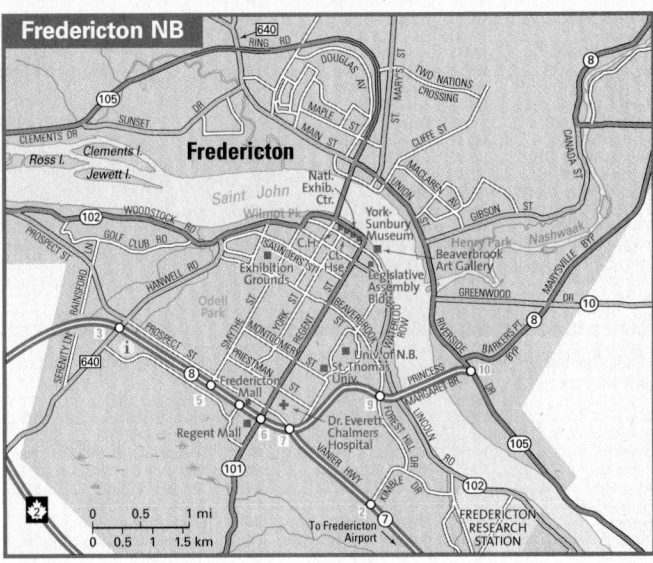

Edmonton AB

Edmonton

Fredericton NB

Fredericton

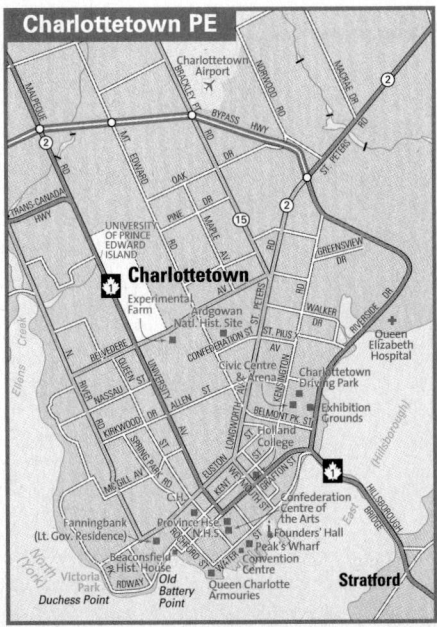

Charlottetown PE

Charlottetown

Stratford

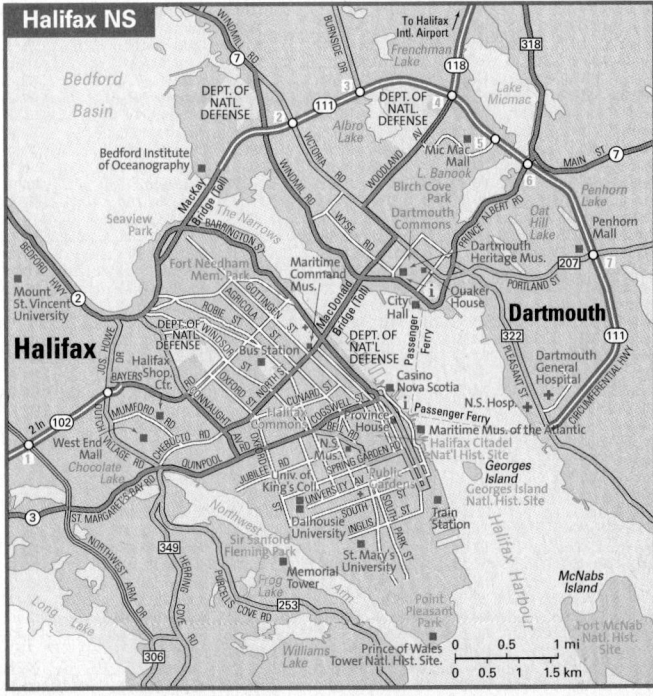

Halifax NS

Halifax

Dartmouth

278 Clarksburg—Linwood

Figures after entries indicate population, page number, and grid reference.

Clarksburg ON, 769 172 C1
Clark's Hbr. NS, 980 180 B4
Clermont QC, 3225 176 C4
Clifford ON, 775 172 C2
Clinton BC, 729 163 E1
Clinton ON, 3216 172 B2
Coaldale AB, 5731 165 D4
Coaticook QC, 6653 175 E4
Cobalt ON, 1401 171 D2
Cobble Hill BC, 1527 163 D4
Cobden ON, 1020 174 A3
Cobourg ON, 16027 173 E2
Cochrane AB, 7424 164 C3
Cochrane ON, 4443 170 C1
Colborne ON, 2054 173 E2
Colchester ON, 1960 172 A4
Cold Lake AB, 4089 159 E3
Coldstream BC, 8975 164 A3
Coldwater ON, 1254 173 D1
Collingwood ON, 15596 172 C1
Comber ON, 1480 172 A4
Comfort Cove-Newstead NF, 597 183 E2
Comox BC, 11069 162 C2
Conception Bay South NF, 19265 183 F4
Conestogo ON, 692 172 C2
Conquerall Mills NS, 549 180 C3
Consort AB, 794 165 D2
Contrecoeur QC, 5331 175 D3
Cookshire QC, 1532 175 E3
Cookstown ON, 1466 173 D1
Coombs BC, 840 162 C3
Coquitlam BC, 101820 163 D3
Cormack NF, 767 182 C2
Corner Brook NF, 21893 182 C3
Cornwall ON, 47403 174 B4
Cornwall PE, 4291 179 E4
Coronach SK, 949 166 A4
Coronation AB, 1166 165 D2
Coteau-du-Lac QC, 1207 174 C3
Cottam ON, 723 172 A4
Courcelles QC, 988 175 E3
Courtenay BC, 17335 162 C2
Courtland ON, 917 172 C3
Courtright ON, 1046 172 A3
Cowansville QC, 12051 175 D3
Cow Head NF, 665 182 C2
Cowichan Bay BC, 1194 163 D4
Cox's Cove NF, 898 182 C2
Cranberry Portage MB, 800 161 D3
Cranbrook BC, 18131 164 B4
Creemore ON, 1285 172 C1
Creighton SK, 1713 161 D3
Creston BC, 4816 164 B4
Crossfield AB, 1899 164 C3
Crowsnest Pass AB, 2118 164 C4
Crystal Beach ON, 6321 173 D3
Crystal City MB, 433 167 D4
Cudworth SK, 752 165 F1
Cumberland BC, 2548 162 C3
Cumberland House SK, 836 160 C4
Cupar SK, 592 166 B3
Cut Knife SK, 585 159 F4
Dalhousie NB, 4500 178 C2
Dalmeny SK, 1470 165 F2
Danville QC, 1796 175 D3
Dartmouth NS, 65629 181 D3
Dauphin MB, 8266 167 D3
Davidson SK, 1105 165 F2
Dawson YT, 1287 155 D2
Dawson Creek BC, 11125 157 F1
Daysland AB, 679 159 D4
Deep River ON, 4491 171 E3
Deer Lake NF, 5222 182 C2
Dégelis QC, 3437 178 A2
Delburne AB, 641 164 C2
Déléage QC, 2036 174 B2
Delhi ON, 4155 172 C3
Déline NT, 616 155 E2
Delisle QC, 4256 176 C3
Delisle SK, 840 165 F2
Deloraine MB, 1041 167 D4
Delta BC, 95411 163 D3
Denare Beach SK, 776 161 D3
Denman Island BC, 866 162 C3
Desbiens QC, 1202 176 C3
Deschaillons-sur-St-Laurent QC, 1060 175 D2
Deschambault Lake SK, 695 160 C3
Deseronto ON, 1811 173 F1
Devlin ON, 678 168 B4
Devon AB, 4496 159 D4
Didsbury AB, 3553 164 C2
Dieppe NB, 12497 179 D4
Digby NS, 2199 180 B3
Disraeli QC, 2657 175 E2
Doaktown NB, 986 178 C4
Dolbeau QC, 8310 176 B3
Dominion NS, 181 F1
Donnacona QC, 5739 175 E2
Dorchester NB, 1179 180 C1
Dover NF, 821 183 E2
Dowling ON, 1979 170 C3
Drayton ON, 1427 172 C2
Drayton Valley AB, 5883 158 C4
Dresden ON, 2589 172 B4
Drumheller AB, 6587 165 D2
Drummond NB, 983 178 B3
Drummondville QC, 44882 175 D3
Dryden ON, 6711 168 C3
Dubuisson QC, 1655 171 E2
Duchess AB, 693 165 D3
Duck Bay MB, 427 167 D2
Duck Lake SK, 667 160 B4
Duncan BC, 4583 162 C4
Dundalk ON, 1776 172 C1
Dunham QC, 3370 175 D4
Dunnville ON, 12471 173 D3
Durham ON, 2641 172 C1
Durham-Sud QC, 988 175 D3
Dutton ON, 1315 172 B3
Earlton ON, 911 171 D2
E. Angus QC, 3642 175 E3
E. Broughton QC, 2489 175 E2
Eastend SK, 616 165 E4
Eastport NF, 557 183 E3
E. Selkirk MB, 599 167 E3
Echo Bay ON, 793 170 B3
Eckville AB, 901 164 C2
Edmonton AB, 616306 159 D4
Edmundston NB, 11033 178 B3
Edson AB, 7399 158 C4
Eel River Crossing NB, 1446 178 C2
Eganville ON, 1319 174 A3
Elie MB, 485 167 E4
Elkford BC, 2729 164 C4
Elkhorn MB, 514 166 C4
Elk Pt. AB, 1403 159 E4
Elliot Lake ON, 13588 170 C3
Elmira ON, 7497 172 C2
Elmsdale NS, 1112 181 D2
Elmsdale PE, 376 179 E3
Elmvale ON, 1860 172 C1
Elora ON, 3346 172 C2
Elrose SK, 557 165 F2
Embree NF, 819 183 E2
Embro ON, 838 172 C3
Embrun ON, 3946 174 B3
Emerson MB, 737 167 E4
Enfield NS, 2588 181 D2
Englee NF, 827 183 D1
Englehart ON, 1703 171 D2
Erickson MB, 507 167 D3
Erin ON, 2633 172 C2
Errington BC, 877 162 C3
Eskasoni NS, 2076 181 F1
Espanola ON, 5454 170 C3
Essex ON, 6785 172 A4
Esterhazy SK, 2602 166 C3
Estevan SK, 10752 166 C4
Eston SK, 1119 165 E3
Évain QC, 3892 171 D2
Evansburg AB, 740 158 C4
Exeter ON, 4472 172 B3
Fairview AB, 3316 158 B2
Falher AB, 1149 158 B2
Farnham QC, 6044 175 D3
Faro YT, 1261 155 E3
Fenelon Falls ON, 2040 173 D1
Fergus ON, 8884 172 C2
Ferme-Neuve QC, 2178 174 B1
Fermont QC, 3234 183 E1
Fernie BC, 4877 164 C4
Ferryland NF, 667 183 F4
Fisher Branch MB, 432 167 E3
Flin Flon MB, 6572 161 D3
Florenceville NB, 707 178 B4
Foam Lake SK, 1303 166 B2
Fogo NF, 982 183 E2
Foremost AB, 556 165 D4
Forest ON, 3020 172 B3
Forestburg AB, 930 165 D1
Forestville QC, 3894 178 A1
Fort-Coulonge QC, 1716 174 A3
Forteau NF, 505 183 D1
Ft. Erie ON, 27183 173 D3
Ft. Frances ON, 8790 168 B4
Ft. Good Hope NT, 644 155 E2
Ft. Liard NT, 512 155 E3
Ft. Macleod AB, 3034 164 C4
Ft. McMurray AB, 33078 159 E1
Ft. McPherson NT, 878 155 D1
Ft. Nelson BC, 4401 155 F3
Ft. Providence NT, 748 155 F2
Ft. Qu'Appelle SK, 1997 166 B3
Ft. Resolution NT, 536 155 F2
Ft. St. James BC, 2046 157 D2
Ft. St. John BC, 15021 158 A2
Ft. Saskatchewan AB, 12408 159 D4
Ft. Simpson NT, 1257 155 F2
Ft. Smith NT, 2441 155 F2
Ft. Vermilion AB, 782 155 F3
Fortune NF, 1969 183 D4
Foxboro ON, 1150 173 E1
Fox Creek AB, 2321 158 B3
Fox Pt. NS, 441 180 C3
Frankford ON, 2096 173 E1
Fraser Lake BC, 1344 157 D2
Fredericton NB, 46507 180 A1
Fredericton Jct. NB, 736 180 A1
Frelighsburg QC, 1048 175 D4
Gabriola Island BC, 2513 162 C3
Gagetown NB, 660 180 B1
Gambo NF, 2339 183 E3
Gananoque ON, 5219 173 F1
Gander NF, 10364 183 E3
Ganges BC, 1457 163 D4
Garden Hill MB, 988 161 F3
Garnish NF, 691 183 D4
Gaspé QC, 16517 179 D1
Gatineau QC, 100702 174 B3
Geary NB, 1084 180 B1
Gentilly QC, 2325 175 D2
Georgetown ON, 26193 172 C2
Georgetown PE, 732 179 F4
Geraldton ON, 2627 169 E3
Gibbons AB, 2748 159 D4
Gibsons BC, 3732 163 D3
Gilbert Plains MB, 748 167 D3
Gillam MB, 1158 161 F1
Gimli MB, 1574 167 E3
Girardville QC, 976 176 B3
Glace Bay NS, 23038 181 F1
Gladstone MB, 927 167 D3
Glenboro MB, 663 167 D4
Glencoe ON, 2178 172 B3
Glenora BC, 760 162 C4
Glenwood NF, 893 183 E3
Gloucester ON, 104022 174 B3
Glovertown NF, 2292 183 E3
Goderich ON, 7553 172 B2
Golden BC, 3968 164 B2
Gold River BC, 2041 162 B2
Gondola Pt. NB, 4324 180 B2
Gore Bay ON, 907 170 C4
Grafton ON, 1134 173 E2
Granby QC, 43316 175 D3
Grand Bank NF, 3328 183 D4
GrandBay-Westfield NB, 3713 180 B2
Grand Bend ON, 1027 172 B3
Grande-Anse NB, 965 179 D2
Grande Cache AB, 4441 157 F2
Grande Prairie AB, 31140 157 F1
Grande-Rivière QC, 3888 179 D1
Grand Falls NB, 6133 178 B3
Grand Falls-Windsor NF, 14160 183 D3
Grand Forks BC, 3994 164 A4
Grand Manan NB, 2577 180 A3
Grand-Mère QC, 14223 175 D2
Grand-Remous QC, 1257 174 B2
Grand Valley ON, 1611 172 C2
Grandview MB, 856 167 D3
Gravelbourg SK, 1211 165 F3
Gravenhurst ON, 10030 171 D4
Great Vil. NS, 477 181 D2
Green Lake SK, 536 159 F3
Greenwood BC, 784 164 A4
Grenfell SK, 1106 166 C3
Grenville-sur-la-Rouge QC, 1443 174 C3
Gretna MB, 538 167 E4
Grimsby ON, 19585 173 D3
Grimshaw AB, 2661 158 B2
Grunthal MB, 733 167 E4
Guelph ON, 95821 172 C2
Gull Lake SK, 1078 165 E3
Guysborough NS, 494 181 E2
Hacketts Cove NS, 413 181 D3
Hagensborg BC, 606 156 C3
Hagersville ON, 2364 172 C3
Hague SK, 688 165 F1
Haines Jct. YT, 574 155 D3
Haliburton ON, 1434 171 E4
Halifax NS, 113910 181 D3
Hamilton ON, 467799 172 C3
Hamiota MB, 847 167 D3
Ham-Nord QC, 959 175 E2
Hampden NF, 651 183 D2
Hampton NB, 4081 180 B2
Hampton ON, 745 173 D2
Hanna AB, 3001 165 D2
Hanover ON, 6844 172 C1
Hant's Hbr. NF, 519 183 E3
Happy Valley-Goose Bay NF, 8655 F1 183
Harbour Breton NF, 2290 183 D4
Harbour Grace NF, 3740 183 E4
Hardisty AB, 808 165 D1
Hare Bay NF, 1224 183 E3
Harrison Hot Sprs. BC, 898 163 E3
Harriston ON, 2008 172 C2
Harrow ON, 2806 172 A4
Harrowsmith ON, 696 173 F1
Hartland NB, 892 178 B4
Hartney MB, 462 167 D4
Hastings ON, 1140 173 E1
Havelock ON, 1352 173 E1
Havelock QC, 811 174 C4
Havre-aux-Maisons QC, 2211 179 F3
Havre Boucher NS, 481 181 E1
Havre-St-Pierre QC, 3020 177 F1
Hawke's Bay NF, 514 183 D1
Hawkesbury ON, 10162 174 B3
Hay River NT, 3611 155 F2
Hearst ON, 6049 170 B1
Heart's Content NF, 538 183 E3
Heart's Delight-Islington NF, 841 183 E4
Hébertville QC, 1514 176 C3
Hebron NS, 716 180 B4
Hensall ON, 1187 172 B2
Herbert SK, 855 165 F3
Hermitage-Sandyville NF, 687 183 D4
Hérouxville QC, 1314 175 D1
Herring Cove NS, 1923 181 D3
High Level AB, 3093 155 F3
High Prairie AB, 2907 158 C2
High River AB, 7359 164 C3
Hillsborough NB, 1272 180 C1
Hillsburgh ON, 1164 172 C2
Hinton AB, 9961 158 B4
Holland MB, 405 167 D4
Holyrood NF, 2090 183 E4
Hope BC, 6247 163 E3
Hopewell NS, 487 181 D2
Hopewell Cape NB, 456 180 C1
Hornby Island BC, 894 162 C3
Hornepayne ON, 1458 169 F3
Houston BC, 3934 156 C2
Hoyt NB, 618 180 A2
Hudson QC, 4796 174 C3
Hudson Bay SK, 1883 160 C4
Hudson's Hope BC, 1122 158 A2
Hull QC, 62339 174 B3
Humber Arm South NF, 1991 182 C3
Humboldt SK, 5074 166 B2
Huntingdon QC, 2746 174 C4
Huntsville ON, 15918 171 D4
Huron Park ON, 969 172 B3
Hythe AB, 712 157 F1
Iberville QC, 9635 175 D3
Ilderton ON, 681 172 B3
Île-à-la-Crosse SK, 1403 159 F2
Indian Head SK, 1833 166 B3
Ingersoll ON, 9849 172 C3
Ingleside ON, 1894 174 B4
Ingonish NS, 607 181 F3
Innisfail AB, 6116 164 C2
Inuvik NT, 3296 155 D1
Invermere BC, 2687 164 B3
Inverness NS, 1785 181 E1
Iqaluit NU, 4220 7
Irishtown-Summerside NF, 1424 182 C3
Iron Bridge ON, 777 170 B3
Iroquois ON, 1278 174 B4
Iroquois Falls ON, 5714 170 C1
Irricana AB, 823 164 C2
Isle aux Morts NF, 988 182 C4
Ituna SK, 743 166 B3
Jarvis ON, 1710 172 C3
Jasper AB, 3815 158 B4
Joe Batt's Arm-Barr'd Islands-Shoal Bay NF, 1028 183 E2
Joggins NS, 491 180 C1
Johnstown ON, 662 174 B4
Joliette QC, 17541 174 C2
Jonquière QC, 56503 176 C3
Judique NS, 444 181 E1
Kaleden BC, 1118 163 F3
Kamloops BC, 76394 163 F1
Kamsack SK, 2264 166 C2
Kanata ON, 56247 174 A3
Kapuskasing ON, 10036 170 C1
Kars ON, 1575 174 B3
Kaslo BC, 1063 164 B4
Kearney ON, 837 171 D4
Kedgwick NB, 1221 178 B2
Kelowna BC, 89442 163 F2
Kelvington SK, 1046 166 B2
Kemptville ON, 3272 174 B4
Kenora ON, 10063 167 F4
Kensington PE, 1383 179 E4
Kent BC, 4844 163 E3
Kentville NS, 5551 180 C2
Keremeos BC, 1167 163 F3
Kerrobert SK, 1109 165 E2
Keswick ON, 17068 173 D1
Keswick Ridge NB, 581 180 A1
Killaloe ON, 669 171 E4
Killam AB, 1048 165 D1
Killarney MB, 2208 167 D4
Kimberley BC, 6738 164 B4
Kincardine ON, 6620 172 B1
Kindersley SK, 4679 165 E2
Kingsey Falls QC, 1329 175 D3
Kingston NB, 689 180 B2
Kingston NS, 7806 180 C2
Kingston ON, 55947 173 F1
Kingsville ON, 5991 172 A4
Kinistino SK, 691 160 B4
Kipling SK, 1004 166 C3
Kippens NF, 1887 182 C3
Kirkland Lake ON, 9905 171 D2
Kitchener ON, 178420 172 C2
Kitimat BC, 11136 156 C2
Kitscoty AB, 643 159 E4
Komoka ON, 1060 172 B3
Kugluktuk NU, 1201 155 F1
La Baie QC, 21057 176 C3
Labelle QC, 1170 174 B2
Labrador City NF, 8455 E1 183
Labrecque QC, 1224 176 C3
La Broquerie MB, 472 167 F4
Lac-au-Saumon QC, 1314 178 B1
Lac-aux-Sables QC, 1441 175 D1
Lac-Bouchette QC, 1445 176 B3
Lac-Brome QC, 5073 175 D3
Lac-des-Écorces QC, 989 174 B2
Lac-Drolet QC, 1133 175 E3
Lac du Bonnet MB, 1070 167 F3
Lac-Etchemin QC, 2488 175 F2
Lachine QC, 35171 174 C3
Lachute QC, 11493 174 C3
Lac La Biche AB, 2611 159 D3
Lac-Mégantic QC, 5864 175 E3
Lac-Nominingue QC, 1930 174 B2
Lacolle QC, 1554 174 C4
Lacombe AB, 8018 164 C2
Ladysmith BC, 6456 162 C3
La Guadeloupe QC, 1772 175 E2
Lake Country BC, 9007 163 F2
Lake Cowichan BC, 2856 162 C4
Lakefield ON, 2444 173 E1
Lake Louise AB, 500 164 B2
La Loche SK, 1966 159 E1
La Macaza QC, 1020 174 B2
La Malbaie-Pointe-au-Pic QC, 4918 176 C4
Lambton QC, 1517 175 E3
Lamèque NB, 1671 179 D2
La Minerve QC, 927 174 B2
Lamont AB, 1581 159 D4
Lampman SK, 648 166 C4
Lanark ON, 865 174 A4
Lancaster ON, 825 174 C3
Landmark MB, 783 167 E4
Landrienne QC, 1007 171 E1
L'Ange-Gardien QC, 2841 175 E1
Langenburg SK, 1119 166 C3
Langford BC, 17484 163 D4
Langham SK, 1104 165 F1
Langley BC, 22523 163 D3
Lanigan SK, 1368 166 B2
L'Annonciation QC, 2085 174 B2
L'Anse-St-Jean QC, 1250 176 C3
La Pocatière QC, 4887 175 F1
La Prairie QC, 17128 174 C3
Lark Hbr. NF, 681 182 C2
La Ronge SK, 2964 160 B3
La Salle MB, 600 167 E4
La Salle ON, 20566 172 A4
La Sarre QC, 8345 171 D1
L'Ascension QC, 1354 176 C3
La Scie NF, 1254 183 D2
Lashburn SK, 674 159 E4
L'Assomption QC, 11366 174 C3
Laterrière QC, 4815 176 C3
La Tuque QC, 12102 175 D1
Laurentides QC, 2703 174 C3
Laurier-Station QC, 2399 175 E2
Laurierville QC, 915 175 E2
Laval QC, 330393 174 C3
Lavaltrie QC, 5821 175 D3
L'Avenir QC, 1274 175 D3
Lavillette NB, 541 179 D3
Lawn NF, 957 183 D4
Lazo BC, 1201 162 C2
Leader SK, 983 165 E3
Leading Tickles West NF, 513 183 D2
Leaf Rapids MB, 1504 161 D2
Leamington ON, 16188 172 A4
Lebel-sur-Quévillon QC, 3416 171 E1
Le Bic QC, 2999 178 A1
Leduc AB, 14305 159 D4
Legal AB, 1095 159 D4
Lennoxville QC, 4036 175 E3
Léry QC, 2410 174 C3
Les Éboulements QC, 1013 176 C4
Les Escoumins QC, 1751 177 D3
Les Méchins QC, 1280 178 C1
L'Étange-du-Nord QC, 3087 179 F3
Lethbridge AB, 63053 165 D4
Lethbridge NF, 594 183 E3
Lévis QC, 40407 175 E1
Lewisporte NF, 3709 183 E2
Lillooet BC, 1988 163 E1
Limoges ON, 1236 174 B3
Linden AB, 565 164 C2
Lindsay ON, 17638 173 D1
Linwood ON, 695 172 C2

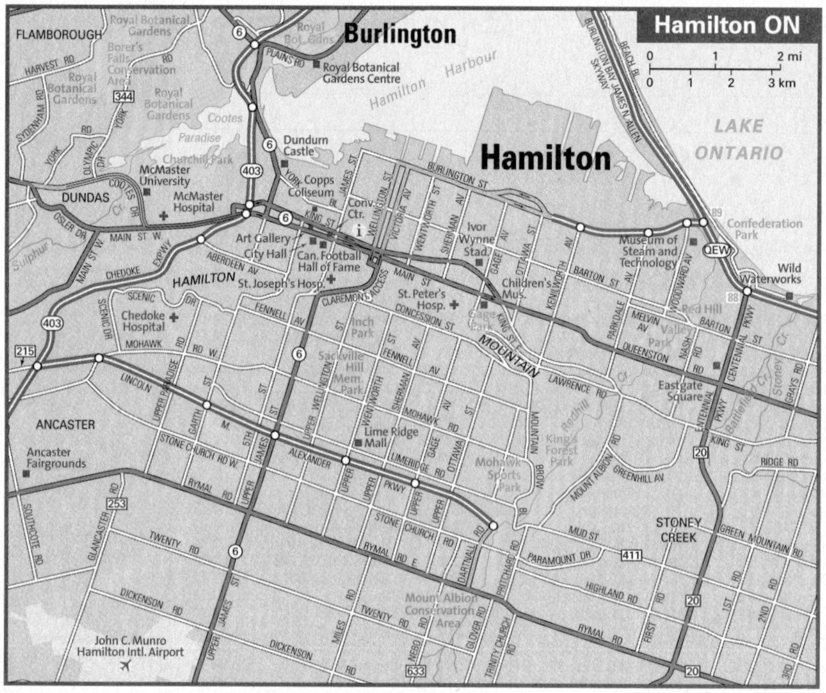

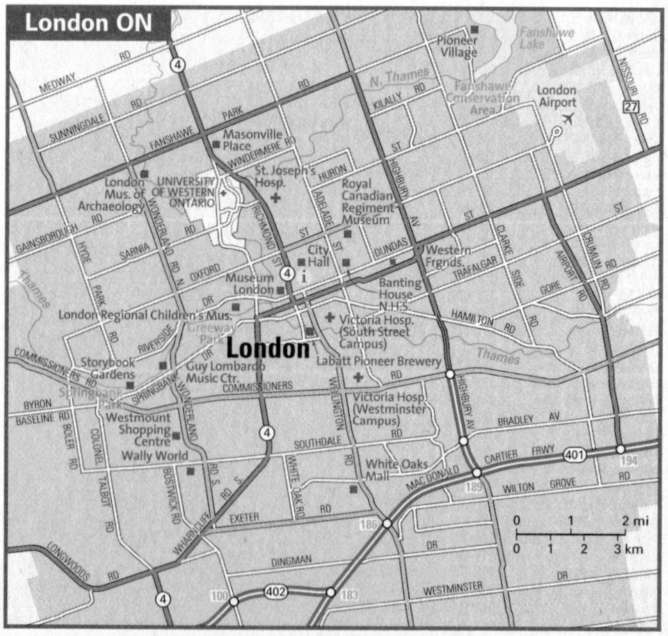

Montréal QC

(map)

Ottawa ON

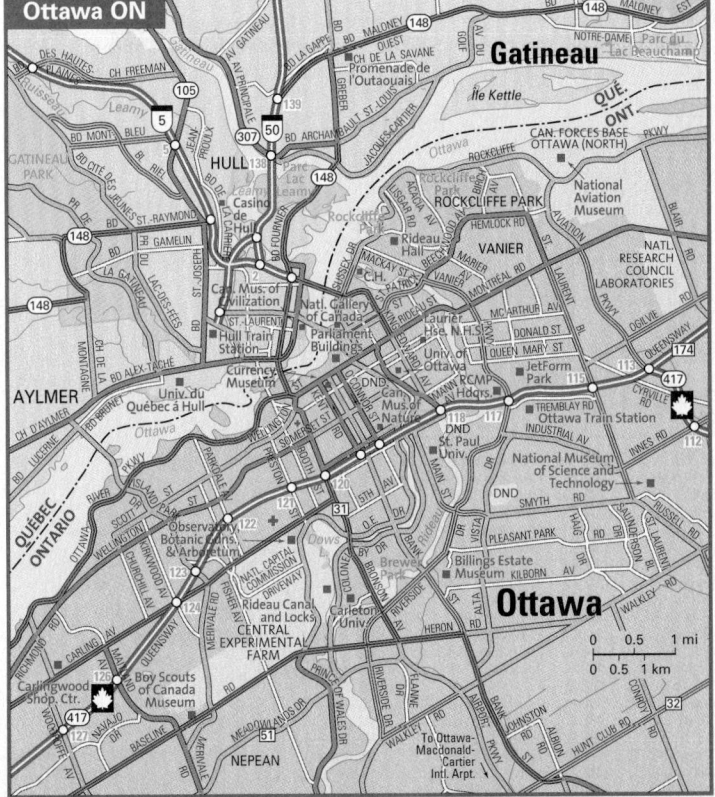

280 | Pointe-aux-Outardes—Ste Agathe

Figures after entries indicate population, page number, and grid reference.

Québec QC

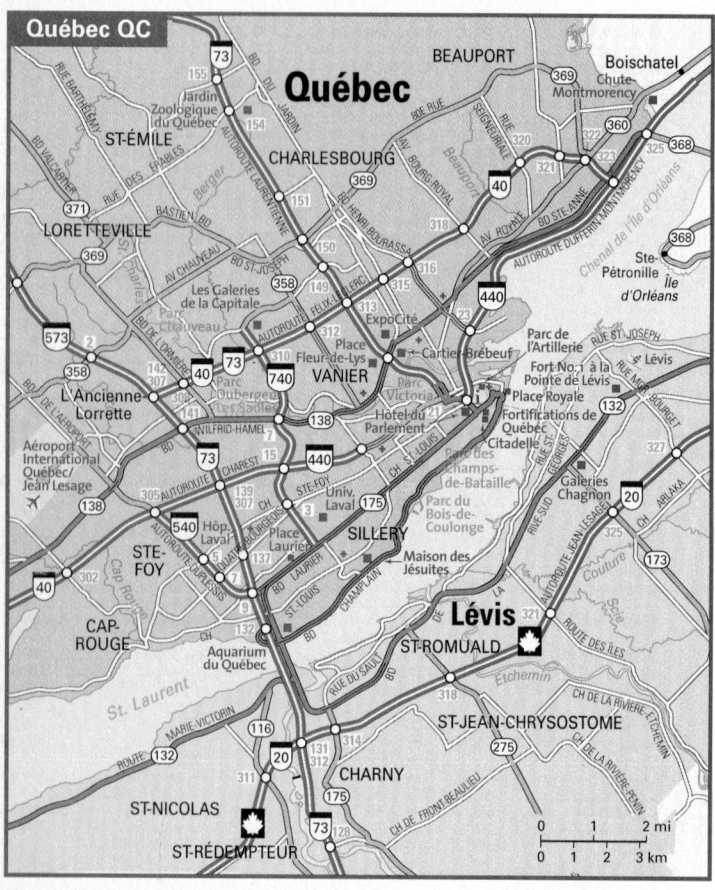

St John's NF

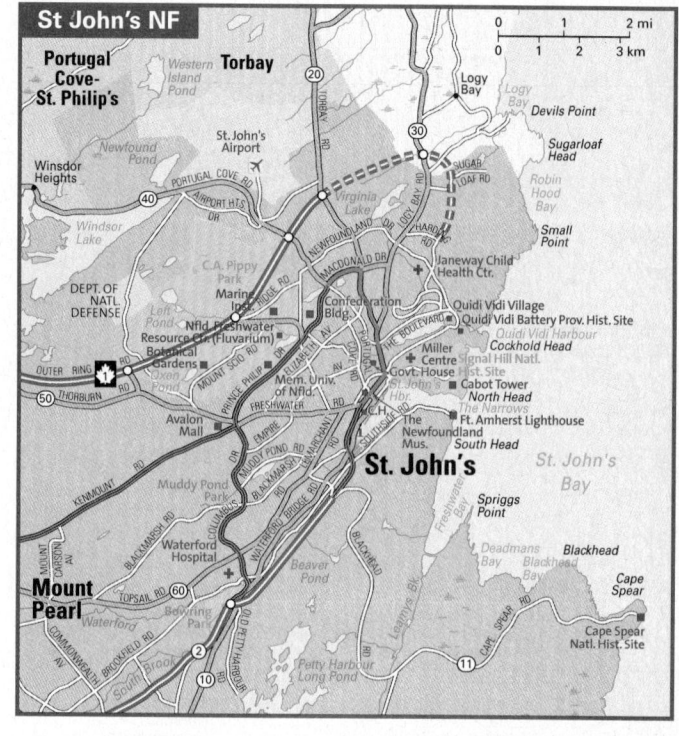

Regina SK

Saint John NB

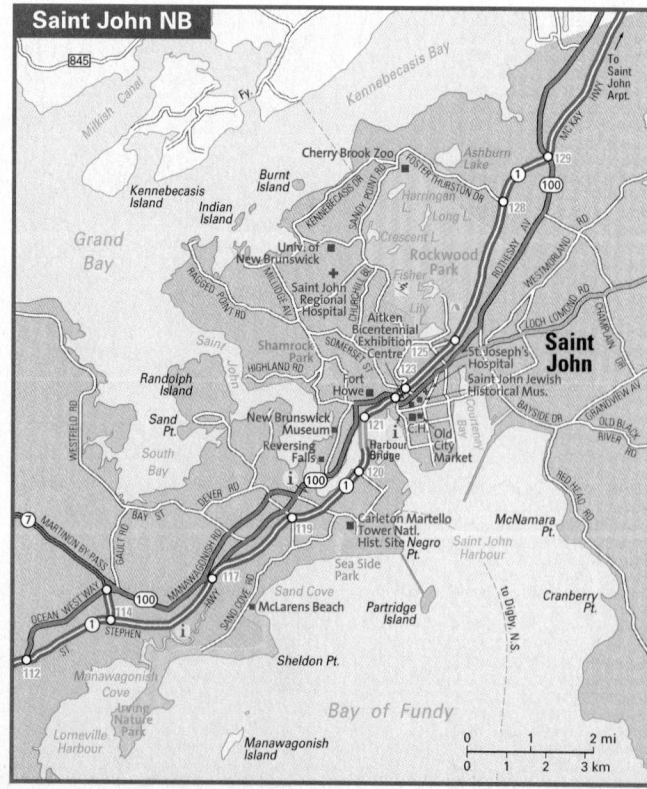

Saskatoon SK

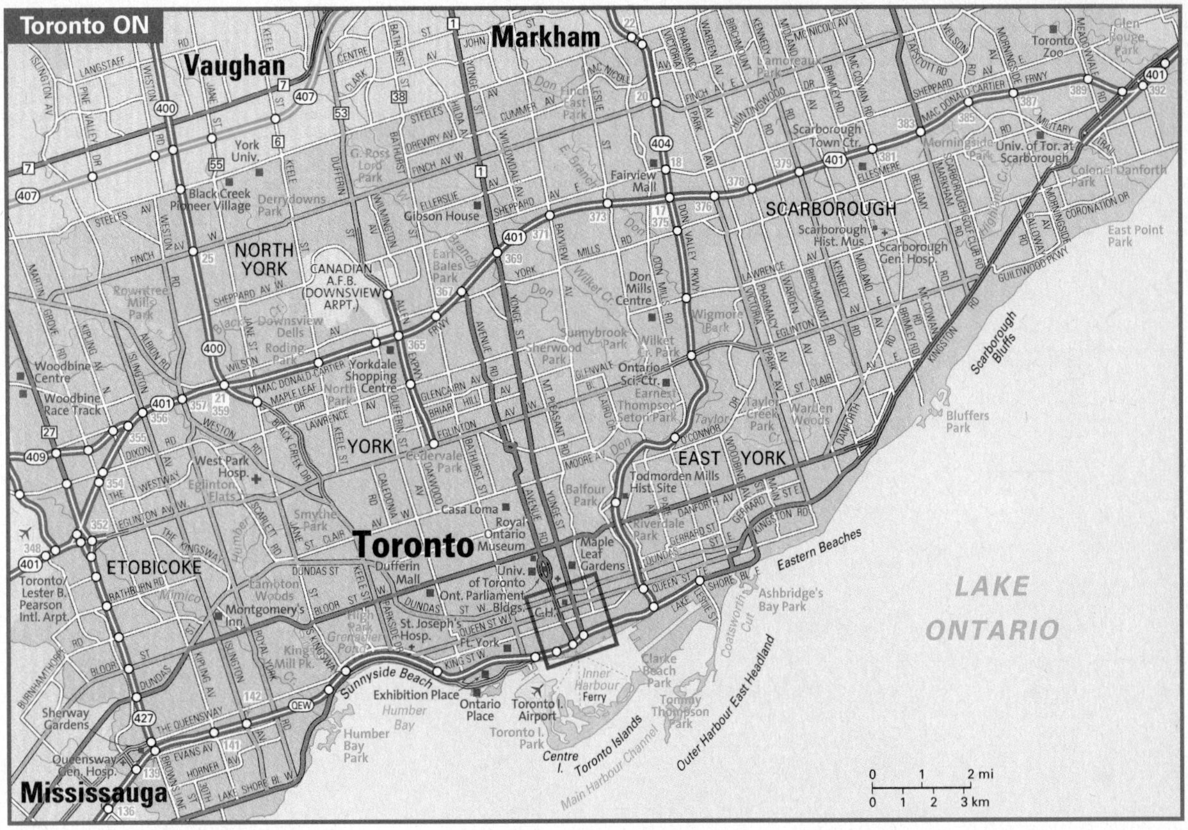
Toronto ON
Markham
Vaughan
NORTH YORK
YORK
EAST YORK
SCARBOROUGH
ETOBICOKE
Toronto
Mississauga
LAKE ONTARIO
Toronto Islands
Eastern Beaches
Scarborough Bluffs
Toronto/Lester B. Pearson Intl. Arpt.
Casa Loma
Royal Ontario Museum
Univ. of Toronto
Ont. Parliament Bldgs.
Maple Leaf Gardens
Exhibition Place
Ontario Place
Toronto I. Airport
Sunnyside Beach
0 1 2 mi
0 1 2 3 km

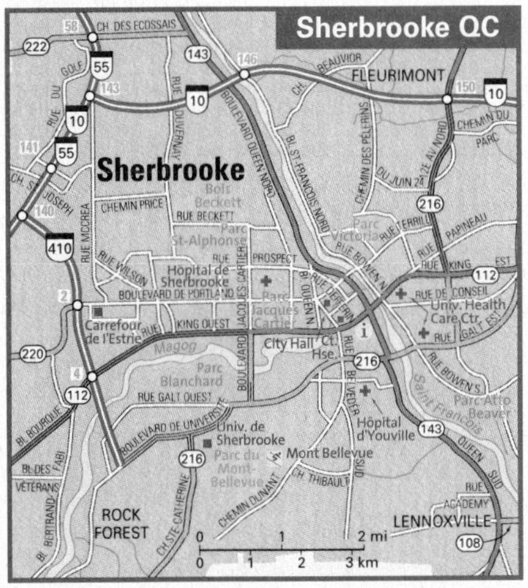
Sherbrooke QC
Sherbrooke
FLEURIMONT
ROCK FOREST
LENNOXVILLE
Univ. de Sherbrooke
Mont Bellevue
0 1 2 mi
0 1 2 3 km

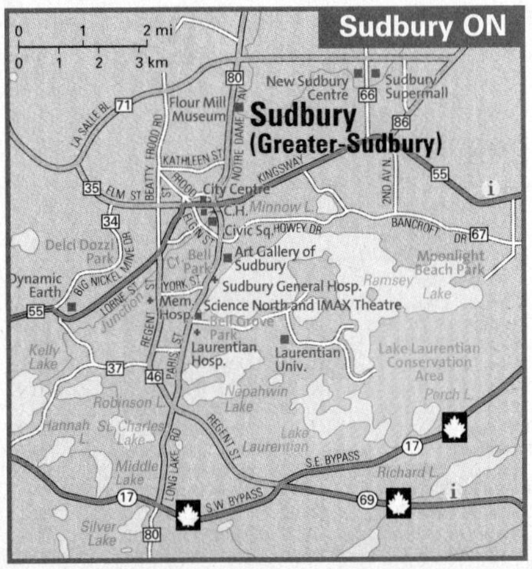
Sudbury ON
Sudbury (Greater Sudbury)
Science North and IMAX Theatre
Laurentian Univ.
Art Gallery of Sudbury
Sudbury General Hosp.
0 1 2 mi
0 1 2 3 km

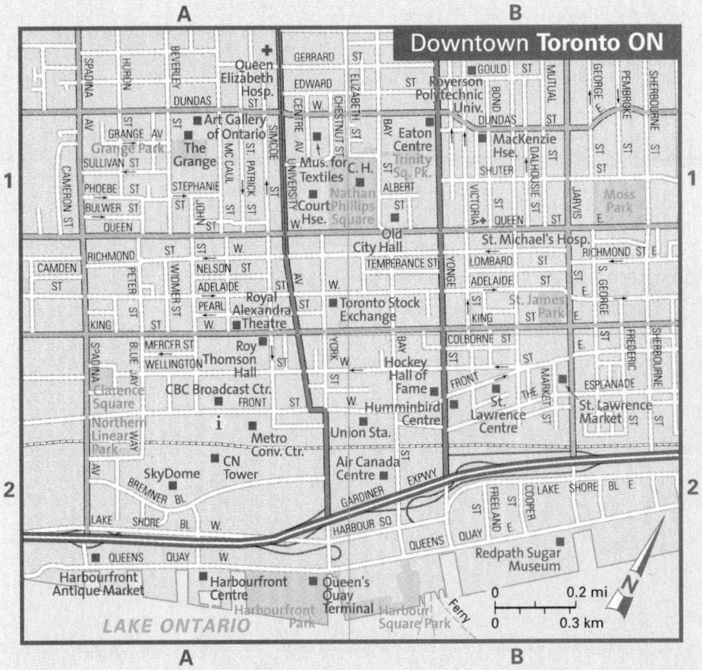
Downtown Toronto ON
A
B
1
2
Art Gallery of Ontario
The Grange
Queen Elizabeth Hosp.
Royerson Polytechnic Univ.
Eaton Centre
MacKenzie Hse.
Mus. for Textiles
C.H.
Court Hse.
Nathan Phillips Square
Old City Hall
St. Michael's Hosp.
Royal Alexandra Theatre
Toronto Stock Exchange
St. James Park
Roy Thomson Hall
Hockey Hall of Fame
CBC Broadcast Ctr.
Clarence Square
Humminbird Centre
St. Lawrence Centre
St. Lawrence Market
Union Sta.
Metro Conv. Ctr.
CN Tower
SkyDome
Air Canada Centre
Redpath Sugar Museum
Harbourfront Antique Market
Harbourfront Centre
Queen's Quay Terminal
Harbourfront Park
Harbour Square Park
Ferry
LAKE ONTARIO
0 0.2 mi
0 0.3 km

Air Canada Centre B2	Hockey Hall of Fame B2	Royerson Polytechnic University B1
Art Gallery of Ontario A1	MacKenzie House B1	Roy Thomson Hall A2
CBC Broadcast Center A2	Metro Convention Center A2	Saint Lawrence Centre B2
City Hall B1	Mus. for Textiles A1	Saint Lawrence Market B2
CN Tower A2	O'Keefe Centre B2	SkyDome A2
Court House A1	Old City Hall B1	The Grange A1
Eaton Centre B1	Queen's Quay Terminal A2	Toronto Stock Exchange A1
Harbourfront Antique Market A2	Redpath Sugar Mus. B2	Union Station B2
Harbourfront Centre A2	Royal Alexandra Theatre A1	

Figures after entries indicate population, page number, and grid reference.

	A	B	C	D
Anmore	...D1	Burnaby...D2	New Westminster...D2	N. Vancouver (DM)...C1	Richmond...C2	Vancouver...B2
Belcarra	...D1	Coquitlam...D2	N. Vancouver...B1	Port Moody...D1	Surrey...D2	W. Vancouver...A1

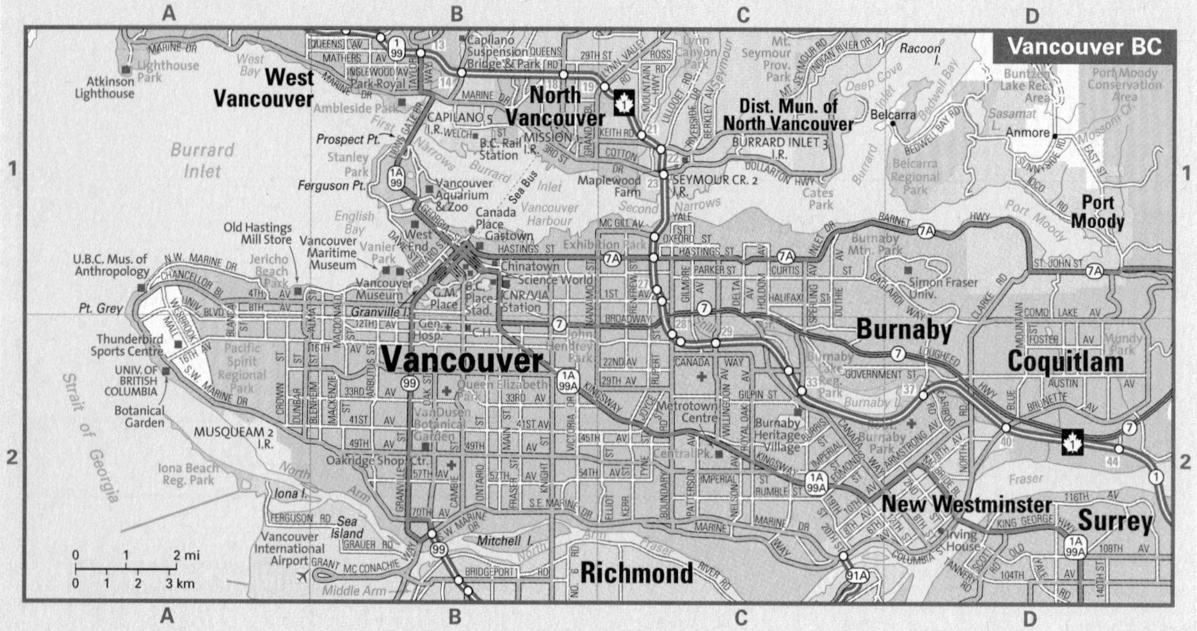

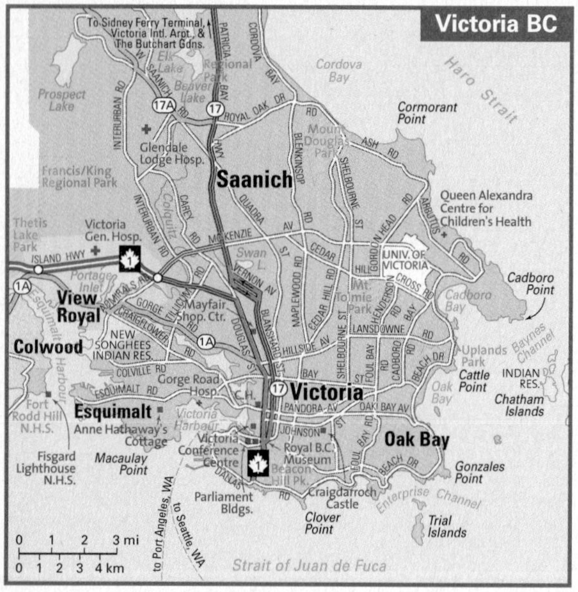

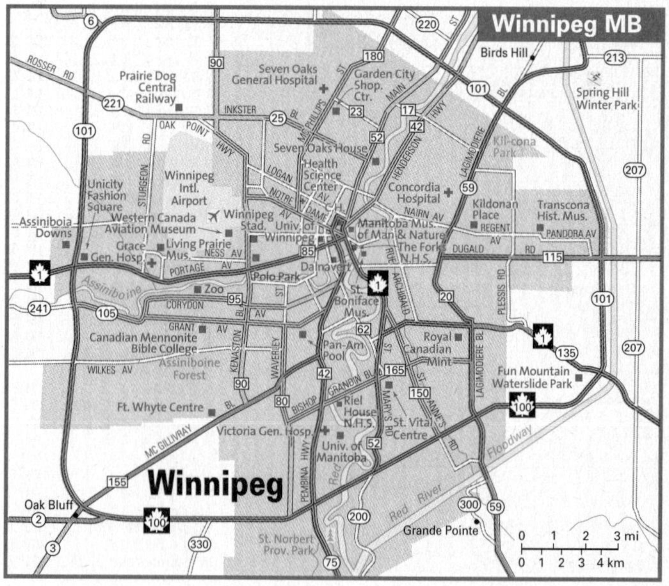

Vancouver BC

Victoria BC

Winnipeg MB

Winnipeg

Victoria

Entries in color indicate cities with detailed inset maps.

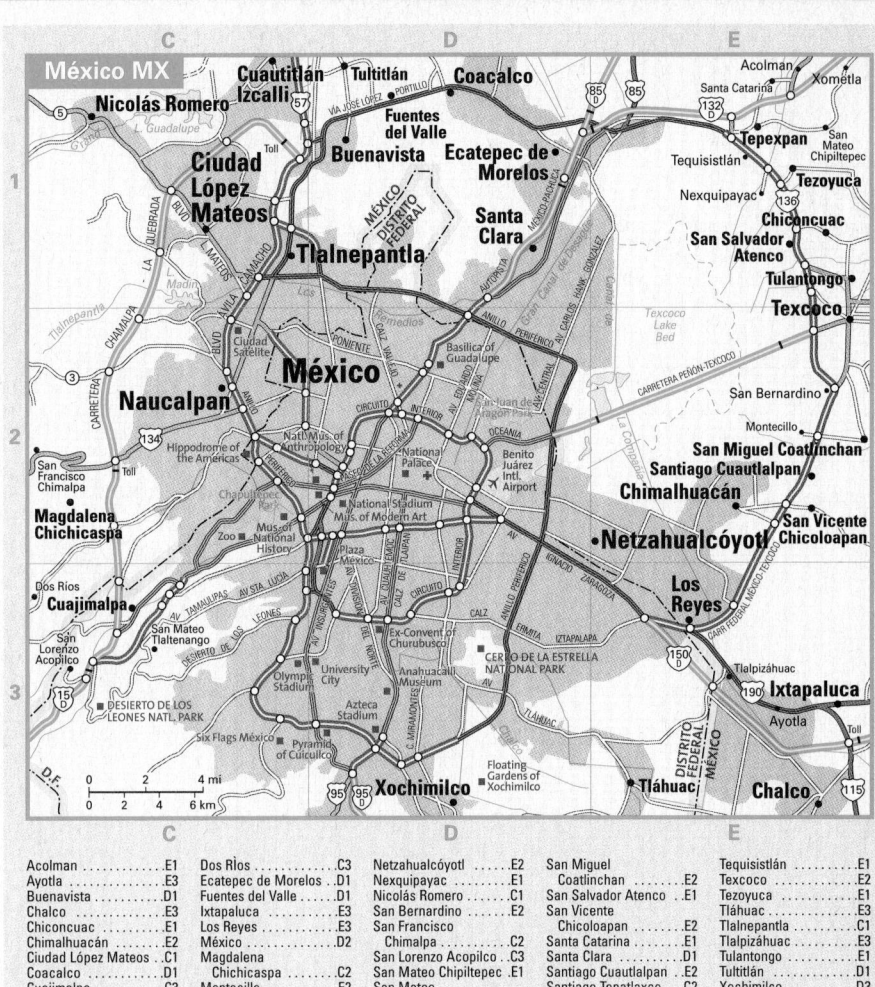

México MX

Cancún MX

(inset map)

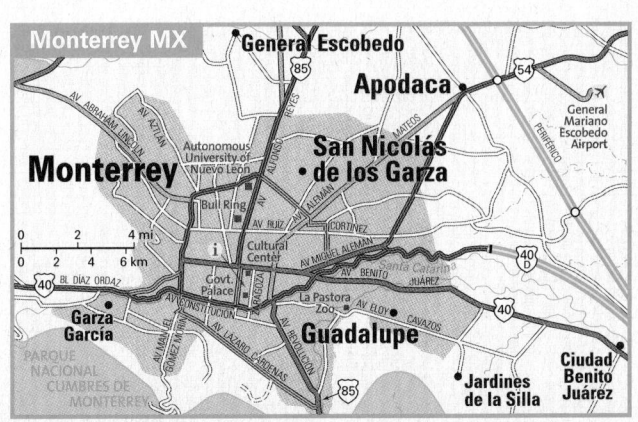

Monterrey MX

284 City to City Distance Chart

Miles

	Albuquerque, NM	Amarillo, TX	Anchorage, AK	Atlanta, GA	Baltimore, MD	Billings, MT	Birmingham, AL	Bismarck, ND	Boise, ID	Boston, MA	Buffalo, NY	Calgary, AB	Charleston, SC	Charleston, WV	Charlotte, NC	Cheyenne, WY	Chicago, IL	Cincinnati, OH	Cleveland, OH	Columbus, OH	Dallas, TX	Denver, CO	Des Moines, IA	Detroit, MI	El Paso, TX	Halifax, NS	Houston, TX	Indianapolis, IN	Jackson, MS	Jacksonville, FL	Kansas City, MO	Las Vegas, NV	Little Rock, AR	Los Angeles, CA	Louisville, KY
Albany, NY	2095	1811	4421	1010	333	2083	1093	1675	2526	172	292	2512	913	634	771	1789	832	730	484	621	1680	1833	1155	571	2326	877	1768	795	1331	1094	1282	2586	1354	2859	832
Albuquerque, NM		286	3563	1490	1902	991	1274	1333	966	2240	1808	1498	1793	1568	1649	538	1352	1409	1619	1476	754	438	1091	1608	263	2945	994	1298	1157	1837	894	578	900	806	1320
Amarillo, TX			3734	1206	1618	988	991	1398	1266	1957	1524	1669	1510	1285	1365	534	1069	1126	1335	1192	470	434	808	1324	438	2662	711	1014	874	1517	610	864	617	1092	1036
Anchorage, AK				4304	4297	2601	4253	2724	2745	4592	4133	2065	4495	4093	4348	3056	3584	3890	3935	3946	4087	3300	3421	3872	4002	4821	4328	3771	4294	4652	3547	3356	3929	3403	3886
Atlanta, GA					679	1889	150	1559	2218	1100	910	2395	317	503	238	1482	717	476	726	577	792	1403	967	735	1437	1805	800	531	386	344	801	2067	528	2237	419
Baltimore, MD						1959	795	1551	2401	422	370	2388	583	352	441	1665	708	521	377	420	1399	1690	1031	532	2045	1128	1470	600	1032	763	1087	2445	1072	2705	602
Billings, MT							1839	413	626	2254	1796	536	2157	1755	2012	455	1246	1552	1597	1608	1433	554	1007	1534	1255	2806	1673	1432	1836	2237	1088	965	1530	1239	1547
Birmingham, AL								1509	2170	1215	909	2346	466	578	389	1434	667	475	725	576	647	1356	919	734	1292	1921	678	481	241	494	753	1852	381	2092	369
Bismarck, ND									1039	1846	1388	794	1749	1347	1604	594	838	1144	1189	1200	1342	693	675	1126	1597	2398	1582	1024	1548	1906	801	1378	1183	1702	1139
Boise, ID										2697	2239	735	2520	2182	2375	737	1708	1969	2040	2036	1711	833	1369	1977	1206	3249	1952	1852	2115	2566	1376	760	1808	1033	1933
Boston, MA											462	2683	1003	741	861	1961	1003	862	654	760	1819	2004	1326	741	2465	714	1890	940	1453	1184	1427	2757	1493	3046	964
Buffalo, NY												2224	899	431	695	1502	545	442	197	333	1393	1546	868	277	2039	1167	1513	508	1134	1080	995	2299	1066	2572	545
Calgary, AB													2586	2184	2441	991	1675	1981	2026	2037	2114	1234	1512	1963	1936	2912	2355	1862	2385	2743	1638	1291	2020	1565	1977
Charleston, SC														468	204	1783	907	622	724	637	1109	1705	1204	879	1754	1708	1110	721	703	238	1102	2371	900	2554	610
Charleston, WV															265	1445	506	209	255	168	1072	1367	802	410	1718	1446	1192	320	816	649	764	2122	745	2374	251
Charlotte, NC																1637	761	476	520	433	1031	1559	1057	675	1677	1566	1041	575	625	385	956	2225	754	2453	464
Cheyenne, WY																	972	1233	1304	1300	979	100	633	1241	801	2513	1220	1115	1382	1829	640	843	1076	1116	1197
Chicago, IL																		302	346	359	936	1015	337	283	1543	1555	1108	184	750	1065	532	1768	662	2042	299
Cincinnati, OH																			253	105	958	1200	599	261	1605	1567	1079	116	700	803	597	1955	632	2215	106
Cleveland, OH																				144	1208	1347	669	171	1854	1359	1328	319	950	904	806	2100	882	2374	356
Columbus, OH																					1059	1266	665	192	1706	1465	1179	176	801	818	663	2021	733	2281	207
Dallas, TX																						887	752	1218	647	2524	241	913	406	1049	554	1331	327	1446	852
Denver, CO																							676	1284	701	2556	1127	1088	1290	1751	603	756	984	1029	1118
Des Moines, IA																								606	1283	1878	992	481	931	1315	194	1429	567	1703	595
Detroit, MI																									1799	1278	1338	318	960	1060	795	2037	891	2310	366
El Paso, TX																										3171	758	1489	1051	1642	1085	717	974	801	1499
Halifax, NS																											2595	1646	2158	1889	2133	3309	2198	3583	1669
Houston, TX																												839	445	884	795	1474	447	1558	972
Indianapolis, IN																													675	879	485	1843	587	2104	112
Jackson, MS																														598	747	1735	269	1851	594
Jacksonville, FL																															1148	2415	873	2441	766
Kansas City, MO																																1358	382	1632	516
Las Vegas, NV																																	1478	274	1874
Little Rock, AR																																		1706	526
Los Angeles, CA																																			2126

Kilometers

	Albany, NY	Albuquerque, NM	Amarillo, TX	Anchorage, AK	Atlanta, GA	Baltimore, MD	Billings, MT	Birmingham, AL	Bismarck, ND	Boise, ID	Boston, MA	Buffalo, NY	Calgary, AB	Charleston, SC	Charleston, WV	Charlotte, NC	Cheyenne, WY	Chicago, IL	Cincinnati, OH	Cleveland, OH	Columbus, OH	Dallas, TX	Denver, CO	Des Moines, IA	Detroit, MI	El Paso, TX	Halifax, NS	Houston, TX	Indianapolis, IN	Jackson, MS	Jacksonville, FL	Kansas City, MO	Las Vegas, NV	Little Rock, AR	Los Angeles, CA	Louisville, KY
Albuquerque, NM	3371																																			
Amarillo, TX	2914	460																																		
Anchorage, AK	7113	5733	6008																																	
Atlanta, GA	1625	2397	1940	6925																																
Baltimore, MD	536	3060	2603	6914	1093																															
Billings, MT	3352	1595	1590	4185	3039	3152																														
Birmingham, AL	1759	2050	1595	6843	241	1279	2959																													
Bismarck, ND	2695	2145	2249	4383	2508	2496	665	2428																												
Boise, ID	4064	1554	2037	4417	3569	3863	1007	3492	1672																											
Boston, MA	277	3604	3149	7389	1770	679	3627	1955	2970	4339																										
Buffalo, NY	470	2909	2452	6650	1464	595	2890	1463	2233	3603	743																									
Calgary, AB	4042	2410	2685	3323	3854	3842	862	3775	1278	1183	4317	3578																								
Charleston, SC	1469	2885	2430	7232	510	938	3471	750	2814	4055	1614	1446	4161																							
Charleston, WV	1020	2523	2068	6586	809	566	2824	930	2167	3511	1192	693	3514	753																						
Charlotte, NC	1241	2653	2196	6996	383	710	3237	626	2581	3821	1385	1118	3928	328	426																					
Cheyenne, WY	2879	866	859	4917	2385	2679	732	2307	956	1186	3155	2417	1595	2869	2325	2634																				
Chicago, IL	1339	2175	1720	5767	1154	1139	2005	1073	1348	2748	1614	877	2695	1459	814	1224	1564																			
Cincinnati, OH	1175	2267	1812	6259	766	838	2497	764	1841	3168	1387	711	3187	1001	336	766	1984	486																		
Cleveland, OH	779	2605	2148	6331	1168	607	2570	1167	1913	3282	1052	317	3260	1165	410	837	2098	557	407																	
Columbus, OH	999	2375	1918	6349	928	676	2587	927	1931	3276	1223	536	3278	1025	270	697	2092	578	169	232																
Dallas, TX	2703	1213	756	6576	1274	2251	2306	1041	2159	2753	2927	2241	3401	1784	1725	1659	1575	1506	1541	1944	1704															
Denver, CO	2949	705	698	5310	2257	2719	891	2182	1115	1340	3224	2488	1986	2743	2200	2508	161	1633	1931	2167	2037	1427														
Des Moines, IA	1858	1755	1300	5504	1556	1659	1620	1479	1086	2203	2134	1397	2433	1937	1290	1701	1018	542	964	1076	1070	1210	1088													
Detroit, MI	919	2587	2130	6230	1183	856	2468	1181	1812	3181	1192	446	3158	1414	660	1086	1997	455	420	275	309	1960	2066	975												
El Paso, TX	3743	423	705	6439	2312	3290	2019	2079	2570	1940	3966	3281	3115	2822	2764	2698	1289	2483	2582	2983	2745	1041	1128	2064	2895											
Halifax, NS	1411	4739	4283	7757	2904	1815	4515	3091	3858	5228	1149	1878	4685	2748	2327	2520	4043	2502	2521	2187	2357	4061	4113	3022	2056	5102										
Houston, TX	2845	1599	1144	6964	1287	2365	2692	1091	2545	3141	3041	2434	3789	1786	1918	1675	1963	1783	1736	2137	1897	388	1813	1596	2153	1220	4175									
Indianapolis, IN	1279	2088	1632	6068	854	965	2304	774	1648	2980	1512	817	2996	1160	515	925	1794	296	187	513	283	1469	1751	774	512	2396	2648	1350								
Jackson, MS	2142	1862	1406	6909	621	1660	2954	388	2491	3403	2338	1825	3837	1131	1313	1006	2224	1207	1126	1529	1289	653	2076	1498	1545	1691	3472	716	1086							
Jacksonville, FL	1760	2956	2441	7485	553	1228	3599	795	3067	4129	1905	1738	4413	383	1044	619	2943	1714	1292	1455	1316	1688	2817	2116	1706	2642	3039	1422	1414	962						
Kansas City, MO	2063	1438	981	5707	1289	1749	1751	1212	1289	2214	2296	1601	2636	1773	1229	1538	1030	856	961	1297	1067	891	970	312	1279	1746	3432	1279	780	1202	1847					
Las Vegas, NV	4161	930	1390	5400	3326	3934	1553	2980	2217	1223	4436	3699	2077	3815	3414	3580	1356	2845	3146	3379	3252	2142	1216	2299	3278	1154	5324	2372	2965	2792	3886	2185				
Little Rock, AR	2179	1448	993	6322	850	1725	2462	613	1903	2909	2402	1715	3250	1448	1199	1213	1731	1065	1017	1419	1179	526	1583	912	1434	1567	3537	719	944	433	1405	615	2378			
Los Angeles, CA	4600	1297	1757	5475	3599	4352	1994	3366	2739	1662	4901	4138	2518	4109	3820	3947	1796	3286	3564	3820	3670	2327	1656	2740	3717	1289	5765	2507	3385	2978	3928	2626	441	2745		
Louisville, KY	1339	2124	1667	6253	674	969	2489	594	1833	3110	1551	877	3181	981	404	747	1926	481	171	573	333	1371	1799	957	589	2412	2685	1564	180	956	1232	830	3015	846	3421	
Memphis, TN	1953	1662	1207	6570	626	1501	2615	388	2151	3144	2177	1492	3498	1223	975	988	1958	867	793	1194	956	750	1796	1158	1210	1789	3311	943	747	339	1179	862	2592	225	2959	621
México, MX	4520	2352	2051	8061	2821	3899	3641	2624	3952	3985	4574	4058	4737	3319	3541	3208	2911	3421	3360	3760	3522	1815	2750	3002	3776	1926	5709	1535	3287	2249	2956	2684	2846	2344	2981	3187
Miami, FL	2315	3467	2951	7997	1064	1784	4109	1307	3578	4639	2460	2293	4925	938	1599	1175	3455	2224	1836	2011	1871	2200	3329	2626	2254	3152	3595	1932	1924	1472	555	2359	4397	1915	4439	1744
Milwaukee, WI	1495	2294	1837	5651	1308	1295	1891	1228	1234	2813	1770	1033	2579	1614	967	1379	1628	143	640	713	730	1625	1697	608	611	2602	2658	1920	449	1344	1866	922	2909	1202	3350	634
Minneapolis, MN	2003	2154	1697	5110	1817	1804	1350	1736	693	2357	2280	1541	2039	2122	1477	1887	1418	658	1149	1223	1241	1607	1487	396	1121	2462	3168	1995	959	1852	2376	710	2698	1310	3139	1144
Mobile, AL	2162	2162	1780	7258	534	1630	3249	415	2840	3704	2306	1874	4187	1033	1347	920	2526	1485	1176	1578	1339	1028	2378	1794	1595	1981	1981	761	1186	301	660	1496	3092	735	3268	1006
Montréal, QC	370	3495	3038	6607	1997	907	3368	2074	2711	4079	504	639	3535	1842	1323	1614	2895	1353	1311	946	1167	2851	2965	1874	907	3802	1150	3044	1403	2436	2132	2187	4177	2327	4616	1480
Nashville, TN	1614	2008	1553	6534	389	1152	2652	312	2116	3179	1828	1152	3463	874	636	639	1995	763	452	854	615	1096	1870	1167	870	2137	2962	1289	462	681	948	899	2938	571	3305	282
New Orleans, LA	2317	2053	1598	7207	761	1837	3146	565	2790	3595	2515	2018	4135	1260	1490	1147	2417	1504	1319	1722	1482	845	2267	1797	1736	1799	3649	579	1329	298	895	1500	2983	732	3084	1149
New York, NY	243	3242	2785	7062	1398	309	3297	1585	2640	4008	346	644	3990	1244	829	1015	2824	1282	1023	750	861	2557	2895	1804	1001	3596	1480	2671	1150	1968	1533	1934	4106	2031	4537	1189
Oklahoma City, OK	2492	879	422	6245	1519	2179	1974	1173	1828	2423	2726	2031	3070	2008	1644	1773	1244	1298	1389	1726	1496	336	1096	879	1709	1186	3862	722	1210	985	2077	560	1809	571	2175	1245
Omaha, NE	2079	1566	1168	5409	1591	1879	1455	1514	991	1986	2354	1617	2338	2076	1532	1841	800	763	1184	1297	1290	1076	870	219	1195	1989	3242	1464	994	1504	2150	302	2082	917	2521	1133
Orlando, FL	1987	3112	2595	7641	708	1455	3754	951	3223	4283	2130	1965	4570	610	1271	845	3099	1868	1480	1681	1541	1844	2972	2270	1899	2796	3266	1577	1569	1117	227	2003	4042	1559	4084	1389
Ottawa, ON	486	3392	2936	6455	1866	842	3265	1971	2608	3977	665	536	3384	1780	1221	1483	2793	1252	1208	845	1064	2748	2862	1772	805	3701	1324	2941	1302	2333	2069	2085	4074	2224	4515	1377
Philadelphia, PA	359	3144	2689	7010	1258	167	3249	1443	2592	3961	516	666	3939	1102	730	874	2776	1236	927	703	763	2415	2806	1755	953	3455	1651	2529	1054	1826	1393	1836	4023	1891	4441	1091
Phoenix, AZ	4121	750	1212	5776	3006	3807	1929	2772	2674	1598	4354	3659	2454	3514	3274	3390	1615	2927	3018	3355	3125	1733	1455	2507	3337	695	5490	1911	2838	2385	3334	2188	459	2200	594	2874
Pittsburgh, PA	780	2687	2230	6526	1088	396	2766	1228	2109	3477	953	349	3455	1033	349	705	2293	751	470	219	306	2005	2349	1273	470	3046	2087	2198	595	1590	1323	1379	3564	1480	3984	634
Portland, ME	434	3762	3305	7546	1926	837	3784	2113	3128	4497	172	901	4475	1772	1350	1543	3313	1772	1545	1208	1381	3084	3382	2291	1348	4124	872	3199	1670	2494	2061	2454	4594	2558	5059	1709
Portland, OR	4753	2245	2727	3902	4259	4553	1430	4182	2093	695	5030	4291	1371	4743	4199	4508	1876	3438	3858	3973	3965	3443	2029	2893	3870	2843	5918	3831	3669	4093	4817	2904	1911	3599	1562	3800
Québec, QC	582	3734	3279	6846	2209	1120	3607	2314	2951	4320	624	879	3775	2055	1564	1826	3136	1595	1564	1187	1406	3091	3205	2114	1147	4043	940	3284	1644	2676	2344	2428	4417	2566	4858	1720
Raleigh, NC	1028	2867	2412	7157	637	497	3395	880	2739	4014	1173	1033	4085	449	504	254	2829	1385	840	914	776	1913	2703	1862	1165	2951	2307	1928	1028	1260	740	1733	3797	1430	4164	907
Rapid City, SD	2816	1353	1347	4795	2431	2616	610	2354	515	1496	3091	2354	1472	2935	2288	2700	491	1469	1961	2034	2051	1733	650	1012	1932	1778	3979	2121	1772	2346	2991	1142	1665	1759	2106	1955
Reno, NV	4420	1641	2101	4843	3926	4220	1545	3849	2208	692	4697	3958	2069	4410	3866	4175	1543	3105	3525	3640	3632	3110	1696	2560	3537	2116	5585	3334	3335	3760	4484	2571	711	3266	835	3467
Richmond, VA	776	3018	2563	7065	848	245	3303	1091	2647	4016	920	780	3994	689	518	465	2832	1290	853	758	832	2106	2716	1812	1009	3146	2055	2140	1031	1471	980	1746	3932	1582	4315	920
St. Louis, MO	1667	1691	1234	6113	883	1353	2158	806	1694	2619	1900	1205	3041	1368	824	1133	1435	473	563	901	671	1022	1376	702	883	1998	3036	1389	385	813	1442	405	2590	669	2986	425
Salt Lake City, UT	3578	1004	1551	4729	3083	3379	882	3006	1545	550	3854	3115	1406	3569	3025	3334	702	2262	2682	2796	2790	2269	854	1717	2695	1390	4742	2655	2492	2917	3643	1728	671	2425	1112	2624
San Antonio, TX	3142	1316	825	6833	1609	2689	2414	1413	2573	2833	3366	2679	3511	2108	2162	1997	1683	2043	1981	2383	2143	436	1522	1623	2397	895	4500	322	1908	1036	1744	1307	2047	965	2182	1810
San Diego, CA	4697	1327	1788	5673	3485	4383	2095	3252	2840	1763	4932	4235	2619	3995	3850	3870	1897	3387	3595	3921	3701	2212	1757	2841	3818	1175	5866	2393	3414	2864	3813	2727	542	2740	200	3450
San Francisco, CA	4769	1788	2248	4940	4212	4570	1892	3977	2814	1039	5044	4307	2409	4721	4216	4439	1892	3453	3873	3987	3981	2940	2045	2907	3886	1900	5932	3118	3685	3591	4541	2919	925	3237	619	3817
Seattle, WA	4664	2354	2837	3623	4352	4465	1313	4275	1977	805	4940	4203	1093	4784	4137	4549	1986	3318	3810	3883	3900	3553	2138	2932	3781	3128	5828	3940	3619	4203	4911	3012	2021	3709	1847	3804
Tampa, FL	2076	3136	2619	7664	732	1545	3778	975	3247	4307	2220	2053	4592	698	1360	935	3123	1892	1504	1772	1667	1868	2996	2294	1921	2821	3355	1601	1593	1141	315	2026	4064	1583	4108	1413
Toronto, ON	644	2962	2505	6595	1541	909	2835	1541	2179	3546	917	171	3524	1619	864	1290	2362	821	779	488	708	2319	2433	1342	375	3269	1681	2512	870	1903	1910	1654	3644	1794	4084	948
Vancouver, BC	4878	2570	3052	3430	4566	4679	1527	4491	2191	1018	5155	4417	899	4998	4352	4763	2201	3533	4024	4098	4116	3768	2354	3147	3995	3358	6043	4156	3834	4418	5126	3229	2237	3924	2077	4018
Washington, DC	594	3051	2594	6903	1023	61	3142	1220	2486	3854	737	618	3831	867	557	639	2669	1128	832	595	669	2191	2713	1649	846	3231	1873	2306	959	1603	1158	1743	3928	1667	4348	959
Wichita, KS	2367	1138	681	5921	1591	2053	1717	1348	1503	2166	2600	1905	2814	2077	1533	1842	986	1171	1263	1601	1371	591	838	628	1583	1445	3736	978	1084	1241	2151	309	2053	747	2434	1134
Winnipeg, MB	2730	2587	2285	4385	2542	2531	1324	2463	668	2336	3006	2269	1313	2850	2203	2615	1821	1384	1876	1948	1966	2193	1892	1121	1847	3010	3361	2581	1685	2526	3102	1324	3012	1939	3453	1870

Miles

	Memphis, TN	México, MX	Miami, FL	Milwaukee, WI	Minneapolis, MN	Mobile, AL	Montréal, QC	Nashville, TN	New Orleans, LA	New York, NY	Oklahoma City, OK	Omaha, NE	Orlando, FL	Ottawa, ON	Philadelphia, PA	Phoenix, AZ	Pittsburgh, PA	Portland, ME	Portland, OR	Québec, QC	Raleigh, NC	Rapid City, SD	Reno, NV	Richmond, VA	St. Louis, MO	Salt Lake City, UT	San Antonio, TX	San Diego, CA	San Francisco, CA	Seattle, WA	Tampa, FL	Toronto, ON	Vancouver, BC	Washington, DC	Wichita, KS	Winnipeg, MB
Albany, NY	1214	2809	1439	929	1245	1344	230	1003	1440	151	1549	1292	1235	302	223	2561	485	270	2954	362	639	1750	2747	482	1036	2224	1953	2919	2964	2899	1290	400	3032	369	1471	1697
Albuquerque, NM	1033	1462	2155	1426	1339	1344	2172	1248	1276	2015	546	973	1934	2108	1954	466	1670	2338	1395	2321	1782	841	1020	1876	1051	624	818	825	1111	1463	1949	1841	1597	1896	707	1608
Amarillo, TX	750	1275	1834	1142	1055	1106	1888	965	993	1731	262	726	1613	1825	1671	753	1386	2054	1695	2038	1499	837	1306	1593	767	964	513	1111	1397	1763	1628	1557	1897	1612	423	1420
Anchorage, AK	4083	5010	4970	3512	3176	4511	4106	4061	4479	4389	3881	3362	4749	4012	4357	3590	4056	4690	2425	4255	4448	2980	3010	4391	3799	2939	4247	3526	3070	2252	4763	4099	2132	4290	3680	2725
Atlanta, GA	389	1753	661	813	1129	332	1241	242	473	869	944	989	440	1160	782	1868	676	1197	2647	1373	396	1511	2440	527	549	1916	1000	2166	2618	2705	455	958	2838	636	989	1580
Baltimore, MD	933	2423	1109	805	1121	1013	564	716	1142	192	1354	1168	904	523	104	2366	246	520	2830	696	309	1626	2623	152	841	2100	1671	2724	2840	2775	960	565	2908	38	1276	1573
Billings, MT	1625	2263	2554	1175	839	2019	2093	1648	1955	2049	1227	904	2333	2029	2019	1199	1719	2352	889	2242	2110	379	960	2053	1341	548	1500	1302	1176	816	2348	1762	949	1953	1067	823
Birmingham, AL	241	1631	812	763	1079	258	1289	194	351	985	729	941	591	1225	897	1723	763	1313	2599	1438	547	1463	2392	678	501	1868	878	2021	2472	2657	606	958	2791	758	838	1531
Bismarck, ND	1337	2456	2224	767	431	1765	1685	1315	1734	1641	1136	616	2003	1621	1611	1662	1311	1944	1301	1834	1702	320	1372	1645	1053	960	1599	1765	1749	1229	2018	1354	1362	1545	934	415
Boise, ID	1954	2477	2883	1748	1465	2302	2535	1976	2234	2491	1506	1234	2662	2472	2462	993	2161	2795	432	2685	2495	930	430	2496	1628	342	1761	1096	646	500	2677	2204	633	2395	1346	1452
Boston, MA	1353	2843	1529	1100	1417	1433	313	1136	1563	215	1694	1463	1324	413	321	2706	592	107	3126	388	729	1921	2919	572	1181	2395	2092	3065	3135	3070	1380	570	3204	458	1616	1868
Buffalo, NY	927	2522	1425	642	958	1165	397	716	1254	400	1262	1005	1221	333	414	2274	217	560	2667	546	642	1463	2460	485	749	1936	1665	2632	2677	2612	1276	106	2745	384	1184	1410
Calgary, AB	2174	2944	3061	1603	1267	2602	2197	2152	2570	2480	1908	1453	2840	2103	2448	1525	2147	2781	852	2346	2539	915	1286	2482	1890	874	2182	1628	1497	679	2854	2190	559	2381	1749	816
Charleston, SC	760	2063	583	1003	1319	642	1145	543	783	773	1248	1290	379	1106	685	2184	642	1101	2948	1277	279	1824	2741	428	850	2218	1310	2483	2934	2973	434	1006	3106	539	1291	1771
Charleston, WV	606	2201	994	601	918	837	822	395	926	515	1022	952	790	759	454	2035	217	839	2610	972	313	1422	2403	322	512	1880	1344	2393	2620	2571	845	537	2705	346	953	1369
Charlotte, NC	614	1994	730	857	1173	572	1003	397	713	631	1102	1144	525	922	543	2107	438	959	2802	1135	158	1678	2595	289	704	2072	1241	2405	2759	2827	581	802	2960	397	1145	1625
Cheyenne, WY	1217	1809	2147	1012	881	1570	1799	1240	1502	1755	773	497	1926	1736	1725	1004	1425	2059	1166	1949	1758	305	959	1760	892	436	1046	1179	1176	1234	1941	1468	1368	1659	613	1132
Chicago, IL	539	2126	1382	89	409	923	841	474	935	797	807	474	1161	778	768	1819	467	1101	2137	991	861	913	1930	802	294	1406	1270	2105	2146	2062	1176	510	2196	701	728	860
Cincinnati, OH	493	2088	1141	398	714	731	815	281	820	636	863	736	920	751	576	1876	292	960	2398	972	522	1219	2191	530	350	1667	1231	2234	2407	2368	935	484	2501	517	785	1166
Cleveland, OH	742	2337	1250	443	760	981	588	531	1070	466	1073	806	1045	525	437	2085	136	751	2469	738	568	1264	2262	471	560	1738	1481	2437	2478	2413	1101	303	2547	370	995	1211
Columbus, OH	594	2189	1163	454	771	832	725	382	921	535	930	802	958	661	474	1942	190	858	2464	874	482	1275	2257	517	417	1734	1332	2300	2474	2424	1036	440	2558	416	852	1222
Dallas, TX	466	1128	1367	1010	999	639	1772	681	525	1589	209	669	1146	1708	1501	1077	1246	1917	2140	1921	1189	1077	1933	1309	635	1410	271	1375	1827	2208	1161	1441	2342	1362	367	1363
Denver, CO	1116	1709	2069	1055	924	1478	1843	1162	1409	1799	681	541	1847	1779	1744	904	1460	2102	1261	1992	1680	404	1054	1688	855	531	946	1092	1271	1329	1862	1512	1463	1686	521	1176
Des Moines, IA	720	1866	1632	378	246	1115	1165	725	1117	1121	546	136	1411	1101	1091	1558	791	1424	1798	1314	1157	629	1591	1126	436	1067	1009	1766	1807	1822	1426	834	1956	1025	390	697
Detroit, MI	752	2347	1401	380	697	991	564	541	1079	622	1062	743	1180	500	592	2074	292	838	2405	713	724	1201	2198	627	549	1675	1490	2373	2415	2350	1194	233	2483	526	984	1148
El Paso, TX	1112	1197	1959	1617	1530	1231	2363	1328	1118	2235	737	1236	1738	2300	2147	432	1893	2563	1767	2513	1834	1105	1315	1955	1242	864	556	730	1181	1944	1753	2032	2087	2008	898	1871
Halifax, NS	2058	3548	2234	1652	1969	1231	715	1841	2268	920	2400	2015	2030	823	1026	3412	1297	542	3678	584	1434	2473	3471	1277	1887	2947	2797	3646	3687	3622	2085	1045	3756	1164	2322	2089
Houston, TX	586	954	1201	1193	1240	473	1892	801	360	1660	449	910	980	1828	1572	1188	1366	1988	2381	2041	1198	1318	2072	1330	863	1650	200	1487	1938	2449	995	1561	2583	1433	608	1604
Indianapolis, IN	464	2043	1196	279	596	737	872	287	826	715	752	618	975	809	655	1764	370	1038	2280	1022	639	1101	2073	641	239	1549	1186	2122	2290	2249	990	541	2383	596	674	1047
Jackson, MS	211	1398	915	835	1151	187	1514	423	185	1223	612	935	694	1450	1135	1482	988	1550	2544	1663	783	1458	2337	914	505	1813	644	1780	2232	2612	709	1183	2746	996	771	1570
Jacksonville, FL	733	1837	345	1160	1477	410	1325	589	556	953	1291	1336	141	1286	866	2072	822	1281	2994	1457	460	1859	2787	609	896	2264	1084	2370	2822	3052	196	1187	3186	720	1337	1928
Kansas City, MO	536	1668	1466	573	441	930	1359	559	932	1202	348	188	1245	1296	1141	1360	857	1525	1805	1509	1077	710	1598	1085	252	1074	812	1695	1814	1872	1259	1028	2007	1083	192	823
Las Vegas, NV	1611	1769	2733	1808	1677	1922	2596	1826	1854	2552	1124	1294	2512	2532	2500	285	2215	2855	1188	2745	2360	1035	442	2444	1610	417	1272	337	575	1256	2526	2265	1390	2441	1276	1872
Little Rock, AR	140	1457	1190	747	814	457	1446	355	455	1262	355	570	969	1382	1175	1367	920	1590	2237	1595	889	1093	2030	983	416	1507	600	1703	2012	2305	984	1115	2439	1036	464	1205
Los Angeles, CA	1839	1853	2759	2082	1951	2031	2869	2054	1917	2820	1352	1567	2538	2806	2760	369	2476	3144	971	3019	2588	1309	519	2682	1856	691	1356	124	385	1148	2553	2538	1291	2702	1513	2146
Louisville, KY	386	1981	1084	394	711	625	920	175	714	739	774	704	863	856	678	1786	394	1062	2362	1069	564	1215	2155	572	264	1631	1125	2144	2372	2364	878	589	2497	596	705	1162
Memphis, TN		1595	1051	624	940	395	1306	215	396	1123	487	724	830	1243	1035	1500	780	1451	2382	1456	749	1247	2175	843	294	1652	739	1841	2144	2440	845	975	2574	896	597	1359
México, MX			2154	2200	2113	1426	2900	1810	1313	2619	1323	1783	1933	2838	2525	1484	2375	2941	2819	3051	2151	2365	2367	2283	1825	2135	853	1683	2233	2996	1948	2570	3139	2386	1481	2477
Miami, FL				1478	1794	727	1671	907	874	1299	1609	1654	232	1631	1211	2390	1167	1627	3312	1803	805	2176	3105	954	1214	2581	1401	2688	3140	3370	274	1532	3504	1065	1655	2246
Milwaukee, WI					337	1019	939	569	1020	894	880	514	1257	875	865	1892	564	1198	2063	1088	956	842	1970	899	367	1446	1343	2145	2186	1991	1272	607	2124	799	769	789
Minneapolis, MN						1335	1255	886	1337	1211	793	383	1573	1192	1181	1805	881	1515	1727	1405	1273	606	1839	1216	621	1315	1257	2014	2055	1654	1588	924	1788	1115	637	452
Mobile, AL							1575	450	146	1203	799	1119	506	1481	1115	1662	1019	1531	2731	1707	730	1641	2545	861	688	2000	673	1960	2411	2799	521	1214	2933	970	958	1787
Montréal, QC								1094	1632	383	1625	1300	1466	121	454	2637	607	282	2963	155	871	1758	2756	714	1112	2232	2043	2931	2972	2907	1522	330	3041	600	1547	1374
Nashville, TN									539	906	703	747	686	1031	818	1715	569	1234	2405	1244	532	1269	2198	626	307	1675	954	2056	2360	2463	701	764	2597	679	748	1337
New Orleans, LA										1332	731	1121	653	1570	1245	1548	1108	1660	2663	1783	871	1643	2431	1002	690	1932	560	1846	2298	2731	668	1302	2865	1106	890	1755
New York, NY											1469	1258	1094	439	91	2481	367	313	2920	515	499	1716	2713	342	956	2189	1861	2839	2929	2864	1150	507	2998	228	1391	1665
Oklahoma City, OK												463	1388	1563	1408	1012	1124	1792	1934	1776	1237	871	1727	1331	505	1204	466	1370	1657	2002	1403	1295	2136	1350	161	1158
Omaha, NE													1433	1238	1228	1440	928	1561	1662	1451	1265	525	1455	1263	440	932	927	1630	1672	1719	1448	971	1853	1162	307	638
Orlando, FL														1427	1006	2169	963	1422	3091	1598	601	1955	2884	750	993	2360	1180	2467	2918	3149	82	1327	3283	860	1434	2025
Ottawa, ON															451	2575	545	382	2901	257	831	1696	2694	675	1050	2170	1981	2869	2910	2845	1483	268	2978	562	1485	1280
Philadelphia, PA																2420	306	419	2890	586	411	1686	2683	254	895	2160	1774	2779	2900	2835	1062	522	2968	140	1330	1633
Phoenix, AZ																	2136	2804	1335	2788	2249	1308	883	2343	1517	651	987	358	750	1513	2184	2307	1655	2362	1173	2075
Pittsburgh, PA																		690	2590	758	497	1386	2383	341	611	1859	1519	2494	2599	2534	1019	321	2668	240	1046	1332
Portland, ME																			3223	264	827	2019	3016	670	1279	2493	2189	3162	3233	3168	1478	668	3301	556	1714	1966
Portland, OR																				3114	2923	1268	578	2925	2057	771	2322	1093	638	170	3106	2633	313	2824	1775	1463
Québec, QC																					1003	1908	2905	846	1261	2381	2193	3080	3122	3057	1654	479	3190	732	1696	1523
Raleigh, NC																						1777	2716	157	825	2193	1398	2563	2894	2926	656	820	3060	265	1266	1724
Rapid City, SD																							1151	1720	963	628	1335	1372	1368	1195	1970	1429	1328	1620	712	792
Reno, NV																								2718	1850	524	1870	642	217	755	2899	2426	898	2617	1568	1867
Richmond, VA																									834	2194	1530	2684	2934	2869	805	660	3003	108	1274	1667
St. Louis, MO																										1326	968	1875	2066	2125	1008	782	2259	837	441	1075
Salt Lake City, UT																											1419	754	740	839	2375	1902	973	2094	1044	1455
San Antonio, TX																												1285	1737	2275	1195	1714	2410	1635	624	1621
San Diego, CA																													508	1271	2481	2601	1414	2720	1531	2209
San Francisco, CA																														816	2933	2643	958	2834	1784	2193
Seattle, WA																															3164	2577	140	2769	1843	1390
Tampa, FL																																1383	3297	916	1448	2039
Toronto, ON																																	2711	563	1217	1375
Vancouver, BC																																		2902	1977	1375
Washington, DC																																			1272	1566
Wichita, KS																																				956

Kilometers

	Memphis, TN	México, MX	Miami, FL	Milwaukee, WI	Minneapolis, MN	Mobile, AL	Montréal, QC	Nashville, TN	New Orleans, LA	New York, NY	Oklahoma City, OK	Omaha, NE	Orlando, FL	Ottawa, ON	Philadelphia, PA	Phoenix, AZ	Pittsburgh, PA	Portland, ME	Portland, OR	Québec, QC	Raleigh, NC	Rapid City, SD	Reno, NV	Richmond, VA	St. Louis, MO	Salt Lake City, UT	San Antonio, TX	San Diego, CA	San Francisco, CA	Seattle, WA	Tampa, FL	Toronto, ON	Vancouver, BC	Washington, DC	Wichita, KS
México, MX	2566																																		
Miami, FL	1691	3466																																	
Milwaukee, WI	1004	3540	2378																																
Minneapolis, MN	1512	3400	2887	542																															
Mobile, AL	636	2294	1170	1640	2148																														
Montréal, QC	2101	4666	2689	1511	2019	2534																													
Nashville, TN	346	2912	1459	916	1426	724	1760																												
New Orleans, LA	637	2113	1406	1641	2151	235	2626	867																											
New York, NY	1807	4214	2090	1438	1948	1936	616	1458	2143																										
Oklahoma City, OK	784	2129	2589	1416	1276	1286	2615	1131	1176	2364																									
Omaha, NE	1165	2869	2661	827	616	1800	2092	1202	1804	2024	745																								
Orlando, FL	1335	3110	373	2023	2531	814	2359	1104	1051	1760	2233	2306																							
Ottawa, ON	2000	4566	2624	1408	1918	2383	194	1659	2526	706	2515	1992	2296																						
Philadelphia, PA	1665	4063	1948	1392	1900	1794	730	1316	2003	146	2265	1976	1619	726																					
Phoenix, AZ	2414	2388	3846	3044	2904	2674	4243	2759	2491	3992	1628	2317	3490	4143	3894																				
Pittsburgh, PA	1255	3821	1878	907	1418	1640	977	916	1783	591	1809	1493	1549	877	492	3437																			
Portland, ME	2335	4732	2618	1928	2438	2463	454	1986	2671	504	2883	2512	2288	615	674	4512	1110																		
Portland, OR	3833	4536	5329	3319	2779	4394	4767	3870	4285	4698	3112	2674	4973	4668	4650	2148	4167	5186																	
Québec, QC	2343	4909	2901	1751	2261	2747	249	2002	2869	829	2858	2335	2571	414	943	4486	1220	425	5010																
Raleigh, NC	1205	3461	1295	1538	2048	1175	1401	856	1401	803	1990	2035	967	1337	661	3619	800	1331	4703	1614															
Rapid City, SD	2006	3805	3501	1355	975	2640	2829	2042	2644	2761	1401	845	3146	2729	2713	2105	2230	3249	2040	3070	2859														
Reno, NV	3500	3809	4996	3170	2959	4095	4434	3537	3911	4365	2779	2341	4640	4335	4317	1421	3834	4853	930	4674	4370	1852													
Richmond, VA	1356	3673	1535	1446	1957	1385	1149	1007	1612	550	2142	2032	1207	1086	409	3770	549	1078	4706	1361	253	2767	4373												
St. Louis, MO	473	2936	1953	591	999	1107	1789	494	1110	1538	813	708	1598	1689	1440	2441	983	2058	3310	2029	1327	1549	2977	1342											
Salt Lake City, UT	2658	3435	4153	2327	2116	3218	3591	2695	3109	3522	1937	1500	3797	3492	3475	1047	2991	4011	1241	3831	3529	1010	843	3530	2134										
San Antonio, TX	1189	1372	2254	2161	2023	1083	3287	1535	901	2994	750	1492	1899	3187	2854	1588	2444	3522	3736	3529	2249	2148	3009	2462	1558	2283									
San Diego, CA	2962	2708	4325	3451	3241	3154	4716	3308	2970	4568	2204	2623	3969	4616	4471	576	4013	5088	1759	4956	4124	2208	1033	4319	3017	1213	2341								
San Francisco, CA	3450	3593	5052	3517	3306	3879	4782	3797	3697	4713	2666	2690	4695	4682	4666	1207	4182	5202	1027	5023	4656	2201	349	4721	3324	1191	2795	817							
Seattle, WA	3926	4821	5422	3204	2661	4504	4677	3963	4394	4608	3221	2766	5067	4578	4562	2434	4077	5097	274	4919	4708	1923	1215	4616	3419	1350	3660	2045	1313						
Tampa, FL	1360	3134	441	2047	2555	838	2449	1128	1075	1850	2257	2330	132	2386	1709	3514	1640	2378	4998	2661	1056	3170	4664	1295	1622	3821	1923	3992	4719	5091					
Toronto, ON	1569	4135	2465	977	1487	1953	531	1229	2095	816	2084	1562	2135	431	840	3712	516	1075	4236	771	1319	2299	3903	1062	1258	3060	2758	4185	4253	4146	2225				
Vancouver, BC	4142	5051	5638	3418	2877	4719	4893	4179	4610	4824	3437	2981	5282	4792	4776	2663	4293	5311	504	5133	4924	2137	1445	4832	3635	1566	3878	2275	1541	225	5305	4362			
Washington, DC	1442	3839	1714	1286	1794	1561	965	1093	1780	367	2172	1870	1384	904	225	3800	386	895	4544	1178	426	2607	4211	174	1347	3369	2631	4376	4560	4455	1474	906	4669		
Wichita, KS	961	2383	2663	1237	1025	1541	2489	1204	1432	2238	259	494	2307	2389	2140	1887	1683	2758	2856	2729	2037	1146	2523	2050	710	1680	1004	2463	2870	2965	2330	1958	3181	2047	
Winnipeg, MB	2187	3985	3614	1270	727	2875	2211	2151	2824	2679	1863	1027	3258	2060	2627	3339	2143	3163	2354	2451	2774	1274	3004	2682	1730	2341	2608	3554	3529	2237	3281	2212	2212	2520	1538

Remember, always wear your safety belt.

STATE/PROVINCE	ROAD CONDITIONS	SPEED LIMIT	MOTORCYCLE HELMET	CHILD RESTRAINT SEAT
ALABAMA	(334) 242-4128	70 mph	Yes, all riders	3 years and younger
ALASKA	(800) 478-7675 (in-state) (907) 723-6037 (out-of-state)	65 mph	17 years and younger, all passengers and drivers with instructional permits	3 years and younger
ARIZONA	(888) 411-7623	75 mph	17 years and younger	Age 4 and under
ARKANSAS	(501) 569-2374 (in-state) (800) 245-1672 (out-of-state)	70 mph/trucks 65 mph	20 years and younger	Age 5 and younger and less than 60 lbs.
CALIFORNIA	(800) 427-7623 (in-state) (916) 445-7623 (out-of-state)	70 mph/trucks 55 mph	Yes, all riders	5 years and younger or less than 60 lbs.
COLORADO	(303) 639-1111	75 mph	None	3 years and younger and less than 40 lbs.
CONNECTICUT	(860) 594-2650	65 mph	17 years and younger	Age 4 and less than 40 lbs.
DELAWARE	(800) 652-5600 (in-state) (302) 760-2080 (out-of-state)	65 mph	18 years and younger	Age 6 years and younger and less than 60 lbs.
DISTRICT OF COLUMBIA	(301) 628-4343	55 mph	Yes, all riders	Age 2 years and younger
FLORIDA Florida's Turnpike Ft. Myers/Bartow Area Lake City Area Chipley Area Ft. Lauderdale Area Orlando/De Land Area Miami Area Tampa Area	(800) 749-7453 (800) 292-3368 (800) 749-2967 (850) 638-0250 (866) 336-8435 (800) 780-7102 (800) 435-2368 (800) 226-7220	70 mph	Under age 21 and those without proof of $10,000 of medical insurance	Age 3 years and younger
GEORGIA	(404) 635-6800	70 mph	Yes, all riders	Age 4 years and younger
HAWAII	(808) 536-6566	55 mph	17 years and younger, reflectorization required	Age 3 years and younger
IDAHO	(888) 432-7623 (in-state) (208) 336-6600 (out-of-state)	75 mph/trucks 65 mph	17 years and younger	3 years and younger and less than 40 lbs.
ILLINOIS	(800) 452-4368	65 mph/trucks 55 mph	None	3 years and younger
INDIANA	(800) 261-7623	65 mph/trucks 60 mph	Under age 18 or instructional permit holders	3 years and younger
IOWA	(515) 288-1047	65 mph	None	2 years and younger
KANSAS	(800) 585-7623 (in-state)	70 mph	17 years and younger	3 years and younger
KENTUCKY	(800) 459-7623	65 mph	21 years and younger, or those without proof of medical insurance	Less than 40 in. tall
LOUISIANA	(225) 379-1100	70 mph	Age 17 and younger, and those 18 and older without proof of medical insurance	2 years and younger
MAINE	(207) 287-3427	65 mph	Riders with learners permit and for one year after obtaining license, as well as passengers under 15 years	Less than 40 lbs. in a child safety seat 40-80 lbs. and less than 8 years in a safety system that elevates the child so that an adult seat belt fits properly
MARYLAND	(800) 327-3125 (winter)	65 mph	Yes, all riders and helmets must have reflectorization	5 years and younger or 40 lbs. or less
MASSACHUSETTS	(617) 374-1234	65 mph.	Yes, all riders	4 years and younger or 40 lbs. and less
MICHIGAN	(800) 381-8477	70 mph/trucks 55 mph	Yes, all riders	3 years and younger
MINNESOTA	(800) 542-0220	70 mph	17 years and younger, drivers with instructional/learner's permits	3 years and younger
MISSISSIPPI	(601) 987-1211	70 mph	Yes, all riders	3 years and younger
MISSOURI	(800) 222-6400 (in-state)	70 mph	Yes, all riders	3 years and younger
MONTANA	(800) 226-7623	75 mph/trucks 65 mph	17 years and younger	Younger than 2 years
NEBRASKA	(800) 906-9069 (in-state) (402) 471-4533 (out-of-state)	75 mph	Yes, all riders	5 years and younger
NEVADA	(877) 687-6237	75 mph	Yes, all riders	4 years and younger and less than 40 lbs.
NEW HAMPSHIRE	(800) 918-9993 (in-state) (603) 271-6900 (out-of-state)	65 mph	17 years and younger	3 years and younger
NEW JERSEY Atlantic City Expressway Garden State Parkway New Jersey Turnpike	(609) 965-7200 (732) 442-8600 (732) 247-0900	65 mph	Yes, all helmets must have reflectorization	7 years and younger and less than 80 lbs. seated in rear seat if available
NEW MEXICO	(800) 432-4269	75 mph	17 years and younger, reflectorization required	Younger than 1 year in a rear-facing infant seat, seated in the rear seat if available, 1-4 years or less than 40 lbs.
NEW YORK	(800) 847-8929 (NY State Thruway)	65 mph	Yes, all riders Reflectorization required	3 years and younger in all seats

Remember, always wear your safety belt.

STATE/PROVINCE	ROAD CONDITIONS	SPEED LIMIT	MOTORCYCLE HELMET	CHILD RESTRAINT SEAT
NORTH CAROLINA	(877) 368-4968	70 mph	Yes, all riders	4 years and younger and less than 40 lbs.
NORTH DAKOTA	(701) 328-7623	70 mph	Drivers 17 years and younger, all passengers	3 years and younger
OHIO	(614) 644-7031 (440) 234-2030 (Ohio Turnpike)	65 mph/trucks 55 mph	17 and younger, novice riders and all passengers	3 years and younger
OKLAHOMA	(405) 425-2385	75 mph	17 years and younger	3 years and younger and 60 lbs. or less
OREGON	(800) 977-6368 (in-state) (503) 588-2941 (out-of-state)	65 mph/trucks 55 mph	Yes, all riders	3 years and younger and 40 lbs. or less in a child safety seat; 4-5 years or 40-60 lbs. in a safety system that elevates the child so that an adult seat belt fits properly
PENNSYLVANIA	(888) 783-6783 (800) 331-3414 (Penn. Turnpike)	65 mph	Yes, all riders	3 years and younger
RHODE ISLAND	(401) 222-5175	65 mph	20 years and younger during the first year of licensure and all passengers	6 years and younger and less than 54 in. and less than 80 lbs.
SOUTH CAROLINA	(800) 768-1501 (in-state) (803) 896-9621 (out-of-state)	70 mph	20 years and younger	1-5 years and 20-40 lbs. in a forward-facing child safety seat; 1-5 and 40-80 lbs. in a booster seat secured by a lap-shoulder belt. LAP BELT ALONE IS IMPERMISSIBLE
SOUTH DAKOTA	(605) 626-2282	75 mph	17 and younger, all helmets must have reflectorization	4 years and younger and less than 40 lbs.
TENNESSEE	(800) 858-6349	70 mph	Yes, all riders	3 years and younger, and 4-7 years and less than 40 lbs.
TEXAS	(800) 452-9292	70 mph	20 and under and those without proof of medical insurance or those who have not completed a training course	3 years and younger or less than 36 in.
UTAH	(800) 492-2400	75 mph	17 years and younger	4 years and younger
VERMONT	(802) 828-4894	65 mph	Yes, all riders. Helmet must have reflectorization	4 years and younger
VIRGINIA	(800) 367-7623	65 mph	Yes, all riders	5 years and younger
WASHINGTON	(800) 695-7623	70 mph	Yes, all riders	Younger than 1 year or less than 20 lbs. in rear-facing infant seat; 1-3 years or 20-40 lbs. in a forward-facing child safety seat; 4-5 or 40-60 lbs. in a booster seat
WEST VIRGINIA	(877) 982-7623	70 mph	Yes, all riders Reflectorization required	2 years and younger
WISCONSIN	(800) 762-3947	65 mph	17 years and younger, or instructional permit holders	3 years and younger
WYOMING	(307) 772-0824	75 mph	18 years and younger	4 years and younger and 40 lbs. or less
ALBERTA	(403) 246-5853	50 km on urban roads. 80 km in rural areas unless posted	Yes, all riders	6 years and under or 18kg (40 lbs.) and under
BRITISH COLUMBIA	(250) 953-9000 (ext. 7623)	50 km on urban roads. 80 km in rural areas unless posted	Yes, all riders	6 years and under or 18kg (40 lbs.) and under
MANITOBA	(204) 945-3704	50 km on urban roads. 80 km in rural areas unless posted	Yes, all riders	6 years and under or 18kg (40 lbs.) and under
NEW BRUNSWICK	(800) 561-4063 (in Canada)	50 km on urban roads. 80 km in rural areas unless posted	Yes, all riders	6 years and under or 18kg (40 lbs.) and under
NEWFOUNDLAND & LABRADOR	No phone number www.roads.gov.nf.ca	50 km on urban roads. 80 km in rural areas unless posted	Yes, all riders	6 years and under or 18kg (40 lbs.) and under
NORTHWEST TERRITORIES	(800) 661-0750 (in NT only)	100 km on paved roads 90 km on gravel roads	Yes, all riders	6 years and under or 18kg (40 lbs.) and under
NOVA SCOTIA	(902) 424-3933	50 km on urban roads. 80 km in rural areas unless posted	Yes, all riders	6 years and under or 18kg (40 lbs.) and under
NUNAVUT	(800) 491-7910	50 km on urban roads. 80 km in rural areas unless posted	Yes, all riders	6 years and under or 18kg (40 lbs.) and under
ONTARIO	(800) 268-4686 (in Canada) (877) 401-8777 (outside Canada)	50 km on urban roads. 80 km in rural areas unless posted	Yes, all riders	6 years and under or 18kg (40 lbs.) and under
PRINCE EDWARD ISLAND	(902) 368-4770	50 km on urban roads. 80 km in rural areas unless posted	Yes, all riders	6 years and under or 18kg (40 lbs.) and under
QUÉBEC	(418) 545-2363	50 km on urban roads. 80 km in rural areas unless posted	Yes, all riders	6 years and under or 18kg (40 lbs.) and under
SASKATCHEWAN	(306) 933-8333	50 km on urban roads. 80 km in rural areas unless posted	Yes, all riders	6 years and under or 18kg (40 lbs.) and under
YUKON TERRITORIES	(877) 456-7623 (in Canada)	50 km on urban roads. 80 km in rural areas unless posted	Yes, all riders	6 years and under or 18kg (40 lbs.) and under

Climate and Collections

Cities	Dec	Jan	Feb	Mar	Apr	May	June	July	Aug	Sept	Oct	Nov
Acapulco, MX												
Anchorage, AK												
Aspen, CO												
Atlanta, GA												
Baltimore, MD												
Birmingham, AL												
Boston, MA												
Calgary, AB												
Charleston, SC												
Chicago, IL												
Cincinnati, OH												
Dallas, TX												
Denver, CO												
Detroit, MI												
Edmonton, AB												
Fairbanks, AK												
Greenville, SC												
Halifax, NS												
Honolulu, HI												
Houston, TX												
Jacksonville, FL												
Las Vegas, NV												
Los Angeles, CA												
Memphis, TN												
México, MX												
Miami, FL												
Milwaukee, WI												
Minneapolis, MN												
Montréal, QC												
Nashville, TN												
New Orleans, LA												
New York, NY												
Oaxaca, MX												
Orlando, FL												
Ottawa, ON												
Philadelphia, PA												
Phoenix, AZ												
Pittsburgh, PA												
Portland, ME												
Portland, OR												
Providence, RI												
Québec, QC												
Richmond, VA												
Salt Lake City, UT												
San Antonio, TX												
San Diego, CA												
San Francisco, CA												
Santa Fe, NM												
Saskatoon, SK												
Seattle, WA												
St. John's, NF												
St. Louis, MO												
Tampa, FL												
Toronto, ON												
Vancouver, BC												
Washington, DC												
Whitehorse, YT												
Wichita, KS												
Winnipeg, MB												
Yellowknife, NT												

California   Canada
Chicago   Florida   Mexico
New England   New York City
Pacific Northwest
Québec   San Francisco
USA East   USA West
Washington DC

Montréal
New Orleans
New York City
San Francisco

USA Road Map
USA Political Map
Mid-Atlantic / Allegheny Highlands Map
New England / Hudson Valley Map
Southeastern USA Map
Western USA / Western Canada Map

Legend

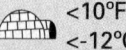 <10°F / <-12°C

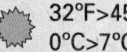 32°F>45°F / 0°C>7°C

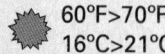 60°F>70°F / 16°C>21°C

 >85°F / >29°C

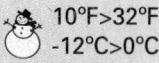 10°F>32°F / -12°C>0°C

 45°F>60°F / 7°C>16°C

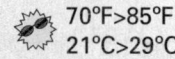 70°F>85°F / 21°C>29°C

 Rain >5 in / >13 cm